MTV

Spain

1st Edition

by Fernando Gayesky, Elizabeth Gorman,
Andre Legaspi & Kristin Luna

Wiley Publishing, Inc.

Fernando Gayesky

Fernando Gayesky (lead writer, The Basics, Barcelona, Catalunya, Valencia, Balearics, Spain in Depth) moved from Argentina to New York City to study film when he was 21 with $800 in his bank account, good fodder for his first travel article on meals for under $5. Since then, he traveled throughout South America and Europe before settling down in Barcelona, Spain. He's also a contributor to *MTV Europe*.

Elizabeth Gorman

After studying abroad in Alicante, **Elizabeth Gorman** (Madrid, Castilla–La Mancha, Extremadura, Castilla y Leon) stuffed a duffel bag and set off for Madrid to help jumpstart an e-zine for young expats and students—She's lived there ever since. A contributor to *Maxim, ELLE Decor, MAP Magazine*, she is currently working on her siesta.

Andre Legaspi

Andre Legaspi (Andalucia, Costa del Sol, Sevilla) was born and raised in Queens, New York, and attended McGill University in Montréal, where he wrote CD reviews and covered the music scene. Andre also contributed to *MTV Europe, MTV Italy*, and wrote *Montréal Day by Day*.

Kristin Luna

Bitten by the travel bug during her first solo backpacking trip through Europe, in which she was cornered by a herd of hungry mountain goats in the Italian Alps, **Kristin Luna** (Basque Country, Pamplona, Aragon) survived, luckily, and has since visited more than 35 countries on three continents and written about her experiences for international publications like *Newsweek*.

Published by:

Wiley Publishing, Inc.

111 River St.

Hoboken, NJ 07030-5774

ISBN: 978-0-7645-8772-6

Editor: Alexia Travaglini

Production Editor: Heather Wilcox

Cartographer: Andrew Murphy

Cover & Interior Design: Eric Frommelt

Wiley Anniversary Logo: Richard Pacifico

Production by Wiley Indianapolis Composition Services

For information on our other products and services or to obtain technical support, please contact our Customer Care Department within the U.S. at 800/762-2974, outside the U.S. at 317/572-3993 or fax 317/572-4002.

Wiley also publishes its books in a variety of electronic formats. Some content that appears in print may not be available in electronic formats.

Manufactured in the United States of America

5 4 3 2 1

Table of Contents

TABLE OF CONTENTS

TABLE OF CONTENTS

List of Maps

An Invitation to the Reader

In researching this book, we discovered many wonderful places—hotels, restaurants, shops, and more. We're sure you'll find others. Please tell us about them, so we can share the information with your fellow travelers in upcoming editions. If you were disappointed with a recommendation, we'd love to know that, too. Please write to:

MTV Spain, 1st Edition
Wiley Publishing, Inc.
111 River St.
Hoboken, NJ 07030-5774

An Additional Note

Please be advised that travel information is subject to change at any time—and this is especially true of prices. We therefore suggest that you write or call ahead for confirmation when making your travel plans. The authors, editors, and publisher cannot be held responsible for the experiences of readers while traveling. Your safety is important to us, however, so we encourage you to stay alert and be aware of your surroundings. Keep a close eye on cameras, purses, and wallets, all favorite targets of thieves and pickpockets.

A Note on Prices

The MTV Guides provide exact prices in each destination's local currency. The rates of this exchange as this book went to press are listed in the table below. Exchange rates are constantly in flux; for up-to-the-minute information, consult a currency-conversion website such as www.oanda.com/convert/classic.

Euro €	US $	UK £	Canadian $	Australian $	New Zealand $
1€ equals	US$1.20	£0.68	C$1.35	A$1.60	NZ$1.75

Star Ratings, Icons & Abbreviations

Every hotel, restaurant, and attraction listed in this guide has been ranked for quality, value, service, amenities, and special features using a **star-rating system**. Hotels and restaurants are rated on a scale of zero (recommended) to three stars (exceptional). Attractions, shopping, and nightlife are rated according to the following scale: zero stars (recommended), one star (highly recommended), two stars (very highly recommended), and three stars (must-see). In addition to the star-rating system, we also use **three feature icons** that point you to great deals, in-the-know advice, and unique experiences. Throughout the book, look for:

 The most-happening restaurants, hotels, and things to do—don't leave town without checking these places out.

 When cash flow is at a trickle, head for these spots: no-cost museums, free concerts, bars with complimentary food, and more.

 Savvy advice and practical recommendations for students who are studying abroad.

The following **abbreviations** are used for credit cards:

AE	American Express	DISC	Discover	V	Visa
DC	Diners Club	MC	MasterCard		

The Best of Spain

by Fernando Gayesky

The Best Places to Drink

- **El Casco** (Zaragoza): With a name that literally translates to "the helmet," you may not know what to expect when diving deep into Zaragoza's core, El Casco, in search of a sweet night out. Which is exactly why El Casco appeals to so many Spanish youth, near and far—it's unpredictable nature and "anything goes" aura make it a recipe for fun and, well, trouble of the best kind. See p. 311.

- **Es Jaç** (Palma de Mallorca): Fashion *wunderkind* Miguel Adrover's joint is an interior designer's wet dream, minus the pretentiousness. Get there early to be able to check it out empty and stay late chilling with the owner and his crew of demented friends, who, if they like you, will point you to the coolest spots in town. See p. 472.

- **Zurriola Marítimo** (San Sebastián): If you're in San Sebastián and have exhausted all of your options in Parte Vieja (or rather they've shut down for the night), Zurriola will never leave you aching for a late-night cocktail, as its doors don't shut until 7am and open again soon thereafter. See p. 268.

- **Malasaña neighborhood** (Madrid): Madrid's Malasaña neighborhood has branded itself a permanent iconic place in Spanish history. During the '80s, it was *the* stomping grounds for cutting-edge artists and musicians during La Movida Madrileña. Today, punks, freaks, and hipsters continue to unite over drinks and rock 'n' roll. Kids party *botellón* style in Plaza Dos de Mayo before meeting for drinks at legendary joints like La Vía Láctea. You can't go wrong; there are more decent bars than hours in a Spanish night out. See p. 81.

- **Medussa** (Cadiz): We don't look for much when we want to drink with friends. We only ask that there's some good tunes, a decent crowd of people, and a trio of eunuchs to pour the beer into our mouths. Surprisingly, we can never find the last but the first two are more than taken care of in Medussa. It's quite possible that the student-favored bar has the best rotation of alternative and '80s rock coming out of its woofers and tweeters—with a focus on musical heroes such as Morrissey, David Bowie, Dinosaur Jr., and Sonic Youth on a nightly basis. See p. 587.

- **Tents at Devesa Park** (Girona): The college crowd that composes most of the noise-making population of Girona and its surrounds has a standing date every summer weekend at the Devesa Park, where trendy city bars and summer-only ventures put up their tents to create a massive outdoor drinking spectacular. Add music, perfect weather, and tons of young people bouncing (and stumbling) around and you've got yourself a perfect summer party. See p. 396.

○ **Bora Bora** (Ibiza): There's a fine line to determine whether a bar with loud music and a gazillion people dancing is just a bar or actually a club in disguise. Bora-Bora walks the line with grace, albeit while staggering at every step. A quintessential Ibiza experience, whether it is pre- or post-club (another distinction that tends to get blurry in this 24-hour party town). See p. 497.

○ **Beach *Chiringuitos*** (Barcelona): Since Catalans decided to turn their faces back to the sea, the simple, wooden decked huts, aka *chiringuitos,* have become a local institution at the beaches as representative as the albino Gorilla Snowflake (RIP). Whether you choose the tourist infested ones on Barceloneta or the electronic music dens of Marbella beach, you can't spend a summer in Barcelona without the taste of a margarita by the sea shore. See p. 368.

○ **Jerez de la Frontera**: Jerez isn't exactly a college town. The majority of the people who come to refine their alcoholic palate with sips of sherry seem to be esteemed members of the AARP. There's nothing wrong with old people, but it's not that fun to get drunk with someone who takes Metamucil with their Miller Lite. However, with age comes wisdom and, when it comes to drinking, few places can compete with a town where the main tourist activity is taking tasting tours of distilleries. See p. 589.

○ **Plaza de la Merced** (Malaga): This is where it's at. If you don't believe us, ask Picasso. Well, if he was alive he'd definitely vouch for the square's importance in Malaga's nightlife. Every Friday and Saturday night in the summer and spring brings hundreds of bag toting locals ready to guzzle their makeshift cocktails and beer. Guests staying at Picasso's Corner Hostel have the added advantage of having their beds a few minutes away from the chaos, so their walk of shame is a nice, short hop, skip, and a stumble away. To see just how prolific the *botellón* in Plaza de la Merced can be, stop by early the next morning before the street cleaners get there. See p. 595.

The Best Cheap Sleeps

○ **Hôme Deluxe** (Valencia): The swankiest in the three-member Hôme family is by far the best value in town. The impossibly friendly staff will point you to your own private theme room, each designed by a different personality with names and decorations as varied as Colonial Alcove and Kyomei. With hostels like this one, even Nicole Ritchie could be a backpacker. See p. 434.

○ **Posada de San Jose** (Cuenca): This is more than just a place to park your stuff. It's an institution, a place for both the rich and the poor to co-exist in one awesome old building, which used to be a 17th-century choir school and one of Velázquez's summer hangouts. See p. 148.

○ **Olga's Place** (San Sebastián): This backpacker's haven located just around the corner from San Sebastián's major surfing beach has the most inviting atmosphere of anywhere along the Bay of Biscay coast. The owner, an ex-pat from Russia, makes you feel right at home, and for the most part, you'll find only English spoken here from your fellow lodgers—a rarity for this part of Spain. See p. 262.

○ **Pension Bellmirall** (Girona): Okay, this is not the cheapest option in town, but for the price of the YMCA in New York you can spend the night at an authentic 14th-century medieval house in the middle of Girona's incredible Call Jueu. The stone walls are decorated with beautiful ceramics and paintings by local artists, giving a new meaning to cozy. See p. 394.

○ **Albergue de Juventud Kabul** (Barcelona): Long before the Taliban put Kabul on the map, this youth hostel was already receiving visitors from all over the world who were ready for action. If not the best place to rest, it's most definitely *the* place to party, located right in the Plaça Reial, the center of Barcelona's nightlife, where you'll find everything from fancy clubs to alternahippy street *botellóns*. The closest you can get to having a party in your backyard in Barcelona. See p. 348.

○ **Lolo Urban House** (San Sebastián): The chill-out vibe this Aussie hostel exudes attracts those looking for a laid-back environment with the possibility of some major partying. If you check in on the right day, you may just get in on one of the frequent pub crawls to San Sebastián's hot spots that the guys running the place initiate. Or if surfing's your bag, you can sign up for one of the ongoing surf trips the hostel offers. See p. 261.

○ **Hostal Catedral** (Salamanca): This hostel is a cut above the rest with bright rooms, impeccable cleanliness, and demure hospitality that you wish you could bottle and bring back home with you. After a lot of traveling it stands out for its sunniness as well as for having more sparkle than a Mr. Clean commercial. See p. 218.

○ **El Beaterio** (Tarifa): Sweet, sweet Carmen. If it weren't for her husband, Verna, we'd be writing dozens of love sonnets for the inimitable Carmen instead of writing about El Beaterio. Then again, if it weren't for her husband, El Beaterio would still be the rundown shell of a monastery that once stood there. Years of blood, sweat, and tears have turned it into a home away from home for hundreds of guests who stay there every year. Some might find the toys haphazardly tossed around the halls strange, but it just adds to the atmosphere and, unknown to the owners and their kids, they provided us hours of entertainment after boozing it up with friends. See p. 580.

○ **Oasis Backpackers'** (Granada): There's too much to say about this place, so to save space we'll forgo some letters: Awsm dnnrs, cmfy bds, frndly ppl, vry chll trrc, xcllnt lndry srvc, tns f thngs plnnd nghtly, png png tbl, vry chp rts. If you'd like to buy a vowel, check out p. 565 for the full review.

○ **Picasso's Corner** (Malaga): By the time this book comes out, all the repairs and renovations to Picasso's Corner might make this one of the best hostels in Spain. While the pristine bathrooms and comfy common areas might sway your opinion toward the positive, the supremely laid-back and friendly staff will knock your opinion on its ass . . . in a good way of course. See p. 600.

The Best Beaches

○ **Ses Illetes** (Formentera): On the paradisiacal island of Formentera every stretch of sand is the best beach you've ever seen, but if someone had a gun to my head, I'd say Ses Illetes is the chosen one. Impossibly clear water, the finest white sand, and no man-made structures whatsoever to get in the way of your perfect tan. And if that's not enough you can cross over to the next beach and take a mud bath in the same place where Paz Vega took hers in *Sex and Lucia*. See p. 512.

○ **Playa de la Concha** (San Sebastián): One of San Sebastián's three main beaches, La Concha is by far the most spacious and, likewise, most populated. Regardless, it's the ideal spot for catching some rays or trying to meet some beachside babes. Girls beware: If modesty's your thing, you might not feel comfortable here amidst the array of topless European beauties. See p. 258.

○ **Platja de Formentor** (Mallorca): The beach at Cabo Formentor is a narrow strip of sand in a bay surrounded by lush mountains of a dark green that merges into the clear green water. The clientele is a little on the posh side, but mingling is not mandatory. See p. 481.

○ **Cabo de Gata Park** (Andalucia): If you do have time to head east for a little extra R&R, Cabo de Gata should be your first destination. The natural reserve not only has some of the most beautiful flora and fauna in southern Spain, but it also has some of the most secluded and breathtaking beaches in the entire country. See p. 568.

The Best Ways to Blow Your Money

○ **Hotel de Londres y de Inglaterra** (San Sebastián): If you're straying from the smelly, cramped hostel scene and forking out a hefty sum doesn't faze you, this four-star located right smack on San Sebastián's most happening beach is your place of choice. The seaside views are spectacular, as is the service and basically every other aspect imaginable about Hotel de Londres y de Inglaterra, which remains one of the country's most popular choices for accommodation. See p. 264.

○ **Gran Hotel Domine Bilbao** (Bilbao): A chef d'oeuvre in itself with its Art Deco furnishings and mishmash of sculptures and paintings, Gran Hotel is located at the most fashionable address with a front-row seat to the Guggenheim. Hands down Bilbao's grandest lodging establishment, the decor of the rooms and overall glamour of the five-star hotel fit right in with the city's revamped contemporary ambience. See p. 279.

○ **Hotel Alfonso XIII** (Sevilla): When you collect your first million as some hotshot CEO, be sure to book a room here to see what all the fuss is about. In the meantime you, the cash-strapped backpacker that you are, can wander in and pretend to be one of the spoiled guests staying in the legendary hotel. Everything, from the light fixtures to the zipper on the bellhop's fly, is gilded and each are worth more than all your possessions combined. See p. 535.

○ **Etxanobe** (Bilbao): The top floor of the Congressional Palace makes for Bilbao's tastiest and most elegant dining experience. Throw on your fanciest attire and sample some of the Basque Country's finest cuisine. See p. 280.

○ **El Bulli** (Costa Brava): You may have to shorten your trip by a day or two, but how many people can say they ate at the world's best restaurant? Star chef Ferrán Adriá's joint gets booked a year in advance, but you may be able to get a last minute spot to try the multi-course tasting menu consisting of the most innovative experiments in taste, smell, and texture, all produced after months of research at Adria's Barcelona kitchen lab. The restaurant itself lies in a beautiful cove about 2 hours north of Barcelona (though for the price tag you'd think it would be, transportation is not included). See p. 406.

The Best Spanish Oddities

○ **Gypsy Weddings** (Mérida): Even Greek weddings have nothing on Spanish gypsy ones. If you're lucky enough to see this sight—and if it's summer you will—you'll see why gypsies have that extra bounce in their step. Clapping, stomping, chanting, singing . . . you'll wish you were a gypsy. Large families gather around a bejeweled bride who is inevitably wearing a tall Spanish comb in her hair. The other women are usually in neon-colored dresses while men are often caught in whacked out tuxes and alligator shoes. Festivities shout, music blares, and I'll be damned if there's a booty not shaking.

○ **Witchcraft Museum** (Segovia): We thought the mummified finger in Avila was weird but we hadn't yet seen the witchcraft museum in Segovia. This private collection exhibits some of the scariest dead stuff you've never imagined. And it's not all hoopla. In the torture dungeon, you can see how so-called witches were intimidated or (gulp) burned during the Inquisition. Admittedly, it was the most disturbing historical account I'd seen thus far, one that made me shriek out loud. Make sure you're firmly planted in your religious beliefs—and your lunch—before you dare to visit. See p. 237.

○ **Paulino/Flamenco Bar** (Tossa de Mar): This bar provides one of the wildest experiences on the Costa Brava. Red lights and velvet, dead animals gracing the walls, and a mix of Spanish kitsch and American pulp that wouldn't be possible anywhere else in the world. The live act involves a flamenco guitar player, a generously proportioned female singer with a voice like Louis Armstrong's, and a team of waiters and locals straight out of a John Waters movie. See p. 411.

The Best Places to Party

○ **Fallas** (Valencia): Valencia is known as Spain's party capital, so it should come as no surprise that they hold the biggest and maddest town party. Four days of incessant noise (Armageddon-worthy firecrackers go off every 6 hr.), drinking, and dancing should take care of the needs of your inner party animal for a while. Picture a Thanksgiving Day Parade, meets pyromaniac Fourth of July, meets St. Patrick's Day, and you'll have an inkling of what the last day of Fallas is like. Did we mention it's 4 days long? See p. 441.

○ **San Fermín** (Pamplona): If nonstop partying for 7 consecutive days sounds good, well, San Fermines might be a bit of a disappointment—it has 8. Spain's eminent Running of the Bulls is no doubt one of the country's most revered annual festivals and with good reason. The city is one chaotic mass of drinking, dancing, and having an all-around good time. See p. 295.

○ **Gay Pride** (Madrid): That's right, the most Catholic country in the world legalized gay marriage. But countries like ours aren't exactly following suit. During Gay Pride week in Madrid, hordes of horny international gays and lesbians come dressed in rainbow fatigues to fight discrimination, inequality, and dreariness, and to celebrate with glitter and gold in the world-renowned neighborhood of Chueca. There are no rules to the game of love during this fiesta; who cares whether he/she is the same sex as you, if you both like it! *La bella vida!* See p. 118.

○ **La Mercé** (Barcelona): Barcelona celebrates its patron saint with a week of cultural events and general partying. The bars put up street vending tables with cheap deals and the streets get packed with people watching the many free concerts throughout the old city until 1:30am, when the party moves on to the Forum, where more bands and DJs keep everybody happy until the sun comes up. During the day museums are free, not that you'll ever make it to see that side of the sun. See p. 377.

○ **La Latina** (Madrid): This neighborhood is more popular on Sunday afternoons than any other spot in the country, and in Spain that's saying something. Everyone and their grandma—no, really,

we're being literal here—arrives in droves for tapas and drinking along La Latina's narrow bar-lined streets leading to the Plaza Mayor. More popular than the bars, however, is parking it in Plaza de la Paja (ironically outside San Pedro church) with a 40 liter of beer and a sparked spliff. Look, I'm just being an observational journalist here. See p. 81.

○ **Primavera Sound** (Barcelona): Growing every year to become one of the most important music festivals in Europe, Primavera Sound is not as popular as Sonar but the musical offer is more varied. The location is unbeatable; the six stages sprawl across the Forum, under the giant solar panes overlooking the beaches, down the hill, next to the saltwater pools, or by the giant Ferris wheel. The acts keep getting better and better, and recent features have included The Yeah Yeah Yeahs, Mogwai, Lou Reed, and Flaming Lips. See p. 377.

○ **Carnaval** (Sitges): Catalunya's biggest gay party takes place in Sitges, where everybody dresses up (or undresses) to the full extent of their flamboyant fantasies. Colorful floats, lots of sequins, boas, and crazy club paraphernalia take over the whole city converting it into, well, a huge club with a beach included. Although Carnaval is mostly a showcase for pretty boys and strong girls, everybody, gay and straight, is welcome to let go of their inhibitions and go ahead with some exhibitions while the music keeps playing on and on. See p. 424.

The Best Clubs

○ **Space** (Ibiza): We can pretty much affirm without fear of being wrong or hyperbolic that this is the best party you'll find in the world on a Sunday at

8am. Space is the mecca for club-goers and if you haven't been there yet you can't claim to be a true one. Only the best DJs in the world work their magic at the turntables for thousands of overeXcited party animals to go crazy to the tune of electronic music at its very loudest. See p. 500.

○ **Pachá** (Ibiza): Although the brand has turned into an international club factory with branches all over the world, we'll still be loving Pachá Ibiza for a really long time. The club that started it all is fancier and less freaky than the others around here, but the music, lights, and fun level are hard to beat, no matter where else you go. See p. 500.

○ **Granada 10** (Granada): If it weren't for the pretentiousness or the absurd covers, the clubs in Marbella would easily compete for this title. But the best everyman's (and everywoman's) dance spot is nestled just north of Granada's busy Gran Via. By day, it acts as a normal theater, but later in the evening it becomes one of the most popular discothèques in town. You might think of wussing out after an exhausting day exploring the Alhambra, but even the weakest of sightseers get a mighty second wind from Granada 10's excellent DJs and music. See p. 567.

○ **Cova d'en Xoroi** (Menorca): Menorca is the sleepiest of the Balearics and of course, it's got nothing on Ibiza, but this club's location makes it an obliged stopover for any self-respecting clubgoer. A huge cave on a majestic cliff is the setting for the wildest parties the island has to offer. See p. 518.

The Best Tapas & Other Cheap Eats

○ **El Tubo** (Zaragoza): Tapas bars aren't scant in Zaragoza's dining district located in the heart of the city center. All early evening activity begins here, primarily on the main tapas drag of Calle Estébanes, a mecca for all lovers of Aragonese delights. See p. 314.

○ **Santa Maria** (Barcelona): If you are adventurous and run away from tradition you'll love this tapas bar with a modern twist by an alumni of master chef Ferrán Adriá. Here you can get a taste of the *nueva cocina* without spending the next 3 days' worth of your hotel budget. See p. 356.

○ **Cervecería Morito** (Burgos): Burgos lays claims to the best tapas bar: Cervecería Morito, where old people dine with the new just because it's so damn good. Sure, there are a lot of good tapas bars in Spain, so competition is steep. But you've got to take into account more than the outer crisp of a *croqueta*. We've done a lot of research on this subject, in particular, and the elements that matter most are 1) quality, 2) price, 3) service, 4) menu, and 5) atmosphere. Morito scores 10 in every regard. That's our story, and we're eating a tapa to it. See p. 210.

○ **Barrio Húmedo** (León): The whole barrio. As in, the best place to go without a map or your *MTV Spain* and trust that you'll still be able to find good eats. In this neighborhood you can bump into a dish of *morcilla* (blood sausage), *croquetas,* or *patatas bravas* blindfolded. It's all locally grown and produced to boot. See p. 199.

○ **Bar El Rinconcillo** (Seville): Despite some of the most miserly bartenders, you'll find some top-notch tapas to go along with your glasses of Cruzcampo. El Rinconcillo has seniority over all others here, bragging on its storefront that its staff has been growling at Seville's denizens since 1670. See p. 536.

○ **Fonda Pepe** (Formentera): This ultra authentic local restaurant serves some of the best seafood available in the island at very decent prices. Expect paper tablecloths, loud families, and young people jumbled together with local workers relaxing after a long day. Spain at its damn best! See p. 510.

○ **La Castañeda** (Granada): La Castañeda is one of the all-time favorites of Granada's locals. Authenticity is never in question since they fulfill all the requirements of our Genuine Tapas Checklist. Hams hanging from the ceiling? Check . . . I didn't say it was a long checklist. See p. 565.

○ **Bonanza** (Sitges): You've come all the way to Spain so you have to try the paella. But paella doesn't come cheap *and* good—except at Bonanza, where after a little strenuous walk uphill you can enjoy a delicious seafood paella that won't go off like a round of bullets in your stomach when you get the check. Yeehah! See p. 422.

The Best Shopping Finds

○ **El Rastro** (Madrid): As if we even had to tell you, duh! The world's biggest treasure hunt takes place every Sunday between the La Latina and Lavapiés 'hoods, where it's possible to dig up everything from antique coffee grinders to old engagements rings. Greater than the goods are the people. Historically it's been a gypsy market, where the ruffians come to make a pretty penny churning tunes out of old street organs or selling their family collectibles. Over the years, however, other nationalities joined the party making it the Ellis Island of flea markets and the world's largest as well. See p. 133.

○ **Mercado de la Ribera** (Bilbao): This multi-tiered permanent establishment located right on the river that dissects Bilbao has everything you could want in terms of food, flora, and fauna. Fresh fish, meat, and vegetables are always on hand, as are flowers, herbs, and anything else under the sun. See p. 283.

○ **Toledo:** Nowhere in the world can you find shopping like in Toledo, where stores sell more steel swords and medieval-style rings than coffee mugs or refrigerator magnets. Toledo's specialty is collapsible daggers cut in an authentic Toledan style that sell for less than 10€, depending on where you

shop. If you've always been dying to own a chain mail suit, here's your golden opportunity—but lots of luck shipping it home. Most important for nerds is the *Lord of the Rings* paraphernalia such as sterling-silver jewelry. See p. 146.

○ **Holalá** (Madrid): Get the Urban Outfitters look for real at this well-stocked vintage store strategically located amidst other fashionable shopping in Chueca. The clothes are hand-picked from around the globe, lending the whole place an internationally funky vibe that beats your frumpy local thrift store hands down any day. There are also locations in Barcelona and Ibiza. See p. 131.

○ **La Condoneria** (Girona): This sexy little shop gives love a good name. Condoms? Latex wear? Bondage gear? Vibrators? Erotic games? Party toys? Whether you like it hot or mild, La Condoneria serves up a wide selection of sex-play goodies to suit your style. See p. 399.

○ **Libreria Beta** (Sevilla): You know that Barnes & Noble by your apartment, the one with the parking lot the size of three football fields, and the multi-storied front of glass windows you look out when you ride up the escalator? Yeah, well this is nothing like that. The only commonality is that Libreria Beta is a bookstore. It is also housed in the old Teatro Imperial, meaning if you ask an employee where to find a book, be it fiction, theater, or otherwise, you may be directed to center stage, the mezzanine, the orchestra, or up the balcony to the nosebleed seats. See p. 548.

○ **Mala Musica** (Jerez de la Frontera): In this octogenarian sherry town comes the improbably awesome Mala Musica, where you will find the best of most types of music, especially indie, rock, electronica, and jazz. Check out Mala for

hard-to-find or older releases as well. We think their new motto should be "So bad we're good." Or wait, is it "So good we're bad"? Suffice to say, they're our new favorite paradox. See p. 593.

○ **Mercat de Sant Josep** (La Boquería; Barcelona): Barcelona's modernista food market is a feast for all senses. Browse through the stalls with every possible kind of fruit, nut, or candy you can imagine. Check out the local fish and seafood in all its edible splendor and finish up by having the most amazing lunch at one of the jam-packed kiosks. See p. 363.

The Best Live Music

○ **La Cruzada** (Mérida): Mérida's like a mini-Rome with the number of ruins and Roman secrets it holds. We discovered one at La Cruzada, where every Friday night you can hear live rock or blues sung to a young, hip audience (that means no white beards). The joint books decent international and local groups that are undoubtedly just passing through—but thank Zeus for that! See p. 183.

○ **Palau de la Música Catalana** (Barcelona): Okay, this is not the place to go see rock 'n' roll or electronic music, but if there's anything that sounds remotely interesting playing while you are in Barcelona, you should not miss the opportunity to catch a show at this marvel of modernista architecture. Arrive early, because you'll spend at least 20 minutes tripping

outside at the ornate balconies with more weird shapes and small statues than cheese factor in a Dan Brown novel; once inside, if the concert is not what you were hoping for, you can spend the rest of your time in your own psychedelic world. See p. 375.

○ **El Eshavira** (Granada): Don't bother going to Sacromonte. The hike up there and the shady venues aren't worth the trouble. The best flamenco is in the heart of the city, and many head to El Eshavira for some of the best performances in the region. If your clapping and shouts are drawing some odd stares from the rest of the audience, you might find yourself in the middle of one of El Eshavira's "off-nights." It doubles as a great jazz haunt and the trumpet players don't react all that well to yelps of "Aya!" and foot stomping. See p. 567.

The Best Must-See Sights

○ **Palacio de la Aljaferia** (Zaragoza): Zaragoza's Islamic palace is one of the city's most visited sites. The dramatic archways and intricate detail work are

truly eye-catching, and the moat and park surrounding the castle are good spots for a leisurely day of lounging. See p. 314.

○ **Parc Güell** (Barcelona): Gaudí's crazy genius is at its best at this trip of a park overlooking the city. Get lost in the freaky structures and gardens until you don't know which way is up. Best of all? It's free. See p. 380.

○ **Guggenheim** (Bilbao): Bilbao's architectural rejuvenation is largely due to the creation of this glass and titanium monster that towers over the River Nervión. One of a series of modern arts museums, the Guggenheim—besides looking cool—also houses an eclectic bunch of temporary and permanent displays. See p. 282.

○ **Museo Chillida-Leku** (San Sebastián): This museum may throw you for a loop, as it appears to be more of a playground than anything else. Set among the lush green hills of outer San Sebastián, the outdoor park displays an entire collection of giant sculptures by the famed Spanish artist Eduardo Chillida. See p. 270.

○ **Basílica de Nuestra Señora del Pilar** (Zaragoza): The city's sprawling and most recognized church is home to some impressive frescoes by Francisco Goya and other well-known Spanish painters. Take a quick ride up one of the towers for a view over all of Zaragoza. See p. 313.

○ **Ciudad de las Artes y de las Ciencias** (Valencia): Valencian star architect Santiago Calatrava designed this amazing complex that is putting Valencia on the map as a true European capital. You can spend a couple of days just visiting this center composed of an aquarium, opera house, botanical garden, science museum, and IMAX theater; but even without visiting each and every exhibit, the general fishlike structure of the complex is worth a picture or two. See p. 441.

○ **Catedral de León** (León): Century-old stained glass isn't exactly a girl's best friend, but it does the trick. León's cathedral has more glass than stone. And more than Gothic it's French, which means a whole new ballpark for cathedral design that's different from any other Castilian cathedral built during the same era. You have to hand it to the architects; they didn't have computers, machines, glasscutters, or any of the strong compounds we use today. The cathedral was built with sheer genius and, one can only guess, a few cuts and scrapes along the way. See p. 201.

○ **Museo de Arte Abstracto Español** (Cuenca): Leaving out the most obvious (Madrid's El Prado) in this category, the contemporary art museum in Cuenca is hailed as one of the best modern art museums in Spain and not just for it's Spanish Abstract collection. The museum occupies Las Casas Colgadas, houses built over a death-defying river gorge that would give even Michael Jordan vertigo. The sights outside each of its large bay windows are just as abstract as the paintings themselves. It's been said that cubism has its roots in Cuenca's abrupt rocky mountains, which artists were inspired by when they started the movement. Whether that's true or not doesn't matter; the influence of Cuenca's vistas is clear as the river below. See p. 151.

○ **Segovia:** A good view takes two perspectives into account: the inward and the outward. The best positioned city is Segovia. Built on a large lookout rock, the city's vantage point enjoys wide, rolling Castilian planes backed by the surreal scenery of the Sierra de Guadarrama Mountains. From the opposite direction, looking into the city, the best view is from Iglesia de la Vera

Cruz, an ancient structure outside the city walls. Segovia's Walt Disney–esque castle surrounded by a tall Roman wall pierces the sky with its pawn-shaped towers straight out of a fairy tale. See p. 232.

○ **Trujillo:** You've heard of "Minnesota nice." But chances are you haven't heard of a village in Extremadura called Trujillo, famous for spawning a dozen or so (probably not so nice) conquistadors. Well familiarize yourself because Trujillo's inhabitants would lay their lives down for you—or at the very least a plate of hot food. In all my travels, I've never been given a more personal welcome: tours, useful tips—hell, the town key! Okay that's stretching it, but I'm sure they'd produce something out of their pockets if I'd asked. See p. 169.

○ **The Ravine** (Ronda): Other than severe beautyphobia, there's no reason you should miss the geologic sight in Ronda. Bandoleros used the ravine and the surrounding hills to escape capture, but I'm pretty convinced that the criminals just had extremely high aesthetic standards. After you catch sight of the unique bridge and canyon, you'll understand why. See p. 570.

○ **Alhambra** (Granada): If you thought Donald Trump or Richard Branson went a little overboard with their self indulgences, you've clearly never met a sultan before. Back in the day, these rulers wouldn't think twice about ordering hundreds of servants to build them a new wing to their palace. With the Alhambra, however, a sequence of sultans ended up creating one of the most fantastic sites in the world—all thanks to their greed. The site is a sprawling showcase of their power, with awesome structures overlooking the rest of Granada below. These sultans had a softer side as well and had the impressive Generalife built to give them a green summer escape. See p. 568.

The Best Ways to Get Your Blood Pumping

○ **Skydiving in the Pyrenees:** Sure, it may put a slight strain on the wallet, and, sure, plummeting more than 3,300m (11,000 ft.) may seem like a risky way to spend an otherwise languid Saturday afternoon. But if you've ever even entertained ideas of hurling yourself out of a six-seater plane to possibly meet your demise (only kidding), you really can't go wrong doing it in the awe-inspiring Pyrenees. See p. 327.

○ **Hitchhiking in Camino de Santiago:** We've had our share of bumps along the road but one in particular involves a sold-out bus and an old couple from Burgos. Technically it was hitchhiking, but I like to say it was socializing in a roadside diner. Little did I know it was nothing out of the ordinary. Pilgrims make this route all the time. Ain't no thang, ma'ma. While the chance of hailing a psycho killer still exists, there are more mom and pop types who'll get you to where you need to be in one piece—and buy you a coffee along the way. Folks are just more trusting in Spain, and that's the way the cookie crumbles. See p. 247.

○ **Kite-Surfing in Tarifa:** You might look like a newborn calf that's trying its damnedest to stand up, but who cares? Kite-surfing (check out the inordinate number of schools in town to get lessons) gives riders a huge rush as they let the whipping winds of Tarifa tow them over the choppy waves of the Strait of Gibraltar. If that's not enough to convince you, you should know that Tarifa is *the* best place for kite-surfing on the planet. Why pass it up if you're already there? See p. 576.

○ **Diving in Illes Medes** (Costa Brava): If you think you've seen it all on earth, try looking below sea level. This seven-islet archipelago is rumored to be the best diving spot in Spain and maybe even the Mediterranean. One thousand three hundred fifty different marine life species say you won't get bored swimming through the multicolored reefs, caves, and underwater rock formations. Your newfound paradise is less than 2 hours away from Barcelona, right across from the Costa Brava resort of L'Estartit. See p. 412.

The Best College Towns

○ **Cadiz:** Let's give the Erasmus program a hearty "Hells yeah!" Sure, if it didn't exist, Cadiz would nevertheless have a decent college crowd partying hard every weekend. But the city wouldn't have the international flavor that makes mingling that much more fun in the city's bars and clubs. So remember to count your blessings as you're chatting up the undergrad from Montana or the cutie from Peru. See p. 582.

○ **Alicante:** This was just another old German tourist haven in the Costa Blanca until the university started gaining respect and, with it, students. Hmm, wide fine-sand beaches, excellent weather, and a neighborhood with more bars than restaurants . . . sounds perfect for Erasmus students! Since the giant European study-abroad organization landed in Alicante, the city has blossomed into a meeting point for Europe's spring breakers year-round. Bars like Havana welcome students from every corner of the Old Continent and, more increasingly, non-E.U. students too. And if you happen to come in the middle of the summer and can't seem to find anyone, take the quick hop to Benidorm, Ibiza's clubbing branch on the mainland, where thousands of youngsters spend their parents' hard-earned money. See p. 443.

○ **Girona:** Unlike the previous two, Girona caters more to local students, which is totally fine with us. The sophisticated Catalonian youth crowds the streets and bars of this enchanting medieval town that, despite housing less than 100,000 souls, breathes the more erudite air of a big city, thanks in large part to the university and its inhabitants. Thursdays are the big university night and if you're lucky enough you'll be able to witness the psychologists versus architects wet T-shirt competition—psychoanalyze the construction of that. See p. 389.

The
Basics

by Fernando Gayesky

*S*unny Spain. The beaches, the food, the booze, the romance. How long have you been dreaming about this amazing trip? But there are details you'll want to work out, things you'll want to avoid, and plenty of things you should be aware of—from the logistical to the cultural—to get ready to enjoy *el sol de España.* And truth is that Spain, as a well-developed country prepared to receive millions of tourists every year, doesn't require ridiculous preparation. But read on, and you'll minimize those moments when you feel like the sorriest sucker in the world for losing time and money, the life force of every traveler, over details you could have taken care of from home.

The Regions in Brief

Spain: The Big Picture

Spain is roughly three times the size of Illinois. It encompasses nearly the whole Iberian Peninsula and is bordered by the Atlantic Ocean and the Bay of Biscayne to the north, and the blue Mediterranean to the south and east. To the west it shares a small part of the peninsula with Portugal, and, over the Pyrenees to the east, you'll find its only other neighbor, France. Talking about Spain as a whole may prove to be quite a challenge since Spain has over 50 provinces, each with its own geography, history, food, and sometimes even language. The country is dominated by high plateaus and mountain ranges like the Cantabrian Mountains in the north, Cuenca's mountains in the east, and the Sierra Morena in the south, and run through by several major rivers like the Tajo, the Ebro, the Duero, the Guadiana, and the Guadalquivir.

Madrid & Castilla–La Mancha

Nearly a hundred years after the Catholic kings expelled the last Moor from the country and unified all of Spain, Madrid was declared, by royal decree, to be the capital city of the Spanish empire. If you check a highway map, you'll see that what is said about the roads and Rome is truer

Spain

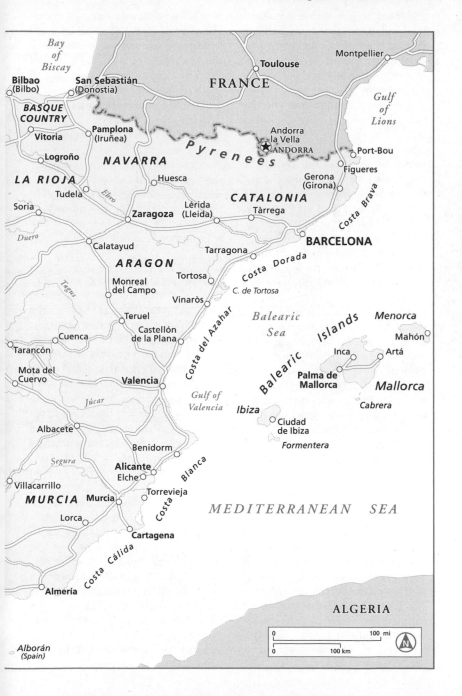

still about Madrid, since every road in Spain indeed leads into its precincts. Even the main international airport and railway stations are located in this city, so, chances are, Madrid will be your first stop. And a good stop it will be. You have to visit El Prado, Madrid's most important museum, where the *Guernica*, Picasso's antiwar masterpiece is located. And as far as museums go, don't forget the Thyssen-Bornemisza Museum, and perhaps the Royal Palace. Or simply wander through the historical quarters and its little medieval mazes around the Plaza Mayor and grab a bite of tapas—remember: You were not in Spain if you didn't have any tapas. While in Madrid you might want to check out "La Movida," the late-night club scene that will keep you partying for days, literally. Provided you don't get trapped in a party spiral for weeks, Madrid will take you at least 2 days to explore. But the region is called Madrid & Environs for a reason. Take a few more days to check out the areas nearby. You can't come this close and not go to **Toledo.** It's at least a day trip to this amazing city, capital of several ancient empires and brimming with monuments, paintings by El Greco, and one of Spain's greatest cathedrals. Check out also the Roman aqueduct in **Segovia, El Escorial,** and the "hanging village" of **Cuenca** (and its museum of modern art).

Extremadura

All over Spain you'll constantly have the sensation that time is messing with you—especially when you adopt the local time and party until 8am, which is when you used to get up for class in your other life . . . That is true for Extremadura more than anywhere else, only this time it's like back to the past. Just alongside your modern day highways some time-warp spots from the

Middle Ages or ancient Rome will pop up unexpectedly making you wonder if you accidentally time-traveled into the age of the *conquistadores,* many of whom called this land home. You want to see what all that gold they sent home turned into? Just visit **Trujillo,** Pizarro´s birthplace.

But it's not only Inca's gold that funded Extremadura´s beauty. **Guadalupe** will receive you with a stunning show of Mudéjar architecture in its monastery devoted to the Black Virgin. We recommend you take 2 days to travel to two additional cities: **Cáceres,** a fortified town built back in the Middle Ages, and **Mérida,** with its stunning ancient Roman theater.

Castilla y León

You've heard of both Old and New Castilla and are a little confused by olds and news and their difference? Well it's not that difficult in fact. New Castilla is a sort of governmental division that actually encompasses a lot more than the medieval Castilla did. Old Castilla, as well as León, in north-central Iberia is the core from which modern-day Spain evolved. As independent kingdoms they both had their own capital cities complete with cathedrals and palaces so each one is full of stuff to see. Don't let the proximity to Madrid fool you. Old Castilla and León's highlights are most definitely not day trips.

You'll want to check out **Burgos,** considered the Cradle of Castille, or see how medieval students lived in **Salamanca,** an ancient university town, or see how today's students go all medieval (or not). And you should also visit the Cathedral in **León** (the capital on the northern plains of the district bearing its name). Have some days left? Maybe a trip to **Zamora,** known for its stunning Romanesque churches, and the historic city of **Valladolid.**

Basque Country

You'll realize instantly you're in the Basque country when people start speaking a language that has absolutely nothing in common with any other European language you've ever heard. Euskara, the Basque language, originated from its own source. It is the oldest language still spoken in Europe and a special and unique culture accompanies it. The Basque people, or Euskotarrak, have been fierce defenders of their cultural identity and being there you'll realize the hugeness of what's at stake.

The Basque country offers a little bit of everything for your itinerary: beaches, mountains, traditions, parties, and the best food in Spain—but you'd better learn to like seafood before going, or you'll be missing out on one of the best things the area has to offer. Basque country's two most visited cities, **San Sebastián** and **Bilbao,** are both interesting mixes of aesthetic architecture and stunning beaches. The nightlife of the two cities leaves little to be desired, as well, and tapas joints and discos are more abundant than breadsticks at the Olive Garden.

Pamplona

Sandwiched between the Basque country and Aragón, when Navarre shows its true colors, you'll see traits of both. There's only one major city here, **Pamplona,** and one major attraction, the annual bull race of **San Fermín,** an 8-day-long party where the main attraction consists of being chased by bulls through the streets of the town. And you may even do it, if you are drunk enough to jump in (bravery usually has very little to do with it).

Cantabria, Asturias & Galicia

Positioned on Iberia's north-central coastline, Cantabria and Asturias are the most verdant (read: wet) regions of Spain, perhaps unluckily for the many pilgrims who pass through here on their way to **Santiago de Compostela,** Spain's rainiest city, which is itself located in the coastal region known as Galicia. Santiago de Compostela is one of the world's most important places of Christian pilgrimage even today, and lots of churches and abbeys mark the way along the routes known collectively as the Camino de Santiago. Galicia's beaches are consistently rainier than those along Spain's southern coasts, making this less of a prime destination for young sun- and fun-seekers. For these reasons we feature only limited coverage of these regions.

Aragón

Aragón is not one of Spain's prime tourist destinations, but still, it has lots to offer. First, its tranquillity. Aragón is the least populated area in Spain, which means there's a lot of peace around here (it also means that public transportation isn't quite that good, so be aware). It's a great spot to recuperate from your party hardy nights in Madrid and prepare for the ones in Barcelona, or vice versa. Aragón also encompasses a good part of the Spanish Pyrenees, making it the proper turf for your winter and extreme sports.

Exactly halfway between Madrid and Barcelona lies **Zaragoza,** the district capital, a youthful city full of university students and hippies. You can also visit **Jaca,** a very lively town that is a winter mountainside base for skiers and snowboarders alike. Another quieter option would be to look for a small mountain village and spend some time wandering and taking in the mountains' fresh air. **Torla** or **Bielsa** are great for just that. Ohhhhhmmmm . . .

Barcelona & Catalunya

Barcelona has everything you need. History: Walk around the Ciutat Vella. Get lost in the narrow streets of this medieval maze; discover the gargoyles and statues that seem to sprout randomly from every nook, cranny, and alley. Check the Gothic churches that lurk around every corner. You want some art? How's about the Joan Miró foundation, the MACBA (contemporary art museum), some of the most exciting theater festivals in Spain, and plenty of music to choose from. Sightseeing? The modernista buildings and developments like Park Güell or La Sagrada Familia make you feel like you're living in a fairyland. You want to party until the sun comes up and then some? Check the clubs in La Rambla, or any number of great outdoor parties in summer. You'll even get your fair share of beaches in this fascinating city that has it all. Take at least 3 days to explore and even then it won't be enough.

Awesome as it may be, Barcelona is not the only thing Catalunya has to offer. A little farther south you'll find **Sitges,** a beach resort that caters to a diverse clientele ranging from freewheeling nudists and gay party crowds to fun-seeking families. Other destinations are **Tarragona,** one of ancient Rome's district capitals; and **Montserrat,** an incredible mountain mass great for trekking and home to a monastery that hosts the "Moreneta," patron virgin of Catalunya.

Costa Brava

Looking for fun in the sun? This is the other zone in Spain where you can find it. A very different place from the Costa del Sol, mainly because of its topography, it is rockier with beaches that spill out right from the foot of the mountains. This produces an infinity of little peninsulas and sheltered coves ready to be discovered by anyone with a spirit for adventure.

Although it gets its fair share of visitors, the Costa Brava will feel a bit less crowded and more unspoiled than the Costa del Sol.

For the most part, it still keeps some of that Mediterranean vibe and those astonishing blue waters.

Sun worshippers usually head for the cute beachfront resorts like **Tossa de Mar.** If interested in the life and works of Salvador Dalí you should take a day trip to **Figueres;** Spain's *enfant terrible* was born here and gave the city one of the most interesting museums in all of Europe. He actually designed the place himself. The jewel of the Costa Brava, not surprisingly, is also related to the artist. **Cadaqués** is the town where Dalí lived most of his adult life. Isolated in the middle of the mountains, Cadaqués is exactly what you imagine when you think of a little fishermen's town on the Mediterranean. White houses, narrow streets, and water so transparent you can see straight down to the bottom of the sea.

Valencia

Valencia, is the third-largest city in Spain, and is not known as a tourist stop, but that may be the good news. In recent years there has been a real revitalization of this city. People don't just come here to see the city's impressive cathedral, the exterior of its worthy Palacio de la Generalidad, or a few of its three important museums. Valencia has always had a highly underrated party scene with great clubs and lots of live music.

The small town of **Elche,** with its proud people who lay claim to the largest palm grove in Europe, is an interesting surprise worth a day trip. To complete your sampler of the region, spend a few days on your back sunbathing in **Alicante, Benidorm,** or any of the other beaches of la Costa Blanca.

The Balearic Islands

Since the ancient times of Carthage, the Balearic Islands have always been populated. It's easy to understand why—just look at its striking beaches, virgin coves, vast countrysides, gorgeous mountains, and beautiful ancient towns. But the secret is way out now and most of northern Europe coordinates a well-timed invasion of its beaches every summer. **Majorca** is overrun when the weather sizzles, especially by sun-starved British and German travelers on package tours. **Ibiza**'s endless parties attract a large gay crowd and party animals who converge from all over the world. **Menorca** is more tranquil, although less convenient to get to, creating a kind of chicken-and-the-egg, catch-22 of logic. Don't think too hard, though; if you're in Los Baleares, you're in one of the max 'n relax capitals of the world!

Sevilla & Andalucía

Andalucía is a dry, fairly unprosperous district. But what spawns wonder in this region is its history. In the 8th century, Muslim armies coming from North Africa overran the Iberian Peninsula. In just a few years virtually all of it was conquered and thus began the 800-year-long retrieval by the Christians, known as La Reconquista. Being closest to the south, Andalucía was the epicenter of various Muslim empires that blossomed big time, only to disappear again, leaving Andalucía to become one of the most advanced societies in the Spanish Middle Ages. Philosophy, mathematics, and arts flourished here like nowhere else at the time, leaving spurs of one of the most enlightened societies in medieval history. Muslims were finally defeated with the fall of Granada in 1942, but 800 years of Moorish administration can't be shaken off lightly, making Andalucía one of the most interesting places in all of Spain.

You'll want to spend a week here visiting the major cities of Andalucía. Start with **Granada,** where you'll see the Moorish legacy in full effect, in what is a true masterpiece of a city. Spend a night in **Sevilla,** capital city of romance in Spain; check out the Mezquita in **Córdoba** and try to recognize all the religions that influenced its architecture along the centuries; and visit **Cádiz,** a seaport famous for being home of one of the most extravagant Carnavals in Europe.

The Costa del Sol

From Algeciras, to the west, to Almería to the east. Beaches! Yeah! Sand, Sun, Sea. Yeah! *Yeah!* Costa del Sol has some of the best beaches in Spain. And who doesn't love the Mediterranean, which has—what else?—*Mediterraneans,* whom we especially like when they are wearing little more than their suntan oil. As all major beaches, it may get a little crowded, but did we mention sand, surf, and nudity??

You'll probably arrive by plane via **Málaga,** the historical city of the region. There are some 28km (17 miles) of beaches here and, at its center, you'll find **Marbella,** a Renaissance city populated by the pretty and wealthy. If you want more of a laid-back fishermen's vibe (one part chill, two parts salt) go to **Nerja.** If you're looking for action, and crowds, **Torremolinos** is your choice. And if you want something a bit different try the Moorish-esque city of **Puerto Banús.**

THE BASICS

Stuff to Figure Out before You Go

◌ **You need to get there.** For the best airfare and flight itinerary, get to know the big travel websites and shop around. In our experience with booking flights to Europe online, Kayak, Orbitz, and Priceline have always had the best prices and the most flights to choose from. You should also try TerminalA.com and Edreams.com, Spanish websites that work with low-cost airlines such as Ryanair and easyJet. In general, try to book your flights well in advance—at least a month before you depart, more for summer travel. While Spain airfares do occasionally go on sale at the last minute, the savings are not usually more than $50 or so—which is hardly worth the anxiety of wondering if you'll get a seat. For domestic traveling, Vueling, Spain's newest low-cost airline, can often be cheaper than driving.

○ **You need a place to sleep.** In a perfect world, you would book your hotel reservations in Spain even before you booked your flight there—during high season, it can be tough to find good-value accommodations on the spot. However, the world is far from perfect. You'll probably end up changing your travel plans somewhat while abroad, and, furthermore, some hostels don't accept reservations until the day before your intended arrival. So, even if you can't book all your accommodations before you leave home, you'd do well to have at least a few beds nailed down in advance. You'll find plenty of helpful tips in the "Staying There" section, later in this chapter, which will give you a feeling for the lay of the land, accommodations-wise, in Spain.

○ **Know what to expect at different times of the year.** Spanish tourism has a rather entrenched seasonal cycle, and, depending on when you go, you're likely to have quite different experiences. Weather, of course, is the most obvious variable. There are also significant differences in traveler demographics during the year, with northern Europeans completely overrunning the

country in August, for example. Rest assured, we'll let you know if a certain hotel has a 90% chance of being full of 100% 80-year-old Dutchmen.

○ **Pay attention to opening hours.** The majority of Spanish museums will be closed 1 day out of every week (usually on Mon or Tues)—though, during summer they might be open the entire week. We'll also give you advice on which days of the week and times of day are best to visit different sights. One rule of thumb though: Whenever possible, book your tickets in advance, either online or by phone.

○ **Embrace the cultural differences.** You won't find all the conveniences of home in Spain, and the language barrier can be frustrating, but part of why you flew thousands of miles to get here was to experience something different, right? So get over all those little differences and challenges because Spain is a great country with an amazing story. Within its borders you'll discover a multitude of Spains, since every region has a unique style and culture to explore.

○ **Be realistic about how much you can do on your trip.** Time flies when you're having fun, and you'll be having a lot of fun in Spain. Don't rush through the country in your quest to send postcards from 10 different cities. Not that you have to milk it completely, but try to enjoy every place for as long as it deserves. If you don't have tons of time to do everything you want, remember, you can always come back—and you'll probably want to anyway.

How Much Time Do I Need in Spain?

To get a full serving of the best Spain has to offer you should spend at least 2 weeks there. A single week or a 10-day trip could work, as long as you travel only to a few

Cuidado! (Watch Out)
....

Throughout this book, you'll find boxes with the heading *"Cuidado!,"* which denotes a fact or warning we think you need to know about (such as legal, cultural, and personal advice gained from hard-won experience). A word to the wise . . . not knowing these things could hinder or derail your trip.

cities and regions. Minor cities can be experienced over a long weekend, but larger cities such as Madrid or Barcelona will require a lot more time. Only problem is, no matter how much time you have, you'll always find out about something you didn't have a chance to see. Or you'll wonder how this city would be in winter, spring, fall, summer, or during that festival you just missed. Spain will always give you more than you bargained for, but in a good way. Also, when you factor in travel time between destinations, checking in at hotels, arriving at the train station in time for your next connection, and so on, you lose a lot of valuable hours that you might have originally dedicated to hanging out, sightseeing, or partying. Moral of the story: You need more time than you think.

We especially recommend that you resist the temptation to do a whirlwind of cities in a week. Taking a picture of your buddy having a local beer is not the same as experiencing a town or a city. Lots of people do it, but it's far more fun to spend more time in each place and get your bearings before you pack up and head to the next city on your TripTik. Unless you're an experienced and insanely laid-back traveler, you'll be wiped out and overwhelmed if you try to see too much too quickly. At a bare minimum, we recommend 3 full days in Madrid, 3 full days in Barcelona, a weekend on the beaches of the Costa Brava, 5 days in Andalucía, 5 in the Basque country, and a long weekend in the Balearics.

In warm weather, definitely dedicate at least 1 full day, if not several, to any

beach or island. And try to spend a few days in less touristy places, such as the Andalucian seaside. Allow 1 full "buffer day" at the start of your trip to recover from jet lag, and remember that you won't be doing or seeing much of anything on the day of your return flight since you'll most likely be heading to the airport in the morning.

WHEN TO GO

The best time to visit Spain? If you require some sun and sand, August and July are your months. May and October are both good months to visit all of Spain and are a little less hot and crowded than the summer season. You can still hit the beaches, but the sun won't fry you on your first beach day.

In summer it's hot, hot, and hotter still, with the cities in Castille (Madrid) and Andalucía (Seville and Córdoba) heating up the most. Madrid has a dry heat; the average temperature can hover around 84°F (29°C) in July and 75°F (24°C) in September. Seville has the dubious reputation of being the hottest part of Spain in July and August, often baking under average temperatures of 93°F (34°C).

Barcelona, while cooler in temperature, can often be quite humid. Midsummer temperatures in Majorca often crest up to 91°F (33°C). The overcrowded Costa Brava has temperatures around 81°F (27°C) in July and August. The Costa del Sol has an average of 77°F (25°C) in summer. The coolest spot in Spain is the Atlantic coast around San Sebastián, with temperatures in the

Weather Chart for Spain

Barcelona	Jan	Feb	Mar	Apr	May	June	July	Aug	Sept	Oct	Nov	Dec
Temp. (°F)	48	49	52	55	61	68	73	73	70	63	55	50
Temp. (°C)	9	9	11	13	16	20	23	23	21	17	13	10
Rainfall (in.)	1.7	1.4	1.9	2.0	2.2	1.5	.9	1.6	3.1	3.7	2.9	2.0

Basque Coast (N. Coast)	Jan	Feb	Mar	Apr	May	June	July	Aug	Sept	Oct	Nov	Dec
Temp. (°F)	45	48	51	52	55	65	67	67	61	53	52	48
Temp. (°C)	7	9	11	11	13	18	19	19	16	12	11	9
Rainfall (in.)	.9	.8	.9	1.3	1.5	1.2	.6	.7	1.0	1.2	1.4	.8

Madrid	Jan	Feb	Mar	Apr	May	June	July	Aug	Sept	Oct	Nov	Dec
Temp. (°F)	42	45	49	53	60	69	76	75	69	58	48	43
Temp. (°C)	6	7	9	12	16	21	24	24	21	14	9	6
Rainfall (in.)	1.6	1.8	1.2	1.8	1.5	1.0	.3	.4	1.1	1.5	2.3	1.7

Málaga (S. Coast)	Jan	Feb	Mar	Apr	May	June	July	Aug	Sept	Oct	Nov	Dec
Temp. (°F)	54	54	64	70	73	81	84	86	81	73	68	63
Temp. (°C)	12	12	18	21	23	27	29	30	27	23	20	17
Rainfall (in.)	2.4	2.0	2.4	1.8	1.0	.2	0	.1	1.1	2.5	2.5	2.4

Seville	Jan	Feb	Mar	Apr	May	June	July	Aug	Sept	Oct	Nov	Dec
Temp. (°F)	59	63	68	75	81	90	97	97	90	79	68	61
Temp. (°C)	15	17	20	24	27	32	36	36	32	26	20	16
Rainfall (in.)	2.6	2.4	3.6	2.3	1.6	.3	0	.2	.8	2.8	2.7	3.2

70s (low to mid 20s Celsius) in July and August.

August remains the major vacation month in Europe as is often the case stateside as well. The traffic from France, the Netherlands, and Germany to Spain becomes a veritable procession, and low-cost hotels along the coastal areas are virtually impossible to find. To compound the problem, many restaurants and shops decide it's time for a vacation, thereby limiting the visitors' selections for both dining and shopping.

In winter, the coast from Algeciras to Málaga is the most popular, with temperatures reaching a warm 60°F to 63°F (16°C–17°C). Madrid gets cold, as low as 34°F (1°C). Majorca is warmer, usually in the 50s (teens Celsius), but it often dips into the 40s (single digits Celsius). Some mountain resorts can experience extreme cold—just how you extreme-sportsmen and -women like it.

The Case for Not Going to Spain in Summer

○ **It can cost 50% more to fly** to Spain in summer than it does in late spring and early fall. Hotels also double their prices in July and August.

○ **Air-conditioning is a rare commodity** in Spain. Not many restaurants and bars have it and, worse still, cheap hotels with air-conditioners are pretty much mythical creatures.

○ **The heat.** Big cities full of asphalt and cement can give you a little taste of the soul-stealing that goes on in hell while simultaneously melting the soles of your sneakers.

If summer's the only time you can travel, however, never fear. You can still have a very good time, and here are some tips to make things cooler in the hot, hot sun.

The Case for Going to Spain in Summer

○ **Get thee to the beach!** This is how everyone, since the dawn of time, survives their sweltering cities—by taking a break from them and heading to the sea, so be sure to incorporate one or more beach, lake, or island getaways into your trip. (You'll be on a peninsula; it's going to be hard not to find a place to get wet.) A bit of snorkeling in Cadaqués is surely the best way to recover from when you almost died of asphyxiation in the streets of Figueres.

○ **Get to know the treasures of Spain's churches and museums** (they have A/C or stay naturally cool year-round), and when you have to tour shadeless ruins like the aqueduct in Segovia, avoid the deadly blazing heat of midday by sticking to the early morning or late afternoon. Don't get too ambitious with the sightseeing, and stay hydrated, especially after a night of heavy drinking.

○ **Take advantage of summer festivals,** like Barcelona's *Grec*. Monitor individual city's cultural information on their websites for details on summer-only rock and hip-hop shows at open-air venues.

○ **In August, avoid the cities.** Seriously, it's miserable. During this month, residents flee Madrid and Barcelona, leaving these normally lively places nearly deserted, or worse, only filled with tourists. Party's at the beach, my friend, till the sun rises from the sea, and then some.

Passports & Visas

For up-to-date passport requirement info for American citizens, visit the passport Web page of the U.S. State Department at **http://travel.state.gov**. This site will be your key to updated travel advisory information and passport requirements/application downloads.

If you don't have a passport yet, allow *plenty* of time before your trip to get one; passport processing in the U.S. normally takes 3 weeks but can take longer during busy periods (especially spring). And keep in mind that if you need a passport in a hurry, you'll pay a higher processing fee.

No matter what country you're traveling from, before your trip, make a few copies of the critical front pages of your passport, with your photo, passport number, and issuing agency info. Keep one copy with you, in a separate place from the passport itself—for example, the bottom of your suitcase—and leave a copy with a trusted friend or family member at home. If you lose your passport, you'll need to visit the nearest consulate or embassy of your native country as soon as possible for a replacement. Replacement passports will be issued much more quickly if you have a photocopy of the vital info passport page handy. Note that there are varying requirements to obtain a passport for travelers under the age of 14 and depending on whether you are renewing your passport or applying for one for the first time.

When traveling between destinations (on planes, trains, boats, and so on), safeguard your passport in an inconspicuous, inaccessible place like the inside pocket of your handbag or daypack. When you've arrived at your destination, it's best to stow your passport in the hotel safe. Even if your individual room doesn't have a safe, the reception desk usually does—ask for the *caja fuerte*.

When you clear Customs and immigration at any Spanish airport, your passport should be stamped with an entry date. From the date that's stamped in your passport, most foreign citizens are automatically given a 3-month tourist visa.

What Kind of Traveler Are You?

One of the most important questions to consider is, "What kind of traveler am I?" Even if you have not had a lot of experience with travel, this is something that shouldn't be too difficult to determine based on your daily life and your expectations for your trip. Take a moment to think about the statements below, and you'll pinpoint your traveling persona.

The *Turistón*

I feel like I must see everything I possibly can while in Spain.

I am less focused on historical details, and more interested in grabbing that photo and heading on to the next major attraction.

I am likely to be the first one up in the morning, ready to grab my coffee, and hit the Prado.

I am likely to plan out my stay prior to arriving to maximize my travel route, excursions, and attractions.

If I could have it my way, I would ski the Pyrenees, shop in Barcelona, walk the road to Santiago, grab a souvenir at El Escorial, swing through La Rioja for a glass of wine, run with the bulls in Pamplona, hit the Theater-Museu Dalí in Figueres, tag the beach, and end my trip with a panoramic shot of Montserrat.

I would feel as though I was missing out if I were to take time out for a 3-hour dinner. After resting my feet for a few minutes, I would be anxious to hit the road again and see more sights.

I'll rent a car, but more so because it is a quick way to get to the next city on my itinerary.

Where is the shopping center? I want to see all the stores!

The *Estudioso*

I am likely to study the history behind major Spanish attractions.

When visiting an attraction I ask questions and explore the architect/painter/sculptor behind it all.

When in a museum, I rent the audio tour that explains what I'm seeing.

I am likely to buy a book and read about what I saw upon returning home.

I would prefer to see fewer attractions and hear more details.

I am more likely to study a few paintings that grab me in a museum than skip over them all to get to the *Guernica*.

I prefer to see the city by way of guided tours so I can get the full scoop.

I am likely to wake up early and spend the first hour of my day with a leisurely *chocolate con churros* while planning the day ahead.

I must have a travel book with me so that I can read up on the attractions as I see them.

I prefer to see fewer cities/regions of Spain and spend more time in each.

I'll rent a car to travel to a nearby city, and enjoy the countryside on my way. I can always come back!

The Sensory Wanderer

I am less likely to read up on my city prior to arriving.

I feel that a map is merely a tool to get you home at the end of the day.

I am more focused on the aesthetics of a city and its treasures than its details and history.

I can spend a day in a museum enjoying painting after painting, without the need to memorize who painted them.

I am looking forward to capturing the feel of my destination as opposed to the best photos of its tourism icons.

When choosing a restaurant I walk around in the less touristy part of town until I see something that inspires me.

I would enjoy spending an afternoon of my trip with a bottle of wine and a book in a monastery's garden.

I like to get out of the *centro* and explore the outer limits of the city.

I would like to take a leisurely drive through La Rioja with no particular agenda besides enjoying the countryside.

I am not likely to wait in line at the Prado for 4 hours to see the *Guernica.*

I am more likely to shop when I stumble upon an outdoor market than to hunt down the nearest Adolfo Dominguez store.

The Partier

The first thing I look for in a travel guide is hot clubs and bars.

When packing, I think mostly about what I will be wearing at night.

I would rather stay out late and sleep in. I can see the attractions in the afternoon.

I plan on getting drunk on the plane ride over! I'm on vacation!

I'll have more money for the cover at the club if I don't spend it on entrance to this museum.

I really want to hook up with a Spanish *chico/chica!*

The Spain Lover

I didn't speak Spanish, but started studying when I decided to go to Spain.

I really want to make Spanish friends and let them show me around.

I don't want to go to bars that are going to be filled with Americans.

What do Spaniards do on the weekend?

How do I get away from the tourists?

I would hate to be in a Spanish city in August when everyone is on holiday.

I would prefer an intimate home-stay setup over an impersonal hotel of my own.

I would eat a dinner that goes on for hours in an ancient family-owned restaurant rather than swing by a hot spot in the *centro.*

Now that you've determined the type of travel you will be doing, it's important to think about *who* you will be traveling with. Choosing a travel buddy is a lot like finding a new roommate. Traveling with your closest friend always seems like the best option, but make sure he/she wants to do the same type of things that you do and has the same type of travel style! Your time may be limited, so minimizing potential for debate and conflict is a great way to maximize your experience.

U.S. & Canadian Embassies & Consulates in Spain

Madrid: U.S. Embassy, Serrano 75, 28006 Madrid (☎ **915-872-200;** fax 915-872-303; http://madrid.usembassy.gov). **U.S. Citizen Services** Monday to Friday 8am to 1pm.

Barcelona: U.S. Consulate General, Paseo Reina Elisenda de Montcada 23, 08034 Barcelona (☎ **932-802-227;** fax 932-806-175). **U.S. Citizen Services** Monday to Friday 9am to 1pm.

Seville: U.S. Consulate Agency, Plaza Nueva 8-8 duplicado, 2ª planta, E2, N° 4, 41001 Sevilla (☎ **954-218-751;** fax 954-220-791). **U.S. Citizen Services** Monday to Friday 10am to 1pm.

Valencia: U.S. Consulate Agency, Doctor Romagosa, 1, 2, J, 46002 Valencia (☎ **963-516-973;** fax 963-529-565). **U.S. Citizen Services** Monday to Friday 10am to 1pm.

Las Palmas: U.S. Consulate Agency, Edificio ARCA, Calle Los Martínez Escobar 3, Oficina 7, 35007 Las Palmas (☎ **928-271-259;** fax 928-225-863). **U.S. Citizen Services** Monday to Friday 10am to 1pm.

La Coruña: U.S. Consulate Agency Consular Agency, Cantón Grande 6 – 8°-E, 15003 La Coruña (☎ **981-213-233;** fax 981-228-808). **U.S. Citizen Services** Monday to Friday 10am to 1pm.

Fuengirola (Málaga): U.S. Consulate Agency, Avenida Juan Gómez "Juanito" 8, Edificio Lucía 1°-C, 29640 Fuengirola (Málaga; ☎ **952-474-891;** fax 952-465-189). **U.S. Citizen Services** Monday to Friday 10am to 1pm.

Palma de Mallorca: U.S. Consulate Agency Edificio Reina Constanza, Porto Pi 8, 9D, 07015 Palma de Mallorca (☎ **971-403-707** or 971-403-905; fax 971-403-971). **U.S. Citizen Services** Monday to Friday 10am to 1:30pm.

The **Canadian Consulate** in Barcelona is at Elisenda de Pinos 10 (☎ **932-042-700**). The **Canadian Embassy** in Madrid is Goya Building, 35 Nuñez de Balboa (☎ **914-233-250**). The **Canadian Consulate** in Málaga is at Horizonte Building, Plaza de la Malagueta 2, First Floor (☎ **952-223-346**).

FOR RESIDENTS OF AUSTRALIA You can pick up an application from your local post office or any branch of Passports Australia, but you must schedule an interview at the passport office to present your application materials. Call the **Australian Passport Information Serv-ice** at ☎ 131-232, or visit the government website at www.passports.gov.au.

FOR RESIDENTS OF CANADA Passport applications are available at travel agencies throughout Canada or from the central **Passport Office,** Department of Foreign Affairs and International Trade, Ottawa, ON K1A 0G3 (☎ **800/567-6868;** www.ppt.gc.ca).

FOR RESIDENTS OF IRELAND You can apply for a 10-year passport at the **Passport Office,** Setanta Centre, Molesworth Street, Dublin 2 (☎ **01/671-1633;** www.irlgov.ie/iveagh). Those under age 18 and over 65 must apply for a €12 3-year passport. You can also apply at 1A South Mall, Cork (☎ **021/272-525**), or at most main post offices.

FOR RESIDENTS OF NEW ZEALAND
You can pick up a passport application at any New Zealand Passports Office or download it from their website. Contact the **Passports Office** at ☎ **0800/225-050** in New Zealand or 04/474-8100, or log on to www.passports.govt.nz.

FOR RESIDENTS OF THE UNITED KINGDOM
To pick up an application for a standard 10-year passport (5-year passport for children under 16), visit your nearest passport office, major post office, or travel agency or contact the **United Kingdom Passport Service** at ☎ **0870/521-0410** or search its website at www.ukpa.gov.uk.

WHAT IF I WANT TO STAY LONGER?
If your plans do change midstream (for example, you started out in Spain with purely touristic intentions but then decided to stay longer for Spanish language classes or bullfighting school or whatever), you should apply for a *prórroga de estancia* at the main police station *(comisaría)* or foreign offices *(oficina de extranjeros)* of the nearest major city. The immigration line is bureaucracy at its most convoluted—and filled with remarkable immigrants who just brought the whole family from Bangladesh in hopes of a better life. In your quest for a *prórroga,* you'll end up making several early-morning trips back to the *comisaría,* as no one can ever seem to assemble all the required documentation on their first try.

For your *prórroga* to be processed, you'll need a very good reason that justifies the extension, proof that you have enough money to sustain yourself for the period of the extension, proof of medical insurance for said period, and proof of return flight back home (a non-changeable plane ticket). Getting a work permit

Planning for a Longer Stay . . . before You Leave
If you're planning to stay in Spain for more than 3 months, and you want to do it legally, you'll need a proper visa. To get one of these, you must appear in person at a Spanish consulate in your home country with required documentation (Spanish-government-approved letters of employment, or letters of enrollment in Spain-based study programs) to obtain either a work visa or a study visa, good for anywhere from 3 months to 2 years. Visit **www.spainemb.org** or contact your local Spanish consulate for further information on obtaining a visa.

involves a lot of red tape, a company willing to sponsor you, and going back to the States to get your visa in a process that can last 4 months to a year. Student visas are easier to get, but still involve going back home to get the stamp.

Customs Info
WHAT CAN I TAKE WITH ME?
You can bring into Spain most personal effects and the following items duty free: one video camera or two still cameras with 10 rolls of film each. One portable radio, one tape recorder, and one laptop PC per person are admitted free of duty provided they show signs of use; 400 cigarettes, or 50 cigars, or 250 grams of tobacco are admitted; and 2 liters of wine or 1 liter of liquor per person over 17 years of age are admitted. For sports equipment you are allowed fishing gear, one bicycle, skis, tennis or squash rackets, and golf clubs.

THE BASICS

ᴍᴛᴠ🖑 Study Abroad

Salminter, Calle Toro 25, 37002 Salamanca (☎ **923-211-808;** www.salminter. com), conducts courses in conversational Spanish, with optional courses in business Spanish, translation techniques, and Spanish culture. Classes have a 10-person maximum. Courses are offered in 2-week, 1-month, and 3-month increments, at seven progressive levels. The school can arrange housing with Spanish families or in furnished apartments shared with other students.

Another good source of information about courses in Spain is the **American Institute for Foreign Study (AIFS),** River Plaza, 9 W. Broad St., Stamford, CT 06902-3788 (☎ **866/906-2437;** www.aifs.com). This organization can set up transportation and arrange for summer courses, with bed and board included. It can help you arrange study programs at either the University of Salamanca, one of Europe's oldest academic centers, the University of Granada, or Pompeu Fabra University in Barcelona.

The biggest organization dealing with higher education in Europe is the **Institute of International Education (IIE),** 809 United Nations Plaza, New York, NY 10017 (☎ **212/883-8200;** www.iie.org). A few of its booklets are free, but its more definitive (and pricey) works such as *Academic Year Abroad* are available at many university libraries or foreign studies departments.

One well-recommended clearinghouse is the **National Registration Center for Study Abroad (NRCSA),** 823 N. 2nd St., P.O. Box 1393, Milwaukee, WI 53201 (☎ **414/278-0631;** www.nrcsa.com). The organization maintains language-study programs in 14 cities throughout Spain. Most popular among university students are the org's programs in Sevilla, Barcelona, and Madrid. Lodgings in private homes are included as part of the intensive experience.

A clearinghouse for information on at least nine different Spain-based language schools is **Lingua Service Worldwide,** 75 Prospect St., Suite 4, Huntington, NY 11743 (☎ **800/394-5327** or 631/424-0777; www.linguaservice worldwide.com), which represents organizations devoted to the teaching of Spanish language and culture in almost two dozen cities in Spain.

For more information about study abroad, contact the **Council on International Educational Exchange (CIEE),** 7 Custom House St., Third Floor, Portland, ME 04101 (☎ **800/40-STUDY** or 207-553-7600; www.ciee.org).

WHAT CAN I BRING HOME WITH ME?

U.S. Citizens

Returning U.S. citizens who have been away for at least 48 hours are allowed to bring back, once every 30 days, $800 worth of merchandise duty-free. You'll pay a flat rate of duty on the next $1,000 worth of purchases. Any dollar amount beyond that is subject to duties at whatever rates apply. On mailed gifts, the duty-free limit is $200. Be sure to keep your receipts or

purchases accessible to expedite the declaration process. *Note:* If you owe duty, you are required to pay on your arrival in the United States—either by cash or check, and, in some locations, a Visa or MasterCard.

To avoid paying duty on foreign-made personal items you owned before your trip (like your laptop), bring along a bill of sale or receipts of purchase. Or you can register items that can be readily identified by a permanently affixed serial number or marking—think laptop computers, cameras, and iPods—with Customs before you leave. Take the items to the nearest Customs office or register them with Customs at the airport from which you're departing. You'll receive, at no cost, a Certificate of Registration, which allows duty-free entry for the life of the item.

For specifics on what you can bring back and the corresponding fees, download the invaluable free pamphlet *Know Before You Go* online at **www.cbp.gov**. (Click on "Travel," and then click on "Know Before You Go! Online Brochure.") Or contact the **U.S. Customs & Border Protection (CBP),** 1300 Pennsylvania Ave. NW, Washington, DC 20229 (☎ **877/287-8667**), and request the pamphlet.

Canadian Citizens

For a clear summary of Canadian rules, write for the booklet *I Declare,* issued by the **Canada Border Services Agency** (☎ **800/461-9999** in Canada, or 204/983-3500; **www.cbsa-asfc.gc.ca**).

U.K. Citizens

For information, contact **HM Customs & Excise** at ☎ **0845/010-9000** (from outside the U.K., 020/8929-0152), or consult their website at **www.hmce.gov.uk**.

Australian Citizens

A helpful brochure available from Australian consulates or Customs offices is *Know Before You Go.* For more information, call the **Australian Customs Service** at ☎ **1300/363-263,** or log on to **www.customs.gov.au**.

New Zealand Citizens

Most questions are answered in a free pamphlet available at New Zealand consulates and Customs offices: *New Zealand Customs Guide for Travellers, Notice no. 4.* For more information, contact **New Zealand Customs,** The Customhouse, 17–21 Whitmore St., Box 2218, Wellington (☎ **04/473-6099** or 0800/428-786; **www.customs.govt.nz**).

Money Money Money Money (Money!)

Old Spaniards will cry a lot about how in Spain you could have a meal for half a dollar. Those were the good old days, and now Spain is no longer that cheap. In major cities you'll find that accommodations are not a lot cheaper than in London or Paris. Of course, drop off the tourist radar and you'll see how quickly prices plummet. All in all, Spain is still a little bit under other European destinations like England or France. Since 2002, the official currency has been the euro (€), which is the standard currency in all European Economic Community countries—for more information, visit **http://europa.eu.int/euro/entry.html**.

Yes, the old pesetas are gone. So be careful with anyone trying to get a last profit on grandma's savings at the expense of imprudent tourists! There are eight euro coins in circulation, ranging from 1 cent pieces to 2€ coins, as well as seven different euro bills from 5€ to 500€. Every country in the European Economic Community mints its own euro coins (which are standardized in color and shape, but differentiated by images of national landmarks or historical figures on the reverse), so you might come across a French or German 2€ coin here and there, but for the most part, euro coins tend to stay in their country of origin. All euro coins, regardless of the country where they were minted, are good throughout the EEC. At the time of writing, US$1 is approximately .78€; and 1€ is $1.28. This

What to Bring . . . & What to Pack It In!

"Backpacker" is a figurative term. You can be a young, carefree, budget-oriented traveler even if you drag a rolling suitcase. In most cases, a rolling bag is just as convenient to carry around as a backpack, if not more so, and it can be easier to keep organized. However, when it comes to climbing stairs or navigating rough terrain and covering longer distances on foot, the classic backpack can't be beat.

To maximize the space in any bag, the key words are **rolling** and **compartmentalizing.** Rolling your clothes will keep you more space-efficient and you'll fit more. As for compartmentalizing, you want to be able to access those things that you need most, more readily, and others not so much. Put toiletries, and so on, near the top or in their own compartment. Keep film, camera, and so on, in a separate compartment that is easily accessible, and, for the love of God, make sure you have a separate compartment for dirty clothes. Another thing to keep in mind is that **you don't have to look like a schlep to be a backpacker!** Nice(r) clothes don't necessarily take up more room, so ditch the hiking boots and pack some wrinkle-free clothes so that you can look presentable when you hit the town.

The reality is, unless you're taking an adventure/eco-tourism trip, you won't *really* be hiking too much. Mostly, you'll be traipsing around cities where the locals look effortlessly chic year-round. And you'll want to keep up with the Joneses (or Espinozas), at least a little bit.

Lastly, we all know that shoes can take up the most room in our bags. Keep in mind when choosing a backpack that there are straps on the outside for larger items such as shoes, sweatshirts, coats, and blankets. Regardless of whatever else you pack, you'll want that favorite, flattering pair of jeans; trendy sneakers (comfortable but cool); comfy, nonskimpy sleepwear (for those shared hostel rooms); and a pair of rubber flip-flops for the shared bathrooms and showers you'll encounter at hostels and other budget hotels.

Keep the inside of your bag free for anything fragile that you might need to insulate with protective packing. And remember: Since you may want to bring

will fluctuate, of course, so make sure to check the exchange rates at **www.oanda. com/convert/classic** to see how your money will hold up during your stay in Spain. Europe is not exactly cheap right now, so make sure you budget accordingly. It is all too easy to think that US$1 is *more or less* equal to 1€ and get yourself into trouble. Trust me, those decimals make a big difference.

Cash

Except at hotels, fancier restaurants, and mass retailers, cash is still the preferred method of payment throughout Spain. Most smaller hotels, restaurants, and boutiques will accept credit cards (or debit cards with the Visa or MasterCard symbol), and they're used to dealing with tourists who only have plastic, but they'll love you forever if you can flash some cash. However, carrying mass quantities of cash in heavily touristed Spanish cities is neither smart nor practical. So, use your card where you can—just be prepared for a little attitude from time to time (as well as the all-too-common "our credit card machine is out of order" line).

a few things home, it doesn't hurt to leave a few compartments empty or pack a collapsible empty bag for the goodies. And if you arrive in Spain and realize you forgot to pack socks, never fear: There are plenty of places to shop here!

What to Bring

→ Clothes that suit the season and your activities. Check the weather, but the key here is comfortable city clothes, not summer camp gear (unless you're hiking the Pyrenees or spending the whole trip on the beach).

→ Comfortable shoes and sandals. You'll be doing a ton of walking.

→ Camera and memory card. Film and batteries can be easily purchased in Spain.

→ Digital-camera link for downloading your photos onto your iPod (check for compatibility).

→ Extra bag to bring stuff home in.

→ Electrical plug adapter (for computers and iPod, camera, and cellphone chargers).

→ Basic medicine kit.

→ Copies of your prescriptions for medicines you take regularly.

→ Sunblock, sunglasses, and hat.

→ A change of clothes (or at least a clean T-shirt and underwear) in your carry-on bag. (Luggage frequently misses its flight when you're connecting through another European airport.)

→ Passport (and visa if necessary).

→ ATM and/or credit cards, and some cash to keep you going upon arrival.

→ Driver's license or driving permit (in case you decide to rent that Vespa after all).

THE BASICS

That said, you will definitely need to have cash on hand for the following: local public transportation (including buses and taxis), museum and monument admissions, on-the-go snacks and drinks, and other small incidentals like postcards and postage. When you do get cash from the Spanish ATM (see next section), try to break down the 50€ and 100€ notes into smaller bills as soon as possible. (Museum admissions and restaurant checks are good for this.) The quickest way to piss off a small business cashier is to present a 50€ bill when paying for a 2€ beer. Yes, it's

the banks' own fault for not stocking their ATMs with smaller denomination bills, but bars (and other places where nothing costs more than a few euros) hate to be in the business of making change for tourists. If you have no choice, just be as apologetic as you can, and they'll accommodate you (albeit begrudgingly).

ATMs

The easiest and best way to get cash when you're in Spain is from a local ATM. ATMs are all over Spain, and nearly every bank card in the world can be used to withdraw

From Cheap to Splurge . . . from Low Rent to Top Euro

Throughout the book we divide the hostels/hotels and restaurants by price range, from "Cheap" to "Doable" to "Splurge."

You know what your budget is, and what's important for you to experience on your trip, so you can plan accordingly.

And even if most of your nights will be spent in hostels or budget hotels, and your meals consist of *bocadillos* and tapas, we also think you should budget for, and treat yourself to, something deluxe you *know* you will enjoy, whether it's a meal at a world-class restaurant, or a night in a grande dame hotel. A constant stream of second-class travel, shared bathrooms, and meals consumed standing up can wear you out, and keep you from enjoying *el sol de España* as you should.

Here is a very general price range for each category (and prices can, of course, vary widely depending upon what city or town you are in, the season, and even the day of the week):

Accommodations
Hostel: Dorm-style, 17€–25€; single/double/triple, 30€–75€

Cheap: Single, 20€–60€; double, 40€–100€; triple/quad, 60€–150€

Doable: Single, 75€–120€; double, 80€–200€; triple/quad/suite, 150€–300€

Splurge: Single, 150€ and up; double, 200€ and up; triple/quad/suite, 300€–1,000€ and (way) up

Meals (not including wine)
Cheap: 5€–15€

Doable: Lunch 7€–20€; dinner 10€–25€

Splurge: Lunch 15€–25€; dinner 25€–50€ and up

cash as long as you have a compatible PIN (many ATMs in Europe require a four-digit PIN). If you're unsure, check with your bank, and while you're at it, inquire about your daily withdrawal limit. Truth be told, we've never changed money before landing on Spanish turf, and the first Spanish ATM we've encountered has usually worked fine, but you can spare yourself that unpleasant suspense of wondering whether your ATM card will work abroad by exchanging at least some money—just enough euros to cover airport incidentals and transportation to your hotel—before you leave. (Just don't expect the exchange

rate to be ideal.) If you decide to go that route, you can exchange dollars for euros at your local American Express or Thomas Cook office, or at your bank.

American Express also dispenses traveler's checks and foreign currency via www.americanexpress.com or ☎ **800/ 807-6233,** but they'll charge a $15 order fee and additional shipping costs, and nobody really uses traveler's checks anymore anyway—in fact, fewer and fewer places of business accept them. You can also just bring $100 or so cash in your wallet, so that if—God forbid—all your cards get demagnetized or your bank's computer

What Things Cost in Spain

As you'll see in this handy box, the cheapest way to fill your stomach is with a tortilla, and the cheapest way to get drunk is with wine or canned beer. As an added bonus, a ton of world-class art and architecture can be seen for free.

Café con leche + pastry	2€	Plate of paella*	8€–15€
Bus/metro ticket	1.10€	Main meat or fish dish*	6€–15€
Monuments and museums	Free; or 2€–5€	Gelato cup or cone	1.50€–3€
Small bottle of water	.80€	Caña of beer	1€
Can of soda	1€	Pint of beer	3€–4€
Tortilla sandwich (takeout)	1.50€–3€	Glass of wine*	1.50€–4€
Tapas	1.50€–8€	Cocktails*	4€–10€
		Postcard + int'l postage	1.15€

*(*prices can go a lot higher at fancy establishments)*

THE BASICS

system crashes, you can exchange U.S. dollars for euros at the airport to tide you over. If you never need the $100, you'll be that much richer when you get back to the States.

Because your bank will impose a fee of 1% plus $1 to $5 or more every time you withdraw from an international ATM (and the bank from which you withdraw cash may charge its own fee), be strategic about how much you withdraw and how often. (The minimum withdrawal is usually 20€; the maximum is usually 300€.) Start by withdrawing, say, 200€ or 250€ at the airport or train station, and see how much of that you're spending on average per day. If you're using a credit or debit card to pay for your bigger-ticket expenses like hotel bills and restaurant meals, you may well find that you only need to make two or three trips to the ATM (spending $15–$25 in fees) over the course of a 10-day trip to Spain.

You can also use your credit card to receive cash advances at foreign ATMs, again, provided you have a compatible PIN (see "Credit Cards" section below). And do

keep in mind that you'll pay interest from the moment of your withdrawal, even if you pay your monthly bills on time.

Credit Cards

Credit cards are another safe way to carry money. They also provide a convenient record of all your expenses, and they generally offer relatively good exchange rates. You can also withdraw cash advances from your credit cards at banks or ATMs, provided you know your PIN. If you don't know yours, call the number on the back of your credit card and ask the bank to send it to you. It usually takes 5 to 7 business days, though some banks will provide the number over the phone if you tell them your mother's maiden name, the last four digits of your Social, and whether or not you laugh (or cry) when you watch the ending of *Dirty Dancing*.

MasterCard and Visa are commonly accepted in Spain, and as in the U.S., most storefronts will post the logos of the cards they accept in the windows. Do note, however, that small businesses in Spain (even in big cities) far prefer cash payment (they have to pay a fee for card transactions) and will often lie about their credit card machine being out of order if they sense that you have enough cash to cover the purchase. If you really need to use the card, stand your ground, and you'll be amazed how quickly these credit card machines can spontaneously fix themselves! Deep down, shopkeepers know that the rest of the world's money is card-based, and they'd rather not lose the sale altogether. *Note:* In the case that no credit cards are accepted by a certain establishment, we'll note it for you next to the prices.

Keep in mind that many banks now assess a 1% to 3% "transaction fee" on all charges you incur abroad (whether you're charged in local currency or U.S. dollars). But credit cards still may be the smart way to go when you factor in things like exorbitant ATM fees and the higher exchange rates and service fees you'll pay with traveler's checks.

Traveler's Checks

Back before international ATMs and global bank networks, and when Pan Am was still in business, there were these quaint things called traveler's checks. (Ask your grandparents to explain.) When you had an upcoming trip abroad (or even out-of-state), you'd go to your bank or American Express office and buy these checks in set denominations (of $20 or $50, usually), and then bring them with you on vacation. You could use them to pay for things like train travel and hotel bills, or you could trade them in during shop hours for cash at the local bank or Amex office in your destination. Because the traveler's checks were numbered and protected, even if you lost them or they were stolen, your money would be protected.

Change Is Good!

When you change money, ask for some small bills (5€, 10€, and 20€) or loose change (1€ and 2€ coins). Petty cash will come in handy all the time in Spain. Consider keeping the smaller bills separate from your larger bills, so that they're readily accessible and you'll be less vulnerable to pickpockets.

Well, guess what? Good ol' traveler's checks are still out there! Nowadays, they're less widely accepted at hotels and other businesses, but the fundamental idea behind traveler's checks is still a good one: You can cash them as you go along, and your money is protected in case of loss or theft of the checks. And given the fees you'll pay for ATM use at banks other than your own, this old-fashioned method of carrying money on the road maybe isn't such a crazy idea.

If you want to go old school, you can get traveler's checks at almost any bank. **American Express** offers denominations of $20, $50, $100, $500, and (for cardholders only) $1,000. You'll pay a service charge ranging from 1% to 4%. You can also order American Express traveler's checks over the phone by calling ☎ **800/221-7282;** Amex gold and platinum cardholders who use this number are exempt from the 1% fee.

Visa offers traveler's checks at Citibank locations nationwide, as well as at several other banks. The service charge ranges between 1.5% and 2%; checks come in denominations of $20, $50, $100, $500, and $1,000. Call ☎ **800/732-1322** for information. **AAA** members can obtain Visa checks for a $9.95 fee (for checks up to $1,500) at most AAA offices or by calling ☎ **866/**

Cuidado! It's Not a Handful of Change, It's a LOT of Money!

With common denominations like .50€, 1€, and 2€, those euro coins in your pocket can add up to a lot of "real" money. It's certainly a beautiful thing that you can pay for a glass of wine in many places with a single 2€ coin, but if you let yourself be brainwashed into thinking, "It's just a coin," you might suddenly find that you've spent the next several days' food budget. Take it from us: It can happen alarmingly fast when happy hour has no clear start or end time!

339-3378. **MasterCard** also offers traveler's checks. Call ☎ **800/223-9920** for a location near you.

Foreign currency traveler's checks might be useful when traveling to Spain as they're accepted at locations where dollar checks may not be, such as bed-and-breakfasts, and they minimize the currency conversions you'll have to perform while you're on the go. American Express, Thomas Cook, Visa, and MasterCard offer foreign currency traveler's checks. You'll pay the rate of exchange at the time of your purchase (so it's a good idea to monitor the rate before you buy), and most companies charge a transaction fee per order (and a shipping fee if you order online).

Getting There

We've said it before: Madrid is Spain's heart, so you'll almost certainly mainline straight into there. From Madrid there are connecting planes to every airport in Spain. Nevertheless, if you mistrust connections, you can get a nonstop flight to Barcelona as well as Málaga. Girona is also an airport where you could arrive, that is, if you are flying with Ryanair from departure cities elsewhere in Europe.

All major flights from North America to continental Europe are overnight flights; flight time from anywhere on the East Coast of the U.S. is about 7 hours. Because most hotels and hostels won't let you check in until lunchtime or later, try to book a flight that arrives in Spain in the mid- or late morning. If you arrive at 7 or 8am, you'll have several uncomfortable hours before you can shower, change, and freshen up. As for the trip back, flights from Spain to the U.S. depart in the late morning or early afternoon. Do your best to book a return flight that leaves at 10am or later—remember that you'll probably

need to arrive 2 to 3 hours before your flight is scheduled to depart in order to secure your seat, and the only way to get to the airport in the early morning is by taxi, which is much more expensive than the airport train or bus services, which don't start running 'til 6:30am or so.

Airfare to Spain is highest in the summer (June–Aug) and lowest from November to March (with the exception of the Christmas and Easter periods, which fall in late Dec and some time between Mar and Apr, respectively).

Daily nonstop flights to Spain depart from New York (Newark and JFK), Philadelphia, Washington, D.C. (Dulles), Miami, and Atlanta. If you're coming from the West or Midwest, common practice is to change planes at one of those airports on the eastern seaboard before crossing the Atlantic to Madrid.

Whatever you do, you'll want to **maximize your time on international segments,** since that's where the movies and the alcohol are free (and sometimes even video games), the cabins are more comfortable, and the flight attendants are cooler and better looking.

For those whose trips originate on the East Coast, keep in mind that nonstop flights to Spain don't cost much more than flights that connect through a European hub like London, Paris, Frankfurt, Amsterdam, or Munich. So, if at all possible, we recommend that you go nonstop from the U.S.: You'll obviously get there faster (and get a decent night's sleep, if sleeping on planes is one of your talents), and you'll eliminate the risk of your luggage not making its connection at Heathrow (all too common, unfortunately).

Booking Your Flight Online

Of the big online travel agencies—Expedia.com, Travelocity, and Orbitz—we've had the best experiences with **Orbitz.** (Priceline has also come through for us more than once.) We also like **Kayak.com,** an under-the-radar travel-booking site that uses a sophisticated search engine (developed at MIT). Each has different business deals with the airlines and many offer different fares on the same flights, so take the time to shop around. Open several Web browsers at once and do side-by-side searches for the same destination and dates, and you'll get a feel for how different sites behave. A nice feature of Expedia.com, Kayak, and Travelocity is that you can sign up for e-mail notification when a cheap fare becomes available to your favorite destination. Also check out **johnnyjet.com,** which has loads of travel tips and links to airline booking and flying-related resources, but also fun things like a webcam of the week, a blog, and, oddly, a tribute to his mom.

Remember to check the **individual websites** for those carriers that fly from

Getting Money from Home (Quickly!)

If your pocket is picked, if you blow your budget, or if you just need more money in a hurry, you can have funds sent to you by a money-wiring service like **Western Union** (often attached to phone or Internet centers that serve the city's immigrant population) or a financial services institution like **American Express,** which has offices in major Spanish cities. For Western Union, scan the streets around the train station for a shop front bearing the Western Union sticker, and go in and inquire about the procedure. You can then relay a message to your parents (or whomever) by phone or e-mail from that same shop.

the U.S. to Spain; they sometimes have online offers that you won't get in the online search sites—Iberia (www.iberia.com), Air Europa (www.air-europa.com), American (www.aa.com), Continental (www.continental.com), Delta (www.delta.com), United (www.united.com), and US Airways (www.usairways.com). The fares at the airlines' own sites can often be shockingly high, too. If you come across a $2,000 fare, don't give up hope; the same flight on Orbitz might only cost $700.

If you want to get really creative (and you don't mind changing planes several times), you can scout out **low-fare carriers** such as Southwest (www.southwest.com), JetBlue (www.jetblue.com), AirTran (www.airtran.com), WestJet (www.westjet.com), easyJet (www.easyjet.com), Ryanair (www.ryanair.com), Vueling (www.vueling.com), Transavia (www.transavia.com), German Wings (www.germanwings.com),

cuidado! ATM is for Monster

ATMs in Spain will usually hold your card during the beginning of your transaction, returning them before giving you the money. This is great, because it's really hard to forget your card this way, but there are some that'll only give you your card back once the money is in your hands, like Citibank, for example. After a few times receiving card and then money it is stupidly easy to forget the card when the ATM works the other way around, spitting out your money, which you just grab and go. Then, after a few idle moments with the card dangling on its lip, the machine will eat your card, passing it on to a bank employee for shredding. And, mark my words, it will be shredded—no matter how nicely you beg them to give it back.

and Air Nostrum (www.airnostrum.com), which can take care of your short hops in North America and Europe but not the transatlantic leg of your trip. Travel websites that work with these carriers, are TerminalA.com and Edreams.com. It won't hurt to check them out.

Great last-minute deals (for example, half of what you'd pay by booking in advance) are often available through free weekly e-mail services provided directly by the airlines. Most of these are announced on Tuesday or Wednesday and must be purchased online. Most are only valid for travel that weekend, but some (such as British Airways) can be booked weeks or months in advance. Sign up for weekly e-mail alerts at airline websites or check megasites that compile compre-

hensive lists of last-minute specials, such as **Smarter Travel** (www.smartertravel.com). For last-minute trips, **www.site 59.com** and **http://us.lastminute.com** often have amazing air-and-hotel package deals, for much less than the major-label sites (however, 90% of the hotels they offer are located miles from the heart of town).

If you're willing to relinquish some control over your flight details, use what is called an "opaque" ('cuz you can't see the details 'til after you buy) fare service like **Priceline**'s "Name-Your-Own-Price" feature (www.priceline.com). Opaque travel sites offer rock-bottom prices in exchange for travel on a "mystery airline" at a mysterious time of day, often with a mysterious change of planes en route. The mystery airlines are all major, well-known carriers. And, if you're not as flexible (or daring) with your travel plans, Priceline does offer specific fares for specific flights. If you do decide to see how low you can go, first visit **BiddingForTravel** (www.biddingfortravel.com) an online forum of experienced travel bidders that help demystify Priceline's inner workings and offer strategic advice on how to get the best fare.

Other Cash-Saving Travel Ideas

- Keep an eye on the travel section of your local newspaper/s for promotional specials or fare wars, when airlines lower prices on their most popular routes. You rarely see fare wars at peak travel times, but if you can travel in the off-peak months, you may snag a bargain.
- Several reliable consolidators are worldwide and available online. **STA Travel** (☎ **800/781-4040;** www.

THE BASICS

Cuidado! Dear Visa, the Balearics Await Me . . .

Banks and credit card companies often freeze accounts for suspicious activity (for example, a 250€ withdrawal from the Caixa at the Madrid Barajas airport when your usual activity is a $3.25 Starbucks charge in San Francisco), so before you leave home, make sure you call your bank or credit card company and let them know of your upcoming trip. Have the phone rep make a detailed note of when and where you'll be abroad so that your card doesn't get denied when you're trying to buy that amazing pair of boots in Barcelona. If you don't call your credit card company in advance, you can still call the card's toll-free emergency number if a charge is refused—provided you remember to carry the phone number with you—but it usually takes 24 hours for your account to be reactivated. Perhaps the most important lesson here is to carry more than one card so you have a backup.

statravel.com) is the world's top consolidator for students, but their fares are competitive for travelers of all ages. **ELTExpress** (☎ 800/TRAV-800; www.flights.com) has excellent fares worldwide, particularly to Europe. They also have "local" websites in 12 countries.

ECONOMY-CLASS SURVIVAL TIPS

Air travel is one of the last bastions of segregation—if you stop and think about it, the blatant classism in the skies is really pretty shocking. While expense accounters and hip-hop artists are maxin' and relaxin' up in the front of the plane, the rest of us are stuck in coach or economy— mere euphemisms for the cramped, stuffy, and downright inhumane conditions airlines subject the unwashed masses (that is, me and you) to. Okay, I'm exaggerating, but unless you're flying first or business class, you will feel like a faceless wretch in an airborne herd of cattle fighting over elbow room on long-haul flights. But with a little advance planning, you can make an otherwise unpleasant experience almost bearable.

○ **Know the layout:** Your choice of airline and airplane will affect your comfort and amenities. Boeing 747s and 777s are much roomier than 767s, for example. All passengers on 777s have their own TV screen and controls for movies and games. Older aircraft models only have a few TV screens hung every 10 rows or so in the center aisle, which makes for difficult viewing. Find more details at **www.seatguru.com**, which has extensive details about almost every seat on six major U.S. airlines. For international airlines, research firm Skytrax has posted a list of average seat pitches at www.airlinequality.com.

○ **Emergency exit seats and bulkhead** seats typically have the most legroom. Emergency exit seats are usually left unassigned until the day of a flight (to ensure that someone able-bodied fills them); it's worth getting to the ticket counter early to snag one of these spots for a long flight. Many passengers find that bulkhead seating (the row facing the walls at the front of each cabin section) offers more legroom, but keep in mind that bulkheads are where airlines often put baby bassinets, so you may be sitting next to a screaming infant for

Traveler's Reality Check

If you do choose to carry traveler's checks, the key is to keep a record of their serial numbers *separate* from your checks in the event that they are stolen or lost. You'll get a refund faster if you know the numbers.

9 hours while you enjoy all that extra legroom.

○ **To have two seats for yourself** in a three-seat row, try for an aisle seat in a center section toward the back of coach. If you're traveling with a companion, book an aisle and a window seat. Middle seats are usually booked last, so chances are good you'll end up with three seats to yourselves. And in the event that a third passenger is assigned the middle seat, he or she will probably be more than happy to trade for a window or an aisle.

○ **If you're intent on getting some sleep,** avoid the last row of any section or the row in front of an emergency exit, as these seats are the least likely to recline. Avoid seats near highly trafficked and potentially smelly toilet areas, which also tend to be noisy as people hang out and chat as they wait for the loo. Avoid seats in the back of many jets—these can be narrower than those in the rest of coach. You also may want to reserve a window seat so you can rest your head and avoid being bumped in the aisle. If you have trouble falling asleep on planes, pop a Benadryl (it works for some people!) or ask your doctor for a sleeping pill (like Ambien or Lunesta) or sedative (like Valium or Xanax) to help you chill out (be sure to bring a prescription with you as well if

you are staying awhile and might need a refill). As a sleep and jet-lag aid, melatonin caplets—available over-thecounter at any drug store or herbalist—also work well for many travelers.

○ **Get up, walk around, and stretch** every 60 to 90 minutes to keep your blood flowing. This helps avoid "economy-class syndrome" and may prevent you from stabbing your snoring neighbor with your dinner spork. Other preventive measures include drinking lots of water and avoiding alcohol. See "When Your Body's Still in Another Time Zone," p. 47.

○ **Hydrate.** Drink water before, during, and after your flight to combat the lack of humidity in airplane cabins—which can be drier than the Sahara. Bring a bottle of water on board, and make frequent trips aft to the galley (the airplane's rear kitchen) where most airlines have a self-service mineral water and orange juice station set up for passengers throughout the flight.

○ **Detox.** Eat healthy, light portions (that is, about half of what they serve you) and minimize your alcohol and caffeine intake. Air travel is stressful enough without having to deal with bloating and palpitations. Think of your flight as a healthy detox, and you'll arrive at your destination feeling surprisingly fresh even if you're somewhat sleepdeprived.

○ **Roll the dice for an upgrade.** At check-in, turn on the self-deprecating charm and ask about any free upgrades to business class they might feel like offering little old you. Hey, don't laugh—I've gotten lucky twice using this stratagem. Madrid is not an especially big business destination, so many of those VIP seats in the front of the plane need to be filled at the last minute.

THE BASICS

Before You Leave

The Checklist!

Here are a few things you might want to do before you walk out the door to ensure the most efficient and drama-free trip to Spain. We all love the idea of packing a bag and heading to the beaches, but it never hurts to take a moment and check into the details.

→ Do you have the address and phone number of Spain's U.S. embassy and consulates? There are consulates in Madrid and Barcelona and a U.S. embassy in Madrid. There's a list of addresses/phone numbers of the consulates on p. 26, earlier in this chapter, or you can visit http://madrid. usembassy.gov/cons/offices.html.

→ Do you need to book any museum, theater, or special travel in advance? Almost all tourist attractions have websites—it never hurts to check 'em out!

→ How's the weather? Is it 100°F (38°C) in Seville? Is it raining in San Sebastián? Obsessively log on to weather.com every day for 2 weeks before your trip and be sure to pack accordingly.

→ Did you check to make sure all of your favorite hot spots and tourist destinations are open? Is The *Guernica* being restored? Is the Sagrada Familia still under construction? Did they find new drawings in the caves of Altamira? You never know!

→ Have you checked the current exchange rate at www.oanda.com?

→ Did you find out your daily ATM withdrawal limit? Do you have your credit card PINs? If you have a five- or six-digit PIN, did you obtain a four-digit number from your bank?

Staying There

Read this section carefully: Knowing the lay of the accommodations land in Spain (and being a bit anal about it) will be one of the most important factors in making your trip a stress-free success.

From castles converted into hotels to basic hostels overlooking the Mediterranean, Spain has some of the most varied accommodations in the world—with equally varied price ranges. After reviewing the basic definitions below, you'll want to check out our listings within each city as well. Accommodations are broadly classified as follows:

One- to Five-Star Hotels

The Spanish government rates hotels by according them stars, from one to five, with five being at the high end of the scale. A one- or two-star hotel is relatively inexpensively priced, but there are plenty of other types of accommodations available that may be even less expensive (see below). Note: The government grants stars based on such amenities as elevators, private bathrooms, and air-conditioning. If a hotel is classified as a *residencia,* it means that it serves breakfast (usually) but no other meals.

→ Did you notify your bank/credit card companies that you will be traveling overseas to avoid automatic account freezes for suspicious activity?

→ Do you have the credit card with which your ticket was purchased? Do you have your frequent-flyer card or number for the airline you'll be traveling with or their partner airline (for example, Iberia is partnered with American Airlines, Qantas, Aer Lingus, and British Airways)?

→ If you purchased traveler's checks, have you recorded the check numbers, and stored the documentation separately from the checks?

→ Did you pack your camera, an extra set of batteries/charger, and enough film/memory?

→ Do you have an international power converter to charge your iPod and other electronics?

→ Do you have a safe, accessible place to store money?

→ Did you bring any ID cards that could entitle you to discounts, such as student ID cards, ISIC cards, and so on, as well as your driver's license for any car or scooter rentals?

→ Did you bring emergency drug prescriptions and extra glasses and/or contact lenses?

→ Did you leave a copy of your itinerary with someone at home in case you decide to reenact the plot of *Turistas* on La Jungla in Madrid's Parque de Atracciones?

→ If using a mobile phone from the U.S., did you check to make sure it can make/receive calls to/from Spain? Did you check into international long-distance rates with your carrier?

THE BASICS

Hostales

The most common type of accommodation in Spain are *hostales,* which shouldn't be confused with hostel, in English. A *hostal* is a modest hotel without services, where you can save money by carrying your own bags and the like. You'll know it's a *hostal* if a small s follows the capital letter H on the blue plaque by the door. The term *hostal* actually implies a standard higher than what we think of when we hear hostel; for example, a *hostal* with three stars is about the equivalent of a hotel with two stars. *Hostales* usually entail a story or two of an old building that has been converted into guest rooms.

Pensiones

These boarding houses are among the least expensive accommodations, but you're required to take either full board (three meals) or half-board, which is breakfast plus lunch or dinner. *Pensiones* are your most basic fare, offering a mattress and not much else. However, lucky for you, Spain has the highest lodging standards in Europe for their prices.

Casas Huespedes & Fondas

These are among the cheapest places in Spain and can be recognized by the light-blue plaques at the door displaying

Cuidado! Avoid an Airport Headache

Check with the airports you will be flying through for any additional requirements regarding items that are prohibited in your carry-on bags, and how many
carry-on bags you are allowed. Heathrow, for example, has been extremely
strict (since the exposure of the alleged Aug 2006 transatlantic aircraft plot)
about enforcing the rule of only one carry-on per person—as in, not even a
small purse and a laptop. Some flights in Europe have been reported to have
additional security checkpoints at random places, such as at the end of the
gangway onto the plane, where they may confiscate even those items you
bought *after* the first security check: for example, that bottle of water or duty-
free lipstick. Airport requirements may even be different airport to airport within
the same country, so save yourself some major grief and call ahead. At the very
least, be ready to check bags or items you can't carry on, or to stuff things at
the last minute into the bag/s you intend to check.

CH and F, respectively. They are invariably basic but respectable establishments.

Youth Hostels

Spain has about 140 hostels *(albergues de juvenil)*. In theory, those 25 or under have the first chance at securing a bed for the night, but these places are certainly not limited to young people. Some of them are equipped for persons with disabilities. Most hostels impose an 11pm curfew. For information, contact Red Española de Alberques Juveniles, Calle José Ortega y Gasset 71, 28006 Madrid (☎ 915-437-412).

Paradors, Albergues & Refugios

The Spanish government runs a series of unique state-owned inns called paradors *(paradores* in Spanish), which now blanket the country. Deserted castles, monasteries, palaces, and other buildings have been taken over and converted into hotels. Historic and charming though they might be, they are quite expensive and advance reservations are usually necessary. Contact Paradores de España, Requeña 3, 28013 Madrid (☎ 915-166-666).

The government also operates a type of accommodation known as *albergues:* These are comparable to motels, standing along the roadside and usually built in hotel-scarce sections for the convenience of passing motorists. A client is not allowed to stay in an *albergue* for more than 48 hours, and the management doesn't accept reservations.

In addition, the government runs *refugios,* mostly in remote areas, attracting hunters, fishers, and mountain climbers. Another state-sponsored establishment is the *hostería,* or specialty restaurant, such as the one at Alcalá de Henares, near Madrid. Hosterías don't offer rooms; decorated in the style of a particular province, they serve regional dishes at reasonable prices.

Some key points to keep in mind:

○ **It pays to book early.** We can't stress this enough. Spain is popular year-round and the good, affordable beds go fast. If you know you'll be traveling to Spain in 3 months, get on the Internet *now* and start sending e-mails to prospective hotels and hostels. You can

Building a Multi-City Itinerary

If you're planning to visit several cities or regions in Spain, multi-city flight structures (for example, flying into Madrid and out of Barcelona) are a great option. All the big online travel agencies have a function that allows you to build a multi-city itinerary. Best of all, multi-city trips are priced about the same as regular round-trips—great news, since you used to pay quite a premium for this convenience.

always cancel, penalty-free, if your plans change.

○ **Reconfirm** all bookings several days before you arrive, and **carry documentation** (that is, a printout of the e-mail the hotel sent you) to prove your reservation exists.

○ **What cheap sleeps?** We'll be blunt: Hotel prices are high in Spain's major tourist destinations. Even those that we categorize as "cheap" in this book (for example, 60€ for a no-frills double room with shared bath down the hall) might strike you as pricey if you're used to what similar lodging costs in Colorado or Cambodia. Know what to expect and plan accordingly, and you won't be blindsided by your cumulative hotel expenses, which may be anywhere from 25% to 50% of your daily budget.

○ **Playing the hostel game.** With prices starting at 12€ per night, dorm beds in hostel-style accommodations are the cheapest way to go in Spain's top tourist destinations. However, most hostels do not accept reservations more than 12 or 24 hours before your planned check-in

time. (This is not because they're deliberately being pains in the ass—it's because they don't know how many beds they'll have free until their current guests inform them that they're moving out.) The best way to handle this is to call the hostel a few days before you're thinking of staying there, and get a clear understanding of how their reservations system works. Often, they'll ask you to call back at 9pm the night before your arrival to make a reservation, and then arrive by 3pm the next day to pay for your bed. Play by their rules, and everybody wins. If you're a member of **Hostelling International** (www.hihostels.com), you can often book days or even weeks in advance, but many private hostels/backpackers don't offer the same service.

○ **Location, location, location.** We're all for saving money, but we're also for living the Spanish *fiesta,* which often means forking over a little extra cash for a room in a great location. It doesn't have to be fancy, but life's too short to sleep by the train station when you could have breakfast in a terrace over Barcelona's Barri Gotic. Believe us, it makes a big difference in your quality of life. So even if you're traveling on a tight budget, try to plan for at least one "splurge," generally at the end of your stay in a city; otherwise, you'll really feel like you're slumming when you make the downgrade.

○ **Make the most of your "free" breakfast.** Most Spanish hotels offer some kind of continental buffet breakfast to their guests at no additional charge. Breakfast rooms can be windowless, depressing salons with tourists talking in too-soft voices, noshing on lifeless croissants, and sipping burnt coffee, true. But if you're running on a budget, you'll want to make good use of your first meal of the day, filling your belly on the spot and perhaps slipping some fruit, napkinful of cereal, or a yogurt into your bag for a pre-lunch snack (since lunch doesn't really get going until about 2pm).

○ **Consider short-term apartment rentals.** As more and more Spanish city-dwellers move out of the historic neighborhoods and into the more livable and affordable suburbs, there are more vacant apartments in the hearts of cities like Madrid and Barcelona than ever before. Most of these apartments are rented out as (furnished) short-term tourist accommodations. These properties, which were probably someone's family home for generations, can be booked through tourism and accommodations agencies easily found online. Simple Internet searches (for example, Google: "Barcelona apartments") will yield hundreds of results, with pictures and prices clearly posted.

Booking Your Hotel Online

Shopping online for hotels is generally done one of two ways: by booking through the hotel's own website or through an independent booking agency (or a fare-service agency like Priceline; see below). These Internet hotel agencies have multiplied in mind-boggling numbers, competing for the business of millions of consumers surfing for accommodations around the world. This competitiveness can be a boon for those who have the patience and time to shop and compare the online sites for good deals—but shop they must, for prices can vary considerably. And keep in mind that hotels at the top of a site's listing may be there for no

Cuidado! Paper or Plastic?

Most airline tickets to Europe are paperless e-tickets these days—meaning you present your passport or a credit card when you check in, and the computer pulls up your travel records—but a few airlines and online agencies still issue paper tickets from time to time. If you do book a paper-ticketed itinerary, *remember to bring the paper ticket with you to the airport,* or you will not be allowed to check in. Period.

other reason than that they paid money to get the placement. In our experience, most hotels offered in package deals to Spain are soulless chain-style monstrosities far removed from the city center.

Of the "big three" sites, **Expedia.com** offers a long list of special deals and "virtual tours" or photos of available rooms so you can see what you're paying for (a feature that helps counter the claims that the best rooms are often held back from bargain booking websites). **Travelocity** posts unvarnished customer reviews and ranks its properties according to the AAA rating system. **Trip Advisor** (www.tripadvisor.com) is another excellent source of unbiased user reviews of hotels. While even the finest hotels can inspire a misleadingly poor review from picky or crabby travelers or that one person who really did get screwed, the body of user opinions, when taken as a whole, is usually a reliable indicator.

Other reliable online booking agencies include **Hotels.com** and **Quikbook.com**. An excellent free program, **TravelAxe**

cuidado! In the Event of Bankruptcy

Airlines sometimes go bankrupt, so protect yourself by buying your tickets with a credit card, as the Fair Credit Billing Act guarantees that you can get your money back from the credit card company if a travel supplier goes under (and if you request the refund within 60 days of the bankruptcy). Travel insurance can also help, but make sure it covers against "carrier default" for your specific travel provider. And be aware that if a U.S. airline goes bust midtrip, law requires other carriers to take you to your destination (albeit on a space-available basis) for a fee of no more than $25, provided you rebook within 60 days of the cancellation.

(www.travelaxe.net), can help you search multiple hotel sites at once, even ones you may never have heard of—and conveniently lists the total price of the room, including the taxes and service charges. Another booking site, **Travelweb** (www.travelweb.com), is partly owned by the hotels it represents (including the Hilton, Hyatt, and Starwood chains) and is plugged directly into the hotels' reservations systems—unlike independent online agencies, which have to fax or e-mail reservation requests to the hotel, a good portion of which get misplaced in the shuffle. More than once, travelers have arrived at the hotel, only to be told that they have no reservation. To be fair, many of the major sites are improving in service and ease of use, and Expedia.com will soon be able to plug directly into the reservations systems of many hotel chains—none of which can be bad news for consumers. In the meantime, you should definitely get a confirmation number and bring along a printout of any online booking transaction.

SAVING EUROS ON ACCOMMODATIONS BEFORE YOU GO

The rack rate is the maximum legal rate that a hotel can charge for a room. Hardly anybody pays this price, however, except in peak season or on holidays. To lower the cost of your room:

○ **Book early**—as in, as soon as you know you'll be taking the trip. If you make a habit of showing up without a reservation, you'll inevitably get stuck paying more than what you'd planned on spending. After all, the best-value accommodations in good locations tend to be fairly well known. We've listed the best budget hotel and hostel options in this book, but many of them are small, with fewer than 20 rooms. If you wait too long to call or e-mail for a reservation, these rooms (and others in the same price range) could be all gone, and all that's left might cost 50% to 100% more, or have an inconvenient location.

○ **Book online.** Many of the hotels we've listed in this book offer Internet-only discounts, so check their websites for the most advantageous rates and special seasonal offers. Conversely, other hotels supply rooms to Priceline, Hotwire, or Expedia.com at rates lower than the ones you can get through the hotel itself. Shop around. And if you have special requests—a quiet room, a room with a view—call the hotel directly and make your needs known after you've booked online.

○ **Remember the law of supply and demand.** Resort hotels are most crowded, and therefore most expensive, on weekends, so discounts are available for midweek stays. Business hotels in downtown locations are busiest during the week, so you can often expect discounts over the weekend. Almost all Spanish hotels have high-season and low-season prices, and booking the day after their "high season" ends can mean big discounts.

SAVING MONEY WHEN YOU'RE THERE

○ **Before you start dialing away** on the in-room phone, find out from hotel staff how much they charge per call. Some hotels charge astronomical rates, while other, more honest hotels only charge you what the phone company charges them—that is, a humane .10€ to .20€ for a local call. In the former case, use prepaid phone cards, pay phones, or your own cellphone instead of dialing direct from hotel phones.

○ **If your hotel offers Internet access** (in-room broadband or Wi-Fi, or a public terminal in a common area), find out if there's a charge for using it. Some hotels don't disclose that they charge 10€ an hour for online access, so you stay logged on for hours, and then they slap you with an outrageous bill upon checkout.

○ **In summer, if your hotel has airconditioning,** be sure to find out upfront if there's an additional charge for using it. (At smaller, budget hotels, it's usually something like 10€–15€ per day.)

○ **Stock the minibar yourself.** If for some reason you can't resist the siren song of the boozy and salty treats in the minibar, just remember that hotels charge through the nose for water, potato chips, and those adorable little bottles of everybody's favorite Tennessee whiskey. If you want to keep

Cuidado! Don't Flink & Dry

As tempting as it is to kick off your vacation by hitting the airport pub for beers and tequila shots, there are a number of reasons you should keep the alcohol intake to a minimum on travel days. A celebratory cocktail or glass of wine with your meal is great, but save the binge drinking for when you're on terra firma.

→ Too much merriment at the airport pub can cause you to miss your flight.

→ No one on the plane wants to be stuck next to your liquor breath for hours.

→ Altitude lowers your tolerance; turbulence messes with your stomach.

→ The midflight hangover onset— 'nuff said.

food and drink in the room, buy your own snacks and drinks and store them in the minibar. (But do it on the sly; most hotels don't condone this behavior.) Otherwise, if you drink a can of Coke from the minibar, just remember to go out and buy a new can at the cafe down the street and replace it before you check out.

○ **Always ask about local taxes** and service charges, which can increase the cost of a room by 15% or more. Smaller, family-run hotels include the tax (IVA) in the room charge, while larger, more expensive hotels often tack the IVA charge on top of the already exorbitant room rate, so check it out before you check in.

When Your Body's Still in Another Time Zone . . .

Jet lag is a pitfall of traveling across time zones, not just spending 9 hours in an airplane (which is why jet lag is not acute when traveling north-south). When you travel east-west or vice versa, your body becomes thoroughly confused about what time it is, and everything from your digestion to your brain feels out of whack. Traveling east, say from Atlanta to Málaga, is more difficult on your internal clock than traveling west, say from Barcelona to New York, because most peoples' bodies are more inclined to stay up late than fall asleep early. Spain, as with the rest of mainland Europe, is on Greenwich Mean Time +1 hour, which means it's 6 hours ahead of (later than) Eastern Time, 7 hours ahead of Central Time, 8 hours ahead of Mountain Time, and 9 hours ahead of Pacific Time. Just like most of North America, Spain observes Daylight Saving Time from late March/early April to late October.

Tips for Avoiding Jet Lag

→ Exercise and sleep well for a few days before your trip.

→ Drink lots and lots of water before, during, and after your flight. Avoid alcohol.

→ Reset your watch to your destination time before you board the plane. Think in that time zone before you even get there.

→ Daylight is the number-one key to resetting your body clock. As soon as you arrive at your hotel, ditch your bags and go for a long, invigorating orientation walk around town. Stay outside, in the sun, for as much of that first day as possible.

→ Get on the local clock right away. As tired as you might feel, resist midday naps, as they will only screw you up even further. Keep moving, eat at the normal local meal times, and drink as much caffeine as you need to stay up until at least 10pm your first night.

→ Over-the-counter melatonin caplets can work wonders in helping you adjust quickly to a new time zone. Start by taking one the night of your flight, and then take one each following night at bedtime.

○ **If a hotel insists upon tacking on any surprise charges** that weren't mentioned at check-in or prominently posted in the room, or a "resort fee" for amenities you didn't use, you can often make a case for getting it removed. You can always take any accommodations-related complaints to the local tourism board—mention that to an ornery hotel staffer, and they're sure to back down.

Dining There

First and foremost, don't use plastic. Try to pay in **cash** whenever possible. Establishments won't accept your credit card unless you're a big spender whose meals cost more than a typical night's stay in Spain.

Cuidado! When Your Luggage Misses Its Flight

If your luggage doesn't immediately show up on the ol' baggage carousel, try not to freak out. Busy airports like London Heathrow and Paris–Charles de Gaulle are notorious about not getting checked bags to their connecting flights on time, so if you've flown through one of those cities, there's actually a better-than-we'd-like-to-admit chance that your luggage might not have made it onto your flight. The good news is, your bags aren't really "lost," just delayed. File a report at the office in the baggage claim hall — be prepared to give an address where your stuff can be delivered, and a phone number where you can be reached, when it does arrive in your city (usually 6–10 hr. later). It sounds sketchy, I know, but this has happened to me several times, and someone from the airline has always shown up with my bag at the specified address later that afternoon or evening. Watch out, though, there are several companies that handle baggage in every airport, and each of them works with more than one airline. In the baggage claim area you can find out which was the one working with your company. Most important, do not leave the baggage claim area before making a report. You can always make it at your airline desk but it will certainly complicate matters.

Next, prepare yourself for the fact that Spanish people talk about food as much as Americans talk about the weather. Often, while Spaniards are eating a meal, they'll verbally judge and debate its merit until the full review is in, then proceed to discuss *past* meals. Food is serious business here, and asking about the hottest restaurant, or best quality for the lowest price, is the perfect icebreaker. In the last couple of years, Spanish cuisine has seen a renaissance, partly from the hand of big-time chefs like Ferrán Adriá, in Barcelona.

For **budget eating** in general, your options are 1) something that came from a pig; 2) Spanish tortilla (a tasty, thick, omelet-type thing made of eggs and potatoes); and 3) fast food (like everywhere). (Also remember that you can drink in any restaurant in Spain—even Burger King and KFC serve beer. Now that's finger lickin' good!) Some other inexpensive dining options are the *alimentación* stores (convenience stores), outdoor markets, and supermarkets. If you want something

cheap, go about three steps in any direction and walk into the nearest . . . pub! Nearly all bars and cafeterias are open from about 7am till 2am and serve tapas (small sandwiches or portions of food) like tortillas, calamari, olives, or something with bacon. In the afternoon, usually from around 1 to 4pm as lunch in Spain is the main meal, the larger of these cafeterias will serve *el menú del día* (about 8€–12€) which includes about 2 hours of eating a first-course dish (such as soup or salad), a second or main course (fish or meat), plus bread, dessert, and a drink (wine, beer, or water). Coffee is usually charged separately or can be sometimes exchanged for dessert. If you've eaten late enough, dinner will be just a matter of a few tapas in your favorite *tasca*. All in all, it's a pretty sweet deal.

Like the majority of Europeans, Spaniards generally aren't big on **tipping**. That's probably because the IVA tax (VAT) tacks on a substantial wad of cash to any meal. For the most part, IVA is included. Check the bottom of your bill to make sure. If it isn't, you should always leave a few coins behind, as long as the service was good; but forking out anything more than 5% to 10% is unheard of.

Health & Safety

Staying Well

Holidays and traveling are good for your health. At least your soul's health. As for the body, don't worry, Spain is not particularly hazardous for it. There are no special vaccines needed to travel *Plus Ultra* (or "Further Beyond," Spain's official motto) and water is normally quite safe to drink. Nevertheless, you can always avoid risks by drinking bottled water and choosing your foods carefully. The main problem for travelers is biting off more than they can chew. Literally. Spaniards eat things you won't be used to, so try not to sample it all during your first meal (it probably won't end all that well if you do!). One thing's for sure: Almost everywhere in Spain you'll be sure to get a lot of food for your money. Don't take it as a challenge, and try not to eat more than you can digest. In all likelihood, if you experience any, uh, *discomfort* from Spanish food, it will probably be mild and pass in less than 24 hours. Nevertheless you might want to carry some of those chalky bright pink wafers and other tummy fixers in case you find Spain delicacies too hard to eat moderately.

Although there are no required vaccinations when entering Spain, it is important that you are up-to-date with all immunizations as defined by the Advisory Committee on Immunization Practice (ACIP). Major vaccinations include tetanus, hepatitis B, MMR, and chickenpox if necessary. It is also always a good idea to see your doctor 4 to 6 weeks prior to your departure for a regular check-up and to make sure you have enough prescription medications to last your entire stay.

For more information, contact the **International Association for Medical Assistance to Travelers (IAMAT; ☎ 716/ 754-4883** or in Canada 416/652-0137; www. iamat.org) for tips on travel and health concerns in the countries you're visiting, and for lists of local, English-speaking doctors. The United States **Centers for Disease Control and Prevention (☎ 800/311-3435;** www.cdc.gov/travel) provides up-to-date information on health hazards by region or country and offers tips on food safety. The website **www.trip prep.com**, sponsored by a consortium of travel medicine practitioners, may also offer helpful advice on traveling abroad. You can find listings of reliable clinics overseas at the **International Society of Travel Medicine** (www.istm.org).

If you suffer from a chronic illness, consult your doctor before your departure. For conditions like epilepsy, diabetes, or heart problems, wear a **MedicAlert identification tag (☎ 888/633-4298;** www. medicalert.org), which will alert doctors to your condition and give them access to your records through MedicAlert's 24-hour hot line.

Pack **prescription medications** in your carry-on luggage, and carry prescription medications in their original containers, with pharmacy labels—otherwise they may not make it through airport security. Also carry copies of your prescriptions in case you lose your meds or run out. Know the generic name of prescription medicines, just in case a local pharmacist is unfamiliar with the brand name.

THE BASICS

It's also a good idea to pack an extra pair or two of **contact lenses** or a back-up pair of **prescription glasses.** If you need new contact lenses or saline solution, or you need to repair a broken pair of glasses, stop in at any *optica* (optician's shop).

What If I Get Sick?

Don't panic. Spanish medical facilities are among the best in the world. If you get sick, consider asking your hotel concierge or (more likely) desk attendant to recommend a local doctor—even his or her own. If needed, your foreign consulate can provide a list of area doctors who speak English.

LA FARMACIA

If you need a pharmacy while in Spain, look for the neon green cross sign. In addition to being the place where you get prescriptions filled, the *farmacia* can also hook you up with tampons, over-the-counter painkillers like ibuprofen or aspirin, condoms, and sunblock. Pharmacists in Spain have the license to sell some prescription drugs without a prescription. You can just walk in and tell them what's wrong, and if it is simple enough, they'll sell you the necessary medication. Note that the *farmacia* does not stock contact lens items—for that, head to the *optica.*

Pharmacies can be found everywhere in most cities and towns in Spain, and are normally open Monday to Saturday from 8am to 8pm, sometimes breaking for the midday *siesta* from 1 to 4pm. In every city, pharmacies take turns staying open late and on Sundays; so if you find a pharmacy and it's closed, look for the sign in the window indicating the nearest pharmacy on duty for that particular shift. In big cities like Madrid and Barcelona, there are 24-hour pharmacies, usually near the main train station. You will have little problem

CUIdado! Cash, Cash, or More Cash . . .

Nobody sleeps for free—and sometimes not even on credit for that matter. Mind those hostels and hotels that are cash only: You'll find the words "No credit cards" after the price listings throughout this book. Be sure to hit up the nearest ATM or bank so you don't get caught short on dinero. See p. 33 for more information on using plastic in Spain.

filling your foreign prescriptions, though be advised that format (for example, drops instead of pills) and name brands of prescription drugs are often different from what you're used to back home.

Playing Safely

With so many parties and beaches, and parties at beaches, so many Spanish gods and goddesses and foreign worshippers of beauty, it is very probable that you'll hook up with someone. If you're going to partake, just remember they have STDs and sperm in Spain, too. And that Dutch hottie from the hostel in Girona might be a walking gonorrhea case. Nothing ruins romance like those very private aches and irritations. *Always* use a latex condom (or polyurethane if you're allergic) when engaging in sexual activity abroad (or anywhere for that matter).

Condoms that are not latex are less effective against disease transmission and pregnancy and should be avoided. If you are unsure as what the condom is made of or it is not clearly marked, it's not worth the risk. Latex condoms *(preservativos)* are widely available in Spain at supermarket checkout lines or any pharmacy, and many bar and club restrooms.

Cuidado! When Is a Star Not a Star?

When booking a hotel through an online agency, keep in mind that star ratings are subjective, and that comments in the feedback section are often listed by the hotels themselves. Although a picture is worth a thousand words, it can also be very deceiving. We're not saying that these hotels are fleabag inns full of junkies, but they may have posted photos of the one room that's been renovated, giving you a skewed sense of the overall quality of the place. A bigger issue is that you'll never get a sense of how well located a hotel is from these websites, because everyone will advertise that their hotel is "steps from the "Plaza Mayor" or "minutes from the Plaça Catalunya." How many steps? How many minutes? You'll find us repeating it often in this book: Hotel location is key in Spanish cities. More often than not, you get what you pay for—and if that online hotel deal seems too good to be true, it probably is.

As with any destination, you should always avoid shared needles for tattoos, piercings, or injections of any kind. Always make sure that you watch the establishment open a fresh needle—again, it's not worth the risk.

Covering Health Care Costs

Medical and hospital services in Spain are not free so be sure to be covered before you travel. Make sure that you have a U.S. health insurance policy and that you have checked with your carrier to see how they may or may not cover medical attention in Spain. Most health plans (including Medicaid) do not provide coverage, and the ones that do often require you to pay for services upfront and reimburse you only after you return home. As a safety net, you may want to buy travel medical insurance, particularly if you're traveling to a remote or high-risk area where emergency evacuation is a possible scenario. If you require additional medical insurance, try **MEDEX Assistance** (☎ 410/453-6300; www.medexassist.com) or **Travel Assistance International** (☎ 800/821-2828; www.travelassistance. com; for general information on services, call the company's Worldwide Assistance Services, Inc., at ☎ 800/777-8710).

Personal Safety

Spain is a highly toured country and that means, as with every other major destination, you'll have to be alert to potential crime. Most of Spain has a pretty moderate crime rate, but in the last few years it has been on the rise in places like Madrid and Barcelona. Luckily, crimes tend to be of the non-violent type. You have to watch out for pickpocketing mostly. Criminals frequent tourist areas and major attractions such as museums, monuments, restaurants, hotels, beach resorts, trains, train stations, airports, subways, and ATMs. In Barcelona, violent attacks have occurred near the Picasso Museum and in the Gothic Quarter, Parc Güell, Plaza Real, and Mont Juic. In Madrid, reported incidents occur in key tourist areas, including the area near the Prado Museum and Atocha train station, and areas of Old Madrid like Sol, El Rastro flea market, and Plaza Mayor. Crowds are crook's natural habitat so exercise caution when in a mob of people. Carry limited cash and credit cards; and leave extra cash, credit cards, passports, and personal documents in a safe location.

Crooks can be very sophisticated, they might work in pairs, one of them snatching your attention by asking for directions or spilling something on your shirt, while the other fishes for valuables in your pockets, although the grab and run is also quite typical. Small medieval passages, like the ones in Barcelona's Barri Gothic, are quite adequate for this kind of activity. This M.O. is usually the one used for grabbing cellphones. Be careful when you're on the phone, since they are one of the most looked for bounties for petty thieves in Spain.

As with any part of the world, you should also keep an eye out for other scams and use common sense to avoid any situations that could sacrifice your safety.

We also recommend the following **safety tips:**

- **Never give out your credit card information** unless you're using it to pay for something.
- **Solo travelers, beware** of those who are very eager to befriend you in a crowded tourist area. Just as in the U.S., if someone seems abnormally nice or generous, you should smell a rat.
- **Always stay by your drink.** It's rare, but we've heard a few stories about someone being slipped a roofie or other substance in their drink and having their stuff stolen (or worse). Stay aware.
- **Watch how much you drink.** Being drunk makes you an even easier target.
- **Stay in well-lit, populated areas at night.** Walking around Spanish cities at night is quite safe, but you don't want to find yourself alone and far off the beaten path.
- **Keep your money, visa, and passport in a secure location,** preferably on your body and in front, not in a secondary bag or backpack.
- **Always keep copies** of your passport, visa, and so on in a location other than that of the originals. These are the only

Getting the Best Room

Always ask if there's a corner room available. They're often larger and quieter, with more windows and light, and cost the same as standard rooms. When you make your reservation, ask if the hotel is renovating; if it is, request a room away from the construction. Ask about nonsmoking rooms, rooms with views, rooms with balconies, rooms that face an interior garden (versus rooms that face a busy street). Ask for the room that has been most recently renovated or redecorated.

If you aren't happy with your room when you arrive, politely ask for another one. Most lodgings will be willing to accommodate you if they have something else available.

documents you have that prove your (legal) presence in Spain.
- **Use common sense.**

Keep in mind that Spain is not quite the melting pot that the U.S. prides itself on being. There may be some anti-American or anti-Bush sentiments—in the form of graffiti or political demonstrations—that may make you uncomfortable. Remember that you are a guest in their country, and be respectful of their opinions. For further information regarding female and minority travelers, see the relevant sections below.

Most importantly, maintain respect for the country and its moral and legal statutes. Americans may have reputations as partiers, but that does not give us carte blanche to behave like idiots, nor does it exempt us from being held accountable for our actions under a law that may be different from our own.

Questions to Ask about Your Accommodations

→ Will I be sharing a room with someone (as with most hostels)?

→ Will I be sharing a bathroom?

→ Are there safes for my personal valuables?

→ Is there a curfew (a few hostels or small hotels still have lock-in or lock-out)?

→ Is there air-conditioning or ceiling fans? (From June–Aug, this is *key*.)

→ Does the hotel serve breakfast, and, if so, is there an extra charge? If there is an extra charge, you probably don't want to pay it if they only serve those crappy, pre-bagged croissants. Ask about that, too.

→ Are there airport transfers to and from my hotel?

→ How far is the hotel from the train station? If it's not walking distance, how will I get there?

→ What is check-in/checkout time? Is there an hour after which they'll cancel my reservation if I haven't arrived yet?

→ Do they have Internet access—either a public terminal in the lobby or Wi-Fi throughout the property?

Last but not at all least, although all drugs are technically illegal, **drug laws** are not very harsh in Spain, as long as its for personal use only (a half gram or less) and you're not selling, in which case all bets are off. Legal penalty for possession of marijuana is merely a fine and most often just a warning, especially in tourist areas. In big cities, people smoke *purros* (tobacco rolled with very strong hash) like they're going out of style, and drugs are quite prevalent in clubs and discos. We certainly do not recommend your doing drugs, but if you decide to do it you should at least be informed. Check the website of **Energy Control** (www.energycontrol.org) for unbiased information about illegal substances. It's good advice, even if you're not traveling.

Staying Connected

Whether or not you bring your own computer, you'll have many opportunities to check your e-mail, update your travel blog, tweak your MySpace page, and so on, while in Spain. If you feel like toting your PowerBook along, you'll find Wi-Fi coverage in a lot of places, and broadband cable connections in some hotels, but chances are your backpack is stuffed enough without having to squeeze in your laptop (and worry about its theft). If you don't bring your own computer, you'll still find plenty of Internet points (the local term for Internet cafes and kiosks) in Spain.

If you don't already have one, you may want to open a free, Web-based e-mail account with Yahoo!, Hotmail, or Gmail, which you can access from any computer in the world with an Internet connection. If you already have an AOL account, you can log on to www.aol.com and check your AOL mail from there.

Cuidado! Don't Blow It

Spain uses 220-volt electricity, whereas the U.S. uses 110-volt. Using any appliances with the wrong voltage can fry them. Hair dryers are a classic casualty of this common traveler's mistake, but most lower-voltage electronics (like laptops and iPods and cellphone chargers) will do just fine with 220-V electricity. That being said, it's still a good idea to check with the manufacturer to see how your appliances will handle the voltage switch. If they're at risk, then be sure to use a **voltage converter.** (Those are the clunky, boxy contraptions you can buy at gadget stores like Brookstone or Radio Shack.) Smaller, simpler **adaptors** change a plug from American flat prongs to European round prongs so you can fit it into the socket, but they do *not* work as electrical converters. Adaptors can be purchased at almost any hardware store *(ferreteria)* in Spain for a few euros. Converters, however, are harder to find in Spain, so, if you need one, buy it before you leave home.

Without Your Own Computer

Almost all hostels and some budget hotels have at least one Internet terminal set up for guests' use. Some places offer this service for free; others charge up to 5€ an hour. (Whatever you do, avoid logging on at any large hotel's business center—their rates for Internet use are ridiculously high, and usually not very well posted.)

If your hotel does not have a public computer, you'll need to track down an Internet cafe, or Internet point. In larger cities, a good place to start your search is at the train station, where there is often a small officelike space with several public terminals. Otherwise, you can canvas the area immediately around the train station, where there are usually a bunch of *locutorios* set up to serve budget travelers (whose hotels are usually nearby) and an immigrant population that needs to communicate easily and cheaply with their family back home. Any city's tourist-heavy old town is also full of Internet spots. This is especially true of any city with a university and a large student population. Another idea is to stop in at the local bar or pub—those with an expat clientele, especially, are likely to have a computer hooked up to the Internet for patrons'

convenience. For each destination in this book, we've listed the addresses of some of the better and more popular Internet points. As you might expect of any computer that's touched by dozens of hands daily, the keyboards are sticky, the mouse often doesn't work, and so on, so make sure you sit down at a decently functioning terminal before you waste valuable minutes trying to get the space bar to work.

Most major airports now have Internet kiosks scattered throughout their terminals. These kiosks, which you'll also see in hotel lobbies and tourist information offices around the world, give you basic Web access for a per-minute fee that's usually higher than regular Internet cafe prices. The kiosks' clunkiness and high price means you should avoid them whenever possible.

With Your Own Computer

If you're going to haul along your laptop, make sure that at least some of the places you'll be staying offer in-room broadband connections or Wi-Fi coverage on the property. Hotels that offer Wi-Fi often have some convoluted password-protected network that may be down half the time; in fact, hotels that offer the some-what more old-fashioned broadband/Ethernet cable connection are often more reliable. If you have a wireless card, just open your laptop and see what happens. With so many unprotected wireless networks in such proximity, you'll often be able to get online automatically. We've been in many a nonwired hotel where we've managed to poach off a neighboring network (from the apartment across the street or law offices next door) that wasn't password-protected.

Although they're not nearly as wide-spread as in the U.S., there are more and more Wi-Fi "hot spots" cropping up at cafes and bars throughout Spain. The website **wifi411.com** has a remarkably comprehensive list of all the wireless Internet networks throughout the world (including Spain); select your desired city, and then select "All Networks" and "All Locations," and you'll get dozens of results.

Mobile Phones

Cellphones are not necessary, true; you can totally get through your trip without having a cellphone, but how damn handy are the things? It's really a good idea to have at least one of them among yourself and your traveling companions for when you need to make hotel reservations, coordinate travel plans with other people, and/or be easier to locate for that cutie you met at the club last night.

Spain, like most of the world, is on **GSM (Global System for Mobiles),** a big, seamless network that makes for easy cross-border cellphone use throughout Europe and dozens of other countries worldwide. In the U.S., T-Mobile, AT&T Wireless, and Cingular use this quasi-universal system; in Canada, Microcell, and some Rogers customers are GSM, and all Europeans and most Australians use GSM. If your cellphone is on a GSM system, and you have a world-capable multiband phone such as many Sony Ericsson, Motorola, or Samsung models, you can make and receive calls across civilized areas around much of the globe, including Spain. Just call your wireless operator and ask for "international roaming" to be activated on your account. Unfortunately, per-minute charges can be high—usually $1 to $1.50 in western Europe. When you speak to your service provider, make sure you check to see if there is a per-month charge for international calling capability. T-Mobile, for example, doesn't charge you a per-month fee; Cingular does. If your provider does charge you for this service, remember to call and cancel it when you return from your trip. If traveling with your own phone, it may pay to simply buy a Spanish chip with a number for your phone, if your phone is liberated, that is. Most likely it's not and it is illegal (though very easy) to liberate it. It is rumored to be done in non-official sell points, the dodgier the better.

If you don't have a GSM phone, you can always **rent a mobile phone** for your trip. There are dozens of cellphone rental outfits on the Web—including www.planetfone.com, www.worldcell.com, www.cellhire.com, www.cellularabroad.com, and www.rentcell.com—which are all pretty competitive with each other. You'll fill out an online form (or call their toll-free customer service line) and provide your credit card number, and they'll ship you a box that contains your rental cellphone, extra battery, charger, and dorky cordura cases, to the address of your choice. When you've returned from your trip, you just put everything back in the same packaging and ship it back to them in the pre-addressed and prepaid FedEx or UPS package. The whole process couldn't be easier—just remember to do it at least a week in advance of your trip. Phone rental isn't cheap, however. You'll usually pay around $50 per week, plus airtime fees of anywhere from 15¢ to a dollar a minute. (Most have free incoming calls, however.) The bottom line: Shop around for the best deal.

While you can rent a phone from any number of overseas sites, including kiosks at airports and at car-rental agencies, we suggest renting the phone before you leave home. That way you can give loved ones and business associates your new number, make sure the phone works, and take the phone wherever you go—especially helpful for overseas trips through several countries, where local phone-rental agencies often bill in local currency and may not let you take the phone to another country.

For trips of more than a few weeks, **buying a phone** makes more economic sense than renting one, as Spain has a number of cheap, prepaid phone systems. Once you arrive, stop by a local cellphone shop and ask about the cheapest package; you'll probably pay less than $100 for a phone and a starter calling card. Most providers have plans where calls to land lines and text messages are as low as 10¢ per minute.

Using a Land Line

If you don't plan on taking a mobile phone with you or renting one while abroad, you can still make phone calls from a public telephone on the street. Pick up a phone card at any *tabaco,* many newsstands, and coffee bars. If you plan on calling the States a lot, however, this can get rather pricey.

TELEPHONE TIPS: FROM YOUR CELL OR A PAY PHONE

❍ To call Spain from the United States, dial the **international prefix, 011;** then Spain's **country code, 34;** and then the city code (for example, **91** for Madrid

and **93** for Barcelona), which is now built into every number. Then dial the actual **phone number.**

❍ A **local phone call** from a pay phone in Spain costs around .20€. **Public phones** accept coins, precharged phone cards, or both. You can buy a card at any *tabaco* (tobacconists) in increments of 5€, 10€, and 20€. Spain has also recently introduced a series of **international phone cards** for calling overseas. They come in increments of 50, 100, 200, and 400 units, and they're available at *tabacos* and bars.

❍ **To make a call,** pick up the receiver and insert .20€ or your card. Most phones have a digital display that'll tell you how much money you've inserted (or how much is left on the card). Dial the number, and don't forget to take the card with you after you hang up.

❍ To **call from one city code to another** is the same as to dial locally since, for a few years now, Spain has reorganized their phone numbers. Now you have to dial the 9 digit number to make local and long distance calls.

❍ To **dial direct internationally,** dial **00** then the country code, the area code, and the number. The country code for the United States and Canada is 1.

The general emergencies number—the number that is comparable to 911 in the U.S.—is **112** for all of Spain. The **national police** can be contacted by dialing ☎ **091.** (Note that these numbers do not have a prefix; they're the same no matter where in Spain you're dialing from. These numbers will work from any phone—land line, pay phone, or cell—even if you have no credit on a calling card.)

Whatever you do about phone use in Spain, try to keep the chitchat with friends and family back home to a minimum. Don't get so caught up with being in touch with the U.S. that you don't step out of your comfort zone and let yourself really experience Spanish culture. The same goes for iPods and portable game devices—they're great for the plane ride over and long train rides, but stow them away when you're riding on a city bus and walking around town. Enjoying Spain is all about stimulating all your senses, which is why you'll never see locals walking around with white earbuds in their ears.

Getting Around Spain

By Train

Spain is crisscrossed with a comprehensive network of rail lines. Hundreds of trains depart every day for points around the country, including the fast TALGO and the newer, even faster AVE trains, which reduced rail time between Madrid and Seville to only 2¹/₂ hours.

If you plan to travel a great deal on the European railroads, it's worth buying a copy of the *Thomas Cook Timetable of European Passenger Railroads.* It's available exclusively online at www.thomascookpublishing.com.

The most economical way to travel in Spain is on Spanish State Railways (RENFE), the national railway of Spain. Most main long-distance connections are served with night express trains that have first- and second-class seats as well as beds and bunks. When booking with RENFE (www.renfe.es), remember that your unpaid reservation will expire 24 hours before the train leaves—so pay for it by then or you'll lose it. At the ticket counter in the station you can only buy tickets for trains departing that day, and you'll normally have to stand in line for a long time just to get them. If you have a reservation though, you can get your tickets at the customer service counter, where you'll have less of a wait. RENFE also operates comfortable high-speed TALGO, TER, and Electrotren trains. The Spanish railway is one of the most economical in Europe, and, in most cases, is the best way to go.

Note that cities that appear to be close to each other on a map might involve inconvenient train changes and slow regional lines—for the best connections, travel through big train hub cities like Madrid or Barcelona.

SPANISH RAIL PASSES

RENFE, the national railway of Spain, offers several discounted rail passes. You must buy these passes in the United States prior to your departure. For more information, consult a travel agent or **Rail Europe** (☎ 800/4-EURAIL; www.raileurope.com).

The **Eurail Spain Pass** is good for unlimited travel on Spain's national rail network. Passes are available in denominations from 3 to 10 days within a 2-month period. Prices start at $238, plus $38 for each additional day for first class. Second class starts at $186 with additional days costing $31. (Children 4–11 pay half-fare on any of these discount passes.)

Be forewarned that some trains in Europe won't accept any rail pass. You'll have to buy point-to-point tickets for these trains in Europe whether or not you have a pass. Regional trains in Spain not run by RENFE (along the northern coast, in the Basque country, around Valencia, and FGC-run trains around Barcelona) don't take passes. You'll have to pay cash for these tickets, and you can't buy the tickets from Rail Europe.

The **Eurail Portugal-Spain Pass,** good for both Spain and Portugal, offers 3 to 10 days unlimited first-class train travel in a

2-month period. Prices start at $272; add $38 for each additional day. **Eurail Spain 'n Portugal Saverpass,** again including both Spain and Portugal, offers any 3 to 10 days unlimited, first-class train travel in a 2-month period starting at $229, and $30 for each additional day.

The **Eurail France-Spain Pass,** good for both Spain and France, offers 4 to 6 days unlimited train travel in a 2-month period. First-class prices start at $331, plus $38 for each additional day, while second-class rates are $288, plus $33 per extra day.

A **Eurail Spain Rail 'n Drive Pass** offers any 3 days of unlimited first class train travel, within a 2-month span, starting from $355 for a standard economy car. Additional rail days cost $44, and additional car-rental days, $40.

EURAIL GLOBAL PASSES

Many travelers to Europe take advantage of one of the great travel bargains of our time, the **Eurail Global Pass,** which permits unlimited rail travel in any country in western and northern Europe (except Great Britain, though Ireland is a go) and Hungary in eastern Europe.

The advantages are tempting: There are no tickets; simply show the pass to the ticket collector, then settle back to enjoy the scenery. Seat reservations are required on some trains (see box below). Many trains have couchettes (sleeping cars), for which an extra fee is charged. Obviously, the 2- or 3-month traveler gets the great-est economic advantages. To obtain full advantage of a 15-day or 1-month pass, you'd have to spend a great deal of time on the train.

Eurail Global Pass holders are also entitled to considerable reductions on certain buses and ferries as well.

In **North America,** you can buy these passes from travel agents or rail agents in major cities such as New York, Montreal, and Los Angeles. Eurail Global Passes are

also available from **Rail Europe** (☎ 877/272-RAIL; www.raileurope.com). No matter what everyone tells you, you *can* buy Eurail Global Passes in Europe as well as in America (at the major train stations), but they're more expensive. Rail Europe can give you information on the rail/drive versions of the passes.

A **Eurail Global Pass** is $635 for 15 days, $829 for 21 days, $1,025 for 1 month, $1,449 for 2 months, and $1,789 for 3 months. If you're under 26, you can buy a **Eurail Global Pass Youth** entitling you to unlimited second-class travel for $415 for 15 days, $539 for 21 days, $669 for 1 month, $945 for 2 months, and $1,165 for 3 months. Even more freedom is offered by the **Eurail Global Pass Saver Flexi,** which is similar to the Eurail Saverpass, except that you are not confined to consecutive-day travel. For travel over any 10 days within 2 months, the fare is $639; any 15 days over 2 months, the fare is $839.

Eurail Global Pass Saver, valid all over Europe for first class only, offers discounted 15-day travel for groups of three or more people traveling together from April to September, or two people traveling together from October to March. The price is $539 for 15 days, $699 for 21 days, $869 for 1 month, $1,229 for 2 months, and $1,519 for 3 months.

The **Eurail Global Pass Flexi** allows you to visit Europe with more flexibility. It's valid in first class and offers the same privileges as the Eurail Global Pass. However, it provides a number of individual travel days you can use over a much longer period of consecutive days. That makes it possible to stay in one city and yet not lose a single day of travel. There are two passes: 10 days of travel in 2 months for $715, and 15 days of travel in 2 months for $940.

Having many of the same qualifications and restrictions as the Flexipass is the **Eurail Global Pass Youth Flexi.** Sold only

¡Cuidado! Before You Put the Pedal to the Metal

When renting a car in Spain, make sure that you have a valid driver's license and remember that most rental cars are manual transmission (stick shift). Automatic transmission cars are available in much smaller numbers and at a higher rate, so it's not a bad idea to practice with your grandpa's old Peugeot before getting there—you don't want to be messing around with the clutch in the middle of Madrid's insane traffic.

Once on the road, be sure to only use the left lane if you are passing someone. If you and your little Fiat hatchback make the mistake of hanging out in the left lane, you'll find an endless convoy of black BMW SUVs crawling up your ass (at about 90 miles an hour). If that's too subtle an indication that someone wants you to pull over, he'll also flash his headlights at you until you get out of the way. Obnoxious, yes, but this will happen to you over and over, so get used to it.

- Most train trips in Spain are under 4 hours, but if you're going to be covering a long distance on a particular trip, **consider booking your train travel overnight.** This will help you maximize your daylight time in Spain and save you money that you'd otherwise have spent on a night's lodging. Overnight train trips must be booked at least 24 hours in advance to guarantee a seat or sleeping compartment.
- **Spanish trains have smoking sections,** so if you're going to smoke, be sure to smoke in the special smoking cars only, not just in the corridor of a nonsmoking car with the window open.
- **Unfortunately, theft can be a problem** on trains. Keep your bags near you at all times, and if you're going to sleep, make sure you have a hand or arm on valuables.

By Car

Nothing beats the flexibility of having your own rental car. Especially when traveling rural areas and the Pyrenees where trains might not take you where you need to go. Not so much for cities like Madrid or Barcelona where traffic can be a bit too congested for you to really enjoy the ride.

Spain's express highways are known as either *autopistas,* which charge a toll, or *autovías,* which don't. To exit the *autopista* in Spain, follow the SALIDA sign, except in Catalunya, where the exit sign says SORTIDA. On most express highways, the speed limit is 120kmph (75 mph). On other roads, speed limits range from 90kmph (56 mph) to 100kmph (62 mph), but you will see many drivers far exceeding these limits. The greatest number of accidents in Spain is recorded along the notorious Costa del Sol highway, Carretera de Cádiz.

U.S. and Canadian drivers don't need an **international driver's license** to drive a rented car in Spain. However, if you're

to travelers under 26, it allows 10 days of travel within 2 months for $489, and 15 days of travel within 2 months for $639. Nevertheless if you're traveling with a Eurail Global Pass Flexi you'll have to get tickets. (You won't pay for them but you have to get them anyway.)

These prices are valid as of early 2007; please check www.raileurope.com to confirm current prices.

Keep the following tips in mind when using the Spanish rail lines:

- **Keep your schedule somewhat flexible:** Spanish train schedules are not that precise and trains may run late.

THE BASICS

driving a private car, you need such a license. You can apply for an International Driver's License at any **American Automobile Association (AAA)** branch. You must be at least 18 and have two 2×2-inch photos and a photocopy of your U.S. driver's license with your AAA application form. The actual fee for the license can vary, depending on where it's issued.

RENTING A CAR

Many of North America's biggest car-rental companies, including Avis, Budget, and Hertz, maintain offices throughout Spain. Although several Spanish car-rental companies exist, we've heard of difficulties resolving billing irregularities and insurance claims, so you might want to stick with the U.S-based rental firms.

Note that tax on car rentals is a whopping 15%, so don't forget to factor that into your travel budget. Usually, prepaid rates do not include taxes. Be sure to ask explicitly what's included when you're quoted a rate. Don't forget to factor in toll charges and gas, which are quite expensive in Spain.

Avis (☎ 800/331-1212; www.avis.com) maintains about 100 branches throughout Spain, including about a dozen in Madrid, eight in Barcelona, a half dozen in Seville, and four in Murcia. If you reserve and pay for your rental by telephone at least 2 weeks before your departure from North America, you'll qualify for the company's best rate, with unlimited kilometers included. You can usually get competitive rates from **Hertz** (☎ 800/654-3131; www.hertz.com) and **Budget** (☎ 800/472-3325; www.budget.com), so it always pays to comparison shop. Budget doesn't have a drop-off charge if you pick up a car in one Spanish city and return it to another. All three companies require that drivers be at least 21 years of age. To be able to rent a

car, you must have a passport and a valid driver's license; you must also have a valid credit card or a prepaid voucher. An international driver's license is not essential, but you might want to present it if you have one; they're available from any North American office of the American Automobile Association (AAA).

Two other agencies of note include **Kemwel Holiday Auto** (☎ 877/820-0668; www.kemwel.com) and **Auto Europe** (☎ 800/223-5555; www.autoeurope.com).

Many packages include airfare, accommodations, and a rental car with unlimited mileage. Compare these prices with the cost of booking airline tickets and renting a car separately, in order to see if these offers are good deals. Internet resources can make comparison shopping easier. Sites like **Expedia** (www.expedia.com) and **Travelocity** (www.travelocity.com) help you compare prices and locate car-rental bargains from various companies nationwide.

By Bus

BETWEEN CITIES

There is a fairly developed bus system to transport you between cities in Spain. Of course trains are faster, and more comfortable, but they will not get you everywhere—there are places in Spain that can only be reached by bus. See the relevant regional or city chapters for more information on getting around.

IN THE CITIES

Once you're in a city, the most efficient and cost effective way to get around, other than using your own two feet, is by bus, metro, or tram. Pick up a public transit map from the local tourist office and head on out. Bus lines are named by numbers and their final destination.

By Plane

The main Spanish airline is **Iberia,** which flies pretty much to every airport in Spain (for reservations, call ☎ **902-400-500**). By European standards, domestic flights within Spain are relatively inexpensive, and considering the vast distances within the country, flying between distant points sometimes makes sense.

In recent years the Spanish multi-destination passes offered by Iberia and Spanair have given way to extremely cheap domestic tickets from new low-cost companies such as Air Berlin, Air Madrid, Futura, and Vueling. By booking a couple of weeks in advance, you can score one-way tickets within Spain and to other European destinations for as low as 15€ including tax and service charges. Most of them allow changes for a small fee, but last-minute tickets cost the same or more than with traditional airlines. Iberia, however, has felt the heat and now too offers some competitive seasonal rates.

For Travelers with Special Interests or Needs

Student Travelers

Before you leave, get an **International Student Identity Card (ISIC),** which offers substantial savings on rail passes, plane tickets, and many entrance fees. It also provides you with basic health and life insurance and a 24-hour help line. The card is available for $22 from **STA Travel** (☎ **800/781-4040** in North America; www.sta.com or www.statravel.com). If you're no longer a student but are under 26, you can get an **International Youth Travel Card (IYTC)** for the same price from the same people, which entitles you to some of the same discounts. **Travel CUTS** (☎ **800/667-2887** or 416/614-2887; www.travelcuts.com) offers similar services for both Canadians and U.S. residents.

Almost all of Spain's monuments and museums offer reduced rates to students. At a less official level, many pubs and bars offer discounted drink prices for students, and some clubs will waive a cover if you can produce a valid student ID.

Single Travelers

Ah, the joys of solitude. No one there to tell you what to do. No annoying companion who would drag you into/away from a museum. No incredibly inappropriate remark about the human needs of monks when you're trying to absorb some Zen from a monastery. Traveling alone can be a great experience.

Safety issues concerning solo travelers are minimal in Spain. Believe it or not, a foreign woman walking alone is less likely to be harassed than two foreign women walking together (for what to expect if you're a woman going solo, see "Women Travelers" below).

If you stay at hostels and go on group walking tours, bike tours, and so on, you're bound to meet a ton of young, like-minded people, whom you can join for dinner, nights on the town, and the like. In every major city, there are also plenty of bars and pubs that have a high backpacker or expat quotient. We've listed the best ones in each city chapter in this book. Don't feel weird about hitting the town on your own—it'll give you an exhilarating sense of freedom, and you might stumble into adventures that never would have happened if you'd just stayed at the hostel reading a book.

Spaniards can be quite open and are more likely to strike up a conversation with you if you're by yourself. So, if part of your plan in Spain is to meet some fine young locals, going around solo can be a great strategy! One exceedingly common pitfall of traveling for too long on your own, however, is that when you do finally interact with people, you're so relieved for the human contact that you tend to talk too much. Don't let this happen to you—you'll come off as a crazy person, even if you're not!

To save money as a solo traveler, always stay in hostels, as single rooms in budget hotels usually cost almost as much as double rooms.

If you do get sick of talking to yourself, you can always scope out the scene at www.tripmates.com to find a new traveling companion.

Travelers with Disabilities

Spain's many hills and endless amount of stairs can prove to be challenge to a visitor with disabilities, but in the last few years, conditions have been improving. Newer hotels and restaurants are wheelchair friendly or at least, more sensitive to your needs. However, since most places have limited, if any, facilities for people with disabilities, you might consider taking an organized tour specifically designed to accommodate travelers with limited mobility.

Flying Wheels Travel (☎ 507/451-5005; www.flyingwheelstravel.com) offers escorted tours and cruises that emphasize sports and private tours in minivans with lifts. **Access-Able Travel Source** (☎ 303/232-2979; www.access-able.com) offers extensive access information and advice for traveling around the world with disabilities. **Accessible Journeys** (☎ 800/846-4537 or 610/521-0339; www.disabilitytravel.com) caters specifically to slow walkers and wheelchair travelers and their families and friends.

Avis has an "Avis Access" program that offers such services as a dedicated 24-hour

toll-free number (☎ 888/879-4273) for customers with special travel needs; special car features such as swivel seats, spinner knobs, and hand controls; and accessible bus service.

Organizations that offer assistance to disabled travelers include **MossRehab** (www.mossresourcenet.org), which provides a library of accessible-travel resources online; the **American Foundation for the Blind (AFB; ☎ 800/232-5463;** www.afb.org), a referral resource for the blind or visually impaired that includes information on traveling with Seeing Eye dogs; and **SATH** (Society for Accessible Travel & Hospitality; ☎ 212/447-7284; www.sath.org; annual membership fees: $45 adults, $30 seniors and students), which offers a wealth of travel resources for all types of disabilities and recommendations on destinations, access guides, travel agents, tour operators, vehicle rentals, and companion services.

For more information specifically targeted to travelers with disabilities check out the quarterly magazine *Emerging Horizons* (www.emerginghorizons.com; $14.95 per year, $19.95 outside the U.S.); and *Open World* magazine, published by SATH (see above; subscription: $13 per year, $21 outside the U.S.).

Gay & Lesbian Travelers

In 1978, Spain legalized homosexuality among consenting adults. In April 1995, the parliament of Spain banned discrimination based on sexual orientation. You probably know by now that not experiencing any legal discrimination is hardly the same as not being discriminated against at all.

However, in Spain in general, particularly in its big cities, you'll find it hard to believe that merely 30 years ago this was an ultradogmatic Catholic country. It's not an unusual event today to see same-sex couples walking hand in hand or kissing in the streets of cities such as Barcelona. And that is even more true in the most popular resorts for gay travelers like Sitges (south of Barcelona), Torremolinos, and Ibiza.

All this being said, if you are gay, and looking to hit up the scene in Spain, here are some valuable resources to make it happen:

First of all, the word *entender* (to understand) has special significance in many gay communities in Spain. If you say that you *entiendo,* you're saying that you're gay. It's kind of like saying that you *really* understand. So go on, don't be shy—say you *entiendo* him or her too.

And since you've already picked up one of our guides, we'd like to recommend *Frommer's Gay & Lesbian Europe* (Wiley Publishing, Inc.), which is an excellent travel resource for the top gay and lesbian cities and resorts in Europe.

The International Gay and Lesbian Travel Association (IGLTA; ☎ 800/448-8550 or 954/776-2626; www.iglta.org) is the trade association for the gay and lesbian travel industry, and offers an online directory of gay- and lesbian-friendly travel businesses; go to their website and click on "Members."

Many agencies offer tours and itineraries specifically for gay and lesbian travelers. **Above and Beyond Tours** (☎ **800/397-2681;** www.abovebeyondtours.com) is the exclusive gay and lesbian tour operator for United Airlines. **Now, Voyager** (☎ **800/255-6951;** www.nowvoyager.com) is a well-known San Francisco–based, gay-owned and -operated travel service. **Olivia Cruises & Resorts** (☎ **800/631-6277;** www.olivia.com) charters entire resorts and ships for exclusive lesbian vacations and offers smaller group experiences for both gay and lesbian travelers.

Gay.com Travel (☎ **800/929-2268** or 415/644-8044; www.gay.com/travel or www.outandabout.com) is an excellent online successor to the popular *Out & About* print magazine. It provides regularly updated information about gay-owned, gay-oriented, and gay-friendly lodging, dining, sightseeing, nightlife, and shopping establishments in every important destination worldwide. It also offers trip-planning information for gay and lesbian travelers for more than 50 destinations, along various themes, ranging from sex and travel to vacations for couples.

The following travel guides are available at many bookstores, or you can order them from any online bookseller: *Spartacus International Gay Guide* (Bruno Gmünder Verlag; www.spartacusworld.com/gayguide) and *Odysseus: The International Gay Travel Planner* (Odysseus Enterprises Ltd.), both good, annual, English-language guidebooks focused on gay men; and the *Damron* guides (www.damron.com), with separate, annual books for gay men and lesbians.

Women Travelers

As in other countries in western Europe, Spain, on the whole, is quite safe for women to travel around. Spanish men are very respectful of women and also quite shy, so don't expect them to come begging for your attention like in other Latin countries. With that said, there are a lot of men from other nationalities living in Spain, particularly in the big cities. Although violent crimes and sexual assaults are not that common, women should avoid walking alone at late hours of the night in dark areas of Madrid, Barcelona, Valencia, and Bilbao. Purse-snatching is alarmingly common in the cities and although no physical aggression is usually involved, it's definitely a violent and unpleasant situation.

THE BASICS

Spanish women are extremely liberated, especially so in the big cities. It is perfectly normal for single women to go out partying, just as in New York, Sydney, or London. Speaking of which, with the strengthening of the British pound, many travel agencies in the U.K. offer "Weekend Bachelorette Parties" for sex-starved British girls. You'll see them in groups of 4 to 15 girls making fools out of themselves all over the Mediterranean coastal towns.

As you go farther south men tend to be more flirtatious and overt with women. Just make sure you set boundaries to avoid unwanted situations. A simple *"no, gracias"* should be enough in most cases.

At the beach, topless sunbathing is by far the norm for women of all ages, but none will say anything if you keep your bikini top on. Going out at night girls dress more conservatively in the smaller towns but you won't stand out at all if you wear a skimpy blouse or micro-mini in the big cities.

Among older people, Franco's old-fashioned machismo is still an issue, as shown in the alarming indexes of domestic violence—but fortunately the future looks brighter for the younger generations.

Minority Travelers

Even though Spanish society is not nearly as ethnically heterogeneous as the U.S., minority travelers shouldn't really encounter any problems. One thing that can take some getting used to is how ignorant/curious Spanish are about how integrated other ethnicities are in other countries. Immigration is growing at a fast pace in Spain, and Latin Americans tend to blend in pretty well thanks to the language; but African and Middle Eastern immigrants are usually more segregated. Although it doesn't translate into violent action or outright discrimination, Spanish people are very un-PC when referring to people from other races. Also, for some reason, the Spanish have a hard time thinking of Asians as "Americans" even if, like so many Chinese or Indian Americans, they were born and bred in the U.S. And if you're African American, you might find people asking you about "what that's like," and assuming you are an aspiring hip-hop artist or basketball player. This curiosity isn't meant to be offensive, so take it as an opportunity to educate them—as their own population grows more diverse, Spaniards could certainly use some enlightenment on this front.

On the Web, there are a number of helpful travel sites for African-American travelers: **Black Travel Online** (www.black travelonline.com) posts news on upcoming events and includes links to articles and travel-booking sites. Agencies and organizations that provide resources for black travelers include: **Rodgers Travel** (☎ 800/825-1775; www.rodgerstravel. com), a Philadelphia-based travel agency with an extensive menu of tours to destinations worldwide, including heritage and private-group tours.

The following collections and guides are also useful resources: *Go Girl: The Black Woman's Guide to Travel & Adventure* (Eighth Mountain Press), a compilation of travel essays by writers including the likes of Jill Nelson and Audrey Lorde, with some practical information and trip-planning advice; *Travel and Enjoy Magazine* (☎ 866/266-6211; www.travelandenjoy. com; subscription: $38 per year), which focuses on discounts and destination reviews; and the more narrative *Pathfinders Magazine* (☎ 877/977-PATH; www.pathfinderstravel.com; subscription: $15 per year), which includes articles on everything from Rio de Janeiro to Ghana as well as information on upcoming ski, diving, golf, and tennis trips.

Eco-Tourists

If you're leaning more on the green side of things, Spain is flowing with eco-tourism options. A visit to www.responsibletravel.com will show you trips and offers for greener travel throughout Spain.

The International Ecotourism Society (TIES) defines eco-tourism as "responsible travel to natural areas that conserves the environment and improves the well-being of local people." You can find eco-friendly travel tips, statistics, and touring companies and associations—listed by destination under "Travel Choice"—at the TIES website, **www.ecotourism.org**.

Ecotravel.com is part online magazine and part eco-directory that lets you search for touring companies in several categories (water-based, land-based, spiritually oriented, and so on). Also check out **Conservation International** (www.conservation.org)—which, along with *National Geographic Traveler,* annually presents the World Legacy Awards (www.wlaward.org) to those travel tour operators, businesses, and organizations that have made a significant contribution to sustainable tourism.

Surf the Turf

Useful & Necessary Sites to Check Out

Here's a list of sites you might want to bookmark as you plan your trip to Spain, and pages to pull up as you sit at the Internet point in Girona, figuring out which club you want to go to that night.

GOVERNMENT

◔ **United States Diplomatic Mission to Spain:** Information regarding U.S. embassies, consulates, and travel information for U.S. citizens in Spain: **http://madrid.usembassy.gov**.

◔ **U.S. Department of State Website:** Information regarding passports, visas (including forms and applications), travel advisories, and much more: **http://travel.state.gov**.

OFFICIAL TOURIST BOARDS

◔ For general info on the Net, check out **www.okspain.org**, the official page of the Tourist Office of Spain; **www.red 2000.com**; or **www.cyberspain.com**. You'll find more details on Spanish travel at: **www.softguides.com**.

TRANSPORTATION

◔ **National Railway Service of Spain:** Official site for the national train system. Comprehensive timetable, prices, and online booking: **www.renfe.es**.

MONEY

◔ **X-Rates:** A good site to see how far your U.S. dollar will take you: **www.x-rates.com/calculator.html**.

Travel Blogs & Travelogues

More and more travelers are using Web logs, or **blogs,** to chronicle their journeys online. You can search for other blogs about Spain at **Travelblog.com** or post your own travelogue at **Travelblog.org.** For blogs that cover general travel news and highlight various destinations, try **Writtenroad.com** or Gawker Media's snarky **Gridskipper.com.** For more literary travel essays, try Salon.com's travel section **(Salon.com/wanderlust),** and **Worldhum.com,** which also has an extensive list of other travel-related journals, blogs, online communities, newspaper coverage, and bookstores.

THE BASICS

Frommers.com—the Complete Travel Resource

For an excellent travel-planning resource, we highly recommend **Frommers. com** (www.frommers.com), voted Best Travel Site by *PC Magazine*. No doubt, you—like us—will find the travel tips, reviews, monthly vacation giveaways, bookstore, and online-booking capabilities to be thoroughly indispensable. Special features include our popular **Destinations** section, where you can access expert travel tips, hotel and dining recommendations, and advice on the sights to see in more than 3,500 destinations around the globe; the **Frommers. com Newsletter,** with the latest deals, travel trends, and money-saving secrets; and our **Travel Talk** area featuring **Message Boards,** where Frommer's readers post queries and share advice, and where our authors sometimes show up to answer questions. Once you finish your research, the **Book a Trip** area can lead you to Frommer's preferred online partners' websites, where you can book your vacation at affordable prices.

For smaller blogs exclusive to Spain, check out a search on http://dir.blogflux. com/country/Spain.html or www.blogfinds. com/Spain. These can be a great resource for finding out what people like *you* are really doing. Listen to your fellow travelers and take their advice.

Books, Music & Movies for a Spain State of Mind

You know the deal with guys like Hemingway. But before you head off to Spain, take in some other new culture to get a preview of what awaits you (or, in some cases, hopefully doesn't) during your travels.

Books

The Quest, in which Pio Baroja dissects life in Madrid during the 19th century, is considered to be a Spanish classic. It belongs to the author's trilogy, *The Struggle for Life,* which offers a complete picture of Madrid's horse-and-buggy slums. *Valle-Inclán Plays* (*Divine Words, Bohemian Lights,* and *Silver Face*) by Ramón del Valle-Inclán attacks bourgeois playwrights of his time by taking a hack at the ruling class, patriotism, religion, and machismo. His weapons were obscenity, vulgarity, and a wet pen. *Fortunata and Jacinta* by Perez Galdos is a commentary on the social

classes in Madrid during the 1875 Alfonsine restoration. Galdos deserves to be a household name outside of Spain, like Dickens, to whom he's often compared. If you're interested in the Balearics, check out *A Winter in Mallorca,* by George Sand. Thirty-four-year-old writer George Sand spent the winter of 1938–39 in Valldemossa, on the northwestern side of the island. Her witty and sometimes cruel depictions of the locals are balanced out by her vivid descriptions of the fabulous landscapes.

In Castilla y León, Burgos is home to El Cid, the greatest Spanish *campeador* (warrior) in history. There are more than a baker's dozen stories about El Cid, spurred with the first written in the 1200s, *El Cantar de Mio Cid.*

Movies

If you're not a bookworm or if you've already read his full collection of works, check out the American classic about the Spanish classic, *El Cid* (1961), starring Charlton Heston and Sophia Loren.

During La Movida, Spanish cinema became an important vehicle for personal expression. Above all others, however, stands out Pedro Almodóvar, who, with his gay and liberal vision of Spain, revolutionized Spanish cinema with his film *Pepi, Lucy, Bom, y Otras Chicas del Montón* (1980), starring none other than Spanish singer Alaska as a teenager. With his film *Laberinto de Pasiones* (1982) Almodóvar presciently reflected a Madrid of violent language, sex changes, modern music, and a sense of uncertainty, which is in direct relation to the current climate in Spain.

El día de la Bestia, by Alex de la Iglesia, is a completely wacked-out and hysterical science-fiction version of Madrid, in which the son of Satan descends upon Spain's capital. And, oh yeah, a Basque priest, who is an avid heavy metal fan, is on a quest as his friends try to stop him.

The sun bleached beaches of Formentera play a main role in *Sex and Lucia,* by Julio Medem. This sexually charged story is about a waitress who goes to the island to discover her boyfriend's past. The beaches are still there, but Lucia . . .

It's All Gone Pete Tong, by Michael Dowse, is the hilarious story of a DJ who makes it big in Ibiza and then starts going deaf. It did very well in the indie movie circuit and is a funny description of life on the edge in Ibiza.

And then there's *More.* This 1969 movie by Barbet Schroeder *(Desperate Measures, SWF)* about a German heroin addict who follows an American girl to Ibiza is not your classic '60s drugs movie, but it is very entertaining and depicts life in Ibiza before Pachá. The score is by Pink Floyd—enough said.

Music

Joaquín Sabina could perhaps be best described as the Bob Dylan of Madrid. If you understand Spanish (and words sung sometimes so that even Spaniards can't), the lyrics in *Malas Compañías* will give you a tour of Madrid that no travel guide ever could.

Of course before coming to Madrid, you should study your music history and check out **Alaska,** the wickedest witch of Madrid. She opened up a whole new can of La Movida movers, such as **Tequila** and **Mermelada. Secretos** offered the most American sound while new wave reverberated with **Los Pistones, Nacha Pop,** and **Radio Futura.** Punk crashed La Movida's party with **Aviador Dro** and the **Zombies.**

Ibiza is known as the center of electronic and club music of the world. From Buddha Bar to Space to simple Best of Ibiza Summer compilations, they all have their own **club mix** of summer favorites for each year. An essential chill-out franchise is the **Café del Mar's mix.** Get the CD and then go to the real deal in San Antonio.

Priceless Spanish Experiences (Done Dirt Cheap)

Some of the most memorable things you can do when traveling in Spain won't cost you a dime. The Spanish don't capitalize on their attractions as we would in the U.S., which means that many of the most important **artistic and architectural attractions** in Spain are readily visible just by

walking down the street. If you're on a tight budget, try to avoid getting sucked into trendy clubs. Instead, partake in the authentic, if not that glamorous, urban ritual of the *botellón,* which consists of sitting around in groups in public spaces—usually parks—with something to

THE BASICS

drink—either bottles of beer, coke, and red wine for making *calimoxto,* or a bottle of hard liquor and a mixer—with some ice and plastic cups. Although not every city government approves of this practice, it is widely enforced by youngsters all over the Iberian Peninsula.

Most attractions offer **discounts to college students** and the like. Always mention any discount cards that you may have. ISIC Cards, AAA, college IDs, and so on, can save you a bundle.

Food & Drink

○ **Do most of your indoor drinking in bars;** they are less than half as expensive as clubs. And since you won't go there until at least 3am anyway, you probably won't need to drink anymore by then. Also, more often than not your club admission will include a drink—so don't throw that pass away!

○ **Buy a bottle of wine and take it with you.** Yes, open containers are permitted on the streets in Spain. Sitting on a bench with a pal and a bottle of wine can be a good way to pass hours of downtime. Just remember to be respectful, as this is a privilege of the Spanish culture and should not be abused.

○ **Tapas are a great way of tasting many different things** without paying exorbitant amounts of money. Try the more expensive restaurants with a three-course *menú del día* for lunch and snack on tapas for dinner. Also, many bars will serve you free tapas as you nurse a few drinks.

○ **Grab some fruit, vegetables, or a nice cheese** at one of Spain's endless outdoor markets—this makes for a satisfying and cheap snack or meal.

Shopping, Sightseeing & So On

○ **Don't be afraid to bargain** in one of Spain's outdoor markets. You'll find everything from cellphones to *castañuelas,* all for a negotiable price.

○ **Don't phone home;** use the Internet to keep in touch with friends and family. Although there is a fee for using the Internet at a cybercafe, the rates are much cheaper than an international mobile phone. Save yourself time and send a mass e-mail, bcc'ing the recipients—your friends and family will understand! You can also post a blog about your adventures abroad. You can even get crazy and send a few postcards.

○ **Walk!** The cheapest and often most enjoyable way to get around is to walk. It might be a novel idea for some of us who live places where we need to drive everywhere, but it's a great way to enjoy all that Spanish cities have to offer.

Festivals & Holidays: What's Open? Santo *Who?*

You're in Catholic country now, so keep in mind that on local feast days, many shops, museums, and government offices close down completely—and in many cases, they have a great big party that's a lot of fun. See the list below to make sure you're in the right city at the right time.

WHAT TO DO WHEN EVERYTHING'S CLOSED

○ **Wander.** Sometimes the best experiences in Spain can be those that are uncharted and unplanned. Explore the city you're in, and enjoy this sense of mystery—just always make sure you know how to get home!

○ **Angels in the Architecture.** Figure out the major architectural attractions in your city and go on a treasure hunt. Many of Spain's most famous pieces of art are scattered through its streets. There is no charge to look, so keep your eyes open and discover what defines the beauty of so many Spanish cities.

○ **People-Watch.** Some of the best people-watching in Spain is right in the middle of a plaza. Sit back, relax, and enjoy the view 'cuz there's plenty to see. This is also a perfect opportunity to study your travel guide and maps to chart out your next adventure.

○ **Join in the Siesta.** Take a break, pick a spot, be it the beach or a bench in the plaza, and adhere to Spain's most beloved habit. Everything stays open late here, so you'll have more time to do stuff afterward.

○ **Church Hop.** Spain is known for its unlimited supply of *iglesias* that are almost always open during the day. You will find some of the most amazing medieval and Gothic architecture, and a cool place to take a break from the summer heat.

○ **Go on a Photo Hunt.** Wait for that moment when the moon rises from the ocean or the Tibidabo illuminates! It's worth a thousand words, and the memory is priceless.

HOLIDAYS

Holidays include January 1 (New Year's Day), January 6 (Feast of the Epiphany), March 19 (Feast of St. Joseph), Good Friday, Easter Monday, May 1 (May Day), June 10 (Corpus Christi), June 29 (Feast of St. Peter and St. Paul), July 25 (Feast of St. James), August 15 (Feast of the Assumption), October 12 (Spain's National Day), November 1 (All Saints' Day), December 8 (Immaculate Conception), and December 25 (Christmas).

No matter how large or small, every city or town in Spain also celebrates its local saint's day. Madrid big day is May 15 (St. Isidro). You'll rarely know what the local holidays are in your next destination in Spain, but you can always ask at the local tourist office. Try to keep money on hand because you may arrive in town only to find the banks and stores all closed. In some cases, intercity bus services are suspended on holidays.

Spain Calendar of Events

The dates given below may not be precise as the exact days are sometimes not announced until 6 weeks before the actual festival. Check with the local tourist office if you plan to attend a specific event.

January

Granada Reconquest Festival, Granada. The whole city celebrates the Christians' victory over the Moors in 1492. The highest tower at the Alhambra is open to the public on January 2. For information, contact the Tourist Office of Granada (☎ **958-247-128**). January 2.

Día de los Reyes (Three Kings Day), throughout Spain. Parades are held around the country on the eve of the Festival of the Epiphany. Various "kings" dispense candy to all the kids. January 6.

Día de San Antonio (St. Anthony's Day), La Puebla, Majorca. Bonfires, dancing, revelers dressed as devils, and other riotous events honor St. Anthony on the eve of his day. January 17.

February

Bocairente Festival of Christians and Moors, Bocairente (Valencia). Fireworks, colorful costumes, parades, and a reenactment of the struggle between Christians and Moors mark this exuberant festival. A stuffed effigy of Mohammed is blown to bits. Call ☎ **902-123-212** for more information. First week of February.

ARCO (Madrid's International Contemporary Art Fair), Madrid. One of the biggest draws on Spain's cultural calendar, this exhibit showcases the best in contemporary art from Europe and America. At the Nuevo Recinto Ferial Juan Carlos I, the exhibition draws galleries from throughout Europe, the Americas, Australia, and Asia, that bring with them the works of regional and internationally known artists. To buy tickets, contact Parque Ferial Juan Carlos I at ☎ **917-225-016.** The cost is 24€ to 55€. You can get schedules from the tourist office closer to the event's date. For more information, call ☎ **917-225-017;** www.arco.ifema.es. Dates vary, but the event usually takes place mid-February.

Madrid Carnaval. The carnival kicks off with a big parade along Paseo de la Castellana, culminating in a masked ball at the Círculo de Bellas Artes on the following night. Fancy-dress competitions last until Ash Wednesday, when the festivities end with a tear-jerking "burial of a sardine" at the Fuente de los Pajaritos in the Casa de Campo. This is followed that evening by a concert in the Plaza Mayor. Call ☎ **915-881-636** or log on to www.gospain.org for more information. Dates vary. Normally 40 days before Easter.

Carnavales de Cádiz, Cádiz. The oldest and best-attended carnival in Spain is a freewheeling event full of costumes, parades, strolling troubadours, and drum beating. Call ☎ **956-227-111** or go to www.carnavaldecadiz.com for more information. Late February or early March.

March

Fallas de Valencia, Valencia. Dating from the 1400s, this fiesta centers around the burning of papier-mâché effigies of winter demons. Burnings are preceded by bullfights, fireworks, and parades. For more information, contact ☎ **963-521-730** or go to www.fallasfromvalencia.com. Mid-March.

Semana Santa (Holy Week), Seville. Although many of the country's smaller towns stage similar celebrations (especially notable in Zamora), the festivities in Seville are by far the most elaborate. From Palm Sunday until Easter Sunday, processions of hooded penitents move to the piercing wail of the *saeta*, a love song to the Virgin or Christ. *Pasos* (heavy floats) bear images of the Virgin or Christ. Again, make hotel reservations way in advance. Call the Seville Office of Tourism for details (☎ **954-592-915;** www.turismo.sevilla.com). The week before Easter.

April

Feria de Sevilla (Seville Fair). This is the most celebrated week of revelry in all of Spain, with all-night flamenco dancing, entertainment booths, bullfights, horseback riding, flower-decked coaches, and dancing in the streets. You'll need to reserve a hotel early for this one. For general information and exact festival dates, contact the Office of Tourism in Seville (☎ **954-592-915;** www.turismo.sevilla.org). Second week after Easter.

Moros y Cristianos (Moors and Christians), Alcoy, near Alicante. During 3 days every April, the centuries-old battle between the Moors and the Christians is restaged with soldiers in period costumes. Naturally, the Christians who drove the Moors from Spain always win. The simulated fighting takes on almost a circuslike flair, and the costumes worn by the Moors are always absurd and anachronistic. Call ☎ **965-537-155** for more information. Late April.

May

Feria del Caballo, Jerez de la Frontera. The major wine festival in Andalucía honors the famous sherry of Jerez, with 5 days of processions, flamenco dancing, livestock on parade and, of course, sherry drinking. For information, call ☎ **956-331-150.** Mid-May.

Festival de los Patios, Córdoba. At this famous fair, residents decorate their patios with cascades of flowers. Visitors wander from patio to patio. Call ☎ **957-201-774** for more information. First 2 weeks of May.

Fiesta de San Isidro, Madrid. Madrileños run wild with a 10-day celebration honoring their city's patron saint. Food fairs, Castilian folkloric events, street parades, parties, music, dances, bullfights, and other festivities mark the occasion. Make hotel reservations early. Expect crowds and traffic (and beware of pickpockets). For information, write to Oficina Municipal de Información y Turismo, Plaza Mayor 3, 28014 Madrid; or call ☎ **915-881-636.** May 15.

Romería del Rocío (Pilgrimage of the Virgin of the Dew), El Rocío (Huelva). The most famous pilgrimage in Andalucía attracts a million people. Fifty men carry the statue of the Virgin 15km (9 miles) to Almonte for consecration. Third week of May.

June

Corpus Christi, all over Spain. A major holiday on the Spanish calendar, this event is marked by big processions, especially in Toledo, Málaga, Seville, and Granada. June 2.

Veranos de la Villa, Madrid. This program presents folkloric dancing, pop music, classical music, zarzuelas, and flamenco at venues throughout the city. Open-air cinema is a feature in the Parque del Retiro. Ask at the tourist office for complete details. (The program changes every summer.) Sometimes admission is charged, but often these events are free. Mid-June until the end of August.

International Music and Dance Festival, Granada. Celebrating its 57th year in 2007, Granada's prestigious program of dance and music attracts international artists who perform at the Alhambra and other venues. It's a major event on Europe's cultural calendar. Reserve well in advance. For a complete schedule and tickets, contact El Festival Internacional de Música y Danza de Granada (☎**958-221-844;** www.granadafestival.org). Last week of June to first week of July.

Las Hogueras de San Juan (St. John's Bonfires), Alicante. On June 20 to 24 during the summer solstice, bonfires blaze through the night to honor the event, just as they did in Celtic and Roman times. The bonfire signals the launching of 5 days of gala celebrations with fireworks and parades. Business in Alicante comes to a standstill. Call ☎ **981-202-406** or log on to www.hoguerassanjuan.com for more information. June 20 to 24.

Verbena de Sant Joan, Barcelona. This traditional festival occupies all Cataláns. Barcelona literally lights up—with fireworks, bonfires, and dances until dawn. The highlight of the festival is the fireworks show at Montjuïc. Late June.

July

La Rapa das Bestas (The Capture of the Beasts), San Lorenzo de Sabucedo, Galicia. Spain's greatest horse roundup attracts equestrian lovers from throughout Europe. Horses in the verdant hills of northwestern Spain are rounded up, branded, and medically checked before their release into the wild again. For more information, phone ☎ **981-221-822.** First weekend in July.

Festival of St. James, Santiago de Compostela. Pomp and ceremony mark this annual pilgrimage to the tomb of St. James the Apostle in Galicia. Galician folklore shows, concerts, parades, and the swinging of the *botafumeiro* (a mammoth incense burner) mark the event. July 15 to 30.

Fiesta de San Fermín, Pamplona. Vividly described in Ernest Hemingway's novel *The Sun Also Rises,* the running of the bulls through the streets of Pamplona is the most popular celebration in Spain. It includes wine tasting, fireworks, and, of course, bullfights. Reserve many months in advance. For more information, such as a list of accommodations, contact the Office of Tourism, Calle Eslava 1, 31002 Pamplona (☎ **848-420-420;** www.san fermin.com). July 6 to 14.

San Sebastián Jazz Festival, San Sebastián. Celebrating its 42nd year in 2007, this festival brings the jazz greats of the world together in the Kursaal. Other programs take place alfresco at the Plaza de Trinidad in the Old Quarter. The Office of the San Sebastián Jazz Festival (☎ **943-440-034;** www.jazzaldia.com) can provide schedules and tickets. Late July.

August

Santander International Festival of Music and Dance, Santander. The repertoire includes classical music, ballet, contemporary dance, chamber music, and recitals. Most performances are staged in the Palacio de Festivales, a centrally located auditorium custom-built for this event. For further information, contact Festival Internacional de Santander (☎ **942-223-434;** www.festivalsantander. com). Throughout August.

Fiestas of Lavapiés and La Paloma, Madrid. These two fiestas begin with the Lavapiés on August 1 and continue through the hectic La Paloma celebration on August 15, the Day of the Virgen de la Paloma. During the fiestas, thousands of people race through the narrow streets. Apartment dwellers hurl buckets of cold water onto the crowds below to cool them off. There are children's games, floats, music, flamenco, and zarzuelas, along with street fairs. For more information, call ☎ **915-881-636** or go to www.go spain.org. Two weeks in early August.

The Mystery Play of Elche. This sacred drama is reenacted in the 17th-century Basilica of Santa María in Elche (near Alicante). It represents the Assumption and the Crowning of the Virgin. For tickets, call the Office of Tourism in Elche (☎ **965-452-747**). August 11 to 15.

Feria de Málaga (Málaga Fair). One of the longest summer fairs in southern Europe (generally lasting 10 days), this celebration kicks off with fireworks displays and is highlighted by a parade of Arabian horses pulling brightly decorated carriages. Participants are dressed in colorful Andalucían garb. Plazas rattle with castanets, and wine is dispensed by the gallon. For information, call ☎ **952-213-445** or go to www.andalucia.com. Always the weekend before August 19.

La Tomatina (Battle of the Tomatoes), Buñol (Valencia). This is one of the most photographed festivals in Spain, growing in popularity every year. Truckloads of tomatoes are shipped into Buñol, where they become vegetable missiles between warring towns and villages. Portable showers are brought in for the cleanup, followed by music for dancing and singing. For information, call ☎ **963-986-422.** Last Wednesday in August.

September

Diada de Catalunya, Barcelona. This is the most significant festival in Catalunya. It celebrates the region's autonomy from the rest of Spain, following years of

The Most Important Planning You'll Do

→ Plan to spend a day walking through the city without a map. Plan to wander and you will discover the kinds of treasures that only Spain can hide.

→ Plan to have a 2-hour *menú del día* lunch at your favorite restaurant, where you can taste everything from classic to creative Spanish cuisine while paying fast-food prices.

→ Plan to relax and enjoy life like it should be—trying to apply your American efficiency to Spain will only give you a headache.

→ Plan to meet Spaniards. One of the easiest ways to learn about a country is to spend time with its people. Spain's people are its warmest and finest assets.

→ Plan to stare out the window as you travel. There's no better front row seat to some of the most beautiful and varied landscape in the world.

→ Plan to take pictures, but not too many. Forget about the future or the past; take heed and just enjoy the moment as much as possible.

→ Plan to party. Be it at a mega club(s) for days or at one of the many town parties, partying is as much a part of Spanish culture as eating.

→ Plan to fall in love. Be it with a Spaniard, a city, or a meal, you can't help but feel the love that dominates this culture.

→ Plan to come back again!

THE BASICS

repression under the dictator Franco. Demonstrations and other flag-waving events take place. The *senyera,* the flag of Catalunya, is everywhere. Not your typical tourist fare, but interesting. September 11.

International Film Festival, San Sebastián. The premier film festival of Spain takes place in the Basque capital, often at several different theaters. Retrospectives are frequently featured, and weeklong screenings are held. For more information, call ☎ **943-481-217** or go to www.sansebastianfestival.com. Second week in September.

Fiestas de la Merced, Barcelona. This celebration honors Nostra Senyora de la Merced, the city's patron saint, known for her compassion for animals. Beginning after dark, and after a Mass in the Iglesia de la Merced, a procession of as many as 50 "animals" (humans dressed like tigers,

lions, and horses) proceeds with lots of firecrackers and sparklers to the Cathedral of Santa Eulalia, then on to Plaza de Sant Jaume, and eventually into Les Rambles, Plaza de Catalunya, and the harbor-front. For more information, call ☎ **933-179-829** or go to www.bcn.es. Mid-September.

October

St. Teresa Week, Avila. *Verbenas* (carnivals), parades, singing, and dancing honor the patron saint of this walled city. October 8 to 15.

Autumn Festival, Madrid. Both Spanish and international artists participate in this cultural program, with a series of operatic, ballet, dance, music, and theatrical performances from Strasbourg to Tokyo. This event is a premier attraction, yet tickets are reasonable. Make hotel reservations early. For tickets, contact Festival de Otoño, c/o Teatro de Madrid,

Avenida de la Ilustración, 28013 Madrid (☎ **917-301-750;** www.madrid.org). Late October to late November.

November

All Saints' Day, all over Spain. This public holiday is reverently celebrated, as relatives and friends lay flowers on the graves of the dead. November 1.

December

Día de los Santos Inocentes, all over Spain. This equivalent of April Fools' Day gives people an excuse to do *loco* things. December 28.

Madrid

by Elizabeth Gorman

While Americans ate Reaganomics for breakfast, a new-wave revolution gripped Spain: Madrileño punks unzipped their pants and partied; '80s dives like Rock Ola and La Vía Láctea became a sanctuary for Madrid's degenerates and *rockeros;* Alaska's music, Costus's art, and Pedro Almodóvar's films—they were all part of La Movida Madrileña. Everyone wanted a piece of it, and who could blame them? After 36 years of Franco's fascism finally went to its grave, Spain had managed a peaceful transition to democratic monarchy. Things calmed down long enough for La Movida to seize the day like a dog in heat—shaping the open-minded, freethinking society Madrid is today.

There have been certain setbacks, like the Islamic terrorist bombing on March 11, 2004, at the Atocha-Renfe train station. Apart from causing major devastation and mass fear, the terrorists succeeded in turning the Spanish elections. While Partido Popular (PP) was too quick to blame the Basque terrorist group, ETA, the Socialist party (the PSOE) was smart enough to keep quiet and win the people's trust—creating a sudden, unanimous swing vote for President Losé Luis Rodríguez Zapatero to take his throne.

That's how Spain's biggest city finds itself today: a socialist capital in the midst of the E.U.'s economical bubble—pulling troops out of Iraq, legalizing gay marriage, passing Catalunya's constitution, and, sadly, facing heavy car pollution (which will be even worse once the large M-30 freeway is finished). Madrid's high altitude and dry climate mean cool Mediterranean nights and hot, sticky afternoons for you.

The Best of Madrid

○ **Best Tapas Bar:** Sure, there are more tapas bars in Madrid than there are Starbucks in Manhattan, but the best of the best, not to mention Pedro Almodóvar's favorite, is **El Bocaito.** See p. 100.

○ **Best Place to Find Nazi Daggers and 19th-Century Diving Helmets: El Rastro** is the world's biggest flea market—you never know what you're gonna find. See p. 133.

○ **Best Restaurant to Try New Spanish Cuisine: Finos y Finas** offers a very modern and creative Spanish menu at a price that won't reduce your shopping list. See p. 104.

○ **Best Hostel Ever: Mad Hostal** has got the art of the youth hostel down to a T. Great location, beautiful building, a bar, and a pre-going-out club to hook up before heading out. See p. 92.

Talk of the Town

Eight Ways to Start a Conversation with a Local

1. Bullfighting: For years now, there's been an anti-bullfighting movement. In fact, entire newspapers have been dedicated to the cause, as well as nude protests in the streets. To some extent, the younger generations in Spain are less enchanted by fights and recognize it as animal cruelty, while others support it as vital to Spain's tradition and the national bull market.

2. Madrileños love to diss their counterparts up in Barcelona. They'll tell you that the folks in Barcelona are *más cerrado* (close-minded), *separatistas* (separatists), and *más europeos* (more European than Spanish). Congress recently passed an *estatut* (law) giving Cataluña an unprecedented level of financial autonomy, causing a boycott of Catalan products in the rest of Spain.

3. The recent smoking ban in public places, though not fully enforced, is sure causing a stir. Ask someone for a cigarette or ask them to put one out, and you're bound for some heated discussion.

4. ETA: Should the Spanish government continue to negotiate with ETA terrorists in support of the recent cease-fire? Or should the Spanish government persecute suspected terrorists and send them to prison? Careful, you could cook a chorizo on the flames you'll be fanning.

5. In the States, it's who makes the best apple pie; in Spain, it's who makes the best *tortilla* (potato omelet). Almost everyone in Spain is willing to put up a fist to defend his/her mom's, sister's, or grandma's secret recipe.

6. Major legislation was passed to restructure Spanish universities. Majors such as Humanities and other studies that don't scream "job placement" got the axe. Needless to say, some pretty smart people are pissed.

7. Twelve strikes and you're out. Spain passed a new law giving all licensed drivers a total of 12 points to start. After each infraction, depending on their gravity, points are taken away. Spaniards love to bitch about this one.

8. The living expenses are skyrocketing in Madrid, making it impossible for young adults to move out of mom 'n' dad's. Twenty-somethings are going berserk and want the government to subsidize cheaper living.

○ **Best Lunch Special:** This Spanish cultural advantage (aka *menú del día*) is best experienced at **La Austríaca.** The sassy family that runs it will not let you go until you clean your plate—not that you'll need any incentive. See p. 102.

○ **Best Museum to Get Your Art History Together:** Of the three biggies, the collection at **Thyssen-Bornemisza Museum** is the one that reflects almost every period in the history of art, from El Greco to de Kooning. See p. 123.

○ **Best Bar to Feel the Spirit of Flamenco without Seeing a Show:** **Candela** is dark, gritty, and dangerous (not really, not anymore). The polar opposite of your average tourist Flamenco show, its walls breathe the spirit of all the big guys that perform at the exclusive back-room "cave." If you manage to get in, please tell us how. See p. 116.

Getting There & Around

Getting There

BY AIR

Barajas International Airport, about 13km (8 miles) northeast of the city, is Spain's largest airport, with domestic and international flights arriving daily, some docking at its shiny new Terminal 4. The airport made Spanish headlines when its same old inefficiency continued and people running down its long, rainbow-colored corridor missed their flights. Walking from one terminal to the other is faster than taking the bus and is facilitated by the hundreds of meters of automated walkways. All major airlines are to be found here along with ATMs, a tourist office (in terminal 2), post office, and, of course, shops and bars.

The best way to get in and out of the airport is the **Metro service** (1€) that runs directly from the airport via line 8 and takes less than 20 minutes to reach the commercial city center. Also, on your way out, you can check your bags at the Nuevos Ministerios station at the beginning of your line-8 ride. A **city bus** (No. 200) for 1€ runs about every 15 minutes to and from outside arrival gates Terminals 1, 2, and 3 to Avenida de América and it takes about 30 minutes; you can switch to the Metro or a taxi from there. A **taxi** to the center will set you back around 18€. The information number for the airport is ☎ **902-353-570** (www.aena.es; Metro: Aeropuerto).

BY BUS

Of course most people would rather fly or take the train than sit cramped for hours on a bus. But if your trip isn't too long and you're trying to save money, it can be a good option. Located south of the M30 ring road, **Estación Sur de Autobuses** (C. de Méndez Álvaro 83; ☎ **914-684-200;** www.estaciondeautobuses.com; Metro: Méndez Álvaro) is the main bus station in Madrid. Most bus lines with service to the south and other parts of the country depart from here, and even the bus lines that don't usually have offices here. To and from Sevilla, travel time is 6 hours, 18€; to and from Granada, about 6½ hours, 15€.

AutoRes (☎ **902-020-999;** www.autores.net) runs through Extremadura and Portugal (43€; travel time to Lisbon: 7½ hr.) and has its own bus station at Calle Fernández Shaw 1 (Metro: Conde de Casal). **Alsa** (www.alsa.es) includes companies that serve the south of Spain and neighboring provinces with routes to and from Barcelona (25€; trip time: about 8 hr.). **Continental** (☎ **925-223-641**) buses head

MADRID

either south to Toledo (4.25€) or north toward the Basque regions such as Bilbao (25€). **Herranz** (☎ 918-904-122) has service to Escorial (3.20€).

BY TRAIN

As in most European capitals, Madrid has more than one central rail station. Both have easy-to-read signs that will direct you to the Metro, but take the "Cercanías" commuter train if you're going from station to station—it's much faster than the Metro. For times and fares contact **Renfe** (☎ 902-240-202; www.renfe.es). Buying your ticket in advance is always recommended, as well as buying round-trip. Round-trip tickets can save you up to 20%. You can make your reservation on the phone as long as you give Renfe 24 hours in advance to book it. Internet sales, however, can be processed with less than 24-hours notice; pick up your tickets at the station. If you have a Eurail pass, you still must make your seat reservation and pay the few euros it costs to do so. The newest train is Spain's pride, the lightning-fast AVE, which runs to certain cities like Toledo (8.30€; trip time: ¹/₂ hr.) and Sevilla (70€; trip time: 2¹/₂ hr.). To and from Barcelona, the trip time is about 5 hours (63€). Toward the north, to and from Bilbao will cost 37€ one-way and the trip time is about 6 hours. Toward the south, to and from Málaga will cost 58€ each way (trip time: about 4¹/₂ hr.).

Estación Puerta de Atocha (Glorieta del Emperador Carlos V s/n), older, prettier, and bigger, is the more centric—just steps away from the museum triangle and a hub for most of your travel connections in Spain. The AVE train joins Seville and Madrid in 2¹/₂ hours every day (70€), or you can take an extra hour and save some money on the Altaria (55€). Ticket booking is open every day 7am to 9:30pm (Metro: Atocha Renfe).

Estación de Chamartín (Agustín de Foxá s/n) is the station for most international trains and a few northbound national trains. Staying at a hostel near Chamartín, however, isn't as practical as you might think, as it's nearly 20 minutes from downtown. Instead, take the Metro to Tribunal, Antón Martín, Sol, or Gran Vía and enjoy the center of town. The ticket booth is open every day during the hours of 8:30am to 9pm (Metro: Chamartín).

BY CAR

Spain's six main expressways (N-I to N-VI) shoot outward from Madrid, so intranational traveling is easy. Two circulating roads pulse outward from the city; the hellish inner road is M-30, which is interminably under construction and an endless nightmare; the outer is the M-40.

Getting Around

BY FOOT

Madrid's central neighborhoods and pretty much everything you'd want to visit are within walking distance of each other. Choose an area per day and you won't even have to worry about the subway. Walking around is the best way to see the street vendors, the dealers, the ladies on Calle Montera, the punk kids, and the Rastafarians. In general, be very careful with cars as you're crossing the street—they don't necessarily respect pedestrians. And be quick: The moment the red trafficlight dude starts blinking, run for your life; you barely have enough time to make it to the opposite sidewalk.

BY METRO

It all boils down to the Metro (subway) and the EMT (buses). Both use the same tickets, but the Metro is infinitely easier to use. Plus, it's (usually) fast, safe, and clean. Buy your 10-trip MetroBus pass in the subway stations at booths or automated machines

Madrid & Beyond

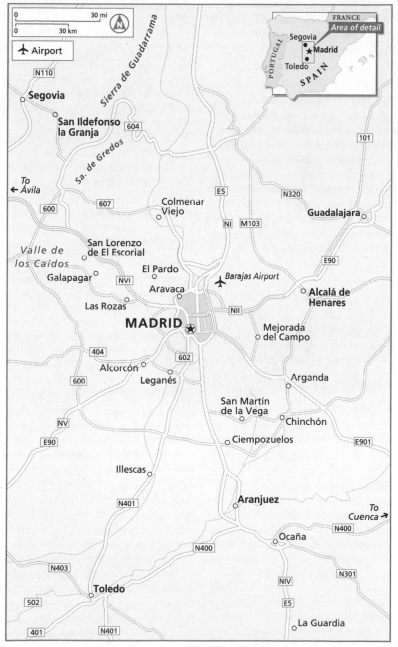

0 30 mi
0 30 km

✈ Airport

N110

Segovia

San Ildefonso
la Granja

604

Sierra de Guadarrama

Sa. de Gredos

101

To
← Ávila

600

607

Colmenar
Viejo

E5

N320

Guadalajara

NI M103

San Lorenzo
de El Escorial

E90

Valle de
los Caídos

Galapagar

NVI

El Pardo

✈ Barajas Airport

Alcalá de
Henares

Aravaca

Las Rozas

NII

MADRID ★

Mejorada
del Campo

404

602

Alcorcón

Arganda

Leganés

600

San Martín
de la Vega

Chinchón

NV

Ciempozuelos

E901

E90

Illescas

N401

Aranjuez

To
Cuenca →

N400

Ocaña

N400

N403

N301

NIV

Toledo

502

E5

401

N401

La Guardia

FRANCE
Area of detail

PORTUGAL

Segovia

★ **Madrid**

Toledo

SPAIN

for only 6.15€ or pay 1€ for each single ride. Metro-system *planos* (maps) are located at the ticket windows; otherwise check out **www.metromadrid.com** beforehand. The subways are closed from 2am till 6am.

BY BUS

The **EMT** (Empresa Municipal de Transportes; **www.emtmadrid.es**) bus service in Madrid is the second-best option for getting around town. Buses run from 6am to midnight. Night buses take off from Cibeles and run from midnight to 6am, but fewer operate at night than during the day. Major bus hubs include Sol, Principio Pio, and Plaza de Castilla. Prices are the same for the Metro as for the bus; however, tickets are not interchangeable.

BY TAXI

Taxis are fairly easy to find and pretty cheap. If you're having a hard time flagging one down, you can call **Radio Taxi** (☎ 914-055-500) or **Tele Taxi** (☎ 913-712-131; www.tele-taxi.es). Fares are set in stone, but make certain that the meter is running and your driver isn't taking you for a proverbial ride.

BY BICYCLE

Madrid is a great city for riding a bike. You can probably go all around the central neighborhoods in 1 day, but you have to deal with pedaling up and down the many hills and crazy drivers. (Recently nudist cyclists protested the traffic with a massive in-the-buff ride.) Because people from Madrid are not so into exercise (besides bumping and grinding) there aren't many bike paths or racks. But if you are a bike activist, or just want to enjoy a Sunday ride around El Retiro, check out **Bike Spain** (Carmen 17 no. 2; ☎ 915-223-899; www.bikespain.info). An outlet for rentals is **Bicimania** (Palencia 20; ☎ 915-331-189; www.bicimania.com); they charge 15€ per

MADRID

cuidado! A simple plan

....

Pickpockets on the Metro are notorious and often work in tag teams of up to three, especially in Sol and Gran Vía. One bumps into you, stealing your attention for a mere second, while the other goes for your wallet or purse.

day, 24€ per weekend, or 75€ per week. Otherwise, **Bravo Bike Tours** (☎ 915-595-523 or 607-448-440; www.bravobike.com) offers a half-day tour that takes you to all the important monuments for 25€; call 1 day in advance to reserve.

BY CAR

If you're thinking about cruising on wheels, know that Madrid is not ideal for driving. Gas is expensive and hard to find in the city, parking is scarce, and the roads are crammed and disorienting. If you still want to go for it, try to drive between 2 and 4pm and park in lots, unless you want to risk parking in reserved spots. (People in Madrid do it all the time and tickets are not terribly expensive, but wasting a day trying to get your car back may not be worth it.)

The big car agencies are in town, as well as the airport and train stations. For reservations try **AVIS** (☎ 902-135-531; www.avis.com); **Europcar** (☎ 917-211-222; www.europcar.com); **Hertz** (☎ 913-937-228 or 917-330-400; www.hertz.es). For a cycle or scooter, call **Motoalquiler** (☎ 915-420-657). Rentals from most of these companies will set you back about 50€ to 80€ for 2 days; all you need is a passport and a valid U.S. driver's license. The best bargain is definitely **pepecar.com** (☎ 902-360-535), where you can find deals beginning at 7€ per day for a tiny Smart car or van.

Orientation: Madrid Neighborhoods

PUERTA DEL SOL This is the geographical center of Madrid and since many big arteries converge there, you'll find yourself visiting it more than you would like to. The neighborhood names and borders are not very clear, but they tend to be defined by the area surrounding a Metro stop of the same name. Look at trendy stores and restaurants for the **Dibuk guides** to the neighborhoods (www.eldibuk.com), which contain maps with hot spots for each area.

SOL The very center of downtown Madrid. Most buses and Metro lines converge here, as do the thousands of travelers who come to gawk at the impressive **Plaza Mayor.** Good shopping and good drinking (at bar haven Plaza Santa Ana in the Huertas area, recently dubbed Barrio de las Letras, or the "Neighborhood of Letters") are also in this area with sidewalks engraved with quotes and passages from Spain's greatest thinkers and writers. The **Puerta del Sol,** which used to be located at the eastern limit of the city and is now the center, is sort of Madrid's Times Square on New Year's Eve, as thousands of people embark on the arduous task of eating one white grape with each of the first 12 bells of the New Year.

EL PRADO This is the ultimate cultural neighborhood, former home of many great Spanish writers. The impressive heritage is still alive in the magnificent Fuente de la Cibeles and the city's three main cultural attractions: **El Prado, Reina Sofia,** and **Thyssen-Bornemisza.** Madrid's three world-class museums are simply too good to miss. They are very close to each other and not far from the other gem in this neighborhood: **Parque del Buen Retiro,** Madrid's green lung, great for outdoor fun or people-watching on a Sunday. It's not as big as Central Park but the blissful feeling of getting out of the city is just as sweet.

LA LATINA One of the oldest neighborhoods in Madrid, this former working-class area is turning into Madrid's newest hot spot (on Sun, especially), thanks to a combination of bars, restaurants, and a new wave of entertainment-industry hipsters making it their home. On Sundays, when the 'hood comes to life, with its massive *Rastro,* it's the best day to stroll around the jam-packed tapas bars and spot local film and TV celebrities.

LAVAPIES The Brooklyn of Madrid, this multi-culti 'hood has been the center for **underground arts and culture** for the past decade. In its hundreds of bars and restaurants you are likely to find Manu Chao or any of the anti-corporate citizens of the world. Here, you'll also find some of the most authentic and grimy flamenco bars in town.

MALASANA The '80s heart of the "Movida Madrileña" (together with Chueca) is now full of artists, musicians, and associated poetry readings, coffeehouses, vegetarian restaurants, and, most significantly, drinking holes. The famed, funky, and fabulous **Calle Fuencarral** begins in this neighborhood and continues out to the Gran Vía Metro stops.

CHUECA West of Calle de Fuencarral is the epicenter of Madrid's **gay and lesbian** communities. This groovy neighborhood has great cafes and shopping by day and perhaps some of the wildest bar scenes in Madrid by night. Chueca is also home to Madrid's most pompous Gaudí-esque building, Sociead General de Autores y Editores.

AUSTRIAS This neighborhood is where you will find Madrid's most grandiose buildings, from the times when royalty were more than just the grinning faces on

MADRID

the cover of *Hello* magazine. Around the Opera metro station you'll find the **Palacio Real, Plaza de Oriente,** and **Plaza de la Villa,** among other landmarks.

SALAMANCA & RUBEN DARIO The *pijo* (yuppie) part of town; a modern neighborhood with straight streets and more designer stores than you can fit in a *Vogue* catalog. Some very interesting museums, like the **Museo Arqueológico** and **Museo Sorolla,** are also in this area of preppy guys and gals. The border—a hell of a border indeed—is **Plaza Colón,** Madrid's skater's cathedral.

Tourist Offices

A good place to pass by at the beginning of your visit is the tourist office at **Barajas airport** (☎ 913-058-656; Mon–Sat 8am–8pm, Sun 9am–2pm). There you can pick up a map and some free English magazines such as *In Madrid* (www.in-madrid.com), which may prove very helpful for a short trip or even if you consider staying longer. The offices at both train stations have the same opening hours as at Barajas, and if you realize you forgot your map where the Spanish sun don't shine, you can get another one at the **Central office** (☎ 902-100-007 or 915-881-636; www.esmadrid.com; daily 9:30am–8:30pm) at Plaza Mayor 27, which moved outside while the building is under construction. You can't miss their kiosks on the Plaza.

Recommended Websites

Some great places to plan ahead on the Web:

- **www.turismomadrid.es**: Official website of the city. Available in Spanish.
- **www.mapmagazine.com**: The premier underground music, arts, and politics e-zine in Madrid for young expats.
- **www.tripfamily.com**: The site with the most ins on the best clubs and DJs in the area.

Cuidado! Smoker's Law

In a small bar, patrons should use their judgment before sparking one up—if you're not sure, smell around or ask. Hash, or *chocolate*, is legal to possess in small amounts for personal use only (a half-gram or less). Smoking tobacco and drinking outdoors is fine with the law—usually, as long as you're cool and in control. Be forewarned, there's a reason that the hash here is always smoked with tobacco: To smoke it solo in a bowl will take you to Planet WhupAss in approximately 5 minutes.

- **www.in-madrid.com**: The English-speaking newspaper and guide to Madrid.
- **www.guiadelocio.com/madrid**: The Web version of the entertainment bible in Spanish.
- **www.webmadrid.com**: A good English-language travel guide to the city.
- **www.madridman.com**: An American-in-Spain's website. Very detailed, if with a little too much advertising.
- **www.madaboutmadrid.com**: A blog-style website in English.
- **www.multimadrid.com**: A comprehensive and English-speaking forum for Madrid.
- **www.lecool.com**: Here's a Web 'zine in Spanish with an updated events calendar.
- **madrid.loquo.com**: Madrid's version of Craigslist with the best classified section.
- **madrid.lanetro.com**: Find directions, street maps, restaurants, clubs, and more on Spain's biggest database for reviews and recommendations.

Johann's Madrid Top 10

Who is Johann, you ask? Only the hottest Spain MTV Veejay from Holland, who has been living in Madrid for umpteen years. He offers this is as his Top 10 Musts for Madrid.

1. **Creperie Ma Bretagne.** Madrid's oldest, most romantic creperie. (San Vicente Ferrer 9; ☎ **915-317-774;** Tues–Sun 8:30pm–1am, Fri–Sat open until 2am; closed Mon.)

2. **José Alfredo's Cocktail lounge.** See p. 113.

3. **La Vía Láctea.** Rock-'n-roll and vintage-soul bar. See p. 113.

4. **Nasti.** Indie music club. See p. 115.

5. **El Parnaso.** Decadent bar with loads of antiques. See p. 112.

6. **Plaza Colón.** Madrid's skate spot. Now more restricted by police, but still cool. Metro: Colón.

7. **La Latina.** One of Madrid's oldest neighborhoods, full of bars and restaurants, good for hanging out on Sunday afternoons. Lots of ladies mingling around. See "Orientation: Madrid Neighborhoods," p. 81.

8. **Cisne Azul.** A tapas bar specializing in mushrooms and flower salads. Succulent. (Gravina 19; ☎ **915-213-799;** raciones 12€–15€; daily 1–5pm and 8pm–midnight; closed Sun.) See p. 104.

9. **Le Garage.** Dingy, sleazy karaoke bar, which turns into an electro/rock club on Thursdays. See p. 117.

10. **Viuda de Vacas.** Spanish restaurant in La Latina. See p. 106.

Culture Tips 101

The legal drinking age in Madrid is 18, but the police certainly don't enforce that law with vigor. For years, the common law in Spain was if you're tall enough to reach the bar, you're served. Although all drugs are illegal, the entire city (and country) smokes *porros*—a joint rolled with tobacco and hash or marijuana—as if their lungs depended on it.

Though a few restaurants have banned it since the no smoking law was passed in Spain, smoking is as prevalent as the old man bars that it fills. Old man bars are so common in Spain (especially Madrid), you're more than likely to stumble into more than one of them daily in order to use the john, order a beer, a tapa, a glass of wine, or just take in the local flair on the skinny. They're located on almost every block in every neighborhood. Old men convene, talk sports and politics, or take their morning shot of *pacharán,* a fruity Spanish liquor. Ah, it's good to be an old man.

Although Madrid is famous for its bars, most young people prefer to drink outdoors. Picking up a 40 *(litro)* at the local *chino* (corner store) and heading to any plaza is local practice here; technically it's considered "A-legal" (a grayish term that's also applied to prostitution). *Macrobotellones* (lots of people drinking in the plaza) and *microbotellones* (a few people) are organized by obsessive text messaging on cellphones and sometimes turn into forms of protest when local whippersnappers, angry that the price of a cocktail in Madrid is so high, demand that loitering in parks with friends and alcohol

MADRID

is their God-given, Spanish right. That is the tradition, and most people agree.

When you're hanging out with the Spaniards, keep in mind that they like to get close—real close. At first, it's a bit uncomfortable when people shove their cheerful faces right up to yours while speaking to you. You may recall Seinfeld's "close-talkers" and instinctually lunge backwards, but try to resist the urge. If you look around, you'll see that Spanish guys often have a hand on their buddy's shoulders and that many women walk arm in arm together—this is a touchy-feely nation. Spanish closeness, does of course, have its own etiquette: Men shake hands when meeting for the first time, while women kiss each other (and men) on both cheeks when first introduced. Does this imply some lovin' later on? Absolutely not. The tradition of *dos besos* (two kisses) is as old as the culture itself, and you'll seem cold and stand-offish if you don't kiss the cheeks of a woman to whom you've been introduced. So don't sweat all the Spanish physical contact. Go with it, you'll like it.

Madrid Nuts & Bolts

Cellphone Providers & Service Centers The main cellphone providers in Spain are **Amena, Movistar,** and **Vodafone.** You can find them all over the city on the main drags. To buy a new cellphone, get a line or service, check out **The Phone House** (Malasaña branch: Fuencarral 66; ☎ **917-014-690;** www.phonehouse.es; Sat–Thurs 11am–9pm; Metro: Gran Vía), a chain that has a catalog with more models than a New York catwalk.

Currency As anywhere else, if you have an ATM card, use it. You'll get the best rates out of those green-eyed monsters. If you like carrying around big wads of dead presidents or just want to complain to someone about the rising price of the euro, banks are open weekdays from 8:30am to 2pm. And finally, if you are really inclined to supporting the Spanish economy in the form of ridiculous exchange rates and fees, there are plenty of exchange booths in or around Puerta del Sol and Plaza Mayor. For your traveler's checks, visit American Express at Plaza de las Cortes 2 (☎ **915-720-320;** Metro: Banco de España).

Embassies If you're in need of some good metal detection and x-ray action, you can always say "hi" to good old Uncle Sam at the U.S. Embassy in the Salamanca neighborhood. It's located at Serrano 75 (☎ **915-872-240;** for after-hours emergencies, ☎ **915-872-200;** www.embusa.es; Mon–Fri 8:30am–1pm; Metro: Rubén Darío, Nuñez de Balboa, Gregorio Marañón).

Emergencies Emergency: ☎ **112.** The two main hospitals in Madrid are **Ciudad Sanitaria la Paz** (Paseo de la Castellana 261; ☎ **917-277-000;** Metro: Begoña) and **Hospital General Gregorio Marañón** (Doctor Esquerdo 46; ☎ **915-868-000;** Metro: Ibiza, O'Donnell). For help with substance abuse, call the **Dirección sobre Drogas** (Recoletos 22; ☎ **918-226-121**). If you're not a tax-paying socialist, credit cards are accepted. For STDs such as possible exposure to HIV, public hospitals run free tests.

Internet & Wireless Hot Spots   Internet cafes, which pop up all over town, are often cramped with kids playing Web games; for special needs, you have a couple of options. The heaps of computers and the little-higher-than-average prices at **Bbigg** (C. Mayor 1; www.bbigg.com; Metro: Sol) guarantee no line when you need to empty your camera's flash card. The ambience is like a computer supermarket; but the connection is fast and you can scan, fax, Xerox, print, and e-mail that picture of your butt in the Plaza Mayor to anyone who could bear to see it. It's open 24 hours and charges 2.20€ per hour and 5€ for 3 hours.

If checking your e-mail is more of a pretext to meet new people than a business requirement, you will find that **Natura Gran Vía** (Gran Via 16; ☎ 915-217-573; 1€ per hour; daily 8am–2am), a ground-floor bar and restaurant with coin-operated computers in the basement, is a better-than-average option (the keyword here being "caipirinha"). The computers work just fine and that guy/girl with the big backpack on the computer next to you may just be your soul mate in disguise.

Laundry   With so much partying, who has time for doing laundry? Not the Madrileños. It shouldn't be hard to find a laundromat near your hotel. If you are in Malasaña, check **Wash Wash** (C. Beneficencia 9; ☎ 914-456-078). This creatively named laundromat will do your dirty work for 9.25€ per 6.5kg (14 lb.) load. Service is usually overnight, but if your plane is leaving for Milan tonight and there's an urgency to your fabulousness, they'll make an exception and do it same-day.

Luggage Storage   Partied Kate Moss–style and got kicked out of your hotel? No worries. Go to **Atocha** or **Chamartín** train stations and you can leave your bags in a *consigna* for 3€ a day. Now you can walk around Madrid with nothing weighing down your hangover. If you've just bought presents for your entire extended family plus the neighbors, and you need a little more breathing room in your hostel, contact **Spain Storage** (Correo 4, 3rd floor, Office 9; ☎ 669-804-530; www.spainstorage.com) in Sol.

Pharmacies   Out of uppers? Head toward the nearest blinking green cross with your written prescription. Though, oftentimes, Spaniards skip the whole doctor thing and head straight there for medical advice. This could be a good solution if you've met up with Montezuma's Revenge. For non-Spanish speakers, pointing works and so does noise-making. Emergency pharmacies are required by law to be open 24 hours a day, on a rotating basis. The daily newspapers tell you whose turn it is to pull the graveyard shift. Condoms are sold in pharmacies, bar bathrooms, and in vending machines on the street.

Post Offices   What happens in Madrid stays in Madrid. But eventually you'll have to go back home to your honey, and nothing says "I Love You" like one of those postcards with the fabric flamenco dresses. To send it, go to your local post office or the main one, **Palacio de Comunicaciones** (Pl. Cibeles; ☎ 913-962-443; www.correos.es; Mon–Sat 8:30am–9:30pm).

Restrooms Don't be a tourist and use a restaurant's restroom without ordering a beer afterward—unless it's a McDonald's, where the code of ethics is universally altered. There are hidden public bathrooms at the top of most major Metro stops. If an upscale club has bathroom staff, tip them some pocket change for their dookie work.

Safety Economic stability has brought Madrid to a state of safety comparable to most European cities. However, with the increase of tourism there's also been an increase in pickpocketing. Just use your common sense. Try to leave your passport locked up in the hotel and make sure you have your credit card numbers somewhere else, in case you have to cancel them. Avoid the less populated areas of Lavapiés at night; some streets near Puerta del Sol, where the professionals of the night offer their services, are probably not the best place to stop and ask for directions. (Unless that's the way you're looking to go.)

Telephone Tips Madrid's city code is **91**; to call the operator, dial ☎ **1009**; you'll get an international operator by dialing ☎ **1008**. You will have to dial oo (like everybody else) so the operator knows it's an international call, then dial the area code and number. Note that recent changes in Spain's phone system now require all local calls within Madrid to be dialed with the 91 prefix. Nearly all pay phones in Madrid have a chart that lists all that info, so don't worry about committing it to memory. All pay phones in Spain take *tarjetas telefónicas* (phone cards), which can be bought at tobacco stores and *estancos* (newspaper stands). Remember to take your card out of the phone after your call! For collect calls, you can call AT&T by dialing ☎ **900-990-011**; MCI by calling ☎ **900-990-014**; and Sprint at ☎ **900-990-013**.

Tipping Waiters here get paid decent wages, so tipping is 10% or less. Only foreigners tip at bars, and you don't tip the masseuse. Cabbies are sometimes tipped .50€.

Sleeping

There are friggin' great places to stay in Madrid—this is a huge city, after all. If you have more than a week's notice of your trip, you won't have to stay in a sucky dump with a dirty toilet seat and warped shower. Dozens of smart places offer you a place to stay for the price of a cab ride in New York. So use common sense and book ahead. Don't sweat trying to find a hostel in the "right" area, either—the various zones are surprisingly close together, and if you're centrally located, you'll never have to walk for more than 20 minutes to get to your destination (5 or 10 is usually more like it). There are an abundance of *pensions* (hotels with very basic rooms) all over Sol, Gran Vía, and Chueca. Most hostels in Madrid keep their main doors locked and buzz their tenants in. Although annoying and inconvenient, it's true that your backpack is a lot safer this way. So, even though most hostels will tell you that they don't have a curfew, be patient when you are ringing the bell at 6am.

Hostels

➔ **Barbieri International Hostel** With not as much personality as Cat's (see below), this hostel inside a typical Madrid building will make you feel like you're back at your dorm, minus the lava lamp. The mixed or single-sex rooms are small and have two, four, or eight beds. The pastel-colored, parquet-floored common spaces are IKEA cozy, with big multi-colored couches and furniture. There's a fully equipped kitchen, a computer with Internet access, lockers in most rooms, and a safe in reception. The ambience is friendly and the bathrooms are sparkling clean, most of the time. However, the best feature, besides the lowest prices around, is the location, smack in the center of fun-filled Chueca. *Barbieri 15, 2nd floor. ☎ 915-310-258. www.barbieri hostel.com. 15€–16€ per person. Breakfast included. Amenities: Internet, kitchen, laundry, shared bathrooms, sheets, telephone, towels (1€), travel info, TV, DVD, movies (.50€). In room: A/C, locker. Metro: Chueca, Gran Vía.*

→**Cat's Hostel** Walking into this 18th-century Andalucian-style palace makes me wish I were 20 and single again. Aside from the sultan-worthy tile and glasswork, plus a fountain from the original building, this place is a backpacker's wet dream. The dorms sleep between 6 and 14 people (a little crowded, but who's sleeping anyway?) and are either girls, guys, or mixed. There are coin-operated washers and dryers on both floors. A cool bar by the entrance is probably one of Madrid's better pickup spots, topped, or rather bottomed, by the underground "cave," with DJs, live music, and computers with free Internet access. The bar is open from 7pm to midnight, so you can start your night there, meeting people and drinking 2€ pitchers of beer. Breakfast, sheets, towels, private lockers, and a great location are all rolled into a price that seems too good to be true. *Cañizares 6. ☎ 913-692-807. www.catshostel. com. 17€ per person. Breakfast included. Amenities: Internet, kitchen, laundry, shared bathrooms, sheets, telephone, towels, travel info, TV (in common room). In room: A/C, locker. Metro: Anton Martín, Sol.*

→**Colors Hostal** ★★ If you're willing to spend a little more than you normally would for a hostel, make this one of your first calls. Located in the trendiest neighborhood, Malasaña, on the main drag with budding design shops and cafes, this brand-new, Isaac Mizrahi–esque hostel is a clean-edged, Fiestaware haven for tourists who appreciate a bit of comfort, design, and flair. In fact, we have no idea why it's not called a hotel, instead. The service is up to par, and even better is the value for your money. Single rooms are date-friendly with a double bed. Try to request room No. 1 (out of only nine rooms), as it's the only room with a glass-encased hanging balcony, for about 5€ more. Candy bars and bottled water treat and greet you in rooms decorated in different colors, with bright bedding, private bath, and flatscreen plasma televisions. You'd never guess the owner is colorblind, but he is. *Fuencarral 39, 4th floor. ☎ 915-214-646. www.colorshost.com. Double 65€–70€. Amenities: Breakfast (3€), elevator, free Internet and Wi-Fi, telephone, towels. In room: A/C, plasma TV, fridge, hair dryer, Internet access, safe. Metro: Tribunal or Gran Vía.*

→**Hostal Alonso** ★ This hostel has more personality than the Church Lady on *SNL.* Although old and traditional, its personal touches, ticks, and quirks won us over within a few seconds, especially considering that it's a government-rated one-star hostel. It's located almost equally near Sol, Plaza Mayor, Calle Huertas, and Plaza Santa Ana, on a quiet street, the kind you imagine when you think "Europe," and right next to an anarchist political group, an Internet cafe, and a used-CD store. Go figure. The building is more than 200 years old and the stripped, wooden floors look original. The building just installed a new elevator, and the owners are constantly repainting and cleaning for the mostly

Sleeping in Madrid

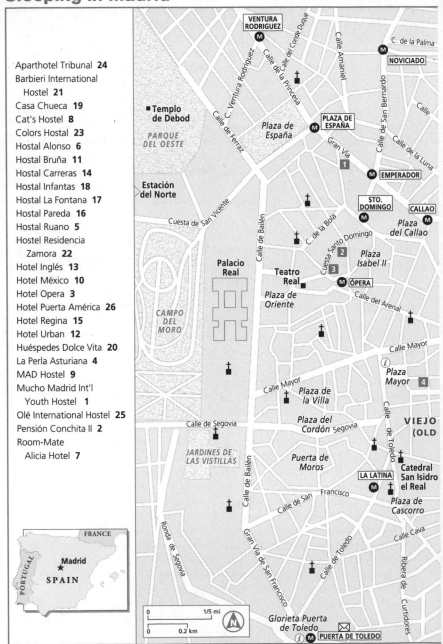

Aparthotel Tribunal **24**
Barbieri International
  Hostel **21**
Casa Chueca **19**
Cat's Hostel **8**
Colors Hostal **23**
Hostal Alonso **6**
Hostal Bruña **11**
Hostal Carreras **14**
Hostal Infantas **18**
Hostal La Fontana **17**
Hostal Pareda **16**
Hostal Ruano **5**
Hostel Residencia
  Zamora **22**
Hotel Inglés **13**
Hotel México **10**
Hotel Opera **3**
Hotel Puerta América **26**
Hotel Regina **15**
Hotel Urban **12**
Huéspedes Dolce Vita **20**
La Perla Asturiana **4**
MAD Hostel **9**
Mucho Madrid Int'l
  Youth Hostel **1**
Olé International Hostel **25**
Pensión Conchita II **2**
Room-Mate
  Alicia Hotel **7**

FRANCE

Madrid
★
SPAIN

PORTUGAL

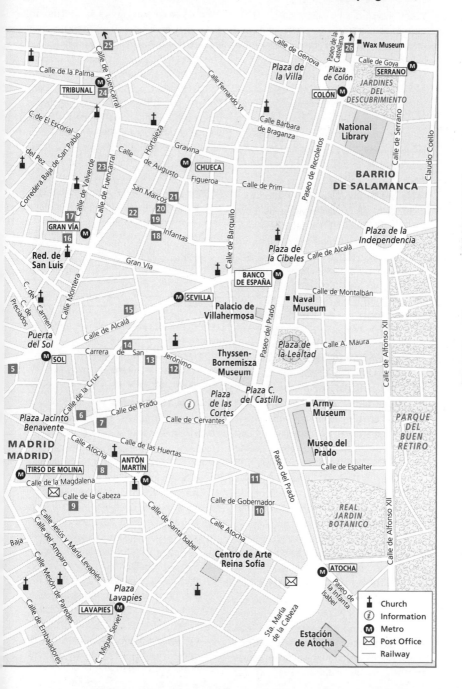

young travelers who pass through. (That means bed frames are new and not creaky.) Ask for an exterior room with a balcony. *Espoz y Mina 17, 3rd floor (corner of Plaza del Angel).* ☎ *915-315-679. Single with sink and shared bathroom 20€, double with sink and shared bathroom 30€, double with private bathroom 40€, triple with sink and shared bathroom 50€. Amenities: Elevator, luggage storage, shared bathrooms, sheets, towels. In room: TV. Metro: Sol, Antón Martín.*

➜**Hostal Bruña** If you're in Madrid for 1 night, then this is your best bet, as it's in the same 'hood as all the major museums, such as Reina Sofia and El Prado, not to mention El Parque del Buen Retiro (Madrid's Central Park). It's also near the Atocha train station so you'll waste no time in scouting out the hostel. The drawback is that it's in a decayed building, lost in the midst of expensive restaurants. The rooms themselves are large but plain, with absolutely no frills (unless you count the hair dryer). You're paying for location and that's it, Bucko. Completely outfitted apartments are also available for 55€ per night and are the only rooms with private bathrooms, kitchen, and laundry services. The youngish woman who runs it has all her marbles and will help you out with anything you need in the area. Lavapiés and Calle Huertas are within a short walking distance, so your night isn't totally shot by the time you have to hop the train, as long as you can pull an all-nighter. *Moratin 50, 2D.* ☎ *914-294-701. www.ctv.es/hostal bruna.com. Single 38€, double 45€, triple 65€. Amenities: Shared bathrooms, sheets, telephone, towels. In room: TV, hair dryer. Metro: Anton Martín.*

➜**Hostal Carreras** Located in the area near Huertas (translation: party central), this hostel is quaint and welcomes guests to their rooms with art such as *Las Meninas*—a copy of course, but still nice to wake up to in the morning. Freshly painted walls and original molding lend an aristocratic air to the place, as if it's a real home rather than a bare-bones hostel where you're afraid to look under the bed. There's more than sufficient furniture, including a wooden writing desk to plan your nightly itinerary. The naturalist iron balconies of the exterior rooms are the most attractive on the street. The catch is there are only eight rooms, so you've got to book at least a week in advance, or else wait for a cancellation. Not all rooms have bathrooms, just a sink and a few with showers, but the place is so homey that walking down the hall to the john is no biggie. *Principe 18, 3 Izda.* ☎ *915-220-036. Single with only sink 21€, single with sink and shower 27€, double with sink and shared bathroom 36€, double with sink and shower 42€, double with private bathroom 54€, triple with sink and shower 54€, triple with private bathroom 60€. Amenities: Shared bathrooms, sheets, telephone, towels. In room: A/C, TV, safe. Metro: Sol, Sevilla.*

➜**Hostal La Fontana** ★ Nobody would ever know from its gritty, unassuming entrance right across the street from a *puti club* (strip joint) and a few seedy bars that this is perhaps the hippest, most design-savvy hostel in the area, on an offshoot of Gran Vía. Inside, bright yellow floors sparkle with embedded glitter and orange, nearly offensive Mod furniture decorates the entrance. Rooms are equally modern and in keeping with the building's historical architecture; double-thick glass windows halt the strains of loud traffic on Gran Vía. The only thing else you could ask for in this gay-friendly joint is a free lap dance. The attractive, multilingual staff would most likely refuse, but they do their best to make sure your stay is more than pleasurable. Bedrooms are modern and clean, and the majority have private bathrooms. *Valverde 6, 1st floor (but really 2nd floor, in American terms).* ☎ *915-218-449 and 915-231-561. www. hostallafontana.com. Single with sink and shared bathroom 23€, single with private bathroom 30€, double with sink and shared bathroom 40€, double with private bathroom 50€, triple with private bathroom 60€. Amenities: Internet (1€ for half-hour), shared bathrooms, sheets, telephone, towels. In room: A/C, TV. Metro: Gran Vía.*

→ **Hostal Pareda** This is a three-star hostel so the prices are a little higher than what you're used to in Madrid, but check out the Hollywood glam rooms with glass chandeliers, original wood floors, porcelain bathtub, and oh yeah—it's right on Gran Vía. This old house is a historic building made up of more than one hostel, though this one, with its grand foyer decorated in period-style furniture, was our ultimate favorite. The best room has its own salon—a little more expensive but worth the extra euros you'd otherwise spend on a few cocktails. The desk clerk is young and helpful. *Valverde 1 (corner of Gran Vía).* ☎ *915-224-700. www.hostalpereda.com. Single 54€, double 67€, double with salon 79€, triple 86€. Amenities: Breakfast (3.20€), elevator, sheets, telephone, towels, TV (in common room). In room: TV (10€ deposit is required for remote control). Metro: Grand Vía.*

→ **Hostal Ruano** This hostel is for that person who always wants to be the center of attention. Perched above Sol, with no elevator to lift you or your luggage, the historical building goes back to 1846, when it was originally El Monasterio de San Felipe. The hostel's entrance greets you like an old '20s movie, with Charlie Chaplin prints and roaring furniture. Its white hospital corridors are impersonal but the rooms are bright with lofty ceilings, funky bedspreads, and sunny rooms that overlook Sol. Obviously, the exterior rooms are noisy but you're asking for it in a hostel with windows open to Madrid's central system. There must've been a special on white lace because it's everywhere here. Rooms without a private bath have sinks and shower stalls. The shared toilets are barely big enough for Tiny Tim and Thumbelina. There's an Internet cafe on the top floor of the building called Euronet, open every day 10am to 10pm. *Mayor 1, 3rd floor.* ☎ *915-321-563. Double without private bath 30€, double with private bath 45€. Amenities: Shared bathrooms, sheets, towels, telephone (in common area). In room: TV. Metro: Sol.*

→ **La Perla Asturiana** You can't get any closer to Plaza Mayor than this, and the prices are super-economical considering your vantage point—although, the fittings in the bathrooms, the furnishings, bedspreads, and vinyl floors are all extremely outdated and worse than a neglected suburban house on antidepressants. But give it a break—it's more than 70 years old. The rooms are dreary, but they're extremely clean smelling and well maintained, sporting new foam mattresses. Rest assured, you'll get a good night's sleep, as long as you can acclimate to the toxic smell of cleaning chemicals. The highlights are the large, luminous '70s globe, no doubt original, and the bright-blue, tiled private bathrooms. Right downstairs from the hostel is bohemian-shopping Buddha heaven and an array of cafes near the Plaza. Call at least a week in advance to secure a reservation with the English-speaking staff. *Plaza de Santa Cruz 3.* ☎ *913-664-600. www. perlaasturiana.com. Single 36€, double 48€, triple 65€. Amenities: Internet (1€ per half-hour), fax, sheets, telephone, TV (in salon), nonsmoking rooms available. In room: A/C in all exterior rooms, hair dryer, safe (1€). Metro: Sol, La Latina.*

MADRID

MTV (Best ☺) →**Mad Hostel** ★★ Owned by the same people as Cat's Hostal, this party hostel was built in a newer building that offers better services and more amenities, though it's not as glam, nor published in as many surface guides. Originally, it was an old *corrala*, a large apartment building with an interior patio. The structure hasn't changed, creating an open, everyone-wants-to-meet-everyone kind of environment—everyone meaning mostly back-packers wearing college T-shirts. The other advantage is the neighborhood. It's off the beaten path and close to less tourist-trod-den areas, yet still close to hot night spots (like Calle Huertas, El Rastro flea market, and Lavapiés) and museums. A little secret is that the employees actually recommend this over Cat's, Europe's No. 1-rated hostel. The upstairs gym, rooftop deck, terrace bar, flamenco *tablao,* pool table, free food, and organized pub crawls, are certainly proof of its superiority. Dorms are all bunked, and you can choose between male, female, or mixed rooms. *Cabeza 24.* ☎ *915-064-840. www.madhostel.com. 17€ per person. Amenities: Bar, breakfast, free Internet, kitchen, laundry, share bathrooms, sheets, telephone (in common area), towels (deposit is required), travel info, TV (in common room). In room: A/C, hair dryer, locker. Metro: Anton Martín.*

→**Mucho Madrid International Youth Hostal** Voted the safest hostel in the world by www.hostalworld.com, this hos-tel is run like a tight ship. That doesn't mean you can't have fun. It simply means that the *señora* has a sixth sense about whether the person you take home is a good choice or not—and you'll thank her in the morning. Rooms are big, airy, sani-tized, bleached, scrubbed, and held to a mother's high standard of cleanliness. There's a place for everything, and every-thing in its place. Mattresses are new and

the four bathrooms look like they've just been scrubbed by the military. Despite all this, the hostel retains its hipness. Rooms with balconies overlook Gran Vía, near theaters, restaurants, and cafes. *Gran Vía 59, 7D, between Plaza Callao and Plaza España.* ☎ *915-592-350. www.muchomadrid.com. 20€ per person. Breakfast included. Amenities: Elevator, Internet, kitchen, laundry, shared bathrooms, sheets, telephone, towels, travel info, TV (in common room), Wi-Fi. In room: Locker. Metro: Gran Vía, Plaza España.*

MTV (Best ☺) →**Olé International Hostel** This hostel works like a backwards mullet: party in the front, business in the back. It's an international breeding ground of trav-elers between 18 and 26 years old, from every corner of the world, who prefer an international (non-hippy) commune right in the heart of Malasaña. In fact, it was difficult to distinguish the guests from the righteous Argentineans who run it. Everyone is your friend and willing to offer you a hand or a recommendation. What its pea-size bunks lack in space, its salon and kitchen make up in breadth. Bathrooms are all exterior, and showers are hot. *Manuela Malasaña 23, 1st floor (again, really the 2nd).* ☎ *914-465-165. www.olehostel.com. 17€ per person. If you make the reservation online, it's even cheaper (15€). Breakfast included. Amenities: Internet, kitchen, laun-dry, shared bathrooms, sheets, towels (1€), TV (in common room), vending machine, lockers. Metro: San Bernardo, Bilbao.*

Cheap

→**Aparthotel Tribunal** This apartment-style hotel is a great option if you are a vegetarian, organic food freak, or just pre-fer to cook your own meals without shar-ing with four other backpackers. There's a sober big reception in a lobbylike area by the elevators. Each fully furnished one- or two-bedroom apartment has a kitchenette with utensils, a small fridge, and a big '60s modern couch; some have a view to Fuencarral. The walls' colors are a little dim—ambience is not exactly springing from every ochre surface—but the Malasaña neighborhood has plenty to make up for it. English is spoken and groups fit right in; you can add a third bed for 20€. *San Vicente Ferrer 1 (corner of Fuencarral).* ☎ *915-221-455. www.aparthotel-tribunal.com. Single 50€, double 80€. Amenities: Kitchen, laundry, sheets, towels, parking. In room: A/C, TV, fridge, hair dryer, safe. Metro: Tribunal.*

→ **Casa Chueca** Though this guesthouse is either gay, metrosexual, or somewhere over the rainbow, it welcomes all sexual orientations with pizazz and flare. Exceeding where other hostels lack, you can't do much better in Chueca, or in Madrid for that matter. Inside the individually styled rooms with private bathrooms, biscuits and tea are set out with the preciseness of a four-star hotel. Bedspreads are straight from IKEA. There's a computer with free Internet access in the front hall, and three rooms have balconies overlooking one of the hottest streets in Chueca, nightly laden with people of all colors and sexual preferences. *San Bartolomé 4, 2 Izda. (corner of San Marcos).* ☎ *915-238-127. www.casachueca.com. Single 40€, double 55€, triple 75€. Amenities: Internet. In room: A/C, TV, Internet hookup. Metro: Chueca.*

→ **Hostal Infantas** Enter this classic Madrid building, go through a dark and massive lobby, walk up the majestic wooden stairs, and ring the bell on apartment 1I. Inside you'll find a quiet and safe little hostel featuring seven rooms with showers and sinks (shared toilets), some with full bathroom including bathtub. Most rooms have balconies, a night table, a

closet and desk, and are very clean. The modern 20th-century Formica furniture has that kind of interesting-without-trying charm, the common areas have new parquet floors, and the shared bathrooms are as clean as only your grandmother could keep them. Speaking of grandmother—try to deal with the lady taking care of the place; grandpa has a little attitude. *Infantas 30, 1st Izquierda.* ☎ *915-210-673. Double with shared bathroom 30€, double with private bathroom 40€. Amenities: Elevator, sheets, towels. In room: A/C, TV. Metro: Gran Vía, Banco, Chueca.*

→ **Hostel Residencia Zamora** Renovated only a few years ago, all the rooms now have private bathrooms, television, heat, air-conditioning, and really nicely patterned hardwood floors, too. Because the rooms overlook the Plaza Vázquez de Mella, they are all bright, as well as quiet. If you don't have a reservation and are worried about getting stranded, check out this hostel first because there are several others in the same building. Convenient to Gran Vía, Sol, and Calle de Fuencarral. *Plaza Vázquez de Mella 1, 4th floor.* ☎ *915-217-031. Single 36€, double 45€. Amenities: Elevator, sheets, towels. In room: A/C, TV, safe (1€). Metro: Gran Vía.*

→ **Hotel México** Ready for a Mexican-deco break in the museum area? Hotel Mexico feels a little past its time of splendor, staff included, but its simple homage to Mexican culture makes it a good option for a quiet night in the crazy city. The bright marble lobby has comfy couches and a very welcoming vibe. Rooms are furnished Mexicana-style with reproductions of famous south-of-the-border paintings, and all have clean, white private bathrooms. They don't offer much of a view though, so you'll have to settle for the TV; but the mattresses are firm and the sheets are soft. Basically, come here just to sleep, or to have breakfast at the cute little dining room with a wooden bar. *Gobernador 24.* ☎ *914-292-500. www.hotelmexico.es. Single 55€, double 65€–70€, double with extra bed 75€. Amenities: Elevator, fax, sheets, towels, parking (10€). In room: A/C, TV, safe. Metro: Anton Martin.*

➜ **Huéspedes Dolce Vita** Out of the hundreds of hostels you can find on single floors of buildings around Malasaña and Chueca, this guesthouse may be one of the most fun, if not most comfortable. Right out of an Almodóvar movie, your room may have three blue plastic stars on top of your bed serving as night lamps; a bathroom with yellow, orange, and white striped walls; or a hot pink shower curtain. Try to get a room with a balcony, which may be noisier, but less dark. The furniture is cheap but has in personality what it lacks in sturdiness. Each room has a tenement-house-style shower and sink, while some have a full bathroom. They offer a 3€ breakfast, but the windowless "dining" room is not the hotel's best feature; better to go downstairs to a bar and have a *chocolate con churros* served by your neighborhood drag queen. *Note:* Minimum stay of 2 nights on the weekend. *San Bartolomé 4, 3rd floor.* ☎ *915-224-018. www.hospedajedolcevita.com. Single with shared bathroom 25€, double with shared bathroom 40€, single with private bathroom 35€, double with private bathroom 55€. Breakfast included. Amenities: Internet, laundry, sheets, towels. In room: A/C, TV. Metro: Chueca, Gran Vía.*

➜ **Pensión Conchita II** ★ If you know a good deal when you see it, this *pensión* will knock you over the head with a plunger. The quaint, naturally bright apartment is totally outfitted with new furniture and everything you could possible need for a few nights in Madrid on a

budget, including a microwave in each room for Easy Mac and a minifridge for the leftovers. Each room has a fair-size bathroom, with an actual bathtub and shower head instead of your average shower closet. It's also in a more-than-unique area near the Opera house and a 5- to 10-minute walk to Sol, Plaza Mayor, or the Royal Palace. Below the small balconies is a narrow and picturesque street without too much thru-traffic. *Campomanes 10, 4 Izda. (between Callao and Santo Domingo).* ☎ *915-475-061. Single 30€, double 44€, triple 66€. Amenities: Elevator, laundry service, sheets, telephone, towel. In room: TV, fridge. Metro: Opera.*

Doable

➜ **Hotel Inglés** This hotel defines "classic Madrid." More than 150 years old, its walls virtually breathe history. Unfortunately, the decor has been recently renovated to adhere to the boring E.U. standard, but at least that includes spotless rooms and friendly, 24-hour English-speaking staff. The great thing is the location, 1 block from Puerta del Sol and within walking distance of every neighborhood that matters. There are 58 rooms; the ones in the front are brighter and louder than the ones in the back. Moreover, if you want to burn off all that *cerveza,* you can always use the gym. *Echegaray 8.* ☎ *914-296-551. Single 75€, double 95€. Amenities: Elevator, fax, Internet, laundry services, rooms for those w/limited mobility, sheets, telephone, towels. In room: A/C (half the hotel), TV, hair dryer, safe. Metro: Sol.*

➜ **Hotel Opera** A modern classic in the middle of the Asturias neighborhood, this hotel offers more wood than the Amazon, with parquet floors, wood-panel walls, and classy dark furniture. You can hang out in one of the six conference rooms, the requisite marble lobby, a cafe with a lovely marble bar, an English bar straight out of a *Sherlock Holmes* tale, or the huge restaurant with a grand piano. The rooms also have parquet floors, chairs, and comfy beds. The ones with terraces have views of old Madrid, which is worth the whole price of the stay itself—especially in low season, when they offer great deals. The quirky feature of this hotel is the dinner, served by their staff of "singing" waiters, making it a full-on Broadway experience. *Cuesta de Santo Domingo 2.* ☎ *915-412-800. www.hotel opera.com. Single 65€–110€, double 75€–140€. Amenities: Breakfast, Internet, sheets, towels, Wi-Fi. In room: A/C, TV, hair dryer, Internet hookup, safe. Metro: Opera.*

→**Hotel Regina** If you want to experience chic living at mid-range prices, you may want to check out this swanky three-star hotel with a lot of blow for the buck. A bright, modern lobby with comfy couches and reception area welcomes hordes of American tourists yearning for comfort à la Marriott. There's a modern, street-level cafeteria, classic dining room, conference room, and a beautiful, brick-walled, bodega-style winery. The 180 rooms are plush and spacious with huge beds, modern wooden furniture, and dark marble bathrooms with double sinks. Try to get the *buhardilla* (attic) rooms, with slanted ceilings and thick wooden beams, with great views of the city. They'll also pick you up and drop you off at the airport—perfect for your parents. *Alcalá 19.* ☎ *915-214-725. www.hotelreginamadrid.com. Single 120€, double 150€, triple 180€. Amenities: Internet, laundry service, rooms for those w/limited mobility, sheets, telephone, parking, room service. In room: A/C, TV, hair dryer, Internet hookup, safe. Metro: Sevilla.*

→**Room-Mate Alicia Hotel** Kitty-corner to Plaza Santa Ana, this hotel will scratch your itch for pop with decor straight out of a Lichtenstein comic book. Minimalism is taken to new heights with apples on display as art and see-through shower stalls in the middle of the room—so you better like your roommate. On the bed, there's a note telling you the next day's weather forecast, so you can dress as inappropriately as you like. The staff speaks English and has a New Age attitude similar to the lobby's decor. Flatscreen TVs and modern lighting won't let you forget you're on vacation. *Prado 2.* ☎ *913-896-095. Single from 80€, double from 90€. Amenities: Bar, breakfast, sheets, towels, A/C, Wi-Fi. In room: A/C, TV, hair dryer, safe, minibar. Metro: Sevilla.*

Splurge

→**Hotel Puerta América** If you have the money and you care at all about interior design, don't stay anywhere else. If you can't afford it, at least go check it out. Don't be fooled by the facade; Puerta América is to hotels what the pyramids are to caskets. Twenty celeb architects and designers (for example, Isozaki, Norman Foster, Zaha Hadid, Ron Arad) took on the design of one full floor each, plus the common spaces and even the garage, creating 12 different auteur hotels in one. When you walk into this huge hotel, through a tiny electric door hidden in the wall, the staff will take you on a tour in a glass elevator for you to pick your favorite world. Some of the creations include a room made out of a single piece of Corian (a mix of resin and marble); a Feng Shui room that includes Inoki wood bathtubs from Japan; round beds and projectors instead of TVs; leather walls, you name it. The rooms aren't too big and the location isn't the best, but the list of amenities—including a menu of different baths (romantic, relaxing, and so on) that you can order to be prepared for you—makes up for everything. All of this doesn't come cheap, but at least you'll save some money on design magazines. *Av. de América 41.* ☎ *917-445-400.*

MADRID

www.hotelpuertamerica.com. Double 150€– 170€ (low season depends on promotions), 200€–250€ (high season depends on promotions). Amenities: Elevator, Internet, laundry service, rooms for those w/limited mobility, sheets, towels, health club, parking, pool, room service, safe. In room: A/C, TV, hair dryer, minibar, Wi-Fi. Metro: Cartagena.

→ **Hotel Urban** A great exercise in modern luxury, this hotel's method seems to be contrasting the old with the new. Built in 2005, with a flashy style worthy of any New York superstar hotel, Urban features antique Buddhist and Egyptian artifacts everywhere, even in your room, matching your oak floors and walls. The main collection though, is in the "Egyptian museum" (also serving as a conference room) with original pieces imported directly from Tut's land. An internal glass elevator takes you from the super-cool lobby, with "C"-shaped leather couches, to the rooftop pool, where you can swim while overlooking the city or have a drink at the outdoor bar, open also to the public. The rooms are big and slick, with all the amenities you'd expect at a five-star hotel, but with local touches like sherry and *jamón Ibérico* (Spanish ham). Aside from the regular rates, special packages include all sorts of cultural and gastronomical perks, so check their website. *Carrera de San Jerónimo 34. ☎ 917-877-770. www.derbyhotels.com. Double 180€–350€ depends on hotel occupancy each night. Amenities: Bar, breakfast, elevator, fax, laundry service, rooms for those w/limited mobility, sheets, telephone, Wi-Fi, parking, room service. In room: A/C, TV, fridge, hair dryer, Internet, safe. Metro: Sevilla.*

Eating

Madrid is a big part of the recent Spanish foodie movement, and with increased immigration, the variety of "ethnic" restaurant options in town is ever-growing. For example, if you're in the mood for authentic Indian food, you don't need to travel 7,000km (4,340 miles) to Bombay, just Calle Lavapiés (Metro: Lavapiés). For just about 10€, Little India serves more spiced rice than you can put away, and it's served on terrazas near trendy bars in the area. If it's the finer tapas you're in the country for, you can't miss with Calle Cava Baja in La Latina. Be sure to avoid Plaza Mayor against all odds, or it will cost you.

For budget dining in the city, **Día** is a particularly low-cost chain grocery store with several locations. A handful of restaurants at Plaza Emperador Carlos V/Ronda de Atocha (Metro: Atocha) stay open 24/7 on weekends, but other than that, you will have to settle for the Spanish equivalent of a 7-11, VIPS, when you get the munchies for some local *chocolate* at 3 in the morning.

Hot Spots

→ **La Musa** SPANISH This is probably one of the trendiest places to eat, but surprisingly, doesn't reek of superficiality. Its earthy tones and wooden folding chairs lend its dining room a down-to-earth comfort zone, to eat decently priced meals in peace. But, that's not to say that the servers here don't have tattoos or super-stylish hairdos or retro sparkly uniforms. Or that they don't play house music till your ears bleed. But people flock here for the high-end cheap meals and good tapas, such as *jabalí glaseado con bombas* (meat stuffed potatoes). For 15€ you can get a tapa sampler for the table. It's worth a go, as long as you're willing to alter your plans if the line gets nasty. *Manuela Malasaña 18. ☎ 914-487-558. Metro: Tribunal. La Musa Latina. Costanilla de San Andres 12 (Pl. de la*

Paja). ☎ *913-540-255. Metro: Latina. www.la musa.com.es. Menú 9.50€. Both restaurants" hours are Mon–Thurs 9am–5pm and 6pm– midnight; Fri 9am–5pm and 6pm–12:30am; Sat 1–5pm and 7pm–12:30am; Sun 1–5pm and 7pm–midnight.*

→ **Maceira** ★★ GALLEGO   If Paul Bunyan were Spanish, he'd squeeze his bod in here. Wood butcher-block tables, tin plates and bowls, and antique saw tables fit together in this rustic Galician eatery. Starfish are glued to the ceiling and fish baskets are used for lampshades. The menus are also wooden—painter's palettes, which boast of foods and wines strictly from the Galician province. Start with a salad, and for your main course, order the squid, clams, or mussels, along with a Gallegan wine. This is one of the most buzzing spots in Madrid, so get there early to ensure a table. *Huertas 66. ☎ 914-295-818. 4€–13€. No credit cards. Daily 1–4:15pm and 8pm– 1am; Fri–Sat until 2am. Metro: Antón Martín.*

→ **Palentino** SPANISH   Here's an old-man bar that's not afraid to get down with the young cats lickin' up the 1€ beers, cheap eats, and prime, party real estate. It's got all the classic criteria: a cigarette-littered floor, fluorescent lighting, and a vat of questionable gazpacho. It's the most popular meeting place in Malasaña to load up on calories and carbohydrates, coating the stomach with a preventative layer before hitting up the area's dozens of bars (around 11pm). Finding bar space is tough, let alone catching the attention of the bar-keep. However, these old-timers manage to keep the pace, and by the same token of old-fashioned manners, not bother you about paying until you're ready. *Calle del Pez 8. ☎ 915-323-058. Bocadillos 1.50€–3€. Beer 1€. Mon–Sat 7:30am–2am. Metro: Noviciado, Santo Domingo.*

→ **Taberna Alemendro 13** SPANISH   Getting a table here is harder than the Yankees on steroids but that doesn't mean it's impossible—unless it's a Sunday. But it's worth a shot for the *roscas* (large hot, doughnut paninis) that they're famous for. Nobody mans a waiting list so be like a vulture and attack freshly vacant tables. You have to order at the kitchen, where the cook miraculously remembers which plate is whose and calls your name when your food is ready. His helper elves distribute the food on busy nights. *Los huevos morcillones* (simply put: damn good scrambled eggs mixed with fries and greasy meat) is a good alternative and/or addition to your meal. *Almendro 13. ☎ 913-654-252. Meal 12€–18€. Mon–Sat 1–4pm and 7:30pm–12:30am; Sun 1–5pm and 8pm–1am. Metro: La Latina.*

→ **Vesubio** ★★ PIZZA   Here's an authentic *pizzaría* for the busted Godfather on the run. It's swarming with hungry youngish proles, so take a deep breath, pretend you've packin' heat with a finger in one pocket, and head toward the bar. Do not speak, in case anyone should discover you're a *guiri* (stupid American tourist in tube socks) and push you out of the way. If you follow those basic rules, you'll come out fine with a steaming, thin-crusted pizza covered in gooey cheese, for no more than 6€. There are no tables here, just bar space, and the secret spot is at the end of the bar, where there's usually a space or two to wedge your slice. If the impenetrable throng makes you go all *Waterboy*, you can always order your pizza at the take-away window. *Hortaleza 4. ☎ 915-215-171. Pizza 4€–6€. Open late daily. Metro: Gran Vía.*

Tapas

MTV Best ✔ → **Automático**   In the competition for best tapas bar, not many can challenge this '60s mod Lavapiés classic, which also houses one of the most popular terrazas. In the winter, the slick sounds of jazz and blues accompany the even smoother tastes of *croquetas, migas* (fried

Eating in Madrid

Automático Bar **17**
Bazaar **42**
Café Antik **25**
Café Comercial **35**
Cafeina **30**
Casa Lucio **13**
Casa Mingo **1**
Chocolatería San Gines **4**
Cisne Azúl **43**
El Bocaito **40**
El Pez Gordo **29**
El Restaurante
   Vegetariano **34**
El Tigre **39**
Finos y Finas **45**
Giangrossi **11**
Juana La Loca **10**
La Austríaca **27**
La Bola **3**
La Botillería de Maxi **7**
La Broche **44**
La Finca de Susana **22**
La Fondue de Tell **32**
La Gloria de Montera **23**
La Ida **28**
La Mallorquina **21**
La Mi Venta **2**
La Musa **9, 31**
La Taberna de Madrid **18**
Las Mañanitas **36**
Maceira **20**
Maoz **5**
Nuevo Café Barbieri **16**
Ojalá **33**
Palentino **29**
Restaurante
   la Sanabresa **19**
Sobrino de Botín **6**
Taberna Alemendro 13 **8**
Taberna Carmencita **41**
Taberna de Vinos **12**
The Mini Bar **26**
Txueca **38**
Vegaviana **37**
Vesubio **24**
Viuda de Vacas **14**
Viva Chapata **15**

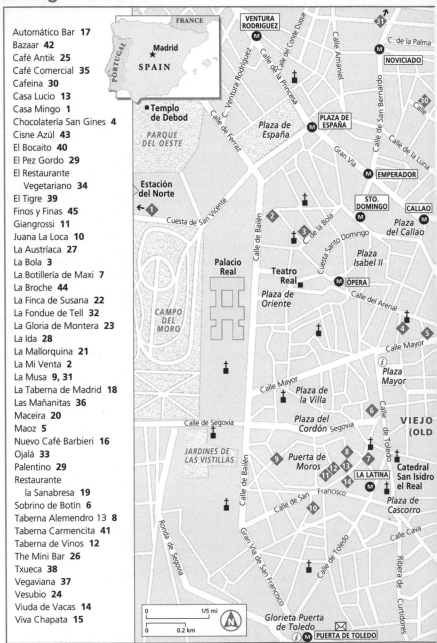

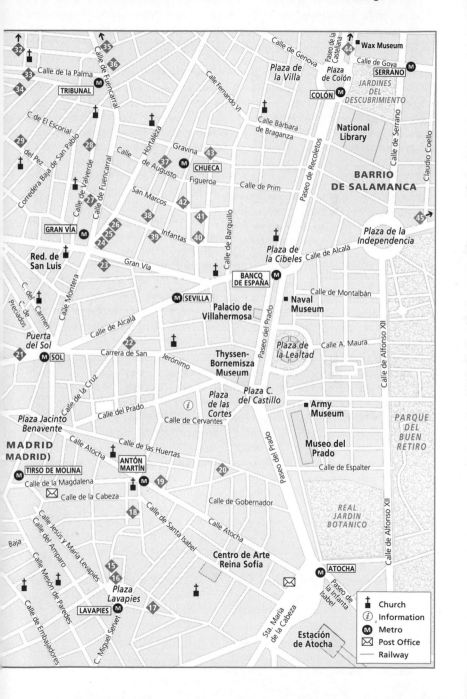

bread crumbs like Thanksgiving stuffing), *dátil con bacón* (dates with bacon), and a bunch of homemade pâtés. On weekend mornings you'll find the lingering party animals from the night before. In the afternoon, Madrileños tired of bargaining at El Rastro come here for well-deserved wine and deliciousness. *Argumosa 17.* ☎ *915-309-921. Tapas 4€–6€. Mon–Fri 6pm–1:30am; Sat–Sun noon–1:30am. Metro: Lavapiés.*

➜ **Casa Mingo** ★★ Finally, a tapas bar for the existentialist. Actually it's a lot simpler than that, but the smooth taste of homemade *sidra* (cider) is just as complex. This *sidrería* dates back to 1888—when the building was used to manufacture trains—and so do its recipes. The *sidra dulce* (sweet cider) is bottled in the same place it's drunk and tastes a bit like ginger ale with a dash of lemon juice. If you're the type who thinks sweet drinks are for pansies, have a glass of *sidra natural,* and you'll be singing another tune. Make sure to get your waiter to pour it into the glass from high above, for the full experience. The bench tables provide a cafeteria-style tavern for the locals and the university students who attend class nearby. The most popular dishes are the Asturian roasted chicken, which feeds three people for 8.50€, the chorizo marinated in *sidra,* and *queso de cabrales* (a type of goat cheese). Reservations are not accepted so get there early to claim sufficient butt space. In the summers, ask the waiter to bring you up to *el parte nuevo,* and you'll be escorted to a new terrace unknown to most (until now, of course). *Paseo de la Florida 34.* ☎ *915-477-918. Tapas 2.80€– 8.50€. Glass of sidra 1.10€. Bottle 4.40€. Bottles to go 3.30€. Daily 11am–midnight. Metro: Príncipe Pío.*

MTV (Best ✪) ➜ **El Bocaito** This 150-year-old house is clearly, hands down, the best tapas bar in Spain, and a good place for novice tapas eaters to start training. Even the strange anatomies of animals, which Spanish people eat and Americans don't, are oh so good. It's also filmmaker Pedro Almodóvar's favorite joint. Sandra Bullock and Hugh Grant were spotted here, as well as Penelope Cruz (though that almost goes without saying). Popular tapas are *ajos tiernos en aceite* (tender garlic in olive oil), cured Serrano ham, *gambas fritas* (fried shrimp), and green asparagus in scrambled eggs, which is a must-order. The famous *mejimecha* (marinated mussels with ham and onions in béchamel sauce) is a beefier meal. Make it easy and order a sample plate for your whole group (feeds four) for 30€. Now is the most important part, so read carefully: Order the fruit plate. It's an orgasm in the form of fresh fruit, sorbet, and white wine. Before you leave, check out copies of Goya's sketches on the wall. *Libertad 4-6.* ☎ *915-321-219. www.bocaito.com. Tapas 5.40€–7.20€. Mon–Fri 1–4pm and 8:30pm–midnight. Closed Aug. Metro: Chueca.*

➜ **El Pez Gordo** Hailed as one of Malasaña's originals, El Pez Gordo is more than just tapas—it's an institution. Sometimes it's over-packed, but that's only because the eats are some of the best in town. The ambience is lively with local intellectuals and regular city dwellers, without any of the salty pretentiousness. Even the bartenders are regular Joes who don't really know why people insist on coming here. Bohemians and local actors from the Alfil theater next door are permanent installations. The menu is short but high caliber: *migas de Almería* (fried bread crumbs similar to turkey stuffing), *solomillo de cerdo al cabrales* (a thick, pork spread), and *ventresca encebollada* (tuna with onions) are all recommendations. It's best to hit this spot around 10pm or a bit before, to snag a table. *Pez 6.* ☎ *915-223-208. Tapas about 6€. Mon–Sat 8pm–2am; Fri and Sat until 2:30am. Metro: Noviciado.*

→ **El Tigre** According to the young bucks in gold chains who run the joint, this *sidrería* (Asturian beer cider joint) is one of the last real tapas bars in Madrid that gives away more tapas and tostadas than you know what to do with—all for the price of just one *caña*-size drink (1.50€). In fact, if you're in a real *pintxo*, you might as well plan on eating, or rather drinking, a light dinner here. You can't beat the ambience: young, attractive Spaniards and stuffed deer heads all under one roof. Just imagine the possibilities. Get here late to meet the after-dinner crowd before the bars. *Infantas 30.* ☎ *915-320-072. Tapas free with drink. Mon–Thurs and Sun 10:30am–1am; Fri–Sat 1pm–2:30am. Metro: Gran Vía, Chueca.*

→ **Juana La Loca** Aptly named, this nouveau tapas bar can get pretty crazy, and, especially on Sundays, you may be disappointed if you were planning on sitting. But if you don't mind being elbow to elbow with super-trendy Madrileños from the film and entertainment business, you'll be rewarded by some of the most creative and delicious tapas in town. The purple tile walls, large wooden tables, and old-tavern style give the place a contradictory feel, which perfectly reflects the cuisine. The tapas vary daily, but if you're lucky, you'll be able to try the exquisite pumpkin won ton or the mushroom risotto, which is truly cinematic. If you go during the week you can enjoy their value meal *(menú)* and go as *loca* (or *loco*) as Jauna herself. *Puerta de Moros 4.* ☎ *913-640-525. Tapas 6.50€–9.20€. Tues–Sun 1pm–midnight. Closed Mon and Aug. Metro: La Latina.*

→ **La Taberna de Madrid** Much like the Lavapiés neighborhood, the crowd in this lively and typical tapas bar is a mix of recent immigrants, South American bohemian intellectuals, and hip underground artists. What brings them all together? Why, mojitos, of course. A menu of creative, not-your-average tapas, at your-average tapas prices, also helps (the tuna carpaccio alone is worth the trip). The walls feature detailed ironwork and antiques, and the big tables welcome large groups. *San Simón 3.* ☎ *915-398-980. Tapas 2.40€. Daily 11am–12:30am. Metro: Lavapiés.*

→ **Ojalá** ★★★ This neon-green, vintage-fan-filled dining room and cafeteria screams New Age—not as common in Madrid as in places like Berlin or New York. Japanese food such as salmon sashimi and California rolls are served along with Indian curry chicken. Its traditional Spanish tapas are twisted versions of their originals, in true La Movida Madrileña spirit. Now for the best part: Venture downstairs (but only with reservations, which are only available to parties of 6 or more) and enjoy the feel of sand beneath your feet as you make for your low-sitting table with fluffed Asian pillows, while video art is projected onto the walls. A feast for the senses. *San Andres 1.* ☎ *915-232-747. Tapas about 6€. Mon–Thurs 9am–12:30am; Sat–Sun 1:30pm–2:30am. Metro: Tribunal, Noviciado.*

→ **Taberna de Vinos** Besides coffee and cigarettes, there's no better combination than tapas and *vino*. Here's where you can get them both. The hard part is finding a table 'cause there's only six. So come here relatively early, and plan on tapas-hopping because you won't want to stay and hang with the older crowd it attracts. There are no reservations, so your best bet is to put your name in with the bartender or stand at the bar like everyone else, admiring the tavern's enormous wine rack. Do not leave until you've ordered the mouthwatering *magret de pato con cebollitas confitadas.* This duck meat is rare and garnished with sautéed onions; listed on my top-five fastest scarfed meals in Spain. If you're squeamish about red meat, go for the *cetas* (mushrooms). Here, Spanish wine is the main course. Experiment with reds: The Toro or the Bierzo are *tintos* that are recommended by the house. *Cava Baja 38.* ☎ *913-641-532. Tapas and raciones 4.50€–13€. Wine by the glass 2€–4€. Daily 1–3:45pm and 8pm–midnight. Metro: La Latina.*

Cheap

→**Bazaar** ★★★ MEDITERRANEAN Martha Stewart would have a spontaneous orgasm here. The two-level restaurant looks like a dry-goods store in Nantucket, with noodles, expensive bottled water, wine, and the like, all stocked on shelves that surround a crisp-white, country-chic dining room. Despite its dozens of tables, the place fills up by 9pm and does not take reservations, so it's essential to arrive by 8:30pm in order to dine at one of the hottest, youngest restaurants in Madrid. For starters, order the *brochette de ternera picante* (spicy meat) and for dessert, *postre Madagascar* (chocolate cake with ice cream and caramel). *Libertad 21.* ☎ *915-233-905. Menú 9.10€. Daily 1:15–4pm and 8:30–11:45pm. Metro: Chueca.*

📺 (Best ♦) →**La Austríaca** SPANISH This homey, small restaurant gets packed during lunch hours with a mix of Spanish office workers in-the-know and trendy young artists from Malasaña. Don't mess with *la familia*—Juan, Antonio, Mary, and Chus have been feeding Madrid for 52 years and they'll make sure that you finish your plate. Their *lentejas* (lentils) are like nothing else in the city, and be sure to try the *marmitaco,* the delicious *tartas* (cakes) that give this place the reputation for having the best *menú del día* in town. Sit at the bar or one of the communal tables and experience lunch Madrid-style. *San Onofre 3.* ☎ *915-313-174. Menú del día 8€. No Credit Cards. Daily 8am–4pm. Metro: Gran Vía.*

→**La Botillería de Maxi** SPANISH Even if you don't like bullfighting, chances are you're going to like bull's tail stew, the dish that makes this 1930s Andalucian dining room famous in La Latina. *Callos a la Madrileña* is another hot item (tripe, in English); the recipe hasn't changed one pinch in the past 50 years so you know they're doing something right. Sundays tend to be overcrowded, and it's difficult to get a table (a problem anywhere in La Latina on a Sun), but it's worth the wait and a drink at the busy bar before sitting in the salon, which is surrounded by cookie-jars with beans, and cooking utensils hanging on the brick walls. The service, once you're seated, is surprisingly quick by Spanish standards. Stay away from the hummus and other lesser quality Middle Eastern tapas, and start with the hot salad, instead. Finish with the *tarta de Santiago* with muscatel. *Cava Alta 4.* ☎ *913-651-249. Main courses 7.50€–17€. Tues–Fri 12:30–4pm and 8:30pm–midnight; Sat–Sun 12:30–6pm. Closed Aug. Metro: La Latina.*

→**La Finca de Susana** MEDITER-RANEAN There's a rumor floating around that this restaurant is actually filled with chefs in training who practice their culinary crafts and hawk it off for cheap. That's about as accurate as your horoscope. Madrileños and tourists alike must accept the fact that even the little guy can get fine dining sometimes. Sell quality for cheap, and they will come. So much so that if you're coming for dinner, you must arrive at 8:30pm to snag a table. Although not as trendy as its sister restaurant Bazaar (above), its refinement still reflects a modern edge. *Tempura de verdures* (vegetable tempura) is the most prized dish, as well as the *gambas peladas con ajo* (peeled shrimp with garlic). There's also a vegetarian menu for non-meat-eaters. To help you weed through the large wine menu, order Doña Beatriz for your choice of white, and Abadia Retuerta or Riscal Tempranillo for red. *Arlabán 4.* ☎ *913-693-557. Menú 8.10€. Mon–Sun 1pm until lunch is over, and 8:30–11:35pm. Reservations are not accepted. Metro: Sol, Sevilla.*

➜**La Gloria de Montera** ★★★ MEDITER-RANEAN   Cheap chic is what's for dinner at this upscale yet weirdly inexpensive restaurant. MoMA-like design chairs and jumbo lampshades create a classy ambience for thin wallets and grumbling stomachs. There are more than a dozen starters that look like Picasso masterpieces, including pumpkin and leek soup, a damn good mixed salad, or crab-and-avocado salad, for no more than 5€ each. A steal, folks! For dinner take your pick from a long menu (in Spanish and English) of fish and meat dishes. The chicken 'n' cheese is the most popular dish. The catch? There are no reservations, so get there by 9pm or better luck next time. *Caballero de Gracia 10.* ☎ *915-234-407. Meal 10€. Daily 8:30pm–close. Metro: Sevilla, Gran Vía.*

➜**Maoz** VEGETARIAN/FAST FOOD   Are you two *centavos* away from selling your body on the street? Never fear, Maoz is here. It's the cheapest option you've got in Madrid, and easily the healthiest fast-food chain in the Western Hemisphere. Eat inside its itsy-bitsy, teeny-weeny restaurant and enjoy the all-you-can-eat vegetarian buffet on the go: hot pita pockets stuffed with fresh veggies and cold salads. Falafels are fried to order by the gregarious, English-speaking cooks, who look more like Mexican guitar players than falafel flippers—part of the chain's young, modern theme. Load up on the buffet like it's the last meal you'll eat for days (it very well could be), and head toward Plaza

Mayor, 2 minutes away, to park it. *Mayor 4.* ☎ *647-408-731. www.maozveg.com. Meal 4€ and under. Daily 11am–2pm. Metro: Sol.*

➜**The Mini Bar** AMERICAN   This hole in the wall, unmarked and hidden under a barber sign, is an olden goldie, and the only rock 'n' roll bar in Madrid with enough Elvis Presley memorabilia to make you puke on your blue suede shoes. Situated smack dab in the middle of going-out world, it's the perfect place to grab a burger and fries before (or after) you get loaded. Everything is made on the spot and served on the outdoor terraza. The old man who runs it around the clock, twists and shouts in English. And boy does he *love* American '50s culture. Pretty soon he's installing Internet—look out. *Hortaleza 10. No phone. Burgers 4.50€ small, and 6.50€ large. Daily 7pm–1am. Metro: Gran Vía.*

➜**Restaurante la Sanabresa** ★SPANISH Restaurants like this one, where the same waiters in black bow ties have been serving the same tables for the past 12 years, are rapidly disappearing in this world. That is why La Sanabresa is considered a gift to Madrileños; it's where conversation is devoured more than food. The restaurant is sparsely decorated, and a peek inside its dull interior might be discouraging at first. But don't let that fool you into thinking it's a lame duck. Instead, go during the day for lunch when it's quieter and when you'll have a better chance of striking up a conversation with Joaquin, the famous, bushy-mustached character who serves the front tables. The menu is one of the cheapest in town: Order the No. 2, which includes a three-course meal (fried eggplant, beef stew, and grilled trout) and a small bottle of wine. *Amor de Dios 12.* ☎ *914-290-338. Menú 14€. Mon–Sat 1–4pm and 8:30–11:30pm. Metro: Anton Martín.*

➔ **Vegaviana** VEGETARIAN Being a vegetarian in Madrid isn't easy—you bump into some sort of dead animal product everywhere. Fortunately, the modernization of Madrid has brought a few new places like this quiet, cozy restaurant where you can take a break from the carnivorous ruckus of neighboring Chueca. Enjoy a large menu of vegetarian dishes like the succulent vegetarian paella or tasty integral pizzas, served with Zen-like manners. *Pelayo 35.* ☎ *913-080-381. www.accua.com/vegaviana. Main courses 7€–9€. Tues–Sat 1:30–4pm and 9–11:30pm. Metro: Chueca.*

➔ **Viva Chapata** SPANISH Here's a bang for your euro, smeared with tomato, cheese, and mayo. *Chapata,* a large sandwich made with panini-like bread, is sold for the price of a Starbucks frappé. The place, popular for its outdoor seating, attracts mostly young local professionals and exudes a *tranquilo,* artsy vibe, so you can eat your mongo-sandwich in peace. This is an excellent spot for a late lunch or a snack to hold you over until the Spanish finally get around to eating dinner at about 10:30pm. The Chapata's hottest seller is the *Natach,* similar to a hamburger with lettuce, tomato, and cheese. *Arepas* (hot, stuffed cornmeal pockets) are also sold at a bargain price. In the evening, the terrace becomes a popular place for *primera copas* (first drinks). *¡Viva la Chapata vida loca! Ave María 43.* ☎ *915-301-093. Chapata 3.50€. Daily noon–1am. Metro: Lavapies.*

Doable

➔ **Cisne Azul** VEGETARIAN Vegetarians rise up! Carnivores sharpen your teeth! If the mouthwatering effect of a menu could be measured, this tiny, unassuming bar with a few tables would rank *very watery.* The pale blue walls and '70s bar are cute, but you're not coming here for the decor. Every day, chef-owner Julián Pulido Vega finds the most exquisite products from the countryside, shown in crates by one of the walls. With 14 types of mushrooms, zucchini flowers, duck foie gras, and the delicious lamb ribs and cold cuts, this place is an irresistible temptation for Joe Schmo and connoisseurs alike. The ration-style servings are simply made—you don't need anything fancy when it's all about the fresh, natural flavor. Come with a group of people so that you can try it all! *Gravina 19.* ☎ *915-213-799. Main courses 9€–18€. Daily 1–5pm and 8pm–2am. Metro: Chueca.*

➔ **El Restaurante Vegetariano** ★★★ VEGETARIAN You know things are good when the first thing handed to you is a shot of pure (non-alcoholic) watermelon juice. Granted, it's not a free *chupito* (shot of liquor) but hey, maybe later. This is probably one of the better vegetarian restaurants in Madrid, and it doesn't hit meat-eaters over the head with them crazy words like tofu, seitan, or soy. Instead, fruit and cheese salads are recommended, as well as the gazpacho soup. Ingredients like pumpkin are used instead of meaty flesh, as well as quiche instead of steak. Reservations are recommended. *Marqués de Santa Ana 34 (corner of Espíritu Santo).* ☎ *915-320-927. Menú Mon–Fri 8.90€. Tues–Sat 1:30–4pm and 9–11:30pm. Closed Sun and Mon. Metro: Tribunal, Noviciado.*

🅜🅣🅥 **Best** ● ➔ **Finos y Finas** SPANISH Although some members of the royal family have been spotted here, you don't have to be as rich or inbred yourself to enjoy the *nueva cocina.* You can find out what all the buzz is about at this modern spot, without spending a week's wages in the process. The clientele can be on the *pijo* side, but once you read the menu you won't care about anything but the food. Executive chef/owner Luis Barrutia travels all over the country looking for the best ingredients for his creative Spanish dishes: mouthwatering creations like *salmorejo* (a traditional tomato mousse of sorts) with herring caviar and cockles, the best *Ibérico* you'll ever get, and a won ton ravioli that seems to compress all of Spain in a tiny square, with mushrooms, ham, Manchego, and truffles. They also have a tasting menu that takes you on a culinary journey throughout regions in Spain for 32€, including coffee and dessert. *Espartinas 6.* ☎ *915-759-069. Main courses 14€–20€. Mon–Sat 12–4:30pm and 8pm–midnight. Metro: Goya, Velazquez, Príncipe de Vergara.*

➜ **La Mi Venta** SPANISH We're going to let you in on a little secret: This old *mesón,* right next to the Royal Palace and the Spanish Senate, is (quasi) below the tourist radar and serves some of the most generous, flavorful dishes in town, on a terrace even. The place has been around since 1962 and so have some of the waiters. Whole pigs are cooked in the dining room's wood-burning stove, which you can peer into you, if you ask politely (though not recommended for weak stomachs). And the paella is fresher than at most places in Madrid. The crowd it draws isn't exactly the youngest or hippest, but that doesn't matter much when all you want is good Spanish food. Either pull up a stool at the bar and order a beer with your meal-size *raciones* (large-size tapas), or head to the back for finer tablecloth dining. Whatever you do, don't leave before ordering the finger-licking *jamón Ibérico*—chances are you won't have much choice because the enthusiastic owners will make you try it anyway. *Plaza de la Marina Española 7.* ☎ *915-595-091. Tapas 6€–20€. Mon–Fri menú 10€. Sat menú 15€. Mon–Sat 9am–midnight. Metro: Opera, Plaza España.*

➜ **Las Mañanitas** MEXICAN If you're feeling a little New World and hungry, try this lively *tortilleria,* in the middle of busy Fuencarral. Despite the common language, many Mexican restaurants in Spain are, how do you say, um . . . crappy. Las Mañanitas, however, is *muy bueno.* The maize-colored floor tiles, Mariachi music, and simple but comfortable furniture—along with great nachos, quesadillas, and margaritas—will make you happy to be there. Try their special *guisos* (stews) and you'll feel like you never crossed the Atlantic. *Fuencarral 82.* ☎ *915-224-589. Main courses 9€–17€. Mon–Fri 1:30–4pm and 9–11:30pm; Sat 9–11:30pm. Metro: Bilbao or Tribunal.*

➜ **Taberna Carmencita** SPANISH Tucked away on a trendy street lined with new, retro-modern bars, is this enchanting corner restaurant, decorated with antique chandeliers and old white lace (more fitting for grandma's house than a well-known spot where famed poet Federico García Lorca frequented). The building is 150 years old and embellished with Spanish tiling and an atmosphere that's not hoity-toity, despite its international popularity. The handwritten menus offer decently priced meals, served to you in four-star-restaurant fashion. Our favorite was the *rosbif* (roast beef) served with an onion mustard and red peppers; the house red fits like a glove. If it's Thursday, order the *cocido,* the hearty stew Madrid is famous for. *Libertad 16.* ☎ *915-316-612. Meal 15€–20€. Mon–Fri 1–4pm; Mon–Sat 9pm–midnight. Metro: Chueca.*

➜ **Txueca** BASQUE Decorated like an ad for Target, this trendy restaurant makes a splash on Plaza Vazquez de Mella, in the heart of Chueca. It's most popular for its terraza, modern tapas, and gastronomical artistry. The mozzarella salad is a culinary and visual delight but even better (and cheaper) is the choice between hot and cold *pintxos* (Basque for tapas) such as the *solomillo con queso y setas pintxo* (sirloin steak with cheese and mushrooms). There's a menu in English, the bread is served hot, and the service ain't bad. The *menú del día* takes care of two entrees, dessert, and a drink, but the terreza costs 1€ extra. Also remember that Spanish people eat din-din late (about 9:30–10:30pm), so timing is everything in Chueca. Reservations are recommended but not necessary. *Plaza Vazquez de Mella 10.* ☎ *915-221-691. www.txueca.com. Tostadas 2.65€–3.70€. Menú 10€. Sun–Thurs 1–4pm and 9pm–midnight; Fri–Sat 1pm–1:30am. Metro: Chueca.*

➜**Viuda de Vacas** CASTILIAN It doesn't get more Castilian than this old *taberna,* housed in a XVII-century building in trendy La Latina. Its ornate, tile walls have seen more history than the Met and so have the Cánovas, who've been running this place for three generations. Sit at the zinc bar or at one of the little wooden tables and enjoy the best Spanish traditional food, including, of course, all sorts of animal parts like the infamous bull's tail, which is pretty good if you can forget about what you're actually eating. Come early or make reservations, unless you want to wait for hours with the 30-something Madrid hipsters. *Cava Alta 23.* ☎ *913-665-847. Main courses 9.50€–19€. Mon–Wed and Fri–Sat 1–4:30pm and 9pm–midnight. Closed Thurs and Sun. Metro: La Latina.*

Splurge

➜**Casa Lucio** SPANISH Bill Clinton has been to Spain five times. He has also been to Casa Lucio—you guessed it—five times. The Spanish Royal Family, Kofi Annan, Barbara Bush, the President of Monaco, Fergie, the prime minister of Japan, and yes, even Bruce Willis have all eaten here, among notable others. But the real celebrity is, and has always been, Lucio himself—an old man who grabs you by the elbow to point out the fresh shrimp, squid, fruits, and vegetables. "The best! The very best of all of Spain is shipped here to me!" he exclaims. The fact that Spanish presidents occasionally dine here doesn't faze him; it's the waiting list that animates him most. He pulls out a book the size of the King James Bible and runs his finger down the long list of reservations. Why do people come here? Fried eggs. Star menu items are the hake, garlic shrimp, and *churrasco de la casa,* which is a nice, juicy steak. But if you ask Lucio, he'll tell you the *huevos estrellados* (potatoes and eggs) are the house specialty. If you don't have enough dough, or a reservation for that matter, try the tapas bar across the street, Casa Lucas. The food is pretty much the same. You don't need a reservation, as it's standing room only, and the prices are a bit cheaper. *Cava Baja 35.* ☎ *913-653-252. www.casalucio. es. Menu 35€. Sun–Fri 1–4pm and 9pm–midnight. Closed Aug. Metro: La Latina.*

➜**La Bola** ★★ MADRILENO If you want to chow on *cocido Madrileño* (a medley of garbanzos, ham, blood sausage, sausage, chicken, and other stuff), this should be your *only* choice, as they prepare it for you individually 3 to 4 hours before you arrive and serve it in a nifty ceramic pot. Infanta Isabel and her brother Afonso XII were big fans of La Bola's *cocido* back in the day and would sometimes order carry-out to the palace nearby. The restaurant is painted blood red and has been owned by the same family for the last 100 years or more; its *cocido* recipe is just as old. Of course, they offer other mushy things, as well as grilled sole, salmon, and hake, all served by a friendly staff that likes to hug. *Calle de la Bola 5.* ☎ *915-476-930. Menú 35€. Mon–Sat 1–4pm and 8:30–11pm; Sun 1–4pm. During July and Aug, closed on Sun. Reservations required. No credit cards. Metro: Opera, Plaza Santo Domingo.*

wwwired

M̄ Best● **Café Comercial** (Glorieta de Bilbao 7; ☎ 915-215-655) is the Humphrey Bogart of coffee houses. Its old-fashioned charisma has lasted over 100 years, and just keeps on truckin'. Last time I was there, I saw a fashion advertisement being shot, as well as a famous poet alone reading a newspaper, and it's not unusual to see it pop up on the big screen, either. Go upstairs and find the smoker's den, as well as old men with their faces screwed, leaning over card tables and interminable games of chess. In the farthest room is an Internet cafe, and with luck your monitor works. This is the quintessential meeting place in Madrid, at any time of the day or night. Its popularity means you're going to pay a few cents more for you're *café con leche.* Open Monday to Thursday 8am to 1am, Friday and Saturday 8am to 2am, Sunday 9am to 1am (Metro: Bilbao).

→ **La Broche** CATALAN This place has gained a quick reputation as one of the most creative restaurants in Madrid, and possibly even in Spain. Opened in 1997 by superstar-chef Sergi Arola, it is a necessary stop for food connoisseurs looking to experience the best of the Costa Brava regional cuisine. The waitstaff is young and speedy (an oddity around here), and the nouveau Mediterranean dishes are served in small portions, allowing you to try more variety without fear of indigestion. The menu changes periodically, but see if you can get the confit potatoes with tomato and aioli or the otherworldly mushroom carpaccio with fresh pasta and pignolia vinaigrette . . . mmm. Pull out your credit card, close your eyes, and open your

mouth. *Miguel Angel 29.* ☎ *913-993-437. Main courses 30€. Mon–Fri 1:30–3:30pm and 9–11:30pm. Closed in Aug. Metro: Gregorio Marañon.*

→ **La Fondue de Tell** SWISS This is a cheese-lover's heaven. Well worth the few extra bucks, it's the only Swiss restaurant in Madrid and it attracts ambassadors (primarily Swiss diplomats) and Erasmus students alike. A popular item on the menu is the mother of all cheese plates, *tala de quesos varios,* which can come as a platter or as small rosettes of cut cheese. Our favorite was the *cabeza de monje.* All the cheeses are straight off the boat from Switzerland and so is the decor ("Riii-colaaaa!!!"). Bring your cheesy friends. *Divino Pastor 12.* ☎ *915-944-277. www.lafonduedetell. com. Menú 25€–30€. Daily 1:30–4pm and 8:30pm–midnight. Reservations required. In Aug, only open for dinners. Metro: Tribunal, Bilbao.*

→ **Sobrino de Botín** SPANISH This old-fashioned *taberna* nestled up to the Plaza Mayor is *the oldest restaurant in the world*—a fact duly noted by the *Guinness Book of World Records.* The bell-ringing year was 1725, when El Botín first opened its doors. Ernest Hemingway helped immortalize this landmark in *The Sun Also Rises,* when Jake invites Brett here for the roast suckling pig. (It wouldn't be Hemingway if he didn't also have them drinking Rioja Alta.) As if this place needed more reasons to be famous, Francisco Goya worked here as a freakin' dish washer. (This somehow did *not* make it into *The Guinness Book.*)

The original carbon oven and kitchen shelved with baskets of ham and goods look like something from a Hans Christian Andersen fairy tale. And be sure to sneak a peek at the caves downstairs from the 1590s, which are nice and cool. Last but not least, there's, ah yes, the food: Start with the salad Botín or the gazpacho, or the garlic

Sweet Fix

With its fat rump sitting on top of Metro Sol, **La Mallorquina** ★★ (Puerta de Sol 6; ☎ **915-211-201;** daily 9am–9:15pm; closed during Aug; Metro: Sol) demands attention not only by the wafting smells of pastries and baked goods, but by the large case windows filled with chocolate balls, flan cakes, and pastries the like of which you've never seen before. The place has been stuffing people's faces with sweets since 1894. Take a seat in its upstairs cafe, a great way to get off your feet. What to get: *café con leche, ensaimadas,* or *napolitanas* (two types of pastries, the latter has custard inside), *medianoche con jamon serrano* (baked roll with cured ham), and Madrid's specialty, *rosquillas* (a flat sugar cookie). Everything is decently priced.

Chocoholics will lose their minds here at the **Chocolatería San Gines** ★★★ (Pasadizo de San Gines 5 [near Calle Mayor]; ☎ **913-656-546;** cup of chocolate and six *churros* 3€–3.20€ depending on the hour; daily 10am–7am; Metro: Sol), the same place where famous Spanish writers of the 19th century convened and philosophized over hot cups of thick chocolate and fried *churros.* It's most popular at 5am, when the bar hour grinds down to a halt. During summer, sit outside on the terraza, or downstairs in its dark mirrored tunnel salon for stolen chocolate kisses. Check your diet at the door.

For the best ice cream and gelato in Madrid, go to **Giangrossi** (☎ **902-444-130;** ice cream and specialty drinks about 3.50€–7€; Mon–Thurs 9am–1am, Fri–Sat 9am–2:30am, Sun 10am–1am; Metro: La Latina), aka "Get Fat." The cool sofas and first-class decor make you feel good about yourself while binging on artisan fat. Calories are packaged on-site, disguised as yummy sundaes and shakes. Try over 40 different flavors—admittedly better (but way more expensive) than Baskin-Robbins. The newest and nearest one is at Cava Baja 40.

soup with egg. For the main dish, your best bets are the clams, roast suckling pig, or the baby lamb. If you're not sure, confer with the dozens of English-speaking tourists who'll certainly be dining here, too. *Cuchilleros 17.* ☎ *913-664-217. Reservations recommended. Main course 10€–28€. Menú 35€. Daily 1–4pm and 8pm–midnight. Metro: La Latina, Sol.*

Cafes/Tearooms

➜ **Café Antik** This gay-friendly, charming cafe is a ragbag of so many antiquated styles, it's hard to classify the look. If you put a gun to my head, I'd say Old French hodgepodge, and you might just pull the trigger anyway. The dark, romantic downstairs is more like an Oriental tearoom mixed with some old Auntie, garage-sale authenticity. There's a full tea menu, wine, and some cocktails such as mojitos and daiquiris. Makes for a great G-rated place to cuddle up and smooch. (It fills up during the day, as well as early evening.) *Hortaleza 4.* ☎ *915-232-784. Drinks 6.50€–7€. Daily 11am–late. Metro: Gran Vía.*

➜ **Cafeina** Although more of a stylish, mid-priced nighttime bar/cafe than an afternoon java stop, this popular corner dive has got more chill than a Minnesota winter. The interior is dark and inviting, and downstairs is a dungeonlike sitting room with scarlet velvet seating and cool brick walls. This place is more for the 25-and-over intellectual philosophy student than the beer-drinking American frat boy, but definitely a local hangout. (Most people know to skip the coffee and order a gin and tonic, the house specialty.) A DJ plays a down-beat house/jazz mix. *Calle del Pez 18.* ☎ *915-220-331. Drink 6€. Mon–Sat 3pm–3am. Metro: Tribunal.*

➜ **La Ida** Sport your leather hippie sandals or Erykah Badu head wrap and stop in for an Asian brew or an afternoon mojito at this alternative, word-of-mouth hotspot in the heart of Malasaña; you'll fit right in. Its bright green walls are decorated like a funky Mexican bar with shabby-chic art. A new exhibition is installed whenever the go-with-the-flow owner feels like it. Banked seating, large open windows, and pillows galore add to the laid-back rustic style. *Colón 11.* ☎ *915-229-107. Daily 1pm–2am. Closed the 2nd and 3rd weeks Aug. Metro: Tribunal.*

➜ **Nuevo Café Barbieri** Make this place your early evening destination in Lavapiés and reward yourself with a cup of coffee or better yet, a chocolate cocktail. On Fridays and Saturdays, singers and poets convene to perform in the backroom for 4€ plus a drink. Part of its charm is that the building is crumbling—a fact that complements it's yellowed mirrors, warped velvet seat banks, and old wood. If it hasn't sunk in that you're in Europe, head here. The waiters hate tourists so be patient and do everything possible not to act like one. Most importantly, don't take photos—they're not allowed. *Ave María 45.* ☎ *915-273-658. Coffee, specialty drinks, or wine about 2€–4.50€. Mon–Thurs and Sun 3pm–2am; Fri–Sat 3pm–2:30am. Metro: Lavapiés.*

Partying

Yeah, the Spanish dance their flamenco, they fight their bulls, and they have their Goyas and Dalís . . . but they don't rock 'n' roll very well, tending instead to marinate in La Movida's leftovers. Sometimes you get lucky with Madrid-based bands like Sex Museum or Los Zodiacs, but most rock tunes usually exhibit uninspired, unoriginal, high school–level musicianship. The jazz scene is a lot better, as are the reggae, salsa, and other world-beat bands. And, of course, a lot of big-name tours stop in Madrid. The Rolling Stones, Depeche Mode, Franz Ferdinand, and Method Man are just a few of the big acts that have recently played in football stadiums or venues around Madrid. As always, consult the entertainment bible, *Guía del Ocio* (and the thousands of posters around the city), to see who's playing and where. For the most part, the clubs here open at about 9:30pm, the live music starts between 10 and 11pm and ends at around 2am, and—in traditional Madrid style—the clubs remain

open till 6am with a DJ kickin' it. Keep in mind, though, that the Spanish invented arriving fashionably late. Midnight is when things are hottest for live music in this town. You can also skip the live music and just swing by around 3am for the DJ session. If Euro electronica isn't exactly your Friday night schtick, the Gothics in the city give you somewhere else to worship. Bars like **Cripta** (in sala Ya'sta at Calle Valverde 10; ☎ **915-218-833** and 651-894-200; www.lacripta.livejournal.com; open Sat 10pm), **Dark Hole** (C. Mesonero Romanos 13; ☎ **915-593-684;** cover 8€; open Sat 1am), and **666** (C. Aduana 21; no phone; www.gothic666.net) are the best Goth bars that attract more than just partiers dressed in black, who stopped scaring people along time ago in Madrid. However, the best way to party is by starting at the tapas bars and weaving your way through neighborhoods such as La Latina and Malasaña, where low-vibed pubs are a dime a dozen. These places do not accept plastic unless noted

MADRID

Partying & Sightseeing in Madrid

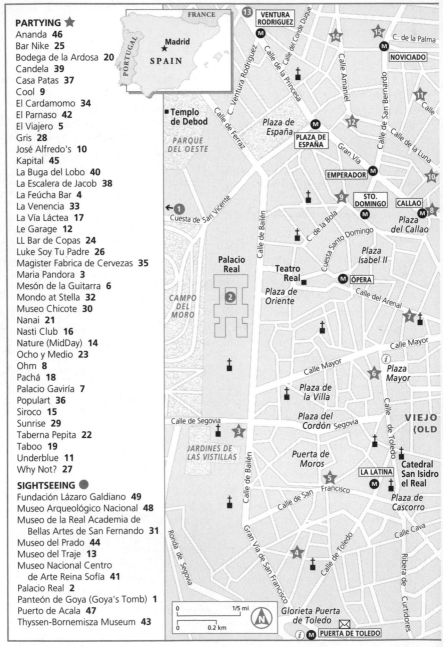

PARTYING ⭐
Ananda **46**
Bar Nike **25**
Bodega de la Ardosa **20**
Candela **39**
Casa Patas **37**
Cool **9**
El Cardamomo **34**
El Parnaso **42**
El Viajero **5**
Gris **28**
José Alfredo's **10**
Kapital **45**
La Buga del Lobo **40**
La Escalera de Jacob **38**
La Feúcha Bar **4**
La Venencia **33**
La Vía Láctea **17**
Le Garage **12**
LL Bar de Copas **24**
Luke Soy Tu Padre **26**
Magister Fabrica de Cervezas **35**
Maria Pandora **3**
Mesón de la Guitarra **6**
Mondo at Stella **32**
Museo Chicote **30**
Nanai **21**
Nasti Club **16**
Nature (MidDay) **14**
Ocho y Medio **23**
Ohm **8**
Pachá **18**
Palacio Gaviría **7**
Populart **36**
Siroco **15**
Sunrise **29**
Taberna Pepita **22**
Taboo **19**
Underblue **11**
Why Not? **27**

SIGHTSEEING ●
Fundación Lázaro Galdiano **49**
Museo Arqueológico Nacional **48**
Museo de la Real Academia de
    Bellas Artes de San Fernando **31**
Museo del Prado **44**
Museo del Traje **13**
Museo Nacional Centro
    de Arte Reina Sofía **41**
Palacio Real **2**
Panteón de Goya (Goya's Tomb) **1**
Puerto de Acala **47**
Thyssen-Bornemisza Museum **43**

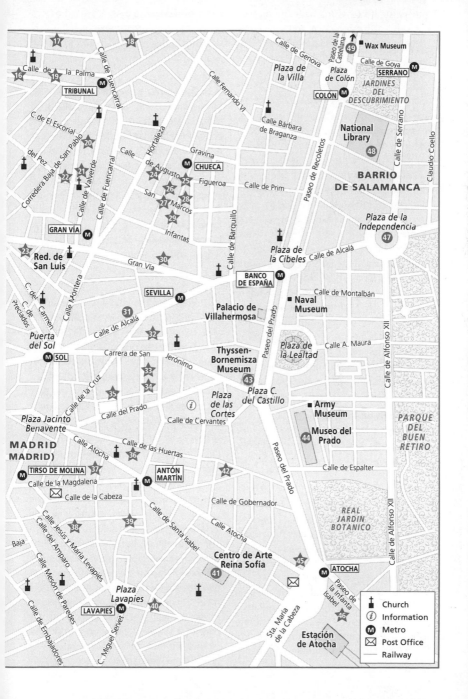

otherwise. If you're still hell-bent on seeing some Spanish rock 'n' roll, check out some of the recommendations below.

Bars & Lounges

Spanish call their nightlife *la marcha* (the march) because they typically prefer to have a single drink in a bar before moving on to the next—and the next, and the next. Madrileños are the most notorious members of *la marcha*'s fan club, as the number of bars almost outnumbers the city census. So, trying to sum up Madrid's bar scene by describing only a few bars is like trying to tell someone about a beach by showing them only a few grains of sand. Add to that the fact that thousands of people are in "the streets and the bars don't close until 3am, and it's easy to see why Madrid is the undisputed champion of European nightlife, and also why Madrileños are nicknamed "cats." Use the following bars as highlights and *marcha* your butt off—it's the only way to get the full effect. All of these bars have a similar prime time of around 1am on the weekends. The only exception is El Viajero, which usually sees action by 11pm.

→ **Bodega de la Ardosa** This bar existed even before Malasaña turned too cool for school. With mostly standing room only, the classically Spanish bar is famous for not just its ripe-old age, but also for its Records Guinness de la Ardosa drinking contest, recently banned because of Guinness's heightened alcohol content. But the scoreboard still stands: U.S.A. ranks fifth; Spain beat it with second. Needless to say that people drink a helluva lot of Guinness here, as well as other international beers on tap and good vermouth. But that's not the only reason why locals both young and old flock to its beer-barrel tables—the salmorejo (thick tomato spread) and homemade *croquetas* are some of the best in town (tapas

and raciones from 2.95€–6.95€). The Goya prints that decorate the walls and the classical music during the day add to its old Spanish charm. *Colón 13.* ☎ *915-214-979. Metro: Tribunal.*

→ **El Parnaso** Discover the eighth wonder of the world and get toasted doing it. Buried beneath a pile of old knight-errant collectibles and antique Spanish Civil War memorabilia, plus a helluva lot of other odd thingamajigs, lies "the Weird Bar," which serves frosted mugs of beer and specialty drinks, accompanied by Turkish pastries, if you rub shoulders right with the bartender. Order one of their sumptuous banana, coconut, or chocolate *batidos,* with or without alcohol, and play the game "I Spy." *Moratín 25. No phone. Metro: Anton Martín.*

→ **El Viajero** A great bar and restaurant in the very cool La Latina district. Get an aerial view of this artist's community while eating on the third-floor terrace or relax on the second floor, which is lit almost entirely by candles—both are potentially very romantic. A little more expensive than average, but so worth it. *Plaza de la Cebada 11.* ☎ *913-669-064. Metro: La Latina.*

→ **Gris** ★★ When gays were freaks and Chueca was a rundown stain on the city, Gris was there. Now it's enjoying its golden age, with all its hideous '80s decorations and cheap drink prices still intact. The crowd is mostly underground edgy: gay guys and friends, and some who don't fit nor like the music, but go there because it's cheap (and you can get shots of absinthe). It's near one of the busiest streets in Chueca, but it could just as well be in the rock 'n' roll neighborhood of Malasaña. After midnight, you can hardly get to the bar, but it's worth fighting for, so stick your elbows out and charge. *San Marcos 29. No phone. Closed Mon. Metro: Chueca.*

➔ **José Alfredo's Cocktail Lounge** If you had to define the quintessential cocktail bar for a police sketch artist, the end result would probably look a lot like José Alfredo's. The couches are big and comfy in dark earthy tones, the lights are dim, and there are lots of mirrors where the young and fabulous patrons can admire themselves and each other in all their trendsetting glory. The lounge music is barely audible, for the place is always packed with thirsty patrons enjoying excellent cocktails while getting ready to start the nightlife. Get there early and score a table with couches, and you're very likely to make some new friends—it's like buying a convertible to pick up girls, only much cheaper. *Silva 22. No phone. Metro: Noviciado.*

➔ **La Buga del Lobo** Probably the most popular hole on the most bohemian street in Lavapiés, is this scallywag's drinking hole that looks more like a colorful tattoo than a bar. Named after a legendary ship that sank off the coast in Guatemala, it specializes in cordials, but most people come for its fashionable Greenwich Village–esque terraza, even though prices are 15% higher for that honor. Paired with its sister cultural space, **La Boca,** located just down the street, it practically owns the block. What to order: *croquetas, huevos caribeños,* and fried plantains or yucca, matey. *Argumosa 8.* ☎ *914-676-151. www.labocadellobo.com. Metro: Tirso de Molina, Lavapiés.*

➔ **La Escalera de Jacob** The patchwork of degenerates that frequent this new-ish dive has one thing in common: They're broke. So the next time it's your turn to buy a round, bring your crew here, where a few cents more than a euro buys a shot or a beer. The tall ceilings and sparse furniture mean it's a sociable place; chances are you'll walk out with a few new phone numbers and e-mail addresses, but only if you want to. This drinking hole is for late night imbibing (and fresh, late-night tapas) so don't stop by until midnight at the very earliest. *Lavapiés 7.* ☎ *915-391-044. Metro: Tirso de Molina, Lavapiés.*

➔ **La Feúcha Bar** For the 20-something hipster crowd with a penchant for partying on holy Sundays, this "Ugly Girl Bar" is a comfortable neighborhood establishment that serves cheap beer, wine, *bocadillos* (3€), and classic, feel-good rock. We heard the Pogues' "Lullaby of New York" on two occasions, making this spot an okay joint in our repertoire of Madrid rock roadhouses—its generic IKEA furniture aside. The dancing DJ with his white afro got the crowd singing with Madness's "Must Be Love." This place is one of the only places in town where you'll find people busting a move at 3pm on a Sunday. *Calatrava 14.* ☎ *620-206-705 and 676-486-977. Metro: La Latina.*

➔ **La Venencia** The old bottles lining the walls of this ancient sherry bar have more dust on them than my Rick Astley tapes. The dozen different types of sherry are stored in dark, wooden barrels behind the bar and served directly into your glass. Sample different kinds of this Jerez province specialty, accompanied by great cold cuts and juicy olives brought straight from Andalusia. The bartender will write up your bill with chalk on the bar and trust that you won't erase it. Don't miss this authentic sample of Madrid's pre-Franco past; talk in whispers and don't tell anyone about it. *Echegaray 7.* ☎ *914-297-313. Metro: Sol.*

➔ **La Vía Láctea** The milky way of this bar is composed of old posters of rock 'n' roll stars, many of which probably had a go at the pool table or a drink at one of the two bars. One of the main scenes during the Movida in the '80s, this bar is now considered an authentic classic by the made-up girls and glam boys who populate it.

MADRID

There's a little area with couches in the front, a tiny DJ cabin, and, apart from the pool table, a couple of booths that have probably seen more action than a Jet Li movie. Good rock 'n' roll blasts from the speakers, and funky bartenders with multicolored hair pour a good selection of drinks. *Velarde 18.* ☎ *914-467-581. Metro: Tribunal.*

→**Luke Soy Tu Padre** As a tribute to the galactic wars, this bar beams in people by the hordes, just because of its title. But it turns out Luke has more to offer than just a cool name and neon lightsabers—it's one of the only places in Chueca that plays good rock, such as the Pixies, the Yeah Yeah Yeahs, The Velvet Underground, Nick Cave, Sonic Youth, and David Bowie continuously, with an emphasis on '70s and '80s British music. Many *extranjeros,* or foreigners, find their way inside the cramped space, and almost all of them are below the age of 26. It's clear that people don't stop by because it's a popular bar, or that it's decorated like a bathroom; if you're inside this joint, it's because you know the day when the music died. *San Bartolomé 14. No phone. Metro: Chueca.*

→**Magister Fabrica de Cervezas** Mahou and Aguila are two beers that are produced locally. Those along with your cheapie beers such as Cruzcampo, Estrella, and San Miguel are poured into small glasses called *cañas* and are almost always crap, depending on your standards. Forget these skunky beers. You've got to draw a line someplace so why not here, one of two microbreweries in Madrid. Although nobody claims the beer is spectacular, it does offer a refreshingly (if not too) light alternative, accompanied with beefy tapas for 2.25€. There's lots of room to mill around so it'll make a great start to the evening on the most popular streets near Plaza Santa Ana. If this place is full, head down the street to its competition, **Cervecería Alemana,** for the same spiel on microbrewed beer and drink prices. *Principe 18.* ☎ *915-210-140. Metro: Anton Martín.*

→**Maria Pandora** ★★ Ching-ching with royalty, or at least in its vicinity, at this champagne room just past the Royal Palace. It might be a walk but it's darn well worth it. Decorated to look like a cozy living room, there's no place like *this* home while sipping 3€ cava next to a large fireplace, dripping candles, and small library, where books are on sale. Dots, chocolate-covered raisins, kiwis, and cherries are free with each glass. There's no doubt this is a destination place with a special someone you'd like to impress or make out with later. The locale is Las Vistillas, a bar-lined street just over the bridge past the palace. *Plaza Gabriel Miro 1.* ☎ *913-664-567. Metro: Opera.*

→**Museo Chicote** Voted by MTV as the best bar in Europe in 2004, it's our duty to mention it here. Banked seating and a revolving door are part of the Deco design constructed in 1931 for the international press crew who soireed while Civil War swelled on Gran Vía. Almodóvar, Alaska, and even Hemingway came this way, until prostitutes took it over during the Franco era. Hustling later slowed to a screeching halt and once again it became a place for locals, internationals, and people of all sexual orientations to drop by for an (understandably) over-priced cocktail (Mojito, 8€). This institution is sans-terraza and most popular in winter months. Don't get here before midnight; otherwise, you'll think you're in the wrong place. *Gran Vía 12.* ☎ *915-326-737. www.museo-chicote. com. Metro: Gran Vía.*

➜ **Nanai** This place looks more like a smoky, underground KGB bar than a cultural association serving drinks. But that's what it is—a bleeding liberal (in U.S. terms) speakeasy that sometimes offers free performances, video art, exhibitions, and speakers. It originally began as a feminist establishment, but don't let that confuse you. There are plenty of heterosexual good-looking men, and clean-shaven women who make good use of the large, more-than-intriguing space. It's a forum for hipster intellects and potato fondue (5€); an underground dive with mismatched furniture and an enchanting vibe, just when you need a dose of "real people" in Madrid. For a relaxing way to kick off the night, drop by for a drink before heading out to the bars later. *Barco 26. No phone. Closed July and Aug. Metro: Tribunal, Gran Vía.*

➜ **Taberna Pepita** For less than a collect call to your parents to ask for more money, you can get a *mini* of either *calimocho*, beer, or sangria, in a glass the size of your head, and a ración of *patatas bravas* ("brave" potatoes). Of course it depends on how difficult your parents are, but you'll probably be able to spring for a ración of *croquetas*, too. The coupla old geezers who run the place have figured it out: Cheap eats, lots and lots of sit-down space (we're talking at least 20 tables here), and colossal-size drinks equals euros and Madrid fame. Start your evening here around 11pm, and pick up some dins, too, if you've got the munchies. *Corredera Baja de San Pablo 20. ☎ 915-319-743. Metro: Tribunal, Noviciado.*

Live Music
ROCK/POP

➜ **Nasti Club** Nasti is everything an indie music venue should be: small red doors covered in graffiti; a very simple, smoky,

dark, black-and-white hall; and tons of hipsters hanging out. Add to that a good amount of grime and dirt, and musical acts that go from guitar/bass/drums garage bands to crazed-out, paint-covered, electro-punk performance combos, and you've got yourself a great exponent of the Madrid underground. Formerly known as Maravillas, it is a stepping stone for many soon-to-be-bigger acts, the difference being that many of these rising stars aren't from Spain. Local bands play at floor level and bigger foreign ones get a small stage. If you're lucky enough you may catch shows like Peaches or Kula Shaker, which, in a 300-people venue, have a lotta flava. *San Vicente Ferrer 35. ☎ 915-217-605. www.nasti. es. Cover 8€. Metro: Tribunal.*

➜ **Siroco** This venue is small, dark, and loud—the way a rock club should be. The upper floor adds some space, but the stage and most of the action is crammed into the basement. The 18- to 30-year-old clientele is dressed in 1976 AC/DC (Back In) Black, the preferred attire of Spain's rock 'n' rollers. This is a very popular venue on weekends, and a lot of times it's better to skip the live shows and arrive after 1am to enjoy the awesome DJs who spin hip-hop, breaks, and funky styles. *San Dimas 3. ☎ 915-933-070. www.siroco.es. Cover varies. Metro: San Bernardo.*

JAZZ/BLUES

➜ **Populart** This is the place for Madrid's lukewarm blues, but its small stage is also graced by "live music of all types," including swing, salsa, reggae, and flamenco. Decorated with old horns and photos of American blues and jazz heavyweights, this midsize bar attracts a mix of 25- to 40-year-old yuppie types and college-age Spanish artists and musicians (many of whom can speak a little English). Upcoming acts are listed by the entrance. Because it's a smaller venue, you'll want to get a good seat by showing up on time (more or less), usually about 10pm. There's no cover but drinks are pricey because of it. *Huertas 22.* ☎ *914-298-407. Metro: Sevilla or Antón Martín.*

→ **Underblue** Right in the heart of Malasaña is this trendy corner space, seemingly a tranquil tearoom with living-room furniture and an assortment of fruity cocktails, teas from all over the world, and blended smoothies. There's even a funky, Malasaña-style clothing designer who sells clothes during the day. But venture down its windy stairs, and you'll find a rhythm-and-blues club that's better than the cat's pajamas and plays music on a nightly basis starting around 11pm (except for Aug). The longhaired owner played the U.S. circuit for a number of years and loves talking to Americans who like to kick around the blues. Order the absinthe and tea. *Minas 1 (on the corner of Calle del Pez).* ☎ *676-559-322. Cafe is open daily noon—2am; clothing is sold noon—6pm; live music 11pm—12:30am. Cover for live music 1€. Metro: Noviciado.*

FLAMENCO

MTV Best ● → **Candela** This is flamenco at its darkest: a grimy, dirty place that was shut down a couple of times for heroin, the drug of choice among *cantaores.* Now they're trying to stay clean, but the faces are still the same. The walls feature beautiful flamenco posters and photos of the biggest luminaries in the art, which used to, and still do, play at the back room, *la cueva* (the cave). Unfortunately, not everybody can get in and, unless you come with somebody who knows somebody, your chances as an outsider are pretty slim, so act inconspicuous and don't worsen our stupid American tourist rep. The local fauna and ambience at the bar still make it worth a visit or two. *Olmo 2.* ☎ *914-673-382. Metro: Antón Martín.*

→ **Casa Patas** Some say that you can't see the real-deal flamenco in a heartless slab of stone like Madrid, but this *tablao* (Flamenco stage) is considered to be one of the best if not the top flamenco joints in Spain. Don't tell Dorothy we're not in Andalusia anymore. Skilled and heart-wrenching classical guitar will impress you even before the dancers come out. When they do come out, you'll realize that any flamenco dancer worth her salt is at least as tough as Ice T (but obviously a lot more graceful). The locals come here and they all know that the delicious meals are definitely secondary compared to the show. Entrance is expensive but well worth it. *Cañizares 10.* ☎ *913-690-496. Restaurant daily noon—5pm and 8—3am; show times Mon—Thurs 10:30pm, Fri—Sat midnight. Cover 30€. Metro: Tirso de Molina or Antón Martín.*

→ **El Cardamomo** This often over-crowded, flamenco-pop nightclub is where young Spanish gypsy hipsters hang out, clapping and stomping to flamenco's newest fusion music. Order an absurdly over-priced drink (after all, they're aware we're gawking) and shake what your momma didn't give you in spur-of-the-moment dancing circles, which will undoubtedly commence close to midnight. There is no *tablao. Echegaray 15.* ☎ *913-690-757. Metro: Alonso Martinez or Sol.*

→ **Mesón de la Guitarra** Reality check! You're in Spain. And no other caveman bar says it better than this one, with ceramic wine jugs and ham carcasses hanging above your head, in a dark tavern where sangria by the liter is more common than the local barflies it attracts. Although it's touristy, it's authentic. Old men play flamenco starting at 9:30pm, Monday to Friday. Calamares are the specialty of the house but the tortilla feeds four. There is no *tablao. Cava de San Miguel 13.* ☎ *915-599-531. Closed in Aug. Metro: Sol, La Latina.*

Nightclubs

Best → **Ananda** ★★ You can't get a better stargazing seat in the city or any closer to the beautiful people than at Ananda, Madrid's premier terraza in the spring and summer. The main club, attached to the Atocha Renfe station, is decorated Moroccan style with enough outdoor furniture for an arranged wedding: swinging sofas, incense, candles, and slickly dressed Spaniards of all shapes and sizes. If you're not enjoying its enormous patio, you're inside one of two gymnasium-size rooms; DJs spin chill out and house in one room while the other is reserved for classic Spanish pop. Both rooms are equally skintight on a Friday or Saturday night. Make sure you call and make a reservation ahead of time with marketing guru Oscar Rubio, and he can put your name on the list and hook you up with free invites. (He does not speak English.) Get there about midnight for the Eastern clubbing action. *Estación de Atocha. Ciudad de Barcelona s/n (next to Atocha station parking, near stairs to street). To get on the guest list,* ☎ *630-579-239. Otherwise cover is 15€ with drink. Metro: Atocha Renfe.*

→ **Kapital** So, you like deep house but not enough to listen to it for hours? You can try some salsa steps, but after a while, everyone can tell you're bluffing? You miss the beat of the drum-box and the rapping? Well search no more. Head to this dance supermarket, a seven-story megaclub with options for every taste. Discover each floor and pick the one you like the most, browsing between hip-hop, techno, Latin, and pretty much everything that you can shake your tail to. If you thought you would never be able to listen to Eminem, Moby, and Celia Cruz at the same venue, think again; everything goes in Madrid. *Atocha 125.* ☎ *914-202-906. Cover Thurs 12€,* Fri 15€, Sat 17€, price includes 1 drink. Metro: Atocha.

→ **Le Garage** What makes a city's nightlife above average are those unusual parties that you can't find anywhere else. Le Garage takes place in a Chinese karaoke house, inside a parking lot, on Thursday nights. After singing your guts out, you can dance your butt off to the best electro and techno this side of the English Channel—compliments of David Kano, from Spanish electronic wonders, Cycle. The ambience is something out of Manchester in the '90s with the cool and the beautiful mingling together and keeping Madrid's night real and unique. *Plaza de los Mostenses (in the parking lot). No phone. Cover varies. Metro: Plaza España.*

→ **Mondo at Stella** Walking into Mondo you'll understand why Madrid is one of the world capitals of techno partying. Dance the night away under a universe of mirrored balls, to the (better than decent) electronic music mixed by guest foreign DJs. Its two dance floors, a couple of bars, and all the music you can handle make this an obliged stop for laid-back, hard-partying Madrileños. The tourist quotient here is surprisingly low, so come meet your nightlife guides and maybe something else. *Arlabán 7.* ☎ *915-316-378. Cover 10€, includes 1 drink. Metro: Sevilla.*

→ **Nature (Mid-Day)** Nature (pronounced Nah-two-ray) is absolutely worth a visit, especially on Thursdays. Unlike the normal club scene, this place is laid-back and dreaddy, with a very open, hole-in-the-wall atmosphere, and DJs spinning mostly house and the occasional (relatively good) techno. The metallic decor and low, red lighting make it seem like Han Solo might show up later on. Little TVs show Japanese anime; wear your old T-shirts, sunglasses, and comfortable sneakers. Try to score a

118 ❀ Madrid

flyer (usually thrown around on the ground nearby) to get two drinks included in the cover. *Amaniel 13 (Covarrubias at Luchana). No phone. www.naturemadrid.com. Cover 10€ includes 1 drink. Metro: Bilbao.*

➜ **Ocho y Medio** The best underground party on Friday nights happens here, just in front of Zara's Lefties on Gran Vía, and attracts more than just one sexual orientation. So no matter what team you're dancing for, cakewalk to Clap Your Hands Say Yeah and Bloc Party. Its gayness is a mild undertone, and isn't the overall statement it makes. The crowd is very moderno between 18- and 30-years-old. Gays can bring their straight friends and everyone has a good time. Arrive late (or early—who can tell anymore?). *Mesoneros Romanos 13. ☎ 915-413-500. Cover 10€ with 1 drink. Metro: Callao, Gran Vía.*

➜ **Pachá** The Madrid branch of this mega-club signature franchise is housed in a beautiful 1930s theater that won many architecture prizes before becoming Madrid's dance cathedral in the '80s. As it is a trademark for this house, you will find the biggest international names behind the turntables; the hottest locals, if a little on the *pijo* side; and, of course, you and a bunch of other tourists that come attracted by the synonym of loud, mm-chh, mm-chh nonstop fun that the two cherries have come to represent (although some say they are actually the dilated pupils that characterize its patrons). Bounce your way in for an all-night extravaganza or visit Pachá Light, their early evening sessions for those who keep going, and going, and going . . . *Barceló 11. ☎ 914-470-128. www.pacha-madrid.com. Cover 12€ with 1 drink. Metro: Tribunal.*

➜ **Palacio Gaviría** How do you turn a beautiful XIX-century Renaissance palace into a giant cheese ball? Just fill it up with lights, a huge sound system, half-naked studs and babes, do a different thematic night every day of the week, and get as many tourists as possible to come. If you do want to meet fellow foreigners in an all-you-can-dance environment, this is probably your best bet. The majestic stairs and beautiful frescoes make it almost worth the entrance fee, and on Thursdays, the International Exchange Party is like a UN convention on X. They also have Reggaetón, Brazilian, and Latin nights with four dance floors and 13 different rooms to practice the international language of love. *Arenal 9. ☎ 915-266-069. www.palaciogaviria.com. Cover 9€–15€. Metro: Sol.*

➜ **Taboo** Dropping like flies is part of the fun at this club where electric beats pop more tops than petri dishes in a high school science lab. Its urban-chic international hotties go at it in a sweaty orgy until the sun comes up, which is why it's called Taboo. Okay not really, but that's my best shot at explaining its illicit name. Arrive around 3am when the party gets going, or a little early to avoid long lines. The place is right in the heart of Malasaña (full of hipster bars) so it's easy to start the night nearby and mosey on in when club hours begin. *San Vicente Ferrer 23. ☎ 915-241-189. Cover 8€, includes 1 drink. Metro: Tribunal.*

Gay Nightlife

Chueca is a world famous uni-sexual neighborhood, a place where gays and lesbians are more than just accepted—they hit the switch to the brightest, most colorful porch lights in Madrid. Its gay pride has overflowed into Green Vía and elsewhere in the center with glorified rainbow flag waving. Just take one step onto Plaza Chueca and walk forward. During **Best** **Gay Pride week,** toward the end of June and the beginning of July, heteros and homos join in parades, protests, and sexual intermingling, kicking off arguably the best party in Madrid.

MADRID

For serious until-dawn clubbers, head toward **Ohm** on Friday and Saturday nights only (Pl. del Callao 4; ☎ 915-413-500; midnight–6am), or else **Cool** (C. Isabel la Católica 6; ☎ 915-423-439; midnight–6am), but make sure to arrive fashionably late or you'll wonder where all the girls in heels and sparkly lipstick are.

→ **Bar Nike** For young, alterna-hip gays still working on the right way to slap an ass, here's a late night noshery that's ugly as sin but prettified with cute young boys. With its cheap prices and bigger-than-God drinks, you can afford to get a little tipsy now, in order to lose that closet inhibition later. Most people stand outside with their drinks, due either to the hideous decor or lack of table space. *Augusto Figueroa 22 (on the corner of Barbieri and Augusto Figueroa), near Plaza Chueca. ☎ 915-211-684. Metro: Chueca.*

→ **LL Bar de Copas** For the guy who likes to sing naked in heels, this is the hottest spot for him and a guaranteed good time. There's no cover, as long as you purchase a drink (4.50€). After a Chuecan supper elsewhere, catch the midnight drag show for big packages in small skirts. Young men under

30 start pickup conversations easily in this tightly packed, friendly atmosphere. There's a dark room downstairs for you know what; use protection, people! The party starts at midnight sharp. *Pelayo 11. ☎ 915-233-121. Metro: Chueca.*

→ **Sunrise** No matter what city, it seems that young, creative, professional, and good-looking gays find each other in one club playing tasteful house music. This is what we're dealing with here, folks. Thick-rimmed glasses, collared shirts, and beautifully tanned Spanish faces make this red-roped club worth the stop, as long as you're in the right market. *Barbieri 7. ☎ 915-775-576. Cover 8€ on weekends. Metro: Chueca.*

→ **Why Not?** Anytime after midnight, this old Hollywood-style bar/club is popular for most sexual preferences between 25 and 30 years old; the space is used by everyone and is known for being extremely social. The low-arched ceiling and narrow dimensions feel a little claustrophobic, but it's likely the person next to you will open you up. Just don't cause too many fireworks (there are no emergency exits) and arrive fashionably late. *San Bartolomé 6. No phone. Metro: Chueca.*

Performing Arts

If you're a single 20-something, the idea of sitting through a Spanish play doesn't sound like the most appealing way to spend time in Madrid, one of the cities with the most bars per person in the European Union, but it is the best way to cut yourself a slice of Madrileño culture when all you have is a few nights to taste it. After all, Madrid is the home of **La Zarzuela,** a type of non-heavy, light-hearted 17th-century theater, in which a pair of Jack McFarland's jazz hands is slapped together with local Madrid humor. The best place to catch a show is **Teatro de la Zarzuela** (C. de

Jovellanos 4, Huertas and Santa Ana; ☎ 915-245-400; admission 7.20€–27€; daily noon–6pm; Metro: Banco de España, Sevilla). Pick up a *Guia del Ocio* at any newsstand and see what's in store because, besides classic theater, Madrid is full of *freakies* who lash out on society with smaller avant-garde theater.

→ **Teatro Real** Earning its title as the Royal Theater, this hall has finally gotten over its awkward teen years and matured into an established opera house, which the city spent more than a 100 million euros to rear. Thanks to a certain guardian angel

MADRID

and opera master, Jesús Lopez Codos, the theater has finally become internationally recognized not just for its vibrating lungs, but also for its pink tutus and flat toes. The year 2007 boasts of Ballet del Teatro Mariinsky de San Petersburgo, the return of the Ballet Nacional, and opera romances such as *Madame Butterfly*. Of course, if Teatro Real's eyebrows are too high for you, just take a stroll around the neighborhood, and you're bound to hear its loudest stars' rising voices warming up in the comfort of their own homes. *Plaza de Isabel II.* ☎ *915-160-600. www.teatro-real.com. People under 26 years old can get 60% off tickets. If they buy last minute, prices are slashed 90% with ID. Admission 25 and under 6€–8€, all other tickets 13€–136€. Daily 10am–1:30pm and 5:30–8pm. Metro: Ópera.*

Sightseeing

If you get bored of drinking, eating, and dancing, you should know that a couple of other attractions draw people to Madrid— for example, the festivals, which usually involve people in costumes . . . drinking, eating, and dancing! You can also feed those few remaining brain cells with world-class museums and historic buildings.

Museums & Art Galleries

Madrid's art museums are awesome and they're half-off if you have a Spanish student card (anything from a foreign school— particularly if it doesn't have a date on it—usually won't fly). But even at full price, most venues are only about 6€. The following days are free for all museums: May 18 (International Day of Museums), October 12 (Fiesta Nacional de España), and December 6 (Día de Constitución Española). If you're walking everywhere, you may want to do the three biggies (Prado, Reina Sofía, Thyssen) together because they form a surprisingly small triangle. The Palacio Real and the Museo de la Real Academia de Bellas Artes de San Fernando are also relatively close to each other. The other museums listed here are a little farther out and may not be worth it if you don't have at least a few days in Madrid. It depends on how much of an art-fiend you really are.

➜**Fundación Lázaro Galdiano** Over looked by tourists with their eyes set on the Thyssen, this little gem of a private collection stands out as one of the best—a good find off the beaten path. Lázaro Galdiano was a Spanish entrepreneur from the 19th century who collected more than 15,000 works of art (there's an English explanation for each), as well as an extensive library. And each room has a picture of what the room used to look like when he lived there, a major bonus when hours of gallery hopping begin to get old. Artists on exhibit include big cheese such as Goya, Velázquez, El Greco, Murillo, Zubarán, Constable, Reynolds, and Gainsborough. *Serrano 122.* ☎ *915-616-084. www.flg.es. Admission 4€ adults, 3€ students. Wed–Mon 10am–4:30pm. Metro: Rubén Dario.*

➜**Museo Arqueológico Nacional** Calling all history buffs! This museum will satisfy your craving for prehistoric artifacts while adding some baroque flair. The most important piece of rock here was discovered on the southeastern coast of Spain and dubbed *The Lady of Elche,* carved in the 4th century B.C. when humans had a lot more hair. Another much-admired keepsake is the collection of reproduction Altamira cave paintings of bison, horses, and boars (oh my!), found in Santander in 1868. *Serrano 13.* ☎ *915-777-912. Admission 3€, free on Sat 2:30–8:30pm. Tues–Sat 9:30am–8:30pm; Sun and holidays 9:30am–2:30pm. Metro: Serrano, Colón.*

Cuidado! The Art of Pickpocketing

While you are ogling the Museo Nacional Centro de Arte Reina Sofía, with its huge glass elevators hanging over the giant plaza surrounded by cafes, the pickpockets are ogling you and thinking, "easy prey." So, remember to always wear a fanny pack nice and high up around the front of your tummy—okay, just kidding about the fanny pack. But do secure your goods at all times.

→ **Museo de la Real Academia de Bellas Artes de San Fernando** Madrid's fine arts museum is a lot less congested than the Avenue of Art. Plus, it's surrounded by large artistic buildings, bank headquarters, and corporate giants. This former baroque palace (lots of gold) houses paintings by Goya, Velázquez, El Greco, Rafael, Rubens, Zurbarán, Ribera, Cano, Coello, Murillo, and Sorolla. The interesting part is these paintings aren't as overplayed as the ones by the same heavy-hitters hanging in the big houses. *Alcalá 13.* ☎ *915-240-864. Admission 2.40€ adult, 1.20€ student, free Wed. Tues–Fri 9am–7pm; Sat–Mon and holidays 9am–2:30pm. Metro: Sol, Sevilla.*

[MTV] Best ☻ → **Museo del Prado** ★★★ Where does an 800-pound Museo del Prado sit? Anywhere it wants. If you miss the enormous collection of moody Goyas and trippy Boschs, classic medieval and Renaissance work, or the other 7,000+ paintings in this top-notch museum, your parents will never send you anywhere again. If this is your first visit, don't spread your legs for the entire museum—unless you know it's the one—otherwise you'll regret it later. So map out the greats to cover first before you get too zealous:

Velázquez, Goya, El Greco, Ribera, and Murillo, which are mostly located on the ground floor. Velázquez' *Las Meninas* is a masterpiece of perception (and ego)—he incorporated a self-portrait into the portrait of Princess Margarita. In the foreground is a mirror reflecting her parents, the king and queen, who are onlooking from our point of view. On the main floor, among the Flemish works, *The Garden of Earthly Delights* by Hieronymus Bosch, King Philip's (II) pet, is a must-see. The triptych (three painting-series on shutters) depicts the history of the world's sins, beginning with the original one by original bad boy and girl Adam and Eve on the left, that ends in Hell on the right (whose imagery was understandably used in a Metallica video). In the middle, is a 16th-century crash course on Kama Sutra—r-r-r-r-R-R. **The Casón del Buen Retiro,** annexed in 1971, houses the bulk of 19th century art though it's currently under renovation. *Palacio de Villanueva, Paseo del Prado.* ☎ *913-302-900. museoprado.mcu.es. Admission 6€. Tues–Sun 9am–8pm. Metro: Banco de España or Atocha.*

→ **Museo del Traje** If you're a fashionista with time on your gloves, head over to the costume museum located in University City. Featured designers include Chanel, Fortuny, Balenciaga, and Paco Rabanne. Exhibitions are on a rotating basis so call ahead of time. *Jean de Herrera 2.* ☎ *915-497-150. www.museodeltraje.mcu.es. Admission 2.85€. Mon–Sun 10am–5pm. Metro: Ciudad Universitaria.*

→ **Museo Nacional Centro de Arte Reina Sofía** ★ With a whole lot of Picasso, Dalí, and Miró, it's like a modern-art superstore. Price check on the Guernica at register six! The old building was originally a hospital but was renovated for the sole purpose of housing 20th-century art. Whether you have a half-day

MADRID

Free & Easy

1. **Modern Art Galleries** are concentrated in one part of town sandwiched between Chueca and Salamanca. For modern-art freaks, they're easy to cover in 2 hours. Some galleries, however, don't appreciate your not forking over the 100s of thousands of euros needed to buy their modern merchandise, so stick your nose up, and oh do behave, dahling. Streets that shoot off Plaza de las Salesas are thick with galleries. For maps, hours, and specific locations, go to **www.artemadrid.com**, or just get off the Metro at Chueca and Alonso Martinez and walk around. You're sure to bump into a few on Calle Barquillo, Calle Almirante, and Calle General Castaños.

2. Every summer from June to July, Madrid hosts **PhotoEspaña,** an international festival of photography and visual arts. Photo expositions are held all over the city and are *the* ticket for gallery hoppers. Projections and large outdoor expositions take over Barrio de las Letras (on and around Plaza Santa Ana and Calle Huertas). For venue info, visit www.phedigital.com.

3. **La Casa Encendida** in Lavapiés is a *gigantísimo* avant-garde cultural center offering free exhibitions, dirt-cheap documentaries (2€), and expos every weekend for the most plugged-in people in the city (Ronda Valencia 2; ☎ **902-430-322** or **916-024-641;** www.lacasaencendida.com; daily 10am–10pm; Metro: Embajadores).

4. **La Fundación Telfónica** is a corporate giant's oasis on Gran Vía that features international artists and free expositions (Gran Vía 28; ☎ **915-226-645;** www.fundacion.telefonica.com; Tues–Fri 10am–2pm and 5–8pm, Sat 11am–8pm, Sun and holidays 11am–2pm; Metro: Gran Vía).

5. **Círculo de Belles Artes** is where timid tourists and/or intellectual locals with thick books under their arms hang out. It has it going on with several

or half an hour, you can't leave Madrid without glimpsing the greatest piece of art that surfaced during the Spanish Civil War: Picasso's *La Guernica* (see box p. 125). *Santa Isabel 52.* ☎ *917-741-000. museoreina sofia.mcu.es. Admission 6€, free Sat after 2:30pm and Sun all day. Mon and Wed–Sat 10am–9pm; Sun 10am–2:30pm. Metro: Atocha.*

➔**Palacio Real** While American presidents walked dogs in front of a wedding cake White House, the Spanish Royal Family walked theirs around the largest palace in all of western Europe. It was built over the original 10th-century site of an Arab alcazar, like most major sites in Spain. Although the Royal Family doesn't live here anymore (they live in the outskirts of Madrid in a palace a tad more modest), it's still used for stately ceremonies. Part of the house is open to the public and is worth the visit, even if for an afternoon quickie. The most important rooms to scope out are the Reception Room and Sate Apartments, which are mostly rococo in style and contain a clock that's a girl's very best friend: diamonds. There's also a porcelain salon, The Royal Chapel, and the Throne Room. Artists like Velázquez and Goya pitched in with the decor. In the Royal Armory weapons date back to the 13th century, making for some exciting games of royal cops and impressive exhibition spaces (okay, it's not *exactly* free—it costs 1€ to see the art, but c'mon!), and even a cafe (Marqués de la Casa Riera 2; ☎ **913-605-400;** www.circulobellasartes.com; schedule varies; Metro: Banco de España).

6. **Subaquatica** is where you spray, not say it. This underground urban art space displays original artwork by local and international street artists from Spain and around the world (Caballero de Gracia 9; ☎ **915-218-415;** www.subaquatica.com; Mon–Sat 11am–2:30pm and 5–8:30pm; Metro: Gran Vía, Sevilla).

7. **Panteón de Goya,** Goya's Tomb, is a church where the artist painted the ceiling shortly before his death. Although considered his finest moment, it is, after all, only one moment. Unless Goya is your god, if your time is limited, best stick to the museums downtown (Glorieta de San Antonio de la Florida 5; ☎ **915-420-722;** Tues–Fri 10am–2pm and 4–8pm, Sat–Sun 10am–2pm; Metro: Príncipe Pío).

8. **Museo del Libro,** the Museo del Prado of paper, is Spain's national library housing sketches by Goya, Velázquez, Rembrandt, priceless bibles, and one of the first grammar books. It's a lot more interesting than a book museum sounds, with interactive tours and hands-on sexy librarians—we mean exhibitions (Paseo de Recoletos 20; ☎ **915-807-825** or 915-807-803; Tues–Sat 10am–1:45pm, Sun 10am–1:45pm; Metro: Colón).

9. **Museo Naval** is for jarheads or wannabes interested in Spain's naval history including shark tooth weapons and the first original map of the Americas (Paseo del Prado 5; ☎ **913-795-299;** Sept–July Tues–Sun 10am–2pm; closed Aug; Metro: Banco de España).

robbers. The palace treasure also includes the world's only complete quartet of Stradivarius stringed instruments (each one valued at hundreds of thousands of dollars). On Wednesdays, hang around for the changing of the guards. Below the palace steps, you'll find the royal gardens, Campo del Moro, where there is no admission fee to roam around. Right next to the Palace is Catedral de Nuestra Señora de la Almudena (☎ **915-422-200;** daily 10am–2pm and 5–9pm), Madrid's holy mamma, which wasn't finished until the 1990s, 110 years after the church and state finally agreed to let Madrid host a cathedral. *Plaza de Oriente, Bailén 2.* ☎ *914-548-700 and 915-*

420-049. Admission 9€ adults, 3.50€ students. Oct–Mar Mon–Sat 9:30am–5pm, Sun 9am–2pm; Apr–Sept Mon–Sat 9am–4pm, Sun 9am–3pm. Metro: Opera, Plaza de España.

📺 **Best☺** → **Thyssen-Bornemisza Museum** ★★★ If you were going to be stranded on a desert island for the rest of your life, which museum would you want with you? Well, the Thyssen would make good company because it's got a little bit of everything: from Renaissance to Realism to Cubism to Pop Art. It's art for dummies. Showcased in chronological order, art history will needle your brain like Atari, bouncing between artists who played off one another's styles and

MADRID

schools of thought. Starting from when artists could only paint iconographic crucifixions for royalty, leading all the way to Georgia O'Keefe's erotic iris, you can't help but marvel at humans' expression in art through the ages—preserving a chunk of what was back then considered pop culture—from Jesus to pornographic flowers. The most impressive started as a private collection of Baron Hans Heinrich Thyssen-Bornemisza. He married former Miss Spain 1961, Carmen Cervera, who painted the walls pink and started collecting Impressionists such as Monet, Renoir, and van Gogh. The couple then made an agreement with the Spanish government in 1992, to open its doors to the public. *Palacio de Villahermosa, Paseo del Prado 8.* ☎ *913-690-151. Admission 6€. Tues–Sun 10am–7pm. Metro: Banco de España.*

Festivals

Madrid has a bunch of festivals that correspond with Christian holidays, including the **Entierro de la Sardina,** in which a sardine is placed in a small casket, paraded about Madrid, then buried at Paseo de la Florida. This all takes place on Ash Wednesday (mid-Mar), for some reason, and thousands participate in the adventure. Despite the lack of ceremonial fish, however, the best festivals take place in the spring/summer, particularly in May.

Apart from all that, every surrounding city, pueblo, and anthill has its own Saint Day. This fact is one of many reasons why Madrid, or Spain for that matter, is a party town—simply for being Catholic. Cheers to that!

During **Christmas,** Plaza Mayor is traditionally the site of stalls upon stalls of junk: party wigs, costumes, stuff kids want and then chuck 5 minutes after their parents bought it. It's on Spain's version of April Fool's Day, **Day of the Innocence,** where practical jokes are played.

During May and June, bookworms go to the **Madrid Book Fair,** an all-month event in El Retiro, that allows publishers to present their books to the public. Dozens of stalls sell Spanish books, and authors stop by to sign jackets.

February

ARCO (Arte Contemporáneo) ★★★. ARCO (www.arco.ifema.es) is the mother of all modern art exhibitions in Madrid. Tickets are very expensive but the onslaught of international artists who come to town spur a citywide frenzy lasting 1 week. It takes place in the middle of February. Admission varies.

May

San Isidro festival. Madrid is at its best during the third week of May. San Isidro is the patron saint of the city, and man, do they love him. The weeklong event in his honor is like New Year's, Fourth of July, and Halloween all rolled together. Women and kids wear traditional *Castizo* costumes, a tremendous amount of hoopla ensues (including live music, carnival food such as *rosquillas* [thin, crispy-brown sugar cookies], street markets, dance performances, and more), and partiers drink and dance in the streets (particularly in the Las Vistillas neighborhood). Be sure to check out the fireworks at Las Vistillas. The local tourist offices and *Guía del Ocio* will have all the info.

Dos de Mayo. If you've got at least one tattoo or multiple earrings (bonus points for other piercings), you won't want to miss the Dos de Mayo celebration in the Plaza Dos de Mayo in Malasaña, on, you guessed it, the second of May! This holiday commemorates Madrid's rebellion against Napoleon's occupation of Spain, but the only people who bother to celebrate are those who live in the plaza of the same name. It's a type of neighborhood party with food and bands, but *what* a neighborhood!

June

Metro Rock Madrid ★. In just its second year, this indie-rock festival attracts big headliners like Franz Ferdinand, Sexy Sadie, and Orthodox Jew reggae guru Matisyahu, with local groups trying to make it big. The

Picasso's La Guernica

At the end of the day, it was Franco's decision to bomb the hell out of the Basque city of Guernica during the Spanish Civil War. Perhaps it was because the city was a forerunner for Basque freedom, which was standing in Franco's way to complete dictatorship. Others speculate that he green-lighted Nazi bombers to trash the civilian city as training for World War II. But one thing is crystal clear here: That's when Picasso exiled himself to Paris, and began to paint his bleak and cold, anti-Franco message: *La Guernica.*

For non-speakers of Cubism, the flower in the bottom center, growing from a splintered vase, is representative of Franco's repressive stronghold on the country. The central horse is suffocated by the mayhem of war. Lady Liberty offers her lamp of Democracy. There's a light bulb/eye that plays on the Spanish word *bombilla,* meaning either freedom or the actual bomb itself. Franco is depicted to the left of the horse, as well as his brethren Hitler and Mussolini, rendered as part men, part bulls.

The painting spent most its years at the Museum of Modern Art in New York. (Little good MoMA did during those years: During the Vietnam war, the painting was defaced with red spray paint by a peace demonstrator who chose the words, "KILL LIES ALL," after Richard Nixon turned a blind eye to the My Lai massacre.) According to Picasso's will, it was only to be returned once Spain had finally become a republic. MoMA had a hard time giving up its baby when Franco died, and went so far as to point out that Spain was not a democratic republic, as stipulated in the will, but rather a constitutional monarchy. That didn't fly, and Spain got its painting.

A copy of Picasso's *Guernica* is now hung as a tapestry at the Security Council room in the United Nations, with the hopes that its presence will warn policymakers of the horrors of war. However, while Colin Powell briefed his nation on the Iraq war in 2003, UN officials, pressured by the Bush administration who deemed the image inappropriate, covered it with a blue cloth during the broadcast.

festival takes place usually around the third weekend of June (www.metrorock. net; admission 35€–55€).

July

🎵 ⬛Best❀**Summercase Festival** ★★★. Simultaneous with the festival in Barcelona, this party in the July heat is the biggest in Spain for anyone who gives a bean about music—attracting the likes of

Fatboy Slim, The Chemical Brothers, and New Order (www.summercase.com; admission 70€–80€).

October & November

Fiesta de Otoño. Theaters and opera do big business in the fall (middle of Oct through Nov) during this festival dedicated to the arts. The best way to stay tuned is with the daily newspaper.

Playing Outside

Of course the easiest place to go running is the huge city park, **El Retiro** (Metro: El Retiro). The only problem is that you might

be running from pickpockets and panhandlers as much as for your health. The Calle de Moyano is the best entrance for

MADRID

Bullfighting

Well, well, well. So you wanna see a bull gored, tortured, dragged, and its balls ripped off and eaten by a small man in tights. I don't blame you, man. Matadors are to Madrid what blood is to Dracula. The Mozarabic stadium, **Plaza Monumental de Toros de las Ventas** (Alcalá 237; ☎ **913-562-200;** admission 1.25€–111€; Metro: Ventas), is stunning itself, with a capacity to seat 25,000, making it arguably the world's home of bullfighting. The ring is divided into 10 *tenidos,* or seat sections. The Royal Family sit in a luxe box a little more modest than a manager's suite at any ballpark, but a helluva lot more symbolic, and decorated in arabesque design. On the other side of the royal box is the ring's clock. Between the first two tenidos, there's a door leading to the butcher's, otherwise known as the skinning room. Between tenidos 3 and 4 is a door leading to where horses are kept. It's also where the *paseíllo* (parade) starts and from where *picadors* (lancers on horseback) enter the ring, tiring the bull with punishing blows. The Door of Madrid between tenidos 7 and 8 is what matadors dream about at night; in fact, Plaza Monumental de Toros de las Ventas is sorta the bar mitzvah for a young matador. Once he's walked through those doors and killed, he's one of the big boys. Through the same doors are two operating rooms and a church, just in case the worst should happen.

While some sections are shaded, others roast in the sun. The latter seats *(filas)* cost a lot less than *sombras* and afford us commoners a chance to see fights all season long. Bullfighting season begins in March and doesn't end until December, and *corridas* are held every Sunday and holiday. However, the majority of Madrileños attend fights during San Isidro Fiesta (Madrid's saint's celebration) starting on May 15, when they take place every day. Bring a butt cushion: Fights last 3 hours, starting at 6 or 7pm. What many people don't know is that there are moonlit matador matches. The bullring holds spot-lit shows on Saturdays at 11pm.

To score tickets, go to www.taquillatoros.com or call ☎ **902-150-025.** Tickets are also available to the general public at the Plaza de Toros (Alcalá 237; ☎ 913-562-200; www.las-ventas.com; Metro: Ventas) on Friday 10am to 2pm and 5 to 8pm.

running and in-line skating because it is far from all of the pond-related hype (gypsy card readers, vendors, screaming kids high on cotton candy, crowds, and rowboats for rent) that goes down in the central part of the park. See p. 130.

The high altitude of the **Parque Juan Carlos I** (daily 9am–11:30pm; Metro: Campo de las Naciones), and its removal from the city makes it worth the half-hour Metro ride from downtown. A weird mix of nature, huge modern statues, and bridges gives the park a post-apocalyptic, *Planet of the Apes* vibe that is somehow very calming. Without a doubt, this is Madrid's best location for **biking, running, Rollerblading, skateboarding, kite flying, Frisbee throwing, and day-tripping.** You might even enjoy the *espectáculos* on Thursday through Sunday nights at 10:30pm; they include music, fireworks, and synchronized fountains. As with most things, consult the *Guía del Ocio* for specific times and prices of events. Here's a little secret: The park offers free bicycles for an hour (even double bicycles!). To get

12 Hours in Madrid

1. **Stroll down Calle de Fuencarral.** Start at the McDonald's (for God's sake, don't go in!) on Gran Vía (Metro: Gran Vía), cross the street, and you'll pass cramped stores selling everything from wristwatches and Walkmans to pornography—but the street quickly transforms into a hipster's wet dream. You'll first come across clothing stores of all shapes and sizes. Many of the windows have gallery-style displays, including mannequins with TV-heads and far-out latex fantasies. As you continue, the stores will fill in with restaurants and bars, where living, breathing walks of art strut their smoking fannies. Both the stores and the cafes come to a climax at the plaza right next to Mercado Fuencarral, which is full of cafe tables (Starbucks! Keep a safe distance! This is Europe, damn it!), more stores, and a whole lot of people just hanging out.

2. **Enjoy a small cup of good coffee at La Glorieta de Bilbao,** where you can sit at the sidewalk tables of Café Comercial, one of those most famous and original cafes, where the city's biggest literary stars from the 19th century convened. There's an Internet cafe upstairs to confirm your reservation or write your parents a quick note telling them you've arrived in Madrid (see "Cafes/Tearooms").

3. **Shop the Plaza de España,** for a dose of modern—decidedly un-hip— Madrid consumer culture. Plaza de España borders Calle de Princesa (whose name changes to Gran Vía as you get closer to Sol), which is full of fast food, movie theaters, and a VIPS. Once you get to the Plaza de España proper, the beautiful fountains and trees offer a welcome place to sit and relax for a few moments. Underneath the park are a parking garage and the city's best (translation: cheapest) underground Chinese restaurant serving homemade noodles and dumplings. Shh!

4. **Climb up to El Templo de Debod** whose Egyptian artifacts were given to Spain and other countries in exchange for financial assistance in the building of Egypt's Aswan Dam. You can pay to go into the small museum at the top of the hill, but you'll have just as much fun taking in the view of the city below, including El Palacio Real and its gardens.

5. **Madrid's Teleférico** is nearby (Pl. del Pintor Rosales s/n; ☎ **915-417-450;** www.teleferico.com; round-trip 4.65€; daily noon–2pm and 3–9pm, hours vary slightly depending on month and holiday; Metro: Argülles). Climb into one of the cable cars and relax. Go to the cafetería and have a drink.

6. When you return, cross Calle de Ferraz again and **walk down Calle de Marqués de Urquijo,** where most of the trendy little pubs accept credit cards and serve authentic Spanish cuisine.

your own municipal wheels, head toward one of two rental buildings: at the northern access to the park, closest to the Metro station Campo de Naciones, or at the Glorieta (roundabout) de Don Juan de Borbón. *FYI:* Parque Juan Carlos I is completely safe for single women during the day. Nobody hangs out here unless they've come for one of the specific activities listed above. The weirdness/sliminess factor is zero.

MADRID

M T V Ⓤ Arty Facts

(FREE) **Escuela de Fotografía y Centro de Imagen** (EFTI; Fuentearrabía 4–6; ☎ 915-529-999; www.efti.es; free admission; Mon–Fri 10am–2pm and 4–10pm, Sat 10am–2pm; Metro: Menéndez Pelayo) is half school and half gallery. The featured work is occasionally by students, but prize-winning photography is also often on display (such as winners from the recent Hasselblad Open, an international contest sponsored by the Swedish camera manufacturer). Displays on the first floor intermingle with studios, students, and a common room, with some exotic photography, design, and style magazines that you may not have seen back home. A great way to spend an hour or two, and also a very likely place to strike up a conversation with a local art student. Set in a pleasant neighborhood with tranquil street-side cafes.

(FREE) **Facultad de Bellas Artes** (El Greco 2; ☎ 913-943-626; free admission; Mon–Sat 9am–10:30pm, gallery Mon–Sat 10am–1pm; Metro: Moncloa and then bus no. 46 to Av. de Juan de Herrera) is the school for fine arts at Madrid's huge Complutense University. You can only get here by bus, but it's not too bad, and the reward is that you will be right smack in the middle of the Madrid student art scene! The big, ever-changing gallery here displays paintings, sculptures, and interactive works by students. A second, smaller room hosts plays, discussions, and occasional films. In addition to a lot of books, the library here is home to nearly 300 drawings from students who studied here in the 18th and 19th centuries.

El Capricho (Almeda de Osuna; weekends 9am–9pm; Metro: Alameda de Osuna), where Goya painted his famous *Witches' Sabbath*, is the site of romantic French gardens and considered the best-kept secret of Madrid (it has a lot to compete with). Maybe it's because it's only open to the public on the weekends and on bank holidays. There's **a maze and a beehive**, in front of which royalty stuffed their faces with chocolate. The story goes the duchess and duke paid a hermit to reside in the gardens. Conditions were that he had to grow his nails and hair long to fulfill mythic expectations. *Doctor Zhivago* was also filmed here.

For extreme tourism, check out **Ecoparque Aventura Amazonia** (Ctra. De la Fuenfría Km 3.9, Las Dehesas, Cercedilla; from Madrid, take A-6 to Coruña and exit on Salida 47 Guadarrama; ☎ 902-511-462; www.aventura-amazonia.com; admission 18€ adult; Mon–Sun 10am–8pm, Sat until 9pm), a 35-minute drive outside the city, to El Valle de la Fuenfría, that brings you to a maze of **canopied obstacle courses** that are kilometers off the forest floor, so you can swing from tree to tree and howl like Tarzan. Whether you're an amateur tree-house squatter or an expert mountain scaler, the eco-park challenges everyone in a completely natural environment (no fun houses), but you'll need a car to get there.

Gardens & Parks

Although the parks in Madrid are fun, they're not a place to be at night if you are alone.

➜ **Casa de Campo** ★ This east-side park is a lot wilder than Retiro and it's great for riding your bike and feeling a little closer to nature. Its 1,200 hectares (2,965 acres) used to be the kings' hunting grounds until it was opened to the public in the '30s. It houses a

MADRID

Board Talk

If you're jonesing to skate, you've come to the right city. Spanish kids have taken to skateboarding like Shakira to ass-shaking, and the government approves, more or less. The cops take their laxatives around skaters and go so far as to stop and watch them land tricks without an iota of tsk tsk. It's hard to get used to, but hey, that's Spain.

For street action, start at the **Plaza de Colon** (Metro: Colón), the best place to hook up with a chain gang of local skaters who'll no doubt take interest in a foreigner. Colón is what first made the city famous for its skateboarding scene, and all Madrileño greats probably got their start here. Skate north on Paseo de la Castellana until you hit **"The Bridge,"** the first one you pass on the right about a mile and half down the way. And though it might not be totally legal, nobody's going to lynch you, much less in Spain, for skating around **Reina Sofía** and **Museo del Prado** (C. Recoletos), asphalt stretches offering makeshift parks.

The best skatepark is **Alcobendas.** Take the No. 127 bus from Plaza de Colon to Plaza Castilla (the two leaning skyscrapers), and transfer there to the No. 153 bus. Let the bus driver know where you're going; he'll no doubt know where and what it is. In any case, keep an eye out for a baseball field, that's your stop. Another well-known skatepark is at a rec center in the Madrid suburb of **Mósteles at the Polideportivo Los Rosales** (Lila c/v Margarita s/n; ☎ **916-645-723;** 2€ for 2 days, 6€ for a membership). Take the Metro to Principio Pio and transfer to the No. 523 bus to Mósteles. Get off at the Plaza del Toros.

Need to do some board-related shopping? Get all the Volcom, Etnies, and Suspect you can handle at the small but powerful **Triburbana** (San Felipe Neri 1; ☎ **915-429-433;** Mon–Thurs 11am–2pm and 5–8:30pm, Fri–Sat 11am–2pm and 5–9pm, closed Sun; Metro: Sol, Ópera). The music is loud, the staff knows their stuff (well-known skaters hang out there), and they have a hip-hop store around the corner where they sell graffiti supplies. We have no idea where **San Francisco Skate Farm** ★★ (Argensola 3; ☎ **913-086-975;** Mon–Fri 10:30am–2pm and 5–8:30pm; Metro: Colón) got the weird name from, but it is unarguably the best skate store in Madrid, with the most imports and selection. Its founder is a celebrity in the Madrid punk skate scene. Mega skateshop **Sk8land** (Manuel Cortina 3; ☎ **914-458-131;** www.sk8land.com; Mon–Sat 10:30am–2pm and 5–8:30pm; Metro: Colón) is another important biggie in the city if you need to replace a board on the fly or spring for new treads, in order to blend with the local ruffians. It's located next to Plaza Colón, so it's easy to shop on the go.

MADRID

zoo-aquarium and an amusement park. Getting there is the most fun; you have to catch the *teleférico* (Pl. del Pintor Rosales s/n; ☎ **915-417-450;** www.teleferico.com; round-trip 4.65€; Mon–Sun noon–2pm and 3–9pm [hours vary slightly depending on month and holiday]; Metro: Argúlles), a gondola that stretches the city. The park is open 24 hours but you don't want to be caught there after dark, when it becomes Madrid's "green" red zone—not a place for a girl by herself unless she's got another agenda entirely. ☎ *914-796-002. Metro: Casa de Campo.*

→**Jardín Botánico** People like to take spliffs inside (despite the number of guards) and lose themselves in the maze of trees, shrubs, and flowers with unpronounceable names (thousands of others got sucked away by a cyclone in the 19th c.) of Madrid's royal botanical gardens. Don't miss the greenhouse with the cacti; it's like a sauna, and will transport you to Bora-Bora. *Plaza Murillo 2. Admission 2€ adults. Daily 10am–sunset. Metro: Atocha.*

📺 Best ☻ →**Parque del Buen Retiro** ★★★ The locals enjoy running and in-line skating through this enormous park with its tall trees, peaceful lawns, and ornate fountains. It was formed after the Royal Palace was destroyed during the Napoleanic wars during Felipe IV's reign, which created an open plain, subsequently opened to the public. It becomes a real spectacle on weekends when the streets swell up with families, musicians, performers, and vendors. A great attraction here and the best way to impress a girl are the **rowboats** that you can rent in the huge man-made pond (it's a small lake, really) located in the center of the park (☎ **915-744-024;** 45-min. rentals for 4€; daily 10:30am–dusk). Also there's a massive greenhouse, **Palacio de Cristal** (free admission; Mon and Wed–Sat 10am–6pm, Sun 10am–4pm, closed Tues), where walk-in art expositions are sometimes housed. For **photo expositions,** go to **Casa de Vacas** (☎ **914-095-819;** Mon–Fri 11am–8pm, schedules vary in the summer). It's best to enter near **Puerta de Alcalá.**

May–Sept daily 7am–midnight; Oct–Apr daily 7am–10pm. Metro: Retiro.

Skiing & Boarding

Spring fever has its clutches on you and you're dying to get back on the slopes? Just because you're in the big city doesn't mean you can't escape for a day with the bunnies. From December to February, make a day trip to the Sierras, north of the province to **Navacerrada** (Puerto de Navacerrada ski and Mountain Resort, Puerto de Navacerrada s/n; ☎**918-523-302, 915-943-034,** or **018-521-435;** www.puertonavacerrada.com) or **Cotos** (Valdesqui, Carretera De Cotos s/n; ☎ **918-523-311;** www.valdesqui.es), where there are ample opportunities to carve in Spanish style. You can reach the areas from either Chamartín or Atocha stations on the Renfe Cercanías line (8b) north to Cercedilla. You'll have to change lines there to the C-9 for Puerto de Navacerrada or to Cotos (the final stop).

→**Xanadu Comercial Centre** Ski indoors on a slope boasting 50cm (about 20 in.) of artificial snow and a capacity of about 500 people. There are alpine trees, a cold temp, and everything you need to get rid of your cabin fever, along with ski shops, restaurants, and bars. *Located on Carretera N-V Km 23 (Carretera de Extremadura). ☎ 902-361-309. www.millsmadridxanadu.com. For 1 hr. during peak time 15€. Mon–Fri 10am–2pm and 4–8pm. Bus: 496, 498, 524, 528 (from Principio Pío), 529, 531, 536 (Méndez Álvaro).*

Shopping

Fashion

Make your first shopping destination Sol, where credit cards reign. Calle Preciados is the franchise-shop-laden pedestrian street leading from Sol to Gran Via that attracts teeny-boppers and princesses with stores like Miss Sixty, H & M, Zara, and El Corte Inglés. Gran Via is just as fashion conscious, but especially noteworthy is Lefties (Carretas 10; ☎ **915-312-188;** daily

10am–8:30pm; Metro: Callao, Gran Via), the Zara outlet, where you'll find last season's hot leftovers for next to nothing. If you are looking for young, high-fashion designers, head to Chueca, particularly the streets Almirante, Prim, and Monasterio. If your Louis Vuitton purse got snatched, replace it in Salamanca on Calle Serrano, which looks like a spread-out Barneys, then head down José Ortega y Gasset for more of designers' dead animals. For urban wear and funky designers, there's nothing like Fuencarral Street, and there's even a street that specializes in shoes: Augusto Figueroa, former residence of none other than Imelda Marcos.

Most shops are open Monday through Saturday from late morning (10- or 11-ish) 'til about 9pm, some closing between 2 to 5pm for siesta. Call ahead as some shops are closed on Sunday.

MTV **Best ✦** → **Lotta Vintage** What do you get when you mix two Scandinavian designers and Madrid? Madrid's most design-infused vintage retro-tique and high prices. Polka-dot tank dresses give way to striped skirts and shirtwaists. Printed shoes to match. *Hernán Cortes 9.* ☎ *915-232-505. Metro: Chueca.*

Vintage

MTV **Best ✦** → **Holalá** This is old-school vintage: Zip-up hoodies and thinned T-shirts with Midwestern softball logos flirt with '60s style sweaters; old Levi's jeans roughhouse among German army surplus. The owners rummage the largest, hippest cities, in order to stock the store. *Hortaleza 42.* ☎ *915-325-423. Metro: Chueca, Gran Vía.*

→ **Pepita Is Dead** If you're a hypochondriac who likes vintage clothing, never fear. These pieces have never rubbed skin with anyone more than the time it takes to

try them on. Pepita broadcasts the '60s, '70s, and '80s like a rock 'n' roll radio station, making bank with never-worn shoes, hip-huggers, cords, trench coats, and suspenders. *Doctor Fourquet 10.* ☎ *915-288-788. www.pepitaisdead.com. Metro: Atocha, Lavapiés.*

→ **Templo de Susu** No rock 'n' roll neighborhood would be complete without a cheap, well-stocked vintage store with a little something for everyone. Men go over the moon for inexpensive bomber/army jackets. Women are tickled pink by high-waisted '70s short shorts and sundresses. *Espíritu Santo 1.* ☎ *915-233-122. Metro: Tribunal, Noviciados.*

Mall

→ **Mercado Fuencarral** This three-story-high mall is a must-see for those who wanna get with it in Madrid. This throbbing core of coolness features nearly 50 stores that sell young designers' clothes, jewelry, smoking equipment, music, and other (sub)culturally relevant items. Also has a (sometimes free) movie theater and two bars but don't spend your time there. The mall also houses the biggest, most frequently used bulletin board in town—second only to the University—for edgy Madrileños to find apartments, drummers, roommates, dogs, boyfriends, and, yes, even sex. *Fuencarral 45.* ☎ *915-215-985. Metro: Tribunal, Gran Vía, Chueca.*

Books

→ **Casa Del Libro** This huge, corporate-feeling mega bookstore will have any book that you could ever want, especially maps and dictionaries. They have some titles in English, too. Much like Borders or Barnes & Noble, you can sit and read for as long as you want without anyone bothering you. Large posters in the stairwell quote famous

MADRID

people from the Marx Brothers to Einstein to Cervantes; reading them is a great way to practice your Español. *Maestro Victoria 3.* ☎ *915-214-898. Gran Vía 29.* ☎ *915-421-900. www.casadellibro.com. Metro: Ópera.*

➜**J & J Books and Coffee** This cafe bar in Malasaña was started by an American-Spanish couple who wanted a spot in Madrid to curl up with a book and hot cup of coffee. Upstairs is a cozy cafe, and downstairs is a stellar bookshop with English titles. English professors love to come here to buy their teaching texts. It's also a meeting place for language exchange, shoptalk, and maybe a little homesickness when it strikes, not to mention the perfect place to pick up a Hemingway novel for your plane ride home. The bar also arranges events like Quiz night and TV night. Intercambio night is on Wednesdays and Thursdays from 8pm to close. If you have no desire to see other Americans while on your trip, stay clear; the bar staff insists on speaking English (American) here. *Espiritu Santo 47.* ☎ *915-218-576. www.jandjbooksandcoffee.com. Metro: Noviciado.*

Music

If you're not heading to **FNAC** in Plaza Callao (Preciados 28; ☎ **915-956-100** and 902-100-632) for new music, then you're scouting the Madrileña streets for used album museums, where buying CDs is still a national pastime. The best used-CD stores are all jammed in one area near the center, Metro Callao, or Santo Domingo.

➜**Bangla Desh** This shop specializes in secondhand material. They carry mostly 1970s and 1980s albums in great condition and have a big vinyl singles section. Finds include vintage Talking Heads or David Bowie. *Costanilla de los Ángeles 5.* ☎ *915-595-056. Metro: Opera, Santo Domingo.*

Gifts That Keep On Giving

If the airline is going to charge you for the extra bottles of Spanish wine you're toting back, then think again. An essential gift is a **Spanish fan** that no woman can be without during hot months. Spanish traditions say women flirted with men by the flick of their wrist. These are everywhere, especially in Plaza Mayor and Sol, and fall anywhere between 1€ and 50€, depending on the quality of hand painting. **Leather wallets** and **Spanish embroidered shawls** are a must, as well as **espadrille shoes** for women: They're sold cheaper here than in any other part of the world. Just outside Plaza Mayor on Calle Toledo are stores specializing in them; however, get there early because there's sometimes a line to get in. If you're shopping for a man, pick up a pair of **leather gloves** or support the local soccer team and buy a **Real Madrid hat** on Plaza Mayor. Artists convene on the plaza to sell **original artwork** for low prices, so think about rolling a canvas into your bag; art is a gift that appreciates with time. Don't forget airport liquor shops make great last-minute shopping when only a bottle of **absinthe** will do.

➜**Discos Babel** Here's a good shop for both secondhand and reissued records, focusing on 1960s and 1970s material. You can find gems such as Suicide's first album or luxurious editions of Turbonegro's albums. *Costanilla de los Ángeles 5.* ☎ *915-481-082. Metro: Opera or Santo Domingo.*

➜**Manuel Contreras II, Luthier** You can't leave Spain without a Spanish guitar!

¡Cuidado! An Ounce of Prevention

El Rastro is often called "thieves market" because slippery hands skillfully crawl everywhere. Most women wear backpacks and purses on their bellies, no matter how much it makes them look fat or pregnant. Unattended bags are sure to be pursued. The same goes for cameras. Make sure they're strapped around your neck or in your hand. Wallets in back pockets are a no-no, which goes without saying.

Manuel Contreras comes from a family that's been making fine instruments for over 40 years, and though not cheap, you can get a much better price for his guitars here than back home. *Calle Mayor 80.* ☎ *915-422-201. www.manuelcontreras. com. Metro: Sol.*

→ **Rock and Roll Circus** ★★ This is heaven for collectors of quality reissues. They also carry rare vinyl editions of recent albums and have a good second-hand selection. Here you can find special editions of Kings of Leon, Captain Beefheart, or Television. *Conchas 4.* ☎ *915-426-644. Metro: Opera or Santo Domingo.*

Tattoos

→ **Chemical Tattoo** Does the idea of getting a new piercing or tat stress you out a bit? Then get it here (from Mon–Sat 11am–9:30pm), together with a sauna or massage, and get rid of the tension that you get from having your privates perforated. *Augusto Figueroa 11.* ☎ *915-323-500. www.chemicaltattoo.com. Metro: Tribunal or Gran Vía.*

Markets

If you haven't got your fill of meat in Spain, head toward the nearest **fruit market** for whole pig heads, skinned baby pigs, pig snouts, full-size squid or octopus, and oh yeah, some fresh fruit. It's the most conventional Spanish experience you'll find in Spain, so make sure you stand alongside an old señora, who'll probably be willing to help you figure out how to order meat or even share a secret way to spice it. The best in the center of town are alongside Plaza Mayor, Mercado de San Miguel. A little pricier but a lot prettier is a few minutes away in La Latina at Mercado de la Cebada, just above the Metro La Latina.

🆄 Best ❶ → **El Rastro** The infamous outdoor (gypsy) market, one of the largest and most famous in the world, is a seething concoction of bootlegged T-shirts, questionable antiques, and won't-find-anywhere gifts for friends back home. It's one of the most fun things you'll see in Madrid, as long as you don't lose your passport along the way. Pick up a fan, a wine casket, and a jar of olives: the essentials for any Rastro trip. The real reason tourists go, however, is to take pictures of the oddities. Antique diving helmets, European furniture, and dismembered dolls rolling in the streets cater to good photo ops for people back home. Yes, Madrid is exotic. The favorite game here is Let's Make a Deal and it's totally acceptable to drive a hard bargain.

Once you've worked up a good appetite, no doubt caused by the secondhand hashish you'll smell throughout, stop in one of the jumble of bars for a small *caña* of beer. Don't hold out for food here though. For lunch, mosey into La Latina along with the hordes of others and play the odds for a table. Smart travelers will plan ahead and make reservations for a nearby eatery. But that's not easy, as the Rastro offers enticing eye candy that makes it impossible to navigate its streets or keep on schedule. Try and check out the scene on Sundays before noon—the place becomes unbearably crowded by 12:30pm. The Rastro comprises many streets but mainly Plaza Cascorro and Ribra de Curtidores. *Metro: La Latina, Tirso de Molina.*

Castilla–La Mancha

by Elizabeth Gorman

W hen Americans think of Spain, Castilla–La Mancha provides the imagery and backdrop for what most likely springs to mind. Dry, baked land interrupted by twisted olive trees and dry bush sweeping across high mesas and low-lying hills. It's the place where Don Quijote and his squire, Sancho Panza, fought off giant windmills and resurrected knight errantry. Today, Pedro Almodóvar takes advantage of the waterless scenery for his main plot in *Volver*. Even the countryside's most dreary expanses conjure up the imagination on rainy days. Anyone making the drive from Madrid to Toledo will appreciate El Greco's bleak renditions of his hometown centuries ago.

Best of Castilla–La Mancha

- **Best Place to Start an Artists' Commune:** Decades ago, a goosey group of creative artists moved to the geographic jewel of **Cuenca** and set up a studio because rent was cheap. Now they're the talk of the town. See p. 150.
- **Best Way to Take a Knight:** In Toledo, chess is the name of the game. If that's too nerdy for you, opt for the steel **swords,** my friend. See p. 146.
- **Best Place to Ride a Donkey:** After a few shots of Chinchón's anis, this will sound like a really good idea. Trust me. See p. 162.

- **Best Place to Pay Your Respects:** The **Royal Pantheon** in El Escorial is the town's class act. See p. 160.
- **Best Place to Pack a Picnic:** **Aranjuez** is the most ideal place to play house, or make whoopee. See p. 151.
- **Best Place for PDA Action:** In Philip II's pursuit to create the picturesque place to play, he and his buddy Juan Bautista de Toledo imported trees from all sorts of places and developed the island along the river Tajo into an Italian-Flemish garden park. **Jardín de la Isla** grew more extensive as the

river's sediment did, so kings kept the pace with more gardens, fountains, and paths. The final product yields a romantic walk, along which inhibitions are easily lost. See p. 153.

○ **Best Way to Get High in Toledo:** It's not the stairway to heaven but on a hot day with a heavy pack on Toledo's steep incline, it damn well feels like it. The *remonte peatonal* escalator was built just for this purpose: Starting near the Puerta de Alfonso VI and ending at the Monestario de Santo Domingo El Antiguo, it makes the run Monday to Friday 7am to 10pm and Saturday and Sunday 8am to 10pm.

○ **Best Moment of Zen:** It's free, it's easy to get to, and it's the most important thing you'll do in Cuenca. Climb from the river's ridge to the farthest, highest point, in order to contemplate the meaning of life and your role in it. Yoga mats not included. See p. 146.

Toledo ★★

Just 1 hour by bus outside Madrid is Toledo, which could have doubled as the picture-perfect setting for *Lord of the Rings,* with cobblestone streets too narrow for senior tour buses. But as tempting as it could have been, Toledo never went all-the-way Disney. Souvenir shops sell real ninja swords instead of snow globes, and nowhere can you find T-shirts with "I Heart Toledo." Sorry, Ma. It is, however, flooded with tourists from all over the world and is by no means one of Spain's secrets. With the advent of the high-speed AVE train linking Toledo to Madrid in a half-hour, Toledo is a new, but very old, suburb of Madrid. Many of its citizens make the commute to work and back every day.

What you have here is a city with legends of mythic proportions: Arabs, Jews, and Christians, all living together peacefully. Well, sort of. The Inquisition put a damper on things in 1492. But the city perked up again when a semi-dejected painter named El Greco began painting scenes of Toledo's gloomy skylines from a hillside overlooking the Tagus River. *View of Toledo,* his most famous work from this series, currently hangs in the Metropolitan Museum of Art in New York. In Toledo, however, his work is spread thin, hanging in almost every monument in the city, a ploy to get you into every single last one of them.

The city stands on top of a hill overlooking New Castile, which made it the logical choice for Spain's capital city. And it was, but only until the 16th century, when it lost its mojo to Madrid. Previously, it had also been the capital for the Visigoths, Muslims, Arabs, and Christians—pretty much in that order. The historic city is protected by a large fortress wall and beyond that is the new city—though there's no need to venture there. Plaza Zocodover is the main meeting point, contrary to the Plaza Mayor protocol in other Spanish cities. If you're so inclined, **Etur** (☎ **925-216-780;** www.e-tur.es) rents Segway scooters (30€ for 1½ hr.) fitted with GPS systems for a basic tour around town, but you'll look like an idiot.

Getting There & Around

BY TRAIN
Hot off the assembly line are the high-velocity AVE trains. Sleek, white, and futuristic, they are the sole trains that depart Madrid's RENFE Atocha train station bound for Toledo 10 to 12 times daily, from 6:50am to 9:50pm. AVE trains leaving Toledo for Madrid run 10 to 12 times daily from 6:55am to 9:25pm. Traveling time is

Toledo

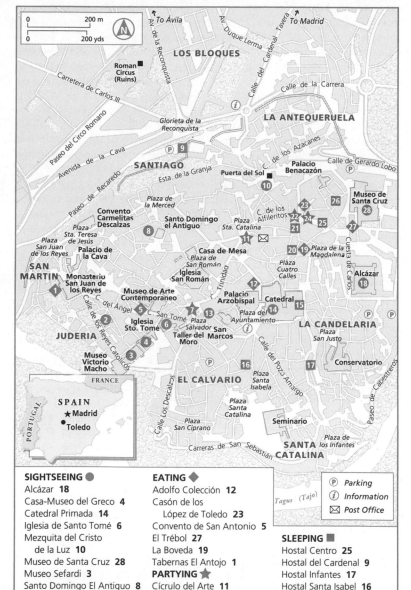

0   200 m
0   200 yds

↑ To Ávila   ↗ To Madrid

Av. de la Reconquista

Av. Duque Lerma

Calle del Cardenal Tavera

LOS BLOQUES

Carretera de Carlos III

Roman ■
Circus
(Ruins)

Paseo del Circo Romano

Calle de la Carrera

Glorieta de la
Reconquista

ⓘ

LA ANTEQUERUELA

Avenida de la Cava

Paseo de Recaredo

Ⓟ 9

Esta. de la Granja

SANTIAGO

C. de los Azacanes

Calle de Gerardo Lobo

Puerta del Sol

Palacio
Benacazón   Ⓟ

Plaza de
la Merced

10

Museo de
Santa Cruz

Convento
Carmelitas
Descalzas

8

Santo Domingo
el Antiguo

C. de los
Alfileritos   23   26

22 24   28

Plaza
Sta. Catalina   21   25   27

Plaza
Sta. Teresa
de Jesús

Plaza
San Juan
de los Reyes

Palacio de
la Cava

Casa de Mesa

Plaza de
San Román

Iglesia
San Román

20 19 Plaza de la
Magdalena

Plaza
Cuatro
Calles

Cuesta de Carlos

Alcázar
18

**SAN
MARTIN**

Monasterio
San Juan de
los Reyes

1

Museo de Arte
Contemporaneo

C. del Ángel

Trinidad

Palacio
Arzobispal

12

Catedral   15

Calle de los Reyes Católicos

2   5   C. San Tomé

Iglesia
Sto. Tomé   6

7

13

Plaza del
Ayuntamiento

14

ⓘ

LA CANDELARIA

Plaza
Salvador San
Taller del Marcos
Moro

Plaza
San Justo

4

3

Museo
Victorio
Macho

Ⓟ

16

Plaza
Santa
Isabela

17

Conservatorio

JUDERIA

EL CALVARIO

Calle del Pozo Amargo

Paseo de Cabestreros

Plaza
Santa
Catalina

Seminario

FRANCE

Plaza
San Ciprano

SPAIN

★ Madrid

● Toledo

PORTUGAL

Carreras de San Sebastián

**SANTA
CATALINA**

Plaza de
los Infantes

SIGHTSEEING ●
Alcázar **18**
Casa-Museo del Greco **4**
Catedral Primada **14**
Iglesia de Santo Tomé **6**
Mezquita del Cristo
    de la Luz **10**
Museo de Santa Cruz **28**
Museo Sefardi **3**
Santo Domingo El Antiguo **8**
Sinagoga de Santa María
    La Blanca **2**
Toledo Interpretation
    Center **13**

EATING ◆
Adolfo Colección **12**
Casón de los
    López de Toledo **23**
Convento de San Antonio **5**
El Trébol **27**
La Boveda **19**
Tabernas El Antojo **1**
PARTYING ★
Círculo del Arte **11**
El Pícaro **24**
Garcilaso Café **7**
La Abadia **22**
La Distilería de Whiskey **23**

Ⓟ *Parking*
ⓘ *Information*
✉ *Post Office*

Tagus (Tajo)

SLEEPING ■
Hostal Centro **25**
Hostal del Cardenal **9**
Hostal Infantes **17**
Hostal Santa Isabel **16**
Hotel Imperio **21**
La Posada de Manola **15**
La Posada de Zocodover **20**
Pensión Castilla **26**

approximately 30 minutes (that's record breaking). In Madrid, you should arrive at the train station 45 minutes before your train leaves, in order to wait in foreseeable long lines to purchase your ticket. Although you won't have the problems of long lines in Toledo, it's best to purchase your return ticket as soon as possible, because they sell out fast. One-way fares are generally 8.30€. In order to get to the historic center from the Toledo train station, head out the front door and go right until you see a bus shelter. The no. 5 will take you in (.80€). For more information on train times and fares from Madrid, call Renfe at ☎ **902-240-202;** in Toledo call ☎ **925-223-099.**

BY BUS

The main bus company that handles trips between Toledo and Madrid is **Continental** (☎ **925-223-641;** www. continental-auto.es). Buses depart from **Madrid's Estación Sur de Autobuses** (South Bus Station), Calle Méndez Alvaro (☎ **914-684-200**), every day between 6:30am and 10pm at 30-minute intervals. One-way fares cost 4.10€. The fastest buses leave Monday to Friday on the hour. Those that depart weekdays on the half-hour, and those that run on weekends, might take an extra half-hour depending on how many villages they hit along the way (travel time: 1 hr.–1 hr. 20 min.). In order to get to the historic center from Toledo's bus station, you could either walk uphill, though it's a trek, or else catch the no. 5 (or no. 6) bus towards Plaza Zocodover (.80€). The bus stop is directly under the bus station.

The city buses that run to and from the bus or train stations are the nos. 1, 5, and 6, with a 15- to 20-minute frequency until 11pm. You'll get dropped off just above Plaza Zocodover.

BY CAR

It's easier to take public transportation, as driving doesn't get you there any sooner, not to mention that parking in Toledo is about as easy as driving an SUV into Los Angeles at rush hour. Exit Madrid via Cibeles (Paseo del Prado) and take the N-401 south.

Toledo Basics

Upon entering the city, pick up a city map at the **Zococentro tourist information desk** at Calle Sillería 14, directly off Plaza Zocodover (☎ **925-220-300**). The official information office is at Puerta de Bisagra (☎ **925-220-843**). It's open Monday to Friday from 9am to 6pm, Saturday from 9am to 7pm, and Sunday from 9am to 3pm. However, that location is all the way outside the old city's gates. If you fall and can't get up, help will come from **Virgen de la Salud Hospital** (Av. Barber s/n; ☎ 925-269-200) in the new part of town. You could also call **Red Cross** (☎ **925-222-222**) for an emergency. For an **ambulance,** dial ☎ **925-221-522.** There's always a **pharmacy** with the same nocturnal hours as a New York corner store. Just take a look at the sign outside of any one to see which location is standing guard. To slip a postcard in a giant lion's mouth, go to the **Correos** (☎ **925-251-066;** Mon–Fri 8:30am–8:30pm, Sat 9:30am–2pm) at Calle la Plata 1.

RECOMMENDED WEBSITES

- **www.ayto-toledo.org**: The official page to the city. It's Spanish only, but chock-full of info, maps, and links to other online resources.
- **www.twotoledos.com**: Two filmmakers from Toledo, Ohio, made a documentary linking the sister cities. Check out the trailer at this site.

Sleeping
HOSTELS

➜ **Hostal Centro** Located near Plaza de Zocodover, this is as close as you're gonna get to the central starting point for the suggested walking tours through Toledo— hence its name. The rooms are a great bargain—they're huge and newly renovated with enough blond-oak furniture to air out your clothes and rid all their funk. The bathrooms are like hotel bathrooms, clean and tiled, with a shower stall. Although there is neither a restaurant nor a bar attached, it's surrounded by (overpriced) cafes. *Nueva 3 (near Plaza Zocodover).* ☎ *925-257-091. Single 30€, double 48€, triple 65€. Amenities: Sheets, telephone, towels. In room: A/C, TV, Internet.*

➜ **Hostal Infantes** ★★ The bright interior plaza is the main attraction at this familiar hostel that spills over the brim with flowers and plants. The all-around friendly feeling and young attitude that this Old Toledan place exudes makes up for the rooms without a view or the smallest hint of style. There's a picnic table and an umbrella for 24-hour use on an upstairs *terraza*, perfect for store-bought *cerveza* first thing in the evening. The rooms are generous with comfy mattresses. The best part is the free breakfast. *Barco 15.* ☎ *925-255-700. www.hostalinfantes.com. Single 38€, double matrimony 48€, double (2 twin beds) 51€, triple 65€. Breakfast included. Amenities: Elevator, sheets, telephone, towels. In room: A/C, TV.*

CHEAP

➜ **Hotel Imperio** This government-rated one-star hotel has large light-pink rooms with big window balconies facing San Nicolas church. The interior is clinically austere with clashing furniture, as if you were in a sanitarium instead of a hotel, but at least that means everything is probably well cleaned. The incredibly efficient staff assures me renovations will take place in the coming year. Until then, it's still a good deal for your money and should be one of the first places you call to book on a tight budget. A cafe is attached, and the best cocktail lounge in town is across the street, while the Alcázar and Cathedral are within short walking distance. *Cadenas 5.* ☎ *925-227-650. Fax 925 25 31 83. Single 28€, double 43€, triple 58€, quadruple 66€. Amenities: Cafe and restaurant, elevator. In room: A/C, TV.*

➜ **La Posada de Zocodover** This hostel has such a great location near the Cathedral that you must call at least a week in advance to reserve one of its mediocre rooms. The ceilings are low, and the bedspreads are all faded, but consider that a small trade-off for its prime real estate. Room nos. 1, 101, 210, and 301 have views of the cathedral (leaning out the window and craning your neck slightly) so make sure to request one of them from the perky receptionist who likes to make the place smell nice. All the rooms have a bathroom so there's no waiting your turn to pop a squat. Doors get locked around 11:30pm or midnight, but people who have come to Toledo to party are given a key to let themselves in quietly. *Cordonerías 6.* ☎ *925-255-814. Regular season double 39€, triple 50€; fiestas and Aug double 45€, triple 55€. Singles are not available. In room: A/C, TV.*

➜ **Pensión Castilla** This is another good option for the busted traveler who nonetheless still appreciates small luxuries. With polished wood floors and beamed ceilings, this historic building offers dollhouse-size rooms with built-in shelves, step-up bathrooms, and comfortable beds dressed in aqua bedding. All the rooms have ceiling fans but no A/C. We can't help but like this place, run by an old woman who's not afraid to tell you doors get locked at 1am. That probably means no visitors, too, you sly dog. You won't find cheaper prices in town, and it's centrally located near Plaza Zocodover. *Recoletos 6.* ☎ *925-256-318. Single with private bathroom 17€, double with shared bathroom 24€, double with private bathroom 27€. No credit cards. Amenities: 1am curfew, some rooms have shared bathrooms.*

DOABLE

➔ **Hostal Santa Isabel** ★★ This historic 15th-century hostel is no-nonsense accommodations for travelers who want quiet, clean, straightforward rooms. It's situated near the cathedral, toward La Judería, a little off the beaten path and right next to the Santa Isabel convent selling homemade jams and *mazapán,* and occasionally exhibiting modern art. There's a recently built annex with 19 extra rooms for overflow book-ing. The rooms are well done in typical European modern with tile flooring. The hotel surpasses its two stars by a galaxy and is the cheapest option for high rolling in Toledo. *Santa Isabel 24.* ☎ *925-253-120. www.santa-isabel.com. Amenities: Breakfast room, lounge, private bathrooms, rooms for those w/limited mobility. In room: A/C, TV.*

➔ **La Posada de Manola** On each of its three floors is a representation of the three cultures that co-existed during the Middle Ages. The 14 room keys are labeled with a specific profession such as bricklayer, dyer, potter, farmer, or translator. Authentic tools associated with each trade decorate the rooms, along with salvaged wood from the original structure. (The website gives you a good idea what your room will actually look like.) It sounds cheesy but it was done without too much overkill. The rooms, however, are small

and overpriced when the novelty wears off. Its saving grace is the romantic terrazas where you can eat breakfast with a view of the city. Make sure you confirm your reservation before it gets lost—like ours was. *Sixto Ramón Parro 8.* ☎ *925-282-250. www.laposadademanolo.com. Single 36€, double 66€. Amenities: Breakfast, library use, rooms for those w/limited mobility. In room: A/C, TV.*

SPLURGE

➔ **Hostal del Cardenal** ★★★ This gem of a hotel, sitting just outside the Bisagra gate on the old fortress wall, was originally an 18th-century pavilion belonging to a cardinal, Señor Lorenzana, of Toledo. Most of the woodwork was kept intact during renovation; however, embellishments were added along the years, such as artisan Mudéjar doors to create wardrobes, and *mucho* antique furniture that seems to overtake the mansion. It's almost sickening how perfectly decorated and well run the hotel is. Sisal carpets run along the corridors, into interior patios drowning in ivy. The gardens leading into the restaurant outside give way to an irrigation system and fountains modeled after the gardens in La Alhambra. *Paseo de Recaredo 24 (outside Puerta de Bisagra).* ☎ *925-220-862. www.hostaldelcardenal.com. High season (Apr 1–Oct 31, Dec 5–9) single 66€, single with extra bed 95€, double 106€, triple 138€; low season (Jan 1–Mar 31 and Nov 1–Dec 31, except Dec 5–9) single 52€, single with extra bed 75€, double 84€, triple 109€. Amenities: Breakfast (7.60€), rooms for those w/limited mobility. In room: A/C, satellite flat-screen TV, hair dryer.*

Eating

TAPAS

➔ **El Trébol** If you can snag a picnic table in the sun on the outside terraza, it's a job well done. Your next challenge is catching the attention of the waiter running around with his ass on fire. Now you deserve a reward. Try the *bombas,* potatoes fried with crumbs with a mushy, minced meat filling, or else the *roscas,* traditional doughnut-shaped hot sandwiches. Specialty drinks such as sangría are served in mug-size glasses. *Sante Fé 5 (under the arch in Plaza Zocodover).* ☎ *925-213-702. Raciones 4€. Daily 11am–4pm and 7pm–12:30am.*

→ **La Boveda** This is the best old-man bar in the city, and every local knows it. (Be sure you go to La Boveda and not La Boveda Rincón next-door, as there is a very large difference between the two.) Stop here either for a cheap dinner or for the late-night munchies. This hole in the wall is known for raciónes (larger portions of tapas) such as *carcamusas* (medley of meats and cooked veggies) and pâté, both typical of Castilla–La Mancha. Make sure to wash it all down with a jar of sangría, said to be the best in town. *Plaza Solarejo 2. No phone. Raciónes 5.50€–12€. Sangría (1.5L) 6€. Daily 8:30am–2:30am.*

→ **Tabernas El Antojo** ★★ This corner wine bar is a perfect joint to start the evening in moderation and in class, but for a price that won't break the bank. The bar features a weekly wine that costs 1.90€ per sizable glass. The tapas are a little more expensive but can be ordered for more than just one person. Start with *la torta del Casar,* a smelly-but-good cheese spread from Extremadura, or a meat-and-cheese plate for a tidbit of everything. The wicker tables and chairs on the sunny patio look out to La Puerta de Cambrón and El Palacio de la Cava. Pop a chill pill and don't forget your shades. *Bajada de San Juan de los Reyes 11.* ☎ *617-364-329. Tapas 6.50€–12€. Mon–Sat 6pm–1am. Closed Sun.*

CHEAP

→ **Adolfo Colección** ★★ This trendy new *vinoteca,* part of a family of other well-known restaurants in Toledo, is designed to attract the 25-and-under bourgeois hipster with an inkling for wine, unique tapas, and reasonable prices. If you fit the requisites, then enter through its sliding glass doors and get seated on a comfortable spring chair at a large wine-tasting table, that lights up for the purpose of watching wine swirl. A cheap, good wine is the Syrah Pago del Ama Collección. Tapas are minimal but filling. Start with the *Jarrete de ciervo* (deer meat) which is best finished off with an almond mousse dessert. Downstairs, you can purchase Adolfo brand oils, coffee, wines (so you can show off what you tasted), cheeses, and desserts. It's an interesting stop even if you don't sit down and eat its semi-stuck-up food. *Nuncio Viejo 1.* ☎ *925-224-244. www.adolfo-toledo.com. Meal 10€–15€. Daily 11am–2am.*

DOABLE

→ **Casón de los López de Toledo** ★★ SPANISH This 16th-century building, now one of the best restaurants in town, is famous for multiple reasons: the smallest window in the world, recorded in the *Guinness Book of World Records;* the only corner balcony in Toledo, right over a crucified Christ found excavated under its foundation; and of course, its eats. Start with a gazpacho and move onto *lomo de venado* (a venison sirloin) or else *solomillo de buey* (ox tenderloin). If you're less than hungry, or rich, have a seat at the bar downstairs for stellar wine and light tapas such as *salmorejo con virutas de jamón y perejil* (a tomato spread served with bread and ham) for 4€. If you time it right, you'll get the leftover tapas the waitresses give away to the lucky patrons sitting at the bar at the end of the night.

After stuffing your gourd, head to the club downstairs for early *copas* (alcoholic drinks). **La Destilería de Whiskey** ★ has nothing to do with its name but on Tuesday nights there's free live flamenco that you can't miss if you're in town. *Sillería 3.* ☎ *925-254-774. Reservations:* ☎ *902-198-344. www. casontoledo.com. Menú without wine 12€. Restaurant: Daily 1:30–11pm. Cafeteria: Daily 9am–noon.*

Partying

As in many Spanish cities, part of partying is the eating you do beforehand. The rule of thumb is to start your evening late (around 10pm), eat slowly, and little by little throughout the night. By midnight, the nocturnal life in Toledo is hopping enough for you to settle back into your old drinking habits again. Toledo offers a relaxed nightlife where jeans are perfectly acceptable. The best places in town are relatively low-key. Calle Sillería and Calle de los Alfileritos are some of the loudest streets for those of university age, as well as those around the Cathedral.

📺 (Best ●) → **Círculo del Arte** ★★ If you're not the clubbing type, that's a real shame because this space is so unique, it should be listed as a Toledan monument. Instead, the 13th-century San Vicente church has been renovated into a dance club, as well as a cultural space for concerts and art exhibitions. During the day, it's a popular cafe and tapas bar so even grandmas can tap a tapa, too, for 5€. When the night owls arrive, however—gelled, powdered, and lipsticked together—it turns into the hottest club in town, smacking of electro, hip-hop, and DJ-altered beats. The only thing left to do is down a mojito (5€). If you're the designated map holder, then play it safe and order a non-alcoholic *granizado de limón* (lemon

Sugar High

Tons of specialty stores pawn sweet treats such as *mazopán* and *horchata*, the milky drink that tastes like an almond slushy. **El Café de las Monjas** (C. Santo Tomé 2; ☎ **925-213-424;** daily 9:30am–8:30pm) makes its own brand of *mazopán* and sells them individually wrapped, so you can taste-test them without having to commit.

For ice-cream cravings, the best popsicle stand we scouted was (surprisingly) a European chain that buys its gelato from Italian artisans. **Il Caffé di Roma** is at Calle Comercio 22 (☎ **925-214-455**). Its ice cream window faces the street. Hours are daily 7:30am to 11pm.

slushy) with mint. Daiquiris are also available. The club stays open until dawn so stick around for breakfast: coffee, OJ, and a croissant for 1.90€. *Plaza de San Vicente.* ☎ *925-214-829.*

→ **El Pícaro** ★★ This split-level concert venue, cafe, and club, owned by the same group as Círculo del Arte and also Garcilaso, is probably the most cosmopolitan of the three and the most crowded before 2am. Its scene is unassuming, friendly, and casual (jeans are okay) putting pretentiousness in check. Even the doorman is incredibly polite, and that's not small cheese. People aged 23 to 30 come here from all over Spain, primarily Madrid, and most often return for the eclectic mix of people and decent hip-hop music (mixed with Spanish pop). *Cadenas 6.* ☎ *925-221-301. www.picarocafeteatro.com.*

→ **Garcilaso Café** With a shag-covered stage and giant bean bags, it's hard not to get comfortable here. During the day it's not a bad place to grab a coffee either, but we'd advise coming here late night for a cocktail or two, especially if you're the *alternativa* type. The two-story lounge is studded (literally) with red, white, and black decor. The exposed beam balcony is set up as a bistro during the day, and at night creates many dark corners overlooking the stage in which to disappear with new language-lab partners. The dancing space is plentiful. On Thursdays through Saturdays, a DJ spins electro music. There's a gay-friendly environment, though not exclusively so. *Rojas 5.* ☎ *925-229-160.*

➔ **La Abadia** This will probably appear in most guidebooks in the eats section, but we didn't like its stuffy, cavelike dining room (well, they actually *are* caves so make sure to check them out before you leave). That doesn't mean you shouldn't rule it out for dinner, but we sided on the upstairs bar instead, which is loaded with people after dinnertime—around midnight. Besides a down-to-earth environment, the upstairs establishment also offers snack food such as *pulgas* (mini-sandwiches), tapas, and fried potatoes, all at a more economical price. It's also on one of the most popular streets for students and younger people to go out, so it's easy to hit while tapa-ing. *Plaza de San Nicolás 3.* ☎ *925-251-140. www.abadia toledo.com.*

Sightseeing

The three cultures that supposedly lived together in harmony and whose relationship was painted pretty in history books but not in real life means there's triple duty for the tourist who likes to hit all the major spots whether he/she paid attention in history class or not. You know who you are. The **Toledo Interpretation Center** just opened its doors (Trinidad 7; ☎ **925-221-616**; admission 4€; Tues–Sat 10am–10pm,

summers until 10:30pm; Sun 10:30am–2:30pm) and is a good way to pick up some background info through audio-visual media and dioramas before charging the brigade of Toledan monuments and monuments.

Museo Sefardi (see below) is another good place to start, as the museum (however lethargically) walks you through Spain's religious wars. Worthwhile doors to the city are Puerta del Sol, Puerta del Cambrón (which sounds a lot like the Spanish word for asshole, the reason why everyone likes it), and Puerta de Bisagra. Greco fans will want to plan their itineraries around his art. No matter what path you take, pace your route with tapas and wine, but stay away from the pointy swords while doing so.

MUSEUMS

➔ **Casa-Museo del Greco** This is only a must-see if you're an El Greco fan. Located in Toledo's *antiguo barrio judío,* this is not actually his real house. He wasn't really that big of a hotshot back in his day so instead, he moved into frayed apartments (granted they were in a palace) owned by the Marquís of Villena in 1585 and a few other pads around town until his death. Only a small chunk of the original structure pulled through after hundreds of years; this and its neighbor now make up the museum that houses a few of his paintings and his so-called life, a diorama-like version of his hypothetical daily routine in Toledo. *Samuel Leví s/n.* ☎ *925-224-405. Admission 2.40€; free admission Sat evenings and Sun mornings. Winter Tues–Sat 10am–2pm and 4–6pm, Sun 10am–2pm; summer Tues–Sat 10am–2pm and 4–9pm, Sun 10am–2pm. Closed Mon.*

🅜 Best ♥ FREE ➔ **Museo de Santa Cruz** ★★ If you're on the El Greco tour, then this museum of art and culture (originally a Renaissance hospice) is a spot you'll want to hit up mainly because it's free. For all the architecture nerds, however, take important note that the decorative facade is in the Plateresque style, famous in 16-century Spain for looking like silverwork. The ground level proves the most important with a bunch of El Grecos: *La Asunción de la Virgen* (his last known piece), *La Veronica,* and a painting dedicated to Goya, *Cristo Crucificado.* Paintings by Goya and Ribera are thrown in there for good measure, too. *Cervantes 3.* ☎ *925-221-036. Free admission. 3€ for guided tour. Mon 10am–2pm and 4–6:30pm, Tues–Sat 10am–6:30pm, Sun 10am–2pm.*

➔**Museo Sefardi (Sinagoga del Tránsito)** ★ Once upon a time in Toledo, men like Samuel Levi ate his matzo balls in peace and built a Mudéjar-style synagogue without anyone bothering him. Today, Sinagoga del Tránsito is a museum outlaying the history of Judaism, leading all the way up to their expulsion in 1492. First you'll enter through the original synagogue, which is impressive for its carved wooden ceiling and stucco Hebrew inscriptions, including psalms inscribed along the top of the walls. After the Jews left, the synagogue was converted to a hospital, then a church, military barracks, and now, a museum. The exhibition is text heavy, in Spanish, and you'll for sure get a headache squinting your eyes through its Plexiglas, but you will leave with a better understanding; it's definitely worth the trip and better than the other synagogue if you're pressed for time, as long as you splurge for a tourist's walkie-talkie thingy. *Samuel Leví n/a.* ☎ *925-223-665. Admission 2.40€; free admission Sat evenings and Sun mornings. Winter Tues–Sat 10am–2pm and 4–6pm, Sun 10am–2pm; summer Tues–Sat 10am–2pm and 4–9pm, Sun 10am–2pm. Closed Mon.*

RELIGIOUS SITES

➔**Alcázar** Although closed for renovation at the time of this writing, there's no question that Alcázar has seen more blood than a butcher on acid. In fact, not too much remains of the ancient building after such a hefty number of sieges and bombardments. The biggest casualty it suffered was more recently, however, in 1936 during the Spanish war when Republicans briefly gained a stronghold in Toledo. Franco's Nationalist troops held ground in the Alcázar along with women and children hostages for 2 entire months. The story goes that a Republican officer reached the National Colonel by telephone within the Alcázar, in order to let him know Republicans had kidnapped his 16-year-old, and unless he surrendered immediately, his son would be executed. The boy was put on the phone next, and his father uttered these famous words: "Then commend your soul to God, shout 'Viva España' and die like a hero." The boy was shot in the head, but the telephone is still on display. Today, the Alcázar is an army museum that's under renovations and won't reopen until 2008. *General Moscardó 4.* ☎ *925-221-673. Closed until 2008.*

➔**Catedral Primada** ★★★ When you've seen one Gothic Catholic church, you've seen them all, or so we thought after one too many. But the cathedral in Toledo left us with more oohs and ahs than fireworks on the Fourth of July. Toledo's Cathedral, which was constructed from 1226 to 1493, is pretty much the Hummer of Catholic churches in Spain, especially when you consider that Toledo was the capital before everyone and their great-great grandma moved to Madrid. Here, it was proclaimed that Joanna "The Mad" and her husband, Philip "The Handsome" were heirs to the Spanish throne. El

Transparente altar stands out as the most genius work by sculptor Narciso Tomé, constituting a wall of marble and florid baroque alabaster. It had been ignored for years because of the bad lighting—every artist's nightmare. So he thought why not cut a hole in the ceiling and let some light in? That really pissed off some Toledans, but the illuminating effect finally gave light to the angels in the nosebleeds who couldn't be seen before, a Last Supper, and a floating Virgin, at certain hours of the day. Take a gander at the doorway to the Treasury. The Spanish style is called Plateresque, named after its comparison to silverwork. The Cathedral's other main attractions are **Goya**'s *Arrest of Christ on the Mount of Olives* and **El Greco**'s *Twelve Apostles* and *Spoliation of Christ (El Espolio)*. El Greco took some major heat for the latter after some head honchos of the Inquisition said he painted Christ with less importance than the onlookers above him. El Greco's hide was saved only because he knew people in high places without their shorts in such a bunch. Elsewhere, red cardinal hats hang from the ceiling: They mark the spot where a Spanish cardinal is buried. *Cardenal Cisneros s/n.* ☎ *925-222-241. Admission 6€. Daily 10am–6:30pm.*

→ **Iglesia de Santo Tomé** ⋆ This 14th-century church in La Judería is famous for only one painting, El Greco's ***The Burial of the Count of Orgaz*** ⋆⋆, which he painted in 1586. It hangs as a total loner in the church that would have otherwise been ignored if it weren't for the masterpiece. People arrive in hordes as if it were the *Mona Lisa,* so get there early in the morning and Hakuna Matata. *Plaza del Conde s/n.* ☎ *925-256-098. Admission 1.90€. Winter daily 10am–6pm; summer daily 10am–7pm.*

→ **Mezquita del Cristo de la Luz** There was probably always a Visigoth temple here but the Arabs took it over when they got control and converted it to a Muslim mosque. When the Christians won ground temporarily, they hid a lit lamp along with a painting of Christ behind a wall so that it wouldn't be ruined when the Arabs invaded again. Legend has it that after the Christian's reconquest, King Alfonso II's horse knelt in front of the building demanding the king to dismount. When he did, the king found the painting, as well as the lamp—miraculously still burning. According to legend, the lantern continued to burn 369 years after the incident. This is a 10-minute trip but worth a quick peek, if even from the outside. *Cuesta de Carmelitas Descalzos 10.* ☎ *925-254-191. Admission 1.90€. Winter daily 10am–6pm; summer daily 10am–7pm.*

→ **Santo Domingo El Antiguo (convento)** ⋆ This ancient convent houses a large El Greco collection that is uninterrupted by the works of any other artist. The surroundings of the convent itself are haunting and inspiring—a place for quintessential Spanish romantic writer Gustavo Adolfo Bécquer to write his famous poems about Toledo. It's a small monument, and won't take you long, but walking through is definitely worth your time, especially toward 6:30pm (around sundown), right before it closes. *Plaza Santo Domingo El Antiguo s/n.* ☎ *925-222-930. Admission 1.50€. Mon–Sat 11am–1:30pm and 4–7pm; Sun 4–7pm.*

→ **Sinagoga de Santa María La Blanca** This Jewish temple is characteristic of Toledo's Mudéjar style with horseshoe arches and Andalusian-looking ornamentation. In the 15th century, after the Jews were kicked out, St. Vincent Ferrer led a

Christian mob high on holy water to convert it into a church. Ironically, it was used later as a center for reformed prostitutes. This synagogue is much older than the first, though not as intricately designed. *Reyes Católicos 4.* ☎ *925-227-257. Admission 1.90€. Winter daily 10am–6pm; summer daily 10am–7pm.*

ⅯⅤ ⬤Best⬤ Shopping

The number of tourist and knickknack shops in Toledo will make your wallet spin. Ceramics, swords, and knives are all big sellers. A folding knife with a bullhorn handle and a Toledo-cut blade makes an excellent gift for any hunter or fisher back home, if you get it past airport security. Lighters (that won't get past the airport security), plates, sword sheaths, and other odds 'n' ends decorated with an Arab design called damascene, are popular, too. Moving on to the baked goods, Toledo is most famous for its *mazapán.* If you're buying to take home, be wary of the brand. Santo Tomé and Casa Telesforo are trusted marks, but your best bet is to frequent one of the many nunneries that bake them the freshest. **Convento de San Antonio**

Hecho en Toledo

Forget light sabers. The original is always better: ⅯⅤ ⬤Best⬤ steel Toledan swords. For centuries, Toledo has held an international reputation for its Mudéjar sword smiths. **Casa Bermejo** (Airosas 5; ☎ 925-285-367) is a factory and store dating back to 1910 that engraves West Point swords, as well as outfits armies all over Europe with their steel. Watch over 50 artisans at work Monday to Friday from 9am to 1pm and 3 to 6pm, and Saturday from 10am to 2pm. There are literally dozens of other shops that metalize the tapered cobblestone streets in Toledo with sheaths, swords, knives, armor, and heavy chain-mail suits, resurrecting medieval heroes like El Cid from his grave.

(Pl. de San Antonio 1; ☎ **925-224-047**) sells mazapán, *corazones de almendra, yemas, rosquitos,* and other nun stuff, for very good prices, daily, from 11am to 1:30pm and 4 to 6:30pm.

Cuenca ★★★

Famous for its **casas colgadas** (hanging houses), the old city has more character than your kid sister's charm bracelet. Both parts of the town (old and new) are located in the mountainous area of the Serranía, which, along with a few other mountain ranges, forms the mid-meridian Iberian Mountain Range. This is all just to say that Cuenca is the heart of it all. Huge, jagged rocks are carved out by two rivers on either side, setting the scene for houses whose floating balconies jut out into open air. The old city sits above the new on the highest point. It's uphill so, smokers, hook up your oxygen tanks because ⅯⅤ ⬤Best⬤ this trek is a must for

anyone exploring the area. Tourists are free to walk through narrow alleyways up to the open-aired castile ruins and rocky walking paths.

Getting There & Around
BY TRAIN

RENFE Cercanía trains leave Madrid's Atocha Railway Station about eight times a day. Trains pull into Cuenca at Paseo del Ferrocarril in the new part of the city (☎ **902-240-202**). The trip time is about 2¹/₂ hours, the length of a few playlists on your iPod. A one-way ticket from Madrid costs 9€. Outside the train station, you can walk north to the old city but don't sweat it—there's an alternative to walking. Buses no. 1 and 2 (.80€) travel up to the make-out point, we mean, parking lot on the ridge above the old city, making several stops within the old town, like Plaza Mayor. The closest bus stop to the train station is serviced by bus no. 1 and is 75m (246 ft.) away on Calle Mariano Catalina. It runs every half-hour on the hour.

BY BUS

There are eight buses from Madrid every day, two being express; the last bus back to Madrid is at 10pm, and they run about every 2 hours. These buses fill up fast so don't procrastinate buying your ticket. Buses to Cuenca begin their journey in Madrid at the Auto-Res bus terminal (C. Caballero 20; ☎ **969-227-087**). Buses arrive at Calle Fermín Caballero s/n (☎ **969-227-087,** or 969-221-184 for information and schedules). A one-way fare costs 9.75€. The closest bus stop to the bus station in Cuenca is serviced by bus no. 1 (.80€), right outside the bus terminal, which makes its run to Plaza Mayor and the old city.

BY CAR

So you scored some wheels. From Madrid, take the N-III to Tarancón, then the N-400, which leads directly into Cuenca. You can also rent cars in the Renfe train station. Try Europcar at ☎ **969-233-924** (www.europcar.com). If you'd rather buy American, there's also **AVIS** (Fermín Caballero 20, near the bus station; ☎ **969-241-458**).

Cuenca Basics

Cuenca's **tourist information office** is conveniently located at Plaza Mayor 1 (☎ **969-232-119;** www.aytocuenca.org and www.turismocuenca.com; Mon–Sat 9am–2pm and 4–9pm). The good city maps cost about .50€.

Sleeping

The fact that you're in Cuenca means you have an inkling for heights or modern art, or were dragged by a friend—but no doubt pleasantly surprised. For the practical type who likes to party anywhere, any time, book a place to sleep in the new city; if you're a romantic, however, or just appreciate a damn good vista, book a room at the top of the hill. The prices are the same, but the old town tucks itself in at about midnight while the new part is just getting primed for the night. The distance from the old to the new is difficult without wheels.

HOSTEL

➜ **Hostal Canovas** ★★ Located in the new city, a hop, jump, and skip away from the biggest bar strip near Plaza España, you can't get a better bang for your buck anywhere else in the city. Don't let the fact it's in the new part of town put you off. It's a close walk to both stations and easy to crawl into bed after a long night of hard drinking next door in La Zona (see "Partying"). The buffed wood floors seem fitting for this mountain town, and so do the large corner bedrooms good for claustrophobics. The bathroom is squeaky clean and pimped out with a bathtub and modern shower, both of which are novelties for a hostel. *Fray Luís ded León 38. ☎ 969-213-973. Single 30€, double 45€–50€, triple 70€. Rates are higher during Semana Santa (Apr). Amenities: Elevator, sheets, telephone, towels. In room: TV, hair dryer (inquire at front desk).*

CHEAP

➜ **Pensión Tabanqueta** ★★ This new-ish hostel with only six rooms perched over the ravine fills up fast due to its good, red-and-white-checkered tablecloth restaurant with more than modest prices and a stellar view, as long as you ask for it. Walking paths are easily accessible, as well as the Castile ruins. Rooms are no-frills without bathrooms, but they're clean and each has a writing desk. We'll excuse its bare bones for the panoramic vistas on the wraparound terraza. The staff roster is incredibly small—one lone woman mans both the hostel and the restaurant, so have some patience; you'll probably have to wait your turn. *Trabuc 13.* ☎ *969-211-290. Double 30€, single 15€. No credit cards. Amenities: Restaurant, shared bathrooms only.*

MTV **Best ☯ →Posada de San Jose** ★★★ This 17th-century choir school was also where Diego Velázquez's daughter lived, and it's rumored he began painting *Las Meninas* here. Both suites and conventlike hostel rooms are available depending on the number of wads in your wallet. The suites are Clorox-bleached and honeymoon-ready with a larger than normal bed and two glass-encased breakfast nooks overlooking the river gorge. The hostel rooms, on the other hand, are on the top floor, like the servants' quarters, with sinks and shared bathrooms—still not a shabby deal for the price. There's a small lookout window and a writing desk for when the mood strikes. *Julián Romero 4.* ☎ *969-211-300. www.posadasanjose.com. Spring–summer and weekends year-round single with full bathroom 50€–55€, double with full bathroom 73€–76€, double with full bathroom and view 83€–87€, single with shared toilet 25€–27€, double with shared toilet 38€–40€, triple with shared toilet 50€–55€; winter consult the website. Amenities: Breakfast room (8€), shared bathrooms, laundry service, telephone (in common area), travel info. In room: TV in some rooms, hair dryer, Jacuzzi in suite, shaving mirror.*

Eating

TAPAS

→**Dédalo** ★ This trendy spot on Plaza Mayor was recently opened by two hipster cats wanting to offer 20- to 30-somethings a restaurant and tapas bar with a BIC's razor edge. In other words, this is not another old-man *mesón* (tavern). Cubist orange-and-black furniture is fitting for a Halloween party (Spain, which does not celebrate ghoul's day, is generally not aware of this overplayed color scheme). Even their tapas are modern, straying from traditional recipes found most places; try something new, like *zarajos*, a regional, Castilla–La Manchan treat of lamb intestines. The music is the best you'll find in the Plaza—after all there's nothing to compete with. And all the food is homemade—as in, not frozen. Start your night early here on the terraza with drinks and tapas. *Severo Catalina 7 (Pl. Mayor). No phone. Tapas 4€–12€. Open early and closes late.*

CHEAP

→**Mesón La Tinaja** ★ CASTILLA–LA MANCHA It's probably the most unpretentious bar in Cuenca, a hot spot for gypsies and locals alike. Looming drunks are a constant factor to contend with, but they're surprisingly well received by the bar staff. Cozied up to the cathedral, this tavern is also an easy place to hit pdq. Castilian barbecue is the starring headline on the menu here. Start with *morteruelo* (hot game pâté), then move on to the chops (they're so good that even Mary would eat her lamb if it were from Cuenca). Salads and pastas are also available for non-carnivores. The place is also popular for breakfast. *Obispo Valero 4 (Pl. Mayor). No phone. Menú 12€. Tues–Sun 9:30am–late. Closed Mon.*

➔**Restaurante Ronda** ★★★ CASTILLA—LA MANCHA While the actual dining room is on the lower half of Calle San Pedro, keep hiking uphill until you reach the terraza with its seasonal seating, umbrellas, polite waitstaff, and magnificent view. The restaurant serves *gazpacho pastor,* a hearty porridge of game, omelets, grapes, and unleavened bread, made famous by Sancho Panza in *Don Quijote.* Tapas is served on fancy compartment plates to share. *San Pedro 20 (Casco Antiguo).* ☎ *969-232-942. Menú 13€—17€. Mon—Sat 1—4pm and 8—11pm; Sun 1—4pm.*

DOABLE

➔**Mesón Casas Colgadas** CASTILLA—LA MANCHA If you're going to spend all your money in one place, you might as well do it in high fashion at the top restaurant in town and halfway off a cliff. You'll know exactly where to jump if your parents call mid-meal about your credit card bill. Start with the *Ajoarriero;* dating back to when cod was the only fish imported inland, this traditional dish is served as a purée served along with potatoes, oil, and garlic. If that doesn't make you wet, try a juicy Castilla—La Mancha hot meat plate or a roasted suckling pig. Finish off with hazelnut cream desserts and regional liquors. Pass the drool bucket, please. *Canónigos s/n.* ☎ *969-223-552. Menú 26€. Meal 20€—40€. Daily 1:30—4pm and 9—11pm.*

Partying

In Cuenca, there's one street to party on, and that's **La Zona,** though technically it's Calle Doctor Galíndez (in the new city off Pl. España). The bar-lined street reeks of cigarette butts during the day and aftershave at night. Thursday is when the university students party, and on Friday and Saturday everyone else does. The under-25s gather for the *botellón* parties (40s 'n' blunts) thrown in the plaza across the street. If you want a more civilized scene, head uphill, back toward the old city. At the tip of the ridge near the castle's ruins, you'll find another string of bars, popular on the weekends for low-priced dinners, tapas, and late-night drinks accompanied by a view overlooking the river gorge. One such place is **El Torreón** ★ (Larga 23; ☎ **969-237-345;** tapas 3€—7€, bocadillos 2.25€—4€; daily noon—2am), which serves *morteruelo* (hot game pâté). Packed to the gunwales with calories, this is the most famous meal in Cuenca to eat in winter. So order a plate, load up on drinks, and head over to the edge of the cliff to face your fear of heights without inhibition. People party here until about 2am and head back down the mountain—or home. It's a small town.

Sightseeing

With the number of art galleries in Cuenca, there is no shortage of things to see, nor will the view get old. You can easily tour the city in a day, but a night's stay is recommended in order to rid your body of stressful toxins; don't doubt the fact Cuenca has that effect. While admiring the mountainous view at the tip of the old town, scan the rocks (the Huécar Gorge) to the east for a giant pair of eyes looking back at you, like the man on the moon only freakier.

The **Casas Colgadas** ★★★, or "hanging houses," are Cuenca's most emblematic point of reference. The fact that they appear to be perched precariously over the gorge is what merits their gawk appeal. Experts hypothesize that they bear Muslim heritage, but their adversaries give credit

Contemporary Art in Cuenca

It's totally backward that a small town like 🏛️ Best 😊 **Cuenca** excels in the modern arts, but this was where a lot of Spanish contemporary artists settled. Like San Francisco during the flower-powered '60s, it was an experiment that led to lots of colors on canvas and probably some dead brain cells. Either way, the pueblo of Cuenca is a little-known secret among art aficionados.

FREE **Fundación Antonio Pérez** ★ (Ronda de Julién Romero 20; ☎ 969-230-619; www.dipucuenca.es; free admission; June and Sept Mon–Fri 10am–9pm, Sat–Sun and holidays 11am–9pm; July–Aug Mon–Fri 10am–1am, Sat–Sun and holidays 11am–9pm; Oct–May Mon–Fri 10am–8pm, Sat–Sun and holidays 11am–8pm), the former convent de las Carmelitas Descalzas, was converted to an odds-and-ends art gallery with works collected by its namesake over the years.

Gustavo Torner, an important artist in Spain during the '60s, was given the key to **Espacio Torner (Antigua Iglesia de San Pablo)** ★ (Hoz de Huécar s/n; ☎ 969-238-373; admission 5€; Tues–Fri 11am–2pm and 4–6pm, Sat 11am–2pm and 4–8pm, Sun 11am–2:30pm; closed Mon) in order to exhibit his minimal work. It's a little pricey but worth a peek inside at least.

Fundación Antonio Saura ★ (Casa Zavala [Plaza San Nicolás]; ☎ 969-236-054; admission 2€; Mon–Tues and Thurs–Sat 11am–2pm and 5–7pm, Sun and holidays 11am–2pm; closed Wed) showcases modern exhibitions of works by Saura, Andy Warhol, Zóbel, and others.

to the noblemen of the 14th and 15th centuries. Nobody really knows (or cares) except for that today they consist of three nice houses to look at: The **Museo de Arte Abstracto Español** makes up two houses while **Mesón Casas Colgadas** occupies the third (see "Eating," above). The best view is from under the houses, beneath **Puente de San Pablo,** the footbridge leading to the government-run four-star El Parador.

→ **Catedral de Cuenca** ★ The first monument to go up after the Muslims were conquered was the cathedral, not surprisingly built on top of an Islamic mosque. The church, started in the beginning of the 12th century, is said to be the earliest example of Gothic architecture in Spain. The structure today, however, suffers a multiple personality syndrome. After hundreds of years of repairs and restorations,

it has become a hodgepodge of Gothic, Romanesque, Renaissance, and modern design. Many people aren't impressed by its modest grandeur but that's because they're missing its most intriguing points. For example, the stained-glass windows are Spanish Abstract and were added as Hail Mary flair. In the Bishop's Chapel, the relics you see here are genuine, as in real body parts of deceased holy people. There's a small museum, **Tesoro Catedralico,** that's worth a quick peek for two canvases by El Greco. *Plaza Mayor.* ☎ *969-224-626. Free admission. July–Sept Mon–Fri 10:30am–1:30pm and 4–6pm, Sat 10am–7pm, Sun 10am–6:30pm; Oct–June daily 10:30am–1:30pm and 4–6pm; May–June Sat 10:30am–2pm, Sun 10:30am–2pm and 4–6:30pm. Admission 2.50€ adults. Museum* ☎ *969-212-011. Admission 1.50€. Tues–Sat 11am–2pm and 4–6pm; Sun 11am–2pm.*

Detour: Road Trippin'

North of the city 35km (22 miles) is **Ciudad Encantada** ★, a geologic phenomenon and the suitably crazy backdrop for Governator Schwarzenegger's *Conan the Barbarian*. Colossal rocks the size of Manhattan skyscrapers carved by water and time tower above a labyrinth of arches and bridges. Pools of water spawn ecological systems whose flora and fauna are not traditionally seen in these parts. From Cuenca, take the CU-912, before turning northeast onto the CU-913. The Ciudad Encantada is signposted.

📺 Best❶ →**Museo de Arte Abstracto Español** ★★★ If you don't see anything else in Cuenca, at least check out the modern art museum, not only for its collection of the best-known artists from the Spanish Abstract movement (including Torner, Saura, Rueda, Chillida, and Tapiés), but also for its primo real estate; it's your ticket into the hanging houses of Cuenca. The museum was jump-started by artist Fernando Zóbel when he donated his personal collection that still dominates the exhibition. Although fabulous, the view is still a helluva lot better. A hippie flute player who took post near a window lulled us through the galleries. *Canónigos s/n.* ☎ *969-212-983. Admission 3€ adults, 1.50€ students. Tues–Fri 11am–2pm and 4–6pm; Sat 11am–2pm and 4–8pm; Sun and holidays 11am–2:30pm.*

Playing Outside

Make like Pee-wee Herman and rent a bicycle from a brand new English-speaking bike shop, **Rodri Bikes** (☎ **687-662-044**). They'll outfit with you with maps, routes, and also repair your own bike. Bike rental is 12€ per day. Because of its ace topography, Cuenca also offers some of the best extreme sports. Choose between **hang gliding, river SCUBA, kayaking and canoeing, canyon rappelling, rock climbing,** and **hiking.** And if those aren't your bag, there's also **horseback riding, orienteering, mountain biking,** and **dirt biking.** With over a dozen companies in town, you can have your pick. For contact information go to www.turismoactivodecuenca.com and www.alcarriaventura.com, or contact the tourist office.

Shopping

Cuencanites are known for their ceramics. The best regional shopping can be done right on Plaza Mayor and down along Calle Alfonso VIII. Tourist knickknack shops are more rare in Cuenca, compared with other Spanish cities. Besides, your mom will appreciate an authentic bowl from a city she's never heard of before more than a refrigerator magnet of the hanging houses. Although near those houses, you'll find bohemian artisans hawking their hanging houses watercolors. The best print and poster shopping can be done in the gift shops at all major modern art galleries.

📺 Best❶ **Aranjuez**

The Royal Palace and its expansive gardens are good enough reasons to stop in Aranjuez, a strawberry lover's la-la land, while en route to Toledo or Madrid.

Ferdinand and Isabella first staked this plot out for their spring retreat, and all the Spanish blue bloods followed suit. The draws of this Hamptons for the royalty

Strawberry Fields

Any fan of Strawberry Shortcake—the doll or the cake—will appreciate the **Strawberry Express,** traveling from Madrid's RENFE Atocha station (p. 136) to Aranjuez on a creaky old steam train. Train attendants in traditional clothing bring frumpiness to an all-new level as they turn back the clock to a time when the first Madrileño train made the same trek across country more than 150 years ago to deliver the strawberries every weekend. The train you see now is about 2 decades old and commemorates its granddaddy that, as legend has it, was silver. The **Tren de la Fresa** runs every weekend between April and June and takes 50 minutes for the one-way only from Madrid to Aranjuez (24€). The price includes a **strawberry tasting** and a guided tour of the Royal Palace and Museo de Falúas, as well as a panoramic ride from the depot to the center of town. Reservations recommended. Purchase tickets with RENFE (☎ **902-240-202**). For more information, contact Museo del Ferrocarril (☎ **902-228-822;** www.museodelferrocarril.org).

were the elaborate labyrinthine gardens that hugged the Tajo river. Even today, it's a breath of fresh, fragrant air and a break from big, bad Madrid, where pollution is at an all-time high. There's not much in Aranjuez in terms of sightseeing; it's a small town that survives seemingly on tourism and postcard sales. Nor is there much in terms of nightlife; urbanites come here for the chlorophyllose greens. Cafes, restaurants, and hotels are within walking distance of each other, but wear good shoes because there's a lot of cultivated ground to cover. Word to the wise: Pack a lunch, a wine bottle, and a blanket, and park it in the gardens with a book. Don't stay longer than a day unless you have to. Those with hay fever do not proceed.

Getting There & Around

BY TRAIN

Trains depart about every 20 minutes from Madrid's Atocha Railway Station to make the 50-minute trip to Aranjuez, a one-way fare costing 3€. The Aranjuez station (☎ **902-240-202**) lies about a 15-minute walk outside monumental city. If you've got lots of gear, there is a bus outside the train station that will take you into town.

BY BUS

AISA (☎ **902-198-788**) runs Aranjuez-bound buses every 30 minutes from 7:30am to 10pm (trip time: 30–40 min.) from Madrid's Estación Sur de Autobuses, Calle Méndez Alvaro (Metro: 6). In Madrid, call ☎ **915-304-605** for information. Buses arrive in Aranjuez at the City Bus Terminal, Calle Infantas 8 (☎ **918-910-183**).

BY CAR

It's easier to take public transportation, as driving doesn't get you there any sooner. Once you're outside Madrid, it's about a 30-minute drive. Follow the signs to Aranjuez and Granada, taking highway N-IV. To rent, contact **Be Smart** (Almíbar 181; ☎ **635-602-030** and 918-011-591).

BY TAXI

Aranjuez is one of those cities you walk. However, if you're stuck without a ride, or you got sunstroke in the park and couldn't find your way out of the maze, call the main switchboard for all the private taxi companies in town at ☎ **918-911-139,** or head toward the Palace to Av. Infantas 8, to the taxi stand where they all convene.

Green Peace

After so many filthy spoils in the palace, it's time to take a breather inside one of the many royal gardens and regain your center of (checkbook) balance. The garden right in front of the palace is **Jardín del Parterre,** small but well-groomed, like a pampered poodle. You can skip this one, as it's directly in the sun and not worth getting dehydrated over. Directly northwest of the palace along Río Tajo is MTV Best● **Jardín de la Isla** ★★, romantically kissed with French design. It's easy to navigate your way through its hedges and a good place to eat a *bocadillo,* if you were smart and thought ahead. Keep an eye out for the "Ne Plus Ultra" fountain, the black-jasper fountain of Bacchus, and the fountain of Apollo, Neptune (god of the sea), and Cybele (goddess of agriculture). Last but not least is the mazelike **Jardín del Principe** ★★, the Prince's Garden that likens to the town's Central Park. Visit the Chinese pond and gazebo. There are three entrances along Calle de la Reina, the third of which leads to **Casa del Labrador.** Gardens open every day in winter, 10am to 6:30pm; in summer, 8am to 8:30pm.

Aranjuez Basics

This very helpful **tourist information office** (Pl. de San Antonio 9; ☎ **918-910-427;** www.aranjuez.es) is staffed with young, good-looking people who will recommend places to go and stay (daily 10am–6pm). In order to ship fresh strawberries home, make for the **Correos** at Peñarredonda 3 (☎ **918-911-132**). But there's no way they're gonna taste the same as they do in Aranjuez.

Sleeping

HOSTELS

➜ **Hostal Castilla** ★★ Normally a hostel with mostly interior rooms is a letdown, but the trellis-topped terraza—along with a small bistro-style cafeteria—is one of Castilla's many highlights. This 19-room, centrally located hostel comes fully equipped with turbo-cleaned, super-big bathrooms, so nobody has to wait in line for the showers. Rooms are modest sized and so are the windows, but the iron-post beds are comfortable enough. It's right next to the hottest going-out area near

Plaza del Toros and student-priced food—though your breakfast is already covered. *Ctra. Andalucía 98. ☎ 918-912-627. Single 39€, double 54€, triple 77€. Amenities: Breakfast, sheets, telephone, towels, travel desk. In room: A/C, TV.*

DOABLE

➜ **El Cocheron Hotel** ★★★ Walking into this place made me want to redecorate my apartment and book another trip to Aranjuez. Built inside an old *corala,* this modern-rustic luxe hotel, known by locals as the *hotel con encanta* (enchanted hotel), treats guests as if they were home with a hot cup of tea and soft slippers (or a cocktail depending on your lifestyle). Each room is individually designed according to what looks most comfortable. The Crate and Barrel—esque patio sucks you in with chaise longues and teak wood. Forget the Parador, and book a night here. The price is more than fair for services rendered. *Calle Montesinos 22. ☎ 918-754-350. www.el cocheron1919.com. Single 85€, double 95€, triple 115€, quintet 125€. Amenities: Bar, cafeteria, laundry service, patio, rooms for those* w/limited mobility, telephone, Wi-Fi. In room: A/C, TV, hair dryer.

Eating

At the tourist office, pick up a small booklet the city publishes called, "Tapas por las Plazas de Aranjuez." It's a handy guide to tapa hopping that fits in your pocket and is available for free at many of the eating establishments it recommends. It's in English and Spanish with pictures and keyed maps. Otherwise, take it from us. Good eating in Aranjuez comes at a price.

➔ **Carême** ★★ INTERNATIONAL   Located right next to the Royal Palace, this brand-new hot spot is the best bet for your buds. Celebrity chef Jesus del Cerro serves up modern dishes at decent prices, in an area that drowns in a stampede of over-priced livestock options. Downstairs is a brightly lit cafe, decorated with toile wallpaper, and upstairs is the dining room that leads to a balcony overlooking the royal palace. Start off with *Carpaccio de Boga-vante* (shrimp) or just play it safe with the artichokes. For your main meal, order *Corazón de Solomillo con foie* (steak with foie gras). There's also an overwhelming list of regional red wines, so add wine tasting to your itinerary—the spitting is not necessary, so don't be fooled into submission. *Av. de Palacio 2.* ☎ *918-926-486. www.careme jesusdelcerro.com. In dining room, meal 16€– 20€. In cafe, menú 17€. Tues–Sun 10:30am to close. Closed Mon.*

➔ **Casa Pablo** ★★ SPANISH   Is that a cigar in your pocket or . . . ? Walking into this splurge-worthy place had me thinking I accidentally entered a gentlemen's smoking lounge. But apparently, it's the best restaurant in town, fitted with white-linen tables and enough wineglasses for a street performer's symphony. The restaurant has

Chiquitrén

So it's totally immature, but who the hell cares. The **Chiquitrén** train tours throughout the city's gardens, an undertaking impossible to do on foot. If you're above that, however, then cool off on the **Barco turís-tico** that takes you upriver, in order to see how not one detail was forgotten in beautifying the gardens for the Nile-like perspective. Trains depart from Palacio Real (☎ **902-088-089;** www.arantour.com; 5€ adult). Trains run each hour in winter, 11am to 5:15pm; every half-hour in summer, 10am to 8pm. Boats depart from Puente de Barcos, costing 7€ adult. Joint ticket for train and boat, 10€ adult. Boats run in July only, 11am to 9pm.

been in the celebrity-status owner's family for 65 years and is famous for its fresh fish and seafood—so start with the shrimp. The asparagus is also recommended, and for a gluttonous finale, try the lemon cream. Of course, you can also just stand at the bar with a beer and tapas, in order to take in the atmosphere without taking out a loan. *Almíbar 42.* ☎ *918-911-451. Meal 20€–40€. Daily 1–4:30pm and 8:30–11:30pm. Closed Aug.*

Partying

Thursdays, Fridays, and Saturdays are the main nights to head out for *copas*. Bars are usually open late afternoon for coffee or *primera copa* (first drinks). The main party zone is near **Plaza del Toros,** bordering the old city. Head up Calle del Almíbar, which is one of the main drags. Intersecting streets such as Calle la Rosa, Calle de las Eras, and Calle de la Calandria are all laced with cafes, bars, and clubs.

What Would Martha Do?

If you're like me, you're going to eat half a strawberry and drop the other half on your pants, or under separate circumstances, your woman's white skirt. Try boiling water. If that doesn't do the trick, here's what Martha Stewart would do:

1. Soak in tannin solution.
2. Beat the stain out with a carpet brush.
3. Flush stain with H_2O.
4. If the stain still sticks, try some hydrogen peroxide and then a few drops of ammonia right after that.
5. Flush it again with cool water and add some vinegar before giving another go with the old wash 'n' spin.

→ **El Laurel de Baco** ★★ This is our favorite place, a historical building with stained-glass windows and a faux fireplace that attracts beautiful people. During the day it's a friendly pub with fair-priced drinks while at night, it's a club playing mostly house and some Spanish pop. Often there's a line to get in but it moves fast. *Eras 6.* ☎ *918-913-943. Café Teatro Thurs at 10pm.*

Sightseeing

Aranjuez is peculiar in that it was never intended to be a civilian town. Rather it was a playground for the Richie Riches and Suzy Q's, when Spanish royalty was "in." What you have here is a whole lot of green, in terms of both grass and money. Strap on your walking shoes and don't forget to stop and smell the flowers. They were expensive.

→ **Casa del Labrador** ★★ Charles IV copied the design of the Petit Trianon at Versailles, in order to build "The House of Workers" in 1803 for the purpose of a hunting lodge (let's face it: party house) for all his royal frat boys. The Billiards room was where Spanish aristocracy held guys' night. Ironically, the queen had the last laugh when she brought her younger lover Godoy for rendezvous (and later promoted him to prime minister). For a palace, it's small but loaded: precious clocks, marble floors, brocaded walls, and a platinum-covered bathroom, where the king took royal dumps in public. *Parque del Principe.* ☎ *918-910-305. Admission 3€ adult, 1.50€ students. A reservation is needed for guided tours starting every half-hour. Winter Tues–Sun 10am–5:15pm; summer Tues–Sun 10am–6:15pm.*

→ **El Palacio Real** ★★ It's Queer Eye for the Royal Guy. Each room in this regal springhouse is completely different from the other, having been rearranged and gutted more often than Joan Rivers, not to mention having suffered a fire in the 17th century. When Ferdinand and Isabella decided they wanted a sweet springtime escape (they already had one for summer), they set up their own version of Camp David here, and, later, Philip II, Philip V, and Charles III made their nest. The same architect who worked on El Escorial, Juan Bautista de Toledo, began planning the palace, but it was Juan de Herrera who finished the project. The most striking rooms are The Porcelain Room (1763) decorated with Madrid-made chinoiserie motifs that cover the entire wall (nice to look at but definitely not livable). The Hall of Mirrors is also worth a second take. At the end of your tour, you'll run into the **Museo de la Vida en Palacio** ★, which gives you great insight as to how filthy rich the clan really was. *Plaza Palacio.* ☎ *918-910-740. Admission (includes museum): 4.50€ adult, 5€ guided tour (50 min.), half-price for students. For tour of private rooms 6€ adult, 5€ student. Winter Tues–Sun 10am–5:15pm; summer Tues–Sun 10am–6:15pm.*

Shopping

Small stalls around town sell the region's strawberries. An Aranjuez *fresón* is claimed to be completely different from a normal strawberry, but it's ostensibly not, other than its larger-than-life size. When they're in season you can buy boxes of them on the street. **Sabores de Aranjuez** ★ (Almíbar 127; ☎ **918-922-780**) is a one-stop wonder for everything Aranjuez. Canned asparagus, strawberry jam, strawberry wines, and regional sweets to take home to your roommate who is cat-sitting, all are reasonably priced. The store's oven-baked smell alone will convince you to buy something.

San Lorenzo de El Escorial

Philip II was so bummed out about the death of his father, Charles V, that he went and built an entire monastery dedicated to preserving the Spanish monarchy until death did it part. The monastery, 50km (31 miles) outside of Madrid, is located in the heart of town and is a must-see for any half-morbid person who appreciates a good dose of dark culture like *Six Feet Under.* Franco's **Valle de los Caídos** is an automatic 3-hour chunk out of your day so it might be worth your while to spend the night (or two) outside of Madrid, in order to cover it all.

Getting There & Around

BY TRAIN

There are Cercanía trains leaving from Madrid's Atocha, Nuevos Ministerios, and Chamartín train stations (☎ **902-240-202**; www.renfe.es) about every half-hour. (*Beware:* Our first train mysteriously never came.) You can purchase your ticket right before departure so no worries buying it in advance. It takes a little over an hour to get there. A one-way fare costs 2.60€. The railway station for San Lorenzo de El Escorial (☎ **918-900-714**) is about a mile outside of town on Carretera Estación. You could walk, but it'd be better to save your legs. Parked outside should be a shuttle bus that meets trains and brings tourists to and from the Plaza Virgen de Gracia, near the monastery. Bus fare is 1.10€. To get back to the train is difficult unless you decide to hoof it. Shuttle buses leave outside the bus station in synch with the trains heading back to Madrid, leaving you about 10 minutes to buy a ticket before it's full steam ahead.

BY BUS

Taking the bus is by far the best option because it drops you off in the dead center of town. The Office of Empresa Herranz, Calle Reina Victoria 3, in El Escorial (☎ **918-904-122** or 918-969-028), runs about 40 buses every day to and from Madrid, except on Sundays when there's only about 10, so make sure you plan accordingly like we didn't. Trip time is an hour, the same as the train, but a round-trip fare will set you back a few cents more, 5.50€.

BY CAR

Take the N-VI highway (aka A-6) from Madrid toward Lugo, La Coruña, and San Lorenzo de El Escorial (nicely marked). After about a half-hour of driving, hopefully accompanied by cheesy Spanish pop

Best Place to Pump Billy Joel's "We Didn't Start the Fire"

··································

📺 Best❗ Franco's memorial is sure to give you the heebie-jeebies when you stop and think about the fact that the people who built the monument were actually Franco's prisoners.

Technically, it's been converted into a monument for both the Republicans and the Nationals who fought against each other in the Spanish Civil War. Many people want to rip it down while others respect it as a national monument, essential to preserving Spain's history. (See "Sightseeing," below.)

songs on the radio, veer left on C-505, toward San Lorenzo de El Escorial (trip time: 1 hr.).

San Lorenzo de El Escorial Basics

The best darn-tootin' **tourist information office**—and we mean it—in Castilla de la Mancha is at Calle Grimaldi 2 (☎ **918-905-313;** www.sanlorenzoturismo. org; Mon–Fri 10am–6pm, Sat–Sun 10am–7pm). It is open all day (that's the exciting part, as they don't take a siesta stranding tourists during lunch). For staying in touch on e-mail, **Quality Call** (☎ **918-901-533;** daily 9:30am–11pm) has two locations: Plaza de San Lorenzo 2 (Galería Martín) and Calle Juan de Leyva 11.

Sleeping

The hotels in the center are not what they seem. Take **Hotel Victoria,** for example. Seemingly the best joint in town (even royalty has stayed here), its outdated arrogance could use a reality-TV makeover.

HOSTEL

➜**Hostal Vasco** ★ This economical hostel tucked inside the center city gets our vote for the most personality. Just by walking up its four creaky flights of stairs, we stopped on each, allured by sofas, lamps, and oddities more fit for the Addams Family than a funky (if by accident) hostel. Finally getting to our room, we recognized our own college dorms. Except these have magnificent views of the city's rooftops and of the hills peaking over them from a small hanging balcony—a perk no state university could afford us. Cast-iron beds, worn couches, and a grandparent's touch win us over with integrity though perhaps not with freshness. Rooms without bathrooms all have sinks. *Plaza de Santiago 11.* ☎ *918-901-619. Double with shared bathroom 32€, triple with shared bathroom 45€, double with full bathroom 38€. Single rooms are not available. No credit cards. Amenities: Restaurant, sheets, towels.*

CHEAP

➜**Parilla Principe** Interestingly enough this cheap hotel is attached to one of the best restaurants in town, though they couldn't be more different in excess, or lack thereof. The simple, clean-cut rooms (some with a great view of the monastery) are more than satisfactory so don't hesitate to book despite its absence of appeal. The staff works just as hard for both its clashing establishments. We saw the locals pour into the restaurant at lunch time so if you've got enough bills left over, splurge for a lavish meal in the enclosed dining room. *Calle Floridablanca 6 (entrance behind restaurant on C. Mariano Benavente 12).* ☎ *918-901-611. Mar 21–Oct 16 single 44€, double 59€; Oct 17–Mar 20 single 42€, double 59€; extra bed 8€. Amenities: Restaurant and bar. In room: TV.*

SPLURGE

→ **Posada Don Jaime** ★★★ We give this small, bright, beaming 19th-century abode tucked away in narrow residential streets four stars for peppiness and to-the-point luxuriousness. The friendly owners are a laid-back mother and son, English-speaking for the most part, who have restored its all-wood attic to a romantic suite and the rest of the house with warm colors and large beds. The junior suite has a porch that makes all the neighbors jealous with a glass-front facade hanging over the street. But the best part is the hidden pool the size of a one-car garage. Exercise machines are haphazardly scattered around its perimeter. Note to self: Next time in El Escorial, stay at Posada Don Jaime. *San Antón 24.* ☎ *619-308-936. Double and for single use only 120€. Breakfast 6€. Amenities: Breakfast room, exercise machines, swimming pool. In room: Jacuzzi.*

Eating

TAPAS

→ **Alaska** ★★ CASTILIAN/TAPAS/BAR   This central restaurant's large patio is shaded under a tree-topped canopy near the hub of quaint shops and an art gallery, providing patrons with the most picturesque scene in town and all major food groups: beer, tapas, Castilian steak, and dessert (the Alaska pastry shop is next door). The cheap prices on the menu don't interfere with the view of the monastery or the mountains, either. *Plaza San Lorenzo 4.* ☎ *918-904-365. Menú 11€. Daily 8am—midnight.*

→ **La Cueva** TAPAS   This is one of the oldest places in town, and the grumpy old men behind the bar help solidify that fact. The tapas are classic, and the terraza ain't bad either, so if you don't have a problem with your anger management and/or your shrink is on international speed dial, relish

the compromised but good-tasting hospitality with a hefty plate of Castilian meats such as *morcilla* (the best bloody blood sausage in town) and spiced sausage de La Mancha. *Sobral 4. No phone. Tapas 2.90€– 13€. Daily 9:30am—midnight.*

DOABLE

→ **La Taberna de Florida** ★ FRENCH   Take a date and choose between cheese, meat, and chocolate fondues for two. Its homey French decor will make you forget you're in Spain (the host is quick to inform you she does *not* serve Spanish cuisine). There's also a full menu though on the pricey side so better to just fondue and flee. *Floridablanca 28.* ☎ *918-960-696. Fondues to share 12€–18€. Summer daily 8:30pm—midnight; winter Fri–Sun.*

SPLURGE

→ **Charolés** SPANISH/FRENCH   I'd never felt like such a bumbling caveman in the presence of red juicy meats as they made their way to white-linen tables. It's a sight that could put PETA activists into convulsions. This restaurant, however, is one of the top-notch restaurants in town specializing in French fish and meats, winning it national acclaim and dozens of newspaper write-ups. It's a little more expensive than most and more attractive to older people with starched collars and gold cufflinks, but that's perfectly explained by its choice cuts and delicate desserts. The tables along a private walkway look over the main drag, shaded under a flower trellis. (There were no animals killed during the writing of this review). *Floridablanca 24.* ☎ *918-905-975. Main course 18€–26€. Reservations required. Daily 1–4pm and 9pm—midnight.*

Partying

By Madrileño terms, El Escorial is not a bad place to party. The city, so close to Madrid, attracts city dwellers and, along with it, their starched collars and smart party know-how. Most bars are conservative, intimate, and geared toward young urban professionals. Eating and drinking action is concentrated on Calle de la Floridablanca and its offshoots.

📺 (Best ●) →**El Sapo Rojo** ★★ It's not an Irish pub but it's damn close, offering the same low-key environment, big screen TV, and oh yeah—the vintage Schweppes bus turned into a wet bar and parked right smack in the middle. If that's not enough to make this place spectacular, bring your laptop for free Wi-Fi access, smack down a Guinness, and open your office hours until late night. *Calle Ventura Rodriguez 7.* ☎ *918-909-163.*

📺 (Best ●) →**Kame Café** ★★★ Besides being the best cafe and bar in town, this unique, not-to-be-missed hot spot hidden in a plaza's corner is a cool reservoir for cheap international cuisine (hummus, miso soup, and veggie-friendly dishes), drinks (caiparina and mojitos), and design-savvy seating. Even the rustic-minimalist bathrooms are worth a peek; actually everything is see-through anyway so you won't have to leave your too-cool-for-school seat. The husband and wife who own the oasis are a jet-setting duo to be reckoned with, and you should. They speak perfect English and love international chin-wag. DJs spin here occasionally. *Calvario 4 (near movie theater).* ☎ *918-960-722.*

→**Move It** This is the only big dance club in town if you absolutely need to trip the light fantastic; otherwise, do yourself a favor and just stay clear. It's filled with a lot of teeny-boppers not afraid to break curfew. I wouldn't go in there if I were paid (which I technically am, so that should tell

you something). *Plaza Santiago 11.* ☎ *637-813-007.*

→**Piano Bar Regina** Offering kegs, too much wine, and an ambience more appropriate for a '70s strip bar, this classic hot spot is just the thing when you're in the mood for drunk people-watching. The lounge is enormous, with waiting room seating and a stage for a band in the back. Sit at the bar, smoke a *cigarro* for the hell of it (everyone else is), and be comforted by the fact that everyone else here is older than you. *Floridablanca 2.* ☎ *918-906-843.*

Sightseeing

→**El Valle de los Caídos** ★★★ So you weren't exactly paying attention in history class while your teacher resembling Ben Stein explained the Spanish Civil War? That's okay, because this monument, 8km (5 miles) away from El Escorial in the middle of the Sierra de Guadarrama, hits you over the head with a crash course in Spanish history. The mere mention of Franco's monument located at El Valle de los Caídos elicits discussion, as it's solely associated with the winning side, as in the fascists, and not with the losers who had to build it. Over time, lobbying groups demanded that it not only be a memorial for the Nationalists, but also for the Republicans. Technically that's true now, but ask any Spaniard, and they'll offer their own version of what the monument stands for. (Duh! Franco.)

One thing that everyone agrees on is that it makes a damn good tourist attraction. Underneath lies the **crypt,** by far the most interesting part of the entire structure. Franco is buried behind the high altar. Take a **funicular** to the base of the cross at the very top of the mountain and yodel (2.50€ adult; Apr–Oct 11am–5:30pm, Nov–Mar

11am–4:30pm). Behind the monument is the posh **Benedictine monastery,** aka the Hilton of monasteries and the envy of all its monkish neighbors. Cuidado Herranz runs only one bus a day to El Valle de los Caídos—the only way to get there unless you're driving. It leaves San Lorenzo de El Escorial at 3:15pm with a return trip at 5:30pm. The ride takes only 15 minutes, and a round-trip fare is 8€. Get to the station early, as there's usually a very long ticket line. By car, head north toward Guadarrama Mountains. The underground basilica is located 6km (3³/₄ miles) west from there. ☎ 918-905-611. Admission 5€ adults, 2.90€ students. Apr–Sept Tues–Sun 10am–6pm; Oct–Mar Tues–Sun 10am–5pm. Closed Mon.

→ **Real Monestario de San Lorenzo de El Escorial** ★★★ To say it's the eighth wonder of the world, like the San Lorenzo tourist office claims, might be stretching it. But at least it gives you an idea of the importance of what you're about to see, perhaps the most important crypt ever constructed. It's also a nice reminder that one day you, too, will die, to put it lightly. The entire burial site, which took 21 years to build, first by Juan Bautista de Toledo and then later by Juan de Herrera, is for Spanish kings and their clans, and is the best representation of Renaissance architecture that exists in Spain, if not the world.

First we have the **New Museums,** stone-arched apartments housing big-timers such as Velázquez and Greco. Ironically, Philip II was disappointed with Greco's artwork and hung them in the most unpopular rooms while favoring Titian's work instead. (It's safe to say Philip's rolling in his grave.) The collection here, and also in **Salon Capitulares,** is just as impressive to someone who doesn't

appreciate art—or Christianity, for that matter—as to someone else who does. Follow the hoards of people to Philip II's apartment, in order to get a glimpse of the actual bed where he died. There's a back door to his apartment that overlooks a humongous basilica, arranged just so Philip could hear the gospel even on his deathbed (who needs sheep when four organ pipes will do?). Note that Philip did not sleep with his wife. They only got married for political reasons, and that his apartment is very Plain Jane. He was a religious fanatic who didn't like frill, apart from the one around his neck. In comparison, the next few apartments belonged to the Bourbon kings who fancied anything expensive.

Descend the marble stairs and you're at death's door, literally: The 🔲 Best 🔵 **Royal Pantheon** is where Spain's monarchs are buried. You'll need a tour guide, in order to get it straight who everyone is, but it's just as imposing to admire the quantity of tombs. The "Wedding Cake" tomb for children, for example, stands icily on its own, calling your respect for heirs who never came into fame. Juan de Borbón. ☎ 918-905-903. Admission 8€ adult, guided tour: 9€. Apr–Sept Tues–Sun 10am–6pm; Oct–Mar Tues–Sun 10am–5pm. Closed Mon.

Shopping

The pedestrian streets of Juan de Leyva, Reina Victoria, Floridablanca, Del Rey, Las Pozas, San Lorenzo, and Joaquín Costa all make up the slim-picking shopping zone of San Lorenzo de El Escorial. If you're in town for more than 1 day, it's worth a trip to the **Mercado** on Calle Rey; and la **Casa de las Columnas,** between Reina Victoria and San Lorenzo, is a good bet to find local artisans, too.

Chinchón ★

Chinchón is for the traveler who prefers eating and drinking his/her way through a new city, to sightseeing. The **Plaza Mayor** is the most unique portico plaza in Spain perfect for just sitting, or riding donkeys (see box, below). Originally the Plaza was used as a stomping ground for cattle fairs. In the 16th century, however, legendary cowboys elevated the town's regional status when bullfights became the main attraction. Green balconied houses create its abnormal shape, providing an amphitheater-like venue for theater, dances, and, in its dark past, executions. Goya and Orson Welles were both huge fans of Chinchón. In fact, Orson was here in the mid-'60s filming two reels, *The Immortal Story* and *Chimes at Midnight.* He liked to take shots of anis (liqueur flavored with aniseed) first thing in the morning with the locals. The second most mind-bumbling attraction is the *cuevas,* antiquated wine cellars located underneath *mesónes.* All you have to do is ask to see the caves (*¿Puedo ver las cuevas?*), in order to descend into their dark, cool depths (see "Eating," below). The 15th-century **Chinchón Castle** seated the counts of Chinchón, but too bad it's closed to the public. The town's 16th- to 17th-century cathedral, **Nuestra Señora de la Asunción** houses a painting by Goya.

Getting There & Getting Around

BY BUS

If you're leaving from Madrid, the bus company that travels to Chinchón is **La Veloz** (Av. del Mediterráneo 49; ☎ **914-097-602;** Metro: Conde de Casal). During the week, it runs about every half-hour, and on the weekend about once every hour. In order to catch the bus, walk to Avenida del Mediterráneo from Metro Conde Casal and you'll see the large green buses lining the street. Bus fare one-way is 3.15€ (trip time: 50 min.). It will leave you off in Chinchón about a 5-minute walk to the Plaza Mayor.

BY CAR

You can drive from Alcalá to Toledo, bypassing Madrid by taking the C-300 in a southwesterly arc around the capital. About halfway there, you'll see signs for Cuevas de Chinchón. Another option is to take the E-901 southeast of Madrid toward Valencia, turning southwest at the turnoff for Chinchón.

Chinchón Basics

The **Oficina de Información Turística Municipal** is at Plaza Mayor 6 (☎ **918-935-323;** www.ciudad-chinchon.com), open Monday to Friday 10am to 8pm, Saturday and Sunday 11:30am to 8pm.

Sleeping

There aren't a lot of reasons to stay the night in Chinchón, other than you drank too much anis or broke your ankle falling off a donkey. Most people park it in Madrid and catch the bus into Chinchón for the day. If you do decide to roll out a bed in Chinchón, here's one main squeeze in town.

→ **Hostal de Chinchón** There's a rooftop pool and garden. If that doesn't say it all, this homey hostel right off the plaza's main drags has a view of said plaza. The rooms are spacious with cool tile floors for the summers though they're out-of-date, so don't expect the Hilton. Bathrooms are clean, and most have bathtubs for soaking travel-worn feet. The family who runs it is extremely polite and hospitable. Breakfast is thrown in for 4€ extra; we recommend taking it poolside. The website is an excellent representation of the hostel. *José*

Antonio 12 (next to Pl. Mayor). ☎ *918-935-398.*
www.hostalchinchon.com. Single 35€, double
42€, triple 54€. No credit cards. Amenities:
Breakfast, laundry service, sheets, telephone,
towels. In room: A/C, TV.

Eating

The restaurants and taverns surrounding
Plaza Mayor and the streets leading above
Chinchón are the city's best highlights, and
almost all the fare is the same so it's difficult to go wrong. Large caves run mazelike
under the older *mesónes,* and all it usually
takes is one inquiry with the bar in order to
be let down into them, either guided by a
member of the waitstaff or on your own.

➔ **Mesón Cuevas del Vino** ✦ SPANISH
Though perhaps out of the way on an
uphill street, it's an oasis worth the trek.
Orson Welles thought so when he ate here
during the filming of a movie. The building
was first used as a winery, still evident by
the ceramic casks, wine presses, and
grinding thingamajigs. The house wine is
served out of a large synthetic wineskin
slumped on a table in the dining room so
make sure to order some. Commit to a big
meal because it's your best bet in town
for the money: gazpacho (the best I've
ever had), homemade garlic potato chips,
spiced chorizo, La Mancha cheese, roast
suckling lamb, ham, and regional game.
Leave room for dessert, in order to sample
miel sobre hojuelas (a honey pastry) sure
to hit your sweet spot. *Benito Hortelano*
13. ☎ *918-940-285 or 918-940-206. www.*
cuevasdelvino.com. Main courses 6€–18€.
Reservations recommended on holidays.
Wed–Mon 1:30–4pm and 8–11pm.

Don't Be an Ass . . . Ride One Instead

[TV] [Best ☺] Donkeys cart patrons
around the Plaza (Rutas en Burro
por Chinchón, Pl. Mayor; ☎ **918-
940-664**), providing the perfect photo
op. You don't have to be a kid to
enjoy it; it's not totally unusual for
adults to mount, too. During the
weekends only, 1 to 6pm.

Partying

Most likely you are in Chinchón for no
longer than a day, so why not pass the time
drinking anis on Plaza Mayor? **El Ruedo**
(Pl. Mayor 44) is choice. In summer
months, *botellónes* pop up all over town;
just listen for the clanking of bottles or
follow the smell of *porros* (spliffs). The
terraza hugging the perimeter of the castle
is a hot spot for mingling and drinking.

Shopping

On **Plaza Mayor** there is a surplus of artisan shops selling pottery and regional
foods such as pungent garlic. (*Advisory:*
Pack a toothbrush—things might get
nasty.) Artisan bread takes on a number of
weird shapes. The most popular is *Torta
de Chicharra,* a sweetbread infused with
Chinchón's most popular herb, anise (with
the taste of black licorice), also found in
locally brewed liquors. The best way to
sample anis is to walk into a local bar for a
tasting session and an explanation of all
the different types.

Alcalá de Henares

Don Quijote de la Mancha by Miguel
Cervantes is quintessential so why not
pick up an abridged copy and at least give
it a half-assed read before coming to the

city that's devoted to him. Alcalá de
Henares (a half-hour outside of Madrid) is
a lively university town that has a rich history for spawning genius like Cervantes,

Alcalá de Henares

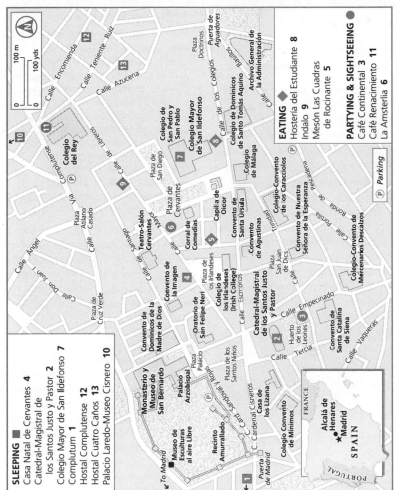

SLEEPING ◼
Casa Natal de Cervantes **4**
Catedral-Magistral de
los Santos Justo y Pastor **2**
Colegio Mayor de San Ildefonso **7**
Complutum **1**
Hostal Complutense **12**
Hostal Cuatro Caños **13**
Palacio Laredo-Museo Cisnero **10**

EATING ◆
Hostería del Estudiante **8**
Indalo **9**
Mesón Las Cuadras
de Rocinante **5**

PARTYING & SIGHTSEEING ●
Café Continental **3**
Café Renacimiento **11**
La Amstería **6**

Lope de Vega, Tirso, Quevedo, Ignacio de Loyola, Luis de León, Jovellanos, and Calderón de Barca, just to name a few. **El Colegio Mayor,** where they all attended school, and the well-kept historic quarter, earned the city the title of World Heritage Site in 1998, and you'll be reminded of this fact on many occasions.

Alcalá de Henares is a golden example of Medieval tolerance in Spain, proving

that yes, everyone can just get along. El Barrio de la Morería claims the zone above Calle Santiago and the northern region of the original Roman wall. El Barrio Judío constitutes Calle Mayor. And last but not least, is El Barrio Cristiano, that makes up the rest of the town.

Most of the monuments are huddled together in one zone so touring the city is easily manageable. If you have an inkling to overdo it, you could visit Roman ruins on the outskirts of town but it's not totally necessary. The city should take you no longer than an afternoon to tackle, but when planning your itinerary keep in mind the city keeps strict nap time hours during the afternoon siesta.

Getting There & Getting Around

BY TRAIN

Renfe Cercanías trains (C1, C2, C7) travel between Madrid's Atocha or Chamartín station and Alcalá de Henares all day long, running every 15 minutes (trip time: 30 min.). Round-trip tickets from Madrid cost 3.35€. The train station (☎ 902-240-202) in Alcalá is at Paseo Estación. Once there, it's an easy, breezy walk to the center of town. Just head down Paseo Estación until you reach Calle de los Libreros, which will lead you straight into the heart of Alcalá de Henares.

BY BUS

Buses from Madrid depart from Av. América 18 (Metro: América), every 15 minutes. A one-way ticket is 1.75€. Bus service is provided by **Continental-Auto** (☎ 918-881-622), and the Alcalá bus station is at Av. Guadalajara 36, 2 blocks past Calle Libreros. If you head south on Guadalejara and keep straight, the road will eventually turn into it.

BY CAR

Heading out of Madrid, look for signs to Barajas Airport and Barcelona. Get yourself onto the N-11, go past the airport, and exit on Canillejas. That will get you to the Alcalá de Henares exit.

Alcalá de Henares Basics

The Oficina de Turismo (☎ 918-892-694) is located at Plaza de Cervantes 1, and is open every day from 10am to 2pm and 4 to

Cervantes Train

For the inner-child in you, there's the shiny new **Tren de Cervantes,** which leaves Madrid's Atocha train station at 11am bound for Alcalá de Henares on the weekends only from March 18 to December 10. Instead of conductors, actors dressed in Cervantina gear give you the scoop on Alcalá (plus traditional sweets) before you even arrive there nonstop. Contact the tourism office (☎ **918-821-354**) for more info. Tickets are sold at Renfe (Atocha). One-way tickets cost 17€ adults.

6:30pm. The second office (☎ **918-810-634**) is at Plaza Santos Niños, and is open with the same hours. The website for tourism in Alacalá, in order to case the scene upon arrival, is www.turismoalcala.com.

Sleeping

➜ **Hostal Complutense** ★★ If you're too imbibed to hop the train back to Madrid, there's no other place to stay than this clean, villalike hostel. Opened in 2006, you can rest assured that everything is clean and seemingly unused. The stone-clad bathrooms are surprisingly stylish and modern for a hostel. The best part is, there's free Wi-Fi and surround-sound music for counting sheep. The desk attendants are young *uni* students so if you need a recommendation, don't hesitate to ask them. *Calle Encomienda 9.* ☎ *639-388-370. Single 36€, double 45€, triple 55€. Amenities: Parking garage, sheets, towels, Wi-Fi. In room: A/C, TV.*

➜ **Hostal Cuatro Caños** Although not as cutting-edge as Complutense, this is another good option for crashing in Alcalá.

The rooms are smaller without a view but there are large windows that let in a lot of light. All rooms have full bathrooms. It is an up-kept, shiny (but bland) hostel with attentive service. *Calle Divino Figueroa 10.* ☎ *918-813-844. Single 36€, double 45€, extra bed 10€. Amenities: Sheets, towels. In room: A/C, TV.*

Eating

→**Hostería del Estudiante** ★★ CASTILIAN
This restaurant located in the Parador of Alcalá is dressed to the nines for the high rollers who want to dine in style. The 16th-century collegiate building now serves Alcalá pastries and tea (Sun 6–9pm) and melted chocolate along with fried croutons. It's the kind of place you'll see upper-class stiffs in tweed suits and pinstripes dip with the pinky finger extended. Onion soup, *cocido Madrileño*, and San Isidro salad are all beefy options assured not to spoil your dinner. Try to save room for dessert, if you can afford it. *Calle Colegios 3.* ☎ *918-880-330. Menú 33€ (includes dessert). Shared plates 12€–25€. Daily 1–4pm and 9–11pm. Closed Aug.*

Best ✿ →**Indalo** CASTILIAN/TAPAS
There's no doubt about it—this is the hot spot in town for tapas. As soon as the clock strikes 2 in the afternoon, it's hard to squeeze through to the bar, but trust us there's light at the end of the tunnel. Famous for its attractive, inexpensive tapas and raciónes, this bar is known throughout the Castilla–La Manchan region, even in Madrid, as having the best grub, at the best price. This is a good place to kick off your day trip in Alcalá, but try to get there as early as possible, in order to grab a prime table in the back sunroom. *Calle de Libreros 9.* ☎ *918-824-415. A beer and tapas 1.80€. Daily 9:30am–1am.*

→**Mesón Las Cuadras de Rocinante** ★
CASTILIAN/TAPAS Situated just down the way from Cervantes's crib, you'll find this classic Castilian kitchen serving the same blessedly inexpensive dishes *para picar* (to pick at) for which Don Quijote craved way back when. Antiquated in style and offering the same tostadas, tapas, and raciónes, the only difference between this *mesón* and those of the Golden Age is the inflation rate. Still, it's a steal for the money. The only thing that's missing is outdoor seating, but the large cozy tables inside make conversation easy. *Calle Carmen Calzado 1.* ☎ *918-800 888. Raciónes (large tapas) 3€–8€. Thurs–Tues 11am–11pm. Closed Wed.*

Partying

Off the less-beaten path is **La Zona,** popular for university students looking to rumble. Along Calle Vaqueras is a multitude of other watering holes.

→**Café Continental** ★★ Surrounded by more plants than Yosemite, this is an excellent place to marinate in the sun with the locals on the best patio in Alcalá, strongly recommended by the local university students who frequent it. It's a cafeteria and a bar, known for both things depending on the time of day. People are friendly and outgoing perhaps because most everyone there is a foreign student, which makes searching for a language-exchange partner (ah-hem) or two, not that difficult. Drink prices are cheaper at the bar than they are at tables. *Empecinado 23.* ☎ *918-789-359.*

→**Café Renacimiento** If beer gardens don't appeal to you, then settle for a Renaissance chapel, converted into a bar cafe. The holy watering hole plays disco

ᴍᴛᴠ🅤 There Goes My A-Plus

Colegio Mayor de San Ildefonso ★★ (Pl. San Diego; ☎ 918-856-487; guided visits admission 2.50€; Mon–Fri 11am, noon, 1pm, 5pm, 6pm, 7pm, Sat–Sun and holidays 11am, 11:30am, noon, 12:30pm, 1pm, 1:30pm, 2pm, 5pm, 5:30pm, 6pm, 7pm, 7:30pm), the best-conserved Renaissance university in Europe, was founded by Cardinal Cisneros in 1499, with an extravagant facade you'll need a guide to interpret, which is also the only way you'll get indoors. If you don't speak a lick of Spanish, take note of the three interior courtyards: the courtyard of Santo Tomás de Villanueva, the courtyard of the Philosophers, and the third, the Trilingual courtyard where Latin, Greek, and Hebrew were taught. From here it is possible to go to the auditorium in which the **Cervantes Literature Prize** is given away every year. Next to the university is the chapel of San Idelfonso with an impressive wood Mudéjar ceiling, dating back to the 15th century. It marks the final resting place for famous people such as Antonio Nebrija, Pedro de Gumiel, and the physician of Felipe II, the Divine Vallés. It's also the place where Miguel de Cervantes was baptized in 1547. Today, however, it's used as a place for alumni and staff to get hitched.

In the front is the sepulcher of Cardinal Cisneros (sans his bones, against his dying wish to be kept there). You'll see it has deteriorated after a rumor spread it was good luck on tests to steal a piece of marble from the monument. You can't steal a chunk anymore—we already asked.

music and serves tropical drinks garnished with paper umbrellas—as if you couldn't have guessed that. The best part is, everything was kept intact when it was renovated: The high, dome ceilings, the stone, and even the general church-y feeling remain unscathed. Raise your glasses and say, Amen. *Cuatro Caños 2 (Puerta de las Martires)*. ☎ *918-891-826*.

➜ **La Amsterlia** ★★ Cafes and bars are literally tripping down Calle Mayor's cobblestone streets. But this joint beats the competition by offering private kegs and free tapas. Each table inside this franchise—a corporate shoot-off from Heineken—has its own tap, controlled by the bartender who regulates the quantity. All you have to do is pull. But don't stop there because the tapas are refreshingly modern, doing away with the traditional staples and piling on some of their own such as steak, soft cheese, and fruit. Patio seating. *Calle Mayor 5*. ☎ *918-898-436*.

Sightseeing

FREE ➜ **Casa Natal de Cervantes** Supposedly the place where Miguel Cervantes was born in 1547, this refurbished, renovated, and restored historic monument has little to do with him, in our humblest opinion. However, it's a trip through time, in order to see how his family *might* have slept, eaten, and even used the bathroom. It's a must-see, only 'cuz it's free. The building is two stories high and will take you 45 minutes tops to wander through. Rooms they didn't know what to do with are filled with *Don Quijote* books published in every language, just in case you weren't sure it was a classic. *Calle Mayor 48*. ☎ *918-899-654*. *www.museo-casa-natal-cervantes.org. Free admission. Tues–Sun 10am–6pm. Last chance to enter is at 5:30pm. Closed Mon.*

➜ **Catedral-Magistral de los Santos Justo y Pastor** Originally a small chapel sitting on the grave of the two sainted children who were martyred in A.D. 305 on the same spot, its style is late Gothic. The other reason to mark this church on your map is because of its magisterial significance, meaning two-thirds of its chapter hold a Ph.D. The only other church in the world that shares the magisterial name is the Saint Peter Church in Belgium. *Calle de la Tercia.* ☎ *918-880-930. Admission depending on each service. Mon–Fri 10am–1pm and 6–8pm; Sat 9:15–11:30am and 5:45–7pm; Sun 10–10:45am, 11:45am–12:15pm, and 6–7:45pm.*

FREE ➔**Complutum** ★ A little farther out of the center, this Roman city was originally located on El Viso hill about 300 years ago, but moved to this site in the 1st century B.C. What you can still see are the basilica, the commercial center, the court, and the baths. The site most worth seeing, however, is the **Casa de Hippolytus** archaeological complex, the former youngsters' school of the city. A bus leaves from Plaza de Cervantes and returns each hour. *Camino del Juncal.* ☎ *918-771-750. www.complutum.com. Free admission. Mon–Fri 9am–9pm.*

➔**Palacio Laredo-Museo Cisnero** ★★ Placing Cisnero's manuscripts under glass is a pitiful excuse to charge admission to one of the most whimsical and fairy-tale-like houses you've ever seen from the Spanish 19th century. Manuel José de Laredo was its designer and architect (and later, Alcalá's mayor) who turbo-blended styles such as neo-Mudéjar, Goth, Renaissance, Roman, and modernista, turning this old house into the talk of the town. *Paseo de la Estación 10.* ☎ *918-802-883. Admission 3€ adult, 1.50€ students, seniors. Tues–Fri 10am–2pm and 5–8pm; Sat–Sun and holidays 11am–2pm and 5–8pm.*

Playing Outside

Feel like packing a picnic? Or getting a piece? Head toward the river and throw down a blanket at Alcalá's natural preserve, **Parque de los Cerros,** for bird-watching, wine drinking, or if you're luckier than us, an afternoon quickie. The park lies south of the city. Take the Pastrana road (M-300). The main entrance lies next to a cemetery's garden. There is a parking lot, as well as access to walking and bicycle paths to the park.

Extremadura

by Elizabeth Gorman

What the Extremaduran region in Spain lacks in coastline and topless beaches, it more than makes up for with green mountainous vistas stretching across the Portuguese border. Its name means "extreme frontier," some say for its Arizona summers and North Dakota winters. This autonomous community made up of mostly whitewashed, fairy-tale *pueblos* (villages), was dubbed conquistador country when in the 15th century men like Hernán Cortés, Francisco Pizzaro, and their greedy brethren up and left an impoverished Extremadura in search of gold and riches to bring back home. And they did. While many travelers who pass through Extremadura are pilgrims heading north to Santiago, a few others know Spain's best kept secret: that Extremadura is an untapped vacation wonder-world, where mass consumerism and corporate giants don't dare wet their toes. Americans are especially seldom and rare. Spaniards, however, take advantage of Extremadura's great outdoors (albeit redneck country) and low profile, opting for quiet weekends at the base of the Sierra de Gata.

Best of Extremadura

- **Best Super-Size Lunch:** Trujillo's **La Troya** is better than any American all-you-can-eat buffet because they don't even make you get up. In fact, they hardly even let you order. See p. 172.
- **Best Outdoor Hippy Festival:** The **WOMAD** festival takes over the city with *botellónes* (40s 'n' blunts parties), dreadlocks, and stray dogs. See p. 192.
- **Best Italian Vacation in Spain:** **Mérida** is the site of so many Roman ruins, there's no reason for you to travel anywhere else. See p. 178.
- **Most Red-Carpet-Worthy Saint:** **La Virgin de Guadelupe** could knock Tyra Banks off her high heels. See p. 177.

- **Best Game of "I Spy":** In Extremadura, **giant storks** drop more than bundles of joy. See p. 184.
- **Best Place to Get Yourself Lost: Cáceres's old city** is a time warp, with not one shiny sign of modernization. See p. 185.
- **Best Music for Moshing:** Metal heads bang to Extremoduro, the most famous hard rock band in this neck of the woods with a strong cult following.
- **Best Public Pick-Up Spot:** Although loads more shabby than anything chic, the **Trujillo bus station** is the only depot in town; that means anyone going anywhere is going to pass through for a small town affair—and it wouldn't be

the first time love was in the air. The bartender in the adjoining cafe pays for your coffee date if you show him your outbound bus ticket, and there's plenty of seating to break the ice. See below.

- **Best Place to Come Out as a Thespian:** Built in ancient times (between the years A.D. 15 and 16) this granddaddy of an **amphitheater** entertained all the social classes and, surprisingly, could seat 6,000. Since there were no mikes back then, they used acoustics, in order to get its sub lifer sound. Stand on center stage and yell up to your buddy at the top to hear how voices traveled without a string and a can. See p. 184.

MTV Best ❽ Trujillo

I left my heart in Trujillo. It is the most unexpectedly charming town in Extremadura, an ancient Arabic city made rich with hot money swiped from the New World. With its cohesive cityscape untouched by modern architecture, it's probably a good thing it's overlooked by tourists, leaving well enough alone. High medieval walls lead through a maze of monochromatic stone palaces and leafy church ruins. The Plaza Mayor sets the main stage while the Castile is the crowning centerpiece spiked with cacti like a poisonous bug warding off predators. The Pizarro family, who discovered Peru; Francisco de Orellana, who discovered the Amazon; and a slew of others, many of whom became traitors or died in the process, made this hometown famous, and nobody here is going to tell you right off the bat they were bad guys. Trujillo's royal pads and palaces were constructed in their honor, incorporating unusual bay

windows that jut out from the building's stone corners, classic courtyards, crests, and busts of all sizes. Tattered remnants from Roman and Arabic times dot the landscape as well. City tours are packaged cheap so head to the tourist office first.

Getting There & Around

BY BUS

From **Madrid's Auto-Res bus station** (Fernández Shaw 1; ☎ **902-020-999;** www.auto-res.net; Metro: Conde de Casal), there are 16 buses per day to and from Trujillo (trip time: 3½–4½ hr.). From Cáceres, there are six buses daily (trip time: 45 min.), and six from Badajoz (trip time: 1 hr. 45 min.). A one-way ticket from Madrid costs 15€ to 21€; from Cáceres, 2.80€; and from Badajoz, 8.90€ to 13€. **Trujillo's bus station,** Calle Marqués Albayda (☎ **927-321-202**), is on the south side of town, on a side street that intersects with Calle de la Encarnación.

BY CAR

To Trujillo from Cáceres, take the N-521; to Lisbon and Madrid, go via the N-V super-highway. Trip time from Madrid is around 2¹/₂ hours, much faster than the bus so worth it to rent a car.

Trujillo Basics

TOURIST INFORMATION

The **tourist office** on Plaza Mayor (☎ 927-322-677; www.ayto-trujillo.com or www.trujillo.es) is open daily 9:30am to 2pm and 4 to 7pm. The city walking tour lasts 1 to 3 hours.

ORIENTATION

Banks to exchange your money and **stores** to blow it in are found along Calle Encarnación, and boutiques string Calle Tiendas.

Sleeping

Finding a bed in Trujillo is easier than spotting a stork's nest. It's not necessary to make a reservation beforehand, and most of the establishments are large enough to handle the city's capacity during festivals. Like most small towns in Spain, hostels are family-owned and paired with *mesónes* (taverns). Hotels on the other hand are charming and almost all high-end, thematically decorated like a nerdy role-playing game, keeping the city's rich conquistador or monastic history in mind.

➔ **Hostal Cadena** ★★ Back in the day, this hostel was the residence of Philip II confessor; that meant that Bad Boyz such as robbers and thieves could enter the house and not be persecuted for their crimes. You can't get more bad-ass than that, not to mention the fact the hostel is in Plaza Mayor, a part of your city tour, and next to arguably the best restaurant in the region, La Troya. Motel-size rooms are spread along a maze of corridors surrounding an

wwwired

Reminiscent of *Happy Days,* the only thing **Ciberalia Café** (Tiendas 18; ☎ **927-659-087;** www.ciberalia.org) lacks is The Fonz. Serving ice cream, tapas, and drinks, it's one of the only places in town for Internet access and by far the best outfitted. Order a *cubre libre* while e-mailing your posse back home. Daily 10:30am to 1 or 2am.

interior patio; the regal decorations, private bathrooms, king-size wardrobes, and bed hangings are the most stylish you'll find in town and a steal for your money. Request a room with bird's-eye views of the Plaza and balcony bliss at sundown. The bar downstairs will give you free coffee and juice in the morning. *Plaza Mayor 8.* ☎ *927-321-463. Double 43€, single 34€, triple 58€. Breakfast included. Amenities: Restaurant and bar, sheets, telephone (in common room), towels. In room: A/C, TV.*

➔ **Boni Pensión** ★ Come home to this economical and centrally located local favorite run by a German couple and their 20-something son who are keen on making you feel at home. As the cheapest place to stay in the city, scruffy young backpackers and families often return to the pension as friends. The salon looks like Roseanne's living room with the added bonus of an instant coffee machine. The five rooms are straightforward with private baths, clean tile-lain floors, and a few love marks such as water stains on the walls. Hugs are accepted. *Domingo Ramos 11.* ☎ *927-321-604. Single 14€, double 25€–30€.*

➔ **Parador de Trujillo** ★★★ In this converted Santa Clara convent, you've got your seven deadly sins covered. Arguably

Extremadura

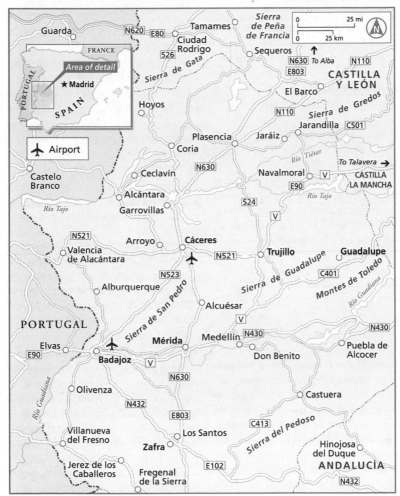

Spain's best parador, this is the best place to fornicate in style. Be the envy of all your friends and enjoy a gluttonous feast of roast suckling pig on the convent's terraza. Pizarro's got greed covered, as many of the rooms are decorated in gold in his honor. Its giant rooms and massage shower will easily turn you into a sloth; and pride will arrive on the scene when you bring down your wrath on the credit card. Whatever dirty sins you commit will be voided at checkout. It's absolutely necessary you ask for a room in the old quarters, where the monks really slept. Old wooden doors were kept to their midget proportions so, prithee, don't hit your head. *Santa Beatriz de Silva 1. ☎ 927-321-350. www.parador.es. Double 110€–120€. Amenities: Bar, restaurant, elevator, telephone. In room: A/C, TV, minibar, hair dryer, safe.*

EXTREMADURA

Eating

CHEAP

→**Cafeteria Hermanos Marcelo** TAPAS Of all the other places to choose from on the Plaza, this is your neighborhood cafeteria that happens to have a great view for not such an expensive price. If you're the adventurous type, try the house specialty: frogs' legs. *Plaza Mayor.* ☎ *927-320-150. Bocadillos (baguette sandwiches) 3€–4€. Summer daily 8am–midnight; winter daily 8am–3pm.*

→**Pizzaría Bocatería La Tahona** PIZZA/BOCADILLOS If Spanish food is getting to your stomach, take a break with pizza at this small joint just off the plaza. Thin crust pizza is served fully loaded in small, medium, and plus sizes, as well as baguette sandwiches that are inches better than Subway back home. Jared has no idea what he's missing. *Afueras 2.* ☎ *927-321-849. Meal 5€–6€. Hours vary, so call ahead.*

DOABLE

MTV (Best ♦) →**Restaurante La Troya** ★★★ SPANISH If you're in the mood for a Hungry Man meal, there is no restaurant in Trujillo better than La Troya. In fact, there's no need to eat anywhere else. Heavy in local flavor, it's where all the young townsmen go for beers and tapas during siesta. One of its founders, Concha, is the hideous-looking woman you see in all the pictures decorating the wall, along with camera-worthy patrons who visit the 16th-century noble's house for breakfast, lunch, and dinner. La Troya's secret to success? Serving tortilla, chorizo, and salad, as soon as you sit down and without your having to say a word. Cha-ching! Only after is the Extremaduran *menú del día: migas* (fried bread crumbs), *cordero caldereta* (lamb), *carden de cerdo* (pork), auctioned

off for the meager price of 15€. *Plaza Mayor 10.* ☎ *927-321-364. Daily 1–4:30pm and 8:30–11pm.*

Partying

If you're looking to get drunk in Trujillo, start in **Plaza Mayor** and work your way down **García de Paredes.** Keep in mind, however, that Trujillo is a small town and chances are you're going to see the same people the next morning you crushed on the night before. So remember who you are and where you come from, son.

→**El Cabo Verde** If you're in the mood for Shakira and Wyclef, head to this narrow neighborhood tavern that feels more like a catwalk than a bar. It's wall-to-wall *pijo* (yuppie), so wear your sexy drawers and *ligar* (find someone to hit on) between the ages of 25 and 40. Make it your late-night destination, as it's a tad out of the way but still on the main drag and one of the hottest places to drink starting at midnight. *Merced 9. No phone.*

MTV (Best ♦) →**La Abadia** During the 17th century, this is where the monks hung out. Now it's more punk than monk, the "it" place for cats to worship house and Spanish pop beats. You won't find better preying material anywhere else than here. A bar was added to the Abby's grassy-green courtyard in back, along with large wicker chairs. It's nothing the monks would do but it's the perfect place for a mixed drink (4€) and hosts a sacred party under the stars starting at 2am. *García de Paredes 20.* ☎ *927-322-036.*

Sightseeing

Trujillo makes tourism easy—and cheap with packaged deals purchased beforehand at the tourism office. Tickets are sold in *bonos* (vouchers). The blue *bono* includes entrance to the castile, Museo del

Los Trece de la Fama

In 1526, Francisco Pizarro (born in Trujillo, Spain) arrived on the island of Gallo (today known as Tumaco, Colombia) to hunt down the Incan kingdom. His expedition was so costly and such an ordeal that the governor of Panama ordered Pizarro and his men packing. Like a kid in a toy store, Pizarro pulled a tantrum and refused to leave. He drew a line in the sand from east to west, crossed it, and told his men whoever had enough balls to do the same: "There lies Peru with its riches; here, Panama and its poverty. Choose, each man, what best becomes a brave Castilian." *Los trece de la fama* (the famous 13), who crossed the limbo line, were knighted by Carlos V of Portugal.

The Fab 13 and their men made a few more trips along the Pacific and after looting, murdering, and destroying the Incan capital of Cuzco, Pizarro founded Lima. Not too ironically, that's precisely where he was violently murdered in 1541 by followers of his old traveling buddy, Pedro de Almagro.

Queso y el Vino, Casa-Museo de Pizarro, Iglesia de Santiago, and a guidebook to the city for 4.70€; the green *bono* adds on the Iglesia San Martín for 5.30€. However, the best deal is the guided tour, which lasts about 2 hours and is in Spanish, of the entire city with entrance to all the above in addition to the Museo del Traje and the Aljibe Altamirano for 6.75€.

PLAZA MAYOR & AROUND

The biggest bow-wow of town is the **Plaza Mayor,** where the majority of the nobles set up camp. The city's main market took place under the arches of the plaza, which also included the Jewish produce department. "The Bread Porch," for example, hangs off the **Palacio de los Marquises de Piedras Albas.** The statute in the middle is by an American artist of **Francisco Pizarro,** the guy who killed off the Incas and discovered Peru along with 13 other men. There's one just like it in Lima. In front of the horse is the **Palacio de la Conquista,** commissioned to be built by Pizarro's brother Hernando. He was the only guy who made it home from the Americas alive (kept safe in the big house for murder). Look for the family busts on the corner of the building; they include

Pizarro's Incan princess Inés Yupanqui and their love child. The church is **Iglesia San Martín;** inside there's a fine looking baroque organ that can still play a pretty tune in one of the only churches that still sees Sunday action. On the west side of the Plaza is the **Casa de las Cadenas,** now a modern hostel (see "Sleeping"). Not only was it the home of Philip II's confessor and a refuge for escaped convicts on the run, the chains on the facade also meant the king gave it a tax break. **Palacio de los Duques de San Carlos** was a duke's residence in the 1500s but it is now a working convent; the double-layered courtyard is a classic. (Ring the doorbell for a tour, 9am–1pm and 4:30–6pm. Admission 1.20€.) **Palacio Juan Pizarro de Orellana** is now a school for poor children, but it was a mansion built for one of Pizarro's cousins who returned to Spain to enjoy the spoils. Situated right next to **Iglesia de San Andrés, La Alberca,** now a littered cistern, was allegedly a public bath in Roman times. The nearby **Alijibe Árabe** (Arab well) is from the 10th century and can still be visited with a tour guide as part of a tour package purchased at the tourist office.

➔ **Castillo** The perimeter of the castile is guarded by a thick blanket of cacti, just as effective as a large mote. Its strategy was to scare off the enemy before it had a chance to charge the fortress. Legend has it that in 1232, the Virgin Mary appeared on the castile walls to root on the soldiers fighting the Arabs, which is how Trujillo got its patron saint. You can walk on top of them for a panoramic view of Trujillo's paint-by-numbers landscape; of course, the vistas are sweeter at sunset. During the summer, the city organizes concerts with a wet bar in the castle's courtyard. Just go uphill from the Plaza, and you'll hit the fortress. There are dungeons below, but you're not allowed in. *Admission 1.20€. Daily 10am–2pm and 4–6:30pm.*

➔ **Iglesia de Santa María** This most interesting church to visit was the first to be built in Trujillo; Isabella and Ferdinand once attended church here. Tourists like it mostly for its climbable Roman tower and impressive views of the city under giant bells that *will* blast your head off. Important Trujillan families are buried in the church such as he-man Diego Garcia de Paredes (b. 1466) who, legend has it, fought off the French army with only one sword. Locals say that somewhere behind the church walls lies a Virgin altarpiece hidden during the Dark Ages from intruding robbers. The problem was, the ecclesiastics couldn't find it again. Do'h! To the right of the entrance is a switch that lights the entire church with a small coin. *Calle de Ballesteros. ☎ 927-320-211. Admission 1.25€. Daily 10am–2pm and 5–8:30pm.*

MUSEUMS

➔ **Casa-Museo de Pizarro** This was where the murderer's—I mean, explorer's family lived. It is now a boring museum documenting his life and the Incan empire. *Calle del Convento de las Jerónimas 12. ☎ 927-322-677. Admission 1.30€. Daily 10am–2pm and 4–7:30pm.*

➔ **El Museo del Queso y el Vino de Trujillo** This is an old church converted into a museum of cheese and wine. History never smelled so bad or tasted so good. The best part is you can try samples of regional wine or, better yet, cheese for .50€ each sample. *Calle Francisco Pizarro s/n. ☎ 927-323-031. www.quesovino.com. Admission 1.30€. Summer daily 11am–3pm and 6–8pm; winter daily 11am–3pm and 5:30–7:30pm.*

➔ **El Museo del Traje** This place exhibits regional clothing, 20th-century Spanish designers, and dresses of famous flamenco singers. It's part of the city tour but by no means a necessary stop otherwise. *Calle Jerónimas 2. ☎ 927-320-184. Admission 1.50€. Daily 11am–2pm and 5–8pm.*

Guadalupe

Guadalupe's whitewashed houses and patios taken over by bizarro species of cacti will win you over easy. So will the old women and their daughters outside knitting, and the grumpy old men who snore loudly under the glare of the sun. Guadalupe is about 50 years behind the times with vintage Euro cars and old-timer allure. It's the kind of place where locals stare at tourists like they're escaped wackos from the next pueblo over. Walk its narrow roads that lead to rolling forest hills, dusty plazas, occasional goat farms, and tightly strung portico houses. Its life vein is the Virgin Mary of Guadalupe, a small statue housed in the monastery that's almost as big as the town it was built in. The city specializes in religious souvenirs and

Monk-Spotting

The **Real Monasterio** is crawling with monks, and they actually take over the tour when the time comes for the show's big event: the Virgin Mary statue that's locked carefully away in a small closet.

metalwork so it's a great place to buy that genuine tin bed warmer or soup ladle for your Aunt Bessie.

Getting There
BY BUS

The bus company **Sepulvedana** (☎ 902-222-282) runs two buses from Madrid's Estación Sur de Autobuses at Méndez Álvaro, the first at 11:45am, the second at 6:45pm, and a third on Fridays, which leaves at 10:45pm. The trip time is about 3 hours, and a one-way fare is 15€. From Guadalupe to Madrid, catch the bus at the bus shelter on Avenida Conde de Barcelona. Purchase your ticket on the bus. Buses leave for Madrid at 8:45am and 3:35pm. **Mirat** (☎ 927-234-863) has service to and from Trujillo and Cáceres (Estación de Autobuses; ☎ 927-232-550) about two times daily.

BY CAR

Look for directions to the town of Navalmoral de la Mata. From Madrid, take the C-401 road that will give you vertigo weaving in and out of the mountains. The trip time is 3$^1/_2$ to 4$^1/_2$ hours, depending on whether you drive like Fernando Alonso, or your grandpa.

Guadalupe Basics

The **tourist office** (☎ 927-154-128) is located in Plaza Mayor s/n. It is open April to October, Tuesday to Friday 10am to 2pm

and 5 to 7pm, Saturday and Sunday 10am to 2pm; November to March, Tuesday to Friday 10am to 2pm and 4 to 6pm, Saturday and Sunday 10am to 2pm.

In addition to metal, the city also boasts some of the best **specialty goods** around: honey, wine, jam, and cheese by the **Villuercas y Ibores** brand, in particular. **Carnicería Marce** (Pl. de Santa María de Guadalupe 18) will give you a good start on your grocery or gift shopping.

Sleeping

We won't lie to you. If you're staying in Guadalupe for the night, you're going to want to stay at the Hospedería del Real Monasterio (see below), if you can swing the few extra euros. It's the starlet of the city and attached to the main attraction—the monastery.

HOSTEL

➔**Hostal Isabel** Low quality and cheap price meet best location. This one-star hostel is for fickle travelers who want Plaza Mayor action but have more peanuts than *centavos* in their pockets. Although the private bathrooms are clean, mattresses are lumpy and mattress pads are absent. Some rooms are windowless save for a small porthole-size skylight. The doors lock when the restaurant below does, so if you come home late, you'll have to wake up the old woman who can barely walk—not a problem, if you don't have a conscience. The restaurant offers the same good value. *Plaza Santa María de Guadalupe 13.* ☎ *927-367-126. Single 18€, double 30€. Amenities: Bar, restaurant, TV in restaurant. In room: Sheets, towels.*

DOABLE

📺 Best ☻ ➔**Hospedería del Real Monasterio** Attached to the monastery and with every God-given right to be

EXTREMADURA

called a parador, it was justly kept for the working class man. Dating from the 16th century as a weigh station for pilgrims visiting the shrine, it demands your respect upon entering rooms in the oldest part of the original cloister (which you should request). Everything was preserved including heavy wooden doors and soaring trestle ceilings with low-hung chandeliers. Its many impressive salons are the perfect place to pop the question if the occasion should arise because, besides tourists, most people who stay here are part of wedding parties. Say a big "I do" to this place, and you'll for sure get lucky. *Monasterio.* ☎ *927-367-000. Single 43€, double for single use 49€, double 61€, triple 82€, quadruple 91€. Amenities: Bar, restaurant (meal 20€, breakfast 6.50€), telephone, travel info, TV, rooms for those w/limited ability. In room: A/C, TV.*

➜ **Hotel Rural Posada del Rincón** Although you're not in the monastery (see above), this is as close as you're gonna get, Bubba, with windows and skylights that practically look into the Catholic mother of all monasteries. Its new renovation accents original exposed brick, wood beams, and slanted ceilings. Huge, inviting common salons come complete with fireplaces and cozy corners to play cards during winter months. The hotel is also attached to the best restaurant in the city (see "Eating"). *Plaza Santa María de Guadalupe 11.* ☎ *927-367-114. www.posadadelrincon.com. Doubles 65€–72€, singles 42€–46€, extra beds 18€. Amenities: Bar, breakfast room (3€), laundry service. In room: A/C, TV, hair dryer.*

Eating

What you see is what you get in Guadalupe, where the best eating is at the foot of the monastery in the Plaza Mayor. Read on 'cause some are better than others and almost all of them are slightly overpriced.

CHEAP

➜ **Hostal Taruta (Copas Gollum)** PIZZA/CAFE What do you get when you cross a hostel, a bar, an ice-cream parlor, a cybernet cafe, and a *pizzaría?* Whatever it is, it ain't Disney World, sugar. Located on the only hopping street in Guadalupe, this late-night noshery is set up for cyber-folk with thin wallets. Beware of the drunks who like to harass American girls. *Alfonso el Onceno 28.* ☎ *927-367-465. Pizza 6.50€. Daily 6pm–3am.*

DOABLE

➜ **Hotel Rural Restaurante** ★★ MODERN EXTREMADURAN This is the restaurant for folks fixing for flavor on the plaza. The award-winning Spanish chef/owner is a local celebrity for the dishes he serves up, such as his justifiably famous *patatera* mixed with honey (9€). The meaty spread has to be prepared in advance so let Pedro know you're coming. The house specialty is a succulent grilled goat, but order the *menú del día* as, clearly, it's the best deal in town. *Plaza Santa María de Guadalupe 11.* ☎ *927-367-140. Menú del día 10€. Meal including wine 35€. Daily 1–4pm and 8–11pm. Reservations recommended.*

➜ **Mesón el Cordero** EXTREMADURAN This mom and pop restaurant is a 20-year-old has-been, but it is still well known for serving some of the best *asado de cordero* (roast lamb) in the region. Miguel and Angelita also serve up some mean *sopa Guadalupana* (a creamy soup with ham and egg). Don't leave the place without trying the house dessert: *flan casero.* Your taste buds will thank you, but the old-fart ambience won't. *Alfonso el Onceno 27.* ☎ *927-367-131. Menú del día 20€. Tues–Sun 1–4pm and 7–11pm. Closed Jan. Reservations recommended.*

Partying

The best and only street for partying in Guadalupe is Calle Alfonso el Onceno, where you'll find a few cafes and bars that serve ice cream and drinks until late night.

➜ **Casa Malia** This is the best place for 20- and 30-somethings to hang out; it's an old theater that left its big screen on display. Jumbo games are broadcast, as well as MTV music videos on Saturday nights. Bingo, a foosball table, a dartboard, and a pool table will keep even the worst case of ADHD occupied for a night. The same owners also run a dance club on the same street, **Discoteca Vértice,** open on weekends. *Alfonso el Onceno 14. No phone. www. casamalia.net.*

Sightseeing

➜ **Real Monasterio de Santa María de Guadalupe** ★★★ This monastery is a shrine to the ⓂⓉⓋ Best✪ **most holy doll** in existence, the patron saint of the entire territory. The story goes that at the end of the 13th century, a shepherd from Cáceres, Gil Cordero, came across a clothed sable statue of the Virgin Mary hidden by Christians who fled the Arabic reconquest. The shepherd built a small shrine inside a church in town. In 1330, Alfonso XI was disgusted to see the church had fallen into disrepair and demanded a new church be built in the doll's honor. The church, rolling in monies from outside contributions, continued to undergo further expansion for the rest of the 14th century. The first baptisms documented in the church's registry were Columbus's Indian servants 4 years after he discovered the Americas.

The tour starts slow, in the **Museo de Bordados** where woven vestments are on display. The **Museo de Libros Miniados** showcases giant choral books—track lighting wasn't an option then so the monks made fonts giant-size. In the **Museo de Pintura y Escultura,** there's a crucifixion supposedly done by Michelangelo and paintings by El Greco and Goya. The **sacristy** houses paintings by Zurbarán and a Turkish lantern taken by the Christians in a game of capture the flag at the Battle of Lepanto. The **Relicario-Tesoro** holds relics and a crown suited for Miss Universe (it's actually for the Virgin Mary) made of ice, ice, baby. The tour ends in the statue's own booty room, the **Camarín** ★★, where you'll find nine paintings of women from the Old Testament by Italian painter Luca Giordano. A monk will stop you here to bow for prayer. Don't feel bad for not knowing it; just clasp your hands and close or lower your eyes to be respectful. He'll dig for a key in his robe, unlock the door to the main attraction, and ask that everyone form a line, in order to kiss the silver medallion encasing a piece of her mantle. Stay calm, atheists; it's not mandatory. Enthusiasts also bring everyday objects to be blessed such as pens or rosaries. It's rumored the statue was carved by St. Luke in the 1100s, but historians believe it belonged to the *Virgenes Negras de la Europa Occidental* (Black Virgins of the Occident—great name for a chick band) from the 1st and 2nd centuries. *Plaza de Juan Carlos 1. ☎ 927-367-000. Admission 3€. Tickets are sold in gift shop. Guided tours only. Daily 9:30am–1pm and 3:30–6:30pm.*

Playing Outside

If you're homesick for your **dirt bike** on the range, get a hold of **Quads Villuercas** (☎ **636-264-382**) for guided tours of the Extremaduran extremities.

For naturalists, become a mounted tourist with **Chalrro** (☎ **927-367-186** and **608-926-037**) and explore Spain's wild outback on **horseback.**

EXTREMADURA

📺 Best ✿ Mérida

Why go to Rome when Mérida will do? Declared the winner of the *Patrimonio de la Humanidad,* a prestigious award granted by the United Nations Educational, Scientific, and Cultural Organization, in 1993, Mérida, like Rome, is a tourist town for its righteous ruins, not to mention one of the most important cities in Extremadura, as it now seats the regional government.

It began as a retirement town, a sort of Florida for veteran soldiers during the time of Augustine's Roman Empire. Its Roman theater, amphitheater, forums, water, and regular chariot races drew settlers (an estimated 40,000) to the region's capital, as well as crowds from outlying suburbia. Mérida developed into a political, cultural, military, and economic heartthrob of Hispania until the Visigoths rained on its parade centuries later. In the 6th century, ownership changed to the Christians for 200 years, until the Arabs took interest. Once the Catholic kings reconquered the region, Mérida's ruins were safe until the French jacked everything up in the 19th century. Modern restoration didn't get rolling until the late 19th century, and many Spaniards today criticize their harried upkeep.

Getting There & Around

BY TRAIN

Trains depart from and arrive at the **RENFE station** (☎ 902-240-202) on Calle Carderos, about a half-mile north of the Plaza de España. Trains run to Cáceres, Monday to Friday six times per day, four times on the weekend (trip time: 1 hr.); to Badajoz, Monday to Friday fives times per day, three times on the weekend (trip time: 1hr.); to Zafra, Monday to Friday four times per day, three times on the weekend (trip time: 1 hr. 10 min.); to Seville, Monday to

You Might Be an Extremaduran Redneck If . . .

1. You drive a four-wheel dirt bike and leave it parked outside your door.
2. You finish all adjectives with *-ino,* the Spanish likes of a Texas twang.
3. You enjoy eating all parts of the pig—head, ears, and tongue included.
4. You sport a faded "Extremoduro" metal-head T-shirt more often than not.
5. You drink *calimotxo* (wine and coke) mixed with *licor de bellota* (acorn liquor).

Friday six times per day (trip time: 5 hr.); to Madrid, Monday to Friday five times per day, four times on Saturday, and three times on Sunday (trip time: 5–7 hr.). The fare from Madrid to Mérida ranges depending on the train, from 25€ to 30€. From the train station in Mérida, head out the door uphill on Calle Carderos until you hit Calle Extremadura. If you keep heading straight, you'll run right into the center of town, about a 10-minute walk.

BY BUS

The **bus station** is on Avenida de la Libertad (☎ 924-371-404), near the train station. Every day, five to six buses go to and from Madrid, two of which run express (trip time: 5¹/₂ hr.); seven buses cruise to and from Seville (trip time: 3 hr.); one to five buses run to and from Cáceres (trip time: 1 hr.); and 5 to 10 buses go to and from Badajoz (trip time: 1 hr.). From Mérida to

Mérida

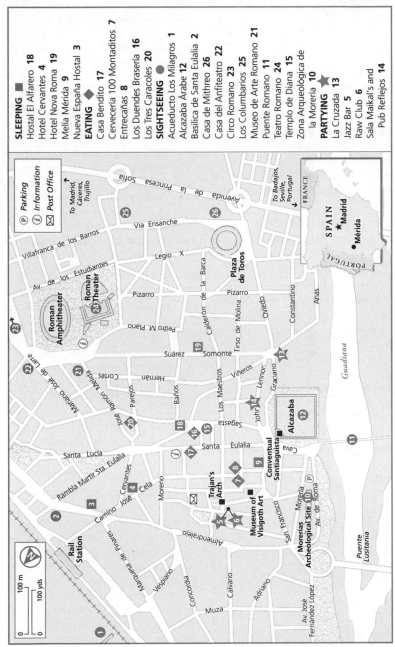

SLEEPING ■
Hostal El Alfarero **18**
Hotel Cervantes **4**
Hotel Nova Roma **19**
Melia Mérida **9**
Nueva España Hostal **3**
EATING ◆
Casa Bendito **17**
Cervecería 100 Montaditos **7**
Entrecañas **8**
Los Duendes Brasería **16**
Los Tres Caracoles **20**
SIGHTSEEING ●
Acueducto Los Milagros **1**
Alcazaba Árabe **12**
Basílica de Santa Eulalia **2**
Casa de Mithreo **26**
Casa del Anfiteatro **22**
Circo Romano **23**
Los Columbarios **25**
Museo de Arte Romano **21**
Puente Romano **11**
Teatro Romano **24**
Templo de Diana **15**
Zona Arqueológica de
la Morería **10**
PARTYING ★
La Cruzada **13**
Jazz Bar **5**
Raw Club **6**
Sala Maikal's and
Pub Reflejos **14**

Madrid, the fare is 19€ to 24€; Mérida to Seville, 11€; Mérida to Cáceres, 4€; and Mérida to Badajoz, 4€.

BY CAR

To drive, take the N-V superhighway from Madrid or Lisbon. Driving time from Madrid is roughly 5 hours; from Lisbon, about 4¹/₂ hours. It's best to park in front of the Roman theater and hike it from there. *Ten cuidado* (watch out) for the mopeds; they're crazy fast and furious in this city. If you've got a lead foot, you'll fit right in. The only chance you've got to get in the race, however, is **AVIS** (☎ **924-373-311**) at the bus station.

BY BICYCLE & MOPED

You can always rent a boring bike, but we recommend bumping like the Romans in a Ciclosport (two-person bike with hood), or the Ciclobus (four-person bike with hood). At **Cyclotour** (below the Puente Lusitania in Parque del Molino de Pancaliente; ☎ **646-216-341**; www.cyclotouristic.com; open daily 11am–sunset), a Ciclosport costs 4€ for a half-hour and 6€ for 1 hour; a Ciclobus costs 6€ for a half-hour and 10€ for 1 hour; a regular Roman bike is 6€ for 2 hours, 10€ for 4 hours, and 18€ for 8 hours. Tours of the city are available in English. We also spotted dirt bikes parked outside apartment buildings, a fact that doesn't help Extremadura's redneck reputation. Popping wheelies is popular for tourists, as well.

A company called **Cuadrigas Tour** (C. Sagasta 9; ☎ **609-104-020**; www.cuadrigas.com) offers Mérida tours—on scooters for about 15€ per hour. We think this is genius, especially for hung-over afternoons when your feet aren't made for walking.

BY FOOT

Walking tours of the city are available in Spanish only. Contact the tourist office or find the booth outside the entrance to the Roman theater. For the full day (10am–7pm), sound equipment costs 15€ plus a 20€ deposit you'll get back when you return the gear. For half a day, it's 10€, plus the 20€ deposit.

Mérida Basics

ORIENTATION

The train station is north of the city. The river Guardiana runs west of the city. Plaza España is the largest square in Mérida and lies on the western side. The bigger Roman ruins such as the theaters are all on the east side of town, though there are others that are scattered throughout Mérida's well-labeled streets. The city is small so it's easy to hoof it. It will take you about 20 minutes to walk from one end to the other.

TOURIST OFFICE

The **Oficina Municipal de Turismo** (☎ **924-330-722**) is at Santa Eulalia 64. The **Oficina de Información Turísticas** (Paseo Sáenz de Buruaga, near entrance to Roman Theater; ☎ **924-009-730**) is just as helpful though probably farther from your hotel. Tourist offices are open June to September 9:30am to 1:45pm and 5 to 7:15pm; October to May, 9am to 1:45pm and 4 to 6:15pm. On weekends all year-round, they are open Saturday and Sunday 9:30am to 1:45pm.

RECOMMENDED WEBSITES

At **www.merida.es**, the main site for the city, you'll find news, restaurants, hotels, local fun facts, and information regarding La Ruta de la Tapa (The Tapa Route), an annual city-sponsored tapa-hopping event usually April through September; we're kicking ourselves for having missed it.

I would walk 500 hundred miles, and I would walk 500 more because Mérida is one of many pit stops on the **Ruta de la Plata** (www.rutadelaplata.com), the pilgrimage commonly known as **El Camino** de Santiago (p. 248). This site gives information and important dates for the long walk ahead. The site is in five languages, including English.

Sleeping

Mérida offers an abundance of places to hang your boots. The problem is finding the quality of hostel that's found in other parts of Spain. Mérida is famous for its ruins, and in many cases its accommodations resemble them.

HOSTELS

➜ **Hostal El Alfarero** ★★★ The only thing missing from this sweeeet abode is a flamenco guitar strumming me to sleep—or else cured ham, but that's found at its namesake tapas bar across the street. The cheery flower-drenched patios, the bright common salon, and the unique ceramic artisan sinks and mirrors will have you snapping your fingers and stomping your feet all the way home. Rooms on the first level have balconies while the rest have large ceiling-to-floor windows, all with bathrooms. This is clearly the best place to stay in a city without many promising options and for a price you can afford. The hydromassager puts the icing on the cake. *Sagasta 40.* ☎ *924-303-183. www.hostalelalfarero.com. No single rooms. Double 45€, triple 61€. Amenities: Sheets, telephone, towels. In room: A/C, TV.*

➜ **Nueva España Hostal** This is the hostel that frequently pops up in most literature because it's cheap and closest to the train station, but those are its only selling points. The hostel is a dour building sitting on a busy street, a 5-minute walk from the center. Rooms are bleak with standard dorm room furniture and fittings. You might want to pack your Prozac, but you can't ask for anything more on a budget than its economical price and standard cleanliness. All rooms have full bathrooms, but make sure to tote your own shampoo. If you are really pinching pennies, the single without a number or a TV is 5€ less expensive than the rest. *Extremadura 6.* ☎ *924-313-356. Single 25€, double 35€, triple 50€. Amenities: Sheets, telephone, towels. In room: A/C, TV.*

DOABLE

➜ **Hotel Nova Roma** This place is so brand new we got high off the paint fumes. Decorated with (fake) Roman busts, it's impossible to forget the Roman theater and the National Museum of Roman Art are only 100m (328 ft.) away. The staff wants to make a good first impression and is very polite to non-Spanish-speaking foreigners. There's a restaurant and cafe attached if you're too lazy to drag yourself somewhere else to eat. The rooms themselves are your typical biz man's home away from home: comfortable but lacking personality. The bathrooms, however, are CEO with inlaid marble and lots of drying-off room. *Suárez Somonte 42.* ☎ *924-311-261. www.novaroma.com. Rates depend on hotel capacity. Double 50€–84€, double with extra bed 84€–111€. Amenities: Bar and restaurant, elevator, kitchen, laundry service, telephone, travel info. In room: A/C, satellite TV.*

SPLURGE

➜ **Meliá Mérida** This five-star hotel located on Plaza España is the crème de la crème of hotels in Mérida. It's actually a chain, but all signs of corporate branding are tastefully swept under the beds. Perhaps that's why it's one of the only hotels I've seen in this part of the country

wwwired

To hotwire, go to **@rroba.com,** Camilo José Cela 28 (near Av. de Extremadura). Daily 11am to 2pm and 5pm to midnight.

with a swimming pool on the roof, a fact worth the steep price when it's summer in Extremadura. The haute dining restaurant also cooks up small snacks, and the bar cafeteria spreads a breakfast buffet. Rooms are straightforward four-star luxurious with comfortable beds and vacation elegance. *Plaza España 19.* ☎ *924-383-800. www.solmelia.com. Single 100€, double 155€, extra bed 50€. Breakfast is 15€. Amenities: Cafeteria and restaurant, elevator, Internet (ADSL connection), laundry service, telephone, travel info, rooms for those w/limited mobility, room service, rooftop swimming pool, gymnasium. In room: A/C, TV, minibar, hair dryer, Internet connection, safe.*

Eating

Who said grazing was bad? In Spain, snacking is the key to a Mediterranean diet, and it's no different in Mérida, where some of Extremadura's best tapas are served. Mérida locals spend their nights in terraced tapas bars near Roman ruins and stuff themselves to the gills. Tapas joints with a view are easy to find, and some bars serve tapas on private patios.

HOT SPOTS

→**Casa Bendito** EXTREMADURA Disguised as an antiquated outdoor market, this jumbo outdoor patio serves food and major ambience for Mérida's newbies; head down for a beer upon arrival and shake the travel lag. They also serve food such as salads, eggs, and brochettes, albeit a little overpriced and extremely touristy. *Calle San Francisco 3.* ☎ *924-330-769. Tapas of the day 2.20€. Platters and raciónes 4€–15€. Daily noon–midnight.*

→**Los Duendes Brasería** ★★ EXTREMADURA Forget your ancient Lite-Brite . . . this restaurant's nightlight is centuries old: the Roman forum, a surreal site by night that brings together locals and tourists in a harmonic symbiosis. Serving

all the right Extremaduran foods, you can't find a better terraza to eat on, as long as you can snag a table and chair to park it. Better to beat the late-night dinner crowds and drink your morning coffee where the Romans might have. *Berzocana 1 (near Templo de Diana).* ☎ *924-301-824. Tapas 5€–15€. Mon–Fri 7:30am–midnight; Sat 9am–1am; Sun noon–midnight.*

CHEAP & TAPAS

→**Cervecería 100 Montaditos** TAPAS One hundred choices of tapas on the wall. Take one down and pass it around, 99 choices of tapas on the wall. You get the idea. Homemade tapas take the form of small sandwiches, served Lazy Susan-style on a wooden wheel and decorated with chips for the entire table to share. This corner joint is a chain but the best place to start your night eating—and drinking—all in moderation, *of course. Felix Valverde Lillo 3.* ☎ *902-197-494. www.cerveceria100montaditos.es. Mini sandwiches .90€–1.20€. Daily 8am–midnight.*

→**Los Tres Caracoles** ★★★ TAPAS/EXTREMADURA This bustling, newly reformed, minimalist tapas bar for adult hipsters is the best buy in town for your money. Serving high-class, inexpensive tostadas such as duck and fruit, cold soups such as melon and gazpacho, and it's namesake platter, snails, all for unbeatable prices, it wins a blue ribbon for best dive. Matching its artistic, steely appearance, The Three Snails' art gallery upstairs occasionally opens during the busy season. *Sagasta 21 (near Foro Romano). No phone. Tapas and tostadas 1€–4€. Snails 3€. Mon–Sat 1pm–12:30am.*

DOABLE

→**Entrecañas** TAPAS Right across the street from Cervecería 100 Montaditos is another noshery with a hefty Extremaduran wine collection, tapas, and outdoor seating. It's brand spankin' new and attractive to young people who want to ching-ching with their loose change. Start by ordering a glass of the Ribera del Guardiana wine, with a ham and egg tostada. *Felix Valverde Lillo 4.* ☎ *924-301-742. Half ración of tapas 1.20€–2€. Full ración 4€–11€. Daily 8am–midnight.*

Partying

Clearly, the plan of attack is divided into two parts: **John Lennon Street** (for those who want to cut a rug) and Plaza Constitución, better known as **Plaza Parador,** for nocturnal cafes and jazz clubs. These are both areas studded with bars and clubs, sexy, seedy, and/or super *bueno.* These are our picks.

CLUBS

➜ **Raw Club** ★ DJs traveling through town might stop here to turn tables or kick back a rum and coke (the secret's in the raw sugar). Although the cocktail prices are on the pricey side (about 7€), it doesn't matter because the video art and the view of the Plaza Parador more than makes up for it. During the day, the '70s-Euro-style cafe throws out its bistro chairs for chatty coffee drinkers, and at night, the club pumps up the volume for electro-imbibed Méridians of all ages. Arrive here after 1am to get action on your hook. *Plaza de la Constitución 2 (2nd floor).* ☎ *699-532-799.*

➜ **Sala Maikal's and Pub Reflejos** For the hard-core partiers, or for the night that unexpectedly keeps going, here's a place that really offers something for everyone. Known for its concert venue, **Sala Maikal's** plays a li'l of everything, but mostly Spanish pop. Inside Maikal's is **Reflejos,** a tiny bar for *heavies,* or hard rockers. The floors and the counters are sticky, and undoubtedly there's no toilet paper in the bathrooms, but it's just that kind of place. *John Lennon 19. No phone. www.saladiscoteatro.com. No cover Thurs and Fri, 6€ cover on Sat, includes 1 drink.*

LIVE MUSIC

➜ **Jazz Bar** ★ Right next door to Raw Club is this smokin' bar. Every Tuesday there's live jazz music, making it the most jiving bodega in town for the 30-something crowd. You don't have to be a jazz aficionado or wear an artsy-fartsy beret to have a good time, as long as you dig its chilled-out vibe. The space is large and the bartenders are attentive so you won't have to wait too long before you get served. *Alvarado 10 (Pl. Constitución, near EL Parador).* ☎ *666-709-263.*

Ⓜ Best ➜ **La Cruzada** ★★★ Enter Camelot where you'll find the best music in town (rock, blues, and jazz) plus live music on Fridays. The medieval decor is cheesy but the beautiful people in tight T-shirts and miniskirts prancing behind the bar make delicious eye candy. Its patrons are 20-something and super hip, making this the hottest late-night club in town for locals and students who like good music and to shake a drum bone. *Atarazanas 2 (next to billiard hall).* ☎ *695-160-018. www. lacruzada.es.*

Sightseeing

Many Spaniards complain that the **Roman ruins** in Mérida haven't been conserved as well as they should have been; however, the amount of objects and ancient architecture unearthed is an impressive fact that should not be underestimated. I mean, give 'em a break; the ruins have had a string of indifferent proprietors following Spain's flip-flopping religious regimes: Romans, Visigoths, Muslims, and finally Christians. In their wake are monuments that withstood centuries of religious wars.

MUSEUMS & MONUMENTS

Tickets are sold in many different ways. To buy a **pass** for the entire city (including the Teatro Romano, Anfiteatro, Casa del Anfiteatro, Casa del Mitreo, Los

Columbarios, Alcazaba, Basilica de Santa Eulalia, Circo Romano, and Zone Arqueológica de Morería), a ticket is 8€ for an adult. Monument visiting hours are June to September 9:30am to 1:45pm and 5 to 7:15pm; October to May, 9am to 1:45pm and 4 to 6:15pm. Basilica de Santa Eulalia is closed on Sundays, and opens a half-hour later than the other monuments (10am). To buy a ticket for only the Teatro Romano and the Anfiteatro, admission is 5.50€ for an adult. You can buy separate tickets for each monument as well, at 2.80€ per adult.

The three emblematic buildings that comprise the **roman monuments** ★★★ made for a killer weekend during Emperor Augustine's reign: **El Teatro Romano,** ▓**Best☻** **El Anfiteatro** (amphitheater), and the **Circo Romano** (ring). Gladiators battled wild animals, or wild animals fought each other, in the amphitheater (built in 8 B.C.) while chariots drag-raced in the ring that held a capacity of 30,000 spectators—the only one like it in Spain.

Next to the entrance on Calle José Ramón Mélida is the **interpretation center** that's worth a gander. In 3D (and in Spanish), learn about the life of a Roman speed racer fit for a Wheaties box who kicked it in the Hipódromo ring during Diocletian times.

Preferred Roman sport aside, for a more cultured evening, Romans might have attended a play, a concert, or a political forum at the theater, an activity more representative of the pragmatic times emphasized by its fine architecture and iconographic sculpture. The Romans raised the roof with an orchestra pit in the front of the theater and acoustics bouncing from center stage.

Outside the theater in the **Casa del Anfiteatro** is where the cake-eaters lived; the richest people in town set up camp here, leaving authentic foundation, floor mosaics, and walls with traces of high-quality Roman art depicting Venus and Eros.

In the same 'hood are the **baths,** a site proving Roman life was filled with small pleasures. Kitchens, ovens, wells, and gardens surround the site that was also used as a cemetery after the 5th century.

El Acueducto de los Milagros was built in I B.C. and finished in A.D. 3. Its large arches, 25m (82 ft.) high, were built to bring water to the city. Perhaps even more impressive are the ▓**Best☻** gigantic **stork nests** that look like something out of *Neverending Story.*

Zona Arqueológica de la Morería was an immigrant settlement used by every establishment: Romans, Visigoths, and Arabs. Explaining everything in Spanish layman's terms is the Center of Interpretation of the Vía de la Plata. On Avenida de Roma, you'll bump into the **Roman bridge,** constructed around 25 B.C. as one of the longest ever made.

Head northeast on Calle Sagasta, and you'll run into **Templo de Diana,** the only religious temple still standing from the Ist century B.C. Later during the Renaissance, it was converted into a count's palace. Just across the way is the **Pórtico del Foro,** where statutes excavated from the site are on open-air display.

South of the city on Calle Oviedo is **La Casa de Mithreo,** the ruins of a 2nd-century Roman residence consisting of three patios, frescoed bedrooms, gardens, and baths. The jewel of the house, however, is the Mosaic Cosmologic.

Nearby is **Los Columbarios** where the gravesite of two leading families has been restored. A center for interpretation at the site delves 1.8m (6 ft.) under, more or less according to Roman tradition.

➔ **Basilica de Santa Eulalia** Head down Avenida de Extremadura and pass by the basilica of Santa Eulalia, a national monument originally built in honor of the god Mars. The Christians later converted it to pay respects to its namesake saint, who was martyred on the spot in A.D. 303. Rumor has it the saint is buried here, but other churches have made the same claim. *Extremadura s/n.* ☎ *924-303-407. Admission 3€. June–Sept daily 10am–1:45pm and 5–7:15pm; Oct–May daily 10am–1:45pm and 4–6:15pm.*

→ **La Alcazaba Árabe** The Muslim fortress, dating back to A.D. 835, was strategically built near the bridge as probably the first military building build in Spain. Take note of the Aljibe (a huge well). Of course, it was conquered when the Christians took over, and now its 15th-century monastery is used as Extremadura's presidential office. You can scale its walls for a photo op of the river. *Graciano s/n.* ☎ *924-317-309. Admission 3.50€. Aug daily 9:30am–1:45pm and 5–8:15pm; June–July daily 9:30am–1:45pm and 5–7:30pm; Sept–May daily 9:30am–1:45pm and 4–6:15pm.*

→ **National Museum of Roman Art** ★★ This must-see museum's Roman heads, monuments, and excavated tools such as ceramics, glass, hair clips, and dice are just as interesting as the building in which they're exhibited. Make sure you wind your way down to the dark crypt, where the frescoed walls of old Roman houses are still intact. It's a quick trip that won't hog your entire day. *José Ramón Mélida (near the entrance to Teatro Romano).* ☎ *924-311-690*

and 924-311-912. www.mnar.es. Free admission Sat after 4pm, Sun, May 18, Oct 12, and Dec 6; regular admission 2.40€. Dec 1–Feb 28 Tues–Sat 10am–2pm and 4–6pm; Mar 1–Nov 30 Tues–Sat 10am–2pm and 4–9pm; year-round Sun and festivals 10am–2pm. Closed Mon.

FESTIVALS & EVENTS

Mérida is the best place in Extremadura to spend **Semana Santa.** The religious processions wheel around the ancient Roman monuments toward the Anfiteatro creating a religious juxtaposition that would make Medusa's head spin. However, Mérida is most known for its **Festival de Teatro Clásico** (www.festivaldemerida.es) during the hot months of July and August. Thousands of theater buffs flock to the Roman theater and watch as real performances are re-created in front of the marble busts of ancient times. Between October 9th and 12th, the gypsies all over Spain shake their booties in the streets of Mérida during **Feria de los Gitanos.**

Shopping

Mérida has lots of commercial shopping in the heart of the city—though sorry, dude, it's mainly for chicks. Start your spree at **Puerta de la Villa** (where the fountain is, also a good meeting spot) and stroll down **Calle Santa Eulalia.** For tourist relics, search artisan shops that lace the streets near the Roman theaters along **Calle José Ramón Mélida.**

Cáceres

It's a tale of two cities, the new and the old. Chances are if you're in Cáceres, you're there to see the latter, 🎵 Best● **Ciudad Monumental,** which is chock-a-block full of regal palaces. Built in the 13th century, it was a safe haven for aristocrats to roll around in their New World money with the condition they supported the

Catholic kings. Many of the impressively conserved buildings are still occupied by the city's well-to-doers.

On the other hand, if you're a beatnik like Jack Kerouac, there's another reason to make this your destination, and it involves thousands of international, 20-something hippies, 40s of beer, and hash: WOMAD

Save Those Euro Cents

If I had a euro for every four-star 14th-century parador in Spain, I could afford to spend a night in one. The **parador** (Ancha 6, in the old town; ☎ **927-211-759;** www.parador.es) in Cáceres is special because, unlike most medieval towns in Spain, the ancient city is completely protected from modern progress. That means no vinyl siding or graffitied phone booths. Even if you don't have the cash to book a room, then at least pass by for a *café con leche* on the enclosed patio encrusted with ivy and Gothic splendor or in the hotel's bar, all formally part of the Palacio de Torreorgaz. Depending on the day and the month, the parador offers young people between the ages of 20 and 30 a special discount.

(World of Music, Art, and Dance), where *botellónes* (informal outdoor drink-ups) and free concerts run rampant throughout the old city.

We should also mention Cáceres is the capital city of its own region, a resting place for *peregrinos* (pilgrims) of El Camino de Santiago (p. 248), and the second biggest town in Extremadura. The pride and joy of Cáceres is Ciudad Monumental, the walled-in historic district.

Getting There

BY TRAIN

Don't sweat catching the train to Madrid. There are seven leaving the station for Madrid daily (trip time: 4–5 hr.). A one-way ticket costs 16€ to 24€. One train per day also runs from Seville (trip time: 6 hr.) for 15€. The station in Cáceres is on Avenida Alemania (☎ 902-240-202), near the main highway heading south. Exit the train station and cross the bridge to the other side near the gas station. The no. 1 bus at the bus shelter there will take you into town. The bus driver is used to tourists taking this route and can likely advise you when to get off.

BY BUS

Bus connections to Cáceres are much more frequent; the bus terminal (☎ 927-232-550) is situated about a walkable half-mile south of the city's center on Carretera de

Sevilla. Buses arrive and depart for Madrid (trip time: 5 hr.) and Seville (trip time: 4¹/₂ hr.) every 2 to 3 hours. Buses also run to Guadalupe (one per day); Trujillo (six or seven per day); Mérida (four per day); Valladolid (two a day); and Córdoba (two per day).

BY CAR

Driving time from Madrid is about 4 hours. If you're coming from the east, take the N-V (main highway) to Cáceres until you reach Trujillo. Exit onto the N-521, and drive another 45km (28 miles) west until you see Cáceres. Here are your two options for renting: **AVIS,** Estación de Autobuses (☎ 927-235-721 and 653-581-270). If that doesn't work, which it often doesn't, then try, **EUROPCAR,** Plus Ultra 1 (☎ 927-212-988).

Cáceres Basics

Inside the fortress wall is the old town of Cáceres, a tightly wound world of its own. Outside the wall to its northeast is the heartbeat of the city, Plaza Mayor and the new city. Offshoot streets that will lead you to Avenida de España are Gran Vía and Calle Pintores. Parque del Principe, the cities outlaying park, is directly northwest of the city, and on the clear other side is Parque del Rodeo. Avenida Alemania does the job of getting you to both the bus station and the train station.

Cáceres

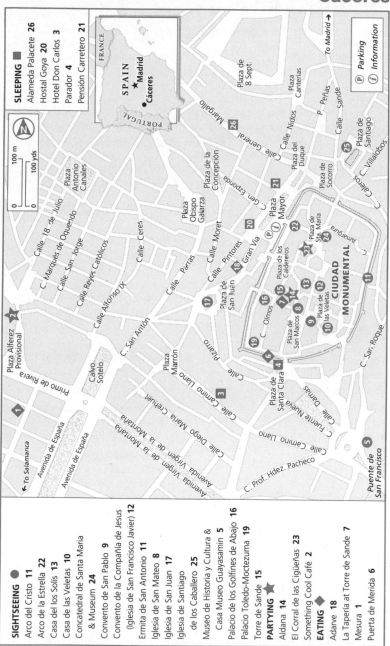

SIGHTSEEING ●
Arco del Cristo **11**
Arco de la Estrella **22**
Casa del los Solís **13**
Casa de las Veletas **10**
Concatedral de Santa María & Museum **24**
Convento de San Pablo **9**
Convento de la Compañía de Jesus (Iglesia de San Francisco Javier) **12**
Ermita de San Antonio **11**
Iglesia de San Mateo **8**
Iglesia de San Juan **17**
Iglesia de Santiago de los Caballero **25**
Museo de Historia y Cultura & Casa Museo Guayasamin **5**
Palacio de los Golfines de Abajo **16**
Palacio Toledo-Moctezuma **19**
Torre de Sande **15**

PARTYING ★
Aldana **14**
El Corral de las Cigüeñas **23**
Something Cool Café **2**

EATING ◆
Adarve **18**
La Tapería at Torre de Sande **7**
Mesura **1**
Puerta de Mérida **6**

SLEEPING ■
Alameda Palacete **26**
Hostal Goya **20**
Hotel Don Carlos **3**
Parador **4**
Pensión Carretero **21**

Ⓟ Parking
ⓘ Information

To Madrid →
To Salamanca →
← To Madrid

SPAIN
★ Madrid
● Cáceres
PORTUGAL
FRANCE

0   100 m
0   100 yds

Talk of the Town

Six Ways to Start a Conversation with a Local

1. It's a scorcher! If you think it's hot in hell, then you've never been to Extremadura, where skin sizzles. People talk about the heat like Americans talk about the NFL; it's the most generic way to start a conversation with a local. .

2. Madrileños are to Extremadurans what New Yorkers are to Texans. From their perspective, Madrileños roll through town acting like they own the joint (and like New Yorkers, many times they do). Start ragging on the city slickers, and yokels will warm right up.

3. Where can I find the best *licor de bellota?* This regional acorn liquor has its roots in Extremadura, and most likely there's a local joint where it's poured more than water.

4. Where's the *botellón?* Translation: Where's the outdoors 40s 'n' blunts party?

5. Is that a *burro* I see? Some types of donkeys like the Andaluz donkey are extinct or going that way, but in Extremadura, donkeys still . . . do whatever it is they do.

6. Where is everyone? At around 3pm, the siesta party starts in Extremadura. The streets are so empty you expect tumbleweeds to blow through. Ask a local *Donde está la gente* (Where is everyone?) and he'll point you in the direction of a bar, to which you can invite him/her.

The **tourist office** (☎ 927-010-834) is centrally located at Plaza Mayor 10. It is open for biz June to September Monday to Friday 9am to 2pm and 5 to 7pm; October to May Monday to Friday 9am to 2pm and 4 to 6pm; open year-round Saturday and Sunday 9:45am to 2pm. The second office (☎ 927-247-172), on Calle Ancah 7, keeps the following schedule: Monday to Saturday 9:15am to 2pm and 4:30 to 6:45pm; Sunday 10am to 2pm.

Just because you're in a medieval town doesn't mean you have to smell like a touring knight. Take your dank clothes to **Tintorería-Lavandería Zeus** (Plaza de Noruega 3; ☎ 927-236-463; Mon–Sat 9:30am–2pm and 5–8pm; closed Sun), the only laundromat we found that agrees to touch your panties, boxers, or briefs.

Drop a letter to your family telling them you've joined the Spanish circus. The **correos** is at Paseo de Primo de Rivera 2 (Mon–Fri 8:30am–8:30pm; Sat 9am–2pm).

RECOMMENDED WEBSITES

For a lowdown on all the events in Cáceres, as well as history, government, and tourist information such as restaurants, monuments, and even a street finder, check out **www.ayto-caceres.es**, only in Spanish.

With **www.paseovirtual.net/caceres**, you can take a virtual tour through Cáceres before you even get there.

To get the who, what, when, and where of WOMAD in Cáceres, visit this site: **www.bme.es/womad**.

Sleeping

It's not hard to find central accommodation unless it's during festival or WOMAD (World of Music, Art, and Dance) And many hostels and even hotels will offer

wwwired

....

The closest place near the center to hit up Internet access is a dimly lit storefront with no A/C called **Ciberjust** (C. de Diego Maria Crehuet 7; ☎ **927-214-677**). It costs 1€ for 30 minutes. Open Monday to Friday 10am to 11:30pm; Saturday and Sunday 5 to 11:30pm.

discounts to younger travelers or those who are walking el Camino de Santiago. So make sure to ask before booking your reservation.

HOSTELS

➔ **Alameda Palacete** ★★ Next to the Parador and Plaza Mayor, this renovated 19th-century mansion is the best place to stay in the city. In the upstairs suite, full light, zebra rugs, and fresh-cut flowers welcome relieved guests old and young with backpacks. The gigantic bathroom is more than enough room for three (obese) men in a tub. Coffee and orange juice are served on the patio. The woman who owns the palace treats all her guests with the reserved grace of a Gatsby aristocrat. It's enough not to want to leave, and you'll be sinking your nails into the place when it's time. *Calle General Margallo 45.* ☎ *927-211-674 and 927-211-262. www.alamedapalacete.com. Single 44€, double 65€, triple 75€, quadruple 85€. In Jan and Feb, prices are 5€–10€ cheaper, depending on reserved dates. All rooms have full bathroom. Amenities: Sheets, telephone (in common room), towels, travel info. In room: A/C, TV.*

➔ **Hostal Goya** ★★ If hearts are worn on sleeves, than this staff is sporting bright yellow T-shirts with huge smiley faces. We wanted to jump up and down, too, when we saw the classic Spanish novels randomly placed in each room and the view of the Plaza Mayor. The rooms are large with lots

of walk-about space, and there's even a suit rack to hang your delicates and/or crinkled-and-wrinkled travel trousers. *Calle Plaza Mayor 11.* ☎ *927-249-950. www.hotelgoya.net. Single 42€, double 50€. Amenities: Fax, laundry service, sheets, telephone (in common room), towels, travel desk, TV (in common room), medical services, veterinary services (in case you're toting your checkbook Chihuahua). In room: A/C, hair dryer, shaving mirror.*

CHEAP

➔ **Pensión Carretero** ★★ Walking into this 70-year-old, family-run pension is like walking into Old World Spain complete with white-lace curtains and rocking chairs. Furniture and finials are sparse but less is more in this grandmalike lodging, snuggly nestled over the Plaza Mayor. The common room's fireplace that burns in the winters adds to its hospitable decor in the summer. All rooms share bathrooms but a few rooms have sinks. *Plaza Mayor 22.* ☎ *927-247-482. Winter months single 15€, double 25€, extra bed 10€; spring and summer months single 20€, double 30€, extra bed 10€. Specials are given to youth walking the Ruta de la Plata (Camino de Santiago). Amenities: Shared bathrooms.*

DOABLE

➔ **Hotel don Carlos** ★★ Another centrally located, 19th-century option that's wicked good for the price is this regal hotel and its professional staff that treats you as if it were a four-star accommodation. Rooms are laundered and scrubbed, and those with balconies look over a small street popular for going out. The Spanish tile floor and original stone arches are a nice touch, reminding you what country you're in after a long night boozing. You're not going to find a better hotel in town for the money. *Calle Donoso Cortés 15 (C. Pizarro).* ☎ *927-225-527. www.hoteldoncarloscaceres. net. Low season (part of Dec, Jan, Feb, and*

July) single 36€, double 42€; high season (spring and summer months) single 45€, double 62€. During long weekends and festivals double 70€–74€. Extra bed 18€. Amenities: Sheets, towel, safe. In room: A/C, TV, hair dryer, Internet (ADSL).

Eating

Spain is known for its quirky service, but in Cáceres there can be an exaggerated case of the slowpokes, particularly if WOMAD is taking place while you are there, taxing the city and its labor force, and leading you to many quick-trip *bocadillos* (sandwiches) to go. In any case, I recommend hitting up the tapas bars; as an outsider you'll have a much better chance of getting noticed.

TAPAS

➜ **Adarve** ★★ TAPAS/BAR Great for tourists who don't speak Spanish, this downtown dive offers pictures of their dishes so you know whether you're ordering tongue or blood sausage before it's under your nose. Usually that means foods come prefabricated, but not here, where everything is made to order. This place is a one-stop wonder for everything Extremaduran *(migas, patatera, torta del casar),* so finish off your checklist of must-try foods. Avoid it at 2pm when it's standing room only. *Calle Sánchez Garrido 4 (off Gran Via or C. Pintores).* ☎ *927-244-874 and 927-248-245. Tapas and tostadas 2€–6€. Mon–Fri 10:30am–midnight; Sat–Sun 9am–5pm and 7:30pm–midnight.*

➜ **La Tapería at Torre de Sande** TAPAS/BAR Attached to the monumental Castillo de la Arguijuela Abajo is a fine-dining banquet hall so beautiful that passersby peer in its gates for a gander at its grandness. Keep dreaming; that's not it. Right next door is its economical protégé, an Extremaduran tapas bar that offers the same first-class atmosphere, but you won't have to wash dishes to foot the bill. This is a great place to stop for a beer and tapas on your tour through the old town. *Calle Condes 3 (Ciudad Monumental).* ☎ *927-211-147. www.torredesande.com. Tapas 4.50€. Daily 12:30pm–4pm and 8:30pm–midnight.*

DOABLE

➜ **Mesura** MEDITERRANEAN Recommended by cute, 20-something students, this hip, ultramodern restaurant, a little out of the way, offers meats, seafood, and veggie-friendly dishes for an unbeatable price, catering to budding professionals with class. Start with a salad and move on to the *tarta de cebolla* or *bacala* (codfish). Best to call ahead for reservations; it's popular. *Calle Obispo Segura Sáez 9 (off Av. España).* ☎ *927-627-515. Platters 7€–13€. Tues–Sat 2–3:45pm and 9–11:15pm. Closed Sun and Mon.*

➜ **Puerta de Mérida** ★★★ MEDITERRANEAN This summer spot is by far the coolest place to get a good dinner. Outdoor seating is set against a flower trellis, a classy look that is only toned down by friendly heavy-metal punk servers. Tuna, asparagus, and *tarta del casar*–drizzled (a strong Extremaduran cheese spread) pork are recommended dishes to share. *Puerta de Mérida 10 (Ciudad Monumental, near Pl. Santa Clara). No phone. Shared platters 12€–20€. Daily noon–12:30am.*

Partying

Cáceres is a great place to get your groove on. It's a university town with lots of traffic to and from its world music festival. Lots of students means fairly priced drinks everywhere. Bar-saturated areas include **Plaza Mayor** (such as Farmácia de Guardia, usually over-packed after 1am on the weekend); **Calle de Pizarro;** streets stemming from **Plaza del Duque** (including C. Gabriel and C. Galán); and for late-night dancing (after 2am); **La Madrila** (namely Pl. Albatros) is loaded with clubs.

➔ **Aldana** ★★★ One of the two hot spots in Ciudad Monumental. Part bar, part venue, this scarlet-red drinking parlor is also used as a cultural center for art exhibits. Its namesake who built the 14th-century house was a high-ranking general under Alfonso VI, and it doesn't seem to have changed one bit. The stately furniture and huge paintings decorate the dignified locale like they might have hundreds of years ago. Although I seriously doubt the general had a taste for hip-hop, jazz, or flamenco. *Orellana 1.* ☎ *927-260-283.*

➔ **El Corral de las Cigüeñas** Another happenin' place in the old city is this cultural center, restaurant, and club, named after the storks that have taken over Cáceres. Its ivy-covered patio and outdoor disco ball will peak your curiosity for a drink. It's also a music venue with a show almost every weekend in the summer, and a good part of them are free. To top if all off, they serve cheap, all-inclusive breakfasts for early risers—or hard-core partiers. *Cuesta de Aldana 6 (near Concatedral de Santa María).* ☎ *647-758-245. www.elcorralcc.com.*

➔ **Something Cool Café** The newest, trendiest dance club in town has a pinewood dance floor that's stick-free, clean smelling, and dotted with New York–style covered sofas. Open as a cafe during the day and disco by night (don't show up until at least 2am), it's refreshing interior and nicely dressed staff attracts clubbers with the same appeal. *Plaza de Albatros. No phone.*

Sightseeing

Locals will tell you **Ciudad Monumental** needs two visits, one during the morning (summer afternoons are too hot) and one at night, which shouldn't be too hard to do, given its nightlife. A few important places are worth checking out, if only in passing (you're not allowed entry in most, as they're either private or gubernatorial).

In the 15th century, **El Convento de San Pablo** and its church with the same name were built (in Pl. de San Mateo) for the Franciscan monks. Now it's famous for its artisan sweets, so stop by and ring the bell to see if their window is open. **Convento de la Compañía de Jesus** is baroque in style and was built just before its members got the boot from Spain. Today it is used for art exhibitions. **Iglesia de San Mateo** is a 15th-century church built on the site of a former mosque. **Iglesia de San Juan** is a huge church, which took 5 centuries to complete, starting in the 13th century. **La Iglesia de Santiago de los Caballero** was probably built on an older existing structure dating all the way back to the 12th century. It's a clear example of the Gothic style converting to the Renaissance. In the old Jewish neighborhood, which once was pretty big, is the modest **Ermita de San Antonio,** built in the 15th century, right on top of an old synagogue.

The main entrance to the Ciudad Monumental is off Plaza Mayor, **Arco de la Estrella,** built for wide loads, in order to let the merchants through. **Torre de Sande** is right in front of **La Casa del los Solís.** The patio is now the residence of a beautiful restaurant bearing the tower's name, centuries after having been badly damaged by orders of unsatisfied Catholic kings, as were many other monuments in the city. Its most impressive keystone is the Gothic window. In the old Jewish barrio is the only Roman entryway that still remains, **Arco del Cristo.**

Palacio de los Golfines de Abajo (C. de los Olmos) is a fine-dining restaurant now, but back in the day Isabella and Ferdinand lived here. It was also Franco's post shortly during the Civil War. **Palacio Toledo-Moctezuma** is where the Aztec princess was brought, in order to live in

Cáceres with her new Spanish conquistador hubby, Juna Cano de Saavedra. **Palacio de Carvajal** is a 15th-century mansion; **Palacio de los Cáceres-Ovando** and **Palacio de Mayoralgo** are both strictly Renaissance in style; **Casa de los Solís** is the most elevated part of the old town, punctuated with the family crest on its Gothic entrance. **Casa Mudejar** (Cuesta de Aldana) has obvious Arab characteristics, rare in these parts.

MUSEUMS

FREE → **Casa de las Veletas** This is an obligatory visit, as it is one of the old 12th-century Alcázars, where a famous *aljibe* (Arab cistern) in its basement still remains. It also houses the **Museo de Cáceres,** exhibiting prehistoric artifacts dating back to the land before time, 7th century B.C. *Palacio de las Veletas.* ☎ 927-010-877. www. museosextremadura.com. Admission 1.20€, but with a E.U. passport, it's free (no love for America). Apr 14–Sept 30 Tues–Sat 9am–2:30pm and 5–8:15pm, Sun 10:15am–2:30pm; Oct 1–Apr 13 Tues–Sat 9am–2:30pm and 4–7:15pm, Sun 10:15am–2:30pm. Library Mon–Fri 9am–2pm. Closed Mon and certain holidays.

→ **Concatedral de Santa Maria and Museum** Plaza Santa Maria is the most important plaza so if you're not minding the crests or signs, make sure you at least note where this Roman-Gothic church is, erected in the 15th and 16th centuries over an older one and crowned with stork nests. Inside the church are three naves containing the gravesite of many conquistadors and a *retablo* (altar) that lights up when you put in some coins. The small museum is nothing special unless you're into religious art and need your fix before the next stop. Once in a while, they'll let people up into the bell tower for a euro, but you'll have to ask once you're there. *Plaza de Santa María.* ☎ 927-215-313. Museum admission 1€.

Mon–Sat 10am–2pm and 5–8pm; Sun 10am–2pm and 5–7:30pm.

FREE → **Museo de Historia y Cultura and Casa Museo Guayasamin** For art lovers, the history and culture center showing Extremaduran art is okay, but much more impressive is the Casa Museo Guayasamin that exhibits 20th-century South American modern art by its namesake, Oswaldo Guayasamin of Ecuador, which creates an interesting snub to the city known for its conquistadors. *In Casa Pedrilla, Puente de San Francisco.* ☎ 927-241-633. Free admission. Tues–Fri 11am–2pm and 5–8pm; Sat–Sun 11am–2pm. Closed Mon.

Festivals & Events

In April, the fiestas dedicated to the city's patron saint, **San Jorge,** kick off on the 22nd and the 23rd. Bullfights ensue. **WOMAD** festivaling usually takes place in mid-May. Stay clear if you're an agoraphobic; there's lots of people, booze, music, and smelly Johnny-on-the-spots. But admittedly, it is one of the best parties in Extremadura, if you like the *botellón* (bottles of beer on the street) scene. At the end of May, the city celebrates **Fiesta de San Fernando** and its ferias: fireworks, bullfights, and drinking. **Festival de Teatro Clásico** takes place in June, commemorating El Siglo del Oro de Cáceres. Finally, the **Mercado Medieval** takes place in November, when undoubtedly there are men in tights.

Shopping

If you're wanting to take home a wheel of *tarta del casar* or any of the other sweets and wines that make Extremadura so extreme, head toward **El Gourmet de la Bellota** specialty foods store (Pl. San Juan 6; ☎ **927-240-724;** Mon–Sat 10am–2pm and 5–9pm, Sun 10am–2pm). To find local crafts, walk along **Plaza Mayor,** but for an outdoor market, breeze by the stalls at **El Mercadillo,** located at Plaza del Indio (Wed 7am–2pm). A hefty shopping zone with something for everyone is **Cruz de los Caídos,** which includes Avenida de Alemania, Calle Gil Cordero, and Avenida Antonio Hurtado. For fashion and accessories, both Spanish and international, go to **Paseo de Cánovas.** Avenida San Pedro de Alcántara, Calle Goméz Becerra, Calle Primo de Riviera, and Avenida Virgen de la Montaña are all offshoots popular for clothing sprees. However, the paseo, itself, along Avenida de España, often turns into a fair for handmade artisan gifts. For the mall rats, there's the **Centro Comercio Ruta de la Plata** housing big clothing franchises. Most shops are open from 10am to 2pm and 5:30 to 8:30pm, though many stay open for siesta, too.

Road Trips

SIERRA DE GATA

The northern region of Cáceres (south of Castile) is **Sierra de Gata,** an area composed of green valleys and pine-fresh northern exposure. The main point here is rainwater collects in the mountains and runs off into small natural swimming pools and damned canals that are as clear as Crystal Light. Rent a car, a rural house, and drive 20 minutes to 1 hour from pool to pool. Just an hour and a half outside of Cáceres, it's the hottest way to explore Extremadura in the summer and still keep your cool. Because you don't pay admission to access the pools, you can spend your money at the canal-side bars. Here are the best in the region:

- **Acebo:** Piscina naturales de Acebo (at Rivera Acebo; ☎ **927-141-677**).

- **Hernán-Peréz:** Piscina natural de Hernán-Pérez (at Río Arago; ☎ **927-445-127**).
- **Hoyos:** Piscina natural de Hoyos (at Rivera Hoyos; ☎ **927-514-002**).
- **Villasbuenas de Gata:** Piscina natural de Villasbuenas de gata (at Valverde-Hervés; ☎ **927-673-078**).
- **Robledillo de Gata:** Piscina natural de Robledillo de Gata (at El Machio s/n; ☎ **927-671-107**).
- **Descargamaría:** Piscina natural Descargamaría (at Cr. Robledillo; ☎ **927-671-021**).

LOS BARRUECOS

South of Malpartida, 14km (8²/₃ miles) outside of Cáceres, is **Los Barruecos,** a natural phenomenon of granite rock, in which rain and time have created small ecosystems. It's a national monument that has preserved white storks, one of the most important species in Europe. This is where you'll also find the **Museo Vostell-Malpartida** (Ctra. de Los Barruecos, Malpartida de Cáceres, Cáceres; ☎ **927-010-812;** www.museovostell.org), an outstanding modern art museum that strangely fits right in with its environment. Created by Wolf Vostell in 1974, it is a vanguard enclave, built from an ancient building used to clean wool. This is a guaranteed good time. Wednesdays are free; otherwise admission is 2€ adults, 1€ students. It is open in the spring from 10am to 1:30pm and 5 to 7:30pm; in the summer from 10:30am to 1:30pm and 5 to 8pm, on Sunday from 10am to 2:30pm; and in the fall and winter from 10am to 1:30pm and 4 to 6:30pm. Closed Mondays.

Castilla y León

by Elizabeth Gorman

Ask anyone and they'll tell you the Leónese know how to host a guest—they've had centuries of practice. During the Middle Ages, those traveling the Camino del Santiago made the region a major pit stop for free food, generous housing, and a wild party on their way along the Jacobean route. Royalty built them hospices, convents, and military stations to lodge and protect the pilgrims, remnants of which can still be seen today at El Convento de San Marcus (now the most expensive place to hang your Armani boots). León hasn't skipped a hostessing beat, even after changing dominions (Roman, Muslim, Christian) more times than Sim City. It was constantly rebuilt until it was finally made the royal seat for the kingdom of León. As to the hostessing skills of Old Castilla, it depends whom you talk to. The region rolls out the red carpet for its local hero El Cid, who took it to the national level, achieving superstar status as a warrior against the Moors. On the other hand, everyone's favorite colonialist, Columbus, didn't fare so well, dying in poverty and disfavor in his later years in Vallodolid (although he's wildly celebrated in modern Spain). But we're pretty sure whichever region you chose, Spain'll bust out the royal treatment for you—just don't go getting wrapped up with any kings and queens on any points of geography, or all bet's are off.

Best of Castilla y León

○ **Best Place to Have a Religious Experience:** The kaleidoscope stained-glass windows in the **Cathedral of León** are out-of-this-world stunning—not to mention dangerous, considering the weak structure and bad quality of stone supporting them. The Gothic shapes and colors put you in a drooling trance while they imprint on your memory for as long as your brain computes. See p. 201.

○ **Best Thirst Quencher for the Wino:** Hailing from Rueda, Valladolid, **Rueda del Duero,** the local Pabst Blue Ribbon of wines, will deliver a dozen fresh roses to your slutty palette. It's the house wine in most restaurants in Valladolid and is cheaply bought by the bottle (7€–14€) at any of the overabundant specialty food shops selling wine and regional foods like olives and oil to tourists on the main drags. See p. 236.

○ **Best Place to Study Abroad:** It's easy to fall in love with Salamanca, and it's easy to come back, as long as it's on a student visa. **Salamanca** is one of the prime party cities in Spain in which to study abroad, so if you think learning is all about lectures and exams, think again. All it takes is a Google and some gonads. See p. 215.

○ **Best Chill Out Scene:** Besides being the political and social meeting point of Salamanca, the **Plaza Mayor** is the best place to plop down and do absolutely nothing or check out the cute prospect licking an ice-cream cone next to you. Perhaps that's what the baroque architects had in mind in 1729 when construction began for the plaza, considered to be one of the most impressive in Spain. See p. 226.

○ **Best Place to Start Worshiping the Devil:** The **Antiguo Museo de Brujería** will make you pee your pants and run to the nearest priest to get blessed. Quick, go to the nearest bar and pick up a bedfellow because you will not want to go to sleep alone. Don't miss it. See p. 237.

○ **Best Attraction:** The legendary **fortress walls** around the city are a key photo op for camera-crazy tourists. Tired of attacks by the Muslims during the 11th century, locals constructed the great wall in Avila where a Roman wall was before, in order to protect the city from intrusions. Most of the wall today remains unchanged since Felipe II restored it in 1596. Now that's *machismo.* Visitors can climb the wall for a panoramic of the outlying country interrupted only by mountains; it's a view that will knock the wind out of you—though the stair climbing will, too. See p. 243.

CASTILLA Y LEÓN

León

León is the gateway city from Galicia, and many people here say the city has more to do with its green Asturian neighbors than its flat-chested Castilian sisters, both in personality and looks. The region outside of the main city is loaded with jewels such as the Picos de Europa, a limestone mountain range marking the spot where León, Asturias, and Cantabria provinces meet. The city of León is more urban than you'd expect, but no doubt the huge welcome mat at the cathedral and wafting smells of cured *cecina* will relax you. The city is manageable on foot with places to *tapear* (take tapas) and drink condensed in one important area, so if there are two words to remember in León, they are: **Barrio Húmedo** (Wet District). Okay, four including the translation. You can *do* it!

Getting There

BY TRAIN

Plenty of trains run from Madrid to León, about five daily and a few more on Fridays and Sundays (trip time: 4–5 hr.). León's train station, **Estación del Norte,** is at Av. de Astorga 2 (☎ **902-240-202**) on the western bank of the Bernesga River. It's an easy 15-minute walk to town. Cross the bridge near Plaza de Guzmán el Bueno and head up Avenida Ordoño II to the old part

Talk of the Town

Five Ways to Start a Conversation with a Local

1. **Lions.** This is an easy one because every local will tell you what the symbol stands for; user beware: The length of the conversation may be predetermined by whether he or she reeks of garlic sauce—that tapa-time favorite.

2. **San Genarin.** Once upon a time there was a revered town drunk, and he was sadly sacked by the city's first garbage truck. So what did the city of León do? They made him a saint to celebrate during Semana Santa. Ask a local how they like to honor him.

3. **Cathedral envy.** The Cathedral in León is one of hundreds that will stick in your craw longer than an episode of *Law & Order*. That said, it's good to find out from locals what other cathedrals they consider to outdo their big daddy among places of worship.

4. **Pigs.** Point one: A Leónese cook doesn't let anything go to waste: blood, ears, tongue—nothing! Ask any local what their favorite joint or member is, and they'll tell you with a watery mouth. Point two: Every year, families on the range celebrate *la matanza del cerdo*, the night all pigs go to heaven. We won't go into further detail.

5. **Trout.** Leónese love their river fish, and in its honor, they host an Iron Chef–style competition, *El Concurso de la Trucha*. If you're a fisherperson or a cook sniffing around for a new culinary experiment, there's bound to be brethren in the area.

of town. A one-way ticket from Madrid is 21€ to 24€, but prices fluctuate.

BY BUS

León's buses arrive and depart from the **Estación de Autobuses** at Paseo Ingeniero Saenz de Miera (☎ **987-211-000**). Three to five buses per day link León with Zamora and Salamanca, and about 13 per day depart from **Estación Sur Méndez Álvaro** (☎ **914-684-200**) in Madrid (trip time: 4¼ hr.) via the Alsa bus company (☎ **902-422-242;** www.alsa.es). A one-way ticket on a direct regular bus from Madrid is 20€ or 33€ for the *supra* (leather reclining seat, catering, TV screen).

BY CAR

León is a hub for connecting cities, five to be exact. Starting from Madrid, head northwest on the N-VI superhighway toward La Coruña. At Benavente, bear right onto the N-630.

Getting Around

BY BUS

León is well connected with buses, though the city is doable on foot. There are three bus companies that run routes throughout the city. For .80€ you can hop a ride. For routes and information, go to **www.aytoleon.es**. Line 7 runs to and from the RENFE train station, as well as the bus station. All lines end up at Plaza de Santo Domingo in the historic city.

BY CAR

Parking is difficult in León so ask whether your hotel provides parking before you get into town. For **Radio Taxi,** call ☎ **987-261-415.**

León Basics

For **tourist information** (☎ **987-237-082;** www.jcyl.es/turismo), look for the big blue

Castilla y León

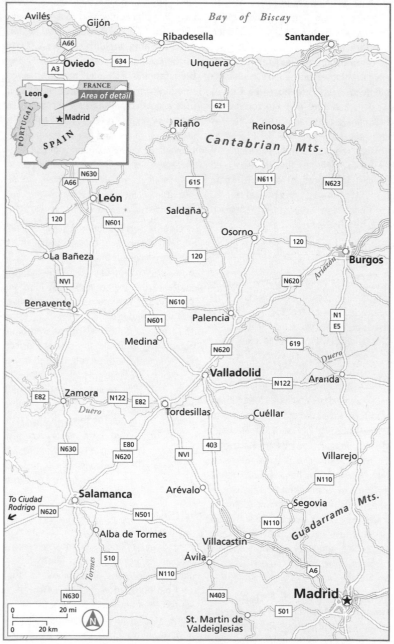

"I" near the Cathedral at Plaza de Regla 3. The hours are Monday to Friday 9am to 2pm and 5 to 7pm, Saturday and Sunday 10am to 2pm and 5 to 8pm (during summer, no siesta).

To **e-mail** your folks back home and let them know you've landed in León undamaged, head toward **Locutorio La Rua** at Calle de la Rua 8 (☎ **987-230-106**; Mon–Fri 9:30am–2:30pm and 4–10:30pm, Sat 10am–2pm and 5–9:30pm).

To send them postcards as evidence of your having been to the glass-encased Cathedral (and not just an Amsterdam cafe), and for all your other **postal needs,** go to **Correos** at Jardín de San Francisco s/n (☎ **987-876-081**).

Sleeping

HOSTELS

📺 **Best** ✦ ➔ **Hostal Albany** This economical place to crash, with its minimalist modern decor, is perfect for those with a subscription to *Architectural Digest*. The building, which was renovated a few years ago, looks like a large ship and alternates between primary colors on every floor. Picasso would have loved the cubist furniture. Philippe Starck, on the other hand, would have loved the clear plastic chairs (they're replicas of his Louis Ghost chair), and the designer bathroom hardware. Each room features a plasma television screen. Room no. 102 has a great balcony; interior patio rooms get a bird's-eye view of the trendy restaurant below. *La Paloma 13.* ☎ *987-264-600. www.albanyleon.com. Triple 80€–90€, double 50€–60€, single 35€–45€. Amenities: Restaurant, bar, elevator, room service, sheets, towels, Wi-Fi. In room: A/C, TV, minibar.*

➔ **Hostal Boccalino (I and II)** ★★★ Sandwiched between the Real Basilica Panteón Real and pedestrian streets, this high-end hostel is actually two kitty-cornered buildings. What they lack in

style, they make up for with spectacular views and a turbo massage shower. Rooms have large balconies that look out over a plaza, the basilica, fountains, and pigeon-filled terrazas. Building number I squats inside Boccalino's restaurant, where free breakfast and fair-priced meals are served. In building no. II, the elevator empties out into a downstairs bar that serves drinks until late night. Travelers have a place to store their bikes, and free Internet access is available in the common room. *Plaza de San Isidro 1.* ☎ *987-220-017. Double 64€, single 40€. Breakfast included. Amenities: bar, restaurant, breakfast, elevator, Internet, sheets, towels, travel desk. In room: A/C, TV.*

➔ **Hostal San Martín** ★ After a long day of hauling your gear cross-country, this is the place to check into for a quiet, friendly atmosphere with big, sunny rooms. The laid-back owners are extremely kind and will let you store your gear, pay whenever you want, and use their Internet access at the front desk. Rooms with shared bathrooms are available for cheaper prices. Double rooms with private bath that face the front have large balconies and full-size tubs (but don't forget your soap—you'll need it to scrub-a-dub). The hostel is situated in the center of town, near restaurants, cafes, and bars. *Plaza Torres de Omaña 1, 2nd floor on the left.* ☎ *987-875-187 and 987-074-186. Triple 51€, double 39€, single 19€. Amenities: Internet (front desk), laundry service (6€), sheets.*

CHEAP

➔ **Pensión Puerta Sol** ★★ This pension owned by a kind, soft-spoken Spanish woman is perched conveniently above Plaza Mayor, one floor above a funk and hip-hop dance studio. The owner is extremely attentive to her guests and has done a stellar job of maintaining this historic building, even keeping its original wooden floors intact. Each room is decorated with secondhand period furniture. Guests haul a small card table out the glass doors onto the large balcony for quiet book reading, travel logging, or, on the weekends, people-watching over Plaza Mayor's fruit market. Although the building is old, its wiring is modern, with lots of places to plug in. *Puerta Sol 1, 2nd floor. (Entrance is around the corner from the plaza.)* ☎ *987-211-966. No credit cards. Double 22€, single 15€. Amenities: Shared bathrooms.*

DOABLE

→ **La Posada Regia** ★★★ This government-rated three-star posada offers the most enchantment you'll find in the region but the best part is, it's good people. The rusticated posada is located right off the main drag and built over an old turret of the original fortress wall (ask the owner for a tour to the look-out tower). Every unique room features exposed beams and feels cozy-warm, painted in deep earthy colors and decorated with antiquated cabinlike furniture. Bathrooms are built for a king, some with moon-shaped Jacuzzis. Rooms in both the original hotel and its more private annex are named after different Spanish rivers and the birds that characterize them. The large family who runs the posada also staffs the kitchen, cooking up a meaty menu that's popular with locals at lunch. The Big Papa delivers the food to the table in the flesh— not because it's super fancy, but just because he's that kind of guy. *Regidores 9-11 (Barrio Húmedo).* ☎ *987-213-173. www.regialeon.com. Double 90€, single 61€, extra bed 20€. Amenities: Bar, restaurant, breakfast included, elevator, travel info. In room: A/C, TV, minibar, hair dryer.*

Eating

On your marks, get set, eat tapas. It's the only way to go in León. Tapas bars start to fill up around 8 to 10pm. The most saturated area is 📺 Best❗ **Barrio Húmedo** (www.barriohumedo.net), aka Plaza Bicha; both names refer to the same area south of Calle Ancha and concentrated around Plaza San Martín. Most bars here specialize in serving one tapa perfected over the years, and it's a cakewalk to sample them all. On Plaza San Martín, **Taberna Lionesa El Liar** is standing room only and famous for its *patatas* (fried potatoes) drizzled in either cheese or garlic sauce; **El Rebota,** also on the plaza, is famous for its *croquetas* (croquettes).

TAPAS

→ **Bar Flechazo** For either the drunken munchies or for an admittedly non-nutritious but cream-your-pants dinner, order a ration of homemade potato chips with salt or cayenne pepper that sink to the bottom and stick to your ribs. Your mom never made them like this: lightly fried over a hot mushy center. You can also order a paper cone loaded to go. This place is infamous so make sure someone in your gaggle orders a plate so you can say you've eaten here. *Platerías 2. No phone. Ración de patatas 2.50€. Hours vary.*

→ **La Bicha** You know a restaurant has to be good when they name the town's most popular plaza after it. The thing is, it's famous for serving the best blood sausage in town. Now hold on, folks. Don't blow it off because you don't like the idea of wrenching blood from pigs, frying it, and slopping it on to a plate like soggy Sloppy Joes. After all, you did agree to visit a city where nothing on a pig goes to waste. The grumpy old man behind the counter gives you some bread to buffer the taste, and you better not complain because he'll serve you a can of whoop-ass for seconds. If you're too scared to try the blood bath, order a *bocadillo* (sandwich). Inside is standing room only. *Plaza San Martín.* ☎ *987-257-518. Meal 7€. Open late.*

CHEAP

→**La Competencia** ★★ PIZZA *Mama mía!* More students come to eat here than there are fixed Italian soccer games. It's a modern, gourmet pizzeria situated in a mess of skinny streets off Plaza Mayor in the old part of town. The menu far surpasses your grocer's freezer in taste and selection: Order the Quiche, Tropical, Mexicaly, Light, or a masterpiece Michelangelo. Pizzas are thin crust and generous on the toppings. This is a perfect option for vegetarians on the go or young tourists looking for a slice of real Leónese life. *Conde Rebolledo 17 and Mulhacín 6.* ☎ *987-849-477. www.pizzerialacompetencia. com. Pizzas and salads 8€–10€. Daily 1–4pm and 7:30pm–12:30am.*

→**La Garea** FAST FOOD Here's an eatery cheaper and open later than tried-and-true Taco Bell, and at least an ocean closer in the hottest going out area in León. In the summer, most people take a seat on the popular terraza for the best people-watching and table service. Take your pick between tapas, hamburgers, and baguettes in the 3€ range. Don't leave without ordering your football-size "mini" liter of *calimotxo*, which is a mixture of coke and wine (when in Spain . . .). This is the perfect place to start the night on a tight budget. Make sure to ask about the free drink with the purchase of any baguette. *Zapaterías 9. No phone. Mini 3€; sandwiches, burgers, baguettes about 3€. Thurs–Sun 10am–early morning.*

CAFES

→**Café Ekole** Ekole is short for the Leónese word *equilocual,* which means either way. That seems to be the philosophy here, where at any hour 18-year-olds rub elbows with 60-year-olds over a large menu of specialty coffees. With the best terrace in the city, Ekole is well known by locals who want a chilled-out environment in which to meet friends, bring dates,

or hold class (an East Coast American university class actually finished a semester here). Rotating art exhibits adorn the walls in one of two large rooms good for drinking your java, mojitos, or homemade fruit shakes like the house Ekole (apple sorbet, raspberry, and lemon). *Fernando Glez. Regueral 1 (Plaza de Torres de Omaña).* ☎ *987-225-702. Specialty drinks 4€–5€. Sun–Thurs 4:30pm–1:30am; Fri–Sat 4:30pm–3:30am.*

→**Café Europeo** It's as if the cathedral hawked up this cafe and spewed it out a few meters away. Terraza views can't get much better for a trendy cafe serving specialty coffees to rastas, punks, hippies, hipsters, jet-setters, and regular Joes between the ages of 25 and 35. After a long day of walking and sightseeing, head this way around 8pm for sundown at the cathedral—the best hour for people-watching on the plaza. *Plaza de Regal 9. No phone. Coffees under 5€. Daily until late.*

Partying

Head toward **Barrio Húmedo** (around Plaza San Martín and neighboring streets such as Calle Zapaterías) and you'll hit the jackpot for dance clubs and bars. On the eastern wall of the cathedral, **Calle San Lorenzo** is full of swankier drinking holes and dance clubs such as **GPS** (Av. de los Cubos 8-10, entrance on Calle San Lorenzo; ☎ **987-875-346**). After a late night in the Barrio Húmedo, head toward **Calle Lancia,** another crowded dimension of disco, or the after-hours hot spot (5am or later) at **Club Lolita** (Burgo Nuevo 10).

BARS

→**Barris** The in-house DJ at this catch-all Irish tavern on Plaza Mayor plays a popular mix of international, house, French hip-hop, and Spanish music for the 20- to 40-year-olds who arrive at all hours of the night to drink and dance. *Plaza Mayor 23.* ☎ *987-209-797.*

ᴹᵀᵛ🐛 Arty Facts

The hottest and most talked-about member of León's culture club among plugged-in Castilian art students is (FREE) **MUSAC** ★★, or Museo de Arte Contemporáneo de Castilla y León (Av. de los Reyes Leóneses 24; ☎ 987-090-000; www.musac.org.es; free admission; Tues–Sun 10am–3pm and 4–9pm). This modern art museum, with its rainbow facade, takes a broad view of contemporary art with installations that rival the MoMA in New York City. Free pop concerts and highbrow international documentaries make this venue definitely worth your positive space and time.

The hugely successful 20th-century Catalan architect Antonio Gaudí, famous for his naturalist lines and giant fruit in Barcelona, left his mark in León when he designed the (FREE) **Casa de los Botines** (Plaza San Marcelo 5; ☎ 987-292-712; www.cajaespana.es; free admission; Mon–Sat 7–9pm, Sun noon–2pm), which is now a private headquarters of the giant corporate bank Caja España. The outside is a warped interpretation of Gothic architecture that is very typical of his whacked-out style. The inside is closed to tourists, but the first floor is open for sporadic art expositions. Check the website for details.

➔ **Chupito Sabor** This small franchise is a hit and run: Down your shot, and don't stay for a second one. In León, you've got a long night ahead of you. The most popular *chupitos* (shots) are sambuca, probably because it's lit on fire, and the margarita, which they pour in your mouth, and then your body is shaken—not stirred. The bar has a massive website offering specialty deals and prices, as if you needed more of an excuse. *Zapaterías 9 (Barrio Húmedo) and Puerta Sol 1 (Plaza Mayor). No phone. www.chupitosabor.com.*

CLUBS

ᴹᵀᵛ (Best ⚑) ➔ **Glam** Living up to its name, the hottest dance club in town attracts the best-looking students, *pijos* (yuppies), and 20-somethings dressed and bedazzled to get lucky. The disco globe spins to house, Spanish, Brazilian, and African beats while beautiful people mingle over mixed drinks in the spaced-out lounge. Don't get there until 1am when the real party starts. *Platerías 10. ☎ 987-201-024.*

➔ **Korova Disco Bar** ★★ This club, named after the infamous milk bar in *A*

Clockwork Orange, is reminiscent of a 1970s disco (which it probably was), with a retro ambience and plenty of dancing space. Rockers will enjoy a range from classic soul and rock 'n' roll to indie faves such as The Strokes or The Pixies. The crowd, mostly youngsters in their mid-20s, show up here to finish the fiesta, so you can make this your last club of the night (3–4am). *Plaza San Martín 13. No phone.*

Sightseeing

León has a few other things to see besides some tapas on your plate. It holds its own in terms of museums, but the star attraction is the world-class cathedral. The city is compact. While covering all the ground it has to offer in 1 day might be hard on your heels, it's definitely doable.

ᴹᵀᵛ (Best ⚑) ➔ **Catedral de León (Santa María de Regia)** ★★★ This house of the Lord is the Hope Diamond of cathedrals. What makes this church different from all the others in Spain are its plethora of stained-glass windows, 182 in all. Since the weight of the church's roof is shifted onto the structure's buttresses, not its walls like

Roman structures, the 13th- through 16th-century designers were able to use more glass than stone, an unbelievable feat back in the medieval day. The church is best appreciated from a seat in the pews for a kaleidoscopic view of the French-Gothic stained-glass art. In the central chapel's apse, there's the *White Virgin*, a 13th-century statue brought to the church for preservation. There's also the tomb of King Ordoño II of León situated dead front and center; it was the Cathedral's way of thanking him for donating the land where his palace originally sat for this holy-cow church (originally it was Roman baths). Also on the main altar is a silver reliquary with the remains of León's patron saint, San Foilán. In the center of the nave is the Renaissance-style retrochoir; you're ·not able to enter, but you can see through to the Gothic east end and the west-end rose. The cloisters cost a euro extra but are worth it for the faded frescoes and old Gothic Roman tombs. However, unless you're a crazed cathedral zealot wearing a pair of Nike Airs, you can skip the museum: The mandatory tour lasts 1¼ hours. *Plaza de Regla.* ☎ *987-875-770. Admission 2€ (an additional 1€ for cloisters) and 3.50€ for museum and tour. Museum hours: Oct–May Mon–Fri 9:30am–1:30pm and 4–7pm, Sat 9:30am–1:30pm; June Mon–Sat 9:30am–1:30pm and 4–7pm; July–Sept Mon–Fri 9:30am–2pm and 4–7:30pm, Sat 9:30am–2pm and 4–7pm. Cathedral hours: July–Sept Mon–Sat 9:30am–2pm and 4–7:30pm, Sun 8:30am–2:30pm and 5–8pm; Oct–June Mon–Fri 8:30am–1:30pm and 4–7pm, Sun 8:30am–2:30pm and 5–7pm.*

→**Panteón y Museos de San Isidoro** Housed in León's basilica, the pantheon contains 23 tombs of Leónese kings, the remains of the church's namesake, and his not-to-be-missed mummy finger. The 10th-century building is open day and night, as part of a longstanding royal edict. The **panteón** ★★ is an eerie tomb decorated with original, untouched Romanesque frescoes from the 1100s, shrouding old coffins of ancient royalty who are now resting in peace. The ceiling art depicts biblical scenes mixed with vegetative decoration; and the cloister and treasure house, though looted throughout history, still contains big gems such as the Chest of the Ivories (1059), St. Isidore's Reliquary Chest (1063), and the Chalice of Agates (Queen Urraca's chalice, 1063). *Plaza San Isidoro 4.* ☎ *987-876-161. www.sanisidorode leon.org. Admission 3€, Thurs night is free. Sept–July Mon–Sat 10am–1:30pm and 4–6:30pm, Sun 10am–1:30pm; July–Sept Mon–Sat 9am–8pm, Sun 9am–2pm.*

Playing Outside

SKIING & SNOWBOARDING

→**San Isidro Ski Resort** This ski resort is the best in northeastern Spain for snowboarders and skiers of all levels. The medium-size winter resort is located in the Cantabrian Mountains that tear across the border between León and Asturias. Lift lines are usually short and renting equipment here is a steal (under 15€), though watch out for the ski school mobs. The site, which is surrounded by forests as well as lakes such as Maraña, Cofiñal, Ausente, and Isoba, is a great spot for nature lovers year-round. On your way up, check out Puebla de Lillo for its walking paths, and stop for coffee in the quaint town of Boñar. *Puerta San Isidro. (From León, take N-601 towards Valladolid until Puente Villarente. Head towards Boñar on the provincial road P-1. From Boñar, hop on 331 towards Puebla de Lillo. The resort is signposted 15km/9⅓ miles from town.)* ☎ *987-731-115 and 902-474-376. www.san-isidro.net.*

Shopping

Every Wednesday and Saturday, the Plaza Mayor plays host to the **fruit market.** This is the perfect solution to your need for a fresh cheap breakfast. Every Sunday from 9am to 3pm on Calle Papa la Guinda is **El Rastro,** the open-air flea market reminiscent of Madrid, where you can find anything from old shoes to antique pocket watches. Shops are a dime a dozen on **Calle Ancha,** the main drag leading up to the cathedral. My favorite by far was

Buenas Intenciones ★★★ (Ancha 10; ☎ 987-073-789; daily 10am–2pm and 5–8:30pm, until 9pm in the summer). Exactly like its name suggests this shop is full of good intentions. First the company contacts NGO (nonprofit) groups such as those for mistreated women, the mentally challenged, or the blind, and then works with individuals to create a product such as clothing, ceramics, jewelry, and knick-knacks; a percentage of the proceeds are donated back to the NGOs.

Valladolid

There's no doubt about it, Valladolid is a university town jam-packed with cheesy dance clubs, restaurants, and cosmo living, a fact that has brought it into full swing with the modern world. Perhaps because it lacks communication barriers: Folks in Valladolid speak the purest form of Castilian Spanish. The Podunk city didn't become important, however, until Isabella of Castile and Ferdinand of Aragon were secretly married here, an illegal alliance that changed the course of history. Valladolid blew up like Dr. Strangeloves's atomic bomb—and so did the Inquisition, when Isabella's Hitleresque Fray Tomás de Torquemada was appointed confessor and put the "stake" in burning. Talk about zealots: On this side of the Atlantic, Izzy and Ferdi's boy toy, Christopher Columbus, is an unequivocal hero today. Valladolid just celebrated the quincentennial celebration of Columbus's death, as this is where he took his last breath.

Getting There

BY TRAIN

It's best to get to Valladolid by train, as more than 14 trains make the trip to and from Madrid daily (trip time: 3–4¹/₂ hr.).

Fares cost 12€ to 21€ for express trips. Another 16 trains to Burgos run every day. The train station, **Estación del Norte,** is at Calle Recondo s/n, by the Plaza Colon (☎ 902-240-202), about a mile south of the center of town.

BY AIR

If you're a real jet-setter, Aviaco's daily flights to and from Barcelona make landfall at Valladolid's **Vallanubla Airport** (Hwy. N-601; ☎ 983-415-500). From there, a taxi will take you to town in about 15 minutes.

BY CAR

Valladolid's highways are connected to Burgos, León, Segovia, and Salamanca, like a cat's cradle. From Madrid, take the A-6 northwest of the city to get on north 403.

BY BUS

Valladolid is a hub for buses, and it's easy to travel to and from surrounding cities. It'll take you about 8 minutes more or less to walk to the **bus station** (Puente Colgante s/n; ☎ 983-236-308). Lines are short for the dozen-plus daily buses to and from Madrid (trip time: 2¹/₄ hr.). Eight buses per day arrive from Zamora (1¹/₄ hr.), and three buses per day from Burgos (1¹/₂ hr.).

Getting Around

The main depot from which to catch a **bus ride** in the historic center is on Plaza España. For information on routes, contact AUVASA (☎ 983-457-720; www.auvasa.es). A one-way ticket will cost you a pretty .95€, and on weekends, there's a night owl service for partiers on the go.

The two main **taxi stops** in the historic center are outside Plaza Mayor and Plaza España. There are two 24-hour companies: **Agrupación de Taxistas de Valladolid** (☎ 983-207-155) and **Radio Taxi** (☎ 983-291-411).

Valladolid Basics

The **tourist office** (Calle de Santiago 19B; ☎ 983-219-310; www.diputacionde valladolid.es) is open daily from 9am to 2pm and 5 to 7pm.

When the guilt trip hits with a vengeance, you can send that postcard from the **post office** (Plaza de la Rinconada, next to Plaza Mayor).

For **emergencies** more serious than a nosebleed, call Hospital de la Cruz Roja Española (☎ 983-222-222).

Sleeping

HOSTELS

➔ **Hostal Los Arces** For a taste of home, check into this historic building in the center of the city. It's one of the originals in Valladolid, where nobles trotted their hot rod carriages through its giant wooden entranceway. Each room is decorated with papered ceilings, lacy curtains, Renoir prints, and framed pictures of the owner's family. The polished-wood floors creak under your feet like you're back home at grandma's—except the mattresses are firmer. Request room no. 102 for the glass-encased balcony overlooking the square. Rooms are fitted with a (accidental) mini-malist stainless-steel sink and a slim-trim

shower stall. In the hallways, there's a dis-penser for toothbrushes just in case yours stinks like ham. *San Antonio del Padua 2.* ☎ *983-353-853. Double 39€, single 28€. Amenities: Sheets, telephone, towels, TV (in common room). In room: TV.*

➔ **Hostal Paris** ★ This towering building a hop, skip, and jump away from Plaza Mayor is a hostel with hotel services, put-ting personal touches such as a cactus or a candle in each room. All rooms are extremely clean and sanitized, with that new-car smell. There's even a love seat that flips out into another bed for extra guests, a minibar, goody basket, and an alarm clock to get your butt in gear. The locked hallway and 24-hour desk atten-dant ensure that it's the safest option for storing smuggled diamonds—just don't hide them under the mattresses, which are way too soft and could easily blow your cover. *Especeria 2.* ☎ *983-370-625. Triple 79€, double 60€, single 44€. Amenities: Elevator, laundry service, sheets, towels. In room: A/C, TV, minibar, shaving mirror, hair dryer.*

➔ **Hostal Teyla** For the cheapest accom-modation in town paired with the best view, rest up at this hostel-pension. The restored house has wood floors, Big & Tall ceilings, and good feng shui. Each room is exterior with a balcony where you can let down all your hair like Rapunzel; in fact, the glass, wraparound balcony in room no. 2 is so exceptional, you'll want to find a Spanish prince (or princess) who'll climb up for a good time. Most rooms share bath-rooms (with up to seven other rooms), but the walk down the hall isn't bad. The com-mon room is uncommon for its large size and serious comfort factor. *Correos 7. 2nd floor.* ☎ *983-341-968. Double with private bath-room 38€, double with shared bathroom 28€, single with shared bathroom 19€. Amenities: Shared bathrooms, sheets, towels, TV (in com-mon room).*

DOABLE

→ **Hotel Olid Melia** ★ This four-star hotel is your class-A option in Valladolid, overshadowing a half dozen other multi-starred hotels with quality and intrigue (one of us saw a ghost but it could have been too much wine, or too little sleep). The bedrooms are generously sized considering Europe's small-room syndrome—and the bathrooms are downright huge—but what you're really paying for here is the excellent service and class. If you forget your toothbrush, a bellhop will run it up faster than you can squeeze the tube. The breakfast buffet is a king's feast with fresh meats and cheeses and can last you most of the day if you stash some leftovers in your bag on the DL. Walking outside, you'll find yourself smack in the center of town with an old-fashioned terraza restaurant (Taberna Pradera) across the street, which is well worth the wait. *Plaza de San Miguel 10.* ☎ *983-357-200. www.solmelia.com. Weekends double 91€; weekdays double 102€, single 75€; 32€ for extra bed with breakfast included in price. Amenities: Bar, breakfast (13€), Internet, laundry service, Wi-Fi, gymnasium, sauna, room service, parking. In room: A/C, TV, hair dryer, minibar.*

Eating

If you're surviving on the candy dish at the hostel's front desk, do your digestive system a favor and head toward **Plaza Universidad,** where there are many fast options costing less than a big bottle of Evian. If students aren't eating their mother's leftovers, then they're spending laundry money on *pintxos* (tapas) and tostadas at their local tapas bar. In fact, it's rare to see anyone younger than 26 in a "real" restaurant in Valladolid.

TAPAS

→ **La Tasquita II** The most well-known tapas bar in town is La Tasquita (Fernández

de la Torre 5; ☎ **983-351-669**) but we're not going to recommend it because the line to get in is even longer than your large intestine. Instead, its cousin the II, who is not too far away, makes the perfect solution for grumbling stomachs. Serving the same food but with less hassle, the staff is a lot more accommodating and there's tons more elbow room. Choose either tostadas or baguettes for less than a phone call home. Recommended picks are the roast beef and the *solomillo piquillo Roquefor* (a gazpacho spread with pepper and Roquefort cheese). For the classicist, shrimp and sangria are available, too. Take your grub outside for seats. *Caridad 2.* ☎ *983-351-351. Tostadas 1.50€. Bocadillos 1.90€. Tues–Sun noon–4pm and 7pm–midnight.*

→ **Vinotinto** (and **Vintotinto Joven**) ★★★ TAPAS/SPANISH Start your tapa streaking here at this buzzing, Soho-ish, metrosexual love-child tapas bar where the young waiters are just as pretty to look at as the artisan plates they conjure up. Choose from skewers of three grilled shrimp wrapped in zucchini or rare slices of duck lightly grilled with an orange for combustible flavor. The waiters will help you choose a wine depending on your mood or their selection (rotated weekly). After teasing your buds with tapas, head across the street to its franchise parent, Vinotinto, for an all-out meal. Start with a mixed salad and if you like fish, don't leave without trying the Portuguese cod. If you're a meat-eater, go for the *chuletón* (a big beef chop). *Vinotinto Joven. Campanas 1.* ☎ *983-378-026. Tapas about 2.20€. Vinotinto. Campanas 4.* ☎ *983-342-291. www.vinotinto. es. 2-course meal including wine 20€. Both restaurants Mon and Wed–Thurs noon–4pm and 8pm–midnight; Fri–Sat noon–4pm and 8pm–12:30am.*

CHEAP

→ **Las Patatas de Blas** BURGERS For the traveler in a pinch, dine where the students do at this mom-and-pop's burger cafe that's cheaper than a Happy Meal—but, sadly, sans the toy. It's one of a kind though, which means there's nothing generic about it except for its grease-stained counter and Church's Chicken fast-food appeal, very reminiscent of home. If you're not a fan of burgers but need a fat meal on the skinny, the cafe specializes in potatoes and sandwiches, too. Get here late, and you'll witness the wave of youngsters who begin their night of debauchery on the same street. This place is also key for the drunken munchies. *Pasión 6. No phone. Meal 4.70€. Burger 1.95€–2.70€. Patatas bravas 1.30€. Daily 1pm–11:30pm; Fri until 2am; Sat until 3am.*

DOABLE

→ **La Taberna del Herrero** SPANISH Popular with the locals, this is gonna be your best bet for your money—as long as you're really hungry and don't order the tomato gazpacho (the melon is okay). It's an especially good choice for lunch but get here early, like when it first opens, or call in advance to reserve a table, especially if the group is larger than two. The rule of thumb here is to share and share alike. Plates are heaping, and Spain knows not the doggie bag, so you're going to have to eat up, son. The seafood melody is a good bet, as well as the *huevos rotos* (damn good scrambled eggs with other greasy stuff like meat). Don't hesitate with the house's red wine; get it while the gettin's good. *Fernández de la Torre 4.* ☎ *983-342-310. Meal 10€. Shared plates 12€. Daily 12–4:30pm and 7:30pm–close.*

Partying

Practically every other street is popular for its drinking holes, but for a sure bet,

head down to **Plaza Mayor** for terraza action (specifically Café Continental), **Plaza Universidad** for dancing and beer, and **Calle Parnaíso** for anything having to do with liquor, dancing on dry bars, or indecent exposure.

BARS & NIGHTCLUBS

→ **Bar Morgan** As the long-haired, leather-vest-wearing bartender said, this bar is anti-*pijo* so don't even think about wearing your Polo colors or your white alligator shoes inside. You'd stick out among the multitude of anti-establishment patrons overflowing the smoky rock joint. The bar faces the cathedral and is in the midst of a gazillion dance clubs and bars, though this one gets packed early and stays that way throughout the night. Art expositions are hung on a rotating basis. *Solanilla 7.* ☎ *983-150-671.*

→ **El Minuto** Each El Minuto minute will last forever because the flaming *carajillos,* or cognacs (1.30€), are so memorable. Baristas carefully measure sweet alcoholic ingredients like a Missouri methamphetamine lab and with the same intoxicating results. The bar is open later than most so it's a great place to polish off a nightcap. *Macías Picavea 15.* ☎ *983-150-671.*

→ **OHM** Feel like a catnap? Stop by this cafe early and make your reservation for some time in an Oriental bed big enough for a sexy romp. We don't know whether to say club or cafe (it's both), but the chill-out Eastern decor is good enough for 7 years in Tibet, as long as you get past the doorman and red carpet outside. Stop by around 1:30am, and Buddha your way to the not-so-friendly bar. *San Lorenzo 7. No phone.*

→ **Taj Mahal** On the drunkest street in the city, university students throw sobriety, and diets, to the wind at Taj Majal. This *chupetería,* or shot bar, is famous for its *comestibles*—a pure chocolate shot glass filled with vanilla cream and cinnamon liquor (1.50€). Better than the evil witch in Hansel and Gretel, the old woman behind the bar knows exactly what students crave and entices them to stay the night with sweets and loud house music. Dancing ensues late-night so make sure to leave a trail of bread crumbs for the way home. *Paraiso 11.* ☎ *983-259-001.*

Sightseeing

As a former Spanish capital, the regal city boasts a Madrid-size Plaza Mayor and a list of monuments thick enough to stick a tack into, such as the **Palacio de Pimentel** (☎ **983-427-100**), where Philip II was born in 1527. **Casa-Museo de Colón** (Calle de Colón s/n; ☎ **983-291-353;** free admission; Tues–Sat 10am–2pm and 5–7pm, Sun 10am–2pm) is a house that was supposedly Columbus's, but it was absolutely not. Rather it's a museum housing fake maps and Aztec, Mayan, and Incan artifacts.

ATTRACTION

FREE ➔ **La Catedral** Rock star architect Juan de Herrera (the same guy who did El Escorial) was called upon by Philip II to build this Gothic mammoth for the king's birth city. Unlike El Escorial, however, Herrera chose hard lines and not a lot of decoration. But then Philip croaked, and the hard hats forgot about the building for 18 years. When things got going again, it was Alberto Churriguera who picked up the pieces, respecting Herrera's original austere design on the inside and adding some flare to the exterior. The best part about the place is the 1551 altarpiece by Juan de Juni, whose realistic work leaves a good first impression. *Plaza de Universidad 1.* ☎ *983-304-362. Free admission to Cathedral. Admission to Cathedral museum: 3.50€. Cathedral and museum Tues–Fri 10am–1:30pm and 4–7pm; Sat–Sun 10am–2pm.*

MUSEUMS

➔ **Casa y Museo de Cervantes** So it's a re-creation, who cares. At least the building is original, which is a lot more than Columbus can say about his "house" in Valladolid. The ceilings and floors are original, dating to when the house was rented out by the king to people like Miguel Cervantes who, believe it or not, had to pay rent just like his neighbors, even at the end of his career. Although not his exact same furniture, historians did a great job using 400-year-old antiques that they found to match descriptions passed down by the generations. This is a pretty-darn-quick museum pit stop, and it'd be wise to visit on a Sunday when you don't have to pay to see it. The beautiful garden outside makes it easy to appreciate the original building in all its literary-genius splendor. *Rastro s/n.* ☎ *983-308-810. Admission 2.50€; free on Sun. Tues–Sat 9:30am–3pm; Sun 10am–3pm.*

➔ **El Museo Nacional de Escultura** ★★ "This one time, at the National Sculpture museum. . . . " Okay, polychrome wood sculptures are not half as boring as they sound. Actually, you should definitely check it out, even if it's just to see the famous realist Flemish sculpture of *Death* by Fray Rodrigo de Holande, commissioned in 1570 to scare the living daylights out of everyone. All-stars here include Alonso de Berruguette, Juan de Juni, and Gregorio Fernández, who all sculpted melodramatically. Another reason for the visit is the diorama scene depicting the city in which Jesus was born through everyday events that would have taken place there. There is an impressive collection of bullfighting statues as well, which were the royal playthings of Charles IV in the 18th century. The tour also includes the Isabelline Gothic

Iglesia de San Pablo ★, with a silver-smithed facade so intricate in design you'll rush to the nearest postcard stand. *Cadenas de San Gregorio 1 and 2.* ☎ *983-254-083. www.mne.es. Admission 2.40€ adult, 1.20€ student. Tues–Sat 10am–2pm and 4–6pm (Mar 21–Sept 30 until 9pm); Sun and festivals 10am–2pm.*

Shopping

➔ **Abalorium Abalorii** For cheap clay (1.90€), beading (1.90€/box), cord (.50€–.90€), string, eyes, and hooks, or anything else for making necklaces or bracelets, stop here and get your money's worth of creative beading supplies to fiddle with on the roadside. *Platerías 9-15.* ☎ *983-378-610. Mon–Sat 10am–1:45pm and 5–8:30pm.*

➔ **Sportland** ★★ This store makes spontaneous camping trips possible. Sure, it's a chain, but you can't find better deals anywhere in the world. You can find packs for under 20€, and small roll-up sleeping bags for the same price. The employees also fix bikes if you're on the go with wheels. *Duque de la Victoria 3.* ☎ *983-209-831. www.sportarea.es. Mon–Sat 10am–2pm and 5–9pm.*

Burgos ★★

Here's another city credited for its perfected lisp (lithp), en ethpañol. Peeps from Burgos potentially make the perfect Spanish news anchors, enunciating without an accent—that is, from the perspective of a lisping Spaniard. The 9th-century city, nestled along the Arlanzón River in the shape of a giant fan, was founded around a soaring cathedral, the kind of cathedral you would find in a fairy tale with witches' hats and schools of bats. In fact, you can—Sleeping Beauty. More on that later. Burgos is also home to El Cid, the greatest Spanish *campeador* (champion) in history; he's buried in the cathedral along with his woman. The biggest party of the year lasts for 2 weeks starting on June 29 and celebrates Peter and Paul (Mary has her own fiesta during Semana Santa). Parades, tapas fairs, daily bullfights, and free concerts ensue. The party climaxes on the first Sunday of July, Día de las Peñas.... *Olé!*

Getting There & Around

BY TRAIN

It's best to take the train to Burgos; there are regional and express trains, and it's worth it to spring for the latter. Trip time from Madrid is about 3¹/₂ to 4 hours (19€–23€); from Barcelona, 8 to 9 hours (34€–43€); and from Valladolid, 1¹/₂ hours (6€–13€). The **Burgos railway station** (☎ 902-240-202) is at the end of Avenida de Conde Guadalhorce, about a half-mile from the southwest of the center. First go to the Plaza Castilla roundabout, then walk due south across the Arlanzón River and bingo.

BY BUS

You'll have no problem hailing a bus to Burgos, as **Continental** (☎ 902-330-400) operates 12 to 17 buses from Madrid. The drop-off in Burgos (trip time: 3¹/₂–4 hr.) is the **bus depot** on Calle Miranda (☎ 947-262-017). Fare one-way is 13€. There's a taxi stand outside or you could hike it: Calle Miranda crosses the Plaza de Vega; cross the river, and you're near the cathedral.

Once you are in the city, you'll find it quite walkable. For those venturing past the old city, city buses are .75€ a ride, though .50€ cheaper if you purchase the *bono* pass. There's also a night bus that runs during off hours. All buses lead to Avenida del Arlanzón. For more information, call **Autobuses Urbanos** ☎ 947-288-829, the city bus system.

BY CAR OR TAXI

From Madrid, follow the N-I north for about 3 hours, and don't get sidetracked with the attractive scenery. If you're traveling from Barcelona, expect the road signs to change a few times while you're not looking, from the A-2 to the A-68, and finally E-4. The road, however, is phat and easy-riding especially with cruise control.

If you've saved your riding for a rainy day, dial up **Radio Taxi** (☎ 947-277-777 and 947-481-010). In the city center, the closest **taxi stand** is at Plaza Mio Cid.

BY BICYCLE

For information on renting bikes in town, go to the tourist office or contact **Bicibur** (Plaza Santo Domingo de Guzmán; ☎ 618-581-718; www.bicibur.es; winter hours 8am–5:30pm, summer hours 8am–9pm).

Burgos Basics

The **Castilla y León tourist information office** is at Plaza Alonso Martinez 7 (☎ 947-203-125), but they have all the information you'll need for Burgos, too. It's open every day from 9am to 2pm and 5 to 8pm. During summer (July–Sept), the office is open all day from 9am to 8pm and an extra hour later on Fridays and Saturdays.

The **Burgos tourist office** is located at Plaza del Rey San Fernando (☎ 947-288-874) and has the same schedule. For more planning info, go to www.ayto burgos.es.

To send home news of your latest escapades, the **post office** is at Plaza del Conde de Castro.

cuidado! Hostile Hostels

Be extremely wary of hostels in Burgos. These listed have been thoroughly checked out and get our full approval. Other hostels in the same area (that will remain nameless) have either housed ETA terrorists (as reported in newspapers) or been accused of alleged sexual harassment (nobody was charged, but that doesn't mean the owner isn't a total weirdo). Do yourself a favor and trust us on this one.

For *ER* reenactments, God forbid, visit **Hospital General Yagüe** at Av. del Cid Campeador 96 for treatment (☎ 947-281-800).

Sleeping

In Burgos, you're much better off springing for a hotel rather than frugally booking a hostel. *Hostales* are available just outside the historic center, offering meager accommodations for high prices. We've listed the few exceptions here.

CHEAP

→ **Hostal Manjon** ★★ In need of a major revamp, this hostel doesn't match up to the two stars the government awarded it; however, it's the best bet in the triad of nearby hostels to which it belongs. The staff is friendly, offering recommendations and good city maps. The furniture doesn't match and wood floors are worn and torn, but the rooms are bright and all of them are exterior—a good or bad thing depending on how deeply you sleep. Mattresses are new and hot water runs 24-7, a Spanish luxury. Nonsmoking rooms are available (and highly recommended in this smoke stack). The center of the city is about a 7-minute walk along the river esplanade. *Gran Teatro 1, 7th floor.* ☎ *947-208-689. Oct–May double with private bathroom 38€, double with shared bathroom 30€; May–Sept double with private bathroom 46€, double with shared bathroom 37€; single 33€ with private bathroom all year; single 22€ with shared bathroom all year. For Peregrinos (Camino del Santiago): 3€ less. Amenities: Laundry service (10€).*

➔**Hostal Teyla** ★★ Not too many hostels occupy the center part of town (hotels have completely taken over the main terrain), and this two-star option is the safest and cleanest. The owners are extremely careful that only guests enter the establishment so no worries of vagabond junkies rumored to visit other establishments in the area ruining your buzz. The *hostal's* rooms are a cut above the competition, each with its own bathroom and stocked minibar with cold emergency hangover remedies. Having been just renovated on the first floor (which you should request), this hostel is a breath of fresh air and should be on the first-call list for any tourist looking for a good deal near the center. *Puente Gasset 4.* ☎ *947-205-916. Double 40€–55€, single 25€–45€, depending on hostel capacity. Amenities: Laundry service (9€), parking. In room: TV, minibar.*

➔**Pensión Peña** ★ For a no-frills, cheap place to park your packs for a night or two, this is the best bang for your buck, especially if you like to party. It's located on one of the hottest, quaintest streets in the city center and is always hustling and bustling with shoppers and boozers. The floors are a little dirty but at least they're bug-free. It's family owned and lived in (Peña was a founding father's surname), so you know the hospitality is good and the

hearts are warm. *La Puebla 18.* ☎ *947-206-323. Double with sink 26€, single with sink 19€, double without sink 25€, single without sink 18€. Amenities: Shared bathrooms.*

DOABLE

➔**Hotel Norte y Londres** ★★★ Don't bust your wallet if it's already broken. This is the best accommodation in town, and you can't beat the price. Facing north as its name suggests, it's located in the city's heart, sharing the same scenic square as the region's tourist office. Each medium-size room is a blast from the past, decorated in period-style furniture dating way before its facade was erected in 1904. The huge bathrooms, on the other hand, are modern with tubs and a basketful of goodies. Exterior floor-length windows open to one of the (loudest) main drags below. It's a romantic view for anyone who can appreciate European architecture but don't expect the Sandman if its festival and punks are on the streets until the cows come home. This hotel is an institution hosted by an accommodating English-speaking staff that can fake a convincing smile no matter what the hour. *Plaza Alonso Martinez 10.* ☎ *947-264-125. www.hotelnorteylondres.com. Double 50€–90€, single 54€–64€, extra bed 13€. Amenities: Breakfast room (6.50€), A/C, TV (in salon), Wi-Fi (in salon), room service. In room: TV, hair dryer.*

Eating
TAPAS

MTV Best ✿ ➔**Cervecería Morito** ★★★ If there's going to be another Last Supper, please God, let it be here. What bread is to civilization, tapas are to Morito. The corner tavern is overflowing at every hour with people of all ages ordering tapas on trendy plates that are too modern for the oldie-but-goody dive. It's the best tapas bar in a sea of others to choose from though you're almost—but not quite—as well off at each. The menus hang from cozy wooden tables more comfortable than a broken-in pair of jeans, and tent seating is available outside. There's a butcher shop's selection of meats; *calamares* and mushrooms are grilled or fried. *Sombrerería 27.* ☎ *947-267-555. Raciones 1.10€–8€. Mon-Thurs and Sun noon–3:30pm and 7–11:30pm; Fri–Sat noon–3:30pm and 7pm–midnight.*

CHEAP

➜ **Royal** ★ BOCATERIA/CAFETERIA Here's the place where punk moms with purple hair bring their preteen kids for a cheap meal. Besides being cut-rate, it's a hot spot on the Huerto del Rey square decked with bars and clubs. Thumb-size sandwiches such as the Sputnik (ham and cheese) are the most popular items on the menu, which also features the *hamburguesa Royal* (don't let Burger King catch wind). Salads are exotic with pineapples and kiwis. Last but not least are soaring mini shish kabobs with shrimp and your usual tapa fare skewered with toothpicks. *Huerto del Rey 25.* ☎ *947-202-611. Meal 8€–10€. Daily 9am–1am; Fri–Sat until 2am.*

DOABLE

➜ **Buenas Noches Burgos** ★★★ INTERNATIONAL This creative newfangled restaurant just opened its doors—and dozens of windows—as a kitchen, bar, cafeteria, and dance club, overlooking the entire city, just yards away from the old castile in El Parque del Castillo. Like a college freshman afraid of commitment, the restaurant cooks up a little bit of everything from Spanish dishes to Japanese maki—and finding sushi rolls in Spain is even rarer than the fish itself. There's a veggie wok for vegans and *risotto de bambú y gambas* for mollusk heads. Dessert might be the perfect excuse for the venture uphill to the best lookout spot

in the city (camera: Don't leave the hostel without it). Arrive after-hours on Saturdays and sweat it off dancing until early in the morning (3–4am), but call a cab home 'cuz it's a long walk. Up the road is another bar and cafe, **El Vagon** (☎ **947-264-383;** daily 11am–3am), run by the same owners. *Parque del Castillo (just follow the road up, about a 10–15 min. walk).* ☎ *947-266-259. Main dish 10€–12€. Dessert 5€–6€. Daily 10am–3am.*

➜ **La Favorita Taberna Urbana** SPANISH This self-proclaimed urban tavern will live up to its cheeky name and become one of your favorites, as long as you can get over the testy service. High ceilings and home-baked smells will drag you in by the nostrils if the big burly chefs behind the glass don't first. Grab a table in front (there's no need to enter the dining room) and order a goat cheese salad or the grilled red peppers and vegetables to start. A few fishes of the day and a huge variety of hearty tapas are written on the giant chalkboard (you'll have to translate). Even the house wine is a *favorito.* It's a popular choice for a late dinner, and there's plenty of seating to go around. *Avellanos 8.* ☎ *947-205-949. www.lafavoritaburgos.com. Cheese plates 5€. Raciónes 10€–12€. Daily 10am–midnight.*

SPLURGE

➜ **La Oveja** SPANISH The rich get fatter and the poor mouths water at this historic culinary gem with Mudéjar ceilings, located right on Plaza de la Liberta and famous for its *cordero* (lamb). Let's face it, highfalutin' cake-eaters are the only people who can afford a meal here. That doesn't mean it's out of reach for the thrifty traveler; you can have it, too, as long as you sit at the cafeteria downstairs. The atmosphere is admittedly less stuffy, and the *horno de leña* is just meters away, which is where the real action takes place (dead pigs, big oven: You get the picture). *Vitoria*

5. ☎ *947-206-440* and *947-209-052. www. grupojeda.com. Raciones 5€–11€. Main dish about 20€. Plato combinado 12€. Tues–Sun 1:15–4pm and 9–11:30pm; Mon 1:15–4pm.*

CAFES/TEAROOM

→ **Café Mármedi** ★★ Avoiding the more touristy cafes on Calle Lain Calvo, I was at a loss for a local cafe until I stopped looking (love is always that way), and Mármedi came into my life along with her voluptuous mojitos. It wasn't love at first sight, but I knew she had something more to offer than a good wine rack and late nights at the bar. Turns out, she's really into video art and has friends at the University of Chicago with whom she exchanges shows. Hot dog, she's an exhibitionist, too! She loves group action and gets down to jazz and soul. Between you and me, low-lit nightcaps at her place are the hottest. *La Puebla 20.* ☎ *947-260-909. Specialty drinks 4–7€. Mon–Thurs 5pm–1am; Fri–Sat until 4am.*

Partying

Burgos gets cold at night and its party habits reflect the cool attitude. Indoor cafes or pubs make for a comfortable night out in this high-altitude town. For streets with condensed action, head toward **Calle La Puebla** and around **Plaza de la Libertad.** Leading into Plaza Alonso Martínez, **Calle Avellanos** is full of students who're beginning their prowl. For clubbing, there are wall-to-wall discos off of **Plaza San Juan** between Iglesia de San Lesmes and El Antiguo Convento de Benardas, but the sleazy-looking men at the bar inside are discouraging. **Huerto del Rey** (Las Llanas) is a more central option for cutting a rug, but don't arrive before 2am because the plaza is filled to the brim with teeny-boppers. The **Bernardos** area near Plaza España, especially around **Calle de los Calzados,** is where you can

wwwired

Café Cabaret (La Puebla 21; ☎ 947-202-722; www.cafecabaret. com; Mon–Thurs 4pm–2am, Fri–Sat 4pm–4am) is your one-stop wonder in Burgos: beer, drinks, huge TV screen for watching games, and an Internet cafe in back for drunken IMing. The sports bar, specializing in Jameson and draft beer, is packed on game nights making it difficult to reach the bar. It's a good thing the bartenders move like Tom Cruise in *Cocktail* so you don't have to wait long for your turn whether it's for a drink or an hour of Web surfing. It's located on a bar-packed street so start off your night early here; get all your traveling research done in back and join your friends to party in front.

dance to the same beat as the early-morning street cleaners.

BARS & NIGHTCLUBS

→ **Ram Jam Club** A laid-back atmosphere and classic rock music like Jimmy Hendrix and Neil Young (hard to find in small-town Spain) make this the perfect setting for groups of traveling friends who still want to be able to hear themselves talk. Get there at midnight and grab a table, a few beers, and dish up stories like it's Seinfeld goes to Spain. Once every 3 weeks or so there's a rock show. *San Juan 29.* ☎ *947-276-683.*

→ **Sohho** This brand-new club is where Burgos gets its groove on late-night. Nicely dressed guys 'n' dolls pour in at about 1am for Spanish pop and house music. It will take you about 5 to 10 totally doable minutes to walk from the city's center and taxis are not necessary for your way home as it's a busy and brightly lit street. If you're in the market to meet that special someone for the night, you'll have no problem picking up a partner for a slumber party here, where the conversation flows as easily as the vodka. But you'd better know how to move to Latin music; otherwise you're the square one out. *Reyes Católicos, 10. No phone.*

Sightseeing

In Burgos, the main attractions are spread out and not necessarily coupled in the historic city center like in most Spanish towns, so expect to do some walking. Plan your route in advance and take advantage of the walking paths along the river.

ATTRACTIONS & MONUMENTS

FREE ➔ **Cartuja de Miraflores** ★★
This royal convent, where Isabella's parents are buried, about an hour's walk east of town, is one of Burgos's highlights. The church was originally built in the late 15th century in order to fulfill her father's wish that he be buried in Cartuja, along with his wife and his son, the young Infante Alfonso, who died before he was 15. Gil de Siloé undertook the project and proved himself to be one of the best artists in history, building an incredible polychromatic **altarpiece** and alabaster **sepulcher** ★★★ for the royal family. It's the largest and most ornate this author has ever "seen"; it was closed during my visit, and I could only glimpse it by virtual camera. Having undergone serious restoration in the past years, other parts of the monastery may still be closed off; so call before committing to the trip out. Bus no. 27 (.70€) leaves Plaza Mayor, near the fountain, at 9:30am, 12:30pm, 4:15pm, and 7:15pm. However, only one bus returns at 4:30pm so you're better off biting the bullet and walking home or hitching a ride from someone else on the tour (which isn't so terrible; you're visiting a religious establishment after all).

Carretera de Burgos a Cardeña Km 3. ☎ *947-252-586. Free admission. Mon–Sat 10:15am–3pm and 4–6pm; Sun 11am–3pm and 4–6pm. 1.50€ for recommended guidebook (in English).*

➔ **Catedral de Santa María** ★★★
Towering above the city, this Gothic Godzilla, built in 1221, belittles anything that comes in sight of it. It's only appropriate then that El Cid and his wife Doña Ximena are buried here in a marble grave. In the Corpus Christi chapel, Cid's chest is hanging on display, supposedly holding documents from the Cathedral Archive. Legend has it, however, that El Cid filled it with gravel that he used to trick moneylenders who came to collect debts. Highlights in the nave and chapels include the effigy of Bishop Alonso de Cartagena (by the aforementioned Gil de Siloé) in the Chapel of the Visitation. The 14th-century image in the Chapel of the Holy Christ of Burgos of Christ being crucified has a cult following and is worth the investigation. Directly across from the entrance on the other side of the church is the Golden Stairway, built by Diego de Siloé in true Italian Renaissance spirit. The oldest chapel in the cathedral dating back to 1240 is the Chapel of St. Nicholas, on the right of the Golden Stairway. You can see the remains of an altar and two tombs from the 12th century days of Roman rule. Choir stalls depict the stories of new and old testament saints as well as the church founder, Bishop Mauricio. The most intricate of all chapels is behind the main altar, the Chapel of the High Constable, or Purification of the Virgin, to which a handful of darn good artists like Siloé contributed. Check out the painting by Leonard da Vinci's class pet Gianpetrino, who painted Mary Magdalene. If you can appreciate religious art, you shouldn't skip the museum, entered from the upstairs

Macho Macho Hero

El Cid (Rodrigo Díaz), born about 1043, was Commander in Chief for King Sancho II of Castile when the king began fighting his brothers and sisters for more territory. El Cid was a military genius and led Sancho's troops using unorthodox methods such as reading Roman and Greek aloud, brainstorming with soldiers from the front, and psychological warfare. But what goes around comes around, and when Sancho was murdered in 1072, Alfonso, the very brother Sancho and El Cid were fighting against, abdicated Castile and León. For obvious reasons, El Cid was not at all liked by Alfonso's posse, and he was exiled 7 years later. So he did what any good businessman would do: He joined up with the Moors and began winning their wars against the Christians. After proving himself again to Alfonso, he was pardoned by the king, who conveniently needed a good commander at the time. A few years later in 1094, there was a siege in Valencia, and you better believe El Cid was there with his Muslim army to gain control of the entire Mediterranean in the name of Spain. When he died at home 5 years later, legend has it his wife Ximena strapped his corpse to a horse and set it loose on the field to conceal his death. El Cid's troops rallied, and the enemy was so terrified they retreated to their ships. His body was moved more times than he has bones but was finally put to rest in Burgos in 1921. Today young lads like to touch the horse's big 'nads on El Cid's sculpture. They think it will make 'em macho.

cloister, where you'll find sculptures, chalices, and stained glass. *Plaza de Santa María.* ☎ *947-204-712. Admission to cathedral and museum: 4€ adults, 2.50€ students. Phone tour: 3.50€. Spring and fall daily 9:30am–1:15pm and 4–7:15pm; winter daily 10am–1:15pm and 4–6:45pm; summer daily 9:30am–7:15pm (Sun closed 3–3:30pm).*

→ **Real Monasterio de las Huelgas** ★★ Before there was El Escorial, there was El Real Monasterio, the place where the Spanish monarchy got sent when they bit the dust. Attached to it is the Cistercian monastery, whose nuns had more power than Madonna. Built in the 12th century by King Alfonso VIII, it holds the sepulchers of him, his wife Doña Leonor Plantagenet, King Henry I, Queen Doña Berenguela, Prince Don Fernando de la Cerda, and other Castilians. The only way one could assure his/her body got sent here, however, was to be a female heir to the Castilian throne, her son, or married to

her. The chapter rooms, vaults, and cloisters are all decorated with Moorish designs since the best artists of the time were, in fact, Moors. Make sure to find the pennant of La Naves de Tolosa in the chapter room. **The Museum de Ricas Telas** ★ has robes nicer than all of Elizabeth Taylor's wedding dresses combined. *Compás de Adentro (outside the center and west across the river).* ☎ *947-201-630. Admission 5€ adults, 4€ students. Tues–Sat 10am–1pm and 3:45–5:30pm; Sun 10:30am–2pm. Closed Mon.*

MUSEUMS & CHURCHES

→ **Castillo de Burgos** There's not much here that's original because Napoleon Bonehead blew it all up when he got kicked out of Spain. But the walk up the hill is worth the view and a drink at one of two watering holes located at the top (see "Eating"). Call ahead for a tour; otherwise just take a look at the ruins for yourself. ☎ *947-288-874. Admission 1.20€. Nov–June*

Sat–Sun 11am–2pm and 4–7pm; July–Oct daily 11am–2pm and 5–8:30pm.

➜**Iglesia de San Esteban** This Gothic church from the 12th century is best known for the *Museo de Retablo* (Altarpiece Museum), which shows gilded and very gaudy altarpieces from all over Burgos from the 15th, 16th, and 17th centuries. It was mysteriously closed at the time of writing (and infamous for never being open) so confirm first. The museum lies at the foot of El Parque de Castillo and is a good stop on your way up the hill to the castile. ☎ 947-273-752. *Admission 1.20€ adults, .60€ students. Summer Tues–Fri 10:30am–2pm and 4:30–7pm, Sun 10:30am–2pm; rest of the year Sat 10:30am–2pm and 4:30–7pm, Sun 10:30am–2pm.*

FREE ➜**Iglesia de San Nicolas** This church just opposite the cathedral is worth a quick peek when you've got some downtime. The austere Gothic structure is so dark and heavy you half expect Lancelot to stride in on horseback—if it weren't for the cheesy religious music blaring from the speakers. But its altar by Francisco de Colonia depicting St. Nicolas is what makes people create such a fuss over the old thing. *Fernán Gonzales s/n.* ☎ *947-207-095. Free admission Mon; Tues–Sun 1€. May–Sept Mon 9am–2pm and 4:30–8:30pm, Tues–Fri 10am–2pm and 4:30–7pm, Sat 10am–noon and 5–7pm, Sun 9am–1:30pm and 5–6pm; Oct–May Mon 9am–2pm and 4:30–8:30pm, Tues–Fri 11:30am–1:30pm, Sat 11am–1:30pm and 5–7pm, Sun 10am–noon and 5–6pm.*

Shopping

Burgos is a bull's-eye for those in the market for decorative spoons or collectible thimbles. If your collection's full up, our time-honored suggestion is jarred olives, wine, and olive oil. The wines are some of the best in the region (the most prestigious being Ribera del Duero), and it's worth a peek inside the many specialty shops on Calle de la Paloma to scout them out for moms, dads, or goosey aunts back home.

📺 Best ☺ Salamanca ★★★

Salamanca is the Ivy League of Spain. Hell, our IQs jumped points just for dragging our butts to town. Greats such as Fray Luis de León, Menéndez Valdés, Miguel de Unamuno, and Miguel Cervantes all passed through in some form or the other, gracing the city with their wit and celebrity. However, this is and always will be a student's town: cheap eats, drinks, mucho fiesta, and a high-caliber university attracting a hybrid of students.

On the Northern Plateau, in the southwest corner of Castile and León, bordering Portugal and the province of Extremadura, Salamanca has a long history of wars and relentless conquerors. After the last Christian takeover by Alfonso VI, the town was finally given its charter in 1096. A few decades later, the university was built, and Salamanca got its groove back. The school soon became so renowned that the Pope classified the University of Salamanca in the same bracket as Oxford, Paris, and Bologna. That name has gotten the boot to the back seat but the language departments are still as strong as ever, attracting international students who supposedly come here to study Spanish, but c'mon man: What they're really researching are the clubs steaming with the city's young horny energy. It only takes about 10 minutes to be enchanted by the city's sights: a modern city with Gothic spiraling buildings that time warps you hundreds of years.

MTV🎵 Arty Facts

Salamanca wouldn't be a university town without a cutting-edge cultural center for the contemporary arts, (FREE) **Domus Artium 2002** (Centro de Arte de Salamanca, Av. de Aldehuela s/n; ☎ 923-184-916; free admission; Tues–Fri noon–2:30pm and 4–9pm, Sat–Sun 11am–9pm), showcasing new artists and their hot creations such as graffiti and hip-hop. A great restaurant cures the gallery-hopping munchies (see "Eating"). Did we mention it's free?

(FREE) **Patio de Escuelas** (Universidad de Salamanca, Pal. de Maldonado, Pl. de San Benito s/n; ☎ 923-294-400; free admission; schedule varies) is an open-air patio run by the University of Salamanca and headquarters for the **Centro de Fotografía.** Exhibitions include sculpture and deserve your attention whether you're totally into it or just jetting through.

(FREE) **Palacio de Abrantes** (Sala de exposiciones de la Universidad de Salamanca, Pal. de Maldonado, Pl. de San Benito s/n; ☎ 923-294-480; free admission; Mon noon–2pm, Tues–Sun noon–2pm and 6–9pm) started out as a 15th-century mansion, but today it's a bustling cultural center. Fine arts such as sculpture, photography, and contemporary installations all find their place here, thanks to a series of young vanguardian artists.

Getting There & Around

BY CAR

You have a car, you lucky dog. From Madrid, take freeway A6 toward La Coruña to Sanchidrian (100km/62 miles), where you will exit and take road **N-501** toward **Avila.** Follow N-501, not yellow nor brick, all the way to Salamanca.

BY TRAIN

Six trains run daily from Madrid's Chamartín train station to Salamanca's Ferrocarril (☎ 902-240-202), leaving at 8:45am, 11:00am, 1:45pm, 3:45pm, and 7:45pm. The price is 14€ one-way, and 25€ round-trip (trip time: about 2½ hr.).

Once in the nicely outfitted Salamanca train station, cross the street to where the bus stop is. The no. 1 bus (black line) comes every half-hour or so (except during siesta, 2–4pm) and will take you directly into the city for .80€. All buses pass near Plaza Mayor eventually so you really shouldn't have a problem.

BY BUS

The express coach service **Auto Res (www.auto-res.net)** to Salamanca leaves Madrid every hour from 7:00am until 10pm for 14€ each way (trip time: 2½ hr.). The cheaper (11€) service is also slower (trip time: 3 hr.) and less frequent—we don't recommend it. The main **bus terminal** (☎ 923-236-717) is at Avenida Filiberto Villalobos, northwest of the old town. Any city bus will take you to the center (Plaza Mayor).

City buses (☎ 923-190-545) depart at regular 10- to 20-minute intervals from Plaza del Mercado. Buses that cut through the center of Salamanca are the 1, 2, 3, 4, 6, or 8; those that go to the train station are the 1, 11, and 3; and those to the bus station are the 4 or the 7. A one-way fare costs .80€. Numbers and prices are subject to change and hikes in the next year.

BY FOOT

By far the number one best way to kick it in Salamanca is with your feet. Period.

Salamanca

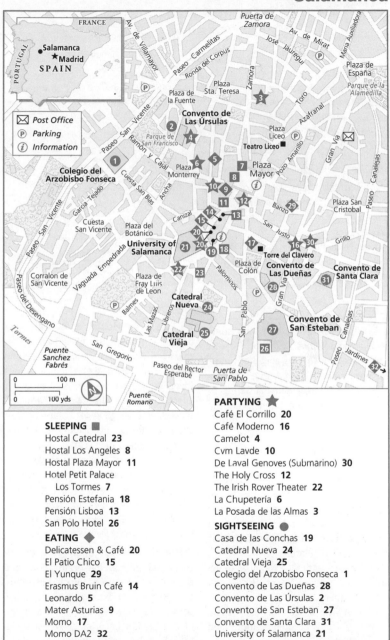

PARTYING ⭐
Café El Corrillo **20**
Café Moderno **16**
Camelot **4**
Cvm Lavde **10**
De Laval Genoves (Submarino) **30**
The Holy Cross **12**
The Irish Rover Theater **22**
La Chupetería **6**
La Posada de las Almas **3**

SIGHTSEEING ●
Casa de las Conchas **19**
Catedral Nueva **24**
Catedral Vieja **25**
Colegio del Arzobisbo Fonseca **1**
Convento de Las Dueñas **28**
Convento de Las Úrsulas **2**
Convento de San Esteban **27**
Convento de Santa Clara **31**
University of Salamanca **21**

SLEEPING ■
Hostal Catedral **23**
Hostal Los Angeles **8**
Hostal Plaza Mayor **11**
Hotel Petit Palace
    Los Tormes **7**
Pensión Estefania **18**
Pensión Lisboa **13**
San Polo Hotel **26**

EATING ◆
Delicatessen & Café **20**
El Patio Chico **15**
El Yunque **29**
Erasmus Bruin Café **14**
Leonardo **5**
Mater Asturias **9**
Momo **17**
Momo DA2 **32**

Salamanca Nuts & Bolts

Emergency The **Red Cross** (☎ 923-216-824) is at Plaza de San Vicente 1. There's hella drinking in Salamanca so it's good to have this phone number on you, just in case.

Laundry If your clothes are skanked from too much traveling, it's time for a wash 'n' spin. **Lavasec** (☎ 923-242-120; Mon–Fri 10am–1pm and 5–7pm, Sat 10am–1pm) is located at Calle Asturias 6.

Post Office Go'head, make your parents' day with a postcard. The main **Correo** is at Calle Gran Via 25.

Taxi Just in case you need a designated driver home, call ☎ 923-250-000.

Tourist Information The tourist office is at **Oficina Municipal de Turismo** (Plaza Mayor 32; ☎ 902-302-002). Its summer hours are Monday to Friday 9am to 2pm and 4:30 to 8pm, Saturday 10am to 8pm, Sunday 10am to 2pm; in winter Monday to Friday 9am to 2pm and 4:30 to 6:30pm, Saturday 10am to 6:30pm, Sunday 9am to 2pm. Just as helpful is the one at **Casa de las Conchas** (Rúa Mayor 20; ☎ 923-268-571; summer Mon–Thurs and Sun 9am–8pm, Fri–Sat 9am–9pm; winter daily 9am–2pm and 5–8pm).

Sleeping

The heart of Salamanca offers up some nice accommodations, but the trick is to call 2 weeks or 10 days ahead of time—otherwise you're screwed. High season begins in April during Semana Santa, or Easter week. Prices are often jacked up during these months, as well as during fiesta, or holiday. It's nearly impossible to find decent accommodation last-minute unless you settle for an over-priced dump near the train station, or a pueblo outside the city as a last resort. Many students find private residents who rent out their rooms, which is an attractively cheap option though *ten cuidado* (be careful), as this trade is not regulated.

If you're stuck without a room, go to the tourist office in Plaza Mayor. Hotels and hostels call there first when they have a cancellation. The office will also supply you with a list of accommodations and phone numbers.

HOSTELS

MTV **Best** ➔ **Hostal Catedral** ★★★
You can't find a better place to stay than this glam guesthouse—a bright, heavenly abode with crisp embroidered sheets. Bling, bling. The hostess is attentive to guests' needs and fills the salon with fresh flowers and her good ol' fashion Spanish charm. Better yet, the *hostal* sits on top of the main street with a crystal clear view of the cathedral. All rooms have bathrooms and new mattresses. Don't hesitate making this place your first call—just remember the early bird gets the room. *Rúa Mayor 46, 1B.* ☎ *923-270-614. With full bathroom, single 30€, double 45€, triple 55€.*

➔ **Hostal Los Angeles** Situated right smack dab in Plaza Mayor, this hotel pins the tail on the donkey for its prime location. Request an exterior room for a balcony looking over the plaza, and groggy mornings will seem brighter over an (over-priced) coffee on the giant Plaza Mayor

wwwired

E-mail your friends back home and tell them you've decided to transfer to Salamanca: Your first option is **Ciberspace** (Plaza Mayor 10; ☎ **923-212-596;** Mon–Fri 11am–midnight, Sat–Sun noon–midnight). The second is **Cyber Anuario** (Calle de la Latina 8; ☎ **923-261-354;** Mon–Fri 9am–1am and Sat–Sun 10am–1am).

below. Rooms with full bathroom have a view of the plaza. For overseas chats, an Internet cafe in the same building is open late for cyber rendezvous. *Plaza Mayor 10, 2nd and 3rd floors.* ☎ *923-218-166. With shared bathroom 18€ single, 32€ double; with full bathroom 28€ single, 38€ double. Amenities: Wi-Fi.*

➜ **Hostal Plaza Mayor** ★★ This well-run, very clean hotel is buried deep in cafes, bars, and restaurants just outside the Plaza Mayor. Walking home in a drunken stupor was never so easy. In fact, its stairs lead directly to the cafe bar next door for easy-access coffee or tapas. The dark-wood furniture and bright rooms lend the place its good taste. The basket of bathroom goodies and extra toilet paper is a plus, and all rooms have full bathrooms—though the corner shower is super small, so be careful bending down for the soap. *Plaza del Corrillo 20.* ☎ *923-262-020. High season and holidays single 36€, double 60€, triple 90€; low season single 30€, double 50€, triple 75€. Amenities: Laundry service. In room: A/C, TV.*

CHEAP

➜ **Pensión Estefania** This family-run hostel just off Calle Rúa Mayor has its own attitude: a mix of Asian, Spanish, and we're-not-sure-what-else decor that leaves a dark, Gothic aftertaste in our mouths we

can't help but like. The owner loves wood and has literally "decked" it out as such using none other than wood-panel siding. Rooms without a bathroom are equipped with their own shower and sink, and sleep up to three people in a private room. Shared bathrooms are shiny clean, and there's a sunny patio. *Jesús 3-5.* ☎ *923-217-372. Double with shared toilet or full bathroom 30€, triple with shared toilet 40€. Amenities: Rooms for those w/limited mobility.*

➜ **Pensión Lisboa** ★ A young couple runs this joint with smiles, and their dirt-cheap, centrally located pension is a reflection of their happy-go-lucky attitudes. Not only that, but there's a terraza on the top floor, where you're invited to eat your bag lunch or catch some rays. Request room no. 8, for a private balcony with a killer view, though the room is smaller than most. Rooms without bathrooms have sinks and mirrors. *Meléndez 1.* ☎ *923-214-333. Shared toilet single 16€, double 24€; with full bathroom single 31€, double 32€. Amenities: Laundry service (6€). In room: TV.*

DOABLE

➜ **Hotel Petit Palace Los Tormes** It might be worth shelling out the dough for a three-star room in this luxe hotel that sits a stone's throw away from Plaza Mayor. The spotless rooms are modern without traces of cheeky Spanish decor. Although all the views aren't of the plaza (request a suite or a *doble superior*), we suggest this place for its affordable sleekness. Pull-down beds are available for extra overnight guests in a family room, or *habitación familiar*, though they'll have to pay extra—for the bed, wise guy. *Concejo 4 (Plaza Mayor).* ☎ *923-212-100. www.hthoteles.com. Weekdays single 65€, double 75€; weekends and holidays double 110€, single 90€; habitaciónes familiars 100€ (week) or 180€ (weekend). Amenities: Restaurant, breakfast buffet (8€), elevator,* *laundry service. In room: A/C, TV, hair dryer, PC with Internet.*

➜ **San Polo Hotel** Situated in the old part of town on the site of the 11th-century ruins of the church of the same name, this modern hotel stands in stark contrast to its historic surroundings. We like its '50s California appeal, sans the outdoor pool. Outside large glass windows is a cafe serving up java where the old church once held holy services. If you have the money, honey, this is the best place in town to rest your noodle. *Arroyo de Santo Domingo 2.* ☎ *923-211-177. www.hotelsanpolo.es. High season (Apr–May, weekends in Sept, and holidays) single (with double bed) 76€, double 96€, triple 114€. See website for other listed prices. Amenities: Restaurant, bar, elevator, sheets, towels. In room: A/C, satellite TV, safe.*

Eating

With all the inexpensive places to eat in Salamanca, choosing just one is difficult. Most restaurants will offer a *menú del día.* As in all Spanish cities, this is the cheapest route. Salamanca is famous for its *salchicha* (sausage) as well as its meaty *hornazo* pastry, typically filled with ham, sausage, and lamb. They're only served in large portions, so if you want to sample but don't feel like lugging leftovers home, pick up an *empanada,* which is a close, pie-crusted relative. Besides serving cheap-ass *cañas* (beer), Salamentine bars are most famous for dishing up a generous portion of tapas to help wash everything down. This is great when all you want is a small snack to tie you over until late in the evening for a night of drinking until early in the morning. **Plaza Mayor** is a great place to start your tapas crawl.

TAPAS

➜ **El Patio Chico** ★ You can't get more hard-core Spanish than this popular tapas bar serving all the classics under hanging hams and antique Castilian thingamajigs, plus a full menu on the terraza. Named after the small plaza where the new cathedral joins the old, it's where the Spanish men feast. It's also good for cheap *churros* (fried dough) and coffee after a macho night out. *Meléndez 13.* ☎ *923-265-103. Breakfast: 1.80€. Main course 7.20€–12€. Tapas 4.10€–12€. Daily 8am–3:45pm and 8–11:30pm.*

Ⓜ Best ☺ ➜ **Momo and Momo DA2** ★★ TAPAS/WINE BAR Possibly the best food we've ever tasted: Both restaurants cook up *tapas modernas* (there are no generic Spanish tortillas on the menu as a rule of thumb) hailed by the international culinary world, all for the cost of whatever is left in your lint-filled pockets. Don't skip out on the cheese-and-pepper tostada; these tapas are dressed to kill. Swing by Momo DA2 for contemporary art exhibitions, live music, and its terraza. *Momo, San Pablo 13-15.* ☎ *923-280-798. Momo DA2, Av. de la Aldehuela s/n.* ☎ *923-180-782. Tapas .80€. Raciones 9€. Daily from 11am–3pm and 9:30–11pm.*

CHEAP

Ⓜ Best ☺ ➜ **El Yunque** FAST FOOD/ SPANISH This is the best buy for your money, offering portions of *patatas bravas* and *bocadillos* the size of your head for only a few euros. *Calimotxo* (coke and wine) is drunk in a gigantic glass for 3€, which is another reason why it's so popular with young Spaniards. That, and it cures the hunger pangs during the wee hours of the night. *Calle Hovohambre (between Calle Varillas and Calle Obispo Jarrín, near Gran Vía).* ☎ *923-219-936. Bocadillos 2€–4€. Weekdays 1:30pm–3:30am; weekends 1:30pm–4am.*

➜ **Leonardo** FAST FOOD We won't blame you Americans for craving a burger 'n' fries. Here's your chance for cheap fast food at the touch of a button, literally. You order from an archaic tape machine that looks like an old jukebox, and it magically computes it back to the kitchen. It's great for a midnight snack and the drunken munchies on Saturday nights. *Iscar Peyra 2.* ☎ *923-212-664. Hamburgers, sandwiches 2.70€–4€. Menú 5.50€. Daily 10pm–1am; later on Sat.*

DOABLE

→**Erasmus Bruin Café** INTERNATIONAL Although this restaurant/bar has its roots in Holland, it's a hot spot among international students for its decent music and big plates: Think Irish pub. The entire bar is decorated like Amsterdam with tons, if not too much, of TGIF "flair." The reasonably priced restaurant, famous for fondue, converts to a popular bar around 11pm. Beware, this is a conservative bunch; you will not find an Amsterdam cafe that's friendly to tokers or mushroom eaters in these parts, but there is a wine corner for those who are into experimentation. *Méléndez 7.* ☎ *923-265-742. www.erasmuscafe.com. Meal 10€–15€. Daily noon–4pm and 8pm–midnight.*

→**Mater Asturias** TAPAS/EURO Stop blaming Eve for the apple and take a bite for yourself. Right off Plaza Mayor, this sinful food bar is a veritable Garden of Eden serving tapas and *sangria de sidra* (Austurian beer cider) on economy-size tables, all fitted with *sidra* dispensers that pour evenly measured drinks—like a modernized and more social version of the beer helmet. Watching *fútbol* games is the second most popular event here. Toward the back, typical Austurian dishes are served. *Calle Prior (right outside Plaza Mayor).* ☎ *923-218-386. Bottle of sidra 3.60€. Main course 9€–16€. Daily 1–4pm and 9pm–midnight.*

CAFE

→**Delicatessen & Café** If you're looking for trendy tapas, you need look no further. Here, beautiful people (mostly tourists) eat fabulous food under a covered patio that

we love. There's a baby grand piano to boot. Order coffee or a piece of chocolate cake and take a seat near the piles of fashion magazines. Otherwise don your fake Gucci's—granted it's not the snazziest place to wear your authentic ones—and dig in. Like at many restaurants in Spain, the bar staff can be slow. *Méléndez 25.* ☎ *923-280-309. Main course 8€–15€. Desserts 3.50€–4€. Menú 10€. Daily 10am–5am. Reservations recommended.*

Partying

This is a university town and though we didn't find an Animal House, Salamantinos might have easily pledged Bar None. Places fill up at midnight, right after a late-night Spanish dinner, and clubs get jumping at 2am. Best part is, there's never a cover—anywhere! Salamantinos dress up to the nines, and unless it's cold, never wear jeans or tennies.

Tuesdays and Wednesdays are the official day for foreigners, when "language exchange" parties are promoted in many bars with drink specials. Thursday is the day par excellence for college students, and on Fridays and Saturdays, everyone and their grandmas party. Holla!

The main areas to hit are Calle Compania for clubbing and hard drinking, Calle de San Justo, Calle de Varillas, and Calle del Consuelo for *chupeterías* (great shot bars—but full of young'ns), and Gran Via, Plaza Mayor, and Plaza de San Juan Bautista, which is famous for its cheap 40s of beer *(litros).*

BARS

→**Café Moderno** Decorated like a small town complete with barbershop and cool vintage radios, it was one of the first dance clubs in Salamanca to promote unconventional activities, such as its own cultural program, El Gallo. Literary superstars like Gonzalo Torrente Ballester and poet Mario

Benedetti have even been spotted here. Join the paparazzi and tote your camera just in case. Get here really late and stay the night for coffee and *churros* in the morning. *Gran Vía 75.* ☎ *923-210-760.*

➔ **The Holy Cross** If you think a bar that looks exactly like a cathedral, albeit on a smaller scale, is pure nirvana, you'll love this heavenly Irish bar with Spanish clientele and great ways to sin—uh, start the night. A jaunt through its pearly gates is worth the ambience of American music and mixed age groups that nix pretentiousness. Its website advertises drunken monks, which just might bring Communion to a whole new level on Sundays. Wednesday is international night. *Poeta Iglesias 17.* ☎ *923-614-419. www.the-holycross.com.*

📺 Best ⭘ ➔ **La Chupitería** Some bars in Salamanca need warning labels, and this is one, serving shots of alcohol for dangerously cheap prices. The shots range from .90€ to 1.30€, and include a wide variety including absinthe-cannabis—proceed with caution! The house specialty is a treat of Bailey's and Kahlua in a chocolate-dipped ice-cream cone with whipped cream— good recipe for a body shot, though a little sticky. *Calle Companía in Plaza Monterrey. No phone.*

➔ **La Posada de las Almas** Large cathedral doors will make you think you're in the wrong place, but its intimidating doormen and highly entertaining decor will put you where you belong: near the bar. Look for the dollhouse with surprising detail on the wall near the main entrance. The bar throws theme parties (Thurs is international night) with guest DJs more times than you can say Hail Mary, and the extremely talented bartenders pour drinks more slick than Sam in *Cheers. Plaza San Boal, down Calle Zamora from Plaza Mayor. No phone. www.posadadelasalmas.com.*

LIVE MUSIC

➔ **Café El Corrillo** This place, a legend in its own right for international jazz shows and big-time headliners, has continued to book solid since it opened in the '80s. Groups that cruise across the downstairs stage, shake, rattle, and roll their way around the globe to places like the U.S., Brazil, Cuba, and Africa. During the day, the cafe is hopping with students who scan posters and bills for upcoming Corrillo events. Show times are Thursday and Friday nights; try to catch the owner during the day for one of his fruit smoothies, and he'll fill you in with the goods. *Meléndez 18.* ☎ *923-271-917. www.cafecorrillo.com.*

➔ **The Irish Rover Theater** Every town has a generic Irish bar, and this is our fave when we need our Guinness fix. It's good for coffee and cheap food during the day, and surprisingly, there's decent pop dance music at night; a DJ spins on the weekends. The bar is set up to look like an old theater complete with velvet-upholstered banks and was the pioneer in hosting live shows (plays, comedy, cabaret, concerts), which it does on Tuesdays (no admission). The roomy dance floor doesn't fill up until about 2am. Keep away if you don't want to be near Americans, especially on Wednesdays, which is international night. This is where the young study-abroad students gather, and you better believe they're sporting their Abercrombie & Fitch. *Serranos 9. (Rúa Antigua towards Casa de las Canchas.)* ☎ *923-210-035. www.theirishrover.com.*

NIGHTCLUBS

➔ **Camelot** Mecca is the wrong word for this club as it's actually a Catholic church, the Convento of Úrsulas, but the point is that it's the best-known dance club in all of Salamanca. The two-story dance floor is packed by 1am with hoards of Spanish and internationals grinding to Spanish pop music. Good luck fighting your way to the bar. There's a war out there, soldier! And two for one drink specials. *Bordadores 3.* ☎ *923-219-091. www.camelotsalamanca.com.*

→**Cvm Lavde** Best known by locals to attract *pijos* (rich socialites), it offers a setting just as distinguished. The dance floor looks exactly like Plaza Mayor, built using the same authentic Villamayor sandstone. Saturday at 2:30am is the best time to see and be seen. *Prior 5-7, near Plaza Mayor.* ☎ *923-267-577. www.cvmlavde.com.*

GAY NIGHTLIFE

→**De Laval Genoves** The club that is really known as Submarino is seasick with fresh underwater decor (it's also rumored that hash gets handed off outdoors). The best DJs spin here, primarily electronic beats. The party starts at 2am in a serious-looking submarine ship with exposed pipes and thingamabobs that sink it as one of the premier dance clubs in all of Salamanca. If you're looking for one place to stay the night, then this is your rave scene. Leave your drunken goggles in your suitcase; besides offering an equal opportunity lover, Submarino is awash with the 20-something and the beautiful. *San Justo 27. (Up from Gran Via. Watch for its porthole doors, as it's easy to miss.)* ☎ *923-260-264.*

Sightseeing

Salamanca is one of those towns you go to for a slice of old Spain. Its skyline is pierced with Gothic buildings and an outstanding cathedral that will take you to another place and time. The amount of things to see and do in Salamanca is overwhelming so sit down with a *café con leche* and plan your itinerary beforehand, in order to keep with Spain's weird siesta schedule and still get everything in. And keep in mind that everything—that includes monasteries and convents—are best in moderation.

Festivals

February

Clear the streets on February 13, **Dia de San Blas,** the day of the old lady, and she ain't no saint. This is the day when women take over—even the mayor's wife gets a shot at her husband's top position. The best part? The men must obey. Someone tell Snoop Dogg, it's Señoras Gone Wild!

March/April

Although historically a Catholic country, Spain seems to do more partying than praying, and this is especially true during Semana Santa, Spain's Catholic version of Spring Break. This is also the time when everyone jacks their prices, in order to make some extra cash off of tourists. **Lunes de Aguas** (Monday of Waters) is the Salmantine celebration when people gather in the country near Rio Tormes to feast on *hornazo*. Interestingly, this is to commemorate the city's prostitutes, exiled during Lent by King Phillip. In those days, students welcomed them back with open arms, and good business.

June

San Juan de Sahagun (June 12) is a celebration in honor of that patron saint of Salamanca; it's a 4-day holiday of music and novice bullfighting.

September

On September 8, the town throws a party for the pilgrims dressed in old *charro* peasant gear. The rest of the month (until the 21st) Salamanca holds fiestas for the **Virgen de la Vega** (Virgin of the Valley) and St. Matthew.

ATTRACTIONS & MONUMENTS

(FREE) →**Casa de las Conchas** This architectural jewel has more than 300 seashells decorating its facade. Why all the shells? Don Rodrigo Arias Maldonado, its first owner, was a member of the Order of

Santiago, and seashells are associated with its patron saint, St. James. There are romantics, however, who say the real reason is that Don Rodgrigo was whipped by his wife, Doña María, whose family crest incorporated seashells. The interior courtyard is framed by arches, which are so typical of Salamanca that the style has been dubbed *Salmantino.* Las Conchas also houses the Tourist Office and regional library. *Calle Companía 2.* ☎ *923-269-317. Free admission. Mon–Fri 9am–9pm, Sat 9am–2pm and 5pm–8, Sun 10am–2pm and 5–8pm. Library Mon–Fri 9am–9pm, Sat 9am–2pm.*

FREE → **Catedral Nueva** Salamanca actually has two cathedrals, the new and the old. The new structure was built in 1513 when the city decided that Isabella and Ferdinand needed more elbowroom while they prayed. Originally it was designed in the Gothic style, but over time, Renaissance and baroque styles also crept in. The main facade, facing Calle Cardenal Plá y Deniel, is an example of Flamboyant Gothic. When masons were repairing the church's deteriorated stone, they added an anachronistic astronaut among the Gothic carvings—see if you can find it first. (If you're sick of Salamanca's "I Spy" games, then here's your answer: The astronaut will be just above your head on the left-hand side of the massive doors, incorporated in the leaf engraving on the farthest column to the left.) Inside the cathedral, look for the Golden Chapel and the Retable of Christ of the Battles, containing the Romanesque carving that El Cid supposedly brought with him during his exile. *Plaza Juan XXII.* ☎ *923-217-476. Free admission. Daily 9am–8pm.*

→ **Catedral Vieja** In order to get to the old church, you must enter through the new, as they're interconnected. Construction started way back in 1140, and included not just Gothic architecture, but

I Spy a Frog!

Who knows why people from Salamanca are obsessed with hiding things in cement like frogs or astronauts, but it attracts schools of tourists who want to crack the case and makes loads of euros in T-shirt, key chain, and knickknack sales. Some people say that Salamanca was once infested with frogs. Another theory is that it has to do with the evils of prison life. We'll stick to the princess and the frog fairy tale, thanks. But there is one Salamantino legend we'll bite into. If you can find the little frog, eroded as it is on the facade of the University Civil, you will either a) Pass all your classes b) Return to Salamanca in the future or c) Have an amazing sex life while in Salamanca. We vote for c. But without any clues, it's damn hard to find the little bugger. Cheat and croak!

also Romanesque influences. Take a look at the popular scallop-tiled Cock Tower *(Torre del Gallo),* a famous Salamanca landmark. The ribbed umbrella lantern is direct Byzantine influence. The altarpiece in the central chapel is by Nicholas of Florence in the 15th century, consisting of frescoes depicting the story of Jesus and Mary, Judgment Day, and Jesus condemning souls to hell. Ouch. Try to spot Salamanca's patron saint, the Virgen of Vega, who has center stage in the same gallery. *Plaza Juan XXII.* ☎ *923-217-476. Admission 3€ adult, 2.50€ student. Daily 10am–7:30pm.*

→ **Colegio del Arzobisbo Fonseca** We checked this place out for the antique clock collection and its peaceful courtyard. It was originally built as a convent in 1527, but in 1838 it turned into a school for Irish

ᴍ ᴛ ᴠ🎸 Geeking Out

Alfonso IX built the **University of Salamanca** (C. de los Libreros; ☎ **923-294-400,** ext. 1125; admission 4€ adults, 2€ students, free Mon [note: Fee also includes entrance to Patio de las Escuelas Menores]; Mon–Fri 4–7pm, Sat 9:30am–1pm and 4–6:30pm, Sun 10am–1pm), the oldest in Spain, in 1218 for the men of León. The most important architectural aspect of the school is the door. Here lies the frog. If you don't want to know where it is, stop reading here. The frog rests high on the right-hand side. It's sitting on top of the left-most skull. If you don't see it by now, stop looking so hard. Next take a look at the medallion above the two doors, which shows Catholic kings holding an ornamented staff representing the unity of Spain.

Inside Fray Luis de Leon Hall, you can see how students have worn down the wooden tables by centuries of arduous note scribbling. Their favorite professor who lectured here won his student's respect for sticking it to the man. After translating the Song of Solomon into Spanish, the hall's namesake was jailed for 5 years by the Inquisition. Back in the saddle again, he began class with: "As we were saying yesterday . . . " Smartass.

Whether you're a student or not, university libraries are daunting; this one is among the oldest in Europe and houses about 160,000 musty volumes. Crane your neck upward to the ceiling; the carved wooden ceilings are worth the strain. From the Patio de las Escuelas Menores, a grassy square, you'll see the entrance to the Museo de la Universidad, which has an impressive zodiac fresco (free if you pay to see the university).

CASTILLA Y LEÓN

Catholics, operational until 1936. *Fonseca 4.* ☎ *923-294-570. Admission .60€ adult, .30€ student. Daily 10am–2pm and 4–7pm.*

→ **Convento de las Dueñas** This small cloister has one of the most beautiful gardens so take a book or a lover. Dozens of eerie faces are uniquely carved on stone columns upstairs, which makes the cloister more entertaining than most. You're also allowed to peek into the former room of La Negrita, an African slave who entered the convent in the early 18th century. Pictures and relics inside repaint the chilling history of the international slave trade. The nuns who run the convent bake delicious sweets (sold by the box for 4€) that help soothe turned stomachs. *Plaza del Concilio de Trento s/n.* ☎ *923-215-442. Admission 1.50€. Mon–Sat 10:30am–12:45pm and 4:30–6:45pm; Sun 11am–12:45pm and 4:30–6:45pm.*

→ **Convento de Las Úrsulas** Northeast of the Colegio Fonseca is the Convento de las Úrsulas, a late-Gothic convent of Ursuline nuns that houses the alabaster tomb (by Diego de Siloé) of Archbishop Alonso Fonseca. The must-sees include works by Michelangelo Morales, Juan de Borgoña, and some other really important guys. So what makes these nuns so cool? They rent out part of their pad to Camelot, the hottest nightclub in town. Now that's a kick-ass Sister Act. *Calle de las Úrsulas 2.* ☎ *923-219-877. Admission 2€. Daily 11am–1pm and 4:30–6pm; closed the last Sun of every month.*

→ **Convento de San Esteban** This must-see in Salamanca is worth the price of admission. Belonging to the Dominican Order (the group of monks who traveled to Central America, in order to convert natives to Catholicism), this impressive church is a solid example of Spanish Renaissance Plateresque style. Walk inside and take note of the mirrors strategically placed on the floors, giving you a bird's-eye view of the intricately carved ceilings. Upstairs are the choir stalls, El Claustro de los Reyes and La Sala Capitular, as well as an exhibition of Central American artifacts kept by monks returning from the New World. *Plaza del Concilio de Trento s/n.* ☎ *923-215-000. Admission 1.50€. Wed–Sat 9:30am–1pm and 4–8pm; Sun 9:30am–1pm; Mon–Tues 4–8pm.*

→**Convento de Santa Clara** The Roman-like building was built by monks from the Santa Clara Order in the 13th century. It's gone under many face-lifts to get it into the shape it's in today. The only way you can climb the tower and catch a glimpse of the fancy ceilings, however, is if you pay for a private tour. *Santa Clara 2.* ☎ *923-269-623. Admission 2€. Mon–Fri 9:30am–1:40pm and 4–6:40pm; Sat–Sun and holidays (except for July–Aug) 9am–2:40pm.*

Shopping

Salamanca is known for its silver and, like most other Spanish cities, its leather. Keep an extra eye out for Salamanca's provincial symbol, a filigreed silver emblem. The best shopping is down **Calle Zamora**—it's lined with both inexpensive and pricey shops. The street opens up to a large **outdoor market** that hosts frequent artisan fairs that attract artists from all over Castilla y León. While you're in this neck of the woods, try **Calle Sol Oriente,** which turns into **Calle Bientocadas,** both known for their shop-lined streets. For souvenirs and T-shirts, the best street is **Calle Rúa Mayor.** Pick yourself up some ubiquitous frog souvenirs, easy gifts for parents and friends. Also, University of Salamanca T-shirts and sweatshirts are dirt-cheap. There are also a few specialty food stores where you can pick yourself up a box of

hornazo, wine, or ham to smuggle home. For fresh fruits and vegetables, explore the **Mercado Central,** just east of the Plaza Mayor.

Road Trip

CARNIVAL DE LOS TOROS IN CIUDAD RODRIGO

Ciudad Rodrigo is a frontier city laden in coats and arms that lies about 30km (19 miles) from the Portuguese border. Not much happens here except during February, when the entire town swells with mad *toro* disease; the town grabs life by the horns during its **Carnival of the Bull,** and, as in the running of the bulls in Pamplona, bulls raid the streets, citizens dance in traditional clothing, and there is mucho, mucho fiesta. It's an event that should not be missed.

The city built on a hilltop is known for its quaint town houses erected by the conquistadores in the 16th and 17th centuries. Take a stroll along one of the narrow paths in the old city for a glimpse of the mansions and churches. In the center of the city is MV Best❶ **Plaza Mayor,** an attractive example of 17th-century architecture that showcases two Renaissance palaces. The city's pride and joy is the Roman-Gothic **cathedral** (☎ **923-481-424;** daily 10am–1pm and 4–7pm), which often gets placed on the back burner during bull season.

The most direct route to Ciudad Rodrigo is from Salamanca. **El Pilar** (☎ **923-222-608**) runs about 12 buses daily (trip time: 1 hr.) and drops you off at **Calle Campo de Toldeo station** (☎ **923-460-217**). A one-way fare costs about 5.40€. If you're driving, the N-620 is the superhighway linking Salamanca and Portugal. The **tourist office** is located at Plaza Amayuelas 5 (☎ **923-460-561;** www.ciudadrodrigo.net; Mon–Fri 10am–2pm and 5–8pm, Sat–Sun 11am–2pm and 4:30–8:30pm).

Zamora

The city of Zamora, capital of its own province, lies high above the Duero River on a prime location used by all of its inhabitants as far back as the Celts as a strategic post. It was called "closed one" because of its no-nonsense approach to invaders. It wasn't until the Golden Age, the 10th to 13th centuries, that they built the monumental biggies you see today. Zamora has so many churches, in fact, that the city is regionally known as a Roman museum. Since Roman times, the city has been a pit stop for pedestrians on the Vía de la Plata, the southern offshoot of the Camino de Santiago. Zamora is also where the king of Castille, Sancho II (Cid's number-one honcho), was assassinated. A lot of modern Zamora has been urbanized, and not all of it is pretty. Once you pass the ugly *moderno* (on your way from the train and bus stations) you'll reach the old town, where the architecture stays true to its ancient self— though I still can't say I was totally impressed apart from its Roman monuments. Zamora lacks . . . charm, like your brother when he first got braces.

Getting There & Around

BY TRAIN

There are about two trains from Madrid every day (trip time: 3½ hr.). Zamora is hardly accessible to other cities by rail. From Avila, three to four trains run daily (trip time: 1½ hr., 18€ one-way). The **railway station** (☎ 980-521-110) is at Calle Alfonso Peña, about a 15-minute walk from the edge of the Old Town. Follow Avenida de las Tres Cruces northeast of the center of town. One-way fare from Madrid to Zamora is 25€. There's a taxi stand, but no taxis—**Taxi Zamora** ☎ 980-534-444 is your best bet.

BY BUS

Auto-Res (☎ 902-020-052; www.auto-res.net) runs one to four buses daily to Zamora from Salamanca. A one-way ticket is 3.20€. There are about seven buses (trip time: 3¼ hr.) to and from Madrid. A one-way fare costs 9.20€ to 13€. The town's **bus station** (☎ 980-521-281) neighbors the railway station at Calle Alfonso Peña 3. No urban buses pass through the center, but walking to the historic center isn't hard— except on your eyes.

BY CAR

If you're passing through Zamora to or from Portugal or headed to northern Spain, Zamora has no problem accommodating you with its eight hospitable highways: north to León, south to Salamanca, and east to Valladolid are the biggies. From Madrid, take the A-6 superhighway northwest towards Valladolid, cutting west on the N-VI and west again at the turnoff onto 122.

What lies outside of Zamora, such as natural reserves and small villages, is just as interesting as the city itself, if not more (see "Road Trips," p. 231). It's worth it to rent a car: **Avis** is at the train station (☎ 980-557-685 and 980-557-566).

Zamora Basics

The main **tourist office** is located on Calle Santa Clara 20 (☎ 980-531-845; July 1—Sept 15 Mon—Thurs and Sun 9am—8pm, Fri—Sat 9am—9pm; Sept 15—June 30 daily 9am—2pm and 5—8pm). Most of the action is on **Plaza Mayor** and the streets that branch off it, such as Calle Santa Clara. The **castle and the cathedral** are next to each other at the farthest end of the old town, and the city's monuments can be surveyed in 4 hours. The **old center** is for pedestrians only, which means no public transportation. **Monuments and**

churches are free, so you can send your proceeds to Zamora's booze and food. Not many streets rival **Calle Herreras,** bar heaven. As long as you time it right, your night is set, and you didn't even have to look like a stupid tourist or drunk and read a map to find out. **Los Lobos,** on the other hand, is an area saturated with tapas joints. Throw South Beach to the wind.

Sleeping

The pickings are slim in Zamora in terms of places to rest your noggin, but if you want a decent deal, then a hostel is going to be your best bet. Even the three-star and four-star hotels in the area are not up to par and only attract businessmen on the run. The nicest, trendiest rooms in town are the double suites at Hostal Trefacio (see below). The city is most popular during Semana Santa (Easter). The onion fair (you wouldn't want to pick up anyone there) and the ceramicist fair during the last week of June are also big days to celebrate in Zamora. If you're coming through town during any of these times, make your sleeping reservations well in advance.

CHEAP

→ **Hostal la Reina** Right on Plaza Mayor, Hostal La Reina is one of the choicest hostels in town, as long as you luck out with the right room. Four rooms have views of the plaza, and they're not bad with a small balcony. But the other rooms are straightforward, a little drab, and barely worth the price—you might as well spend the night some place just as crappy for the same price or cheaper. Service is slow and not always organized; make sure to confirm your reservation at least once before arrival. Get your key at check-in and take care of your business (in cash) before they leave for the night. *Calle de la Reina 1.* ☎ *980-533-939. Summer rates, with private bathroom, triple 45€, double 35€, single 25€;*

summer rates, with shared bath, triple 35€, double 25€, single 16€; summer extra beds 10€; winter rates, with private bath, triple 35€, double 26€, single 20€; winter rates, with shared bath, triple, 25€, double 16€, single 13€; winter extra beds 7€. Breakfast: 2.50€. Amenities: Shared bathrooms, sheets, towels.

→ **Hostal Sol and Hostal Luz** For bargain hotel shopping, this is your best bet. These two hostels are owned by the same landlord and are bunked on top of one another for an overflow of out-of-town guests. That means they rarely run out of room, even during festivals. The high-rise business building is near the main drag Calle Santa Clara and tapas central. Rooms are bright with large windows looking over a not-so-busy side street. All the rooms have private bathrooms with full-size tubs, the mattresses are springy new, and hot water runs all day. There is no difference between the two hostales other than a flight of stairs and a few euros. *Benavente 2.* ☎ *980-533-152. Hostal Sol: double 42€, single 32€; Hostal Luz: double 37€, single 26€. Amenities: Elevator, TV.*

DOABLE

📺 Best ☻ → **Hostal Trefacio** Pilgrims know best in Zamora. One of the most popular places to lodge on the road, Hostal Trefacio dwarfs other establishments in town, including the four-star hotel Dos Infantes nearby, because of its individual style and exceedingly edgy sensibility. The hostel is located in Los Lobos zone, midway between the bus and train stations and Plaza Mayor, and in the popular hub of tapas bars. Creative hardware, spendy wood floors, original art, and thrifty Mod furniture has IKEA eating dust. What more could a pilgrim—or anyone else for that matter—need? There's a massage shower in the bathroom. Ding ding ding! *Alfonso de Castro 7.* ☎ *980-509-104. www.hostaltrefacio. net. June 1–Nov 2 and Semana Santa double* superior 54€, double 48€, single 29€; Nov 3–May 31 double superior 48€, double 42€, single 27€. Breakfast: 2.95€. Amenities: Restaurant, elevator, laundry service, telephone, travel info, Wi-Fi (on 1st floor), common room. In room: A/C, TV.

Eating

If you're in the tapas mood, then clearly the area you'll head for is **Los Lobos,** which includes Calle Alfonso de Castro, Horno, Puebla S. Torcuato, and Flores de S. Torcuato, right off of Calle Santa Clara where it meets with Alfonso IX. There you'll find a handful of small bars offering up *pintxos* and plates of fried food like pig ears—yes, really. Bars fill up around 9pm or later, Spanish dinnertime. Other tapas bars are around Plaza Mayor and designate the starting point for a looong night out.

CHEAP

→**Bocateria** SANDWICHES   The truth be known, I ate the majority of my meals at this homespun sandwich factory. It's a simple-Simon's sub shop that wins hearts and stomachs over with cheap prices, great service, and take-away food. It's open late, and next-door are a few of the city's premier spots (though they don't get started until about 2am). The *papeo* (chicken and egg), *Argentino* (steak), and *Escandinavo* (hamburger) are the most popular *bocadillos,* but they also serve salads, desserts, and raciónes. There's a terraza, but the prices are hiked up 10%. Plaza del Fresco s/n (near Plaza Mayor). ☎ 980-530-863. Bocadillos 2.60€–4€. Platos combinados 6€. Tues–Sun 1:30–4pm and 8pm–midnight.

→**El Jardín** CASTILIAN   Around 9pm, this terraza is a summer hot spot for its cheap *menú del día*. Tables surround a large fountain on Plaza del Maestro in the zone of Los Lobos. There's lots of seating but still try to get there early because it fills up on nice summer nights. In the fall,

you can sit in a dining room upstairs though that's where part of its charm gets lost. The *mollejas a la plancha* (grilled mussels) hit the bull's-eye. Plaza del Maestro 8 (Jardincillo de S. Torcuato). ☎ 980-531-827. Main 3.50€–8€. Menú del día 8.50€. Daily 8am–midnight.

→**Hacienda Nahuatl** ★ SPANISH/MEXICAN/ITALIAN   This place runs zigzag across the border. A mixed bag of Mexican, Spanish, and Italian food has been served to youngish patrons for the past 12 years. A good choice in fall and winter months, when it doesn't lose business for its lack of an outdoor terraza, its funky Aztec decor and a dirt-cheap crossbreed of food (tacos, chicken enchiladas, lasagna, paella) will assure everyone a good night and still leave enough chump change for another round of beers. It's located about a 3-minute walk from Plaza Mayor in an old building that weirdly looks as Old Western as the food it serves. Try the Puntas Mexicanas or the ceviche Nahuatl first. Plaza del Mercado 1. ☎ 980-536-436. Main 3.95€–13€. Daily 10:30am–4:30pm and 8:30pm–12:30am.

DOABLE

→**Restaurante Sarafín** CASTILIAN Arguably the best restaurant in town, its reasonable prices (for high-grade Zamoran meat) mean you can eat like a Castilian king without having to spend like one. It's also a seafood joint, with fresh shipments from Galicia, making it a great place to smack your mackerels. Its indoor seating is cozy for cool fall evenings, and during summer, there's a terraza, where they only serve drinks and tapas. Order a *menú del día,* or if you're a grill lover, the house recommends the *lechazo asado* (roasted baby lamb chops) or the *tostón asado* (roasted chickpeas). Plaza Maestro Haedo 10. ☎ 980-531-422. Meal 6€–18€. Menú del día 16€–23€. Daily 1–4:30pm and 8:30pm–midnight.

Partying

Partying in Zamora is a barrel full of drunken monkeys, as long as you follow the right timetable. Start your evening on **Plaza Mayor** (the hottest place is **Ocellum**) or thereabouts, or **Los Lobos** for tapas and beer. At about midnight, make your way to **Calle Herreros,** a street with more bars than a state penitentiary. At 2am or 3am, clubs in **Plaza Fresco** get going, especially **Embrujo** (☎ **980-535-899**), a nationally recognized club that students love with an in-house DJ who spins Spanish pop.

BARS & NIGHTCLUBS

➔ **Bar Juma** Chances are if you're in Europe, you're listening to electro and house. Of all the places to choose from on bar-struck Calle Herreros, this is the best place with the most marinated ambience. During the week, lounge to chill-out music and sip beer at the bar. During the weekend, the system gets turned up a decibel and electric-static dancing ensues. *Herreros 13. No phone.*

➔ **Freeway** For the after-hours party for cats on the prowl, head toward Los Lobos. This split-level club specializes in good-looking people and house music, easy to dance to with or without the drinks (mixed: 4.50€). It's one of the choicest places in town, but the catch is it's only open on Friday and Saturday at 4am. *Alfonso de Castro 1.* ☎ *980-530-942.*

➔ **Pub Serumura** Named after the Arabic word for Zamora, this club draws a younger crowd early in the evening but the 25-plus-somethings dribble in around 2am. Natives come here for the upbeat '80s and '90s music the 40-year-old DJ spins; but don't discriminate, it's good stuff like Frankie Goes to Hollywood, old-school Madonna, Pink, anything pop but no Reggaetón (Spanish hard-core clubbing

music) is his rule of thumb. The building is a converted 16th-century wheat mill that's kept its old-world integrity, adding the large screen for videos. You'd be holding back if you didn't shake a JLo booty here so get your move on. *La Reina 17. No phone.*

Sightseeing

ATTRACTIONS & MONUMENTS

Fernando I redid the entire **castillo** with his team of top designers back when Zamora saw a lot of action fighting the Moors, and then later clashing with the Castilians and Portuguese. Just recently, the city decided to move **El Museo de Baltasar Lobo** (currently at Iglesia de San Esteban; ☎ **616-929-577;** free admission; Tues–Sat noon–2pm and 7–9pm, Sun noon–2pm) to the castile, in order to create a better space for the modern sculptures. It will be an enormous improvement to this empty space lacking any remnant of what it used to be, save for the deep moat and trapezoidal shape. Baltasar Lobo was a Spanish sculptor in the same class as Matisse and Picasso who became famous for his mother-and-child shapes. Until his museum is implanted here (sometime in 2007), there's nothing to check out besides a Plateresque entrance, parks, and a pretty good view of the river. The castile was closed at the time of writing but can be reached through the entrance of the cathedral.

➔ **Cathedral** Have another big church, they're good for you. The Romans made Zamora's from scratch in 1151, but because of delays, the cathedral has a very Gothic aftertaste. The only Roman ingredient is the Puerta del Obispo. The main attraction is the **Museo Catedral** ★★, where the Flemish tapestry collection would make your grandma do wheelies. Most of the work is from the 16th century Renaissance days and depicts stories like David and

Goliath. It's also worth it to take a second look at the biggest *altar de monumento* in Spain. Made of solid silver and gold, this hunk of metal is made to move. *Plaza de la Catedral s/n.* ☎ *980-530-644. Admission 3€ adult, 1.50€ student. Apr–Sept 10am–2pm and 5–8pm; Oct–Mar 10am–2pm and 4:30–6:30pm.*

CHURCH

Iglesia de San Pedro and San Ildefonso (Plaza de San Ildefonso) is a small, narrow Roman church constructed in the 12th and 13th centuries, in honor of the city's patron saint; it deserves your attention if you're walking by **Iglesia de San Juan de Puerta Nueva,** which sits square in Plaza Mayor with its rose window facing south. **Iglesia de San Claudio de Olivares** (Plaza de San Claudio) was probably the first Roman church that was built in the city. The dullest church is **Iglesia de Santiago de los Caballeros** (Calle de Santiago el Viejo), but legend has it this is where El Cid said his prayers when passing through town. **Iglesia de Santa María la Horta** (Plaza de la Horta) is a hodgepodge of Roman and Gothic architecture. **Iglesia de San Vicente** (Plaza del Fresco) is a well-groomed church with the best looking tower in town. Churches are open July 1 through September 30 Tuesday through Sunday 10am to 1pm and 5 to 8pm (free admission).

MUSEUM

➔**Museo de Semana Santa** If you haven't gotten over Spain's most devout Catholics marching in white sheets and wearing pointy hats like members of the KKK, or you just want to understand it all (hint: It has nothing to do with the American group, which copied Spain's customs and maliciously adopted them as their own), here's an entire museum dedicated to the week of silent processions and festivals during Spain's holy Semana Santa (Easter). This was the first Semana Santa museum to see the light of day, exhibiting processional statues of carved Virgins and Jesuses who make the route each year. For a non-expert on the subject, it'll take a quick 20 minutes to get through the museum. *Plaza Santa María, La Nueva s/n.* ☎ *980-526-072. Admission 3€. Mon–Sat 10am–2pm and 5–8pm; Sun 10am–2pm.*

Road Trips

SANABRIA & AROUND

Taking a road trip in Zamora's province is just as much fun—if not more—than going to Zamora in the first place. The Sanabria area, home to the only glacier-fed lake in Spain, is a natural park popular for daytripping. When heading north to either Galicia or León, plan a romantic stopover in **Puebla de Sanabria,** the most important village along the old Roman road and Rio Tera in the northeast corner of the Zamora region, not too far from the Portuguese border.

Narrow cobblestone roads weave uphill overspilling with flowerpots and ivy, which make you believe in this village. **La Iglesia de Nuestra Señora del Azogue** (Plaza Mayor s/n), castle, and El Macho lookout tower are more than worth the 2€-admission fee to get in and snoop around. Head down the walking path behind the castle and cross the bridge below to get to **Playa La Chopera.** The river is clean, shallow, and good for dips on hot days. The posada's riverside bar, **El Chiringuito de Virgilio** (☎ 620-154-591; June–Oct 10am–1:30am), serves cheap tapas (1€), coffee, and beer, and usually gets hopping around 6 to 7pm in spring and summer. The **tourist office** is located at Calle Rúa 13 (☎ 980-620-734). Open daily 11am to 2pm and 5 to 8pm.

By car, head northeast from Zamora on N-631 to N-525 all the way to Puebla de Sanabria. The road is signposted. Two daily

buses (trip time: 1¾ hr.) leave from Zamora's bus station (Av. Tres Cruces 18; ☎ 980-521-281 or 980-521-282; Mon–Sat 1:30pm and 5:30pm, Sun 9am) toward **Ribadelago** (one-war fare: 8€). Buses for **Lago de Sanabria** depart from Calle Arrabal (Puebla de Sanabria) on Monday through Saturday at 3:05pm and 7pm. You must stay the night because they don't return until the next morning.

La Posada de la Villa is a comparatively inexpensive rural house with a view of the Portuguese skyline. Rooms have stone walls, religious paraphernalia, and wood floors; there's a bar and restaurant on-site (Plaza Mayor 3; ☎ 980-620-347; www.laposadadelavilla.com; double 65€, breakfast included, no singles). Visit one of a string of charming cities near the lake such as **San Martín de Castañeda** ★★, where there's a large monastery and an interpretation center.

📺 ⟨Best⟩ Segovia ★★

If you like Toledo, chances are you'll like Segovia even better. It has all the charms of a medieval city with half the tourists and more local flair. Plus, its nickname is Stone Ship (its hull being the Disney-worthy alcázar perched on the rocks while the jutting cathedral's tower is the mast). Besides being the capital of a few Moorish kingdoms, Segovia was the reigning site where Isabella I was crowned queen of Castile. When Carlos V took over the country, Segovia had a hard time stepping down from the ring, so to defend its title, the city waged an uprising against the Imperial government called the Revolt of the Comuneros. Broken and bleeding, Segovia lost one to nothing in 1521.

Situated between the two rivers Eresma and Clamores with a front row seat to the Sierra de Guadarrama mountains, your viewfinders can't find more attractive than this. You should spend at least 1 night if not 2, in order to appreciate everything the city has to offer—from monuments, cathedrals, nightlife, oh my.

Getting There

BY TRAIN

Fifteen Cercanías trains leave Madrid's Chamartín Railway Station per day for the 2-hour trip to Segovia, but you can pick up the train from Atocha when it pit-stops there. Outside the train station, board the city bus that departs every quarter-hour for the Plaza Mayor. The **train station** at Segovia lies on the Paseo Obispo Quesada s/n (☎ 921-420-774), a 20-minute walk southeast of the town center.

BY BUS

Buses arrive at the **Estacionamiento Municipal de Autobuses** (Paseo de Ezequiel González 10; ☎ 921-427-707), near where Avenida Fernández Ladreda and Paseo Conde de Sepúlveda meet. There are 10 to 15 buses a day to and from Madrid (one-way fare: 5.35€). Buses depart from Paseo de la Florida 11 (Metro: Principio Pío), and about four a day between Avila, Segovia, and Valladolid.

BY CAR

Take the N-VI, also called A-6 on some maps, or the Autopista del Nordeste northwest from Madrid, toward León and Lugo. Turn northeast at the junction with Route 110.

Getting Around

BY BUS

City buses (☎ 921-462-727) pass through the center on the outskirts only near Plaza Mayor or the Aqueduct. Ask the bus driver to let you know when to get off. Heading into town from the bus station, catch the no. 6 bus; if you're arriving by train, hop on

Segovia

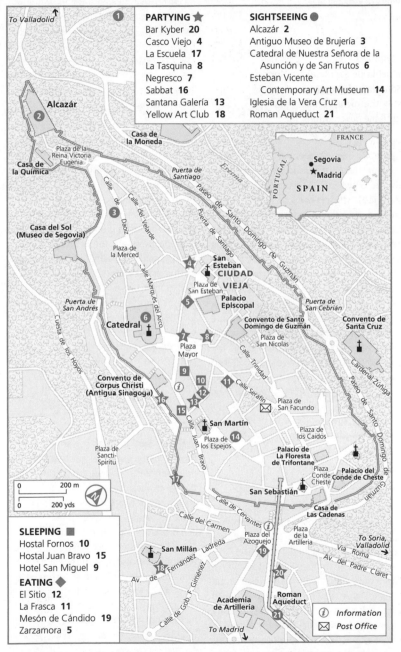

PARTYING ⭐
Bar Kyber **20**
Casco Viejo **4**
La Escuela **17**
La Tasquina **8**
Negresco **7**
Sabbat **16**
Santana Galería **13**
Yellow Art Club **18**

SIGHTSEEING ●
Alcázar **2**
Antiguo Museo de Brujería **3**
Catedral de Nuestra Señora de la
   Asunción y de San Frutos **6**
Esteban Vicente
   Contemporary Art Museum **14**
Iglesia de la Vera Cruz **1**
Roman Aqueduct **21**

To Valladolid ↑

1

Alcázar

2

FRANCE

Segovia ●
★ Madrid

PORTUGAL

SPAIN

Casa de
la Moneda

Plaza de la
Reina Victoria
Eugenia

Casa de
la Química

Calle de Daoiz

Calle del Velarde

Puerta de
Santiago

Paseo de Santo Domingo de Guzmán

Eresma

Casa del Sol
(Museo de Segovia)

3

Plaza de
la Merced

Calle Marqués del Arco

4
San
Esteban
CIUDAD
VIEJA

Plaza de
San Esteban

5
Palacio
Episcopal

Puerta de
San Andrés

Catedral

6

Convento de Santo
Domingo de Guzmán

Plaza de
San Nicolas

Puerta de
San Cebrián

Convento de
Santa Cruz

Cardenal Zúñiga

Cuesta de los Hoyos

7 **8**

Plaza
Mayor

Calle Trinidad

9

Convento de
Corpus Christi
(Antigua Sinagoga)

ⓘ

16

10

11 Calle Serafín

12

13

15

Calle Juan Bravo

✝ San Martín

Plaza de
los Espejos

14

Plaza de
San Facundo

✉

Plaza de
los Caidos

Paseo de Santo Domingo de Guzmán

Plaza de
Sancti-
Spiritu

Palacio de
La Floresta
de Trifontane

Plaza
Conde
Cheste

Palacio del
Conde de Cheste

17

Calle de Cervantes ⓘ

San Sebastián

Casa de
Las Cadenas

0   200 m
0   200 yds

N

Calle del Carmen

Plaza del
Azoguejo

Plaza
de la
Artillería

To Soria,
Valladolid →
Via Roma

✝ San Millán

Calle de Gob. F. Giménez

Av. de Fernández Ladreda

18

Av. del Padre Claret

19

20

Academia
de Artillería

Roman
Aqueduct

21

To Madrid ↓

ⓘ *Information*
✉ *Post Office*

the no. 8, to catch a ride into town with your rock-heavy luggage (.80€).

BY TAXI

The largest taxi stand is just outside the Aqueduct. To hail a cab, call **Radio Taxi** ☎ 921-445-000.

Segovia Basics

The **tourist information office** is at Plaza Mayor 10 (☎ 921-460-334). It is open daily from 9am to 3pm and 5 to 7pm. In the summer, it's open all day from 9am to 9pm. There's a second welcoming center at Plaza del Azoguejo 1 (☎ 921-466-720), which is open daily year-round from 10am to 8pm. Postcards can be sent from the main **post office** at Plaza de los Huertos 5. You'll need a **cybercafe** to brag to your buds back home, and the best one in town is near the Roman aqueduct: **Internetcafé.es** is at Calle Teodosio el Grande 10 (☎ 921-425-158; daily 9am–1 1pm). If an aqueduct a day didn't keep the doctor away, head toward **Hospital General** (1.5km/1 mile southwest on the Avila highway) or quicker yet, just call **Red Cross** (☎ 921-440-202).

Recommended Website

A helpful site for finding everything Segovian such as happenin' restaurants and bars is **www.viasegovia.com**.

Sleeping

HOSTELS

➜**Hostal Fornos** This utterly unique 19th-century two-story hotel is so cute looking, it's straight out of an Anne Geddes photograph. Centrally located in the old city, each room is hand-painted to look like a girly beach house with floral motifs and organic soaps. Whimsical design is matched with teak patio furniture so guests don't have to leave the room to enjoy a taste of the outdoors. It's a little more expensive than what you'd pay elsewhere in town,

but the service, hand-painted decor, and its surprisingly young, rock 'n' roll guests (a spillover from the owner's rock bar Santana nearby) seals the deal. *Infanta Isabel 13.* ☎ *921-460-198. www.hostalfornos. com. May–Nov double 51€, single 39€; Dec–Apr double 45€, single 32€; extra bed 12€. Amenities: Telephone. In room: A/C, TV.*

MTV (Best ❂) ➜**Hostal Juan Bravo** ★★ Sitting on the old wall above Paseo del Salón, you can have views to die for, as long as you can snare one of three to-die-for rooms in back with French windows facing the rolling hills of the Sierra de Guadarrama mountains. The sweet old man who owns the hotel (along with his cranky wife) told me the sight never gets old. The views are the best you'll find in the city, and along with the cleanliness and quaintness of each room, you will be convinced to stay an extra night if your timetable affords it—we did. But watch out for the Señora, she's got major 'tude, but only because she spends her days scrubbing the place. It sparkles. *Juan Bravo 12, 2nd floor.* ☎ *921-463-413. Double with private bathroom 38€, double with shared bathroom 32€. Doubles are for single use. Amenities: Shared bathrooms. In room: TV.*

DOABLE

➜**Hotel San Miguel** For someone who likes to party, you can't get a better location than this. Cozy masculine rooms feature large beds dressed in plaid linens that your younger brother probably had on his bunk. Its rustic furniture all matches and complements the high-beamed ceilings. The non-English-speaking staff is incredibly polite and also runs the bar and restaurant down below. It's a tad overpriced, but let's face it: You're paying for location and not having to sleep in a hostel for the night—and for that private bathroom. *Infanta Isabel 6.* ☎ *921-463-657. www. sanmiguel-hotel.com. High season double 72€,* *single 40€; low season double 60€, single 30€. Breakfast included. Amenities: Cafeteria, bar, laundry service. In room: A/C, TV.*

Eating

TAPAS

➜ **El Sitio** Literal translation: The Place. And you better believe it is hard to find room at the bar, which is packed with 20- to 24-year-olds around dinnertime or before, to order your standard fair of Spanish tapas. A more sophisticated dining room in back serves *cochinillo* and *judiones de la granja* (baby pork and beans) as the *menú del día* (18€). It's located on a bar-saturated street, so if you plan right and eat late, you'll be a most efficient partier, making the most of your barhopping time. *Infanta Isabel 9.* ☎ *921-460-996. Raciónes 9€–12€. Mon–Sat 9pm–3am or 4am; Sun 1:15–11:30pm.*

CHEAP

➜ **La Frasca** ★ SPANISH Complete with a terraza and a view of the cathedral, this is the most economical place you're going to find for services rendered. The food ain't bad either. The corner joint specializes in *bocadillos* and salads served by waiters in penguin suits, but the best deal for your money is the *menú del día* (sit inside, as the *menú* outside will cost you a few *céntimos* more). Start with La Frasca salad and order the house wine or vermouth on tap. Raciones are either full- or half-size portions. *Plaza de La Rubia 6.* ☎ *921-461-038. Menú 12€. Daily 9am–1am.*

DOABLE

[MTV] Best☺ ➜ **Zarzamora** FUSION Miss ma's cooking? Here's a snack bar that tastes better, Junior. Although the small restaurant has a down-to-earth, homey concept, the food is outta this country with healthy pitas, exotic salads, and cheesy quesadillas. Even at the few tables outdoors, don't worry—the prices stay the same. Start with a tomato and avocado pita, the Zarzamora salad (feeds three to four people), or a pasta dish with shrimp and mango. Sorry Miss Piggy, it's a match made in heaven for vegetarians. *Travesía de Escuderos 1.* ☎ *921-461-247. Meal about 15€. Wed–Sun 6pm–close.*

SPLURGE

➜ **Mesón de Cándido** ★★★ SEGOVIAN Forget the fact that Henry Kissinger, Marlon Brando, and Bill Clinton have eaten here. This restaurant has enough old-world charm to hold up an aqueduct, and what do you know?! There's one a few meters away from its popular terraza seating. Since 1905, this institution has served the best lookin' *cochinillo* in town with more antiquated style than it has dead baby pigs in the kitchen—and that's a lot. The upstairs dining rooms are for royal treatment and are lined with French windows with fine views of the aqueduct. *Azoguejo 5.* ☎ *921-425-911. Meal with house wine 35€–40€. Daily 12:30–4:30pm and 8–11pm.*

Partying

Most folks gather around Plaza Mayor during siesta and early evening hours. If you're in the mood for cocktails first, head towards **Negresco** (Plaza Mayor 16; ☎ **921-460-882**) for mixed drinks (4€–5€) and major terraza action first. Besides just Plaza Mayor, the zone near Iglesia San Millán, beginning on Calle Fernández Ladreda, is rich with terrazas and tapas. Your next move: Calle Infanta Isabel (aka Bar Street) or **Bar Kyber** (near the aqueduct on Calle Fernán García). After bars begin to die down, head toward Paseo del Salón to a hot dance club specializing in *pijos* and electro music, **Sabbat** (☎ **921-462-316**), around 2am. After still a longer night (bleeding into morning), make for **La Escuela** (at the bottom of the stairs from Paseo del Salón on Calle San Millán) at dawn on Fridays and Saturdays for more dancing, if your system can handle it.

BARS & NIGHTCLUBS

→ **Casco Viejo** ★★ You'd miss this mysterious jazz bar tucked away near Plaza de San Esteban if you didn't know it was there. Inside, it emits a young vibe against an old tavernlike bar scene, tended by a long-haired dude behind the counter. The smell of hashish wafts in the air and everyone knows everyone else's name—yes, it's *that* kind of place. Trippy Alice-in-Wonderland stairs go up (sideways) to an attic room where groups play cards, smoke, and drink. *Vallejo 6.* ☎ *921-461-031.*

MTV **Best ●** → **La Tasquina** ★★ This wine bar and restaurant attracts people by the barrel load for its serious wino ambience and regional digs. The prices are incredibly reasonable for the quality you're getting, and the complimentary tapas are gourmet. If you're not sure which kind of bottle to bring back to the folks, taste-test a few here with the swirling bar aficionados who like to educate tourists. It's a local favorite, too, and a sure thing in between long takes of sightseeing. If you're clueless about wine, start with a local. **MTV** **Best ●** **Rueda del Duero.** *Valdeláguila 3.* ☎ *921-461-954.*

MTV **Best ●** → **Santana Galería** This historical rock bar serving free tapas has nothing to do with the famous band of the same name. The laid-back owner has been at it for 15 years, supporting local and international artists and musicians along the way, as well as serving coffee to the old-timers who frequent it in the morning. By night, classic rock is king and the cafeteria floor gives way to a punk dance club and occasional concerts. It's absolutely unpretentious, just like good rock should be. Why aren't there more places like this in the world? *Infanta Isabel 18.* ☎ *921-463-564.*

→ **Yellow Art Club** This is arguably the best, most important house music club in town, and it's situated on a main drag near Iglesia San Millán. But if you're heading out, make sure you don't get all dressed up for nothing; the only nights it's open are Thursdays, Fridays, and Saturdays, when it's packed with well-groomed university students around 2am. They might be offering two-for-one drink deals, if you're lucky. *Fernández Ladreda 25.* ☎ *921-443-246.*

Sightseeing

ATTRACTIONS & MONUMENTS

→ **Alcázar** ★★ If you like your head in the clouds, spend some time here, the castle that inspired Disney's Sleeping Beauty—so they say. Admittedly, the resemblance is uncanny. Sharp soaring spires, a moat deep enough for a fleet of alligators, and regal rooms dripping with gold pineapples take you into a world where miracles can happen. It's no surprise then that this isn't the original. The oldest section dates back to the 12th century, but nasty community wars destroyed most of it in the 19th century. So what's so magic? This is the place where Isabella and Ferdinand first made eyes at each other, and you can walk through the dark room where Isabella prudishly daydreamed of her life with the king. Phillip II married for the fourth time Anne of Austria here, as well. Highlights include the tower, which smokers might have problems climbing. *Plaza de la Reina Victoria Eugenia.* ☎ *921-460-759. Admission 3.50€ adult. Mar–Aug 10am–7pm; Sept–Feb 10am–6pm.*

→ **Catedral de Nuestra Señora de la Asunción y de San Frutos** ★★ This is not the original Roman cathedral, as the first one was burned down during the Wars of the Communities in 1521. But it only took Carlos V 4 years to begin construction of this mother church in honor of Segovia's patron saint, San Frutos, and the Virgin

Segovia ❀ 237

Mary. It wasn't finished until more than 200 years later. The architect Juan Gil de Homtañón recycled the old Gothic structure from the first, as well as other old relics such as the choir stalls, a Hispano-Flemish Gothic cloister (El Claustro) by Juan Guas, and the church's front facade, which is the biggest ooh-and-ah of the place, all making it the last Gothic church ever built in Spain. A museum showcases sculpture, tapestries, and a collection of primitively printed books, including the Synod of Aguilafuerte. *Plaza Catedral, Marqués del Arco.* ☎ *921-462-205 and 921-460-694. Admission to cathedral, cloisters, museum, and chapel room 2€ adults. No admission to cathedral only, on Sun morning. Spring and summer 9:30am–6:30pm; winter 9:30am–5:30pm.*

→Iglesia de la Vera Cruz It's a hike to get to this church, north of the center city, but it's worth it to see Segovia from outside the wall and not to mention the weird-shaped church, older than the Knights of the Round Table. The 12-sided structure, a copy of the Church of the Holy Sepulcher in Jerusalem, was solely for the use of knights; the double-decker inner temples are where they pulled all-nighters for their initiations. A piece of wood claimed to be from Jesus' cross was here for many years, which is how the church got its name, but was moved, and now only the chapel remains. *Carretera de Zamarramala.* ☎ *921-431-475. Admission 1.75€. Fall–winter daily 10:30am–1:30pm and 3:30–6pm; spring–summer daily 10:30am–1:30pm and 3:30–7pm.*

→Roman Aqueduct ★★ The legend goes that a small girl fetching water got tired of her chore so she sold her soul to the devil as long as he could find an easier way to transport water from the well. Poof! There was an aqueduct. The holes you see are where the devil stuck his fingers. More likely, the Romans built it 2,000 years ago out of granite. Take a closer gander and

you'll see that not one cup of mortar was used to build the seamless, 118-arched structure. *Plaza de Azoguejo.*

MUSEUMS

📺 Best ☻ →Antiguo Museo de Brujería If you've never been to a witchcraft museum, here's your chance to descend the stairs of Hell. Specializing in torture devices used on accused witches during the Inquisition and complete with a torture cave (don't worry, it's not hands-on), in addition to corpses, antique masturbation devices, and loads of hallucinogenic drugs, this museum should not be missed. The collection was a donation from a private party in Italy; and it's only appropriate that the museum is now housed in Segovia, in the same province as the zealots who burned women at the stake and ripped apart their insides. This is not for the weak stomached. *Daoíz 9.* ☎ *921-460-442. Admission 4.50€ adult, 4€ student. Daily 11am–2:30pm and 4:30–8pm.*

→Esteban Vicente Contemporary Art Museum For the traveler who doesn't like to go between the lines, here's a contemporary art museum featuring Segovian artist Esteban Vicente, the only Spanish member of the New York School of abstract expressionism, and a big baller along with contemporary greats such as Pollock, Rothko, and de Kooning. As the last of the Mohicans in his movement, he recently brought it back to his motherland in the form of his own gallery. His colorful paintings, which also hang in the halls of MoMa, will leave you feeling *satisfecho.* *Plazuela de las Bellas Artes.* ☎ *921-462-010. Admission 1.40€ adults, 1.20€ students, free on Thurs. Tues–Fri 11am–2pm and 4–7pm; Sat 11am–7pm; Sun 11am–2pm.*

Shopping

Shopping in Segovia is fruitful; the **clothing** is brighter and bolder than most cities in

CASTILLA Y LEÓN

this neck of the woods, so it's worth it to cruise the side streets packin' the heat of your credit cards, especially along **Calle Daoiz.** For avid music collectors who favor heavy metal and hard-core punk, check out **Totem Vértigo** (Plaza del Corpus 3; ☎ 921-429-962; www.totemvertigo.com; Mon–Sat 10am–2pm and 5–8pm).

Avila

This ancient city is built on a rocky hill overlooking mountainous wilderness and arid mesas, transporting you to a time when chivalry was alive and kissing, and all just an hour outside of Madrid. Today, however, its mix of audacious 21st-century architecture and medieval ruins is unsettling, and so is the disproportionately large percentage of old people moping around and sagging off park benches. But don't let any of that fool you. Avila is filled with small surprises, which include its sights, specialty food, and handful of eclectic bars. And while said village elders are grumpy toward tourists, the younger ones are quick to give you a recommendation, directions, or even a free drink. The main attraction is the ancient defense wall that surrounds the old part of the city, which is why the majority of tourists make the trip from Madrid. Avila is also the birthplace of Saint Teresa of Jesus, the mystic nun with a cult Christian following. The last reason people head toward Avila, however, is to beat the heat. Avila sits at a little more than a thousand meters above sea level, the highest capital in Spain, a fact that makes summers less miserable than in the rest of the country.

Getting There
BY TRAIN

Twenty-four Cercanías trains travel to Avila from **Madrid's Chamartín railway station** (☎ 902-240-202; www.renfe.es; Metro: Chamartín) leaving every 2 to 3 hours. You can also pick up the Cercanías train at Atocha (Metro: Atocha Renfe), as it's on the same route. An Express train

(trip time: 1½ hr.) will cost 6.05€ while a regular train (trip time: 2 hr.) will cost 6.90€. The Avila train station is a 15-minute walk to the east end of the old town. Follow Avenida Jose Antonio to where it ends by the large church of Santa Ana and bear left up Calle Duque de Alba to reach Plaza Santa Teresa.

BY BUS

From Madrid, buses are less frequent than trains (eight on weekdays, three on weekends). Buses depart Madrid from **Estación del Sur de autobuses** (Metro: Méndez Alvaro). Daily buses run at 7:15am, 8:30am, 10:00am, 12:00pm, 1:30pm, 3:45pm, 5:30pm, and 8:00pm. In Avila, buses use a terminal on the Avenida de Madrid (☎ 920-220-154): Walking from here, cross the small park opposite, then turn right up Calle Duque de Alba. Fares cost 6.50€ one-way, 12€ round-trip (trip time: 1½ hr.).

BY CAR

From Madrid, take the A-6 out of the city. Take the Villacastín exit and then follow the N-501 national road to Avila.

Getting Around
BY BUS

To get into town from the bus station, you can walk or take the no. 2, 3, or 5 bus. From the RENFE train station, hop aboard either the 1, 3, 4, 5, or 7. Bus nos. 7 and 1 pull up right in front of the cathedral. Buses swing by every 25 minutes, except on Sundays when they come every 45 minutes. There are no night buses, and each way will cost you .70€. For more information, call the **urban transportation service** ☎ 920-252-411.

Avila

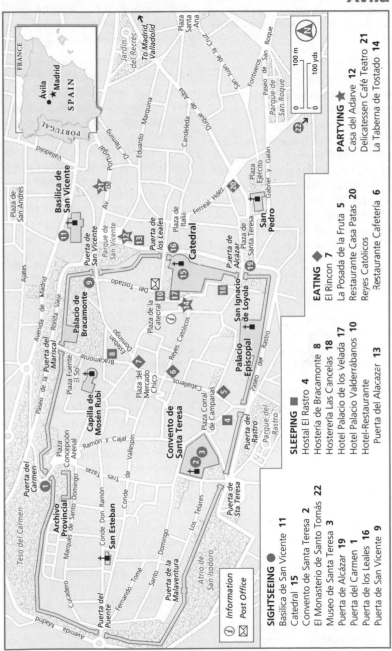

SIGHTSEEING ●
Basílica de San Vicente **11**
Catedral **15**
Convento de Santa Teresa **2**
El Monasterio de Santo Tomás **22**
Museo de Santa Teresa **3**
Puerta de Alcázar **19**
Puerta del Carmen **1**
Puerta de los Leales **16**
Puerta de San Vicente **9**

SLEEPING ■
Hostal El Rastro **4**
Hostería de Bracamonte **8**
Hostería Las Cancelas **18**
Hotel Palacio de los Velada **17**
Hotel Palacio Valderrábanos **10**
Hotel-Restaurante
Puerta del Alacázar **13**

EATING ◆
El Rincon **7**
La Posada de la Fruta **5**
Restaurante Casa Patas **20**
Reyes Católicos
Restaurante Cafetería **6**

PARTYING ★
Casa del Adarve **12**
Delicatessen Café Teatro **21**
La Taberna de Tostado **14**

BY TAXI

Pick up a taxi at the stop in the old part of town at Plaza de Mercado de Grande (**Radio Taxi;** ☎ **920-353-545**).

Avila Basics

In Avila, your bases are covered. **Oficina de Turismo** (☎ **920-211-387;** daily 9am–2pm and 5–8pm) is at Plaza de la Catedral 4. In the summer months, you'll find a tourism hut at the **Estación Renfe** (Paseo de la Estación; no phone; daily 9am–2pm and 5–8pm). A second hut is right outside **Puerta de San Vicente** (☎ **920-357-126;** Fri 4–7pm, Sat 10am–2pm and 4–7pm, and Sun 10am–2pm). For the tech-style low-down on Avila, get yourself connected to **www.avilaturisma.com**. You can find Internet access outside the wall, but it's a walk. Try **Cibernet Games** (☎ **920-352-352;** daily 11:30am–2:30pm and 4:30pm–1am) at Av. de Madrid 25.

Let me guess! You're sending a postcard of the wall home to your folks? The **post office** (☎ **920-211-354**) is located at Plaza de la Catedral 2. You broke more than a nail and need medical assistance? Either call **Red Cross** (☎ **920-222-222**) or head toward **Hospital Provincial** (☎ **920-357-200**) at Calle de Jesús de Gran Poder. In terms of **shopping,** every Friday, a **market** is held in **Plaza Mercado Chico** where fruit, vegetables, and pottery are sold. The atrium of **St. Isidro** sells fabrics, bags, clothes, fish, birds, and other random stuff.

Sleeping

Avila has thrown pensions to the birds; there are none. There are, however, a large number of *hostales* that surpass their two-star rating. For Paris Hilton wannabes, there is the **Hotel Palacio de los Velada** (Plaza Catedral 10; ☎ **920-255-100;** velada hoteles.com) and also the **Hotel Palacio Valderrábanos** (Plaza Catedral 9; ☎ **920-211-023;** www.palaciovalderrabanoshotel.

com), which both have been turned into outrageously expensive four-star hotels, rich with history and tourist moola.

CHEAP

→ **Hostal El Rastro** ★★ There should be no reason you don't stay here unless the rooms are all booked, which they won't be because it's a large, empty posada, a Spanish version of *The Shining.* More than 300 years ago, it was an inn for *caballeros.* There were no beds so instead weary knights slept on the floor. Today, the large salons have been converted into dining rooms, one that leads to its own chunk of the medieval wall (this won't be obvious, and you'll have to ask). The current family in residence has been there for the past 140 years and knows all the secret ins and outs. Make sure to request a room with a view of the wall. All rooms have full bathrooms. Redrum! *Plaza del Rastro 1.* ☎ *920-211-219. Single 29€, double 35€, triple 46€. June–Aug: single 30€, double 41€, triple 56€.*

DOABLE

→ **Hospederia de Bracamonte** ★★ Forget about *Back to the Future*—this is back to the past, as lived by Spanish noble knights right in the comfort of your tight-ass rented pad. Each room is dressed to look as if it were another chamber in what was once the palace of Regidor D. Juan Teherán Monjaraz during the 16th century with stone walls, canopy beds, tile floors, and trimmings. Did we mention there's also a view of the Monasterio de Mosén Rubí and the great wall? *Bracamonte 6.* ☎ *920-251-280 and 920-253-838. www.hospederia debracamonte. com. Single 36€–50€, double 61€–73€, extra bed 15€. 6€ breakfast. Amenities: Sheets, towels. In room: A/C, TV, hair dryer.*

📺 Best ☻ → **Hostereria Las Cancelas** ★★ These rooms are king size, and the crown jewels are the fireplaces—or where there used to be fireplaces, as they've all been filled in. The 15th-century inn exceeds our expectations with a decor that doesn't stray from its medieval roots. The high-priced restaurant downstairs is highly recommended in all the guidebooks though it attracts an older crowd, a gold mine for the Golden Girls. *Cruz Vieja 6.* ☎ *920-212-249. www.lascancelas.com. Single 45€, double 65€, extra bed 30€. In room: A/C, hair dryer.*

→ **Hotel-Restaurante Puerta del Alcazar** ★★ Situated on an ancient street speckled with patio seating and nightlife and running along the most popularly used entrance to the wall is this newly renovated hotel that's an economical and smart place to crash. The rooms are bright and spotless though a tad overpriced. *San Segundo 38. ☎ 920-211-074. www.puertadelalcazar.com. Single 43€, double 55€, extra bed 22€. Breakfast included. Amenities: Laundry pick-up, TV.*

Eating

You'd think this little town was in the center of Manhattan with its steep food prices. Inside the walls, you can't find quality grub for less than the price of your hotel. Get outside the box and try to plan your meals ahead of time, in order to avoid a tourist trap on a hungry stomach. Avila specializes in steak, beans, and sweets called *yemas;* these are all products found outside the famous walls.

TAPAS

→ **El Rincon** One local tipster told us this was a good, inexpensive choice near the center. The typical tapas bars, with more seating than the Last Supper, turned out to be worth the investigation 'cuz of its cheapskate prices. You'll find a tapa for every craving, including scrumptious *patatas bravas* with a winning recipe (the secret's in the sauce). Careful you don't order twice, the bartenders are twins. If you're interested, they also have a pretty

decent two-star hotel and restaurant attached, all recently renovated. *Plaza de Zurraquin 4 (right next to Plaza del Mercado Chico). ☎ 920-213-152. www.plaza-zurraquin. com. Tapas 4€–6€. Tapas bar 10:30am–4pm and 7pm–midnight. Restaurant 1:30–4pm and 8:30–10:30pm.*

→ **Restaurante Casa Patas** Here's a cheap solution to the expensive situation of being trapped inside the city walls. It's also one of the only places in Avila that sympathizes with vegetarians, offering a truly green menu. The LCD-screen TV in front and dinner-size tapas are reasons why it's popular with the locals. Don't get put off by the stares when you walk in; the dining room is in the back so smile politely and just keep going. *San Millán 4. ☎ 920-213-194. Raciónes 5€–15€. Menú 10€. Bar (tapas and raciónes) 10am–11pm. Restaurant (lunch only) 1:30–4pm. Closed Wed.*

CHEAP

→ **La Posada de la Fruta** SPANISH Here's where you can sample what Avila has to offer (steak and beans) without having to panhandle for your train ticket back to Madrid. Order a small plate with benefits of the effulgent patio or a full-out dinner, but don't forget your Blue Blockers. The natural light flooding in is like the second coming of Christ. There's not a better spot except that all the other tourists know about it, too. *Plaza de Pedro Dávila 8. Cafeteria ☎ 920-220-984. Restaurant ☎ 920-254-702. Small platters, bocadillos, and tapas 3€–7€. Main course 5€–16€. Menú (includes dessert and glass of wine) 8.25€. Cafe daily 9am–1am. Restaurant daily 1–4pm and 7:30–11:30pm.*

SPLURGE

→ **Reyes Católicos Restaurante Cafetería** SPANISH If your *padre* (or your credit card) is footing the bill, this is the best restaurant—and terraza—in Avila. The prices are major league but the food makes mouths water: Avila steak, bean dishes, *morcilla* (blood sausage), and your basic fare of Mediterranean fish. *Reyes Católicos 6 (near Plaza del Mercado Chico). Reservations recommended.* ☎ *920-255-627. www.restaurantereyescatolicos.com. Menú (includes 2 courses and a dessert) 25€–30€. Weekdays 10am–11pm; weekends until late.*

Partying

Avila has some great dives but most are outside the city walls so take a deep breath, plug your nose, or hold a hand. We promise it's cheaper once you reach the other side. In fact, we found that Avila has a standardized price on beer for about 4€. Mixed drinks stay in the 5€ to 6€ range.

BARS & NIGHTCLUBS

➜ **Casa del Adarve** The local vanguard and artistic-minded tourists alike gather in this large space with its own eclectic style—and pool table—to whisper very intelligent things to each other. There's outdoor seating, too, with a view of Avila's backlit wall. The chilled-out soiree goes 'til 4am on the weekends and 2am during the week. *San Segundo 40.* ☎ *920-228-176. www.barelbar.com.*

➜ **Delicatessen Café Teatro** ★★ What can we say about hung-upside-down grandma furniture, international music, antique toys, and a dance floor with good looking people, other than it's our favorite cocktail bar, club, and cafe, all rolled crookedly into one? Lug your cameras to this destination hot spot, you're gonna want pics. The best night to suss things out is Saturday. *Portugal 7. No phone.*

➜ **La Taberna de Tostado** Here's your chance to duck into a royal palace of the 14th century, the Palace of los Velada, where it's rumored that Queen Isabella

stayed in 1531. Now it's a fancy hotel upstairs, and downstairs is a dark-lit, sophisticated watering hole, authentic in royal aspects. Saturday is the night to head out to this laid-back, seemingly older person bar. But that's not to say there wasn't a young couple in the back room totally going at it. *Plaza Catedral 10 (the entrance is on Calle Tostado).* ☎ *920-255-100.*

Sightseeing

ATTRACTIONS & MONUMENTS

➜ **Basilica de San Vicente** According to urban legend, the Romanesque church located just outside the city's walls pays special homage to the place where Saint Vicente and his two sisters were martyred when the Romans killed them in the 4th century. Built in 1130 on top of a funerary crypt, it became the premier religious venue for taking important Castilian oaths. A few yards ahead of the massive church is a small garden, where Romans used to bury their dead. It's a short visit and very nearby. *Plaza de San Vicente.* ☎ *920-255-230. Admission 1.40€ adult, 1.20€ group. Daily 10am–1:30pm and 4–6:30pm.*

➜ **Catedral** Deeply embedded in the fortified wall on an old Roman site is a huge granite church that looks more defensive than it does religious. The wall and the 12th-century cathedral are melded into one, making it the most obvious—and earliest—example of a Gothic cathedral-fortress in Spain. The red-and-white limestone column inside is an unusually French style. It's worth the few euros to wind the cathedral's depths; inside there's an El Greco, as well as a famous monstrance by Juan de Arfe. The Chapel of Saint Nicholas houses a Renaissance portrait asking for "alms to marry orphaned ladies on the Day of Saint Nicholas." It was a socialized dating service back then offering betrothals of 12 women without families of their own.

Santa Teresa (1515–82)

As a girl, Teresa was fascinated by the Catholic saints and was caught sneaking out in an attempt to be martyred to the Moors. Unlike most angsty teenagers today, she rebelled by entering into a convent of Carmelite nuns in 1534. Once there, she fell extremely ill for no reason at all, to the point that she felt spiritual "ecstasy" from all her pain. High on holy E, Teresa wrote her first book based on the spiritual suffering she felt during her sickness. By 1559, she became convinced that Christ had presented himself to her. Most of her writings were controversial at the time and had to be read between the lines (the Inquisition was raging). She later went on to found her own monastery in Avila, reforming the Carmelite order.

Plaza de la Catedral. ☎ *920-211-641. Admission for museum: 4€ adult. Mon–Fri 10am–7.30pm; Sat 10am–8pm; Sun and holidays noon–6:30pm. Last ticket is sold 45 min. before closing.*

→ **Convento de Santa Teresa** In all honesty, the church is small, but Santa Teresa's Carmelites Descalzadas weren't short-changed any gold. Catholics and the like flock to Saint Teresa's convent built on her birthplace, in order to give props to the mystic who reportedly saw visions of Mary and Jesus. (She also was an exceptional writer.) The entire church, built in 1636, sits on a **crypt-turned-museum.** Exit the church and swing to the left, in order to enter the souvenir shop and the room of relics. Head past the postcards and take a gander at none other than the finger of Saint Teresa, encased in glass and donned with a ring. Legend has it, Franco guarded the finger on his nightstand and prayed to it at bedtime. Alongside her finger is a piece of bone from San Juan de la Cruz, her monk friend who was another brilliant writer. *Plaza de la Santa.* ☎ *920-211-030. Free admission. Church Tues–Sun 9am–1:30pm and 3:30–8pm. Room of relics Tues–Sun 9:30am–1:30pm and 3:30–7:30pm. Closed Mon.*

→ **El Monasterio de Santo Tomás** This Dominican convent was built in 1492 when Columbus sailed the ocean blue. Although none other than King Ferdinand and Queen Isabella who used it as their summer residence commissioned it, it was actually María Dávila and Tomás de Torquemada who founded the convent in 1483 when Torquemada was appointed as the first Grand Inquisitor of Spain. You may have heard of the devil—he liked to burn people at the stake. People say he's also buried here though there is no tombstone to prove it. From the outside the facade looks bare-bones, but take a look at the emblem of the Catholic monarchs: a yoke and a sheaf of arrows. Especially noteworthy inside is the marble monument, carved by the 15th-century Florentine sculptor Domenico Fancelli, over the tomb of Prince Don Juan, King Ferdinand's only child. *Plaza de Granada 1.* ☎ *920-220-400. Admission 3€ adult. Tues–Sun 10am–1pm and 4–8pm. Closed all day Mon and Tues morning. Last tickets are sold 30 min. before closing.*

MTV **Best ◑** → **Los Muralles** Ironically, everything about Avila is what surrounds it—and it's no wonder. The wall is 2.5km (1½ miles) in perimeter (you can walk 1km/⅔ mile of it, split in two sections), with 86 towers and nine enemy-eating gates. The Romans actually started the project, but Christian and Islamic slaves finished off the wall in the 12th century; the Muslim influence is indicated by the Mudéjar ruins found on the northern and western stretches; the iron was donated by the Jews. Early in the day or in the evening are the best times to walk, as there are fewer people and better lighting. Slam an espresso and go to the bathroom beforehand; we wish someone had told us. The best city wall access is from **Puerta de Alcázar, Puerta de los Leales, Puerta de San**

Vicente, and **Puerta del Carmen.** The last tickets are sold at 7:15pm, an ideal time to head up. ☎ *920-255-088. Admission 3.50€ adults, 2€ students. Tues–Sun 10am–8pm. Closed Mon.*

Santiago de Compostela ★★★

If there's a popularity contest for Catholicism's holiest cities, Santiago de Compostela takes the bronze medal, ranked right behind Jerusalem and Rome/Vatican City. But this city has got a lot more going on for it than a bunch of religious fanatics wearing giant seashells (we'll explain the mollusks later). Over 100,000 pilgrims flock to the Iberian Mecca each year, and they're not all Catholic.

Santiago University attracts 33,000 students, and praying is the last thing on their minds at the city's plethora of rock 'n' roll infused bars. If you're wondering why some of them aren't speaking Spanish, it's because Galician, which sounds a lot like Portuguese, is still taught in schools. The region was originally Celtic before it was Romanized but stayed fairly autonomous under Castilian rule, albeit suffering occasional Viking raids—which explains all the redheads.

The **feast of Santiago** takes place on July 25th and is one of the most important fiestas in Christian Palm Pilots. Saint James is Galicia's patron saint and the guy who wipes the slate clean for sinners when they pay respect among the carnies, pyrotechnics, and papier-mâché *cabezudos* during the week's festivities.

The **tourist office** is at Rua del Villar 43 (☎ **981-555-129**) and is open during the winter Mon-Sun 9am-2pm and 4pm-7pm. During summer June 1-Sept 30, every day, 9am-9pm.

Getting There

BY PLANE

If your holy walking staff's broken, sell your soul to the devil and fly into the Lavacolla **airport** (☎ **981-547-501**), about 11km or 7 miles from the center on the road to Lugo. **Iberia (800/772-4642)** has six daily flights to Santiago, and there are three daily flights from Barcelona.

BY TRAIN

From A Coruña, more than a baker's dozen of **trains** (☎ **981-520-202** or www.renfe. es) make the 1-hour trip daily at a cost of 3.60€–4.85€. Express Talgo trains are available for about 10€ more. Three trains arrive daily from Madrid; the 8-hour trip costs 42€.

BY BUS

Buses leave on the hour, connecting A Coruña with Santiago (1 hr.), and cost 6.15€ one-way. For information, call **Castromil** (☎ **981-589-700;** www.monbus.es). Seven buses arrive in Santiago daily from Madrid (8-9 hr.); the trip costs 38€ one-way. For schedules, call **Alsa** (☎ **981-586-133;** www.alsa.es).

BY CAR

Take the express highway (A-9/E-50) south from A Coruña to reach Santiago. From Madrid, N-VI runs to Galicia. From Lugo, head south along N-640. Be careful not to run over any of the pilgrims hitchhiking along the Camino del Santiago route.

Santiago de Compostela

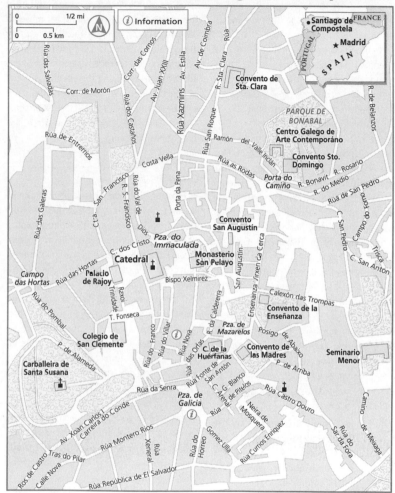

① Information

Santiago de Compostela
★ Madrid
FRANCE
PORTUGAL
SPAIN

0   1/2 mi
0   0.5 km

Convento de
Sta. Clara

PARQUE DE
BONABAL

Centro Galego de
Arte Contemporáno

Convento Sto.
Domingo

Porta do
Camiño

Convento
San Augustín

Pza. do
Immaculada

Catedral

Monasterio
San Pelayo

Palacio
de Rajoy

Campo
das Hortas

Bispo Xelmirez

Calexón das Trompas

Convento de la
Enseñanza

T. Fonseca

Colegio de
San Clemente

Pza. de
Mazarelos

Convento de
las Madres

Seminario
Menor

Carballeira de
Santa Susana

C. de la
Huérfanas

Rúa da Senra

Pza. de
Galicia

①

Sightseeing

→**Cathedral of Santiago de Compostela** Like a mirage in the desert, this cathedral is the final destination for the hordes that make the trek each year; and most likely, it won't disappoint. As soon as the city was hailed as holy in 1075, the oldest remnant of the church, the **Capilla del Salvador** was constructed. Enter the Old Cathedral through the Obradoiro door,

where lies the Romanesque **crypta** with the first groined vaults (an arched ceiling longer than a football field) ever built in Spain. A silver urn in the crypt supposedly contains the remains of the Apostle St. James. In the cathedral's **Capilla del Relicario** is a gold crucifix, from the year 874 A.D., reportedly containing a piece of the cross—*His* cross. Near the entrance, Maestro Mateo's **Portico de la Gloria** was considered to be Europe's cream of the crop during the 12th century. The central pier of the grandiose doorway is still the end-all for pilgrims, who either touch or kiss the **Tree of Jesse** column, marking the end of the finish line. Kneeling at the ground is a **statue of Master Mateo,** the brains behind the masterpiece. Since the Middle Ages, mothers wishing their sons to bear Mateo's genius, or else students seeking the same for themselves, bump foreheads with the stone-aged architect. One last, more modern tradition is the **Butafumeiro,** a giant swinging incense urn, which sets you back 240€ if you wanna see it in action. Reportedly, it swings about twice per week. However, during Jubilee year (when the Feast of Santiago, July 25th, lands on a Sunday), the urn swings every day at noon. The next Jubliee is July 25th, 2010, so there's no excuse for last-minute planning. *Plaza del Obradoiro.* ☎ *981-583-548. Free admission to the cathedral; admission to the cloisters 3€. Daily 7am–9pm. Cathedral's museum:* ☎ *981-560-527. Admission 5€. July–Oct Mon–Sat 10am–2pm and 4–8pm, Sun 10am–20m; Nov–June Mon–Sat 10am–1:30pm and 4–6:30pm, Sun 10am–1:30pm.*

➜ **Visita de las Cubiertas de la Catedral** If you've ever dreamed of jumping roofs, this tour will help you gain inspiration for your Criss Angel routine. In the Middle Ages, pilgrims climbed the 84-step stairwell to burn their rankly peon (and frankly, just rank) clothes. The cathedral now offers safe-guarded tours on the hour from Plaza del Obradoiro. For reservations, call the cathedral (☎ 981-552-985). *Admission 10€ adults, 8€ pilgrims and students. Daily 10am–2pm and 4-8pm.*

FREE ➜ **Centro Gallego de Arte Contemporáneo** If contemporary art gets you off, then take a break from all the religious hoopla and head here, to the Galician Center of Contemporary Art. The creation of this gallery was the first time in the entire Galician region an art museum dared to color outside the lines putting antiques and classicism second to contemporary art. The terrace is perfect for open-air exhibitions during the summer, as well as a great view—so tote that digital camera. Better yet, it's totally free. *Rua Valle-Inclán, s/n.* ☎ *981-546-629. www.cgac.org. Tues-Sun 11am–8pm.*

Sleeping

CHEAP

➜ **Hostal Pazo de Agra** If your last name doesn't ring any royal bells then skip the Hostal de los Reyes (below) and book a room at this low-budget but highly recommended hotel, located just a few minutes' walk from the cathedral. The price is such a steal that some travelers are suspicious, but the service proves Pazo de Agra to be a worthy bargain. Located in a three-story house, rooms are modest, clean, and promise hot water after your long and (quite literally) cross-country walk. The husband, wife, and son who run the *hostal* also own a restaurant nearby called Zingara, a perfect place for breakfast. **Hint:** You can charge your meal to your room. *Rua da Caldereira 37.* ☎ *981-583-517. Apr 1–Oct. 31 double 36€, single 26€; Nov 1–Mar 31 double 32€, single 20€. Amenities: Internet, private bath, towels and sheets included.*

SPLURGE

➜ **Hostal de los Reyes** This building is better for gawking at than booking a room in, though we can't not mention it because of its historic importance. It's considered by proud Spaniards to be the oldest in the world. (Though we checked, and it's not— Japan owns that claim.) Right next to the cathedral, this parador was once a royal hospice and then a pilgrim's hospice in the 15th century. Isabella and Ferdinand's favorite architect Enrique de Egas built it, and now tourists can roam around its gardens, while guests roll around in the sheets. A tour guide must accompany visitors without a room key from the cathedral. *Plaza Do Obradoiro.* ☎ *981-582-200. www.parador.es. Tours daily 10am–1pm and 4–7pm. Double 232€; single 176€. Breakfast included. Amenities: Everything. Seriously! It's got five stars and has more than 500 years of experience.*

Eating

The Saint Jacob's Shell, Viera, is the symbol of the city, as well as that of El Camino de Santiago, but its contents are also eaten at many of the restaurants in town. *Pulpo á la Gallega,* cuttlefish prepared with paprika, as well as *empanada Gallega,* a fish, meat, or vegetable pie, are other Galician musthaves. For desert, *la tarta Compostelana,* an almond cake, is the regional integument. To wash it all down, the Ribeiro wine of the Galician region, one of the most famous in Spain, will make you feel holy indeed.

Instead of *tapas,* or small appetizer plates, the Galician city specializes in *raciones,* larger portions of the same foods. Get your eats down Franco and A Raíña streets, A Troia street, and Rúa de San Pedro and the surrounding streets. Other areas rich in *raciones* are Porta do Camiño, Rúa Travesa, Plaza de Santo Agostiño, and San Roque.

➜**Casa Manolo** GALICIAN If you're a pilgrim, chances are you're in Santiago de Compostela on a budget. This is the best and least-expensive meal in the city, famous for feeding pilgrims in a building that is at least a hundred years old. Things are made easy here where only one *menú del dia* is offered, consisting of a two-course meal that'll stick to your ribs. Don't ask to hold the mayonnaise or put it on the side; what you see is what you get. Expect a line at lunchtime (around 2pm). *Plaza Cerrantes, s/n.* ☎ *981-582-950. Meal 6.50€. Daily 1–4pm; Mon-Sat 8:30–11:30pm.*

Partying

Perhaps it's the sea breeze off the coast or all those fir trees that make for a good muse, but Santiago de Compostela is laden with rock bars. **Ruta 66** (Pérez Constanti 4) is a true-blue rock bar that's worth the extra steps it is from the center, as long as you're not wearing Gucci shoes or JLo jewelry, in which case these aren't your people. Juliette and the Licks, White Stripes, Hives, and the like are all regulars on the sound system. It's quite easy to *ligar* (hit on someone) and usually packed with the right kind of people—those with good music taste. Get there at 3am.

If counterculture is not what you're looking for, **Casa de las Crechas** (Via Sacra 3) is as classic as the chipping art hanging in the cathedral, which it sits directly behind. Ironically, it was supposed to have been an old brothel—the club, not the cathedral. The word *crechas* refers to the women's blonde streaks in their hair, or so the story goes. Now folk music and Celtic music (hello, bagpipes!) work the floors; on Wednesdays there are live jam sessions.

📺 Best✪ Detour: Camino de Santiago ★★

It all started with a beheading. That's how Apostle James was killed in Jerusalem in 44 A.D., supposedly the first of Jesus' apostles to get bumped. Legend has it that James's remains were transported in a stone boat to Spain, where the apostle had preached, to Galicia, the northwest corner pocket of Spain before they were brought inland to Santiago. When his remains were reportedly rediscovered in the 9th century,

Sally Sells Sea Shells by the Galician Seashore

They're everywhere—on churches, sidewalks, and roads, tattooed on bodies, sewn to backpacks, glued to staffs, and even on plates in restaurants. The world's most famous mollusk—also the symbol of Saint James—directs pilgrims along the often vaguely marked Camino de Santiago. Coincidently, the shell is also the pagan sign of fertility, a much less prudish reason to make the journey, but the reason nonetheless why young couples wishing to reproduce themselves commonly make the trek.

pilgrims from all over Europe came by land and sea, making the path El Camino de Santiago the most important Christian pilgrimage of the Middle Ages. Whether you've got a religious bone in you or not, El Camino de Santiago is the best way to see the back roads of Spain. Period.

Pilgrims usually take 20 to 30 days to complete the peonage on foot or bicycle and stay in free *hostales, refugios,* and sometimes convents along the way. Pilgrims must have a **Pilgrim's Credential,** which they can get at any of the albergues along the way or by contacting the **Santiago de Compostela Oficina de Peregrino** (Rúa do Vilar, 1. ☎ 981-562-419, www.archi compostela.org. Open daily 9am-9pm). This document gets stamped in churches, albergues, and even bars along the way. Iberia Airlines offer discounts, as well as many other Spanish establishments along the route, so always ask. At the end of the journey, request a certificate to hang in your trophy room back home.

Recommended Websites

○ **www.mundicamino.com**: An "official" Camino del Santiago site, featuring places to eat, sleep, and plan your route.
○ **www.santiagoturismo.com**: The city's website is surprisingly helpful (in terms of government-sponsored sites, that is) and it's in English. You'll also find info on all of the pilgrim albergues in town to crash after a hard month's walk.

○ **www.xacobeo.es**: This is one of the most famous, multilingual websites and is considered an official one at that. It's extremely good for planning routes.

Camino Frances (Ruta Jacobea)

This road most traveled has more nicknames than a high-school linebacker. Our favorite though is Milky Way, as its path stretches horizontally from either Saint Jean Pied de Port or Somport, depending on which route you choose, across northern Spain through Navarre and Castile y León, all in perfect accordance with those curious stars and the swath they cut through the sky to form what we know as the Milky Way. Who needs a compass when a galaxy will do?

If you're in a hurry (like most Americans who are likely on limited vacation time—did you know Spaniards get a whole month's vacation compared with our measly two weeks?), monumental pit stops long the route include Pamplona, Burgos, León, and, finally, Santiago de Composotela.

In **Pamplona,** you can find pilgrim's lodging between June 1 to October 31 (closed July 5–15) at either **Convento de las Adoratrices** (Calle Dos de Mayo 5; ☎ **948-211-366** and 662-570-716; 5€ per peregrino; amenities: microwave, showers, hair dryer) or **Casa Paderborn** (Playa de Caparroso 6; ☎ **660-631-656;** 5€ per peregrino; amenities: kitchen, microwave, laundry service, hair dryer). Of course the best (or worst) time to be in Pamplona is during San Fermin, or the running of the bulls, July 7 to 14 (p. 295).

An hour's walk west of Pamplona, near the town of **Estella,** the company Bodegas Irache has donated a fountain to parched pilgrims—one tap for water, the other for wine. Ingenious.

There are three albergues for pilgrims in **Burgos** (Asociación de Amigos del Camino de Santiago de Burgos, Santander 13, 2nd floor, 09004 Burgos; ☎ 947-268-386). **Albergue de Burgos** (Finca del El Parral, en La Salida de Burgos; 3€ per night) is located just outside the city gate in an enchanting park, El Parral, near Hospital del Rey and the river. Rustic log cabins make unusual barracks for bunked sleeping; bring your own soap and towel. For more information call **Asociación Amigos del Camino de Santiago** (☎ **947-460-922**).

The best time to pass through Burgos is in August when the city celebrates **Festival Mix,** an electronic musical cocktail served with an audiovisual twist; it's some of the most progressive stuff you'll see in this area. At the end of June, Burgos celebrates **Festival de San Pedro y San Pablo,** the biggest event of the year. An entire 10 days is packed tight with bull fights, and—you better believe it—a four-star tapas fair that merits Michelin's rubber stars.

In **León,** the municipal **albergue** (Campos Góticos s/n; ☎ **987-081-832** or 987-081-833; 3€ per night) is an eyesore but better outfitted than most, with laundry service, bathroom toiletries, and even a coffee machine, but no place to put your bike. It opens at 12:30pm and does not lock its doors at night, meaning no curfew for you. For more info on peregrino services in León, contact **Asociación de Amigos del Camino de Santiago Pulchra Leónina de León** (Plaza Santa María del Camino 7, 24006 León; ☎ **987-245-763**).

Leon celebrates **Festival de San Pedro y San Pablo** at the end of June, just like Burgos, with all the bull drippings along with a giant bonfire and a satisfying display of pyrotechnics. There's a tapas fair (León is known for it's better-than-most tapas), and a Car Park Rock Festival, which thankfully is more modern than its vintage sounding moniker.

Camino de Madrid

Starting from none other than Madrid, this route makes its way north toward Segovia and through the Valladolid province before meeting up with Sahagún and the Camino Frances (see details above). Contact the city's **Asociación de Amigos del Camino de Santiago de Madrid** (Carretas 17, 7th floor, 28012 Madrid; ☎ 915-232-211) for additional tips and info on the Camino de Madrid. Also, see p. 86 for where to stay in Madrid if you are starting your walk or ride from here.

In **Segovia,** your options are slim when it comes to free lodging. **Hípica Eresma,** however, offers all of the basic necessities for no cost at all (Carretera Palazuelos km 2; ☎ 921-120-042). In **Valladolid,** the **Red Cross** (☎ 605-041-394) has stationed a pilgrim's post at Albergue de Peregrinos, 47800 Medina de Reioseco, and **Asociación Jacobea Vallisoletana** (Real 105, 47152 Puente Duero) can assist you with planning your trek. Also see Segovia, p. 232 and Valladolid, p. 203 for more on those cities.

Ruta de la Lana

One of the oldest routes, Ruta de la Lana has probably been in use since before Visigoth rule and on through the centuries when Burgos became a large exporter of wool. It used to be bumpin' with places to eat and relax while on the road. But ever since the locomotive was invented, the area has fallen into a slump, even though the Castilian mesas are some of the most *bellas* in the country. Starting in Cuenca, the route heads north through Guadalajara until it joins with Camino Frances in the providence of Burgos (see above).

Cuenca's **Hospital de Santiago** (Mateo M. Ayllón s/n; ☎ **669-934-272**) is a resting place for pilgrims on the run, offering all the basics including hot showers, towels, soap, and Spanish nurses. It's also the headquarters for the **Asociación de Amigos del Camino de Santiago de Cuenca.** The best time for a pilgrimage in Cuenca is the last week of August, which lucky for you cuts down on the heat factor significantly. **Feria y fiestas de San Julian** takes place, as well as bull runs, parties, and the normal fiesta fare.

Via de la Plata (The Silver Route)

Popular belief is that this route is called silver because of the old silver-trading empire that ran between northern and southern Spain. But actually, the word *plata* is Arabic, referencing a road that would be taken into battle with the Muslim neighbors. Scorching hot in the summer and with poor infrustructure, in direct accordance with the entire region, it's the only route that extends through Extremadura running north along the Portuguese border into Sanabria (national park territory) and the thick green forests of Galicia. This is the route for rugged pilgrims, who will feel rewarded for having experienced what Extremadurans call the *real* Spain. We don't disagree. Major worthwhile cities along this route include Sevilla, Mérida, Cáceres, Salamanca, and Zamora.

The **Albergue Juvenil de Sevilla** is at Calle Isaac Peral (☎ **955-035-800;** single 7.15€, double 12€). The best time to be alive and in Sevilla is during **Feria de Abril,** arguably Spain's best Flamenca fiesta, which is held in—when else?—April.

Mérida has two albergues, but the newest puts the yellow brick in the road with its state-of-the-art facilities, which include a kitchen. **El Antiguo Molino de Pancaliente** just opened its doors for pilgrims, but walk fast; there are only 12 beds. The best time to do it up in Mérida is during **Festival Teatro Clásico,** which runs July through August. Sure, a theater festival sounds nerdy but Romans built the actual venue, as in an amphitheater older than your grandma's great, great, great, and über-great grandmother. Get thee there! For more information on lodging and attractions, contact the tourist office in Mérida (p. 180).

Cáceres is pilgrim-friendly and a good many of its pensions offer small discounts to those who are passing through. The **Asociación de Amigos del Camino de Santiago de Cáceres** (Ronda del Carmen 35, 8th floor, 10002 Cáceres) can tell you about some of them, such as **Las Valetas** (Margallo 36 [near Plaza Mayor]; ☎ **927-211-210**), which offers shared rooms and bathrooms (towels and sheets included) with breakfast for 20€ per night. The **municipal albergue** for pilgrims was closed during the time of writing but will reopen at the start of the year. Contact the Cáceres **tourism office** for updates and more information (p. 188). If you're a smart planner, you'll pass through this bustling town the second week of May during **WOMAD** (World of Music, Art, and Dance). WOMAD translation: Spanish hippies who toke up, beat their bongos, and drink 40s and *calimotxo* (coke and wine mix) in the historic district of Cáceres. This party is a'ight in our book though watch out for the rivers of piss flowing through the old city.

Salamanca's **municipal albergue** (☎ **652-921-185**) for pilgrims is one of the most charming we've seen thus far, located right in the heart of the historic center next to the big mama of a cathedral. The albergue's are the only digs in the city that are dedicated to Catholic beatniks on the road. For more information on the route in this region, dial the **tourist office** in Salamanca (p. 218) or the **Acasan Vía de la Plata** (Gran Vía 54, Entreplanta D, 37001 Salamanca; ☎ **923-151-083**).

Zamora lays claim to one youth hostel (Calle Villapando 7; ☎ **980-512-671**) but has no albergues specifically dedicated to the pilgrims' cause. The youth hostel offers double rooms, shared bathrooms, and breakfast, all for 8.25€ per pilgrim under the age of 30. **Asociación de Amigos de la Vía de la Plata** (Santa Clara 33, 49002 Zamora; ☎ **980-531-664**) offers up additional info. The **Saint James the Apostle fiesta** takes place annually on July 25th. Events that ensue are novice bullfights, a running of the bulls, and herds of students trying to walk home while being not too sober.

Camino del Norte ★★

Contrary to what the experts say (what do they know anyway?), this is a choice route stretching across the northern edge of Spain along the Bay of Biscay and the Spanish Cantabrian sea. It's considered the oldest route, first taken by the Christians descending from the North—but it won our respect for its coastal surfing towns that are known throughout the world.

Critics of the Camino del Norte complain of badly marked roads, many of which are heavily traveled highways. Hoofing it parallel to the sea also means that there are a number of rivers you'll have to cross, as well as long stretches without ocean views. Those are all good points to consider, so we recommend renting a Volkswagon bus instead, which is technically cheating but way cooler.

Major stopping points along the route include San Sebastian, Guernica (the same Guernica you read about in your art history books), Bilbao (don't miss the Guggenheim), and finally Santander.

In **San Sebastian,** the **Albergue Ondarreta** (Paseo de Igueldo 25; ☎ **943-310-268;** www.donostialbergues.org), aka La Sirena, is an attractive and peaceful youth hostel that rents rooms with private bathrooms to pilgrims for a discounted price: in the summer, 16€ per person; winter, 12.50€. Towels are 1.10€, sheets are 2.75€, and breakfast is included. It's hard to go wrong in San Sebastian, as there are major events year-round. Its **film festival** (**www.sansebastianfestival.ya.com**) is held in late September, as well as the **Regatta de Traineras,** which are boat races you can check out every Sunday. The **International Jazz Festival** is held every July. (See p. 254 for San Sebástian basics.)

The **Albergue de Gernika** (Carretera Kortezubi 9; ☎ **685-752-286** or 656-762-217; www.alberguegernika.com) in **Guernica** (spelled differently in Castillian Spanish) offers bunked boarding with shared bathrooms for 13€ per person. Towels cost 1.50€ and sheets cost 2.50€.

Experts say crossing through Basque country proves more difficult for pilgrims trying to find *refugios*. But what **Bilbao** doesn't have in quantity, it makes up for with sheer quality. **Albergue Bilbao Aterpetxea** (Ctra. Basurto-Kastrexana 70; ☎ **944-270-054;** http://albergue.bilbao.net) was rated the top albergue in all of Europe. Although sterile looking, the state-of-the-art, 8-floor complex is a sure-fire bet for an air-conditioned, Windex-induced night's sleep. Prices range from 16€ to 20€ per person for bunked rooms and shared bathrooms, with breakfast and sheets included. Towels cost an extra 3.50€. Amenities include a gym, table tennis, Internet access, a common room, and a washer/dryer. Bilbao's biggest week, and a good time to pass through the city, is called exactly that, **Aste Nagusia,** which takes place in August. (See Bilbao, p. 273.)

In **Santander,** the **Albergue Santos Mártires** (Rua Mayor 9; ☎ **942-219-747;** open year-round) is free for pilgrims, but you should donate a small amount. Cantabria's **La Asociación Amigos del** **Camino de Santiago** is also located there, with the same contact information as listed for the albergue. Head toward the **tourism office** if you don't get any answer (like the rest of the country, they're probably enjoying a quick siesta).

Basque Country

by Kristin Luna

Beaches, mountains, traditions, parties: You'll find it all in this tiny corner of Spain bordered by France and the Bay of Biscay. Basque Country's two most visited cities, **San Sebastián** and **Bilbao,** are both interesting mixes of aesthetic architecture, stunning beaches, and thriving nightlife. As one of the most artistic areas of northern Spain, Basque Country—or **Euskadi** as it is called locally—has a seductive romance to its cultural vitality. The Basque people pride themselves on their identity, one that is completely separate from that of Spain. The region itself is autonomous, meaning it has its own government; you'll notice Basque flags flying high and a peculiar language you're not familiar with spoken in most parts.

Pilgrims heading west in a quest to reach Santiago will pass along one of two routes that split at Irún and traverse different areas of Basque Country: The Coastal Road takes you along the beaches and through Bilbao, while the Inland Road veers southwest and through Vitoria-Gasteiz. Each one has stop-off points at some impressive churches, sanctuaries, and basilicas in rural Euskadi.

One of the Basque Country's greatest draws is its beaches. With 252km (150 miles) of coastline, there are more than a few spots to hit the coast, not to mention places galore to go surfing, yachting, or windsurfing on the uncultivated Bay of Biscay.

But perhaps what Basque Country is most known for globally is its gastronomy. Some of the world's most famed and skilled chefs originate here, and they take full advantage of their proximity to the Bay of Biscay by cooking up every underwater delight imaginable. If seafood's not your bag, other regional favorites are beans and corn, and game like fresh lamb and pork.

Local beverages include home-brewed cider or *txakoli,* a dry sharp-tasting wine.

Best of Basque Country

○ **Best Day Excursion: Fuenterrabía.** A short bus ride from San Sebastián, Fuenterrabía, just over the bay from France, makes for a nice daytime getaway. See p. 271.

○ **Best Regional Dish: Bacalao.** I'm not even a seafood lover—in fact, I'm about as far from it as you can get—and even I immensely enjoyed this codfish dish, typical of the Basque region. You can find it pretty much anywhere, as both a tapa and main course.

○ **Best Museum: The Guggenheim.** One of a series of similar museums constructed by New York architect Frank O. Gehry, the glass and titanium colossus is responsible for the recent surge of tourism that Bilbao has seen since the Guggenheim's construction just less than a decade ago. See p. 282.

○ **Best Beach: Playa de la Concha.** Spilling over with vacationers and locals during summer months, this is *the* social spot in San Sebastián and a great place to catch some rays. See p. 258.

○ **Best After-hours Venue: Zurriola Bar** (San Sebastián). A bar, restaurant, cafe, and disco all rolled into one. if you're looking for somewhere to go when all the other bars close down, you'll find the doors open at this beachside joint. See p. 268.

○ **Best Backpackers' Haven: Olga's Place.** The sweet smile of the Russian expat for whom this hidden gem is named will win you over every time. And the atmosphere is the most social of any hostel in town. If you speak just a bit of Spanish (or better yet, Russian), you may even find yourself being invited for a free meal by the hostess-with-the-mostest herself. See p. 262.

○ **Best View: Monte Igueldo.** As if the ride up the funicular isn't enough already, the spectacular sights of San Sebastián from above will bring you back to this delightful city time and again. See p. 271.

○ **Best Surfer Spot: Playa de la Zurriola.** With its crashing waves and youthful vibe, you'll find surfers dotting the ocean of this beach year-round. See p. 258.

○ **Best Hike: Monte Urgull.** Not too taxing, but a good half-hour walk with rewarding views, you can pick one of many different marked paths that will lead you to the top of this "mountain" (more accurately, small mound). See p. 271.

○ **Best Living Art Display: Museo Chillida-Leku.** Set among a fertile park, this hillside museum of sculptures is an astonishing, yet pleasing, diversion from your everyday museum. See p. 269.

San Sebastián (Donostia)

With some of Europe's most fabulous beaches, a nightlife to rival that of Ibiza, and a welcoming, seaside atmosphere, it's no wonder San Sebastián is a favorite

destination for travelers from around the world. Just 20km (12 miles) from the French border, San Sebastián has an ideal setting

Useful Basque Phrases

No one seems to know exactly where the Indo-European language originates. One thing is for sure—it sounds and looks nothing like Spanish, so don't expect to go there and understand a word. With the exception of the main touristy spots in San Sebastián and Bilbao, English speakers are few and far between (and likewise Spanish speakers, too, at times).

Bai/Ez = Yes/No

Kaixo!, Agur/Agur!, Adio = Hello/Goodbye

Ikusi arte = See you

Eskerrik asko/Ez horregatik = Thank you/You're welcome

Egun on = Good morning (literally: Good day)

Egun on, bai = Standard reply to *Egun on*

Arratsalde on/Gabon = Good evening/Good night

Mesedez = Please

Barkatu = Excuse (me)

Aizu! = Yo! (not polite, to be used with friends)

Kafe hutsa nahi nuke/Garagardoa nahi nuke = Can I have a coffee? / . . . a beer?

Non dago . . .? = Where is . . .?

Komuna, non dago? = Where are the toilets?

Non dago tren-geltokia?/Non dago autobus-geltokia? = Where is the train station? . . . bus station?

Ba al da hotelik hemen inguruan? = Where is the nearest hotel?

Ez dut ulertzen = I don't understand.

Ez dakit euskaraz = I don't speak Basque.

Ba al dakizu ingelesez? = Do you speak English?

Gazteleraz badakizu? = Do you speak Spanish?

Zein da zure izena? = What is your name?

Pozten nau zu ezagutzeak = Nice to meet you.

Jakina!/Noski! = Sure! OK!

Nongoa zara? = Where are you from?

Neska polita/Neska ederra = You're hot.

Bizi gara! = We're alive! (handy to know the morning after!)

Topa! = Cheers!

One = bat/ **Two** = bi/ **Three** = hiru/ **Four** = lau/ **Five** = bost/ **Six** = sei/ **Seven** = zazpi/ **Eight** = zortzi/ **Nine** = bederatzi/ **Ten** = hamar

BASQUE COUNTRY

with three main beaches nestled among a series of verdant mountains.

While you'll find a decent amount of English spoken in San Sebastián thanks to the summer tourist influx, you'll also hear your share of Euskera. Whereas the language seems to be dying out in some parts of the region, half of the *Donostiarras*—residents of San Sebastián—still speak Euskera, thanks to a solid sense of national pride. In the Basque language, San Sebastián is **Donostia**. So don't get confused when you are on a bus and find out that its final stop is Donostia, when you were meant to be headed for San Sebastián.

Home to just 180,000 inhabitants, San Sebastián still maintains a big-city feel without the overpopulation of permanent residents. In fact, the majority of its people seem to be tourists, especially in summer months when the city center is heavily congested with a jumble of nationalities. If the sound of this alone gives you a panicky feeling of claustrophobia, you'd be best off visiting San Sebastián sometime other than July and August, the city's peak season.

San Sebastián residents live by the saying that "doing nothing is doing something," and after a week soaking up the lazy lifestyle, you'll get the meaning of the paradoxical philosophy. Aside from the city's rich artistic patrimony and a few museums scattered here and there, daytime activities include lounging on the beach or on a bench at one of the city's many green spaces. Yet, you'll find yourself wondering exactly how the time flew in the lethargic city.

Getting There

BY AIR

Airports at San Sebastián, Bilbao, Vitoria-Gasteiz, Biarritz, and Pamplona all offer **flights** through a host of low-cost carriers. From Madrid, there are flights to San Sebastián on **Iberia Airlines** (☎ 902-400-500; www.iberia.com), with three to

six flights daily and three flights from Barcelona. The domestic airport is 20km (12 miles) away at Fuenterrabía. From there, **Interbus** (☎ 943-641-302) services San Sebastián's center every 20 minutes from 6:45am to 9:05pm Monday through Saturday. Tickets are 1.40€.

BY TRAIN

From Madrid, you can hop one of the three daily **Renfre trains** (☎ 943-641-302; www.renfe.es) in the direction of Irún at the French border that stop at San Sebastián (35€, trip time: 6½ hr.). An overnight train from Paris stops in San Sebastián, and RENFE also provides two daily trains from Barcelona to San Sebastián and on to Bilbao (35€, trip time: 8½ hr.). The train station lies on the eastern side of Río Urumea, south of Playa de la Zurriola at Paseo de Francia 22 (☎ **902-240-202** or 943-649-637).

BY BUS

San Sebastián has a number of **buses** passing through at any given time. The main bus station, **Continental Auto** (Av. de Sancho el Sabio 31; ☎ **943-469-074**), runs seven to nine buses daily from Madrid (27€, trip time: 6 hr.), though the train is more convenient. **Vibasa** (Po. De Vizcaya 16; ☎ **943-457-500**) operates three buses from Barcelona (25€, trip time: 7 hr.), and **Transportes PESA** (Av. de Sancho el Sabio 33; ☎ **902-101-210**) runs buses every 30 minutes to Bilbao (8€, trip time: 1¼ hr.).

BY CAR

From Madrid, take the **N-1** toll road north to Burgos, then follow **A-1** to Mirando de Ebro. Continue on the **A-68** north to Bilbao and then the **A-8** east to San Sebastián. From Pamplona, take the **A-15** north to the **N-1** route, which leads right into San Sebastián.

Basque Country

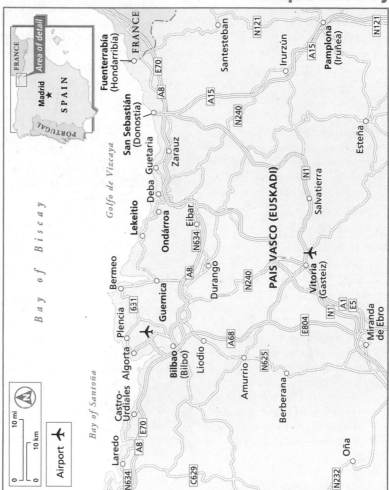

Getting Around

BY BUS

San Sebastián is well connected by local **bus** services, so, though it's so small, you'll only need to take **Bus 26** or **28** (1€, trip time: 20 min.) if heading out of town or arriving from the bus terminal, which is a bit of a hike from the center.

BY BIKE

You can rent **bicycles** or **motorbikes** from **Bici Rent** (Av. de Zurriola 22; ☎ **943-290-854** or 655-724-458), which has two locations along Playa de Zurriola; the second is at Paseo de Colón 54 (☎ **943-469-074**). Bike rentals are 4€ for 1 hour or 16€ for the day; 6€ an hour for a two-seater or 30€ a day. The shop is open Monday through Friday 10:30am to 2pm and 4 to 8:30pm, Saturday 11am to 2pm and 4 to 8:30pm. Or try **Comet** (Av. de la Libertad 6, San Sebastián; ☎ **943-422-351**).

BY CAR

If you must have your own mode of transportation (advisable if you plan on taking day trips to surrounding villages), you can rent a car at **Avis** (C. del Triunfo 2; ☎ **943-461-556**; www.avis.com), open Monday to Friday 8am to 1pm and 4 to 7pm, Sat 9am to 1pm, or at **Donosti-Net** (C. de Embeltrán 2; ☎ **943-425-870**), an all-purpose one-stop shop, open daily 9am to 9pm.

San Sebastián Basics

ORIENTATION

You'll hear the main drag in town referred to simply as **"The Boulevard"** and discover a smattering of shops and restaurants along the wide street that heads north from the train and bus stations. The Boulevard ends near Playa de la Concha and is a gateway to **La Parte Vieja,** the old town quarter that is home to a mix of cheapie shops, tapas bars, and pensions. You'll find your main bar scene here, as well as your best shot at cheap accommodation. Heading west from La Parte Vieja are the elegant streets of **El Centro,** with boutiquey stores, four- and five-star hotels, and classy cafes galore.

The city's three main beaches are 📺 Best❶ **Playa de la Concha, Playa de Ondaretta,** and **Playa de la Zurriola.** La Concha Bay, which cuts into Playa de la Concha, is one of the most reproduced snapshots in Europe and, without a doubt, one of Spain's most beautiful spots. This is San Sebastián's most populated beach, and a good place to go for topless sunbathing.

Just west of Playa de la Concha is Playa de Ondaretta, every bit as attractive though not quite as popular except among families

who take their children to the beachside playground. If you want to get away from the crowds, Ondaretta is pleasant enough and just a 5-minute walk away from la Concha. And if you venture just far enough west, you can catch a glimpse of some fascinating works of modern art by famous sculptor Eduardo Chillida, which make a stunning picture at sunset with the waves crashing into them. If you like his work, you can also visit his museum (p. 269).

The hot spot among students and young people is 📺 Best❶ **Playa de la Zurriola,** just to the east of where Río Urumea divides the city. With stronger waves produced by the untamed Bay of Biscay, Zurriola is one of the best surfing spots on the west coast of Spain.

TOURIST OFFICES

Stop by the **Centro de Atracción y Turismo** (Boulevard Reina Regente 3; ☎ **943-481-166**) for information and maps on the city and surrounding area. The tourist office is open June through September from Monday to Saturday 8am to 8pm and Sunday 10am-2pm, and October through May from Monday to Saturday 9am to 2pm and 3:30 to 7pm. **Tourist info** can also be found at the train and bus stations in the summer months (open daily June–Sept 9am–9pm).

RECOMMENDED WEBSITES

○ **www.basquecountrytourism.net**: This website with an English-language option is worth a browse as it has explanations on a variety of Basque subjects, including gastronomy, culture, sports, and spas, among other things.

○ **www.donostia.org**: This site also has some useful info about San Sebastián in English, as well as maps and transportation links.

○ **www.enjoyss.com**: This link is more targeted toward students and young

San Sebastián

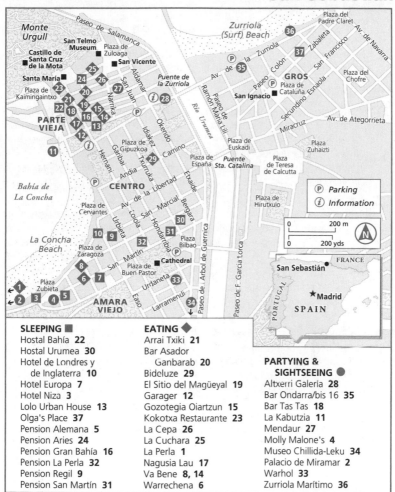

Monte Urgull

Paseo de Salamanca

Castillo de Santa Cruz de la Mota

San Telmo Museum

Plaza de Zuloaga

San Vicente

Zurriola (Surf) Beach

Plaza del Padre Claret

Av. de Navarra

Santa María

Puente de la Zurriola

Av. de la Zurriola

Plaza de Kaimingaintxo

San Juan

Aldamar

Narrika

Río Urumea

Paseo Colón

GROS

Plaza de Cataluña

San Francisco

Esnaola

Plaza del Chofre

PARTE VIEJA

Hernani

Garibai

Idiakez

Txurruka

Okendo

Camino

Plaza de Gipuzkoa

San Ignacio

Secundino

Miracruz

Av. de Ategorrieta

Bahía de La Concha

CENTRO

Andía

Av. de la Libertad

Extxaide

Bergara

Plaza de España

Puente Sta. Catalina

Plaza de Euskadi

Plaza de Teresa de Calcutta

Plaza Zuhaizti

Plaza de Cervantes

Urbieta

Loiola

San Marcial

Hondarribia

Plaza de Hirutxulo

📍 Parking

ⓘ Information

La Concha Beach

Plaza de Zaragoza

San Martín

Plaza de Buen Pastor

Plaza Bilbao

Cathedral

Paseo de Árbol de Guernica

Paseo de F. García Lorca

0   200 m

0   200 yds

Plaza Zubieta

Urdaneta

Easo

Larramendi

AMARA VIEJO

FRANCE

San Sebastián

PORTUGAL

★ Madrid

SPAIN

SLEEPING ■
Hostal Bahía **22**
Hostal Urumea **30**
Hotel de Londres y de Inglaterra **10**
Hotel Europa **7**
Hotel Niza **3**
Lolo Urban House **13**
Olga's Place **37**
Pension Alemana **5**
Pension Aries **24**
Pension Gran Bahía **16**
Pension La Perla **32**
Pension Regil **9**
Pension San Martín **31**

EATING ◆
Arrai Txiki **21**
Bar Asador Ganbarab **20**
Bideluze **29**
El Sitio del Magüeyal **19**
Garager **12**
Gozotegia Oiartzun **15**
Kokotxa Restaurante **23**
La Cepa **26**
La Cuchara **25**
La Perla **1**
Nagusia Lau **17**
Va Bene **8, 14**
Warrechena **6**

PARTYING & SIGHTSEEING ●
Altxerri Galería **28**
Bar Ondarra/bis 16 **35**
Bar Tas Tas **18**
La Kabutzia **11**
Mendaur **27**
Molly Malone's **4**
Museo Chillida-Leku **34**
Palacio de Miramar **2**
Warhol **33**
Zurriola Marítimo **36**

travelers. It has links to about every page that has anything to do with the area.

○ **www.paseosvirtuales.com**: This site in Spanish isn't the best, though it does have maps, photos, and movies about Basque Country's prime destinations if you're more of a visual planner.

CULTURE TIPS 101

One of Spain's most culture-infused areas, Basque Country is known for its folklore

and artistic presentations. If you're lucky, you may witness a performance by a *bertsolaris,* a poet who improvises verse in the Basque language; a dance by a *dantzari,* an entertainer of folkloric interpretations; or a show by *txalapartaris,* a percussionist of ancient tradition.

Even stranger are the *harrijasotzailes,* or stone-lifters, and *segalaris,* or grass-cutters—people dedicated to preventing

Talk of the Town

Three Ways to Start a Conversation with a Local

1. **"Dude, where can I go to catch a sweet wave?"** Okay, maybe go soft on the Californian lingo if you want to be understood in the land of non-English speakers, but surfing is often the talk of the town among students in this surfer's haven.
2. **"Where does all the partying take place in this joint?"** You and I both know that La Parte Vieja is the place to be after dark, but if you act like an ignorant tourist, maybe you'll be asked along for a *zurrito* with the locals.
3. **"What are some useful Euskera phrases?"** Take an interest in their heritage—Donostiarras are a prideful bunch—and just maybe they'll take an interest in you, too.

the extinction of these ancient "sports." And don't forget *pelota,* the popular sport that is a sort of cross between lacrosse and handball.

Two major annual events draw in thousands of visitors from around the world, packing the streets, and accordingly the hotels. The biggest party of the year, **Aste Nagusia,** which takes place in mid-August, celebrates traditional Basque music and dance with festive displays and happenings. The following month, the **International Film Festival** attracts the cinema lovers

from around the world to participate in the 2-week-long event.

Culinary arts play a large part in Basque culture, as well. Like any ocean city, San Sebastián doesn't have a shortage of seafood. A plethora of fresh aquatic options including hake, tuna, and prawns, to name a few, fill any menu. If you're particularly adventurous where gastronomy is concerned, you can try one of the two peculiar regional specialties: squid cooked in its own ink and baby eels that look like shriveled up worms, fried with hot pepper in an enameled clay dish.

San Sebastián Nuts & Bolts

Currency   You can get your dollars changed into euros at a post office, though you'll get the best exchange rate by withdrawing money directly from any ATM.

Emergencies   If you need medical attention, call ☎ 112 or take Bus 28 to **Hospital de Gipuzkoa** (Paseo del Dr Begiristain 115; ☎ 943-006-000).

Internet Access   Uda.berri, a lively bar and cafe at Larramendi 8 (☎ 943-451-538), offers free wireless, as well as a mix of electro, house, and hip-hop music at all times. If you don't have a computer of your own, it has one for public access, though it's oftentimes occupied. Open daily 8am to 3am. Other Internet points are **Donosti-Net** (☎ 943-425-870), one of the biggest and best Internet cafes in town, on Calle de Embeltrán (open daily 9am–11pm) or **Zarranet** (☎ 943-433-381) at Calle San Lorenzo 6 (open Mon–Sat 10am–10pm, Sun 4–10pm). Or check your e-mail at one of the plentiful *locuturios* that dot the streets of San Sebastián.

If you're staying in San Sebastián more than just a few days and plan on doing *mucho* Web surfing, you can get a library card at **Biblioteca Central** next to Jardines de Alderdi-Eder at the beginning of Playa de la Concha that enables you to access the Internet for free. Once you sign up for your card, you must wait 3 days to use it. Library hours are Monday through Friday 10am to 8:30pm, and Saturday 10am to 2pm and 4:30 to 8pm.

Laundry   Have your clothes washed for 3.80€ a load and dried for 2€ a load at **Lavomatique** downtown (Iñigo 14; no phone; Mon–Fri 9:30am–2pm and 4–8pm, Sat–Sun 10am–2pm). Or if you're on the other side of the bridge near Zurriola, you can drop by **Wash 'n Dry** (Iparragirre 6; ☎ 943-293-150) and wash your clothes yourself at this coin-op, Aussie-run laundromat, or take advantage of the convenient drop-off service. Open daily 8am to 10pm.

Pharmacies   If you need over-the-counter medication for that nasty traveler's diarrhea or just need something to relieve the lingering pain that resulted from too many tequila shots the night before, you can head to one of the many pharmacies, denoted by a large green cross. Just have your Spanish dictionary handy. You'll be served by someone behind the counter who most likely doesn't speak English—and having to explain your symptoms by mere hand gestures can be downright awkward at times.

Post Office   The **central post office** is located on Plaza del Buen Pastor (☎ 902-197-197) and is open Monday through Friday 8:30am to 8:30pm and Saturday 9:30am to 2pm. Another branch can be found on the Zurriola side of town on Paseo Colón and is open Monday through Friday 8:30am to 8:30pm and Saturday 9:30am to 1pm.

Telephone Tips   Calls within and to San Sebastián begin with **943.** Cellphone numbers can begin with **615, 675,** and **678.** For more info on dialing to and from Spain, see p. 56.

Sleeping

Pensions and hostels are a dime a dozen in this touristy town. Most of the cheapest lodging can be found along San Martín leading up to Playa de la Concha or in Parte Vieja where all the action takes place. High season in San Sebastián typically lasts from July to September, but booking ahead is always advised, as many festivals and conferences throughout the year leave free rooms scant.

HOSTELS

MTV Best ☺ →**Lolo Urban House** ★
I walked into this unassuming Aussie-run joint and was surprised to hear all English spoken within. The crowd, mostly of the surfer genre, is an easygoing, light-hearted one, and you can always find someone to go out with if you hang out in the chill-out room long enough. You couldn't find a better location, as the hostel overlooks the main square below. Rooms sleep two to four people, and there is a kitchen should you

choose to cook your own meals (although breakfast is included). The only drawback is the two shared hall bathrooms, each with a low-pressure shower stall that requires you to hold down a button in order for it to keep running. Other than that, this place gets an A+. Two other branches in the neighborhood are run by the same fun-loving crew, and they'll place you in rooms there should this one be filled to capacity. The staff also runs an activity program which includes outdoor excursions and pub crawls. *Kursaal Center, Boulevard 26. ☎ 943-428-154 or 943-003-447. www.enjoyss.com. 22€–25€ per person in a double with shared bathroom or triple; 17€–30€ per person in dorm room. Amenities: Elevator, sheets, towels.*

MTV (Best 🏅) → **Olga's Place** ★★★ You wouldn't find this place if you weren't looking for it, as there is no sign or any indication that a fantastic backpackers' oasis is located on the fourth floor. The owners Olga and Rafael are as nice as they come, and you won't find a more welcoming reception anywhere else. The rooms are painted in vivid, contrasting colors and each lodges up to six people. You can cook your own meals in the kitchen (if you're lucky, Olga will sometimes invite you to dine with her), and a bathroom with several shower stalls is shared, though there is one private bath for all to use on a first-come, first-served basis. *Zabaleta 49. ☎ 943-326-725 or 678-977-230. Reservations through www.hostelworld.com. Dorm bed 14€–18€, single 18€, double 30€. Amenities: Elevator, sheets, towels.*

CHEAP

→ **Hostal Urumea** ★ The owner of Hostal Urumea, Conchi, is as sweet and friendly as they come. Her pension located on a quixotic, apple tree–lined lane in the heart of the city's Romantic Zone in the middle of town only has six rooms (five doubles, one single) and is more family-oriented than your normal hostel. If you do desire a more low-key, homey environment, you won't be disappointed by Urumea. All the rooms are modest, but recently renovated and decorated with a floral, antiquey motif. The road below is pedestrian only, so you won't be kept up by late-night traffic. *Guetaria 14. ☎ 943-424-605. www.hostal urumea.com. Single 22€–30€, double 45€–60€, extra bed 12€–15€. Amenities: Elevator, rooms for those w/limited mobility. In room: TV, fridge.*

→ **Pension Alemana** One step inside this hostel made me wonder if I'd come to the right place. Fancy is the first word that came to mind, particularly for a budget accommodation in a beachy town. I found the English-speaking staff extremely welcoming and would stay here again, as it is warm, eye-pleasing, and right near Playa de la Concha. The rooms are colossal—and the bathrooms as well—and house up to four people. Call 2 weeks in advance for booking. *San Martín 53. ☎ 943-462-544. www.hostalalemana.com. Single 51€–55€, double 63€–93€. Amenities: Bar, breakfast room, elevator, parking (11€ a day). In room: A/C, TV, hair dryer, Internet, iron, minibar, safe.*

→ **Pension Aries** If traveling alone, Aries is the best deal you'll find in town. It's dirt cheap—especially for the single rooms that are often double the price elsewhere—and right in the midst of all the action. What more could you want? *San Jerónimo 22. ☎ 943-426-855. www.pension aries.com. Single 13€–25€, double 35€–60€, add an additional 15€–20€ for an extra bed. In room: TV.*

→ **Pension La Perla** The staff at La Perla is extremely helpful, and the 10 rooms and accompanying bathrooms of this pension are impeccably clean. Not the most social of environments, but if you're in San Sebastián more for the beaches and shopping, Le

Perla is the perfect location for you, as it is situated on one of the main shopping streets right near the Cathedral and within a short walking distance (90m/300 ft.) from Playa de la Concha. *Loyola 10.* ☎ *943-428-123. www.pensionlaperla.com. Single 25€–35€, double 35€–50€. Amenities: Elevator. In room: TV.*

→**Pension Regil** This place is absolutely nothing extravagant, but the interior decoration is cheerful, although the rooms are quite closetlike. Regardless, the place is clean, cheap, and with wireless Internet if you require nothing more. The location's not so bad either, as it's in the center near a plethora of stores and not far from the beach either. There is a kitchen that is only open in the summer. *Easo 9.* ☎ *943-427-143 or 615-178 143. www.pensionregil.com. Single 30€–45€, double 35€–65€, extra bed 7€–15€. In room: TV, Internet.*

→**Pension San Martín** The rooms in this humble hotel are quite small, but bright and inviting and fine enough if you're staying only a few nights. Because the pension only has six rooms, singles are only available during the summer months. *San Martín 10.* ☎ *943-428-714. www. hagi.entrewebs. com/sanmartin/index.htm. Single 36€, double 48€–59€, double with extra bed 63€–77€. Amenities: Elevator. In room: TV.*

DOABLE

→**Hostal Bahía** ★ Don't be fooled by the outward elegance of Hostal Bahía. The reception and lobby area is striking in its Belle Epoque romance, and boasts marble floors and countertops and romantic mood lighting. As far as the appearance of the rooms themselves, Bahía is nothing exceptional. However, the beach is just around the corner, and the rooms are spacious with nice, big, furnished balconies. It's a comfortable enough option right in the center of town if you're on a budget and don't mind noise at all hours of the

night (or rather not planning on sleeping a wink in the first place). *San Martín 54.* ☎ *943-469-211. www.hostalbahia.com. Single 49€–99€, double 59€–119€, extra bed 15€–25€. Breakfast included. Amenities: Restaurant, cafe, elevator, Internet, sheets, towels. In room: A/C, TV, hair dryer, Internet.*

→**Hotel Europa** This central hotel that occupies one of the city's oldest buildings is a government-rated three-star with four-star appeal and services. The rooms are all decorated similarly but constructed in different odd shapes, which we found engaging. Hotel Europa has everything you need—a cafeteria, restaurant, wireless Internet, and even a pool in summer months. Continental breakfast is included in the price, and you can opt to have your food brought up via room service at no extra charge. Booking in advance is advisable. *San Martín 52.* ☎ *943-470-880. www. hotel-europa.com. Single 110€–165€, double 110€–165€, double with extra bed 150€–210€ (only available June–Sept). Amenities: Restaurant, cafeteria, elevator, Internet, swimming pool, TV, valet parking. In room: A/C, TV, hair dryer, Internet, minibar, safe.*

→**Hotel Niza** ★★ Hotel Niza has a certain style and grace that you won't find at most of San Sebastián's more contemporary hotels. The antique elevator, whitewashed floors and furniture, and bright beachy tones are just a few of its lures. At the end of Playa de la Concha, Hotel Niza is ideally situated between the beach and all the waterfront cafes. All rooms have balconies, some with stunning views of the ocean. A breakfast buffet is available for 9.50€. *Zubieta 56.* ☎ *943-426-663. www.hotel niza.com. Single 52€–102€, double 108€–128€, extra bed 20€. Amenities: Restaurant, cafeteria, coffee shop. In room: A/C, TV, hair dryer, Internet.*

→**Pension Gran Bahía** ★ If the guest book filled with positively raving reviews and the table overflowing with thank-you letters is any indication of the welcoming environment this pension exudes, you'd be lucky to stay here a night. The owner Teresa is more than eager to ensure you'll have the most pleasant of stays in San Sebastián and has, therefore, decorated the 10 rooms (six downstairs in Gran Bahía I, four upstairs in Gran Bahía II) to make you feel right at home. Each room has its own character (my favorite was the one decked out in retro leopard print), with shag rugs and beautiful photography and paintings adorning the walls. With interior rooms that face a courtyard instead of the main street, you won't be kept up at night by the bustling nightlife of La Parte Vieja. The rooms are quite big, as are the floor-to-ceiling closets. There is no kitchen, but breakfast is included. As Gran Bahía already has a steady stream of regular clients, you'd be wise to phone ahead, particularly from July to September. *Embeltrán 16.* ☎ *943-420-216 or 675-717-408. www. pensiongranbahia.com. Single 39€ (only available during off season), double 50€–85€, triple 75€–118€, extra bed 20€. Breakfast included. In room: A/C, TV.*

SPLURGE

📺 Best 💡 → **Hotel de Londres y de Inglaterra** ★★★ If you're saving up for one major splurge at the end of your vacation, here's the place to do it. How can you not love a place where the staff turns back your comforter at night and leaves chocolates on your pillow? If you're given a seafront room, you'll have the best seat in the house, as you can sit out on your balcony and take in all of Playa de la Concha from above. Londres remains a revered favorite among Spaniards throughout the country—thus, it is often booked solid far in advance—and is fully worth the (many) extra pennies it will cost to stay there for a night or two. *Zubieta 2.* ☎ *943-440-770*

or 900-429-000. www.hlondres.com. Single 120€–186€, double 144€–270€. Amenities: Restaurant, bar, breakfast room, elevator, parking. In room: A/C, TV, hair dryer, Internet, minibar, safe.

Eating

Eating is an event in itself here in Basque Country. Like elsewhere in Spain, both lunch and dinner are three-course ordeals, and each takes place over the span of a few hours. In the bigger Basque cities, it's quite common to begin your evening out with a *txikiteo,* which entails going from bar to bar drinking small glasses of wine, or *zurito,* the same except with beer.

If you're a seafood lover, you'll be in heaven among the aquatic dishes that top the menu of every restaurant. Sea bream, squid, hake, eel. Lobster, crab, squid, prawns. And when the weather heats up, you won't see many people without an ice cream in their hand. Here's one time when it's perfectly acceptable to be a follower, not a leader. **Heladerias** with exotic flavors (try the Spanish specialty *crema catalana*) are plentiful on and around **Alameda del Boulevard,** so do some sampling of your own.

If you're just looking for a midday cup of coffee, head for the Cathedral, as cafes line **Reyes Catolicos** and encompass **Plaza del Buen Pastor.**

HOT SPOTS

→ **La Cuchara** ★ TAPAS La Cepa may be the talk of the town (see below), but those who really know San Sebastián will tell you that La Cuchara is the place to be. My one qualm with this tapa-lovers' place of choice is that it is so popular it is often difficult to elbow your way to the front of the bar to order. *31 de Agosto 28.* ☎ *943-420-840. Tapas start at 2€. Mon–Tues 7:30pm–1:30am; Wed–Sun 12:30–3:30pm and 7:30pm–1:30am.*

Cuidado! Dishwashers Wanted

One thing to note when eating out in San Sebastián is that credit cards are rarely accepted anywhere, and when they are, it's usually only MasterCard and Visa. During my visit, I encountered some drunken American boys who only traveled with AmEx and, stupidly enough, did not ask if it was accepted beforehand—they were stuck in the kitchen washing dishes after dining. For real. Moral of this story? Keep an ample supply of cash handy at all times.

➔ **La Perla** ★★★ BASQUE My taste buds were spoiled after sampling the epitome of fantastic cuisine at this seaside culinary heaven. Though fancier than some of its neighbors, the inside still emits a bit of an informal maritime air with its wave etchings and seashells scattered about at random. Go for the grilled foie gras with sweet onion and sautéed apple, and satisfy your sweet tooth with the chocolate cake with hazelnut ice cream, doused in warm chocolate sauce. You can dine on the terrace, though the inside also offers magnificent sunset views over La Concha with its wall-to-wall window. *Paseo de la Concha s/n.* ☎ *943-462-484. www.la-perla.net. Entrees 14€–18€. Daily 1–3:30pm and 9–11pm.*

TAPAS

➔ **Bar Asador Ganbarab** With specialties like grilled crab pie, spider crab and prawns, and garlic sausage, the dishes here are more complex than most. With prices like these, you can afford to be adventurous and try them all. *San Jerónimo 21.* ☎ *943-422-575. Tapas from 2€. Bar open Tues–Sun 11am–3:15pm and 6–11:45pm; restaurant open Tues–Sun 1–3:15pm and 8–11:15pm.*

➔ **La Cepa** Quite famous around these parts, La Cepa has been in existence for nearly 60 years and deserves the hype it receives for its hearty ambience and dazzling display of tapas. The place is most known for its sausage and Jabugo ham (a regional specialty), so try a sample or two of each, then wash them down with some *vino tinto* (red wine) from the La Rioja region, Spain's own wine country. *31 de Agosto 7.* ☎ *943-426-394. www.barlacepa. com. Tapas around 1.80€–3€. Daily 11am–midnight.*

➔ **Nagusia Lau** With its constant buffet of *pintxos* (Basque-style tapas), you can grab a snack at anytime of the day in this old-style tavern on La Parte Vieja's main street. If you want more to fill your belly, tasty meals are available for 8€ to 18€. *Mayor 4.* ☎ *933-433-991. Daily 10pm–midnight.*

CHEAP

➔ **Va Bene** HAMBURGERS/SANDWICHES With its location right on the city's main drag and its terrace dining, you'd rather expect this burger and sandwich joint—which tries its hand at being somewhat of an American '50s diner—to be on the upper end price-wise. But all of the tasty meal and snack options are between 2.50€ and 4.50€, a veritable bargain. *Boulevard 14.* ☎ *943-422-416. Another branch of Va Bene can be found at Blas de Lezo 4.* ☎ *943-454-699. Sun–Thurs 11am–12:30am; Fri–Sat 11:30am–1:30am.*

➔ **Warrechena** BASQUE The greasy food isn't great and the waitress lurked around me the whole time (I was the only one dining in the restaurant, perhaps not the best sign?), but if cheap's the question, Warrechena is the answer. Whereas in most restaurants in San Sebastián, full meals are upwards of 20€, you can get the menu of the day at Warrechena for just

10€. *San Martín 42.* ☎ *943-423-162. Daily noon–4pm and 8–11pm.*

DOABLE

➔ **Arrai Txiki** BASQUE For the hippies among us, this bar and restaurant prides itself on its biological farming. But non-hippies, don't be deterred: Just because it's good for the environment doesn't mean it doesn't taste good, too. *Campanario 3.* ☎ *943-431-302. Entrees 10€–14€. Mon, Wed, Thurs, and Fri 1–4pm; Sat–Sun 1–4pm and 8:45–11:30pm.*

➔ **Bideluze** SPANISH Bar on the top, restaurant on the bottom, you can find reasonably priced meals at this downtown eatery. Try the *solomillo, pimientos del piquillo,* and *setas y patatas* (sirloin, sweet red peppers, and mushrooms and potatoes). *Garibai 24.* ☎ *943-422-880. Other Bideluze branches can be found at Plaza Guipúzcoa 14 and Plaza Bideluze 2. Main courses average 12€. No credit cards. Bar upstairs Mon–Thurs 8am–1:30am; Fri–Sat 8am–2:30pm. Downstairs restaurant daily 1–11pm.*

➔ **El Sitio del Magüeyal** MEXICAN This isn't your usual south-of-the-border cuisine, so don't order the fajitas expecting something off Taco Bell's value menu. Rather, the food is cooked with a sort of Spanish flair, the presentation is impressive with the brightly colored sauces drizzled artistically over the main course, and the flavored margaritas leave little to be desired. The stark white walls and minimalistic decor with orange furniture add to the attractiveness of the restaurant. *Fermín Calbetón 45.* ☎ *943-424-866. Average entree 6€. Daily 1:15–3:30pm and 8:15–11pm.*

SPLURGE

➔ **Kokotxa Restaurante** If you're itching for some high-end Basque cuisine and have the extra dough to spend, you can try a little of everything the region has to offer with Kokotxa's *menú degustación* (42€).

Cider House Rules

A new daytime trend among the Basque and tourists is visiting *sidrerias,* where cider is made. Cider season is from January until May, and during this time, the taps flow freely for visitors, and you can drink your fill while munching on tapas. Normal cider house etiquette means you stand while eating. It may be uncomfortable, but it makes it easier to travel to and from the *kupela* (cider barrel) for replenishment. Ask the tourist office for a list of local *sidrerias.*

Or opt for the more reasonably priced menu of the day, which is just 17€ and includes three courses plus wine. Although it has a hearty fish menu, Kokotxa also caters to the non-seafood lover with a large selection of meat and vegetable dishes, as well. *Campanario 11.* ☎ *943-421-904. www.restaurantekokotxa.com. Entrees 16€–20€. Closed for dinner on Sun and all day Mon.*

CAFES

➔ **Garager** Garager is a nice outdoor joint for grabbing a morning pick-me-up and croissant. It's out in the middle of things along the main boulevard and is just one of many similar competing cafes that all offer comparable menus and prices. The breakfast menu is served until noon and costs 2€ to 4€. *Boulevard Zumardia at San Jerónimo. No phone. Daily 9:30am–2am.*

➔ **Gozotegia Oiartzun** Stop your stomach from rumbling with a breakfast pastry from this central cafe (or homemade chocolates if you're not calorie-counting). Or just grab a cup of coffee and people-watch from the outdoor terrace. Baked goods range from 2€ to 5€. *Igentea 2.*

☎ *943-426-209. Mon—Fri 7:30am—9pm; Sat—Sun 8am—9pm.*

Partying

On most days of the week, the partying all takes place on the streets of La Parte Vieja, just off the main boulevard. You'll find a wide variety of people, ranging from the very-young-shouldn't-even-be-allowed-inside underagers to the very-old-shouldn't-even-be-allowed-out-after-dark fogies. Still, no matter your musical tastes or party style, you'll find something to please you in the diversity of San Sebastián's nightlife.

A typical night out in San Sebastián should begin with a *poteo-ir-de-pinchos* (referred to as *tapeo* in the rest of Spain), a native custom that sends you on an extensive tapas crawl searching out morsels on toothpicks. A ritual that is unique to Basque Country, you'll be presented with a platter of tapas, which you can spear with toothpicks. When you're finished, the servers will tally up the toothpicks and you fork over your money accordingly. The best tapas street is **Calle 31 de Agosto.**

The area just west of Monte Urgull in Parte Vieja is where the rest of the night action takes place, with **Calle Fermín Calvetón** as the most popular for disco barhopping.

BARS

➜ **Bar Ondarra** Even on weekdays, this happening bar draws a mix of internationals from all over the globe, and the atmosphere is cozy—but weekends are when it really gets rockin'. Upstairs, there is a quieter, more low-key bar, **bis 16,** that is also part of Ondarra. *Zurriola 16. No phone.*

➜ **Bar Tas Tas** ★ Moments after stepping into this loud, crowded bar, someone plopped a cowboy hat on my head and handed me a free shot. Not bad for my first night in San Sebastián. Ask any local or

international student where to begin your weekend partying, and they'll point you in the direction of Bar Tas Tas. Beers aren't that cheap, but the bar often has two-for-one specials or deals that include free shots. *Fermín Calbetón 35. No phone. www.tastas.net.*

➜ **Mendaur** A free shot with any drink every day from 10pm to midnight? I'm there. Although this is just like all of its neighbors on Fermín Calbetón—if you've been to one, you've been to them all—Mendaur ensures it stays packed by ongoing drink specials. So even if you don't stay longer than it takes to do a shot, there's no harm in mooching a free drink. *Fermín Calbetón 8.* ☎ *943-422-268.*

➜ **Warhol** We were drawn into this swanky establishment based on the name alone. Sure enough, it is decorated just as Andy himself would have liked it—in bright reds, blues, and yellows, with multicolored light fixtures, Warholesque paintings and photographs, and leather seats and couches in the back. *Pintxos* are served just in the mornings, and drinks range from 2€ to 5€. While Warhol caters toward San Sebastián's gay population, anyone can enjoy him- or herself here, even if they don't fall under the aforementioned category. *Sánchez Toca 3. No phone.*

LIVE MUSIC

➜ **Altxerri Galería** This live jazz club tends to attract an older, classier crowd, but if you've removed your beer goggles and discovered that every one of your fellow bar-goers in La Parte Vieja is underage (and that bothers you), Altxerri might be a refreshing alternative. *Reina Regente 2.* ☎ *943-421-693. Cover charges vary, depending on the night and performer.*

➜ **Molly Malone's** Sure, it's not the most original of names, and sure, you've most likely had your fill of Irish pubs. But Molly's has a cozier atmosphere than most with its three staggered floors and pleasant ambience. It's one of the few bars in town that you'll find consistently has a crowd, even on the odd Sunday or Monday night. Just don't expect the bartenders to speak English—they're not *actually* Irish. Meals are also served throughout the day, and live music is often on the night's agenda. *San Martín 55.* ☎ *946-469-822.*

CLUBS/DISCOS

➔ **La Kabutzia** If you're itching to break loose after a few too many beers, head to this floating disco after 8pm. The club is located at the end of the boulevard on a real docked boat. And although there is not much as far as decoration goes, that may be because not much is needed: The wood paneling, neon strobe lights, and just knowing you're dancing on the sea should be enough by way of a fun evening out. *Bahía de la Concha, next to the Ayuntamiento. No phone. www.lakabutzia.com. 12€ cover includes 1 drink.*

🅼 (Best ❂) ➔ **Zurriola Marítimo** ★★★ What's not to love about a cafe/restaurant/discothèque that is located right on the waterfront and virtually never closes? During the day, Zurriola is an enjoyable locale for grabbing a bite to eat on the beach, but at night, the real action happens. Tourists and residents of all walks of life flock to this popular disco once the music starts thumping. *Plaza de la Zurriola 41.* ☎ *943-297-853.*

Shopping

There's not a shortage of shopping in San Sebastián, but the nicer stores are outside of the tourist eyesores in La Parte Vieja and scattered throughout the center along **Avenida de la Libertad** and the smaller streets that dissect it. Most stores are open from Monday to Saturday from 10:30am to 1:30pm and 4 to 8pm, with a few slight variations.

FASHION

➔ **Apache** At this gift boutique near the main boulevard, you can find that wooden necklace or mustard-yellow handbag you've been dying for, as it offers a good assortment of accessories. *Garibay 1.* ☎ *943-432-214.*

➔ **Boon Boutique** With clothing from London, this trendy boutique sells clothes for more casual occasions, such as cotton skirts, T-shirts, tanks, and funky dresses. **Wicca** in Parte Vieja also sells from the same line. *Easo 14.* ☎ *943-425-036.*

➔ **Hermes** Not the classy French designer label that may come to mind, this Hermes is decorated in a comic book theme with a unique style all its own. Clothes are cheaper than most, as well—always a plus for the traveler on a budget. *Fermín Calbetón 33. No phone.*

➔ **Malas Pulgas** For dressier designer duds for the girl with daddy's credit card in tow. You could max your plastic here as the clothes are cute and original. *Garibay 4.* ☎ *943-421-318.*

➔ **Pukas Surfshop** Meet all your beachy needs—boards, suits, and the like—at this surfer's paradise. Pukas has another branch on Zurriola Beach where you can rent surf equipment or enroll in surfing school (see "Board Talk," below). For the non-athletic shopaholic, the downstairs hosts a collection of funky casual wear. *Mayor 5.* ☎ *943-427-228.*

BOOKS

➔ **Elkar** If you're clean out of beachside reading material, you just may find something to suit your literary craving in this two-story bookstore. Although most books are in Spanish or Basque, there is a lone English-language shelf, as well as an extensive section of travel books in a variety of languages. *Fermin Calbeton 21-30.* ☎ *943-420-080 or 943-420-930. www.elkar.com.*

Board Talk

If surfing's your thing or you simply want to test the waters for the first time, you can take advantage of one of the surf vacays offered by **Urban House** (☎ 943-428-154;** www.urbansurfsansebastian.com); packages for surfers of all levels consist of 2- to 14-day trips that include accommodation, equipment rental, daily surf instruction, and excursions to nearby beaches. Or if you just want to rent a board and wetsuit or take a lesson or two, head to **Pukas Surfeskola** (☎ 943-320-068) at Av. de la Zurriola 24. Board rentals begin at 10€ an hour and are cheaper the longer you rent them for, and wetsuits start at 5€ an hour. A 5-hour instruction course is available for 60€ including the cost of equipment, and private lessons are also possible. Open 9am to 9pm in the summer; and Monday through Saturday from 10am to 2pm and 4 to 8pm, Sunday 11am to 2pm and 4:30 to 7:30pm throughout the rest of the year.

➜**Lagun** With bookshelves that span the height of the store, you're sure to find a suitable assortment of classics in English here. *Urdaneta 3.* ☎ *943-444-320. www. librerialagun.com.*

MALLS

One of the bigger shopping centers in town, **San Martín** is located in the heart of the city center on the street of the same name and houses supermarkets, cafes, and clothing stores like Bershka and Zara.

➜**Brexta** This American-style mall along the Boulevard is a bit daunting in size, but does have a hodgepodge of clothing, accessories, and tourist stores. ☎ *943-421-520.*

SOUVENIRS

➜**Txapela** For regional accessories and handicrafts, head to this artisan outlet, which sells souvenirs and the rough cotton shirts for which the Basquer are famous. *Puerto 3.* ☎ *943-420-243.*

Sightseeing

Besides San Sebastián's natural wonders, you can see everything else worth seeing in just half a day's work. If you want the more involved kiddie tour of the city, you can jump on the cute **tourist train** (☎ 943-422-973), which takes you on a 40-minute whirlwind tour of the city, disclosing its

history and culture with commentary in various languages. Tours depart every half-hour from **Calle Andia** from 11am to 9pm in the summer, 11am to 1pm and 4 to 7pm during the rest of the year.

Palacio de Miramar. This former palace stands alone on a hill opening onto La Concha. Queen María Cristina opened the place in 1893, but by the disorderly 1930s, it had fallen into disrepair and the city council eventually took it over in 1971. Because you can't go inside the palace, you must settle for a stroll through the lawns and gardens. The palace stands on land splitting the two major beaches of San Sebastián: Playa de la Concha and Playa de Ondarreta. ☎ *943-219-022. Daily 8am–9pm.*

Museo Chillida-Leku. If you want to see just one museum in San Sebastián to make momma happy, you won't be disappointed by this unique sculpture park. Basque sculptor Eduardo Chillida, whose work appears in many museums around the world, created each of the odd-looking pieces of art that dot the gardens, as well as the outdoor museum itself. The museum lies a 10-minute drive from the heart of San Sebastián, in the little mountain town of Hernani. The hillside around the park is sprinkled with some 40

12 Hours in San Sebastián

1. **Visit the Chillida-Leku.** Start your day off with some cultural satisfaction by taking in the work of Basque sculpting legend Eduardo Chillida.
2. **Taste the tapas of Parte Vieja.** If you're in the need for a mid-afternoon snack, head to the old part of town and try a tapa or two at a few of the ubiquitous tapas joints.
3. **Hike up Monte Urgull.** A variety of trails for every preference and skill level creep up and wind there way through the oversize mound.
4. **Have coffee at Plaza del Buen Pastor.** A great local meeting point, this square that surrounds one of the city's major churches is not lacking in quality cafes and eateries.
5. **Hit the beach.** You could easily spend 12 hours just sitting on the beach watching the surfers as well as masses of scantily clad (or unclad) sunbathers.
6. **Cool off with ice cream on the boulevard.** You won't be the only one sating your taste buds in San Sebastián. Once the mercury rises ever so slightly, the whole city seems to migrate to one of the many *heladerías* that sprinkle the streets.
7. **Watch the sunset from Monte Igueldo.** If you time it right, you can hop on the last funicular of the day that takes you to the top of the westbound mountain overlooking Playa de la Concha and the rest of San Sebastián.
8. **Dine at La Perla.** This beachside restaurant has a stunning view of La Concha and is the perfect place to enjoy traditional Basque cuisine while catching the last few minutes of post-sunset light.

Chillida monoliths set among magnificent beech trees, oaks, and magnolias. In the center of the property is a 16th-century farmhouse, which the artist designed to display some of his smaller pieces. *Caserío Zabalaga 66, Jáuregui Barrio, Hernani.* ☎ *943-336-006. www.eduardo-chillida.com. Admission 8€ adults, 6€ students with ID. Guided visits are an additional 5€. July–Aug Mon–Sat 10:30am–8pm, Sun 10:30am–3pm; Sept–June daily 10:30am–3pm. Bus G2 takes you here from San Sebastián.*

FESTIVALS/CALENDAR OF EVENTS

January

San Sebastián Day. Partying for 24 hours straight has never seemed to faze the Spaniards. This annual festival is no different. From midnight on January 19 until midnight the following evening, the city flag is hoisted, and uniform-clad, drum-beating companies take to the streets playing melodies in honor of the city's patron saint. At noon on January 20, the children take their turn at the drum playing.

July

Jazzaldia. Music lovers from all over flock to San Sebastián during the last 2 weeks of July to participate in this open-air cultural spectacle in Plaza de la Trinidad (www.jazzaldia.com).

Aste Nagusia. Never passing up a chance for a fiesta, San Sebastián stages its annual party in mid-August each year, which is a celebration of traditional Basque music and dance, along with fireworks, cooking competitions, and sporting events.

September

International Film Festival. San Sebastián has its time to shine in the spotlight, as it transforms into mini-Hollywood for the film festival, the only internationally competitive event of its kind in Spain. Visit www.sansebastianfestival.com for more info.

Playing Outside

Obviously, the best way to take advantage of San Sebastián's mild seaside climate is by visiting its spectacular beaches. However, outside of the sandy banks and south of the city center, green oases abound if you fancy a day away from the sunbathing masses.

We spent many an hour after our beachside ventures recovering from sun meltdown in the well-kept gardens of **Jardines de Alderdi-Eder.** We were not alone, as the rest of San Sebastián had the same idea, or so it seemed. Overlooking Playa de la Concha and with plenty of benches for resting, these gardens are the perfect spot for reading a book or cooling off with an ice cream from one of the boulevard's prevalent *heladerias.*

It's worth a trip to the top of 📺 Best ●**Monte Igueldo** simply to see the views of Playa de la Concha from the top of the "mountain" (more like a large hill in my opinion). You can easily hike up in half an hour or choose to take the **funicular** from the west end of Playa de Ondaretta. The funicular makes the journey up and down every half-hour on Monday through Friday from 11am to 8pm and Saturday from 10am to 10pm. It only takes 2 minutes and costs 1.10€ one-way or 2€ round-trip. Once up Monte Igueldo, you can see the views from every which way, or if you're really desperate for entertainment, visit the mountain's amusement park with roller coasters, bumper cars, and all the sort of cheap pursuits these type places have to offer.

The wide promenade of **Paseo Nuevo** almost encircles 📺 Best ● **Monte Urgull,** one of the two mountains between which San Sebastián is nestled. Even if you've taken in the views from Monte Igueldo, it's still worthwhile to hike up one of the various trails that take you to the top of Monte Urgull to see the views of Playa de la Concha to the west and Playa Zurriola to the east. A fortress stands at the top of the hill and offers panoramic views of both beaches.

Fuenterrabía (Hondarrabía)

A big seaside resort and fishing port near the French frontier, 📺 Best ● **Fuenterrabía** (Hondarrabía in Basque) makes for a delightful day away from the floods of tourists in San Sebastián and is just 23km (14 miles) up the road.

Fuenterrabía Basics

GETTING THERE

The only way to visit this border town other than renting a car is by bus. **Interbus** (☎ 943-641-302) goes from Plaza Guipúzcoa near the city hall in San Sebastián to Fuenterrabía every 20 minutes (1.50€, trip time: 45 min.). Call for more information. If you're traveling by **car,** take the **A-8** east toward the French border. Fuenterrabía doesn't have a train station, but is serviced by the **RENFE** station in nearby Irún (☎ 902-240-202; www.renfe.es). Trains depart Irún's Plaza de San Juan

BASQUE COUNTRY

for Fuenterrabía at 10- to 15-minute intervals. Irún is the end of the line for trains in northern Spain. East of Irún, it's all about the French trains.

VISITOR INFORMATION

Fuenterrabía is a town that can be explored without direction, though if you do want pamphlets on the history, culture, and major attractions in the area, you can stop by the **tourist office** at Calle Javier Ugarte 6 (☎ 943-64-13-02; www.bidasoaturismo.com), which is open July to August Monday 4 to 8pm and Tuesday to Friday 10am to 8pm. Off-season hours are Monday to Friday 9am to 1:30pm and 4 to 6:30pm, Saturday 10am to 2pm and 3 to 8pm, Sunday 10am to 2pm.

ORIENTATION

I was surprised to arrive in Fuenterrabía and be able to see Hendaye, France, just feet over Txingudi Bay, as there are absolutely no recognizable differences between the two towns (except maybe the language spoken in each). You can take a ferry (1.50€, trip time: 5 min.) just across the harbor from Jaizkibel to visit Hendaye beach, a popular surfing spot due to the strong winds and equally as appealing to sunbathers as the coastline is wide and sandy. Ferries leave each side every 15 minutes.

The most eye-appealing part of town is the **medieval quarter** roosting high above the harbor, where some of the villas date from the early 17th century. The fishing district in the lower part of town is called **La Marina;** its old homes, painted boats, and marine atmosphere attract many visitors.

Wander for an hour or two around the old quarter, taking in Calle Mayor, Calle Tiendas y Pampinot, and Calle Obispo, and stopping by the castle, now a luxury hotel, in the Plaza de las Armas. The most impressive church in the old quarter is **Iglesia de Santa María,** a Gothic structure that was vastly restored in the 17th century and endowed with a baroque tower.

If you have a car, you can take a side trip to **Cabo Higuer,** a promontory with panoramic views, reached by going 4km (2½ miles) north via the harbor and beach road. You can see the French coast and the town of Hendaye from this cape.

Sleeping & Eating

You can easily make it to and from Fuenterrabía in 1 day with no need whatsoever to stay the night. However, if you feel like delaying your reentry into the fast pace of San Sebastián, a number of hostels can be found in the medieval quarter, on and along the road leading up to Plaza de Armas—and there's one hostel across from the tourist office on Calle Javier Ugarte—most of which do not require reservations in advance.

Fuenterrabía is studded with restaurants and pavement cafes, so if you're looking for some chow, you can dine at one of the outdoor terraces along **Calle San Pedro.** Because restaurants in Fuenterrabía tend to be very expensive, you can also fill up on seafood tapas in the many taverns along the waterfront. If you want to escape the crowds for just a light snack, head to **Gaxen** on Matxin de Arzu Zuloaga for a sandwich, crepe, and homemade shake or glass of freshly squeezed fruit juice.

➔ **Parador de Hondarribia** This refurbished castle, standing at the Plaza de las Armas, has been turned into one of the smallest and most desirable paradors in Spain. It still maintains much of the original structure of the Castillo de Carlos V, and is adorned with arches, wrought iron, and coffered ceilings. If you do decide to splurge and go this route, be sure to call a month or two in advance to reserve your place. Even if you don't stay the night at this magnificent hotel, you can stop by the parador for a peek at the stunning gardens and terrace and enjoy the bird's-eye view over both Spain and France. The parador also offers an array of outdoor activities like golf, horseback riding, parapente, surfing, canoeing, and fishing, to name a few. *Plaza de Armas 14.* ☎ *943-645-500. www.parador.es. Single 144€, double 190€, suite 256€–354€, extra bed 70€. Amenities: Bar, breakfast room, elevator, gardens, money exchange, parking. In room: TV, hair dryer, minibar, safe.*

Bilbao

Most Spaniards will tell you Bilbao is an industrial wasteland that has little to offer. And though the omnipresent towering buildings and smokestacks can be a bit daunting at times, the artistic values that have made Spain's sixth-largest city the cultural hot spot it is today make up for its few shortcomings.

After an industrial crisis in the 19th century that stretched well into the next, the last few years of the 20th century were devoted to social development in Bilbao, hence the construction of the Guggenheim and other artistic landmarks for which the city is now recognized. It's safe to say Bilbao has become the cultural mecca of northern Spain, and rightfully so with its various museums and pieces of art that dot the city at random.

The Basque Country's capital is home to more than 350,000 people and is the most economically prosperous city in the region as a result of the industrial revolution. You seem to run into water anywhere you go in Bilbao thanks to its function as a seaport along the Bay of Biscay and the River Nervión that dissects its center.

Bilbao is a pleasant place to visit any time of the year, as it is never too cold or too hot (temperatures hover around 50°F/10°C in the winter, 70°F/21°C in the summer). And if you're coming off the lingering high from

Of Politics & Peace

Geographically, the Basque Country occupies part of both France and Spain in the western foothills of the Pyrenees. During the Spanish Civil War (1936–39), the Basques fought alongside the Republicans who were defeated by Franco's Nationalists. The oppression that developed during the Franco years has led to deep-seated resentment against the policies of Madrid by the Basque people. Many Basque nationalists still ardently wish that their region could be united into one autonomous state. In 1961, a separatist movement backed by the **ETA—Euskadi Ta Askatasuna,** meaning Basque Homeland and Freedom— took effect, and many Basque people began fighting for the independence of their "country" by carrying out a series of violent attacks. ETA, which is not to be confused with all Basque people, is considered a terrorist organization by the U.S. and the E.U. However, March 2006 witnessed a move that was internationally publicized as a monumental step toward peace when the group declared a permanent cease-fire with the objective of promoting a democratic process in the Basque Country. The car bombing staged at the Madrid airport in January 2007 was a disappointment to peaceseekers, but the prime minister announced only a suspension of peace talks with ETA, so it still may not be a total wash. One giant step forward, a few stagger steps back . . .

San Sebastián's party atmosphere you won't lose momentum in Bilbao, with bars and discos scattered in every direction.

Getting There

BY AIR

Bilbao Airport (☎ 944-710-301) is served by **Iberia** (☎ 902-400-500; iberia. com) whose main booking office at the airport is open daily from 5am to 10pm, along with low-cost carriers like **easyjet** (☎ 902-299-992; www.easyjet.com) and **Air Berlin** (☎ 902-320-737; www.airberlin.com). Other nearby airports that offer additional low-cost options include **Santander** and **Vitoria-Gasteiz.**

Bilbao Airport is 8km (5 miles) north of the city. From the airport into town, take **bus no. A3247** to the heart of the city (1.50€, every 30 min.).

BY TRAIN

The Spanish railway network operates four commuter lines from the city, three lines in metropolitan Bilbao via **RENFE** (☎ 902-240-202; www.renfe.es) from Bilbao-Orduña, Bilbao-Santurzi, and Bilbao-Muskiz. **FEVE** (☎ 944-232-226; www.feve. es) also offers one from Bilbao-Balmaseda. The Basque railway network **Euskotren** (☎ 902-543-210; www.euskotren.es) runs three lines from Bilbao-Lezama, Bilbao-Ermua, and Bilbao-Bermeo.

Estación de Abando (☎ 902-240-202; www.renfe.es) is on Plaza Circular 2, just off Plaza de España. From here, you can catch short-distance trains within the metropolitan area of Bilbao, and long-distance trains to most parts of Spain. For longer trips, you usually have to switch lines in Mirando de Ebro, about an hour and a half south of Bilbao.

Two trains per day run to and from Madrid (trip time: 7 hr.); two per day run to and from Barcelona (trip time: 9¹/₂ hr.); and one train per day goes to and from Galicia (trip time: 12 hr.). Also, two night trains per week run to and from the Mediterranean Coast: one toward Alicante and Valencia (daily during the summer months), and the other toward Málaga (three times a week in summer).

Talk of the Town

Three Ways to Start a Conversation with a Local

1. **"Where did the Basque language originate?"** Though the origins of Euskera are little known, anyone will give you their own opinions of the language, its Indo-European roots, and how it's important for the identity of the Basque people.

2. **"What are your thoughts about ETA?"** Like anywhere else, bringing up politics can be an extremely touchy subject. But if you are brave and truly want to know the local consensus (odds are, there isn't just one) on the separatist group and political violence in the region, you won't be met with silent reactions.

3. **"How has the addition of the Guggenheim affected Bilbao?"** The exterior of this shiny, metallic art museum is so reflective, you can spot it from miles away. The construction of the monument in 1997 helped pave the way for Bilbao's transformation into a modern art rapture. Still, despite its relative newness, the Guggenheim has already become symbolic of the revamped city, as it is one of Bilbao's most recognized buildings.

BASQUE COUNTRY

Bilbao

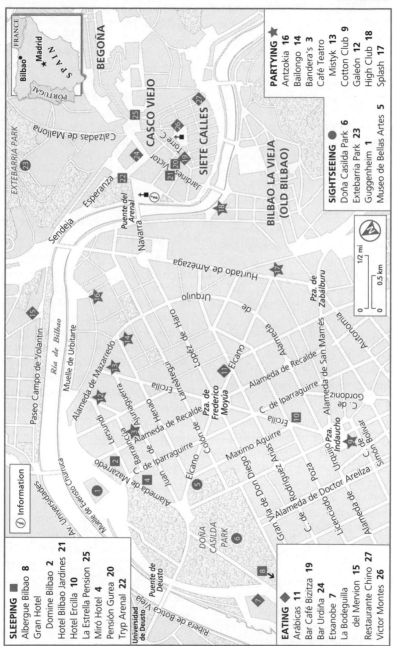

SLEEPING ◼
Albergue Bilbao **8**
Gran Hotel
  Domine Bilbao **2**
Hotel Bilbao Jardines **21**
Hotel Ercilla **10**
La Estrella Pension **25**
Miró Hotel **4**
Pensión Gurea **20**
Tryp Arenal **22**

EATING ◆
Arábicas **11**
Bar Café Bizitza **19**
Bar Urdiña **24**
Etxanobe **7**
La Bodeguilla
  del Mervion **15**
Restaurante Chino **27**
Victor Montes **26**

PARTYING ★
Antzokia **16**
Bailongo **14**
Bandera's **3**
Café Teatro
  Mistyk **13**
Cotton Club **9**
Galeón **12**
High Club **18**
Splash **17**

SIGHTSEEING ●
Doña Casilda Park **6**
Extebarria Park **23**
Guggenheim **1**
Museo de Bellas Artes **5**

(i) Information

BEGOÑA

CASCO VIEJO

SIETE CALLES

BILBAO LA VIEJA
(OLD BILBAO)

BY BUS

The main bus station, **Termibus,** south of the center at Calle Gurtubay 1 and Calle Luis Briñas 12 (☎ **944-395-077**), offers several daily buses to most major cities in Spain. **Continental Auto** (☎ **944-274-200**) operates from here with nine buses daily from Madrid (trip time: 5 hr.). To get to the city center from the terminal, hop on the Euskotran or metro, both of which have stations directly outside of the bus station.

PESA (Estación de Buses de Garillano; ☎ **902-101-210**) operates more than a dozen buses per day to and from San Sebastián (trip time: 1¹/₄ hr.). If you'd like to explore the nearby villages of Lekeitio or Guernica by bus, use the services of **Bizkaibus** (☎ **902-222-265**). Fifteen buses per day go to Lekeitio (trip time: 45 min.) Monday to Saturday, two on Sunday. Ten buses make the 45-minute run on weekdays to Guernica; on weekends, five make the trek.

BY CAR

If coming to Bilbao from the north, take the **A8** motorway. From other parts of Spain, head toward Bilbao on the **A68.**

BY FERRY

If you're in the mood for a very long seaside journey, you can take a ferry offered by **Acciona Trasmediterranea** or **P&O Ferry** all the way from Portsmouth in the United Kingdom down to Bilbao (or vice versa). The ferry office is at **Cosme Echevarrieta** 1 and can be reached by calling ☎ **944-234-477.**

Getting Around

BY METRO

Relatively new to Bilbao—its construction only began in 1995—the **metro** (☎ **944-254-025;** www.metrobilbao.com) has two lines that connect both banks of the city. A third line is currently being built.

BY BUS

Bilbao is well connected by **buses,** and you shouldn't have a problem finding one to your intended destination. The city has 30 efficient **Bilbobus** (☎ **944-484-080;** www.bilbao.net) lines, 25 for normal buses and 5 that travel to areas a normal bus can't access. If you're traveling to other places along the Bay of Biscay, **Bizkaia** (☎ **902-222-265;** www.bizkaia.net) has more than 100 lines that connect to nearby cities.

BY TRAM

A **tram** system, **Euskotran,** just opened in 2002 offers yet another option for traveling around the city. Visit www.euskotran.es (☎ **902-543-210**) for more information.

BY CAR

A **car** is quite handy if you're heading out of the city, even for a day, as the bus and train lines can be major time-killers. You can hire a car through **Europcar** (☎ **944-422-226;** www.europcar.com) and **Atesa** (☎ **944-423-290;** www.atesa.es), which both have offices for car rentals inside Bilbao-Abando, the central train station. Try **Hertz** (Plaza Pio x 2; ☎ **944-153-677;** www.hertz.com) or **Avis** at Licenciado Poza 56 (☎ **944-275-760;** www.avis.com). Or visit **Alquilobilbo** at General Eguía 30 (☎ **944-412-012**) or **A-Rental** at Pérez Galdós 24 (☎ **944-270-781**).

BY TAXI

There is no shortage of **taxis** at any given hour in Bilbao. However, in the unlikelihood that you should have trouble finding one, you can phone one of the many taxi services such as **Radio Taxi** (☎ **944-448-888**), or **Tele Taxi** (☎ **944-102-121**).

Bilbao Basics

ORIENTATION

A sprawling city, Bilbao is divided into eight districts, which are then broken down even further into specific neighborhoods. **Abando**—stretching from Ría de Bilbao in the northeast to Gran Vía in the southwest—is one that you'll hear about often, as it encompasses some of Bilbao's greatest monuments like Iglesia de San Vicente and Museo de Bellas Artes.

If you're either a clothing, food, or art connoisseur, you'll likely spend most of your days perusing the streets of ritzy **Indauxtu** in the 6th District which covers much of the city center, is bordered by Gran Vía and Calle Juan de Garay, and is home to some fine dining, shopping, and museums.

Casco Viejo, the late-night place to be, is where all of Bilbao's youthful residents migrate after dark. This old part of town spans from Parque Etxebarria in the northeast to Ría de Bilbao in the south and is the social heart and soul of the city, as well as the best place to go for cheaper stores and eats.

Though not as visited as the aforementioned parts of Bilbao, **Uribarri**—from the bridge Puente de la Salve in the northwest to Parque Extebarria in the southeast—is a great place for bird's-eye views of Bilbao.

TOURIST OFFICES

The main **tourist office** can be found on **Plaza Arriaga** and is open Monday to Friday 11:00am to 2pm and 5 to 7:30pm, Saturday 9:30am to 2pm and 5 to 7:30pm, Sundays and holidays 9:30am to 2pm. The tourist office at the Guggenheim (Av. Abandoibarra 2; ☎ 944-795-760) is open Monday through Friday from 11am to 6pm, Saturday from 11am to 7pm, and Sunday from 11am to 2pm. The office opens an hour earlier and shuts an hour later during summer months.

RECOMMENDED WEBSITE

○ **www.bilbao.net**: This city website in English has just about all the information you could possibly need to plan your trip to Bilbao, and links to anything else it doesn't touch on.

Bilbao Nuts & Bolts

Currency   You can get your dollars changed into euros at any post office, though you'll get the best exchange rate by withdrawing directly from any ATM.

Emergencies   The **SOS hotline** in Bilbao can be reached by dialing ☎ 112 or ☎ 944-441-444. You can seek police assistance by calling ☎ 092 or receive health help by calling ☎ 944-100-00 or ☎ 902-212-124 for urgent matters.

Internet Access   Check your e-mail at **Laser Internet Center** (☎ 944-453-509), a mega-cafe at Sendeja 5. Open weekdays from 10:30am to 3:30am and weekends from 11am to 3:30am.

Luggage Storage   If for some odd reason, you can't drop your bags off early before check-in time or leave them after you've checked out, luggage storage is available at the **Bilbao-Abando** train station.

Pharmacies   **Green crosses** denote **pharmacies,** where you can seek medical advice and purchase over-the-counter drugs. Just have your Spanish dictionary handy to describe your symptoms or needs so you don't have to pantomime condoms.

BASQUE COUNTRY

Post Offices   Bilbao has no fewer than eight **POs.** With the exception of the **Carretera Zorroza-Castrejana** branch (open Mon–Fri 8:30am–2:30pm, Sat 9:30am–1pm), all keep the same hours from Monday through Friday 8:30am to 8:30pm and Saturday from 9:30am to 1pm (except for summer months, when they close at 2:30pm on weekdays). You'll find other branches at **Alameda de Mazarredo** and **Plaza Casilla,** among other places.

Safety   Like any big city, Bilbao sees its share of crime. Just exercise normal precautions, and avoid the Guggenheim parking lot after dark—more than a few muggings have occurred there.

Telephone Tips   All telephone numbers in Spain have nine digits, including the provincial code. Calls within and to Bilbao begin with a **944.**

Sleeping

Bilbao has an overabundance of hotels due to its art and business operations that draw in people for conferences and exhibitions at all times of year. You won't find too many cheap options, though a couple relatively inexpensive pensions are sprinkled here and there in Casco Vieja. A range of four- and five-star lodges can be found throughout Indauxtu and along the river and Alameda Mazarredo, near the fabulous Guggenheim. Booking in advance is recommended at any time of the year.

HOSTELS

➔ **Albergue Bilbao** If you're looking for a more social experience than that of pensions and hotels, you'll find your fellow backpackers here. One of the few traditional hostels in town, this *albergue* designed for the young person on a budget is located just 5 minutes from the city center. There are rooms with one, two, three, and four beds, and bathrooms are shared on each floor. Just don't forget your youth hostel card, which is valid in many different countries and costs around 5€ to 15€ (depending on where you purchase it), as it is required to stay here. If you don't already possess a card, you can buy one at any HI-affiliated hostel. All those under 25 receive a discounted price. *Carretera*

Basurto-Castrejana, Basurto. ☎ *944-270-054. albergue.bilbao.net. Single 16€, double 14€ per person, triple 4€ per person. Amenities: Bike rental, Internet, laundry service, money exchange, parking, safe deposit, TV, VCR. In room: A/C.*

CHEAP

➔ **La Estrella Pension** The rooms in this one-star are a bit utilitarian, but functional—not to mention relatively cheap. The pension is classier than most, and the staff is very helpful. Plus, did we mention the awesome location right smack in the heart of Casco Vieja? *María Muñoz 6.* ☎ *944-164-066 and 944-150-731. Single 35€, double 48€, triple 65€, extra bed 15€. Amenities: Bar, breakfast room. In room: TV.*

➔ **Pensión Gurea** This basic pension located in Casco Vieja is attractive with its large, open bedrooms, wooden floors, and pink and peach interior. All rooms have their own bathrooms, and some have balcony views overlooking the old city. Call a week or two in advance to assure booking. If the place is booked solid, rooms in a cheaper, more minimalistic hostel upstairs are often available. Though they may not be as aesthetically pleasing, they do provide a convenient place to lay your head. Upstairs rooms have shared baths and cost 5€ to 10€ less than their downstairs neighbors. Singles are only available during the week. *Bidebarrieta 14.* ☎ *944-163-299. Single 40€, double 45€–50€, triple 65€–70€, triple with extra bed 80€. In room: TV, hair dryer, free Wi-Fi.*

DOABLE

➜ **Hotel Bilbao Jardines** ★ This hotel held true to its name, reminding me of some sort of flashy botanical gardens with its contemporary decor, jade green accents, and unique rooms of all shapes and sizes. A continental breakfast in the cheerful salon downstairs is available for an additional 3€. *Jardines 9.* ☎ *944-794-210. www.hotelbilbaojardines.com. Single 50€–60€, double 65€–74€, triple 80€–90€, family room 95€–105€. Amenities: Elevator, TV. In room: A/C, TV, hair dryer, Internet.*

➜ **Hotel Ercilla** ★★★ Hotel Ercilla is more the size of a theme park than an average hotel (I got lost on more than one occasion). One basic double room could house a small army, and the bathrooms are accordingly built for kings. It's no wonder why this royal hotel is a favorite among politicians, journalists, and movie stars. The only qualm I had with Ercilla was that I could hear every rattle, every door creak, and every (ahem) noise from my feisty neighbors. Other than that, Ercilla offers services galore, and I could have happily stayed for weeks without ever needing to leave. *Ercilla 37-39.* ☎ *944-705-700. www.ercillahoteles.com. Single 68€–129€, double 95€–191€, suite 180€–382€. Amenities: Restaurant, bar, disco, elevator, gym, parking, sauna, shops. In room: A/C, hair dryer, Internet, minibar, safe.*

➜ **Miró Hotel** ★★ Bilbao's first boutique hotel is unlike any I've ever experienced. Opened in early 2006, Miró is located just across the street from the Guggenheim and decorated appropriately. It is a work of art in itself with its boxy and minimalistic, yet enticing rooms decked out in striking contrasts of white, black, and red. The staff is extremely accommodating and will gladly deliver your heavy bags to your room for you. Of all the city's four-stars, this one gets my vote. *Alameda Mazzaredo.* ☎ *946-611-880. www.mirohotelbilbao.com. Single 92€–135€, double 116€–185€. Amenities: Restaurant, bar, gym, Jacuzzi, parking, sauna, spa. In room: A/C, TV, DVD player, hair dryer, Internet, minibar.*

➜ **Tryp Arenal** This three-star chain hotel is nothing particularly special, but ought to do in a pinch. Its greatest feature is the double-paned windows that block all noise of Casco Vieja below, a big plus if you're actually trying to get some sleep in Bilbao. The rooms and bathrooms are large and comfortable and the staff is friendly. A buffet breakfast is included in the price. *Fueros 2.* ☎ *944-153-100. www.solmelia.com. Single 70€–82€, double 149€. Amenities: Restaurant, breakfast room, elevator, Internet. In room: A/C, TV, hair dryer, minibar, safe.*

SPLURGE

Best ➜ **Gran Hotel Domine Bilbao** ★★★ A sharp knock on my door was accompanied by a five-woman lineup rushing into my room to tidy up, replace my complimentary toiletries (which, it must be said, filled up three small shoeboxes), and turn back my covers, leaving chocolates and a squeaky toy sheep on my pillow—and I had only just arrived an hour earlier. It took me just seconds to figure out why this hotel is heralded as the most glamorous joint in town. The bathrooms are mammoth with their old-fashioned bathtubs separate from the showers. The downstairs entranceway itself is stunning with splashy modern art embellishing the walls and cubic-style furniture dressing up the place. Personally, I most appreciated the stereo and miscellaneous mix of CDs that each room boasts. *Alameda Mazzaredo 61.* ☎ *944-253-300. www.granhoteldominebilbao.com. Single 125€–230€, double*

160€–260€, suite 200€–900€. Amenities: Restaurant, bar, elevator, Internet, Jacuzzi, parking, sauna, Turkish bath. In room: A/C, TV, hair dryer, Internet, minibar, stereo.

Eating

TAPAS

➜ **Bar Urdiña** Popular among tourists, you'll be in good company at Urdiña with its great selection of tapas, many Basque delights, as well as a terrific location right in the middle of Plaza Nueva. The bar boasts a scrambled egg and seafood platter as one of its main specialties—it's a hangover helper on a plate. ☎ 944-150-874. Tapas start at 2€. Daily 10am–midnight.

CHEAP

➜ **Restaurante Chino** CHINESE   I know, I know, why would you want Chinese in Spain? But if you're sick of Basque game and seafood or just seeking an inexpensive meal, it's always nice to have options. The inside is quite large and much nicer than your average cheapie Chinese joint. Somera. ☎ 944-159-976. Entrees 4.50€–9.50€. Menu of the day 6€. Dinners for 2 starting at 16€. Daily noon–4:30pm and 7:30pm–midnight.

DOABLE

➜ **La Bodeguilla del Mervion** ★ BASQUE Although I almost passed right by it, as it's not showy or the slightest bit obvious from the outside, I was seduced into this Basque joint by the taunting smells that wafted out to the riverside. Bodeguilla, a vision right out of the days of Old Spain, is decorated accordingly. The walls are of a red-orange claylike substance, (faux) bricks are inlaid around the fake yet depictive windows, and the tiles painted with rural scenes are quintessential of times past. Start with the lamb stew in almond sauce and try the cuadaja, a typical Basque dessert that is a sort of a mix between custard and yogurt. Finish with pacharan, the

Let's Make a Deal

For low prices at restaurants, cheap transportation, and discounts at museums, shops, shows, and more, you can take advantage of the city's **Bilbao Card,** which is well worth the few euros it costs. Cards are available for 1, 2, or 3 days at 6€, 10€, and 12€, respectively, and can be purchased at any of the tourist offices or at Albergue Bilbao Aterpetxea.

house liqueur. Campo Volantín 14. ☎ 944-453-093. Entrees 12€–15€. Full menu for 2 people 30€. Tues–Sun 1–3:30pm and 8:30–11:30pm.

➜ **Victor Montes** BASQUE/SPANISH   Right in the heart of the Casco Viejo lies this bustling restaurant and tapas joint well known for its large portions of local fresh eats, including the likes of grilled squid and traditional Basque roasts and stews. Take your meal at a table in one of the bistrolike dining rooms or at one of the few tables positioned peering out at the square, grab some tapas at the bar with the harried locals, or to make an even faster exit back into the fray of the Plaza Nueva, check out the regional meats and produce at the downstairs deli. Plaza Neuva 8. ☎ 944-157-067. www.victormontes bilbao.com. Tapas 1.50€. Mains 9€–19€. Mon–Thurs 1–4pm and 8:30–11pm; Fri–Sat 1–4pm and 8:30–midnight.

SPLURGE

📺 Best ☺ ➜ **Etxanobe** ★★★ BASQUE Situated atop the Congressional Palace in Spain's most contemporary city, Etxanobe is the dining venue of choice for politicians and high society—not to mention the perfect spot for sampling some of the Basque Country's most exquisite cuisine. The room's great height is accentuated by a charming mishmash of old-fashioned

French touches and gold lamé curtains, as well as drapes billowing from the ceiling and a lone wall decorated with Dalí-esque flair by Spanish artist Joaquin Gallando. You'll be hard-pressed to find a tenderer lamb than this succulent *cordero* served with an artistic accoutrement of edible garnishes. For a more regional specialty, opt for the *bacalao* (codfish), Bilbao's most revered dish. Or try a bit of everything with the *menu gastronomico* (65€). For dessert, the *leche caramelizada* is a decadent caramel flan, topped with crystallized *muscovado,* an unrefined sugar with hints of molasses. And chocoholics, take note: Specialties include triple-chocolate mousse and mini-chocolate bombs with mango ice cream. Still not convinced? The wine list is more extensive than the menu itself and specializes in reds and whites from the neighboring Rioja region, otherwise known as "Spain's own wine country." Call in advance, or book your table online. Ah, dare to dream! *Abandoibarra 4.* ☎ *944-421-071 and 636-702-161. www.etxanobe.com. Entrees start around 16€. Mon–Sat 1:30–4pm and 8pm–midnight.*

CAFES

➜ **Arábicas** Coffee is not just coffee, but rather an experience at this pioneering cafe that offers an extensive menu of favorites from all around the globe. Pastries and tapas are also served throughout the day for 2€ to 4€. *Rodríguez Arias 4, Indauxtu.* ☎ *944-151-603. Mon–Sun noon–1am.*

➜ **Bar Café Bizitza** With typical Bilbao flair, this cafe mixes gastronomy with art, and delightfully so. At this quiet double-decker cafe, you can enjoy a cup of coffee (2€) and slice of homemade cake (3€) while taking in the latest photo exhibition on display. *Torre 1, Casco Vieja.* ☎ *944-165-882. Mon–Sun 5pm–1:30am.*

Partying

You'll never be lacking for things to do once the sun goes down in this party-hardy city that seems to really come alive around midnight or so. Bars generally close between 3 and 5am, while the clubs stay open much later. With the most eclectic crowd in northern Spain, Bilbao caters to every walk of life, from the artsy-fartsy, tree-huggin' partier to the beer-drinkin', dart-flingin' pub-goer. **Casco Vieja** is often the site of early-evening drinking and tapas crawls, particularly along **Calle Pozas** and **Calle Barrencalle,** before the discos and clubs in the city center really get going after midnight. The gay crowd typically fills the bars and clubs of **Calle Barrencalle.**

BARS

➜ **Galeón** ★ I have a confession to make: I'm a total sucker for theme bars. And I wasn't the slightest bit disappointed by Galeón. With a pirate theme and greeting sign that says "Welcome aboard," some may find the whole Disney-World factor more than a bit cheesy. I, however, appreciated the steel anchor, rope ladders, large barrels, and everything else even remotely *Pirates of the Caribbean* about the cheerful bar. The only thing missing, in my opinion, was an appearance by Johnny Depp or Orlando Bloom. *Alameda de Mazarredo 25.* ☎ *944-231-462.*

LIVE MUSIC

➜ **Antzokia** ★★ Stumble into this refurbished theater with the intriguing abandoned playhouse exterior and bouncers guarding the doors. Inside, you will discover a massive dance floor with a stage and wraparound balcony where everyone is doing their thang—break dancing, having private jam sessions, no one paying attention to the next. The music is a mix of rock and heavy metal. Not the greatest place for an evening of socializing, but for drunken festivities it is the place to be. *San Vicente 2, Plaza Circular.* ☎ *944-244-625.* *www.kafeantzokia.com.*

➔**Café Teatro Mistyk** This colorful bar with a Cirque du Soleil–like vibe offers an array of free shows—ranging from concerts to comics—during the week, and a groovy, dance scene on the weekends. *Ercilla 1.* ☎ *944-236-342. www.pubmistyk.com.*

➔**Cotton Club** More than 30,000 beer caps line the walls at this Harlem-esque joint. With a DJ on hand and catchy Spanish music reverberating through the place, Cotton Club is hopping with the 20s and 30s crowd, particularly on weekends. *Gregorio de la Revilla 25.* ☎ *944-104-951.*

NIGHTCLUBS

➔**Bailongo** Another place to dance the night away, this psychedelic disco is decked out in mirrors and orange decor with a circular bar in the center. A beer goes for about 2.50€, while cocktails start around 4€. *Henao 6, Gran Vía.* ☎ *944-247-003.*

➔**Bandera's** This cozily lit, fashionable joint is trendy because, if nothing else, it is in the same neighborhood as the Guggenheim, offering great night views of the titanium giant reflecting off the river. The twinkling lights that speck the wooden bar area are warm and intimate, and the bar has an interesting mix of pop and indie music. *Barraincúa 12.* ☎ *944-240-742.*

➔**High Club** The city's gay crowd congregates at this bumping night club, where Spanish music abounds. Check out the hyperactive dark room in the back or go upstairs where XXX-rated films are shown. Definitely not for the faint of heart. High Club is filled with eligible, young, queer bachelors, though it has been known to draw a few women, as well. *Naja 5. No phone.*

➔**Splash** If you're truly hard core, even by Spanish standards, and aren't ready to hit the sack when all the other bars and clubs close, you'll find the doors open and an overabundance of energy at Splash. The place doesn't even open until 8am on Saturday and Sunday (which are the only days it operates). Yawning is prohibiting, and the bar even has coffee available to prevent exhaustion of any degree. *Iturriza 7. No phone.*

Sightseeing

🅼 Best 🔖 ➔**Guggenheim** You can spot the glistening metallic exterior from the Basque Country's most famous museum from miles away. Situated right on the Nervión River, the 104,700-sq.-m (1,127,000-sq.-ft.) museum is uncontestedly Bilbao's number-one attraction. Designed by internationally known architect Frank Gehry, the Guggenheim and its neighboring bridge, Puente de la Salve, are symbolic of the new Bilbao, a modern-art sanctuary. The Guggenheim primarily displays artwork by 20th-century greats, including Picasso

---

cuidado! Thieves at Work

Bilbao ain't NYC but this might remind you of the ugly side of the Big Apple . . . Apparently, thieves patrol the Guggenheim parking lot preying on those tourists who are passing through by permanently separating them from their luggage left in the car. I know, right? It sounds just like that time you road-tripped to see your friend at NYU and left your luggage in the car for just a minute— oh no, wait, that was me. So be smart and put your bag (along with any food items that you don't want to be confiscated by security) in coat-check for safekeeping.

and Warhol. It also houses new pieces by local Basque and Spanish artists and features traveling exhibits from New York. If you don't see anything else in Bilbao but the Guggenheim, it was still a trip worth making. If you need a lunch break in the midst of your hours of browsing, the cafeteria downstairs serves snacks and light meals for surprisingly reasonable prices. *Abandoibarra 2. ☎ 944-359-000. www.guggenheimbilbao.es. Admission adult 13€, student 7.50€ with presentation of ID. Sept–June Tues–Sun 10am–8pm; July–Aug daily 10am–8pm.*

➜ **Museo de Bellas Artes** Bellas Artes is to Bilbao what the Prado is to Madrid. An important collection of both medieval and modern works, Bellas Artes features work by Spanish greats such as Picasso, Velázquez, Gaugin, and Goya, placing particular emphasis on 19th- and 20th-century pieces by Basque artists. If you've done the Guggenheim, this should be the next stop on your tour de arte. Afterward, take a stroll around the pictorial exterior English gardens that surround the museum. *Plaza del Museo 2. ☎ 944-396-060. Admission 4.50€ adults, 3€ students, free on Wed. Tues–Sat 10am–8pm; Sun 10am–2pm.*

Playing Outside

The green space in Bilbao is 7 sq. m (75 sq. ft.) per resident, meaning you should never have a problem finding a plot of grass to call your own. Bilbao's main park is the Romantic-style **Doña Casilda Park,** which, now a century old, has become a center of entertainment with its pond of ducks and biscuit sellers, basketball courts, merry-go-round, Fine Arts Museum cafe, and stage for live performances. Or head to the equally as relaxing **Extebarria Park,** which formerly housed a steel factory before its transformation in the '80s. Situated on an incline, Extebarria is a great spot for viewing the city from afar. Or you can take a stroll along **Memorial Parkway,** a lovely boulevard along the river that was constructed in 2002 and passes the Palace of Congress and Guggenheim.

Shopping

A self-professed shopaholic, I was rather overwhelmed by Bilbao's offering of chain stores and boutiques. If you're looking for mainstream places like Zara, United Colors of Benetton, and the like, you'll find them on or around **Gran Vía,** the primary shopping promenade, as well as a hodgepodge of overpriced designer shops. Most shops keep hours from 10:30am to 1:30pm and 4:30 to 9pm on Monday to Saturday.

Casco Vieja is home to a good deal of shopping, too, and prices are more reasonable here. Start out on **Somera** with its random configuration of shops. You'll find bohemian-inspired clothing and ethnically infused knickknacks at **La Luna** (Somera 8) or be able to satisfy your outdoor needs at **La Casa de la Montaña** just down the way on Somera (no number). **Safo de Lesbos** (La Torre 7; www.safodelesbos.com) has a random mix of books, posters, and trinkets for the gay and lesbian crowd.

If you're cooking for yourself or just need an early afternoon snack, the multi-level ☆ Best ● **Mercado de la Ribera,** open Monday to Saturday 7:45am to 1:45pm, is the biggest in town and never runs short of fresh fruits, veggies, fish, and meat.

BASQUE COUNTRY

Pamplona

by Kristin Luna

The capital of Navarra is home to just under 200,000 people, a small percentage of whom are students at the local university. Pamplona is located near the Pyrenees and is sandwiched by Aragón to the east and Basque Country to the west, and exhibits discernible traces of each culture as a result.

But the way I see it, tourists come to Pamplona for two reasons and two reasons alone: 1) to join the drunken masses of bull chasers for the annual San Fermín and 2) to stop over on their trek across Camino de Santiago. (Perhaps this is why Pamplona town folk are known for being a rather closed society, and not extremely accepting of newcomers and tourists?) Like any town, it has its good points—the many lush, green parks, for example—but overall, we found Pamplona to be the most unwelcoming and overrated of all Spanish cities. But if you must do your Hemingway thing, my suggestion is to come during San Fermín and get the hell out of Dodge as soon as it has ended.

The Camino de Santiago is responsible for bringing many people to Pamplona. The trail starts at the Puente de la Magdalena northeast of town, passes through the walls of the Portal de Francia or Portal de Zumalacárregui, goes through the cathedral, Plaza Consistorial, and church of San Saturnino, on to the parks skirting the castle, and across the Puente de Zizur. From there, it heads west for the final 700km (420 miles) of the journey.

Best of Pamplona

○ **Best Budget Option: Hotel Eslava.** Tucked away from the noise of the old city, but close enough to reach all main attractions within minutes, this quaint, family-run hotel is comfortable and won't break the bank. See p. 290.

○ **Best Alternative to Tapas: Finzi.** The Italian-inspired decor, monthly wine runs to Italy's finest vineyards, and hearty and delectable Italian cuisine keep this place packed night after night. See p. 292.

○ **Best Nonstop Party: San Fermín.** You are almost never going to have another (legitimate) excuse to party from sunrise to sunrise for 8 days straight. See p. 295.

○ **Best Local Flair: Hotel Maisonnave.** Brand spanking new with a delightful staff and rooms that aren't too pricey, you'll find a vigorous San Fermín atmosphere at Maisonnave with its vintage art and paintings of the famed festival. See p. 291.

○ **Best Natural Experience: Parque de la Taconera.** With chickens, peacocks, and goats galore, you'll be intrigued by this park where mammal and avian friends alike convene in the middle of the city. See p. 296.

Getting There & Getting Around

Getting There

BY AIR

During the week, four to six flights through **Iberia** (☎ 800-772-4642) arrive from Madrid and Barcelona. **Aeropuerto de Noaín** (☎ 948-168-700 or 948-317-512) is 6.5km (4 miles) from the city center and is accessible only by taxi (10€).

BY TRAIN

Three **trains** arrive daily at **Plaza de la Estación** from Madrid (48€, trip time: 4 hr.) and three from Barcelona (32€, trip time: 6 hr.). Three daily train connections arrive in Pamplona from San Sebastián (17€, trip time: 2 hr.) and six daily from Zaragoza (16€, trip time: 2 hr.). **RENFE** timetables and information can be obtained by visiting www.renfe.es or calling ☎ 902-240-202 or 948-130-202. There is also a railway **ticket office** in town on Estella 8 (☎ 948-227-282).

BY BUS

Daily **buses** connect Pamplona to many of Spain's major cities: four from Barcelona (23€, trip time: 5½ hr.), six from Madrid (24€, trip time: 4½ hr.), eight from Zaragoza (12€, trip time: 2 hr.), six from Bilbao (12€, trip time: 2½ hr.), and at least 10 from San Sebastián (6€, trip time: 1½ hr.). Stop by the **Estación de Autobuses** at Calle Conde Olivetto (corner of Calle Yanguas and Miranda) for a full timetable or check out one of the bus carriers' websites: **www.autobusesdenavarra.com**, **www.laburundesa.com**. At the time of publication, a new bus station was being built on the other side of the street. For more bus information, call the bus station at ☎ 948-223-854.

Getting Around

BY BUS

Pamplona's a relatively small city, and very walkable. However, if you're arriving by train, you'll find yourself on the outskirts of town—not so close if you're hauling a considerable size backpack. Hop the **bus** (1€) just outside the main entrance to the train station to go directly into town.

PAMPLONA

BY TAXI

If you do need a taxi to shuttle you to and from the train station, airport, or your hotel, you can phone ☎ 948-232-300 for a pickup.

Pamplona Basics

ORIENTATION

Pamplona's heart and soul is its **Plaza del Castillo,** a lively square in the middle of the historic part of the city that was constructed in 1847. During San Fermín, this is a popular spot for those without lodging to crash; during warm months, it's a good place to scarf down an ice-cream cone to cool off. Between **Plaza del Toros**—home to the annual San Fermín—and Plaza del Castillo is **Calle Estafet,** the street where the bulls thunder down during the festival.

But you'll most likely spend your days roaming the primarily pedestrian streets of the historic part of town—the area that begins with Plaza del Castillo and stretches westward, and is home to a surplus of shops, restaurants, and bars.

Tourist Office

The main **tourist office** is at Calle Eslava 1 (☎ 948-420-420), with another branch located on Duque de Ahumada s/n (☎ 948-220-741).

Recommended Websites

○ **www.navarra.es**: If you're fluent in Spanish, you may find some useful information on this government website. If you're not, you can still use the maps and weather reports for reference.
○ **www.sanfermin.com**: For info, pics, and the full program for San Fermín, see this site which does have an English option.

Culture Tips 101

If bulls aren't your thing and you still want to be cultureified Navarran style, you can check out **pelota,** a sport that, while unique to northern Spain, is similar to tennis. Professional matches take place at **Frontón Euskal-Jai Berri** (☎ 948-331-159), 6km (3 1/2 miles) outside of town along Avenida de Francia. Game times are Saturdays at 4pm, some Sundays and holidays. Admission is 12€ to 15€ for bleacher seats.

Pamplona Nuts & Bolts

Currency Get your BPs and dollars changed into euros at any post office in Pamplona, though—as in the rest of the country—you'll get the best exchange rate by withdrawing directly from any ATM.

Emergencies If you need help from the **Navarra police,** you can phone ☎ 088. To reach the **municipal police** (Mtrio. De Irache 2), call ☎ 948-255-150 or ☎ 092 for very urgent matters. To get a hold of the **national police** (General Chinchilla 3), call ☎ 948-224-008 or ☎ 091 for immediate assistance. If you require medical care, you can phone or visit the **Hospital of Navarra** (Iruñlarrea 3; ☎ 948-102-100 or ☎ 061), **Hospital Virgen del Camino** (Iruñlarrea 4; ☎ 948-109-400 or ☎ 061) or the **Spanish Red Cross** (Yanguas y Miranda; ☎ 948-226-404).

Pamplona & Beyond

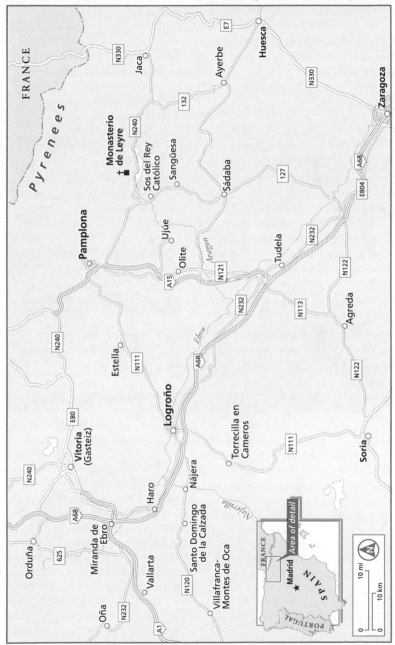

Internet Access You can visit the kind owner of the friendly, English-speaking **Kuria.net** (Curia 15, near the cathedral; ☎ **948-223-077**) during the long hours when everything else is shut down for siesta. There are several computers with fast connections, and fax and printer services are also available. Internet use is 3€ per hour. Open Monday to Saturday 10am to 10pm. Across the street from Kuria.net, the charming cafe/bar/art gallery **Café Curia** (Curia 4; ☎ **948-210-765**) has two flatscreen computers with high-speed Internet. You can enjoy a cup of coffee and the colorful paintings by local artists while you check your e-mail, and sit out on the newly constructed terrace and bask in the sun when you're done. Open Monday to Friday 9am to 1:30pm and 5 to 9:30pm. Prices are 3€ for an hour of Internet use. There are also a few random *locuturios* on Calle Tejeria and Calle St. Nicolas where you can get online or use fax and international telephone services.

Laundry & Public Showers Pamplona has no traditional *lavanderías,* but if you stink and are in need of a fresh wardrobe, you can get a load done for you at **Casa de Duchas** (Eslava 9; ☎ **948-221-738**) for 5€. And if your clothes aren't the only thing smelling and you're visiting during San Fermín without a hotel room, you can scrub down in one of the many **showers** for 3€. Towels and soap are available for an additional .40€. Open Tuesday through Saturday from 8:30am to 10pm, Sunday and holidays 9am to 1pm. Hours are extended just a bit for San Fermín, though washing service is not available then.

Pharmacies Remember: **pharmacies** are denoted by a large **green cross.** Look for the referral sign on the door if it is after hours.

Post Office The **central post office** is located on **Paseo Sarasate** and is open Monday through Friday from 8:30 to 10:30pm and Saturday from 9:30am to 2pm.

Telephone Tips Calls within and to Pamplona begin with a **948.**

Sleeping

If you're thinking of heading to Pamplona for San Fermín spur of the moment, don't expect to find anywhere to lay your head. Most hotels are booked 7 to 8 months in advance, with many taking reservations as far as a year ahead of time. Prices for rooms throughout the city are three to five times as much during the famed festival, so you'd be better off camping or staying in a nearby town and busing in each day. Ladies with rooms to rent swarm the bus and train stations like bees on honey, but you'll likely find these overpriced, as well.

Due to the high volume of Camino a Santiago trekkers who pass through at all times of the year, accommodation should be booked 2 to 3 weeks prior to your arrival, particularly for weekend stays.

Hostels

➔ **Arriazu Hostal** The chandelier at the entrance of this hostel is a welcome greeting for those more used to dirty backpackers than chic furnishings. With a prime location just off the main tapas drag of San Nicolás, as well as Plaza del Castillo, this hostel is unbeatable in terms of convenience—though I can't say the same for its price. *Comedias 14.* ☎ *948-210-202. www. hostalarriazu.com. Single 47€–55€, double 55€–65€, triple 78€–90€. Amenities: Breakfast room, sheets, towels. In room: A/C, TV.*

Pamplona

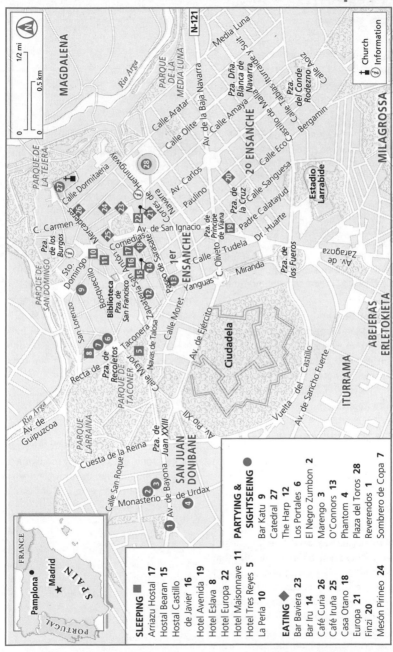

0   1/2 mi
0   0.5 km

N-121

MAGDALENA

MILAGROSSA

ABEJERAS

ERLETOKIETA

ITURRAMA

SAN JUAN
DONIBANE

PARQUE DE
LA TEJERA

PARQUE DE LA
MEDIA LUNA

2º ENSANCHE

Estadio
Larrabide

PARQUE DE
SAN DOMINGO

PARQUE DE
TACONER

PARQUE
LARRAINA

Ciudadela

1er
ENSANCHE

Rio Arga
Av. de
Guipuzcoa

Cuesta de la Reina

Pza. de
Juan XXIII

Calle San Roque

Av. de Bayona

Monasterio

Calle de Urdax

Av. Pio XII

Calle San Francisco
Zapateria

Navas de Talosa

Calle Mayor

Calle Moret

Calle Taconera

Recta de San
San Lorenzo

C. Carmen

Pza. de los
Burgos

Sto.
Domingo

Bosquecillo

Pza. de
Recoletos

Biblioteca

Pza. de
San Francisco

Mercaderes

Comedias

Calle Mayor

Paseo de Sarasate

Pza. del
Principe
de Viana

Yanguas

C. Oliveto Tudela

Calle

Miranda

Av. de Ejército

Vuelta del Castillo

Av. de Sancho Fuerte

Calle Dormitaeria

Calle de Hemingway

Navarra

Cortes de Navarra

Av. de San Ignacio

Av. Carlos
Paulino

Calle Aratar

Calle Olite

Av. de la Baja Navarra

Av. Calle Amaya

Pza. Dña.
Blanca de
Navarra

Media Luna

Pza. de
la Cruz

Calle EcoCas

Calle Sanguesa

Padre Calatayud

Dr. Huarte

Pza. de
los Fueros

Av. de Zaragoza

Castillo de Maillia
Calle Tablas Inuradi

Pza.
del Conde
Rodezno

Bergamin

Calle Conde Aroz

SLEEPING ■

Arriazu Hostal **17**
Hostal Bearan **15**
Hostal Castillo
de Javier **16**
Hotel Avenida **19**
Hotel Eslava **8**
Hotel Europa **22**
Hotel Maisonnave **11**
Hotel Tres Reyes **5**
La Perla **10**

EATING ◆

Bar Baviera **23**
Bar Iru **14**
Café Curia **26**
Café Iruña **25**
Casa Otano **18**
Europa **21**
Finzi **20**
Mesón Pirineo **24**

PARTYING &
SIGHTSEEING ●

Bar Katu **9**
Catedral **27**
The Harp **12**
Los Portales **6**
El Negro Zumbon **2**
Marengo **3**
O'Connors **13**
Phantom **4**
Plaza del Toros **28**
Reverendos **1**
Sombrero de Copa **7**

✚ Church
ⓘ Information

SPAIN

FRANCE

Madrid
★
Pamplona ●

PORTUGAL

Cuidado! These Bulls Are Pissed

Chasing after the angry, large-horned beasts may sound like fun at the time (especially after a few *cervezas*), but can be a dangerous activity that causes many injuries and oftentimes even death. Although the Navarran government tries to exercise precautionary measures, there are still too many runners, and at times the bulls are even fully blocked in by the young people who invade the course. You can still enjoy all the excitement from the sidelines, but if you're dead set (no pun intended) on running along beside the animals, be careful. One cheap thrill isn't worth a visit to the hospital, or worse—the morgue.

→**Hostal Bearan** If you decide to make the trek to San Fermín late in the game and have yet to book accommodation, you might just find an opening at this downtown budget hotel, which often doesn't completely fill for the festival until a month in advance. The older couple who runs it is charming, it's filled with English-speaking backpackers from all over the map, and you'll find the prices much more reasonable than those of its neighbors. *San Nicolás 25. ☎ 948-223-428. thegallipot@terra. es. Single 36€–106€, double 42€–120€, triple 54€–160€. Amenities: Elevator, Internet, sheets, towels. In room: A/C, TV.*

→**Hostal Castillo de Javier** This hostel not only looks new, but still maintains that fresh paint smell. Opened in 2004, the 17 rooms are pristine and sensual, and the building is located on the main tapas drag. The interior is one of the most attractive of all hostels and pensions in town, and, to my surprise (and delight), the price doesn't reflect the place's high caliber. Just don't expect the red carpet to be rolled out upon your arrival; like many other lodges in Pamplona, the staff isn't particularly welcoming. Book 1 to 2 weeks in advance. *San Nicolás 50-52. ☎ 948-203-040. www.hotel castillodejavier.com. Single 40€, double 55€, extra bed 20€. Amenities: Bar, breakfast room, elevator, sheets, towels. In room: A/C, TV, hair dryer, Internet, safe.*

Cheap

MTV (Best ♥) →**Hotel Eslava** You'll find the nicest service in town at this cozy, family-run hotel on the northwest corner of the historic part of Pamplona. Resting between Plazas Virgen de la O and Recoletas, the hotel is a bit hidden, but well worth the search. It is quieter than many other areas of the city (save during the running of the bulls and on big football match nights), has more character with its homey fashion, and the prices are unbeatable. *Recoletas 20 at Plaza Virgen de la O. ☎ 948-222-270. www.hoteleslava.com. Single 37€, double 65€, triple 73€. Amenities: Break-fast room, elevator, Internet. In room: TV, hair dryer.*

Doable

→**Hotel Avenida** ★ This charming, sophisticated three-star's room decor is a little old-fashioned, with white wood and floral furnishings, but if you're traveling in a larger group, the connecting rooms make it a good option. The main problem with Avenida is it only has 24 rooms, and much of the year, those are filled with regulars. Still, if it's within your price range and you're planning your trip far enough in advance, it's worth a try. The only other downfall is the location—in the industrial center of town, it's a bit of a hike to the bars in the old city. *Av. de Zaragoza 5. ☎ 948-245-454. Single 70€, double 106€. Amenities: Restaurant, bar, breakfast room, elevator. In room: A/C, TV, hair dryer, Internet.*

→ **Hotel Europa** I would rather crash in Taconera Parque with the aggravatingly loud chickens than spend 1 night in this stuffy, uptight snob sanctuary. The staff acts as if they are doing *you* the favor by allowing you to stay there, and the rooms are boxy and rigid. Europa's only saving grace is its locale right off Plaza Castillo; however, you'll find many hostels and pensions in the same neighborhood where you'll get more bang for your buck. But if everywhere else in town is booked and you prefer claustrophobia and insolence to a Discovery Channel night with some avian friends, then maybe Hotel Europa is the place for you. *Espoz y Mina 11.* ☎ *948-221-800. Single 72€, double 86€. Amenities: Restaurant, cafe, elevator. In room: TV, Internet, minibar.*

📺 **Best ●** → **Hotel Maisonnave** ★★ Brand shiny new and decorated with vintage artwork from the running of the bulls, Maisonnave is contemporary and attractive, not to mention one of the few places in town you'll be treated like a guest, rather than a pest. And how's this for a sweet deal: If the hotel is fully booked save the luxe Jacuzzi suites, the kind staff will place you in one for the price of a normal room. *Nueva 20.* ☎ *948-222-600. www.hotel maisonnave.es. Single 65€–71€, double 75€–85€, with cheaper prices on weekends, extra bed available for an additional 20€–24€. Amenities: Restaurant, cafe, elevator, Internet, parking (11€ a day). In room: A/C, TV, hair dryer, Internet.*

→ **La Perla** "The Pearl" doesn't exactly live up to its name, as—unlike Madonna—it hasn't seen a renovation in years. However, it becomes quite a hot spot regardless come San Fermines thanks to its spot on the main square in the heart of Pamplona, as well as its view of the path the bulls run. *Plaza del Castillo 1.* ☎ *948-227-706. Double 65€–120€, suite 150€. In room: A/C, TV.*

Splurge

→ **Hotel Tres Reyes** ★★★ Can I just say that there's a hairdresser on one floor and a pianist permanently stationed downstairs? I think that should tell you the caliber of lodging we're talking about at Pamplona's fanciest hotel. You'll wish you had your prom outfit nearby when you set foot in the elegant lobby. The place absolutely reeks of pretentious, high-class Spanish society. However, the English-speaking staff is kind, the rooms look like they're made for royalty, and you'll no doubt sleep like a king (that is, after all, the translation for *reyes*). You will pay a pretty penny if you choose to lodge here, although weekend prices (which tend to be much lower) are surprisingly reasonable. *Jardines de la Taconera s/n.* ☎ *948-226-600. www.hotel3reyes.com. Single 148€, double 191€, weekend 99€ for single or double, executive single 172€, executive double 222€, weekend 130€ for all executives. Amenities: Restaurant, bar, garden, gym, massage services, sauna, swimming pool (summer only). In room: A/C, TV, DVD, hair dryer, iron, minibar, safe.*

Eating

If there is such a thing as "cheap dining" in Pamplona, I sure didn't come across it. Lunchtime *menú del día* prices are fixed around 10€ to 12€ including wine, while dinners typically start at 15€. Navarran food consists of many Basque-inspired seafood dishes, thanks to the influence of its western neighbor, as well as game from its own Pyrenees. Though tasty and satisfying, menus don't vary much from restaurant to restaurant.

Tapas

➔**Casa Otano** ★ A favorite of sports enthusiasts who want to grab a bite to eat while watching the big game, this tapas bar has an extensive choice of different *pinchos,* all fresh and equally as tasty. If you are into some more serious sit-down dining check out the upstairs restaurant (see below). *San Nicolas 5.* ☎ *948-225-095 and 948-227-036. Tapas start around 2€. Sun–Thurs 9am–11pm; Fri–Sat 9am–4:30am.*

Doable

➔**Bar Iru** ★★ NAVARRAN This unsuspecting bar will leave you feeling more satisfied than many other joints in Pamplona. Start with the *milhojas de verduras* (an attractive presentation of assorted vegetables), follow with the *lasaña de hongos* (lasagna), and finish with the *pastel de crema catellana* (a sort of caramel crème brûlée concoction). *San Nicolás 25. No phone. Menu of the day with wine 11€. Daily 1–4pm and 8:30–11pm.*

➔**Casa Otano** ★ NAVARRAN This enjoyable restaurant is situated above the bar of the same name. The decor is more traditional than on the tavernlike ground floor, with lighter wood paneling and a collection of china plates hanging on the mango-colored walls. The place is often packed (if it's any indication how good the food is, tables constantly have to be added to the crowded room), and the service is accordingly slow. But the tasty Navarran dishes like *pochas con chorizo* (beans with sausage), *confit de pato* (duck), and *torta helada con salsa chocolate* (a decadent ice-cream cake) make it well worth the wait. Arrive before 10pm to avoid rush hour. Reservations recommended on weekends. *San Nicolas 5.* ☎ *948-225-095 and 948-227-036. Entrees 10€–24€. Mon–Sat 1–4pm and 9–11:30pm; Sun 1–4pm.*

➔**Mesón Pirineo** ★ NAVARRAN Warning: It is advisable to not eat for many hours before visiting this restaurant of Navarran specialties, or you'll run the risk of having to be wheeled out due to belly-busting consumption. The food is phenomenal, service is friendly, and you must check out this exquisite culinary experience for yourself before leaving town. Fifteen euros gets you a feast, complete with starter, main course, wine, bread, dessert, and complimentary shot of liqueur. Try the *ensalada con codorniz* (salad with quail) or *alubias de tolosa* (bean stew) to start, followed by the *confit de pato al opozto* (duck) or *estofado de ciervo* (beef), and topped off with the flan or *delicia de limón. Estafeta 41.* ☎ *948-020-702. Entrees start at 15€. Mon–Sat 1–4pm and 8–11pm; Sun 1–4pm.*

Splurge

➔**Europa** BASQUE This local favorite specializes in the finest of Navarran and Basque eats. The menu is ever-changing according to what is seasonal at the time, and the chef is quite famous in the area. The restaurant itself has a rather sophisticated air to it despite the more casual, old-fashioned feel of the rest of the city. And don't choose now to calorie count and pass on sweets—in fact, skip the main dish if you so desire and simply start with one of Europa's decadent desserts, accompanied by a glass (or whole bottle if you splurge) of one of the extensive cellar's many world wines. Reservations are recommended. *Espoz y Mina 11.* ☎ *948-221-800. Entrees 12€–22€. Tasting menu 48€. Mon–Sat 1–3:30pm and 9–11pm.*

MTV Best ➔**Finzi** ★★★ ITALIAN You can't come to Pamplona and not try the gourmet delicacies of this perfect alternative to Spanish food. The restaurant only serves two shifts of people per night, so reservations are always necessary. The *insalate Finzi* and a glass (or entire bottle if you like) of *Sangre de Judas* are tasty ways to start the evening off right. Order the *farfallone di tartuffo blanco* (pasta with white truffles) or *malfatti di melanzane* (pasta with eggplant) for a main and splurge on *profiterolles con chocolate caliente* or *tartuffo di cioccolate gianduia*—both, little pieces of chocolate heaven. Make friends with the owner, who is fluent in English and has lived all over the world (including North America), and you may just receive a complimentary *limoncello* as a nightcap. If you're around on a Wednesday, Finzi offers live music at the weekly "Noche de sabor Napoletano" with a set menu at 20€ per person. Just don't forget to book a day or more in advance. *Paulino Caballero 12.* ☎ *948-153 263. www.finzi.es. Set menu 20€. Tues–Sun 1:30–3:30pm and 8:30–11:30pm.*

Cafes

→ **Bar Baviera** Not the cheapest lunchtime venue, but the locale is great for people-watching and catching some rays in warmer months. The waiters aren't in any hurry to serve you; often, you have to track them down. But if you have time to kill and you're looking for a light meal as opposed to the typical *menú del día,* try one of the salads (starting at 5€) like *ensalada ruta,* a small, creamy chicken dish with mayonnaise, potatoes, avocados, and asparagus. *Plaza del Castillo 10.* ☎ *948-222-048. Entrees 5€–11€. Daily until 10pm.*

→ **Café Iruña** ★★ You can almost imagine you're Ava Gardner or Ernest Hemingway sipping a *café con leche* whilst sitting beneath the fancy-schmancy high ceilings and gold trimmings of Café Iruña. Despite the fame the cafe has received via Hemingway's recs, Iruña's prices remain surprisingly reasonable. You can get a cup of coffee for 1€, a complete lunch for 9€, the menu of the day for 12€ and, most importantly, a beer for under 2€. The cafe is open daily from 8am to 11pm—with lunch served from 1 to 3:30pm—but the millisecond dinner begins at 8:30pm, the dining room fills up. So arrive early, hover at the bar pre-dinnertime, and grab your seat ASAP. *Plaza del Castillo.* ☎ *948-224-293. Entrees start at 12€. Daily 8am–11pm.*

Partying

The bulk of pre-partying takes place in the historic quarter, with the late-nighters shifting when the bars close between 3 and 4am to the discos just south of **Plaza de Juan XXIII.** Early evening when the weather is nice, students often congregate in **Plaza de los Burgos** for a few *cervezas con limón* (beer mixed with lemonade).

Thursday night is the prime night for university partying, while on Fridays all people, young and old, make the pilgrimage—no, not to Santiago—to the bars of the Old Town. On Saturdays you'll primarily find your high school–aged crowd out and about, especially along **Calle Navarrería.**

Our suggested going-out itinerary: Start out with a beer at one of the cafe terraces on **Plaza del Castillo,** migrate over to **Calle San Nicolas** for more drinks and *pinchos,* move on to **Navarrería** where all those under 30 make an appearance at some point in the evening, and end your night (or possibly morning) at one of the **Avenida Bayona** area's hopping discos.

Bars

It doesn't really matter if you start off at **Bar Navarrería, Bar Cordovilla, Bar Ezkia, Bar Aldaba,** or one of the many other drinking establishments that comprise **Calle Navarrería;** all the youthful nomads only end up buying a beer and drifting outside to the plaza in the center of this buzzing mecca for bar-goers.

➜ **Bar Katu** You won't find your international crowd here, but if you're looking to get off the beaten bar track, this crowded, smoky place, where the locals come to mingle amid comic caricatures of famous figures on the walls, won't disappoint. *Jarauta 9. No phone.*

➜ **The Harp** Irish, Scottish, American, Scandinavian—all the internationals in town convene at the Harp for football and rugby matches and just about every other odd occasion. Unlike many other Irish pubs in Spain, English is spoken exclusively here (the owners are, gasp, actually Irish). The restaurant upstairs, El Arpa, offers pricier yet filling meals for 35€. *San Gregorio 12.* ☎ *948-211-549.*

➜ **Los Portales** Popular among international students (and with beer for just 1€, it's no wonder why), this underground bar is small and dungeonlike but comes alive on Thursdays (University Night) and on Fridays after midnight. If you're nostalgic for home, you can hear English spoken and American music played here. *Plaza Recoletas.* ☎ *653-198-926. www.barlos portales.com.*

➜ **O'Connor's** The only thing Irish about this pub is its name. Though one time owned by imports from the land of Celtic folklore and leprechauns, the light-hearted bar is now run by locals. Tapas are served all day long should you need something to feed your tapeworm. *Paseo Sarasate 13. No phone.*

➜ **Sombrero de Copa** For a younger, more casual crowd of university students, this bar off of Plaza Recoletas is unbeatable. The atmosphere is lively, yet friendly, and there's a roomy dance floor and occasional live music. *Recoletas. No phone. www. pagina.de/sombrerodecopa.*

Discos/Clubs

➜ **El Negro Zumbon** I prefer this sexy lounge to its more publicized neighbor Marengo due to the starlit ceilings and linear modern art drawings on the walls. The music is a mix of house and techno, and there's never a cover charge to get in. Tip for the ladies: If you're looking particularly hot, you may get an invitation for free drinks from the owner. *Monasterio de Cilveti 2.* ☎ *948-173-975. www.negrozumbon.com.*

➜ **Marengo** Chances are if you're chatting with locals, they'll send you to this underground discothèque for late-night action. With catchy, hip-swingin' Latin flava and plenty of room to dance, Marengo remains a favorite among travelers and residents of all ages. Although the cover charge is a bit steep (6€ on Thurs, 10€ on Fri, 12€ on Sat), students get in for free on Thursdays. *Av. de Bayona 2 off of Plaza de Juan XXIII.* ☎ *948-265-542. Cover Thurs 6€, Fri 10€, Sat 12€.*

➜ **Phantom** One glance at my plain tank top, jeans (designer, not that it mattered to them), and flip-flop-clad feet got me nothing but upturned noses from both guests and staff upon my entrance into this apparent breeding ground for svelte should-be models and Spanish hipsters. Still, the contemporary ambience of the disco bar further enhanced by the formation of bright, sharp colors and minimalistic decor made me want to come back here again—only next time I'll pack my miniskirt and stilettos. *Monasterio de Usun 1.* ☎ *609-408-878.*

➜ **Reverendos** The trendy 20- and 30-something crowd populates this late-night watering hole in search of someone new to go home with that night . . . So if you don't like the vibe at Marengo (or just aren't seeing the action you desire), you can flirt to

San Fermín

It's 10am on the morning of July 6. Like a zombie in a trancelike state, you follow the masses of white-clad people—natives and visitors alike—through the winding streets of historic Pamplona to convene at the city hall. You're most likely in a severely hungover state, but you don't care. You're just waiting to see what will unfold in the coming 8 days.

At precisely noon, a member of the city council lights a rocket which explodes over the heads of the thousands of people below waving red neck scarves in their hands. The crowd goes mad. MTV Best⦿ **San Fermín** has officially begun.

San Fermín has always been an important part of Pamplona heritage, but it wasn't until Ernest Hemingway popularized the cultural event in his acclaimed novel *The Sun Also Rises* that foreigners from near and far began to flock to the Navarran region in July of each year out of yearning to see the eminent **running of the bulls,** as well as follow in the beloved writer's footsteps.

For 8 days straight, the city is a frenzy of drinking, dancing, praying, and partying. The festive spirit unites everyone, and no one is an outsider. As the Spanish say, "Pamplona becomes the world capital of happiness"—at least for a brief time.

Although technically the festival is a religious celebration in honor of the patron saint San Fermín, you can expect a lot of drinking to go along with it, as nothing in Spain is accomplished without the presence of *muchas bebidas.* If you're feeling compelled to make up for your sins of the night before, you can attend mass or one of the other religious services held throughout the 8 days.

Or just spend your time partying in the streets of Pamplona. Each day begins at 6am with a joyful awakening by pipers and the municipal band, and the festivities more or less continue until the same time the following morning. Basically, it's 192+ hours of ceaseless *fiestas.*

The *encierro,* or bull run, is without a doubt the most popular aspect of San Fermín. At 8am on the morning of July 7, a rocket is launched as the bulls are released from their corrals and set out to run the course that leads to the bullring, where they await their fate. The run lasts approximately 3 minutes, and crowds of people gallop alongside the bulls as they travel through the streets of the old city to the **Plaza del Toros.**

The running of the bulls tradition dates back to when herdsmen used to bring their bulls across country from the pastures to fight in the famous ring. The bulls would spend the night in the nearby city and at dawn on the day of the fight, run across the town accompanied by oxen or fellow bulls. All the while, men on horseback would chase them into the stalls with sticks.

According to historians San Fermín was not born spontaneously but arose out of the conjunction of three separate fiestas: those of a religious nature in honor of San Fermín and that have taken place since time immemorial, the commercial fiestas organized since the 14th century, and the *taurine* festivals that were centered around the bullfights.

But fun with bulls isn't the only thing the **famous festival** has to offer. Throughout San Fermín, you'll find folk dances, musical performances, and rural sports, like the athletic feats of the stone-lifters and wood-cutters. On July 14, all the festivities wind down, and it's like the *encierro* never happened—until people begin preparing again for next year.

PAMPLONA

your heart's content at this bumping night club. Cover is 6€, which includes the price of a drink. *Monasterio de Velate 5.* ☎ *948-222-064. Cover 6€, includes 1 drink.*

Sightseeing

Don't get too excited should you be visiting Pamplona at any time other than San Fermines. You can't actually go inside the stadium at **Plaza de Toros,** as it is only open during the festival and occasional holidays and special events. You can still snap your picture in front of the arena, but you may be disappointed as the outside of the bullring is quite unimpressive.

FREE → **Catedral** Pamplona's most important sight, dating from the late 14th century, the cathedral is a mix of neoclassical and baroque and was the product of Ventura Rodríguez, architect to Charles III. At the center is the alabaster tomb of Charles III and his Castilian wife, Queen Leonor. The 14th- and 15th-century Gothic cloisters are a highlight, and the Barbazán Chapel, off the east gallery, is noted for its vaulting. The Museo Diocesano, housed in the cathedral's refectory and kitchen, displays religious objects, spanning the era from the Middle Ages to the Renaissance. *Curia and Dormitalería.* ☎ *948-210-827. Free admission to cathedral; museum 4€. Mon–Fri 10am–1:30pm and 4–7pm; Sat 10:30am–1:30pm.*

Playing Outside

It took me days to actually figure out where the constant crowing was coming from. And when I did finally pass [MTV][Best●]**Parque de la Tarconera,** I about fell over the side of the wall in my clamor to make out all the forms of wildlife below. Chickens, roosters, and even peacocks make their homes in the luxuriant moats of this pleasant park. So if you've exhausted Pamplona's few minor touristy sites (and you will quickly), you can spend some time among the greenery and wildlife of the city's natural fine points.

The striking **Parque de Tejera** is close to the most monumental part of Pamplona. Here you'll see towers of the town walls and the square of Plaza de Santa Maria la Real, with the baroque Archiepiscopal Palais. Following along the walls, you'll likely stumble upon Puerta de Zumalacarregui, one of the six old doors of the town, and the Santo Domingo Park.

ᴍᴛᵥ🖤 The University Scene

While Pamplona itself isn't the biggest city (population roughly 185,000), its university scene is one of the most bumping in northern Spain. The University of Navarra's main campus is located south of the city center, so you'll never go far without running into a crew of talkative university students, particularly in the bars and clubs along Avenida Bayona. However, the most popular late-night hangouts are found inside the walls of Pamplona's old town, primarily around Calle Navarrería, as well as the streets trailing off from Plaza del Castillo. Thursdays are prime-time party nights for the university crowd, when you'll find cheap drink specials and occasional discounts—though the students pack the bars on Fridays and Saturdays, as well.

If you want to be in the midst of all the action, you can enjoy the hustle and bustle of the city's main plaza from the comfort of one of its many benches or cafes along the **Plaza del Castillo.** In the summer months, there are often artistic performances that take place here, as well as festivals of all sorts.

If you still need more green, right smack in the center of the industrial part of town, the **ciudadela,** built in the 16th century, hides beautiful gardens within its interior. This pentagonal fortification is also a perfect picnicking locale.

If rafting, canoeing, hydrospeed (sort of like white-water rafting on a boogie board), and kayaking are on your to-do list in Navarra, outdoor guide company **Nattura** (Marcelo Zelaieta 75; www.nattura.com; ☎ 948-131-044) can hook you up with the action.

Shopping

Many local artisans sell their goods in the handicraft stores scattered throughout the Old City along **Calle Mercaderes** and its surrounding arteries. For clothing and more expensive merchandise, head east of Plaza del Castillo to the ritzier part of town.

Fashion

→ **Diagonal** I was drawn into this hip store by the gorgeous dresses on the mannequins, but was quickly deterred after one look at the price tags. However, if you have the dough to spend and want an alternative to chain stores, Diagonal is worth perusing. *García Castañón 8 at Esquina and Estella.* ☎ *948-256-082.*

→ **Ella's** For funky, unique clothing that doesn't necessarily have to cost an arm and a leg, head to this trendster boutique on the main square. It may be small, but has a lot to offer. *Plaza del Castillo 42.* ☎ *948-212-121.*

→ **Unzu** Another major Spanish department store chain, but nowhere near as daunting as El Corte Ingles, Unzu is much more manageable and houses apparel from a host of designers and apparel companies on its numerous floors. *Mercaderes 3 at Plaza Consistorial.* ☎ *948-209-100.*

Sports

→ **Basati Kirolak** On the edge of the Old Town, this shop for gear junkies sells an assortment of outdoor equipment should you be in need. Rental equipment for canyoning is also available. *Recoletas 8.* ☎ *948-212-345.*

Gifts

→ **Etc.** Arts, gifts, clothing, and more can be found at this bohemian lover's delight. If you want to embrace your inner hippie (or at least pretend like I do), you may just find what you're looking for at this incense-infused shop. *Mercaderes 8.* ☎ *948-207-765.*

PAMPLONA

Aragón

by *Kristin Luna*

Y ou won't find your envisioned Spain in landlocked Aragón, but the diverse
region is quickly gaining popularity among adventurers and those looking for a
break from the big cities. Perhaps it's due to its tranquil and inviting atmosphere—a
result of the region being so sparsely populated. Or maybe it's the fact that Aragón
itself is a hodgepodge of neighboring cultures—French influence from the north,
Catalonian flavor from the east, and Basque and Navarran inspirations from the west.

You'll never be lacking in things to do in Aragón. From mid-November until Easter,
the snowy peaks of the Spanish Pyrenees are chock-full of boarders and bunnies,
while the lush, green valleys are just as crowded from mid-June to mid-September
with hikers, canyoners, and adrenaline junkies alike. The region boasts some of the
country's best walking trails, including the GR-11, which stretches from coast to
coast. Ever heard of the little-known *Camino de Santiago?* You will after visiting
Aragón. The two primary pilgrimage paths begin in or around the lively town of Jaca
(a winter mountainside base for skiers and snowboarders alike), and Benasque, so
keep your eyes peeled for those making the 1,000km (620-mile) journey.

En route to or from the Pyrenees, you can stop over at Jaca, or go right on south to
Zaragoza, the region's active metropolis and capital. If you prefer a quieter setting for
reflecting (ahem, recovering from one long Spanish hangover), the Pyrenees are home
to several quaint, off-the-beaten-path villages like Torla and Bielsa, as well, and are
also a great excuse for giving extreme sports like parapente and canyoning a go.

Best of Aragón

○ **Best Adrenaline Rush: Sky diving in Santa Cilia.** It ain't cheap, but the best things in life never are. Venture over to the tiny Aragónese town from your base in Jaca to hurl yourself 3,500m (11,500 ft.) out of a plane and see panoramic views of the Pyrenees you'll never forget. See p. 327.

○ **Best Road Trip: Monasterio de Piedra.** This lush oasis in the middle of dry, desertlike Aragón is worth perusing, at least for a day. See p. 318.

○ **Best Spanish Sport: Parapente.** A cross between paragliding and sky diving, this custom sport isn't for the faint of heart. In fact, more accidents occur through parapente than any other sport in the region, but if you're seeking that much-needed rush, parapente won't disappoint. See p. 334.

○ **Best Mountainside Town: Benasque.** With a scenic setting, a ski resort just 4km (2¹/₂ miles) up the road, and nightlife you won't find elsewhere in the Pyrenees, why wouldn't you drop in on Benasque on your next trip through the area? See p. 331.

○ **Best Spot for Spanish Hot Chocolate: Café Babel.** Even if you're not a self-professed chocoholic, you really can't visit Spain and not try a cup of the signature creamy, souplike hot stuff. While you can find *chocolate caliente* at nearly any cafe along Paseo de la Independencia around Zaragoza's Plaza de España, Babel offers a variety of 32 flavors in a modern setting. The only problem is which one to choose. See p. 310.

○ **Best Chill Out Spot:** Whether it's tea or tequila that gets your mouth a watering, **Mombasa Café** will satisfy. The African ambience is soothing and exudes an über-chill sort of vibe. See p. 312.

○ **Best Late-Night Hot Spot: La Casa del Loco.** All of Zaragoza's pretty little things (and even the not-so-pretty) make the journey to this party asylum at some point in the evening. It's one of the few joints open past 4:30am, so if you want to *fiesta*, be sure and arrive just before the crowd does to avoid the lines. Just don't get there too early or you'll be committing social suicide. See p. 313.

○ **Best Place for Sampling Regional Tapas: Bodeguilla de la Santa Cruz.** If this eight-tapas-for-11-euros deal in Zaragoza isn't a steal, I don't know what is. The food is always fresh and service is speedy. Just heed this simple advice: Don't ask what's in 'em until you've tasted for yourself . . . unless you have a stomach of steel. See p. 308.

○ **Best Locale for a Siesta: Parque Primo de Rivera.** If you don't have a hotel room to go back to for your mid-afternoon zzz's or it's daily lockout time in your hostel, grab a bench or a patch of grass and crash in this pleasant park. See p. 315.

○ **Best Bang for Your Buck: Hotel Las Torres.** With clean, affordable rooms, a welcoming staff, and a location to kill, Hotel Las Torres is definitely deserving of a night's stay. See p. 307.

○ **Best Wine Selection: Algo Más.** Though actually a tapas bar, Algo Más has an extensive wine wall of regional delights that stretches from the ceiling to the floor. See p. 309.

○ **Best International Vibe: La Tierra.** You may even forget you're not in your homeland after visiting one of La Tierra's three branches and hearing English spoken all night. This fun-loving bar attracts tourists and expatriates from all over the globe. See p. 313.

Zaragoza

Prior to my arrival in one of Spain's largest cities, I'd received mixed reactions from Spaniards hearing of my pending trip. Some said it was a hellhole; others said it was party central. Some raved about the abundance of parks; others complained about the Zaragoza accent. But I found Zaragoza every bit as pleasant and charming as the few who did give it two thumbs up. True, this capital of Aragón is a bit rough around the edges, but in an endearing sort of way.

Zaragoza lies directly between Barcelona and Madrid, making it a convenient and worthwhile break in your journey between the two. Though not massive by other city standards (pop. 660,000), Zaragoza has a bustling student population and an even more booming nightlife thanks to the local Universidad de Zaragoza. Although Zaragoza has something for everyone, it is particularly a hippie haven. Dreadlocks, body piercings, and tattoos run rampant, and more often than not, you'll find folks smoking marijuana in cafes around town (despite drugs not being legal in Spain). If you run out of things to do, mullet-hunting should provide you with ceaseless hours of entertainment.

If you want to be mistaken for a native, you first and foremost need to learn how to pronounce the city name in the local dialect. That's "Thah-rah-*goh*-thah" spoken with the accent on the third syllable and as if possessed by some odd lisp with a cotton ball stuffed in your mouth. Got it? Good. You'll score immediate brownie points if you get that down pat.

Getting There

BY PLANE

From Madrid, Tenerife, Palma, and Almería, you can hop a direct flight to Zaragoza via **Iberia. Ryanair** (☎ 976-712-300) flights also go to Zaragoza from Milan and London Stansted. The small airport is 10km (6 miles) from the city center, and **buses** (☎ 976-554-588) run frequently from here to **Plaza de San Francisco** and **Plaza de Aragón** (1.70€). **Taxis** are available at the door to the arrivals hall and cost 17€ to 20€ to get into the center.

BY TRAIN

As Aragón's capital, Zaragoza is easily accessible by train from nearly every other major Spanish city. Fourteen trains arrive daily from Barcelona (22€, trip time: 3½ hr.), 18 from Madrid (40€, trip time: 1½ hr.), and 5 from Pamplona (17€, trip time: 2 hr.). The train station **Estación Zaragoza-Delicias** (☎ 902-116-680 or 902-240-202; www.renfe.es) is on **Calle Rioja** a bit west of town, and if you're headed for the center, you can take **bus no. 51** from the station to **Paseo de la Constitución** (.80€, leaves approximately every 12 min.).

Note: If you're traveling by rail pass, remember your pass is only valid on the slower-than-Christmas regional trains, and

cuidado! Know before You Go

Public transportation in Aragón is virtually nonexistent in most places save Zaragoza, so car rental is really the only way to see everything worth seeing. Just remember, like elsewhere in Europe, the majority of rentals are stick shifts. So unless you want to be like me and rent a car having never driven a manual before, only to end up stranded and broken down in the middle of an abandoned canyon, you should be sure to practice in advance of your trip.

Aragón

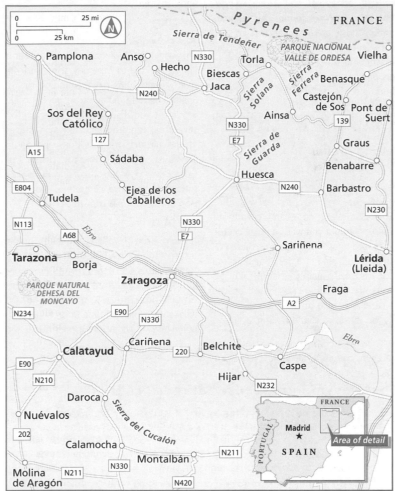

that should you go the high-speed route, you'll have to fork over additional cash by making a reservation in advance.

BY BUS

If you don't already possess a rail pass and are heading to Zaragoza from the Pyrenees, you might choose the **bus** instead. It's quicker, cheaper, and runs more frequently. Buses run frequently to all other major cities, including to and from Madrid every half-hour from 4:15am until 10pm (16€, trip time: 4 hr.), Barcelona at least 15 times a day (11€, trip time: 4 hr.), Pamplona eight times a day (11€, trip time: 2 hr.), Huesca every half-hour (5.50€, trip time: 1 hr.), Jaca five times daily (12€, trip time: 2½ hr.), and Tarazona four times daily (6€, trip time: 1 hr.).

The primary **bus station** (Paseo de María Agustín 7; ☎ **976-300-045**) is where the two main operators, **Ágreda Automóvil (www.agredasa.es)** and **Alosa (www. alosa.es)**, can be found. In summer months, Alosa provides services to and from select French cities including Lourdes and Pau.

BY CAR

If you're **driving** from **Madrid** to Zaragoza, take the **E90** headed east. From **Barcelona**, take the **AP2** or **E90** west.

Getting Around

BY BUS

The city has an extensive **bus service** (☎ **976-592-727**; www.tuzsa.es) with lines that reach every nook and cranny of Zaragoza. Should you want a more scenic as opposed to practical bus ride, there is a **tourist bus** from Plaza del Pilar that hits all of Zaragoza's main tourist attractions. Tickets are 4€, can be purchased on the bus, and are valid all day. Buses depart only on Saturday, Sunday, and holidays every 15 minutes from 10:30am to 1:15pm and 5 to 8pm.

BY CAR

You certainly don't need a **car** to get around within Zaragoza's city limits, but if you're looking to take day trips into the nearby mountains or surrounding towns, Spain's shoddy public transport system won't get you there quickly. Zaragoza has several car-rental agencies like **Avis** (offices at the airport, train station, and Santa Orosia 21; ☎ **976-489-236**), **Hertz** (Av. Goya 61; ☎ **976-320-400**), and **Europcar** (offices at the airport, train station, and Hernán Cortés 31; ☎ **902-105-030**).

BY TAXI

If you're tired of walking and taking public transportation, **tourist taxis** offer broad tour services (☎ **976-751-515**). For more information, call central **tourist information** (☎ **902-201-212** or **976-201-200**). On weekends, 5am is a prime time for heading home once most bars shut their doors and

Talk of the Town

Four Ways to Start a Conversation with a Local

1. **"Where's the best party in this town?"** If you're lucky, and happen to throw this question across the path of a student, you may just be invited to one of the exclusive, never dull, university parties around Plaza de San Francisco. Zaragoza locals are friendly and always happy to invite a foreigner along for a wild night, so don't be shy.

2. **"Why do the bars in Zaragoza close earlier than other Spanish cities?"** Just prepare for an angry outburst about how unfair it is that bars shut down at 4:30am when they used to never close, how it's disrupted the party vibe in a city that never slept, and how the government has no respect for the Spanish youth. Hang in there through the whining, and you might snag a tip on where you can party after hours.

3. **"So what's the deal with this Virgen del Pilar chick?"** If you want the 411 on *Nuestra Señora del Pilar,* her significance to Zaragoza, and why the city's biggest festival is in her honor, who better to ask than a native?

4. **"What exactly is with all these mullets?"** On second thought, maybe it's wise to not mention the fact that many Zaragozans—male and female— were born in the wrong decade . . .

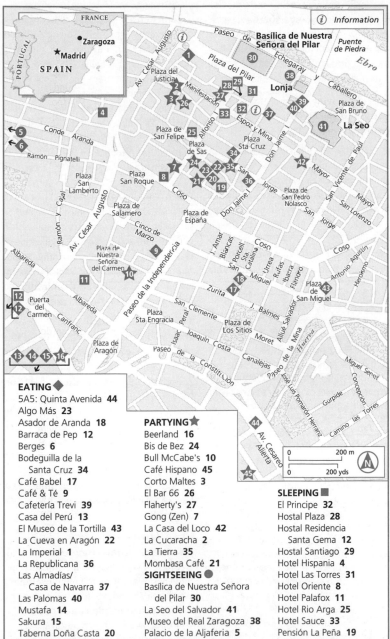

EATING ◆

5A5: Quinta Avenida **44**
Algo Más **23**
Asador de Aranda **18**
Barraca de Pep **12**
Berges **6**
Bodeguilla de la
  Santa Cruz **34**
Café Babel **17**
Café & Té **9**
Cafetería Trevi **39**
Casa del Perú **13**
El Museo de la Tortilla **43**
La Cueva en Aragón **22**
La Imperial **1**
La Republicana **36**
Las Almadías/
  Casa de Navarra **37**
Las Palomas **40**
Mustafa **14**
Sakura **15**
Taberna Doña Casta **20**

PARTYING ★

Beerland **16**
Bis de Bez **24**
Bull McCabe's **10**
Café Hispano **45**
Corto Maltes **3**
El Bar 66 **26**
Flaherty's **27**
Gong (Zen) **7**
La Casa del Loco **42**
La Cucaracha **2**
La Tierra **35**
Mombasa Café **21**

SIGHTSEEING ●

Basílica de Nuestra Señora
  del Pilar **30**
La Seo del Salvador **41**
Museo del Real Zaragoza **38**
Palacio de la Aljaferia **5**

SLEEPING ■

El Principe **32**
Hostal Plaza **28**
Hostal Residencia
  Santa Gema **12**
Hostal Santiago **29**
Hotel Hispania **4**
Hotel Las Torres **31**
Hotel Oriente **8**
Hotel Palafox **11**
Hotel Rio Arga **25**
Hotel Sauce **33**
Pensión La Peña **19**

ARAGÓN

the lines for clubs have become a discouraging length, so if you're looking to catch a cab, call ahead (☎ 974-362-848, 976-751-515, or 976-424-242) or start your search a half-hour before the rush. Most taxis pass through El Casco, but if you're not having any luck, head farther down to Plaza España or Plaza Aragón instead.

Zaragoza Basics

ORIENTATION

The majority of what's happening in Zaragoza takes place south of Río Ebro within the old city limits between Avenida César Augusto and El Coso in Casco Histórico. The majority of backpackers spend the bulk of their time in Casco Histórico (often referred to as Casco Vieja), home to most of Zaragoza's historic buildings and monuments. Plaza del Pilar

A Euro Saved . . .

If you're planning a whirlwind tour of the city, the Zaragoza Card could be the way to go. At 12€ for 1 day, 17€ for 2, or 22€ for 3, you gain admission to all of the city's sites and museums for a consecutive 24, 48, or 72 hours, respectively, from the first time you use the card. Keep in mind that many of Zaragoza's main attractions are free (like it's central draw, El Pilar), and unless you're planning on visiting every tourist hot spot the city has to offer, it could end up being a waste of money. However, it may be worth it if you travel by public transit because, along with the card, you receive a number of free trips on the local bus. You also get discounts at many restaurants, bars, hotels, and car-rental agencies, as well as travel on the two tourist bus lines that stop at all the major sites.

is the center of daytime motion and a great place to nurse that looming hangover.

Zona Centro is the very center of town, surrounding the twin squares Plazas de Aragón and Paraíso and including the city's main promenade, Paseo de la Independencia. Here you'll find a good number of the city's finest hotels as well as a scattering of street-side cafes. The tapas zone is El Tubo, bordered by Calle el Coso to the south, Río Ebro to the north, Calle de San Vicente de Paúl to the west, and Avenida de Augosto to the west.

As far as nightlife is concerned, El Casco, Zaragoza's party central just south of Plaza del Pilar, is the place to see and be seen. Beside the university campus south of Gran Vía, you'll also find a collection of unassuming bars, cafes, shops, and restaurants around Plaza de San Francisco and along Calle Corona de Aragón and Calle Tomás Bretón.

TOURIST OFFICES

Walk-in offices are at Plaza del Pilar (☎ 976-393-537; www.turismozaragoza. com; daily 10am–8pm) and inside Zaragoza-Delicias Railway Station (☎ 976-324-468; daily 9am–8pm). Other branches are located at Glorieta de Pio XII (☎ 976-201-200; Mon–Sat 10am–2pm and 4:30–8pm, Sun 10am–2pm), the auditorium of the Conference Palace at Calle Eduardo Ibarra 3 (☎ 976-721-327; Mon–Fri 8am–3pm), and Zaragoza Trade Fair Centre (☎ 976-764-700; open when trade fairs are held).

RECOMMENDED WEBSITES

○ www.zaragozaturismo.es: An overall review of what to do in the city, this is the best place to go to familiarize yourself with Zaragoza before you arrive.

○ www.aragonguide.com: One of the most detailed websites on Zaragoza, don't hesitate to visit Aragón Guide for more history on the region and the

wwwired

If you're toting around your laptop, you can pick up a **wireless** connection just about anywhere in Zaragoza. Official Wi-Fi zones are **Plaza del Pilar, Plaza San Francisco,** and **Centro Independencia** (on Paseo de la Independencia). If you don't have your own computer handy, **Cyber Café El Navegante** (C. Mayor 53) charges 1.20€ per half-hour of surfing. You can get online at **Conecta-T** (Murallas Romanas 4; ☎ **976-205-979;** Mon–Fri 10am–11pm, Sat 11am–11pm) next to the central market, where you can also **change your money** or use one of the headsets to call home over the Internet.

Pyrenees, as well as additional monuments, historical sites, and alternative attractions.

- **www.aragonturismo.com**: If my recs aren't enough for you, you can find further things to do and see on this regional tourist site with an English version.
- **www.ayto-zaragoza.es**: Amid the local politics on this government website, you will find useful maps and public transportation information.

- **www.redaragon.com**: An overview of what's going on in Zaragoza, this is a Spanish-only guide to festivals and concerts in the area, as well as other cultural trivia.
- **www.turismozaragoza.com**: This one-stop tourism website covers pretty much everything you need to know about traveling in Zaragoza.
- **www.unizar.es**: This home for *Universidad de Zaragoza* will provide you with some insight into the haps around town, as well as a bit of background info about the region.

CULTURE TIPS 101

The region's most revered artist Francisco Goya was born near Zaragoza in 1746. After studying here and there around Spain and journeying to Rome where he won a painting competition, Goya returned to Zaragoza and painted part of the cupola at the Basilica del Pilar. Goya then ventured into the world of royalty after painting portraits for many Spanish counts, dukes, and duchesses before he left Spain for Bordeaux, France, where he eventually died. Many products by the famed painter and printmaker can be seen all over Aragón—including inside El Pilar—although his most well-known works are housed at the Museo del Prado in Madrid.

Zaragoza Nuts & Bolts

Currency At **Internet Change** (C. Jardiel just beside El Pilar; Mon—Wed 10:30am–10pm, Thurs–Sun 10:30am–2:30pm and 5–10pm) you can exchange or transfer money, check your e-mail (prices start at .60€ per 15 min.), or use the fax or telephone services. You can also head to **Western Union** (on César Augusto) should you need to have money wired to you, though you'll obviously get your best exchange rate by using one of the city's many **ATMs**—however, take note: Some services like **Caja Madrid** don't except foreign cards.

Emergencies If you catch a bout of the Spanish flu or have other burdensome ailments, high-tail it to **Hospital Miguel Servet** on **Paseo de Isabel la Católica**

(☎ 976-765-500) or **Hospital Clinico Universitario** at the university (☎ 976-556-400). For immediate assistance, the **Policía Local** (☎ 092) is on **Calle de Domingo Miral.**

Luggage Storage   Most respectable hostels or hotels will let you leave your bags there before or after you check out. Many places have luggage rooms, so if you arrive hours before check-in, you can still drop off your stuff and head out to see the sights.

Pharmacies   If you need over-the-counter medication for that nasty traveler's diarrhea or just need something to relieve the lingering pain of last night's tequila shots, **pharmacies** are denoted by large, lit **green crosses.** Just have your Spanish dictionary handy—having to explain your symptoms by hand gestures can be awkward.

Post Office   Don't forget to send a letter home every once in awhile so your momma doesn't post your stuff on Craigslist. Head to the **main post office** (Paseo de la Independencia; ☎ **915-963-006**) just south of Plaza de España, open Monday through Friday from 8:30am to 8:30pm and Saturday 9:30am to 2pm. You can also **change money** at the Western Union inside. For post office **information** or to find other branches, phone ☎ **902-197-197.**

Safety   Zaragoza is generally pretty safe for a big city. Just exercise typical precautions—like keeping your personal belongings close to you and making sure you're not alone when headed home late at night.

Sleeping

Should you not phone ahead for a room prior to your visit, get ready to hear the phrase *están completos* (we're fully booked), no matter the time of the year. You'd be wise to book weeks, sometimes months, in advance. Still, accommodations are plentiful and range from the three-, four-, and five-star hotels around **Plaza España, Paseo de la Independencia,** and **Paseo de le Constitución** to many hostels and pensions in Zaragoza's prosperous **Casco Histórico.** Pick up a list of all hotels and prices in the tourist information office.

HOSTELS

➔**Hostal Plaza** The same crotchety old man who runs Hostal Santiago owns this hostel, just meters away from the other. He's not the friendliest—in fact, I found him rude and completely unpleasant—and

will pretend to not understand a word you say. Amenities and decor are similar to Santiago, though this hostel seems to fill up more quickly and is a tad bit pricier. *Plaza del Pilar 14. ☎ 976-294-830. www.hostal plaza-santiago.com. Single 25€, double 38€. Amenities: Elevator, sheets, towels. In room: A/C, TV. Bus: 22, 23, 30, 33, 36, 45.*

➔**Hostal Santiago** The deep green interior of the rooms is alluring, as is this three-star hostel's location right in the middle of all the activity. Every room but two has a shower, some with bathtubs, though toilets are shared. As far as hostels go, there's nothing special about Santiago, and it has no frills to offer other than its cleanliness, relatively inexpensive prices, and sheer convenience. *Santiago 3-5, right beside Plaza del Pilar. ☎ 976-394-550. www. hostalplaza-santiago.com. Single 20€, double 36€. Amenities: Elevator, sheets. In room: A/C, TV. Bus: 22, 23, 30, 33, 36, 45.*

CHEAP

➜ **Hostal-Residencia Santa Gema** The rooms provoked memories of my childhood nursery at my grandmother's house, but they are cheap. The trade-off is you'll be a bit of a distance from the bars of Casco Histórico, though just a 5-minute walk from the university campus and its surrounding attractions. *Santander 3.* ☎ *976-353-090. Single 18€–24€, double 23€–31€. Amenities: Parking, TV. In room: TV. Bus: 22, 23, 30, 33, 36, 45.*

➜ **Hotel Sauce** The name of this two-star alone is misleading, as there's definitely nothing saucy about it. In fact, as far as accommodation goes, I'd say it's the diet, low-calorie, sodium-free option. But just 100m (330 ft.) from Plaza del Pilar, this place is often full anyway. Bottom line: You can get more for your money elsewhere. *Espoz y Mina 33.* ☎ *976-205-050. www.hotel sauce.com. Double 91€. Amenities: Cafeteria, laundry, parking. In room: A/C, Internet, safe, TV. Bus: 22, 23, 30, 33, 36, 45.*

➜ **Pensión La Peña** With chipping paint, peek-hole skylights that seem to have materialized after someone dropped a wrecking ball through the roof, and the occasional hair on the pillow from last night's visitor, La Peña isn't exactly the Hilton. The one hall shower can't decide between hot and cold, off or on, and the owners aren't exactly speedy with things like payment, fixing the hot/cold–off/on shower, or on-the-ball with things like not temporarily misplacing passports. However, at this price, what more can you expect? La Peña is one of the cheapest joints in town and its location—directly in the center of town just feet from El Casco's hopping bars—makes up for what it lacks in appeal. *Clinegio 3.* ☎ *976-299-089. 15€ double bed with single occupancy (18€ double occupancy). Amenities: Breakfast room. Bus: 22, 23, 30, 33, 36, 45.*

DOABLE

➜ **El Principe** Part of the Best Western chain, this government-rated three-star is next to Plaza del Pilar and comfortable enough, though more catered toward businesspeople and definitely lacking in originality and character. If you're looking for ambience, search elsewhere. If you simply don't care, then El Principe is a satisfactory, affordable option in a nice part of town. It's full much of the time due to congressional activity, so always call ahead. *Santiago 12.* ☎ *976-294-101. www.hotel-el principe.com. Single 59€, double 78€. Amenities: Restaurant, cafeteria, elevator, Internet, parking (9€ per day). In room: A/C, TV, hair dryer, Internet, minibar. Bus: 22, 23, 30, 33, 36, 45.*

➜ **Hotel Hispania** ★ This hotel isn't that big, yet I was continuously lost due to its various staircases, corridors, and elevators. With more personality than most, this stylish yet affordable two-star has a central location and an atmospheric charisma with a sort of romantic air to its coziness. What it lacks in outward appearance, it makes up for in comfort. And its ongoing promotional prices aren't anything to scoff at either. *Av. César Agosto 95-103.* ☎ *976-284-928. www.hotelhispania.com. Single 55€–90€, double 55€–90€, extra bed 12€. Parking available for 12€ a night. Amenities: Bar, breakfast room, elevator, TV. In room: A/C, TV, hair dryer, Internet. Bus: 22, 23, 30, 33, 36, 45.*

[MTV] **Best** ➜ **Hotel Las Torres** Who doesn't want to wake up each morning greeted by a balcony view of the magnificent towers of El Pilar? The rooms are all decorated alike in a fertile green that evokes pastoral images, but nonetheless, the main draw of this two-star is its proximity to, well, everything. *Plaza del Pilar 11.* ☎ *976-394-250 or 976-394-254. www.hotellas torres.com. Single 41€, double 55€, triple 65€.*

Amenities: Breakfast room, parking. In room: A/C, TV, hair dryer. Bus: 22, 23, 30, 33, 36, 45.

➔**Hotel Oriente** ★★ One of the classier (yet reasonably priced) lodges of its kind, Hotel Oriente is a more sophisticated option for the traveler with a little more dough to spend. Situated right dead in the city center just off Plaza de España, you'll always find a congressman or two lurking in its hallways. If you didn't bring a computer of your own, there is free Internet use on the computer in the lobby. This place is often filled to capacity during the week, so booking a month or more in advance is advised. Coso 11-13. ☎ 976-203-282. www.hotel-oriente.com. Single 57€–69€, double 57€–81€, triple 69€–96€, with the cheaper rates on the weekends. Amenities: Restaurant, breakfast room, bike rental, car rental, currency exchange, elevator, health services, Internet, laundry service, parking. In room: A/C, hair dryer, Internet, minibar, safe. Bus: 22, 23, 30, 33, 36, 45.

➔**Hotel Río Arga** ★ The rooms in this two-star are big and inviting, though the hotel is on the modest side. Still, it's convenient, some of the staff speak English, and the location is in one of the city's loveliest neighborhoods near El Pilar. Contamina 20. ☎ 976-399-065. Single 37€, double 56€, triple 70€. Amenities: Elevator, parking. In room: A/C, TV. Bus: 22, 23, 30, 33, 36, 45.

SPLURGE

➔**Hotel Palafox** ★★★ If you want to stay among the ranks of the Rolling Stones and Shakira, this is your hotel of choice. By far the swankiest place around, Palafox is the only five-star in Zaragoza and will put a slight dent in your wallet should you decide to crash there. The rooms have a seductive flair and are worth every penny. The stained glass of the corridors is stunning, as are the mirrored ceilings. All rooms are equipped with state-of-the-art entertainment systems complete with PlayStation. But even if you can't afford to live among the rich and famous for a night or two, you should stop by for a meal in one of the magnificent salons or a drink at the bar. Palafox also shares the building with Casino Zaragoza if you're looking for a little gambling action. Casa Jiménez s/n. ☎ 976-237-700 and 976-468-075. www.palafox hoteles.com. Single 150€ during the week, 101€ on weekend; double 178€ during the week, 101€ on weekend. Amenities: Elevator, garage, gym, Internet, laundry service, medical services, sauna, solarium, swimming pool (open June–Sept). In room: A/C, TV, hair dryer, Internet, iron, minibar.

Eating

At times, there seem to be more places to eat than there are people in Zaragoza, yet the majority of spots to grab a bite are tapas joints. **Calle de Estébanes** is the prime location for tapas, and you can easily start at one end and make your way to the other by having a *pincho* ("tapa" in northern Spain) and *bebida* (drink) in each one like the Spaniards do.

HOT SPOTS

MTV **Best** ➔**Bodeguilla de la Santa Cruz** MUDEJAR/ANDALUCIAN If you're plenty hungry or sharing a meal with a friend, head to Bodeguilla for the eight-tapas-for-11€ deal. However, your eyes may be bigger than your stomach, as the waitress presents you with an array of different regional delicacies, and I guarantee you'll be set for the evening. Just make sure to slip on your roomiest pants before taking on this tapas challenge. Bodeguilla is open for breakfast as well, with food-and-coffee combos starting around 2€. The rustic, mellow environment is good for socializing at the beginning of the evening. Santa Cruz 3. ☎ 976-200-018. www.bodeguilla santacruz.net. Mon–Sun noon–3pm and 7–11pm. Combos from 2€; tapas platter 11€. Bus: 22, 23, 30, 33, 36, 45.

➜**Las Almadías/Casa de Navarra** ★ NAVARRAN This quiet and sophisticated restaurant is hidden just off Plaza del Pilar and is open daily except for Monday with no particular hours. Rather, food is served when you're hungry. *Santiago 27.* ☎ *976-291-320. Entrees 12€–15€; tasting menu 18€. Bus: 22, 23, 30, 33, 36, 45.*

TAPAS

📺 (Best ●) ➜**Algo Más** With a wide-ranging selection of regional wines, Algo Más has plenty of options to quench your thirst after those platters full of tapas. If you know enough Spanish to get by and are interested in the neighboring wine region Rioja, from which many of the Algo Más products originate, you can pick the brain of the guy behind the bar and he'll give you the detailed history. *Estébanes 2.* ☎ *976-205-595. Tapas prices begin at 2€ a pop. Mon–Fri 8:15am–3pm and 7:30–11pm; Sat noon–4pm and 7:30pm–midnight. Bus: 22, 23, 30, 33, 36, 45.*

➜**El Museo de la Tortilla** Make your own tapa at this bar, which specializes in, what else, but concoctions involving tortillas. Many are omelet-like (hence the tortilla part) on bread. A typical custom of Basque Country, the waiter will set out plates in front of you, and you take what you like, paying for each toothpick you leave behind. *Plaza San Miguel.* ☎ *976-293-911. Tapas prices begin at 2€. Mon–Sun 1–4pm and 7:30–11pm. Bus: 22, 23, 30, 33, 36, 45.*

➜**La Cueva en Aragón** This illuminated, smoky tapas paradise is always packed to the brim, with people spilling out onto the streets. Try the house specialty, a tapa that consists of a piece of bread drenched in garlic sauce and topped off with mushrooms and shrimp. *Libertad 16 at the intersection of Call Estébanes.* ☎ *976-204-645. Tapas prices begin at 1€. Open daily except Mon. Bus: 22, 23, 30, 33, 36, 45.*

➜**La Republicana** Owned by the same people as Bodeguilla, La Republicana has a more Spanish retro flair than its sister establishment with its wall decorations and old-fashioned piano. Though it also offers eight tapas for 11€, you can also try more exotic dishes like the *courgette* (zucchini) or curried chicken with pineapple. *Méndez Núñez 38.* ☎ *976-396-509. www.la republicana.net. Sun–Thurs 8:30am–4:30pm and 6pm–midnight; Fri–Sat 8:30am–4:30pm and 6pm–2am. Bus: 22, 23, 30, 33, 36, 45.*

➜**Taberna Doña Casta** If you're working your way down Calle Estébanes, make this tapas bar one of your stops and sample the house specialty, *setas,* a piping hot bowl of assorted mushrooms. *Estébanes 6 at the corner of Libertad.* ☎ *976-205-852. Tapas prices begin at 2€. Open daily, even Mon when its neighboring tapas bars aren't. Bus: 22, 23, 30, 33, 36, 45.*

CHEAP

➜**5A5: Quinta Avenida** ★ BOCADILLOS If you need a break from tapas and full-course meals in the middle of the day, Quinta has an extensive sandwich menu with more than 100 choices. My biggest dilemma here was choosing which one. Most sandwiches cost between 4€ and 6€ and are made with a type of potato flat bread. Dine outside at one of the tables right next to Paseo de Constitución. *León XIII 2.* ☎ *976-238-193. Mon–Fri 1–4:30pm and 7:30pm–midnight; Sat–Sun 1–4:30pm and 7:30pm–1am.*

DOABLE

➜**Barraca de Pep** VALENCIAN Mmm, paella. You won't find this delightful mishmash in a whole lot of places in Aragón, as it is typical of the south and east coasts. So if you haven't ever tasted the seafood-and-rice mixture, I suggest you get on that. Take-away is also an option. *Pamplona*

Escudero 34. ☎ *976-555-943. Average entree 12€. Daily 1–4pm and 8:30pm–midnight. Bus: 35.*

➔ **Casa del Perú** PERUVIAN   If the sight of yet another tapas place gives you pangs of agony, try out a tasty alternative at this South American joint. If you're adventuresome or simply a self-professed alcoholic, order a *pisco sour* (an interesting combo of egg white, lemon juice, and grape brandy) to wash down your meal. *Santa Teresa de Jesús 2.* ☎ *976-563-873. Average entree 15€. Daily 1:30–4pm and 8:30pm–midnight.*

➔ **Las Palomas** ★ SPANISH   I can assure you that you won't stumble across an open-ended buffet of this magnitude elsewhere in Zaragoza (or possibly in Spain). So if you're famished to the brink of delirium, there's nowhere better to satiate your hunger than this all-you-can-eat buffet for just 10€, which includes paella, salads, tapas, desserts, and other regional food. Lunch is served beginning at 1pm, and dinner starts at 8:30pm. *Plaza del Pilar 16 at the corner of Calle Don Jaine I.* ☎ *976-392-366. Buffet 10€. Bus: 22, 23, 30, 33, 36, 45.*

➔ **Mustafa** LEBANESE   Fans of *Arabian Nights* will appreciate the themed embellishments at this relatively new restaurant featuring typical Lebanese dishes like hummus, couscous, and kabobs. Just don't forget to save room for dessert—the baklava is fab. *Latassa 32.* ☎ *976-355-201. Average entree 10€–14€. Daily 1–4pm and 8:30pm–midnight. Bus: 30, 40, 45.*

➔ **Sakura** JAPANESE   If you can't go long without your fill of sushi, or simply want a takeout option (they're rare in Spain), you can try out the Spanish version of the popular raw cuisine at this Japanese restaurant near the university. *Fernando el Católico 51.* ☎ *976-562-721. Average entree 12€. Daily 1–4pm and 8pm–midnight. Bus: 30, 40, 45.*

SPLURGE

➔ **Asador de Aranda** SPANISH   It's no secret that a big draw to this dressed-up Castilian inn is the decor, like a real live version of something you would read about in *Don Quixote.* The restaurant does offer a selection of regional game, with the house specialty being the roast spring lamb. *Arquitecto Magdalena 6.* ☎ *976-226-417. Average entree 24€. Mon–Sat 1–3:30pm and 9–11:30pm; Sun 1–3:30pm.*

➔ **Berges** SPANISH   Open for more than 40 years and still operated by the same family who founded it, this enormous restaurant near the train station fits 400 people but caters more toward the business crowd. But if you are looking to stray from the tapas mob and try some more regional cuisine like paella or monkfish marinara in a more urbane setting, maybe the business suits and over-40 crowd won't deter you. *Av. de Navarra 34.* ☎ *976-331-020. Average entree 18€. Daily 1–4pm and 9–11:30pm. Bus: 26, 35.*

CAFES

➔ **Café & Té**   With branches scattered throughout the country, this Spanish answer to Starbucks is even decked out in the signature green color. The coffee, tea, and Spanish hot chocolate are all quite good, even if prices are a bit steep. But Café & Té does serve food all day, so when you're not accustomed to Spanish hours and looking for something to eat before the standard opening time of 9pm, here's your place. Drinks range from 2€ to 5€ depending on how fancy you go, while food is 5€ to 10€. *Paseo de la Independencia.* ☎ *976-235-209. Sun–Thurs 6:30am–12:30am; Fri–Sat 6:30am–2:30am.*

Best ➔ **Café Babel**   Sugary sweet mugs of piping hot chocolate (3€) greet you at this fashionable joint that boasts 32 flavors of the thick creamy stuff. The contemporary decor and melodic jazz tunes make for a cozy cafe night should you need a mellow break. *Jerónimo Zurita 21.* ☎ *976-236-115. Mon–Thurs 8:45am–1am; Fri–Sat 8:45pm–3am.*

➔ **Cafetería Trevi** One of the few places you'll get a full meal for a reasonable price, this cafe near La Seo unbelievably offers a three-course menu with wine for under 10€, while a cup of joe goes for 2€. *Plaza de la Seo 2. No phone. Hours vary. Bus: 22, 23, 30, 33, 36, 45.*

➔ **La Imperial** This cafe just off of Plaza del Pilar is an ideal place to sit on the terrace away from the tourists in the square and enjoy a nice cup of coffee and a *churro.* Just don't expect personal attention (or friendly service) from the servers—with the response you receive, you'd think you were doing them a favor by picking their cafe to dine in among the hundreds of others Zaragoza has to offer. Coffee costs roughly 2€ a cup, while *churros* go for 1.50€ a pop. *At the intersection of Plaza de Cesar Augusto and Calle Salduba.* ☎ *976-294-549. Sun–Fri 8am–2am; Sat 11am–3:30am. Bus: 22, 23, 30, 33, 36, 45.*

Partying

"We were just wondering what happened to you last night? Is everything all right? Why did you go in so early?" That was the phone call I received the morning after partying with my new Spanish friends for the fourth consecutive night. True, I had gone in early—early in the morning, that is. After starting the evening at 8pm, bar-hopping to practically every disco, pub, and club in Zaragoza, and finally hitting the pillow at 6:30am, I thought I'd done well for myself. Apparently not, according to Zaragoza standards.

You could live in Zaragoza most of your life and still not visit half of the bars, clubs, and discothèques hidden in the never-ending, interlaced side streets of

📺 ⓑ**Best**❶ **El Casco** (literally meaning "the helmet"). From Thursday to Saturday, the city center absolutely explodes in a cheerful, drunken frenzy. Prior to 2006, the bars rarely, if ever, closed, but a recent law enforced a city-wide closing time of 4:30am, upsetting the predominant youth population of Zaragoza and rightfully so. A favorite pastime of Zaragoza students is staying out until breakfast, grabbing a bit to eat and sober up, then finally hitting the pillow at 9am or so. A few select discothèques have managed to stay open until morning, and the city's relentless partiers frequent these venues once the other bars and clubs close down for the night.

BARS

➔ **Beerland** If the name alone doesn't draw you in, maybe the Bavarian style of this traditional German beer hall will. Right next to the university campus, you'll always find a student or two here grabbing a pint of the house specialties on tap like *Augustijn* or *Franziskaner,* or watching whatever sporting event is on at the moment. Just make this your first stop for the night, as it shuts down early. Native German dishes are also available if you skipped out on tapas earlier in the evening. *Plaza de San Francisco 17.* ☎ *976-560-603. Bus: 30, 40, 45.*

➔ **Bis de Bez** This dimly lit, swanky lounge looks like it belongs more in Manhattan than amid the monotonous tapas bars of Calle Estébanes. It's more than a bit suggestive in its vaguely phallic art and decor, but if you're going upscale, it might be worth trying out. Its slogan is "No strangers, but friends you've not met yet," which in my opinion translates to "No strangers, but people you've not slept with yet." So if you're looking to sample the local, ahem, flavor, you just might get the opportunity at Bis de Bez. *Estébanes 2. No phone. Bus: 30, 33, 36, 45.*

➜**Bull McCabe's** You didn't think I forgot about the cliché Irish bar, now did you? This cheerful pub remains a popular midtown watering hole due to its two floors and immense volume, and like any other European city, you'll find your hodgepodge of nationalities here, though it is more a starting point for the evening than anything else. *Cadíz 7.* ☎ *976-225-016. Bus: 30, 33, 45.*

➜**Café Hispano** For live music by talented professionals and not-so-talented crowd members, this lively bar is a good place to get your drink on. *Camino de las Torres 42.* ☎ *976-222-161.*

➜**Flaherty's** "With every pint, there's a lot of love." Such is the motto of the bartenders at the friendly bar near El Pilar. The best draw of this atypical Irish pub is its weekday happy hour from 7 to 9pm in which you can down all the Budweiser and Amstel your stomach can hold in 2 hours time for 1€ a bottle. Irish breakfasts and light snacks are also available. *Alfonso I 39.* ☎ *976-298-094. www.paddyflaherty.com. Bus: 30, 33, 36, 45.*

➜**Gong (Zen)** This Asian-infused bar is extremely trendy and modern with a diverse assortment of world music and minimalist, yet colorful decor. If you prefer cocktails to pints, Gong (Zen) is your man. Popular with the gay crowd and those not so keen on pub atmosphere. *Alfonso I 13.* ☎ *976-392-590. www.gongzgz.com. Bus: 30, 33, 36, 45.*

➜**La Cucaracha** ★ You enter the smoky establishment, and it doesn't take you long to figure out why its name literally translates to "the cockroach." Sketchy men grinding up next to you make it hard to penetrate (excuse the verbal selection) the sweaty masses, and *"Tienes un novio?"* ("Do you have a boyfriend?") will be thrown your way more than once. Yet, for some reason, this bar is always packed—especially with foreigners and those looking for one-night stands—though it remains a favorite of permanent Zaragoza inhabitants as well. *El Temple 25. No phone. Bus: 30, 33, 36, 45.*

📺 **Best ●** ➜**Mombasa Café** ★★ The first thing I noticed about this eccentric place is its hot (mostly female, guys take note) waitstaff and animal print tables and chairs. The choice of music, which ranges from Doors favorites to American hip-hop, is a bit odd given the bar's ambience, but this colonial cafe is a suitable alternative to the bump-and-grind Spanish disco bar. It's also open on Mondays, while many other places in Zaragoza aren't, which is a definite plus if you're a 7-days-a-week type of socialite. *Cuarto de Agosto 9. No phone. Bus: 30, 33, 36 45.*

DISCO PUBS/CLUBS

➜**Corto Maltes** ★ If the roaches on the entryway and the eye-catching artwork behind the bar (naked women adorn the walls) aren't enough to draw you in, perhaps the music will—or the fact that this dance bar is roomier than its stuffy next-door neighbor La Cucaracha. Beers cost 3€, while the bar's specialty shots can be purchased for 2€. The music's not bad with a wide range of hot Spanish tunes. *El Temple 21-23. No phone. Bus: 30, 33, 36, 45.*

➜**El Bar 66** ★★ Formerly a monastery, this Bat Cave of a music bar is worth a trip if you're up for a night of dancing and a suitable mix of native Spanish and popular American/English music. Drink prices are a bit steep (5€ for a cocktail) after enjoying cheap beer and tapas earlier in the evening, but the medieval feel of the stone-walled multi-levels of El Bar 66 is appealing and the dance floor more spacious than most. *Entrances on both Calle Santa Isabel and Calle el Temple. No phone. Bus: 30, 33, 36, 45.*

📺 Best♀ → **La Tierra** With three branches in town, the most popular located in Casco Histórico, La Tierra is your typical American dance bar with that familiar American music from the past 3 decades, typical English speakers, and your typical crowd of international students. The drinks are cheap, and if you're looking to speak in your native tongue, you can almost be guaranteed this is the place you'll excel. *Mendez Nuñez 16-18.* ☎ *976-232-030. www.latierra.org. Bus: 30, 33, 36, 45.*

LIVE MUSIC

📺 Best♀ → **La Casa del Loco** ★★ Should you need another reason to visit one of the only places open till first light, the name of this most popular club in town translates to "The House of the Crazy." The late-night/early-morning hot spot really fills up beginning around 4:30am when all the other bars in the area begin to shut their doors, so head there a bit earlier to avoid the line that snakes its way all the way down the street and around the corner. Every Thursday features live concerts. *Mayor 10.* ☎ *976-396-771. www.lacasadelloco. com. Cover 5€–10€. Bus: 30, 33, 36, 45.*

Sightseeing

Zaragoza's sights are more or less framed by Río Ebro to the north, Avenida Cesar Augosto to the west, and Paseo Constitución to the south. Museums and churches generally open between 9:30 and 10:30am and close their doors mid-afternoon for siesta, reopening between 4 and 5:30pm. Admission to all sights is included with purchase of the Zaragoza Card (p. 304), though many of them are free in the first place.

📺 Best♀ → **Basílica de Nuestra Señora del Pilar** Without a doubt the city's most recognizable monument, this 16th- and 17th-century church should be

Get Connected . . .

Want to experience a bit of the local flava but don't know anyone in town? Check out a backpacker service like **hospitalityclub.org** or **couchsurfing.com**, which allow you to create profiles and browse through those of others living in the city you're visiting. If you view a profile that sparks your interest, you can send the person a message and maybe even schedule a (platonic) rendezvous. (*Note:* This is not a dating service and the webmasters will trash any amorous messages.) If you're skint on cash and don't mind taking up lodging with a complete stranger, you can also find someone to host you for a night or two while in town. Sign up a few weeks before your trip, as it often takes awhile for membership to go through.

your first stop. Thousands of people visit the chapel each year to pay homage to the tiny statue of *Virgen del Pilar* in the Holy Chapel. The name "El Pilar" comes from the pillar upon which the Virgin supposedly stood when she asked Santiago (St. James) to build the church. During the second week of October, the church is a backdrop for an important festival devoted to the Virgin, with parades, bullfights, fireworks, flower offerings, and street dancing. Locally born Goya is responsible for painting some of the church's awe-inspiring frescoes. The **Museo Pilarista** in the back of the church houses a rich, ancient collection of stunning jewelry, as well as sketches and other artwork by Goya, Bayeu, and others. *Plaza del Pilar 19.* ☎ *976-299-564. Admission to the cathedral is free; museum 2€. Cathedral Tues–Sun 7am–8:30pm. Museum daily 9:30am–2pm and 4–6pm (4–7pm in the summer). Bus: 22, 23, 30, 33, 36, 45.*

12 Hours in . . .

1. **Devour a mug of thick, piping-hot Spanish chocolate.** If you can do without your coffee fix, substitute your morning cup of Joe for Spain's famous soupy hot cocoa.

2. **Wander around Plazas del Pilar and La Seo.** Admire the stunning architecture of two of Zaragoza's most visited churches—Basílica de Nuestra Señora del Pilar and La Seo del Salvador—or just soak up the sun while people-watching in the plazas that surround them.

3. **Visit Aljaferia.** If there's one tourist attraction you don't want to miss, it's this magnificent Islamic palace chock-full of works of Mudéjar art.

4. **Siesta in Parque Primo de Rivera.** When everything else shuts down for mid-afternoon siesta, don't be the only one not catching your zzz's (you'll need it for the pending night). With hundreds of acres of green, you can always find a plot of grass to lay your head.

5. **Shop along Paseo de la Independencia.** Memories, priceless. For everything else . . . break out your plastic and take home a souvenir of your time in Spain.

6. **Sample the best tapas Zaragoza has to offer.** Visit ▥ Best❂ **El Tubo** and fill your belly by meandering down Calles Estébanes while trying a tapa or two at each native joint.

7. **Explore el Casco.** There's a reason all of the city flocks here once the sun goes down. Discover it for yourself by barhopping in Zaragoza's lively party district.

➔**La Seo del Salvador** Just as impressive, if not more so, than its neighbor El Pilar, La Seo is a reflection of Aragónese art. The construction of the cathedral commenced during the late 12th century, and important architectural elements from the period still remain. The north wall on the exterior of the church is a fine example of **Mudéjar** intricacies and a lingering reminder of one of the past royal families. Also worth a visit is **Los Tapices de La Seo,** a collection of remarkable Flemish and French tapestries within the church. *Plaza de La Seo s/n.* ☎ *976-291-231. www. cabildodezaragoza.org. Admission to museum 2€. Nov–Apr Tues–Fri 10am–1:30pm and 4–5:30pm, Sat 10am–noon and 4–5:30pm, Sun 10–11:30am and 4–5:30pm; May–Oct Tues–Fri 10am–1:30pm and 4–6:30pm, Sat 10am–noon and 4–6:30pm, Sun 10–11:30am and*

4–6:30pm. The museum is closed during the afternoon on Sun. Bus: 22, 23, 30, 33, 36, 45.

➔**Museo del Real Zaragoza** Soccer enthusiasts or Real Zaragoza fans can drop by this stadium and see all sorts of sports paraphernalia. Guided visits of the stadium and its various components are also available by phoning in advance. *Eduardo Ibarra.* ☎ *976-567-777. Admission 1€. Mon–Sat 10am–2pm and 5–8pm; Sun 11am–2pm. Bus: 20, 30, 35, 40, 45.*

▥ Best❂ ➔**Palacio de la Aljaferia** The seat of the Regional Assembly of Aragón, this Islamic palace is perhaps Zaragoza's most historical monument and one of the most emblematic reflections of Mudéjar art. The walls and archways are absolutely stunning in their detailed carvings and designs, and the open-air courtyard with pool is pleasant to visit during summer months. The moat surrounding the palace is also a nice place for relaxing or tossing around a Frisbee. *Los Diputados s/n.* ☎ *976-289-684. Admission 3€ adults, 1€ students with ID. Nov–Mar Sat–Wed 10am–2pm and 4–6:30pm, Fri 4–6:30pm; Apr–Oct Sat–Wed 10am–2pm and 4:30–8pm, Fri 4:30–8pm.*

FESTIVALS/CALENDAR OF EVENTS

May

Primer Viernes de Mayo. The first Friday of every May, you can join in on the religious festival that celebrates Count Aznar's victory over the Moors in the 8th century thanks to help from the Jaca women. If you're contemplating a trip to Jaca, here's your time to go. The environment is friendly, and the beer flows freely.

June

Camino de Santiago Folk Festival. Every other year in Jaca, this international musical feast brings thousands of visitors to town for the last 2 weeks of June.

October

Fiestas del Pilar. On October 12, thousands of people in Zaragoza dress up for this national holiday of patriotism to pay homage to the Madonna el Pilar by bringing flowers to her in the plaza. The festivities last 9 days and include fireworks, street brass bands, dances, concerts, exhibitions, parades, and bullfights. The Mass of Infantes (child singers) also takes place on October 12 at dawn, and the street procession of 258 lanterns and 15 crystal floats—the Crystal Rosary—can be seen the following day.

Playing Outside

For a city its size, Zaragoza is surprisingly green. You won't have trouble finding a

International EXPOsure

If you're in Zaragoza before summer 2008, you can't miss the tents, signs, and buildings galore advertising **Expo 2008** (www.expozaragoza 2008.es). The International Bureau of Expositions granted Zaragoza the honor of hosting the 2008 conference on water and sustainable development, which will be attended by representatives of more than 80 countries. Sounds boring, right? Not necessarily so. Along with the expo comes scheduled activities and festivals. And just think: More people coming to the area means an even more promising nightlife experience.

place to spend the afternoon picnicking or resting up for another night out. To escape the city noise, 📺 Best ❾ **Parque Primo de Rivera** (Av. San Sebastian; Bus: 20, 30, or 40) is the place, with its combination of manicured landscape, natural ponds, and even a cascading waterfall. Leading from Sagasta Avenue to the Imperial Canal, **Parque de Pignatelli** (Bus: 33) is smaller and not quite as populated, but a nice lounging point if you find yourself south of the center. Snaking its way through the more cosmopolitan streets in town, **Paseo de la Constitución** (Bus: 33) has sufficient benches for relaxin' and munchin'.

At the end of Paseo de la Independencia, **Plaza de Aragón** (Bus: 30 or 40) was built to glorify Aragón as an autonomous region. Though the center of much daytime traffic, Plaza de Aragón is surrounded by green gardens where you can have a rest. **Plaza España** (Bus: 23, 30, 33, or 40), at the meeting of Avenida Independencia and Calle Coso, is the very center of Zaragoza and a great place to take a coffee at one of the many sunny sidewalk cafes and make fun of all the mullets that pass you by. If you're looking for fellow boarders or want to kick around a ball for a few, skateboarders and footballers crowd **Plaza de San Bruno** (eastern end of Plaza de la Seo; Bus: 22, 23, 30, 33, 36, or 45), particularly in midto late afternoon.

Shopping

If you've saved up your travel allowance for a shopping spree, Zaragoza won't disappoint. You'll find your large chain stores like **Zara, Mango,** and **Clockhouse** along **Paseo de la Independencia** and many cheaper options in Casco Histórico along Calle Don Jaimie III, Calle Alfonso I, and their intersecting streets. **El Corte Ingles,** *the* department store of Spain, has two branches right off of Independencia where you can surely find anything you're looking for in the overwhelming tall towers. East of **Paseo de la Constitución** are the more expensive boutiques and designer clothing stores. The most exclusive stores can be found on **Francisco de Vitoria, San Ignacio de Loyola, Cadiz,** and **Isaac**

Lights, Camera, Action!

Want to give your friends and parents back home visual proof that you have made it to Spain in one piece? Have your moment in the spotlight via the **webcam** in **Plaza del Pilar.** Arrange a time in advance that they'll be online and you'll be out and about, and give them a show-stopping performance. Just don't be surprised when you get weird looks for cartwheeling through the square . . . not many people are aware of the strategically placed camcorder. To view the live webcam, visit **www. turismo.ayto-zaragoza.es.**

Peral. Most shops keep business hours from 10am to 1:30pm and 5 to 8:30pm daily except Sunday.

➜**Alejandro** Smart-dressing men (aka metrosexuals) can invest in Spanish fashions at this popular male fashion stop. The store often has some pretty stellar sales and is the official supplier for the local soccer team. *Royo Urieta 20.* ☎ *976-220-225.*

➜**A Todo Trapo** You vintage lovers can check out the secondhand finds at this clothing shop and also contribute to a charitable cause—providing funds for reintegration projects—should you decide to purchase anything. *Méndez Núñez 9.* ☎ *976-297-747.*

➜**B60** B60 lodges an array of brightly colored and unique designer clothing for women, though they're not at all easy on the wallet. *Pedro Maria Ric 1.* ☎ *976-228-062.*

➜**Coronel Tapiocca** If you're heading into the mountains post-Zaragoza and need to stock up on outdoor goodies, you can most likely find all you need in this gear shop. *Centro Comercial Augusta at Av. Navarra 180.* ☎ *976-349-305. Another branch is located at the commercial center on Gran Casa.* ☎ *976-349-305.*

➜**Esenzia** A bit more punk rock than most of its neighbors in the area, Esenzia has alternative clothing selections for both males and females. *San Vicente de Paúl 23.* ☎ *976-201-676.*

➜**Lolita** Geared toward teeny-boppers and fashionable university students, this outlet aims for a mixture of sophistication and practicality through its assortment of clothes for women, as well as accessories galore. *Jerónimo Zurita 13.* ☎ *976-231-432.*

➜**Salam** Ethnic clothing, accessories, gifts, and other imported products can be found at this exotic store. With Peruvian, Aztec, Indonesian, and Kenyan objects,

Outdoor Explorer

Spain is the second most mountainous country in all of Europe, and accordingly, the Pyrenees are home to some of the nation's greatest outdoor sports. For **general information** on getting some fresh mountain air, we recommend Club Ibón de Orientación ☎ 976-372-311, Club de Montaña Pirineos, ☎ 976-298-787, Polideportivo de Caspe, ☎ 976-730-441, and Club de Montaña Peña Guara, ☎ 974-212-450. Other helpful contacts are listed by activity below.

→ **Mountain Excursions.** Federación Aragonesa de Montañismo, ☎ 976-227-971.

→ **Equestrian.** Federación Hipica Aragonesa, ☎ 976-730-904.

→ **Canyoning.** Federación Aragonesa de Espeleología, ☎ 976-730-434.

→ **Skiing, Snowboarding, and Mushing.** Federación Aragonesa de Deportes de Invierno, ☎ 976-742-968; and Club Mushing Litera, ☎ 974-420-142.

→ **Air Sports.** Federación Aragonesa de los Deportes Aéreos, ☎ 976-214-378.

→ **Watersports.** Federación Aragonesa de Actividades Subacuáticos, ☎ 976-730-120; and Federación Aragonesa de Piragüismo, ☎ 976-731-236.

→ **Cycling.** Federación Aragonesa de Ciclismo, ☎ 976-730-733.

you won't find this shop the slightest bit dull. *Lorente 50.* ☎ *976-561-138.*

Markets

El Rastro (Glorieta de José Aznarez; Sun 8:30am–2pm) is a flea market situated outside the bullring with a random hodgepodge of antiques and other household goods. Ideal for bargain hunters and lovers of bric-a-brac. Cheaply priced clothing, accessories, and linens can be found at **Mercadillo La Romareda** (outside Romareda Football Stadium; Wed and Sun 9am–2:30pm), Zaragoza's largest open-air market. On Sunday mornings, paintings and crafts are on display at **Plaza de Santa Cruz.** In case you have room to fill in your bag, **Plaza de San Bruno** unleashes an antiques market on Sunday mornings.

Calatayud

When I told Zaragoza locals that I was headed to Calatayud next, I was met with obvious stares that said more than words. I understood every unspoken word when I arrived in the ramshackle town. Calatayud's dilapidated interiors and ongoing construction around every corner do nothing whatsoever to enhance its already understated outward appearance. Its scant offerings are its works of Mudéjar art and an attractive church scattered here and there, like **St. Peter of the Francos, Sepulchre, St. Andrew's,** **College Church of St. Mary,** and **St. John the Royal.** And oh yeah—Calatayud is the closest stop to **Monasterio de Piedra,** just 28km (17 miles) from one of the region's most beautiful settings. For all you eternal optimists dead set on making the most of the town, you can drop by the **tourist office** at Plaza de la Fuerte (☎ **976-886-322),** open Tuesday through Saturday from 10am to 1pm and 4 to 7pm, and Sunday from 10am to1pm.

Calatayud is a stop on the main rail line from Madrid to Zaragoza. Fifteen **trains** a day chug in from Madrid (29€, trip time: 1¹/₄ hr.), nine from Zaragoza (6€, trip time: 1 hr.), and 15 from Barcelona (45€, trip time: 5 hr.). Three or four **buses** make the run from Zaragoza (6€, trip time: 1¹/₂ hr.). If you can afford to have your own **car,** take the **E-90** toward Madrid.

Eating & Sleeping

If you're planning a day at the monastery, Calatayud is a good place to lay your head as hotels are a dime a dozen. If you prefer to snooze in a nature lover's paradise (which is perhaps the way to go), you can book a room at the **Monasterio de Piedra Hotel** (see "Sightseeing," below).

➜**Hospederia de los Dolores** I felt like I was on the set of a colonial movie while staying at this elegant inn. The rooms have an old-fashioned style, some with four-poster beds and canopies, others with iron frames, the lobby has decorative pieces like wells and wheelbarrows, and the staff dress accordingly in period costumes. Even if you choose not to stay but your stomach's growling, you'll find the best food in town at the hotel's classy restaurant. This *hospederia* is definitely one of the only enticing things about Calatayud and even has its own wine museum—a huge bonus. *Plaza de los Mesones 4.* ☎ *974-889-055. www. mesonladolores.com. Double 53€–65€, suite 75€–88€. Amenities: Restaurant, bar, cafeteria, elevator, gift shop, laundry service, museum, parking (6€). In room: A/C, TV, hair dryer, Internet, safe.*

Sightseeing

M Best ◑ ➜ **Monasterio de Piedra** There's no doubt that this 12th-century monastery and outstanding park are an oasis in an otherwise unimpressive area. The waters from the River Piedra carved the park into the landscape, leaving behind a series of serene lakes, rocky grottos, and free-flowing waterfalls. A variety of plant and animal species enhances the biological wonder, while the 50m (164-ft.) Cola de Caballo waterfall reveals a stunning natural cavern. Lose yourself in the winding tunnels and stairways or see the multi-level views by taking one of the two pathways, either the red or the blue. You can take a tour of the monastery itself, or pop into the on-site wine museum. If you don't care to pack your own lunch and dine outside at the picnic area or by El Lago del Espejo (Mirror Lake), you can grab a bite at either **Piedra Vieja Restaurant** or **Reyes de Aragón.** Just make sure and plan ahead to enjoy the vast beauty of this natural attraction, because buses only go there from Zaragoza (leaving at 9am, returning at 5:30pm) or Calatayud (leaving at 10:30am, returning at 5:30pm) on Tuesday, Thursday, Saturday, and Sunday. *Monasterio de Piedra.* ☎ *902-196-052. Admission 11€ adults, includes entrance to the park, monastery, and museum. Park winter daily 9am–6pm; summer daily 9am–8pm. Monastery winter daily 10:15am–1:15pm and 3:15–5:15pm; summer daily 10:15am–1:15pm and 3:15–7:15pm.*

Jaca

Didn't your mama tell you to not judge a book by its cover? Well, just remember that when you stumble into the mountainside municipality of Jaca (pronounced *Hah*-kah). You won't find flamenco or salsa dancing in Jaca, but you will find unexpected personality in this gem tucked away among its sprawling mundane residential areas. Were it not for the road signs and people speaking in Spanish, it could easily be any large town in the Swiss Alps or the nearby French Pyrenees. Though not big by most standards (it barely surpasses 15,000 permanent inhabitants), Jaca's narrow streets and rustic charm offer a tempting "city" break for those who've spent too much time in the sparsely populated surrounds with only birds of prey for company.

On any given day, so many elderly people crowd the streets that Jaca could be mistaken for a retirement community. But Jaca, a contender to host the Winter Olympics the past four times around, has served as the site for the University Olympics and will bring in youthful athletes from all over the world in the 2007 Youth Olympics. And at night, its more than pleasing assortment of bars and clubs draws in a fair share of students and partiers. It takes more than an evening to sample the nightlife, so give yourself a few days to immerse yourself in the local culture.

Getting There & Around

BY PLANE

Although Jaca doesn't have an airport of its own, you can fly into Zaragoza ($2^1/_2$ hr. by bus), Vitoria ($3^1/_2$ hr. by bus), San Sebastian (3 hr. by bus), and Bilbao (3 hr. by bus), all of which have airports that offer low-cost carrier options and flights from all over Europe.

BY BUS

By **Alosa's bus service (www.alosa.es),** Jaca is easily accessible from Zaragoza (12€, trip time: $2^1/_2$ hr., 6 times daily), via Huesca (6€, trip time: $1^1/_2$ hr., 8 to 11 times daily), or from Pamplona (6.50€, trip time: 2 hr., twice daily). For more timetables, visit the **bus station** on Avenida Jacetania (☎ **974-355-060**).

If you want off the beaten path, which I suspect you do, **buses** are often the only way to travel around Jaca.

BY TRAIN

The only **train** that goes to the **Jaca station** (Calle Ferrocarril; ☎ **974-361-332**) is a rickety old three-car carrier that runs from Canfranc to Zaragoza with stops at

Jaca three times daily—it takes an hour more than the bus. The station is a bit out of town so you might want to hop on Jaca's only bus that travels from the station to the front of Paseo de la Constitución.

BY TAXI

Unless you're starting off in a bigger city, car rental is not an option, as the closest rental agency is located south of Jaca in Huesca. Should you be in a bind and need to get somewhere unreachable by other means, you can phone **Pedro Peral Porrua** (San Marcos 5; ☎ **974-362-848** or **620-660-776**) for a **taxi.**

BY BIKE OR BY FOOT

Bicycles are handy to have if you're carless, especially if you want to explore the surrounding valleys of **Echo** and **Ansó,** which have some breathtaking forests and old-world stone villages. You can **rent** a bike for the day at one of the city's outdoor companies downtown like **Barabú** (C. Mayor 42).

If you're planning on staying within the city, there's really no need for public transportation as everywhere is easily reached by foot. Should you go that route, you won't be the only one exploring the city *a pie* (by foot) as Jaca is a stop on Camino de Santiago.

Jaca Basics

Jaca is so small, it doesn't even have neighborhoods. Instead, everything worth seeing is contained in the historic part of the city center. You can't get lost in the miniscule town, so feel free to wander mapless and see what you discover. Pick up a list of hikes, day trips, and other info on the area at the **tourist office** (Plaza Ayuntamiento 1; ☎ **974-360-098**). Open daily from 9am to 1:30pm and 4:30 to 7:30pm.

RECOMMENDED WEBSITES

○ **www.aetda.com**: This organization, based in nearby Huesca, has listings of all outdoor sports and companies in the area to fulfill your climbing, hiking, and generally outdoorsy needs.

◌ **www.jaca.es**: The main government website, which is actually quite in depth, will help you plan your trip to Jaca accordingly so you can be full steam ahead in no time.

◌ **www.valledelaragon.com**: Read about important logistical information you gotta have as well as about nearby monuments in the Aragón Valley.

◌ **www.lospirineos.com**: If you're planning on visiting some of the smaller nearby towns, this is the most useful website for planning your excursions.

CULTURE TIPS 101

If traveling during May, be sure and hit up Jaca for **Primero Viernes de Mayo** (the First Friday of May), a celebration you won't want to miss. As early as 8am (a time of day most Spaniards are not accustomed to seeing unless on the way home from the night before), locals and visitors alike travel en masse to the cemetery for this religious procession in honor of Count Aznar's 8th-century victory over the Moors. Later, a drunken musical procession takes place on Calle Mayor, before everyone goes home to pass out midday.

Jaca Nuts & Bolts

Emergencies   If you need to report something lost or stolen or have other troubles, you can phone the **local police** at ☎ **974-355-758** or ☎ **974-355-092.** For **medical emergencies,** call the **regional hospital** at ☎ **974-355-331.** To reach the **Red Cross,** call ☎ **974-361-101.**

Internet Access   **Cibercafé Santi** is located on **Calle Mayor 42-44,** but the main entrance is through the shopping center at Calle Mayor 4. Hours are Monday through Saturday from 10am to 1:30pm and 4:30pm to midnight, Sunday and holidays 4:30pm to midnight. Prices are 1.40€ per half-hour. **Ciberciva,** beside the tourist office on **Plaza Ayuntamiento,** is a bit cheaper at 1€ per half-hour (Mon–Sat 11am–1:30pm and 5pm–midnight; Sun 5:30pm–midnight).

Money Exchange   **Caja Madrid** (corner of C. Mayor and Av. del Primero Viernes de Mayo) is the most convenient place to change your currency should you not have access to a cash card to withdraw money directly from an ATM.

Post Office   The old home of the *correos* (Av. Regimento de Galicia) is still marked, but the **post office** (☎ **974-355-886**) has moved to Calle Pirineos 8 off Paseo de la Constitución (Mon–Fri 8:30am–2:30pm; Sat 9:30am–1pm).

Sleeping

Hostels may not abound in Jaca, but a plethora of budget and relatively inexpensive choices are at your disposal. Due to its proximity to the ski resorts and location as the starting point for Camino de Santiago, Jaca often spills over the brim in peak season, so book well in advance if traveling during summer, Easter, or ski season. High-season prices usually take effect from Christmas until Easter and from mid-July to mid-September, depending on the hotel.

HOSTELS

➔ **Albergue del Pelegrino** If you are one of the brave souls making the pilgrimage to Santiago, you can stay at this hostel, which is the cheapest option in town, but only with presentation of your actual pilgrim's credentials. For prices and information, visit the local tourist office (see "Jaca Basics," p. 319) or pick up a guide to pilgrim accommodation beforehand. *Conde Aznar s/n.*

➔ **La Casa del Arco** This enchanting hostel occupies Jaca's oldest building, a charming house with 14th-century origins. Neatly tucked away just across from the bus station, La Casa houses up to 14 people in its two-, three-, and four-bed chambers. And if rooms are hard to come by in the summer and you're desperate enough, the incredibly kind and accommodating staff may just open up the private rooftop room for your lodging convenience. Showers and bathrooms are shared, though one double room has its own *baño* for an additional 7€ per person per night. The ground-floor bar exudes a cozy feel with its ethnic music and African decor. Sit down and have a beer, or ask the bartender to whip you up a cup of his specialty Indian tea. For the breathing friendly, La Casa del Arco is one of two places in Jaca where smoking is completely prohibited. *San Nicolás 4.* ☎ *974-364-448. www.lacasadelarco.net. 18€ per person. Amenities: Restaurant, sheets, towels.*

➔ **Hostal Somport** This is more hotel-like than the hostels you are most likely accustomed to. The rooms are inviting, the help is friendly, and you are just feet away from the main bar streets and other major attractions. Some rooms have their own bathrooms; others are shared. A fine option if going the budget route. *Echegaray 11.* ☎ *974-363-410. 25€ per person. Closed Sun. Amenities: Bar, cafeteria, sheets, telephone, towels. In room: TV.*

CHEAP

➔ **A Boira Hotel** You won't find a larger hotel with more atmosphere and reasonable prices than this. The hotel was completely refurbished in 2006, and it shows. Each room is vividly painted, and the light wooden decor looks brand new. Although only a government-rated two-star, this place gets five stars from me in terms of price (manageable), cleanliness (impeccable), and friendly nature of staff (the finest). It may not have the greatest location, though situated right next door to the Palace of Congress, but everything in Jaca is just a short walk anyway. Some rooms have balconies, but if it's character you want, opt for the skylights and slanted ceilings of the top-floor rooms. Each room has its own bathroom. The comfortable lobby and sitting room are a bonus, and the breakfast-only restaurant is pleasant. *Valle de Ansó 3.* ☎ *974-363-528 or 974-363-848. www.pirinet.com/aboira. Single 33€–36€, double 47€–56€. Amenities: Breakfast room, Internet, parking (8€), TV (in common room). In room: A/C, TV, fridge, hair dryer, Internet.*

➔ **Ramiro I** A prime location for those who may want to party yet don't necessarily want to be kept up each night by the other revelers. Ramiro is smack in the city center, a street or two away from all the bar action, making it quieter if you're taking the night off or easily accessible when stumbling home in the wee hours of the morning. The rooms are not spectacular, but they're sanitary, have their own bathrooms, and some, their own balconies. For the price, you could perhaps find a better steal, but breakfast is included. *Carmen 23.* ☎ *974-361-367. Single 35€–39€, double 64€–72€, triple 84€–95€. Amenities: Restaurant, TV and video (in common room). In room: A/C, TV, hair dryer.*

DOABLE

➜**Hotel Jaques** There's nothing truly worth noting about this two-star in one of the town's main plazas. For the price, it's surely one of the nicer places if you don't give a damn about uniqueness or quality of staff. The rooms are bright and airy, the decoration is cheerful, and the location is ideal. Still, I would only stay at Jacques were everywhere else in town full. *Unión Jaquesa 4.* ☎ *974-356-424 and 974-355-018. www.hoteljaques.com. Single 32€–45€, double 55€–70€, extra bed 20€. Amenities: Restaurant, bar, elevator, parking. In room: A/C, TV, hair dryer, minibar, safe, wireless Internet.*

➜**Hotel La Paz** The cold stares and attitude at the reception desk make you wonder what exactly you did wrong in the 5 seconds since stepping through the doors to Hotel La Paz. Yet despite the rudeness and the fact that the ambience is certainly lacking, this isn't a terrible option if you're traveling with more than just yourself. The hotel offers singles, doubles, triples, even quads, and each is minimalistically furnished and has a nice, spacious bathroom. Some have pleasant balconies, as well. Both the restaurant decorated with vintage drawings and downstairs bar are convenient if you don't want to leave the hotel again after a long day of sightseeing. *Mayor 41.* ☎ *974-360-700. Single 31€–37€, double 45€–54€, triple and quadruple 60€–80€. Amenities: Restaurant, bar. In room: A/C, TV, hair dryer.*

➜**Hotel Mur** There's no beating Hotel Mur in terms of comfort and convenience. Built in 1875, the establishment is located right on Jaca's main drag just feet from Ciudadela. It's a great choice if you're hangin' with a couple pals because some of the brightly painted rooms hold up to four people and won't put a strain on your wallet. The desirable balcony views further enhance the hotel's lure. Bathrooms are fancied up with painted tiles, and the hallways and staircases are ritzier than the room prices suggest. If you pulled a Britney last night, the hotel offers an over-the-top "honeymoon" suite, complete with fully stocked bar, plush leather couches and chairs, Jacuzzi in the room, TV, sauna, and three balconies. The price is a bit high at 200€ a night, but since the hotel has no limit on how many people can crash in the suite, the wedding party can join you. *At the intersection of Santa Orosia and Primer Viernes de Mayo/Francia.* ☎ *974-360-100. www.hotelmur.com. Single 34€–47€, double 51€–63€, triple 63€–76€, quadruple 75€–88€. Amenities: Restaurant, breakfast room. In room: A/C, TV, safe.*

Eating

TAPAS

➜**Aleda Ños** ★ Strangely out of place among the hodgepodge of modest eateries in Jaca's city center, Aleda Ños's modern interior decoration and outdoor dining option aren't its only appeals. The staff is more than eager to help a foreigner in need, and prices are much lower than outward appearance would imply. From 8am to 3pm, you can sample whatever tapas the cooks happen to conjure up that day or come back later at night for a real meal from 8 to 11pm. The bar serves alcohol until closing time at 2am. *Plaza Aragón. No phone. Tapas 2€ and up. Meals 8€.*

➜**Cafeteria Astun** Astun is just another ever-present tapas bar, but it stands out for its central location with a pleasant terrace ideal for relaxing and people-watching. If you do grab a bite to eat here and are adventurous, try the *pulgo vinagretta* (a mix of onions, peppers, tomatoes, and octopuses) or *caracoles a la llauna* (snails). If the thought of slimy food on your palette frightens you, you can't go wrong with the *pimiento relleno de bacalaoo carne* (red pepper stuffed with codfish or meat). *Plaza Cortes de Aragón 7.* ☎ *974-364-641. Tapas prices start at 1.50€. Daily 8am–1am.*

→**La Portaceta** The pace is slow, and you're likely to find Jaca's elderly population dining here in similar fashion, but Portaceta is pleasant, cheap, and less packed than tapas joints on the main squares. Try a regional dish like the *albóndigas con tomate,* which simply means meatballs with tomato sauce. *Unión 4.* ☎ *974-361-471. Tapas and toasties 1€–3.50€. Daily 1–3:30pm and 8–11:30pm.*

CHEAP

→**Pista Lynch** ECLECTIC The menu is diverse, the service is speedy, and you'll find about anything you're looking for at this semi-fast food joint. If you're sick of tapas, try the Burrito Tajin or Paella Mexicana. *Av. Primer Viernes de Mayo 7.* ☎ *974-355-698. Combination plates 7€–8€. Hamburgers 2.50€. Pizzas 6.25€. Sandwiches 4€. Daily 1–3:30pm and 8–11:30pm.*

DOABLE

→**El Picaro** ★ PARRILLA The atmosphere is friendly at this native Spanish joint (the owners cooked me a meal even after they shut their doors for fiesta), and the food is good but not overpriced. Try the *codorniz* (a decadent quail accompanied by fries). The restaurant also serves tasty *sidra natural de barril,* a house cider that is distilled on-site. *Bellido 11.* ☎ *974-360-017. Menu of the day 9€. Thurs–Tues noon–4pm and 8pm–midnight. Closed Wed.*

→**La Casa del Arco** ★★ VEGETARIAN Take a break from the meat and head to this hippie haven for some of the best food in town. Located on the second floor of the hostel of the same name, the restaurant with its African groove tunes and tavern-like coziness offers a strictly vegetarian menu of Mediterranean-inspired exotic

dishes. *San Nicolás 4.* ☎ *974-364-448. www. lacasadelarco.net. Prices start at 5€ a course; you can eat a full meal for just 10€. Daily 1–3:30pm and 8:30–11:30pm.*

SPLURGE

→**Restaurante el Portón** ★★★ ARAGONESE The elegant old-world charm of el Portón keeps it crowded, especially during peak season; book a table in advance should you arrive in Jaca amid the ski crowd or summer pilgrims. Regional game like duck, quail, and the like are popular dishes at this classy establishment. Dishes are pricier than most, with the majority falling upwards of 15€. *Plaza Marqués de la Cadena.* ☎ *974-355-854. Thurs–Tues 1:30–4pm and 8:30pm–midnight. Closed Wed.*

→**Restaurante Serbal** ARAGONESE If you're sick and tired of impersonal service, Serbal is a welcome return to hospitality. You can tell the staff genuinely wants you to have an enjoyable dining experience, as their attentiveness and willingness to coach you through your selection are evident. Likewise, the refined dining room is just as charming as the help. Some of the restaurant's specialties are *migas al estilo de echo* (a bread crumb starter), *hojalde de verduras y salmón* (vegetable and salmon), *bacalao al ajoarriero* (codfish), and *jarretes de cordero* (lamb). *Carmen 22.* ☎ *974-363-892. Menu of the day 10€–16€ for 3 courses. Daily 1:30–3:30pm and 8:30–10:30pm.*

CAFES

→**El Rincón de la Catedral** CAFÉ For the best cup of coffee in town and mouthwatering pastries, head to this cafe just outside the cathedral. If you want to eat dinner here, book in advance, as reservations are often necessary during summer months and holidays. *Plaza de la Catedral.* ☎ *974-355-920. Entrees 8€–13€. Tapas start at 1.50€. Daily 11am–3:30pm and 7–11:30pm.*

➜**Pilgrim Café** CAFE/BAR Perhaps it's the speedy service or ideal location that attracts so many diners to this just average restaurant/bar. It could be because it stays open all day, while other establishments close their doors for several hours for siesta. Or maybe it's the fact that the entire menu is priced below 10€. The salads are quite massive and tasty (and just 6€ a pop), but some of the other plate combinations are a bit strange. And though open and beer-hall-like inside with an outdoor dining area overlooking the lawn of Ciudadela, it doesn't offer any magnificent adornings or ambience. Whatever the reason, Pilgrim Café remains a favorite of locals and travelers alike and is rarely, if ever, empty. *Av. Primer Viernes de Mayo 7.* ☎ *974-363-337. Hamburgers and sandwiches 3€–5.50€. Main dishes 6€–10€. Tack on .60€ per plate if you opt to dine on the terrace. Daily 8am–2am.*

Partying

If you're not visiting Jaca during its peak (ski season—the optimal month is Dec—or at the height of the summer tourism run), you won't find too bumping of a party scene. In the off season, bars are only open from Thursday to Friday. You won't find a true blue Spanish discothéque in Jaca; however, many **disco bars** offer similar environments without the exorbitant cover charges. You'll find these primarily on **Calle Gil Berges** and **Calle Bellido.** Bars typically close between 3 to 5am. For a more relaxed evening, have a round of tapas and take a beer in one of the two main plazas, **Plaza Cortes de Aragón** or **Plaza del Marques de la Cadena.**

BARS

➜**Camelot** The cobwebs, as well as medieval paintings and hangings, make this theme pub one of the most visited in town. A hipper crowd than that of neighboring establishments frequents Camelot—even still, a mullet or two isn't a rare sighting. *Gil Berges and Puerta Nueva. No phone.*

➜**El Corral** Judging from the name and pictures of cowboys on its business cards, you might be fooled into thinking this punky bar is Western themed. However, upon arrival, you'll find loud heavy metal music, a crude sign behind the bar that says "Vagina Ensalata," and an alternative crowd not lacking body piercings and tattoos. *Gil Berges. No phone.*

➜**La Bodeguilla del Medio** This fun Cuban bar is decorated with photography from the Latin American country and plays music accordingly. Good margaritas, daiquiris, and mojitos are among the house specialties. *Gil Berges. No phone.*

➜**Viviana** The artistic decor, including soothing purple walls, cartoonish flower paintings, and the illuminated framed drawings, are the lure of this chill pub that is set away from the noise of the two main bar streets. *Plaza Marques de la Cadena. No phone.*

NIGHTCLUBS

➜**Bertoni** By far the most popular kid on the block, you'll find your college-aged crowd in this bar that hosts a mix of mostly pop and Spanish music and students and young people from all walks of life. *Gil Berges 3. No phone.*

➜**Bogart** This sort of galactic setting is roomier than most with starlight substitutions peeking out of the aluminum walls and illuminating the place. A good mix of people and music makes for a worthwhile stop on your nightly rounds. *Bellido 19. No phone.*

➜**La Trampa** If you're a card-carrying member of the 24 and over club, you'll fit right in at this place where the early-30s crowd comes to get laid. Even though I was in the age minority, I dug the music and had a good time anyway. *Ramiro I 1. No phone.*

➜ **Obsesion** When I walked in the door to Obsession, a line of *chicos* was sitting on the floor in a rowing pattern, doing some sort of odd chant and dance. Mmkay. Needless to say, there's a fun-loving, if not eccentrically wacky, feel to this loud bar with plenty of neon strobe lights. *Gil Berges. No phone.*

➜ **Santa Locura** If Bertoni is too full for your liking, head just a few doors down to Santa Locura, a disco bar that is quite similar in crowd and atmosphere, but not nearly as claustrophobic. *Gil Berges 9. No phone.*

Sightseeing

➜ **Ciudadela or Castillo de San Pedro** This magnificent crumbling stone fortress that forms a star pattern in the center of the city must be viewed two ways: from within and from above. As one of the few pentagonal citadels with its original shape preserved, Ciudadela was declared a monument of cultural interest in 1951 and restored in 1968. You can only enter Ciudadela with a tour guide (tours in Spanish only) at 11am or 5pm. It costs 4€, but if you're really hard up, you can follow in one of the groups of school children that frequently drop in. If you miss tour times or don't feel like paying, you can admire the citadel's exterior with its deep moat that houses an entire herd of deer that permanently inhabit it. If you have a car, drive the 6.4km (4 miles) outside of town to the Mirador Peña Oroel. From there, you can climb to the top and see the citadel's stunning star formation from above. *At the crossing of Primer Viernes de Mayo and Av. Francia. Nov–Mar daily 11am–noon and 4–5pm; Apr–June and Sept–Oct daily 11am–noon and 5–6pm; July–Aug daily 11am–noon and 6–8pm.*

Playing Outside

PARKS & GARDENS

When the sun comes out, so do Jaca's residents, particularly at the **ciudadela lawn,** a lush, green haven for chronic loungers. The lawn surrounding the citadel on all sides is ideal for sunbathers and those who want to just people-watch. Just look out for the local children and their relentless games of football/soccer in which you're just an invisible obstacle—I learned this the hard way after a flash of black and white smacked me between the eyes, and a herd of squirmy kids trampled over me and my laptop without so much as a second glance.

Alternately, ample benches, greenery, and shade make **Paseo de la Constitucion** a prime spot for lazing about and nursing that weeklong hangover.

CLIMBING & HIKING

➜ **Alcorce Pirineos Aventura** Rent your harnesses and some of those damn-handy *carabineers* here, or check out the outdoor activities the company has planned. *Av. Regimento Galicia 1. ☎ 974-356-437 and 974-363-972. www.alcorceaventura.com. Nov–Mar Mon–Sat 10am–1:30pm; Apr–Oct Mon–Sat 10am–1:30pm and 5–8:30pm.*

➜ **Barabú** This outdoor guide company offers canyoning, hiking, trekking excursions, as well as a place to purchase or rent gear for all outward-bound-style activities. *Mayor 42. ☎ 974-356-016. Mon–Sat 10:30am–1:30pm and 5–8:30pm.*

ICE SKATING

➜ **Ice-Skating** Spaniards come from all over to take a turn around this impressive year-round rink. Admission is 7€ including skates; 5.50€ without. *Located south of the center on Av. Perimetral.* ☎ *974-355-192. Mon–Fri 7–9pm; Sat 5:30–10:30pm; Sun 11:30am–1:30pm and 4:30–7:30pm. Closed Mon Oct–Nov.*

Other Attractions

➜ **Dead Sea Natural Therapy** If you've had just about all the sightseeing and nature you can handle (hey, it's bound to happen at some point) and just welcome a relaxing day, take a dip in the thermal baths at Natural Therapy, or pamper yourself with a massage, manicure, pedicure, or other treatment offered at this swanky spa. No excuse necessary. *Av. Regimiento de Galicia 3.* ☎ *974-356-132.*

➜ **Jaca Bowling** Need a break from Jaca's omnipresent disco pubs? Try your luck at cosmic bowling. The alley also houses a bar/restaurant so you can get your hair-of-the-dog for the evening, as well as an arcade in case rolling a 10-pound ball down an oily lane just doesn't get your heart a racing. *Polígono Campacian s/n.* ☎ *974-362-109. Mon–Thurs 5pm–1am; Fri 5pm–3am; Sat 11am–3am; Sun and holidays 11am–1am.*

Shopping

When it comes to shopping, Jaca is no Milan. Although you'll come across occasional clothing stores sprinkled throughout the city, outdoor and gear stores are more prevalent than any. You'll find your select clothing stores on and around **Calle de Carmen** and **Plaza de Aragón,** with a few also on **Calle Mayor.** Store hours are much the same as elsewhere in Spain, opening from 10:30am until 8:30pm with a generous siesta sometime mid-afternoon. For women's designer apparel, try out **Abad Boutique** (Mayor 4; ☎ **974-361-149**), **Carlota I** and **II** (Carmen; ☎ **974-363-210**), and **Julia Palacin** (☎ **974-363-229**). If you dig tight-fitting, cheap, and

Cuidado! Internet Inaccess

If you're heading from Jaca directly into the Pyrenees, you may want to check your e-mail one more time and drop Mom and Pops a line saying that you may be inaccessible for some days. You'll find few, if any, places to get online in the Pyrenees, save the select hotels that offer connections if you have your own laptop. If you're worried about being out of touch and have a GSM phone, you can purchase a SIM card in Jaca. Many different providers service the area, though you'll get the best reception in the mountains with Movistar.

trendy attire for wannabe trendsters, you might find something among the assortment of male and female teeny-bopper wear at **Lenny King** (Av. Francia at C. Mayor).

Road Trips from Jaca

CANDANCHÚ & ASTÚN

If you've come to Jaca to hit the slopes, your nearest resort is in Candanchú, 34km (20 miles) north of Jaca. With 23 chair lifts, equipment rentals, a ski school, and more than 50 trails, Candanchú should satisfy skiers of all skill levels. The highest run is 2,400m (8,000 ft.). **Buses** leave from **Plaza Biscos** in Jaca for Candanchú at 8:20am each morning (2€, trip time: 45 min.). A few **hostels, pensions,** and some pricier **hotels** are located near the ski station should you not want to travel to and from Jaca each day. For more information, call ☎ **974-373-194** or visit the website **www.candanchu.com**. If you've tired of Candanchú's *pistes* (ski runs), you can head just 3km (2 miles) east to Astún and give those trails a go. Just don't plan on staying over—accommodation in Astún (☎ 974-373-088; www.astun.com) is scarce, and way overpriced.

SANTA CILIA

I stared distractedly at my full coffee cup as my heart pounded loudly in my chest and people all around me drank beer—and it was just 11am after a major party night. My reasons for wanting to hurl myself 3,500m (11,500 ft.) out of the side of an airplane were beginning to get a bit fuzzy as the mercury hit a stifling 97°F (36°C). After a training session that was much briefer than I would have liked, I was harnessed up and stowed inside the plane. As we climbed higher, my fear began to diminish, just like the people who were now ant-size dots more than a mile below. In what felt like moments, we reached maximum altitude. Before my tandem guide had counted to three, he shoved me out the plane door and we were free-falling toward the ground below. After about 20 seconds, I felt a pop as my guy pulled the parachute chord—and we were hanging stationary in the air. Less than 10 minutes later, we were on the ground again. It went by so quickly and now only seems like a dream. But if you're an ultimate adrenaline junkie like I am and haven't given **sky diving** a try, there's no better opportunity to do it than with the magnificent Pyrenees as your backdrop.

Your hookup is at 📺 Best❀ **Centro de Paracaidismo Pirineos** (☎ 609-401-800 or 609-060-622; www.paracaidismo pirineos.com), located at **Aeródrome de Santa Cilia** just 15km (9 miles) to the west of Jaca. Just don't forget to phone in advance—space is limited as the center normally only offers jumps on Saturday and Sunday most of the year (though every day in July and Aug). You can easily get there by **car** via the **N240,** and a **bus** traveling from Jaca to Pamplona stops on the

town's outskirts a few times a day. If you want to get your blood pumping before you take the plunge, you can always rent a **bike** in Jaca and make the hilly journey to the airfield yourself.

PARQUE NACIONAL ORDESA Y MONTE PERDIDO

If you're looking for a relaxed daytime atmosphere and a party-hardy nightlife, head east of Jaca and into the twisting, turning mountain roads that lead up into the famed range of tall peaks and national parks. I'm going to give it to you straight: There's simply no way you'll get around in

What to Bring: A Sky Diver's Journey

I arrived in a tank and shorts, thinking I would be outfitted in one of those jazzy neon parachute suits. Wrong. Even if it's a sweltering summer day, you'll be glad you threw on your warm duds once you're more than 3,000m (10,000 ft.) in the air and the wind is violently lashing against your body. So be sure and take a **fleece, jeans,** and **sneakers,** of course. Although the kindly owner in charge of the center often takes pictures with his snazzy professional **camera,** if you bring your own, you can always find someone who will snap a few shots for you as you're gearing up and making the descent. Take your own **portable USB device** or **blank CD** and you can take home the photos the owner snaps of you. As a small business, **credit cards** are not accepted. So don't forget to have the exact amount in **cash** (185€ for a tandem jump) and maybe a little extra if your stomach's stronger than mine and you want to grab a bite to eat at the cafe beforehand, or also purchase a video of your jump (an additional 70€).

the Pyrenees without your own mode of transportation. Distance-wise, all the towns and villages that cover the vast expanses of mountains and valleys aren't far from one another. However, buses are few and far between and if you're relying on **public transit,** logistically it is often impossible to get where you want to go within a day, sometimes even 2 or 3. The **bus schedule** is illogical, and even **bicycle rentals** aren't possible in most places. At the same time, you don't want to miss out on the sheer beauty and immense opportunities the famed mountain range has to offer. So I suggest you get yourself on over to a car dealer and get set up with a nice, jazzy Spanish rental. You'll find your best deals online obviously, and most **car-rental companies** require you to book at least 24 hours in advance (most ask for 48), but if you haven't planned ahead, drop in to **Avis** (☎ **974-218-249** or 650-885-449; Mon–Fri 8:30am–1pm and 4–7:30pm, Sat 9:00am–1:30pm) inside the bus/train station of Huesca and try your luck. To get to Huesca, take a bus (11 daily, trip time: 1 hr.) or train (three daily, trip time: 1¹/₂ hr.) from Jaca. Or if you're coming from Zaragoza, a plethora of rental agencies are headquartered there.

Torla

Torla is one of those atmospheric towns that can't be described, only experienced. While Torla is quiet by nature and doesn't have any particular monuments of note, the aesthetically pleasing layout of the town, as well as beauty and proximity of the national park that surrounds it, make it well worth the trip.

Getting There & Around

Only one **bus** leaves from Sabiñanigo, just south of Jaca, to Aínsa daily, leaving at 11am and reaching Torla at noon. In the opposite direction, the bus leaves Aínsa at 2:30pm and arrives at Torla at 3:30pm. But reaching Torla *por coche,* by **car,** is the easiest way to go. **Taxis** offer daily excursions into the mountains if you can't get there by other means (☎ **974-486-243**).

Basics

Spend a day wandering through the picturesque cobblestone streets of Torla with no agenda. You won't need a map to navigate the tilting town, though at times, the streets do seem to form an intricate labyrinth that only leads to dead ends. Signs marked TORLA HISTÓRICA have descriptions of the main sites in English. The main tourist office is on **Calle Fatas** at Plaza de Aragón, the other at **Av. Ordesa 19** (weekdays from 8am–3pm and weekends from 9am–2pm and 4–7pm). Right next door to the main tourist office, you'll find **Turismo Rural,** which will set you up with a *casa rural* if you so desire. There is a **post office** in Plaza Mayor that is only open from 9 to 11am on weekdays.

Sleeping

For a town its size, Torla isn't lacking in hotels. *Refugios* (cheaper bunkhouselike options that lodge many backpackers in each room) and hostels are scattered around the center of town, all relatively the same in price (beginning around 20€–25€ a room) and quality. One- and two-star options dot **Avenida Ordesa** and offer stunning views of the nearby national park. **Calle Fatas,** the main street that splits the town's center, houses the remaining lodging, including the brand new **Hotel Villa Russell** (Fatas; ☎ **974-486-770;** www.hotelvillarussell.com; single 55€–77€, double 75€–109€, triple 105€–139€, apartment 140€–160€), a three-star that is arguably the nicest in town. On-site amenities include a restaurant, bar, elevator, and parking. The rooms are comfortably large and furnished with couches, hardwood floors, minikitchens, safes, TVs, A/C, Internet access, and DVD players, and the showers have so many nozzles (nine to be exact), that you won't be sure what to do with them all. Some of the rooms open onto a courtyard terrace which doubles as an outdoor bar in the summer. Access to the basement sauna, Jacuzzi, and gym is 6€ per 45 minutes. Prices include buffet breakfast. Advanced booking is necessary in July and August.

Eating

➜ **El Taillon** BASQUE   While you can find a hodgepodge of tourist eyesores in the way of restaurants, El Taillon a cafetería, terrace, bar, and restaurant all rolled into one—will provide you with a menu of regional dishes and *bocadillas* and has a suitably attractive perch above the valley just on the edge of town. *A Ruata.* ☎ *974-486-304. Menu of the day 15€. Open at 7:30am. Dinner is served daily from 8:30pm.*

Partying

Surprisingly, for a town of roughly 200, there's no shortage of **bars** here either, though they're often a bit hidden with basement entrances or the like. Most are located along Calle Fatas and hopping during summer's climbing/hiking season and winter ski time, but sometimes closed at other times of the year. Torla even has its own nightclub, **Discoteca As Proas,** and bar with karaoke, **Arcos Iris Pub,** both located at the west end of Fatas.

Playing Outside

As you most likely didn't come to Torla to sit on your ass all day, venture out into the surroundings for a bit of nature fun. A multitude of **hiking trails** start at the edge of Torla and wind all throughout the valley and neighboring mountains. For **canyoning, rafting, hydrospeed,** and the like, stop by **Compañia Guias de Torla** (A Ruata s/n; ☎/fax **974-486-422;** www.guiasdetorla.com) and sign up for a day trip to the nearby national parks. Prices start at 35€ and range according to activity and skill level.

Bielsa

A typical morning in Bielsa. There you are, sitting on your hotel balcony, soaking up the morning sun and enjoying the fresh mountain air, when out of nowhere a medley of misplaced barnyard bells goes *clankety-clank.* You curiously peer around the corner as a herd of sheep and goats laggardly pass you by. They're in no hurry. No one leads them, and where they're going, I'm not sure. The cars coming down the street—the main road into the center of Bielsa—pull onto the side of the road to make way for the furry friends, as they disappear over the horizon. Approximately 6 hours later, the same thing happens, only this time, the mammals head back to where they came from. And that's about as exciting as it gets in this northern village that is just 13km (8 miles) south of the French border. Bielsa is so small, they don't even need street signs, and it's rare to see one. It has a cute, kid-sister aura, though tacky tourist shops full of nonsensical knickknacks make the town look more run-down than it really is. While you may tire of the town's quaintness itself after a day or so, Bielsa lies in the heart of the Pyrenees and is a prime starting point for exploring the trails and outdoor opportunities of the nearby mountains and canyons in Ordesa and Monte Perdido.

ARAGÓN

Getting There & Around

The only **bus** to and from Bielsa is actually a large minivan that runs to and from Aínsa, leaving from **Plaza Mayor** at 6am on Monday, Wednesday, and Friday (2.50€, trip time: 40 min.) and returning at 8:45pm on the same days. You can easily travel Bielsa and the surrounding trails by **foot**, but a **car** is necessary to reach Valle de Pineta and other parks.

Basics

The **tourist office** for the national parks is in the Plaza Mayor (weekdays 8am–3pm and 4–7pm, weekends 9am–2pm and 4–7pm). Another tourist booth at the entrance to Valle de Pineta within the national park (daily 7am–9pm) offers a list of marked trails and helpful advice.

Sleeping

The handful of budget accommodations in the city center like **Hostal Marbóre** and **Hotel Valle de Pineta** are mostly only open during high season. Book in advance if you're coming to Bielsa in July or August. Even then, look for places advertising *habitaciones* or *chambres*—often homes of families or widows who rent out a room(s)—and you should be fine. The nicest inn around by far is **Hotel Bielsa** (Carretera de Francia s/n; ☎ **974-501-008;** www.hotel-bielsa.com; single 50€–56€, double 60€–66€, extra bed 16€), a three-star that is open year-round and has a ski lodge feel. The rooms are beautiful with deep color schemes and hardwood floors, and you can't beat the views, no matter on which side of the hotel your room is located. The staff is more than accommodating and attentive and has been known on occasion to drive visitors out to the national parks if they don't have their own transportation. Not to mention, the hotel has **wireless Internet** and is one of the few places in town where you can actually go online. The

other option is at the **Pineta Restaurante Bar,** right next to the tourist office in the main square. It has an old-school dial-up connection on its sole computer that takes ages to load a single page and costs 2€ per hour.

If you prefer to stay out of town and in the wildlife, you can **camp** for free in the foothills of Valle de Pineta during the summers, or at the magnificent **Parador de Bielsa** (Valle de Pineta s/n; ☎ **974-501-011;** www.parador.es) if you don't mind forking over a larger chunk of cash. The *paradores* do often offer discounts of 20% or more if you stay in the same one for at least 2 nights, so check for seasonal deals.

Eating

"Oh no, you can't order the chicken when you have the lamb on the menu. The lamb *es muy bueno,*" the owner of **Hotel Bielsa and Restaurante** sighs. Go with what she says—you'll be glad you did. If you're sick of the ever-present tapas bars, the restaurant at Hotel Bielsa does indeed serve up the best meals in town. Dinner comes complete with bread, starter, main dish, wine, and dessert. For the town, 15€ may be on the higher end price-wise, but portions are meant for two and will leave you stuffed until your next meal. Try the *canalone de pescado* (fish wrapped in pasta and doused in a creamy cheese sauce) to start, follow with the restaurant's specialty *cordero* (the lamb *muy bueno*), and finish with *crema de platanos* (a bowl of rich banana cream with chocolate shavings) or *tarte de manzanas* (a decadent apple pastry drizzed with a delightful cherry topping). Hotel Bielsa serves breakfast from 8:15 to 10am, lunch from 12:30 to 3pm, and dinner from 8:30 to 10pm. Breakfast 7.50€; dinner with wine 15€. If you want to go cheaper, bars and restaurants are aplenty in Bielsa, though the majority are holes-in-the-wall or dives that don't put a lot of effort into food preparation.

Playing Outside

If you want to hop over into one of the nearby national parks but don't have your own set of wheels, **Capra** (☎ 626-608-066;** www.monteperdido.com/capra) offers taxi and 4×4 excursions. Guide companies like **Esquiruelo** (La Cruz s/n; ☎ 626-608-066) will show you the ropes while you try your hand at **canyoning** or **rafting,** or you can simply **rent ski equipment** if you're a seasoned veteran of the slopes.

Benasque ★★★

Just over the mountains east of Bielsa is ▨ Best● **Benasque** whose unspoiled beauty and laid-back vibe made it my favorite town in the Pyrenees. Its engaging cobblestoned lanes and delightful mountain lodges are perfect for wandering during lazy summer days. The town has a good *après ski* atmosphere, with lively bars that are open until the early hours of the morning. An array of hotels and restaurants in Cerler are an option, as well.

Getting There & Around
BY BUS

The only way into Benasque by **bus** is via **Barbastro** (7€, trip time: 2 hr., twice a day). Buses from other destinations like **Huesca, Zaragoza,** and **Barcelona** connect in Barbastro. If you want to reach **Cerler,** buses make the trip to and from Benasque four times daily.

BY CAR

The best way to travel to and around Benasque is by **car,** as the public transportation in the area is scant. You can rent a car in one of the bigger nearby cities like **Huesca, Barcelona,** or **Zaragoza** then arrive in Benasque by the **A139** that runs north from Barbastro. The road ends just beyond Benasque and takes some winding turns through the mountains, so if you fear you're lost, worry not, you're most likely just nearing your final destination.

BY BIKE

Once you're settled in Benasque, you can rent **bikes** at **Vits** on the main square (☎ 974-552-036) or at **Casa de la Montaña** on Avenida de los Tilos (☎ 974-552-094).

Basics

For tips on what to do around Benasque, head first to the **turismo** (☎ 974-551-289; July–Aug daily 9am–2pm and 4–9pm; Sept–June Thurs–Mon 10am–2pm and 5–9pm, Tues–Wed 5–9pm) located at San Sebastían 5. If you need immediate **medical care,** phone ☎ 608-536-882 for emergencies. Or head to **Centro Sanitario** (☎ 974-552-138) from noon to 2pm when no appointment is necessary. Appointments can be scheduled from 9am to noon. The nearest hospital is **Hospital de Barbastro,** 90km (54 miles) south of Benasque on N240 (☎ 974-313-511). The only **post office** in town is at Plaza del Ayuntamiento (☎ 974-552-071). Not a whole lot of places offer **online access,** except for the **locoturio** (☎ 479-551-459) on Calle los Huertos, open daily from 11am to 11pm.

RECOMMENDED WEBSITES

○ **www.benasque.net**: This splashy website has basic information on the area, so long as your Spanish is up to par.

○ **www.fedme.es**: Again in Spanish, the website of the Federación Española de Deportes de Montaña y Escalada provides information on sporting opportunities in the mountains.

○ **www.rfedi.es**: Perhaps more detailed than the FEDME site, this link specializes in winter sports, with history and tips on each.

○ **www.turismobenasque.com**: This link is the official site for the Aragónese government and Benasque tourist office.

Sleeping

A base for skiers and snow bunnies in the winter, Benasque is not lacking in the hotel department. In fact, it seems to have more hotels than people, but if you're traveling in between seasons (from Easter to summer), you may have a hard time finding a room as many of the hotels shut down until late June. During late summer or ski season, book weeks in advance as Benasque is often filled to capacity, especially on weekends.

CHEAP

➜ **Hotel Puente I and II** These two hotels located on each side of Benasque's main road don't look like much from the outside but may very well be the most economical choice in town. Rooms are faultlessly clean with appealing hardwood floors, and are a good cheap place to crash. The restaurant and salon are spacious, the basement has pool and foosball tables, and there are two computers with Internet access for .50€ per 15 minutes. The hotel also arranges excursions to the nearby mountains. *San Pedro s/n.* ☎ *974-551-279 and 974-551-211. www.hotelelpuente.com. Single 27€, double 42€–55€. Amenities: Ski storage, TV, VCR. In room: TV.*

DOABLE

➜ **Hotel Aragüells** ★ Right smack in the center of all that's going on in Benasque, Hotel Aragüells is cozy and convenient. The owner is a bit skeptical of English-speaking foreigners, and the rooms are small, but each has its own bathroom. If

you're traveling in a pack, Aragüells is the way to go—you can rent a quad and even cram in additional beds for an extra 15€ a night. *Los Tilos s/n.* ☎ *974-551-619. www.hotel araguells.com. Single 35€–45€, double 45€–70€, triple 60€–81€, quadruple 70€–90€. Amenities: Bar, cafeteria, parking, TV.*

➜ **Hotel San Marsial** ★★ A mother-daughter operated hotel, San Marsial's 28 cute and cottagelike rooms are tasteful with an old-fashioned charm. If you're traveling in a pack, ask for one of the family lodgings that come with connecting bedrooms and separate baths. A filling buffet breakfast is included in the price. *Av. de Francia 75.* ☎ *974-551-616. www.hotelsan marsial.com. Single 45€–63€, double 58€–98€, double with sitting room 88€–130€, apartment 100€–220€, extra bed 30€. Amenities: Cafeteria, Internet, parking, TV. In room: Hair dryer, minibar, TV.*

➜ **Hotel Solana** With its rustic stone exterior, deeply colored walls, hardwood finishings, and unique paintings, Solana has a sort of romantic air about it—if you're lucky, maybe it will inspire the rest of your evening. The hotel has dining and drinking options should you be too tired from a day on the slopes to venture back out again. Rooms with Jacuzzis are available for extra. *Plaza Mayor 5.* ☎ *974-551-019. www.hotelsolanabenas.com. Single 28€–50€, double 38€–100€, triple 50€–100€. Amenities: Restaurant, bar, cafeteria, TV. In room: TV.*

SPLURGE

➜ **Hotel Ciria** ★★★ Situated in the heart of Benasque, this rustic mountain lodge is surely the nicest in town. Family-run and friendly, Hotel Ciria has duplexes with living rooms that fit four or more people, as well as suites with Jacuzzis. The perfect place to meet fellow skiers, this hotel caters to those hitting the slopes as it has a place for ski equipment storage. If you plan on staying a week or more, the hotel has an exclusive 7-day offer starting at 304€ or a 5-day special for 217€ (not applicable in July and Aug). Book weeks, if not months, in advance, especially for weekends. Closed for a few weeks in May each year. *Los Tilos s/n.* ☎ *974-551-612 or 974-551-080. www. hotelciria.com. Price per person 38€–78€. Amenities: Restaurant, cafeteria, elevator, parking, massage, money exchange, solarium (open only in summer). In room: A/C, TV, hair dryer, Internet, minibar, safe.*

Eating

➜**Borda Roldanet** ★ TAPAS Snowboarders and mountain-biking types flock to this appealing Pepto-Bismol pink building on Benasque's main street. Borda Roldanet is the perfect place to drop by for a *primera copa* (first drink) or light tapas before a big night out. Try the *lentejas* and wash them down with an *orujo de hierbas* (a shot of a specialty type of Spanish liquor). If you happen to be in the right place at the right time, you may even catch some random dance party action at this original joint—the owners and regulars have been known to clear out the tables, set up the turntables, and start a techno club of their own. *Av. de Francia s/n.* ☎ *974-552-834. Tapas start at 2€. Daily 3pm–1:30am.*

➜**Cantaloope** ARAGONESE Amid the array of the usual tapas bars and pizza eateries, Cantaloope is one of the more modern joints in town with local game and offerings. *Av. de Francia 74.* ☎ *676-123-021. Meals 7€–15€. Open 1–4:30pm for lunch; dinner is served from 8pm.*

➜**El Fogaril** ALTOARAGONESA With specialties from the surrounding valley, this restaurant on the ground floor of Hotel Ciria is a favorite of locals and visitors alike. The staff hunts and fishes for the majority of ingredients used—how's that for eating local. Meat-eaters take note: Try the grilled lamb, partridge stuffed with

truffles, or wild pork. *Los Tilos s/n.* ☎ *974-551-612. Average entree 18€. Daily 'til closing.*

➜**El Rebost** ★ IBERIAN/TAPAS You won't find this hidden tapas bar unless you go in search of it, as it's located right at the northern edge of town near Hotel San Marsial, but it offers a variety of *bocadillos* and regional food. Open-topped *torta* sandwiches are a filling lunchtime endeavor, as are the wide range of tapas available. If you're dining with at least one other person, opt for the yummy fondue. *Mayor 53.* ☎ *685-994-549. Tapas begin at 2.50€. Full meal 9€–12€. Wed–Mon 10am–11:30pm. Closed Tues.*

Partying

Like everything else in Benasque, the bulk of the bars and clubs are only open during high season or on weekends. But fear not, you'll always find somewhere to go for a drink (or many) in the small yet lively town. Oftentimes, the local partiers and music lovers travel in packs to raves and field parties that take place nearly every week in neighboring towns like Graus and feature bands and DJs. If you're a raver or just like loud, thumping music and a good time, ask around; *"Conoces una fiesta a cerca de Benasque?"* may just be your ticket to join in the fun. Most of the bars and nightclubs open between 10:30 and 11:30pm and don't close until the last person straggles home for the night (or the morning).

➜**Agente Naranja** This disco pub is popular with the skating and snowboarding crowd, and oftentimes all those hanging around Borda Roldanet will head here once the tapas place shuts its doors. DJs spin great music, with an eclectic mixture of house, techno, and funk. *Las Plazas s/n. No phone.*

➜**Chema** For those looking to rob the cradle, you'll find all your local underagers in this juvenile club. However, before prime partying hours (midnight in these parts), you can sometimes find the 40+ crowd and oldies tunes at this paradoxical venue. *Av. las Plazas s/n. No phone.*

➜ **La Nit** The more alternative crowd—La Nit isn't lacking in body piercings and tattoos—can be found just around the corner from Petronilla and Chema. Music is louder and more heavy-metal style, and the bar is capacious enough for getting your groove on. *Plaza Mayor s/n. No phone.*

➜ **Petronilla** Next door to Chema, Petronilla aims more for the older (but not necessarily more sophisticated) clientele. The west wing of the disco pub offers a roomy dance floor and loud house music, while the east wing has pool tables and darts and caters to those looking for a quieter environment of socializing. *At the intersection of Los Huertos and San Marsial.* ☎ *974-551-071.*

➜ **Pub Surcos** If you want to meet the locals, they all drop in to Surcos at some point in the evening. You can't blame them really, as the music is hip and catchy, and the prices aren't bad either. Learn some key Spanish phrases beforehand, and you'll be a hit with the crowd. Surcos is open daily in the winter and summer from 10:30pm until whenever the last bar-goer heads home for the night (or morning). Closed on Mondays in the spring and fall. *San Pedro s/n. No phone.*

Playing Outside

Just 4km (2½ miles) above Benasque sits **Cerler** (☎ 974-551-012; www.cerler.com), the highest **ski resort** in the whole Pyrenees. It has the first six-man chairlift to be installed in Spain, and a skiable drop of 800m (2,624 ft.) from El Gallinero, at 2,700m (8,856 ft.), to Ampriu below. If you want to venture into the nearby Posets-Maladeta but don't want to do it alone, you can sign up for one of the many activities **Barrabes** (☎ 974-551-056) offers including **trekking, climbing, rafting,** or

Para what?

If you've never heard of a little sport called 📺 (Best❢) *parapente,* that's probably because you're used to it being referred to as paragliding (differing slightly from the more popular hang gliding). This sport, where you strap on a parachute and fling yourself over the side of a mountain, is particularly popular in Spain, and the best spot to do it is just 12km (7 miles) south of Benasque in Castejón de Sos. Companies like **Parapente Pirineos** (☎ 974-553-567) and **Volar en Castejón** (☎ 974-553-504) offer tandem jumps and introductory courses. To get to Castejón de Sos by **car,** head south on the **A139.** If you don't have transportation, you can always call a **taxi** from Benasque (p. 331).

canyoning. The office is located on the first floor of the Barrabes equipment store. If Barrabes doesn't have what you're looking for, you can drop by **Sin Fronteras** on Carretera Benasque (☎ 974-550-177; www.sinfronterasadventure.com) or **Compañia de Guías Valle de Benasque** (☎ 974-551-336; www.guiasbenasque.com) at Av. de Luchón 19.

Shopping

Like most ski towns, the bulk of Benasque's stores are outdoor clothing and gear shops, like **Barrabes** (☎ 902-148-000;www.barrabes.com), a four-story gear paradise on the main street in the center of town with a host of popular outdoor brands, and **Khurp** (Edifício Comercial Los Tilos; ☎ 974-551-421; www.khurp.com) across the street, which offers an assortment of essentials for the outdoor lover, with an emphasis on clothing. If you're sick of shops for gear junkies, there are a couple clothing shops like **Poupee** (C. Los

Huertos 4; ☎ **974-552-044**), one of the only boutiques you'll find around. A bit pricey, it does offer some designer names if that's your thang.

Llanos del Hospital

On the map, there's not much to indicate signs of life between the northern cities of Spain and the French border. But if you do make the journey through the winding, dangerous paths of the Posets-Maladeta, you'll catch a glimpse of a sign announcing the presence of Llanos del Hospital, nestled snugly at the base of the Posets. A hospital may be the last thing you expect to find in the glacial gorge; however, the word "hospital" may just be the slightest bit misleading.

The Benasque Valley, which is home to the Spanish peninsula's highest peak, has long been a starting point for travelers trekking the duration of the **Camino a Santiago** and is a necessary crossing for those coming from France. The first refuge built in the Pyrenean area was on the French side in 1200. By the 18th century, the hospital in Benasque had been opened but was destroyed by a tragic avalanche at the end of the century. Several people were killed, and a new refuge took its place to prevent mishaps and deaths.

Nowadays, it is far from your vision of candy stripers and sterile operating rooms. For more than 15 years now, this hospital has served as one of the area's most historical and popular **hotels**. Open for lodging in 1994, **Llanos del Hospital** (Camino Real s/n; ☎ **974-552-012** and 608-536-053; www.llanosdelhospital.com;

single 61€–68€, double 74€–83€, triple 176€–193€, quad 186€–204€) was completely renovated in 2005. In the winter, the hotel serves as a **cross-country ski resort;** in the summer, a base for **climbers** and **hikers.** Although only a government-rated three star, Llanos del Hospital is truly stunning with its richly decorated rooms and mahogany furnishings. The elegant woodcarvings on the doors—each one unique—spacious interiors, and romantic mood lighting make for a blissful sleeping experience. The rooms are furnished with king-size beds, a rarity in a country of twins, and the stone interior lets you relive the days when the hospital was just a small hut—but in complete and utter luxury. Two-story duplex suites are available with two bedrooms, two baths, if you're in a larger group. The resort is a popular venue for weddings, so book your room in advance, especially if you'll be there on a weekend. If you can't afford an evening in one of the luxurious suites, treat yourself to a meal in the hotel's popular restaurant, where the average price of a dinner is 20€, or a drink in the bucolic bar of this living example of centuries' worth of history.

The easiest way to arrive at Llanos del Hospital is by **car** by way of the A139. A **bus** does make the trip to and from Benasque a couple times a day should you not have your own means of transportation.

Alquézar

This Moorish town of just 310 inhabitants seems a bit out of place among the other mountain villages in Aragón. And it's not the easiest place to get to either. Still, it's a nice stop-off point for a day or two and the most popular spot for **canyoning** in all of Spain. Alquézar overlooks El Parque Natural de la Sierra de Guara right smack in the center of the province of Huesca.

The **tourist office** (Arrabel s/n) is located immediately on the left as you enter the town from the southern route. It's open daily June to October from 10:30am to 1:30pm and 4:30 to 8pm (weekends only during the other months).

Getting There & Around

The only way into the town sans car is on one of the twice daily **buses** from Barbastro at 7:30am and 3pm Monday to Friday, 9:30am and 2:30pm Saturday.

By **car,** head into Barbastro, then follow the signs that mark the windy narrow road and lead 28km (18 miles) north to Alquézar. The village can be accessed two ways—via the high road, which offers panoramic views, or the lower road that deposits you directly in the main square. If you do arrive by car, you'd be wise to park above and enter the village via one of the many stone paths that lead downward.

By **foot,** you can travel into the bordering canyons by taking one of the **S4 Pasarelas del Vero,** a series of intertwining paths that leads you down into Barranco de La Fuente and Rio Vero.

Sleeping

Due to the adrenaline junkies that flood Alquézar during warm months and the large number of middle-aged tour groups that pack the town on weekends, accommodation can be hard to find if you don't phone ahead.

HOSTELS

➜ **Albergue Refugio La Era** If you don't mind sleeping shoulder-to-shoulder with other smelly backpackers, this *albergue* is for you. Located on the edge of the cliff overlooking the canyons below, Refugio La Era has the best view in town and is the place for canyoners to crash. A parking lot, indoor restaurant, and terrace dining are all favorable features. Guests are housed

¡Cuidado! Cash Out

Make sure you have ample cash with you when arriving in Alquézar. The town only has one ATM, which runs dry in summer months due to the tourist influx. Even if you do make it to the cash machine before it's empty, it may not accept your card anyway unless you're withdrawing from a Spanish account.

in the only room and share the two toilets and two showers. Outdoor excursions are available through the refuge, as are equipment rentals. *Camino Eras Bajas s/n.* ☎ *974-318-431. Price per person 22€–33€.*

➜ **Alquézar Camping** This rustic hostel with its old-fashioned stone and wood interior has three rooms with private bathrooms that each house six people. Ideal for the traveler on a budget, there is a kitchen where you can cook your own meals, and rooms cost just 10€ a person. Or if you prefer a place of your own, you can rent one of the cabin bungalows starting at 34€ for two people, 70€ for four, 81€ for five, and 90€ for six. If you have your own tent, you can rent a space and pitch it at the campsite for 4€ a night. Canyoning guides and equipment rental are also available. *Barbastro s/n.* ☎ *974-318-300. www.alquezar.com.*

➜ **Escuela-Refugio Alquézar** With 75 beds within the two-, three-, four-, and eight-people rooms, this hostel may be your best bet of finding a room should you arrive in peak season with no place to stay. *San Gregorio 30.* ☎ *974-318-966. www. prames.com/era. Price per person 20€–38€.*

CHEAP

➜ **Pensión Fonda Narbona** The greatest appeal of this centrally located place is its youthful staff, rare among hostels in Spain. With tastefully decorated rooms, most of which are doubles, you'll sleep peacefully at Fonda Narbona. A few of the rooms share a hall bathroom, while others have their own. The restaurant downstairs specializes in paella and Aragonaise dishes. *Baja 19.* ☎ *974-318-078. www.pirineo.com/ fonda_narbona. Single and double 28€– 40€, quadruple 60€–64€, extra bed 10€. Amenities: Restaurant, bar, money exchange, parking, TV.*

DOABLE

→ **Villa de Alquézar** This medieval establishment perched above the Plaza Mayor offers the most spectacular views from each room's balconies, particularly on the top floor. Some of the rooms are quite basic, but clean and comfortable, while others have intricate woodcarvings and pleasant paintings with richly colored walls. Each has a full bathroom, and prices include breakfast, which constitutes a feast that is laid out nicely for you in the first-floor restaurant. A parking lot and garage are around the back side. *Calle Pedro Arnal Cavero 12.* ☎ *974-318-416 and 608-030-207. www.villadealquezar.com. Single 50€, double 58€, triple 75€. Closed 1 week each in Dec, Jan, and Feb. In room: A/C, TV.*

Eating

A smattering of competing restaurants greets you as you enter the town, all quite similar in price and menu. For lunch and light meals, try out **Bar Restaurant O'Cabo** on the main square, with prices from 3€ to 5€. Dinner is best enjoyed at

Restaurante La Cocineta on Calle Arrabel (☎ **974-318-278** or 974-229-646; Thurs–Tues 12:30–4pm and 5:30–10:30pm). The atmosphere is soothing after a tiring day in the *barrancas* (canyons), the food and service are *fantasticós,* and the choice of music (the *Breakfast at Tiffany's* theme played during my meal) is *tranquilo.* Full meals are available for 13€, 21€, or 25€, depending on how fancy you go. Start with the *alubias de auila* (a white bean soup with seasoning), follow with the *pollo de corral estico tia visitacíon* (chicken dripping with a sweet-and-sour sauce and accompanied by fried potatoes), and for dessert, you can never go wrong with tiramisu. Don't forget to sample the house wine or sangria, both homemade and lip-smacking good.

Playing Outside

If you fancy hurling yourself off towering cliffs and into the frosty river below, you can't miss out on the chance to go **canyoning** in Spain's prime location for the sport. **Avalancha** (☎ **974-318-299**) is one of Alquézar's few guide companies that offer daily excursions to the nearby canyons. Sharing a building with **Hotel Santa Maria** on Calle Arrabal, Avalancha is open from March to December. Or make your reservations with **Casa Jotab** (C. La Iglesia; ☎ **974-318-458;** www.jotab.com), another canyoning company based in Alquézar.

Barcelona

by *Fernando Gayesky*

I heard folks in Barcelona are more interested in being clear-headed at work the next day than they are in downing their fifth whiskey and Coke. Yet it's 4am on a Wednesday morning and the colorfully decorated streets of the bohemian Gràcia neighborhood are still packed with kids jumping in the rain. Huge speakers blast ska music, wet curls and soggy dreads slosh atop bouncing heads, and everyone but me seems to know the words. I can't help but wonder, "Don't these people have to work in the morning?"

Good thing I don't have to clock in anytime soon. Since my wanderings through Barcelona began, I've partied from Thursday through Monday morning, hit the beach, and sat at cafes to drink up the electric Kool-Aid that is Barcelona along with thousands of other travelers and expats who invade this cosmopolitan city each summer. Invasions are nothing new to Barcelona, which has been dealing with travelers for the last 1,500 years thanks to its prime location on the Mediterranean. Therefore, becoming friends with out-of-towners and non-Spanish locals is an inevitable part of an authentic local experience.

I came to Gràcia's yearly street fest with a Colombian, an Argentine, a dread-locked Cuban, and a proud *gitano* (gypsy). I've met more kids from Latin America in Barcelona than actual Catalans—maybe the Catalans are as cold as they say—or maybe there are just so many South Americans here.

Other Spaniards say that Barcelona is the most European of Spain's cities—and it's not always said in a complimentary manner. But the people here are proud of their rebellious, edgy coolness that traces its routes back to ancient history. Wander the Barri Gòtic, one of the best-preserved medieval quarters in Europe, then take in Gaudí. Check out the city's amazing street murals, then Goya. Fado, bullfighting history, and now *mestizaje* and hip-hop enrich this city that's so close to the beach it hurts.

The Best of Barcelona

○ **Best Hotel:** The quirky boutique **Hostal Gat Xino** will give you a flavor of Barcelona's minimalist style without breaking the bank. See p. 352.

○ **Best Unusual Meal:** Keep your balls intact at **Foodball,** a new dining concept pioneered here by the Camper shoe company. You can get balls—whole grain rice balls, that is—stuffed with organic mushrooms, chicken, chickpeas, or tofu and algae. It's near the MACBA, and the crowd is as interesting as the food. See p. 359.

○ **Best Cafe to Get in Touch with Your Inner Self:** Follow the trails of incense onto the patio of the Maritime Museum for a late-night cup of savory tea at the **Spiritual Café** in Raval. Breathe in the rich surroundings and smoke of the hookahs. See p. 363.

○ **Best Way to Use Your Elbows: Can Paixano** has it all, excellent champagne, dirt-cheap and tasty sandwiches, and a vibe so upbeat it could make Dick Cheney crack a smile. Getting to the bar, though, will require all the elbow training that you've earned at concerts. See p. 356.

BARCELONA

Talk of the Town

Five Ways to Start a Conversation with a Local

1. **Do you speak Catalan as well as Spanish?** Ask this, sit back, and let your new Barcelona buddy go on about how the Catalans are truly bilingual. If you really want to set them off (and don't mind risking your rep), just add, "So why don't y'all just speak Spanish?" (See "Cata-*What?*" below.)

2. **Do you think Catalonia should separate from Spain?** In this fiercely independent state, separatist politics remain a hot-button issue.

3. *Mi amigo* **in Madrid said that people in Barcelona are close-minded and snooty. Why is that?** After cursing the "ignorant monkeys that spawned" the Madrileños, they'll say it's not true and counterpoint that Madrid has no sense of art, fashion, or business—especially business. As the epicenter of trade for over 2,000 years, Catalonia has been a thriving economic region that has circumvented the political bungles of Madrid.

4. **What's your favorite museum?** If you're lucky, maybe they'll even take you there. If your new friend doesn't have a favorite, shake 'em off, because in the home of some of the last century's most influential artists, everyone ought to have a *número uno.*

5. **Espanyol or Barça?** Even though FC Barcelona is by far the biggest soccer team in town, there's a smaller team, Real Deportivo Espanyol, which plays at the Olympic Stadium in Montjuïc and fights every year not to lose the category. Some Catalans hate the fact that it's called Espanyol, but true ones know that Espanyol was originally the local team while Football Club Barcelona was founded by *guiris.*

cata-What?

Barcelona is the capital of **Catalonia** (Catalunya in Catalan, Cataluña in Castilian), a region that continues to forge its identity apart from that of Spain. Many Catalans think of their region as a separate country, with its own language, traditions, and turbulent history. In the late 19th and early 20th centuries, Catalonia was a hotbed of socialist and anarchist activity. Catalan separatists established an autonomous republic (1932–38) that opposed Francisco Franco's loyalist forces during the Spanish Civil War (1936–39). Over 65 years after the end of the Spanish Civil War, Catalonia is dominated by leftists, and officials are debating a proposal that says the region has a right to separate from Spain. However, most Spaniards do not agree with recognizing Catalonia as a separate nation.

○ **Best Sunset Cocktails:** Visit Gaudí's masterpiece, **Casa Milà (La Pedrera),** and watch the sunset as you drink *cava* (chilled wine) from the whimsical rooftop terrace bar. Time it so you can catch the live music at 9pm from July to September. See p. 379.

○ **Best Mega-Club:** Partying with a group? **Razzmatazz** has several rooms playing different styles that will please nearly everyone bumping and grinding in this huge entertainment complex. See p. 371.

○ **Best Club to Find a Companion: Club 13** is a prime pick-up spot if you can shake your booty half-decently. Hip-hop Tuesdays will give you a little home advantage over all those groove devoid Europeans. See p. 370.

○ **Best Home-Grown Music:** Immigration from both within and abroad has created the Barcelona sound, **mestizaje,** a multicultural blend of Latin, Spanish, and African rhythms with a dose of hip hop and electronica. See p. 370.

○ **Best Amusement Park with a View:** Take a funicular ride up **Mount Tibidabo,** which forms the northwestern boundary of the city. When the weather's good, you can catch breathtaking views of Montserrat and the Pyrénées—and even Mallorca on the clearest days. See p. 381.

○ **Best Trip Not Involving LSD:** Explore the nooks and crannies of Gaudí's strange and enchanting **Parc Güell** that sits atop a hill and offers great views of the city. See p. 380.

○ **Best Yearly Beach Party:** The Summer party of **Sant Joan** starts with huge bonfires at the beach and ends with everybody skinny-dipping in the water at sunrise. See p. 376.

○ **Best Weekly Beach Party:** If you miss Sant Joan, don't worry. The party goes on all summer at the **Chiringuitos** in Nova Mar Bella and Barceloneta. See p. 368.

○ **Best Church You Won't Attend Mass at:** The **Sagrada Familia** is almost as surreal as those pictures of a blinking Jesus on the cross. But in full medieval fashion, it's been in the works for over 100 years and won't be finished anytime soon. See p. 381.

Getting There & Getting Around

Getting There
BY PLANE
El Prat de Llobregat Airport (☎ 932-983-838; www.barcelona-airport.com or www.aena.es) is 13km (8 miles) southwest of the city. Most people fly to Madrid and change planes there for Barcelona, although Delta has direct flights to Barcelona.

Barcelona & Beyond

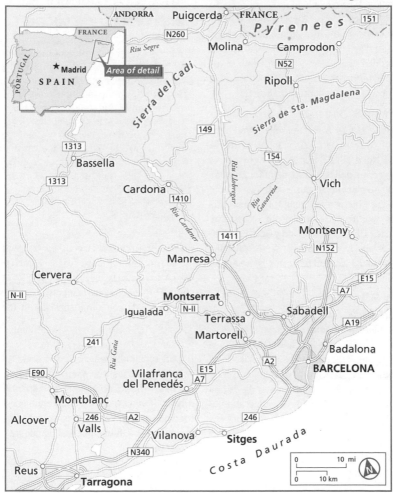

The **Aerobús** is the easiest way to get into town from El Prat; it leaves from all three terminals (A, B, and C) every 12 minutes from 6am to midnight Monday through Friday and 6:30am to midnight Saturday, Sunday, and holidays. It costs 3.60€ one-way and takes about 30 minutes to get to Plaça Espanya, Plaça Universitat, and Plaça Catalunya.

The **train** (☎ 902-240-202) also connects the airport to town. It runs from El Prat to Estació Central de Barcelona-Sants, daily from 5:38am to about 10pm. The half-hour ride costs 2.25€.

A 20-minute **taxi** ride from El Prat into town will cost about 20€ to 30€.

BY TRAIN

RENFE (☎ 902-240-202) is Spain's national train line. **Estació Sants** (Metro: Sants-Estació) handles most trains traveling within Spain. Although if you're leaving for or coming from elsewhere on the continent, you'll usually end up at the **Estació de França** (Metro: Barceloneta); look for showers, visitor info, first-aid, and shops there. The Metro goes to both stations, so you can hop aboard, get off in the Barri Gòtic (either the Liceu or Plaça Catalunya stops), and start hunting for hostels.

BY BUS

Take a bus to Barcelona only if you have time to spare. The main station, at **Estació del Nord** (Alí Bei 80; ☎ 932-656-508), is the arrival and departure point for **Entecar** (☎ 902-422-242), buses that come from southern France, Italy, and Madrid. **Linebús** (☎ 932-650-700) makes the Paris run, while **Julià Via** (☎ 934-904-000) caters to travelers from Frankfurt and Marseille. Estació del Nord's Metro stop is the Arc de Triomf.

BY BOAT

Barcelona's harbor is the biggest in the Mediterranean, with passenger services to the Balearic Islands and Genoa, Italy. **Transmediterránea** (Moll de Barcelona Station; ☎ 932-959-100 or 902-454-645) is the major ferry line between Barcelona and the Balearic Islands (trip time: about 8 hr.). There's no Metro stop here, but it's

Cuidado! Closing Times

Most people in Spain take vacation time during August. That applies also to Barcelona, where a lot of stores close their doors for 2 or 3 weeks of the month. It's a great time for driving, since locals take off and only tourists are left to cram the narrow walk-only streets of the old city. If you want to meet locals or visit tourist attractions, though, this wouldn't be the best time.

And You Thought It Was Only for Talking

In this modern day and age there are no limits for the uses you can give to your cellphone. Not only can you talk, send messages, browse the Internet, and hear some music with it, in Barcelona you can also check when the next bus is coming! Just send an SMS to 7412 with the word Temps, the code of the stop you are at (a four-digit number you'll see at the pole at the stop), and the bus line number and, *voilà!* The TMB will answer.

only a 10-minute walk from the Drassanes Metro stop at the base of Las Ramblas. Take a taxi if you're lugging around a lot of stuff. *Tip:* Make your reservation as far in advance as you can, especially in the summer.

BY CAR

Driving tip number one: Do not drive here! As in Madrid, it's not worth the hassle—too much traffic, no parking, and Spanish drivers. If you do decide to take the coast road during the high season, expect to be slogging through bumper-to-bumper traffic at times.

Getting Around
BY SUBWAY

The Metro (subway) is clean and efficient, but doesn't have any stops in the Ciutat Vella, so the stops closest to where you want to get on/off are on Las Ramblas or Port Olímpic. A single ticket (valid for both the Metro and buses) costs 1.15€, but if you intend to take more than five journeys, it's best to buy the T10 ticket for 6.30€ that is good for 10 trips. And yes, as in just about every city, you'll see locals jump the turnstiles. Before you're tempted, keep in mind the squares in the red pinstripe shirts. If you're caught by them without a Metro ticket, you'll be fined 40€. The Metro runs from 5am to midnight Sunday through Thursday and 5am to 2am Friday through Saturday.

BY TRAM

There are four tramlines. They run from near central parts of the city to towns on the outskirts. They work from 9am to 2pm and 4 to 7pm, Monday to Thursday, 9am to 2pm Friday. For information call Trambaix ☎ 902-193-275.

BY BUS

There are plenty of buses with routes and timetables clearly marked at each stop. Be aware that most buses stop running well before the Metro closes and you'll be at the mercy of nasty traffic jams. As with the Metro, a single ticket costs 1.15€.

BY BICYCLE

There are a few bicycle lanes in the center of the city, along with places that will rent bikes, including **Un Coxte Menys** (Espartaria 3; ☎ 932-682-105), and **Biciclot** (Verneda 16; ☎ 933-077-475). You are not required by law to wear a helmet, so you don't have to worry about smashing your weave—just your brains.

Barcelona Basics

Orientation: Barcelona Neighborhoods

Pushing up against the Mediterranean Sea, Barcelona's coastline runs from southwest to northeast. It'll only take you 10 minutes to walk from the beach's cool breeze to city-slicker sleaze once you pass the **Mirador de Colón** (p. 379) and hit Las Ramblas.

📺 Best❖ **Las Ramblas,** a wide promenade that is the city's main artery, stretches all the way to **Plaça Catalunya.** From end to end, it's about a 20-minute walk, but that doesn't count all the time taken to snap a photo with the silver chick statue (how she gets the paint out of her hair is beyond me), peruse the newsstands, buy a gerbil, or just sit at one of the many cafes and watch the herd shuffle along. It can get pretty crowded sometimes. Keep drifting northward on Las Ramblas, and the **El Raval** neighborhood will be to your left and the **Barri Gòtic** to your right. Put the two together and you get a meaty portion of the **Ciutat Vella (Old City),** where most of what you want to see awaits.

Cuidado! Wallet Watch

I wouldn't say Barcelona is a dangerous city (there's almost no violent crime), but with the increase of tourism, the levels of pickpocketing and bag-snatching have become a little alarming. You should be cautious, especially at night. The neighborhoods of Raval and Sant Pere, with their dark, narrow alleys and lots of corners to hide, are a snatcher's paradise, particularly after bars' closing hours (3am). Stick to main streets, like Via Laietana or Ronda Sant Pau. The rule of thumb is, if cars go by, it's safe. Barri Gòtic and el Born tend to be safer because of increased police presence. The airport is another quick-finger's turf and the most likely place for you to get your passport stolen, so be aware of your bags at all times—the police station is a really awful place to start your vacation.

El Raval is a multicultural mash of mazelike streets that smell like tandoori chicken and pee. This neighborhood used to be the Dirty South of Barcelona, full of hookers, hard drugs, and muggers. But, like Mariah Carey, this place has experienced a remarkable comeback. Thanks to gentrification (aka "urban renewal") and police crackdowns, the place has been cleaned up. It's still a little grimy, but the construction of the sleek **Museu d'Art Contemporani** (see "Museums," later in this chapter) brought in trendy new galleries, shops, and artsy bars. You should still keep your eyes open and hold on to your bags on L'Arc del Teatre which points south in the area known as **Barri Xinès** (literal translation: Chinatown; actual meaning: red-light district). Since the cops came stomping through, the worst that will probably happen to you is an old prostitute named Tita might suck her teeth at you by the port. But still be wary of your wallet, and women should not wander through here alone, especially on Carrer de Hospital.

The **MTV Best♦ Barri Gòtic** is the city's oldest quarter; here you'll find the **Cathedral de Barcelona** (see "Performing Arts," later in this chapter). It's best to wander through the narrow, winding cobblestone streets at dusk when the buildings warm up to the fading Mediterranean light and the street musicians come out to play. On the northeastern edge of Barri Gòtic (about a 15-min. walk northeast from the center of Las Ramblas) is the must-check-out bohemian neighborhood **El Born,** with some good eats and drinks, as well as the **Museu Picasso (Picasso Museum;** see "Museums," later in this chapter). The Born is the latest up-and-coming neighborhood whose gentrification includes coffee and pastry shops, old-style delis, and designer shops.

Important streets to know about in case you get lost are the east-west **Gran Vía** (officially Gran Vía de les Corts Catalanes), which runs through Plaça Espanya and is just a few blocks north of Plaça Catalunya. **Avinguda Diagonal** runs northwest to southeast and cuts the whole city in half 10 blocks northwest of the Ciutat Vella. Passeig de Gràcia begins at Plaça Catalunya and runs north to Avinguda Diagonal. Besides the Gaudí buildings on Passeig de Gràcia, there really isn't much to see on the other streets.

Gràcia, about an hour's walk to the northwest of Ciutat Vella, was once a separate village outside the city walls erected by the Romans. Those walls are long gone, yet this mildly bohemian and chill community still has a strong sense of identity and neighborhood pride ("Gràcia for life, holmz")

A Euro Saved . . .

The **Barcelona Card** is worth every penny if you plan on hitting up a lot of attractions. It offers steep discounts on admissions and free, unlimited use of public transportation. You can buy this card to cover 1 to 5 days. The price ranges from 17€ to 30€. For adults, it's 17€ for 1 day and 22€ for 2 days, for example.

The 24-hour card includes the Metro and the bus, and unlimited travel on all public transport. You can also use the card to get discounts of 10% to 100% in 29 museums; 10% to 25% off some theaters and shows; and discounts at other venues. In addition, there's a 10% to 12% savings at about two dozen stores and 18 restaurants. Check the cards for specifics when you buy one. They're for sale at the tourist offices at the airport, at Sants Station, and in the Plaça de Catalunya. See "The Ruta del Modernisme: L'Eixample & Gaudí" on p. 380 for another discount offering.

wwwired

You'll find access to the Internet throughout town but especially in Ciutat Vella. Many *locutorios* (see below) also have Internet access.

EasyInternetCafé has over 300 terminals in this modern center. Just don't let the bright orange walls blind you—a few travelers have lost their wallets to thieves here. You can burn CDs, scan, copy, and fax. It's located at Las Ramblas 31 (**www.easyinternetcafe.com**). They charge 1.80€ per hour; a 1-day unlimited pass is 4€, a 7-day pass is 10€, 30 days is 20€. It's open daily from 8am to 2:30am (Metro: Liceu). A branch at Ronda Universitat 35 is a little less expensive (daily 8am–2am; Metro: Catalunya).

Bcnet's Internet cafe also doubles as a gallery, at Carrer Barra de Ferro 3, down the street from the Museu Picasso. Call ☎ **932-681-507.** It's 2.40€ per hour, and a 10-hour ticket is 18€ (Mon–Fri 10am–10pm, Sat–Sun noon–10:30pm; Metro: Jaume I).

Euro NetCenter is at Carrer Marqués de Barbera 19, a block off Las Ramblas. It charges .50€ per 30 minutes (daily 11am–10pm; Metro: Liceu).

MS Internet, at Carrer Pintor Fortuny 30, is 3 blocks off Las Ramblas in El Raval. Call ☎ **933-175-562.** You can surf here for 1€ per hour (Mon–Sat 9:30am–9:30pm; Metro: Liceu or Catalunya).

marked by its annual street parties in August (p. 377). Grab a drink at the Plaça de Sol and act like you're from *el barrio, vato.*

North of Plaça Catalunya is **L'Eixample,** which means "the expansion," and is simply a huge grid of commercial streets void of any character with the exception of Gaudí's mutant modernista behemoths— **Sagrada Familia, Casa Milà,** and **Casa Batlló**—and the **Quadrat d'Or (Golden Triangle).**

Don't bother walking through the **Sants-Montjuïc,** a plain middle-class neighborhood on the west end of the city. Go straight to the summit of Mont Juïc (the big mountain and Barcelona's highest point) which is crammed with museums, botanical gardens, a fortress, and the 1992 Olympic grounds. **Plaça de Espanya** on the southeastern end is also cool, with its wild fountains. The **Poble Espanyol** area has a handful of good clubs—most notably/ notorious La Terrrazza (see "Clubs & Discos," later in this chapter). And if you must,

there's Epcot's unwanted stepchild, the Poble Espanyol mini—theme park (see "Top Attractions," later in this chapter).

Back to the beach, follow Colombus's lead, head east and cross the **Rambla de Mar** footbridge to Maremagnum, a "waterfront development area" (read: mall with a boardwalk). Here you'll find shops, an aquarium, overpriced restaurants, an IMAX, and pimply teenagers. There are several clubs offering free entrances and drinks, but unless you're broke or a middle-aged white guy looking for prostitutes, it's best to avoid them. Further down you'll find the old fishermen's neighborhood of **Barceloneta,** a necessary stop for good fish, seaside bars and restaurants, and the most crowded and dirtiest beaches. Avoid eating at the boardwalk restaurants in **Sant Joan de Borbó,** unless you like paying high prices for bad food. But leave the boardwalk and enter the matrix of narrow streets, and you'll find an excellent array of local favorites.

Keep walking northeast along the coast for 5 minutes and you'll hit the **Port Olímpico.** Wow. How terribly *un*exciting. But hey, at least the beach starts here. After passing the Hotel Arts and the Torre Mapfre and the *guiri-* (foreigner-) infested **Villa Olimpica,** you'll get to the bohemian seaside enclave of **Poble Nou,** the typical former-industrial-neighborhood-slowly-being-taken-over-by-artists that you can find in most big cities, except that this one is only a few blocks from the best beaches in Barcelona. Save the streets by the beach, this is the quietest area of Barcelona, with a nice *Rambla* and beautiful old fishing village.

TOURIST OFFICES

The main office is located underground at the Plaça Catalunya. Look for the sign with a big, red "I." The office has free magazines and fliers, including info on the big clubs and bars, and will make hotel reservations for you. The **Barcelona Card** (see p. 344) can also be picked up here. Call ☎ **807-117-222** from inside Spain or ☎ **933-683-730** from outside (www.barcelonaturisme.com; daily 9am–9pm; Metro: Catalunya).

Recommended Websites

- **Barceloca.com**: An all-round guide to what's on or available in the city. Restaurants, bars, clubs, and everything else you can think of.
- **GoGayBCN.com**: In Spanish and Catalan, this caters to LGBT travelers, with apartment listings and a Gay Guide.
- **Barcelonareporter.com**: A news, opinion, and information resource on Catalonia.
- **bcn.es**: The city's bilingual website.
- **Lifestylebarcelona.com**: Specializes in offering "unique experiences" in and around the city, from parachute jumping to chocolate massages.

Culture Tips 101

Catalan is one of Spain's four native languages and the regional (or national, depending on your politics) language of Catalonia. It's somewhat of a half-Spanish, half-French love child of the Pyrenees and you can get the gist of what's going on if you speak either of the two. After years of being outlawed during the Franco dictatorship, Catalan has returned to Barcelona and the rest of the region in full force. All of the signs, menus, and TV and radio shows are in Catalan. Fortunately, everyone also speaks perfect Spanish. It's totally cool to address someone in *castellano* (Castilian, aka Spanish) without first asking if they speak it, but you'll definitely make them crack a smile if you spit out a few Catalan phrases.

Useful Catalan Phrases

- **Hola** (hello) **Adéu** (goodbye)
- **Perdoni/disculpi** (pardon me/excuse me)
- **Merci/grácies** (thank you) **De res** (you're welcome)
- **Ho sento, no parlo català** (I'm sorry, I don't speak Catalan)
- **Parla anglès?** (Do you speak English?)
- **Si'us plau** (please)
- **Molt bé** (very good/okay)
- **Quant és?** (How much is it?)
- **Jo estimo als animals, per això no me'ls menjo** (I love animals, so I don't eat them)

Barcelona **Nuts & Bolts**

Cellphone Providers   The three main cellphone companies are **Amena, Movistar,** and **Vodafone,** and they have offices everywhere. To recharge your phone, you can do it at ATMs, locutorios (see below), and there are also some cellphone ATMs in drugstores and cellphone stores. If you have an American phone, head to the Pakistani cellphone stores in Raval. They'll unblock it and sell you a SIM card for local calls only with your own Spanish number and 10€ credit for 15€.

Crisis Centers   If the partying got a little out of hand and you need assistance with drugs call **Narcotics Anonymous** (☎ **902-114-147**; www.na-esp.org), for info on drugs call **Energy Control** ☎ **902-253-600** (see "Testing 1-2-3," p. 376).

Currency   There are several **banks** around Plaça Catalunya, Las Ramblas, and on Plaça de Sant Jaume in Barri Gòtic. General banking hours are Monday through Friday from 8:30am to 2pm. You'll probably get the best rates at **ATMs** (you'll need a four-digit PIN, so call your bank before you leave home to get one). Many **exchange stations** stay open late in Las Ramblas, but you won't get a good rate. Hotels should be your last resort; they give the poorest rates.

Embassies & Consulates   If you lose your passport, are really sick, fall into the hands of the law, or get into some other serious trouble, the embassy can help. The **United States Consulate,** Passeig de la Reina Elisenda de Montcada 23 (☎ **932-802-227**; FFCC train: Reina Elisenda), is open Monday to Friday from 9am to 1pm.

Emergencies   In an emergency, dial ☎ **112** for the main number for the municipal **police,** to report a **fire,** or to request an **ambulance.** To dial for an **ambulance** directly, use ☎ **061.** If you are the victim of a crime and want to call the **police** directly, dial ☎ **091.** If you've been pickpocketed, go to **Turisme Atenció** at Carrer Nou de la Rambla 80 (☎ **933-441-300**) in El Raval, 3 blocks from the port; this police stations deals specifically with tourists.

Laundry   There are several self-service **laundromats and dry cleaners** in the **Ciutat Vella.** Some hostels have laundry facilities and charge an average of 7€ a load, wash and dry. **Lavomatic** is at Plaça Joaquim Xirau 1 (☎ **933-441-300**), 1 block to the right of Las Ramblas and 1 block below Carrer Escudellers. A wash is 3.75€ and a dry is .75€ for 5 minutes of hot air. It's open Monday through Saturday from 10am to 10pm. **Wash @ Net** is at Carrer les Carretes 56, near Las Ramblas in El Raval. A wash is 4€ to 6€ and a dry is 1€ every 10 minutes. You can surf the Internet for .50€ per 30 minutes. It's open daily from 10am to 11pm.

Luggage Storage   Estació Barcelona-Sants (☎ **934-956-200**) rents lockers for 4.50€ a day. It is open daily from 5:30am to 11pm. **Estació de França** (☎ **934-963-464**) rents lockers for 3.50€ per day, daily from 7am until 10pm.

Pharmacies   Look for signs with green neon crosses. They rotate the 24-hour shift, so check any pharmacy window to see the nearest one on duty.

Post Office   The **main post office** is on Plaça d'Antoni López, facing the water at the end of Passeig de Colom (☎ **902-197-197**), and is open Monday to Saturday

8:30am to 9:30pm and on Sunday from 8:30am to 2:30pm. You can also pick up stamps at *estancos* (the kiosks that say TABACO) and just drop off your postcards or letters in any of the bright yellow mailboxes throughout the city.

Restrooms Call them *aseos, servicios, lavabos,* or whatever. Make a beeline to the back of any restaurant or bar and be sure to go through the correct door—CABALLEROS or SEÑORES means men, and DAMAS or SEÑORAS is for women.

Safety Unlike the folks in Madrid, Barcelona locals won't constantly remind you to walk with your handbags in front of you—but don't get too comfortable. Tourist-infested zones like the Ciutat Vella and on or around Las Ramblas and on the Metro are prime hunting grounds for pickpockets. **Petty theft and pickpocketing** are problems, so avoid being a target and keep a limited supply of your money in a secure place on your body. Be especially careful around the Picasso Museum, Parc Güell, Plaza Real, and Mont Juïc.

Telephone Tips To use a phone booth, it's best to buy a *tarjeta telefónica* from a newsstand or *estanco,* as many do not take coins. All have dialing instructions in English. If your family likes to pass the phone around so everyone in the house can say "hi," it's better you look for a *locutorio* (call center). They're all over Ciutat Vella, give better rates, and offer a booth for privacy. For **directory assistance,** dial ☎ **1003** for numbers within Spain, **1008** within Europe, and **1005** for the rest of the world. **Toll-free numbers** are phone numbers that begin with **900.** Calling an **800** number in the States from Spain is *not* free and costs the same as an international call.

Tipping Prices shown on menus have to include any **service charge.** Only when the menu indicates *"IVA no incluido"* (VAT not included) can this be added to the bill. **Tips** are not compulsory, but plan to dish out an additional 5% to 10% when you're happy with the service. **Taxi drivers** don't expect tips.

Sleeping

What is it that makes sleeping in Barcelona so much more expensive than Madrid? Well, it could be that the population nearly doubles with young tourists during the summertime. Expect to pay around 80€ for a double and 50€ for a single, and you'll just have to learn to deal with the cramped, overpriced hostels if you're on a tight budget. If you want to stay in the touristy areas like Las Ramblas or Barri Gòtic, make reservations weeks, even months in advance. If you didn't plan ahead, your best bet is to show up at hostels around 11am when they know exactly who's sticking around another night and who's taking off (there are several on Carrer de la Unió). You could also try staying in Gràcia which will have more vacancies and is not too far from Ciutat Vella. If all else fails, go to the tourist office—they can make reservations for you.

Hostels
MTV Best ● →**Albergue de Juventud Kabul** If you want a good night's rest, steer clear from this animal house. But if it's an all-night party you're looking for, about 200 frat boys and sorority gals are crammed into rooms of four to eight people; you can expect to be awoken in the

middle of the night by drunks looking for their bunks. Smack dab in backpacker central, the party leaks in from the streets to the common rooms that blast American music. *Plaça Reial 17.* ☎ *933-185-190. www. kabul.es. Single bed 15€–23€. Key deposit 15€. No reservations. Amenities: Bar, free Internet, laundry (2.50€), pool table, TV (in common room). In room: A/C. Metro: Liceu.*

→ **Backpackers BCN** This small hostel is far away enough from the center of Barcelona to be safer and quieter, but still within walking distance of Las Ramblas (10 min.). On your down time, grab a book from their library and chill on the terrace, check out a DVD in the common room, or cook dinner in their full-service kitchen. Nice place to stay if you want to relax and get a good night's sleep. Max four people to a room, 18 beds total. *Carrer Diputación, 323 principal 1a.* ☎ *934-880-280. Single bed 22€. Breakfast included. Amenities: Curfew 3am–7:30am, kitchen, lockers (5€ deposit), patio, PlayStation, sheets, TV (in common room), free Wi-Fi. Metro: Passeig de Gràcia.*

→ **Centric Point Youth Hostel** We feel odd listing three hostels in the same chain, but this new one has really outdone itself. If your sleeping sardine style days are over, this is your spot. In a modernista building and offering a wider range of sleeping options than the other Point Hostels, this place is chill and the interior design merits the exterior; arched windows with views around the Rambla and Passeig. Common areas have a more refined decor than most youth hostels and the atmosphere is less chaotic. *Passeig de Gràcia 33.* ☎ *932-312-045. www.centricpointhostel.com. Per person 12 bed 22€, per person 6 bed 23€, quad 25€, triple 34€, twin 50€, double 55€. Breakfast included. Amenities: Bar, bike rental, common area, Internet, organized events/ tours, sheets, towels (2€), TV. In room: A/C. Metro: Passeig de Gràcia.*

→ **Gothic Point Youth Hostel** Comfy couches, a large TV, colorful decor, and free Internet make the lobby a great place to hang out and meet other backpackers. There are 150 beds in dorm-style rooms, but each bed has its own shelf, outlet for plugging things in, and reading light and can be curtained off for added privacy. About a 10-minute walk from the most popular bars. Sea Point Youth Hostel is its sister hostel on the beach nearby. *Plaça del Mar 4.* ☎ *932-247-075. Carrer Vigatans 5.* ☎ *932-687-808. www.gothicpoint.com. High sea-son single bed 22€; low season single bed 17€. Breakfast included. Amenities: Free Internet, lockers (1.20€ per day), fridge, rooftop terrace, sheets (1.80€), towels (1.80€), vending machines. In room: A/C. Metro: Jaume I.*

→ **Sea Point Youth Hostel** The second of the Point hostel trio in BCN, this one lacks the privacy of Gothic Point but makes up for it with beach access, yes that's correct a youth hostel in front of the Platja San Sebastia. So we won't blabber on about the other perks, except to say it's clean too. *Plaça del Mar 4.* ☎ *932-247-075. www.sea pointhostel.com. Per bed 17€–22€. Breakfast included. Amenities: Bike rental, common area, Internet, organized events/tours, sheets (2€), towels (2€), telephone, TV. In room: A/C, lockers (1.50€). Metro: Barceloneta.*

Cheap

→ **Hostal La Terrassa** You get what you pay for, so don't expect spectacular views and chocolate on your pillow. The 50 sparely decorated rooms are claustrophobically small. Some rooms have terraces (only .6m/2 ft. deep), but everyone can use the outdoor terrace on the main floor. The friendly staff speaks English. People gather in the large and impeccably clean eating/chilling area, where you can watch TV, bring in food from outside, or grab a

Sleeping & Eating in Barcelona

SLEEPING ■

Albergue de Juventud Kabul **26**
Backpackers BCN **48**
Bany's Orientals **37**
Casa Camper **17**
Centric Point Youth Hostel **49**
Gothic Point Youth Hostel **39**
Hostal Gat Xino **6**
Hostal Goya **47**
Hostal La Terrassa **10**
Hostal Malda **22**
Hotel Arts **33**
Hotel Peninsular **12**
Mesón Castilla **19**
Park Hotel **35**
Sea Point Youth Hostel **31**

EATING ◆

Agua **32**
Arola **33**
Bar Jai-ca **29**
Bar Jardí **21**
Bar Mundial **45**
Bon Bocat **25**
Can Maño **30**
Can Paixano **28**
Candela **46**
El Café que Pone
  Muebles Navarro **7**
El Foc **2**
El Rosal **41**
El Sortidor **1**
Els Quatre Gats **20**
Foodball **17**
Kashmir **11**
King Döner **9**
Kiosco Universal **16**
La Báscula **40**
La Reina del Rava **8**
Laurel **5**
L'Economic **43**
Machito **50**
Mercat Sant Antoni **4**
Mercat Santa Catarina **44**
Mercat de Sant Josep/
  La Boqueria **16**
Origen 99.9% **38**
Papitu **15**
Pla dels Angels **18**
Quimet-I-Quimet **3**
Ra **14**
Romesco **13**
Santa Maria **42**
Shunka **23**
Spiritual Café **27**
Teranga **36**
Vaso de Oro **34**
Venus **24**

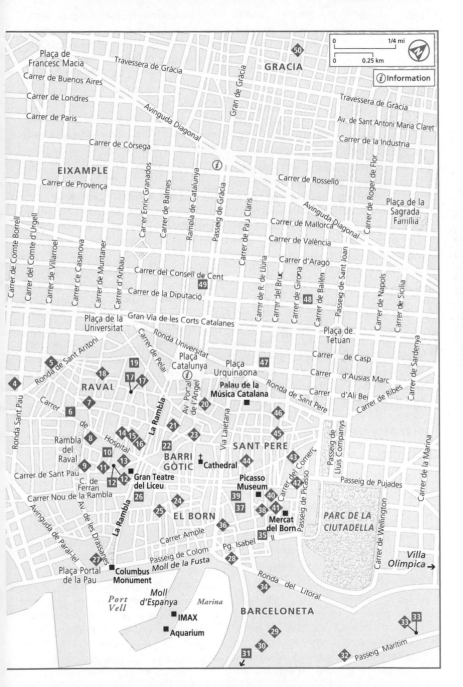

Plaça de Francesc Macia
Carrer de Buenos Aires
Carrer de Londres
Carrer de Paris
Travessera de Gràcia
Avinguda Diagonal
Gran de Gràcia
GRACIA

50

Travessera de Gràcia
Av. de Sant Antoni Maria Claret
Carrer de la Industria

Carrer de Còrsega

EIXAMPLE
Carrer de Provença

Carrer de Rosselló

Carrer Enric Granados
Carrer de Balmes
Rambla de Catalunya
Passeig de Gràcia
Carrer de Pau Claris

Avinguda Diagonal
Carrer de Mallorca
Carrer de València

Carrer de Roger de Flor

Plaça de la Sagrada Família

Carrer de Còrsega

Carrer del Comte Borrell
Carrer del Comte d'Urgell
Carrer de Villarroel
Carrer de Casanova
Carrer ce Casanova
Carrer de Muntaner
Carrer d'Aribau

Carrer del Consell de Cent
49
Carrer de la Diputació

Carrer de R. de Llúria
Carrer del Bruc
Carrer de Girona
Carrer de Bailèn
Passeig de Sant Joan

Carrer d'Aragó

48

Carrer de Napols
Carrer de Sicilia

Plaça de la Universitat
Gran Via de les Corts Catalanes
Ronda Universitat
Plaça Catalunya

Plaça de Tetuan

Carrer de Sardenya

Carrer de Sant Antoni
Ronda de Sant Antoni
5
18
RAVAL
19
17 17
Carrer de Pelai

Plaça Urquinaona
47
Plaça Catalunya

Carrer de Casp
Carrer d'Ausias Marc
Carrer d'Ali Bei
Carrer de Ribes

4
Carrer
7
6
de
8
Rambla del Raval
9
10 11
12 17
13
14 15 16
22
La Rambla
Av. Portal de l'Angel
20
21
23

Palau de la Música Catalana
Ronda de Sant Pere
Via Laietana
46
45

SANT PERE
43
44
Carrer del Comerç
Passeig de Lluís Companys

Carrer de la Marina

Rambla del Raval
Carrer de Sant Pau
Carrer de Sant Pau
13

BARRI GÒTIC
† **Cathedral**

Picasso Museum
39
40 41
42

Passeig de Pujades

PARC DE LA CIUTADELLA

Carrer de Sant Pau
26
C. de Ferran
Gran Teatre del Liceu
Carrer Nou de la Rambla
Avinguda de Paral·lel
La Rambla
Av. de les Drassanes
25
24
36
EL BORN
37
38
35
Mercat del Born
Passeig de Picasso

Carrer de Wellington

27
Carrer Ample
Pg. Isabel
28
Plaça Portal de la Pau
Columbus Monument
Passeig de Colom
Moll de la Fusta
Ronda del Litoral
34

Villa Olímpica →

Port Vell
Moll d'Espanya
Marina
■ **IMAX**
■ **Aquarium**

BARCELONETA
29
33 33
32 Passeig Marítim
31 30

0   1/4 mi
0   0.25 km
ⓘ Information

ⓘ

snack from the vending machine. *Junta de Comerç 11.* ☎ *933-025-174. Double 46€–50€, triple 50€–66€. Amenities: Dining area, terrace. In room: A/C, TV. Metro: Liceu.*

➔ **Hostal Malda** These are the cheapest, cleanest beds in Barri Gòtic, hands down. The only drawback is that the hotel is on the third floor (no elevator) and they don't give you your own key (you have to be buzzed in), but the location within the hustle and bustle of the Barri Gòtic and price more than make up for that. No reservations, so show up by 10am to snag one of the 30 rooms. *Carrer Pi 5 (entrance inside small shopping center).* ☎ *933-173-002. Single 15€, double 30€, triple with shower 45€. Amenities: Shared bathrooms, TV (in common room). Metro: Liceu.*

Doable

➔ **Bany's Orientals** ★★ There are reasons all the guidebooks and travel mags rave about this establishment. Here are some of them: high ceiling loft style suites with patios, dark wooden floors and refined modern furniture, marble bathrooms so clean you could lick them, primo location in the Born and a stone's throw away from the Barri Gòtic—and the list goes on . . . On the downside, it's usually booked and lacks common areas—but who needs them when you're in the heart of it all? *Calle Argenteria 37.* ☎ *932-688-460. www.hotelbanysorientals.com. Single 80€–90€, double 95€, suite 125€, extra bed 40€ Amenities: Breakfast room, elevator, Internet, travel info, rooms for those w/limited mobility. In room: A/C, TV, hair dryer, Internet, safe. Metro: Jaume I.*

➔ **Casa Camper** Like any good rebel, Camper knows how to use the color red, ration its water, and treat its troops. Mallorcan peasant mantras are integrated into Barcelonian progressive design and translated as spacious, red-walled yet understated rooms with lounges, hammocks, and plasma TVs. All this brought to you with environmental awareness and an easy spirit. Best place to stay if you hang in front of the MACBA and right next to their shoe store and cafe Foodball (p. 359). *Elizabets 11.* ☎ *933-426-280. www.casacamper. com. Single 185€–215€, double 200€–235€, suite 205€–255€. Breakfast/snacks included. Amenities: Breakfast bar, free bikes, rooms for those w/limited mobility, Wi-Fi. In room: A/C, TV, DVD and CD players. Metro: Catalunya.*

📺 **Best ●** ➔ **Hostal Gat Xino** ★★ Centrally located in the Barri Xinès of the Raval district, this modern hostel is stylish and comfortable with its groovy green decor, en-suite flatscreen satellite TVs, high-power jet showers, and incredibly soft sheets. The best rooms have private terraces. There's also a breezy breakfast area, a wood-decked patio, and a roof terrace perfect for an afternoon smoke. *Hospital 155.* ☎ *933-248-833. Single 64€–75€, double 96€, quad suite 128€. Breakfast included. Amenities: Breakfast room, patio, roof terrace. In room: A/C, TV, Internet. Metro: Sant Antoni.*

➔ **Hostal Goya** ★★ The address may be posh, but the service is comforting. You can make yourself at home with free tea, coffee, and hot chocolate in the Scandinavian-looking communal TV room. Half the rooms have been renovated and have that minimalist IKEA look, with comfy beds, plush duvets, and throw pillows. The best rooms are doubles with balconies and the worst are small, dark singles. Be sure to reserve in advance because it fills up quickly. *Pau Claris 74.* ☎ *933-022-565. www. hostalgoya.com. Single with shared bathroom 34€, double with shared bathroom 73€, double with private bathroom 88€. Amenities: Terrace, TV (in common room). In room: A/C (in some rooms). Metro: Urquinaona or Catalunya.*

➜ **Hotel Peninsular** ★ Maybe it's good karma from once having housed a convent that makes this hotel genuinely one of the nicest places to stay in Barcelona. The iron railings, relaxing courtyard, and plant-draped atrium extending to the glass ceiling make this an oasis within the grimy Barri Xinès. The rooms are spacious and clean, and the hotel serves a decent continental breakfast. *Sant Pau 34.* ☎ *933-023-138. Single with shared bathroom 30€, single with private bathroom 50€, double with shared bathroom 50€, double with private bathroom 70€. Breakfast included. Amenities: Breakfast bar, safe, TV (in common room). In room: A/C. Metro: Liceu.*

➜ **Mesón Castilla** The photos you take of yourself having breakfast in the charismatic tiled courtyard or leaning against the baroque painted headboards on the damask covered beds or under the Catalan flag in front of Mesón Castilla are going to bring back fonder memories than the ones of you on a Habitat couch in an all too common design hotel. Since Méson is government-rated and owned by the megachain Husa it has all the creature comforts and it's surprisingly quiet for the location. *Calle Valldoncella 5.* ☎ *933-182-182. hmeson castilla@teleline.es. Double 120€. Amenities: Breakfast room, courtyard, fax, laundry service, lounge, parking, rooms for those w/limited mobility, TV. In room: A/C, TV, hair dryer, minibar, safe. Metro: Catalunya, Universitat.*

➜ **Park Hotel** Blame the gringo in us, but we love the 1950s design of this hotel. The long tiled bar, glass bricks, and spiral staircase make us swoon. The bedrooms, although more neutral, still have a bit of retro feel. Just across the street from Estació de França, on the edge of the Born, and very convenient to Barceloneta and Parc de la Ciutadella, you can't beat the location. *Av. Marques de l'Argenteria. 11.*

☎ *933-196-000. www.parkhotelbarcelona.com. Single 120€, double 155€. Breakfast included. Amenities: Restaurant, bar, breakfast room, fax, laundry service, parking, rooms for those w/limited mobility, TV, Wi-Fi. In room: A/C, TV, hair dryer, minibar, safe, Wi-Fi. Metro: Liceu.*

Splurge

➜ **Hotel Arts** Most Catalans view this 44-story luxury hotel as an obstruction to their view of the sea, and they can't understand why architect Bruce Graham chose to surround it with a white frame obstructing the views from inside as well. However, once inside, another world opens up. A world where execs close million dollar deals on roof deck pools and Juicy Couture track suits blend with Burberry golf pants in the Salon de Té. This is the first Ritz-Carlton in Europe after all. The five dining options including Arola, BCN's sexiest tapas bar (p. 356) and the more laid-back Bites, where you and your friends can share a salad and sneak a peek at who's checking in or marvel at how much better Frank Gehry's *Fish* looks from this side. If you're really lucky you can get a Chromotherapy treatment next to fashion's new It Girl at the spa on the 42nd floor (maybe she'll invite you back to her duplex suite and ask her personal butler to light your cigar). The incredibly comfortable neutral palette rooms are decked out with Bang and Olufsen entertainment systems and Aqua di Parma products. You would be hard-pressed to see the rest of the city when you could just stay in this hotel all day. *Calle Marina 19-21.* ☎ *932-211-000. www.hotelarts barcelona.com. Suite 370€–10,000€, apt. 1,300€–2,600€. Amenities: Restaurants, bars, fitness center, Jacuzzi, laundry service/dry cleaning, pool, rooms for those w/limited mobility, spa. In room: A/C, TV, DVD and CD players, hair dryer, Internet, minibar, room service, safe. Metro: Ciutadella-Vila Olimpica.*

12 Hours in Barcelona

1. Dive headfirst into Barcelona's signature modernista architecture by following the **Ruta del Modernisme.** Start by figuring Gaudí out in **La Pedrera,** then finish at his never-ending masterpiece in **Sagrada Familia** (p. 381).

2. Relive the times of knights and princesses in the **Barri Gòtic's** (p. 344) stone alleys. Keep your eyes open and you'll also see Roman aqueducts and ruins.

3. Take a swim at the beach in **Nova Mar Bella** (p. 383). Dry off with a drink at one of the *chiringuitos,* sweat and dance for a while, then jump back in the water for a moon bath.

4. Trip your brains out without ingesting any substances at **Parc Güell's** dreamy gardens and landscapes (p. 380).

5. OD on seafood at **Universal** in Mercat de la Boqueria or **Mundial** in El Born; top it off with the best ice cream this side of the Pyrenees at **Cremeria Toscana** (see "Eating," p. 354).

6. Start your night raid sipping *cosmos* at **Bar Bodega Teo** (p. 365), warm up those dancing feet at **Club 13** (p. 370), and finish with a sunrise splash at **Liquid** (p. 371).

7. Take the tram up to **Montjuïc** (p. 381) and get lost in a sea of green landscaping, then suck in some culture at **Fundación Miró** and get soaked at the **magic fountains.**

8. Visit neighboring museums **MACBA** and **CCCB** (p. 378) for some modern art and cool exhibitions. Once you're all cultured-out try and pick up a skater boy or girl in the Plaça.

Eating

As skinny as the women may be, Barcelonians know how to eat. Whether Cuban, Indian, Basque, American, or a ubiquitous multinational chain, Barcelona offers every kind of food you could desire, yet at less-than-desirable prices. The cheapest way to fill your belly is to hit up the *mercats* (markets) for fresh foods and pick up other staples at *supermercats/supermercados* (grocery stores).

Most restaurants, even some expensive ones, have a *menú del día* (lunch menu), with a price range from 6€ to 15€ for an appetizer, entree, dessert, and wine. Have a really good, big lunch at a reasonable price, and then just have tapas for dinner.

The downside is that you waste two sightseeing hours right in the middle of the day; but since the sun doesn't set till 9:30pm in the summer, it's no big deal.

Another option: Pick up a *bocadillo,* a no-frills baguette filled with meats, cheese, or an omelet. For late-night snacks (overpriced chips and candy), check out the news kiosks on Las Ramblas. And then there's *döner kebab*—everywhere!

Lunch is eaten from 2 to 4pm and is followed by a long siesta to rest and digest, drinks at around 10pm, and dinner at 11pm. You'll have more than enough time to make it out to the clubs by 2am when the party starts jumping.

Barcelona Metro

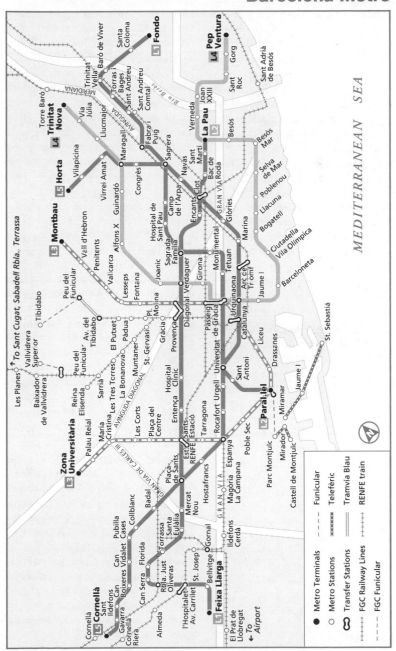

Hot Spots

→**Arola** ★★ TAPAS Wait for a good hair day before you attempt the terrace at Hotel Art's Arola. Even if the decor is white-washed-lounge-by-the-sea casual, the crowd is Euro-glam, everyone-is-looking-at-me happenin'. When you get over yourself and the eye-candy staff, settle down to the live DJs dub and enjoy a *guaracha* (Diego Cabrera's interpretation of the mojito) along with Sergi Arola's tapas. To much critical acclaim, Arola takes time from his reality TV show to oversee his capricious interpretation of the classics; so indulge in unforgettable *patatas bravas* (spicy fries), gazpacho, and the like . . . They will never taste nor look the same at the *chiringuito* (vending cart). *Hotel Arts, Calle de la Marina 19-21.* ☎ *934-838-065. www.hotelartsbarcelona.com. Tapas 5€–19€. Entrees 27€–35€. Wed–Sun 2–5pm and 8–11:30pm. Metro: Citutat Vella-Port Olímpico.*

📺 Best ❢ →**Can Paixano** WINE BAR Look up "bubbly" in the dictionary and you will find the definition "sparkling wine"—as in *cava*—as well as a reference to "feeling and exhibiting cheerful excitement"—as in *you,* after a visit to the insanely cheap and superbly fun, Can Paixano. Experience the mayhem along with hordes of locals and travelers as people shout their orders for house-made *rosada* or *blanc* and pass *entrepans* (sandwiches) of a wide selection (mostly meat) over your head. It's not for the tired (standing room only) or the timid, so shout out your order, swill it down, then throw your napkin on the floor. If you enjoyed your experience grab a bottle or two at the in-house store. *Calle Reina Cristina 7, Barceloneta.* ☎ *933-100-839. www.canpaixano.com. Sandwiches 1.50€–3.80€. Cava per cup .40€–.70€, per bottle 2.35€–4.15€. Mon–Sat 9am–10:30pm. Metro: Barceloneta.*

📺 Best ❢ →**Santa Maria** ★★ NOUVEAU TAPAS Give your palate a treat at this tastefully decorated modern tapas restaurant in trendy Born. The mouthwatering creations by Ferran Adria's disciple Paco Guzmán change periodically but some memorable tapas include stockfish ragout with pumpkin, garlic, and asparagus or marinated sardines with eggplant and curry yogurt. You'll need a lot to fill you up, since the tapas are not overly large and you'll be very hungry by the time you get a table. *Calle de Comerç 17.* ☎ *933-151-227. www.santamania.biz. Tapas 2€–6.80€. Tasting menu 36€. Daily 1:30–3:30pm and 8:30pm–midnight. Metro: Jaume I.*

Tapas

→**Bar Jai-ca** Why go to the tourist traps around Passeig Joan de Borbó when just a few blocks away this exciting corner tapas bar awaits. Come to Bar Jai-ca to enjoy the fresh seafood specialties and drinks at half the price and double the quality as those you left behind. Young locals pack the small tables and the bar, devouring *berberechos* (cockles), fried shrimp, and some of the spiciest *padrón* peppers around. *Calle Ginebra 13.* ☎ *932-683-265. Tapas 1.80€–9.20€. Mon–Sat 9am–11:30pm. Metro: Barceloneta.*

📺 Best ❢ →**Papitu** ★ Behind the Boquería Market on a little Plaça lies this hole-in-the-wall counter bar with a bunch of umbrella-covered tables. The tapas are classics (*padrón*, a type of peppers, *chorizo, croquetas, chipirones,* fried baby squid, *tortilla*) nothin' fancy, but the way the owner's grandmother makes them, the most delicious Spanish comfort food is available to you for the price of a Happy Meal. *Plaça Galdric. No phone. Tapas 3€–6.90€. No credit cards. Daily 8am–11pm. Closed in winter. Metro: Liceu.*

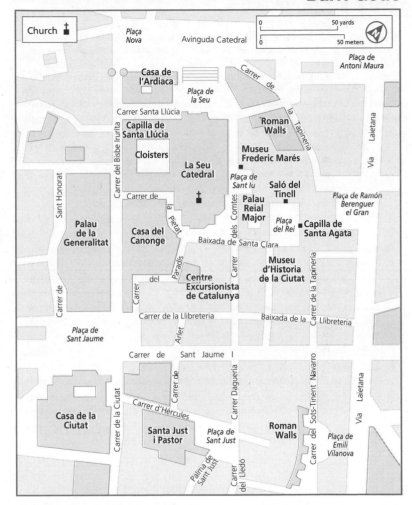

Map labels:

Church ✝

Plaça Nova

Avinguda Catedral

0   50 yards
0   50 meters

Plaça de Antoni Maura

Casa de l'Ardiaca

Plaça de la Seu

Carrer de

la Tapineria

Laietana

Carrer Santa Llúcia

'Roman Walls

Capilla de Santa Llúcia

Museu Frederic Marés

Via

Carrer del Bisbe Irurita

Cloisters

La Seu Catedral

Plaça de Sant Iu

Saló del Tinell

Plaça de Ramón Berenguer el Gran

Sant Honorat

Carrer de

la Pietat

Palau Reial Major

Carrer dels Comtes

Plaça del Rei

Capilla de Santa Agata

Palau de la Generalitat

Casa del Canonge

Baixada de Santa Clara

del

Paradís

Carrer

Centre Excursionista de Catalunya

Museu d'Historia de la Ciutat

Carrer de la Tapineria

Carrer de

Plaça de Sant Jaume

Carrer

Arlet

Carrer de la Llibreteria

Baixada de la

Llibreteria

Carrer de Sant Jaume I

Casa de la Ciutat

Carrer de

Carrer de la Ciutat

Carrer d'Hércules

Carrer de

Carrer Dagueria

Sots-Tinent Navarro

Via Laietana

Santa Just i Pastor

Plaça de Sant Just

Roman Walls

Carrer del

Plaça de Emili Vilanova

Palma de Sant Just

Carrer del Lledó

→**Quimet-I-Quimet** You better arrive at this tiny wine bar early before it gets packed from wall to wall with locals who know the deal. Pick your wine from the hundreds of bottles lining the walls (or choose a nice draft beer) to go with the awesome *montaditos* (tapas on bread) with smoked salmon, cream cheese, and truffle honey or any of the other scrumptious creations the busy barman conjures

up. *Calle Poeta Cabanyes 25.* ☎ *934-423-142. Tapas 2.25€–8.50€. Mon 8–11:45pm; Tues–Sat 1:30–4pm and 8:30–11:45pm. Closed Aug. Metro: Paral-lel, Poble Sec.*

→**Vaso de Oro** The platinum goes to the Golden Cup as the hordes standing at the long wooden bar can attest. The only way to get any food is to yell at the lively staff who will in turn give you a hard time while pouring one of the tastiest *flautas* (home

Top 10 Local Favorites

When **Quentin de Briey** is not competing on a board, he's traveling around the world taking photographs of other skaters doing so. You've probably seen his snaps in mags such as *Kingpin* (U.K.), *Freestyler* (France), *Dogway* (Spain), *Skateboarder* (U.S.), or at his website, www.quentindebriey.com. Born in Belgium in 1976, Q moved to Barcelona in 1999 to become part of a movement that has turned the city into what many consider Europe's skateboarding capital. Here's why he's not planning on leaving anytime soon.

1. El **MACBA** (see "Museums," p. 378) is easily my favorite place to go when I have nothing to do. I go there to meet new people, watch the skaters or skate myself, have a coffee, or just enjoy the sun. The square is closed to traffic making this a relaxing haven in the heart of Barcelona.

2. El **Flamingo** (see "Bars," p. 365) wins my vote for favorite bar in the city. It's a small cocktail bar with a permanently good atmosphere.

3. **Ra** (see "Eating," p. 362) is where I like to go for lunch during the week for the good food, sun, and lack of city traffic.

4. **Parc de la Ciutadella** (see "Playing Outside," p. 381) is a perfect spot to relax on the grass or take a date on a romantic boat ride.

5. **Playa de Bogatell** (5km east of Ciutat Vella in Barcelona; Metro: Bogatell) is a great place to go for a swim at lunchtime.

6. **Libreria Ras** (Doctor Dou 10; ☎ **934-127-199;** www.rasbcn.com) should be visited once a week to check out the latest arrivals in art books and mags.

7. **Club 13** (see "Clubs & Discos," p. 370) is a nice place for some booty shakin' during weekdays after midnight.

8. At **El Rosal** (see "Eating," p. 359) they cook my favorite food: chutney chicken and moussakas. Perfecto for Sunday lunch.

9. Riding through the empty streets of **Poble Nou** (see "Orientation: Barcelona Neighborhoods," p. 346) on a bicycle is a highlight that is not to be missed.

10. If your new (not sketchy) friend has access to a rooftop terrace in the **Gótic,** do not hesitate (see "Orientation: Barcelona Neighborhoods," p. 344).

brew served in flute glasses) in town. If you don't know what to order, just point at what looks tasty as it is dished up onto the bar. Some of our favorite tapas here are the potatoes *bravas* (spicy square-cut fries), the *granjero* (aka surprisingly yummy egg sandwich), the *mojama* (a cut of dried tuna), and the variety of cooked and cured meats. *Balboa 6.* ☎ *933-193-098. Tapas 2.20€–11€. Daily 9am–midnight. Closed Sept. No credit cards. Metro: Barceloneta.*

Cheap

→ **Bon Bocat** MIDDLE EASTERN/GOTIC For the best falafel in town, check out one of these two joints on either side of Plaça del Tripi (aka George Orwell). They had the brilliant idea of adding mint to their sandwiches and that, plus a secret recipe for the famous chickpea croquettes, makes it the perfect late-night or mid-day snack. *Calle Escudellers 31 and 58.* ☎ *933-172-791. Falafel 3.50€. Sun–Thurs 1pm–2:30am; Fri–Sat 1pm–3am. Metro: Drassanes, Jaume I.*

➜**Can Maño** SEAFOOD/BARCELONETA Don't let the fact that it has entrances on two streets fool you. This restaurant is tiny, and the sexiness of its decor (not very) is inversely proportional to the quality of its food. The impossibly bright fluorescents make even the hottest tan look pale, but once you try the just-reeled-in *dourada*, masterfully grilled or fried and see the pittance of coins that they ask for it, the color will return to your cheeks in a heartbeat. *Calle Baluard 12.* ☎ *933-193-082. Entrees 4€–6€. Mon–Fri noon–4pm and 8–11pm; Sat noon–4pm. No credit cards. Metro: Barceloneta.*

➜**El Rosal** INTERNATIONAL/BORN In the mega-trendy **Passeig del Born,** few places are as popular on a Sunday afternoon as this tiny bar with large outdoor seating and a curious kitchen built in two stories of an old corner store. When you finally get a table, enjoy some Middle Eastern–inspired dishes like baba ghanouj, moussaka, or, our favorite, chutney chicken. Everything is prepared with the utmost attention to detail, and the vibe is hip and mostly hungover. *Passeig del Born. No phone. Entrees 5€–11€. Daily 9:30am–3am. Metro: Jaume I.*

➜**El Sortidor** ★ ITALIAN When owner Claudio came from Torino he knew exactly what he wanted to do: a lunch-only family restaurant with a different prix-fixe menu every day, plus Friday and Saturday dinner specials. He found the perfect place for it in this turn-of-the-20th-century bar with vintage wooden refrigerators and vitraux glass doors in the quiet Plaça del Sortidor, at the base of Montjuïc. How did he get it to work? By making perfect homemade tagliatelle and spirit-invoking Italian classics like braised leg of lamb with couscous and cream of zucchini soup. *Plaça del Sortidor 3.* ☎ *934-418-518. Menu 8.50€. Dinner*

menu 19€. Mon–Sat 1–4pm; Fri–Sat 8–11pm. Metro: Poble Sec, Paral-lel.

📺 Best ❶ ➜**Foodball** ★ HEALTH FOOD Located near the MACBA, this quirky new dining concept by the Camper shoe company caters to the neo-hippies in the neighborhood. The food is presented in, yes, balls. The whole grain rice balls stuffed with either organic mushrooms, chicken, chickpeas, or tofu and algae, are actually good. Take a couple to go or plant yourself on the colorful tiered concrete benches. *Elisabets 9.* ☎ *932-701-363. Foodballs 1.75€ each. Main courses 5€. Daily noon–11pm. Metro: Liceu.*

➜**King Döner** ★ MIDDLE EASTERN This city has more *döner kebab* joints than 50 Cent has gunshot wounds, but King Döner in the Rambla de Raval tops them all. Shawarmas, affectionately known as "Arab tacos," come 3.50€ a serving. You can order them with chicken, lamb, or fresh veggies. They also serve veggie falafels for the PETA-minded. *Bajos 39, Rambla de Raval. No phone. Sandwiches 2.50€–5€. Daily 11am–1am. Metro: Liceu.*

➜**Laurel** ARGENTINEAN/RAVAL Sick of pork derivates and frightening insects from the bottom of the sea? Get over to this Argentinean enclave across from the Renoir Cinema and satisfy your need for a juicy grilled steak without leaving your wallet as a ransom. Enjoy the best *empanadas* (big turnovers with varied fillings) this side of the Atlantic and, for a change of pace, fresh good-looking salads. Top it off with flambéed *dulce de leche* crepes and you'll know where to go on your next vacation. *Calle Floridablanca 140.* ☎ *933-256-292. Entrees 7€–12€. Hours vary, so phone ahead. Metro: Urgell, Sant Antoni.*

➜**L'Economic** CATALAN This very simple, home-style restaurant serves lunch only on its cute patio or at marble tables in the low-ceilinged hall, surrounded by ornate Andalusian tiles and oil paintings. The menu varies every day but is sure to include Catalan classics like *butifarra* (sausage) or *lomo* (pork loin) with french fries or a "salad" consisting of three leaves of lettuce. The appetizers are usually more tempting and less-meaty dishes like lentils, or paella on Wednesdays. *Plaça Sant Agustí Vell 13.* ☎ *933-196-494. Entrees 5€–7.50€. No credit cards. Mon–Fri 12:30–4:30pm. Closed Aug. Metro: Jaume I.*

➔ **Romesco** CATALAN It's like *abuela* (grandma) is in the kitchen serving up huge portions of home-style food in this small restaurant popular with locals and back-packers on a budget. Try the *menú del día*, aka the Cuban Grand Slam: Fill up on rice and beans, fried plantains, *carne en salsa* (beef stew), and a fried egg for only 4.50€. *Sant Pau 28 (1 block off Las Ramblas).* ☎ *933-189-381. Main courses 5€–12€. Mon–Fri 1pm–midnight; Sat 1–6pm and 8pm–midnight. Closed Aug. Metro: Liceu.*

➔ **Teranga** SENEGALESE/BORN Don't be distracted by the other Senegalese restaurant around the corner. This one is bigger, better, and more attractive. Start with a refreshing ginger or *bissaø* (hibiscus) drink, while you wait for a table. Once you are seated on one of the three levels, pick one of the five dishes presented in cute multicolored disc-menus and let your taste buds do the rest. Sautéed spinach with yucca is an ideal vegetarian option, while relentless meat eaters can get satis-fied with sumptuous lamb or veal with couscous or rice. *Calle La Nau 3.* ☎ *933-103-365. Entrees 5€–6€. Wed–Mon noon–5pm. Metro: Jaume I.*

➔ **Venus** MIDDLE EASTERN/CAFE A veg-etarian's paradise—choose from 14 differ-ent veggie salads, couscous, and hummus, plus meat dishes like moussaka and lasagna. Packed with artists, students, and sales clerks from the trendy shops, you can't help but feel like part of the gang since they cram as many tables as physically possible into the small space. The walls are just as crammed with colorful paintings and artist expos that rotate every 2 months. Try the Alexandria couscous with chicken, chick-peas, raisins, and the works. *Avinyó 25.* ☎ *933-011-585. Main courses 4.90€–8.50€. Mon–Sat noon–midnight. Metro: Liceu.*

Doable

Best ❂ ➔ **Bar Mundial** ★ SEAFOOD In this canteen with tiny tables crammed full of people, the plan is very simple: Sit down, order a bottle of cheap but decent house white, then start ordering every-thing on the menu. Ideally, you want to come here with three other people. That way, you can order the largest amount of seafood *raciones* (portions) to share; also, you won't have to wait too long for a table. It's all delicious, but not ordering *tallari-nas* (cockles) or *navajas* (razor clams) braised with butter would be like going to Ibiza and skipping the clubs. *Plaça Sant Agustí Vell 1.* ☎ *933-199-056. Entrees 9€–15€. Tues–Fri 2–4pm and 8:30–11:30pm; Sat noon–4pm and 8:30pm–midnight; Sun noon–3:30pm. Closed 2 weeks Aug. Metro: Jaume I.*

Best ❂ ➔ **Candela** ★ MODERN CATA-LAN A neighborhood classic, Candela's outdoor seating in front of the humble St. Pere church is perfect for lunch or dinner. For a more vibrant meal, sit inside by the bar or in the mod back room with all the local hipsters, including the waitstaff. The menu fits the clientele, with healthy cre-ations like quinoa *timbales* or the ultimate Spanish combination of lentils with melon, chorizo, and *manchego* (a rich, Spanish, sheep's-milk cheese). If you see it on the menu, try the mind-blowing *fideuá* (noo-dles with seafood). The delish desserts are all homemade. *Plaza Sant Pere 12.* ☎ *933-106-242. Entrees 4.50€–15€. Mon–Sat 9am–12:30am. Metro: Arc de Triomf, Urquinaona.*

→ **El Foc** MARKET At this modest place on a narrow side street off Paral-lel, with red-checked tablecloths, average decor, and piped-in elevator music, homemade bread is served hot from the oven along with lip-smacking entrees. The weekly menu offers delights such as cod in a bittersweet sauce that's kiss-the-chef perfect. El Foc had a classic British-style kitchen before, but whatever they did, it's great now. *Calle Blasco de Garay 8.* ☎ *934-422-253. www.elfoc.com. Entrees 10€–15€. Mon–Sat 8pm–midnight; Sun 1:30–5pm and 8pm–midnight. Closed 2 weeks Aug. Metro: Poble Sec, Paral-lel.*

→ **Kashmir** PAKISTANI With plenty of Pakistani and Indian restaurants in Barcelona, Kashmir consistently tops every local's list. This small, no-frills restaurant serving up great food at reasonable prices is a good lunch break after a day of gallery walking and thrift shopping in El Raval (it's very busy from 2–4pm). They're a little conservative with the *picante*, so you might have to ask them to kick it up a notch if you want enough curry to set your mouth on fire. *Sant Pau 39.* ☎ *934-413-798. Main courses 6€–10€. Daily 1–5pm and 8pm–midnight. Metro: Plaça Catalunya.*

→ **Kiosco Universal** ★ SEAFOOD/RAVAL Of the many places to eat inside the rumble-tumble of the Boquería Market this is our favorite. Sit by the huge bar with market workers and savvy locals and order plates of some of the best seafood in town. Impossibly fresh *navajas* (razor clams), crispy *chipirones* (fried baby calamari), *tallarinas* (cockles)—anything that lives in the sea makes it straight to your plate. Although not as cheap as it used to be, the taste-bud excitement factor is still well worth your buck. *Mercat San Josep (Boquería).*

Parada 691. ☎ *933-178-286. Entrees 8€–16€. Mon–Sat 9am–4pm. Metro: Liceu.*

→ **La Báscula** VEGETARIAN/BORN What happens when an American cook and an Argentinean neo-hippie marry? A cooperative like La Báscula, which features a large menu with many international vegetarian options, drinks that only your nature-loving vegetarian aunt in Colorado could come up with, and desserts that add a touch of healthiness to their sweet decadence. Wait for a table in the front lobby with dozens of parked bikes and doors turned into tables and enjoy an exotic tea or drink a *curalotodo* (literally, a "heal it all") while you wonder if the world could really be a better place. *Calle Flassaders 30.* ☎ *933-199-866. Entrees 5€–13€. Tues–Sat 1pm–midnight. Metro: Jaume I.*

→ **Machito** ★ MEXICAN/GRACIA This may be the only place a Mexican would recommend for authentic Mex in BCN. An homage to Frida's house in Coyoacan, the inner patio is bright and inviting. You may think it's too cute to be true, but they ain't messin' around in the kitchen. The mole, quesadillas with pumpkin flower, or *huitlacoche* (a mushroom that grows on corn), and the Micheladas (Mexican beer with lemon, salt, and Tabasco) are delectable and, like all true south of the border *comida, muy grande, guey* (very righteously big, dude)! *Calle Torrijos 47.* ☎ *932-173-414. Entrees 6.50€–8.50€. Daily 1–4pm and 7pm–12:30pm. Metro: Fontana.*

→ **Origen** **99.9%** CATALAN Catalan Cooking 101 would also be an apt name for these two small, well-designed (note the colander lamps) bistros around Plaça Born. The didactic magazine-like menu walks you through the origins (hence the name) of many Catalonian classics, from simple tostadas loaded with local cheese or the vegetarian-friendly stuffed eggplant

BARCELONA

to the hearty duck with plums and pignolis. The plates are not miniscule as you might expect judging from the fancy decor, and are high quality and full of flavor. So pace yourself or you won't have room for the classic desserts, which go well with coffee or sweet wine. *Passeig del Born 4.* ☎ *932-956-690. Entrees 2.40€–5.40€. Daily 12:30pm–1am. Metro: Jaume I.*

➔**Ra** INTERNATIONAL Summer's here and you don't want to be indoors. Ra is what you need with its sunny terrace on Plaça de la Gardunya, just behind the Boqueria Market. The colorful, hand-painted tablecloths give the place a party feel, and the international menu ranges from Argentinean steak to chutney duck or parsley risotto. Add one half-Brazilian DJ and you'll have yourself a very Bossa Nova dinner. *Mil Vuit-Cents 15.* ☎ *933-014-163. Entrees 6.50€–11€. Mon–Fri 10am–2:30pm. Metro: Liceu.*

Splurge

➔**Agua** ★★ MEDITERRANEAN Whether you sit on the terrace right smack on the beach or inside the sunny dining room with huge windows, simply watching the waves crash ashore from either venue makes this one of the most relaxed places to eat. Order heaping portions of meats and fish grilled over an open fire or try the fresh pasta with succulent prawns. Wines are a tad expensive, but the food is reasonably priced for the quality. It's a very popular spot, so make reservations for the weekends. *Passeig Marítim de la Barceloneta 30.* ☎ *932-251-272. Main courses 13€–16€. Daily 1:30–4pm and 8:30pm–midnight (Fri–Sat 'til 1am). Metro: Ciutadella–Vila Olímpica.*

MTV **Best** ✿ ➔**La Reina del Raval** ★ MARKET CUISINE This chic restaurant among all the kabob joints in the *Rambla del Raval* shines with its slick interiors featuring incredible paintings by local painter Oriol Moragrega. The creative menu varies

according to what's market fresh, and the tasting menu (32€) is nothing short of spectacular. Bulgur salad with clams, market fish with eggplant, green beans and ginger, and a heavenly peach cream with forest fruits and mint are some of the salivation-inducing marvels. *Rambla de Raval 3.* ☎ *934-433-655. www.lareinadelraval.com. Entrees 7.50€–20€. Mon 8:30pm–2:30am; Tues–Sat 1:30pm–2:30am. Metro: Liceu.*

➔**Pla dels Angels** MODERN INTERNATIONAL Opposite the MACBA, this trendy restaurant explodes with a kooky kaleidoscope of colors and imaginative dishes. Pick up the wine bottle; the menu's glued to it. Take your pick from the high-quality and reasonably priced salads, meat, pasta, and gnocchi. Try the octopus carpaccio or just stick with the bourgeois White Castle miniburgers if you're not as adventurous. You can fill yourself up by ordering one of their generously portioned appetizers. Be sure to book in advance for the weekends. *Ferlandina 23.* ☎ *933-294-047. Main courses 13€–16€. Menu 5.35€. Daily 1:30–4:30pm and 9–11:30pm (Fri–Sat 'til midnight). Metro: Universitat.*

➔**Shunka** ★★ JAPANESE/GOTIC When I said the thing I missed most in Barcelona was good sushi, my Japanese friend sent me here, to eat the "best sushi in Europe." Unfortunately word got around (thanks a lot, Ferran Adriá!) and nowadays getting a table can prove more strenuous than dealing with the DMV. Once you are seated, though, check out the blade-waving masters and take a break from all that cured meat with some good ol' raw fish. *Templers 6-10.* ☎ *934-124-991. Entrees 8.50€–15€. Menu 14€. Mon–Fri 1:30–3:30pm and 8–11:30pm; Sat–Sun 2–4pm and 8:30–11:30pm. Metro: Jaume I.*

Cafes & Tearooms

➔**Bar Jardí** CAFE This outdoor cafe is a refuge from the shopping madness on the street. Look out for the big camel by the doorway, walk through to the back of the market and head upstairs to an unexpected spot for an afternoon beer and *bocadillo* (sandwich). The trees, chirping birds, and hanging surf boards—not to mention the hotties with flared bangs and shaved heads peppered throughout the open courtyard—are a welcome distraction from the sensory overload on the street. *Portaferrissa 17. No phone. No credit cards. Mon–Sat 11am–9pm. Metro: Universitat.*

➜ **El Café que Pone Muebles Navarro** CAFE If you're wondering where the long name came from (aka Muebles Navarro, Café Muebles), it used to be a furniture store, which explains the bizarre collection of chairs and sofas to sink into with your new Barça-buddy. Grab some coffee and NY cheesecake, and check out the art, the alterna-cool clientele, or spoken-word artists on select nights. *Riera Alta 4–6.* ☎ *607-188-096. Tues–Wed 2pm–2am; Thurs 6pm–2am; Fri–Sat 6pm–3am. Metro: Liceu.*

➜ **Els Quatre Gats** ★ CAFE Step back in time at this former turn-of-the-20th-century artist's lair, where Picasso hung his first exhibit and Gaudí chilled out with other members of the modernista movement. "The Four Cats" (Catalan slang for "just a few people") was a center point in the city's intellectual and bohemian life and its history comes alive on the mosaic-tiled walls and dozens of black and white pictures of famous customers. Your best bet is to order a coffee and take in the *fin de siècle* atmosphere, and the mixed crowd, because the prices are inflated and the service is snooty. *Montsió 3.* ☎ *933-024-140. Daily 1pm–1am; cafe daily 8am–2am. Metro: Plaça de Catalunya.*

📺 ⬭Best⬭ ➜ **Spiritual Café** ★★ CAFE Lounge on comfy cushions, breathe in the sweet incense, and watch the performers spit fire, perform Chinese theater and

Dessert Anyone?

The Spanish really have their seafood and cold cuts down, but when it comes to gelato, no one does it like the Italians. There are a few *gelaterias* around town and they all look appetizing, but don't waste your time with cheap imitations: The best gelato in Barcelona has a home and it is 📺 ⬭Best⬭ **Cremeria Toscana,** with two branches, one in Eixample (Muntaner 161; ☎ **935-393-825**) and one tucked into a small street in Born (Canvis Vells 2; ☎ **932-680-729**). The ice-cream flavors vary daily: The mango, melon, or coconut made with fresh fruit are out of this world, and the *nocciola* (hazelnut) gives a whole new meaning to nuts. The pleasure can be attained from noon to midnight; the memories will last much longer.

acrobatics, or even let them give you a massage. The Chinese pottery, Arabic scrawled tables, hanging plants, and patterned rugs add to the feeling of an Oriental oasis. After a few cups of tea and puffs of the flavored tobacco in the hookahs, you'll feel like your aura is hot pink with purple polka dots. *Museu Marítim, Av. Drassanes.* ☎ *933-175-256. Thurs–Sat 9:30pm–3am. Metro: Drassanes.*

Markets

📺 ⬭Best⬭ ➜ **Mercat de Sant Josep/ La Boqueria** Be sure to bring your camera to this bustling market. Dozens of stalls spill over with fresh vegetables, fruits, nuts, spices, meats, and seafood, along with hundreds of people chattering and haggling, and it's all packed underneath an impressive vaulted glass and iron structure. If you or any of your friends get a kick out of the skinned rabbits, pig heads, and guts hanging off hooks, seek professional help. Seriously. *La Rambla 89, between Carrer de Carme and Carrer de L'Hospital in El Raval.* ☎ *933-182-584. Mon–Sat 8:30am–8:30pm. Metro: Liceu.*

➔ **Mercat Santa Catarina** In 1848 Santa Catarina became the first covered market in Barcelona, setting in motion a new trend around the city. Again in 1999 a new wave hit—the redesigned undulating mosaic roof by Enric Miralles. As seen in every architectural design magazine, the renovated Mercat Santa Catarina is now more tourist attraction than local market. The prices are a bit higher and the selection smaller than at most neighborhood markets, but you can still find some deals. Pick up what you can't find in the stalls at the small supermarket; **Cuines de Santa Caterina** is an upscale pan-world tapas bar brought to you by Grupo Tragaluz (Hotel Omm) with models turned waiters to help you decipher the menu. *Francesc Cambó 16, Ciutat Vella. Market Mon 7:30am–2pm; Tues–Wed 7:30am–3:30pm; Thurs–Fri 7:30am–8:30pm; Sat 7:30am–3:30pm.* ☎ *933-195-740.*

www.mercatsantacaterina.net. Restaurant daily 1–4pm and 8pm–12:30am. ☎ *932-689-918. Metro: Jaume I.*

➔ **Mercat Sant Antoni** If you want to know what a real Catalan market is all about, try the elegant Mercat Sant Antoni. The late-19th-century-style wrought iron-work makes it a local landmark, but the unbeatable prices and wide selection of fresh foods is the reason why the whole neighborhood shops here. The outer loop is full of clothing and *merceria* (sewing notions) stalls; the middle circle is set up with prepared and packaged foods and fruit/vegetable stalls; then the inner circle is saved for what may be the best selection of fish in the city. A smattering of bars and cafes also offer the prepared market food. Nerds of all ages come on Sunday mornings to swap comic book collections, old maps, books, and postcards. *Comte d'Urgell 1 bis.* ☎ *934-234-287. Mon–Thurs and Sat 7am–2:30pm and 5:30–8:30pm; Fri 7am–8:30pm. Metro: Sant Antoni.*

Partying

It doesn't match the madness of Madrid and Ibiza, but you can easily be initiated into the night owl tribes' ritual club hopping. Thursdays through Saturdays are the busiest nights, yet you can find a joint any night of the week. Clubs open after 11pm but aren't jumping until 3am. You can go to "afters" until 10am—so don't expect to get much sightseeing done once you fall into the clubbing cycle.

You can also save beaucoup bucks by looking for promoters passing out flyers after 10pm on Las Ramblas granting free or discounted entrance to the major clubs, such as Moog and City Hall. If you have no clue as to where to go, start your search off at Plaça Real and then walk through nearby Carrer Escudellers in Barri Gòtic

where you'll find several clubs, bars, and stumbling drunks, *ahem,* party people.

The club scene relies heavily on electronica—house and electro, in particular—but hip-hop heads, indie rockers, and *salseros* can also find their spots to bug out. Barcelona isn't really known for its live music scene, but you can catch some international acts and homegrown talent (p. 370) in venues half the size of those in major American cities. For up-to-date listings check the *Guía del Ocio,* available at newsstands; snag free mags like *Go, Metropolitan, Mondo Sonoro,* and *AB* at bars or music shops; or check out the websites in "Recommended Websites: Music & Nightlife," below. Spanish-titled sites and

Recommended Websites: Music & Nightlife

→ www.barcelonarocks.com
→ www.lecool.com
→ www.atiza.com
→ www.salirenbarcelona.com
→ www.clubbingspain.com
→ www.guiadelocio.com

publications are in Spanish, but listings are straightforward and easy to understand.

The dress code isn't nearly as froufrou and pretentious as in New York or Paris. Jeans are the norm, but why be boring? Now is the time to wear the quirky threads you bought at the *mercadillo*—you might hesitate to wear those orange, poofy, Ali Baba pants at home. You can wear sneakers at most clubs (be careful at moody Terrrazza and Discotheque, where bouncers double as the fashion police), but flip-flops are a definite ticket back to your hotel room.

Bars

→ **Absenta Bar** A breath of fresh air from the too fabulous BCN bars. The scene here is quality live music, mostly blues, jazz, tango, or swing brought to you by a friendly international staff. In between sets enjoy one (or more) of 20 types of absinthe and an Argentinian *empanada* in the outdoor seating area with all the other unpretentious music lovers in Barceloneta. *Sant Carles 36, Barceloneta.* ☎ *932-215-785. Metro: Barceloneta.*

🎬 Best ◐ → **Bar Bodega Teo** ★ The "bar with the couches" in the heart of the Gótic serves some of the best cocktails in town. Wonder-couple Rafa and Lizzie perfected their bartending art all over the world and now serve Barcelonans international favorites like Cosmos with fresh cranberry juice, Pisco Sours, and Lychee Martinis. The bar in the front room is topped with working wine barrels, and photos and paintings by local artists adorn the walls; the back room is extra-chill. *Ataúlf 18.* ☎ *933-151-159. Metro: Jaume I.*

→ **Bar Mudanzas** When this bar first opened, they had a hard time keeping the junkies out. Times have since changed—and with them the neighborhood. Its ground floor and mezzanine, with tiled floors, dark wood, and marble-top tables, are packed each night with those who know better than to elbow for a drink at the bars in the neighboring Passeig del Born. *Vidriería 15.* ☎ *933-191-137. www.mudanzas.barceloca.com. Metro: Jaume I.*

→ **Curtis** Like a little black dress in a ballroom full of sequins, Curtis stands out from the Port Olímpico glitz for its demure and elegant structure. The smiling faces of the mixed, "less is more" crowd spilling out onto the beach are testament to its high-quality groove. *Trias Fargas 2/4.* ☎ *932-681-473. Metro: Ciutadella.*

→ **Dr. Astin** A red door on a tiny street in El Born is all that identifies Dr. Astin, a big, smoky bar for the alternative crowd, with good DJs spinning Latin rock from the disciples (and mentors) of Manu Chao. South Americans love dancing, and that's what usually happens later in the night when spirits get high on mojitos and cuba libres. *Abaixadors 9.* ☎ *933-101-058. Metro: Jaume I.*

→ **Flamingo** A small cozy place with a huge cocktail menu, Flamingo is a good place to have a drink and meet lots of different people from around the globe. Be there for happy hour (8–10pm) and ask Nicola, the bartender, for a mojito, one of her specialties. *Pintor Fortuny 15.* ☎ *933-012-322. Metro: Liceu.*

→ **Kentucky** This smoky dive in Raval is a nighttime classic and, since it "opens" at 6am, a favorite after-party when the clubs

Partying & Sightseeing in Barcelona

PARTYING ⭐
Absenta Bar **48**
Arena **19**
Arena Madre **19**
Arena Vip **20**
Bang Bang **17**
Bar Bodega Teo **38**
Bar London **26**
Bar Mudanzas **40**
Café Dietrich **16**
Catwalk **46**
City Hall **21**
Club 13 **33**
Curtis **7**
Discotheque **5**
Dr. Astin **39**
Fellini **30**
Flamingo **25**
Fritz Hot Club **11**
Harlem Jazz Club **37**
Jamboree **33**
Kentucky **29**
KGB **12**
L'Antic Teatre **42**
La Luna **14**
La Macarena **32**
La Paloma **24**
La Terrrazza **5**
Les Fatales **15**
Liquid **8**
Mau Mau **28**
Metro **18**
Moog **29**
O'Hara's Irish Pub **36**
Otto Zutz **9**
Razzmatazz **45**
Sala Apolo **27**
Salvation **43**
Tarantos **33**
Travel Bar **34**

SIGHTSEEING ●
Caixa Forum **7**
Casa Milà (La Pedrera) **13**
Catedral de Barcelona **35**
Centre de Cultura
   Contemporània de
   Barcelona (CCCB) **23**
Fundació Joan Miró **2**
La Font Màgica
   (Magic Fountain) **6**
Museu d'Art Contemporani
   (MACBA) **22**
Museu Nacional d'Art
   de Catalunya (MNAC) **3**

Museu Picasso **41**
Mirador de Colón **31**
Olympic Stadium **1**
Parc Güell **10**
Poble Espanyol **4**
Sagrada Família **44**

FRANCE
Barcelona
★ Madrid
PORTUGAL
SPAIN

TIBIDABO

Carrer de Numància
Carrer de Berlin
Carrer de la Infanta Carlota Joaquima
Carrer de Còrsega
Carrer de Rosselló
Carrer de Provença
Avinguda de Roma
Carrer de Tarragona
Carrer d'Entrença
Carrer de Rocafort
Carrer de Calàbria
Carrer de Viladomat

Carrer de Sants de la Creu Coberta
Carrer de Sant Antoni
Carretera de la Bordeta
Carrer de Sant Fructuós

PARC
JOAN
MIRÓ

Plaça de
Espanya
Gran Via de les Corts Catalanes
Carrer de Sepulveda
Carrer de Floridablanca
Carrer de Tamarit
Carrer de Manso
Carrer del
Parlament

Av. de Marqués de Comillas
Av. de la Reina Maria Cristina

Poble
Espanyol

Palau
Nacional **3**

POBLE-SEC

Avinguda de l'Estadi

Avinguda de Paral·lel

Estadi
Olímpic **1**

PARC DE MONTJUÏC

Avinguda de Miramar

PARC D'ATRACCIONS
DE MONTJUÏC

Castell de
Montjuïc

Passeig de Josep Carner

0   1/4 mi
0   0.25 km

ⓘ Information

Plaça de
Francesc Macia

Travessera de Gràcia

GRACIA

Carrer de Buenos Aires

Carrer de Londres

Carrer de Paris

Avinguda Diagonal

Gran de Gràcia

Travessera de Gràcia

Av. de Sant Antoni Maria Claret

Carrer de Còrsega

Carrer de la Industria

EIXAMPLE

Carrer de Provença

Carrer de Rosselló

Avinguda Diagonal

Carrer de Mallorca

Plaça de la
Sagrada
Família

Carrer de València

Carrer d'Aragó

Carrer del Consell de Cent

Carrer de la Diputació

Gran Vía de les Corts Catalanes

Plaça de
Tetuan

Carrer   de Casp

Plaça de la
Universitat

Ronda

Plaça
Universitat

Plaça
Catalunya

Carrer   d'Ausias Marc

Ronda de Sant Antoni

RAVAL

Plaça
Urquinaona

Ronda de Sant Pere

Carrer   d'Ali Bei

Palau de la
Música Catalana

Carrer de Ribes

La Rambla

Av. Portal de l'Angel

Via Laietana

BARRI
GÒTIC

SANT PERE

Rambla
del
Raval

Hospital

Gran Teatre
del Liceu

C. de Ferran

EL BORN

Mercat del Born

PARC DE LA
CIUTADELLA

Carrer de Sant Pau

Carrer Nou de la Rambla

La Rambla

Passeig de Picasso

Passeig de Pujades

Avinguda de Paral·lel

Carrer Ample

Passeig de Colom
Moll de la Fusta

Pg. Isabel II

Ronda   del   Litoral

Villa
Olímpica →

Plaça Portal
de la Pau

Moll
d'Espanya

Marina

BARCELONETA

Port
Vell

IMAX

Aquarium

Passeig   Marítim

Sand, Drinks & Rock 'n' Roll

At least a dozen 📺 (Best☻) *chiringuitos* are scattered along the Barcelona coastline, blasting reggae, house, or chill electronic lounge. During the day, you can rent out chairs and umbrellas on the sand and wait for the girls to come around with free *chupitos* (shots). Stick around after dark, grab a table, and mingle with the mixed tourist-and-local crowd over drinks. Cocktails go for about 6€; canned beer, 3€. If you're not down with the 300% markup, pick up cans of beer at the supermarket across the street for .60€ each and listen to the music from the shoreline. **Beach Bar 23** on Barceloneta (☎ **933-190-472**) plays a good mix of old-school salsa on Fridays (7–11pm) that gets everyone dancing on the sand. If you are up for some late night, electronic booty-shakin', head to the last beach, **Nova Mar Bella,** where the fantastic threesome of **Mochima, La Nueva Ola,** and **Amparo** features DJs spinning from 4pm until well after midnight. Guests have included Groove Armada and International Deejay Gigolos.

close. The narrow corridor by the bar is usually very crowded, just like the back room, with a London-worthy fog hanging above it all. The bathroom lines, which can be of epic proportions, are a great place to meet new people since they can't escape from you. *Arc del Teatre 11.* ☎ *933-290-020. Metro: Drassanes.*

➜ **KGB** If it's hard it's here. KGB has been *the* hard-core spot in Barcelona for over 2 decades. Hip-hop, punk, hard-core, nu metal: If it makes your ears bleed, you'll probably find it in this dark corner of the earth. Lately it has also experimented with some ska and reggae nights, so you might want to check it out even if you aren't tougher than (nine inch) nails. *Alegre de Dalt 55.* ☎ *932-105-906. Cover 9€, includes 1 drink. No credit cards. Metro: Joanic.*

➜ **O'Hara's Irish Pub** A good place to congregate with fellow Anglos from around the world. It gets jam-packed with sweaty Brits, Aussies, and Irish folk wiggling their way to the bar. Each night has a different theme, but a cowboy hat apparently is acceptable gear any night of the week. And don't get too excited about the beach party; it just means the bartenders

are wearing bikinis—sorry, no foam. *Ferran 18. No phone. Metro: Liceu, Jaume I.*

➜ **Travel Bar** Depending on your luck, it might be packed with huge British jocks or drunk singing Frenchmen on any given night—both are equally entertaining. Decent plates of food like pasta and curry chicken are served every night for 1€ and if you bring one of the flyers they leave at most hostels, you'll get a two-for-one drink special. If you're lucky, the guy in the gorilla suit will come out and do a table dance, free of charge. They also have Internet access, play movies during the day, and it's the jumping-off point for the "Smashed Pub Crawl" on Tuesdays, Thursdays, and Saturdays at 9:30pm. For 18€, drinks included, you're herded to four bars and a nightclub with a group of folks you'll probably be a little *too* familiar with by the end of the night. *Boqueria 27, just off La Rambla.* ☎ *933-425-252. No credit cards. Metro: Liceu.*

Clubs & Discos

Serious drinking at the bars doesn't begin until the clocks strike midnight. Most clubs don't open until 2am, and they are generally empty until the bars close at 3am.

Many clubs stay open as late as 6am. Expect to find cover charges of between 5€ and 20€, if there is one, depending on the night, the DJ, and what the bouncer thinks of you (ladies have the upper hand). Some clubs don't charge to enter or you can use flyers (from bars or given out on the street) to get a discounted admission. But a mixed drink can set you back 5€ to 10€. Don't balk at the price; the drinks here are *strong*. If you are charged to get in, ask if it's *amb consumició* (drink included). If so, take your ticket to the bar to get the first drink free. Tipping is not compulsory, although it's common to leave .05€ to .10€ at bars.

Follow those bright-eyed clubbers who just can't stop to after-hours clubs (aka *el after*) like **Fritz Hot Club** (Autovía de Castelldefels Km 12 no. 6; ☎ **934-146-990**; bus: L95 from Plaça Universitat and Plaça España) on Monday and Sunday mornings or **Bang Bang** (Gran Vía 580; no phone; Metro: Plaça Universitat) to end or begin your day with electro and Latin house.

➜ **Catwalk** If you are at one of the Port Olimpico clubs, keep an eye out for the babe handing out discount passes to this choice *el after* (and maybe the only one in walking distance). Backlit white walls filled with broken champagne glasses welcome you in the entranceway. Gals resembling Peaches at age 19 gyrate in swinging cages to the electronic beats and pulsating lights on the first dance floor, and a good mix of hip-hop, pop, and ethnicities heat up the smaller second floor. Give our regards to the magnificent diva who spins in the upstairs ladies room—she makes us want to powder our nose every 5 seconds. *Port Vell, Ramon Trías Fargas s/n. ☎ 932-216-161. Cover 15€, includes 1 drink. Metro: Ciutadella-Vila Olímpica.*

BARCELONA

Culture Club

In a city where people really love to drink and chill, bars were just not enough. Hence the *asociaciones culturales,* which are basically bars where "members" engage in some type of "cultural activity" (like watching soccer games on a large-screen TV). Membership usually consists of paying the price of a beer plus about 2€. *Asociaciones culturales* are usually cheaper than bars, and the vibe is cooler than a penguin in winter. Here are some of our all-time faves.

The mother of all asociaciones, 🎦 ⬤Best⬤ **L'Antic Teatre** (C. Verdaguer i Callis 12; ☎ 933-152-354; www.lanticteatre.com; daily 5–11pm; Metro: Arc de Triomf) has been around for ages and seen more history than your 10th-grade western civ teacher. A former anarchist enclave, dreads and fragrant smokes are the norm. The backyard is the meeting place for laid-back *Barcelocos* (crazy Barcelonians) who play foosball and drink around the ancient gum tree. The theater shows artsy films, alternative plays, and dance performances, which tend to sell out early.

Another new classic, **Mau Mau** (Fontrodona 33; ☎ 934-418-015; www. maumaunderground.com; Thurs 11pm–2:30am, Fri–Sat 11pm–3am; Metro: Parallel) is more electronic and modern, with lighting installations decorating the walls of a restored underground warehouse. There are big sofas for resting your butt while you sip a beer and listen to the DJs. Check out their website for a complete listing of cultural activities.

The Groove

Barcelona's 📺 Best◑ *mestizaje,* born in the heart of this city, is a syncretic sound that taps into global rhythms, layering flavors of funk into a tasty paella of beats for a fusion of body-moving rhythms. You can catch plenty of *mestizaje* acts during BAM (see "Festivals/Calendar of Events," below) in the summer.

Check out Ojos de Brujo (literally, "eyes of the wizard"; www.ojosde brujo.com), who spread hip-hop, funk, and rumba onto a little flamenco to get the crunchy *cachondeo* that tastes like true multicultural Barcelona. Their DIY, anticorporate approach is very much in line with their egalitarian spirit and the lyrics on their albums *Vengue* and *Bari.*

There's also Raval's 08001 (www.08001.org), a collective of 23 artists who mix reggae, dub, raï, flamenco, and electronic beats with a dose of trip-hop. Their first work *Raval ta Joie* is the culmination of 10 months of music-making spontaneously combusting in their warehouse studio. Both Ojos and Raval's are worth checking out live—their jam sessions combine tripped-out visuals with high-energy beats that guarantee a fun, sweaty show.

➜ **City Hall** *The* place to be partying on Sunday nights. This night is more about the party people than the beautiful people, so leave the heels at home and get ready to jump around until 5:30am. Work up a sweat to electro and deep-house sets by resident and international DJs, or chill outside on the comfy sofas. Once you snag a seat, it's hard to give it up. *Rambla de Catalunya 2–4.* ☎ *933-172-177. Cover varies. Metro: Plaza de Catalunya.*

📺 Best◑ ➜ **Club 13** ★ Although technically it's a bar, Club 13's dance floor sees more action than many clubs do, especially during the week. The slick interiors attract the cool and the beautiful to its two dance floors. Because of its "bar" status, there is no cover, but the door can be more selective than Simon Cowell. The music can be a little tacky on Thursdays but on Hip-Hop Tuesdays (meeting point for homeboys and girls) and Fridays, few places can compete with 13. The only problem is that the night doesn't get going until after 1 and you'll be kicked out of there mercilessly at 3am. *Plaça Reial 13.* ☎ *647-514-788. Sun–Thurs midnight–2:30am; Fri–Sat midnight–3am. Metro: Liceu.*

➜ **Discotheque** During the winter, the fabulous shift rotates next door from La Terrrazza to Discotheque, known to host glam parties, like "F**K Me, I'm Famous!" Expect top international DJs and bags of attitude from the doormen and bartenders. Remember, tipping is compulsory. *Poble Espanyol, Av. Marqués de Comillas s/n.* ☎ *935-115-764. Metro: Espanya.*

➜ **Fellini** If you are dancing at Club 13 (see above) and they kick you out right in the middle of your running man, fear not, just follow everybody to Las Ramblas and then go 2 blocks down (don't confuse it with the strip club next door). The first (and biggest) dance floor is up a flight of stairs, with a smaller one in the back. One more flight up is the "Red Room," which is great in the winter, but can get a little too hot in the summer. Resident DJs alternate with famous guests like Jazzanova and the likes. *Rambla 27. No phone. Cover 12€, includes 1 drink. Metro: Liceu.*

➜ **La Macarena** Formerly *Tablao Flamenco,* Macarena has become one of the meccas for dance music in Barcelona. Its small dance floor gets completely packed after 3am, but the DJs are so good, no one seems to mind an extra elbow in their ribs. *Carrer Nou de Sant Francesc 5. No phone. www.macaronaclub.com. Cover free before 2:30am, 5€ afterwards. Sun–Thurs midnight–4:30am; Fri–Sat midnight–5am. Metro: Drassanes.*

📺 **Best** ❷ → **La Paloma** This elegantly restored theater and dance hall will transport you back to the Belle Epoque with its red velvet foyer and chandeliers. If you get there early enough, stand in the balconies and catch Grandma and Grandpa in full formal regalia practicing their cha-cha until the ballroom session finishes and the house music begins. They have live performances and mix up techno, pop, and hip-hop later in the evening. *Tigre 27.* ☎ *933-016-897. Cover 7€. Metro: Universitat.*

→ **La Terrrazza** This mega-club has reopened its doors, welcoming the buff and the beautiful to romp in its extravagant playground under the stars. Unless you spent all winter in the gym or recovering from plastic surgery, expect a long wait at the door. *Poble Espanyol, Av. Marqués de Comillas s/n.* ☎ *934-231-285. www.laterrrazza.com. Cover 18€, includes 1 drink. Metro: Espanya.*

→ **Liquid** *Chiringuitos* are great, but the party doesn't last all night. Although a little bit out of the way and more on the *pijo* (conservative) side, Sundays at Liquid are anything but conservative. An incredible pool, complete with bridges and an island, plus some big names behind the turntables (Ellen Allien, Miss Kittin, The Hacker, to name a few) make for some W-I-L-D summer parties. *Tip:* Everybody ends up in the pool; if you are shy, don't forget your bathing suit. *Complex Esportiu Hospitalet Nord, Manuel Azaña.* ☎ *639-420-156. www.liquidbcn.com. Cover 15€ with 1 drink, 20€ with 2 drinks. Sun midnight–6am. Metro: Zona Universitaria.*

→ **Moog** Known as the *"catedral del techno"* (techno cathedral), this granddaddy of Barcelona electronica clubs is like Mick Jagger—a little old, but can still wiggle and make the girls jiggle. It has deep house and techno on the roster and gets ridiculously packed by 3am, especially on their best nights—Monday and Wednesday. They play NuWave upstairs and the scene is full of alterna-kids with their printed T-shirts and Converse kicks, so the dress code is cool and comfortable. *Arc del Teatre 3.* ☎ *933-191-789. Cover varies. Metro: Drassanes.*

→ **Otto Zutz** If hip-hop is your thing, this former textile factory cum mega-club is your place to be in BCN. Two different dance floors, one lounge in between, and not one, but *two* VIP sections provide for an all-encompassing night surrounded by glitter and bling-bling. *Carrer de Lincoln 15.* ☎ *932-380-722. www.ottozutz.com. Cover 15€. Wed midnight–5am; Thurs–Sat midnight–5:30am. Metro: Fontana.*

📺 **Best** ❷ → **Razzmatazz** This mega-warehouse entertainment complex can house up to 10,000 dilated pupils (give or take a few Cyclops and eye patches). About 5,000 clubbers can take in the five clubs housed here for just one admission price. The indie rock concert space is considered to be the best venue in town. Concert prices vary; check listings or call ahead. *Almogavers 122.* ☎ *932-720-910. Cover 12€. Metro: Marina.*

Gay Bars

→ **Arena** Get your hand stamped in one of the four Arenas in Barcelona and switch freely among all. They all have great and spacious dance floors. Classic gets its visitors moving Abba-style with some bulletproof dance-floor fillers. Madre will lure its younger prey with house and chart hits and offers all the good sins from its dark room including Monday strip shows. Arena

Rules of Engagement

The legal minimum drinking age in Barcelona is 16, but who's counting? Like everywhere else in Spain, no one cares about your drinking problem and it's okay to drink alcohol in public, unless you step out of line and pick a fight or mistake a flower stand on Las Ramblas for the loo. When staggering out of bars or clubs, be courteous to the folks living in Ciutat Vella. If you make too much noise, the club bodyguards will do a good job of shutting you up.

And if there aren't any around, you are likely to get a bucket of water or worse thrown on your Polo shirt by the old lady upstairs. Since 2006 both drinking and smoking joints in public is supposed to be penalized with fines. So are the prostitutes on Ronda Sant Pau, smoking in clubs, and the dudes that sell beer on the street or at the beach. Truth to be told, the only ones that we've seen being penalized are the guys at the beach, and it's only because the *chiringuito* owners call the cops on them. Use your common sense. No one will get scandalized if you roll one up at the beach, but asking a cop or a bouncer for a light is pushing it a bit. Heavier drugs are widely used in clubs and some bars, but in the restrooms and behind closed doors.

VIP will be the Spanish retro paradise, home to the queens and divas, and Dandy, the newest addition to the group, offers tackier house music and a more mixed crowd. Add to the group Aire, a lesbian mega-club, and Punto BCN, a classic gay bar, where you can pick up free passes to the clubs on Wednesdays. *Arena Classic. Diputació 233. ☎ 934-878-342. www.arena disco.com. Cover Fri 5€, Sat 10€. No credit cards. Fri–Sat and holidays 12:30–6am. Metro: Passeig de Gracia or Universitat. Arena Madre. Balmes 32. ☎ 934-878-342. Cover Tues–Fri and Sun 5€; Sat 10€, includes 1 drink. No credit cards. Daily 12:30–5am. Metro: Passeig de Gracia or Universitat. Arena VIP. Gran Via de les Corts Catalanes 593. ☎ 934-878-342. Cover Fri 5€, Sat 10€, includes 1 drink. No credit cards. Fri–Sat and holidays 12:30–6am. Metro: Universitat. Aire. Valencia 236. Thurs–Sat 11pm–3am. Metro: Passeig de Gracia. Punto BCN. Muntaner 63. Daily 6pm–2:30am. Metro: Universitat.*

➔ **Café Dietrich** Everything shines in Dietrich. It might be because of the golden lighting. Or maybe Marlene´s spirit is still around sharing some glamour with the whole place. Dietrich is Barcelona´s gay *teatro* cafe par excellence. Drag queens from all over the world will offer the best shows in town and, if you´re lucky, you might even receive a deep kiss on the mouth from one of these silver-screen-style divas. *Consell de Cent 255. ☎ 934-517-707. No credit cards. Metro: Verdaguer.*

➔ **La Luna** Perfect for late bloomers or nonstoppers. Get there between 6 and 8am when you´ll find the dance floor shaking to the sounds of current hits and old club favorites. It has a quiet bar and not so quiet dark room and hosts the Ursus Cave on Sundays, one of the best-known bear lairs in Barcelona. *Av. Diagonal 323. No phone. Cover 20€. No credit cards. Metro: Verdaguer.*

➔ **Les Fatales** Les—which was founded when a group of women from the electronic scene decided to get together to promote lady DJs—offers everything from pop to electronica for girls who want to meet girls. You can also catch occasional performances and a very interesting and politically aware cabaret. Check out their website for more information on special events. *Balmes 90. No phone. www.lesfatales.*

org. Cover 3€–6€. No credit cards. Metro: Passeig de Gracia.

➜ **Metro** Still one of Barcelona's bests for the contemporary clubber. Pass the caged Venus and get the party going. One dance floor stays alive with all the great songs disco has to offer, and another one gets you off on Spanish pop and traditional Spanish music. A notorious back room known as "the labyrinth of lust" features even a video lounge room. Metro offers what you need to have fun, from drag shows on Mondays to foam parties and, if you're there at the right time, they even have bingo. *Sepulveda 185. ☎ 933-235-227. www.metrodiscobcn.com. Cover 10€. No credit cards. Metro: Verdaguer.*

➜ **Salvation** Gay boys and their minions strut their stuff on the two floors of this industrial space. Nineties music and house beats throb in the air, so you can "pump the jam" on the packed dance floor or get a little closer to your new boy-toy in the chill-out area. The door policy isn't as strict as at other places, so bring your ugly friends, too. *Ronda Sant Pere 19–21. ☎ 933-180-686. Cover 11€, includes 1 drink. Metro: Urquinaona.*

Live Music

➜ **Bar London** This smoky, bright bar with a dark back room has been around for almost a century, and won't be closing anytime soon. As a matter of fact, it rarely closes at 3am when other bars do. The booths in the back are great for watching the live shows, which range from Latin rock to Catalan folk, but are always an experience. *Nou de la Rambla 34. ☎ 933-185-261. Metro: Liceu.*

➜ **Harlem Jazz Club** One of Barcelona's oldest and best jazz clubs is also one of the smallest and most sterile looking. But you're not here for dorm-room decorating tips, right? Get a little chummy with the international student crowd and enjoy an eclectic variety of music. Despite the name, you can hear everything from live jazz to African rhythms to klezmer to Romanian gypsy music on any given night. *Comtessa de Sobradiel 8. ☎ 933-100-755. Cover Fri–Sun 5€, includes 1 drink. Metro: Jaume I.*

➜ **Jamboree** If you think Barcelona ain't got no soul, then come out on Monday nights for the "What the Fuck" (WTF) jazz jam session that gets packed with a wild, funky crowd and b-boys/-girls getting ready to mash up the dance floor during the funk/hip-hop DJ set that follows. Daily jazz or blues performances. The drinks run from 8€ to 10€ each, so pregame it. Upstairs, the attached club Tarantos (☎ 933-183-067) has flamenco shows (3€). *Plaça Real 17. ☎ 933-017-564. Cover Mon 3€, Tues–Sun 8€. Metro: Liceu.*

📺 Best ● ➜ **Sala Apolo** Rubadub, slither, slide, sweat, and swagger. Girls watch your booties, boys watch your pockets. Everyone watch the stage as, night after night, the music here will take you higher. This dilapidated and massive old ballroom—less grandiose than La Paloma, and more major-live-act-venue than Razz—also sports a cinema. After the headline bands make you scream like a baby, they switch off to the club sessions. Wednesdays at Canibal is mostly live acts with a Latin, ska, and/or world-music vibe. Thursdays at Powder Room bring out the soul, hip-hop, and funkadelic DJs; on Fridays and Saturdays at Nitza is international electronica. If you're in town for awhile, check online for the 18€ (annual fee) discount card for events here and at Mau-Mau. *Nou de la Rambla 113. ☎ 934-414-001. www.sala-apolo.com. Metro: Parallel.*

➜ **Tarantos** Tarantos is to Flamenco what tapas is to cuisine: a taste of Spain in a tiny portion that can ultimately satisfy or disappoint. No matter what, this small and intimate venue is a good gamble for your buck, with a 1-hour show and a sample of very authentic flamenco music and dancing for only 5€. *Plaça Reial 17, Barri Gòtic.* ☎ *933-191-789. 5€. 3 shows daily at 8:30, 9:30, 10:30pm. Metro: Liceu.*

Performing Arts

From classical music to contemporary dance, from Broadway-style musicals to street mime performances, Barcelona offers everything. Arts are a vital part of this city's life, and performing arts are no exception. Most plays are in Catalan, but if you speak Spanish or are pretty perceptive you may be able to follow. Check the all-knowing *Guia del Ocio* or head for the information office at **Palau de la Virreina** where you'll find leaflets and *Teatre Bcn,* the monthly listings guide; or just walk down **Las Ramblas** and see the living statues and street musicians. Once you get bored of waiting for the dudes to

There's the Vanguard & Then There's La Fura

Barcelona is the birthplace and home to one of the best-known contemporary theater companies in the world: La Fura dels Baus. Born in 1979, it has become a central reference for avant-garde Catalan theater without losing its experimental edge, always looking to push the limits of theater even further. Don't really like theater? La Fura will make you question everything you *think* you know about it.

Silver Screen under the Stars

In a city with weather like Barcelona's, outdoor movies are the perfect pastime. In the summer, screenings are everywhere, but nothing beats the **Sala Montjuïc** (Castell de Montjuïc gardens; no phone; www.salamontjuic.com; 4€; July–Aug Fri–Sat 8:30pm). Under the slogan "Picnic and Cinema," Catalan hipsters hang out and watch a good selection of movies in their original language with Spanish subtitles. A perfect way to end a day's excursion to Montjuïc.

Also check out the free screenings at **CCCB** (p. 378), every Tuesday, Wednesday, and Thursday in August. Try to get there very early to sit on one of the lounge chairs in the garden and watch an old classic while sipping a martini in full Hollywood style.

actually move, you can visit the majestic theatres and admire their impressive architecture, or the small, smoky, students' theaters, if you like something smaller. If you happen to be in Barcelona in June and July, be sure to check what the Grec festival has to offer (see "Festivals/Calendar of Events," below).

➜ **Mercat de Los Flors** Something new is blooming in this one-time flower market that is now dedicated to innovation in theater. It presents performances that experiment with unusual formats, new technologies, pop culture and performing arts, film nights, and DJ sessions as well as housing the Marató de l'Espectacle (see "Festivals/Calendar of Events," below). Box office opens 1 hour before show, advance tickets are also available from Palau de la Virreina. *Lleida 59.* ☎ *934-261-875. Tickets 9€–30€. Metro: Plaça Espanya or Poble Sec.*

Ⓜ️ **Best ◑** ➔ **Palau de la Música Catalana** ★★★ The Palau is an obligatory Kodak moment for every visitor to Barcelona, but if you can actually catch a show, you're sure to take home something much bigger than that German tourist's nose dipping into your frame. Arrive very early, not because of tickets selling out (though that's a major possibility, too), but so you can spend some time checking out every detail on the outer walls and inside the hallucinogenic concert hall. Open daily from 10am to 3:30pm. Box office open 10am to 9pm Monday to Saturday, Sunday 1 hour before concerts. *Sant Francesc de Paula 2.* ☎ *932-957-200. Metro: Urquinaona*

➔ **Teatre Lliure** The "free theater" (you actually do have to pay) has two separate spaces where they stage a variety of quality dramas. Some of the most interesting actors and directors in Spain have started here, at the bottom of the Montjuïc mountain. Box office is open Monday to Friday 11am to 3pm and 4:30 to 8pm; Saturday and Sunday 2 hours before show. *Plaça Margarita Xirgú s/n.* ☎ *932-892-770. Tickets Tues–Wed 12€–16€, Thurs–Sun 16€–24€. Metro: Plaça Espanya or Poble Sec.*

Sightseeing

Barcelona transforms the most ordinary of objects into works of art that everybody can experience—benches, sidewalks, and even light posts have a subtle aesthetic quality, not to mention the wild architecture of Gaudí and the Modernistas concentrated in L'Eixample (see the walking tour on p. 380). Barri Gòtic is one of the best-preserved medieval quarters in all of Europe, with quiet plazas, lofty palaces, and a maze of narrow streets. Take a stroll down Carrer Avinyó and you'll be able to see major landmarks and then catch some lunch only a few meters away in one of the city's most popular restaurants and bars.

BARCELONA

Festival Frenzy

That day in Gràcia with my friends, we toasted and sloshed our foamy beer when suddenly a wave of bodies rushed down the narrow street. Some mugs were laughing, most were cursing, and I felt my stomach drop to my knees as I was swept away by the crowd. I had no idea what we were running from or where my friends were, but within seconds the stampede flowed out into the main avenue. The situation was as absurd as the wildly monstrous architecture towering over the crowd. I crossed the street as a van labeled GUARDIA URBANA screeched to a halt and spit out six masked guards swinging batons and shields at anyone running from them.

Some punks threw whatever they could at the cops, but I sat still and watched. I thought violence and the police state were something of the Franco era; apparently, Barcelona kept that tradition when it tried to revive its Catalan identity. The van then left as quickly as it came and I looked around for some recognizable faces. "Let's go to the after-party," said the Colombian as he ran up to me. The madness never ends in "Barce-loca."

Festivals/Calendar of Events

Barceloneses are notoriously hard-working, yet they still manage to find the energy to celebrate before clocking in early to work the next day. The year-round schedule of unique neighborhood *festes* share traditions like the *castelles*, or castles, where groups of up to 400 people pit their strength and balance against each other to build human towers up to 10 stories high, and of course, the *gegantes* (giants) that lead processions, and finally, the freaky *capgrossos* (fatheads) that spark up mischief. Check out www.festivales.com and the cultural agenda section of www.bcn.es for dates and general info.

April

Sant Jordí. The red-and-gold Catalan flag decorates every inch of the city during this celebration of patron saint, St. George. The equivalent of Valentine's Day in the States (sans corporate takeover), lovers exchange gifts—a man gives a rose and a woman gives a book. Most enlightened couples give both. April 23.

Feria de Abril. Barcelona's version of Sevilla's biggest party is a mix of Spanish-ghetto-fabulous and redneck carnival with hams instead of guns. Avoid going during the day, when the sun mercilessly shows the caked makeup dripping down the polka-dotted grandmas' cheeks. At night, though, the party gets going and, tent after tent, the impromptu *cante* and *sevillanas* inevitably build on to dancing on the tabletops until the wee hours. And after all that sangria, "granny don't look so bad, no more." At Fórum de Barcelona. End April/May. Metro: El Maresme-Fòrum.

May

Festival de Flamenco Ciutat Vella. If you thought Flamenco was old and boring, well this is the festival that will make you eat your words. A 5-day vanguard Flamenco Frenzy featuring performers and DJs fusing flamenco with whatever you can think of, from tango to hard-core rock 'n' roll. Not for someone looking for traditional flavor. A whole bunch of related activities like movies, confrences, and exhibitions. www.tallerdemusics.com. Late May. Around the CCCB. Metro: Universitat.

June

Marató de L'Espectacle. Locals love this event that packs in theater, skits, animation, dance, movies, music, and circ (circus-related performances, like fire-eating, and so on) into this 2-day "marathon of the spectacle." Performances begin around 10:30am and don't let up until dawn in the historic and beautiful Mercat de les Flors. Second week of June. Carrer de Lleida 59. Metro: Espanya.

Sónar. If you're into electronic music, multimedia technology, and contemporary urban art, this 3-day international festival of advanced music and multimedia art is a must. There are exhibitions, record fairs, and sound labs by the CCCB by day, and concerts and DJs play at SónarNight. www.sonar.es. Tickets 20€ to 105€. Mid-June.

Best❶ Sant Joan. It's the summer solstice and Barcelona's burning up. Check out the fireworks at Montjuïc, Tibidabo, or L'Estació del Nord. Later, head to the beach for Barceloneta's pyromaniac orgy Nit del Foc (Night of Fire), dance around bonfires until dawn, and then follow the drunken

Testing 1-2-3

If you've been to a big concert lately in Spain, no doubt you're wondering what's up with those guys called **Energy Control.** EC (☎ **902-253-600;** www.energycontrol.org) is an NGO (or non-governmental organization) that tests concert-goers' pills to confirm whether they contain MDMA, the active component in *Extasis* (Ecstasy)—or possibly pack an unwelcome punch.

That's the Ticket

Don't expect a tour guide and bus on this route—the **Ruta del Modernisme**. It's actually a ticket for discount admission at dozens of modernista buildings in the city and includes a map and guide booklet detailing the history of different sites. Passes are 3.60€ for adults and 2.60€ for students, are valid for 30 days, and can be bought at **Casa Amatller** (Passeig de Gràcia 41; ☎ **934-880-139**). See "The Ruta del Modernisme: L'Eixample & Gaudí" on p. 380 for info on walking the route.

lemmings into the ocean for some skinny-dipping fun. June 23.

📺 Best❶ **Primavera Sound.** This new mega-festival is slowly taking the spotlight away from Sonar. It takes place at the Forum, one of the coolest sites in Barcelona. The six stages are on different levels; you can see a band at the main stage, then grab a bite in the food court and a drink at the bar with a view of the sea and the city that is almost worth the ticket price itself. Two stories below, there is a second stage, right next to the saltwater swimming pools and another one between them. The ever-growing 2006 lineup included top indie rock acts like the Yeah Yeah Yeahs, the Flaming Lips, and Mogwai; old glories like Lou Reed, Motorhead, and the Violent Femmes; and electro-popes and DJs such as DJ Rush, Ellen Allien and Apparat, and Justice. At Fórum de Barcelona. www.primavera sound.com. Tickets 40E to 65E per day, 100E 3-day pass. Primavera Bus from Plaça Catalunya. Metro: El Maresme-Fòrum Stop.

GREC Festival. This 5-week summer event brings theater, dance, and music performers from all over the world to over 50 different venues. Pick up a free schedule at the big booth in Plaça Catalunya and try to see at least one show at the beautiful theatre at Montjuïc, aka Teatre Grec. www.barcelonafestival.com. End of June and all of July.

August

📺 Best❶ **Festa Major de Gràcia.** The most popular neighborhood party is distinctive for its wildly decorated streets. Bands play on small stages throughout Gràcia as young crowds sing and scream along, drinks in hand. Just be out before the Guardia Urbana slams through in the wee hours. www.festamajordegracia.com. Third week in August.

September

Festa de la Mercé. This weeklong celebration of Barcelona's patron saint, Our Lady of Mercy, features human towers, *gegantes* and *capgrossos,* dazzling fireworks, and general drunken revelry. There is also free admission to many museums on September 24. Check out BAM (Barcelona Acció Musical; www.bam.es), which hosts free concerts. September 19 to 25.

November

Festival Internacional de Jazz de Barcelona. To get some jazz in Europe this is THE festival you have to check out. You'll find every style jazz has to offer, from bebop to gospel, performed by some of the best mainstream performers in the world, who get together in Barcelona every year. Catch it in theaters all over town and at the Ciutadella park, where they hold big band concerts. www.the-project.net. November. All over Barcelona.

Museums

FREE → **Caixa Forum** ★ Inside an old modernista factory at the bottom of Montjuïc lies this fantastic exhibition hall. Three halls host changing exhibitions of the sort that you usually only see in New

Miró, Miró on the Wall

Did you know that if you pay attention, you can catch Miró on Las Ramblas? No dude, not the actual *man;* he's been pushing up daisies for years. What you can catch, though, is a colorful tile mosaic very close to both the Liceu Theatre and the Liceu Metro and if you look closely, you can even find the tile he signed.

York's MoMA. The best news is that, thanks to Catalunya's biggest bank's (La Caixa) social conscience, you won't have to pay a penny for it. *Av. Marqués de Comillas 6-8. ☎ 934-768-600. www.fundaciolacaixa.es. Free admission. Tues–Sun 10am–8pm. Metro: Espanya.*

➔ **Centre de Cultura Contemporània de Barcelona (CCCB)** Spain's largest cultural center is dedicated to exploring how the urban landscape catalyzes cultural development—highbrow talk for how cities shape art and media, and vice-versa. The CCCB has regular multimedia exhibits, including film series and music performances. *Montalegre 5. ☎ 933-064-100. www. cccb.org. Admission 4.40€ 1 exhibit, 6€ 2 or more exhibits, free 1st Wed of month. June 21–Sept 21 Tues–Sat 11am–8pm, Sun 11am–3pm; Sept 22–June 20 Tues and Thurs–Fri 11am–2pm and 4pm–8pm, Wed and Sat 11am–8pm, Sun 11am–7pm. Metro: Plaça Catalunya or Universitat.*

➔ **Fundació Joan Miró** Joan Miró is yet another Spanish artist who made an impact on the modern art scene. If you find yourself wondering, "WTF? I could've painted this with my eyes closed," think of it this way: His surreal, simple forms, and primary colors collaborate to create vitality and spark the imagination. (Are you

inspired yet?) If you're still confused, check out the cool Mercury Fountain. The permanent collection is well worth a trip. *Parc de Montjuïc s/n. ☎ 934-439-470. www. bcn.fjmiro.es. Admission 7.20€ adults, 5€ students. Oct–June Tues–Sat 10am–7pm; July–Sept Tues–Sat 10am–8pm, Thurs 10am–9:30pm, Sun 10am–2:30pm. Metro: Parallel, then Funicular de Montjuïc. Bus: 50 or 55.*

➔**Museu d'Art Contemporani (MACBA)** ★★ If you're into modern art, you'll totally fall in love with this museum. The temporary exhibitions are really innovative, even more so than the permanent ones, which focus on avant-garde art between WWI and II, and include paintings, sculpture, and photography. The building itself, designed by Richard Meier, is a gargantuan anomalous work of art—kinda like a space station landed in El Raval. The plaza in front attracts dozens of fledgling skaters busting their stuff *Note:* If you skate by the entrance, you *will* get yelled at! *Plaça dels Angels 1. ☎ 934-120-810. www.macba.es. Admission 7€ adults, 5.50€ students. Mon–Fri 11am–7:30pm; Sat 10am–8pm; Sun and holidays 10am–3pm. Metro: Plaça Catalunya or Universitat.*

➔ **Museu Nacional d'Art de Catalunya (MNAC)** Learn the history of Catalonia through its art and artifacts, like Romanesque frescoes and Gothic paintings. Modern art from the Museu d'Art Modern complements the collection. What better way to absorb history than with visual CliffsNotes? *Palau Nacional, Parc de Montjuïc. ☎ 936-220-376. www.mnac.es. Admission 8.50€ adults, 6€ students. Tues–Sat 10am–7pm; Sun and holidays 10am–2:30pm. Metro: Espanya.*

➔ **Museu Picasso** ★ Whether you're a Picasso buff who is familiar with the stuff that made him famous (that is, cubism, blue and pink periods) or not, consider

Gaudí

The most famous of the modernismo architects, **Antonio Gaudí i Cornet** and his wildly amorphous designs have sparked debate for years. He infuses Gothic influences with inspiration from nature and innovative materials into colorful untraditional forms. He constructed two of Barcelona's most visited sites—the **Casa Milà** (see below) and the **Sagrada Familia** (p. 381)—although he wasn't well appreciated during his lifetime. He died penniless at the age of 76 and today some still consider his work a little too, well, gaudy. Yet the city of Barcelona has certainly come around in recent years, even going as far as to proclaim 2002 the Gaudí International Year.

what you'll see at this museum. It doesn't have any of his masterpieces. Most of the work here is from his younger and older years, so if you're interested in seeing how his technique and style evolved, it's worth a visit. If for nothing else, you can pick up some cool mugs, tees, and general Picasso goodies at the gift shop. *Montcada Street 15-23.* ☎ *933-196-310. www.museupicasso. bcn.es. Admission 6€. Tues–Sun 10am–8pm. Metro: Liceu or Jaume I.*

Top Attractions

📺 Best 🍴 FREE → **Casa Milà (La Pedrera)** ★★★ The last work of Gaudí's before he turned to the Sagrada Familia. The building seems to have washed ashore with walls that mimic the ocean's waves and balconies tangled like seaweed. Check out the whimsical rooftop with its views of Barcelona. It's a great place to see the sunset. Live music at 9pm from July to September adds to its charm. *Provença 261-265.* ☎ *902-400-973. www.caixacatalunya.*

es. Admission 8€. Daily 10am–8pm. Metro: Passeig de Gracia.

FREE → **Catedral de Barcelona** ★★ One of Barcelona's most popular and recognizable monuments—yup, it's a cathedral alright. It's near Las Ramblas, so you can take your picture and go on with your day. If you stick around, you can catch a performance of the *sardana* in front of the cathedral on Sunday after Mass; services begin at noon and 6:30pm. *Plaça de la Seu s/n.* ☎ *933-151-554. Free admission to cathedral; museum 1€. Cathedral daily 9am–1pm and 5–7pm; cloister museum daily 10am–1pm and 4–6:30pm. Metro: Jaume I and Liceu.*

FREE → **La Font Mágica (Magic Fountain)** ★★ Designed for the 1929 World's Fair, this enormous fountain comes to life during weekends when streams of water shoot in the air in sync with colored lights and dramatic music. The colorful clouds of mist can be frighteningly trippy, but the hundreds of camera-snapping tourists ferried in by the busload will kill any buzz. *Plaça Carles Buïgas 1 (in front of the Palau Nacional). Free admission. Shows May to early Oct Thurs–Sun every half-hour 9:30–11:30pm; mid-Oct to Apr Fri–Sat every half-hr. 7–8:30pm. Metro: Espanya.*

→ **Mirador de Colón** This tower with a statue of Columbus on top is a city landmark. Pay 2€ and take the elevator to the top to catch a great view of the urban sprawl and the ocean. Take note, Columbus has got it all wrong again: He's pointing east to Libya and not the Americas. *Portal de la Pau s/n.* ☎ *933-025-224. Admission 2€. June–Sept 9am–8:30pm; Oct–May 10am–6:30pm. Metro: Drassanes.*

FREE → **Olympic Stadium** See where all the action took place at the 1992 Olympics. The stadium was originally built in 1929, was remodeled for the Games, and now hosts the RCD Espanyol (team of the Professional Spanish Football League).

The Ruta del Modernisme: L'Eixample & Gaudí

By the mid–19th century, an overcrowded, old Barcelona was bursting at the seams with crime and cholera when it was decided that the city walls had to come down and make way for the "expansion" (*l'eixample* in Catalan). Ildefons Cerdà designed a plan for a utopian space with gridded streets, ample park space, and low buildings that was later ignored by developers who erected tall, fortresslike buildings. However, the building boom coincided with Barcelona's golden age of architecture and provided the setting for modernist experimentation, with its over-the-top curvilinear designs and bright colors.

Grab your camera and get ready to walk the **Ruta del Modernisme.**

1. **Plaça Catalunya.** Start off here at the lower edge of L'Eixample. Get your last dose of A/C at the Corte Inglés shopping mall and pick up a free map.

2. **Passeig de Gràcia.** Walk up the main artery of L'Eixample and you can already notice a big difference from cramped Barri Gòtic. Do some window-shopping at the designer boutiques and check out the wrought iron lamp posts and the spiral, trippy slabs of pavement that were originally designed for the patio of Gaudí's Casa Batlló before they covered the entire boulevard.

3. **Manzana de la Discordia.** The "block of discord" is one of the most notable modernist landmarks, home to three flamboyantly clashing designs—Casa Amatller, Casa Lleó, and Casa Batlló—between Carrer Aragó and Carrer Consell de Cent. You can buy a Ruta del Modernisme pass (p. 344) in Casa Amatller. Gaudí's Casa Batlló opens its first floor, chimneys, and attic to the public. Be careful not to walk around with your eyes raised toward the sky because you might run into a light post like Gaudí ran into a train.

4. **Carrer Aragó.** Head east off of Passeig de Gràcia to take a lunch break in one of the affordable restaurants. It's also a great spot for people-watching.

5. **Casa Milà/La Pedrera.** Get back on Passeig de Gràcia and head 3 blocks north to one of Gaudí's signature works, La Pedrera, which you should go out of your way to see. The building seems to have washed ashore with walls that mimic the ocean's waves and balconies tangled like seaweed. Check out the whimsical rooftop and its views of Barcelona. (See "Top Attractions," above.)

6. **Sagrada Familia.** Get ready for a walk. Turn right on Carrer Provença and follow it for 11 blocks. (Don't turn on slanted Av. Diagonal.) Gaudí's masterpiece-in-the-making sticks out like a sore thumb. (See "Top Attractions," above.)

Woo! You made it! There's a Metro stop here (L5 and L2) to take you back into the city.

Perched atop the hill Montjuïc, it overlooks Barcelona from the southwest. ☎ 934-262-089. *Free admission. Sept–Mar 10am–6pm; May–Sept 10am–8pm. Metro: Espanya (then a 20-min. walk).*

MTV Best ● FREE → **Parc Güell** ★★★
In true Gaudí fashion, construction of the tripped out park he designed wasn't finished until after his death. Initially a

miniature garden city for the rich, only one of his intergalactic gingerbread houses was completed and is now the Casa-Museu Gaudí. Try to get here early in the morning if you plan on taking pictures of the colorfully tiled serpentine structures—you'll be fighting with dozens of parents and their toothless kids to snap a picture of the iguana fountain seen on every postcard. (*Tip:* If you take the Metro, prepare to trek up a huge hill. Pack some water and snacks because a lot of the shops on the outskirts of the park are overpriced.) *Carrer del Carmel 28. ☎ 934-243-809 or 932-193-811. Free admission. Daily 10am–sunset. Metro: Lesseps (then a 15-min. walk). Bus: 24.*

→ **Poble Espanyol** ★★ Built for the 1929 World's Fair, this "Spanish Village" represents each region in Spain with scaled-down versions of their most recognizable attractions. It's definitely a tourist trap with plenty of overpriced souvenir shops,

but it's a great stop if you want to fill your scrapbook with funny, cheesy pics. *Av. Marqués de Comillas. ☎ 935-086-300. www. poble-espanyol.com. Admission 7€ adults, 5€ students. Sun 9am–midnight; Mon 9am–8pm; Tues–Thurs 9am–2am; Fri–Sat 9am–4am. Ticket booth closes 1 hr. before park. Metro: Espanya.*

MTV Best ● → **Sagrada Familia** ★★★ If you see only one thing in this town, it has got to be this glorious, spiraling drippy sand castle in the sky. Love it or hate it, Gaudí's enormous masterpiece, started in 1882 and still incomplete, is an architectural monument to the absurd. Climb up the narrow spiral staircase or wait in line and take an elevator to catch the view from the top of the towers. *Majorca 401. ☎ 932-073-031. Admission 8€ adults, 5€ students, 3€ guide/audioguide, 2€ elevator ride. Nov–Mar daily 9am–6pm; Apr–Sept daily 9am–8pm. Metro: Verdaguer or Sagrada Familia.*

Playing Outside

Parks

Visit the city's main park, **Parc de la Ciutadella** (daily 8am–9pm; Metro: Ciutadella or Arc de Triomf), and jog, ride a bike, or simply veg out by the fragrant gardens or tranquil ponds; just be sure to check out the funky fountain that Gaudí helped create. There are plenty of families with rug rats in tow heading to the city zoo in the park. It's safe during the day, but like most big city parks, use some common sense if you plan on walking through here at night. During the summer, there are free jazz concerts in the little gazebo at 10pm on Wednesdays.

At MTV Best ● **Mount Tibidabo,** breathe in some fresh air and take your last glimpse of Barcelona on this mountain peak. After your moment of Zen, go scream your guts out on the rides at the theme park, **Parc d'Atraccions Tibidabo** (Plaça

Tibidabo 3; ☎ **932-117-942;** 22€ for all rides, 11€ for six rides; summer daily noon–10pm, off season Sat–Sun noon–7pm; Bus: 58 to Avinguda Tibidabo Metro, then take the Tramvía Blau, which drops you at the funicular, round-trip 3.10€).

The most impressive park in Barcelona is the MTV Best ● **Montjuïc.** The tallest mountain in the city is home to many attractions, but the park alone is well worth the trip. The best way to get there is by taking the Funicular (TMB; ☎ **933-187-074**) from the Paral.lel Metro station up. It works daily, from 9am to 10pm, in summer and from 9am to 8pm in winter. The round-trip fare is 2.40€; one-way is 1.20€. For a more exhilarating trip, hop on to the **Montjuïc teléferic** (cable car) from Barceloneta to Montjuïc. Between June 20 and September 15 it works daily from 10:30am to 8pm and in winter, from noon

Board Talk

Skating's been around Barcelona forever, not for nothing it's been called the LA of Europe. The city became famous for its spots in the late '90s, when people started to come from abroad exclusively to skate. Its radical urban architecture full of obstacles, benches, wild fences, and metal bars on the streets make the city seem like it was designed by Jay Adams. Add that it barely ever rains and a great temperature the whole year long and you get the perfect city for skating. Don't forget that, with the Metro, you're less than 20 minutes away from every spot! And, of course, there's the beach, where you can let the board rest and have your eyes do the skating for a while.

The hottest spots are: **Plaça Sants,** in front of the train station. This is the place where it all started, where the locals come to do their ollies and jumps. Heck, this place is so big that it even got its own sneakers by Nike SB. The **MACBA,** with its big cement square and tilted platfom is another rider's dream, except for the tourists and the cops. It's the meeting place for all the *guiri* skaters although some locals come here to show off too. The park by **Paral.lel Avenue** in front of the three chimneys, is not as popular but just as fun, with its weird sculptures and levels, and finally, **Plaça Universitat** presents a couple more options. A few skateparks and ramps specially built for skaters are located by **Platja Marbella** and **Fórum,** but they are nothing like the public places that sprout everywhere in the **Condal town.** Try them, and you might find yourself skating with Marcos Gomez, Jose Noro, Raúl Retamal (Reta), Pablo Dominguez, or Lee Hun Doek. They are Barcelona's finest and have been here since the beginning. You'll find other board-minded youngsters who will be glad to fill you in on what's going on.

Lately the legal situation got a little hairy with the new civic laws. So, be advised that it's supposed to be forbidden to skate all over the city, outside of the government built skateparks. Actually, that means you'll just have to be a little more discreet, like avoiding big groups and places where you can bother people.

If you need gear, the hottest stores for skaters are **Free Barcelona** (Bonsucces 2; ☎ 934-125-645; and Viladomat 319; ☎ 933-217-290) near the MACBA and **Tac Tic,** on Enrique Granados Street in the back of Plaça Universitat.

And to have a drink there's always the **Bar Manolo** (Lancaster 3; no phone), a mythical bar where skaters get together since the dawn of time.

to 5pm. It will set you back 7.50€ one-way, or 9€ round-trip. Once you are at the top, the most fun is to get lost in the maze of trails and find the mind-boggling parks and structures there. The Quarry, the Teatre Grec, and the Font del Gat, are amongst the coolest sites.

Bicycling

Bike Tours Barcelona is a guided bike tour in English that will take you to all the major sites, like Gothic Quarter, the Old Harbour, Ciutadella Park, the Sagrada Família, the Olimpic Port, and Gaudí's architectural landmarks, in 3 hours. No reservations needed; just show up at the meeting point, the Tourist Office of Plaça Sant Jaume at 11am, and grab a bike (Esparteria 3; ☎ 932-682-105; www.bike toursbarcelona. com; admission 22€, includes a drink; daily at 11am year-round; Metro: Jaume I or Liceu). Another awesome biking experience is to rent one (see rental places on p. 343) and ride up the coast toward Mataró. In less than half an hour you'll be at the Maresme coast (see "Beaches," below), ready to jump in the crystal-clear water.

Beaches

The **beaches** in the city are quite nice considering that 2 million people live by them and they are man-made, but can be very crowded and sometimes dirty, especially in July and August. It still can be great to spend the hot summer days sitting by a *chiringuito* (see "Sand, Drinks & Rock 'n' Roll," p. 368) and jumping in the water among the mostly topless and sometimes fully naked girls and boys. Another classic Barcelona experience is to end your night with a skinny-dip in the warm summer water of the Mediterranean. All six beaches in Barcelona have services like lockers, free outdoor showers, public restrooms, lifeguard, and bicycle parking.

Sant Sebastiá (Metro: Barceloneta) is the first beach, a long stretch by an uninhabited area of town, and an unofficial nudist beach. The downside is its proximity to the port, which makes the water quality iffy, despite the humongous stone wall that divides them.

Barceloneta (Metro: Barceloneta) is the closest to the old city, and the most crowded. Finding a spot here in July can prove harder than getting a ticket to the NBA finals. Most tourists come here for a quick dip and the seaside bars and restaurants that offer good food at reasonable prices.

Mar Bella and **Nova Mar Bella** (Metro: Poble Nou or Selva de Mar) are the two beaches farthest from the center, and the least crowded, although that doesn't mean you'll be more than 3 feet away from your neighbor in August. The high dunes make Mar Bella the city's official nudist beach and a major "bear" (see "Gay Bars," p. 371) hangout. The center of Barcelona's beach

Hanging Out

If you've been partying for 3 days straight and want to get away from the crowds, walk from Las Ramblas (more than 15 min.) and just keep walking (and walking) until you hit the **nudist beach** Platja Mar Bella.

Even if you prefer to keep the family jewels under wraps, Mar Bella is worth the trek if you want to check out **skaters** peeling their skin on the popular half-pipe. If you're not ready to take the plunge, take your board to the MACBA (see "Sightseeing," above) and zip around with other novice skaters.

In true Spanish fashion, the best places to chill with a bottle and a group of friends are at the plazas; yet don't let the names fool you. Plaça George Orwell in the Barri Gòtic is anything but Big Brother. Also known as the "Plaza del Trippy," there really isn't anything psychedelic about this grimy concrete enclave at the end of Carrer Escudellers. It's a prime spot for *botellón* (passing around a bottle among friends outdoors), but the crowd can be a bit shady.

The **Jardins Rubio i Lluch** is the perfect spot for bringing a *bocadillo* (baguette sandwich) and a book. Sit underneath the many trees or archways of the Escola Massana, the neighboring school of art and design, and check out the art students smoking cigarettes between classes. Feel free to wander through the two-room student gallery and try to be there around 1pm during their midday break if you're looking to meet José or María del Arte. (Metro: Liceu).

Detour: Castelldefels

Less than half an hour from Barcelona is Castelldefels, a small coastal town with the most amazingly wide **beaches** you've ever seen. During the weekends, it probably has a population equivalent to that of Barceloneta, but if you want to be alone, just go there during the week. You'll have miles of beaches with no beach balls, buckets, or crying kids. Castelldefels even has a small **medieval castle**, a 10th-century **Romanesque chapel,** and some **Paleolithic caves.**

Have a bit of nosh when the day's over at **Rincón de Lola** (Plaza del Mar 1y2; ☎ **936-651-226;** Thurs–Tues 10am–2am). Enjoy the sunset while having a *clara* and some tapas on its huge terrace overlooking the beach and still make it back to Barcelona in time to start the night. (Renfe line 2 from Barcelona Sants or Passeig de Gràcia toward St. Vicente de Calders and hop off at Castelldefels.)

nightlife is at the *chiringuitos* in Nova Mar Bella (see "Sand, Drinks & Rock 'n' Roll," p. 368).

If you want natural beaches with less people and cleaner water, take the Rodalies Line 1 at Plaça Catalunya or Arc de Triomf towards Maçanet to **Mongat,** an endless beach with lots of families and sports. A little longer and you'll get to our favorite, **St. Pol de Mar,** which is 30 minutes away. Besides a clean, fine sand beach with blue water, there's a cute little old town as well.

Swimming

Barcelona has lots of public pools if waves and rough seas are too much of an inconvenience for you. Be advised, though, flip-flops and swimming caps are generally a must. The man-made sea pools by the forum are free and worth checking out, but the crowd of noisy families makes them more of an anthropological experience than good ol' exercising.

➔ **Club de Natació Atlétic Barceloneta** This historical club that just recently turned 100 years old, has everything you need to get exercised. One indoor and two outdoor pools (one of them heated) on a sun packed terrace overlooking the beach, gym, sauna, and Jacuzzi. *Plaça del Mar, Barceloneta.* ☎ *932-210-010. www.cnab.org. Admission 8€ per day for non-members. Membership 28€ per month plus 58€ joining fee. Oct–Apr Mon–Fri 6:30am–11pm, Sat 7am–11pm, Sun 8am–5pm; May–Sept Mon–Sat 7am–11pm, Sun 8am–8pm. Metro: Espanya then escalators.*

➔ **Piscina Bernat Picornell** The huge Olympic indoor pool is not only called that because of its measure—It actually was the main venue for the Olympics in 1992. There's also a 50m-long (164-ft.) outdoor pool with a terrace with views of the city, a climbing wall, and a gym. During the Grec festival they offer late night sessions of swimming and movies and there are also regular sessions for nudists (9–11pm Sat all year; 4:15–6pm Sun Oct–May). *Av. Del'Estadi 30-40, Montjuïc.* ☎ *934-234-041. www. picornell.com. Admission June–Sept 4.50€ per day, Oct–May 8.50€. Outdoor pool June–Sept Mon–Sat 9am–9pm, Sun 9am–8pm; Oct–May Mon–Sat 10am–7pm, Sun 10am–4pm. Covered pool, rest of the complex, Mon–Fri 7am–midnight, Sat 7am–9pm, Sun 7:30am–4pm. Pool and gym Oct–Apr Mon–Fri 6:30am–11pm, Sat 7am–11pm, Sun 8am–5pm; May–Sept Mon–Sat 7am–11pm, Sun 8am–8pm. Metro: Barceloneta then bus 17, 39, or 64.*

Shopping

Most shops don't open until 10am and they close for lunch roughly between 2 and 5pm. Large shops don't take the siesta, though; most stay open until 8pm (and an hour later on Sat). Barca's summer sale season begins the first week of July and goes through the last week of August.

Clothing & Fashion

Catalan style tends toward casual, bright, and cute, and trendy sneakers and tees are what the majority of people wear. Local designers have managed to carve out spots for themselves on **Carrer Avinyó** and around the **Born.** Vintage is not the huge trend it is in England, France, or the States, but you can pick up a few gems in the shops concentrated on **Carrer Riera Baixa** (mostly '60s to '80s styles) in **Raval.**

Spain is a powerhouse of fashion chain stores. **Zara, Women's Secret, Bershka, Massimo Dutti** (all owned by **Inditex**), **Mango, Adolfo Dominguez,** and the quirky **Camper** all call the **Avenida Portal de l'Angel** home. If the prices here aren't low enough for you, try the outlets on **Calle Girona** between **Calle Ausiás Marc** and **Gran Via de les Corts Catalanes.**

Best ❂ → **Como Agua de Mayo** With clothing as poetic and feminine as its name, Agua is by far our favorite women's clothing boutique. Small and selective, Agua packs some of the best up-and-coming European clothing, shoes, and accessories by names such as Miriam Oscariz and Pink Soda. *Calle Argenteria 43. El Born.* ☎ *933-106-441. Metro: Jaume I.*

→ **Humana** A PC way to attire yourself is this Goodwill-style chain that takes donations and gives its profits to poor African countries. They have a selection of '60s and '70s clothes, toys, and home products throughout their nine stores in the city. The largest is at Av. Paral-lel 85.

→ **Holala** For guys and gals with a discerning eye for fun '60s to '80s vintage garb, Holala is by far the liveliest place in BCN to shop for dead stock and one-of-a-kind tees, sportswear, military gear, and more. If you are in Ibiza you can check out their flagship store (p. 503). *Carrer Riera Baixa 11.* ☎ *934-419-494. www.holala-ibiza.com.*

→ **Mango Outlet** The mobbed outlets offer last season's fashions and slightly imperfect women's fashion and accessories with the brand-name bling. *Calle Girona 37.* ☎ *934-122-935. Also Calle Pau Casals 12.* ☎ *932-090-773.*

→ **Rethink Audio Wear** This life-style store offers clothes, music, gadgets, and books, and even has a DJ booth and items geared towards DJs and wannabee waxers. *Carrer Comerç 23, El Born.* ☎ *932-689-907. www.7rethink.com. Metro: Jaume I, Arc de Triomf.*

Books/Visual Arts

The bookstores in MACBA, CCCB, and Caixa Forum have a great selection of art books, but also stock alternative literature and guides. You can find collectible books and vintage posters on Carrer Banys Nous.

→ **Central Bookstore** Stocked with goods by liberal arts and philosophy heavyweights in various languages, this is a good place to finish up a late paper during spring break. Study or fish for cute bookworms at the cafeteria in the back of the Raval locations. *4 locations. www.lacentral. com. La Central: Calle Mallorca 237;* ☎ *934-875-018. La Central del Raval: Calle Elisabets 6;* ☎ *933-170-293. La Central del Lliure: Passeig de Santa Madrona 40-46; No phone. La Central del MACBA: Plaza del Àngels 1; No phone.*

➜ **Mercado** The big white kayak filled with graphic-design and illustration books makes for an impressive centerpiece in this very cool art gallery and store. Rotating exhibits include local and international contemporary artists, all with an edge and highly collectible. *Plaza Comercial 3.* ☎ *932-688-631.* *www.mercadodelborne.com.* *Metro: Jaume I.*

➜ **Montana Shop & Gallery** It's obvious as you walk around BCN that graffiti is respected and damn good. Check out the only graffiti supply and specialty store in the city. You can also catch an art show and buy a book by one of your favorite artists. *Carrer Comerç 6.* ☎ *932-680-191.* *www.mtnshopbarcelona.com.* *Metro: Arc de Triomf.*

Home

➜ **Coses de Casa** The store dates from the 19th century, but the goods are modern, mostly hand-woven fabrics and weavings from Majorca. The appealing textiles, many with bold, geometric patterns, take inspiration from centuries-old Arab motifs. *Plaça de Sant Josep Oriol 5.* ☎ *933-027-328.* *Metro: Jaume I or Eliceo.*

➜ **Habitat** When IKEA grows up, it wants to be Habitat. This Conran chain store is a great place for European home-wares of a better quality and design—like hammock seats designed by Carla Bruni or light up tables by Daft Punk. Most of the time pieces are already assembled (and expensive), so you may want to just window shop. *Centro Commercial "El Triangle," Plaça Catalunya 4, Eixample.* ☎ *933-017-484.* *www.habitat.net.* *Metro: Catalunya.*

➜ **Herbs** You will undoubtedly impress with flowers or a plant from this store. An incredible selection of tropical and couture greenery, plus they sell those cool eggs that crack open and a plant comes out with HAPPY BIRTHDAY written on the leaf. *Carrer Rec 28.* ☎ *932-681-804.* *www.herbs.es.* *Metro: Jaume I.*

Edibles

➜ **Caelum** Abstinence makes the cookie taste sweeter. This shop specializes in homemade and perfectly packaged cookies (most of them contain almonds), jams, and liqueurs by Spanish monks and nuns. Relax over a drink in the charming cafe and sample some of the delicacies. Our favorite is the *tortas de aceite* (looks like a pita, but it's a sweet cracker with fennel seed essence). *Calle de la Palla 8, Barri Gòtic.* ☎ *933-026-993.* *Metro: Liceu, Juame I.*

➜ **E&A Gispert** If you smell roasting almonds as you are walking around the Born, you're not losing it; Gispert has just got their oven burning again. Established in 1851, this specialty food store is the only place in the city where you can watch the antique art of nut roasting. Treat yourself to a paper bag full of them or fill a lovely straw basket with beautiful fancy foods that are perfect for mom's upcoming birthday. *Calle Sombrerers 23, El Born.* ☎ *933-197-535.* *Metro Jaume I.*

➜ **Fargas** Quality chocolate is in abundance here, but Fargas gives you an orgasmic chocolate-covered almond sample when you purchase any of their products. They will caringly package their chocolate truffles or any of their quality *bombones* for you in a little gold box. But after you try the almonds, you're going to end up buying them as well. *Doh! Calle Pino 16, Barri Gòtic.* ☎ *933-020-342.* *Metro: Liceu.*

➜ **Selecció Natural** Here's your chance to ask a million stupid questions about wine and just get a patient informative answer. This small didactic shop run by an effervescent Swedish/Catalan couple specializes in small Catalan wines categorized as *joviales, expresivos,* and *complejos* (roughly translated as young, expressive, and complicated). They will walk you though your selection and set you up with a perfect bottle, no matter your price range. They also run wine tasting tours to the local vineyards. *Calle de la Cirera 7 bajos, El Born.* ☎ *932-681-878. www.seleccionatural bcn.com. Metro: Jaume I.*

Music

➜ **Etnomusic** Pick up some old-school salsa, klezmer, or dub reggae at this small shop that has been catering to eclectic music tastes since 1991. Don't know how to pronounce Youssou N'Dour? Think djembe is a typo? Don't fret—the friendly staff will help guide you through stacks of world music CDs. *Bonsucces 6.* ☎ *933-011-884. Metro: Catalunya.*

➜ **Overstock** This store stands out from the other five record stores on the same street because it definitely lives up to its name. Pick up magazines, biographies, DVDs, apparel, footwear, patches, pins, or buy concert tickets—you name it, they've got it. Oh yeah, they also have CDs and vinyl that you'd have a tough time finding at home in Wichita. *Metro: Universitat.*

Markets

Held during daylight hours every Monday, Wednesday, Friday, and Saturday in Plaça de les Glòries Catalanes (Metro: Glòries or Encants), **El Encants** is an open-air little-bit-of-everything market, once known for its antiques and now predominantly cheap items, from electronics to bolts of fabrics. There are some interesting antique tchotchkes to be found at this dirty and disorganized market. Bargaining is expected.

The higher quality and price-point **antiques** market takes place on Thursdays in front of the Cathedral, Pla de la Seu (Metro: Jaume I). For **coins** and **postage stamps,** check out the trading at Plaça Reial on Sunday from 10am to 8pm (Metro: Drassanes). A **book** and **coin** market is held at the Ronda Sant Antoni every Sunday from 10am to 2pm (Metro: Sant Antoni).

➜ **El Mercadillo** Also known as the "Camello" because of the life-size camel standing guard below the alien spaceship at the entrance to this indoor flea market. It's a great place to get those Turkish MC Hammer pants and whatever else is trendy at the moment at a cheaper price. There's a tattoo and piercing parlor, as well as the chill Bar Jardí (see "Cafes & Tearooms," above) upstairs. If you want more name-brand clothing like Pepe Jeans, Benetton, and Lacoste, keep walking down the crowded street. *Porta Ferrissa 17.* ☎ *933-018-913. Metro: Universitat or Liceu.*

Catalunya

by *Fernando Gayesky*

atalunya is to tourism what Virgin megastores are to music. Girona, the most happening small town since Pompeii, is a pristinely preserved medieval town populated by Barcelona expats with a fresh, university fueled nightlife. This idyllic setting has also raised and attracted many artists such as Salvador Dalí, whose creative genius is on display at his museum in Figueres. This town is the portal to the magnificent Costa Brava, where thousands of coves and rock formations dive into the bluest sea. Follow Dalí's inspiration to the source of his bizarre dreams: isolated coastal Cadaqués, with a history rich in sex, drugs, and rock 'n' roll. Tossa de Mar's endearing beaches, enclosed by a miniature walled historic town, were discovered by artists like Marc Chagall in the '30s and have been packed with sun and culture lovers ever since. The monastery of Montserrat, in the outskirts of Barcelona, is a point of pilgrimage for many Catholics around the world. South of Barcelona boys and girls gone wild flock en masse to the sun-drenched beaches and the party central that is Sitges. The golden beaches turn into the Costa Daurada, with long stretches of fine sand and inviting turquoise water. Tarragona, former capital of the Hispanic Roman Empire, is home to ruins that would have Russell Crowe pulling out his sword and getting ready to rumble. From the human towers of *castellers* to Gaudi's post-human constructions and superstar chef Ferrán Adriá's culinary innovation, Catalans have always been known for living by their own rules and pushing the boundaries.

The Best of Catalunya

- **Best Outdoor Summer Drinking:** The tents at Girona's **Parc de la Devesa** are a magnet for young bar-seekers. See p. 396.

- **Best Hotel for a Good Knight's Sleep:** Pensión **Bellmirall** is housed in a Middle Ages stone building smack in Girona's historic area. It doesn't get any quieter than this. See p. 394.

- **Best Place to Play Medieval Hide and Seek:** The **Call Jueu** in Girona is a fascinating maze of cobblestoned streets and alleys twisty enough to lose your companions—but small enough to find them again. See p. 417.

- **Best Roman Holiday:** In the old Roman capital of **Tarragona** it's impossible to walk 2 blocks without finding a piece of ancient architecture, and when visiting the **Amphitheater (Amfiteatre Romà)** you can almost see the likes of Charlton Heston's Ben-Hur getting down on the Arena. See p. 417.

- **Best Party to Play Dress Up:** Sitges's **Carnaval** is an everything-goes madness of a town party full of floats, costumes, and parades. Check your inhibitions at the city limits. See p. 424.

- **Best Seaside Meal:** Try the tallarinas at the **Chiringuito** in Cadaqués and your taste buds will never be the same. See p. 405.

- **Best Celeb Hangout:** The kind of people that made **L'Hostal** famous in Cadaqués are not your typical E! over-produced media hogs. Only the coolest painters and musicians groove on this joint's comfy seats. See p. 406.

- **Best Fringe Flamenco Show:** Tossa's **Flamenco Bar** (aka Paulino's) features performers, clientele, and decor that even Almodovar, the great Spanish director of kitsch, couldn't dream up. See p. 411.

- **Best Museum to Kill Time in: Teatre-Museu Dalí,** in Figueres, presses the limits of imagination and the boundaries of egotism and erotica. See p. 402.

Best Girona ★★

For years people who are sick of the madness of Barcelona and Costa Brava have come to settle down in this laid-back town where the seamless integration of the old and the new makes even Barcelona's Barri Gotic look tacky. As deep as their Catalan roots are embedded (all you hear is Catalan on the streets), most people are very open-minded to foreigners and more than willing to practice their language skills: Spanish, English, and French are all common second languages. With a mere 86,000 inhabitants, Girona manages to pack more culture, sightseeing, and action into its walls than do many bigger cities. Walking by the medieval gray stone houses along the winding streets of the Call Jueu (Jewish quarter) you almost expect to bump into a knight at the turn of any corner. Yet, on the other side of the Onyar River that divides the city like a time-warp, a vibrant set of trendy bars, restaurants, and clubs makes for a party-worthy night. The expansion of the university's campus and the election of Girona as Ryan Air's main hub this side of the Pyrenees means that the dread-locked backpacker has become more common than screaming teenagers at a Justin Timberlake concert. While in Girona, you shouldn't miss the chance to hang out with fellow travelers, see the sunset over the

CATALUNYA

pink and orange stone houses lining the Onyar River, and have an evening drink at the tents in La Devesa Park. After a very cultural and historical day of learning all about purity in medieval churches and Arab baths, you might want an intense night of gettin' dirty.

Getting There

BY PLANE

Girona's airport, located 11km (7 miles) south of town, was little known until a couple of years ago when low-cost **Ryan Air** (☎ 807-220-220; www.ryanair.com) chose it as its main Iberic hub. A few other airlines quickly followed suit, and a number of daily flights now arrive from all over Western Europe. **Iberia** (☎ 902-400-500; www.iberia.es) links Girona to other destinations within Spain. A taxicab from the airport to the center of town will cost 18€. Barcelona Bus has service to Girona every hour from 5:30am to 12:30am; buses take 25 minutes and cost 1.75€ one-way; 3.30€ return (valid for 30 days).

BY TRAIN

The train station is about half a mile from the historic town center near Plaça Espanya. More than 25 **RENFE trains** (☎ 902-240-202; www.renfe.es) per day connect Girona, Figueres, and Barcelona from 5:45am to 10pm, with most trains running in the early morning and late evening. Trip time is 30 minutes to 1½ hours, and the price varies from 5€ to 23€ depending on the train.

BY BUS

The bus station in Girona is right next to the train station off of Plaça Espanya. **Barcelona Bus** (☎ 902-130-014) runs three to five daily services from Barcelona for 9.50€ and from Figueres for 3.90€. **Sarfa buses** (☎ 972-201-796 in Girona) connects Girona with destinations all over Catalunya and the Costa Brava. You can

also catch buses leaving straight from the airport to destinations in Costa Brava and Barcelona.

BY CAR

Girona lies right off of the A7, the main north-south route. From Barcelona, take the A-2 north to reach the A-7.

Getting Around

BY TAXI

Taxis are not really very necessary in this theme-park-size town, but there are a couple of clubs outside walking distance. That being the case, you can call **Taxi Girona** (☎ 972-222-323 or 972-203-377).

BY BICYCLE OR FOOT

Girona is small enough that you can walk the entire town even if you're from L.A. The old town's streets are extremely narrow and sometimes very steep; but if you want to rent a bicycle to go check out the university campus (p. 397) at the far end of town, you can do so at the **Alberg Residencia Cerveri de Girona,** aka the youth hostel (C. dels Ciutadans 9; ☎ 972-218–003), at a price ranging from 5€ for 3 hours to 32€ for 48 hours.

Girona Basics

ORIENTATION

The **Onyar River** runs north to south and is the natural axis around which the city revolves. The **Parc de la Devesa** and the **Ter River** are the natural northern limits. On the eastern bank of the river lies the magnificent older area of town, with its winding cobblestoned streets that climb the mountain to the old city walls. Most tourist attractions are here among the tattoo parlors and kitschy retail venues like La Condoneria (p. 399). The four walking bridges that connect both sides of the river are perfect for romantic evening walks. A little further south, the **Plaça Catalunya,** in the middle of the river itself, is used as a

Girona & Beyond

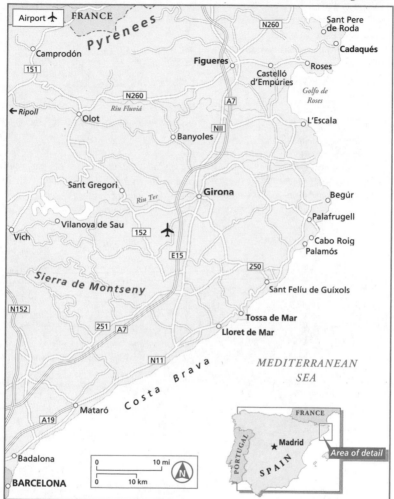

meeting point by locals and foreigners alike. On the west bank, the city turns modern and vibrant. You are likely to find yourself spending your nights in the area from **Plaça Independencia** to **Parc de la Devesa,** where the outdoor summer bars are clustered.

TOURIST OFFICES

You'll find the **Oficina de Turisme** (Rambla de la Llibertat 1; ☎ **972-226-575;** www.

ajuntament.gi/turisme) right after you cross the bridge on Carrer Nou, on the pedestrian boulevard to the left. It's open Monday to Friday 8am to 8pm, Saturday 8am to 2pm and 4 to 8pm, and Sunday 9am to 2pm.

RECOMMENDED WEBSITES

Girona's official website, www. ajuntament.gi/web/eng/index.php, which can be read in English, contains information on everything that goes on in the city as well as links to other English-speaking websites of interest.

Another good website available in English is www.costabravagirona.com. Our beloved and ever-present **Guia del Ocio** has a Girona chapter, www.guiadelocio.com/girona, but it's only available in Spanish.

Culture Tips 101

Being deeper into Catalunya, you will find that Catalan indeed has more of a presence here than in Barcelona. It's all you hear on the streets and see on the signs, and even when people speak Spanish to you (fear not, everybody does) you may notice their thick, Catalan accent. Not too sure about your grammar school Spanish? You're in luck as the last couple of years have witnessed a big increase in the number of British expats, and even American basketball players who play for the local team and now populate the English and Irish pubs in the old town (p. 396). People from Girona are in general highly educated, so don't be afraid to try speaking English to them, especially the younger generations. But, remember: Girona is a quiet town so leave your loud, obnoxious, American self packed in your bags—especially at night, when buckets of water launched from above have been known to cool down loud partiers.

Girona **Nuts & Bolts**

Currency As always, you will get the best exchange rate at an **ATM**. On your way from the train station to the old town you will see a bunch of them, and also in the area surrounding Plaça Independencia.

Emergency For an emergency, dial **112**. If you need a hospital, call Girona's Hospital ☎ **972-940-200**.

Internet The *locutorios* (cybercafes) are easy to find around town. Here is an option to get your fix of e-surf: **Comunica-T** (C. Carreras Peralta 4; Mon–Sat 10am–11pm, Sun 4pm–11pm; 2.40€ per hour, 10€ for 5 hr.), a nicely kept spot in the old town, has all the services you need to stay connected, plus scanning, faxing, and CD-burning.

Pharmacies Look for the big green cross if you need some medicine, lip balm, or whatever. The **Carolina Murtra** (C. Rambla Llibertat 18; ☎ **972-200-191**) is right by the tourist office.

Telephone City code: **972**; operator: **1003**; international operator: **1005**. Note that recent changes in Spain's phone system now require that all local calls be dialed with the 972 prefix.

Sleeping

Girona is not on the main tourist track; therefore, it's pretty easy and cheap to find a place to stay, especially after unsuccessfully trying to get a room on the Costa Brava in the middle of summer. Most cheap hostels and pensions are not very interesting, mostly converted old people's houses, but if you book in advance, you may be able to get a room at the dreamy Hotel Bellmirall, steps away from the cathedral.

Girona

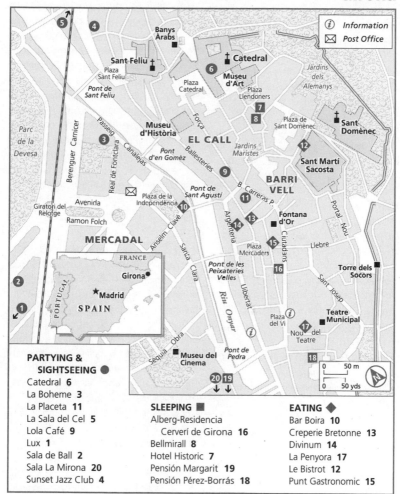

HOSTEL

→ **Alberg-Residencia Cerverí de Girona**
The local branch of the hostelling international chain, which actually doubles as a student residence during school months, looks and feels a lot like a college dorm. A great place to meet both fellow travelers and local students, it provides extras, like free Internet access, a library, a TV room with VHS movies, and bike rental. The dorms fit from two to eight beds and each room has a private toilet and desk. The common showers are not the cleanest and the decor is kind of depressing; but the location, right in the middle of the old town, couldn't be better. *Calle dels Ciutadans 9.* ☎ *971-218-003. 14€–20€ per bed. Amenities: Cafeteria, bike rental, elevator, fax, Internet, laundry, rooms for those w/limited mobility, shared*

showers, sheets, telephone, travel desk, TV. In room: Locker.

CHEAP

➜ **Pensión Margarit** This family hotel that has been around since 1948 recently underwent a bunch of renovations. The shiny and uninspired decor is characterized by the more than 50 framed puzzles scattered all over the hotel, including an 8,000-piece reproduction of a classical painting that is displayed in the dimly lit breakfast room. The rooms are spacious, the beds are comfy, and the bathrooms are pristine. Be sure to ask for a room with a balcony overlooking the tiny Japanese-style patio, the nicest area in the hotel. If you are really bored, ask Jaime to tell you about the puzzles, but don't say we didn't warn you. *Calle Ultonia 1.* ☎ *972-201-066. www.hotelmargarit.com. Double 36€–68€. Amenities: Bar, breakfast room, elevator, fax, Internet, laundry service, rooms for those w/limited mobility, telephone, TV. In room: TV, hair dryer, safe.*

➜ **Pensión Pérez-Borrás** Two pensions run by the same owners and just around the corner from each other. Slightly better is the Borras due to it's renovated and enticing entranceway and the option of private baths with some doubles. Both have a dark sort of Granny's house feeling with a mishmash of not too fancy but sturdy antique furniture, plenty of room, and clean bathrooms. There is no doorman, so don't lose the key. *Plaça Bell-Lloc 4.* ☎ *972-224-008. Single with shared bath 17€, double with bath 40€.*

DOABLE

ⓜ Best ◐ ➜ **Bellmirall** ★ Up the hill leading to the cathedral you'll find an amazing stone house from the 14th century, perfect for the crusader on a holiday quest for chill. It's definitely not a party place, but if you want major Girona style, this is your thing. The seven rooms are decorated with antique furniture, paintings by local artists, and colorful ceramics, and each features windows looking out onto the old quarter. The bathrooms are on the small side and the rooms don't have TV or telephone, but that only adds to Bellmirall's charm—I mean, who wants to admit they stayed in last night watching *The Apprentice?* If you stay here in the summer you can enjoy the pleasure of having breakfast in the courtyard while you plan your next attack on the infidels. *Calle Bellmirall 3.* ☎ *972-204-009. Double 60€–70€, triple 75€–85€. Breakfast included. No credit cards. Free parking (hotel provides permit). Closed Jan–Feb.*

SPLURGE

ⓜ Best ◐ ➜ **Hotel Historic** ★★ A city with the sense of style and taste of Girona could not lack a boutique hotel that reflected it. Across the street from the Bellmirall, this 9th-century house has been restored with great attention to detail to offer all the comforts of a four-star hotel without all the pretense. Each uniquely decorated room is named after a different Girona-related element like "leaves," "manaias (medieval singers)," "giants," or "flies." We like the Cenefas (streams), with the exposed beam ceilings, round bathtub that screams "champagne and bubble-bath," and cute balcony for morning-after mimosas. And because you're in Girona, it'll cost you less than a dingy two-star in Barcelona. Hey, it's almost worth it to commute. They also have apartments available for longer stays. *Calle Bellmirall 4A.* ☎ *972-223-583. www.hotelhistoric.com. Double 114€, junior suite 150€, apt 300€. Free parking on adjoining plaza. Amenities: Restaurant, laundry service, room service. In room: A/C, TV, minibar, safe.*

Eating

Like everything else, the array of food in Girona is very impressive for a town its size. Restaurants are concentrated mainly in the old town and around Plaça Independencia. In the last couple of years *cocina de mercado* (market-fresh cuisine) has taken over the dining scene, giving finer palates and deeper pockets a chance to fulfill their destinies. But beware all that glitters, especially in the newer part of town around Plaça Independencia: The prices live up to the promise, but all that pricey food may not.

HOT SPOTS

MTV (Best 🎵 → **Bar Boira** ★ TAPAS This trendy bar right on Plaça Independencia is the meeting spot for the under-30 crowd. A slick interior with trendy metal fixtures doubles as a bar later in the evening and the outdoor tables are a great place to enjoy vermouth and tapas while people-watching over the plaza. Innovative and mouthwatering tapas like breaded brie croquettes with grapefruit reduction or tuna soufflé with ham at very reasonable prices allow even the poorest of us to enjoy a taste (if not a full meal) of the cuisine that makes *Time* magazine's food section. *Plaça Independencia 17.* ☎ *972-203-096. Tapas 1.20€–3€. Daily 'til closing.*

→ **Le Bistrot** CATALAN PIZZA Amidst the winding streets of the old town you will find this all-time local favorite that has recently lost in quality what it has gained in popularity. However, the medieval building with vintage '40s decor works great for an early bite or late-night snack. The cheap Catalan-bread pizzas with all sorts of fresh local toppings, like pasta or a mushroom mousse, and a vibrant, hectic ambience mean that the place never stops rockin'—from the early evening with the old men playing dominoes, to the late night when their dreadlocked grandsons share tables with college friends. *Pujada de Sant Domenec 4.* ☎ *972-218-803. Entrees 4€– 6€. Daily 1–4pm and 8:30pm–midnight.*

CHEAP

→ **Creperie Bretonne** FRENCH Being this close to France it would be a sin not to get yourself a nice crepe and remember the days of La Revolution. Located in one of the ubiquitous gray-stone medieval structures in the old town, this creperie's interior is a collector's wet dream: The walls are covered in cool vintage French tin posters; half an antique crepe truck is displayed inside the entrance; and, when you go to the bathroom, you'll be powdering your nose in an old train car. Add to this a wide array of wonderful sweet and salty crepes (our favorite is the Bergere, with mushrooms, goat cheese, bacon, and chives), the famous Bretagne cider, and a nice variety of salads, and you will be more than willing to wait for a table. *Calle Cort Reial 14.* ☎ *972-218-120. Crepes 5€–9€. Tues– Sun 1–4pm and 8pm–midnight.*

→ **Divinum** MODERN CATALAN The most original and chi-chi of the Rambla Cafés, this creative bistro offers innovative dishes such as the "5 ways to eat an anchovy." Whether you sit outside or in, get your all-so-rare fix of greens with a tasty goat cheese, nut, raisin, and bacon salad and then challenge your palate with the more complex eel, shrimp, and salmon ravioli or mild *piquillo* peppers stuffed with Gorgonzola and *sobrasada* (chorizo-like Spanish sausage). If you are splurging, pick a wine from their expansive list and try the locally homemade desserts such as the decadent chocolate *coulant* with cassis ice cream. *Rambla Argenteria 12.* ☎ *972-217-990. Entrees 6€–14€. Tues–Sun noon– 5pm and 7pm–1am.*

DOABLE

→ **Punt Gastronomic** CATALAN Emplaced in what looks like a cavern, this tiny restaurant very close to the Ajuntament is decorated so tastefully that even the balloons and Coke-can planes

CATALUNYA

look like they fit in among all of the earthy tones. Speaking of tasty, the delicious market cuisine is what really keeps the few tables constantly packed. The tuna, cod, and veal carpaccio are so fresh they almost breathe, and the *ceps* (mushroom) salad and *escalivada* (typical Catalan dish made of anchovies, red peppers, goat cheese, and eggplant) will make you forget there ever was a chorizo. The homemade apple tartine is not to be missed. *Minali 3.* ☎ *972-227-957. Entrees 8€–15€. Tues–Sat 1:30–4pm and 9–10:30pm.*

SPLURGE

MTV **Best ◉** → **La Penyora** ★★ MODERN CATALAN Husband and wife team Lluis Llamas and Consol Ribas have turned this restaurant/arts venue into one of the top places to eat in Girona. The menu changes daily according to what's available in the market and features art reproductions matching the menu's language (Hollywood photos for English, pointillist paintings for French, and so on). The lentils with Jabugo chorizo are a feast for the senses, and other plates with international influence include the rosemary-smoked *dorada* (sea bream) with tabbouleh, or stuffed pork tournedos with brandy that still makes my mouth water just thinking about it. La Penyora also doubles as an art gallery and hosts book presentations and other cultural events, so be on the lookout for local celebrities (not that you would know any). *Calle Nou del Teatre 3.* ☎ *972-218-948. Menú del día 11€. Entree 7.50€–18€. Daily 'til closing.*

Partying

Girona is a small town, near enough to Barcelona to make it worth taking the hour-long trip to party over there. Yeah, right! The 15,000 students who attend the university need a closer place to blow off steam. Thursday is the big night around here, and

bars are completely packed, with lots of university-inspired parties at clubs and pubs. The best summer party (end of May to Oct) takes place at the **MTV** **Best ◉** **Parc de la Devesa** where many bars set up their tents, and outdoor drinking is not only allowed but encouraged. Try the Glops tent, which is the biggest, or the Nummulit tent, which attracts a younger crowd. Just one warning: The music at bars and clubs in Girona tends to be on the sucky side, with your average top-40 playlist mixed with really bad Spanish pop (the kids here love to sing along). But, have yourself a couple of drinks, put your music snobbiness aside, and you'll be having fun and singing along with Britney in no time.

BARS

→ **La Boheme** This chill bar right off of Plaça Independencia is a good place to start the night and meet some locals. The tables with comfy chairs outside are ideal for people-watching as you enjoy an early aperitif. You can almost picture the weary merchants and travelers of yore sitting at the bar amidst the dark, red, 19th-century-style interiors. Of course the cool rock 'n' roll bartenders kind of kill that vibe, but, as cute as they are, who's complaining? *Plaça Jaume V. i Vives 6. No phone.*

→ **La Placeta** Alterna-hippies of the world unite! This dreadlocked enclave in the middle of the old town has nothing to offer but its vibe: a very simple bar with a bunch of tables outside, cheap drinks, and cool people—what else do you need? Alternative and politically conscious youth chill out in this little plaza while loading up on booze to get ready for the rest of the night. Oh, did we mention the aroma? *Buenaventura Carreras Peralta 7. No phone.*

MTV **Best ◉** → **Lux** ★ If you are in Girona on a Thursday night, you have to check out Lux. Not quite a disco, but definitely more than a bar, the two dance-floors/bars are packed with hotties from the local university letting loose after a hard week of studying. Check out the bathrooms, where girls and boys hang out together and uninformed foreigners go crazy trying to make the faucets work. (Pssst, there's a pedal under the sinks.) *Figuerola 50. No phone.*

→ **Lola Café** Though just steps away from La Placeta, Lola, with its trendy design (like the crazy curving lamps), is like its polar opposite. A fairly *pijo* (conservative) clientele starts to pack the place after midnight, when they move the tables for some buttshaking. Check out the beautiful black-and-white photos on the walls and then the beautiful bartenders . . . any resemblance? "Who's that hot model in the picture? Really? That's you?" will get you a smile and maybe even a free *chupito* (shot). *Força 7. No phone.*

LIVE MUSIC

Although nothing like Barcelona, Girona actually gets some favorable backlash from bands on tour to said illustrious neighbor, especially jazz, local, and smaller international acts. Locals are really fond of live music and many bars (like Lux on Wed) host a live-music night.

→ **Sala La Mirona** Girona's one and only big concert hall, La Mirona is a huge industrial space that has been nicely adapted to host concerts of mostly local big acts, like Ojos de Brujo, or small international numbers, like Maceo Parker, that make it past Barcelona in the summer. Sala La Mirona is open for live concerts only and on Thursdays, when unknown local bands play for university kids. *Amnistía Internacional s/n. Polígono Industrial Torre Mirona. ☎ 972-200-122. Prices vary with concerts.*

→ **Sunset Jazz Club** Sunset has nothing to envy from its New York counterparts like Blue Note—well, maybe just a couple

of acts. But, aesthetically, this is the ultimate jazz club. With red couches, dark smoky interiors, black tables, and vintage hanging lamps, Sunset is an ideal place to bring a date you actually want to talk to. Pictures of jazz legends and Toulouse-Lautrec posters grace the walls. Yep, they did it right. The owners try to bring the biggest names they can for their Saturday live music nights to keep the cool flowing. *Pons I Martí 12. ☎ 872-080-145. www.sunset jazz-club.com. Free or 5€ cover.*

CLUBS

→ **La Sala del Cel** When you think about Spain's nightlife, you picture mega clubs, electronic music, laser lights, smoke, and scantily clad hotties dancing tribally until the sun comes out. In Girona that image is manifest every Friday and Saturday at Sala del Cel, which has been a hot spot in the city's nightlife since 1982; it also claims to

---

M T V ⓤ Hanging Out

Girona is a university town, which means young people are *everywhere*. A good way to make friends, though, is to visit the Montelivi campus. There aren't any bars, other than the cafeteria, where of course they serve alcohol (don't you love Spain?), and the area is not particularly happening; but in the nice weather, the students hang out on the lawns around the university's buildings. It's easy to sit down with a group and start a chat; since they're not really used to foreigners, they might even offer to show you around (as long as you don't act skeevy or anything). The campus is about a 20-minute walk south of the old town on Avinguda Montilivi; or, if you are lazy, you can take the really slow bus that goes there.

be one of the first clubs in Spain to promote electronic music (but who doesn't?). Come shake your tail on the huge dance floor to the rhythms of their team of resident DJs and illustrious visitors like Felix Da Housecat, Ken Ishii, or The Hacker. *Calle Pedret 118.* ☎ *972-214-664.* *www.lasaladel cel.cat.*

➜ **Sala de Ball** Unless you are balding, very nostalgic, or into really cheesy, Latin pop, don't even think of coming here any other day than Thursday. But Thursdays, Sala de Ball hosts university nights and all hell breaks lose. Like the name says, this ballroom features a large dance floor surrounded by comfy couches where you can mingle with your honeys and your homies while you watch all the Spanish kids dancing and singing their lungs out to Latin pop, top-40 hits, club hits, and The Beatles. Yeah, the music is no thrill, but there is no cover; mixed drinks are only 5€; and the party gets going at around 2 and goes on until really late. *Calle Riu Guell 2.* ☎ *972-201-439.*

Sightseeing

📺 Best☻ **El Call,** ★★ the 600-year-old Jewish neighborhood of Girona, is one of the biggest and best-preserved old nabes

Flower Power

If you are lucky enough to be in Girona in mid-May you may be able to catch the 📺 Best☻ **"Temps de Flors."** Basically, Gironans spend all their money on the most ridiculous amount of beautiful flowers you have ever seen and use them to decorate the entire old town, including inside the monuments, like the Banys Arabs and the cathedral. All the magic of the medieval gray-stone buildings gets splashed with a festival of colors and smells that will make you cry, man, I swear.

in Europe. It's fun just to walk around, hang out, and picture the Jewish community living in this neighborhood—until the Catholic kings gave them the boot in 1492. The persecution was always there, hence the winding streets with lots of places to shake off your pursuers. At the center of the neighborhood is the **Bonastruc Ça Porta Center** with the **Museu d'Historia dels Jueus de Girona** (La Força 8; ☎ **972-214-618;** 2€; May–Oct Mon–Sat 10am–8pm, Sun 10am–3pm; Nov–Apr Mon–Sat 10am–6pm, Sun 10am–3pm), which depicts the history of the 'hood and hosts other related exhibitions.

➜ **Catedral de Girona** ★ At the top of a steep set of stairs, Girona's star attraction is a sort of architectural mash-up worthy of a track by M.I.A.'s Maya Arul. Built between the 11th and 18th centuries, it reflects many different architectural styles, like Romanesque, Gothic, and Catalan baroque. If you can do anything on the way up besides catch your breath, check out the bronze angel weathervane on top of the dome. And if you're really into heights, you can climb the bell tower for an extra 2 *tacos* (as in Spanish slang for euros—think outside the bun, man). *Plaza Catedral s/n.* ☎ *972-214-426. www.lacatedraldegirona.com. Admission 4€, Sun free. Mon–Fri 10am–7pm; Sat 10am–4:30pm; Sun 10am–7pm.*

Playing Outside

Girona's charm lies more in its architecture than in its nature. But being in Catalunya, which is the capital of trekking, a decent hike is always nearby. A good way to get in touch with nature is to take a walk along the River Ter, the "other" river in Girona. Start north of the Parc de La Devesa, on the little bridge that crosses the river, and then walk toward where the Ter meets the Onyar. You'll see an amazing variety of vegetation and wildlife, and, once you are there, it's beautiful to just

Board Talk

Like any other city in Spain, Girona has its own board scene. When you get off the train just walk south on Pierre Villar or Barcelona streets. Follow the trail of graffiti (people are so cool about graffiti here that they even light them at night) right under the elevated train tracks. One block down, where Calle Creu meets the elevated tracks, you'll see the grand finale of graffiti and about half a dozen half-pipes, plus a bunch of kids grinding and gettin' some air. Show off your American skills and you will make new buddies in no time.

chill and have a picnic with the cathedral in the background. For more info on trails or to hire a guide ask for the Senderismo (trekking) booklet at the tourist office or call **Punt de Benvinguda** (☎ 972-211-678; www.pb.onyar.net), a nature-related tourist outfit.

Another way to enjoy the river is to get out on it in a kayak. **Caiac i Natura** (☎ 699-770-647; www.caiacinatura.com)

organizes eco-friendly kayaking excursions that leave from the Parc de les Ribes del Ter, right across the river from the Devesa park.

Shopping

If you want to blow the money that you saved by staying here instead of in Barcelona or the Costa, you have plenty of opportunities. The mainstream shopping district is on each side of the Onyar river. On the west bank, walk on Carrer Santa Clara, where you will find local and foreign clothing stores like Adolfo Dominguez and Tommy. The same holds true for Rambla de la Libertat. Further north, check out Carrer Ballesteries where young local designers and urban streetwear are featured in stores like Carme Puigdevall i Plantes (C. Calderers 17; ☎ **649-805-354**; www.carme puigdevalliplantes.com), Underground (C. Ballesteries 12; ☎ **972-410-087**), and Ayumi (C. Ballesteries 50; ☎ **972-485-470**).

If you are in need of a different kind of outerwear, on the same street you will find ▥ Best ♦ **La Condoneria** (C. Ballesteries 34; ☎**972-485-608**; www.lacondoneria. es) with a great selection of latex products and all sorts of "toys."

Figueres

Unless you're an art history major, Figueres is probably not your absolute first choice in the Costa Brava, especially since it's not really *on* the Costa. But even if it is a little out of your way you should get there and experience the Surreal Life. No, not the washed-up stars and lingerie-wearing baseball players of VH1. This is the hometown of Salvador Dalí's Museu-Teatre Dalí. The city itself is pretty dull, but the dreamy museum is worth the short excursion. It's huge and plays enough tricks on your perception that you'll begin to understand why the surrealist master said, "I don't do drugs. I am drugs."

Getting There & Around

RENFE trains (☎ 902-240-202) arrive at the **Estació de Figueres** on Plaça Estació. The 2-hour trip from Barcelona to Figueres costs 8.05€.

All **buses** arrive at the same plaza as **Estació Autobuses** (Plaça Estació; ☎ **972-673-354**). **Barcelona Bus** (☎ **972-505-029**) gets you here from B-town; the 2¹/₂-hour ride costs 13€.

Catch a **cab** from **Taxi Figueres** (☎ **972-505-043**) at the train station, or along the Rambla call ☎ **972-500-008**.

Figueres Basics

Figueres is situated at the northeastern end of Catalonia. With 34,200 inhabitants, it is the largest of the cities bordering France. As the nerve center of the Costa Brava, it's a good place to stop in for a day before (or after) hitting the beaches.

Upon your arrival at the **Plaça de Estació,** cross the plaza and swing a left on Carrer Sant Llatzèr. Walk several blocks to Carrer Nou, and take a right onto the town's tree-lined **Rambla.** On the right side of the Rambla you'll find a bunch of hotels and museums, and a couple of blocks up lies the **Plaça de Gala I Dalí,** which is the reason why you made it all the way here.

The **main tourist office** is on Plaça Sol (☎ **972-503-155;** www.figuresciutat.com). Check out their free listing of accommodations and pick up a map to point you in the right direction. The office is open November through March from Monday to Friday 9am to 3pm; April to June and Oct, Monday through Friday 9am to 3pm and 4:30pm to 8pm, and Saturday from 9:30am to 1:30pm and 3:30pm to 6:30pm; July to August from Monday to Saturday 9am to 8pm, Sunday 9am to 3pm; and September, Monday to Saturday 9am to 8pm.

Ask them how you can catch a free **guided walking tour** of the city Saturdays at 11am. Extra branch offices open during summer: one at Plaça Estació (open July–Sep 15 Mon–Sat 10am–2pm and 4–6pm) and another in a yellow mobile home in front of the Dalí museum.

Don't forget to grab a copy of *La Guía* for hotel, food, and shopping recommendations.

Figueres Nuts & Bolts

Currency   The **ATM** right across from the train station and a couple around the Plaça del Sol and the Rambla will fulfill all your money-related needs.

Emergency   Dial ☎ **112** in an emergency. For medical assistance, get yourself to Hospital Ronda del Rector Aroles ☎ **972-675-089.**

Internet   **Oh!net** is the Internet kiosk at the bus station; the charge is 2€ for every 20 minutes. **Tele Haddi** (C. Joan Reglá 1; ☎ **972-513-099**), has a fee of 1€ per 15-minute increment, 1.50€ per 30-minute increment, and 2.50€ per hour.

Luggage Storage   The **train station** has large lockers where you can stow your stuff for 3€; it's open daily from 6am to 11pm. The **bus station** also has storage for 2€ and is available from 6am to 10pm daily.

Sleeping

Although most visitors plan on staying in Figueres for only a day, it might be worth your while to stay the night considering that rooms are much cheaper here than in Barcelona. If you gave the tourist office a pass, start your search on Carrer Jonquera around the Dalí museum or closer to the Rambla and Carrer Pep Ventura. Don't get too mad if someone spills beer on your bags—most rooms tend to be above small bars and restaurants.

CHEAP

➔ **Hostal La Barretina** This hotel rests on top of the bar, la Barretina, where you can enjoy one last drink before going up to your room. Just a few steps from La Rambla, the location couldn't be more centric. From the train station, walk up the left side of the Rambla to its end and look for Lasauca up ahead. Get reacquainted with the comforts of home: Each room has A/C, heat, TV, and a private bathroom. *Lasauca 13. ☎ 972-676-412. Single 23€, double 39€. Reservations recommended. In room: A/C, TV.*

DOABLE

➜ **Hotel Los Angeles** This hotel has very simple and clean rooms painted in pastel colors and, like everything in Figueres, Dalí reproductions on the walls. Frequented mostly by French and Spanish tourists, Los Angeles features a cafeteria, Internet room, and breakfast room exclusively for its guests. After a long weekend partying on nearby beaches this is the place to give your body a well-deserved rest; and it's probably the most convenient hotel in Figueres. *Barceloneta 10. ☎ 972-510-661. www. hotelangeles.com. Double 42€–54€. Amenities: Bar, breakfast room, elevator, Internet, TV (in common room). In room: A/C, TV.*

➜ **Hotel President** For it's centric position between the Dalí Museum, Plaça del Sol, and la Rambla, this is one of the best choices for lodging in Figueres. From the outside it doesn't look like much, but once inside you'll find it's quite colorful. In contrast with the reception and common areas, the decor in the rooms is quite straightforward—with the mandatory Dalí paintings, of course. Rooms do have TV and A/C, which is much needed in the brutal heat of July and August. *Ronda Firal 33. ☎ 972-501-700 or 972-501-704. www.hotel president.info. Single 45€, double 65€–75€. Amenities: Restaurant, bar, laundry, room service. In room: A/C, TV, hair dryer, safe.*

Eating

Don't expect Asian fusion or Ethiopian restaurants—most of the places here serve *comida típica* (classic Catalan dishes), in other words, meat and fish. Save money by shopping at the markets in Plaça Gra and Plaça de Catalunya (open Tues, Thurs, and Sat 5am–2pm).

➜ **Catalunya Amor Meu!** CATALAN With its doable prices, Amor Meu is one of the newest additions to Figueres's restaurant scene. The restaurant is very modern and elegant, with high ceilings, pastel green walls, comfortable red chairs, and the most dedicated service around. Try the tasty salted pork with curry. Amor Meu has a tapas bar just next door, and on weekends the DJs show up at the bar. So if you don't want to walk any further, stay and have a dinner/late drinks combo. *Magre 7. ☎ 972-502-036. Entrees 8€–16€. Daily noon–4pm and 8pm–11am; drinks up to 2am.*

➜ **Durán** ★ CATALAN This splurge-worthy hotel/restaurant right off the Rambla is another Figueres oldie but goodie, and just guess who used to dine here? Good old Salvador himself would sit among other wealthy Catalans in the amber-colored salon and order typical Catalan specialties like *zarzuela* (fish stew) or pretty much every animal that can be hunted, gathered, and served with a side of fries. Desserts are rich and generous, much like many of the patrons. *Carrer Lasauca 5. ☎ 972-501-250. Main courses 14€–27€. Daily 12:30–4pm and 8:30–11pm.*

➜ **Mesón Asador** TAPAS This tapas joint has been serving traditional Catalan cuisine for over 30 years. The restaurant has even been recognized by the city with a plaque proving its standing as a true classic. *Pujada de Castell 4. ☎ 972-510-104. Tapas 3€–15€. Mon–Sat 11am–4pm and 7:30–11pm.*

Partying

Most people don't stay overnight here since they come to see the museum and leave, but, if you decide to stay 1 extra night, don't worry, you'll find that there are some places for you to make the most of it. Figueres's nighttime scene takes place for the most part around the Plaça del Sol, but Plaça de las Patatas (literally, potatoes square) also has some good places to have a drink, where you can hang with locals and listen to great music while nibbling at tapas.

📺 Best ☺ ➜ **El Café del Barri Velli** Right on the Plaça de las Patatas, this cute little cafe is a great spot to enjoy the breezy nights. It's a bit off the tourist circuit so most of the clients here are locals. Saturdays the cafe transforms the *plaça* into a stage show-casing all types of music. The food here is vegetarian so take advantage of the amazing fruit shakes—they are the closest thing to a beach you'll get in Figueres. *Plaça de les Patates 7.* ☎ *972-505-776.*

➜ **El Local** This is not just a bar, it's a cafe/*galeria*/*mercat de l´art.* Something is always happening here—when there's not an opening, there's live music. And there's always the opportunity to taste some seriously great homemade cakes. Check out the art gallery on the mezzanine to get some of that cultural vibe Figueres is all about. *Muralla 1.* ☎ *972-509-687.*

➜ **Jem Casey´s** One of the best Plaça del Sol has to offer. Jem's has a huge terrace if you want to stay outside. If you fancy some good ol' dancing, get inside where you'll find lots of people shaking it; and every 2 weeks there are live-music acts. There's also a huge screen where they show videos and movies, and a garden in the back, for some insightful political chats with your new friends. *Plaça del Sol 10.* ☎ *972-500-644.*

Sightseeing

📺 Best ☺ ➜ **Teatre-Museu Dalí** ★★★ When the mayor of Figueres asked native Salvador Dalí to donate a painting to a museum the town was planning, the over-achieving artist donated an entire museum. He insisted on using the ruins of an old theater that burned down in 1939 (hence the name "theater-museum"), which was where he had shown his first show as a teenager. The **huge reconstructed theater** is infused with Dalí's character, studded with giant eggs and loaves of bread, and full of his paintings, sculptures, and other creations—even his tomb.

Not only that, if you thought P. Diddy was a shameless self-promoter, the rapper pales in comparison to this self-proclaimed genius—Dalí even personally designed this museum/mausoleum/monument to himself. Check out his **naughty, erotic cartoons** and the many **paintings of his wife** and muse, Gala, including one, which when viewed through a telescope, transforms into Abraham Lincoln—hot! In the remarkable ***Sala de Mae West*** you walk into a regular room with funky furniture. Once up the stairs on top of the plastic camel (surrealism, remember?), you'll see the room morph into the blonde actress's portrait. These are just a few of the tricks Dalí liked to play on reality. **Paintings** not to be missed are *Poetry of America, Galarina,* and *Galatea of the Spheres,* but while you explore the museum, don't just focus on the enormous paintings. Take in every square inch of the floor, wall, nooks, and crannies, to absorb all the maestro's decorative touches and surprises.

Make sure you don't miss the **Joies** ★★★ around the corner, a permanent exhibit of Dalí-designed jewelry where you can appreciate the fusion of his impeccable sense of design and surreal aesthetics with the most exquisite materials. *Plaça de Gala-Dalí 5.* ☎ *972-677-500. www.salvador-dali.org. Admission adults 9€, students 6.50€. July to mid–Sept daily 9am–7:45pm; mid-Sept to June Tues–Sun 10:30am–5:15pm. Visits available various nights July–Aug; call for information.*

Cadaqués ★★

You probably thought those little Mediterranean towns where teens raced their scooters through corridor-size streets, fishermen lay their boats on the beach, and everything was white and bright only existed in movies. Well, I've got news for you. There between the mountains and a deep, bluer-than-Cameron-Diaz's-eyes sea lies the town of Cadaqués, your Mediterranean fantasy town come true.

Cadaqués was also the summer home of Spain's *enfant terrible,* Salvador Dalí, and his notorious wife Gala. Nearby **Cap de Creus** and its astonishing rock formations were a source of inspiration for the artist and you can see them in a number of his paintings featured in his house turned museum.

Speaking of Dalí, haven't you ever wondered how a land ruled under the iron fist of one of the most obscurantist dictatorships of the last century could produce such an outrageous character? Cadaqués's isolation in the mountains is the answer. In the '60s, it became a free haven for hippies, artists, and everyone who felt the need to escape Franco's clutches. Here you have it then, Cadaqués, the kind of place you thought didn't exist anymore.

Getting There & Around

BY BUS

We said it before, Cadaqués is isolated. Locals voted the city to remain train-station free, so the only way to get there is by bus. Two to four daily buses run from Barcelona and up to seven depart from Figueres. **Sarfa** buses (☎ **972-258-713**) leaving from Estacío del Norte in BCN are the ones you'll need.

BY CAR, BIKE & MOPED

Don't try to get around town by **car** here. There are almost no sidewalks, and streets are not wide enough for a car and a human, never mind two cars or a pack of humans, so you will be moving at walking speed behind pedestrians. If you're not a patient and careful driver you'll go crazy and/or kill someone. **Bikes** are probably not your best choice either, unless you are a serious biker; Cadaqués is a town on a cliff-side, which means lots of uphill roads. **Scooters** are probably the best way to move, besides walking, as the hundreds of teenagers going up and down the town at high speed, can tell you. Only, it's not that cheap to rent a Vespa. At approximately 20€ for 2 hours, it might be worth it if you're going to Cap de Creus, but not to move around town. Some local scooter rental places are **Bikes & Boats Cadaqués** (☎ **972-258-027**) or **Cadaqués Rentals Sl.** (☎ **972-159-034**).

WALKING

Cadaqués is really a small town with everything less than a 30-minute walk away. The best beaches as well as some restaurants can be a little further, but you can always look forward to a beautiful walk along the seashore.

Cadaqués Basics

When the bus drops you off at Carrer de l'Horta Vella, take the **Carretera de Roses** to the **Avinguda Caritat Serinyana,** which leads directly to the center of the city. Once in Cadaqués it's very simple to get oriented, although it's also very easy to get lost! Cadaqués is shaped like a horseshoe around a cove. Since the mountains are behind the city, the beach is always downhill. And most places you'll want to go to are by the shore or near it anyway. The town is a beautiful maze of curving streets and alleys. Like NYC's West Village, it's a mess—but, hey, it works.

The **tourist office** (☎ 972-258-315) is located in the back of Bar Casino at Carrer Cotxe 2; it is open Monday to Saturday 9am to 2pm and 3 to 8pm, Sunday 10:30am to 1pm.

cadaqués Nuts & Bolts

Currency Cadaqués may be quite isolated, but even here the best exchange rates you'll get are from the **ATMs** scattered about town.

Health & Emergency Medical assistance: **Dispensario Cadaqués** (Carrer Nou; ☎ 972-258-807). For emergencies dial ☎ 112.

Internet Cadaqués is still a fishing town, but fishermen like modern-day commodities as much as the next guy. Check your e-mails at **Bar Casino** (p. 406) or at **1´ inter@net** (Plaça Dr. Tremols 8; ☎ 972-258-297; .50€ per 15 min.; Mon–Sat 10am–11pm), a small room with a bunch of computers and a wide entrance that integrates it into the square.

Pharmacy Moradel (☎ 972-258-932), on Plaça Frederic Rahola, has all your basic prescription-strength pharmaceuticals.

Sleeping

A small town, voted big-building free, does not have an enormous amount of rooms, so get there early or try to make advance reservations. August and weekends are guaranteed to give you headaches. The camping facilities at **Camping Cadaqués** (Cra. Port-lligat 17; ☎ 972-258-126) might be a little too far away for convenience. Of course, in Cadaqués that means a 20-minute walk through gorgeous little passages and narrow white streets.

CHEAP

➜ **Fonda Marina** Located just a block from the beach, this inn's rooms are pretty plain and clean and have two single beds, some of them with a balcony. The sweetest couple in all of Cadaqués runs the *fonda*, so you'll feel more than welcome here. *Riera de St. Vincent 3.* ☎ *972-258-199. Double 55€–65€.*

➜ **Fonda Vehi** Up a narrow alley toward la Eglésia de Santa María is the hostel Vehi, in a classic white stucco building. The hostel offers the cheapest rooms in town, but it only has four of 'em—so are you feeling lucky? The recently renovated rooms have character, with funky red-tile floors and orange bed covers. *Esglesia 6.* ☎ *972-258-470. Single 25€, double 50€–75€.*

MTV Best ● ➜ **Hotel Misty** ★ This beautiful hotel takes Cadaqués's Mediterranean vibe into full account. A series of little white buildings surround a lush garden with huge trees and a swimming pool. All the rustic wooden details in your room will make you (almost) feel like getting up at sunrise to get your fishing boat ready. Rooms feature glass doors overlooking the garden and bathrooms with bathtubs and showers. *Carretera de Port Lligat s/n.* ☎ *972-258-962. Single 40€–60€, double 50€–73€. Amenities: Bar, swimming pool, ping-pong table, billiard table, private parking. In room: TV.*

DOABLE

➜ **Hostal S´Aguarda** Located in the upper part of Cadaqués, the S'Aguarda has a wonderful view of the sea, but is a bit far away (relatively speaking, for Cadaqués anyway) from the center of town and the beaches. The very bright rooms that open out onto flower-bedecked terraces are spacious, with soft-colored walls decorated with artwork. The full bathrooms have tubs and showers. *Carretera Port Lligat 30.* ☎ *972-258-082. www.hotelsaguarda.com. Double 50€–100€. Amenities: Bar, laundry service, outdoor pool, room service (breakfast only), parking. In room: A/C, TV, hair dryer.*

➜ **Hotel Llane Petit** ★ This small hotel stands in one of the nicest locations in town. All of the rooms have balconies, most overlooking the beach. The staff is very attentive and the rooms are spacious and in very good condition. You'll be sharing the pool with mostly German and northern European families. But, being 20m (66 ft.) away from the beach, why would you want to use the pool anyway? *Doctor Bartomeus 37.* ☎ *972-251-020. www. llanepetit.com. Double 65€–122€. Amenities: Bar, room service, laundry service. In room: A/C, TV, safe.*

Eating

Beaches in Cadaqués are not big enough for *chiringuitos* with the exception of Ses Olivares beach, which has two. The first chiringuitos is average to lame, but the one farthest away from the town (Ses Oliveres 2; no phone; Entrees 5.70€–16€; Mon–Sat 9am–11pm; June–Sept) is run by a local family and, as with everything, Grandma's gazpacho tastes better. If you leave Cadaqués without tasting their 📺 Best ♦ *tallarinas* (cockles), you'll be missing out big time. While you are at it, you might want to try the *chipirones,* and as a dessert, the homemade chocolate cake is so airy it melts in your mouth.

CHEAP

➜ **Bar L´estable** TAPAS This simple place with nautical motifs, carved stone walls, and striped curtains that match the

cook's apron is a perfect place to have some tapas in the evening. Try the *croquetas* or *buñuelos* (dumplings) while you watch the boats gently rock as the sun goes down. *Riba Pixot.* ☎ *972-258-580. Tapas 2.80€–5.70€. Daily 2–11:30pm. Closed in winter.*

➜ **Celeste** ITALIAN More than anything, Celeste has ambience: white carved walls with small framed paintings and pictures, candlelight, small separated tables, and lots of wood details. As far as food goes, pasta here is really good and cheap. Get there early, or you may have to wait for more than an hour for a table. *Calle Nou 1.* ☎ *972-159-420. Entrees 5.60€–16€. Summer daily 1:30–4:30pm and 8pm–2:30am; winter Sat–Sun 1:30–4:30pm and 8pm–2:30am.*

➜ **Tao** ASIAN If you didn't believe us when we said Cadaqués was a haven for hippies in the '60s, this all-out hippie enclave is living proof. Behind its blue door you'll find a cavelike space with short tables and Indian decorations. Have a veggie couscous with basmati rice or the tasty chicken satay with some of the real survivors of Cadaqués´ flower-power days. *Sa Jorneta 1. No phone. Entrees 5€–8.25€. Daily 2pm–midnight.*

DOABLE

📺 Best ♦ ➜ **Tiramisu** MEDITERRANEAN When it comes to outdoor dining, the only thing that beats this restaurant garden is probably eating on the beach itself. Treat your palate to one of the best kitchens in town, run by an Italian guy married to a Spanish chick. Try the perfectly seared tuna or the *carpaccio de buey* (raw ox) that is sliced so thin it's almost transparent. While you wait for a table, order one of Rocco's dry martinis, definitely one of the best in town. *Miguel Rosset 8.* ☎ *972-258-133. Entrees 9€–23€. Easter–Sept Wed–Mon noon–3pm and 8–11:30pm.*

Food for Thought

In a country where eating is one of the national pastimes and a region where innovation is a necessity, it should come as no surprise to find the world's most creative, and possibly best restaurant. When a restaurant gets three stars in the prestigious Michelin guide, an honor that less than 70 restaurants in the world can claim, it usually means business. But when its chef, Ferrán Adriá becomes an international star, making the cover of the *New York Times Magazine,* it becomes a completely different phenomenon altogether.

In an effort to achieve a multi-sensory experience for diners at ★ ★ ★ 📺 ⬤Best⬤ **El Bulli** (Cala Montjoi, Roses; ☎ **971-150-457;** www.elbulli.com; tasting menu 160€; Apr–June Wed–Sun 8–10pm, June–Sept daily 8–10pm) Adriá uses unusual ingredients such as corn flakes and pop-rocks to make unintelligible dishes like pistachio-LYO with black truffle jellied consommé and mandarin air, dulsa angel hair pasta with sea urchins and lime caviar, and white asparagus with virgin olive oil capsules and lemon marshmallow. The experience consists of a tasting menu of more than 30 dishes over the course of 3 hours under the chef's and maitre d's close attention. The by-reservation-only waitlist usually closes a few months before the beginning of the season, but the Bulli empire now sports a few restaurants in Madrid (and even a hotel).

Partying

Nightlife in Cadaqués is actually a lot more fun than you would expect in a small town. As the night wears on, follow the tide of people from the beaches and chill-out places to the more active bars on the Carrer Miguel Rosset, where you can sit outside people-watching or shoot pool and listen to some tunes. Unless you're a wuss, you'll probably end up in at least one of the two places that stay open past 3am.

BARS

→ **Bar Casino** If you actually go into the bar right by the center of town and in front of the beach, you'll find it as empty as Jessica Simpson's bookcase. Action here takes place across the street on the little dock and beach in front of the bar, although you're not *supposed* to bring your glasses out there. In the back of the bar you'll also find some coin-operated computers at your disposal. (*Tip:* They don't charge you for printing.) *Doctor Tremols 1.* ☎ *619-672-710.*

→ **Café Tropical** With scads of places to choose from on the Carrer Miguel Rosset, the Café Tropical is the archetypical Cadaqués drinking estab. It rocks a small garden filled with palm trees, for that authentic island ambience, and a pool table inside, where the blasting music is a lot less chill than the island beats outside. You'll fit in nicely among the healthy mix of locals and tourists of all ages who pack the place nightly in summer. *Miguel Rosset 19.* ☎ *972-258-801.*

→ **La Frontera** Twenty-fivers and up flock to this beautiful Cadaqués-style house to groove to the DJ's beats and take a breather in the front garden. It's one of the largest bars on this street, but it still overflows with a crowd. *Miguel Rosset 22. No phone.*

📺 ⬤Best⬤ → **L'Hostal** Open since 1901, L'Hostal is one of the coolest jazz clubs in Europe, attracting the likes of Salvador Dalí, Gabriel Garcia Marquez, and Mick Jagger. Live music is played until 3am, normally jazz but also some blues and rock 'n' roll. At 3 the live music stops, and the dancing begins to the tune of the Gypsy Kings or the soundtrack to *Dirty Dancing. Paseo 8A.* ☎ *972-258-000.*

→ **Shadows** One of the two possible final stops on your all-night crawl, Shadows is a pub with a preference for black and ultraviolet lights. A younger crowd gets together here to dance till dawn to Spanish pop and a bit of electronica. At 3am the kids congregate here and make the place rock, but don't come before that because you won't find a soul. *Miguel Rosset 15.* ☎ *972-259-171.*

📺 Best ☺ → **S7t** S7t is a great bar for vegging out in preparation for the rest of your evening. Carles, the owner, offers more than 26 different cocktails, and, if you ask him to, he'll probably invent a new one for you. On clear nights, you can see the red moon rising above the cove. *Riva Pichot 7. No phone.*

Sightseeing

📺 Best ☺ → **Casa-Museu Dalí** Growing up, baby Dalí traveled from Figueres to Cadaqués every summer with his family. Years later he claimed that the vision of Cap de Creus was the landscape of his dreams. As soon as he was able, he moved to Cadaqués with his wife Gala and settled

down in Port Lligat for over 40 years. Visiting the house that Dalí designed himself is a crash course on how one of the greatest personalities of our times lived and worked. You'll be able to see the bed where he dreamed and the atelier where he committed those dreams to the canvas. Be aware, though, that you'll have to book your visit beforehand or risk wasting half a day waiting. *Port Lligat.* ☎ *972-251-015. Admission adults 8€, students 6€. Mar 15–June 14 and Sept 16–Jan 6 Tues–Sun 10:30am–5:10pm; June 15–Sept 15 daily 10:30am–9pm.*

Playing Outside

Along the shoreline in Cadaqués you'll find many coves with beautiful **beaches.** Most of them are rock or pebble, although you will find some cramped sand beaches in the center. Our recommendation is **Sa Conca**. It's a 20-minute walk to this rocky cove, but it has the most incredible rock formations and perfectly cerulean Mediterranean waters. If you want to sunbathe in your birthday suit this is the place to do it (anywhere else in the city and you might receive some bruises from stone-throwing old ladies).

One of the coolest features in this area of the Costa Brava is the endless amount of **coves** that unfold one after the other all

CATALUNYA

Boy Meets Girl . . . Finally

So, you're on the beach when you spot the love of your live for the first time, once again. You watch [insert name here] from a distance marveling at his/her beauty and dreaming up the perfect line to make [insert name here] fall forever in love with you . . . and then the sun goes down, or he/she leaves and you've missed your window.

Lucky for you, slowpoke, Cadaqués always gives you a second chance. You'll find [insert name here] again. If not at dinner, he/she'll be at a table in the casino, or cruising through Carrer Miguel Rosset from bar to bar. And if you didn't find the nerve to talk to your true love [insert name here] yet, you'll get a last chance at Shadows or L'Hostal, the only places open after 3am. By now you should've had enough time to come up with a really creative line, or you should at least be drunk enough to think you did.

Surreal Estate

If you're wondering how Dalí put the mad into mad genius, you'll find part of the answer in the nature park of **Cap de Creus** ★. Up the hill beyond Port Lligat, the landscape morphs into a succession of arid rock formations that will twist your sense of reality. The Tramontana (the famous wind that "makes you horny or drives you crazy") sometimes makes it impossible to get there by bicycle, and the vastness of the jagged highlands and cliffs with precious *calas* (coves) at their base would stupefy even the most rugged traveler. When you think of little Salvador coming here every summer and finding monstrous shapes in the rocks you start to get the whole surreal vibe. The **light tower** at the end, which was featured in the 1971 Kirk Douglas film *The Light at the Edge of the World,* nowadays is a hippy restaurant/hostel.

The best way to explore the Cap is by scooter or renting a boat. If those two options escape your budget you can always take a tour boat. **Creuers Cadaqués** (☎ **972-251-057**) offers two different 1½-hour routes to the Cap: One goes all the way to the tip and the other passes by Dalí's house in Port Lligat and other coves, but doesn't stop anywhere—not even to let you get off the boat to take a dip. You'll see the booth right by the seashore and for 12€ per trip you're in.

the way to the Cap de Creus. Some can be reached by land, but most are only accessible by sea. **Rentals SL** (Plaça Dr. Pont 17; ☎ **972-159-034;** www.rentacosta.com) hires out small dinghies for as low as 60€ for 4 hours in high season.

Waters as transparent as Cadaqués's practically scream for some **scuba diving** and **snorkeling,** and, if you know where to look, you might find some morenas, barracudas, and even red coral. Contact **Diving Center Cadaqués** (☎ **652-317-797**) for info on courses and excursions.

Tossa de Mar ★

Only 90km (56 miles) northeast of Barcelona's craziness, surrounded by rocky, green hills lies this calm "blue paradise" (as Marc Chagall, one of the many painters and artists who "discovered" Tossa in the '30s, baptized it). Tossa is the quintessential Costa Brava town. A striking shoreline where small but exquisite sand beaches and rocky promenades are topped off by the walls of a 12th-century medieval town, so amazingly preserved that it seems weird to see people wearing modern day clothes. Walking through its curving, sloped streets filled with multicolored geraniums is like falling into a time warp you won't necessarily want to leave. Maybe thanks to its secluded location, Tossa's personality wasn't too marred by the resort-building craze of the '60s and '70s like its neighboring package-tour neighbors such as Lloret de Mar. It is a large tourist destination in its own right though, and, in the summer months, the beaches are heaving with bodies trying to touch a drop of the unfeasibly clear water. At night the streets burst with young people strolling in and out of the dozens of bars and clubs including some gems that make Tossa unique among its Costa Brava breathren.

Getting There & Around

Tossa de Mar is on the main Barcelona-Palafruggel **bus** route—a good thing too, 'cause there's no train service. **Sarfa** (☎ 902-302-025) provides service along the 1½-hour route from Barcelona's Estació del Nord daily from 8:15am to 8:15pm. The **bus station** is on the road to Lloret de Mar, 10 minutes northwest of the center.

Getting there by **car** is quite simple, just drive north from Barcelona along the A-19.

Tossa de Mar Basics

ORIENTATION

The walled **Vila Vella,** which marks the Southeastern border of the town, was built between the 12th and 14th centuries. It houses the remains of the old castle, a lighthouse, and the museum. Directly north of it you'll find the **Vila Nova,** with cobblestone streets and a bar on every other corner. Further up stretches the newer part of town, which offers nothing more than oodles of hotels and restaurants. **Passeig del Mar** borders the main beach and then turns into **Avinguda de Sant Ramon Penyafort,** which continues

wwwired

A few Internet cafes are scattered around, but you'll have more fun checking your e-mail at the bars that have computers.

The bar/restaurant **Scuba Libre** (Av. Sant Ramón de Penyafort 11; ☎ 678-532-781; .50€ per 10 min.; daily 8am–2:30am) is lively all day. It starts serving divers from the neighboring scuba shop when they emerge from their first immersions and continues through the day, presenting homemade lunches and then, later, mojitos. There are four coin-operated computers for your e-leisure.

bordering the coast as it winds toward the other beaches.

TOURIST OFFICES

The **tourist office** is at Av. El Pelegrí 25 (☎ 972-340-108; www.infotossa.com). April, May, and October, it's open Monday to Saturday 10am to 2pm and 4 to 8pm; November to March, Monday to Saturday 10am to 1pm and 4 to 7pm; June to September, Monday to Saturday 9am to 9pm, Sunday 10am to 2pm and 5 to 8pm. There's also a very convenient info **kiosk** by Platja Gran.

Sleeping

Tossa, oddly enough, has only 2 months of high season and, with heaps of accommodations, it's fairly easy to get a room. But, as always, if you actually have standards (much less high ones), you should book in advance. Heading from the bus station, you'll find many options that are likely to be available, and cheaper than the accommodations by the beach. In front of Platja Gran and on all the surrounding side streets, accommodations range from seriously divey to three stars. If your inner princess is in need of pampering, you'll have to head a little further away from the beach or over onto Platja de la Mar Menuda.

CHEAP

→ **Carmen/Pepi** If you're tight on moolah, you can't do better then this centric and cozy little hostel run by Pepi and her mom Carmen, self proclaimed lovers of the *mochilero* (backpacker). Carmen will even give you a few euros off if you lament to her about your budget, so don't be afraid to squeeze out a few tears. We're not sure if this is a blessing or a curse, but the rooms are a bit cramped due to the big new beds they just installed. The plant-filled central courtyard is a nice place to chill. *Sant Miquel 8.* ☎ *972-340-526. Single 25€–40€,*

CATALUNYA

double   30€–45€.   Breakfast   included.
Amenities: Courtyard. In room: TV, fridge.

DOABLE

➜ **Best Western Mar Menuda** ★ The Mar Menuda is the most popular place to crash in Tossa mostly due to its coveted, entirely white suites that overlook the sea. Recessed tables, beds, benches, and even safes emerge from the walls, and bedding is made from traditionally patterned Mallorcan *ikats,* adding to the Balearic Island feel. Even the standard rooms in the back that face the parking lot and mountain are nicely decorated. The only drawback this hotel possesses is a slight mildewy odor due to its proximity to the water. The restaurant offers great home-cooked Catalan meals for those nights when you can't drag yourself away. *Platja Mar Menuda s/n.* ☎ *972-341-000. Double 136€–190€, suite 180€–235€. Breakfast included. Amenities: Restaurant, bar, breakfast room, fax, Internet, laundry service, pool, room service, rooms for those w/limited mobility, telephone, travel info, TV. In room: A/C, TV, fridge, hair dryer, safe.*

➜ **Hotel Rovira** This large hotel complex in front of Platja Gran offers large, clean, and void-of-decor rooms. It's popular with young people and families due to its in-house faux grotto bar/pizzeria (so bad it's funny) with a big-screen TV and live music. It also houses the Paradis Disco, game rooms, and a front-terrace cafe. All rooms except the singles face the sea. *Pou de la Vila 12.* ☎ *972-340-261. www.hotelroviratossa. com. Single 44€, double 72€–82€. Amenities: Restaurant, bar, breakfast room, disco, elevator, fax, game room, safe 3.70€, telephone, travel info, TV. In room: A/C, TV, fridge.*

SPLURGE

[MTV] (Best 🌙) ➜ **Best Western Premier Gran Hotel Reymar** ★★ The lure of the beach in front and even Tossa itself will likely not be strong enough to get you out of the most comfortable beds in town. If you do manage to leave your room, the views of the sea create a mesmerizing backdrop for the modernly retro, tiled bars and roof-deck pool. The luxury spa includes every form of massage and water therapy you can imagine; but if you don't have time for that, each room has it's own Jacuzzi bathtub also. If you're really a rock star, they even offer a few fantastic and more private California coast–style apartments for an extended stay. *Platja Mar Menuda.* ☎ *972-340-088. www.granhotel reymar.com. Single 77€–147€, double 108€–268€, suite 166€–394€. Breakfast included. Amenities: Restaurants, bars, breakfast room, disco, fax, gym, Internet, laundry service, pool, room service, rooms for those w/limited mobility, solarium, spa, telephone, travel/ activities desk, TV lounge, Wi-Fi. In room: A/C, TV, fridge, hair dryer, safe.*

Eating

Being the tourist town that it is, Tossa offers a great variety of restaurants of generally good quality. Vila Vella offers the most picturesque dining, or choose from among the varied international cuisines in Vila Nova.

➜ **La Lluna** TAPAS   Go medieval on the olives at this picturesque hole-in-the-wall tapas bar in the heart of the historic Vila Vella. Knuckle down at the wooden outdoor tables and enjoy some foodie delights such as an assortment of local pâtés, *piquillo* peppers with cod *brandade,* or a custom-made tortilla. The knowledgeable staff will help you pick a wine from their excellent list. Finding the place is half the fun, since the tiny street it's on doesn't have a name. (*Hint:* On the approach from the lighthouse, take the street that branches off at the T-shaped tree.) *No address.* ☎ *972-342-523. Tapas 2.20€–5.50€. Daily 11am–4pm and 7–11pm. Closed Tues Sept–June.*

→ **La Piccola Nostra** ITALIAN Besides cramming up the beaches and complaining about the weather, there are a couple other things Italians can do really well. Two of them are pasta and pizza. This Olive Garden–looking spot with a big terrace in the Vila Nova delivers thin-crust crispy pies and huge plates of perfectly made pasta (the pear-stuffed *sachetti* with Parmesan shavings will have you kissing the waiter). The wine list is extensive but not Italian, and if doctor Atkins has an influence on you, you can always resort to the grilled meats and fresh salads. *Pou de la Vila 4.* ☎ *972-342-580. Entrees 5.20€–16€. Daily 1–4pm and 8–11pm.*

MTV **Best ☻** → **Vera Mar** ★ SEAFOOD This classic seafood restaurant located 50m (164 ft.) from the beach in Tossa recently changed owners; but we're happy to report that the quality of the food is just as strong as always. Try the best *mejilones a la marinera* (mussels marinara) known to man and the taste-bud-boggling seafood paella. The abundant *menú del día* (15€) is the best deal since the Louisiana Purchase. *Enric Granados s/n.* ☎ *972-344-003. Entrees 6.50€. Daily 12:30pm–midnight.*

Partying

If you like to barhop, Tossa offers a great selection of small (and sometimes just plain freaky) venues where you can tie one on. As far as clubs are concerned, the choices aren't nearly as interesting, but the crowd may be slightly younger than the group of Peter Pan–syndrome folk you'll find in the bars. The highest concentration of watering holes is in the Vila Nova, around **Carrer San Josep** and **Carrer Estalt.** A younger crowd fills **Mar i Cel,** a Parque Güell inspired bar, with a big screen TV. Next door is the friendly little **Don Pepe** where you can dance to the live Flamenco guitar, and around the corner you'll find **Bounty,** maybe the only little

tavern where you can get sloppy to the tune of old men playing cards out front. **El Piratin,** at the foot of Vila Vella, has a great old shipwreck vibe (anyone else sense a continuing theme around here?), good music, and a terrace.

A few surprises can be found off the beaten track as well.

→ **Discoteca Ely** If you're in need of dance music, throbbing bodies, and flashing lights, get your fix here among fellow young tourists and locals from all over Costa Brava. *Bernats 2.* ☎ *972-340-009. 1-drink minimum.*

→ **Don Juan** *Jamón* hanging from the ceiling, walls lined with beer steins, and rough-hewn wooden tables provide all the comforts of a local tavern. Don Juan opens it's doors early for the workers to grab a pre-clock-punch *carajillo* (espresso with cognac), never closes for siesta so the tourists can wash their beer down with a *bocadillo,* and keeps the fire burning late so the waitstaff from all the other bars can enjoy a nightcap—your basic crowd-pleaser. *Pintor Francesc Serra 1.* ☎ *972-340-298.*

MTV **Best ☻** → **Paulino/Flamenco Bar** ★ Sevilla meets Atlantic City in an ambience only Almodovar could attempt to replicate. Red-hued lights, taxidermied animals fighting for wall space next to aged photos of bullfights, and an old wooden bar packed to the ceiling with bottles creates a speakeasy/cabaret atmosphere. The cast of characters includes a tall elderly vocalist, who may have been someone's dad before her destiny dictated that she spend every night singing flamenco-ish covers of 1950s American classics like "Shaboom-Shaboom" (hey, it could happen to anyone); the Mickey Rooney look-alike waiter who gets the crowd going with his soft-shoe dancing; Olés, the Don Juan–mustached guitar player; and, finally, the sassy, suspender-sporting bartender.

CATALUNYA

Scratching the Surface: Illes Medes

Roughly halfway between Tossa and Cadaqués lies **Spain's hottest diving spot:** 📺 Best● **Illes Medes.** This tiny archipelago composed of seven islets houses about 1,350 species of marine life in a protected natural park. The otherworldly landscapes include multicolored, coral-covered rocks, dark and scary caves, a sunken boat, and sandy bottoms, attracting a variety of life forms including starfish, octopuses, scorpion fish, and occasional dolphins, whale sharks, and blue marlins. Snorkeling and glass-bottom boats can also provide entertainment for that sissy of a girl/boyfriend of yours. The touristy town of **L'Estartit** is the best launching point. A bunch of dive centers are based there; shop around for prices, as they often vary. We recommend **Diving Center El Rei Del Mar** (Av. de Grecia 5; ☎ **972-751-392;** www.rei-del-mar.com) or **Aquatica** (Camping Rifort; ☎ **972-750-656** or 609-311-133).

Sarfa (☎ **902-302-025**) runs four daily buses from Barcelona's Estació del Nord to L'Estartit in July and August and one the rest of the year.

Despite (or perhaps because of) the bizarreness of this strange crew, the music is mesmerizing and the crowd goes wild. *Sant Pere 4.* ☎ *972-341-075.*

Sightseeing

Walk up, down, and around the streets of the **Vila Vella,** which remains almost the same as it was 700 years ago, when Shrek used to vacation here. At the top of the hill are the **Far de Tossa** (lighthouse), a few cannons, and other remains of the old castle and church, plus some awesome views of the town and the Costa Brava.

→ **Museu Municipal** This quaint museum in the 600-year-old Governor's house exhibits Roman artifacts found in the city and paintings from the many artists that used to vacation here in the '30s, including a couple of Chagalls. *Plaça de Roig I Soler 1.* ☎ *972-340-709. Admission 3€. June 15–Sept 30 daily 10am–10pm; Oct–June Tues–Sun 10am–2pm and 4–6pm.*

Playing Outside

The **beaches** in Tossa are refreshingly cool and clean, but get very crowded in July and August. **Platja Gran** is the biggest one, with towers at one end and fishing boats waiting to sail to sea on the other. At the northern end is **Platja de la Mar Menuda,** a smaller beach that caters mostly to the people staying at the two hotels set back from the shore. The surreal **L'Illa Island** garnishes the view. **Es Codolar** is a beautiful sandy cove on the other side of Vila Vella, but being quite small, it gets packed faster than a New York City subway car at 6pm.

Tossa's underwater rock formations and its water's visibility make **scuba diving** almost a necessity. **Diving Center Mar Menuda** (Mar Menuda Beach; ☎ **689-785-168;** www.divingtossa.com) offers immersions from the beach or a boat for certified divers. If you want to become one, you can do it in three 8-hour days for 380€.

Tarragona ★

Tarracó was once the capital of Hispania, the Iberic part of the Roman Empire.

Emperor Augustus loved the "city of eternal spring" (that was way before global warming) and a UNESCO-worthy group of ruins have been preserved from that period, making Tarragona a living museum where you can learn more in a day than in a year of high school history. Set on a hill above the aquamarine waters and broad beaches of the Costa Daurada, Tarragona is not flooded with tourism, so you can visit most attractions without waiting in long queues; and the beach is relatively empty even in the summer. Be forewarned: The small university has its fair share of young people, but Tarragona is definitely *not* a party town.

Getting There & Around

BY PLANE

Although Tarragona has no airport of its own it lies merely 7km (4^1/$_3$ miles) away from Reus. Iberia has two daily shuttle flights connecting with Madrid. And low-cost Ryan Air offers flights to Dublin, London, and Frankfurt. **Hispano Igualadina** (☎ 977-770-698) offers service from Reus to Tarragona.

BY TRAIN

The best way to arrive is, no doubt, by train from Barcelona. Fifty-five trains make the 1- to 1^1/$_4$-hour trip to and from the Barcelona-Sants station. (*Note:* Most of the time you can also get on at Passeig de Garcia's or Clots' Renfe station.) If you are coming from Madrid, five trains per day make the 8-hour trip to Tarragona. Once there, the **RENFE** office is in the train station at Plaza Pedrera s/n (☎ 902-240-202; www.renfe.es).

BY BUS

Ten buses per day depart from Barcelona to Tarragona (trip time: 1^1/$_2$ hr.); from Valencia, 10 buses (trip time: 3^1/$_2$ hr.); and from Alicante, six buses (trip time: 6^1/$_2$ hr.). Call the **bus station** at ☎ 977-229-126 for more information.

Inside the city 15 local lines are run by the **Municipal Transportation Agency** (no phone; www.infonegocio.com/emt); each line is identified by a color and a number. The public bus is your best bet for cheap wheels to the farther beaches or the Roman aqueduct. Nos. 1 and 9 go from Rambla Vella to all the beaches; no. 2 goes to the train station, port, and Rambla Nova; and no. 75 goes from the Plaça Imperial to the aqueduct. Rides are 1.05€ a pop.

BY CAR

Take the A-2 southwest from Barcelona to the A-7, then take the N-340, which is a fast toll road. The one-way cost of the toll road from Barcelona to Tarragona is 8€. Traffic in downtown Tarragona is pretty smooth. For parking, many streets offer "blue zones"—the only areas designated for you to park in, but don't forget to get the ticket. Public parking facilities are also available.

BY TAXI

Taxis are unusually expensive here with day fares starting at 3.30€ and nights at 5.75€. But if you are down by the port late at night, you'll pay whatever it takes to avoid climbing the slope back to the hotel. Call **Agrupación Radio Taxis de Tarragona** at ☎ 977-236-064.

Tarragona Basics

ORIENTATION

The train station in Tarragona is right by the beach and the port. West from there is the **Port Esportiu** with many clubs and bars, and further west is the **Moll de Pescadores** (docks) and adjacent fishermen's neighborhood. From the train station, if you go right and up the first set of stairs, that'll get you to the **Rambla Nova,** an opulent boulevard that crosses the city from the **Balcó del Mediterrani,** overlooking the sea, to the **Plaça Imperial Tarracó,** next to the bus station. Two blocks northeast of the **Nova** is the **Rambla Vella,** where the **old town** begins. Most of the sights are in the old town—the museums, cathedral, and tourist info. The center of the old town is the **Plaça de la Font,** in what used to be the Roman Circus. Downhill toward the sea from the old town is the **amphitheater** and the main beach, **Platja del Miracle.** Leaving town, 4km (2¹/₂ miles) away by the route to Barcelona lies the **Pont del Diable,** a 220m-long (722-ft.) Roman aqueduct.

TOURIST OFFICES

The **tourist office** is on the way from the center to the cathedral at Calle Major 39 (☎ **977-250-795;** www.tarragonaturisme. es). It's open Monday to Friday from 9am to 9pm, Saturday from 9am to 2pm and 4 to 9pm. Information Kiosks at the Rambla Nova, Passeig Arqueológico, and on the roundabout at the beginning of the Rambla Vella can also hook you up. They'll give you a map with the location of the original Roman buildings marked in yellow.

Tarragona Nuts & Bolts

Currency Most **ATMs** are on or around the Rambla Nova.

Emergency For medical assistance, **Hospital de Santa Tecla** is at Rambla Vella 14 (☎ **977-259-900**). For emergencies call ☎ **112.**

Internet **Tarraconect@** (Cós del Bou 9; ☎ **977-239-818**) is right off Plaça de la Font and has about 10 PCs (2€ per hour) and some phone booths. You can also recharge your cellphone or send a fax. Hours are Monday to Saturday 11am to 2pm and 5 to 10:30pm; Sunday 5 to 10:30pm.

Right by the Rambla Nova and in the back of a cafe, **Netgaming** (Méndez Nuñez 7, Bajos; ☎ **977-234-552**) features about 30 computers plus a couple of tables where you can have a drink while you wait for your friend to finish his/her e-mails. They also will burn CDs and scan anything daily from 11am to 10pm. Rates are 1.50€ to 1.80€ per hour.

Pharmacies Look for the green crosses in the old town. In Rambla Nova, the closest drugstore is **Farmacia Del Clós** (Rambla Nova 55; ☎ **977-221-430;** Mon–Sat 9am–2pm and 4–9pm).

Sleeping

There aren't heaps of budget sleeping options in Tarragona, as most folks just day-trip here. Try to bed down fairly close to the old city—Tarragona can be eerily vacant at night, especially in the lower half of the new city. You'll find a few decent options around Plaça de la Font as well as on the Rambla Nova in the northern part of the new town. If you come in high season and miss that last train back, you may need to scour around the station, up near the Plaça Imperial Tarraco or east along Via Augusta. The tourist info has a very handy brochure with a map pinpointing each hotel and its digits.

➔ **Aparthotel Alexandra** A very good deal, especially if you're staying more than a day. This streamlined modern hotel features 30 cheery apartments with kitchenettes, living rooms, and a tiny shared pool. Also, being on the tree-lined Rambla Nova, it's less of a schlep from the beach and bars. *Rambla Nova 71.* ☎ *977-248-701.*

www.ah-alexandra.com. Single/double 50€–60€, triple/quadruple add 18€–23€ for adults. Amenities: Bar, breakfast room, elevator, fax, laundry service, pool, room service, rooms for those w/limited mobility, telephone, travel info. In room: A/C, TV, fridge, hair dryer, Internet, microwave, safe.

→ **Forum** Even though you have to walk up a few flights, Forum is a decent deal for its location. The rooms are sunny and spacious; some face the *plaça* and have small balconies, but if you need a good night's sleep we suggest the rooms facing the back. All rooms include very small bathrooms with showers. For the price, you're not going to get anything better, especially not with ceiling fans and an old-city address. *Plaça de la Font 37.* ☎ *977-231-718. Single 21€, double 41€. Amenities: Restaurant.*

→ **Hotel Plaça de la Font** In Tarragona, 15€ gets you upgraded from a crappy pension to a room with a view (and soundproofed windows). Simple and classic design, huge firm beds, impeccable new bathrooms and all the other stuff you need to get your zzzs are here. *Plaça de la Font 26.* ☎ *977-240-882. www.hotelpdelafont.com. Single (only available from Oct–June) 40€, double facing back 50€–55€, double facing front 55€–60€. Amenities: Restaurant, cafe, elevator, fax, parking, rooms for those w/ limited mobility, safe, telephone, travel info. In room: A/C, TV.*

Eating

The restaurants in the old town, many built inside ancient ruins, offer excellent variations on local cuisine in breathtaking settings, and the many *plaças* are nice for an outside cocktail after a day of underground exploration.

TAPAS

→ **El Varadero** Carved wooden doorways lead to display cases packed with the catch of the day and nautical elements abound in this maritime extravaganza. The sad little turtle and tiny fish that fill the tanks in the middle only add to the bizarre, hull-of-a-ship vibe. You'll find many locals downing *chupitos* (shots) in the middle of the day to wash down the inexpensive, yet titanic portions of grilled sardines, catch of the day, and oversize *croquetas de rape* (glorified monkfish tater-tots). We like the outdoor seating here (and at their sister restaurant L'Ancora); but due to major construction going on in the old port, you may opt for the less noisy and more Captain Jack Sparrow–ish interior. *Trafalgar 13.* ☎ *977-242-806. Tapas/Entrees 6€–22€. Tues–Sun 1–5pm and 7:30pm–1am.*

→ **La Nau** ★ A lively crowd fills this popular *cerveceria* (beer house) built inside original Roman and Gothic arches. The decor is hodgepodge, with tinted metallic stone surfaces, basket-woven chairs, and an intense stained glass depicting the city's monuments in cutout relief. Suds by the meter (which looks like a giant, glass, tubular bong covered with an ice pack) is the claim to fame that puts Nau on the party map. Unless you are a complete lush you'll need a few friends to tackle the minimum 2m (6½ ft.) of amber, be it domestic, imported, or *champu* (aka *clara*—beer with lemon soda). If you're a lone wolf, don't fret; you can also order by the glass or from an extensive list of imported bottles. Recommendable tapas are *patatas bravas* (square-cut fried potatoes) with wasabi sauce or the duck carpaccio. Daily specials stray from the classics, and dessert is a chocoholic's wet dream. *La Nau 12.* ☎ *977-230-203. Tapas 3€–18€. Daily 9am–1am.*

CHEAP

→ **Pulvinar** ITALIAN The *pulvinar* was the box seating where the bigwigs would sit away from the plebeians and admire the races. Now it's a lovely patio restaurant named for its position near Tarragona's ancient Roman Circus. It offers thin crust pizzas, fresh pastas with a variety of sauces (only in Tarragona would you find pasta with *romesco* sauce—a Catalan tomato-and-almond sauce used mostly for grilled vegetables), creative salads, and friendly service worthy of an emperor's praise. *Ferrers 20.* ☎ *977-235-631. Entrees 7€–14€. Daily 1–4pm and 8–11pm.*

DOABLE

→**Palau de Baró** ★ CATALAN Constructed in 1867, the Palau building flaunts an original fresco by Catalan painter Mariano Fortuny; it's in the small room reserved for one-party seating (you need to ask to see it). In the three light and airy main dining rooms, the walls have been refurbished with modern stenciling, which works well with the intricate original tile floors. All of this sounds very refined, but an air of shabby chic prevails, especially on the large plant-filled patio. The prix-fix menus have add-ons you'll pay more for—watch out for this! All of the most tempting dishes have a few euros tacked on, but how can you get just a salad for a first when adding another euro gets you a gazpacho or an additional 4€ turns a simple salmon into *fideua* (paella made with pasta instead of rice) with monkfish? *Santa Anna 3.* ☎ *977-241-464. Entrees 13€–28€. Tues–Sun 1–3:30pm and 8:30–10:30pm.*

Partying

Compared to the partying that took place at Caligula's place, things have slowed down a bit in Tarragona. The options are basically: watching a mediocre rock 'n' roll cover band or having an early drink at one of the outdoor terraces in the old town. During school months, Thursdays see some action; but in the summer, only the weekend has anything going on. However, if that white pill you took for your headache ended up not being an aspirin and you desperately need to sweat it out, you can try one of the incomprehensibly cheesy clubs in the port, with such enticing names as Vogue Beach Club and Dance Place—but brace yourself for a runway show of cheap, overdone glitz with music to match. Somehow we weeded through these options and found a few places meriting note here.

→ **Aigua** Offering foosball, an Astroturfed deck looking out onto the port, and a mixed sexual preference, their fauxhawk-sporting clientele have edged Aigua a quarter-notch above the other style-afflicted bars and clubs in the area. *Port Esportiu. No phone. Free before 3am, 5€ after with drink included.*

📺 Best ● → **Café Baraka** Oddly, there is no busting of moves at this, the only bar that Tarragonians consider a hot spot due to its high-caliber DJs. The decor is simple, with outdoor metal seating that doesn't distract from the seaside view. Popping in for just one drink as the sun goes down can turn into a long night of cruising sun-kissed youth to the sounds of deep and chill rhythms. *Platja Miracle. No phone.*

→ **Dejá Vu** On Friday and Saturday the local crowd packs in and grinds down to pop and electronic at this small bar, whose only distinguishing feature is the exposed brick wall. Thursdays, it's just a chill place to swill giant and inexpensive cocktails. Funny, I feel like I've seen this review before.... *Reding 9.* ☎ *610-846-830.*

→ **Groove** A black and white collage of jazz greats behind a long wooden bar, a perfect sound system, and dim lighting from the hanging mosaic lamps provide the ambience for the young rock/soul/blues/jazz buffs of Tarragona, who fill this narrow East Village–style haunt. When the semester starts up, Groove is maybe the only place in Tarragona worth cramming into to check some live bands. *Cardenal Cervantes 4. No phone.*

→ **Scum** If you plan on getting a metal or rock band together but aren't sure where anyone would dare let you play, chances are Scum wouldn't mind you test-driving your U2 cover here. A ready-for-anything, 25+ crowd shows their support in the den-like space regardless of the talent of whomever has the guts to get up on the small stage. The venue offers 8 to 15 concerts per month making it easier to catch Spain's next Springsteen before the agents sign him—that is, if there *is* a Springsteen in Spain. Besides, isn't the name genius? *Fortuny 22.* ☎ *616-959-413.*

Sightseeing ★★

Walking around the old town you'll bump into Roman and medieval ruins around every other corner. Pay special attention to the medieval 📺 Best ● **Call Jueu** in the Plaça dels Angels and the **Voltes Gotiques** an old market on Carrer Merceria. Don't leave without visiting the major historical attractions. Pay for each attraction individually or get the 2-day ticket that's valid for all the Roman ruins for 8.60€ and worth every penny.

📺 Best ● → **Amfiteatre Romà** If you think football is violent, you should see what went on in this arena. The magnificent and well-preserved theater was built on a cliff overlooking the sea, and you can sit on the same grades where those bloodthirsty Romans drank their wine. *Parc del Milagro.* ☎ *977-242-220. Admission adults 2.20€, students 1€. May–Sept Tues–Sat 9am–9pm, Sun 9am–3pm; Oct–Mar Tues–Sun 9am–5pm.*

→ **Catedral** ★ The humongous 12th-century cathedral is located in the highest point of town, where the provincial Roman Forum used to be. Unless you come during mass, you'll have to walk around and enter through the cloisters. The cathedral itself is one of the finest in Spain with a sunny cloister surrounded by elaborately carved capitals, dozens of chapels rich in religious masterpieces, and an exceptionally detailed Catalan gothic altarpiece. The **Museu Diocesá** houses a collection of religious art that spawns 10 centuries and includes everything from statues and reliquaries to paintings and enormous tapestries. Follow the fascinating audio tour (included in the entrance fee) and see if you can find the arch depicting the procession of the mice on your own. *Plaça de la Seu.* ☎ *977-238-685. Admission to the cathedral and museum 3.50€. Mar 16–May 30 Mon–Sat 10am–1pm and 4–7pm; June 1–Oct 15 Mon–Sat 10am–7pm; Oct 16–Nov 15 Mon–Sat 10am–5pm; Nov 16–Mar 15 Mon–Sat 10am–2pm.*

FREE → **Museu D'Art Modern** Are you sick of paying to look at old stuff surrounded by old people? This modern art museum dedicated to Tarragonian sculptor Julio Antonio hosts an eye-opening collection of modern Spanish artists. The centerpiece is said sculptor's *Mausoleo Lemonier,* an astounding marble and bronze sculpture in the museum's patio. *Santa Anna 8.* ☎ *977-235-032. www.altanet.org/MAMT. Free admission. Tues–Fri 10am–8pm; Sat 10am–3pm and 5–8pm; Sun 11am–2pm.*

→ **Museu Nacional Arqueològic (MNAT)** Refresh your high school Latin and art history at this Roman version of IKEA, with columns and mosaics in great states of conservation, music instruments, and even some sexual amulets and stone dildos—apparently the Romans' reputation for partying was very well deserved. An interesting audiovisual presentation in the basement is conducted in many languages, including English. *Plaça del Rei 5.* ☎ *977-236-209. www.mnat.es. Admission 2.40€. June 1–Sept 30 Tues–Sat 9:30am–8:30pm, Sun 10am–2pm; Oct 1–May 31 Tues–Sat 10am–1:30pm and 3:30–7pm, Sun 10am–2pm.*

CATALUNYA

→ **Pretori y Circ Romá (Roman tower and circus)** ★ Right across from the MNAT, through the massive Roman Walls, lies this tower with a Roman base and medieval top. The best part is walking through the tunnels under what used to be the circus, where the chariot races à la Ben-Hur took place. *Plaza Rei.* ☎ *977-221-736. Admission 2.20€. May–Sept 30 Tues–Sat 9am–9pm, Sun 9am–3pm; Oct–Mar Tues–Sat 9am–7pm, Sun 10am–3pm.*

Playing Outside

Ten minutes away from the city lies **Universal Mediterrania,** Spain's and soon Europe's biggest **entertainment center.** The complex encompasses three theme-hotels each with its own set of bungalows and lakes: a **beach park** on the Costa Daurada, the **Caribe Water Park,** and the ginormous **Port Aventura** theme park that consists of Epcot-ish replications of regions such as Mexico, China, Polynesia, and the Mediterranean. Although largely populated by families and teenagers, some of the **rides** are worth checking out, if you're into that kind of thing. Highlights are the Dragon Khan, with eight inverted loops or the Stampida, a two-tracked roller coaster made entirely out of wood so you can puke in the cars next to you, rather than the poor operator at the bottom. The park is open from March 18 to June 17, daily 10am to 8pm (but it often closes at 7pm); in summer, daily from 10am to midnight; from September 12 to January 9, daily 10am to 7pm. Admission costs adults 41€ to 51€. Visit www.portaventura.com for updated info and promos. About 50% of the trains on the Barcelona-Sitges-Tarragona line stop at Port Aventura. From Barcelona, the one-way trip takes 50 minutes and costs 6€ to 11€. A taxi from the center of Tarragona to Port Aventura costs about 14€ one-way.

The sandy, 500m (1,640-ft.) beach of **Platja del Miracle** in Tarragona is inconveniently sectioned off from the city by the train tracks. Walk through the underpass on Mestre Benages or the overpass a little farther down. The sand is not so fine-grain as on the other beaches but the water is clear and, depending on the day, you can catch a wave or two or just fight the smaller surf on your boogie-board. Farther up north are the nicer but shorter beaches of **Savinosa,** with fine sand and some nudists letting it all hang out. Farther up is

Man-chitecture

A curious custom in Catalunya is the mix of physical activity, architecture, and tradition that merge in the *castells:* "stories" of three or four men who pile on top of each other to make human towers that reach death-defying heights. Participants wear classical uniforms with colors that represent their team and always include a waist sash used by the climbers to step on (I once witnessed some kids trying to do it without the sash, resulting in a mass exposure of bare butts). The size of the *castellers* obviously diminishes as the tower gets taller, leaving the higher and most dangerous positions to women and children. Normally they go up six or seven stories, although up to nine-story *castells* have been achieved. The **first Sunday of October** on even-numbered years there's a competition in Tarragona's bullring. *Castellers* from every corner of Catalunya get together and try to outdo each other. The most famous teams come from Valls, Vilafranca del Penedés, and Terrassa. Otherwise you'll see them perform at each town's local party days.

All That Glitters . . . on La Costa Daurada

One of the most stunning stretches of Spanish beachdom is the **Costa Daurada** (the golden coast), named for its golden sand beaches that stretch some 211km (131 miles) along the entire coastline of the province of Tarragona, from Cunit to Les Cases d'Alcanar.

South of Tarragona the coastline stretches for miles toward the stunning beauty of the **Cape of Salou.** Get some friends and a boat and spend the day exploring its coves and hidden-away corners. (You might just be able to find that secret place in the world meant only for you.) South toward Valencia is **Cambrils,** a maritime town with an excellent beach and an important fishing port sandwiched between the impressive Colldejou and Llaberia mountains and the sea. **El Regueral** isn't only one of the finest beaches but it also has a windsurfing club where you can rent boards and kayaks.

To the north of Tarragona you'll find the little towns of **Altafulla** and **Torredembarra.** Their beaches are in a virgin area covered with dunes and low vegetation. During those hours when only the bravest, or the most brain-baked, stay on the beach, you can go check out the medieval castles in both towns.

If what you're looking for is a more secluded beach where you can go and have a romantic picnic with that Dutch hottie you keep bumping into at every hostel, then a bit further north, closer to **Comarruga,** which is itself a magnificent and very cosmopolitan beach, you'll find the perfect hide-out of **Sant Salvador.**

The Costa Dourada's **countryside** is full of large stretches of salt and fresh water, riverbank woods, rice plantations, and miles of beaches. Where the Ebro River joins the sea you'll find an incredible delta filled with 300 different species of birds, among them the picturesque pink flamingos.

La Costa's festivals are also stunners. People in this province have inherited a rich tradition of *festes majors* and they continue to honor them faithfully. Ceremonial processions, spectacular human towers (see "Man-chitecture," earlier), totemic bulls, captivating *jota* folk dancing, essential theatricalities, delicious food, and fireworks invite you to join in the fiesta.

the nicest, **Platja Larga,** with over 3km (2 miles) of fine golden sand, topped by a rocky green hill. All beaches can be reached by bus nos. 1 and 9, which stop at Rambla Vella in the old town.

Sitges ★★

If you've been to Provincetown in Cape Cod, you will experience major déjà vu in Sitges, also a former fishing town discovered by artists and coveted for it's gay and family-friendly vibe. For that matter you could compare it to Mykonos, Fire Island, and maybe San Fran as well, just on a much smaller scale. Though for it's size, Sitges really packs a punch. Its breathtaking architecture, museums, boutique hotels, and beaches attract everyone under the sun and its cuisine can stand toe-to-toe with the bigger cities in the region. Although predominantly frequented by middle-aged gay men, young gay and hetero couples/singles and lesbians also account for the large crowded restaurants and bars. Sitges's discos aren't nearly as tacky as the ones

CATALUNYA

further down on the Costa del Garraf, nor as sophisticated as those in Barcelona, but they are small-town friendly and full-on every summer night. Sitges is a sort of mainland Ibiza for its outrageous mixed sexual orientation parties and the flock of artists who enjoy them—and don't forget the sunny beaches.

Getting There & Around

BY TRAIN

Fourteen trains leave for Sitges from Barcelona each day. Board at De Clot Aragó, Passeig de Gracia, or Barcelona Sants. *Note:* The Renfe station (☎ 902-240-202) at Passeig de Gracia is on the corner of Carrer de Aragó, by Casa Batló, and not easily accessed underground by Metro. The 2.40€ each-way trip takes approximately 35 minutes from Sants or 45 from Passeig de Gracia.

BY CAR

Sitges is a 45-minute drive from Barcelona along the C-246, a winding coastal road. An express highway, the A-7, opened in 1999; it's a much less scenic road, but crucial on weekends when all of Barcelona makes for the beaches.

BY BUS

Monbus (☎ 933-620-020) connects the Oasis commercial center in Sitges with the Plaça Universitat in Barcelona. A night bus to and from Barcelona leaves every hour from 1am to 4am, and service directly to the Llobregat Airport runs every hour from 8am to 11pm.

BY TAXI

In Sitges, you'll be close enough to everything not to need a taxi, but if your trick knee injury from the war acts up again, call ☎ **938-941-329** or 938-943-594. **Taxi stands** are located at the Centro Comercial Oasis and the RENFE station.

BY BIKE

The town itself is usually too packed with tourists to ride a bike through, but it's nice to get one for exploring the beaches further out. **Sitges Bike** (Centro Comercial Oasis, local 34; ☎ **938-944-458;** www.sitgesbike.com), is a full-service bike store that can get you rolling for 10€ a half-day (4 hr.) and 16€ a full-day (8 hr.).

Sitges Basics

Once the Renfe train or bus leaves you across from **Carrer Artur Cornonell,** walk downhill on any perpendicular street into the center of Sitges. **Carrer Sant Francesc** is one of the larger streets that will lead you into **Plaça Cap de la Villa,** a common meeting point. Downhill from there lies the south corner of **Platja San Sebastiá.** Up the hill and through the prettiest part of Sitges along the cobblestoned streets you'll find the **Sant Bartomolmeu i Sant Telca** church; down the steps is **Passeig de la Ribera,** the seafront boulevard with lots of bars and palm trees. The famous **Carrer de Pecat** ("Sin Street") is actually called **Carrer 1er de Maig de 1838** and runs from Passeig de la Ribera, halfway from the beach of the same name, to **Plaça Indústria.** Bars are mainly concentrated along the streets surrounding this *plaça* and off of **Carrer Parelldes.**

The **tourist office** is at Carrer Sinea Morera 1 (☎ **938-945-004;** www.sitgestur.com), west of the train station. From July to September 15, it's open daily 9am to 9pm; September 16 to June, hours are Monday to Friday 9am to 2pm and 4 to 6:30pm. There's another branch by the Museu Maricel, on Fonollar n/n (☎ **938-110-611**). To find your way around town Sitges LGBT scene, grab a **Sitges Gay Map** at any store and you'll get the DL on what's happening where.

Recommended Websites

www.outlet4spain.com and **www.** **sitgesguide.com** are very useful for all general info, for planning to go out, and for booking hotels.

Sitges Nuts & Bolts

Currency **ATMs** can be found everywhere, but for guaranteed choices try **Plaça Cap de la Villa.**

Emergency Call ☎ 112 for general emergencies or get yourself to Hospital Sant Camil ☎ **938-960-025.**

Internet There are a smattering of *locutorios* and cybercafes around the center. The most recommendable is **Café Roy** (Parellades 9; ☎ **938-110-052**), which has a large indoor/outdoor patio where you can get yourself connected. Wi-Fi is free with drink/food purchase. For those of you not packin' there are two house computers as well. Roy is open daily noon to 5pm and 8 to 11pm.

Pharmacies **Gerard Planas,** Calle Artur Carbonell 30, in front of the Renfe station (☎ **938-941-573**), has the usual array of pharmaceuticals, cosmetics, whatever. **www.sitgesguide.com** has a listing of the pharmacies that take turns staying open for 24-hour access.

Sleeping

It's easier to nab a photo of Nicole Richie eating than a hotel room within 10k (6¼ miles) of Sitges in high season, so definitely call ahead. Unlike most other Spanish resort towns, Sitges has very limited space to exploit, so the mega-hotels (hallelujah) are on the outskirts. In the town center, the numerous private homes turned boutique hotels are also worth a peep. Many revelers commute in for the parties from Barcelona and neighboring towns and then grab the early morning train/bus back to sleep. Some hotels close November to May, reopening only for Carnaval. The tourist office or the English-speaking accommodation bookers at www. outlet4spain.com (☎ **938-102-711**) can be of assistance.

CHEAP

→ **Hotel Platjador** Platjador doesn't offer much more then a simple bed, but the rooms are ample and have what you need on a hot summer night (hello, we're talkin' A/C here, people!). Some rooms have balconies facing the sea, but the ones facing the pool have a consolation prize . . . better mattresses. This may be the only place where you'll even find a room without booking in advance. *Passeig de la Ribera 35-36.* ☎ *938-945-054. www.hotelsitges.com. Double 42€–71€. Amenities: Restaurant, bar, breakfast room, elevator, fax, pool, telephone, travel info, TV. In room: A/C, TV, hair dryer.*

DOABLE

→ **Calípolis** If you're not into the old-world charm of the local hotels, preferring a slicker, more exclusive place with a miniscule pool to pose in front of, Calipolís is your best option. Glamorous types of all backgrounds and sexual preferences fill up its spacious, simply furnished rooms and sparkly white restaurant and lounge. The modern circular shape provides perfect balconies for pre-cruising the Passeig Maritím. And its proximity to Platja de la

CATALUNYA

Rodona cuts the travel time to L'Atlantida, Pacha, and Playa del Muerto. *Av. Sofía 2-6.* ☎ *938-941-500. www.hotelcalipolis.com. Double 85€–240€.* *Amenities: Restaurant, bar, beach towel service, bike rental, breakfast room, elevator, fax, Internet, laundry service, room service, rooms for those w/limited mobility, smoking floors, telephone, travel info, TV, Wi-Fi. In room: A/C, TV, hair dryer, minibar, safe, Wi-Fi.*

Ⓜ Best ☻ → **Hotel Romantic/Hotel Renaixença** ★★ Flabbergastingly decorative with turn-of-the-20th-century ceramics, furniture, and art, the three tasteful adjoining villas that make up Romantic and Renaixença should be a mandatory stop for anyone studying Catalan art history and/or interior design. The prices are low due to the lack of amenities such as A/C or elevator, all foregone to conserve the original structure. The service is still tailored, and nowhere will you enjoy a cocktail or breakfast more than in their luxuriant gardens or uniquely decorated lounges. The villas are usually booked solid, but at least stop by for a gander. If you're staying at The Renaixença, which doesn't have its own reception, check in at Romantic and they give you a key. *San Isidro 33.* ☎ *938-948-375. www.hotelromantic.com. Single 49€–75€, double 88€–111€. Breakfast included. Amenities: Bar, breakfast room, garden, lounges, fax, rooms for those w/limited mobility, telephone, travel info, TV. In room: Hair dryer, safe.*

Eating

Sitges offers all kinds of dining variety, from greasy falafel to fine truffles. Restaurants tend to stay open late, and no chef would dream of taking a vacation in August (although many shut their doors from Oct–Apr).

TAPAS

→ **La Croqueta** Bustling with a young, pre-club crowd, this groovy nouveau '60s-style tapas bar is great for late-night munchies. Grab a plate from the bartender and pick your atypical *pintxo* (Basque tapa on bread usually speared with a toothpick) or order a larger *racion* at the bar or one of the small tables. The *hamburgesa boton, huevos rotos,* and the *bacalao* and orange salad taste as good as they look. A surprisingly decent international wine list and equally creative desserts make for a perfect economical meal. Leave your toothpick on the plate and the age-old Basque honor system stays in place—like dim sum dining, they'll add it up and give you your bill. *Marqués de Montroig 8.* ☎ *938-948-668. www.la-croqueta.com. Tapas 1.25€–13€. Daily 12:30pm–midnight (call for winter hours).*

CHEAP

→ **Al Fresco Café** ★ INTERNATIONAL You can have your three meals a day and *merienda* (snack) at this small, all white and wood cafe. In Soho this would be run of the mill, but here, where the salads usually consist of iceberg lettuce, onion, and tomato, it's foodie paradise. The small lunch and dinner menu is made up of classic light fare, and the very popular Angus burger shares the printed page with curries, fancy phyllo-dough empanadas, and fresh salads. Anything you order is the right choice, and you can top it off with a slice of mango cake and an Italian coffee. *Major 33.* ☎ *938-113-307. Entrees 4€–11€. Daily 9am–11pm.*

Ⓜ Best ☻ → **Bonanza** ★ SPANISH Don't go posting this restaurant/pension on your blog—so far it's been fairly easy to get a seat due to the uphill tramp to get there. The prices are unbeatable, plus it's cute in that classic tiled-with-outdoor-seating way. But most importantly, the lip smackin' *fideua* is so good you don't mind having aioli (garlic and oil sauce) breath for the rest of the day. If you plan on looking for love later in the evening, just order something less pungent from the extensive menu. Either way, your stomach will be full and your wallet happy. *Plaça Doctor Robert 2.* ☎ *938-948-121. Entrees 6€–14€. Daily 1–4:30pm and 7–10:30pm.*

DOABLE

→**Beach House** INTERNATIONAL Neither decor nor presentation is comparable to the hot international Abercrombie boys that serve the Aussie/Asian–influenced comfort food. A few dishes that may distract you for a moment are the prawn and avocado crepes and the seafood risotto. A classic English or continental breakfast is worth crowding the roof terrace for, and if you need an excuse for ogling again you should return for the prix-fixe lunch or dinner menu. Dance music keeps the vibe going all through the incredibly sweet desserts. *Sant Pau 34.* ☎ *938-949-029. Prix-fixe dinner 20€. Daily 9am–1am. Closed Dec–Apr opening only for Carnaval.*

SPLURGE

→**Cal Pinxo** SEAFOOD As pretty as the presentation is, not all of us want to attempt ripping open a Mediterranean craw-daddy, so one of the nicest things about Cal Pinxo is you can order a *paella marinera* de-shelled, for the same price as a normal one. Believe me, I was skeptical, but the taste did not suffer one iota; in fact I think I enjoyed it more (or maybe the refreshing *sangria blanca* impaled my better judgment). If you can't squeeze onto the breezy outdoor patio don't worry, the nautical-themed interior is just as comfy. The *royale de passio* for dessert is pure bliss. *Passeig de la Rivera 5.* ☎ *938-948-637. Entrees 15€–65€. Daily 1–4pm and 8–11:30pm.*

Partying

Whether you're into moonlight or dark smoky rooms, Sitges has something up its sleeve for you. The scene here is predominantly gay, but the vibe is mostly welcoming to all. The big annual parties like the wicked **Carnaval** (p. 424) and the girls-only rave of all raves **Legend** at Atlantida (www.thelegendparty.com) get packed beyond compare; so plan ahead for these, it's worth it. If you can't make it, don't come undone—any summer night in Sitges you can still hit 10 times the party you'll find anywhere else on the Catalan coast.

BARS

→**Bar Xatet** This small cafe will transport you back to those days when Rusiñol and the young Picasso hung out in Sitges. Scan the walls for caricatures of all the celebs you studied in art history while you enjoy a vermouth in this homey establishment with more locals than the average pub. *Sant Francesc 1.* ☎ *938-474-471.*

→**Marypili** Really the only joint in town that is more female than male. The owners are as friendly as you can get, so everyone feels snug at this petite spot just off of the hectic Plaça Industria. Marypili's anniversary and the annual Legend party brings über-babes from far and wide to crowd the patio and spill out onto the street to enjoy a proper tea or a perfectly mixed drink. *Joan Tarrida 14. No phone. www.marypili.net.*

→**Pachito** Apparently nothing to do with Pachá, so why do they have those iconographic cherries on their wall? Anyway, of all the small and, let's face it, sort of tacky places on Primer de Maig, Pachito's DJs spin better music for the mixed crowd to sweat to—and when we say mixed, we include the 70-year-old grandpa shaking it to the Pussycat Dolls. *Carrer 1er de Maig 5. No phone.*

CATALUNYA

→ **Pub Voramar** This darkly ambient, nautical-themed watering hole built by a fisherman in the '50s (and still in the family) features Juanito, the silver-haired swashbuckler, who may just take a minute off from pouring drinks to jump up and join in as the band plays. Music is on the jazz/rock side, and if you're lucky you'll get a Bob Dylan type singing the Catalan blues (what do they have to be sorry for?). Sit outside for a sunset *picada* (snack tray) and a beer or a *coco-loco* (their special coconut and vodka cocktail) after a day at Platja San Sebastiá and soak in that Sitges vibe. *Puerto Alegre 55. No phone. www.sitges-pub-voramar.com.*

CLUBS

🎵 Best● → **L'Atlantida** The most fun you can have in Sitges is at the beach, and when you want to dance, why leave the beach? Three kilometers (2 miles) south from town is Sitges's major beach club, with outdoor dance floors plus a terrace, access to the private beach, and even fast food, in case all the dancing and swimming makes you hungry. A bunch of screens in the shape of sails show projections and give the space a nautical vibe. Tuesdays are gay nights and Thursdays host the infamous foam parties, which are not so messy when you can just go wash off at the beach. A free bus leaves from the Hotel Calipolis (Avda. Sofia 2-6) at the San Sebastian beach. *June–Sept. No phone. Cover varies with party.*

→ **Trailer** *The* place to end a very gay night in Sitges. This place is popular every day, but its Sunday foam parties are its most famous. But be aware that to get to the bathroom, you'll have to walk through the darkroom—so if you want to relieve your bladder, you may have to relieve somebody else first. *Angel Vidal 36. No phone. Cover 10€ with drink.*

Sightseeing

The Noucentistas, Romanticos, and Modernistas, among others, have all passed through Sitges, leaving their mark on the numerous galleries, museums, architecture, and culture. Tours of the most architecturally significant sites can be arranged through the tourist office. The museums are incredibly unique and you'd be a dweeb if you let yet another day at the beach or a vicious hangover stand in your way to visiting them. The **entrada combinada** 6.40€, is a great deal since you'll want to hit at least two of these museums; the pass is good for a month.

FESTIVALS & EVENTS

The ancient tradition of 🎵 Best● **Carnaval** that takes place in towns throughout Spain during the week before Lent (usually Mar or Apr), is at its most flamboyant in Sitges, which draws a wild, gay crowd from all over Europe. The celebration, where audacity is more valued than originality, features parades, floats, and all sorts of sexy costumes. But the real action takes place at the hundreds of parties going on nightly in clubs, restaurants, and bars. Leave your shyness at home and join the gay parade that closes the festivities—what happens in Sitges, stays in Sitges. February to March, throughout Sitges (www.sitges.com/carnaval).

At the opposite extreme of the spectrum from Carnaval is Sitges's big cultural event, **Festival Internacional de Cinema de Catalunya,** a film festival focusing on fantasy that includes over 200 new short films, full features, animation, documentaries, and some outstanding retrospectives. You won't find big blockbusters here, but rather indie films from all over the world. Over 100,000 cinephiles join the fun, which converts this 20,000-inhabitant town into a Spanish Cannes. Various venues around town. Second week of October (www.cinemasitges.com).

MUSEUMS

MTV **Best** ◎ → **Museu Cau Ferrat** ★★ Artist and writer Santiago Rusiñol was a tour de force behind the modernista movement, and his estate, Cau Ferrat (den of iron), once two simple 16th-century fishing houses, was transformed into a studio and collaboration space for Catalonia's bohemians. The first floor demonstrates Rusiñols collection of antique ceramics and glass, some of which he dug out himself. The walls are filled with his captivating paintings and those of his idols and contemporaries such as El Greco, Casas, and Picasso. The second floor's elaborately carved ceilings, Gothic arches, stained glass, religious art, and oil paintings provide a backdrop for the craziest collection of wrought-iron and glass pieces you could possibly imagine. Rusiñol's curatorial hand and use of these everyday objects as sculpture is what sets them apart. *Fonollar s/n.* ☎ *938-940-364. Admission 3.50€. Summer Tues–Sat 9:30am–2:30pm and 4–7pm, Sun 10am–3pm; winter Tues–Sat 9:30am–2pm and 3:30–6:30pm, Sun 10am–3pm.*

→ **Museu Maricel** The former residences of North American millionaire Charles Deering and the painter Ramon Casas were combined to form the Museu Maricel. Its collections range from 15th-century wooden altar pieces to 20th-century art and collections from the likes of Roig, whose marine-related paraphernalia, models, and drawings somehow coordinate with the period furniture and modernista works. Though it's completely prohibited, people are constantly getting reprimanded for taking pictures on the first floor, where the sea behind the arched windows creates a dramatic blue contrast to the white marble

sculptures set before it. **Palau Maricel,** across the street, is also dazzling, but it's only open to the public for a few days each summer when for 10€ you can take a tour and enjoy a concert on its rooftop garden. Call Museu Maricel for reservations and times. *Fonollar s/n.* ☎ *938-940-364. Admission 3.50€. Tues–Sat 9:30am–2pm and 4–6pm; Sun 9:30am–2pm.*

→ **Museu Romantic Can Llopis** Get here any hour on the hour and you can take part in a guided tour of toy dolls that would give even Chucky goose bumps. This is not only Europe's largest collection of antique dolls, but a fascinating step back in time to see how the upper class of Sitges sashayed. *Sant Gaudenci s/n.* ☎ *938-940-364. Admission 3.50€. Entrance permitted by guided tour only every hour on the hour Tues–Sat 9:30am–2pm and 4–7pm; Sun 10am–3pm.*

Playing Outside

Sitges has nine golden **beaches** surrounded by breakwater walls and a promenade filled with restaurants and bars stretching alongside of it. You can rent lounge chairs and umbrellas at any of these beaches, but the prices vary, so ask around. The most family/mixed beaches are the Platja de Sant Sebastiá and the mostly covered with boats, la Fragata. Platja la Ribera starts to get more of a party vibe, and by the time you hit Platja de la Bassa Rodona it's late-night cruising and grinding. But you'll have to make the 3km (2-mile, 45-min.) hike (or take a taxi) if you want to hit the nude beaches. Follow the boulevard to l'Atlantida and walk uphill, parallel to the railroad tracks. Beyond a few hills, the two small coves will be on your left-hand side. The first, although mostly gay, may actually have a few women, while the second is officially a gay nude beach, with a cruising area across the railroad tracks in the woods.

CATALUNYA

Valencia

by *Fernando Gayesky*

Valencia is one of the most visited areas in Spain, mainly due to the long, wide beaches of the Costa Blanca. But, unfortunately, like Drew Barrymore, these beaches grew up too fast. The '70s concrete building frenzy hit paradisiacal towns like Benidorm and Alicante like a cinder block, creating an urban landscape of cement boxes fronting blue waters. But now that cheap, impersonal vacation packages are slowly going the way of the dinosaur, these towns are investing in alternatives for the more selective visitor, such as extreme sports and designer restaurants. The tiny town of Benidorm turns into a tourist megalopolis every summer, which means fighting for a spot at the beach, but also a bursting party scene at the level of the big cities. Alicante, the capital of the Costa Blanca, offers a beautiful *barrio viejo* (old town), trademark beaches, and a whole neighborhood devoted to bars and clubs that jump every day of the week thanks to the tireless locals and wide-eyed foreign exchange students. Elche is a small inland jewel, with half the town's surface covered with palm trees and some of the best restaurants in the area. And then, of course, there's Valencia. Spain's third biggest city and probably the most under-visited has been slowly undergoing a transformation that's turning it into a main tourist destination. From the magnificent architectural achievement of the Ciudad de las Artes y de las Ciencias, to the newly posh America's Cup Port and back to the always happening historic quarter of El Carmen, Valencia is adding to its well-earned status as a party capital of Spain (with Las Fallas and the Ruta del Bacalao as its streamer) a much-needed international influence and modernity injection.

Whether this flooding of new people and ideas will in the long term work against its authenticity or not, right now is a time of change, and if you can catch it and take a piece of it back home, your journey will have been worth it.

The Best of Valencia

○ **Best Museum/Aquarium/Concert Hall/IMAX Theater:** The **Ciudad de las Artes y de las Ciencias** in Valencia is not only all that, but also an amazing achievement of modern architecture. See p. 441.

○ **Best Party to Light Your Fire:** Valencia's **Fallas** is the biggest town party in Spain, maybe the world, and after 4 days of nonstop drinking and celebrating, not only the floats will be burnt. See p. 441.

○ **Best Hostel for Couples:** At **Hôme Deluxe** Valencia, you can get your own twin room with a theme and depending on who you share it with it could be "Insomnia" or "Sexy Love." See p. 434.

○ **Best Paella:** Paella is from Valencia, and if with experience comes perfection **L'Estimat,** in Valencia has been dishing out superb versions of rice with saffron since 1927, so they know what they're doing. See p. 437.

○ **Best Neighborhood to Escape the Tourist Frenzy: Barrio Santa Cruz** in Alicante is one of the prettiest in Spain, in a city where tourists go straight from the beach to the bar and back. See p. 445.

○ **Best Tropical Hotel outside of the Tropics: Hotel Huerto del Cura** in Elche features luxury bungalows in the midst of Europe's biggest palm grove. See p. 450.

○ **Best Train Ride:** The **trenet** that connects Alicante, Benidorm, and Denia through sea and mountains gives a whole new meaning to public transportation, and is arguably the best way of knowing the Costa Blanca for no money. See p. 448.

Valencia ★★

Despite being the third biggest city in Spain, the place that claims possession of the Holy Grail has historically been largely overlooked by visitors. Since you can walk around the old town without dodging maps and giant backpacks at every other step, Spanish people come for a weekend of wild partying or relaxing at the beach. During the late '80s and '90s, a phenomenon called the Ruta del Bakalao attracted clubbers from all over Spain who would arrive on Thursday nights and start a route of nonstop parties lasting until Monday morning. And, today, March's Fallas is a primal celebration involving fire, explosions, dancing, and drinking for (here we go again) 4 straight days.

The city beaches, although very crowded and hot in the summer, are wider with finer sand than those in Barcelona, and feature cute '30s/'40s beach-town, two-story hotels, and houses. In the last couple of years Valencia has been undergoing a "Swan"-worthy makeover commanded by its prodigal son, Santiago Calatrava, a superstar architect. The mega endeavor called Ciudad de las Artes y de las Ciencias is the crest of a wave of renovation that is turning this into a cosmopolitan and stylish city. New design hotels and restaurants pop up every week and the food map is being enriched by everything from Mexican and Italian to Thai and Japanese. As if this isn't enough, the town was chosen to host the

Talk of the Town

Five Ways to Start a Conversation with a Local

1. It's very rare that you will hear a local speaking **Valenciano** (the local dialect of Catalan), so if you do, ask them why Valencians are less apt to embrace the mother tongue than their counterparts in Barcelona.

2. **Fallas, Fallas, Fallas.** Valencians have more stories about their fiesta major than a group of potheads reminiscing over their trip to Amsterdam.

3. The clean-up campaign of the city for the **32nd America's Cup** has not gone without controversy and criticism. Ask a local what they think of the planned destruction of the 1930s buildings lining the public beaches of Malvarrosa and the rapid gentrification of Barrio del Carmen.

4. Just what is an *Agua de Valencia?* We have been told it's champagne, gin, and orange juice, but you'll have more fun finding out for yourself.

5. Even if you have found yourself exhausted by trying to start conversations related to **football**, no one is going to get bored talking to you about it, so listen and learn about the guts and glory of Valencia's home team, aptly named Valencia CF.

2007 America's Cup, the oldest and maybe chicest sporting event in the world, turning the port area into a posh complex of seaside lounges and hangouts. Valencia is considered by many to be *the* place du jour in Spain—it's still a diamond in the rough, but hurry! Word is out and everybody and their mother are pulling out their hammer and pick.

Getting There

BY AIR

The airlines operating most flights to Valencia are **Iberia** (☎ 902-400-500; www.iberia.es) and **Air Europa** (☎ 902-401-501; www.aireuropa.com) with many daily departures to Madrid, Barcelona, Palma de Mallorca, and Sevilla. If you want to travel from/to outside Spain, an array of low-cost airlines, including **Ryan Air** (☎ 807-220-220; www.ryanair.com), **EasyJet** (☎ 902-299-992; www.easyjet.com), and **Vueling** (☎ 902-333-933; www.vueling.com) have daily flights to London, Paris, Rome, and Brussels. The airport, **Aeropuerto de Manises,** is located 8km

(5 miles) west of the city. A taxicab from the airport to the center of town will cost about 14€ plus a supplement of 2.75€. The **Aerobus** connects the airport and the center directly every 20 minutes from 6am to 10pm and costs 2.50€. The regular bus line no. 150 (Metrobus; ☎ 963-160-707) takes the local tour (45 min.), costs 1.05€, and leaves every 10 minutes from 5:25am to 11:55pm. You can also walk 3 blocks and take the train into **Estación del Norte.** One runs every 20 minutes and for 1.15€ it'll get you to the center in 20 minutes.

BY TRAIN

Valencia's **Estación del Norte** (Jativa 2; ☎ 902-240-202) is very conveniently located near the center of town. Up to 10 Alaris, high-speed trains, depart daily to Madrid (trip time: 3¹/₂ hr.), eight trains to Barcelona (trip time: 3¹/₂–5 hr., depending on the train), and another eight south to Alicante (trip time: 1¹/₂–2 hr.).

BY CAR

From Barcelona, take the A-7 highway south to Valencia. From Alicante, the A-7

VALENCIA

Valencia & Beyond

north, from Madrid, arrive via the A-3 in direction east, and if you are coming from the southwest your best bet is the N-430.

BY BUS

The **bus station** in Valencia is on the northwestern side of town about a 20-minute walk from Barrio Carmen. Bus no. 8 connects it with the Plaza del Ayuntamiento. There are about 10 daily buses to Barcelona (**Alsa;** ☎ 902-422-242; trip time: 4½ hr.), Madrid (**AutoRes;** ☎ 902-020-999; trip time: 4 hr.), and Alicante (trip time: 2½ hr.).

BY BOAT

Ferries to and from the Balearic Islands leave from the **Muelle de Poniente** (☎ 963-164-859). **Trasmediterranea** (☎ 902-454-645) operates daily ferries to Palma and four weekly to Ibiza during the summer months. **Balearia** (☎ 902-160-180; www.balearia.com) has daily services to Ibiza and Palma, fewer in winter.

Getting Around
BY TAXI

Taxi stops are available at the airport, train station, and bus station. Otherwise, call **Radio Taxi Manises** (☎ 961-521-155), **Radio Taxi Valencia** (☎ 963-703-333), or **Teletaxi** (☎ 963-571-313).

BY BUS OR BY SUBWAY

EMT buses (☎ 963-158-515; www.emt valencia.es) cover the whole city in a network that is fairly easy to figure out. Grab a map at the tourist office or check out the maps on every bus stop. Buses run from 6am to 11pm, with night buses covering some of the routes until 1:40am during the week and 3am on Fridays, Saturdays, and holiday eves. A single ticket costs 1.10€; buy it on the bus, or get a 10-ride ticket for 5€ at kiosks and tobacco stores.

Other than taking the high-speed tram from the university district to the beach, you probably won't be using the **Metro** (☎ 900-461-046; www.metrovalencia. com), because there are no stops in the old city. The most central metro stop is at the train station, and you can transfer at Benimaclet to the beach-bound speedster. A single ticket is 1.20€ and the 10-ride pass is 5.60€.

BY CAR

Driving in Valencia can be just as stressful as in any other European city, but street parking is a definite nerve-wracking experience. All the major car-hire agencies have offices in the airport. Some local cheaper options are **Pepecar** (Paseo Alameda 34; ☎ 807-212-121; www.pepecar. com) and **Autos Golden** (Paseo Alameda 36; ☎ 963-374-480; www.autogolden.com).

BY BICYCLE OR BY FOOT

The old town in Valencia is perfectly walkable, there's no metro service, and the buses in the center are slower than Jack Johnson at 16RPM—so walking is probably your best bet. Going from the center to the beach

---

¡Cuidado! Safe Treks

Ever notice how all the old quarters of major cities can turn all Courtney Love on ya, going from grunge to glamour-puss and back to a state of no return in just a few blocks? Well like Barcelona's Barri Gotic the growing pains of Valencia's old city have left a few stranglers wondering how they got replaced by the likes of you. We were approached by old pervs on bikes on a quiet Sunday afternoon in the middle of the old town. Although a simple flip of the bird usually does the trick (that is if you don't want to hang with the local gentry), if you are a chick alone at night or carrying valuables you may not want to get sloshed and walk alone down a dark alley.

Valencia

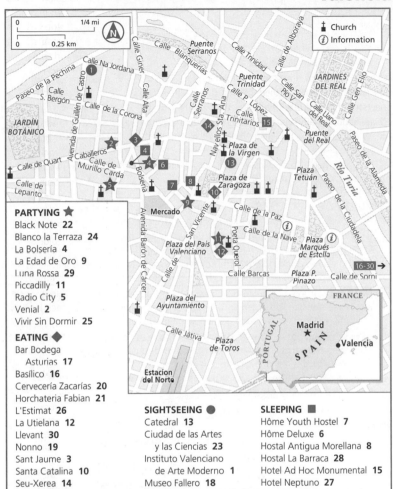

PARTYING ★
Black Note **22**
Blanco la Terraza **24**
La Bolsería **4**
La Edad de Oro **9**
Luna Rossa **29**
Piccadilly **11**
Radio City **5**
Venial **2**
Vivir Sin Dormir **25**

EATING ◆
Bar Bodega
  Asturias **17**
Basílico **16**
Cervecería Zacarías **20**
Horchatería Fabian **21**
L'Estimat **26**
La Utielana **12**
Llevant **30**
Nonno **19**
Sant Jaume **3**
Santa Catalina **10**
Seu-Xerea **14**

SIGHTSEEING ●
Catedral **13**
Ciudad de las Artes
  y las Ciencias **23**
Instituto Valenciano
  de Arte Moderno **1**
Museo Fallero **18**

SLEEPING ■
Hôme Youth Hostel **7**
Hôme Deluxe **6**
Hostal Antigua Morellana **8**
Hostal La Barraca **28**
Hotel Ad Hoc Monumental **15**
Hotel Neptuno **27**

will take about 20 minutes and the Ciudad de las Artes y de las Ciencias is a 10-minute walk away.

Valencia's flatness and size is ideal for bicycles, which rent very cheaply, so it can be worth it to get one if you are here for a few days. **Do You Bike** (Pza. Horno de San Nicolás s/n; ☎ **963-155-551;** www.doyou bike.com; 1 day 7€, 1 week 25€; daily 10am–2pm and 5–8pm) has this location

in Barrio del Carmen, with another one at the port and in the Blasco Ibañez area. They rent bikes and organize tours. **Valencia Bikes** (Paseo de la Pechina 32; ☎ **963-851-740;** www.valenciabikes.com; 1 day 15€, 3 days 36€; Mon–Fri 9am–5pm) does mostly guided bike tours (22€ for a 3-hr. tour), which can be pretty interesting. They also rent guideless bikes, although at much higher prices than Do You Bike.

12 Hours in Valencia

1. Walk over one of the pictorial bridges and gander down at the once dried **Rio Turia,** now turned verdant park; a 50-year-in-progress testament to Mother Nature and Valencian landscape design (p. 442).

2. Soak up the sun and the saffron at one of **Malvarrosa** beach restaurants specializing in **paella** (see "Eating," p. 436) and then continue to feed the buzz at one of the beach clubs lining the boardwalk.

3. Swim with Valencians at the **El Salers** pristine beach, then stay to toast with them and gobble down a lip smacking catch of the day at **Leo's** chiringuito.

4. Get your geek on at Europe's largest Aquarium, Museum of Science, IMAX, or the Opera House (all at once may put you over that 12-hr. limit) at the **Ciudad de las Artes y de las Ciencias** (p. 441).

5. Watch on a giant TV or from one of the tour boats as world-class sailors winch and come-about on million-dollar yachts sponsored by major fashion labels. Then hit the decks with internationally buff mates at one of the many **America's Cup Port** restaurants, bars, and clubs (p. 443).

6. Climb the 47m-high (155-ft.) gothic tower known as **Miguelete** and feast your eyes as far as farms beyond the city itself.

7. Don't miss one of the **IVAM** outposts. **IVAM Julio Gonzalez** if you want to see some familiar 20th-century masterpieces or **Centre del Carme** where upcoming Iberian artists take center stage (p. 442).

8. After browsing around the multitude of shops in the quintessentially Spanish bohemian Barrio del Carmen (lovingly referred to as just **El Carme;** p. 442) stop for an **Agua de Valencia** in one of it's hypnotizing bars or cafes and dive right into *La Movida,* but be careful—there aren't any lifeguards to drag you out of these waters (p. 438).

Valencia Basics

The former river Turia, now turned into a series of parks and green areas with a bike path, goes from the Mislata Park to the port, dividing the town into a northern and southern half. In the northern area you'll find the **bus station,** the **Fine Arts Museum,** and the **university campus.** The juicier area of town is the southern half. Directly across the riverbed from the bus station is the old city, which is bordered by the Turia in the north and the streets Guillem De Castro, Xativa, Colon, and General Palanca to the west, south, and east. In the northwestern corner of the old town lies the **Barrio del Carmen,** the oldest part of town with **IVAM** and the windy streets that you will probably stumble on at night. At the southeastern end of Carmen is the **Plaza de la Virgen,** home of the **Cathedral,** which stretches south to the **Plaza de la Reina.** Continuing south through the "axis of squares" that divides the old town, you'll get to the **Plaza del Ayuntamiento,** the center of town, from where Avenida Sotelo goes straight in to the **train station** and the **Plaza de Toros;** going southeast on the riverbed you'll get to the **Ciudad de las Artes y de las Ciencias** complex and then, toward the coast is the **Port America's Cup** and **Malvarrosa Beach,** another big area of day and night entertainment.

Culture Tips 101

You may notice that some street signs and names are not quite in Spanish. What you are actually reading is **Valenciá,** a version of Catalan spoken in this province. However, before you run to the store to get yet another dictionary, you should know that unlike in Catalunya, people here don't like to speak Valenciá so much. Spoken in the small towns inland, it's not considered very fashionable to speak despite the government's efforts to bring back the heritage. More so, with the affluence of foreign students on exchange programs, the America's Cup crews and their minions, and businessmen in general, English is more widely spoken than in many other Spanish cities.

The **cops** in Valencia follow the same guidelines as they do in most Spanish cities, if you don't bother anybody, they won't bother you (and yes, singing The Pussycat Dolls at the top of your lungs on a small street at 5am falls under that category). If anything, they are a little more relaxed than in Barcelona, although the new mayor has been inspired by Giuliani's New York style of nightlife destruction that seems to be so popular these days. As a consequence, bars have to pull their tables off the streets early and beach parties are not what they used to be, but you can still see the blond dreadlocks on bikes doing business and the long lines at clubs' restrooms.

The **tourist information office** is at Calle Paz 48 (☎ 963-986-422; www.comunidad-valenciana.com, available in English). It's open Monday to Friday 9am to 12:30pm and 4:30 to 8pm. Additional offices are at the airport, train station, and by the America's Cup Port.

RECOMMENDED WEBSITES & MAGAZINES

www.aboutvalencia.com is an English website with everything from apartment rentals, weather, and festivals to bars and clubs. The detailed **www.barriodelcarmen.net** is a valuable guide (in Spanish) to the coolest neighborhood in town. If nothing else, you can always depend on the local chapter of the Guia del Ocio, **www.guiadelocio.com/Valenica,** but this one is only available in Spanish.

A surprising number of English publications abound, starting with the all-encompassing booklet you can get at the tourist office. For the most detailed information on restaurants, bars, culture, and even shopping, get a copy of *Hello Valencia,* a bilingual 200-page manual to the city. It sells at newsstands for 2.40€, but you can get it for free at some bars. *24/7 Valencia* is a monthly mag written by and for English speaking ex-pats, with some interesting articles, short stories, and art, nightlife, and restaurant listings. You can get it in over 100 different places, including Irish pubs and other bars. The trendy *coolcarmen* is one of those map/guides for the neighborhood in Spanish and English—also free and at stores and available at bars in El Carmen.

Valencia Nuts & Bolts

Currency The area around the Plaza del Ayuntamiento is plagued with **ATMs** and the occasional **exchange booth.** As always, prefer the prior.

Health & Emergency Emergencies: **112**. If you can walk, go to **Hospital Clínico Universitario,** Av. Blasco Ibáñez 17 (☎ **963-862-600**). **Crisis Centers: Drug abuse helpline** ☎ **900-161-515; Women's center** ☎ **900-580-888.**

Internet There are Internet cafes and hot spots everywhere. As usual the cheapest are the *locutorios:* **Workcenter** (Xativa 19; ☎ **961-120-830;** 2€ per hour; open 24/7) is a Kinko's-style office away from home store. Tons of computers and everything you need to turn those blurry butt pictures into a beautiful anatomy diorama. **Interlinks** (Pie de la Cruz 16; ☎ **963-922-500;** 1€–1.50€ per hour; daily 10pm–midnight) is a typical *locutorio* (phone parlor) with 15 PCs with cameras and also phones, in case seeing and reading is not enough.

Laundry Do your duds at **Lavandería El Mercat** (Plaza del Mercado 12; ☎ **963-912-010;** Mon–Fri 10am–2pm and 5–9pm, Sat 10am–3pm), a self-service laundromat with coin-operated machines.

Pharmacies Condoms, suntan lotion, baby oil, and other party supplies can be found in those stores with the green cross. **Farmacia Pons Torres** (Pl. Ayuntamiento 16; ☎ **963-524-583**) is open Monday to Saturday 9am to 10pm.

Telephone City code: **963;** operator: **1003;** international operator: **1005.**

Sleeping

The biggest concentration of hotels and hostels in Valencia is in the old town, but our favorites are the small *hostales* by the beach, in the Balneario Las Arenas, where, for a decent rate you can get a room with a balcony overlooking the beach. The rates are usually the same throughout the year; high season is only for special events, like Fallas or trade shows. Valencia is also home to some of the best-rated youth hostels in Europe.

HOSTEL

➜ **Hôme Youth Hostel** From the get-go you will feel at home in this old house turned youth hostel. The rooms are ample with original tiled floors, and an interior patio provides for windows whether you're facing the street or not. The common areas feature big sofas, a decent sort of '50s diner decor kitchen, a roof terrace, and spanking clean bathrooms. When we were asking questions to the very friendly staff a fellow *guiri* (foreigner) approached us and exclaimed, "I've stayed in three other youth hostels in Valencia, this one is by far the best!" So take her word for it. If you are in need of an even cheaper option, albeit more bare bones and crowded, Hôme also has the Backpackers. For info about all of the fine Hôme establishments check their website. *La Lonja 4.* ☎ *963-916-229. www.likeathome.net. Single 22€, double 21€, triple 19€, dorm 17€. Amenities: Bike rental, breakfast room, free small lockers and luggage storage, Internet, kitchen, laundry (or laundry service), roof terrace, shared bathrooms, sheets, telephone, travel info, TV (huge selection of DVDs). Bus: 7, 27, 28.*

CHEAP

MTV **Best** ➜ **Hôme Deluxe** ★ This youth hostel, the nicest and most expensive in the Hôme family, is a backpackers gone Rockefeller. Winner of every possible hostel award, it is located on the second floor of a beautiful old building. Each of the 10 private rooms has a king- or queen-size bed and a balcony and is decorated with a different theme by a different designer, known by such enticing names as

And for Everything Else There's . . .

. . . the **Valencia Tourist Card;** it's is the deal of the century. Seriously, for 6€ to 15€ you can get a 24-, 48-, or 72-hour card that gets you free transportation on the zone A metro, tranvia, and bus, plus big discounts on a huge selection of museums, historical sites, stores, entertainment, bike rentals, Internet cafes, and restaurants to name a few. You can purchase them online at www.europeancitycards.com and www.etmvalencia.es or call ☎ **900-701-818,** but it's just as easy to pick one up at any tourist office, hostel, or kiosk around the city.

Insomnia, Sexy Love, Hotel California, and Safari. There are two full bathrooms and three toilets, a fully equipped guest kitchen, and two lounge areas, one of them with a TV and DVD player. In all, the Deluxe feels like a big apartment that you share with other like-minded travelers, and the staff is as chill and helpful as you could expect from a friend whose pad you crash at, pointing you to the best restaurants and most fun places in town. *Cadirers 11.* ☎ *963-914-691. www.likeathome.net. 22€ per person, breakfast included. Amenities: Bike rental, breakfast room, complimentary coffee, fax, Internet, kitchen, laundry service, shared bathrooms, sheets, telephone, towels, travel info, TV. Bus: 5, 81.*

→ **Hostal Antigua Morellana** Located right in the center of the historical district, this fully renovated hotel in an 18th-century house offers excellent value. The rooms are very bright and clean with new mattresses, although the decor is a little sterile with a mix of vintage furniture and Martha Stewart—esque bed covers and curtains. Some have balconies overlooking the street and a comfortable lobby is crammed with big sofas and a coffee machine. Ninety percent of the people staying here are foreigners of varied ages, so you can always find someone to climb up the *Miguelete* tower with you. *En Bou 2.* ☎ *963-915-773. www.hostalam.com. Single 38€–48€, double 48€–58€. Amenities: Elevator, fax, laundry service, TV, wheelchair friendly. In room: A/C, TV. Bus: 7, 27, 28, 81.*

📺 Best ♥ → **Hostal La Barraca** We love this classic '60s beach town family hotel because of its location and simplicity. The reception walls are tiled in blue and white and the restaurant is a perfect place to dine or drink staring at the sea. The rooms are very simply decorated with small but full bathrooms, white walls, and new pinewood beds. The key here is to get one of the bigger rooms with balconies facing the beach. They cost a little more money but can fit three or four people and the views are well worth it. On top of that, for all of you late bloomers, breakfast is served all day. *Paseo De Neptuno 36.* ☎ *963-716-200. Double 55€, triple to the sea 100€. Amenities: Restaurant, bar, elevator, fax, Internet, laundry service. In room: A/C, TV. Bus: 19, 20, 21, 22, 23.*

DOABLE

📺 Best ♥ → **Hotel Ad Hoc Monumental** ★★ Whoever it was that complained about the lack of sophistication in Valencia never visited this tastefully restored house, dating from 1881. The renovation was conducted with great respect for the original details; some rooms have brick walls, others high vaulted ceilings, mosaic floors, and exquisite new fabrics that blend with the old better than vodka and tonic. The bathrooms are completely new with black and white tiles and full bathtub and shower. Although definitely not a party hotel, you'll feel like you're living large without spending a fortune. The location is also hard to beat, right next to the old riverbed and close to the cathedral and the Palacio del Temple. *Boix 4.* ☎ *963-919-140. Double 122€–175€. Amenities: Restaurant, laundry service, nonsmoking rooms, room service. In room: A/C, TV, hair dryer, safe. Bus: 8, 11, 16, 28, 29, 36, 80.*

SPLURGE

➔ **Hotel Neptuno** ★ If you want to do rock-star living Valencia style, check out this beachfront hotel right across the street from the America's Cup Port. Enter the bright marble and dark wood lobby, take the glass elevator with a view of a water-wall and interior garden to your bright and spacious room, furnished with modern, minimalist furniture, and equipped with everything you may need: a reading room with computers, a modern gym with sauna, steam bath, and mini squash court, a bar, and a luxurious roof deck with Jacuzzi. All bathrooms have fancy fixtures, Etro Milan bath products, and hydro-massage tubs. The service is impeccable and having the buffet-style breakfast on the beach terrace sure beats your company's cafeteria. *Paseo de Neptuno 2.* ☎ *963-567-777. www.hotelneptunovalencia. com. Single 128€–190€, double 141€–232€. Amenities: Restaurant/bar, breakfast room, elevator, fax, Internet, laundry service, telephone, travel info, wheelchair friendly. In room: A/C, TV, ADSL, fridge, hair dryer, safe. Bus: 19, 20, 21, 22, 23.*

Eating

Valencia is located in one of the most fertile areas of Spain and it's always been famous for its produce. Birthplace of *horchata* (see box p. 438) and *paella,* it lacked until not too long ago many options besides that. But the city's architectural and financial revival has also brought a whole new array of creative Spanish cuisine restaurants and a variety of ethnic food joints, catering to the global connoisseur's, such as yourself, every whim.

HOT SPOTS

➔ **Basílico** ★ PAN-ASIAN The chefs/owners of this corner bistro with the requisite brushed metal seats and colorful tables have traveled around the world and brought influences from everywhere to their menu. Being the only sort-of-Thai restaurant in town and your best (and for now only) bet for Sunday brunch, its few tables are always packed with foreign expats and worldly locals. Try the Thai prawn stir-fry, Vietnamese beef rolls, and Middle Eastern yogurt-glazed lamb. The menu varies seasonally but the produce always comes straight from the nearby market, making it a safe bet at any time. *Cádiz 42.* ☎ *963-168-369. Entrees: 11€–14€. Tues–Sat 1–11:30pm; Sun 11am–11:30pm. Bus: 7, 8.*

[MTV] Best ☻ ➔ **Nonno** ★ INTERNATIONAL You will have to be looking at the street numbers to find this dark-storefront restaurant that has turned into a cult place for Valencia's young and clever. The walls are graced with huge pop art paintings that match the minimalist decor of the dining room where locals and foreigners who know their way around pack the tables on a nightly basis. The menu is simple but creative, with such listings as *spaghettini con salmón a la siesta* and guacamole wraps and fish brochette with avocado sauce, but the favorite dish here is the hamburger with mustard sauce. And don't forget to order dessert, the *mousse blandita de chocolate,* which will forever change your notions of cocoa. *Ciscar 56.* ☎ *963-250-949. Entrees: 7.50€–13€. Mon–Fri 12:30–4pm and 8:15pm–midnight; Sat–Sun 8:15pm–midnight. Bus: 13.*

TAPAS

➔ **Bar Bodega Asturias** In a good example of Valencia's culinary transformation, this simple, no-frills tapas bar serves all of your classics plus some. The original Asturian owner is no longer there, but the new Uruguayan ones kept the quality of the original recipes and added their own influences; so now next to the classic potatoes with garlic and *esgarraet* (pepper with cod) you can also have *mollejas a la parrilla* (sweetbreads). *Doctor Sumsi 2.* ☎ *963-331-155. Tapas: 1.50€–10€. Mon–Sat 8am–11:30pm. Bus: 14, 15, 19, 40.*

➜ **Cervecería Zacarías** ✶ Ignore the bright fluorescents, modern decor, and dubious watercolor paintings—you've come here to eat. Try to get a table outside and enjoy some of the most delicious tapas Valencia has to offer among packs of locals who know where it's at. Everything coming from the sea (squid, baby squids in their ink, mussels) is fresh and yummlicious and if you can get a hold of the sassy waiters, make sure you get a bottle of house wine to wash it down right. *Císcar 16.* ☎ *963-950-297. Tapas: 3€–12€. Mon–Sat 8am–midnight. Bus: 13.*

CHEAP

➜ **La Utielana** VALENCIAN   To get to this hidden worker's restaurant you'll have to find the Plaza Picadero de Dos Aguas, right behind the Astoria Palace Hotel. Once there, take the little street that starts at no. 4 and you'll see the ornate entrance of this simple family eatery with typical Valencian blue and white tiles that's been serving dirt-cheap hearty tapas and menus since 1959. Enjoy daily fresh fish dishes and thick soups that would make a Valencian grandma proud. Finish lunch like every other Spanish worker, with a *carajillo* (coffee with cognac). *Plaza Picadero de Dos Aguas 3; San Andres 4.* ☎ *963-529-414. Entrees: 4€–8€. Mon–Fri 1:15–4pm and 9–11pm; Sat 1:15–4pm. Bus: 9, 10, 27, 70, 71.*

DOABLE

📺 Best 🙂 ➜ **L'Estimat** ✶✶ VALENCIAN It doesn't get more classic than this seaside

restaurant founded in 1927. If you enter through the back you'll see the fish tanks with live lobsters and other delicacies of the deep blue. Sit in the main dining area, decorated with classic Valencian tiles, photographs, and oil paintings depicting Mediterranean life, or on the outdoor terrace, inches away from the sand. Of course you'll want to try the paella here, but the *arroz a banda* (rice cooked in fish stew), and *arroz con bogavante* (lobster), are equally mouthwatering. The dessert menu is as extensive as the sea is deep, and the combination menus, while a little expensive, will fill you up for 2 days. *Av. Neptuno 16.* ☎ *963-727-385. Entrees: 9€–24€. Wed–Sat 1–4pm and 9–11pm; Sun–Mon 1–4pm. Bus: 19, 20, 21, 22, 23.*

➜ **Llevant** VALENCIAN   Llevant provides both the cool sea breeze and a phat paella, whether it be a traditional Valenciana (chicken, rabbit, and vegetables), a *marisco* (shellfish), or mixed (with all sorts of things, including snails and sausages). Service is slow, so you'll be tempted to pick on the *tallarinas* (cockles) or toss down a few cold ones, but don't fill up, the wood-oven slow-cooked paella is massive. Reserve in advance or you'll wait even longer. *The last restaurant on Playa Patacona, Malvarrosa.* ☎ *963-564-485. Entrees: 8€–22€. Tues–Sun 9:30am–11pm. Bus: 19, 20, 21, 22, 23.*

SPLURGE

➜ **Seu-Xerea** MARKET   One of those successful mash-ups of Mediterranean and Asian cuisine, Seu-Xerea presents a myriad of combos such as local mussels with coconut milk, or fillet of red bream with rice flour tagliatelle and red pepper sauce, all presented with panache and excellent service. Try to avoid the modern, exposed-brick inside and get an outside table on the much more interesting side street in Barrio del Carmen. *Conde de Almodóvar 4.* ☎ *963-924-000. www.seuxerea.*

VALENCIA

You Say Horchata, I Say Orxata

Not to be confused with the Mexican rice drink, **Horchata de Chufa** is made from the chufa nut (or tiger nut), which, though it dates back to ancient Egypt, is now grown mainly in Valencia. Legend has it a young girl offered a glass of this smooth nutty beverage to the king of Catalunya and Aragon. After sucking it down, he asked her, *"Que es aixo?"* (What is this?) The girl replied, *"Es leche de chufa"* (It's chufa milk). An excited king replied, *"Aixo no es llet, aixo es or, xata!"* (This isn't milk, it's gold, honey). Hence . . . *orxata*, or in Spanish *horchata*.

Don't try it from those Slurpee-looking machines at bars—you want to get the real deal at a traditional *horchateria*. Horchaterias are a unique experience and may also specialize in ice cream, *turrón* (an almond-based sweet nougat), pastries, and other *golosinas* (sweets). This drink is most popular from May to October in Valencia and Catalunya. During Fallas (see "The Roof Is on Falla," p. 441), it's popular to imbibe your cholesterol-lowering *horchata* with artery-clogging but delectable *buñuelos* (fritters sprinkled with sugar). A sure-fire place to get a cold glass is **Santa Catalina** (Pl. Santa Catalina 6; ☎ **963-912-379;** www.horchateriasantacatalina.com), one of the classics. **Horchateria Fabian** (C. Ciscar 5; ☎ **963-349-317**) specializes in both *horchata* and *buñuelos*.

com. *Entrees: 14€–20€. Mon–Fri noon–3:30pm and 8:30–11pm; Sat 8:30–11pm. Bus: 4, 6, 8, 9, 11, 16, 28, 36.*

CAFES

➜ **Sant Jaume** ★ This cafe is like Salma Hayek, tiny and gorgeous. Even if caffeine makes you hyper and stupid you should go by to have a look at all the detail in the Art Deco wooden bar, walls, and ceilings. A bunch of tables outside in the plaza serve as the meeting point for the town's hipsters, who start with a *cortado* (espresso macchiato) and later move on to vermouth and other cocktails. *Caballeros 51. ☎ 963-912-401. Coffee from 2€. Daily noon–1:30am. Bus: 7, 81.*

Partying

Valencians like to party big time. Besides being host to one of the largest town parties in the world (see "The Roof Is on Falla," p. 441) they also forged in the '80s and '90s the every weekend, 3-day-partying phenomenon known as Ruta del Bakalao. The most traditional area for boozing it up is **Barrio El Carmen,** where bar after bar

line the streets and people just wander the streets with drinks in hand. In the summer, Carmen shares popularity with the beach. Bars can be found in Las Arenas, and the mega-chill lounges at the America's Cup Port offer something for the very hip; more clubs and pubs are located on Eugenia Viñes street, by the Metro stop of the same name. Around the Plaza Canovas is another boozy area, and a couple of bars hover by the university. Just choose where you want to start the night, and just let yourself go with the flow of *la movida.*

BARS

➜ **Blanco la Terraza** Wear what you want, you can't clash with the enormous white pleather sectional seats and the all-glass walls facing the port, at this made-for-the-America's-Cup lounge. Expect Café del Mar–style smooth beats from the DJ and micro-mini-goddesses on the arms of ascot-clad perma-tan yachtsmen from the crowd. You can pick on the *tapas frias* and sandwiches from their sister restaurant Mar de Bamboo and indulge in a pricey refreshment while you watch the sky turn all shades of orange over the bay. *No phone.* *Bus: 1, 2, 19, 20, 22.*

➜ **La Bolsería** ★ Another Carmen hot spot, La Bolsería features a long wooden bar with enough space for the young clientele to dance and a mezzanine with iron chairs and tables for a romantic drink. Wednesdays are soul music Erasmus nights, if you want to meet European students on their party semester. DJs keep things going from Wednesday to Saturday with a mix of everything from house to Spanish pop. If you are in need of cheap culture visit the art shows on Sunday nights or live international music shows on the small stage in the back on Tuesdays. *Bolsería 41.* ☎ *963-918-903. www.bolseriavalencia.com. Bus: 7, 81.*

➜ **La Edad de Oro** If you are from the States, this small Route 66 homage bar à la American music emporium will seem cliché and tacky, but it's hapnin' in Valencia. It may also be the only place where you are going to hear The Clash although it may be gut-wrenchingly mixed with K.C. and the Sunshine Band. The crowd is cool though, and drinks are fairly priced and poured well. We'd recommend a few hours here with an occasional break on the bench in the Plaza Collado outside. *Generoso Hernandez 1.* ☎ *963-924-724. Bus: 7, 27, 28, 81.*

📺 (**Best** 🅑) ➜ **Radio City** Every city has an enclave for alternative-minded youth. Radio City covers that niche in Valencia and covers it well. The front-bar area with semi-bright lights and lower music is perfect to chat up a love interest, but it's on the darker dance area in the back where the action takes place. Lots of locals and foreign exchange students heat up the floor every day of the week. Check out the live Flamenco on Tuesdays, or pick up a calendar and get informed about the theater, dance, and film festivals they hold during the week. *Santa Teresa 19.* ☎ *963-914-151. Bus: 7, 81.*

➜ **Vivir Sin Dormir** If you thought you wouldn't be able to practice your aim in Spain, think again. Vivir Sin Dormir has everything that makes your typical bar in Nebraska fun: pool tables, darts, DJs on weekends, and a big dance floor. But unlike at home, here you get a huge terrace and the beach for the price of admission. The patrons are a little older (meaning over 25), but it's a good place to start the night before moving on to the clubs at the end of the street. *Paseo de Neptuno 42.* ☎ *963-727-777. www.vivirsindormir.com. Bus: 19, 20, 21, 22, 23.*

LIVE MUSIC

Live music in Valencia can be a disappointing affair, a Spanish interpretation of American music. But with world music skyrocketing into the mainstream, your best bet is to find a band with some Latin flavor, that way, even if it is bad, you won't know any better. Most bars have live music nights (see above) but some have bands rockin' it almost every day.

➜ **Black Note** Right in the middle of the university district, this concert hall features DJs spinning funk on Fridays and Saturdays and live music the rest of the week. Bands play everything from acid jazz to electro bossa nova and blues. *Polo y Peyrolón 15.* ☎ *963-933-663. No cover. Metro: Aragón.*

Cuidado! Walk of Pain

Before you squeeze into those pinchy Gucci loafers or 4-inch stilettos, know that the taxi-to-reveler ratio in Valencia is about 1–50. You may be taking that *nitbus* or walking for a long time before a Mercedes with a meter rescues your Hush Puppies from the cruelty of dancing all night and wobbling home.

VALENCIA

MTV📺 Hanging Out

The **university district** in Valencia surrounds the Avenida Blasco de Ibañez and Avenida Los Naranjos. Two universities and about 20 colleges inhabit this neighborhood and students swarm the streets 9 months a year. The Plaza Xuquer is the epicenter of the neighborhood with lots of bars and live music venues. Practice your foreign languages with the many students that come to Valencia's university through Erasmus and other European student exchange programs. For more info contact the **Asociación Erasmus Valencia** (☎ **963-828-680;** www.esnvalencia.com).

CLUBS

➜**Luna Rossa** Few places in Valencia have as rich a history as this former thermal bath right by Malvarrosa beach. Opening as a club called Akuarela, it became the last stop in the infamous Ruta del Bakalao, where people in various states of destruction would arrive Monday mornings after partying the whole weekend nonstop. It later became a Latin club with a high level of cheesiness, and since 2006 it has reopened as Luna Rossa, the name of the Italian America's Cup team, which says a lot about the vibe they're goin' for. The setting is fantastic, the original building of the '40s public baths and a huge outdoor space with round drink huts like Tom Cruise's in *Cocktail. Eugenia Vinyes 152. No phone. Thurs–Sat midnight–7am. Cover varies with parties. Bus: N1A.*

➜**Piccadilly** Unleash your inner ho at this former *puticlub* (brothel) converted into a hip disco. All the details where kept so that as you walk in you feel like you are in the middle of a '70s porn flick: the red velvet, the mirrors, the seedy back room, even the bouncer looks like he just came from shooting with Linda Lovelace. Pick your favorite theme from their weekly program, electroclash and sexy on Wednesdays, university night Thursdays, international electro-funk and house on Fridays and Saturdays, and cheesy pop followed by electro on Sundays. *Embajador Vich (next to the Astoria Hotel). No phone. Wed–Sun midnight–7:30am. Cover none–12€ depending on the night. Bus: N2.*

➜**Venial** This gay club is a safe choice for a fun night in Valencia. The abundance of sweaty half-naked Governator look-a-likes doesn't discourage anybody from coming. The ambience is very welcoming and there are go-go dancers and transvestite shows for the enjoyment of people of all preferences. Thursdays are Latin nights, involving a lot of Spanish pop in the Shakira sense. Fridays and Saturdays are house nights, and Sundays are maybe the most hard-core days, with shows and electro heating up the dance floor. *Quart 26.* ☎ *963-917-356. www.venialvalencia.com. Daily 1–7am. Cover varies with parties. Bus: N4.*

Sightseeing

FREE ➜**Catedral** ★ Indiana Jones would have been ecstatic if he knew that all he had to do to get the Holy Grail was visit this cathedral's chapel. Besides the most famous wineglass in history, the cathedral presents an interesting mishmash of baroque, Romanesque, and Gothic architectural styles, and an impressive collection of paintings by Goya and Zurbarán. But the top of the line, literally, is scaling the MTV Best● **Miguelete** Gothic tower to get an unforgettable view of what the city looks like without you in it. On Thursdays, in the plaza you can also witness the 1000-year-old tradition of the **Tribunal de las Aguas,** where farmers discuss and solve

VALENCIA

The Roof Is on Falla

Everyone knows Spaniards can throw a party, but Valencians seem to have outsmoked the rest of their countrymen with the annual 🎵 Best ◗ **Fallas de San José** (www.fallas.com). Imagine combining the Macy's Day Parade with Burning Man and you have something like the Fallas. From March 1 to 19 the fireworks, concerts, bullfights, and other outdoor festivities begin and get successively louder and more elaborate after the 12th. Each neighborhood sponsors artisans who take up to a year to construct the paper, wood, and (less Al Gore–friendly) polystyrene, Disney-esque *fallas* (floatlike mammoth sculptures reaching up to 15m/50 ft. and costing up to 160,000€), which satirize politicians, current events, and celebrities. On March 16 the city starts to display the 350 or so *fallas* in 28 different spots around the center in a fierce competition for becoming best *falla* and *fallera* (beauty queen representing her barrio). **Fireworks** light the night skies over Paseo Alameda and smaller ones boom at 2pm daily at the Plaza de Ayuntamiento. Three-million-plus tourists and locals view and judge the *fallas* while chowing down at the **paella competitions** and the *casals* (food stalls) offering *buñols* (fried dough) and other festival delicacies, simultaneously reveling in alcohol and drug-induced frenzies. Although the fire department has the whole situation very much under control, it's still mayhem on March 19, *La Nit de Foc* (or Night of Fire), when, at midnight, *La Crema de Las Fallas* (the cremation of the *fallas*) begins at the Plaza de Ayuntamiento. The best *falla's ninot* (1.5m/5-ft. figurine) is chosen for the Hall of Fame in the **Museo Fallero** (p. 442), while, much to the thrill of the feverish festival-goers, the rest go up in flames.

their irrigation issues in Valenciano, which holds a way bigger historical than entertainment value. *Plaza de la Reina.* ☎ *963-918-127. Free admission to cathedral; to Miguelete 2€; to Museo de la Catedral 3€. Cathedral Mon–Sat 10am–6pm, Sun 2–6pm; Miguelete Mon–Fri 10am–12:30pm and 5:30–6:30pm, Sun 10am–1pm and 5–6:30pm; Museo de la Catedral Mon–Fri 10am–1pm and 4–7pm. Bus: 9, 27, 70, or 71.*

🎵 Best ◗ → **Ciudad de las Artes y de las Ciencias** ★★★ Valencia's version of a face-lift is this massive complex designed mostly by native wunderkind architect Santiago Calatrava. The fish-shaped trippy buildings come in a set of five: The **Palau de les Arts** is a concert hall à la Sidney's Opera House. **L'Umbracle** is a futuristic botanical garden. **L'Hemisferic** is maybe the world's coolest IMAX Theater, projecting documentaries, laser shows,

and planetarium-style action. The **Museu de les Ciencies** is an interactive science museum where children flip out and you may finally be able to understand what your 12th-grade physics teacher was talking about. Finally, **L'Oceanographic** is the biggest aquarium in Europe with a mind-blowing polar zone, a dolphinarium, and underwater tunnels where you can walk through colossal fish tanks swarming with sharks, giant eels, and other scary creatures without getting your briefs wet. *Av. Autopista del Saler 1, 3, 5, 7. ☎ 902-100-031. www.cac.es. Admission to L'Hemisferic: adults 7.50€, students 5.80€. Admission to L'Oceanografic: adults 22€, students 17€. Admission to Museo de las Ciencias Príncipe Felipe: adults 7.50€, students 5.80€. L'Hemisferic Mon–Fri 10am–2pm and 4–8pm; Sat–Sun 10am–2pm and 4–9pm. Museo de las Ciencias Príncipe Felipe and L'Oceanografic*

Mon–Fri and Sun 10am–6pm; Sat 10am–8pm. Bus: 19, 35, 40, or 95 to Centro Comercio de Saler.

📺 **Best ❂** →**Instituto Valenciano de Arte Moderno** ★★ Aimed at those people who say there's no cultural interest in Valencia, this modern art museum has become one of the most important in Spain, putting the Big V on the map of European art centers. Its shows include a permanent collection of Julio Gonzalez's paintings, drawings, and, most importantly, iron sculptures that will give you goose bumps, plus some remarkable temporary exhibitions of modern art. The main exhibits are in an ultramodern building that is itself worth the visit, and a secondary space is at the Centre del Carmen, a convent dating from the 14th century where ancient and modern art blend without a glitch. *Guillém Castro 118.* ☎ *963-863-000. Admission: 2€ adults, free for students. Both centers June–Sept Tues–Sun 10am–10pm; Oct–May Tues–Sun 10am–8pm. Bus: 5.*

→**Museo Fallero** The museum houses the fascinating prize-winning *ninots* from 1934 to present and other related artifacts, so even if you missed the pyrotechnics you can still marvel at what was salvaged. For more info, see "The Roof Is on Falla," p. 441.

Boɑrd Tɑlk

Valencia's board scene is not as big as Barcelona's, but you can still find some dudes doing their thing. The center of activities is undoubtedly the **Gulliver Skatepark,** in the riverbed park right under the Puente del Reino (Pont del Regne)—you'll recognize it because of the Brobdingnagian statue of Gulliver with slides for kids. Right next to it, Valencian cool cats try their ollies on the several ramps and slopes. Buses no. 15, 19, and 40 will drop you off nearby.

Plaza Monte Olivete 4. ☎ *963-525-478. Admission: 1€. Tues–Sat 9:15am–2pm and 5:30–9pm; Sun 9:15am–1:30pm.*

Playing Outside

The river that used to cross Valencia, Turia, flooded the city one last time in 1957. Its course was detoured south of the city leaving its dry bed unattended. Nowadays it has been turned into **Jardines del Turia** (www.culturia.com), a series of beautiful parks that compose the city's biggest green space where you can leave behind all that traffic and go everywhere on bike or on foot.

Playa de Malvarrosa and **Las Arenas,** with their wide swath of fine white sand, comprise the city's beach. The water used to be too polluted to swim in, and although it is a lot cleaner now, you may want to ask the lifeguard before jumping in. Buses no. 19, 21, 22, and 23 will do the trick.

If your goal is fewer people and cleaner water, head south 10km (6¼ miles) towards **Playa El Salér.** Take the **Autocares Herca** bus (☎ **963-491-250;** www.autocares herca.com) from the corner of Gran Via de las Germanias and Calle Sueca, Plaza Canovas, or across the street from the Ciudad de las Ciencias y las Artes. Buses run every hour from 7am to 9pm and drop you off right by a bunch of ugly hotels; walk a little farther south and you'll find yourself in an almost untouched area, aside from an excellent *chiringuito* that sells the most delicious fresh fish.

Shopping

With no lack of air-conditioned malls and boutiques, shopping may have replaced culture as the major pastime for Valencians. The Old City—**Barrio El Carmen** to be specific—has a wide variety of exclusive to Valencia alta and alterna-moda boutiques along with record, home, and gift stores, and edgy salons. Stores mostly keep the hours of Monday to Saturday 11am to 2pm

Three Sheets to the Wind

Just like Barcelona's face-lift for the '92 Olympics, Valencia is getting a nip and tuck for the **America's Cup 2007** (**www.portamericascup.com** and **www. americascup.com**). The America's Cup Port, part of Valencia's expansive port district has been sectioned off for pimping and preening, featuring dilapidated warehouses turned glam discothèques (p. 438) and beer tents slick enough to draw the attention of the Valencian jet set. Giant TVs (really the only way to watch the races), related activities and exhibitions, and theme stores are a big draw for Valencians and tourists alike, especially in the summer months when touring the old city can lead to heatstroke. The America's Cup Port can be reached by walking from the Las Arenas metro stop on line 4 (blue line) or a multitude of buses (nos. 19 and 22 or night bus no. N1B from the old city).

and 5 to 9pm. Some stores close early on Saturdays and for 2 weeks in August.

Current fashion leans toward retro, quirky, and colorful pop clothing and accessories—you can find stores fitting this description all over **Barrio del Carmen,** some worth skipping lunch for are: **Nacked** (En Sanz 4; ☎ 963-440-083) and **Confecciones Drácula** (Roteros 1; ☎ 963-921-798; www.confecciones-dracula.com).

Head to **Carrer de los Derechos** to shop for local and international young designer labels that kick it up a style notch at: **Zak Kolel** (☎ 963-922-159) and **Bagalú** (☎ 963-918-449). For that exclusive to Valencia oddball T-shirt and those unclassifiable but collectible modern rubber figurines try **Perrolento** (Quart 10; ☎ 963-153-248; www.perrolento.com). Otherwise pick up a classic T with a PC message at **Malasaña** (Plaza Porxets 7; ☎ 963-940-156).

Skaters and lovers of the streetwear look stock up at **Skate World** (Comedias 14; ☎ 963-531-838) and **Beloved** (Alta 32; ☎ 963-915-648). If you're a vinyl junkie, a browse through the collection of classics at **Mardigas** (Mantas 2; ☎ 963-926-372) will not disappoint. And if it's an object d'art you're holding out for, stop by **Studio Vintage** (C. Purisima 8; ☎ 963-924-715), where you can get an original dust collector from the golden age or a reissue of a '70s classic conversation piece.

Known as the second largest market in Spain, **Mercado Central** (Plaza Mercado; Mon–Sat 7:30am–2:30pm) is also one of the most architecturally fascinating, with a high, open, *modernista* roof and a cathedral-like dome. Everything from slippery eels to ceramics and the famous Valencian oranges can be found in its multitude of stalls. The market is photo-op galore, and a perfect place to try the market's fresh produce is at one of the sardine-packed bars.

📺 (Best ❢) Alicante

Alicante (Alacant) is the capital of Costa Blanca and the second largest city in Valencia. The main attractions are the long wide stretches of overdeveloped fine sand beaches big enough to swallow the thousands of tourists that arrive every summer.

The temperature and humidity in July and August make it hard to do anything but laze on the nearest spot of sand, and that's a shame, because on top of a mountain looming over the town, sits one of Europe's largest medieval castles. Once you snap

VALENCIA

out of your D&D fantasy you can head down to a superb modern desert park and back into the wonderful winding streets of the old town.

Then there's the nightlife. Alicante's university is only 30 years old, but it's been growing rapidly thanks in good part to Erasmus and other European study abroad programs where university beach towns are more popular than roses on Valentine's Day. That, mixed with the party-animal gene that's inherent to Valencians, makes for exciting evenings composed of sidewalk-cafe-mingling and beach dancing. With new edgy clubs and restaurants opening, this city is worth visiting for a few days, regardless of the season.

Getting There & Around

BY AIR

Alicante's Airport, **El Altet** (☎ 966-919-100), is located 9km (5¹/₂ miles) southwest of the center and operates with regular and charter flights from all over Europe. Over 10 daily flights arrive from Madrid, five from Barcelona, three from Mallorca and frequent connections are made with Bilbao, Ibiza, Sevilla, and other European cities. A bus service (☎ 902-422-242) connects the airport with the center of town every 40 minutes from 6:30am to 11:10pm (1€).

BY TRAIN

The **Estación de Madrid** (Av. Salamanca; ☎ 902-240-202) receives eight daily trains from Barcelona (trip time: 3–6 hr.) and 12 from Madrid (trip time: 4 hr.). Twelve daily trains connect Valencia (trip time: 1¹/₂ hr.) and up to 20 link Elche (trip time: 1¹/₂ hr.).

From Plaza Puerta del Mar, **Ferrocarriles de la Generalitat Valenciana,** or FGV (☎ 900-720-472), offers tram service north to Benidorm and other locations along the coast. Every half-hour there's a tram to El Campello where

you can transfer to the 🚊 **Best ⓿** *trenet* (see "Small Train, Big Ride," p. 448) to Benidorm (every hour) and Deniá (every 2 hr.).

BY CAR

Alicante lies right on the E-15 expressway that runs along the coast of Valencia. Coming from Murcia, take the N-340 to the northeast. Traffic in Alicante can be tedious at best. Unless you want to drive around the Costa Blanca, it is hardly advisable to get a car, but if you insist, **Javea Cars,** at the airport (☎ 965-793-312), will rent you a three-door Fiat for 135€ per week.

BY BUS

Alicante's **bus station** (Portugal 17; ☎ 965-130-700) is right by the center, just a 5-minute walk from the old town. Hourly buses head to Benidorm and Valencia. The bus to Madrid takes 5 to 6 hours. The **public bus system** in Alicante is fairly easy to understand, although buses tend to take the longest possible route from point A to point B. But on those hot summer afternoons, even in the slow-moving traffic, you'll be glad to spend some time in the A/C. Each bus stop posts a map of the city and one with each bus route. A local ticket is .95€.

BY TAXI

Most areas in Alicante are within walking distance, except for some beaches and a few bars. If you need some wheels, try **Radio Taxi** (☎ 965-910-123), **Tele Taxi** (☎ 965-101-611), or **Area Taxi** (☎ 965-910-757). Taxi stops are all over town (look for the T sign), plus at the train and bus stations.

BY BIKE OR BY FOOT

Walking will get you pretty much everywhere in Alicante. Biking can be a little scary and exhausting, considering that Alicante is in the mountains, but it's good for getting around the beach in San Juan or arriving to Isla Marina (see "Bars & Clubs") in style. At Playa de San Juan, **Rent and Go** (Av. Costa Blanca 95; ☎ **605-272-277**) rents bikes for 4€ an hour, scooters for 35€ a day, and quads for 38€ an hour.

Alicante Basics

ORIENTATION: ALICANTE

Alicante prides itself dearly for its majestic **Explanada de España,** a boulevard with mosaic sidewalks lined with tall palm trees and every tourist trap you can think of. The Explanada goes west to east by the harbor from Plaza Canalejas to Plaza Puerta del Mar, where the port ends and the beach begins. On the west side of the harbor, **Centro Comercial Panoramis** is a mall with stores, restaurants, and everything to attract visitors who want to do the same things they do at home. On the other side lies the **Zona de Ocio,** home of some of the cheesiest bars and clubs known to mankind. Halfway down the Explanada you'll find the **Rambla de Mendez Nuñez,** the center's main artery, packed with loads of traffic. On the western side of the Rambla is the city center, the train and bus stations, and other places you'll only visit if you are in trouble, like the police station and post office. To the east of the Rambla is everything you came here for: The old town, aka **El Barrio,** is the area where all the cheap hotels, nice restaurants, and coolest nightlife are to be found. As you continue going west up the mountain, you'll find the 📺 Best 🏆 **Barrio Santa Cruz** ★★, which with its white and blue houses, narrow, sloped, cobblestone streets, and flowers everywhere may be

one of the prettiest in Spain. Up the arid yet astounding **Parque de la Ereta,** is the mammoth **Castillo de Santa Bárbara,** which peers down at the town like Big Brother. Back at the coast, Plaza Puerta del Mar marks the beginning of the **Playa del Postiguet,** the city's main beach. About 20 minutes down the coast, the **Playa de San Juan** is the province's longest beach.

TOURIST OFFICES

Tourist offices are placed at the major tourist areas (airport, train station, beach, Rambla) although, at the time of writing, many of them were closed for renovations. The main tourist office is at Rambla Mendez Núñez 23 (☎ **965-200-000**); it's open Monday to Saturday from 10am to 8pm from June to September and Monday to Saturday 10am to 7:30pm during winter.

RECOMMENDED MAGAZINES & WEBSITES

The official tourism website **(www. alicanteturismo.com)** is available in English and has info about beaches, hotels, and so on. A local version of **www. guiadelocio.com** is in Spanish and not as complete as in the big cities, but it's good for checking out current events. The free magazines at tourist agencies and cool stores and restaurants are the best way to get in touch with Alicante's culture and nightlife. *Üala* (www.uala.net) is a monthly Spanish-only magazine that packs in tons of information on everything that goes on in Alicante, plus interviews and articles for you to practice your high school Spanish. *Plan A* is a very practical guide, with seasonal info on the coolest restaurants, clubs, bars, and shops in the city.

Alicante Nuts & Bolts

Currency As always, you will get the best exchange rate at an **ATM**. All along Rambla de Mendez Nuñez there's at least one on each block.

Emergencies For emergencies dial ☎ 112. The **drug abuse helpline** is ☎ 900-161-515 and for the **women's center** dial ☎ 900-580-888.

Internet Up Internet (Angel Lozano 10; ☎ 965-200-577; 3€ per hr.; daily 8am–1am, Fri–Sat till 3am) has 19 computers with broadband connection so you don't have to wait to send those drunken pictures—quick! before you sober up and realize how ridiculous you look!

Pharmacies Look for the green neon cross. **Belda Calatayud** is right on Calle San Fernando 51 (☎ 965-206-894) and open Monday to Saturday 9am to 9pm.

Telephone City code: **96**; operator: **1003**; international operator: **1005**.

Sleeping

CHEAP

📺 (Best◐) → **Hostal La Milagrosa** Very similar to Metidja, this hotel is a little bit farther away from the center, but very close to the *barrio,* the castle, and the beach. The small but comfy rooms come with or without private bath. Shared bathrooms are clean, although not that well equipped. You can admire the views, get a suntan, or nap on the shared terrace; or ask the impossibly friendly staff to give you a room with a small balcony facing the impressive Santa María church, and see how many bells it takes to wake you up in the morning. *Villavieja 8.* ☎ *965-216-918. www.hostallamilagrosa.com. Single with shared bathroom 20€, single with bathroom 25€–30€, double with shared bathroom 20€–25€, double with bathroom 25€–30€. Amenities: Paid Internet, terrace. In room: A/C, TV.*

→ **Hostal Metidja** Walk up the first floor of this apartment building on the Rambla to this very simple family run hostel. The wallpaper in the rooms is made of a combination of hairy and shiny material that won't cease to amaze you while checking in to the simply furnished and small rooms with new mattresses, and fortunately, A/C. The location and price are hard to beat, but being on the main drag, it can also get a little noisy. The rooms on the street side have balconies where you can gander at all the girls and boys heading to the beach or bars. Single rooms have shared bathrooms. *Rambla Mendez Nuñez 26.* ☎ *965-143-617. Single with shared bathroom 18€–20€, double with bathroom 32€–40€. In room: AC, TV.*

DOABLE

→ **Abba Centrum** The local member of the Abba chain offers a very good value. Close to the train and bus stations, the lobby decor is bright and modern, if a little cold. Rooms are newly furnished with a definite knack for beige colors. Each one has parquet floors and a firm bed. The bathrooms are sparkling clean and all have bathtubs and showers. Check out their weekend deals, when you can get one of their government rated three-star hotel rooms for the price of a hostel in Barcelona. *Pinto Lorenzo Casanova 33.* ☎ *965-130-440. www.abbahoteles.com. Double 65€–95€. Amenities: Restaurant (Mon–Fri), bar, laundry service/dry cleaning, room service, Wi-Fi. In room: A/C, TV, hair dryer, minibar, safe.*

Eating

In a town as touristy as this one, it can be difficult not to fall into one of the paella tourist traps that line the seafront. However, a few good options include some excellent cheap tapas, and, more recently, a few upscale restaurants, which will cost you;

but you'll dine on excellent food in daz-zling environments. Another advantage is that most Alicante kitchens stay open until 1am, which comes in very handy for the most severe cases of late-night munchies.

CHEAP

📺 (Best ❶) → **Mesón   Labradores** TAPAS   In the middle of the crazy maze of bars and lame restaurants that cater to the taste-disabled northern European tourists in the barrio you'll find this classic Spanish tapas bar, hailed by locals since 1963. When I say classic, I mean it: traditionally tiled walls and floors, antique lamps, cop-per fountains and plates lining the walls, and even massive bags of garlic hanging from the ceiling. The menu doesn't fall short; they'll bring you a pen and paper menu (with no prices) on which you check off what you want. Don't miss the sizzling skillet with *gambas al ajillo* (shrimp), an octopus so tender you'd be able to eat it even if you were 90, and if you're adven-turous, a sumptuous serving of *callos* (tripe) or perhaps some snails. Top it off with some dessert and don't forget to tip, so you can hear them ring the bell as they give each other a hard time. *Labradores 19.* ☎ *965-204-846. Tapas 2.50€–8€. Tues–Sun 8pm–1am.*

→ **Rincón de Antonio** SPANISH   In the heart of the dreamy Barrio Santa Cruz lies this family restaurant with rows of wooden tables in a vibrant hall and outdoor tables for those steamy summer nights. Here you'll eat just like at home, if your mom was Penelope Cruz, that is. Locals pack this place from 10pm until closing to devour the house specialties: cold cuts and more elaborate stuff like monkfish casserole or sea bass with almond sauce. And, for God's sake, drink some beer—you're in a *cerve-ceria* after all. *San Rafael 13.* ☎ *965-202-688. Entrees 3.50€–12€. Tues–Sun 11am–5:30pm and 8pm–1am.*

SPLURGE

→ **La Ereta** ★★ MODERN VALENCIAN Built right next to the castle, in the Parque de la Ereta, this restaurant looks like an L.A. mansion. Resembling a giant luxury deck suspended over the slope of the hills, it's made of thin, dark-wood planks, contrast-ing with the white tablecloths, cream chairs, and black clad staff. The menu varies but includes such creations as gazpacho gua-camole, cod with cuttlefish and romesco, and an out of this world *chocolate con churros*. There are two tasting menus, one with five dishes and another one with seven, so come over with your royal friends and make sure they pick up the tab. The easiest way to get there is to take the elevator to the castle and walk down from there, or take a cab. If you climb up through the park you'll probably feel too sweaty among the swank locals and foreigners who frequent the joint. *Parque de la Ereta.* ☎ *965-143-250. www.laereta.com. Tasting menu: 45€–51€. Thurs–Sat 2–3:30pm and 9–11pm.*

Partying

Alicante's nightlife is surprisingly lively year-round, with students in the off sea-son and tourists making up the difference in the summer. There are two main areas to party: **El Barrio** is to booze what a bee-hive is to honey, with about three or four bars per block in a 10-block ratio. The other party area is the port. And the only thing cheesier than the bars at the port is . . . wait, there's nothing cheesier! Unless you enjoy hard-bodied teenagers line-dancing to Whitney Houston. A smaller area is the one around the central market known as *Ruta de la Madera* (wooden route, since most bars there are decorated in wood); and during the summer months, the *chirin-guitos* at Playa de San Juan have also been known to see some sweaty dancing action.

Small Train, Big Ride

If you are traveling north from Alicante, don't even think of taking the bus. Instead hop on the **⚑ Best ●** *trenet* of the FGV (see "Getting There & Around," p. 444). This tram takes you to El Campello, where you switch onto the narrow gauge little train that goes up the coast and through the mountains. From here you'll get a sensational view of every beach town in the Costa Blanca and, if you see something you like, just step out. Our favorite secluded beaches are in the towns of Amerador and Coveta Fumá. The trenet goes all the way to Deniá passing through Benidorm and Altea on the way.

→ **Glass Club** Locals with a knack for the bling pack this small club with lots of Plexiglas and white surfaces, conveniently situated right in the middle of the Barrio. Resident DJs spin a mix of electronic, house, and sometimes the infamous local top 40. But check on their parties; they have been known to include everything from '80s to live house singers. *Montegón 8.* ☎ *696-474-429. www.glassclub.es.*

MTV ⚑ Best ● → **Havana** Outside the barrio, on Rambla Méndez Núñez, Havana is the preferred meeting point for foreign students and their local friends. During the day it's a cafe, and at night they pull out the tables to make room for a big dance floor. The hottest bartenders in town pour drinks all night, and free *chupitos* (shots) are customary at the door. The house and electronic parties on weekends get a little too crowded after 1am; during the week the party grinds down, and both the music and the people are mellower. *Rambla Méndez Núñez 28.* ☎ *965-216-926.*

MTV ⚑ Best ● → **Isla Marina** The chicest and newest hot spot in Alicante is tucked away from everything—and more exclusive for it. To get to this beach club you'll have to walk about half a mile beyond Playa Postiguet on an enclosed road by the coast. (*Tip:* Take a cab!) Once there you'll find a seaside entertainment emporium, composed of three big comfy areas with beds, hammocks, and lounge chairs; two bars; a restaurant; and a dance floor where things stay rockin' until the wee hours. Although the prices are higher than in El Barrio, you could technically spend your whole day here, if they'd let you. *Av. Villajoyosa, s/n.* ☎ *965-265-728. www.isla marina.com.*

→ **Xiringuito** Few bars can compete with the simple concept of drinks, music, and sun chairs by the beach. Alicante's own *chiringuito* is right at the end of Playa de Postiguet, and lives up to every chill-out expectation. Besides drinks, a deck, and sand, they offer some decent sandwiches, which may be all you need at 4am. The attire is beach casual, with lots of white, sandals, and some hippy prints here and there; but the music is better than at most places in town (check out reggae Fri). *Av. Deniá, Postiguet beach s/n. No phone.*

Sightseeing

Besides walking around the **MTV ⚑ Best ● Barrio de Santa Cruz,** there are a couple of monuments worth leaving bed, beach, and bar for.

FREE → **Castillo de Santa Barbara** One of the biggest medieval fortresses still standing in Europe, this castle presides over the city at the summit of a mountain that seems right out of the *Lord of the Rings* trilogy. The view of the bay is breathtaking and getting there with the underground elevator (2.40€ round-trip) from the footbridge at Playa del Postiguet is just part of the fun. ☎ *965-162-128. Free admission. Daily 10am–7pm.*

FREE → **Iglesia de Santa María** The oldest church in town dates from the 14th century and is a mishmash of European architectural styles, mostly Gothic, with a sculpted baroque portal and golden rococo altar. Yeah, it's another church—but this one is free. *Plaza Santa María.* ☎ *965-216-026. Free admission. Daily 10am–noon and 6–7:30pm.*

Playing Outside

Playa del Postiguet is Alicante's city beach and even though it gets very crowded in the summer, the sand is still incredibly fine and the water clear. Look out at the endless blue horizon and maybe you'll forget about those massive buildings guarding your back. If you want a little (emphasis on the little) more peace, head over to **Playa de San Juan.** Twenty minutes away from the center lies the longest beach in the province, with 5km (3 miles) of white sand, bars by the shore, and every beach activity you can think of. Rather than taking a bus ride through skyscraper hell, get there with the tram, at Plaza Puerta del Mar and be patient: The farther away you get, the nicer the beach becomes.

Elche ★

The first thing an *ilicitano* (local) will brag about is Elche's (Elx) status as a Unesco World Heritage Site twice over. Indeed, this little town a half-hour away from Alicante and a world away from the über-touristy retreats of the Costa Blanca has a lot to offer to the casual visitor. The first legacy is the **Misteri d'Elx,** an ancient theater piece that has been on for so long it makes *Cats* seem like a newbie. The second is much simpler: palms (the trees, not the clapping at the end of the play). How do palms become a heritage to humanity? Well, when you come to Elche and see the humongous **palm groves** that spread over almost half the area of the city you'll understand. Phoenicians are thought to have planted the first ones, which gives you an idea of how long this city's been around. Thousands of artifacts and remains older than JC himself were found in the area and make the **Museo Arqueológico y de Historia de Elche** (MAHE) an Indiana Jones wannabe's wet dream. Elche is also Spain's shoe and sandal manufacturing capital, which brings in a lot of dough and, with it, some excellent restaurants and entertainment to cater to those full-pocketed entrepreneurs. Although the nightlife is not as big as in neighboring Alicante, there are a couple of interesting bars where you can sip a drink after a long day of sightseeing and palm tree climbing.

Getting There

The train station called **Estación Parque** (Av. Del Ferrocarril; ☎ **965-456-254**) is a 10-minute walk from the center of town. Elche is on the Murcia-Alicante route. Trains to/from Alicante pass by at least once an hour. The trip takes 30 minutes and costs 1.75€.

The **bus** station (☎ **966-615-050**) is adjacent to the train station. From there you can catch a ride weekdays every half-hour to Alicante (trip time: 45 min., 1.60€); four daily buses go to Valencia and seven to Murcia.

If you are **driving,** take N-340 highway southwest from Alicante. A **taxi** (☎ **965-427-777**) to Alicante is about 20€ each way.

Elche Basics

The train and bus stations are on the north border of the old town. The city spreads on both sides of the mostly dry Vinalopó River. The old town, palm groves, and most monuments and attractions lie on the east bank of the river.

wwwired

....

Get connected at **Netkeeper Servicios** (J.R. Jimenez 15; ☎ **966-611-805;** Mon–Sat 11am–2:30pm and 4:30–11pm, Sun 4:30–11pm), a typical *locutorio*-style Internet spot where you can surf, fax, and call—all at very reasonable prices (Internet access for about 1.50€ an hour).

As you walk into town from the train or bus you'll bump into the **tourist information office** (Parque Municipal s/n; ☎ **965-452-747;** www.turismedelx.com). It's open Monday to Friday 10am to 7pm, Saturday 10am to 2:30pm, and Sunday 10am to 2pm.

Sleeping

→**Hostal Candilejas** This homey-with-a-vengeance family hotel on the west side of the river offers excellent value a mere 5 minutes away from the center. The old-style lobby with marble rooms, a TV, and vintage couches bring to mind gramma's house, and the arguments between the mother and daughter will make you feel like you've never left Kansas. The rooms are simply but tastefully furnished, with dark wood desks, firm beds, and full bathrooms. *Doctor Ferran 19.* ☎ *965-466-512. Single 34€, double 42€. Amenities: Elevator, parking 8€, TV. In room: A/C, TV.*

MTV **Best** ♥ →**Hotel Huerto del Cura** ★★ For the price of a doable hotel you can treat yourself to this fantastic government rated four-star hotel where every "room" is actually a separate bungalow right in the middle of the biggest palm grove in town. In fact, stepping out of your wood cabin, you will feel as though you are on a tropical island. Spend a night or two in style having breakfast by the pool, playing tennis, or dining at **Els Capellans,** one of the best eateries in town, with an impressive view of the hotel's grounds and gardens. *Porta de La Morera 14.* ☎ *966-610-011. Double 88€–128€. Amenities: Restaurant, bar, dry cleaning, fitness center, laundry service, outdoor pool, parking, room service, sauna, solarium, tennis courts, wheelchair friendly. In room: A/C, TV, hair dryer, minibar, safe, Wi-Fi.*

Eating

The opening of a few modern gourmet restaurants added to the already existing traditional ones, making for a very interesting gastronomical map—to the point where many people from Alicante drive the 20km (12 miles) to Elche just for dinner.

→**Arenal** ★ INTERNATIONAL Of the modern restaurants we mentioned above, this is our favorite. Right across from the MAHE it has a slick black-and-white theme, which runs from the furniture to the over-size photographs on the wall. Enjoy the creative Mediterranean fusion dishes like Thai *solomillo,* or cod fish wrapped in rice leaves with sesame seeds and *mitsunan* (I don't know what it is, but it tastes great). *Diagonal del Palacio 8.* ☎ *966-610-687. Entrees: 9€–20€. Tues–Sun 1:30–4pm and 9:30pm–12:30am.*

MTV **Best** ♥ →**La Tartana** ★ VALENCIAN It doesn't get much homier than this traditional restaurant in a 19th-century Valencian building. Walk across the original tile floors through the house's rooms and pick which one you want to sit in to enjoy an exciting meal composed of meats, fish, or rice, the house specialty. Particularly special is the *arroz con bogabante* (rice with lobster) or the mushroom and tender onion salad. For dessert, don't miss the homemade cakes. *Nueva de San Antonio 17.* ☎ *965-425-787. Entrees 7.80€–16€. Tues–Sun 1–4pm and 8–11pm.*

VALENCIA

A Little Misteri Anyone?

The second world heritage in Elche is the medieval singing drama of the FREE **Misteri D'Elx.** The play, which takes place in the Basilica de Santa María, is composed of two acts, the Vespra and the Festa, that have been played on consecutive days, August 14 and 15, almost every year for over 500 years. Non-professional locals portray the death of the Virgin and her assumption into Paradise to be crowned the Queen of Heaven and Earth with a *mise en scene* (complete with flying angels and a grand finale featuring a downpour of brass foil) that would make Andrew Lloyd Webber proud. Dress rehearsals take place on August 11, 12, and 13, and the night of the 13th the skies are blazed with Independence Day–worthy fireworks. This is a hot ticket in Spain, so reservations are a must. Make them at the **Casa de la Festa** (Carrer Major de la Vila; ☎ **965-456-112**). If you miss the party, check it out secondhand at the **Museu Municipal de la Festa** (C. Major de la Vila 25; ☎ **965-453-464;** entrance: 3€; Tues–Sat 10am–1pm and 5–8:30pm, Sun 10am–1pm).

Partying

The nightlife in Elche pales in comparison with neighboring Alicante, and many people just go to the latter for the night. But if you do stick around town, the main area for clubs is the **Polígono Industrial Altabix,** on the northeastern end of town; but the coolest bars are in the old area of town.

MTV Best ● → **Beat** The hippest bar in town is decorated in a '50s American rock-a-billy style, with a long shiny bar, retro printed wallpaper, and seating composed of chrome bar stools and round lounge couches. Hip locals suck down strong cocktails poured by the expert bartender/owner Felix. Thursdays through Saturdays DJs spin everything from funk and electro to '60s and '70s pop for everybody to shake their booties. *Mare de Déu dels Desamparats 7.* ☎ *966-611-578.*

→ **The Clap** This dark but shiny bar decorated in black and white is popular with Spaniards over 25, despite the unfortunate name. The music is not as good as Beat's (see above), careening from electro to world music and sometimes crashing right into the wall of the much-dreaded Spanish *pachanga* (top-40 dance music). *Puerta del Organo 2.* ☎ *661-811-399.*

Sightseeing

At the tourist office you can pick up two flyers on walking tours: One goes through the historical center and monuments, the other through the **Palm Groves** ★★, composed of 200,000 palm trees that were originally cultivated by the Moors, whose original irrigation system is still keeping the magic alive today. On that route you shouldn't miss the **Huerto del Cura** (Porta de la Morera 49; ☎ **965-451-936;** admission 4€; July–Sept 9am–8:30pm, other times 9am–6pm), an old orchard turned botanical garden of sorts with nicely arranged Mediterranean species and the fabulous **Palmera Imperial,** a sort of Shiva among palm trees, with seven branches coming out of the main trunk (yeah, that's not very common). Also in here is a replica of yet another source of Elche's pride, the **Dama d'Elche,** a beautiful Iberian bust of a woman dating from 500 B.C. and found right at this spot. **Museo Arqueológico y de Historia de Elche,** or MAHE (Diagonal del Palau s/n; ☎ **966-615-382;** daily noon–9pm), is housed in the impressive Alcasser de la Senyoria, which was the residence of the lords of town between the 11th and 18th centuries. Inside, you can have a look at the history of the city from the Visigoth era to current days.

Benidorm

You may think Benidorm is a new brand of sleeping pill, but over five million tourists walk through the infamous, cheap-commerce infested streets every year. A big chunk of them are English blokes on package tours, and not precisely the kind that make Tony Blair proud. Why then do more than half a million people at a time still come here to fight for a piece of beach space? Despite all the tasteless high-rise overdevelopment, Benidorm does have impossibly fine sand beaches, which, like your favorite supermodel, are still pretty, no matter what crap you put on them. The tiny old neighborhood where the Levante and Poniente beaches meet is pleasant enough for an afternoon stroll or late night drink, and the headland produces a breathtaking view of the whole coastline. With hundreds of thousands of youngsters in party mode, the nightlife includes everything from beach bars and traditional taverns to mega clubs with pools and international DJs. As little cultural value as it may have (aside from an anthropological insight into the deep darkness of the UK's youth), Benidorm is a good place for wild partying and beach bumming.

Getting There & Around

The **FGV train** (FGV; ☎ 900-720-472; www.fgv.es) has two stops on the northern border of the town, the Estación Benidorm and the Estación Benidorm Disco. (Yes, clubs are such a big deal here they get their own train station.) Every hour a train makes for Alicante and one every 2 hours goes to Deniá. **Buses** stop at Av. de Europa 8, right by the shopping mall with the **Alsa buses** office (☎ 966-803-955). Seven buses daily run to Valencia and at least one every hour to Alicante. If you have a **car,** take the E-15 expressway south from Valencia or north from Alicante. For **taxi service** call ☎ 965-861-818.

Benidorm Basics

Benidorm stretches west to east along the coast and features two main beaches, Poniente and Levante. The area behind **Playa de Poniente** is full of northern European and Spanish families and doesn't have much to offer the young traveler. The old neighborhood is on the little hill in between the two main beaches, and has its own smaller beach, **Playa de Mal Pas,** and a nice area of restaurants and more "upscale" bars. Most of the action takes place in the area around **Playa de Levante,** with a boardwalk lined with restaurants, bars, and pubs. Young people tend to hang out on the beach between Calle Valencia and Avenida E. Romero. Further east, the area around Avenida de Mallorca, aka "Ground Zero," is where British hotels, bars, and restaurants form their own subcity. Toward the eastern end of the beach is a higher concentration of Dutch, Belgian, and Nordic families.

The main **tourist information office** is right by the beach, at Av. Martinez Alejos 16 (☎ 965-851-311; www.turismedelx.com). It's open Monday to Friday 9:30am to 8:30pm, Saturday 10am to 1:30pm and 5 to 8pm, and Sunday 10am to 1:30pm. Additional **kiosks** can be found at Avenida De Europa, a block away from the bus stop, and in the corner of Gerona and Avenida Del Derramador.

wwwired

Every other store in Benidorm seems to have computers with Internet access. The minigolf and arcade center **Rec. Walker** has an air-conditioned separate room with 12 coin-operated computers a block away from the beach (Av. Del Mediterraneo 54; no phone; .50€ for 10 min.; daily 10:30am–2:30am). A cheaper option is **Vic Center** (Lepanto 9; 1.80€ an hour; daily 9:30am–11:30pm), a *locutorio* where you can also buy calling cards.

Sleeping

Benidorm has more hotel beds than any other city in Spain, but most of them are booked up by tourist agencies for package tourists. Among the ones that aren't, prices are significantly lower when you book a weekly stay and/or full board (meaning meals too).

CHEAP

➜ **Hotel Los Angeles** Located right in the middle of the old town and 100m (328 ft.) away from Playa de Levante, this friendly family owned and operated hotel has small but simple rooms with A/C and TV. Most double rooms have balconies and the ones on the top floors are very bright, but the single rooms are very dark and a little depressing. The best deals involve staying for a week and taking full board, which is served at the restaurant across the street. *Los Angeles 3.* ☎ *966-807-433. Single 23€–50€, double 42€–80€. No credit cards. Amenities: Restaurant, elevator, TV. In room: A/C, TV.*

➜ **Pensión La Orozca** Every room at this no-frills pension faces the exterior, which means they are luminous but can get a little noisy, considering it is located on a busy street in the center of town. The rooms are pleasantly furnished with floral-printed bed covers and the bathrooms have bathtubs and bidets. There are rooms with balconies and with or without TV and A/C—you can afford to miss the rerun episodes of *Flava of Love*, but, if you are here in the summer, don't even consider the ones without A/C. *Ruzafa 37.* ☎ *965-850-525. www.laorozca.es. Double 30€–60€. In room: A/C, TV.*

DOABLE

📺 Best 🅾 ➜ **Hotel Canfali** This white building, on top of the little hill between Playa de Levante and Playa de Poniente, feels almost like one of those villas in the Greek islands. You can enjoy your breakfast with a spectacular view of Playa de Levante and then walk down the little stairway to the beach. From a perch in one of the hammocks in the solarium, you can see the other side of town. The spacious rooms have full bathrooms and are plainly decorated, but if you can get one with a balcony overlooking the shore you're not going to spend any time inside anyway. *Plaza de San Jaime 5.* ☎ *965-850-818. www. hotelesrh.com. Double 45€–87€. Amenities: Restaurant, bar. In room: A/C, TV, safe.*

Eating

Every other building in Benidorm houses a restaurant, and thanks to the influx of multinational tourism, you can find almost every kind of cuisine, from Dutch and Indian to Argentinian and Thai, although the quality can be very uneven. Our favorite spots in town are dedicated to Spanish food.

➜ **La Cava Aragonesa** TAPAS If you happen to find any locals, they'll probably point you to this classic tapas tavern with a far-from-classic variety of hundreds of reasonably priced tapas. They also have *tablas,* combinations of cheeses and cold cuts, that are ideal to pick on at the permanently crammed bar. Ask for the wine of the day, always a good quality at grin-inducing prices. A sit-down, a-la-carte restaurant is located across the street. *Plaza De la Constitución.* ☎ *966-801-206. Tapas from 1€. Daily noon–1am.*

🎵 Best ♪ → **O Conxuro da Queimada** GALICIAN This new small restaurant run by a son/mother team has very few plates on its simple menu, but each is extra delicious. Besides the classic *pulpo a feira* (Galician-style octopus), try the peppers, veal skewers, and chorizo, all brought directly from Galicia. Wash it down with a nice white Albariño and make sure you are there on Fridays at 11pm, when they prepare the traditional *queimada,* a sweet and strong liquor that dates from the times of witches and packs quite a spell. *Pintor Lozano s/n.* ☎ *661-246-422. Tapas 1€–5€. Daily 11am–midnight.*

Partying

Benidorm comes alive at night with thousands of youngsters and adults walking from bar to bar. The main drinking areas are the English part of town, or **Ground Zero,** which spreads around Avenida De Mallorca and should be avoided at all costs—unless you are really into vomiting on the streets, sad live-sex shows, and other self-deprecating activities like eating Cheetos out of someone's ear. Around Avenida Esperanto is the **Zona 9,** or Spanish zone, with lots of (you guessed it) Spanish bars with terrible music and a Spanish version, minus the grossness, of the English area. Our favorite bar crawls are either on Gats, Costa Del Barco, and the surrounding streets in the old town, or the ones by the boardwalk. Most clubs there have loungey beach bars, a couple of rock 'n' roll bars feature live music, and you can score your discount flyers for the clubs, which are all located right at the entrance of town, on the N-332.

BARS

→ **Ku Playa** The chill-out version of the club can sometimes be even more fun than the original. The interiors are decorated in a Buddhist-Balinese style with statues of Ghanesh randomly mixed among the four bars and go-go dancers. The resident DJs spin ambient and chill dance music during the day and weeknights, and heavier international house to warm things up before partiers hit the clubs on weekends. Fridays feature theme nights such as white night, forbidden garden, cabaret, and other hedonistic schemes. *Playa de Levante. No phone.*

🎵 Best ♪ → **Seethesea** This chic bar and cafe, together with the Hotel Canfali, claims the best location in Benidorm. Situated right on the side of the cliff, it is suspended on top of Levante beach, which is connected to the bar by a set of stairs on the rocks. Two resident DJs keep the bodies moving and they occasionally have visuals, performances, and live music. *Médico Cosme Bayona 5. No phone.*

CLUBS

→ **KM DanceClub** With a cheese factor almost doubling that of its neighbors, KM caters to the masses. Its three dance floors include the Main room, the Klasic room, and the Garden, which can hold a total of 5,000 people, not including the dancing muscle men. They also host theme parties like Foam and Ladies Nights. With a ticket to KM you can also access neighboring Penelope and El Divino. *Av. Pais Valenciano, km 122.* ☎ *639-124-376. www.kmdisco.com. Cover 10€–20€ with a drink.*

🎵 Best ♪ → **Ku** In perfect Ibiza style, Ku, although smaller than its older siblings, attempts to bring the island feeling to Benidorm. An all-white building with seven bars, a stage, and a large outdoor area, it even has a pool where patrons get wet 'n' wild. Since bars don't close until 4 or 5, this place doesn't get going until 5:30am. For special nights they fly in DJs directly from Ibiza, and the dancers from Ku Playa (p. 454) do a double duty with more "intense" dance acts on the stage. *Av. País Valenciano, km 121. No phone. Cover 10€–20€ with a drink.*

Playing Outside

Besides lying on the **beach,** you can partake in almost every imaginable watersport in Benidorm. A cheaper and somehow easier alternative to water-skiing is **cable water skiing,** a system where the skier is pulled from a line based on a platform that stretches out 100m (328 ft.) to sea. Get your fix at **Cable-Ski Benidorm** at the end of Playa de Levante (Rincón de Loix, Levante; ☎ 639-612-713; www.cableskibenidorm. com; 1 hr. 20€, 3 passes 10€). **Marco Polo Expediciones** (Av. Europa 5; ☎ 965-863-399; www.marcopolo-exp.es) is a sort of Kmart for outdoor fun, offering everything from bicycle, quad, and jeep rental to scuba diving, horse riding, and catamaran sailing. The prices vary according to the activity but are not too crazy—a mountain bike tour is 14€ per person, a quad 48€ per hour, horses are 33€ for a 1-hour excursion. Everything is multilingual except the horses.

Balearic Islands

by *Fernando Gayesky*

Once upon a time, in the middle of the Mediterranean, there was a group of unspoiled islands. Bathed by an endless sunshine in the middle of a clear blue sea, these islands boasted an idyllic combination of white-sand beaches, rocky coves, and majestic mountains. Multicolored flowers proliferated, happily mixing with orange and olive trees. And then came mankind . . . First the Carthaginians, then the Greeks, the Romans, the Vandals, the Moors—the islands were more popular than Michael Jackson in the '80s. After the Moors were expelled and put together a neighboring kingdom of their own, a new sort of invasion hit these Castilian isles. Only, this time the hordes were not coming to kill and ransack, but, rather, to get tan and wasted on the beaches. Instead of spades and combat boots they sported cameras and Birkenstocks; and, what is more curious, as massively as they came, they left each year along with the summer winds. These bands of (mostly northern European) families still invade the Islands starting at the end of May every year— and why shouldn't they? In the Balearics you can find everything you possibly need for a perfect summer vacation.

Mallorca is the older sister and certainly the more developed one. In Palma, the island's capital, you will find all the amenities a big city has to offer, including an old fort, art galleries, exquisite restaurants, trendy bars, and thriving clubs. Although some of the most striking beaches have been sadly ruined by overcrowded resorts and the influx of thousands of families on package tours, you may still be able to find some virgin coves and less crowded spots by the sea. Mallorca also offers a vast countryside, climbable mountains, and beautiful ancient towns where time seems to have stopped long before the German tourist invasions.

Meanwhile, Menorca—the quiet middle sister—has the longest, least developed beaches and features the sleepy old towns of Ciutadella and Maó. Ciutadella is the more happening town of the two, with its sweetly historic demeanor and proximity to nice, tranquil beaches.

The baby of the family is Formentera, "the last paradise in the Mediterranean," a tiny island you can discover on foot, with caves, beaches, more fine-sand beaches, and lots of Italian vacationers.

And then, of course, there's the young, wild brat of an island, Ibiza, which offers

more party per week than most of us can afford in a lifetime. This is the place where big-city professional clubbers are brought to their knees, where DJs achieve superstar status, and drugs are easier to come by than food. With an affluence of tourists that grows faster than Shakira's fan base, it is very hard to get a room on this burgeoning island in July and August. But forget about a room—people have been stranded on the beach for not getting a round-trip plane ticket. So for once in your life, plan ahead (I know how hard it is, believe me), secure your stay well in advance, and bring money—because popularity doesn't come cheap. The Brits pack pounds and, especially in Ibiza, they set the standard. If you want cheap, go to Morocco. If you want endless fun, ridiculously beautiful beaches, and hot Europeans in party mode, welcome to Baleares.

The Best of the Balearics

- **Best Beaches to Let It All Hang Out:** Pack the sunblock, if nothing else, before you seek out **Las Salinas Beach,** a nudist beach 11km (7 miles) from Ibiza Town; **Cala Xarraca Beach,** up on the north coast; or any of the more unspoiled beaches in **Formentera,** a tiny island 16km (10 miles) south of Ibiza. See p. 506. At **Ses Illetes,** Formentera the water is so hypnotizing that no one will notice if you are wearing a bathing suit. Not that anybody else is. See p. 512.
- **Best Place to Watch the Sunset While . . .**
  - **. . . Chilling with a Drink: Chiringuito Tiburón,** Formentera. It's hard to think of a more relaxed

situation that doesn't involve tranquilizers. See p. 512.
  - **. . . Workin' It with a Date: Son Marroig,** Mallorca. At the top of this cliff, overlooking the strange rock formation with a needle-eye hole and the impossible color palette in the sky, you would have to be a hairy serial killer with garlic breath not to score. See p. 483.
  - **. . . Hangin' in San Antonio:** Check out the beachfront **Café Mambo** in San Antonio while you search for the perfect partner whose "likes" include spending time with friends and long walks on the beaches. See p. 497.

○ **. . . Making It onto an Album Cover: Café del Mar,** Ibiza, comes out with a new chill-out compilation every year. See what the hoopla is all about and if you are lucky. . . . See p. 504.

○ **Best Party to Do Something You Would Never Do at Home:** At Manumission Mondays at **Privilege Club,** Ibiza, everything goes. Find a new boy, girl, or anything in-between, take it all off and jump in the pool, you decide. But don't say we didn't warn you. See p. 500.

○ **Best Excuse for Imbibing:** Ibiza's **Disco Bus** is cheap and probably more reliable than finding a sober friend to drive you home. It runs during the season from every major club to every major hotel on the island. See p. 488.

○ **Best (Legal) Party Involving Animals:** The **Fiesta de Sant Joan,** Menorca, is an amazing display of how people can get crazy without the use of synthetic drugs. Witness the drums beating for 48 hours straight and horses rearing among thousands of .

Talk of the Town

Five Ways to Start a Conversation with a Local

1. There is a **natural rivalry among the islands.** Ask the locals which they like better and why: which beaches are nicer, which one is more fun, which has the best food?

2. Many celebrities have houses on the islands: Elle McPherson in Ibiza, Claudia Schiffer in Formentera, and so on. Everybody has a **celebrity story** that they may be willing to tell you. But the most beloved celeb in Mallorca is Michael Douglas, aka Miquel de S'Estaca, because of the mansion he owns near Son Marroig, Estaca, former property of Archduke Luis Salvador. Just mention Miquel and you are sure to have conversational success.

3. The **new** *autopista* **(highway) in Ibiza**—construction started in 2006—is causing a lot of controversy. Should this modern expansion be built to accommodate the island's growth (and traffic) spurt? Or should the island's physiognomy be preserved at the cost of longer commutes?

4. After you read *A Winter in Majorca,* **by George Sand,** you will realize why it is such a hot-button issue. She describes Mallorcans as being paranoid, closed-minded, and lazy. Seventy years later, the wounds are still fresh. Some residents will tell you they agree, while others will call her everything but pretty.

5. **Rafael "Rafa" Nadal, born and raised in Manacor, Mallorca,** is the island's prodigal son. In case you don't know, Rafa, at 18, was the youngest tennis player ever to win the Davis Cup, and also the youngest to enter the top 100 in the Indesit ATP ranking. He became number 2 at 19 and currently holds the longest streak of wins on clay. But, because of his decreased performance on other terrains, he hadn't been able to topple the number 1 player, Swiss-born Roger Federer, at the time of this writing. Everybody in the islands (particularly in Mallorca) will be willing to discuss his career and future in full detail.

people, in a tradition that dates long before X met Stacey. See p. 522.

○ **The Best Traditional Party:** Renaissance at **Pachá** is still pretty wild, even by Ibiza standards. See p. 500.

○ **Best Party Calisthenics:** Warm up on the beach at **Bora Bora,** in Ibiza. Get your full workout across the street at **Space** (p. 500), and then cool down at **Bora Bora** again. See p. 497.

○ **Best Bar for Having Epiphanies:** At **Es Jaç,** Mallorca, the decor is so perfect and unusual, you may decide you want to give a new stylish turn to your life, career, and so on. But don't worry, after a couple of shots of *Hierbas,* you'll go back to using your necktie as a headband. See p. 472.

○ **Best (or Worst) Restaurant to Lick Your Fingers at:** Order *Arroz con*

Bogavante at **El Chiringuito d'es Cavallet,** Ibiza, and give your taste buds a field trip. But, before you stick your thumb in your mouth, remember: You are in the biggest cruisin' beach in Ibiza. See p. 496.

○ **Best Sea-View Stroll:** Spend a couple of hours strolling the area around Ibiza's **D'Alt Villa,** the Old Fortress, with its beautiful views out over the water. See p. 490.

○ **Best Place to Lay Those Weary Bones: Casa de Huespedes Vara de Rey** is an eye in the storm of Ibiza. The couple who run this hostel use an artist's touch to make each of the 10 rooms a calm and serene nest away from home. See p. 492.

Mallorca

In 1907, the first considerable group of tourists arrived in Palma aboard the steamship *Victoria.* They must have liked it, because tourism hasn't slowed down since. Mallorca is a large island with a varied landscape and pretty much everything a visitor could want, from super-inclusive resorts, where everything is already planned for you, to DIY journeys featuring major cultural and historical sites, watersports, or beach adventures.

The island's capital, **Palma de Mallorca,** has almost half a million inhabitants and a massive offering of cultural and entertainment activities. The overdevelopment of some areas—like the bay, which looks more like a Caribbean resort from hell than a heavenly Mediterranean island—can be ignored in favor of the pleasant, honey-colored stone buildings on cobblestone streets in the old city. You can take a

break from the sun by walking through those narrow streets, imagining the town ransacked by pirates, then turn the corner and bump into yet another contingent of English tourists who are happy to return with interest the monies their predecessors took away. The nearest beaches get packed like a New York subway station at rush hour and scoring a table at a restaurant can prove as hard as getting a flight back to the mainland in August. But beauty is all around, and many of those "tourists" have never left, making Palma's population a vibrantly multicultural mix. People here are used to dealing with foreigners, English will take you almost as far as German, and there's a level of sophistication that you won't find in other places on the continent. Walking through the shopping venues, you'll notice the stores have nothing to envy of those in Barcelona or

Madrid. In classic island fashion, arts and crafts are very popular, from the exhibitions in spectacular old-fortress-turned-art-center **Es Baluard** to the many sculptures scattered around the city's public spaces or the more informal markets. The restaurants range from the typical Spanish tapas at a local hangout to fresh fish by the waterfront, ethnic cuisine, or *nueva cocina* delicacies in Soho-like settings. The nightlife is fueled by the thousands of visitors who venture out every night looking for off-the-beach fun. The megaclubs look small compared to those in Ibiza, but, unlike in Ibiza, you can find other ways to blow your money and squander your sleeping hours here. Cool designer bars, funky drag-queen hangouts, and local rock 'n' roll clubs make Mallorca fun even if you roll at a lower pace than 120 beats per minute. There is also an offering of live music ranging from Flamenco to jazz and rock 'n' roll where performers actually play instruments (if you're into that sort of thing).

Outside of Palma there's a world of options: The hooligan paradise of **Magaluf,** where very young and very drunk ruffians amuse themselves by beating the crap out of each other. The endless coast, from overdeveloped high rises by the beach to almost-virgin coves. The artist communities of **Deiá** and **Valldemossa,** built on the mountains and overlooking the bluest sea. The northern tip of **Cap Formentor** with fine sand beaches surrounded by green mountains. Medieval towns like **Pollença.** And a plethora of fields of olives, grapes, and flowers in the countryside; the list goes on.

In Mallorca it's all about diversity. Everybody can have fun; it's just a matter of choosing your poison.

Palma de Mallorca
GETTING THERE
By Air

The airport in Mallorca, **Son San Joan** (☎ 971-789-000), is huge for a town this size. Even so, it gets way too crowded during the summer months. There are flights arriving from a multitude of countries and, usually, if you are abroad, you should fly directly in, avoiding an unnecessary stop in mainland Spain. Be aware that getting a last-minute ticket in July and August is almost impossible, unless you are willing to pay a small fortune for them. Book your return trip in advance as well and make sure it is a solid reservation. Delays are not unusual during these months.

From peninsular Spain, Valencia and Barcelona offer the most direct flights to Palma. During the summer, **Iberia** (☎ 902-400-500; www.Iberia.com), **Span Air** (☎ 902-131-415; www.spanair.com), and **Air Europa** (☎ 902-240-042) run several daily flights from Barcelona and Valencia and less frequent ones from Madrid, Bilbao, Ibiza, Menorca, Malaga, Sevilla, and other Spanish cities. The new low-cost airline **Vueling** (☎ 902-333-933; www.vueling.com) runs several daily flights from Barcelona and Madrid. If you book in advance you may get tickets for as little as 20€ plus taxes round-trip, even in August. If you are arriving from the U.K., check with travel agencies specializing in the islands like **holiday holiday** (www.holidayholiday.co.uk); charter flights often sell their empty seats at slashed prices. They also offer inexpensive packages including hotel and flights.

The airport is located 8km (5 miles) west of the city. Bus no. 1 takes you to the city from 6:15am to 2:15am. **Buses** leave every 15 minutes during the day for the 30-minute run to the city center. The trip costs

Balearic Islands

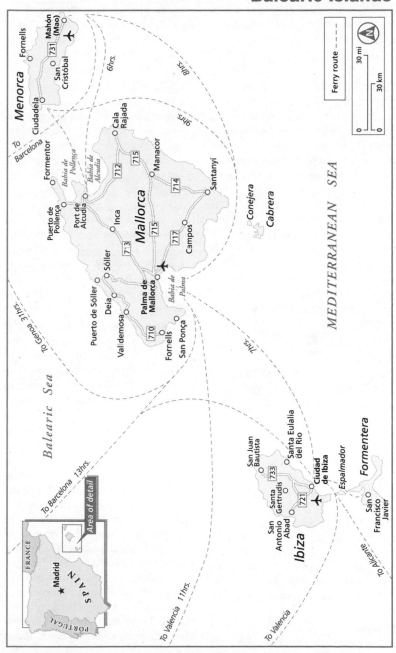

Ferry route -----

30 mi

30 km

Menorca

Fornells
Mahón (Mao) ✈ 731
San Cristóbal
Ciudadela

To Barcelona

6hrs.

8hrs.

6hrs.

Formentor
Bahía de Pollensa
Cala Rajada
Manacor
Puerto de Pollensa
Port de Alcudia
Bahía de Alcudia
715
712
Mallorca
714
Santanyí
Inca
713
715
717
Soller
Campos
Puerto de Sóller
Deia
Palma de Mallorca ✈
Valldemosa
Bahía de Palma
710
Forrells
San Ponça

Conejera
Cabrera

MEDITERRANEAN SEA

Balearic Sea

To Genoa 31hrs.

7hrs.

To Barcelona 13hrs.

Area of detail

FRANCE
Madrid ★
SPAIN
PORTUGAL

San Juan Bautista
Santa Eulalia del Rio
Santa Gertrudis
733
Ciudad de Ibiza
San Antonio Abad
721
Ibiza
Espalmador
Formentera
San Francisco Javier

To Valencia 11hrs.

To Alicante

To Valencia

1.10€. Call ☎ **900-700-710** for more info. A **taxi** costs about 20€ and will get you to the center about 10 minutes faster.

By Boat

Trasmediterránea (☎ 902-454-645; www.trasmediterranea.es) operates two catamarans and a daily **ferry** from Barcelona. They take 3¹/₂ hours or 7 hours, respectively, and start at 70€ one-way. Six ferries per week go to/from Valencia, Monday to Saturday, at 44€ one-way, and cover the distance in 7 hours. A quicker boat makes the journey in 4 to 6 hours and sets you back 70€. Service to Ibiza and Menorca is also available. **Balearia** (☎ **902-160-180**) offers two daily services from Barcelona to Palma (85€–314€ round-trip, trip time: 4 or 7 hr.) and one to Alcúdia. They also have boats connecting Ibiza-Palma and Alcúdia-Ciutadella, in Menorca. These schedules are for the summer; in the winter, sailings are greatly reduced.

GETTING AROUND

By Bus

Buses depart from the **Estació d'autobusos** (C. d'Eusebi Estrada, behind the train station) to most points on the island. For schedules and itineraries, visit the **tourist information office** (see below) for a brochure or contact **Transport de les Illes Balears** (☎ 971-717-190; tib.caib.es). A one-way ticket from Palma to Cala Ratjada, the farthest point in the island, costs 9.05€, and to Cala Sant Vicenç, 1€.

The city bus system is composed of six lines that cover all of Palma. A single ride costs 1.10€ and a 10-ride card costs 7.50€. Contact **Empresa Municipal de Transportes** (☎ **900-700-710**; www.emtpalma.es) for itineraries, fares, and timetables.

By Train

Two different train lines leave Palma from the station in Plaça Espanya. One is the scenic, historic train to Sóller (see "All Aboard," p. 483). The other one is the **Servicios Ferroviarios Mallorca** line to Inca (☎ **971-752-245**). The ride takes 40 minutes and costs 1.80€ each way. There are 40 departures daily Monday to Saturday, and 32 on Sundays.

By Taxi

The city of Palma is walkable, but if you need to get from one side of town to the other in those killer stilettos, you may want to take a cab. If you call from certain areas where an abundance of drunken teenagers congregate at night, like around Plaça Gomila, cabs probably won't come to get you; in fact, be ready to wait at least half an hour at night, no matter where you are requesting a pick-up from. Taking a taxi (☎ **971-401-414** or 971-754-440) to other towns is a costly option. To Cala Ratjada, for example, it clocks at about 60€ one-way.

By Car & Moped

If you'll be staying in Palma, don't worry about renting a car. In typical European fashion, the streets of the old city are so narrow and, in high season, so crowded that you'll be lucky to even walk down them much less navigate a car through the throngs. Parking is next to impossible, and you have to pay for it everywhere; plus the system is complicated and you'll end up spending more in parking violations than if you had rented a limo with a chauffeur.

If you want to get out of town and explore the island, you can always take buses; though it might be nice to make your own schedule instead. Especially if you want to escape the gangs of tourists during the season, a car or moped can be essential in getting that bit of freedom. At the airport you can find all the big names as well as some smaller agencies that will offer you better deals on rentals. **Hasso**

Mallorca

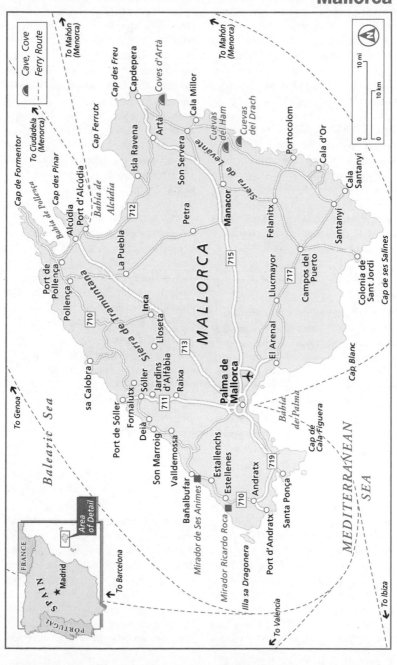

Cave, Cove
Ferry Route

To Mahón
(Menorca)

To Mahón
(Menorca)

To Ciudadela
(Menorca)

10 mi

10 km

Cap des Freu

Cap de Formentor

Cap Ferrutx

Cap des Pinar

Cap de Pollença

Cap de Formentor

Capdepera
Coves d'Artà
Cala Millor
Artà
Cuevas
del Ham
Cuevas
del Drach
Portocolom
Cala d'Or

Isla Ravena

Son Servera

Bahía de
Alcúdia

Port d'Alcúdia
Alcúdia

Sierra de Levante

Cala
Santanyí

Cap de ses Salines

712

La Puebla

Petra

Manacor

Felanitx

Santanyí

715

MALLORCA

Campos del
Puerto

717

Colonia de
Sant Jordi

Port de
Pollença

Pollença

Inca

710

Lloseta

713

Llucmayor

El Arenal

Cap Blanc

sa Calobra

Sierra de Tramuntana

Sóller
Jardins
d'Alfàbia
Raixa

711

Palma de
Mallorca

Bahía
de Palma

Port de Sóller
Fornalutx
Deià

Son Marroig

Valldemossa

Cap de
Cala Figuera

Bañalbufar

Estallenchs
Estellenes

710

Andratx

719

Mirador de Ses Animes

Mirador Ricardo Roca

Illa sa Dragonera

Port d'Andratx

Santa Ponça

Balearic Sea

To Genoa

To Barcelona

FRANCE

SPAIN

Madrid

PORTUGAL

*Area
of Detail*

To Valencia

To Ibiza

*MEDITERRANEAN
SEA*

(☎ 902-203-012; www.hasso-rentacar. com) rents a two-door, standard transmission with no A/C for about 30€ a day and four-door Mercedes automatics from 51€ a day. For scooters go to **Rent Zoom** (C. Perla 2, Playa de Palma; ☎ 971-267-070; www.rentzoom.mallorca.com), where a 50 cc automatic costs 39€ a day. A Honda Legend 125 is 43€ a day and a Transalp 650 is 81€ per day. You will need to be over 18 and have a driver's license to rent anything over 50cc. Helmets are mandatory.

If motors are not your thing, you're in luck. Palma is very bike-friendly and even has some bike paths to nearby beaches. The best place to rent a bike is **Palma on Bike** (Plaça Coll 8; ☎ 971-718-062; www. palmaonbike.com). The cheapest bikes go for 12€ a day, which includes a helmet, lock, tool kit, pump, and insurance.

BASICS
Orientation: Palma de Mallorca

Beyond the impressive **cathedral** stretches the old town, which alternates well-preserved historic buildings with rundown houses and some newer constructions that err more on the tacky side. It's a great place to lose the hordes on an early-evening stroll. Keep your eyes open for the many extremely long-standing stores that are still part of Palma's picturesque trading and seafaring history. At the opposite end of the old town from the cathedral lies **Plaça Espanya,** adjacent to the train and bus stations. From there, the **Plaça Major** tracks due south. Down the steps on the western end of the Plaça Major lies **Plaça Weyler** and the beginning of **Carrer Unió,** one of the most emblematic streets in Palma. Carrer Unió runs into **Plaça Rei Joan Carles I,** sort of Palma's version of Times Square. A nice boulevard lined with trees, **Passeig des Born** marks the end of the old town and

heads south toward the port. On the western side of the boulevard is the neighborhood of **La Llotja,** the old trade market, home now to the highest concentration of bars and restaurants in the city. This neighborhood is where the party is during the off season. The **Avinguda Gabriel Roca** spans the coastline of Palma; its western end, near the **Plaça Gomila,** is the epicenter of nightclubs, gay bars, and *botellón* (passing around a bottle among friends outdoors). Another neighborhood worth checking out for its dining options is **Santa Catalina.** Home to the market of the same name, Santa Catalina is situated west of **Avinguda Argentina.** In the last couple of years a multitude of new restaurants have opened their doors in this neighborhood that comes to life between 9pm and midnight. On the eastern end, the formerly sketchy quarter of **Portixol** is undergoing a process of gentrification worthy of Nolita in Manhattan.

Tourist Offices

Oficines d'Informació Turística (OIT) can be found in Palma and all over the island. A good starting point is the **OIT Aeroport** (Consell de Mallorca, Palma airport; ☎ 971-789-556), which is open every day. Or else stop by the main office, **OIT de Mallorca** (Consell de Mallorca, Plaça de la Reina 2; ☎ 971-720-251), in Palma. Each **OIT** can give you detailed local maps and enough tourist information to wallpaper your entire apartment.

Youth Information Service Office

The **Centre d'Informació Jove de Palma** (C. Ferreria 11-13; ☎ 971-725-501; www.a-palma.es/cij; Mon–Fri 10am–2pm and 5–7pm) offers many services for youth up to 25, like sex-ed and advice, self-confidence workshops, and legal help—though most services are conducted in Catalán and Spanish only. They also offer free

Palma de Mallorca

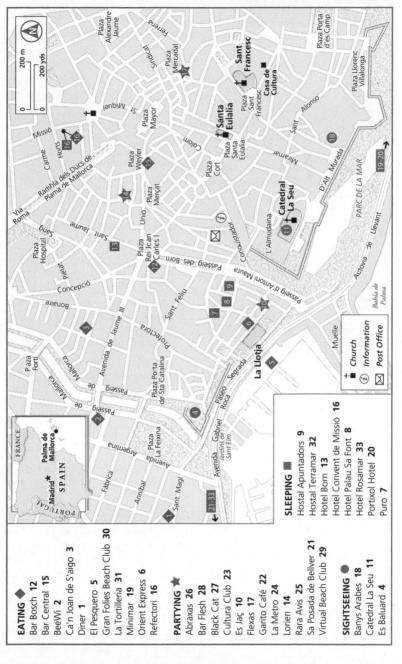

EATING ◆
Bar Bosch **12**
Bar Central **15**
BeeWi **2**
Ca'n Joan de S'aigo **3**
Diner **1**
El Pesquero **5**
Gran Folies Beach Club **30**
La Tortilleria **31**
Minimar **19**
Orient Express **6**
Refectori **16**

PARTYING ★
Abraxas **26**
Bar Flesh **28**
Black Cat **27**
Cultura Club **23**
Es Jaç **10**
Flexas **17**
Garito Café **22**
La Metro **24**
Lorien **14**
Rara Avis **25**
Sa Posada de Bellver **21**
Virtual Beach Club **29**

SIGHTSEEING ●
Banys Arabes **18**
Catedral La Seu **11**
Es Baluard **4**

SLEEPING ■
Hostal Apuntadors **9**
Hostal Terramar **32**
Hotel Born **13**
Hotel Convent de Missió **16**
Hotel Palau Sa Font **8**
Hotel Rosamar **33**
Portixol Hotel **20**
Puro **7**

12 Hours in Mallorca

1. Get a cramped neck checking out Gaudí's *vitraux* (stained-glass windows) at the majestic **Catedral** in Palma (p. 475).

2. Cross the island and visit the paradisiacal beach of **Formentor** (p. 481), where royals like to get their feet wet.

3. Spend a day of pampering and self-gratification at one of the chic **beach clubs** around Palma (p. 472).

4. Take the historic train to **Sóller** (p. 483) and find the Art Nouveau building you'll buy when you retire.

5. Choose your poison and **dance** the night away: mad electronic, funky rhythms, or gut-wrenching rock 'n' roll (see "Clubs," p. 473).

6. Have a gay ol' time with the drag queens at **Flexas** (p. 473); and afterward, follow them to **La Metro** (p. 474).

7. Get inspired in **Valldemossa,** where George Sand and Chopin spent their notorious winter, and then witness a picture-perfect sunset at **Son Marroig** (p. 483).

8. Get a comprehensive tan with hip Mallorcans and tourists on the more than 3km (2 miles) of beach at **Es Trenc** (p. 476).

Internet access and a bulletin board with job postings and apartment rentals, in case you are another one of the many tourists who decide to stay.

Recommended Websites & Magazines

Big city and tourist destination that it is, Palma has loads of magazines and websites touting everything the island has to offer. Our favorite cultural and nightlife mag is *Youthing;* published once a week, this free, Spanish-language publication gives you the 411 on current island happenings. It's available at virtually every hip store in Palma and at the tourist offices as well. *Vámos* (www.vamos-mallorca.com), a decent English-language guide that is issued every season, is filled with info about what to do in Palma, from cultural events to pubs and clubs and more. A less comprehensive but more attractive guide to the Balearics is *looc baleares,* a free English-language monthly featuring plenty of photos and interviews with artists,

musicians, and the like. **Eggcellent.net** also offers info on shopping, dining, playing, and partying in Palma, but better still are the maps they publish, with directions to many bars, stores, and restaurants.

www.illesbalears.es and **www. conselldemallorca.net** are all-encompassing sites (without annoying pop-up ads) run by the official tourist counsel. And we love **www.a2zmallorca.com** for its extensive facts, history, and even a bar guide. For a complete guide with a British perspective try **www.majorca-mallorca. co.uk**.

CULTURE TIPS 101

In the last 60 years Palma has made itself over more than Cher and Madonna put together. The "German invasions" have resulted in a population so rich and mixed that the chorus of foreign languages in the city doesn't really surprise anyone anymore. Particularly so in the summer, when the ratio of tourists to locals rises to ridiculously disproportionate levels. Heck, most of the locals *are* foreigners . . . But that just might make having conversations with them much easier, since they are usually very worldly people with active interests in arts, fashion, and culture.

The same general rule that applies to dealing with the law in most of Spain is good here as well: As long as you don't bother anybody, no one will bother you.

That said, doing stupid things like driving drunk or rolling a big stinker in a bar will definitely not enhance your vacation. So keep your cool and be respectful, and you won't encounter any problems. And really, you can't be too terribly frightened of cops who cruise around in purple, yellow, and red cartoon cars.

Palma Nuts & Bolts

Currency ATMs can be found throughout Palma. Towns outside the city usually have a few on their main drags, depending on the size of the place. If you are visiting the nearby beaches, bring cash; most *chiringuitos* (refreshment stands) don't take plastic.

Emergencies In case of emergencies, call **112**. If you stepped on a sea urchin and aren't feeling that hot, head to the **Clínica Rotget** (C. Santiago Rusiñol 9; ☎ **971-448-500**); or **Clínica Juaneda** (C. Son Espanyolet 55; ☎ **971-731-647**). Both clinics are open 24 hours.

Laundry Get that stubborn Mallorcan dirt out of your clothes at **Lavandería y Tintorería Soft** right off of Plaça Gomila. They take their time (normally 2 or 3 days), but if you ask really nicely they may sud your duds overnight (C. Porres, 2 Bjos; ☎ **971-450-493**; 8.90€ for a 5-kilogram load).

Pharmacies **Farmacia Castaner** (Plaça del Rey Juan Carlos; ☎ **971 711-534**) opens daily from 9am to midnight.

Telephone City code: **971**; operator: **1003**; international operator: **1005.**

SLEEPING

If you show up in Palma in the summer without reserving a room in advance, there are still some indoor options (like a bar stool) and outdoor options (like park benches and port docks) for catching 40 winks in **Palma.** Crawling distance to all the bars, clubs, and late-night bites, **La Gomila** is convenient but it's not exactly what you'd call a quiet neighborhood. In **La Llotja,** you generally find more upscale, centrally located accommodations, but it still offers a few inexpensive places to hang your hat. As you close in on the **Historical Center,** you will find fewer

affordable options and, correspondingly, more breathtaking lobbies. The trendy **Portixol** district is home to numerous designer hotels and their equally chichi restaurants.

Hostels

➜ **Hostal Apuntadors** ★ From the same owners who brought you the Terramar comes this enhanced version of a hostel. The rooms are not filled with lovely antiques, and most likely no one you've ever heard of calls this their home away from home; but it's a great value for the location, large rooms, cleanliness, and spectacular roof terrace. *Calle dels*

Apuntadors 8. ☎ 971-713-491. www.palma-hostales.com. Single with shared bath 33€, single with private bath 45€, double with shared bath 45€, double with private bath 60€, 6-bed dorm with shared bath 20€ per person. Amenities: Cafe with satellite TV, breakfast room, elevator, safe, sheets, terrace, towels.

→**Hostal Terramar** Located across the harbor in La Gomila, this *hostal* offers a clean, sunny place for you and all your buddies to crash after a hard night out, as well as a terrace for you to broil yourselves on the next day. Although one of the least expensive options, it also seems to be the most recently renovated of the area hostels, most of which look like they need a reality makeover show to jump-start them. Select rooms are equipped with private bath, terrace, and furnished kitchen. *Plaça Mediterrània 8. ☎ 971-739-931. www.palma-hostales.com. Single with shared bath 30€, double with shared bath 40€, double with private bath 52€, triple 65€, 5-bed penthouse dorm 20€ per person, apt (minimum 2 people) 60€. Amenities: Breakfast room, kitchen/dining, laundry, shared bathrooms, sheets, terrace, towels, Wi-Fi.*

Cheap

→**Hotel Born** Notoriously famous for its incredible 18th-century details—as well as for being the best location in town—Born is beloved by travelers of all ages. The rooms are just so-so compared to the rest of the hotel, but they are ample; for a good night's sleep, book one facing the quiet courtyard. Enjoy the fresh-brewed coffee and an *ensaimada* (a local pastry fried in pork lard) for breakfast in the Mallorcan-style, palm-tree-lined courtyard. *Calle Sant Jaume 3. ☎ 971-712-942. www.hotelborn.com. Single 50€-65€, double 73€-93€. Breakfast included. Amenities: Bar, bike rentals, courtyard. In room: A/C, TV, hair dryer, safe.*

→**Hotel Rosamar** Depending on the night, a crowd may be gathered on the leafy garden patio in front of a big screen showing Festival Europeo de la Canción (Europe's version of *American Idol*) or grooving to the sounds of a DJ spinning under the stars. The rooftop terraces—all three are excellent spots for sunning—provide superb views, lounge chairs, and showers to recuperate after a night of pain and pleasure. However, truth to be told, the Rosamar is like a vintage leather jacket: It could use a few repairs; but it's broken in just right, and everyone looks good in it. This hotel caters mostly to gay men, but all are welcomed by the knowledgeable staff, who will advise you on all things Mallorcan for those nights when you can't fit this bible in your pocket. *Avinguda Joan Miró 74. ☎ 971-732-723. www.rosamarpalma.com. Single 45€, double/suite 60€-85€, triple 70€. Breakfast included. Amenities: Bar, laundry service, safe, 3 terraces, travel/tourist desk, TV, Wi-Fi. In room: A/C, suites have TV.*

Doable

→**Hotel Palau Sa Font** ★ Good things come in small packages. . . . In this case the package is a former Episcopal palace seemingly designed by Berlin socialites on Mediterranean holiday. Inside, the eclectic decor and furniture mix with local and international art positioned on guest room doors (strangely enough) as well as in common areas. The vibe is a bit early '90s, but the warm colors lend a soft light to the common areas and the precious roof terrace with its tiny wading pool and awesome views. *Calle dels Apuntadors 38. ☎ 971-712-277. Single 97€-203€, double 147€-215€. Breakfast included. Amenities: Bar, fax, pool, safe, terrace, towels, travel desk or travel info. In room: A/C, TV, hair dryer, minibar.*

→**Portixol Hotel** A bit on the pricey side for this category, but worth the extra dough. This posh little hotel and restaurant lies in Palma's new hot-spot. It was built in the '50s and remodeled in 1999, with great Swedish style. The solid details of the rooms are perfect in their simplicity and touches of color and enhance the sea and sky pouring in. The Portixol prides itself in service to your taste arranging yoga classes and throwing in free tickets to the local football games to boot! *Calle Sirena 27.* ☎ *971-271-800. www.portixol.com. Single 115€; double 195€–275€; Atico (loft room with terrace) 350€; extra bed 50€. Breakfast included. Amenities: Restaurant, bar, bike rental, fax, gym, Internet, laundry service, rooms for those w/limited mobility, sauna, spa, swimming pool, terrace, towels, travel desk or travel info, TV. In room: A/C, TV, hair dryer, Internet, minibar, safe.*

Splurge

➜**Hotel Convent de Missió** ★ Though you may not be able to finagle a room here, stop in to admire the lobby or at least visit the website and see what Mallorcan modern architecture and interior design is all about. The use of Japanese design elements give this stripped-down 17th century monastery a Zen-like quality. The vaulted ceiling of the art gallery and snap-a-pic-before-you-eat dishes in the equally au courant restaurant make Convent de Missió a worthy cultural stop. *Calle de la Missió 7a.* ☎ *971-227-347. www.conventdelamissio.com. Double 242€, junior suite 299€, suite 368€. Breakfast included. Amenities: Restaurant, bar, laundry service, room service, sauna, solarium. In room: A/C, TV, hair dryer, Internet, minibar, safe.*

➜**Puro** ★ La Llotja does it up Delano style with Puro World, not just a hotel and restaurant, but a self-nominated way of life for chic global nomads to "see and be seen" (we are quoting this from the website). Like many Ibizan dens of the divine, Puro has it's own label which as of now

mostly consists of spa products, but we are guessing that they will come out with more merchandise as this concept palace grows with popularity. Even with all this hype, Puro standards are high and the Asian influence is used selectively and effectively from the bedding to the fusion cuisine at the trendiest eatery in town. The rooms are so lofty and airy you may not need to go up to the roof deck, but you should not miss out flaunting that YSL tanga in one of the tents by the small but important pool. *Calle Montenegro 12.* ☎ *971-425-450. www.purohotel.com. Single 165€–170€, double 235€–260€, suite 285€–450€. Breakfast included. Amenities: Restaurant, bar, babysitting, laundry service, room service. In room: A/C, TV, hair dryer, Internet, minibar, safe.*

EATING

The quality and variety of the food offered in Mallorca is comparable only to that of the big cities on the mainland. Besides the fantastic tapas and seafood that are the typical fare in the islands, Mallorcan culinary offerings also include a smattering of ethnic food and even a 24-hour diner. The most popular areas to dine are in the neighborhood **La Llotja** and, more recently, in **Santa Catalina,** the neighborhood that spills out from the **Mercat de Santa Catalina** where many *cocina de mercado* (market cuisine) restaurants serve delicious, freshly made food from menus that vary according to the daily crop of produce. The restaurants along the waterfront tend to be very expensive, and—judging by the food—you're paying almost exclusively for the view.

Hot Spots

MTV Best ● ➜**Bar Bosch** TAPAS This classic bar with the sassy waitstaff has been a popular rendezvous for Mallorcans since the days when its name was one of the only German influences on the island. Grab a table in the loud and vibrant marble dining room, or, better yet, sit outside and enjoy this ideal spot for people-watching on Plaça Rei Joan Carles. One of the main draws of the Bosch is that, despite its popularity, the prices are still ridiculously cheap. The tapas, while not quite what you would call delicacies, do represent many Mallorcan classics; try the *frito mallorquin*, a delicious meat scramble, or get a *pica-pica* (combination plate) with everything you can fit on it. But the real specialties here are the sandwiches: Don't ask me how they do it, but a "Bikini" (toasted ham and cheese sandwich) never tasted so good. *Plaça Rei Joan Carles I no. 6.* ☎ *971-721-131. Tapas 1.50€–3€. Combination plate 8.50€. Mon–Sat 7am–2am; Sun 7am–1:30am.*

📺 Best 🌑 → **Minimar** ★★ INTERNATIONAL In nouveau-trendy Portixol, this classy restaurant fits like a glove. Whether you go with friends or a recently acquired love interest, IKEA-modern tables and decor, with a great view of the sea, make for a very pleasant dining experience. The mouthwatering menu of creative tapas and main dishes includes such light and healthy options as sea urchin and truffle scramble, tuna sashimi salad, and grilled octopus with orange aioli (a traditional garlic and olive oil sauce). The menu has huge, magazine-style photos of each dish, which, believe or not, are actually bigger than they look. Don't order too much food, because dessert is a must. The crème brûlée with lime and ginger or the trio of delicate chocolate cups make me wish I were still there. *Vicari Joaquim Fuster 67. Portixol.* ☎ *971-248-604. Entrees 14€–26€. Tapas 5€–15€. Mon–Sat 10am–2pm and 5–9pm.*

Tapas

→ **BeeWi** This modern bar with punch-board ceilings, stenciled graffiti walls, and '60s funk music is an up-and-coming Mallorcan hot spot. Completely decorated in green, orange, and white, BeeWi would be right at home in New York's Lower East Side—only, the prices are much cheaper and Moby is not a regular here. The tapas and *pintxos* (sort of a Spanish bruschetta with all sorts of toppings) are a mix of the classics, like *croquetas* (croquettes) and *tortillas* (Spanish omelette with potatoes), and new creations like squid balls with ink sauce or quail eggs with crunchy *jamón* (cured Spanish ham) and potato chips. Long kitchen- and even longer bar-hours make it great for lunch, dinner, pre-club tapas, or even an afternoon snack while you check e-mail on your laptop over their Wi-Fi connection. *Passeig Mallorca 3.* ☎ *971-956-052. Tapas 1€–9€. Mon–Sat 8am–2am. Kitchen hours Mon–Sat 12:30–4pm and 5pm–midnight.*

Cheap

→ **Diner** AMERICAN You know how it is . . . No matter how good that *jamón* is, sometimes you just can't help but crave a nice, homemade hamburger or a cheesy, hot tuna melt. Especially if it's 3 in the morning and you forgot to eat dinner. Luckily Palma has it's own 24-hour diner, with the requisite bright lights, red booths, and '50s pictures on the walls. We don't need to tell you what to order here—just that the fries are crunchy, the hamburgers juicy, and the shakes thick. And, since it's one of the only joints open 24 hours, everybody eats here, not just homesick expats and tourists. *Calle San Magín 23.* ☎ *971-736-222. Hamburgers 5€. Open 24/7.*

→ **La Tortilleria** SANDWICHES Under the dilapidated building in Plaça Gomila, this large cartlike counter is always surrounded by young'uns satisfying their early-morning munchies on their way out for the day or on their way home for the night. Try the infamous *bocadillo de tortilla de patatas* (omelette sandwich with potatoes)—if you are vegetarian, you will probably become quite familiar with this staple of the non-meat, Spanish diet. Most people scarf down the *jamón, queso, huevo y bacon* (ham, cheese, fried egg, and bacon) on a roll. It's not exactly health food, but it's just what you need to absorb the alcohol and curb that craving; besides, it's open late, and the prices can't be beat. *Plaça Gomila. No phone. Sandwiches 2€–4.50€. Daily 11pm–7am.*

➔**Orient Express** CREPES All aboard! The interior of this cute creperie, with lots of carved dark wood, is decorated to emulate the dining car on an old train. The retro cash register, telephone, and furniture make you feel you've stepped back to the golden years of swing dancing and cigar smoking at the theater. Some interesting vintage posters amp up the golden-age ambience. They have a wide variety of crepes, with good vegetarian options, like *champignon* (mushroom) and cheese, or a delicious vegetable soufflé with Roquefort sauce. The waitstaff is very friendly, and the low prices make it a go-to spot in this neighborhood that—with a restaurant in every other building—has no shortage of choices. *Sa Llotja del Mar 6.* ☎ *971-711-183. Entrees 7€–9€. Mon–Fri 1:30–4pm and 8:30pm–midnight; Sat 8:30pm–midnight.*

Doable

➔**El Pesquero** SEAFOOD Location is key when it comes to this fancy tapas bar and restaurant perched right on the water. Sitting here during the late afternoon, you can sip on a drink while you watch all the boats coming back to port for the night. Your killer view from the wooden deck, with its white umbrellas and nautical-blue deck chairs, almost makes up entirely for the average food. Your best bets are the different varieties of fish, so fresh it's practically

brought from the sea to your plate. Sea bass and sea bream are house classics, but, depending on the day, turbot, red mullet, or swordfish may also be available. Have them grilled or *a la espalda* (open-baked with garlic) with a nice Albariño or Mallorcan white wine. *Moll de la Llotja.* ☎ *971-715-220. www.cafeportpesquer.com. Entrees 9€–20€. Daily 10am–midnight.*

➔**Gran Folies Beach Club** MEDITERRANEAN The food is one of the many reasons to come spend a day at this sunseeker's heaven, only a short bus ride away from Palma. Built in seven levels on the slope of a huge cove, the club beckons you to come early and rent a sun chair by the saltwater pool. After a morning spent diving from the rocks and swimming in the crystal-clear seawater, you'll surely work up an appetite. Luckily, you can either enjoy lunch from your deck chair or walk up a couple of levels and dine on the terrace with a view of the endless blue sea. Start with a creative salad, like the Mimosa (endive, asparagus, avocado, caviar, smoked salmon, and shrimp), and continue with the scrumptious paella or grilled tuna cubes. Digest for a little (remember: Momma always said half an hour!), then rinse and repeat as necessary. *Cala Llamp, Port D'Andratx.* ☎ *971-671-094. www.granfolies.com.es. Entrees 14€–19€. Daily 10am–2am. Bus to Port D'Andratx.*

Splurge

MTV **Best** ☻ ➔**Refectori** ★★★ INTERNATIONAL One of the few things that most people in Palma agree on is that Jaime (pronounced *Hi-meh*, unlike the naked chef) Oliver is the top chef on the island. In this sober dining room with black chairs, white tables, a tree in the middle, and impressive black and white prints covering the walls, the menu dreams up dishes you could never have imagined. Start with a plate of *ceps* (local mushrooms) *al olive-oil comfit* with Kenya beans, the presentation of which is truly museum-worthy. For a main, we highly recommend the stewed monkfish with sobrasada on a bed of potatoes, spinach, sunflower seeds, and raisins with beet oil; or try the red veal *turnedó* with sautéed wild mushrooms. If your taste buds can handle more pleasure, finish with one of the ever-changing, never-disappointing desserts, such as our favorite: the coconut flan with kumquat and cocoa sorbet. Definitely make a reservation though; the hottest ticket in town is not for late-comers. *Calle de la Missió.* ☎ *971-227-347. Entrees 25€–28€. Mon–Fri 1–3:30pm; Mon–Sat 8–11pm.*

Cafes

→ **Bar Central** Another classic Palma hangout, dating from 1945, this tiny cafe right across the street from the modernista Gran Hotel serves the best *café con leche* in the city. Skip the few tables inside and go for one on the sidewalk since this street, right down the steps from Plaça Major, is one of the most picturesque areas in Palma. You can get simple sandwiches here or check out the **Forn des Teatre**, right next door, a 70-plus-year-old bakery, which serves up some of the best *ensaimadas* (pinwheel-shaped Mallorcan pastries) in town. Vegetarians beware: This innocent-looking pastry is typically fried in lard. *Plaça. Weyler 10.* ☎ *971-721-058. Daily 6am–9pm.*

📺 Best ☺ → **Ca'n Joan de S'aigo** ★ Three hundred years ago, Palma did not have quite so many cafes. As a matter of fact, coffee had probably just come across the high seas to Europe from Ethiopa. But when Red Beard was in need of something to quaff his sweet tooth, he probably put in to port at this classic ice cream parlor and pastry shop, where locals still arrive in packs every day to enjoy the fantastic,

only-in-Mallorca duo of fresh-baked *ensaimada* and homemade ice cream served in pretty glasses. Try a sorbet made from seasonal fruit or the luxurious chocolate, if you dare. If sweets are not your thing, the decor alone—with its tiled, Art Nouveau floors and green, blown-glass chandeliers—makes this an obligatory sightseeing stop. *Calle de Ca'n Sanc 10.* ☎ *971-710-759. Wed–Mon 8am–9pm.*

PARTYING

Bars

In Palma, the ratio of bars to inhabitants is one of the highest in Spain, which is saying quite a lot actually. Many are tourist-oriented boozing holes with the monochromatic landscape of lobster-hued multinationals drinking cheap sangria like it's cranberry juice. But if you look a little closer and follow the lead of the locals, you will find some pretty unique authentic bars, where rules are bent and legendary parties are born. From trendy design lounges to crazy drag-queen hangouts and the beach club spectacular, Palma offers a bar for every mood and taste.

📺 Best ☺ → **Es Jaç** Fashion wunderkind Miguel Adrover's version of a bar is a feast of interior design. Every detail in the tiny place has been paid extreme attention to: from the white tiled bar, where every tile was made out of wood covered in clay, to the Egyptian style bathrooms with birdhouses on the top, every lamp, the pillows, and the giant pot in the middle. Come early so that you can see it without too many people in it and enjoy a pomade (gin with lemon) or the classic Hierbas (Balearic herb liquor). It gets packed after midnight with chill arts scene locals and sophisticated tourists that mingle to the sounds of electronic music and old-skool house. *Calle Vallseca 13. No phone. No credit cards.*

📺 (**Best** ❢) → **Flexas** If you haven't seen the video for "Time Gous By Con Loli," Loli's cover of Madonna's "Hung Up," stop reading and check it out online. Once you know what you're in for, come to their bar and see firsthand what the fabulous trio of singer and two dancers is capable of. The decor is sophisticated kitsch, the kind of place where celluloid slumlord John Waters would be happy to have a drink; and—with drag queens and performers encouraged to do their thing—the clientele is anything but boring. Try the surprisingly fantastic tapas, served until midnight. *Calle Llotgeta 12.* ☎ *971-425-938.*

→ **Lorien** To call this dark, wood-happy, basement bar in the old town a "beer heaven" is an understatement. The menu offers over 100 types of beer in bottles and draft from almost 20 countries. Start your tour in Belgium, the heavy hitter with over 50 varieties including both pineapple and banana brews. Continue with a visit to Germany, Holland, the U.K., and so on. By the end of the night you'll be able to say *cerveza* in 12 different languages, or at least you'll think that's what you're saying. *Calle de les Caputxines 5a.* ☎ *971-723-202.*

→ **Virtual Beach Club** ★★ Another paradise of hedonism, Virtual, with its enviable seaside location, just might be the all-day affair you always dreamed of. Just a 10-minute cab ride from Palma, this resort has been one of the hottest places in the island since it opened in 2006. Sit back and choose from a broad selection of drinks made with fresh juices, or dive in as the sound of the sea mixes with the chill-out music in the background. You can also grab a bite at the casual bistro or the white-napkined restaurant and, when the night comes, dance your last bit of energy away in the Zona nightclub, surely one of the chicest caves known to man. All just

for a one-drink minimum. *Passeig Illetas 60.* ☎ *971-703-235. www.virtualclub.es.*

Live Music

Unlike Ibiza, Palma has quite a lively music scene, and most bars offer shows on certain nights. Check *Youthing* **magazine** to see what's up during your stay.

→ **Sa Posada de Bellver** Just about every city we have been to in the U.S. and Spain has their own version of this bar/restaurant. In a Bohemian grunge atmosphere frequented mostly by local 20-somethings who are just making their way out for the night, live acts belt their hearts out on the small stage as partiers shout to each other to be heard above the noise. Even if you come just for the music, you won't be able to resist the delicious combo of Lebanese/Mallorqui chow, especially the *greixonera de brossat* (even better then your granny's ricotta cheese tart). You can also get tarot and palm readings after 9pm on Thursdays and Saturdays. *Calle Bellver 7.* ☎. *971-730-739. Cover 2€. Entrees 5€–12€. Concerts daily at 10pm and 12:30am.*

Clubs

If you are looking for the best international DJs and the most massive clubs in the world, you are on the wrong damn island. However if you want a more laid-back clubbing experience with less drugs and more culture, you may find yourself happily surprised. Palma has a huge variety of clubs that offer everything, from Ibiza-style electronic dance madness to '80s metal and drag-queen electro galore. Most clubs charge a cover of about 10€ to 20€ (that price usually gets you a "free" drink) and are open from midnight to 6am. But some "bars"—with dance floors as hot as anything you can hope for—are also open until 4am, and some of them even have free admittance. Door policies are pretty lax, but dressing up a little will help you cruise in like the Knight Rider.

➜ **Abraxas** Housed in what used to be known as Pachá, Palma's spin on the mega club perches on the side of a cliff overlooking the bay. The place is jam-packed with perma-tan tourists and English kids trying to dress as slick as Italians. A battalion of disco balls and strobes will distract you from the hot go-go dancers who heat up the scene in the main room. Unfortunately, one of the dance floors boasts that downer of a mix of Spanish pop, reggaeton, and Top 40 that has caused so much damage to the musical palate of Iberian youth; but you can always seek refuge on the electronic dance floor, the terrace, or the VIP section, if you can sweet your way into the latter. *Passeig Marítim 42.* ☎ *971-455-908. www.abraxasmallorca.com.*

MTV (Best ◉) (FREE) ➜ **Cultura Club** This multicultural venue could easily be in any subcategory of the partying section. Open since 2005, it has rapidly become the local favorite based on its excellent menu of diverse events: movies on Tuesday nights, live concert videos of Nirvana and the like on Wednesdays, live music and stand-up comedy on Thursdays, and guest DJs on Fridays and Saturdays. After midnight, things get heated up when the real dancing starts. The crowd here is alternative, indie-rock boys, girls, and others—a perfect place to meet locals and follow them to the next party. *Calle Jaume de Santancilia 3. No phone. www.culturaclub.com.*

(FREE) ➜ **Garito Café** ★★ Although it started as a classic local bar in the '70s, after a 1998 renovation it has become a point of reference for Palma's night scene. The party starts here as early as 8pm, when you can go to have a chill drink or eat tasty sandwiches and salads on the terrace to the sounds of jazz or loungey electronic music. At night, resident DJs and international guests the caliber of Peter Kruder have everybody shakin' their booties in the well-preserved Art Deco hall or at the "red room" upstairs. Wednesday night is for funk, soul, and hip-hop; Thursdays electro, techno, and house music take over; Fridays move to old-skool house and disco, and Saturday is guest DJ night. Sundays, you can get into the groove with '80s pop and new wave. And, best of all, since it doesn't have a cabaret license and closes "early," there's no cover charge. *Dársena de Can Barbará.* ☎ *971-736-912. www.garitocafe.com.*

➜ **La Metro** La Metro is a post-Franco Spanish classic. Within kitschy red interiors with a bar in the middle and a stage at the end, boys dressed as girls and barely dressed girls perform periodically to the sounds of irreverent electro clash. Everything goes here after midnight, and a second wind blows at 4am when refugees from Cultura Club and other closing bars come to end the night. Leave your prejudices behind and bring your attitude intact. *Plaça Gomila. No phone.*

(FREE) ➜ **Rara Avis** You definitely won't find a place like this in Ibiza, though you might in Seattle. High heels are replaced by Cons, fishnets give way to jeans, and alternative rock blasts from the speakers. The place is not too big and/or fabulous, and the scene of mostly local youngsters can sometimes get downright rowdy; but if rock 'n' roll is what primes your pump, you'll be jumpin' all night. The first Thursday of every month they hold a *noches raras* (weird nights) dedicated to a particular band or music style. *Plaça Gomila. No phone. www.soyraro.com.*

Gay Nightlife

Gay and straight life in Mallorca are not segregated. Most bars and clubs are very gay-friendly, but particularly so are Es Jaç, Flexas, and La Metro. For gay-only bars, check out the Avenida Joan Miró, near Plaça Gomila. There you can find the following two clubs, which are almost next to each other.

➜ **Bar Flesh** Across the street from Black Cat, this bar is run by two Englishmen and specializes in videos of the don't-tell-your-momma kind. *Av. Joan Miró 68.* ☎ *971-455-146.*

➜ **Black Cat** Palma's favorite gay club is also the biggest and raciest, with an infamous downstairs darkroom. It offers live shows at 3:30am for a mixed crowd of locals and visitors. They also host weekly theme-parties such as Roman parties and an outrageous Carnaval in late February. *Av. Joan Miró 75. No phone. usuarios.lycos.es/blackcatdisco.*

SIGHTSEEING

Most people think of Mallorca as all beaches and nonstop partying, but Palma has a lot of nice landmarks that you shouldn't wait for a rainy day or a sunburn to visit.

➜ **Banys Arabes** While this may not be as impressive as other Arabic baths you've seen around Spain, it's a lovely little diversion if you are crusing around town and need a break from the heat. Duck into the flourishing garden and check out the only thing left in the city that speaks of the once-thriving Moorish community established in the 10th century. In the *caldarium,* or central bath area, light leaks through holes in the ceiling and creates dust-speckled rays of light around the small dim space—it makes for a truly dramatic scene as the half-orange dome and 12 columns catch the sun. *Calle Serra 7.* ☎ *971-721-549. Admission 1.50€. Daily 9am–7pm.*

wwwired

If you can't pass a day without updating your photo log, you have problems. However, we are here to help. **Azul Cybercafé** (C. Soledad 4, basement entrance, right off of Plaça de la Reina, by the cathedral; ☎ **971-712-927;** Mon–Thurs 10am–9pm, Fri–Sat 10am–8pm) opened in 1999 and has ruled Palma's Web life ever since. This cyber-joint offers service for .05€ per minute and features new computers and a super fast 2.4 Mb connection, plus Wi-Fi if you want to bring your own. Add drinks, food, fax, and telephone service, and you've got all you need for the perfect e-experience—whatever that means to you. If you get too excited by your pal's new video on YouTube and drop your laptop, don't worry: They also repair PCs.

➜ **Catedral La Seu** Walking up through the garden paths to la Seu and seeing it from a distance as a beacon of the city is even more impressive then entering it; but since you *should* enter it too, we'll give you the low-down. In 1230, construction began on the site of the former main mosque, and—in case you thought Sagrada Familia in Barcelona is taking a long time to be finished—it was not completed until 1600. There was an earthquake in 1851 that destroyed the original facade of this classic Levantin Gothic structure. Then came the 20th century and with it Antoni Gaudí; everyone in Catalunya had to get a piece of him, so, among other modernista details, he created the odd wrought-iron centerpiece, which hangs from the ceiling. There is also a small museum of massive gold and silver artifacts attached. *Calle Palau Reial.* ☎ *971-231-130. Cathedral free admission. Museum 3.50€. Mon–Fri 10am–6:15pm; Sat 10am–2:15pm.*

FREE → **Es Baluard** The Museu d'Art Contemporani, all lit up at the end of La Llotja with its magnificent old wall and Jorge Oteiza Hilargia's sculpture *La luna como luz movediza* in front, is a site to behold, as are its contents. Works by the prolific European masters such as Picasso, Miró, Magritte, and Giacometti are in the permanent collection along with current artists Rebecca Horn and José Manuel Broto. A section is dedicated to local Balearic artists, and temporary shows often feature video installations or photography. Even if you don't dig contemporary art, the bar in the stylish cafe overlooking the port is a good place to enjoy some live music (mostly classical). Check the website for events, which are scheduled year-round. *Calle Sant Miquel 11. www. esbaluard.org.* ☎ *971-713-515. Free admission. Mon–Fri 10am–6:30pm; Sat 10am–1:30pm.*

Deja Vu

If the Balearic islands remind you of the California coast, well, you have one man to thank for it: Miquel Josep Serra i Ferrer, otherwise known as Father Juniper Serra. A Franciscan monk born in Mallorca in 1713, Father Juniper left the islands for Mexico in 1749. He later made his way up the Californian coast establishing missions from San Diego to Monterey, and dropping plant seeds from his homeland all along the way. The similar climate did the rest, and, hence, the prevalence of cypresses, sycamores, and orange and lemon trees in Mallorca make you feel like you never crossed the Sierra Madre.

PLAYING OUTSIDE

There are no beaches in Palma. The closest public beach is **Playa Nova,** but it's nothing to write home about. Of the beaches nearby Palma, your best bet is probably **Can Pastilla.** This largely overdeveloped beach attracts thousands of people every summer, but the sand is very fine and the water is clear and tourquoise. Take the bus to **Platja de Palma.**

The beaches near Palma tend to be more crowded than others but there are some good options a short bus ride away. Since you'll have to take a bus or drive anyway, you might as well go to a really nice beach. One favorite is **Es Trenc,** a long stretch of white sand where Mallorcans come to take their clothes off and get their tan on. Woods surround the beach, which is fairly isolated, but its popularity has attracted a few *chiringuitos* and restaurants. If you want real nature, walk to the next beach, **Best** **Es Cargols,** which—though not huge—is almost completely undeveloped. You can reach Es Trenc and Es Cargols by taking the bus from Palma to Colonia Sant Jordi.

SHOPPING

It's so hard to resist shopping in Palma, especially on those days when you'll use any excuse to hang out in the air-conditioning. A decent concentration of crafts are available in **Plaça de l'Artesania** and **Plaça Llorenç Bisbal,** and the central market offers a variety of packaged food treats to sneak through customs. If you are looking for clothes to show off—be it on runway or half-pipe—Palma delivers on that front as well. Three areas that offer newcomer and top international labels are **Carrer Argentina,** around **Plaça Born** up to **Plaça Major,** and around **Plaça de Cort.** Stores open from Monday to Saturday, 9:30am to 2pm and 5 to 8pm. However, smaller shops tend to close

Made in Mallorca

There are a few things that, while you may occasionally encounter them elsewhere in Spain, hail specifically from these parts. The *ensaimada,* purchased as much for their eye-catching hexagonal boxes as their spiral shape and sweet, fluffy, powdered dough, are the classic Mallorcan treat, traditionally eaten with *café con leche* or ice-cream. (Be warned vegetarians, these babies are full of pork fat.) Another Mallorcan exclusive that lasts a lot longer is that shoe you see in every shop window and on practically every passer-by: the *avarcas.* Available in every color and dating back to early Spain, this peasant shoe turned trendy is praised for being the most comfortable form of footwear available. The jury is still out on the exact origin of the *Siurell statuettes*—whether Phoenecian, Greek, or Arab—but most Mallorcans will tell you that these clay figurines are part of a game dating back to the Bronze Age or that they have some sort of religious significance. What everyone agrees on is that these whistles and statues—which are most often white with hand-painted bursts of primary colors and usually depict humans and animals—make perfect souvenirs. The Consell de Mallorca offers a handy leaflet (available at any tourist info center) indicating ideal places to purchase theses treasures.

Saturday afternoons, and major stores and shopping malls open from 9:30am until 10pm Monday to Saturday.

→**Calaseu** Considered a city landmark, Calaseu has served Mallorcan shoppers since 1510. *Cesteria* and *aparagaterias* (basketware and woven articles) are crammed into every corner and hanging from the ceilings as well. The stock of woven totes with leather piping, espadrilles in a multitude of colors, hammocks, fishing baskets, and common household products are constantly being updated by the vibrant new German owner. *Carrer Cordelería 17. No phone.*

→**Gordiola** Tour the museum and factory where they have been churning out glass of all shapes and sizes since 1719, and then browse the wares to your heart's content in the giftshop. But don't worry if your agenda prevents you from taking the road trip. Palma has two equally enticing stores where you can snag a goblet or perhaps consider a signature curlicue chandelier to brighten up your room at the hostel.

Factory/museum: Carretera Palma-Manacor Km 19, Algaida. ☎ *971-665-046. www.gordiola. com. Stores: Calle Victoria 6.* ☎ *971-711-541. Calle Jaime II 14.* ☎ *971-715-518.*

→**Pasatiempos** This club-kid favorite packs in a broad selection of international and local street, skate, and surf paraphernalia, like banana bikes, custom-painted Vans, one-of-a-kind appliqué bags, and humorous T's concocted by small Mallorcan labels like La Familia Bien Gracias y Si me Buscas me Encuentras. *Calle Quint 3.* ☎ *971-725-980. www.pasatiempos. net.*

MTV **Best ♥** →**Zest** Zest is our favorite shopping find for it's fantastic cyber murals and its discernable selection of one-of-a-kind, quirky yet sophisticated clothing and accessories for lads and lasses. This store would be right at home in Tokyo, Melrose, or the Brooklyn hipster haven of Williamsburg; but thank goodness it's here so you can get those mint metallic leather sandals by Gios Chippo, or a bag and T by the house label Rita Mutano and make your friends (and enemies) back home green. *Calle Corderia 11.* ☎ *971-495-612.*

Markets

Market day in Mallorca can be one guy with a sausage stand if you're unlucky or fantastic antiques and crafts if your lucky charm is workin' its mojo. Here, as well as at all other markets in Spain, use your bargaining skills; it's expected. One of the noteworthy markets is the **Consell town flea market,** which started as a little Sunday pastime by Aussie collector John Douglas in 1994 and now attracts a massive crowd of up to 300 vendors. This is the place to pick up that collectible you can resell on eBay in a few years (or a few weeks). **Sineu** holds one of the most authentic farmer's markets on the island every Wednesday. To get to both Consell and Sineu take the Palma Manacor train at Palma's main station. **Palma**'s big market is held on Saturday morning, along the streets below El Corte Ingles. Your best bet is to pick up a guide to all Mallorca's markets at the tourist info center, or check the website www.balearnet.com/mallorca for up to the minute stats on what's selling where islandwide. Festivals bring out the best vintage and antiques around the island, so keep your eyes peeled.

Pollença/Formentor/Alcúdia

Pollença is one of those tiny inland towns that are full of history and charm. Once awarded to the Order of the Templars (think *DaVinci Code*) by the King of Spain, every nook and cranny has a story. The big attraction here is **Monte Calvario,** otherwise known as the Calvari. Three hundred sixty-five steps, built in the 18th century and beginning next to the town council on Carrer de Jesus will take you to a small *ermita* (hermitage or small shrine/chapel)

right by the Calvari. The incredible panoramic lookout at the top is very rewarding, and, if you're not up to a bit of devout exercise, you can also reach it by car on the cross-lined Carrer de las Cruces.

In the small town of **Badia de Pollença,** which is accessible from **Port de Pollença,** you will find warmer water and whiter sand than at the southern Mallorcan beaches. This area known for its watersports does not have much in terms of nightlife, but it is a nice place to chill.

The intimidating drive to **Formentor** around winding, cliff-side roads has done little to deter tourists from the furthest northern tip of the island. During the day the drive is slow with traffic, which is fine since you will want to spend as much time as possible looking out the window at the incomparable views. The landscape evolves from lush, green pine forests to jagged rock formations and twisting cypress trees as you climb the curves to **Cap Formentor.** If you chose to drive, which is the easiest way to reach the Cap, watch out for hardcore bikers, buses, and transport vehicles as the roads are not just steep and curvaceous, but also extremely narrow. There are many lookout points along the way. Once you manage to park your car at the lighthouse, you will find a little kiosk offering refreshments near a sign marking a rugged circuit trail to **Moll de Patronet.** This 500m (1,640 ft.) footpath takes approximately 15 minutes each way and brings you to a magical little *cala* (cove). You have to be in fairly decent shape to make the climb back up. Either on the way to the Cap or back be sure to spend some time at some of the accessible calas along the way and experience, along with other day-trippers, the **Platja de Formentor** and its inexplicable beauty.

The charismatic historic center of **Alcúdia** is a worthy alternative to a day at the beach. Built within a still-standing protective wall, the numerous postcard stands and tacky souvenir shops only steal the appeal of one main street, Carrer Major; wander off a bit and you'll find bougainvillea-covered walls, secret gardens, and a few bistro gems. Another benefit to **Alcúdia** is its accessibility to both the **Pollença** and **Alcúdia** bays. With watersports galore and the best nightlife on this side of the island, **Port d'Alcúdia** is the home base chosen by many visitors, despite (or perhaps because of) its Jersey-shore, honky-tonk feel. The heavily touristed Alcúdia bay offers a wide beach that gets cleaner and deeper as you venture away from the port. The boardwalk attractions include duty-free supermarkets selling anything and everything from dildos and booze to beachwear, and booths where you can arrange tours on glass-bottomed boats or catamarans.

GETTING THERE

From the bus station at Plaza Espanya, in Palma, there are five **buses** daily to Port de Pollença via Inca and Pollença (4.80€ one-way). There are also nine buses to Alcudia and Port d'Alcudia (4.20€ one-way), but unfortunately the only way to get to Formentor is by car or catching a cab in Port de Pollença.

If you are **driving**, take the PM-2 Expressway to Inca and continue on the C-713 to Alcudia, or exit on the PM-220 to Pollença and Port de Pollença, from there continue on the windy road to Formentor.

BASICS

The tourist office in Pollença is in a medieval building at **OIT Municipal Pollença,** Carrer Sant Domingo 2 (☎ 971-866-746). It's open Monday to Saturday

8am to 3pm and 5 to 7pm. In Alcudia, **OIT Municipal Alcúdia,** Carrer Major 17 (☎ 971-897-100), opens Monday to Saturday 8am to 3pm, and the big Tourist Booth in the middle of the boardwalk in Port d'Alcudia, **OIT Municipal Port d' Alcúdia,** Passeig Marítim s/n (☎ 971-547-257), is open Monday to Saturday 8:30am to 9:30pm. All of them are pointed to by street signs around town.

SLEEPING

You will have your choice of cheap sleeps on the road parallel to **Alcúdia beach,** which is lined with all manner of hostels. If you are tempted in the early-morning hours to crash out on one of the lounge chairs that are left out on the beach overnight, watch out—even this unassuming little bay has its share of freaks who will be lining up to rouse you from your slumber. **Pollença** and **Alcúdia** feature incomparable *petit hotels* tucked away up on hills and hidden inside secret gardens. **Formentor** has a few options, but only one on its famous headland (see Hotel Formentor, below).

➜**Can Tem** ★★ Nowhere will you feel more like an invited guest than at this intimate and captivating Hotel d'Interior (an antique building converted into a small hotel under strict guidelines as to preserve the historic space). Entered from a cobblestone pedestrian side-street, this renovated 17th-century laborers' home is like a step into the past, with all the comforts of modernity. A grand foyer leads to the open-air courtyard, which most of the accommodations overlook. Each extremely welcoming room will have you contemplating how to get its contents to *Antiques Roadshow* without anyone noticing. If old stuff isn't really your thing, you can stay in the discerningly modern studio loft toward the back off the garden. *Calle de L'Església 14.*

Alcúdia. ☎ *971-243-537.* *www.hotelcantem. com.* *Single 68€–75€, double 77€–100€, suite 108€–120€, extra bed 36€. Breakfast included. Amenities: Breakfast room, fridge, garden, laundry, rooms for those w/limited mobility, telephone, travel desk/travel info, Wi-Fi. In room: A/C, TV.*

➜ **Hostal Calma** Hostal Calma is one of the most popular of the many *hostales* on Carrer Teodoro Canet, possibly due to its friendly staff and lively cafe in the reception area. Most rooms have small balconies and face a quiet inner courtyard; all are clean with private baths, but some have beds that are firmer then others. *Calle Teodoro Canet 25, Porto Alcúdia.* ☎ *971-548-485. www.hostalcalma.com. Single 25€–29€, double 42€–52€, triple 53€–63€. Croissant and coffee free, full breakfast 3€. Amenities: Bar, breakfast room, elevator, Internet, parking, rooms for those w/limited mobility. In room: A/C, TV, safe.*

➜ **Hotel Formentor** ★★★ Perched in one of the most idyllic spots on the island, and now a preserved area, the Formentor has been frequented by the crème de la crème of society, entertainment, and politics since 1929. More graceful than glitzy, this massive hotel complex with its endless surrounding gardens leading to one of Mallorca's prettiest beaches (accessible only from the hotel or the sea) has inspired local and international artists to depict it's beauty in the Louvre-worthy paintings that grace the common areas. The crowd may be a bit silver-haired for your taste, but, darling, with age comes wisdom; they know that after they consume an exemplary dinner on the moonlit terrace they are going to slip beneath high-thread-count sheets and doze off to the sound of soft waves caressing the shore. Make sure you nick the sensuous, cruelty-free bath products and the cozy five-star slippers. *Platja de Formentor.*

Formentor. ☎ *971-899-100. www.hotel formentor.net. Single 135€–270€, double 185€–430€, junior suite 475€–665€, additional bed 30€–75€. Amenities: Restaurant, bar, beach bar, bike rental, boutique, car rental, fax, gardens, gym, Internet, laundry service, minigolf, private beach, rooms for those w/limited mobility, sauna, spa, swimming pool, terrace, towels, travel desk, TV. In room: A/C, TV, hair dryer, minibar, safe.*

➜ **Hotel Juma** Located in sunny, laidback Plaça Mayor, the Hotel Juma maintains its vintage 1907 atmosphere without making you feel like you're turning into an old relic. Each fully equipped room is styled in a smooth blend of new and old that features decorative antiques paired right next to all the modern conveniences (ladies, you can still give your hair that perfect blow-out). The outdoor/indoor restaurant and cafe features beamed ceilings and attractive wooden chairs and marble tables. *Plaça Mayor 9, Pollença.* ☎ *971-535-002. www.hoteljuma.com. Single 63€–86€, double 92€–115€, triple 107€–125€. Breakfast included. Amenities: Restaurant, bar, fax, Internet, travel info, TV. In room: A/C, TV, hair dryer, Internet, safe.*

➜ **Hotel Puerto** A decent budget option, H. Puerto has a bit of a '70s family rec room vibe with large common area lounges to watch TV or go-online. The spacious rooms continue the vibe with flame-stitch bedcovers and clean—if outdated—bathrooms. *Calle Teodoro Canet 29, Porto Alcúdia.* ☎ *971-545-447. Single 20€–25€, double 35€–40€, triple 47€–52€. Continental breakfast 2€. Amenities: Bar and TV lounge, breakfast room, dining room, elevator, parking, rooms for those w/limited mobility, Wi-Fi. In room: A/C, TV, minibar, safe.*

EATING

➜ **Café Español** MALLORCAN Situated in the ex-administrative building of the

Order of The Templars (yep, more Dan Brown–esque action), you can still see the order's shield on the wall facing the Cathedral. People-watch over a mammoth *pa amb oli* (dark Majorcan bread with olive oil) that comes with a choice of *jamon Iberico,* cheese, tomato, or all three. *Carrer Plaça Major 2. Pollença.* ☎ *971-534-214. Pastas, salads, sandwiches 4€–10€. Daily 7am–midnight.*

➜ **La Baguette** SANDWICHES   Of all the quick, cheap options around Badia de l'Alcúdia, this strong contendor opens for breakfast a little earlier than the others. Grab a seat outside and dive into a colossal slice of apple tart with a *café con leche,* while watching the town wipe the sleep out of its eyes. Your obvious lunch choice should be one of a wide variety of baguette sandwiches to grab and take to the beach. *Calle Moliners 13, Port d'Alcúdia.* ☎ *971-549-713. Breakfast pastries or tarts with coffee, salads 3€. Sandwiches 3.20€–5.20€. Daily 7am–noon.*

➜ **L'Arca d'en Peter** ★ MARKET   Carnivores and vegans alike will find something to devour under the umbrellas of the sunlit terrace at this petite hotel restaurant offering a taste of market-fresh cuisine. Catering to people with all types of palates and needs, their creative and talented chefs will even whip something up for you if you have special dietary restrictions. Get a good dose of liver-friendly greens (hey, we know what you did last night) with one of their designer salads or indulge in a brochette of angler fish and prawn. And don't skip on the homemade desserts—once you've finished your salad, of course. *Calle d'en Serra 22, Alcúdia.* ☎ *971-539-178. Menú del día 8.50€. Entrees 7.50€–16€. Daily 12:30–4pm and 6:30pm–midnight.*

PARTYING

The majority of nightlife offered on the northwestern end of the island is concentrated in and around Port d'Alcúdia. All along Carrer Moliners and the surrounding streets you will find a plethora of English and German pubs. On the boardwalk, Spanish-style bars with outdoor seating predominate—good places to enjoy a perfect twilight refreshment, such as *clara* (beer with lemon soda).

➜ **Menta** Alcúdia's answer to the mega-club has a swimming pool in the middle, two DJs, seven bars (including a few that offer snacks), and younger, better-looking Euro-dolls then in the average Alcúdia pub. The best party to hit is Lokita (www.lokita.net), on Fridays, which attracts international wax wonders such as Groove Armada and even imported West Coast specialista Kaskade. *Av. Tucan 6, Port d'Alcúdia. No phone. Cover varies with party.*

PLAYING OUTSIDE
Beaches

If you mixed the trees of Big Sur with the bays of Rio de Janeiro and added a dose of reefs and transparent turquoise water, you would get **ⓜ Best ♦ Platja de Formentor.** If you'd like to experience what lies beneath without getting all wet you can visit some of the finest beaches on the northern coast on a glass-bottomed boat tour from Port d'Alcúdia (see "Watersports," below).

Watersports

Alcúdia is considered the mecca of Mallorcan sporting life. You can rent gear for all sorts of activities and take lessons in everything from windsurfing to paragliding.

   Transportes Maritimos Brisa (Passeig Marítim s/n; ☎ **971-545-811;** www.tmbrisa.com) offers glass-bottomed or sail catamaran tours around Pt. Pollença, Pt. Alcúdia, Formentor, and the little coves in between. The catamaran sailboat will take you (and up to 100 other passengers) to a sunny, white sand cove then throw on a BBQ (all meat/chicken) lunch, and pass out snorkels, masks, and flippers so you can get up-close and personal with the flora and fauna below. Opt for the simple hot dog and fries or a paella lunch on a glass-bottomed (non-sailing) catamaran to Formentor and witness some of Mallorca's most exclusive beaches. You'll have to shove aside a few brats if you want to see the sights through the glass bottom, but you do surprisingly see heaps of fish and coral. Trips last approximately 2 to 5 hours and cost 16€ to 50€.

Wind & Friends Watersports (Apartado de Correos 178; ☎ **627-086-950;** www.windfriends.com) has a basic windsurfing minicourse of 2¹/₂ hours per day for 3 days and includes the wetsuit for 105€. A beginner's sailing minicourse for 3 days at 3 hours per day runs 135€. Wind & Friends also features equipment rentals for those in the know and longer term courses.

If you like the view of the Alcúdia bay from the ground, imagine being suspended over it. After overcoming the first 10 seconds of panic attack when you realize how high you are, the experience turns into a peaceful and unforgettable ride. Paragliding School Alfafábia offers beginners and advanced courses with two seater and tandem rides starting at 80E for the first tandem ride. (Apartat de Correus 95; ☎ **971-891-366.** www.comeflywithus.net.)

Sóller/Deiá/Valldemossa

You are not going to find a place to bust a move or flash your bling in the northwest, but you will come away from any time spent in and around the Tramuntana range with impressions of the natural beauty engraved in your mind for life. **Sóller** and the surrounding valley have been coveted by those trying to get its goodies since the Christians overthrew the Moors in 1231. George Sand in her mostly derogatory account of the time she spent with her lover Chopin in Mallorca notes that the French would revel over the quantity and quality of citrus fruits on the island, if they could just get their hands on it, and in the subsequent years they did. Thenceforth there grew a sort of camaraderie between **Sóller** and France and those palatial houses dotted around the center *plaça* can be attributed to the influencial Parisians blowing their francs on Sóller second homes during the modernista era.

Two impressive sites are the **Banco Central Hispano** and the facade of the adjacent church, **Església Parroquial de Sant Bartomeu,** both designed by Joan Rubió i Bellver, who apparently soaked up a lot from his professor Gaudí. However, the farmers were the original architects of the ancient terraced olive groves and vertiginous road (now paved and bluntly referred to as C-710) that leads you through the dense green valleys of the Serra Tramuntana. As you head south, past the peasant homes turned private paradises that line the 710, toward the Germanically preserved **Deiá,** a known foreign artists' haven, don't forget to stop to smell the roses—or to buy a snack, take a hike, or browse the ceramic ware at a local artisan's studio. Many Brits make the trek here as homage to the poet Robert Graves, who is responsible for turning this out-of-the-way treasure into one of the

All Aboard

As you walk past Sóller's main train station and Plaça Espanya, you don't expect to stumble on the little modernist train station for the **Ferrocarril de Sóller,** or Sóller railway (Castanyer 7; ☎ **971-630-301;** www.sollernet.com/trendesoller). Built in 1606, Can Mayol, the main building of the Railway Station in Sóller, houses two large exhibition rooms that display random works of art such as ceramics by Picasso and Miró.

Since 1912, residents and tourists alike have made the 27km (17-mile) ride (about an hour) from Sóller to Palma. Once on board the old electric locomotive, watch the urban sprawl give way to deep valleys of flowering trees and hillside towns. Then, the little wooden engine that could climbs north through the 13 tunnels of the Serra Tramuntana where the landscape turns rockier. *Note:* A seat on the first or last car makes a great photo op of the train snaking around a ridge above the valley.

The Palma ticket window (Estació Plaça d' Espanya 2, Palma; ☎ **971-752-051**) opens 20 minutes prior to arrival of the train; get there early to snag a window seat. Six trains per day leave from the Palma station and seven per day leave from Sóller (9€ one-way, 14€ round-trip). The tram to Pto. Sóller leaves every half-hour and you can get your ticket from the driver (3€ each way, approximately 15-min. ride). There are three pick-up points dotted along Carrer Marina for the return trip. Another handy website is http://trendesóller.com for train and tram, timetables history, and related pictures.

If you did not get all of your "little wooden trains built in the early 20th century" urges out, there is also the *tranvia* (tram). The tram begins its ramble through town along residential roads (kids run to wave hello and horses stop to nod as it passes) and ends at the not so impressive Port de Sóller, but just for the ride it's worth it.

most desired properties for permatourists. Since these tourists-turned-residents (and everybody else, too) must abide by strict regulations when building their home away from home so that it blends into the existing architecture and landscape, it makes for a lovely stroll down to the small fishing cove and pebble beach of **Cala de Deiá.**

Continue on to 🅼🆅 Best❂ **Son Marroig,** an outlook point over **Foradada.** This former island must have once feared being abandoned by its mother Mallorca and just attached itself (a couple of continental shifts and million years later) like the malformed peninsula it is. Its rocky headland features a few strange orifices, one of which is so large that you could drive a

boat through. We have the Archduke Luis Salvador of Austria, owner of the land, to thank for making sure no one built a mega hotel blocking the lookout. His former house still stands on this point and is now open as a museum honoring the archduke, and there's a reception hall with beautiful gardens—although that's not the reason why you should come here: Even if it's 10am when you arrive, stay to witness a sunset so awesome it will make you wonder if someone slipped you a mickey.

You can't imagine it could get any better than this until you head on to **Valldemossa.** This little village was put on the map by la Cartuja, the 14th-century monastery-turned-private-estate, which opened its doors in the late 1930s to the illin'-with-TB, French composer Chopin and the ahead-of-her-time writer George Sand. Known to be one of the only places on the island that actually gets snow in the winter, this fablelike town with its excess of deep-green cypress trees and stone-clad everything, is off the charts on the Richter scale of quaint.

TOURIST INFORMATION

For maps and information about Sóller and the surrounding area check out the tourist office at **OIT Municipal Port de Sóller** (C. Canonge Olivier 10, Port de Sóller; ☎ **971-865-467**). It's open Monday to Friday 8am to 8pm, Saturday 10am to 5pm, and Sunday 10am to 1pm.

SLEEPING

➜ **Es Petit Hotel** Heidi would feel right at home in this chalet-style stone hotel. Rooms are spacious and decorated in bright colors, but the view, gardens, and walking paths through the middle of two valleys are what makes this place postcard perfect. *Calle Uetam 1, Valldemossa.* ☎ *971-612-479. www.espetithhotel-valldemossa.com. Single 108€–144€, double 120€–160€, extra bed 50€. Breakfast included. Amenities: Restaurant, bar, fax, gardens, Internet, terrace, travel desk. In room: A/C, TV, hair dryer, minibar, safe.*

➜ **La Vila** ★★ Even Posh Spice would be happy hiding out at La Vila with its original Art Nouveau, *trompe l'oeil* walls and spiral marble staircase. But owners Toni and Tania are not divas, just PC folk—they donate a percentage of their proceeds to Oxfam—who take pride in their Sóller valley surroundings and in making sure you have all you need for a relaxing stay in one of their well-dressed suites. Breakfast is not just included; it's made to order and includes fresh-squeezed Sóller orange juice served wherever you like, be it the *plaça* out front or on the terrace overlooking the

tropical garden. *Plaça Constitució 14, Sóller.* ☎ *971-634-641. www.lavilahotel.com. Single 59€–69€, double 85€–95€. Amenities: Restaurant, bar, breakfast room, fax, garden, laundry service, travel info, Wi-Fi. In room: A/C, TV, hair dryer, safe.*

EATING

➜ **Café Sóller** ★ MEDITERRANEAN The art gallery inauguration parties each month and funky, individually painted tables in the main *plaça,* perfect for people-watching, make this bar/cafe/restaurant/art gallery worth your time—but it's the grub that makes it worth your wallet. The epic-size menu includes heaping bowls of pasta, creative salads, and fresh-catch entrees with a side of potatoes au gratin and seasonal vegetables. As if the selection is not already enough for you, they add an extensive specials list to the menu each day. *Plaça Constitució 13, Sóller.* ☎ *971-630-010. Entrees 7€–16€. Daily 8am–noon.*

➜ **Can Lluc** MALLORCAN Once you get down to the *cala* (cove) you won't want to run back up to get yourself some chow and suds, so you basically have two options: Can March or Can Lluc. Lluc is our top pick, mostly for the prices, since the food at both places is your basic, serviceable Mallorqui fare plus some fresh fish options. *Cala de Deià.* ☎ *649-198-618. Entrees 10€–15€. Daily 12:30–5pm.*

➜ **Ca'n Ribes** MALLORCAN We recommend this restaurant above all the others crowding the Port de Sóller for a few damn good reasons: Their terrace is on the flat area of the sidewalk (the precarious seating at the other restaurants will have you falling backwards and rolling down to the sea); they have the best views overlooking the harbor, and a wide, well-priced selection of succulent fish cooked by agile Mallorcan hands. Plus, where else can you

Sleeping Like a Rock

If you embrace the greener side of life, do we have a truly unique destination for you! **La Ruta de Pedra en Sec** (the dry stone route), otherwise known as GR-221, is a 170km (105-mile) trail that passes through the Tramuntana mountain range. The **Consell de Mallorca** can hook up hikers with two rustic stone refuges (three more are under construction and may be finished by the time you get there) that offer all you need in the way of accommodation for just 10€ to 36€ per night (not including a nominal charge for towels and sheets if you need them) as well as food service ranging from 4€ to 25€. The trail is broken up into eight spectacular stages, starting at Port d'Andratx and continuing up to El Pont Romá in Pollença; so if you have time or fitness restrictions you can still enjoy trekking through the diverse geography that only Mallorca can offer. Some routes can only be reached on foot but others are accessible by car. For all general information regarding routes, availability, and pricing, contact **The Environment and Nature Department** of the Consell de Mallorca (C. General Riera 111, Palma; ☎ **971-173-700**), or visit their website at www.conselldemallorca.net (type "dry stone route" in the search window).

get a *paella marinera* (paella with seafood) for just 12€? *Calle Santa Catalina 22, Port de Sóller.* ☎ *971-638-493. www.canribes.es.vg. Entrees 11€–25€. Daily noon–11pm.*

PARTYING

→**Café Sa Fonda** This no-frills terrace bar is a great place to stop for a cold one and admire the rooftops of Deiá. Since the bar plays decent mostly rock music and sometimes features live acts, the crowd here is mostly an assortment pack of young foreigners. *Via Arxiduc Luis Salvador 9, Deiá. No phone. Tues–Sun 10pm–midnight.*

SIGHTSEEING

→**Museo Chopin** This 14th-century Carthusian monastery houses—among other Frederick Chopin memorabilia—the piano that he composed on. The lovingly curated small museum lined with dark-wood cases and frames filled with compositions, portraits, and keepsakes is also the best place to pick up the polemic Aurora Dupin (aka George Sand) novel *A Winter in Mallorca,* describing their lives and experiences while living here in the winter

of 1938–39. Also make sure you take a stroll through the verdant garden facing the sea. *Celda 4 - Museo Chopin, Real Cartuja de Valldemossa.* ☎ *971-612-106. www.museochopin.com. Admission 7.50€, includes entrance to the Museum, the Palau del Rei Sanxo, and summer piano recitals. Mon–Sat 9:30am–6pm; Sun 10am–1pm.*

PLAYING OUTSIDE

All that high-elevation driving making you dizzy? Well then, turn off the C-710 at the 29km (18-mile) marker and go down a mile on an even more impossibly winding road that will eventually deposit you at the crystal-clear waters and striking landscape of **Cala de Deiá.** Better still, from June through September most people prefer to park their cars and walk down due to the incredibly narrow road and insane traffic. When you get there, take a dip and watch the fishing boats going in and out of their tiny shacks, or just relax and clear your head from the drive. The **Camí dels Ribassos** (Ribassos hiking trail) begins at the same point of the main road and goes through the woods taking approximately 40 minutes. When you see the water mill, you know you are getting close. Walk along the stream to reach a road that ends in steps leading directly to the cove. Bring your snorkel and you'll be able to appreciate the gorgeous underwater rock formations and marine life.

Ibiza

Those who appreciate the finer cultural nuances of traveling abroad should not visit Ibiza in the summer. Most points of interest involve gin, strobe lights, and—at least—some sounds of the tide. The **clubs and beaches** are why everyone's here. But if you like to dance, look good, feel good, and ride excess like a bareback horse, Ibiza will knock your socks off. Its sunny, beautiful beaches and good-natured locals in the day appear wholesome. When the sun goes down, though, this island emerges as a wild thing, hard-partying and looking for almost-scary fun. It's a mix of festive, colorful, theatrical elements—plus the relentless thumping of music that seems to never stop, until morning, that is. That's what Ibiza is like every day from the middle of July until the end of August. So, if you want to go to Ibiza, go now, because it might kill you (or your career, or your sanity) when you're older. This is the biggest damn Slip 'N Slide of a party you ever saw.

This small island was once best-known for its beautiful beaches and the small artisan communities that grew from a European hippie invasion in the early and mid-1970s. Ibiza still holds true to this character for 9 months of the year (and year-round in the inland villages). In the past decade, however, Ibiza has become a giant, fire-breathing Godzilla of a party. Each summer, this island rears its head, thumps it chest, and emits a terrifying war cry in the form of electronic music from the world's greatest DJs. Ibiza is one of the epicenters of modern disco/rave culture, and savvy Europeans and Aussies seek the sounds that came out of this island in the late '80s like some people seek Dead tapes

from the early '70s. Young Europeans know this little island as *the* place for summer holiday. You'll find a lot of Americans and Brits now, too, and Germans, Italians, and Spanish, too, but in fewer numbers.

Even at its worst, Ibiza is fascinating to watch: boorish tourists who refuse to speak anything other than English to the locals, who put up with their antics for 3 months every summer so that they can live in peace during the other 9 months of the year. At its best, though, Ibiza is a beautiful, almost spiritual, and very tolerant place. The gay community is so well-established here that it practically merits its own section.

People-watching is free, but everything else here will hurt. A week's worth of nightlife will cost you as much as a new Hyundai. Getting into clubs can cost up to 60€, and most hotels double (and sometimes triple!) their prices in July and August.

Getting There & Around

GETTING THERE

By Air

Iberia and Air Europa fly into **Es Codolar International Airport** (☎ **971-809-000**), which is 5.5km (3½ miles) southwest of Ibiza Town, just above the southern coast. Buses leave from the airport and drop passengers at the Bus Stop Bar in about 15 minutes. Service runs hourly 7:30am to 10:30pm and costs around 1.20€.

By Boat

Trasmediterránea, at Andenes de Puerto Estación Maritimo (☎ **971-454-645**), operates a **ferry service** from

Ibiza

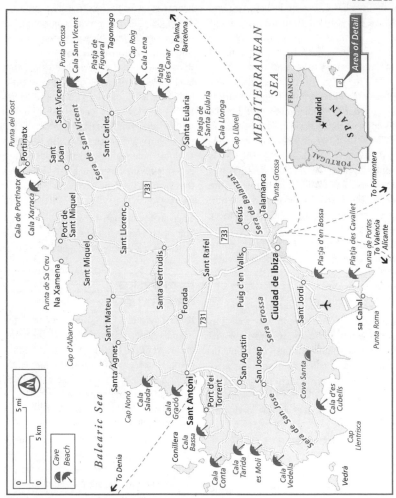

Barcelona four times a week; a one-way ticket costs 50€. One boat per day arrives daily from Valencia (70€ one-way). From Palma, there are four ferries per week, Tuesday to Friday; a one-way ride runs 69€. Boats from Barcelona, Valencia, and Palma de Mallorca leave all day long. If you arrive by boat, you'll be dropped off right in the middle of it all.

GETTING AROUND
By Bus

The only public transportation is the bus system. Buses leave Ibiza Town from the **Bus Stop Bar** on Isidoro Macabich (no phone), which is open daily from 9am to 11pm; you'll pay 1.80€ or less per fare. The service here is slow. Sometimes the woman behind the counter will just close up shop for 20 minutes, while she chats with her friend behind the bar, regardless of the number of people in line. You can always buy a ticket from the actual bus driver, which is recommended, because there are four different bus companies in Ibiza, and it's easy to get confused. Getting back into Ibiza Town is always easy because the buses are the biggest, loudest things around. Missing one would be like missing a marching band in your backyard.

The MTV Best● **Disco Bus** (☎ 971-192-456) is what it's all about here. The fare is around 1.75€ or 2€, and the destinations are every major club and hotel on the island. The Disco Bus hits each location once per hour and runs (like everything else) mid-May through end of September. See www.ibizanight.com to learn more about the Disco Bus and lots of other club-related info.

By Taxi

Cabs are available and recommended for club-hopping if you have the extra cash to spare (☎ 971-307-000). It's more expensive than it should be, but you won't be ripped off any more than you are anywhere else on the island. Here, .50€ or so is plenty for a tip. Like most of the natives here, the cabbies are mellow and safe people.

By Car, Bike & Moped

If you plan to get out of Ibiza Town, it's not a bad idea to rent a car or a scooter. But try to avoid making your exit through the town center during high season; it moves slower than Depeche Mode on Quaaludes. **Valentín Car & Bike** (Avinguda Bmé. Vte. Ramón 19; ☎ 971-310-822; welcome.to/casavalentin; Mon–Fri 8am–1pm and 3:30–8:30pm, Sat 9am–noon and 5:30–8:30pm) rents motor bikes for 25€ to 30€ per day. You pay gas. It has everything from old Vespas to spanking-new 250cc Yamahas. They also have automatic cars for 40€ a

day. Bad news is, you do need a driver's license even for the less than 50cc mopeds, although a learner permit has passed as one before. Helmets are required for anything with a motor and just two wheels. **Bravo Rent a Car** (Avinguda de Santa Eulália, Pachá rotary; ☎ 971-313-901; autos bravo.es; daily 9am–1pm and 4–8:30pm) brings in new cars each year and has offices all over the island. Most rental places have automatics, but you will have to book them well in advance or you will get stuck with the 150€ a day Mercedes that you can't park to save your life.

On Foot

Once in town, plan to walk everywhere. The city is compact and easily covered on foot. You really only need a bus or scooter to get out of town.

Ibiza Basics

ORIENTATION

Ibiza Town is on the southern end of the island's eastern coast and lies to the south and west of the Marina. A small and unremarkable portion of Ibiza Town does curve around to the north of the Marina, but you won't be spending any time there. The **Sa Penya** neighborhood is where the action is—action like you may never have seen before. Dozens of bars, restaurants, street vendors, drag queens, and nationalities converge here and get warmed up for the nightly sacrifice to the club gods. During the day, you can find good fashion shopping, pubs, and groceries here. The beginning of Sa Penya is marked by Plaça d'Antoni Riquer and the street that runs through it, parallel to the Marina, which is called Calle de Lluís Tur i Palau to the west of the Plaça, and Passeig des Moll to the east.

Calle de La Virgen is the most famous of the streets here; it is a long, narrow street that runs parallel to the Marina, from the

Ciudad de Ibiza

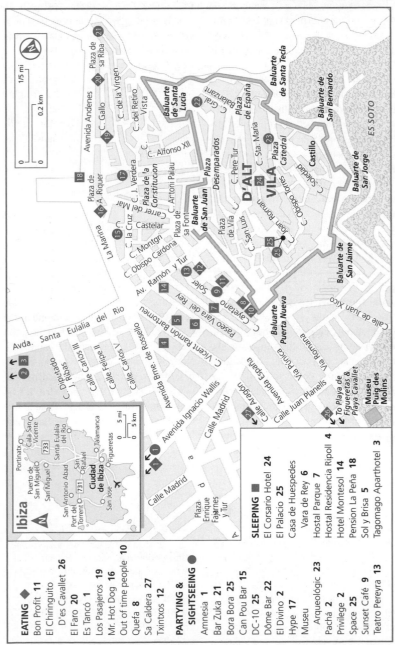

Ibiza

Portinatx

Cala San Vicente

Puerto de San Miguel○

San Miguel○ 733

San Antonio Abad

Santa Eulalia del Río

San Rafael

Ciudad de Ibiza

Figueretas

Talamanca

731

Port del Torrent○

San José

0   5 mi

0   5 km

EATING ◆
Bon Profit **11**
El Chiringuito
D'es Cavallet **26**
El Faro **20**
Es Tancó **1**
Los Pasajeros **19**
Mr. Hot Dog **16**
Out of time people **10**
Quefa **8**
Sa Caldera **27**
Txintxos **12**

PARTYING &
SIGHTSEEING ●
Amnesia **1**
Bar Zuka **21**
Bora Bora **25**
Can Pou Bar **15**
DC-10 **25**
Dôme Bar **22**
El Divino **2**
Hype **17**
Museu
  Arqueológic **23**
Pachá **2**
Privilege **2**
Space **25**
Sunset Café **9**
Teatro Pereyra **13**

SLEEPING ■
El Corsario Hotel **24**
El Palacio **25**
Casa de Huespedes
  Vara de Rey **6**
Hostal Parque **7**
Hostal Residencia Ripoll **4**
Hotel Montesol **14**
Pension La Peña **18**
Sol y Brisa **5**
Tagomago Aparthotel **3**

eastern tip of the city to the equally busy Calle de Pou, which begins right at the Marina and runs north to south. Sa Penya continues south for about 8 misshapen blocks before it runs into the foot of the elevated Old Fortress.

📺 Best● **D'Alt Villa (Old Fortress)** ★ is the one touristy thing you should make time for, if nothing else. Ibiza Town more or less ends at the southern point of the Old Fortress. Paseo de Vara de Rey is the other major landmark in Ibiza Town—several hostels, the tourism office (see below), a travel agency, and a few good shops and restaurants are all on this street. Paseo de Vara de Rey is 3 blocks to the west of D'Alt Villa and runs northeast to southwest. Everything that we've mentioned here can be walked between in 20 minutes or less.

Other villages worthy of a day or half-day trip for some rural relaxation are **Santa Gertrudis** (to the northwest of Ibiza Town, in the very middle of the island, about 30 min. by bus), **Santa Eularia** (to the east of Ibiza Town, on the coast, 20 min. by bus), and **San Rafael** (directly between Ibiza Town and San Antonio). The clubs Privilege and Amnesia (see "Clubs," below) are both just outside of Ibiza Town. No point on the island of Ibiza is much more than an hour from Ibiza Town by bus, or 90 minutes by scooter. **Playa d'en Bossa** is a mere 15-minute bus ride south of Ibiza Town. This is one of the most crowded and commercial beaches on the island, but Space (see "Clubs," below) and Bora Bora (p. 497) are here.

Ibiza is ridiculously small. The villages are even smaller. Venues that aren't in Ibiza Town or San Antonio simply have the village listed for the address because all of the stores, bars, and such are located on one central street. Basic maps and road signs work just fine if you're going to scooter it between beaches and villages, and the buses go to all villages we have

named and many beaches. And the clubs themselves (also reachable by bus) are landmarks that every cab driver and local knows. You'd have to work really hard to get lost on this island.

TOURIST OFFICES

Go to the **tourist office** on Vara de Rey 13 (☎ **971-301-900**) for info; it's open 9am to 1pm and 5 to 8pm Monday to Friday, 10:30am to 1:30pm Saturday. A second, smaller tourist office is right across from where the boats let you off. They won't make hotel reservations for you. *Tip:* Call hotels and make your reservations long before you get here.

RECOMMENDED WEBSITES & MAGAZINES

When you're ready to venture out, you'll have no trouble finding sources of info to help you navigate, red-eyed, through this hurricane of discos and sunshine. *DJ Mag Ibiza* (DJMAG.com) gives you the most info on clubs, bars, restaurants, beaches, and markets in the least amount of words, along with short interviews with the big DJs. *Ministry* in Ibiza is like the *Maxim* of this island: funny articles written by a staff that jumps into the whole Ibiza scene head-first. You're sure to get the inside (read: wasted) view of how the club scene

---

cuidado! Bus-ted Up

Even though Ibiza is a wee morsel of an isle, your travel time may become super-size given the irregularity of bus service between towns. If you're not renting a car or a scooter, decide where you will be spending most of your time on the island and choose a hotel in that area. That way, you won't spend all your money on taxis to get back home after bus service stops.

12 Hours in Ibiza

1. Watch the sunset at **Sunset Ashram** in Cala Conta near San Antonio (p. 505).
2. Take a full day at the **beach,** either S'Estanyol Beach by Ibiza Town, Aiguas Blancas up on the north coast, or Cala Llonga in between.
3. **Party calisthenics:** Warm up on the beach at Bora Bora (p. 497). Get your full workout across the street at Space (see "Clubs," p. 499), and then cool down at Bora Bora again.
4. Take a **scooter ride** through the countryside (pack a picnic . . .).
5. Experience **extreme Ibiza;** go to Manumission at Privilege (p. 500). Don't forget your latex and whips.
6. Look good and feel good while at **Ibiza's traditional party:** Renaissance at Pachá (p. 500).
7. Watch the freaks go by in **Sa Penya,** particularly on Carrer de La Virgen: sock-and-sandaled and sunburned German tourists, English fashion victims, loudmouth drag queens, and many, many beautiful party people from all over Europe.
8. Spend a couple hours walking around **D'Alt Villa,** the Old Fortress (p. 490), with its beautiful views of the sea.

operates. Two smaller magazines that we like are *Party San,* which you can pick up at the Sunset Café (p. 498) and *7,* available at clothing stores and club stores. The website **www.ibizanight.com** gives you basic info on the clubs but is more useful for its detailed info on the Disco Bus (see "By Bus," above), restaurants, and—most importantly—reservation information (make your reservations early!). The site is in English and Spanish. Another very complete website in English is **www.ibiza-spotlight.com**, where you can get anything from discounted club tickets to real-estate advice and detailed beach information.

CULTURE TIPS 101

The official language of the Balearic Islands is Catalán, the language of Barcelona. But, you'll often be able to speak English (and German).

One quick way to lose money here is by handing it over to José Law when he pulls you over for swerving around on your rented scooter. El Hombre isn't really out to get you, but let's face it: If your island were invaded each summer by two million hallucinating British Gen X-ers, you, too, would want to try to control things at least a little bit. Road blocks with breath tests are the newest attempt to keep you and your wasted friends out of harm's way. Take our advice: Use a cab at night.

Ibiza Nuts & Bolts

Currency   As always, you will get the best exchange rate at an **ATM.** Although there aren't many of them right in Sa Penya, there are several scattered all around the Passeig de Vara de Rey, particularly at the southwestern end.

Embassies   For embassy info, see Madrid, p. 84.

Emergencies   Emergencies: **092.** Red Cross 24-hour ambulance service: ☎ **971-390-303;** 971-191-009.

Laundry   Got a little too carried away at the foam party? Don't worry, the good grannies at **Lavisec** have more than their share of experience with hard stains, and if you are pleasant enough, you will have your clothes looking like new overnight (C. Carles III 11; ☎ **971-190-676;** 11€ for a 5-kilogram load).

Pharmacies   The pharmacy on **Passeig de Vara de Rey** has condoms (*preservativos;* Mon–Sat 9am–1:30pm and 5–9pm, Sun 5–9pm). The one in D'Alt Villa is open 24 hours for you and your horny/nauseous/sunburned friends.

Telephone Tips   The city code is **971.** For the operator, dial ☎ **1003;** the international operator is at ☎ **1005.** Note that recent changes in Spain's phone system now require that all local calls be dialed with the 971 prefix.

Sleeping

The thing about Ibiza: People usually don't just pass through. This is their destination. People come to this island for a wild vacation and expect to pay for it. But the prices aren't too, too crazy—it's simply finding a room here that's a big pain. Local government has finally understood that expansion is not unlimited in the Balearics (because they are surrounded by water, which happens often with islands)—and building those 10-story resorts on the beach doesn't really help the skyline either—so they have tightened the rules for new construction, making precious lodging even scarcer. Save yourself a huge headache and make a reservation for a room before you arrive on the island. A little planning ahead will get you a sweet little room at Vara de Rey or something with a view at the Hotel Montesol.

CHEAP

➔ **Hostal Residencia Ripoll** The beds in this 15-room hostel are not the firmest, but chances are, by the time you hit them, you won't notice anyway. The common areas and shared bathrooms are clean and—although most face the street—they are fairly quiet. If you have a party of two or three, it may be worth it to ask about their fully equipped apartments. *Calle Vicente Cuervo 10-14.* ☎ *971-314-275. www. apartamentos-ripoll.com. Single with shared bathroom 30€, double with shared bathroom 42€, apt. up to 3 guests 78€ with private bathroom. In room: A/C, TV, kitchen (in apts).*

➔ **Pension La Peña** This pension seems to have the cheapest rooms in Ibiza Town. The common bathrooms are of questionable character, but many of the rooms (though small and bare) have a beautiful view of the sea. The 10 doubles and three single rooms are rented out almost exclusively to gay guys who want to be near the action that makes the Carrer de la Virgen famous. *Calle Mare de Deu 76.* ☎ *971-190-240. Single 15€–25€, double 25€–35€.*

DOABLE

MTV Best ● ➔ **Casa de Huespedes Vara de Rey** ★ The young couple that runs this hostel is beautiful to look at and fun to talk with. Their artists' touch makes every room a calm and serene haven from Ibiza's madness. Call ahead; many guests have been returning for years. Already a great place to make new friends, because there are only 10 rooms here, things only got better when the rooftop terrace was completed in the summer of 2000. Great, great people and beautifully painted rooms. *Paseo de Vara de Rey 7.* ☎ *971-301-376. www.hibiza.com. Single 27€–45€, double 48€–80€. Amenities: Rooftop terrace, shared bathrooms.*

➔**Hostal Parque** ★ Of the 29 rooms here, many have a pleasant view of the park and *plaça* below, but what's most interesting for tourists is that your neighbors will most likely be Spanish. Try to get a room with a balcony so you can invite people from the *plaça* up to join you. The cafe and restaurant is open 365 days a year from 7am to midnight, making it a great place to start your night. *Plaza del Parque 4, just south of Paseo Vara de Rey.* ☎ *971-301-358. www.hostalparque.com. Single with shared bathroom 35€–50€, single with private bathroom 45€–70€, double with shared bathroom 50€–80€, double with private bathroom 55€–100€, triple with private bathroom 75€–135€. Amenities: TV (in common room). In room: A/C, TV, hair dryer (in some rooms).*

➔**Hotel Montesol** This place has been *the* hotel in Ibiza Town since 1934. Private baths, phones, air-conditioning, and TVs make this place worth the extra bucks. All of the spacious rooms have big closets, bathtubs, and, most importantly, great views either of the harbor, old city, or quaint Passeig de Vara de Rey. The sophisticated bar here is more fashionable in the off season. *Northeastern end of Passeig de Vara de Rey 2.* ☎ *971-310-161. www.hotelmontesol.com. Single 40€–60€, double 65€–106€. Amenities: Bar. In room: A/C, TV.*

➔**Sol y Briso** A relatively reasonable price makes this another option. Rooms are comfy with tasteful, rustic furniture, but getting a bed here can be hard. And, though the location is golden, you'll have to share the bathrooms. *Avinguda B.V. 15.* ☎ *971-310-818. www.hibiza.com/index_e.html. Single 18€, double 30€. Amenities: Shared bathrooms.*

➔**Tagomago Aparthotel** Spanish coeds jam this place and they have come to *party!* Bright modern rooms with full kitchen (save cash by cooking!), living room, balcony (view of harbor), and TV. If you're smooth, you'll be able to get extra folks on the floor—the staff doesn't really pay attention to who's coming and going. Also, the single beds are big, and can comfortably fit two people. The hotel has a cafeteria/snack bar and currency exchange, and will help you rent cars and bikes. Just a 1-minute walk to Pachá and 5 minutes to El Divino and a few paces away from minigolf, paddle tennis, and real tennis. *Paseo Marítimo (opposite side of the harbor from Sa Penya, a 5-min. cab ride from there).* ☎ *971-316-550. www.ibiza-online.com/hoteltagomago/index_e.html. Single 31€–55€, double 50€–100€. Amenities: Cafeteria, darts, Internet kiosk, pool table, pool, TV. In room: A/C.*

SPLURGE

➔**El Corsario Hotel** ★ Legend has it that this intimate, 14-room boutique hotel is the oldest in Ibiza, and that, since its construction in the 17th century, it has hosted

Cuidado! Just Busted

Despite their overwhelming abundance, drugs are still illegal in Ibiza. However, in traditional Spanish fashion, people usually don't get busted unless they get violent. So don't. The standard Spanish chill factor applies here as well, but the locals have become less patient with the rowdy English tourists in recent years, so if you do get in a bind, don't go shooting your mouth off. Also be forewarned that most people get a good searching when traveling from Ibiza to another country.

wwwired

You're a serious addict if you're wasting your time, money, and mind in front of a computer screen in Ibiza when you could be wasting those same things on the beach or at a club. If you need that fix, though, log on at **Centro Internet Eivissa** (Av. Ignacio Wallis 39 Bajos; ☎ **971-318-161;** www.centrointernet eivissa.com; Mon–Sat 10am–11pm, Sun 5–11pm; no credit cards). Along with 14 PCs, scanners and color printers are also available if you need them, you geek.

Surf@net (Riambau 4; ☎ **971-194-920;** 3.60€ per hour; daily 10am–2am) is a nice bright space with 20 or so PCs with flat screens and all sorts of other services, like cellphone recharging, money wiring, and faxing. It is right in the harbor, has cranking A/C, and the connection is fast so you can make the most of your time. They give you a card with a code that you use to log-in to the computer. (Don't forget to return it or you'll get yelled at.)

Like the name says . . . **Chill** (Via Punica 49; ☎ **971-399-736;** 4€ per hour; Mon–Sat 10am–midnight, Sun noon–midnight) is the best place to hang out, have a coffee, play some board games, and check your e-mail. The computers are a little older and not that fast but if you want to share your buddies' party pics with your new friends, this would be the place.

many celebs, including the members of Pink Floyd, who shot part of their classic "The Wall" here. Each eclectic room is completely unique and is decorated by the owner, Beatrice, an art collector who uses the space as a private gallery. Pick the room that best suits your style and your wallet, and don't forget to have breakfast on the terrace overlooking the port. Chances are, the DJ who saved your life last night will be sitting at the next table. *Calle Poniente 5.* ☎ *971-301-248. www.ibiza-hotels.com/CORSARIO. Double 110€–430€. Amenities: Bar, breakfast room, fax (in common area), laundry service, Wi-Fi. In room: A/C, TV, fridge, hair dryer, Internet.*

➔ **El Palacio** The first thing you will notice about El Palacio is the Hollywood-Boulevard style hands and feet impressions on the wall. (Psst! Look for punk legend Nina Hagen's.) The walls in this movie buff's paradise feature photos and posters of movie stars that flank you all the way to the private courtyard with pool. Each of the seven rooms—all with great

views—is named after a different Hollywood star, the Marilyn being the penthouse. The Garbo is the chicest, but, unless you have a serious Snow White fetish, stay away from the Walt Disney room. *Calle Conquista 2.* ☎ *971-301-478. www. elpalacio.com. Double 240€–380€. Open May–Oct. Amenities: Bar, breakfast room, fax, parking, swimming pool. In room: A/C, hair dryer.*

Eating

Pills and thrills aside, try to eat at least one decent meal a day. It will help you go the distance at night. It's sad to note that all-night food in Ibiza is only a little more common than an acoustic "Happy Mondays" song. Although some of the clubs sometimes have a guy in the parking lot vending pretzels and bottled water for a price that would usually get you a case of wine, you really can't count on it. Your best bet is to buy food at a local market (they're everywhere) during the day and stow it away in your hotel room for when you come back at night. Think smart and buy in advance: You'll probably want something salty and a little protein, and I'm a big believer in buying bananas and oranges for those highs and lows (respectively). And some bottled water!

CHEAP

MTV **Best ☻** →**Bon Profit** ★ MALLOR-CAN Even in a *plaça* full of trendy places with outdoor seating, Ibizans prefer this worker-friendly indoor joint to all others. Dig in to a paella appetizer big enough to be a meal in itself or a vegetable soup your grandma would want to call her own. Larger appetites might like the fresh, baked fish with a side of fries or salad. Got a black hole in your belly that just went supernova? Then don't miss the homemade desserts either. How can a baked apple be so scrumptious? *Plaça del Parque 5. No phone. Entrees 5€–10€. Mon–Sat 1–3pm and 8–10pm.*

→**Los Pasajeros** CLASSIC SPANISH You'll never pass for a local in Ibiza; but if you want to eat where they do, check out this trendy second-floor cantina where you can get a full meal for the price of an Evian at Pachá. Owner Maria keeps the place lively and the prices accessible. The clientele is mostly gay, and the food is deliciously classic Spanish fare. *Vicente Soler 6, 1st floor. No phone. Entrees 4€–8€. Sun–Fri 1–5pm and 8pm–midnight; Sat 8pm–midnight.*

→**Mr. Hot Dog** FAST FOOD We like the fair price and good food here. Mr. Hot Dog will serve you a big-ass yummy cheeseburger for 5€. The French bread and chicken breast is also recommended. Their terrace seating is right in the middle of it all, providing you with some great people-watching. *At the Marina. No phone. Daily 9:30am–4:30am.*

DOABLE

→**Es Tancó** ★ SEAFOOD It is possible to eat the most savory fresh fish without spending a small fortune. You have to go to San Rafael, though. A quick 15-minute bus ride away, this unassuming restaurant with wooden tables spread out over two floors is another local favorite and makes a *bullit de peix* (a casserole with three kinds of fresh fish with aioli) that will have you licking the bones. If you ask for it *a banda* (with rice), be prepared: After you're stuffed with all the delicious fish, they bring you a paella-size pan of rice cooked with broth, that you won't possibly finish, but you'll most definitely have to try. *Av. Isidro Macabich 9, San Rafael. ☎ 971-198-599. Entree 8€–24€. Tues–Sun 1–4pm and 8pm–midnight. Autobuses San Antonio No. 3, San Antonio-San Rafael-Ibiza town, or Disco Bus after midnight.*

→ **Quefa** CAFE/TAPAS This small cafe has nothing to do with art, but the old country store sells all kinds of semi-gourmet meats, cheeses, fresh bread, wine, and ready-made tapas—perfect stuff for a picnic at a quiet beach of your choice. Or you can sit outside at the base of the old city and eat at one of the cafe tables. *Cayetano Soler 9. ☎ 971-302-972. Sandwiches 3€–7€. Mon–Sat 10am–2pm and 5–9pm.*

MTV **Best ☻** →**Sa Caldera** ★ SEAFOOD Run by the same native Ibizenco couple for 15 years now, Sa Caldera is the restaurant of choice for locals (even other restaurant owners) of Ibiza Town. The husband cooks, and the wife runs the show. All the food is "down-home," specializing in fresher-than-fresh fish. The paella for two costs up to a whopping 44€, but the *menú del día* for 14€ includes spectacular main dishes like grilled salmon with herbs. Located about a 10-minute walk from the port, you won't see the sunset or hear the tide; but you will be treated right and experience a real slice of life with the locals. *Obispo Padre Huix 19. ☎ 971-306-416. Menú del día 11€–14€. Main courses 14€–44€. Sun–Fri 1–5pm and 8pm–midnight; Sat 8pm–midnight.*

➔ **Txintxos** CAFE/TAPAS This small out-door cafe right next to the old city is nicely away from all the hoopla in the harbor. The staff is pleasant, and the food focuses on classic Basque tapas. Enjoy a monumental selection of *pintxos frios* (Basque chorizo on crusty bread) or *calientes* and rations like fried calamari. Top it off with a cup of *Txacoli* (Basque white wine). *Conde de Rosellón 1.* ☎ *971-399-559. Pintxos 1.20€– 3.60€. Daily 11:30am–3:30pm and 8pm– 2:30am.*

SPLURGE

MTV Best ● ➔ **El Chiringuito D'es Cavallet** ★★★ SEAFOOD If you are not gay, maybe you thought you had no reason to go to Es Cavallet beach. Think again. This restaurant has the best seafood in town, and maybe even in the world. The decor is tasteful and simple and the beach-front setting appeals, but we would still eat here if it were in a tin house under a highway. Ask for the classic *ibizencos,* all made with ingredients right off the boat, like *arroz con bogavante* (rice with lob-ster) or *arroz a la marinera* (a sort of seafood paella) and you will never want to darken the door of a Red Lobster again. *Es Cavallet Beach.* ☎ *971-395-485. Entrees 15€–35€. Daily 1–6:30pm. Autobuses Voramar El Gaucho No. 11 Ibiza-Salinas.*

➔ **El Faro** ★★ SPANISH/SEAFOOD Very touristy, very ritzy. Kings, presidents, rock 'n' roll stars, and famous athletes have been eating here regularly for the last 20 years. Choose your dinner from among the live fish and lobsters scrambling around the tank. Like Se Caldera, you can pay up to 44€ for paella here; but unlike Se Caldera, the atmosphere here is downright swank. The restaurant is right on the water but a few blocks away from the Sa Penya mad-ness. The owner's name is Mercedes, which totally makes sense. Reservations advised. *Plaça Sa Riba 1.* ☎ *971-313-233.*

www.elfaro-ibiza.com. Entrees 12€–44€. May–Oct daily 10am–4am.

CAFES

➔ **Out of time people** Besides being a center of spirituality worthy of Madonna's latest reincarnation (or was it the previous one?), this small cafe with comfy outdoor seating is one of the few places in the city where you can get a very good selection of teas and homemade juices. They have con-coctions for every kind of hangover and illness, together with all sorts of esoteric literature, conferences, and surprisingly good, ohm-less music. *Jaume I, No. 2.* ☎ *971-392-321. Coffee from 2€. Mon–Sat 10am– midnight.*

Partying

BARS

As you would expect with a Spanish island, Ibiza has a bar for every occasion. Some are for cool beachside drinks, others are for hot late-night action, but the bulk of the bars you'll encounter in Ibiza Town are meant to operate like giant cannons that will blast your wasted ass into the disco stratosphere. Keep your chin up, strap on your crash helmet, and head on down to the crowded international big-top may-hem that is the Sa Penya district. It's your job to get there at about 11pm or midnight and to be ready to perform death-defying stunts of fashion and consumption.

Among the extreme clothing, you may notice a fair number of attractive and seemingly coked-up folks who—despite all of their talking—are rather stationary. It's their job to get you into their bar. Here's how it usually goes: A sexy and fast-talking hawker approaches you and says "Hey there, mate. How about tickets for Amnesia tonight?" Be sure that you know where you want to go ahead of time because they will always try and sell you on the less-attractive events first (such as

Hanging Out

You'll have no trouble finding the cool kids on this island, friends. Ibiza is one big party, but go to the **beaches** if you want to really hang out, especially because all of them are topless and many are nude (see "Playing Outside," below). Kids don't mass on the plazas or squares here. With all the beautiful, long stretches of sand around, why would they?

Ibiza's best hangout, however, is difficult to find. Not only are these fabled **full-moon parties** hard to suss out, you also have to accept that they're only going to happen once a month. When they do go down, there will be no flyers, and the Germans and the English won't be able to help, but if you make friends with just a few locals, they'll be able to tell you the day and location of one of the island's best events. Drum circles, booze, bonfires, and more on secluded black-sand beaches that are beautiful enough to make you cry.

Calle de Santa Agnes, in San Antonio, is probably the last place you want to hang out, unless you're 16, belligerent, and culturally void: The scene here is vomiting and groping in the streets, 100% rude, 100% lame.

a foam party [p. 498] instead of a hot dance scene that ends with live sex on stage). So having already done your homework, you say, "How about tickets for Pachá?" What usually happens next is that you'll agree to go in for a drink. Yes, that's right; if you agree to a couple of (relatively) cheap whiskey-and-Cokes, you'll get a big discount or even free admission! What a great system! Make sure that you get your tickets inside the bar; scalpers have been known to sell fakes on the street. As so many of the 20-something party people here already know, looking sexy and freaky will get you what you want because the clubs want beautiful people!

→ **Bar Zuka** The candles, old tile floor, and beautifully painted walls add to the more-refined-less-hectic vibe (until they break out the tequila later at night). Regular attendance by some of England's biggest DJs. Less queeny and painted-up than the rest of Calle de la Virgen. Bring cash, 'cause they don't take credit cards. *Calle de la Virgen 75. No phone.*

🎵 Best ♥ → **Bora Bora** When the MTV beach parties grow up, they want to be Bora Bora. Drink, dance, and chill while coming down from nearby Space (or while gearing up for it, depending on your schedule and stamina). Along with the party people, there are many unaware beach-goers here who have a dim realization that they are not in the same state as everyone else at the bar. This is a very mellow, very appropriate, very Ibiza way to end a disco marathon: 2€ for a beer and usually around 500 people. Open all the time—really. *Playa d'en Bossa, across the street from Space. No phone.*

🎵 Best ♥ → **Café Mambo** This cafe is located in San Antonio, but, hey nobody's perfect. Listen to mellow ambient music, have a drink, and watch a magnificent sunset over the water from the terrace (a must-see while in Ibiza). The rabid British party monkeys that swarm San Antonio do show up later on, but it's fun to slip slowly from the mellow sunset to that high-energy fiesta while getting sauced on gin-and-tonics. Including the surrounding beach, max capacity is about 2,000 people. Around 7€ for a drink. *End of Av. de Vara de Rey, in San Antonio. No phone.*

→ **Can Pou Bar** Has been a local favorite for over 80 years, except that the customers back then were all fishermen, not club and clothing-store owners. There are a few terrace tables and the inside is comfy. It doesn't cram people in here for the extra buck as so many other places do. Coffee, juice, small sandwiches, and breakfasts are served. Walls are lined with beautiful artwork that reflects the local temperament. Right on the marina between Sa Penya and Paseo de Vara de Rey, this is usually the place where you'll get the cheapest club tickets. *Corner of Lluis Tur i Palau and Montgri.* ☎ *971-310-875.*

→ **Hype** What's in a name? This is only one of the very many bars that operate in this way in the Sa Penya district. Drink your way to cheap disco and watch the show pass by from the terrace seating. *Calle d'Emile Pou 11A. No phone.*

→ **Sunset Café** In addition to the usual array of alcohol, the Sunset offers food too. The chicken sandwiches are tasty, and the fresh juice and "breakfast salads" (garden salads with a lot of fruit) for 4.50€ are nothing short of miraculous after a night of partying. A DJ spins good house music from 9pm till 1am. Be sure to say hi to Patrick, the friendly German owner, and whichever hottest-woman-ever happens to be behind the bar with him. Sitting on their pleasant plaza right off the Paseo de Vara de Rey is a great getaway when you are over the Ibiza Town nonsense. *Plaza del Parque 3.* ☎ *971-394-446. www.sunset-cafe-ibiza.com.*

LIVE MUSIC

Live music? Yeah, right. Only the most popular DJs on earth spin here on a nightly basis. Save for a handful of German and Dutch expats who live inland, there's not much of a live music scene on this island. If middle-aged Germans covering the Eagles and the Dead is your thing, though, be sure to rush on over to **Teatro Pereyra** (corner of Calle Conde Rosellón and Calle Aníbal; no phone; daily 7am–4am). The good times get rolling at 11:30pm. Despite everything, they do get points for being open 21 hours a day and for having an enormous and beautiful bar. The big round tables can seat about six stools, and capacity is about 300 European preps. Lord knows why they came to Ibiza.

Good Clean Fun

Amnesia and one or two other clubs host the infamous *espuma* (foam) parties that you've seen on E!, full of scantily clad hotties splashing around and getting it on in over-the-head bubbly goodness. Well, color me soaking wet with soap in my eye! Who thought that being buried alive in foam was going to be a good time? Listen. If you're gonna do a foam party, do it right because—no joke— you'll wind up gagging, getting felt up (which might be what you're lookin' for), and slipping and cracking your head in 2m (6 ft.) of the stuff. Being prepared, though, can make a foam party a lot more fun. The foam pros show up with backpacks containing goggles, bathing suits, beach sandals or old sneakers, and a towel. They gear up before the foam comes to town (it rains down like one of the 10 Plagues, like the fury of God himself, in terrifyingly enormous quantities), and make sure that they're a good 9m (30 ft.) from the center of the dance floor.

club scene

Because they're the big business here, all of the clubs adhere to the same high prices and late schedule. Here's the lowdown (exceptions are noted in the club descriptions):

→ Clubs run from the middle of May until the end of September and are open from midnight till 6 or 8am daily. Prime time is from around 3:30 to 5:30am.

→ Cover is between 40€ and 60€! Discount tickets are easy to come by, though, and bring the price down to 20€ to 35€ (see "Bars," above, to learn more). Little bottles of water are around 6€ and drinks are 10€ to 15€. All of the clubs take at least Visa and MasterCard. They want your money, in any form.

→ None of the clubs is exclusive at the front door. Instead, they have exclusive rooms within.

→ Each club holds between 5,000 (Pachá) and 10,000 (Privilege) people at once! They all have smaller rooms tucked away here and there (especially Pachá), so don't get put off if you don't like the feel of the main room.

→ The crowds are between 19 and 30 years old. Despite the fashion blitzkrieg here, there are also thousands of preps and dorks and family men running around this island. These folks are more likely to not make it past the bar scene at Sa Penya, though.

CLUBS

→**Amnesia** If Pachá is the Sean Connery of clubs, Amnesia, which was full of hippies and liquid acid in the early '80s, is more like Mick Jagger: past its prime and blissfully unaware of it. Yes, it's as big as an airplane hangar. Yes, it has a retractable roof. Yes, it has trees and drag queens and several rooms and dancers and balconies, but big deal—where's the love? Best nights: Godskitchen on Tuesday and Cream on Thursday. *A 2-min. walk south of San Rafael, which is 15 min. by bus or 10 min. by cab from Ibiza Town.* ☎ *971-198-041. www.amnesia.es.*

→**DC-10** The best place to be on a Monday morning—that is, of course, if you have the rest of the week to recover. This new classic hosts CircoLoco, a wild, wild, sunglasses-mandatory kind of party. Located next to the airport under the shadow of a DC-10; legend has it, this was a local music bar before becoming Ibiza's favorite takeoff runway for after-hours astronauts. *Se Salinas 10.* ☎ *971-198-086. www.circoloco.com.*

→**El Divino** Beautiful (almost opulent) and often semi-exclusive. You can get here by taking the boat that leaves every half-hour from the Marina. You can't miss it; it's the one with the flashing lights and the big sign that says EL DIVINO. The best areas of the enormous and ornate deck on the water are usually roped off for the many VIPs that attend this club. One of the main events, Miss MoneyPenny, is basically prom night for a lot of English drag queens. Hed Kandi is on Saturdays. Another night, be prepared to wear your latex and leather and bring a whip, because you're gonna git your freak on tonight! Be prepared for wild costumes, excessive groping, and shagging in the bathrooms. Straight out of a movie—or hell, if you're a Puritan. *On the Paseo Marítimo at the Puerto de Ibiza Nueva, across the harbor from Ibiza Town.* ☎ *971-318-338. www.eldivino-ibiza.com.*

BALEARIC ISLANDS

[MTV] (Best ●) →**Pachá** Open since 1975, this is the original Ibiza disco and is considered to be one of the finest nightclubs on planet Earth. Like Sean Connery or your favorite M.I.L.F., Pachá has aged with elegance over the years and hosts a more noticeable contingent of 30- and 40-year-olds (although they are very far from the majority). Pachá is *muy fashion,* as they say here, and the most international (read: not ²/₃ English and German) of the clubs. The go-go girls are fly and the dance floor gets hot and grimy (the way you like it, baby), but the drag queens and freak-outs that keep the other clubs churning are usually not here (so don't dress out for Pachá—dress *up*). Famous people stop by all the time. You can even come here in winter as it's open year-round. *Av. 8 de Agosto, on the Paseo Marítimo, a 20-min. walk southwest of Ibiza Town.* ☎ *971-310-959. www.pacha.com.*

[MTV] (Best ●) →**Privilege** This place is midgets and strobe lights and 10-foot drag queens on stilts, people shagging on stage (really!), fire-eaters, and an enormous swimming pool, and music, and lord knows what else running around all over the place. And you have to pay money for toilet paper! Privilege tends to be more gay than other clubs, particularly for Manumission

(Mon), which is also its best event. *A 10-min. walk north of San Rafael (15 min. by bus, 10 min. by cab from Ibiza Town).* ☎ *971-198-160. www.privilegeibiza.com.*

[MTV] (Best ●) →**Space** Even on Sunday, this place is still insane and happy from the night before. Whoop! This x-tensive club doesn't even open till the others close, so pretty much the whole island congregates here around 8am. A big open-air room with a semi-translucent tarp for the ceiling gives the whole club a sitting-under-a-shady-tree kind of feel. Space ties with Pachá as our favorite club. Best event: Home, starting Sunday at 8am (the regular hours are 8am–6pm—how wild is that?). *Playa d'en Bossa.* ☎ *971-314-078. www.space-ibiza.es.*

GAY NIGHTLIFE

Gay life here is hard to miss, so we'll just point out that a lot of mostly gay bars are on the Calle de la Virgen and Calle Mayor in Ibiza town.

→ **Dôme Bar** Check this place out for some of the trendiest and queeniest times on the island. *Calle Alfonso XII 3. No phone.*

→ **Es Cavellet Beach** It's 95% gay, 100% nude. Expect bad techno music, a whole lot of drugs, and a lot of naked gay men (and some women). Straight girls sometimes stop by for a bit of sightseeing and weird

Boy Meets Girl?

Yeah, more like boy meets boy on this island. Or girl meets boy dressed like girl, or boy meets girl who looks like a boy dressing as a girl, or . . . whatever. Ibiza is not a place for the shy. The whole point of this island is that you can do whatever you want, baby. Do it loud, do it bright, do it in spandex, and do it topless—you can rest when you get home. When the summer rolls around, the local hippie types will often refer to "the colors returning," referring to the bright clothes, jewelry, and smiles that come to this island each summer. So make sure you play up the part! The gay nightlife here is not a separate entity; it's all swirled together. Our best advice: Be safe (no matter who you end up with), because Lord knows you'll have opportunities here. The one thing we don't recommend is buying too many drinks, especially at as much as 16€ a pop.

fantasizing. *15-min. bus ride south of Ibiza Town, close to the southernmost tip of the island.*

Sightseeing

Ibiza's cultural attractions are outshined by the sunshine that hits the wonderful beaches and the strobe lights that flood the clubs. Ibiza Town, however, is a beautiful old city (that, in fact, has been a Unesco World Heritage site since 1999) with steep winding streets and a humongous **16th-century fortified wall** that is the first thing you will see if you arrive by boat. The wall, which remains pretty intact today, was constructed to protect **D'Alt Vila (the old town)** from a combined Turkish and French invasion. It's a nice walk up the narrow streets through the white houses covered in bougainvillea—besides, it may be the one thing you did in Ibiza that you can tell your parents about. Once you find the **cathedral** (Plaza de la Catedral s/n; ☎ **971-312-774**) you will be rewarded with one of the best views of the city and its harbor. The cathedral, which dates from the 14th century, was built in a mix of Catalán, Gothic, and baroque styles. If your appetite for culture is still healthy, venture across the street and check out the **Museu Arqueológic** (Plaça de Catedral 3; ☎ **971-301-231**; admission 2.40€ adults, 1.20€ students; winter Tues–Sat 9am–3pm, Mar–Oct Tues–Sat 10am–2pm and 6–8pm, Sun 10am–2pm; closed holidays). This former arsenal houses the world's most important collection of Punic artifacts among other prehistoric objects like pottery and vases excavated in Ibiza and Formentera.

Performing Arts

All the performance on this island takes place in the clubs: live sex acts, striptease, midgets, stilt freaks, fire eaters, drag

Is That a Dragon on Your Ass, or Are You Just Happy to See Me?

There are dozens of tattoo shops on the island, but the one that stands above the others is **Inkadelic,** Plaza Constitución 10 (no phone). Its owner, Neil, has a cool studio with objects brought from his trips all over the world. He offers a good variety of tats, from your average dragon to some very cool Japanese designs, but otherwise getting scratched in Ibiza can be tricky. That Mitsubishi symbol probably seemed like a good idea at 9am on a Saturday morning when you were still going from the night before, but the significance will be hard to explain later on when you return home and are trying to get a job that does not involve checking IDs.

queens, go-go girls, aliens, latex—and then there's all the freaks who pay to get in. Just what goes on in the bathrooms during Manumission at Privilege (p. 500) is more "performance" than most people will need in a lifetime.

Playing Outside
BEACHES

The Ibiza tourist office claims that this tiny island has about 56 📺 (Best ❸) **beaches!** If you really want to explore, head to the tourist office (p. 490) and pick up the free *IBIZA: Playas a la Carta.* This catalog describes each of the beaches and tells you how to get there, too.

To get away from the tourist hype that envelops the beaches closer to Ibiza Town, try 📺 (Best ❸) **Las Salinas Beach** (about 11km/7 miles south of Ibiza Town; follow

BALEARIC ISLANDS

Scoot Over

The best way to get away from some of the hype is to rent a scooter. They're cheap, and they're a total blast. Avoid the temptation to drive when f#@!ed up — it's hard to look good when you're picking your teeth up off the pavement. We don't want to sound like Nancy Reagan, but there's really no need to be driving your scooter while blinded by whiskey. The cheapest rentals are just a little out of the beaten tourist path (p. 488). A short cab ride or long walk will reward you with ample savings. A little scooter that maxes out at 40mph can traverse the entire island (east to west) in about 45 minutes. And even during the crowded tourist season, many of the roads are barely populated. Bring a picnic! Find a beach! The locals inland are not likely to speak English; as Catalan is the mother tongue for them, even Spanish is a second language. Note that wearing a helmet is mandatory for anything other than a bicycle, and you'll need to present your hometown driver's license to rent a scooter.

the signs for the airport), a full-on nudist beach that's less than 15 minutes from Ibiza Town by scooter. The attractive crowds here tend to be a little older (as in over 21), more local, and with more money. This beach is the height of cool in Ibiza.

You'll miss 🎵 Best♦ **Cala Xarraca Beach** unless you're looking for the restaurant of the same name. It makes sense, though, because the restaurant is the only thing here besides a few beautiful houses. The super-cool, topless beach is more tiny pebbles and shells than sand. Surrounded by rocky cliffs, the water is very clear with tints of blue and doesn't get deep for quite a while. Bring goggles and a snorkel for collecting stones in the water. **Paddle boats** are rented by the restaurant.

The tiny island of 🎵 Best♦ **Formentera** is about 10 miles south of Ibiza and features dreamy and unspoiled stretches of white sand that seem to go on forever. Its three beaches, Illetes, Levant, and Es Pujols, all outdo anything on Ibiza; they're prettier and the crowds are cooler. Only 5,000 people are permanent residents on this island, and although that number jumps to 20,000 in the summer, this place is still more chill than a penguin on ice.

Boats leave Ibiza Town at least once an hour from 7:45am till 10:30 at night. You'll get to Formentera in about 30 minutes and will pay about 34€ round-trip. Contact **Balearia Lines** (Calle Aragón 71; ☎ 971-310-711, central reservations ☎ 902-160-180; daily 7:30am–6:30pm, later in summer) for more info.

SCUBA DIVING

Ibiza has some of the best diving in the Mediterranean. Some people come here specifically for the clear waters and the unique marine life and mysterious shipwrecks that can be found beneath the surface. For a beautiful adventure, contact **Ibiza Diving** (Puerto Deportivo in the village of Santa Eulária; ☎ **971-332-949;** www.ibiza-diving.com; daily 9:30am–1pm and 2–6pm) or **Figueral** (Playa de Es Figueral, a 45-min. bus ride north of Ibiza Town, on the northeastern coast; ☎ **971-335-079;** daily 9am–2pm and 4–6:30pm). Instructors at both places speak English.

HORSEBACK RIDING

This is a scenic, memorable experience. The **Centro Ecuestre Easy Rider,** Camí del Sol d'en Serra, Cala Llonga, outside Santa Eulalia des Riu (☎ **971-339-192),** offers a 2-hour coastal ride with scenic dips inland.

Shopping

Between the influence of the hippies and the already artistic leanings of the native Ibizan culture, there's plenty of artistry, beautiful pottery, clothes, and jewelry on the island. I'd set aside some money for gifts.

→ **Holala!** "Unique clothing for unique people." In sticking to this creed, it has taken used clothing and brought it into the world of high fashion. Written up in nearly every fashion magazine you can think of (including *Elle*, *Vogue*, and *Cosmopolitan*), this trend-setting place always has something cooking. It sells everything from old kimonos and military surplus to modern clothing like Dickies and Adidas. But bring your wallet—those old 501s don't sell for cheap. *Plaza de Mercado Viejo 12.* ☎ 971-316-537.

→ **Libro Azul** This bookstore and gallery space hosts one or two readings and art expos every month. The art here leans toward the enormous, as in sculptures as big as a fridge. The books, many of them secondhand, lean toward the New Age and are in German, English, Spanish, and Catalán. *Village of Santa Gertrudis.* ☎ 971-197-454.

→ **Mapa Mundi** It's all about the shoes, which are totally unique, not too costly, and make a great gift for Mom, Sis, girlfriends, or yourself. The dresses here are beautiful, but out of the range of most travelers (they begin at 150€). If Indiana Jones and Stevie Nicks opened a store together, it might look like this place: beautiful, flowy dresses set in an old-world setting with maps, old travel trunks, and beautiful tribal-looking jewelry. *Plaza de Vila 13, at the base of the Fortress.* ☎ 971-391-685.

→ **Noon** Sick of the hippie-dippie scene? Need to check out the edgier side of Ibiza? The fashion zeitgeisters have figured it all out for you. Bar, bookstore, cybercafe, and the latest and hottest in local and international fashion, are all offered in this Soho-esque lifestyle space. Noon has two entrances, one known as Funkin'Irie at Bar@Noon, Carrer de Jaume 1, and one just known as Noon, on Carrer Cayetano Soler 9. *Carrer de Jaume 1, and Carrer Cayetano Soler 9.* ☎ 971-394-850.

MARKETS

→ **Hippy Market** This is what the locals call the fun outdoor markets, so if you're asking for directions, don't bother translating it into *mercadillo de hippi* or something like that. The biggest and best of the markets takes place in Es Canar (northeast of Santa Eulária). Unlike many other outdoor markets, this one has some truly beautiful stuff: great hats and sarongs for the beach, all sorts of handmade wind chimes, instruments, ceramics, fans, and also the requisite T-shirts, bowls, and watches. The market at Es Canar is in the middle of a hippie village and has been

what to wear

Platforms, pigtails, and a Stetson will get you real far here. As will pushing yourself to the fashion limits: Dye your hair! Paint your face! Wear just a bikini top! The fashion here goes right with the freewheeling, tripped-out attitude of the island. People might sneer at you if you're walking around in the middle of Des Moines, Iowa, with a micromini pleather skirt and a quarter-ounce of glitter on your face, but people here will love it. Everyone wants you to look wild and feel good about it.

running since the early '70s. Get here by bus (1€) or by scooter (30 min. maximum). It's easy to spend a few hours among the nearly 400 booths here, so give yourself some time. The bright woodcarvings of Paulo Viheira capture the warm and creative essence of non-disco Ibiza. Although he does have his own studio in Santa Eulária, you'll have an easier time tracking him down here. Prices range from about 16€ for something the size of a dinner plate to nearly 238€ for enormous carvings that you could windsurf on. Highly recommended, and easy to find. Ask any of the friendly workers at the market. *In Es Canar (northeast of Santa Eulária, a 20-min. bus ride from Ibiza Town). Apr–Oct Wed 9:30am–7pm.*

Side Trip: San Antonio & Surrounds

San Antonio, on the west coast, is a nightmarish combination of suburban shopping mall, soccer riot, and frat party, where the youngest and most terrible of the tourists come to party. Except for the Café Mambo (p. 497) and the sunset spots (below), it should be avoided at all costs. Staying here is not advisable and rather difficult since most hotels pre-sell their rooms to tourist agencies leaving no space for last minute bookings. But it has been blessed by its primo sunset views (at around 9pm in the summertime), and

Info, Por Favor

You can find the tourist information office in San Antonio at Passeig de Ses Fonts (☎ **971-343-363**). The hours are 9:30am to 8pm, Monday to Friday; 9:30am to 1pm Saturday and Sunday from May to October; 9:30am to 2:30pm Monday to Friday, 9am to 1pm Saturday in the off season.

some of the nicest beaches are in the general vicinity (a mere half-hour bus ride away from Ibiza). As it is sort of an obliged destination, you'll probably find yourself there at one point or another.

EATING

➔ **Zafiro** SPANISH Only 2 blocks away from the beach in Cala de Bou is a completely different world from the San Antonio schlock. Most tourists don't venture this far, leaving this simple restaurant with great food and better prices available for the locals (and you). Sassy waiters and a bustling down-to-earth ambience complete the experience. *Av. San Agustín 118, Cala de Bou.* ☎ *971-343-903. Hours vary, so call ahead.*

PARTYING
Bars

The best reason to go to a bar in San Antonio is to watch the sunset—in fact, that is probably the only reason. Sunset is a really nice spectacle though, and bars on this side of the island exploit that to the max. But, at night, the bars in San Antonio are dirty, lame, and boring, packed with very young and very drunk English kids.

MTV Best ☻ ➔ **Café del Mar** Listen to the ambient music that made this place world-famous, have a drink, and watch a magnificent sun set over the rocks directly in front. The rabid British party monkeys that swarm San Antonio show up later on, but it's fun to slip slowly from the mellow sunset to that high-energy fiesta while getting sauced on gin-and-tonics. The decor by Catalán architect Louis Géll has not been touched since the '80s and that sort of Miami pink and black Deco thing still works for it. Including the surrounding beach, max capacity is about 2,000 people. *Carrer de Vara del Rey s/n.* ☎ *971-342-516.*

➔ **Kumharas** If it only had hammocks this place would be a resort. What started as a great place to watch the sunset has morphed into a mega center of hippie-hedonism. If you're sick of planning out what to do all the time, you could just spend your whole day here. Start off with a healthy brunch with fresh juice and tea by the pool, take a capoeira or yoga class in the afternoon followed by a massage, watch the sunset with chill-out music and cool people, and then have an Asian-influenced dinner in the Middle Eastern tents. To top it off, dance the night away with special music nights like reggae Tuesdays or hip-hop Thursdays. *Cala de Bou, Bahia de San Antonio. ☎ 971-805 740. www.kumharas.org.*

MTV **Best** ☻ → **Sunset Ashram** A better option to watch the sun take a dive is this bar at the relatively more secluded and waaaaaaay nicer beach of Cala Conta. The cement terrace with dome-shaped straw roof glows under the orange light of the magic hour, and you are bound to fill up your camera's memory card with pictures of that big bastard sinking in between the two small islands across the cove. Be warned, the last bus leaves from here to San Antonio at 6:45pm, cellphone reception to call a 12€ cab is not ideal, and hitchhiking is not advisable. *Cala Conta beach. ☎ 661-347-222. Bus Voramar El Gaucho N. 4 from San Antonio-Cala Conta.*

PLAYING OUTSIDE
Beaches

If it's **beaches** you want, avoid San Antonio beach or S'Arenal, the most crowded beaches on the island—you're not likely to find a spot to lie down there. Better take a bus or a quick ride to Cala Conta or Salada (below) and save yourself from losing your sanity before you hit the clubs.

Cala Conta is a long stretch of beach with sand so fine you can almost snort it (don't). It gets pretty packed in the summer, but it is still one of the best places on

the island to see the sunset. The Des Bosc and Sa Conillera Islands add to the view, but be careful, they are much farther away than they seem. Unless you are in really, REALLY good shape, don't try to swim across or your limp body will end up being dragged back to shore by the lifeguards (hey, maybe you want that). You can have a drink at Sunset Ashram (see "Bars," earlier) or eat fresh seafood on the beach at the excellent **S'Illa des Bosc** (☎ **971-806-161**). Take the Voramar El Gaucho bus (no. 4) from San Antonio-Cala Conta. (*Note:* The last bus to San Antonio returns at 6:45pm.)

Two small, fine-sand coves divided by a huge rock formation and surrounded by more rocks and pine trees make **Cala Salada** a nice (and less crowded) option not too far from San Antonio. The first beach on the left is more rocky, go over the rocks to the second beach, which is bigger, sandier, and mostly nude. The bus does not take you here, so it is ideal for scooters or bikes (parking your car in the summer can be an issue). The surrounding woods are great for a nature walk, and if you forgot to pack your picnic, fear not, there is a **restaurant** creatively named Cala Salada (☎ **971-342-867**) that serves up fresh fish and seafood on the beach.

Hiking

The northwestern part of the island is composed of mostly **wildlife preserves,** and trekking the trails that traverse it makes for a great exorcism of all the substances you put in your body the night before. **Trails** are marked with blue, green, and red dots on the rocks, to determine their difficulty (blue being the easiest and red the hardest). One of our favorites, although not very easy to find, is the one at **Puerta del Cielo** (Heaven's Gate). Take the road to Santa Agnes and, once there, look for signs that say Porta d'es Cel, or ask a local. Follow the road for about a mile, and you will see a restaurant and a bunch of parked cars. Leave your vehicle there and walk toward the sea, following the blue marks. After a 5-minute walk through

rocks and vegetation, you'll come to an opening with a view of the sky and the coast that will convince you there really is a heaven.

Formentera

If you want to see what Ibiza was like before the mmm-cha, mmm-cha and the drugs converted it into a den of sin, you should make some time for a trip to Formentera. "The **last paradise in the Mediterranean**" is the *pequeña* (little one) of the Balearic sisters and was, luckily, forgotten until pretty recently. As a consequence, you will see very few big hotels, and the tallest structures are the lighthouses. Formentera is a recovery paradise from Ibiza's workout and even the partying is in chill mode; for maxin' and relaxin' few places in the world could beat this 20km-long (12-mile) island with a population of about 7,000 people on 67km (42 miles) of coastline. The beaches are mostly undeveloped, with ridiculously fine, white sand, and some are so long you could spend half a day walking them from end to end. An incredible amount of light bathes the island in the summer, making it a paradise for diving, with a uniquely preserved underwater vegetation and crystal clear waters that give a whole new meaning to the words "deep blue." The island's limited hotel capacity is maxed out summer after summer by German and English older couples at the beginning of the season and then younger Italians as summer advances. This provides for an interesting nightlife, the kind that you imagine at Caribbean destinations (only minus the calypso music): drinks and dancing by the sea from sunset 'til sunrise.

At many beaches, people are so relaxed they don't even bother to put clothes on and, in just their birthday suits, take mud

baths on the beach alongside the transparent water. The hordes of tourists arriving for the day as an escape from Ibiza's madness mix seamlessly with those who are spending their whole vacation there and the ritzy yacht owners who pick it as their port in the Mediterranean.

Getting There & Around

GETTING THERE

By Boat

Boats to Formentera sail from Ibiza Town's main port at a rate of up to 26 a day from 6am until 9:30pm in the summer months; there are eight daily departures in the winter. Crossing the 5km (3-mile) channel takes anywhere from 25 to 90 minutes, depending on the boat, and will cost you between 18€ and 34€ round-trip (150€ if you ferry a car, though we don't really recommend it). For more information, call **Balearia** (☎ 902-160-180; www.balearia. com) or **Trasmapi** (☎ 971-312-071). The boat drops you off at the port in La Savina, on the northwest side of Formentera.

GETTING AROUND

By Bus

The only public transportation is run by **Autocares Paya** (☎ 971-323-181), which runs small buses connecting all the destinations on the main road. Call them for more info and schedules.

By Taxi

Cabs will be waiting when you get off the boat. A ride to the other side of the island should not cost more than 15€, but make sure to ask beforehand. Each small town has its own cab company. You can call either one of the following companies from anywhere, but they will take their time to come pick you up: **San Francesc** (☎ 971-322-016), **Es Pujols** (☎ 971-328-016), and **La Savina** (☎ 971-322-002).

By Car, Bike & Moped
We recommend getting around the island by bicycle. The island is the perfect size for it, and you won't alter its peace and quiet with the annoying sound of a scooter. You'll be happy to have a bike for those couple of trails that can only be accessed by foot or bike. That said, a scooter can be convenient, especially at night, to move around the pitch-black roads, or, if you are too lazy to go up the 192m (630 ft.) of elevation to get to the lighthouse at Sa Mola. There are a couple of agencies right by the port where you can rent cars, mopeds, and bicycles. Many of the hotels rent scooters and bikes too. Some local agencies are **Autos Formentera** (☎ 971-322-817) and **Proauto** (☎ 971-328-729). Scooters cost between 20€ and 25€ a day and bicycles 6€ to 10€. You can get them at **Moto Rent Migjorn** (☎ 971-322-306) or **Moto Rent Pujols** (☎ 971-322-488). As on the other islands, you need to show your regular driver's license and accept one of their helmets in order to rent a scooter.

Formentera Basics
ORIENTATION
As I said earlier, it would take you just a couple of hours to walk from end to end of the island, and there is just one road. The tiny towns have maybe two or three streets at the most, so, unless you are really messed up (which is possible), you can't get lost here even if you try.

La Savina, Formentera's main port, is located on a harbor on the northwestern side of the island, in between two salt lakes that look beautiful but, well—one of them is named **Estany Pudent (Stinky**

Lake) . . . 'nuff said. Right up north on the coast is **Ses Salines,** the salt mines, which were the main source of income on the island before it became the tourist-driven "last paradise." Nowadays the old mines make for a striking landscape and the nicest bike trails on the island. Further north is the small peninsula that leads to the **Punta des Trucadors,** with some of the most idyllic beaches on both sides, alternating with rock formations. This area is the best to watch the sunset from either the beach or one of the sunset bars (p. 511). North of Punta des Trucadors lies the **S'Espalmador island.** Right across the stinky lake from La Savina lies **Es Pujols,** Formentera's answer to Barcelona's Sant Antoni, with the highest concentration of hotels, restaurants, and Germans; I would suggest you stay away from this overpriced town and head to the more remote areas. (If you miss the crowds, just go back to Ibiza.)

Directly south from **La Savina** is the biggest town and capital of the island, **Sant Francesc Xavier.** The town is worth checking out, with its charming whitewashed houses and nice little *plaças* surrounded by bars where you can sip a vermouth if you are too fried to be at the beach. South of **Sant Francesc** is the road to **Cap de Barbaria.** Down that road and to the west are the white beaches of **Cala Saona** and further down south the actual cap with its lighthouse, which, unless you are really bored of everything else on the island, is not worth the trip.

Continuing on the main road from Sant Francesc (PM-820, which crosses the whole island from west to east and has bike paths on both sides), you will hit **Sant Ferran de Ses Roques,** another small and unassuming little town that houses the liveliest restaurant on the island, **Fonda Pepe** (p. 510). As you continue on the 820, you'll see the endless beach of

12 Hours in Formentera

1. Take a **bike ride** through the lunar landscape of the salt mines at **Ses Salines.**

2. **Beach,** baby, beach. Choose the long and wild stretches at **Migjorn,** the yacht-infested waters of **Illetes,** or the small, secluded ones in **Es Calo.**

3. Take a boat or wade across to **S'Espalmador** and get down and dirty in a **mud bath.**

4. Watch the feast of colors in the sunset sky at **Tiburón.**

5. Eat the quintessential paella with the locals at **Fonda Pepe** and then have a gin-lemon at the front bar.

6. Dance the night away under the stars at **Blue Bar,** then go skinny-dipping in the crystal clear sea.

Migjorn, to your right. This beach has the best beach bars and is our recommendation for trying to find a hotel. A rocky coast flanks you on the north as you continue east toward the cute little fishing town of **Es Calo.** This town is worthy of a stop to check out the timber boat shelters lining the coast or to take a swim at the nearby small coves. Farther along, the road goes up through pine-covered hills and past clearings where the view is so beautiful it might make you cry (and it isn't the wind, silly). At the summit, the old farmlands that are divided by prehistoric walls made of piled stones would make Fred Flintstone proud. Finally, at the eastern end lies the lighthouse, **La Mola Faro,** with breathtaking views of the cliffs and a couple of caves that have been known to shelter stranded tourists in more than one occasion.

TOURIST OFFICES

The tourist office (☎ **971-322-057**) is open Monday to Friday, 10am to 2pm and 5 to 7pm, Saturday 10am to 2pm. It is in one of those storefronts at the port and can be easily confused with a car-rental agency. The ladies working there are adopted locals mostly of the Italian kind who love the island and are fun and helpful.

RECOMMENDED WEBSITES

○ **www.formenteraweb.com**: A pretty comprehensive guide of everything Formentera has to offer, available in English.

○ **www.illesbalears.es**: The official website of the Balearics Tourist Agency is also very complete and available in many languages.

○ **www.guiaformentera.com**: Yet another guide, also in English.

Culture Tips 101

The official winter population of the island is a little over 7,000 people. This number triples in the summer with mostly Italian tourists but a big number of Germans and English too. Locals are used to this and are friendly and courteous. Formentera takes great pride in its unspoiled landscape, so throwing garbage on the beach or playing your boom box at top volume is the easiest way to make some quick enemies. Since pretty much everybody in the island works in tourism-related activities, you won't find it difficult to get by with just English. Also because of its more private nature, most beaches in Formentera are nudist friendly. As in all of Spain, nudity is legal in public spaces, but nowhere is it as common as here. Lastly, police presence is very rare here and they won't bother you unless you are disturbing others. In this center of chill, if you are not, you will stick out like Paris Hilton in a convent, and get voted off the island in no time.

Formentera **Nuts & Bolts**

Currency   As always, you will get the best exchange rate at an **ATM**. All the towns have at least one.

Emergency   Centro Médico (☎ **902-079-079**), on the main road, 3km (2 miles) south from La Savina. For emergencies dial ☎ **112**.

Internet   Internet access seems like a very far-fetched concept in this nature paradise, but if your sister is about to have a baby or something urgent like that, you can check your e-mail on the island. **Café Formentera** (Sant Ferran; ☎ **971-321-842**; www.cafeformentera.com; Mon–Sat 10am–9:30pm), the only Internet cafe on Formentera, offers 11 computers with flat screens and a pretty-fast DSL connection at 5€ per 65 minutes. You can also send faxes and have a nice Italian espresso while you're at it. And if you are enough of a nerd to have brought your notebook, you can get connected too, for the same price.

Pharmacies   You can find one in each town: Sant Francesc, on Santa Maria (☎ **971-322-419**); or Sant Ferran, on Joan Castelló Guasch 21 (☎ **971-328-004**).

Telephone   City code: **971**; operator: **1003**; international operator: **1005**.

Sleeping

Formentera has only 50 hotels and no additional development is permitted. In other words, you are more likely to find a skinhead at a Phish concert than a room here in August. Camping is not allowed and even the caves fill up quickly (though you'd eventually get kicked out of them anyway). Advance booking is more necessary here than in any of the other islands, but most hotels don't open until May. If you want to secure a room before then, call the lovely ladies at the tourist information and they will help you. A lot of hotels pre-sell their capacity to travel agencies for tour packs, but here are some places you can try.

→ **Hostal Ca Mari** This complex, located among the dunes on pristine Migjorn beach, is composed of three different hotels that share a common swimming pool, a '70s style tiled bar, and a restaurant. Buildings are constructed of the typical island, white-washed stone and the rooms are very simple, spacious, and comfy. They have regular rooms, bungalows, and apartments with small kitchens. Try to get the bungalows down by the beach, with small porches and mosquito nets. Earlier in the season the place is filled with mostly older Germans and families; later on is all about the young Italians. *Platja Migjorn.* ☎ *971-328-180. www.guiaformentera.com/camari. Double with breakfast 50€–100€, studio (2 people) 42€–92€, apt. (4 people) 52€–130€. Amenities: Bar, restaurant, bike/scooter rental, breakfast room, fax, parking, swimming pool, telephone, travel info, TV.*

Ⓜ Best ☻ → **Hostal de Pepe** ★ Rosalia, the rambunctious woman who runs Hostal de Pepe, says the owner is threatening to close it down, since, with Fonda de Pepe, the bustling restaurant and bar in front, he is not particularly in need of the cash flow. Let's hope she's just jerking our chain. This bare-bones *hostal* is clean, has spunk, and is a convenient crawl across the street or upstairs for those nights of gorging on paella and wine at Fonda Pepe. All rooms feature a private bath and a few have small balconies. Be warned: At press time they did not have any ventilation; but some renovations are currently underway—maybe they will sneak in a fan or two. *Calle Major 68, Sant Ferran.* ☎ *971-328-033. Single 32€, double 52€, triple 79€. Breakfast included. Amenities: Breakfast room, pool.*

→ **Hotel Riu La Mola** ★ Though probably the biggest structure on the island, Riu La Mola manages to blend in pretty well with the landscape since it is built into the side of a hill. In the same philosophy as other resort chains, this outpost of the Riu group offers a little bit of everything—from live entertainment to table- and real-tennis courts, free kayak and bicycle rentals to diving school (at a fee). The rooms have all the amenities a government-rated, four-star hotel can offer including terraces overlooking one of the most splendid beaches in Formentera. The real deal, though, are the individual bungalows, interconnected by terra-cotta trails and beautifully manicured gardens. *Apartado 23, Playa de Migjorn, Formentera.* ☎ *971-327-000. www.riulamola.com. Single 62€–192€, double 98€–292€, bungalows 43€–165€ per person depending on amount of people and season. Breakfast and dinner included. Closed Nov–Apr. Amenities: Restaurant, 2 bars, dry cleaning, health club, laundry service, minigolf, 2 pools, tennis court. In room: A/C, TV, hair dryer, minibar, safe.*

Eating

Since you will be spending most of your time at the beach, that's probably where you will eat. Most beaches have some sort of *chiringuito* on them, and most *chiringuitos* have some sort of food, varying from simple sandwiches to elaborate fresh-fish dishes. But, since this is a fishing island, you should not miss some of the sit-down seafood restaurants. Prices vary, but they tend to be cheaper than on Ibiza since the restaurants are less pretentious. It is actually worth it to take a day trip, have a delectable *fideua* (paella with fine pasta and aioli instead of rice) then take the last boat back.

CHEAP

MTV Best ● → **Fonda Pepe** ★★ SEAFOOD This unassuming family restaurant is to Formentera what "Stairway to Heaven" is to rock 'n' roll—an absolute classic. With more than 50 years of history, the big dining room is always packed with local workers, German families, and trendy Italian youngsters. But the reason you should come here is the gigantic sizzling plates of sumptuous paella packed with seafood and yumminess, the refreshing gazpacho, or the grilled fresh fish. Top it off with a

The Last Windmill

El Molí Vell was the last working windmill on the Balearics and, though retired, has been restored to working condition today. Built in 1778 it was still grinding grains until the 1960s. If you can babble some Spanish, it is of particular interest to speak to the caretaker, whose husband was the last owner and operator of it before it was finally put to rest and acquired by the local government.

shot of *hierbas* (a local digestive) and then get your night started at the vibrant bar in the front (see "Bars," below). *Calle Major 51, Sant Ferran. No phone. Entrees 8€–20€. Sun–Fri 1–5pm and 8pm–midnight; Sat 8pm–midnight.*

→ **Ma Vie** SPANISH If you have to go to Es Pujols, you might as well grab a bite here. The friendly staff will serve you decent food at fairly low prices (for the area anyway). They specialize in fresh island fish, but they also offer all sorts of meat, salads, and tapas. Don't leave without trying the mouthwatering crepes flambé. The walls display the different wines they offer, and the many shiny, wooden tables get jam-packed every night. You can wait for yours at the long bar where the bartender will tell you everything you need to know about anything. *Es Pujols.* ☎ *971-328-529. www.formenteraonline.com/mavie. Entrees 7€–15€. Mon–Sat 1–3pm and 7pm–midnight; Sun 7pm–midnight.*

DOABLE

→ **Es Molí de Sal** ★★ BALEARIC If you need to impress that Italian boy/girl you picked up at the beach, few places will do like this ancient salt windmill beautifully converted into a restaurant. The hard thing will be to keep your eyes on each other and away from the incredible views of the sea or the beautiful plates of what is possibly the island's freshest fish, which is sold by weight. But if you decide that you've had enough fish, you can choose from their many rice, meat, and pasta dishes, although it would be a shame to miss the *bullit de peix* (fish casserole with aioli) with *arroz a banda* (rice cooked in the fish stew). On second thought, you may want to avoid the aioli on your first date. *Illetes Beach.* ☎ *971-187-491. Entrees 18€–29€. Apr–Oct daily 1–4pm and 8–10:30pm.*

DOWN & DIRTY

North of Ses Illetes lies the island of **S'Espalmador.** The island, which has no permanent structures, offers beautiful beaches and very popular mud baths that add a good deal to the relaxation factor. But if you are a little germophobic, forget about them during the high season, when the mud tends to get "dirty" and overused. To reach S'Espalmador, take a Barca Bahia Boat that makes the La Savina–Ses Illetes–S'Espalmador trip three times a day for 12€ round-trip—just find the boats at the harbor in La Savina or right at the beach in Ses Illetes. A lot of people just wade across, but some of them get caught in the tides and never make it to the island . . . or anywhere else.

Partying
BARS

Formentera is all about the beach bars, where you can hang out all afternoon and usually until midnight or later depending on how cool you (and they) are. If you want more serious nightlife you will have to go to Es Pujols, where tons of sun-kissed European youth fill up the bars in preparation to go dancing.

→ **Blue Bar** You can ask anyone on the island for the best beach bar and 9 out of 10 will point you to Blue Bar. The decor is the kind of borderline ticky-tacky that you can imagine at a hippie-ish beach bar, with blue, sea-inspired murals and a statue of an alien with a peace sign. They also serve good seafood, meat dishes, and salads, and—even though you can't really see the sun dipping into the sea from here—their sunset DJ sets get things moving until early in the morning. *Migjorn Beach Km 7.9.* ☎ *971-187-011.*

→**Fonda Pepe** I know, we already reviewed this in the restaurants and hotels, but the bar at the front of Fonda Pepe is the most authentic on the island. Foreign and local cool cats mingle together along the dark, wooden bar or commune outside in the street. A '70s hippie central, Pepe's has kept the spirit and the pinball machines alive and kickin'. *Calle Major 51, Sant Ferran. No phone.*

MTV **Best ●** →**Tiburón** Your visit to Formentera wouldn't be complete if you didn't watch the sun sinking into the water at one of the bars on the west side of this island. Besides choice seating, this local's favorite offers creative seafood and salad dishes, plus a very laid-back island vibe. Oh, and if you show up with your yacht, they'll come down and serve you right there. *Playa Cavall d'en Borras.* ☎ *659-638-945.*

CLUB

→**Xueno** The only club on the island can by no means compete with Ibiza's biggies, but some DJs, like Frankie Knuckles, take the boat out here for a chiller set in this two-story club packed with wide-eyed Italians. *Es Pujols.* ☎ *971-329-160. www.xueno.com. Mid June–Sept.*

Playing Outside
MTV **Best ●** BEACHES

There are officially six beaches in Formentera, plus a seemingly endless number of coves, each one with its own charm and unique characteristics. Our suggestion, if you have the time, is to explore them and pick your favorite. Be aware that except for **Es Pujols** and **Cala Saona,** most of them are nudist friendly or have nudist areas, whether that is your thing or not.

Migjorn is the longest beach with lots of rock formations and sometimes seaweed. Along the coast there are hostels and *chiringuitos,* hidden in the protected

sand dunes. The **MTV** **Best ●** **Platja de Ses Illetes** and **Platja de Llevant** are beaches on each side of the northern tip of the island. The western side is the chosen site for private yachts to anchor; and at the eastern side, with its rougher waters and coves protected by rock formations you'll find the lowest concentration of bathing suits on the island. By the small fishing village of **Es Calo** a couple of small, very secluded beaches are good for swimming inside the rock formations.

SCUBA DIVING

The waters surrounding Formentera, if not too deep, are extremely clear and populated by the best preserved posidonia forests in the Mediterranean. These seagrass "forests" provide for an incredible underwater landscape. Contact **Vell Mari** (Av. Mediterranea 90, Port de La Savina; ☎ **971-328-035;** www.vellmari.com) or **Orcasub** (Hotel Formentera Playa; ☎ **971-388-035;** www.orcasub.com) for English-speaking info on courses, excursions, and snorkeling.

CYCLING/TREKKING

Over 20 trekking and biking trails snake around the island. A particularly beautiful bike ride is to go around the **salt mines** by Es Pujols. Get the green tours booklet at the tourist office for more info on this and other rides.

Market Fare

If the shopaholic in you can't take the lack of action anymore, wait for Wednesday or Sunday and check out the market at **El Pilar La Mola.** Beside local arts and crafts (pay special attention to the jewelry) the music and a very festive ambience will add a touch of excitement to your dissipated life.

Menorca

The coast of **Sant Lluis,** at the eastern end of Menorca, is the first place where the sun rises in Spain. Maybe that's the reason why the second largest of the Balearic Islands is like the quiet, virginal sister in a family of wild, party-by-night animals. With a much lower profile than Mallorca and Ibiza, Menorca has remained surprisingly undeveloped, and in 1993 it became a Unesco Biosphere Reserve, which means that further development of the island is supposed to be sustainable (in other words, your new Hummer won't cut it here).

The maiden of this natural environment is the **Natural Park S'albufera d'es Grau,** a lagoon and a group of salt marshes with crazy birds and vegetation. About 80% of the coastline is protected, and, for an island with more beaches than the three others put together, that's a lot. It is possible for you to find a secluded beach in the summer and actually be completely alone. And, oh the beaches you will go to: long sandy stretches, rocky, fjordlike coves, and even pebble-covered small bays. You may even be able to catch a decent wave for surfing here. In the north shore, by Fornells (see "Board Talk" box, later), when the famous Tramuntana blows, it is not unusual to see 15-footers breaking on the shore.

When you are sick of lying on your bum, get up and explore some of the many **natural caves** where people lived long before the first baby Hilton was even born. **Hiking** and **horseback riding** are pretty big activities here too. And when you're not riding a horse you may well be trying not to be stepped on by one at Sant Joan in Ciutadella or at any of the other colorful and magical town fiestas that rove the whole island in the summer. And of course, diving and snorkeling in the deep blue waters is unforgettable.

Such peace and tranquillity attracts lots of artists, bringing a bit of cultural life to the old port towns. But if modern art is too new for you, check out some older (actually prehistoric) relics preserved in the area. The nightlife is not really that hot, though. This is more the place where you come to rest or be sporty than for any spring-break type of madness. However, lining the port areas of the two bigger towns, **Ciutadella** and **Maó,** some good bars and restaurants cater to the young and restless, who mix with the older yacht owners and locals. Oh, and did we mention the club with one of the best locations in the world? (See p. 518.)

Menorca is the most English of the islands; it actually belonged to them for most of the 18th century. That can be seen clearly in the architecture, the gin factory in Maó, and the prevalence of that incomprehensible sport, cricket, which is played in some parts of the island. If you thought you would never be able to enjoy the peace and quiet of a Mediterranean beach in the summer without a bunch of German kids kicking sand on your face, or the complaining of a wannabe Italian diva keeping you awake, you were wrong. You will always have Menorca.

Getting There & Around
GETTING THERE
By Air
Menorca's **International Airport** (☎ 971-157-000) is located about 4.5km (2³/₄ miles) southwest of Maó. It operates mostly in the summer months with chartered flights arriving primarily from the U.K. **Iberia/Air Nostrum** (☎ 902-400-500), **Air Europa** (☎ 902-401-501), and **Vueling** (☎ 902-333-933) all offer daily connections to the Spanish mainland. During the summer, there is a bus connecting with

BALEARIC ISLANDS

Maó's bus station every 30 minutes from 5:45am until 10:15pm, and two more at 11:15pm and 12:15am. The ride takes 15 minutes and costs 1.50€. A taxi from the airport's taxi stop to Maó will hurt somewhere from 7.50€ to 9€.

By Boat

Balearia (☎ 902-160-180; www.balearia. com) runs a daily boat to Maó (54€, trip time: 9 hr.) and one to Ciutadella (85€, trip time: 4 hr.) from Barcelona plus one daily ferry from Alcúdia in Mallorca to Ciutadella (55€, trip time: 1 hr.) during the summer months. **Trasmediterranea** (☎ 902-454-645) also runs services from Barcelona (57€, trip time: 8 hr.) and Palma to Maó.

GETTING AROUND

By Bus

Buses tend to be pretty slow, but they do connect most points on the island. **Transportes Menorca (TMSA;** ☎ **971-360-475;** www.transportesmenorca.net) runs buses all over the island, and **Torres Allés Autocares** (☎ 669-483-593; www. e-torres.net) runs the airport bus and buses from Ciutadella to area beaches. For information or schedules visit their websites or grab some brochures at the tourist office.

By Taxi

A cab from Ciutadella to Maó will set you back a whopping 41€. Depending on which you are closer to, you can call one at **Radio Taxi** in Maó (☎ 971-367-111) or in Ciutadella, **Taxi Móvil** (☎ 971-482-222).

By Car, Bike & Moped

If you want to take advantage of all Menorca has to offer, you should ideally have some kind of locomotion, besides the mile-an-hour buses. A scooter or a small car will get you anywhere you need to go, but, if you want to go across the island, a 50cc is probably not enough. To rent a car

at the airport, try **Atesa** (☎ 971-366-213), which charges 50€ and up for its cheaper models. In Maó, **Autos Valls** (Plaça España 13; ☎ 971-354-244; www.autosvalls.com) will rent you a three-door for 90€ to 100€ for 3 days, and they will bring it to the airport for you. They also carry motorcycles. To get a bike or motorcycle in Ciutadella, check out **Velos Joan** (C. Sant Isidre 32-34; ☎ 971-381-576). A bike will set you back 7€ a day or 25€ for 5 days, and a scooter, 30€ a day.

Menorca Basics

ORIENTATION

Menorca is about 15km (9¼ miles) wide and 52km (32 miles) long, which is a little more than the distance separating its two main towns of Maó and Ciutadella. The capital, **Mao,** lies on the eastern tip of the island, on an outstanding natural harbor coveted by many throughout its history. Most boats from the Continent arrive here. The airport is also on this side of the island, 4.5km (2¾ miles) southwest of Maó. There is a main road, the ME1, that connects Maó with Ciutadella and cuts the island in two very different halves: **The northern side** is more rugged and uneven, with a dramatic coastline and smaller beaches with reddish, dark sand. Here the beaches are more secluded and the sea is rougher, and most of them can only be accessed by foot or boat. The **Es**

Cuidado! Prix Fixe

Taxis here work with fixed rates so ask for the price of the ride before getting in the cab to avoid surprises. They have been known to take advantage of foreigners, and once you get to your destination, there's not much you can do to dispute the fare.

12 Hours in Menorca

1. **Find yourself a beach to lie down on.** Choose the north coast if you want more privacy and ridiculously beautiful landscapes or the south coast for that fine, white sand and azure water that makes the cover of travel magazines worldwide.

2. **Take a stroll through the gorgeous historical center of Ciutadella** and finish by getting a pair of *avarcas* (classic Menorcan sandals) in the market at Plaça des Borns.

3. **Surfing in the Balearics?** The up-to-15-feet-tall waves on the north coast say you can.

4. **Run with the bulls?** No, but escape from the horses at the crazy 48-hour-long Festa de Sant Joan.

5. **Have a drink at El Mirador, in Maó,** with cool people overlooking the bay, then walk down for a cocktail and tapas at the port.

6. **Go primal at a party** in the caves of Xoroi.

Grau lagoon is on the north coast too. **The south side** is flatter and made up of calcareous rock. The cliffs are smoother and the beaches are longer, more idyllic, with long stretches of white sand surrounded by pines. From the main road, a bunch of smaller branches spread out to the beaches and resorts on the coast. As you go along the MEI, you will pass a few towns, namely **Alaior, Es Mercadal, and Ferreries,** good for a bathroom stop and little else. At the end of the road you get to **Ciutadella,** the second-largest town and second port too. Most boats from Mallorca and one daily from Barcelona arrive here.

TOURIST OFFICES

The tourist office in Maó (Carrer Sa Rovellada de Dalt 24; ☎ **971-363-790;** www.e-menorca.org) is open Monday to Friday 9am to 1pm and 5 to 7pm, Saturday 9am to 1pm. If you land in Ciutadella, look for the tourist office at Plaça Catedral 5 (☎ **971-382-693**). It's open June to September daily 9am to 9pm; October to May Monday to Friday 9am to 1pm and 5 to 7pm, Saturday 9am to 1pm.

RECOMMENDED WEBSITES & MAGAZINES

Like we said, the nightlife is not the strength of Menorca, so unfortunately there aren't any guides like *Guia del Ocio* or similar here. However two excellent free tourist magazines are available in English. *Menorca Bienvenidos* is a publication of local newspaper *Menorca.* It comes out once a year and packs 102 pages of solid information on everything from beaches and horse racing to arts and crafts. Like those in-flight magazines, it has two columns, an English and a Spanish one, so it's great for practicing your *castellano.* Another nice yearly magazine is *Menorca Magazine.* This one has more photos and less content, and is trilingual, adding German to the mix.

The best website for nightlife is **www. menorcaweb.com**, available in four languages and not that exciting, but very informative. **www.menorcadigital.com** is another local website (available also in English) where you can find good deals on apartments and hotels, plus a weekly guide to the island's cultural events.

BALEARIC ISLANDS

Culture Tips 101

Menorcans retained the politeness and soft manners from their English heritage. Except for the madness that possesses everybody during Sant Joan, people are very cool and quiet here, and crooning "American Pie" on the streets is not seen as a nice diversity trait. Police presence is more decorative than anything, though if you see a red, yellow, and purple car, don't make too much fun of it and try to have some respect. In the first 2 hours in Menorca, I got offered *chocolate* (hash) twice, by teenagers who where willing to give me their phone number for any needs. Provided, I don't look like a cop, but that gives you an idea of how laid-back cops actually are.

Menorca **Nuts & Bolts**

Currency   ATMs are available in Maó, Ciutadella, and other towns. You can always exchange money at the hotels, but they will rip you off big time.

Emergency   Get your boo-boos fixed at Hospital Verge del Toro, Calle de Barcelona, Maó (☎ 971-157-700). For emergencies dial ☎ 112.

Internet   Dry-surfing is possible at the following establishments. There are fancier options, but **Locutorio Miranda** (S'Arraval 30, Maó; no phone; Mon–Sat 10am–9:30pm) is the cheapest way to check if he/she wrote you back. The cost is .60€ for 15 minutes. Since 1998, **C@fé Internet** (Pl. de los Pinos 37, Ciutadella; ☎ 971-384-215; www.elcafe.net) has offered 21 computers, burning and faxing capabilities, as well as food and drinks. Internet access is 5€ per 3 hours.

Pharmacies   In Maó you can get your baby oil at **Escudero Sirerol,** Camí d`Es Castell 9 (☎ 971-363-148). In Ciutadella, check **Cavaller Cavaller,** Plaza Catedral 7 (☎ 971-380-083).

Telephone   City code: **971;** operator: **1003;** international operator: **1005.** Note that recent changes in Spain's phone system now require that all local calls be dialed with the 971 prefix.

Maó

The capital of Menorca is settled on top of a cliff on the southern shore of the astonishing 5km (3-mile) natural harbor that has seen its share of boats sail by since the genesis of navigation. Although not as beautiful as Ciutadella, Maó has an interesting architectural heritage that was inherited from the times of British colonization. Its main attraction is its port and the endless number of bars and restaurants accumulated by the harbor. The main square is **Plaça de l'Esplanada,** right off the bus station. There are a couple of bars and cafes around it and an ice cream parlor to sate your raging sweet tooth. Saturdays and Tuesdays there is a market where artisans from all over the island hawk their wares. From there, walk toward the old town, to **Plaça Bastió,** a cute, smaller *plaça* where locals come for cheaper food and drinks than by the port. Right off of the *plaça,* you'll see the **Arc De Sant Roc,** a massive medieval arch right out of *A Knight's Tale.* Continue walking on the narrow streets to **Plaça Constitució** where you will see the **Esglesia Santa Maria,** house of a massive pipe organ that would make Mozart drool. As you walk past the next square, **Plaça de Espanya,** you will see the former cloisters turned mall of **Mercat Claustre del Carme,** and the picturesque winding street of **Costa de Ses Voltes,** which winds down to the harbor, home of the **Gin Distillery** and hundreds of bars and restaurants that sell its merch.

Sleeping

➜ **Hostal Jume** Don't expect any luxury from this inexpensive, old, and very simple hotel, 2 blocks away from Plaça Espanya. An old man will show you up a flight of stairs to a very simple but clean and comfortable room with a decor that smacks of Gramma's house. The rooms have fans but no air-conditioning. Call in advance to try to get a room facing the outside, with a decent view and the possibility of a breeze. There is a TV room with couches and a small breakfast room, but the main reason to come here is for the prices—probably the cheapest option aside from a cave. *Carrer Concepció 6.* ☎ *971-363-266. Single 22€–30€, double 43€–51€.*

➜ **Hotel RTM Capri** Right on the opposite side of town from Jume, this government-rated, three-star hotel is also on the not-so-much side of the amenities spectrum. The lobby has a central desk reminiscent of an airport info desk and the hallways sport a peppy orange. The bedrooms are sober and not too stylish, but very clean and comfortable with new furniture and sparkling bathrooms. All rooms have balconies and Wi-Fi, since this hotel is preferred by businesspeople. The pool on the sixth floor is small but has a bit of a view of the town, which makes up for any lack of space. There is also a spa and a conference room, where you can host your depositions on beach bumming. *Carrer Sant Esteve 8.* ☎ *971-361-400. www.rtmhotels.*

com. Double 40€–94€ per person. Breakfast included. Amenities: Restaurant, bar, dry cleaning, fitness center, laundry service, non-smoking rooms, outdoor pool, room for those w/limited mobility, room service, sauna. In room: A/C, TV, hair dryer, minibar, safe.

Eating

As in the other islands, the staple in Menorca is seafood. In Maó, the most popular destination for restaurants is the port and harbor. The line of restaurants, bars, and cafes goes on for about 2 miles. It is a nice walk, and you can find everything from cheap tapas to expensive seafood and even Chinese or Indian, but beware of flashy restaurants that are nothing but tourist traps.

🅼🆅 Best ➜ **La Minerva** ★★ CATALAN Okay, this is not cheap, but if you are going to splurge and spend the money that most restaurants ask for on the waterfront, you may as well eat well. This could-be tacky restaurant serves up what may well be the best seafood in all of Menorca. Diners can also sit on a floating deck across the street from the proper restaurant building and kitchen. The decor brings a strongly nautical theme and the patrons are usually older yacht owners or young bons vivants on vacation. From here you can see all the action on the water's surface while you enjoy the marvels from within. Try the mouthwatering lobster with sea eels, grouper with shrimp sauce or if you are really splurging, get the island's specialty, *caldereta de langosta* (lobster stew with herb liquor). If you are all seafooded out, the good selection of meats ranges from meatballs in almond sauce to ostrich steak with sherry. *Moll del Llevant 87.* ☎ *971-351-995. Reservations required. Entrees 18€–30€. Daily 12:30–3:30pm and 8–11:30pm.*

➔ **Latitud 40°** TAPAS Nothing displays the culture mix of Menorca like a Guinness and *boquerones* (unsalted anchovies). This tiny local joint has the old dark wooden bar, the drafts, and everything that you would find at a pub in London, save the open front with a view of the harbor and the excellent tapas. To continue with the Anglo-Hispanic mix, the British owner has hired a team of hot Argentinean bartenders who attract a fun mixed crowd of locals and tourists who range in age from 20 to about 50. Grab one of the few tables or sit at the bar and enjoy the fabulous shrimp *croquetas* or *montaditos* (tapas on bread) with camembert, bacon, and mushrooms. The prices are maybe a little high for tapas, but the portions are also bigger than your usual, and the pleasure of downing them with a good pint is hard to beat. *Moll de Levant 265.* ☎ *971-364-176. Tapas 4.80€–9€. Daily 7pm–3am. Closed Sun in the winter.*

➔ **Lizarran** BASQUE Coming to the Balearics to eat Basque food doesn't seem like the best idea, but the people at Lizarran have developed a formula that is really hard to beat—especially if your pockets are half empty rather than half full. The *pintxos* (Basque tapas on bread) and *cazuelas* (casseroles) are creative and delicious (don't miss the baby octopus with black-eyed peas cazuela) and, at less than 2€ for a glass of good wine, not drinking is not an option. The place gets packed with locals who arrive at Plaça Bastió to escape the hordes of tourists and overpriced eateries at the sea shore. *S'Arraval 1.* ☎ *971-357-151. Entrees 5€–13€. Mon–Sat noon–3:30pm and 7:30–11:30pm.*

Partying

Like with the dining, most nightlife in Maó takes place on the waterfront. The bars are packed in summer with vacationers from the nearby beach resorts, many in their own yachts. Most bars are by the eastern end of the port, and it is fun to crawl from one to the other in search of your nirvana.

➔ **Akelarre** For 25 years this bar has been a Maó classic, and Akelarre is not planning to stop any time soon. Built under big, stone arches and with a high, exposed beam ceiling, it has a historical feeling to it, which makes you feel like you are not only boozing it up, but also soaking up some local culture. Hang by the huge bar with antique jazz instruments on the wall or on the nice patio next to a huge city wall that feels all medieval castle—look, Mom! . . . More history. The ambience is very local, late 20s, and it gets a little more *pijo* (conservative and snobby) during the summer months. They have different DJ sessions and after 1am the dance floor gets started; but they also feature jazz concerts and even stand-up on the second floor. If you need a little fuel for your fire, sandwiches and salads (4€–9€) are available until 2am. *Moll de Ponent 41-43.* ☎ *971-368-520.*

📺 Best 🌢 ➔ **Cova d'en Xoroi** You've heard the stories about Studio 54. But when it comes to legends, nothing beats this cavern complex turned bar/club. Xoroi was a Moor who, after the expulsion of the Moors from Spain, went to live in this cave, stealing food and even a woman from the neighboring village. One winter, he got sloppy and left tracks in the snow, jumping of the cliff, rather than being captured. Whether the tale is tall or not, the fact is you can't leave Menorca without visiting the club. The immense caves on a cliff by the sea are probably one of the most spectacular sights you can see in a club (well, that and RuPaul in a leotard). Remember your yoga breathing while walking down a stairway on the side of the cliff and gaping at the illuminated walls on

Heart of Stone

Menorca has been inhabited for over 6,000 years and most of the earlier locals forgot to clean up after themselves. As a result, there are thousands of prehistorical stone monuments that you can visit throughout the year. The oldest ones are the megalithic sepulchers in **Ses Roques Lises** and **Binidalinet.** But the darlings of stone-constructions in Menorca are the funeral *navetas:* horseshoe-shaped buildings that are exclusive to this island and are thought to have been used for dwellings and burials. The best preserved ones are in **Ses Roques,** near Ciutadella. The other big monuments are the *talayots,* sort of big stone Ts. The most interesting is Taula in **Trepucó,** located near Maó just off the cemetery road.

one side and the endless sea on the other. They have Latin nights, guest DJs, and even foam parties on Thursdays—maybe an allegory to the lack of hygiene at Xoroi's former home. If you are not into dancing or watching hot people dance, just come during the day to have a drink on the view-a-licious terrace. *Cova d'en Xoroi, half a mile from Cala N'Porter.* ☎ *971-377-236. www. covadenxoroi.com. June–Sept. Club cover 15€– 25€.*

📺 Best ⚫ ➔ **Mirador Café** More alternative and laid-back than the bars on the ritzy waterfront, Mirador is ideal for an evening aperitif or a late-night drink while listening to some rock 'n' roll and hanging out with locals. The decor is very simple and the ambience is mellow, with great wooden tables and deck chairs where you can sit back and enjoy some of the best views of the port. They also have tapas, salads, and sandwiches (2€–5.50€). *Plaça Espanya 2.* ☎ *971-352-107.*

Sightseeing

FREE ➔ **Esglesia de Santa María la Major** Goths and music lovers alike will enjoy a visit to Maó's main church. The church, built originally in 1287 but remodeled many times after, is not necessarily impressive from the outside, with only the

belltower adding some attractive to the almost dull facade; but as soon as you step inside you'll bump into the majestic 3,210-tube, four-keyboard organ that would make Jean-Michel Jarré wet his spandex panties. The city's most valuable possession was built over 100 years ago by German masters Otter and Kiburz, and if you are lucky enough to be there between June 30 and August 30 you'll be able to hear it in action, played by one of the illustrious guests that perform at the Festival de Música de Maó (www.menorcaweb.net/ jmdemao). *Plaça Constitució. No phone. Free admission. Daily 8am–1pm and 6–8:30pm.*

FREE ➔ **Xoriguer Gin Distillery** You know you are in an English-influenced town when the main sightseeing attraction is a gin factory. After watching the long process of making gin in giant copper vats, you can do what you really came for: Taste-test the more than a dozen types of local gin, which are very aromatic and tasty. *Moll de Ponent 93.* ☎ *971-362-197. Free admission. Mon–Fri 8am–7pm; Sat 9am–1pm.*

Playing Outside
BEACHES

There are *tons* of beaches in the Maó area and the best thing to do is grab a car or a

Board Talk

Okay, this is not the Mavericks, but when the legendary Tramontana wind blows on the north coast, some pretty decent waves hit the gorgeous beaches. That happens mostly in the winter months, unfortunately, but if you got the itch, hit the beaches at La Vall and you may get some action. And if you don't mind holding a sail, you can try some excellent wind and kite surfing. At **Windsurf Fornells** (C. Nou 33, Es Mercadal; ☎ **971-188-150**), they rent boards and also offer 4-day courses for 152€.

scooter and go find one that speaks to you. If you are on a tight budget, take a bus to the main beaches and then walk a little ways if you are looking for more privacy.

Cala en Porter, protected on each side by two spectacular cliffs, is a not-too-wide but deep beach with fine sand. It was one of the first to be exploited by the Brits, but the scant development doesn't really affect the landscape all that much. In the little urbanization you can find bars, restaurants, and a health center. A short walk from there lies the **Cova d'en Xoroi** (see "Clubs"), and, if you continue walking, you'll come to **Calascoves,** a not so attractive but almost virgin pebble beach that is a center of nudism. On the side of the cliff are a bunch of caves that were inhabited in prehistoric times. Later taken over by hippies, who were in turn kicked out too, now you can visit them on your own. On the way from **Alaior** to **Cala en Porter** is the prehistoric settlement of **Torralba d'En Salort,** definitely worth a stop. Take the Bus to Cala en Porter from Maó.

▶ **Cala Presili** This group of beaches north of Maó is one of wildest (in

a natural sense) in Menorca. Together with **S'Arenal de Morella** and **Playa d'en Tortuga,** they are in the natural reserve area of **Es Grau.** The landscapes are quite spectacular, and we're talking not the naked sunbathers, but about the black rocks and sand that are straight out of *A Trip to the Moon.* They are only accessible by foot, from the road to **Cape Favaritx.**

SCUBA DIVING

The protected area around Es Grau has a remarkable variety of submarine life. **Sotalaigua** (Hotel Pueblo, Punta Prima; ☎ 680-149-057; www.sotalaigua.com) offers diving excursions with kayaks, and/or quads, besides baptisms and courses.

Ciutadella

Ciutadella, with its beautiful small streets and historic center, is more attractive than Maó, and taking a day off the beach to see it is a must. The old town looks, under the summer light, like a wonderland city made of sand, with its gracious 17th- to 19th-century colonial houses and cobblestone streets. The center of the town is **Plaça des Born,** where you can see the main sand castle, the **Ajuntament,** and some other buildings out of a fairy tale, like the **Palau Torresaura.** From there walk toward the **Plaça de la Catedral** and check out the Gothic cathedral with a baroque facade, which dates originally from the 14th century and was built on top of a former mosque. Walk from here around the old city and check out the many churches hiding in the narrow streets, including the **Església del Roser,** on Carrer del Roser, which is sometimes used as a gallery that puts on some cool exhibitions from local artists. To the other side of the **Plaça des Borns** lies the port, smaller than Maó's but also very nice, with animated restaurants and bars.

Sleeping

➜ **Hostal-Residencia Oasis** Through the wide carriage entrance of this oasis lies a bright and cheery flower garden, which once upon a time used to be an orchard. The old couple who owns the property decided to open this small family hotel with 18 simple rooms. Each unit is clean with firm beds, fake wood paneling, and new private bathrooms. You will be much happier if you book one facing the garden. In the summer you can have your breakfast out there, enjoying the smell of the bougainvilleas. The best deal of all is that the prices are not just cheap, they are "negotiable." *Calle Sant Isidre 33.* ☎ *971-382-197. Double 30€–50€. Breakfast included.*

➜ **Hostal Residencia Ciutadella** This hotel has a lively restaurant on the bottom and guest bedrooms upstairs. They are quite modern and functional, if not that big. The furniture is fine and simple, and the bathrooms are spotless and shiny with lots of marble. They also have bigger apartments with kitchenettes that are the best deal. The patrons are more predominately Spanish than at other places, and the owners have four other hotels on the island. *Calle Sant Eloy 10.* ☎ *971-383-462. Double 50€–95€, triple 65€–110€. Breakfast included. Amenities: Restaurant, bar, dry cleaning, laundry service, Wi-Fi. In room: A/C, TV, hair dryer, safe.*

Eating

➜ **Bar Triton** TAPAS In an almost perfect parallel to the rapid modernization of the island, this 1914 fishermen's bar by the port nowadays has a website in six different languages. The quality is still the same, and the fishermen continue to come here at 4am for an early snack before sailing off; but now they share the space with red-eyed youngsters aching for a quick bite before diving into bed. The bar is very simply decorated with old pictures of the port, or you can sit on the terrace and enjoy alfresco din-ing with wonderful seafood tapas such as *chipirones* (fried baby squids), and *navajas* (razor clams), or full entrees and breakfasts. When it comes to ordering, follow the sailors' lead (not advice we usually give unless in reference to seafood!). *Muelle Ciutadella 55.* ☎ *971-380-002. Tapas and platos combinados 4€–30€. Easter–Oct daily 4am–2am; Nov–Easter 4am–2pm.*

📺 Best ❷ ➜ **El Jardín** ★★ MODERN CATALAN Next to the Hostal-Residencia Oasis, this new restaurant is not as cheap as the hostel, but has a kitchen that has already endeared it as a local favorite. Sit outside behind the gorgeous garden and dive mouth first into their exquisite menu, which changes periodically. El Jardín offers such fusion-minded delicacies as duck fig comfit with cardamom sweet potatoes or cured, ham-marinated codfish with garlic sautéed *girgolas*. Vegetarians can also have a field day with dishes like seitan with an olive tapenade. Salads include goat cheese *tropezones* (ladyfingers) with pancetta, mushrooms, nuts, and lentil vinagrette, and if they have it, possibly the most beautiful (and delicious) salad ever: wildflowers with marinated sea bass and honey. *Calle Sant Isidre 33.* ☎ *971-480-516. Entrees 13€–20€. Lunch menu 15€. Tues–Sun 1–3:30pm and 8–11:30pm.*

Partying

➜ **Café El Molino** This popular bar, though atypically located inside a 200-year-old colossal windmill near the old part of town, is a classic venue when it comes to boozing it up. Since it is open all day, like Triton, it caters to local fishermen in the morning and an older crowd in the afternoon. Though from the early evening on, hordes of local and foreign youngsters

BALEARIC ISLANDS

Party On!

Each sleepy town in Menorca wakes up with a bang once a year in the summer, when they throw the 📺 Best● **town party.** It starts with the sound of drums and the *flageolet* (tin whistle), which keep on going for the next 48 hours (yup, sleeping is kind of an issue). Menorcans have a long-standing equestrian tradition, and the horses, together with the farmers who love them, are the real lives of the party. As tradition holds, a representative of nobility presides over the long row of black horses that march on their rear legs in-between the people and around the representative of the clergy, creating a sort of energy reminiscent of the running of the bulls in Pamplona, only much safer. This medieval tradition also involves jousting and more tricks with horses than even the Ringling Brothers could hope for. The *festas* start with Sant Joan on June 23 and 24 in Ciutadella and they go from town to town through the summer until the last one, Mare de Deu de Gracia in Maó, September 8 and 9. They all follow sort of the same structure and although Sant Joan is the biggest and most popular, they all tend to get packed, so reserve accommodations well in advance if you are going to hit one of them. Check out the calendar at the island's official website, www.emenorca.org.

pack the interior, which features extra-high vaulted ceilings, and overflow onto the outdoor tables. It slows down sort of "early" (1:30am), but it is an ideal place to start the night. *Camino de Mao 7 no. 41-43.* ☎ 971-380-000.

→ **Esfera Disco** This portside disco features three bars and five different areas for all of your nighttime needs. Start by having a quiet drink at the tables outside by the water, then enter and drink more at the bar inside an actual cave. Once you're nice and revved up on spirits, go to the mezzanine and check out what's happening on the dance floor below, or oogle at the go-go dancers. When you are ready to take it further, head down to the dance floor and try your best to move to the blend of lame Spanish pop, salsa, and oldies. If you get lucky you may finish the night with a romantic drink in the upper terrace, overlooking the port. All of this, and you just pay for drinks. If only they could get the music right. . . . *Es Pla de Sant Joan. No phone.*

Sightseeing

FREE → **Catedral de la Purificación de la Madre de Dios** This Catalán Gothic church is the biggest in Menorca, and was built on top of the old mosque by order of King Alfonso III right after reconquering the island in the 13th century. Check out the beautifully ornate 18th-century chapel inside, the reconstructed neoclassical facade, added in 1813, and try to find the only remains of the original mosque. (*Tip:* Look up.) *Plaça de la Catedral. No phone. Free admission. Daily 8:30am–1pm and 6–9pm.*

FREE → **Plaça d'es Born** The main plaza in Ciutadella is the heart of the city and also one of the prettiest sites. Standing in the middle surrounded by yellow medieval calcareous stone buildings you'll feel like you somehow woke up in a fairy tale made of sandcastles and paper boats. Check out the market right in the center and by no means enter the McDonald's across the street. *Plaça d'es Born.*

Playing Outside

BEACHES

Some of the nicest beaches in Menorca are on the west side of the island and, unlike Maó, you can walk to the beach from Ciutadella. But of course the most secluded ones are a little further away, reachable by scooter or bicycle.

The ginormous cove of 📺 Best● **Cala Morell** is 8km (5 miles) away from Ciutadella at the end of a trail that starts in Punta Nati, exiting north from Ciutadella. The beach itself is not too big but the landscape is incredibly beautiful. Each side of this cove belongs to a different geological period, which you can see by just looking at them (even if you didn't make it past fourth grade geography). Further west at **La Vall** you'll find some of the most stunning beaches ever, with sand dunes that turn into woods with rock formations separating them. Also nearby are the prehistoric **ruins of Cala Morell** which you should visit if you are already nearby.

About a half-hour (2km/1¼ miles) walk south from Ciutadella, **Cala Santandria** has some development around it and gets crowded in the summer, but the sand is white and fine, the water is cerulean, and it is right around the corner from the city.

📺 Best● **Macarella's** group of untouched beaches—with unrivaled white sand surrounded by lush vegetation on top of gray cliffs—defies being described with mere words. Add to the mix a sea with all possible shades of blue and no manmade structures whatsoever and you've got yourself the paradise you came here looking for. The only problem is you'll need your own means of transportation to get there. It's about 14km (8⅔ miles) southeast from Ciutadella. Take the route to Sant Joan de Missa and from there detour towards Torralbet, where a small trail leads to the parking area right by the beach.

TREKKING

There are many trails all around the island, but if you are into gorgeous beaches, take the bus to Son Xoriguer and from there take the trail that goes east along the **coast to Santa Galdana.** These 12km (7½ miles) of beaches will get stuck in your head like a Britney Spears song—only the beach will actually be really enjoyable. Take water and food, since the mountainous trek will take you about 5 hours one-way.

Shopping

Although Menorca is not precisely a shopping paradise, a few things are worth checking out. Cheese and cold cuts from Menorca are quite famous, and you can get them at street markets or in Ciutadella. Try **Ca Na Fayas** (C. Murada d'Artrutx 32; ☎ **971-381-686**), a nice gourmet store that sells all of the local specialties.

Sevilla

by Andre Legaspi

The unrelenting Spanish sun beats down harder on the winding streets of Sevilla than any other place in the country and, with the mercury averaging triple digits in the summer, it's surprising anything can thrive, let alone survive, in an environment like this. But thanks to its location next to the Guadalquivir River and a revolving door cast of rulers that called Sevilla home, it has grown to become one of the most culturally intoxicating cities in Europe.

And while some of the unsavory aspects of being a city (graffiti, litter, and so on) are in full view, visitors manage to overlook them in what is one of the most visually striking cities in Spain. Slinking your way through the chicaning alleyways and passages that crisscross through the heart of the city, various shapes, bold lines, and colors will grab for your attention. Literally the second your train chugs to a halt in Sevilla, you'll be welcomed by the sharp, modern lines of Santa Justa Station, belying the intricate and complex beauty of the city's 14th- and 15th-century attractions such as the cathedral and Alcázar. These structures are actually made even more breathtaking during Semana Santa when throngs of hooded figures in silken robes glide through the city streets. It's a captivating, and at times sobering, event that brings thousands of pilgrims and tourists to Sevilla. Two weeks later and the city will dive straight into Feria de Abril. Trading in the religious garb for vibrant flamenco dresses, locals throws themselves into this incredible citywide party that lasts for an entire week.

Sevilla's rich history and tradition is a venerable recipe for an incredibly unique destination. Grease up a riverbank, throw in a cup of Roman conquest, a few quarts of Christian influence, and a tablespoon of Arab rule. Preheat to 116°F (47°C) and bake for several hundreds of years. What you're left with is the tasty, cultural paella that is Sevilla, an indescribable city that radiates as much life and vitality as it does heat. Sprinkle some flamenco for some spice and let cool. Serves 700,000.

Best of Sevilla

○ **Best Hostel: Oasis Backpackers Hostel.** I can't think of any other place in Sevilla where you can find an ultra-comfy bed, air-conditioning, laundry service, AND hordes of cute international backpackers for less than 30€. While the math doesn't add up, I'm not one to complain. Hands down, the best place to stay in Sevilla. See p. 531.

○ **Best Bar: La Rebotica.** I don't need a ton of bells and whistles when it comes to boozing. Thankfully La Rebotica puts more thought and effort into concocting shots and mixed drinks than the surroundings. See p. 540.

○ **Best Dress-to-Impress Club: Boss.** The selection process is stiffer than Harvard's, but the undergrads here are much hotter. No offense to those Ivy Leaguers, but Boss is renowned for its attractive and fashionable clientele. Ladies, flutter those eyelashes a little for the bouncers because they're a picky bunch. Gentlemen, unless you have an army of Victoria's Secret models in tow, you might want to flutter those 20€ bills in front of the burly doormen. See p. 541.

○ **Best-Dressed Club: Elefunk.** Sorry, the title is a tad misleading. Whereas Boss had the best-dressed clientele, Elefunk is the club that's best dressed. The urban influence is noticeable, but anything goes in one of Sevilla's best clubs. Known simply as "Funky" by locals, Elefunk is overflowing with awesome house and funk beats as well as off-the-wall decorations. See p. 541.

○ **Best Tapas Bar: El Rinconcillo.** Perhaps it's the sadomasochist in me, but I love the crotchety old dudes here manning the bar. With one hand, they'll chalk down the figures of my bill on the wooden counter while they deftly fill a glass of beer with the other. Even with both hands writing and pouring, they find the time to snarl to the next customer. It's all worth it though when you sink your teeth in one of their incredible tapas. See p. 536.

○ **Best Flamenco: El Arenal.** You might end up paying more for a night of flamenco here than for a bed at a hostel, but at least you can dream of that spiraling polka-dot dress while you curl into fetal position on the sidewalk. See p. 542.

○ **Best Way to Traverse the Guadalquivir: Puente de Isabel II.** There are multiple options when it comes to crossing the Guadalquivir. Some are eye-catchingly modern (Puente del Alamillo), others drab (Puente San Telmo). Puente de Isabel II trumps them all with classy circular supports that are practical and photogenic at the same time. Heading east on the bridge will also bring you right next to Plaza de Toros de la Maestranza. See p. 528.

○ **Best Place to Drain Your Camera Battery: El Catedral.** This one was a tough one. The cathedral barely eked

SEVILLA

out the Casa de Pilatos mainly because of its backpacker-friendly admission fee. Even with an entire afternoon at your disposal, there are an endless number of side rooms full of shiny religious goodies, ancient art, and marble sculptures where you can channel your inner Ansel Adams. You might want to pack a separate battery for the Giralda. See p. 545.

Getting There & Around

Getting There

BY AIR

It's not cheap or advisable, but if you're in a rush to get to Sevilla you can board an Iberia flight to **Aeropuerto San Pablo,** 9.7km (6 miles) from the city center on Calle Almirante Lobo (☎ **954-449-000**). Multiple flights from Madrid and other Spanish cities such as Barcelona, Zaragoza, and Alicante are connected to this hub, but international flights, Lisbon being an exception, are rarely seen at this airport. Thankfully though, not all airlines will end up maxing your credit card. Budget companies like RyanAir connect Sevilla to cities like London, Dublin, Liverpool, Milan, and Pisa. If you plan a few months ahead, tickets can be as cheap as 50€. Otherwise, you're looking at a price-tag of roughly 100€ to 150€ for something within the next couple of days. Getting from the Sevilla airport to the city center obviously costs considerably less. Several shuttles are available to get you from Aeropuerto San Pablo to Sevilla and they shouldn't cost much more than 2€.

BY TRAIN

Years ago, traveling to Sevilla would require an uncomfortable day trip on a painfully slow regional train. Thanks to the high speed AVE trains, those several hours have been trimmed down to less than 3 hours. No less than a dozen trains make the journey to the sizzling city from Madrid, with a few stops along the way, Cordoba being the most notable. From the south, more than 15 trains come to a halt in the gorgeous Santa Justa station (☎ 954-14-111) from cities like Cádiz and Jerez de la Frontera. Check www.renfe.es for timetables and fare information.

BY BUS

If you're afraid of heights or conductor hats, you'll be glad to know that Sevilla is well connected to Andalucia's extensive bus system. The main carrier in the area, **Alsina Graells** (☎ 954-418-811), shuttles folks from Córdoba, Málaga, and Granada daily to one of two bus stations in Sevilla. Most likely, you'll be dropped off in **Prado de San Sebastian** (Manuel Vázquez Sagastizábal s/n; ☎ 954-417-111). The newer one at Plaza de Armas (☎ 954-907-737) usually receives travelers from farther points of origin.

Getting Around

BY FOOT

If it weren't for the heat and the tangled mess of streets, Sevilla would be a walker's paradise: All major attractions aren't more than 10 minutes from each other, streets are small enough to discourage most drivers, and the pretty overhead canopies of fabric do provide some shelter from the sun's vicious rays. However, the arrangement of roads and sidewalks is borderline chaotic. Even those armed with a detailed map and a sharp sense of direction will find themselves lost at some point. If you have neither, your best bet is to locate the Guadalquivir River (most drivable streets are one-way and point in the direction of the river) and walk along the riverbank

Sevilla & Beyond

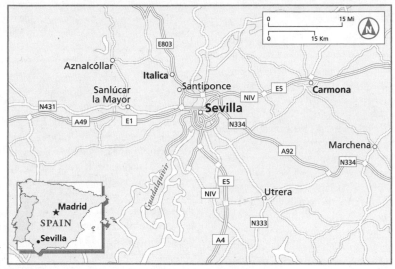

using the bridges as waypoints on the way to your destination. Wandering the heart of the city before you familiarize yourself with the area can be frustrating or even worse, especially at night, unsafe (see "Safety," p. 531).

BY BUS

Believe it or not, **public transportation** (TUSSAM; ☎ 902-45-99-54; www.tussam. es) is an excellent way to see the major sites quickly, cheaply, and comfortably. The only caveat is that you'll only see them from the outside. Otherwise, for 1€ (or 3€ for a day pass, 7€ for a 3-day pass) you can catch one of the C buses (it goes in a circular route) and see the different bridges, Plaza de Espana, Parque Maria Luisa, Torre del Oro, and other worthwhile attractions. However, using the bus for getting around the center of Sevilla is not only limited, it's not recommended. As they make repeated stops and get waylaid by stop lights and traffic, you'll find that you can quickly cover more ground on your own two feet.

BY TAXI

Shuttling around in a cab can be awfully expensive, but it might be your best option if you need to get somewhere far and get there quickly. Here are several decent companies in town: **Giralda** (☎ 954-675-555) and **Taxi Internacional** (☎ 954-293-033).

BY CAR

As you probably have already guessed, driving in Sevilla is only for the skilled and patient. Getting around in an automobile is a downright nightmare with the narrow one-way streets and those who do decide to throw caution and sanity to the wind will end up driving in circles around the same area for hours. Once you arrive in Sevilla, find a parking lot outside of the city center and leave it there for the duration of your trip. Or opt for renting a car from a familiar company like **Avis** (Av. de la Constitución 15b; ☎ 954-215-370; www. avis.com) or **Hertz** (Santa Justa Station; ☎ 954-426-156; www.hertz.com).

Sevilla Basics

Orientation

The neighborhood of **Centro Historico** is sort of like that neon-blue bug zapper in your back patio. Instead of drawing buzzing insects to its sizzling surface, the old section of Sevilla draws noisy tourists to its scorching streets and incredibly beautiful landmarks like the cathedral and the Alcázar. Fight the urge to swat at the passing sightseers—they're relatively harmless.

Those who enjoyed strolling through Cordoba's Barrio de la Judería will enjoy Sevilla's version in what is called the **Barrio Santa Cruz.** Homeowners in the area love to show off their green thumb by creating a picturesque sequence of streets filled with flower boxes, colorfully painted homes, and leafy courtyards open for everyone to admire. Quaint restaurants and cafes are thrown in to the

mix to make what was once the Jewish ghetto into a relaxing and eye-catching neighborhood.

It could be the name. The neighborhood north of Barrio Santa Cruz and Centro Historico shares the same moniker as the embarrassing '90s song that you only hear at wedding receptions and throwback weekends on the radio. Yes, few venture to **La Macarena** and it's actually a good thing: It makes for a nice escape from the groups of tourists walking around the well-worn paths around the cathedral. La Macarena is home to a few interesting churches like the Iglesia de Santa Inés. Legend has it the woman that the church and convent was named after mangled her own face when King Pedro the Cruel's incessant pursuit drove her to the edge. I hear listening to the Macarena over and over again can produce the same result.

Across the Guadalquivir is the area known as **Triana.** Back in the day, thousands of gypsies called it home, fishermen lined its shores, and for many who sailed into the city, it was their first taste of Sevilla. Now, it's where visitors can find top-notch restaurants and bars serving tasty seafood tapas. Strangely enough, many locals don't even consider Triana part of Sevilla—it even has its own (less impressive) cathedral.

Crossing Puente San Telmo or 📺 Best❖ **Puente Isabel II** from Triana, you'll find yourself in **El Arenal.** It's perhaps the liveliest and most active place in Sevilla, especially at night. Most of the city's best bars, clubs, and restaurants are a hop, skip, and a flamenco stomp away from the area. During the day, sights like the Torre del Oro and the bullring at Plaza de Toros de la Maestranza keep locals and visitors entertained until happy hour.

wwwired

Hopelessly addicted to MySpace and need to get your fix? The best place to go to is **Internetia** (Av. Menendez Pelayo 46; ☎ **954-534-003**). It's open 24/7 and they've managed to cram 80 terminals inside so you'll rarely have to wait to use a PC or one of the few Macs Internetia has set up. Rates go as high as 1.90€ per hour. The most convenient spot in the city center is **CiberDucke** (C. Trajano 10; no phone), where over a dozen terminals tap you in to cyberspace. It's open from 9:30am to 10pm Tuesday through Friday and 11am to 10pm Saturday through Monday. And it's slightly cheaper than Internetia (up to 1.50€ an hour)—Ernie was right: CiberDucke, you're the one.

Talk of the Town

Five Ways to Start a Conversation with a Local

1. **Quieres ir a bailar?** The most beautiful thing about Sevilla isn't the magnificent gardens in the Alcázar, the psychedelic walls at Casa de Pilatos, nor the blond Belgian disk jockey at the hostel. Instead, it's the passion that locals have for the graceful art of flamenco. The only thing locals love more than talking about the intricacies of the dance is actually doing the dance themselves. So whip out that Spanish, stow away your inhibitions, and stun them with your own version of the Sevillana. Yipping and wailing optional.

2. **Toro or not to Toro?** In addition to being not much of a tongue twister, the question has always existed in the minds of Spaniards. Many traditionalists might side with the former and defend it intensely so tread carefully. In any case, it always sparks a great debate among locals and tourists alike. It's so steeped in Sevilla's history that it's unlikely you'll find someone who hasn't decided whether the sport is actually a sport or a barbaric spectacle.

3. **Let's get a cold one!** Unless you're the world's worst speed reader you will have gathered, multiple times, that Sevilla gets, as New Englanders would say, wicked hot. Unfortunately, Sam Adams isn't readily available in the super-*mercados* in Sevilla. There is Cruzcampo, however, and tons of it. The tasty brew is enjoyed in the late afternoon when the streets are at their hottest and the locals at their thirstiest. Before they start their tapas binge, and way before they get ready for dinner, Sevillans flock to street-side *cervecerias*. These places pump out ice-cold beers for folks to enjoy, usually street-side at outdoor tables. It's the perfect way to cool off, end a hectic day, and make a few new, inebriated friends.

4. **Sartre es idiota.** Even if you can't distinguish existentialism from eggs Benedict, chances are good that one out of several thousand university students in Sevilla will be able to debate or educate you on the famous philosopher. On the southern edge of the Alcázar, along San Fernando, you'll find college kids hanging around the bookstores and eateries lining the street. Otherwise, you can head into the Antigua Fábrica de Tabacos— the historical structure that is now used as the main university building. After you've exhausted your brain cells, you can exhaust your mojo by bumpin' and grindin' with more co-eds in the town's discothèques.

5. **Can you spare a dime?** Another topic on the minds of Sevillans is the current state of city economics. An unfortunate spell of unemployment has seen small businesses suffer and small crimes spike. Locals will be more than happy to vent about other things that plague Sevilla, but ask where you can find a job and prepare yourself for a diatribe like no other.

Tourist Offices

Once you've made it to Sevilla, head to one of the **tourist information offices** (Av. de la Constitucíon 21b; ☎ 954-221-404; Calle Arjona 28; ☎ 954-221-714) and get your hands on a free map of the city. With the probability of getting lost being in the range of "very likely" to "Wait a sec . . . I'm in Spain?", that map may very well be the most valuable freebie you'll get during your entire trip.

Recommended Websites

○ **www.andalucia.com**: Comprehensive site about Andalucia and its cities, including Sevilla.

○ **www.alsinagraells.es** and **www. ctsa-portillo.com**: The two main bus companies for shuttling between cities in southern Andalucia and Costa del Sol.

○ **www.elgiraldillo.es**: The print version of this can be found in different tourist offices, hotels, cafes, and attractions. Inside both the site and the pamphlet are listings of what concerts, art exhibitions, parties, and movie events are taking place in the coming weeks.

Sevilla Nuts & Bolts

Cellphone Providers/Service Centers   Can't cut the fiber-optic umbilical cord? Stay connected with your friends, both new and old, with one of several cellphone providers in Sevilla. The major ones are **Amena, Movistar,** and **Vodafone** and it seems as though at least one of the companies has an outlet every other block in the city center.

Crisis Lines   To report rape or sexual abuse: **Amuvi,** Alberto Lista 6 (☎ **954-905-649**).

Currency   Finding a **cash machine** in Sevilla is no problem. There's at least one every 2 or 3 blocks in the city center. However, you're better off looking for one along one of the major streets where it's well lit and busy. As you'll read below, crime is slightly higher in Sevilla and common sense will serve you well if you avoid those ATMs on the side streets.

Embassies   Aside from the things that Pepto-Bismol can fix, the only thing that'll put more of a damper on your journey is losing your passport. See if the g-men at the **Consulate of the United States** can help you out. They're located at Paseo de las Delicias 7 (☎ **954-231-885**).

Emergencies   To get in touch with the police quickly, dial ☎ **091** for the national police and ☎ **092** for the local police. In case of fire, ☎ **080** will bring *bomberos* to extinguish any inferno. ☎ **061** should be used for any urgent medical emergency. Otherwise, you can head to Hospital Virgen del Rocío (Av. Manuel Siurot s/n; ☎ **955-012-000**).

Laundromats   People might claim that the heat isn't that bad since it's really just a dry heat. They're right, but spend a few hours out in the convection oven known as Sevilla and it's impossible not to sweat through several shirts. Before you know it, you'll have a stinking pile of T-shirts screaming to be cleaned. Head over to **AutoServicio de Lavanderia Sevilla** (Castelar 3; ☎ **954-210-535;** Mon–Fri 9:30am–1:30pm and 5–8:30pm, Sat 9am–2pm) to get back some form of sartorial respectability.

Luggage Storage   My first mistake was booking my hostel for June 15 instead of July 15. My second mistake was walking around the city with a 40-pound pack looking for one with a vacancy. Save yourself the embarrassment and exhaustion by dropping off your bags at the train station, **Estación Santa Justa.** For a few euro, you can keep your luggage there up to 24 hours. While the station is a short bus trip from the city center, the 1€ fare is well worth it. So is double checking your reservations before you leave.

Pharmacies   If you need some meds, look for the neon green crosses that jut out onto the sidewalk. These little labs have enough prescription drugs to stock a few nursing homes. However, they're not the same pharmacies that you'll find stateside—you'll have to buy your Altoids and get your photos developed somewhere else. Most places close surprisingly early, so make sure your ailments get tended to in the morning or early afternoon.

Post Offices   One sure fire way of getting brownie points with your significant other back home is to send him or her a little something from Espana. Instead of getting embarrassed while Customs personnel sift through flamenco dot undies, mail them from the **post office** located at Av. de la Raza 4 (☎ **954-615-695**). Not only will you have fewer things to carry, you might have a very pleasant surprise waiting for you when you get home.

Safety   Sevilla in many respects, is one of the few cities in Andalucia that actually feels like a full-fledged city. Wide paved avenues are clogged with traffic, graffiti goes unnoticed on storefront gates, and, unfortunately, crime isn't uncommon. Thanks to a rising unemployment rate, petty crimes have spiked in the last year or so. Pickpocketing, muggings, and a few cases of assault have plagued the tourism industry. Use your common sense and keep all your belongings in sight. Drive-by scooter thefts, while rare, still occur. Thieves ride by on a scooter and snatch a pedestrian's handbag and, unless you want to dislocate your shoulder, the only thing you can do is to let your bag go. So keep your bags on the sidewalk side of your body, tuck your wallet in your front pocket, avoid those dark alleys late at night, and you'll leave Sevilla without incident.

Sleeping

Thanks to the massive influx of tourists in the spring and summer, there are scads of budget accommodations in Sevilla. The historic center is where you'll find the bulk of hostels and hotels but you can usually find a slightly better deal on the other side of the Guadalquivir close to areas like Triana.

Hostel

🎵 (Best ●) → **Oasis   Backpackers Hostel** ★ ★ Throw out the 5-second rule. I obliterated that standard when I scarcely hesitated to ingest a chocolate cookie that I knowingly dropped behind my bed a few days earlier. That's how clean the rooms in the Oasis Backpackers Hostel are. By far one of the best hostels in the country, it continues the line of awesome Oasis locations in Spain and Portugal. The hostel is located right off of Plaza de la Encarnación in a converted and fully renovated Andalusian building. Furnished from head to toe with sturdy wooden bunks and modern couches, it feels more like a chic hotel than anything else. As I mentioned before, the rooms all have immaculate wood floors, pristine bathrooms, and key-card entry to each dorm. The biggest perk, without question, is the air-conditioning in each of the dorms. Lumbering back to the

Sleeping & Eating in Sevilla

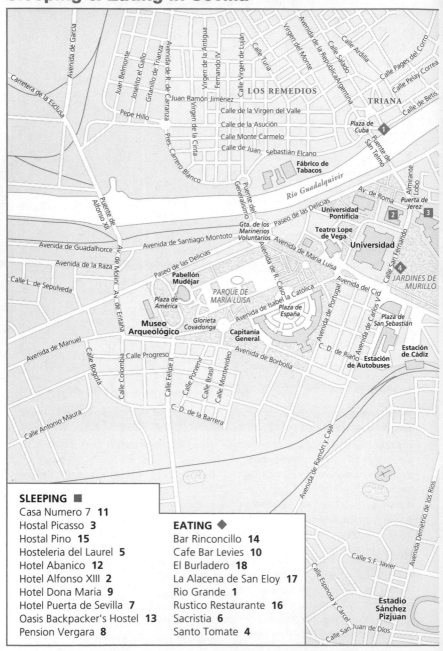

SLEEPING ■

Casa Numero 7 **11**
Hostal Picasso **3**
Hostal Pino **15**
Hosteleria del Laurel **5**
Hotel Abanico **12**
Hotel Alfonso XIII **2**
Hotel Dona Maria **9**
Hotel Puerta de Sevilla **7**
Oasis Backpacker's Hostel **13**
Pension Vergara **8**

EATING ◆

Bar Rinconcillo **14**
Cafe Bar Levies **10**
El Burladero **18**
La Alacena de San Eloy **17**
Rio Grande **1**
Rustico Restaurante **16**
Sacristia **6**
Santo Tomate **4**

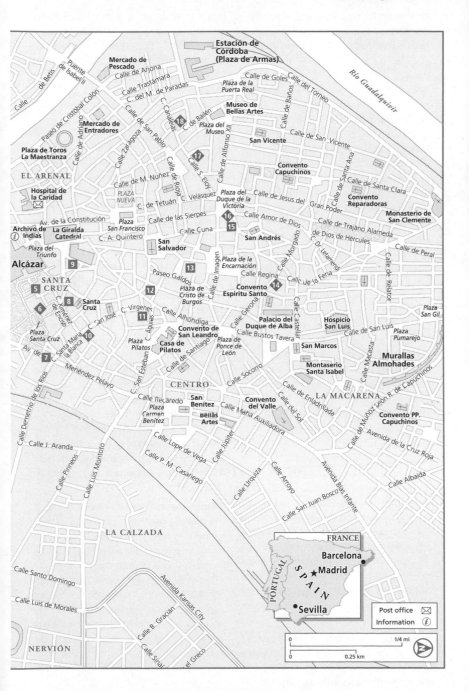

hostel after a long, sweaty day of sightseeing, it's hard not to let out a loud sigh of relief when that wall of cold air first hits you. Plus, it's a super-sociable place where you'll end up meeting tons of travelers thanks to the various activities and dinners set up by the staff. Speaking of which, they're top notch. If you don't have a reservation and all the walk-in beds have been taken, the folks at Oasis will offer the common room couches for you to crash in. Need to get your threads snuggly fresh? Toss your dirty underwear in a basket, hand them 6€ and by the next day they'll have them clean and folded for you. *Calle Don Alonso el Sabio 1A.* ☎ *954-293-777. www. oasissevilla.com. Single bed in dorm room (4 per dorm) 18€, private double room (shared bath) 40€. Breakfast included. Amenities: Internet point, laundry service. In room: A/C, safe.*

Cheap

➔ **Hostal Pino** Chances are if you didn't book in advance at Oasis you won't have much luck finding a bed as a walk-in (unless you come in at the crack of dawn). The staff there will feign sympathy and politely direct you to another place 5 minutes away—Hostal Pino. The hostel seems sketchy at first. It's next door to a gaming haunt full of old men staring at video gambling screens, guests have to be buzzed in AND out, the lobby is dark, and the friendly staff could pass as a modern-day Addams family. Despite all this, Hostal Pino is actually a deal and a half. You get your own air-conditioned room (a rarity for cheap hotels), bathroom, and a surprisingly comfortable bed. *Tarifa 6.* ☎ *954-212-810. Single 27€ with private bath. No credit cards. Amenities: TV. In room: A/C.*

➔ **Pensión Vergara** A backpacker's favorite, this old Sevillan house is in the heart of Barrio Santa Cruz, above a souvenir shop, 4 small blocks from the cathedral. Its

bright interior patio, with tons of plants and atmosphere, may make you feel as if you've gone back in time a bit. Inside are spacious, brick-walled rooms with floral bedcovers, and 8 of the 12 have a view over the cobblestoned street. *Ximenez de Enciso 11.* ☎ *954-215-668. pensiónvergaraSevilla@ yahoo.es. 20€–30€ per person. No credit cards. Amenities: Shared bathrooms.*

Doable

➔ **Hostal Picasso** ★ It's just an assumption, but I'd venture to say that roughly 459 hotels and hostels in Spain alone are named after Pablo. Of them all, none is as homey and affordable as this one. From the minute you enter the colorful foyer all doubts about the safety and comfort of the hostel are washed away by the warm smile of the receptionist and the forest of leafy plants. Some might find rooms a little hard to get to, with the maze of hallways and the series of stairs, but once you do reach it, you'll find it more than acceptable. Soft beds, air-conditioning, and clean bathrooms welcome guests to a pleasant night's stay. The location couldn't be better either. Guests will love the fact that it essentially sits in the shadow of the Alcázar. *San Gregorio 1.* ☎ *954-210-864. www. grupo-piramide.com. Double 50€ with bath, double 40€ without private bath. Amenities: TV. In room: A/C.*

➔ **Hosteria del Laurel** When you can eat and drink to your heart's content and then stumble to your bed without having to navigate through the streets, you know you've found a winner. Such is the case with the Hosteria del Laurel. This incredibly quaint tavern also doubles as an affordable and extremely comfortable *hosteria*. You'll have no problem falling asleep in their soft beds but you might have difficulty standing up if you keep ordering *cervezas* in the bar below. *Plaza* de los Venerables 5. ☎ 954-220-295. www. hosteriadellaurel.com. Single 49€–67€, double 70€–97€. In room: A/C, TV, hair dryer, safe.

➔ **Hotel Abanico** ★ The minute I heard Starship pouring out of the lobby radio, I practically spun on my heels and booked it outta there. Fortunately, the warm *"Hola!"* from the receptionist coaxed me back in. Friendly staff aside, the converted 18th-century house is an extremely comfortable and clean place to spend the night. It's right around the corner from the Casa de Pilatos and also offers a chill patio where you can kick back and enjoy a *café con leche* to start your morning off right. You'll even find yourself singing the crappy '80s song as you stroll out of this place, "Nooooothing's gonna stop us now!" *Calle Aguilas 17.* ☎ *954-228-950. www.hotelabanico. com. Single 77€, double 99€. Amenities: A/C, TV, Internet.*

➔ **Hotel Puerta de Sevilla** This modern, modest hotel on a main street in Santa Cruz offers all the comfort and amenities of its higher consecrated competitors and more. The classical oil paintings and antiques in the lobby, original stairs from the 19th-century building, and Andalusian poems on every door are almost too picture-perfect. Imagine the smell of orange blossoms (goodbye, musty hostel), wafting through your ample Provençal-style room. The über-helpful staff can tell you legends of the city to get in full Sevilla mood. *Santa María La Blanca 36.* ☎ *954-987-270. www. hotelpuertadesevilla.com. Single 50€–55€; double 65€–85€. Amenities: Internet, laundry, rooms for those w/limited mobility, TV. In room: A/C.*

Splurge

➔ **Casa Numero 7** ★★★ The Hotel Alfonso XIII may have more prestige, more rooms, and a bigger suffix, but size ain't everything. 7 seems to personally attend to their guests' every need. Hell, there's

even a butler that heeds your every, well almost every, request. Inside, you'll find that the small 19th-century establishment doesn't cut any corners when it comes to furnishings. The award-winning inn is rife with antique embellishments, luxurious rugs, and uniquely designed quarters where guests can kick off their boots, don their ascot, and call for Jeeves, Alfred, Mr. Belvedere—or whatever name they decide to call him. *Virgenes 7.* ☎ *954-221-581. www. casanumero7.com. Double 177€–250€. Amenities: Honesty bar. In room: A/C.*

MTV Best ✱ ➔ **Hotel Alfonso XIII** ★★★ Unless you have a XIII at the end of your name or you rake in XIII figures annually, you might have to enjoy this hotel from the outside. It's a landmark in itself and the hotel attracts only the wealthiest and most famous of clientele. Every inch in the lobby, rooms, hallways, bathrooms, and probably even the janitor's closet oozes decadence. *San Fernando 2.* ☎ *800/221-2340 in U.S. or 954-917-000. Doubles 295€–500€. Amenities: Restaurant, laundry service, pool, tennis courts. In room: A/C, TV, hair dryer, minibar, safe.*

➔ **Hotel Doña Maria** If you plan on dancing your ass off until the later hours of the morning, you won't be affected by the startling wake-up call in this place. Hotel Doña Maria's inconsiderate neighbor, the cathedral, always decides to test its huge bells every morning, ensuring that most of the guests next door are up and about in the wee hours. Deep sleepers and those who have an incredibly thick skin will otherwise love the antique charm of this hotel. Incomparable views of the cathedral and uniquely designed and comfortable rooms make stays memorable and the slight inconvenience of the morning bell recital forgettable. *Don Remondo 19.* ☎ *954-224-990. www.hdmaria.com. Doubles 100€–200€. Amenities: Laundry, pool. In room: A/C, TV, hair dryer, minibar, safe.*

SEVILLA

Eating

Since this is a full-fledged city, many a backpacker in Sevilla have fallen into the unfortunate, yet financially attractive, trap of frequenting pseudo-fast-food joints to save a euro or two. Stocked with chains like Pans & Company, Burger King, and Starbucks, Sevilla is also full of amazing little eateries where you can sample mouthwatering tapas and Andalusian meals without breaking the bank. At least once though, you should treat yourself to a nice sit-down meal at one of the pricier joints.

Hot Spot

➔ **El Burladero** ★★ SPANISH/ANDALUSIAN It's all bull crap. Really, it is and it's great. Walls are covered with bullfighting memorabilia, the menus have several dishes with bull-butt (oxtail), and even the waiters are extremely bullish. All puns aside, El Burladero is a fixture not just in cuisine, but in Sevilla's steeped bullfighting history. Among the rows and rows of matador and bullring photographs, you'll find the original tiles from the 1929 Sevilla World's Fair adorning the walls of this incredible restaurant. Perhaps lost among the history and bull worshipping is its savory menu. A varied assortment of food is prepared with care and the resulting plates coming out of the kitchen, like the roasted lamb with oxtail, will have you happy as a triumphant matador. Your stomach might even let out an exalting "TORO!"—you might wanna grab some antacid for that. *Canalejas 1.* ☎ *954-505-599. Main courses 15€–25€. Daily 1:30–3:30pm and 9–11:30pm. Closed mid-June to Sept.*

Tapas

🎬 Best ● ➔ **Bar (El) Rinconcillo** ★★ CLASSIC TAPAS Its claim as the oldest tapas bar in Sevilla may be disputed, but it is one of the busiest and best places to scarf down those little dishes. Serving the Sevilla community for years, since 1670 according to the sign, El Rinconcillo is known for its tasty tapas (you can't go wrong with the salty and mouthwatering pork cheeks with potato or with the curry-infused spinach and chickpeas) and brusque, yet endearing, waiters. If you don't order from the right guy, prepare for a scowl and a lecture. Otherwise, they'll chalk up your tab right on the wooden counter and pour you a beer in a matter of seconds. Once you've had your fill and paid your bill, they'll wipe the counter clean, grunt *"Gracias,"* and prepare their photogenic grimace for the next patron. *Gerona 40.* ☎ *954-223-183. Open late.*

➔ **Sacristia** MODERN TAPAS Mateos Gago bubbles with energy in the later hours of the evening when people fill the street side bars, spilling out onto the sidewalk. One popular spot is Sacristia. It may be a little more posh, although not by much, than other traditional tapas joints and the clientele reflect this. Younger, shinier locals come here to pre-drink or they come to settle in for a night of boozing and noshing. *Calle Mateos Gago 18.* ☎ *954-219-207. www.tapearensevilla.com. Open late.*

Cheap

➔ **Café Bar Levies** MODERN TAPAS As you enter this average student hang-out looking place (you know, lame art and decor, small tables, and so on) you'll wonder how so many young Spaniards can look so happy all crammed in together. When you finally get seated and the tapas arrive, you'll understand. The portions are huge (for tapas, of course) and delicious, with vegetarian options that could convert any carnivore. The mushroom-leek au gratin rocks and *papas* (potatoes) *al mojo* are what the '60s were all about. Outdoor seating is in a quaint plaza and the service is lightning fast by Spanish standards. Then you get the check and you'll wonder, like that time your friend took care of the bill at the end, "why didn't I order more?" *San José 15.* ☎ *954-215-308. Tapas 2.60€; combination platters 6€. Daily 9am–1am.*

➔ **Santo Tomate** HEALTH It doesn't take an enterprising genius to realize that opening a cheap, healthy eatery across from a university is a great idea. Poor students who normally subsist on ramen and stale pizza are always in the market for affordable, tasty, and fitness-conscious alternatives. The buffet-style Santo Tomate provides all this across the street from the main university building on San Fernando. For 8€, you can slop as much grub on your tray and make as many return trips to the buffet as your stomach will allow. Early birds will particularly like the breakfast options. You can score coffee, toast, fried eggs, bacon, and sausage for 4€. You don't even need a high-school degree to figure out that Santo Tomate is a pretty good deal. *Calle San Fernando 23.* ☎ *954-563-396. www.santotomate.com. Buffet 8€. Hot meals 4€. Mon–Fri 8am–6pm; Sat–Sun 12:30–6pm.*

Doable

➔ **La Alacena de San Eloy** ★ DELI/ANDALUSIAN This half-deli, half-bistro is fully swank. Don't be deceived by the casual stools, the hanging hams, and the conventional glass displays: La Alacena offers some truly decadent and exotic items on its menu. Duck foie gras (a dish quickly becoming endangered in the States) and sea urchin caviar are a couple

of high-class dishes you can scarf down or you can settle on comfort-zone edibles like pork loin or kidney bean soup with bull tail. For an interesting and delicious combo, give the chestnuts in syrup with Avila goat cheese a whirl. *San Eloy 31.* ☎ *954-215-580. Tapas 1.50€–2.90€. Half ration 4€–7€. Full rations 8€–9€. Daily 11am–4:30pm and 7:30–11:30pm.*

➔ **Rio Grande** SPANISH Views usually come at a premium. Most of the time it's in the form of inflated prices or exclusivity. In Sevilla's Rio Grande, you'll come across more of the latter (reservations are recommended). Otherwise, it's surprisingly affordable. It'll be tough to eat here every night on a backpacker's budget, but one dinner won't force you to live off of bread and water for the rest of your trip. Diners probably won't be wowed by the plates presented to them, which range from the traditional paella to the ubiquitous bull-tail dish, but the view of the Torre del Oro and the Guadalquivir River will easily detract anyone from the decent dishes. *Calle Betis s/n.* ☎ *954-273-956. Main courses 16€–25€. Daily 1–4pm and 8pm–midnight.*

➔ **Rústico Restaurante** ANDALUSIAN/TAPAS Much like the interior and staff, the menu of Rústico Restaurante is modest, warm, and homey. The surroundings won't floor you and neither will the food, but by meal's end you'll find yourself smiling and satisfied. Not feeling particularly hungry? There are plenty of tapas choices if your stomach only has room for a few more bites. *Calle Javier Lasso de la Vega 14.* ☎ *954-379-568. Daily menu 7.90€. Tapas 1.80€–2.20€. Mon–Thurs 8:30am–3:30pm; Fri 8:30am–midnight; Sat 1pm–midnight; Sun 1–7pm.*

Partying

If you have enough fight left in your liver after a few hours of afternoon tapas, Sevilla has plenty of spots to TKO that pesky organ. The hottest spot in town by

Partying & Sightseeing in Sevilla

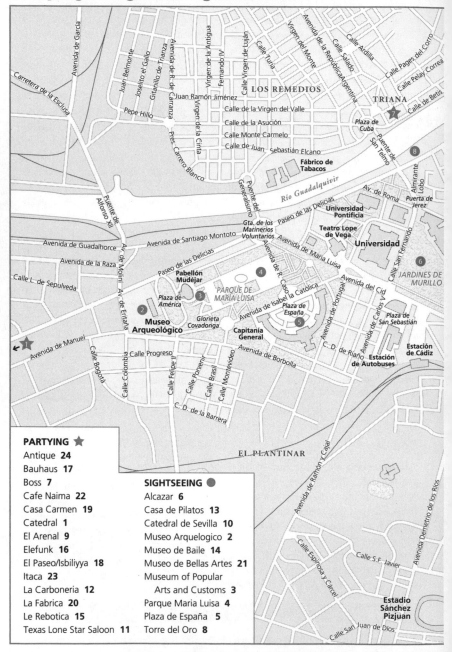

PARTYING ⭐

Antique **24**
Bauhaus **17**
Boss **7**
Cafe Naima **22**
Casa Carmen **19**
Catedral **1**
El Arenal **9**
Elefunk **16**
El Paseo/Isbiliyya **18**
Itaca **23**
La Carboneria **12**
La Fabrica **20**
Le Rebotica **15**
Texas Lone Star Saloon **11**

SIGHTSEEING ●

Alcazar **6**
Casa de Pilatos **13**
Catedral de Sevilla **10**
Museo Arquelogico **2**
Museo de Baile **14**
Museo de Bellas Artes **21**
Museum of Popular
    Arts and Customs **3**
Parque Maria Luisa **4**
Plaza de España **5**
Torre del Oro **8**

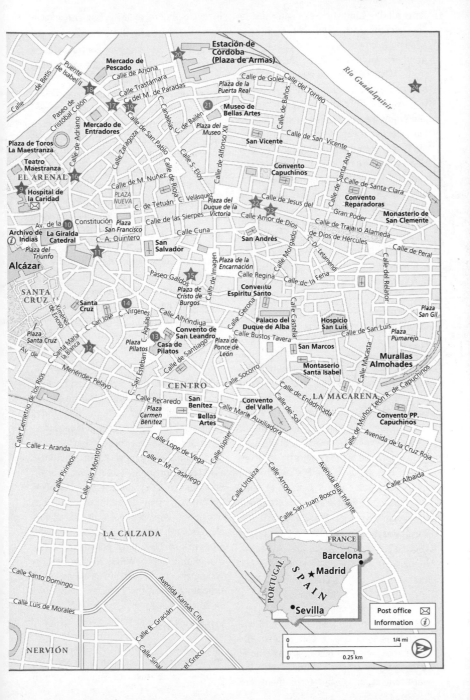

Estación de
Córdoba
(Plaza de Armas)

Río Guadalquivir

Puente de Isabel II

Calle de Betis

Mercado de
Pescado

Calle de Arjona

Calle de Goles

Calle del Torneo

Plaza de la
Puerta Real

Calle de San Vicente

Paseo de Cristóbal Colón

Calle Trastámara

Calle del M. de Paradas

Calle de Baños

Calle de Adriano

Mercado de
Entradores

Museo de
Bellas Artes

Calle de Bailén

Plaza del
Museo

San Vicente

Calle de San Vicente

Calle de Santa Ana

Calle de Santa Clara

Plaza de Toros
La Maestranza

Teatro
Maestranza

EL ARENAL

Hospital de
la Caridad

Convento
Capuchinos

Convento
Reparadoras

Monasterio de
San Clemente

Calle de Zaragoza

Calle de San Pablo

Calle de Rioja

Calle de M. Núñez

PLAZA
NUEVA

Calle de S. Eloy

Calle de Alfonso XII

Calle de Santa Ana

Gran Poder

Av. de la Constitución

C. de Tetuán

C. Velázquez

Plaza del
Duque de la
Victoria

Calle de Jesús del

Calle Amor de Dios

Calle de Trajano Alameda
de Dios de Hércules

Archivo de
Indias

La Giralda
Catedral

Plaza
San Francisco

Calle de las Sierpes

San Andrés

Calle de Peral

Plaza del
Triunfo

Alcázar

C. A. Quintero

San
Salvador

Calle Cuna

Plaza de la
Encarnación

Calle Morgado

Calle D. Letamendi

Calle del Relator

SANTA
CRUZ

Paseo Galdós

Plaza de
Cristo de
Burgos

Calle Regina

Calle de la Feria

Ximénez de Enciso

Santa
Cruz

C. San José

C. Virgenes

Calle Alhóndiga

Convento
Espíritu Santo

Plaza
San Gil

Plaza
Santa Cruz

C. Santa María
la Blanca

C. San Esteban

C. Aguilas

Convento de
San Leandro

Calle Gerona

Calle Castellar

Palacio del
Duque de Alba

Hospicio
San Luis

Calle de San Luis

Plaza
Pumarejo

Av. de

Menéndez Pelayo

Plaza
Pilatos

Casa de
Pilatos

Calle de Santiago

Plaza de
Ponce de
León

Calle Bustos Tavera

San Marcos

Murallas
Almohades

Calle Macasta

Calle Cementerio de los Ríos

CENTRO

Calle Socorro

Montaserio
Santa Isabel

LA MACARENA

R. de Capuchinos

Calle Recaredo

San Benítez

Plaza
Carmen
Benítez

Convento
del Valle

Calle María Auxiliadora

Calle del Sol

Calle de Enladrilada

Convento PP.
Capuchinos

Bellas
Artes

Calle de Muñoz León

Calle J. Aranda

Calle Luis Montoto

Calle Lope de Vega

Calle P. M. Casariego

Calle Júpiter

Avenida de la Cruz Roja

Calle Pirineos

Calle Urquiza

Calle Arroyo

Calle Albaida

Avenida Blas Infante

Calle Santo Domingo

LA CALZADA

Avenida Kansas City

Calle San Juan Bosco

Calle Luis de Morales

Calle B. Gracián

Calle Smail

el Greco

NERVIÓN

FRANCE

Barcelona

PORTUGAL

SPAIN

★ Madrid

● Sevilla

Post office ✉
Information ⓘ

0   1/4 mi
0   0.25 km

SEVILLA

far is Alfalfa. Almost every night sees the area become overrun by giddy night owls hopping from bar to bar and club to club. Another viable option is the Alameda region where you'll find a slew of kitschy bars and exciting clubs as well as a few of the city's best gay clubs. Rather stay outside and enjoy the cool Sevilla night? Head to Plaza del Pan for the town's massive *botellón* (BYOB street party). Once you've guzzled a few more ounces of Cruzcampo and made some new friends, it's time to work off that impending gut. Bring them to Triana, the area on the other side of the river, where you can finally experiment with that flamenco-booty-grinding dance you've been choreographing in your head. Clubs like Boss make Triana *the* prime place to bust a move. Few clubs here open before 11pm and close before 5am (bars are usually open 10pm–3am), so party hardy and hold off on that nap until tomorrow's siesta.

Bars

→ **Bauhaus** ★ Sharing the same name as the art school in Germany, this joint seems to have taken a few courses from the famous Weimar institution. As you'll find out yourself, its ultramodern interior doesn't let the name down. It doubles as a restaurant/cafe but the nocturnal incarnation of Bauhaus sees the DJs switch from spinning up-tempo dinner music to playing awesome house and electronica. *Marqués de Parada 53.* ☎ *954-224-210.*

→ **Café Naima** ★ Obliterating all stereotypes of jazz joints, Café Naima is as unpretentious and easygoing as they come. Instead of a dark, smoky, and cramped underground space, Café Naima has large windows, simple furniture, and bright walls sprinkled with framed photos of jazz legends and albums. Locals in Alameda sometimes frequent the cafe to take in the respectable jazz performances but the warm and friendly staff turns them into

loyal customers. *Calle Trajano 47 (Conde de Barajas).* ☎ *954-382-485.*

→ **La Fábrica** When it comes to beer, Spain doesn't exactly hold a candle to the ales of other European countries. This little microbrewery in Plaza de Armas tries to prove everybody wrong with their sweet artisan beers. Grab a seat at one of their barrel-tables or snag one in their terrace and sample a beer, or a few, with a few friends. *Plaza Legión 1 (Plaza de Armas).* ☎ *954-908-828.*

📺 Best ● → **La Rebotica** ★★ I love dive bars. I love shots. When the two come together in a sublime marriage, well I'm simply in love. Such is the case with La Rebotica. Sometimes overlooked by the shinier, louder bars in Alfalfa, this small haunt shows off its arsenal of shots, all named after aging pop-culture figures, and plays some decent tunes while you knock back a few. If you want to drink, and drink cheaply, this no-frills joint'll get the job done. *Calle Perez Galdos 11.* ☎ *954-221-625.*

→ **Texas Lone Star Saloon** Just north of the cathedral, you'll find this little slice of Texas. Well, there's a Texas flag and a giant-screen TV, although you'll be watching more European soccer matches than American sporting events on the tube. Y'all ready for some *fútbol?* You can down Bass, Bud, and Corona, but no Shinerbock. Even though they dared mess with Texas, this place gets packed with young foreigners and even some locals at night, grooving to throbbing pop/dance music that would make Willie Nelson pee his Wranglers. As of yet, no one has put a shotgun rack on their scooter. *Placentines 25.* ☎ *954-210-384.*

Nightclubs

→ **Antique** ★★ Another posh club for anyone looking to unleash their happy feet, Antique is a favorite among Spanish celebrities. Lesser-known clubbers come here to hopefully catch a glimpse of some famous *futbol* player showing off moves not normally seen on the pitch. It was once the site of the Expo '92, but you would never be able to tell with the massive face-lift it received when owners took over the pavilion. Getting in is almost as difficult as getting into Boss, so dress to the nines or risk getting shown a red card by the bouncers and being escorted out of the queue. *Calle Matematicos Rey Pastor y Castro s/n.* ☎ *954-462-207. www.antiquetheatro.com.*

📺 **Best** ✿ ➔ **Boss** ★★★ Here's a sure-fire way, without using chloroform, to get past the bouncers in Sevilla's best and most exclusive dance club: Surround yourself (this applies to both men and women) with two or three of the most beautiful locals you can find, throw on your finest clubbing clothes, and whip out the most arrogant and confident attitude possible. Needless to say, it's difficult to get into this Triana hot spot on any day let alone the weekend. What's the fuss all about? Well, Boss has some of the best house and hip-hop pouring out of its speakers and the four unique bars pander to clubbers of all sorts—as long as they're jaw-droppingly gorgeous. *Calle Betis 67.* ☎ *954-990-104. www. discotecaboss.com.*

📺 **Best** ✿ ➔ **Catedral** ★★ Make a pilgrimage to this mecca of music if you can. The dance floor is always packed with bodies twisting to cutting-edge electronica, techno, house, and hip-hop with the occasional spiced-up pop hit thrown in for good measure. The ultrapopular discothèque may not be as swank as other clubs in town, but it sure is one of the most exciting. *Cuesta del Rosario 12.* ☎ *954-228-590. www.catedralclubsevilla.com.*

📺 **Best** ✿ ➔ **Elefunk** ★★ Leave it to the Black Eyed Peas to sully the name of one of the best nightspots in town. Long

before they sold out, when they were still a respectable underground hip-hop fixture, Elefunk injected Sevilla with a lethal dose of alternative entertainment. Those who set foot in the club for the first time usually are caught off-guard by the Dalí-meets-Detroit urban decor. Thankfully, the music is enough to turn them into Elefunk loyalists—on a nightly basis, DJs spin an incredible mix of electronica, funk, and hip-hop. *Calle Adriano 10. www.elefunk.org.*

Gay Nightlife

➔ **El Paseo/Isbiliyya** Before you head out to Ítaca, lower those inhibitions at two of the top gay bars in the city. El Paseo and Isbiliyya sit side-by-side and not only have a hell of a view of the Guadalquivir from their terrace, but most who come here admire the view of its attractive gay and lesbian crowd. *Paseo de Colón 2.* ☎ *954-210-460.*

📺 **Best** ✿ ➔ **Ítaca** ★★ Forget that it's Sevilla's top gay dance club. It's probably one of the best discothèques in the city, period. Like many alternative dance nightspots in any city, the clientele are mostly young gay males who strut their stuff to techno, bassy pop, and excellent house music. Straight folks aren't prohibited, but usually stick out and draw some skeptical stares. Sometimes they'll put on shows, but it's of course at its most chaotic and fun during the weekends. Once you've gotten sufficiently worked up, retreat to the darkroom in the back where almost anything goes. Things really get going much later at night, so don't bother coming here before 2am. *Calle Amor de Dios 31.* ☎ *954-907-733.*

Flamenco

➔ **Casa Carmen** Secret, undiscovered flamenco haunts that only locals know about don't exist in Sevilla. Hell, you'd think Britney and her unsightly benign growth . . . er . . . K-Fed were fixtures at each place given the paparazzi like flash-fest from the crowds. Casa Carmen, despite being overrun by tourists, is a decent place to check out affordable flamenco. Tickets cost 14€ (11€ for students), a steal compared to other venues, but it's smart to reserve in advance through their website or by calling. A trio of performers (a guitarist, vocalist, and dancer) plow through various forms of flamenco, giving guests a taste of the different styles. No two shows are the same and Casa Carmen prides itself in changing up performers and shows on a daily basis. Once in a while, the busty bartender and waitress will jump on stage and bounce around as part of the finale. Though not nearly as talented as the performers, they provide an entertaining element that probably garners them a few extra tips. I myself have one: Sports bras aren't just for sports. *Calle Marqués de Paradas 30. ☎ 954-212-889 or 954-215-633. www.casacarmenarteflamenco. com. Tickets 14€ adults, 11€ students. Shows start at 9:30pm; when in demand a second show is put on at 11pm.*

📺 **Best** ◐ ➔ **El Arenal** ★★ Thanks to Tradicional Escuela de Curro Vélez, El Arenal is able to bring some of the most talented and passionate performers to its stage. The intimate setting helps patrons get into the show, allowing them to actually feel the powerful stomping and fiery wails from their seats. Much to the budget traveler's chagrin, all this doesn't come cheap. El Arenal charges up to 30€ for tickets and that doesn't even include dinner. If you have enough scratch and desire for quality flamenco, you won't be disappointed with

El Arenal. *Calle Rodó 7. ☎ 954-216-492. www. tablaoelarenal.com. Performances at 8:30pm and 10:30pm.*

➔ **La Carboneria** ★ Maybe it was the stifling heat, the benches full of tourists, or the constant shushing by the husky flamenco dancer, but La Carboneria didn't stand out as a venue for flamenco. I admit I shouldn't expect a whole lot for a place that doesn't charge for admission but I'd gladly pay a few euros for a more intimate and comfortable setting. Having said that, many of the folks I met along the way ended up loving the place. The flamenco wasn't bad at all and the performers were more than capable in their respective arts of dance, song, and guitar. The terrace in the back is worth the visit however, with performers and patrons mingling and boozing in the breezy, leafy outdoor patio after the show. When the stage is void of polka-dot dresses and nylon-string guitars, La Carboneria is home to various music performances and concerts. *Calle Levies 18. ☎ 954-214-460.*

Classical/Opera

📺 **Best** ◐ ➔ **Teatro de la Maestranza** ★★★ Give up the stomping and wailing for a few nights and expose your eardrums to the more soothing sound of opera. Teatro de la Maestranza has made a name for itself internationally as a venue for the performances of *Marriage of Figaro* (which Mozart composed after being inspired by Sevilla). If you have even the slightest interest in opera, a night at this theater is a must. *Paseo de Colón 22. ☎ 954-226-573. www. teatromaestranza.com. Tickets 7€–84€. Check site or call for showtimes.*

Sightseeing

Sevilla is home to some of the most impressive structures you'll see while you're in Spain. Since they're all conveniently

located in the Centro Historico part of town, you could tackle the main three in an afternoon. If you're here for several days

Free & Easy

Flamenco fees and fine dining can leave your wallet bruised and battered. Fear not, little backpacker, not everything in Sevilla will require you to relinquish those colorful euro bills. Here's a small list of things to do on the cheap while you're in town:

→ **La Carboneria.** Sure it's a tourist trap, but you can stroll in without paying a cent and experience some flamenco. The performance area is a little uncomfortable and the stomping and clapping may be shoddy at times, though you can't really complain since you're not exactly a paying customer.

→ **Botellón in Plaza del Pan.** The most social pre-drinking event in all of Spain also has the most affordable cover charge: zero€. Unless you count the two or three euros you used to buy the ingredients for your *kalimoxto,* aka Coke and wine (convenience stores can also sell you a *lote,* which is an all-in-one-*botellon* kit with drinks and cups), the party in the plaza is the best way to schmooze with locals and prepare for the night ahead without pulling out any cash.

→ **Parque Maria Luisa and Plaza de Espana.** They're the most picturesque public spots in Sevilla and the only thing you'll have to spend is a few calories walking from the city-center to both places. It's well worth the walk though with incredible landscaping, design, and architecture.

→ **Culture du Jour.** With the exception of Casa de Pilatos, many of Sevilla's best sights can be experienced simply by flashing the cashier a smile, student ID, or by dressing up like a derelict. I'll explain the last part in a bit. For places like **Torre del Oro** (Tues) and the **Cathedral** (Sun), admission is free on certain days. Other attractions, **Alcázar, Museo de Artes y Costumbres Populares,** and **Museo Arqueológico,** offer free admission for students with a passable ID (I was able to get in gratis with my expired university ID). The cathedral, according to the signs, also lets in the unemployed for free. I wonder if God has any openings for freelance travel writers . . .

SEVILLA

however, you're better off doing one each day. Otherwise it can get a little overwhelming and tiring (lots of climbing in the Giralda and tons of ground to cover in the Alcázar). Same thing goes for Sevilla's popular outdoor spots. Parque Maria Luisa and Plaza de Espana are both doable in one afternoon since they sit side-by-side along Avenida de Isabel La Católica. When you hit up any of the sights, be sure to bring along a large water bottle with you. You'll be glad you did when you reach the park without collapsing from dehydration.

Festivals

Semana Santa ★★. The time-honored tradition of robed and hooded *cofradías* (brotherhoods) slowly marching through the side streets of Sevilla is perhaps the main reason travelers come to the city during Easter. The period from Palm Sunday to Easter Sunday is filled with these large groups of hooded men making their pilgrimages with several obligatory floats, each depicting a scene from the Passion. Good Friday is the busiest day, when several of the major brotherhoods undertake their procession. Needless to

ᴍᴛᴠ🎵 The University Scene

Practically sitting in the luxurious Hotel Alfonso XIII's backyard, you'll notice another magnificent building. The **Real Fabrica de Tabacos** was once a tobacco factory where the legendary Carmen used to work. Today, it serves as the main building to the Universidad de Sevilla, one of the top universities in Spain. The prestige and historical background might have enticed the thousands of undergrads to come to the Andalusian city, but I'm sure the party scene also tempted the move. The nightlife largely panders to the huge university crowd, and if they're not filling the bars and clubs, they're throwing parties of their own. Head over to the main university area around the Real Fabrica de Tabacos near Menendez Pelayo and San Fernando and scour the postings in the school buildings to see what's going on that weekend. While you're at it, strike up a conversation with passing students. Unless it's the exam period when they can be extremely snarky, most are bilingual and friendly.

say, finding vacancy at nearby hotels during this period is close to impossible. Book months in advance. Easter week.

Feria de Abril ★★. Much less somber than Semana Santa, the Spring Fair turns Sevilla into one large outdoor party. It lasts for about 8 days, filling the streets with lively parades, noisy *casetas* (tents), and happy, inebriated locals dancing and singing. The event started out in 1847 when notorious party-fiend and farm-animal fan Queen Isabel II passed an act allowing a livestock fair to take place in the city. It quickly morphed into a convivial celebration that to this day brings heaps of mirth to Sevilla. Third week of April.

Attractions & Monuments

→ **Alcázar** ★★ From Pedro the Cruel to Isabella the not-so-cruel, many an iron fist have ruled from Sevilla's palace bringing riches and renown to the region. The ancient site is not one to be missed and that's probably why it's still used occasionally by Spain's royalty to this day (note the idle x-ray machines and metal detectors inside the gallery). Similar to the other Alcázars, Alcazabas, and Alhambras in the region, Sevilla's Alcázar is a sight to

behold. The expansive well-maintained gardens are perfect strolling territory on hot days. If the shade's not cool enough for you, you can retreat into the main building and watch an educational movie in the air-conditioned multimedia room. Otherwise, just come later at night when the grounds reopen for a unique Alcázar experience: Lights flicker on and drape the surroundings in dramatic lighting. *Plaza del Triunfo s/n.* ☎ *954-502-323. Admission 7€ adults, free for students. Tues–Sat 9:30am–7pm (later for night show, call for info).*

ᴍᴛᴠ **Best** 😊 → **Casa de Pilatos** ★★★ It's a shame that a place so small and extraordinary should have one of the highest admission fees in the city. My favorite place in Sevilla requires you to fork over 5€ to scope out the ground floor and 8€ for both levels. No matter which option you choose, Casa de Pilatos is an amazingly unique building that incorporates a slew of different architectural and design styles. Dabbling in Gothic influences here, a little baroque there, and a smidge of craziness everywhere, Casa de Pilatos is essentially a kaleidoscope of colors and patterns hell-bent on assaulting your eyes. Some walls are awash with colorful tiles while others have incredible wood detailing and carvings. Don't forget to look up once in a while too. The ceilings can sometimes be more breathtaking than things at eye level. If you can, try to scrounge up the extra 3€ since the second floor has a great deal to offer. There, the duke's residence is fully preserved and a tour guide will describe (in Spanish and English) the various uses of each room and the origins of the pieces of art adorning the walls. Among the canvases are original pieces like Goya's representation of a bullfighter in Ronda as well as a Velázquez painting of the duke and duchess painted as gods alongside Hercules. Photos aren't allowed anywhere on the second level and even if you think you can sneak a shot in when the group goes ahead to the next room, the tour guide's sixth sense will catch you red-handed. *Plaza Pilatos 1.* ☎ *954-225-298. Admission to both floors 8€, ground floor only 5€. June–Sept daily 9am–7pm; Oct–May daily 9am–6pm.*

MTV Best 👍 → **Catedral de Sevilla** ★★★ In case you didn't gather from the *Guinness Book of World Records* plaque in the corner, or if you have incredibly poor depth perception, Sevilla's cathedral is ginormous. The largest Gothic building in the world is also one of the most impressive structures in Europe. While it's not recommended, one doesn't even need to go inside to appreciate the construction and design of the cathedral. Ornate arches and painstakingly detailed statues make the neighboring Alcázar seem almost ordinary. Inside, there are too many breathtaking rooms, sacristies, and altars to describe them all here. Before you try and tackle the side rooms, don't miss (it's incredibly hard to anyways) the gilded main altar and its meticulously sculpted panels. The entire piece soars a few stories up, almost reaching the high ceilings.

Finally there's La Giralda. Not to be confused with the pompous TV personality of similar nameage, this tower is almost as big as the ego of the mustached windbag. The spiraling climb up a gentle ramp rises for more than 20 levels and the journey is well worth it. The view of Sevilla afforded by the balcony atop the tower is spectacular as are the peeks of the cathedral's exterior details through the iron grates from the windows on the way up. *Note:* There's supposed to be a strict dress code (according to a few signs) that doesn't allow shorts or T-shirts, but during the busy summer season it's rarely enforced. *Av. De la Constitución s/n.* ☎ *954-214-971. Admission 7.50€ adults, 2€ students, free on Sun. Sept–June Mon–Sat 11am–5pm, Sun 2:30–6pm; July Aug daily 9:30am–3:30pm.*

→ **Plaza de España** ★★ The inner-nerd in some of you might exclaim, "Naboo!" Yep, one of Sevilla's most beautiful landmarks was used in *Star Wars: Episode II.* When you first arrive, your inner George Lucas will have your digital camera working overtime when you catch site of the picturesque square. A semicircle of marble columned structures (now used as government buildings) surround an open area with an impressive fountain in the center. Separated by a pseudo-moat, you'll have to cross one of several elegant Venetian-style bridges (check out the ceramic columns along the sides) connecting the areas. It was constructed as the centerpiece to the Iberian-American Expo in 1929. Be careful when entering the intermediate buildings, however. The balconies may seem like the perfect spot for a few Kodak moments, but you'll come upon what looks to be pigeon purgatory—you'll have to traverse an obstacle course of bird poop and feathers to reach the popular aviary hangout. For a more spectacular sight, visit Plaza de Espana in the evening.

12 Hours in Sevilla

Spending less than 3 days in Sevilla is ludicrous. Spending 12 hours? Absolute insanity but absolutely doable. All you need is a good pair of running shoes and a quick *café con leche* to give you that caffeine boost in the morning. Let's get crackin'!

1. **El Catedral.** You can't miss this place. No really, you can't. The largest cathedral (according to the folks at the *Guinness Book of World Records*) is just south of the city center and should be the first place on your list of "Places to See."

2. **La Giralda.** Conveniently, it's accessible from the cathedral. The only catch is that you'll have to climb over 20 levels of ramp to reach the top. It's absolutely worth it though. By the time you get to the lookout, you'll have an amazing view of the city as well as buns of steel.

3. **Alacázar.** Hop over to the royal residence next door and see how royalty lived back in the day and how they live nowadays. Occasionally used by the royal family, this old fortress/residence is pretty impressive. Intricate wall details, refreshing fountains, and an expansive garden all show that prior rulers didn't cut any corners when it came to pimping out their digs. If you have an hour left to spare at the end of the day, stop by at night when the Alcázar slips into something a little bit more comfortable--an array of soft, colorful lights.

4. **Barrio de Santa Cruz.** Pick any time of day to visit this quaint neighborhood and chances are you'll cross paths with dozens of tourists. Nevertheless, a stroll through the picturesque neighborhood will make even the butchest hearts feel all warm and fuzzy inside. Perhaps it's the whitewashed buildings and their cute flower boxes overhanging the iron-wrought windows, but most will be powerless over the barrio's charm.

5. **La Carboneria.** Flamenco for the masses. The rows of benches here are almost always packed for the free flamenco performance and, for the most part, it's pretty good. That is, if you can poke your head through the digital camera minefield that seems to be clicking nonstop throughout the show. At the end, cool off in the open-air terrace in the back and chat up the guitarist. Just be careful when shaking hands, those flamenco dudes like to keep their plucking nails, long, sharp, and hard.

6. **Bar Rinconcillo.** Brusque waiters growl at patrons, plates of tapas are shoved in front of your mug, and your tab is scratched on the counter as if it was your bookie reminding you of what you owe. All of this together, believe it or not, makes for one of the best tapas bars in Sevilla. Try their pork cheeks with potato and you'll see why.

7. **Plaza de España.** It's a sight to see during the day, but it's unforgettable at night. If you catch the light and music show that the city occasionally holds in this square, you're in for an amazing evening experience. In the afternoon, take advantage of the sunlight to inspect the plaza's intricate details: carefully painted ceramic columns on the bridges and the colorful panels lining the exterior of the ground level, to name a few.

Once in a while the square becomes filled with colorful lights and music, making it easier to picture its previous incarnation as a Star Wars set. Even if you're not a fan of Yoda, visit the plaza you must. *Entrance along Av. de Isabel la Catolica.*

Museums

→ **Museo Arqueológico** Giant forearms, while useful in tennis or in making sophomoric self-pleasure jokes, aren't something you'd normally find in archaeology museums. Fortunately for forearm fetishists, one remnant from a humongous ancient statue is on full display at the Museo Arqueológico in Sevilla: a donkey-size fragment of a limb. The rest of the museum has your standard and somewhat boring collection of ancient coins and pottery shards, but there are several exceptional statues (the ones of Mercury and Venus in particular) and busts spread throughout the space that are worth checking out. *Plaza de América s/n.* ☎ *954-232-401. Admission 1.50€, free for students. Wed–Sat 9am–8pm; Tues 3–8pm; Sun 9am–2pm.*

→ **Museo de Baile** The jury's still out on whether Museo de Baile is worth all 10€. If you were curious about the history of flamenco and wanted an entertaining education on the dance, then this is your place. The modernly designed museum is relatively new and packed with multimedia displays. Otherwise, you might be better off saving those euros for a night at El Arenal. *Calle Manuel Rojas Marcos 3.* ☎ *954-340-311. www.flamencomuseum.com. Admission 10€ adults, 6€ for children. Nov–Mar daily 9am–6pm; Apr–Oct daily 9am–7pm.*

→ **Museo de Bellas Artes** ★ Here you'll discover important religious works by Spanish masters you've probably never heard of, such as Murillo and Zurbarán. The visit is worth it for Sala V alone, which

has a gorgeous ceiling and giant Murillo canvases depicting religious figures with scary things (like rabid dogs) lurking in the shadows. The *museo* can't match any of the major museums of Madrid (its modern art collection is forgettable), but the air-conditioning is just as strong on hot summer days. *Plaza del Museo 9.* ☎ *954-221-829. Admission 1.50€. Tues 3–8pm; Wed–Sat 9am–8pm; Sun 9am–2:30pm.*

→**Museum of Popular Arts & Customs** I admit, fabrics and ceramics aren't the most exciting things in the world. But when you're on the verge of heat exhaustion, things that normally wouldn't grab your attention suddenly become interesting when air-conditioning is involved. Once inside, however, the Museum of Popular Arts & Customs is actually not that bad. The basement in particular houses several workshop re-creations from different occupations like a luthier's workspace from a few decades ago and a blacksmith's forge. On the main floor, you'll find various temporary exhibitions as well as displays of different fabrics. There might not be any camera-worthy views inside the museum, but the museum itself bookends a picturesque fountain/plaza with the Museo Arqueológico on the other side. *Plaza de América.* ☎ *954-232-576. Admission 1.50€ adults, free for students. Wed–Sat 9am–8pm; Sun 9am–2pm; Tues 3–8pm.*

→ **Torre del Oro** From the outside it seems more like a beige behemoth than a Gold Tower. Back in the day, the tower was a sight to see on the Guadalquivir River with glorious golden tiles covering head to toe. When the blistering sun fell on the golden tiles, 13th-century sailors could spot the tower from miles away. Since then, the Sevillan landmark has lost its shiny skin to age, vandals, and looters but it still manages to draw quite a crowd. Nowadays it serves as a museum, displaying relics and images from the city's nautical past. *Paseo de Cristóbal Colón.* ☎ *954-222-419. Admission 1€. Tues–Sat 10am–2pm; Sun 11am–2pm.*

Playing Outside

→ **Parque Maria Luisa** Whether you're trying to play it cool with your date or just looking to cool off, the shaded promenades of Parque Maria Luisa are perfect for both. Bunches of leafy trees extend just high enough into the Sevilla sky to help shade those traipsing through the cozy courtyards and flowered walkways that cut through the park. It's no wonder that the park was once part of the regal Palacio de San Telmo (now a seminary situated in the park). You might hear about the giant Ferris wheel, Noria Panorámica de Sevilla, which, sadly, was moved from the park to Manchester, England, in October 2006. *Av. de María Luisa.*

Shopping

The best way to cool off on a particularly steamy day is to dip into the stores along Tetuan and Calle Velazquez. Unless you're wandering around during the siesta hours (2–6pm), when everything is dead, the frigid stores always entice sweaty window shoppers with their full-blast air-conditioning. Luckily, you'll find Sevilla's clothing stores are either full of colorful and bright flamenco dresses or trendy couture for the younger population. Spain's hip clothing chains (Pull & Bear, Bershka, and Mango) are all well-represented here.

→ **Discos Latimore** Disco ain't dead, baby! And neither is Discos Latimore. This little music store should satisfy the casual music fan's needs. Browsing though the vinyl you'll find some '70s LPs of the horrendous genre as well as some classic rock gems. *Javier Lasso de la Vega 4.* ☎ *954-382-161.*

→ **El Corte Inglés** I came here to stock up on that wonderful nectar known as Fanta Naranja and I left with an ironing board, a cummerbund, and a goldfish. Okay, so while that might be a slight exaggeration of my shopping experience, you can find almost anything within this mega-store. In a culture where you have to buy your fruit in a *fruteria,* your meat in a meat market, and the rest from a *supermercado,* it's refreshing and a relief to be able to track down the essentials in one ultra-*supermercado.* While I'm all for small businesses, El Corte Inglés is definitely a boon for travelers. *Plaza Duque 6.* ☎ *954-220-931.*

→ **Flamenco Cool** Stop here to load up on kitsch. You'll find locally made and imported gifts, including polka dot magnets, hot pink bull heads, and a pair of flamenco shoes more apt for RuPaul than Carmen. *Amor de Dios at San Andrés.* ☎ *954-184-818. www.flamencocool.com.*

→ **Juan Foronda** This chain store deals with exquisitely embroidered mantillas and flamenco accessories. Who needs a gift back home? *Tetuan 28.* ☎ *954-226-060.*

MTV Best → **Libreria Beta** ★★ In a previous life, Beta was once a theater (Teatro Imperial). When it closed down, the bookstore chain decided to preserve the main parts of the building. The result is a uniquely attractive bookstore whose design doesn't seem forced. Naturally, you'll find books on theater, music, art, architecture, and history on-stage while the balcony contains many fiction titles.

Most of the paperbacks here are in Spanish, but there is a decent selection of English books back where the cheap seats would be. *Calle Sierpes 25.* ☎ *954-293-724. betaimperial@libreriasbeta.com. Closed Sun.*

→ **Munda Interiores** With home decor and objets d'art of such tasteful and modern quality, you just can't fathom they could be useful. Check out the whitewashed serving trays with just a spill of color down the sides, handcrafted by the owner. *Bailen 22.* ☎ *954-565-066.*

→ **Raquel** This is the place for offbeat meets traditional flamenco gear such as Hawaiian prints on classic ruffled dresses. Pick a style off the rack and they will alter it to fit you nice and tight. *Cuna 51.* ☎ *954-217-293.*

→ **Yellow Rat Bastard** Somehow, my favorite store back home made the trans-Atlantic journey and spawned an illegitimate copy-cat. At first glance, it looks like they simply expanded to Spain, but the clothes you'll find in this Yellow Rat Bastard bastard aren't anything like the clothes you'll find in the New York store. Instead of labels like Dickies, Triple Five Soul, and Obey, they simply have the name "Yellow Rat Bastard" emblazoned across their tops and jeans in various styles. Some look hideous while others are actually worthy of being in the original SoHo store. *Calle Puente y Pellón 21. www.ratabastarda.com.*

SEVILLA

Andalucia

by *Andre Legaspi*

A t first, staring out the bus window as you pass through Andalucia may seem like a wasted effort. The parched, dusty hills of southern Spain replay the same pattern over and over again: a perfectly symmetrical grove of olive trees, dry mounds of dirt, olive trees, mound of dirt, olive trees. But once in a while, you'll see an incredible castle pop out of nowhere and then disappear into the same pattern of trees and dirt. That's Andalucia for you—the lone ancient fortress, the dilapidated minaret, or the whitewashed buildings on the faraway hill. Several cultures, over thousands of years, have crashed together in the region, sprinkling the boring landscape with unbelievably breathtaking towns overflowing with unique customs, deep traditions, and legendary landmarks: the awe-inspiring Alhambra in Granada, the mystical columns of the Mezquita in Cordoba, and Ronda's drool-worthy Puente Nuevo to name a few. By the time you reach Jerez de la Frontera though, your mouth will be watering for a different reason. Sherry, the region's biggest and tastiest export, is produced here by the barrel and the pungent aroma of the sweet liquor fills the huge warehouses within the town's numerous bodegas. A visit to Jerez is an intoxicatingly fitting way to end your trip to Andalucia.

Best of Andalucia

○ **Best Hostel: Oasis Backpackers' Hostel.** Incredible staff, cheap and tasty meals, laid-back backpackers, and the best rooftop terrace of any hostel in Spain make the Oasis one of the best, not only in the country, but in the world. See p. 565.

○ **Best Budget Hotel: El Beaterio.** You won't find owners more adorable or hospitable than the ones in El Beaterio.

Their unique character is found everywhere in this spacious *hosteria:* in the intriguing art hanging on the walls, the kooky kitsch in the "lobby," and the loud, shaggy dog Nani. See p. 580.

○ **Best Tapas Bar: La Castañeda.** Authenticity oozes from this tapas joint. From the loud waiters to the ham swinging from the ceiling, La Castañeda is one of the top tapas places in Andalucia. See p. 565.

○ **Best Dive Bar: Medussa.** Just when I thought it couldn't get any better with the awesome music, chill crowd, and Tuesday video concerts, they had to inform me of their 1€ beers on Wednesday. Like I really needed another reason to stop by Medussa. See p. 587.

○ **Best Flamenco: El Eshavira.** The intimate, cavelike performance area puts you face to face with the polka-dot dresses and sweaty guitarists. A must if you're in Granada. See p. 567.

○ **Best Photo Op: Ronda Bullring.** You don't have to be Ansel Adams to realize that an infinite number of beautiful photos can be taken in this circular structure. If you're lucky, you'll have it all to yourself. Head to the stands for the best angles. See p. 575.

○ **Best Dance Club: Granada 10.** The popular discothèque sort of looks like a classical theater. Well, that's because it is. In the afternoon, when the space isn't filled with Andalucia's most energetic and beautiful nightowls, movies are usually shown throughout the week. See p. 567.

○ **Best View (Restaurant): Restaurant Don Miguel.** When your interior decorator has a jaw-dropping ravine in Ronda to work with, you don't exactly need Martha Stewart to make the place look good. Diners on the outdoor terrace can admire the orange colors of the canyon while the sun sets. See p. 573.

○ **Best Attraction: Alhambra.** Considered one of the wonders of the world, Granada's famed complex has so many breathtaking sights that you could easily spend an entire afternoon there and still not see everything. That's when you should buy a second ticket for the illuminated version at night when the indescribable site slips into something more comfortable. See p. 568.

○ **Best Beaches: Cabo de Gata.** Sometimes volcanoes can produce some of the most impressive sights in the world. The shores of Cabo de Gata are evidence of this. The sandy beaches are full of incredibly secluded spots made possible by huge, rocky cliffs. See p. 568.

○ **Best Student Crowd: Cadiz.** Talking to co-eds here, you might think you're in some college town in the states. Thanks to the Erasmus exchange program, there are plenty of American and international students milling about. With so many university kids around, the nightlife in Cadiz is one of the best in Andalucia. See p. 582.

○ **Best Interactive Attraction: The Sherry Bodegas.** You can't visit Andalucia without stopping by Jerez for a few tastings at the bodegas. Each visit always ends with several shots of various sherries and brandies. See p. 592.

Cordoba

Depending on your point of view, the layout of Cordoba can be a marvel or a madhouse. Short-fused tourists will likely agree with the latter when they become disoriented by the knotty streets in the heart of the city. Others will notice the

ANDALUCIA

intriguing geographical timeline as they work their way south from the modern hotels and clubs on Avenida de America to the ancient Puente Romano on the Guadalquivir.

Back in the days when ancient hipsters were sporting leather skirts, spears, and espadrilles, few places in the world were more popular and powerful than Cordoba. They certainly had plenty to brag about with a population reaching almost a million, the honor of being the capital of Muslim Spain, and one sexy river to the south now known as the Guadalquivir. Surprisingly, as you'll see in areas like Barrio de la Juderia, much has been preserved from the city's rich past.

Getting There & Around
BY TRAIN

The easiest and most convenient way to get to Cordoba is by rail. The smaller cities and towns may not be connected just yet, but if you're shuttling between the main cities there's no better way than on the **AVE high-speed train.** The most heavily used route in the region is the one that runs from Madrid to Seville, with all trains making intermediate stops at Cordoba. About 30 leave daily and it takes just over an hour and a half from Madrid and 40 minutes from Seville to get to Cordoba. The **train station** (Plaza de las Tres Culturas; call RENFE for timetables and info, ☎ 902-243-402; www.renfe.es) sits just on the northwest edge of the city and isn't that far from the center of Cordoba; but walking across Avenida de America can be an uncomfortable task in the middle of the day so slap on some suntan lotion and guzzle a bottle of water.

BY BUS

If your next destination is some small Andalusian town, it's likely that you'll have to take the bus. While I'd discourage

Culture Tips 101

You might consider it veggie voyeurism or even floral fetishism, but whatever alliteration you come up with still won't make it wrong. Homeowners don't just condone it, they actually take great pride in showing off their leafy courtyards. While Americans might fight every Christmas trying to out-watt their neighbors with strings and strings of lights, the same competitive spirit applies to Cordoban's green thumbs. Don't be shy when passing by a particularly colorful display—they're there for everyone's enjoyment.

anyone from taking the 4¹/₂-hour bus trip to Madrid, it's a decent option budget-wise for passage to places like Granada, and it may very well be your only one. Several bus companies make the 3-hour drive to the home of the Alhambra from just behind Cordoba's train station. The most reliable and relaxing line is **Alsina Graelss Sur** (☎ 957-278-100). Others include **Transportes Urena** (☎ 957-404-558), usually used by travelers going to and coming from Jaen, and **Secorbus** (☎ 902-229-292), an affordable, yet uncomfortable, way to get to Madrid from Cordoba.

Surprisingly, there are buses that somehow squeeze through the tiny streets of the city and while the fare only costs 1€, you're usually better off doing the pedestrian thing. Not only do the routes get confusing (when in doubt, throw your destination street out to the driver to see if he nods or shakes his head), but the buses easily get caught in a standstill when a delivery truck or a stalled car cuts off the traffic circulation. A 10-minute walk can easily turn into a 45-minute bus trip, so do

Andalucia

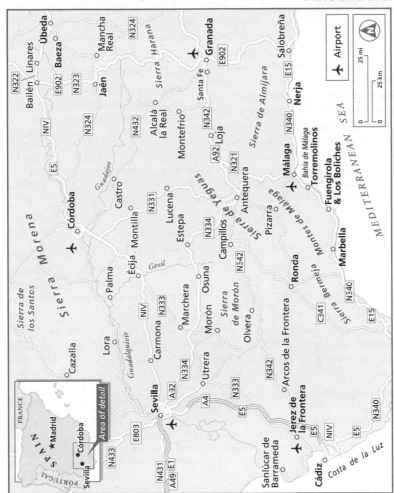

some hamstring stretches and avoid the buses if you can.

Cordoba Basics

It's advisable to stop at the **tourist office** at Calle Torrijos 10 (☎ **957-471-235;** www.andalusia.org) before heading to your hotel unless you're taking a taxi or bus. You can grab a map and get some hotel and travel information Monday through Friday from 9:30am to 6:30pm, Saturday, Sunday, and holidays from 10am to 2pm.

Consider Cordoba's streets a warm-up to Seville's chaotic passageways. With a slightly less dense tangle of roads and alleyways, Cordoba is a bit more navigable than the city further down the

Guadalquivir. Should you get lost, use the tower of the Mezquita as a point of reference and you'll get your bearings back in no time. Heading outside of Barrio de la Juderia, the historical center of the city, without a map, the three sides of Cordoba will let you know when you've gone too far: Avenida de America and Avenida de la Libertad to the north sandwich the green Jardines Renfe and Paseo de Cordoba, Avenida de la Republica

Argentina and Paseo de la Victoria surround the Jardines de la Victoria and Jardines Duque de Rivas to the west, and the Guadalquivir River snakes along the southern edge of Cordoba.

RECOMMENDED WEBSITES

○ **www.andalucia.com** and **www.spain.info**: Both sites overflow with tons of information about the cities in the region, possible activities, and historical write-ups.

cordoba **Nuts & Bolts**

....

Currency   Caixa and Unicaja, just to name a couple, have hundreds of **ATMs** in every major Andalusian city and town, no matter how small. In places like Cadiz (check the streets to the northeast), it seems like the machines outnumber the locals 3:1.

Emergencies   For general emergencies throughout Spain, dial ☎ **006**. Local police can be reached at ☎ **092** or, if you have a medical emergency, dial ☎ **061** to call for an ambulance.

Laundromats   Laundromats can be hard to find. A few chains, like **PressTo** (www.pressto.com), offer laundry and dry-cleaning outlets throughout the region. Otherwise, most of the hostels (save for the ones in Cadiz and Tarifa) offer either laundry services or coin operated machines.

Pharmacies   If you come down with something nasty (a possibility if you decide to take that day trip to Morocco), your first order of business is to seek out the neon-green signs on the street. That's where you'll find a few folks in white lab coats and prescription medicine as far as the eye can see.

Post Offices   Send out those postcards and parcels through Spain's Correos. There are several offices throughout Cordoba, but you can go to Jose Cruz Conde 15 (☎ **957-496-342**) or Puente Genil 1 (☎ **957-296-633**) to ship your souvenirs.

Safety   The cities and towns listed below are either student hot spots or major tourist draws, but aren't notoriously unsafe. Just use common sense when traveling at night and when going into crowded plazas and markets. Keep your belongings in your sight and use caution when strangers approach.

Sleeping

Unfortunately, young backpackers looking to meet other travelers in Cordoba have very limited options. There's no bona fide youth hostel in the city, but there are plenty of very affordable and pleasant hostels where you can bunker down for a few days. Contrary to a traveler's common sense, some of the best values are found right next to Cordoba's most visited and

Cordoba

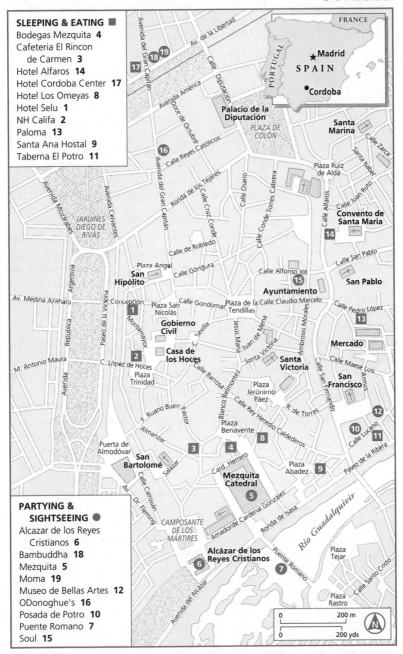

prettiest site: the Mezquita. For those with a bigger budget, many of the ritzier hotels have claimed territory on the city's fringes.

CHEAP

➜ **Hotel Los Omeyas** ★ Getting a personal wake-call from a 1,300-year-old mosque/cathedral is actually kind of nice. Just half a block away from the Mezquita, its morning bells ring gently through the quaint accommodations of the Hotel Los Omeyas. Rooms are relatively small, but all the essentials like air conditioning and a comfortable bed are there. Knowing that tourists would gladly pay twice the amount for the location and basic amenities, it's a mystery why the place has such cheap rates. It's probably because the small family that runs Los Omeyas are very chill and friendly. In the morning, they're always happy to make you a simple breakfast of *café con leche* and tostadas even if you wake up at a ludicrous 6am. It's too bad the Mezquita doesn't have a snooze button. *Calle Encarnación 17.* ☎ *957-492-267. www.hotel-losomeyas.com. Single 35€–41€, double 42€–65€. Amenities: Hotel restaurant nearby, bar, cafeteria, lounge. In room: A/C, TV, safe.*

➜ **Santa Ana Hostal** ★ With fuzzy pictures on the Internet, a dearth of reviews, and prices low enough that even a derelict would have doubts, I was expecting the worst when I walked down Calle Corregidor Luis de la Cerda. The second I spotted the entrance in a cute whitewashed alley, all those suspicions evaporated into the dry Cordoban air. A cordial young girl sped me through the check-in and I was more than pleasantly surprised by my room: air conditioner, a TV with multiple English channels, and, best of all, a recently renovated, clean, and modern bathroom. Although the single rooms are a little constricted, larger rooms feature an enormous space that includes a sunken

common room. As if that isn't enough, the Mezquita is a block and a half from the hostel. *Calle Corregidor Luis de la Cerda 25.* ☎ *957-485-837. www.hostalsantaana.com. Single 30€–40€, double 60€. Amenities: Internet point, laundry service, parking. In room: A/C, TV.*

SPLURGE

➜ **Hotel Alfaros** ★★ Nothing is worse than stumbling out of a club, nauseous, drunk, disoriented, and looking for a cab to get home. Cut out the middle man (not the alcohol) by booking a room at Hotel Alfaros. Literally across the street from a few popular nightspots on Calle Alfaros (Valhalla, R Room, and La Boveda), the upscale hotel draws travelers young and old to the small, quaint street for a comfortable night's stay. Rooms are decorated extremely tastefully and are well furnished. *Calle Alfaros 18.* ☎ *957-491-920. Single 115€, double 140€. Amenities: Restaurant, garage. In room: A/C, TV, minibar.*

➜ **Hotel Cordoba Center** ★★★ Screw being an astronaut or firefighter. When I grow up, I want to be a businessman in Spain so I can spend a few nights at the Hoteles Center Cordoba and expense it. Execs and CEOs love to crash here and it's not hard to see why. After they shower in the chic black and white bathrooms, guests sleep in style on huge, plush king-size beds. The ultramodern building looms over Avenida America for plenty of unique views and there are amenities up the wazoo throughout the hotel: gym, sauna, and a gorgeous rooftop pool with an almost-too-friendly lifeguard. *Av. Libertad 4.* ☎ *957-758-000. Double 130€–180€. Amenities: Bar, fitness center, pool. In room: A/C, TV, hair dryer, minibar, safe.*

➜ **Hotel Selu** Despite mispronouncing the name a total of five times while checking in, the friendly desk staff smiled politely at my idiotic fumbling and showed

wwwired

Whether you need to unload your digital camera's memory card onto a CD or e-mail your mom to plead for more cash, you can get both done at **Tele-Click** (Eduardo Dato 9; ☎ **957-290-587**) on one of their dozen computers (.90€ per half-hour; Mon–Fri 10am–3pm and 5:30–10:30pm, Sat–Sun noon–11pm).

me to my room. I almost didn't leave that evening since the coolly air-conditioned room, comfy bed, and cable television had me in a procrastinating, vegetative state. Luckily, it's not far from the major attractions and it sits in a commercial area with plenty of stores for window shopping. If you have enough cash, you can't go wrong with Hotel Say-loo . . . er . . . See-lyoo . . . forget it. *Calle Eduardo Dato 7.* ☎ *957-476-500. www.hotelselu.com. Single 60€–80€. Amenities: Bar, breakfast room, cafeteria, laundry service, lounge, room service. In room: A/C, TV, hair dryer, minibar, safe.*

→ **NH Califa** Quaint and cozy isn't exactly what every tourist looks for when they come to Cordoba. Those aching for the comforts of modern convenience will be content with the NH Califa. Part of the NH Hotel chain, it sits on the edge of the city, about a 5-minute walk from the train station. Rooms are stocked with the generic, upscale furnishings normally found in luxury chains. *Lope de Hoces 14.* ☎ *957-299-400. www.nh-hotels.es. Double 117€. Amenities: Bar, laundry service, lounge, room service. In room: A/C, TV, hair dryer.*

Eating

The great thing about dining in Cordoba is that it's easy to weed out the tourist traps from the authentic Andalusian eateries.

Most of the over-priced traps blatantly coax sightseers to their tables with chalkboard deals and faux-antique signs. A few of these places near the Mezquita are authentic, but most restaurants elsewhere are more discreet, offering more delicious dishes at half the price. Unfortunately, despite the influx of sightseers, it's impossible to get a hearty meal during siesta. Most eateries open around 11am for lunch, close at 2 or 3pm for siesta and don't open until 9pm for dinner (closing around midnight or 1am).

CHEAP

→ **Cafeteria El Rincon de Carmen** ★ ★ SPANISH/ANDALUSIAN Many of the places in Barrio de la Juderia can get pricey since it's one of the heavily touristed areas in Cordoba. With only 10€, I was ecstatic to stumble upon the sidewalk menu on the non-descript exterior of Cafeteria El Rincon de Carmen, where a mixed salad and sirloin of pork would cost just under 9€. The waiters quickly plopped down a standard (lettuce, tomato, corn, tuna, and onion), but huge, mixed salad and a tender sirloin with a surprisingly tasty sauce drizzled on top. Diners can opt for a comfy wicker chair in the air-conditioned interior or for a seat outside in the charming shaded terrace. *Calle Romero 4.* ☎ *957-291-055. Main course 4.50€–10€. Open for breakfast, lunch, and dinner.*

→ **Paloma** SPANISH If you're craving *pechugas* (chicken breast) and *chuletas* (pork chop) on the cheap, Paloma is a decent place for an inexpensive lunch. Most dishes will cost you around 8€ and if you come a few hours earlier the waiters will gladly pour you a *café con leche* and plop down some greasy *churros* for breakfast. *Plaza de la Corredera 4.* ☎ *957-492-558. Main course 8€. Daily 9am–4pm and 8pm–1am.*

ANDALUCIA

12 Hours in Cordoba

You could easily spend an entire day in the entrancing confines of the Mezquita, but it'd be a gross misappropriation of your time. Cordoba has quite a bit more to offer, so here's a breakdown of the places to check out if you unfortunately have only a day to spend in this awesome city.

1. **Mezquita.** Start off the day here when there's less of a crowd. The rising sun pokes through the windows on the eastern side making it a breathtaking sight. If you're not fully awake, you definitely will be when you finally see the striped arches and the forest of columns underneath them.

2. **Alcazar de los Reyes Cristianos.** Military buffs will get off on this fortress and the imposing structures overlooking the city. If ancient warfare isn't your cup of tea, retreat to the acres of gorgeous gardens—a great oasis to cool off, relax, and catch your breath before heading to the next site.

3. **Barrio de Juderia.** Back near the Mezquita, this neighborhood is the perfect strolling grounds for those without much of an agenda. Simply wander through the quaint, narrow streets of the area and experience Cordoba at its most peaceful.

4. **Museo de Bellas Artes.** Many argue that Goya, along with Picasso, was one of the greatest Spanish artists in history. This little museum has a small cache of his works and for a small fee, visitors can admire the legend's creations.

5. **Puente Romano.** Hopefully, by the time this guide goes to print, the tarps and scaffolding are long gone. The ancient bridge is a rough beauty, especially at night when the moon and stars sparkle on the Guadalquivir River beneath.

DOABLE

→ **Bodegas Mezquita** ANDALUSIAN The restaurant might as well put a huge neon sign outside saying TOURISTS WELCOME. The eatery, as well as a small food shop of the same name, is right smack in the middle of the historic center of the city and you'll always find couples with digital cameras dangling from their necks strolling through with their fanny packs swinging to and fro. Predictable clientele aside, the food is actually pretty good, albeit a little pricey, and it's one of the few eateries around the Mezquita that's open during the early evening (near the end of the siesta period). However, shelve your plans for an Andalusian feast. Up until 9pm, they only serve foods from their tapas menu. *Calle Céspedes 12.* ☎ *957-490-004. www.bodegasmezquita.com. Main course 8€–14€. Dinner daily 'til close.*

→ **Taberna El Potro** SPANISH Sometimes, when your stomach sounds like it's trying to hit on a humpback whale, you'll sacrifice quality for quantity. At Taberna El Potro, I'm talking about the paella. The generic, premade paellas aren't bad and they fill you up but they're an insult to authentic versions of the dish. Instead, try some of their other fish and meat dishes from your outdoor perch overlooking Plaza del Potro. These are actually cooked on-site and are rather tasty. *Calle Lineros 2.* ☎ *957-473-495. Main course 8€–12€. Open for lunch and dinner.*

Partying

If the sole purpose of your trip is to sleep through the afternoon and then rip it up at night, you might want to take the following into consideration: Most **discothéques and clubs** are found north of Avenida America while the **dive bars and lounges** are mostly found close to the town center. **Calle Alfaros,** in particular, has a quartet of interesting bars, Velvet Café, Valhalla (a harder, rock bar), R Room, and La Boveda, all within a few yards of each other.

➔ **Bambuddha** ★ Exclusivity is over-rated. Fake it instead at Bambuddha, a smooth bar/lounge next door to Moma, by calling and reserving the little alcove that floats above the main area. Reminiscent of a sultan's den, plush couches and tons of silky pillows make it perfect for your harem or a group of 20 or so friends. From your perch you can watch the young crowd below milling about and enjoying the Middle Eastern/Asian vibe the bar exudes. If you'd rather sip your cocktail al fresco, head outside to the sidewalk patio, plop down on one of the wicker couches, and kick back under the palm fronds like an Egyptian pharaoh. *Av. Gran Capitan 46.* ☎ *957-403-962.*

➔ **Moma** Everybody knows that fine wines and scotches are much more satisfying when aged. Some find that the same thing is true with members of the opposite sex. That's why you'll find a small contingent of college-aged patrons in the predominantly 30-something crowd at the chic Moma cafe-bar. Red velvet couches and stools usually cradle the bums of businessmen sipping a post-work cocktail in the afternoon, but in the late hours of the evening the place fills up with gorgeous middle-aged singles flirting and mingling. Drinks here can get kind of pricey, so pony up next to a potential sugar-daddy or -mommy and work that charm for all its worth. *Av. de la Libertad (Esquina Miguel Gila).* ☎ *957-271-912.*

➔ **O'Donoghue's** In 115°F (46°C) weather, even the gray, rainy U.K. seems like a more comfortable place than scorching Cordoba. Rather than heading a few hundred miles north on RyanAir, walk a few minutes north on Avenida Gran Capitan for the next best thing: O'Donoghue's Irish tavern. Seek shelter from the blinding sun in the dark, cool pub while gulping down pints of Guinness and watching Premier League soccer on the flatscreens. *Av. Gran Capitan 38.* ☎ *658-788-806.*

MTV **Best ♥** ➔ **Soul** ★★ Mother Teresa was a kind one. James Brown had a ton of it. I sold mine for all encompassing power and free premium cable. And it's also the name of my favorite drinking spot when I'm in Cordoba. Whether you're sipping a *café con leche* in the morning, a refreshing *Fanta naranja* in the sweltering afternoon, or a mojito at midnight, Soul is an incredibly chill bar/cafe where you can sit in one of their retro chairs and listen to awesome tunes (heavy on the '60s R&B and Soul of course) no matter what time of day it is. If you're overdue for a low-key night, your Rx is to head here in the midnight hour and catch some Wilson Pickett spilling out of the speakers. *Calle Alfonso XIII 3.* ☎ *957-491-580.*

Sightseeing

➔ **Alcazar de los Reyes Cristianos** ★★ Much like my current drought, this military fortress hasn't seen any action in years. This impressive beige complex was once an intimidating sight from the river in the 14th and 15th centuries, with its three massive towers (Tower of the Lions, Tower of Allegiance, and the Tower of the River) watching over the surrounding area. Now, it serves as one of Cordoba's most popular tourist attractions. Intriguing turrets and the trio of towers provide awesome photo opportunities of Cordoba but you'll have to exercise a good deal of patience and caution when cruising around the Alcazar. The narrow doorways leading to the towers and the dusty, and sometimes treacherous, staircases end up causing annoying pedestrian bottlenecks. After descending, head to the gardens to let your blood pressure taper off. The huge, verdant oasis is a perfect place to take a breather or to woo a prospective mate. Unfortunately for me, it didn't do much to help break my celibate streak. *Caballerizas Reales s/n.* ☎ *957-420-151. Admission 4€ adults, 2€ students. Mid-Oct to Apr Mon–Sat 10am–2pm and 4:30–6:30pm; May–June and Sept to mid-Oct Mon–Sat 10am–2pm and 5:30–7:30pm; July–Aug Mon–Sat 8:30am–2:30pm; year-round Sun and holidays 9:30am–2:30pm.*

MTV Best ☺ → **Mezquita** ★★★ Usually, stripes are very unflattering. Horizontal ones can make people look thicker while vertical ones make them look tall and lanky. Red and white ones are very *Where's Waldo* or candy-cane-ish. However, slapped on hundreds of arches, they work wonders for this incredible Spanish landmark. Originally built as a mosque, a cathedral haphazardly thrown together in the middle created a small dent in the otherwise overwhelming interior of the structure. Come in the early morning when the rising sun pours through the wrought-iron windows and creates a hauntingly beautiful effect on the army of columns and their faded red and white arches. *Torrijos and Calle Cardenal Herrero s/n.* ☎ *957-470-512. Admission 6.50€ adults, 3.25€ children. Nov and Feb daily 10am–5:30pm; Dec–Jan daily 10am–5pm; Apr–June daily 10am–7pm; Mar and July–Oct Mon–Sat 10am–6:30pm, Sun 9–10:15am and 2–5:30pm.*

Free & Easy in Cordoba

At last count you had 3 euros and change sitting at the bottom of your pocket and wanted to save it for a semi-decent meal at the end of the day. As it turns out though, the end of the day won't come around for another 6 hours or so. Don't worry. Believe it or not, a few things in Cordoba won't cost you a single euro.

→ **Posada del Potro.** For the price, you can't really complain about the small exhibits. The reconstructed inn moonlights as an art exhibit and it usually displays the works of local photographers and artists. See p. 561.

→ **Puente Romano.** While the bridge is always under repair and renovation, it's easy to see why since its one of the oldest structures in Cordoba. Hop down toward the Guadalquivir to check out the ancient bridge gratis. See p. 561.

→ **Museo de Bellas Artes** ★ Not floored by the photographs in the Posada de Potro? Fortunately, across the plaza (a mere 50m/164 ft. away) is a building with some truly legendary Spanish artists. Museo de Bellas Arte contains a number of canvases done by 19th- and 20th-century artists but most come to this modest museum for one name: Goya. A few of his works hang on the walls here and make the 1.50€ admission well worth it. *Plaza del Potro 1.* ☎ *957-471-314. Admission 1.50€ adults, free for children under 12. Tues 3–8pm; Wed–Sat 9am–8pm; Sun and holidays 9am–3pm.*

FREE ➔ **Posada del Potro** The only transients you'll find here are the photographs on the second floor. The Potro Inn, once a lodge for travelers passing through Cordoba, has since been converted into an odd municipal museum. It costs nothing to go inside and explore the area and thankfully so. Almost all of the rooms are closed off to the public and you'll end up climbing the stairs just for the exhibition space that the museum rents out to the artistic community. Nevertheless, the re-creation of the inn's exterior is somewhat interesting as are the little models depicting life back in the old days. *Plaza del Potro 10.* ☎ *957-485-501. Free admission. Daily 10am–2pm and 5–7:30pm.*

➔ **Puente Romano** ★ Perhaps one of the oldest structures in all of Cordoba is also one of the most inexpensive sites to visit. The ancient bridge dates all the way back to the 16th century. However, many of the bridge's elements are not from the original incarnation since it has undergone multiple repairs and restorations. In fact, for much of this year, the famous bridge has been under the cover of large tarps. For something almost as old as Keith Richards it's not surprising that it needs constant restorations. *Just off of Av. del Alcazar and Ronda de Isasa.*

Shopping

➔ **El Corte Ingles** No matter how big or small the town or city is, it always seems as though there's an El Corte Ingles to be found. It's a good thing too, since the mega-market is one of the most useful shops for travelers. You'll find everything from basic toiletries and clothes to housewares and hardware supplies. This branch, conveniently located in the middle of a sprawling shopping center, is a perfect air-conditioned oasis for those seeking refuge from the sun. If you really want relief, you could easily pick up a bottle of SPF 45, a new A/C unit, shady sombrero, and the new Arctic Monkeys album from this superstore. *Ronda de los Tejares 32.* ☎ *957-222-881. Mon–Sat 10am–10pm.*

➔ **Fluid** You probably wouldn't have guessed by the narrow, uneven streets in the center of Cordoba, but skateboarding actually thrives around here. When local boarders look for new threads to possibly catch a sponsor's eye, many of them head to Fluid. Standard names in skateboarding and surfing couture like Volcom are found emblazoned on their board shorts, backpacks, T-shirts, and hats. *Claudio Marcelo 9.* ☎ *957-488-966. Daily 10am–2pm and 5:30–9pm.*

Granada

Strolling through the main avenues of Granada is one of the best ways to experience the eye-catching Andalusian city. During the day, the huge, colorful swaths of fabric over the commercial avenues shield shoppers from the bright afternoon sun and the smaller, less conspicuous side streets conceal small ethnic shops that sell everything from hookahs to costume jewelry. The night is also a good time to experience the vibrant town; the sidewalks along Gran Via de Colon, one of the main avenues of Granada, become imbued with the colorful lights of the festive decorations that hang over the busy street.

Getting There
BY AIR
Very few planes departing from cities outside of Spain touch down on Armilla

ANDALUCIA

Airport's runways (☎ 958-245-200). Iberia is the main carrier that uses Granada's airport, serving the major cities of Barcelona and Madrid. Granada is roughly 16km (10 miles) from Armilla and a taxi will cost you up to 20€. Budget-minded travelers will likely opt for the buses that shuttle to and from Plaza Isabel Catolica. A single fare is about 4.40€ for the almost an hour long trip that leaves several times a day (Mon–Sat 8:15am, 9:15am, 5:30pm; Sun 5:30pm and 7:30pm).

BY TRAIN

Like any other city in Spain, the rail system is the most preferred and efficient way to travel to Granada. Unfortunately, your choices are slightly more limited compared to taking the bus. And because of more frequent stops, the trip to Seville is longer (trip time: roughly 4–5 hr. total) than the trip by bus. Ticket prices are the same, however, costing no more than 20€. Two trains leave daily for Madrid and take roughly 6 hours while only one train, an overnight train taking 12 hours, leaves for Barcelona every evening. Wherever your destination may be, make sure you give yourself some time to get to the **station** (☎ 958-271-272). It's located on Avenida de Andaluces, just off Avenida de la Constitucion, and it'll still take you a good 20 minutes to walk to the train depot with luggage.

BY BUS

Even though the hectic station is just out of walking distance from the city center, **Estacion de Autobuses** (Carretera de Jaén s/n; ☎ 958-185-480) is one of the busiest in Andalucia. Granada is a major hub for all the towns in the region and you can reach most any destination via motorcoach. Both Seville and Cordoba are served by about 10 buses daily. Both trips take just over 3 hours and cost no more than 18€. The Costa del Sol route is shorter and cheaper with a 2-hour trip and about a 10€ fare to get to Malaga and the surrounding beach towns.

Granada Basics

The main **tourist office** in Granada can be found at Calle de Santa Ana 4 (☎ 958-225-990). They're open daily, 9am to 7pm Monday through Friday and 10am to 2pm on Sunday.

For general exploring in the city, a decent map from your hotel, hostel, or the tourist office and a good pair of sneakers are all you need to tackle the streets of Granada. Tempting as it may be, don't pay any credence to the large rectangular signs pointing to the main attractions. A few of them bring you through an annoying, circuitous route to your destination. Some, including a few signs to the Alhambra, bring you nowhere near where you want to be. One word of caution: The maps are void of any topographical information. In other words, an innocent-looking path down a tiny road can easily turn into a 15-minute vertical climb up a painfully steep sidewalk.

Recommended Websites

○ **www.andalucia.com** and **www. spain.info**: These two sites are the best places to find any information about the towns in Andalucia and the country.

○ **www.aboutgranada.com**: General info, hotel links, and all sorts of touristy goodies are hyperlinked from this site.

○ **www.granadainfo.com/english. htm**: Similar to About Granada, but also has a cache of random tidbits about the sites and experiences in Granada.

Granada

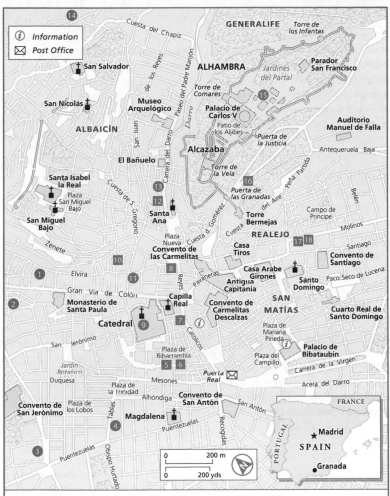

- ⓘ Information
- ✉ Post Office

PARTYING & SIGHTSEEING ●
Alhambra **15**
Aphrodisia **2**
Bohemia Jazz Café **4**
Catedral **9**
El Eshavira **1**
Granada 10 **11**
Sacromonte **14**
Sugarpop **3**
The Upsetter **13**

SLEEPING & EATING ■
Alhambra Cafeteria **6**
Cafeteria/Pasteleria Lopez-Mezquita **7**
Carmen de San Miguel **16**
Heladeria Tiggani **5**
Hotel Molinos **18**
Hotel Zaguan del Darro **12**
La Castaneda **8**
Oasis Backpacker's Hostel **10**
Taberna Lopez Correa **17**

Granada Nuts & Bolts

Currency   Your best bet is to dip down to the major arteries of the city, **Gran Via de Colon, Avenida de la Constitución,** and **Calle Reyes Catolicos,** to find those cash-spitting **ATMs.** If you have other currencies swimming around in your purse or wallet, there are a few currency exchanges on **Gran Via de Colon** and **Avenida de la Constitucion.**

Emergencies   For general emergencies throughout Spain, dial ☎ **112.** Medical emergencies can be addressed by dialing ☎ **091** or ☎ **958-282-000** or calling Granada's **Health Services** (Av. del Sur 11; ☎ **958-027-000**). You can reach the local police at ☎ **092** or 091. The **Red Cross** can be contacted for other emergencies at ☎ **958-222-222.**

Laundromats   For the most part, the hotels and higher quality hostels have laundry facilities or services offered to their guests. Otherwise, you'll be relieved to find that chains, like **PressTo** (www.pressto.com), offer laundry and dry-cleaning outlets throughout the region.

Pharmacies   Like all other cities and towns in Spain, the place to go for strong medicines and ointments is the pharmacy. Along the sidewalks you'll usually find one neon green cross lit up every few blocks. Maybe next time you'll think twice before streaking through a field of poison sumac.

Post Offices   If you need to send stuff out via snail mail, Spain's Correos is what you'll use to ship those packages and postcards: Go to the **post office** at Av. America 55 (☎ **958-133-153**) to stock up on stamps and stuff.

Safety   Again, use common sense when traveling at night and when going into crowded plazas and markets. Keep your belongings in your sight and use extreme caution when approached by strangers. The latter definitely applies when walking around Sacromonte (p. 570) in Granada. The gypsies there are generally harmless, but don't let your guard down if something seems fishy.

Sleeping

➜ **Hotel Molinos** It sounds impossible, but I managed to get lost on the way to the Alhambra, the town's biggest landmark (p. 568). After doubling back multiple times and cursing at the ancient site for having only one entrance, I came upon the Hotel Molinos. Frustrated and tired, the friendly smile behind the desk disarmed me before I should let out a snarl. Amiable staff aside, the hotel is a decent option along the south edge of the Alhambra. It's actually separated into two sections: One is more apartment-like and provides a quieter, more peaceful stay, while the other is in the same building as the reception, more like a true hotel. You'll have no trouble sleeping in the boldly colored rooms, each featuring an A/C and soft beds. The staff also knows a few things as well—after following the receptionist's instructions, I was on the road to the Alhambra within minutes. *Calle Molinos 12.* ☎ *958-227-489 or 958-227-367. www.eel.es/molinos. Double 30€–45€. In room: A/C, TV.*

ANDALUCIA

→**Hotel Zaguán del Darro** ★★★ You might not get much use of the tapas bars right next door. In fact, you might not get much done at all. The rooms, with wrought-iron bed frames supporting soft, ultra cushy mattresses, all have amazing views from the foot of the Alhambra and most feature balconies above the Rio Darro. It's not much of a river but what's above is an awesome perspective of the Granada landmark. If you have enough scratch to cover a night here, you can pretend to be Spanish nobility in this classy hotel on one of Granada's most captivating streets. *Carrera del Darro 23.* ☎ *958-215-730. www.hotelzaguan.com. Single 40€–65€, double 55€–95€. Amenities: Bar, cafeteria. In room: A/C, TV, minibar, some rooms with Jacuzzi.*

📺 **Best ◐** →**Oasis Backpackers' Hostel** ★★★ Thanks to the Oasis Backpackers' Hostel, I almost missed my train. I was laying back on plush pillows, enjoying the unbelievable view of the Granada sunset from the ultrarelaxing terrace and shooting the breeze with an amazing group of travelers when I remembered that the Spanish sun didn't go down until much later at night during the summer. Like many of the hostel's guests, I found it hard to leave. The incredible dinners that the hostel staff puts together and the insanely cool backpackers that call the Oasis their temporary home make it tough. The comfy rooms don't help either, with solid wooden bunks, clean bathrooms, and digital, personal safes for everyone. Nor the laundry service where the staff will clean and fold your dirty duds for 6€. The Internet point, couches in the lobby, kitchen, and dining area, outdoor patio/barbecue, and the hostel bar are only separated from each other late at night, so it's almost impossible not to meet people in this very chill environment. If you don't count the fee for changing the date on your train ticket, the Oasis Backpackers' Hostel is an incredible deal. *Placeta Correo Viejo 3.* ☎ *958-215-848. www.oasisgranada.com. Single bed 15€, double room 36€. Amenities: Internet point, kitchen, laundry service. In room: Safe.*

Eating

Tired? Hungry? Poor? Worry not, weary traveler, Granada's tapas bars won't leave your stomach growling no matter how empty your pockets are. Best of all, you can also get drunk in the process. Just stumble through the door, pay for your pint of ale, and shout for some tapas. Many of the bars here either charge less than a euro or charge nothing at all. Usually, I've found that they bring out the choicest snacks earlier when it's not as busy. If you're hungry for a real meal during the siesta, you're out of luck. Many of the restaurants close during nap time and don't reopen until 8 or 9pm (staying open until 1am or so).

TAPAS

📺 **Best ◐** →**La Castañeda** ★ The only way it can get any more authentic in this place is if you had to swat flies with a slice of ham before they get into your beer. Lucky for us, there aren't any flies in La Castañeda and the only thing you'll swat with their awesome tapas is your taste buds. Bring a few friends, hunker down underneath the cured hams hanging on the walls, shout your order to the surly waiter, and rub your hands in anticipation for the big plates of tapas. It's one of the top joints in town. *Calle Elvira 5.* ☎ *958-226-362. Tapas free with drink. Main courses 6€–9€. Tapas nightly 'til close.*

ANDALUCIA

DOABLE

➜**Taberna López Correa** ANDALUSIAN Just off of Plaza del Realejo, the quaint Taberna López Correa whips up some decent Andalusian plates for an even more decent price. Enjoy the *rabo de toro* (bull tail stew) under old-fashioned iron lamps, and if you're lucky, live musicians will play traditional songs in the background. They've been around for a while (since 1890), so they've definitely nailed the traditional thing down. *Calle Molinos 5.* ☎ *958-222-351. Menu of the day: 8€. Main courses 7€–14€. Daily 'til close.*

SPLURGE

➜**Carmen de San Miguel** ★ SPANISH/ ANDALUSIAN Most diners don't stumble upon this fantastic restaurant given the fact that it's at least 5 minutes removed from any main thoroughfare in Granada. Famished, I was glad to find the Carmen de San Miguel at Plaza Torres Bermejas, a dead-end with a unique view of the Alhambra. The restaurant is only open for the summer, but the mouthwatering vanilla-glazed suckling pig could easily keep the place in business year-round. The good food doesn't exactly come cheap here though, so have your wallet armed the next time you get lost and "stumble upon" Carmen de San Miguel again. *Plaza Torres Bermejas 3.* ☎ *958-226-723. Main course 17€–21€. Open for dinner daily in the summer.*

CAFE

➜**Alhambra Cafeteria** In the evening, it becomes a pizzeria/restaurant, but I love coming here in the morning to enjoy a greasy plate of *churros* and *café con leche*. With the outdoor patio almost always full in the early hours, it seems I'm not the only one. The Alhambra Cafeteria is relatively simple, almost resembling a no-frills Spanish diner inside, but its location in the busy Plaza Bibrambla ensures that there's always a steady flow of hungry, thirsty tourists and locals passing through. *Plaza Bibrambla 27.* ☎ *958-523-929. Morning 'til late.*

➜**Cafeteria/Pasteleria Lopez-Mezquita** When shopping on the charmingly shaded Reyes Católicos, make sure you take a break in this quaint cafe/bakery. Everything, from the glazed mirrors to the old-fashioned glass displays, reeks of the good ol' days when you could buy a coffee and pastry for a few pesetas. Now, a few euros will get you a yummy gourmet Danish. *Reyes Católicos 39.* ☎ *958-221-205. Morning 'til late.*

➜**Heladeria Tiggani** ★ When it comes to sugary treats, few connoisseurs can claim to be as discerning as the Aussie dentist with a giant sweet tooth I met in Granada. Dave somehow knew all the best candy stores and ice cream stands in Granada and pointed me toward Heladeria Tiggani. His rousing endorsement involved an exclamation of, "When they say it's strawberry, *it's frickin' strawberry!*". Sure enough, the cold pink treat was chock full of yummy strawberry fragments swimming in silky ice cream almost as smooth as Florentinian gelato. The other flavors were just as refreshing, with the *straciatella* as a personal favorite. Trust me, when I say Heladeria Tiggani's good, *it's frickin' good*. *Plaza Bib-Rambla 11. No phone. Closed during siesta.*

Partying

Throughout the evening, you never quite know what kind of action is brewing within the small alleyways and streets that snake through the city. Part of Granada's mystique lies in the fact that it feels like a small hill town during the day and a lively medieval city at night. The cobblestone paths might lead you to a secluded and intimate flamenco venue or it may bring you to a dark, smoky hookah bar, a common meeting place in Moorish Spain. In general, if you're hoping to find a bar they're happenin' from 10pm until 1 or 2am, when partiers usually migrate to the dance clubs and discothéques (covers ranging from 5€–15€; try to score a flyer from the many promoters on the streets to get in for free) and do their thing until the early morning hours. Whatever you do, you're sure to come across hordes of smiling locals and an extremely laid-back vibe.

BARS

➔ **Bohemia Jazz Café** ★★ Pay no attention to the gaudy neon Budweiser sign in the corner. While the logo brings up thoughts of watery lager and crushing beer cans on your forehead, the rest of this cafe feels more like your traditional jazz haunt. It's dark, cozy, and full of cool cats. When there isn't a live band kicking around or a performer mashing the piano keys, there's a constant stream of Chet Baker and Louis Armstrong seeping out of the speakers. *Santa Teresa 17. No phone.*

➔ **The Upsetter** ★★ You might be thousands of miles away from the Caribbean, but that doesn't mean there isn't any reggae in Spain. One of the hottest nightspots in Granada just so happens to be this reggae bar/club. The Upsetter is where you'll always find a happy-go-lucky crowd of young Granada locals. While the majority of tunes are of the Toots and The Maytals variety, they change it up every so often to keep it real. *Calle Carrera del Darro 7.* ☎ *958-227-296.*

FLAMENCO

📺 Best ● ➔ **El Eshavira** ★★ Unless you want to stare at a brick column for an hour, you'll want to get here early. No more than 70 people can fit in the main performance area and while it can get uncomfortably crowded, it makes El Eshavira one of the most intimate flamenco venues you'll find anywhere in Andalucia. Three performers squeeze together on the miniscule stage but it hardly restricts them from producing powerful stomping, intricate guitar trills, and passionate singing. Other nights, El Eshavira is home to top-notch jazz concerts. *Calle Postigo de la Cuna 2.* ☎ *958-290-829. Admission around 10€.*

NIGHTCLUBS

➔ **Afrodisia** The folks who thought up Afrodisia must have used the inimitable Pam Grier as some sort of muse when creating this club. Advertised as "black club groove," the discothéque exudes the cool, funky attitude that the '70s icon was known for. The music runs the gamut from reggae to funk and modern hip-hop, but everything that the DJs spins is guaranteed to get those bootays on the dance floor movin' and shakin'. *Calle Almona del Boqueron s/n. No phone. www.afrodisiaclub.com.*

📺 Best ● ➔ **Granada 10** ★★ Those staying at the Oasis Hostel don't have to stray very far to get to Granada's top discothéque. Fifty meters (164 ft.) down the cobblestoned street you'll find the bright lights of Granada 10. The marquee and old-fashioned light bulbs outlining the sign hint at the club's double identity. By day, obscure Spanish movies are usually shown on the screens—but Granada 10 is most exciting by night. You'll always find a flock of gorgeous 20-somethings inside, sipping cocktails and cutting up the rug to Spanish house and trance. I'm sure if the sultans of the city were still around, those horny rulers and their harems would be here on a nightly basis. *Carcel Baja 10.* ☎ *958-224-001. www.granada10.com.*

ANDALUCIA

Cabo de Gata

If you thought the small beach spots in Nerja with a dozen other sunbathers were secluded, then you probably haven't made the trip out to Almería yet. There, just underneath the looming peaks of the Sierra Nevada, lies the protected land known simply as 📺 Best ● **Cabo de Gata.** It may be its remote location on the southeastern edge of Andalucia, but many tourists overlook the region completely and pass by it on their way to Barcelona. Don't make the same mistake. Cabo de Gata is by far one of the best and most unique ecological gems in Western Europe. Sitting on a bed of volcanic rock, the lush coastal environment has become the home of thousands of species of flora and fauna. If you couldn't care less about endangered shellfish or different strains of ferns, then the park's **beaches** are reason alone to visit. The miles of white, sandy shore, sometimes surrounded by impressive cliffs, are rife with extremely secluded coves. It's quite possible that you'll be the only sunbather on the pristine beach for miles. And Mother Nature hasn't forgotten about the adrenaline junkies. They can choose from intense **mountain-biking** trails, **kayaking** adventures, **scuba diving** and **deep-sea photography**—just some of the activities found in Cabo de Gata.

The main visitor center, **Los Amoladeras** (☎ 950-160-435; July 1–Sept 30 daily 10am–2pm and 5–9pm, Oct 1–June 30 daily 10am–3pm), can be found at kilometer 7 on highway ALP-202. Get all the information about the entire park, its activities, and the services provided within. Entrance to the park is limited only to pedestrians. Several surrounding villages, such as those near San Jose and Las Negras all have paths leading to the heart of Cabo de Gata. Simply follow the signs leading to the trails and you'll soon be in paradise.

➔**Sugarpop** ★ It's easy to confuse the chaos inside with your run-of-the-mill rave, though you don't need to be tripping on anything to have a great time at Sugarpop. The intense and excellent electronica pouring out of the speakers is enough to keep the clubbers going until the early morning hours. Once the other clubs and bars shut down for the night, the castaways with energy to burn migrate to Calle Gran Capitán to stretch their weekends out as far as they can. On other days, Sugarpop becomes a much tamer, but just as popular, live music venue for all kinds of bands and artists. *Calle Gran Capitán 25.*

Sightseeing

📺 Best ● ➔**Alhambra** ★★★ Before it became the pimpest palace in all of Spain, the massive complex overlooking Granada was used to keep the nasty, bad guys from sacking the city. As the threat of invaders waned, Moorish big-wigs thought the prime chunk of real estate would be better used as their modest home and quickly booked their interior designers. The following centuries saw a succession of powerful sultans and rulers who left the Alhambra more luxurious and extravagant than they had found it. Today, it's considered one of the wonders of the world, right between the Pyramids of Giza and JLo's rump. Slightly smaller than the latter, the Alhambra is visited by thousands each week. Yes, I said week. It's because of that fact that reserving a ticket beforehand might be prudent. You can try your luck, and probably succeed too, at coming in during the two half-hour periods in the

ANDALUCIA

Las Alpujarras

In 1492, the Moors were purged from Granada. It doesn't have the same ring as "Columbus sailed the ocean blue," but it's an often overlooked fact in Andalusian history. Back then, as Isabella and Ferdinand gloriously came through Granada's gates, thousands of Moors were forced to flee from the city. Most ended up in what is now known as **Las Alpujarras,** a region nestled in the majestic Sierra Nevada mountains initially populated by Berber farmers. Nowadays, thanks in part to the Christians' decision to simply take over the homes that the Moors and Berbers once inhabited, the original Berber architecture has been preserved throughout the tiny towns in the Alpujarras.

Anyone even remotely interested in **hiking, nature,** or **scenic landscapes** should really consider a day trip from Granada. Tourist offices in the city offer maps and information about walking and hiking paths that snake through the verdant valleys and lush gorges that cut through the Sierra Nevada—a stark contrast to the beige, dry scenes of the rest of Andalucia. Journeying through Las Alpujarras, be sure to try their *jamon Serrano,* a specialty that's only made possible by the conditions found in the high grounds and dry air of the mountains. It's just over 50km (31 miles) southwest of Granada, so you'll have to start your day early if you plan on tackling some of the longer hiking trails. All things considered, seeing the snowy Sierra Nevada mountains from the breathtaking valleys will quickly make you forget that you had to roll out of bed at the buttcrack of dawn.

day (call for exact times) where they release another 1,000 or so tickets to those in line at the entrance but save yourself the disappointment by reserving. When you receive your ticket, make note of the time allotted for the Palacios Nazaries—they give you a particular half-hour period when you can enter; miss your half-hour time frame and you won't be able to gain admittance at all. To find the main entrance of the Alhambra, you can take the bus or a taxi, but it's a doable, though steep, climb up Cuesta de Gomérez to the front gate, Puerta de las Granadas. From there, it's another 15-minute hike to the actual complex. You don't actually need a ticket to walk around the main grounds, but you pay for entrance to the separate attractions: Generalife, Palacio Nazaries (Palace of the Nasrids), Alcazaba, and Palacio de Carlos V. You'll want to devote at least an entire afternoon to taking in all the sights in the Alhambra. The luxurious and intricately detailed Patio de los Leonares and the insane landscaping in the gardens of Generalife (the sultan's swanky summer home) are only a couple places that you shouldn't miss—plus the paintings found in the Museo de Bellas Artes, the imposing and impressive Alcazaba (the fortress used to guard Granada), and the residence of the Roman ruler Charles V, who apparently was too good to live in the sultan's old digs. The Alhambra is also open at night when floodlights give the complex a distinctly unique and dreamlike aura. *Palacio de Carlos V (entrance on Cuesta de Gomérez). ☎ 958-220-912. Admission Alhambra and Generalife 10€; Museo Bellas Artes 1.50€; Museo de la Alhambra 1.50€; illuminated visits 6.75€. Mar–Oct daily 9am–7:45pm and 10pm–midnight (for illuminated visit); Nov–Feb daily 9am–5:45pm and 8–10pm (for illuminated visit).*

➔**Catedral** Just when you thought you had your fill of cathedrals in Spain, Andalucia throws another gem at you in Granada. Luckily, it doesn't cost very much to check out the sparkling white marble ceilings and columns. Don't miss the Capilla Real, or Royal Chapel. Take your time though since the two most famous personalities in the chapel aren't going anywhere anytime soon: Queen Isabella and hubby Ferdinand chose Granada as their final resting spot and can be found resting in the Capilla Real. *Gran Vía de Colón 5.* ☎ *958-222-959. Admission 3€ for cathedral, 3€ for chapel. Mon–Sat 10:45am–1:30pm and 4–8pm; Sun 4–8pm.*

FREE ➔**Sacromonte** ★ When real estate in Granada started to get expensive and scarce, these crafty gypsies didn't bother checking out Craigslist. No, they did the next best thing: They settled in the hollowed out caves in the hills of Granada. Located to the north of Albaycin, the hills of Sacromonte quickly became a unique (and heavily visited) neighborhood. Tourists make the hike up just to peer into the strange, yet extremely intriguing accommodations and some of the gypsies take full advantage of this fact by trying to sell you all sorts of trinkets. In the evening, you'll hear about "cave parties" and "authentic cave flamenco," but more often than not they'll end up being a disappointing gathering of the region's youth. Stick to the city proper for the nightlife. *Northeast of Albaicín neighborhood.*

Ronda

Erosion can lead to some funny looking things like **fjords** that resemble genitalia or it can create some unbelievably breathtaking sights. One example of the latter lies just west of Málaga. The town of Ronda is essentially the result of millions of years of the **Guadalevín River** slicing and separating the land that it now sits on. Its unique geography was the reason that the now legendary group of Spanish bandits, or **bandoleros,** sought refuge in the surrounding mountains. They've long been removed, but the mystique of a romantic and dangerous past still lingers in Ronda. A vicious **ravine** cuts across the town separating the old part from the new and forcing some inhabitants to settle in homes built precariously on the edge. The sight most associated with Ronda, however, is not the ravine but the awesome structure that dares to cross it, the **Puente Nuevo.** Impressive by the sheer impossibility of its construction, the bridge not only connects Ronda's citizens, but it gives them an immense sense of pride.

Getting There & Around
BY TRAIN

Options are limited when it comes to using the Andalusian rail system to get to Ronda. However, it's the best way to get there since it's much quicker than weaving through the surrounding highways on a coach. From Granada, there are three trains that make the 2½-hour journey to Ronda. If you're coming in from the south, only one train departs daily from Málaga. The **train station** (Av. Andalucia s/n; ☎ 952-871-673) in Ronda is at the northern edge of town and it's roughly a 15-minute walk to the bridge from there.

BY BUS

Only a few doors down from the train station, Ronda's **bus depot** (Pl. Concepción García Redondo; ☎ 952-187-061) is usually a much busier hub. Coaches rumble in and out shuttling travelers between towns all over Andalucia. Several bus companies serve Ronda's bus station and most have their daily schedules hanging above their ticket windows. The major destinations that you can reach by bus from Ronda include Seville, Málaga, and Marbella.

BY BICYCLE

While a little dangerous in the narrow streets of the old part of Ronda, exploring the town and surrounding region on bicycle is a great option. **Jesus Rosado** on Plaza del Ahorro 1 (☎ **952-870-221;** www.bicicletasjesusrosado.com) rents out bicycles at a decent rate of 2.50€ per hour or 10€ each day (18€ for two, 21€ for three). It's open 10am to 2pm and 5 to 8:30pm Monday to Friday and 10am to 2pm on Saturdays. For Sunday rentals, call ☎ **637-457-756** for special arrangements.

Ronda Basics

Unlike navigating through the madly confusing streets of other Andalusian cities, it's easy to find your way around Ronda, even without a map. The **old town** is quite small and the streets in the newer half form a familiar grid pattern. If you're ever lost in the old part, you only have to locate the main road of **Armiñán.** Almost all of the side streets originate from the street and once you find it, you can follow it all the way to the **Puente Nuevo** and jump over to the other side of town. On the north side, you'll find yourself walking up and down two primary streets: **Carrera Espinel,** the main shopping thoroughfare (void of any motor vehicles), and **Virgen de la Paz** on the westernmost edge of Ronda. The latter continues where Armiñán left off on the bridge and also runs alongside the bullring.

For general information, brochures on local attractions, and area maps you can find the **tourist office** (☎ **952-187-119;** www.turismoderonda.es) near the bullring at Paseo de Blas Infante s/n.

Ronda **Nuts & Bolts**

Currency   They might be a little harder to find in the old part (and will likely have a slightly higher fee), but you won't have a problem tracking down an **ATM** anywhere in the new part. On **Calle Espinel** and **Virgen de la Paz,** machines dot every block or two.

Emergencies   For general emergencies throughout Spain, dial ☎ **112.** For health emergencies, call ☎ **061.** To get in touch with the police you can use one of three numbers: ☎ **091,** ☎ **952-871-370** for the National Police, and ☎ **952-871-461** for the Guardia Civil.

Laundromats   The chain of dry cleaners/laundromats, **PressTo,** has an outlet at Calle Mariano Soubirón 17 (☎ **952-879-177**). Call for rates and hours.

Pharmacies   Compared to other cities, there aren't nearly as many pharmacies in Ronda. Still, you'll find a few illuminated green crosses on the major streets. They usually close well before the sun goes down, so refill your prescription earlier in the day.

Post Offices   Head to the office of Spain's **Correos** at Virgen de la Paz 20 (☎ 952-872-557) for all your mailing needs.

Safety   Just because the *bandoleros* are long gone doesn't mean you should let your guard down in this town. Crime, rare as it is, does occur in Ronda and clueless tourists are a target. Use your common sense and only travel in well lit areas in the wee hours.

Sleeping

→**Hotel Don Miguel** ★★ Talk about a room with a view. Just like its restaurant (p. 573), the Hotel Don Miguel gives a select group of guests amazing panoramas of the gorge below. If you do get a chance to pry your eyes off the window, you'll see that the rooms are comfortably homey. With an excellent restaurant below, fantastic views from some of the guest rooms, and simple, yet plush, furnishings, spending an extra 30 or 40 euros for a night is worth the upgrade. *Plaza de España 4.* ☎ *952-877-722. www.dmiguel.com. Double 85€. Amenities: Restaurant, bar, lounge. In room: A/C, TV, safe (in some).*

→**Hotel Morales** ★ The only negative thing about this awesomely affordable hotel, as the family next door unfortunately learned the hard way when my TV was blasting *Beverly Hills Cop,* is that the walls aren't exactly soundproof. Eddie Murphy in *español* aside, the rooms themselves are immaculate (though the mattresses are kind of stiff), the bathroom sparkles, and the friendly folks at the desk are always happy to tend to their guests' needs. The location is perfect too with the Hotel Morales a 10-minute walk southwest from to the train station or 10 minutes northwest from to the bridge. *Calle Sevilla 51.* ☎ *952-187-002. Single 32€, double 42€. Amenities: Internet point, lounge. In room: A/C, TV.*

Eating

CHEAP

→**Restaurant Hermanos Macias** SPANISH Perhaps it's the affordable prices, its central location, or the fact that it's part of the adjacent hotel, but there's always a tourist to be found somewhere in the Restaurant Hermanos Macias. You might have to look harder with the inordinate number of empty tables (it doesn't seem wildly popular, even in the busy dinner hours) but it really doesn't matter who decides to eat here. Everyone loves an inexpensive meal, especially ones that are actually pretty tasty. The mixed salad and grilled chicken dish with potatoes (under 10€ altogether) isn't bad at all. To my dismay, instead of Fanta naranja they had the vastly inferior Kas. Thankfully, the cheap prices make the soda-pop blasphemy easier to swallow. *Calle Pedro Romero 3.* ☎ *952-874-238. Main courses 5€–9€. Daily 8am–midnight.*

→**Vesubio** ★ PIZZA/ITALIAN In the small towns of Andalucia, it's almost impossible to find good pizza joints, take out places, and self-serve laundromats. On Calle Sevilla you'll find two out of three under one roof. While a laundromat-pizzeria would be genius (wash those tomato sauce stains on-site!), Vesubio is a small, homey eatery that whips up awesome, though non-traditional, pizzas and other Italian dishes with the option of taking them all to go. The Vesubio pizza, in particular, overflows with an incredible combination of

wwwired

Of all the Internet spots in Ronda, the best one, without a doubt, is on Calle Sevilla. The others are uncomfortably hot, sketchy, or both. Thankfully, the five computers in **Informatica Virtual System** (C. Sevilla 43; ☎ **952-870-158**) sit in an air-conditioned room and are connected to a fast provider. They're open Monday to Friday 9:30am to 2pm and 5 to 8:30pm, Saturday 10:30am to 2pm.

ham, bacon, salami, egg, and *cebolla*. The egg, done over easy and slapped on the middle of the pie, erupts once you poke the yolk and gives the whole pizza a uniquely tasty flavor. While the joint stays relatively dormant during the day, it trembles with activity after 9pm with families and other locals. Unlike my volcano references, you won't get sick of the different pizzas in Vesubio. *Calle Sevilla 24. ☎ 952-190-398. Main courses 5.50€–12€. No credit cards. Daily 1–4pm and 8:45–11:30pm (until midnight on Sat).*

DOABLE

→**Los Candiles** SPANISH In the evenings, Plaza de Socorro gets incredibly busy with locals winding down after a long day of work and children playing games in front of the church. It all makes for a lively backdrop to a dinner at Los Candiles. Every conceivable pork dish can be had here for an awfully decent price. *Plaza de Socorro 7. ☎ 952-876-864. Main course 6€–16€. Daily for lunch and dinner (until 12:30am).*

MTV Best ☺ →**Restaurant Don Miguel** ★★ ANDALUSIAN If you're not careful here, your dish could fall victim to gravity or a ravenous bird. Either is worth the risk

when you sit down at one of the outdoor tables at Restaurant Don Miguel. The multi-level terrace teeters over the northeast edge of the canyon, affording patrons an unparalleled view while they dine on savory dishes like breast of duck in a port and prune sauce or the traditional oxtail stew. Once you've finished admiring the bridge make sure you weigh those euro bills down with your plate. I'm sure a ton of imprudent tourists have made a few pigeons either very rich or very constipated. *Calle Villanueva 4 and 8. ☎ 952-871-090. www.dmiguel.com. Main courses 9€–16€. Open for breakfast, lunch, and dinner (closes at midnight, later on weekends).*

Partying

People come to Ronda for the sights, not the nightlife. Unfortunately, there's a dearth of quality clubs and bars even in the newer part of town. Most are gimmicky and not a whole lot of fun. But if you want to grab a few drinks with some friends, there is one place worth checking out in the old part of town.

→**El Choque Ideal** ★ The bright orange furniture seems a bit too modern and too colorful to be in the historic part of Ronda, but it surprisingly fits in with the surroundings. El Choque Ideal is a funky, yet demure, cafe and bar where happy patrons can enjoy a game of pool, chat with friends, or just admire the awesome views of the surrounding valley. Stop by for a quick break in the afternoon when a few hardy souls are sure to be knocking back a few glasses of beer or later in the night when it picks up. It never gets really packed, but that's part of the reason why El Choque Ideal is a great place to hit up if you want to just lay back and chill. *Espiritu Santo 9. ☎ 952-161-918. www.elchoqueideal.com.*

A Hop, Skip & a Click Away

While you were jostling for position on the bridge, channeling your inner Naomi Campbell, and throwing elbows to get that perfect shot of the valley, you might have noticed that one small home on the southwest side of the ravine and the narrow path leading to it. You'll definitely want to be wearing good sneakers or hiking boots, but that path leads to perhaps the best photo opportunity in the entire region. The starting point is near Calle Tenorio and Casa de Don Bosco. Locate the little plaza with the fountain in the middle and look for the staircase to the south. Follow this down until the wide stairs are replaced by a somewhat treacherous and rocky, dirt path. Pass the home that you saw from the bridge, with the Korean flag waving and the ominous sign advertising panoramic photos "gratuit," continuing on for another 10 minutes until the path completely disappears. At that point, you'll be presented with an awesome view from the foot of Puente Nuevo. Snap a few photos and rest before the tiring walk back up. The area is sometimes frequented by young couples looking for a secluded make-out spot, as I accidentally found out when I inadvertently hit a pair of lovebirds with my discarded apple core, so don't worry when you hear rustling in the bushes nearby.

Sightseeing

→ **Baños Arabes** Tempting as it may be in the warm Ronda summers, disrobing in public to cool off will probably draw a few odd stares and the ire of local police. Back in the day though, it was completely acceptable. Although it was within the walls of the Arab Baths and it was done so that they could sweat more, not less. Almost every city and town in the Muslim/Moorish-influenced south had one of these establishments where people could "purify" their bodies. Unfortunately, not much remains of the ancient building, but enough exists to paint a decent picture of what things might have seemed like hundreds of years ago. In what's left of the "hot room" is a small makeshift cinema where a video in Spanish plays a CGI documentary about the baths. You may not understand much of it and the cartoony people in loincloths might make you chuckle, but it's entertaining and informative nevertheless. *Calle San Miguel s/n.*

☎ 677-545-715. *Admission 2€ adults, 1€ students. Winter Mon–Fri 10am–6pm, Sat–Sun 10am–3pm; summer Mon–Fri 10am–7pm, Sat–Sun 10am–3pm.*

→ **Centro Interpretación del Puente Nuevo (Interpretation Center of the New Bridge)** Once you've repeatedly crossed the bridge, shot it to death with your camera, and admired the views from it, it's time to go inside. Yup, you might have guessed from the windows on the sides, but you can explore the innards of the amazing structure. The entrance and ticket counter to the Interpretation Center is at the staircase on the southwest corner of the bridge. Although it's made up of only two relatively small rooms, the fee required to gain passage to the inside is worth all 2€. The displays outlining the design, construction, and evolution of the structure and a few original construction implements from the original 18th-century building are surprisingly interesting. Even if that doesn't appeal to you, checking out

Smokey (the Bear) & the Bandit

The tiny Interpretation Center of the New Bridge and the Museo Taurino are two museums definitely worth visiting while you're in Ronda. Here are two that are worth visiting if you either own a gun rack or stole one.

Unless you really like antique guns or reading about the history of *bandoleros* in every language *but* English, you'll want to report the *bandolero* that took your 3€ at the front desk to the Guardia Civil. Yes, long ago the Guardia Civil purged the mountains around Ronda of the sneaky bandits hiding out and avoiding capture, but many have been immortalized in this small museum, the **Museo del Bandolero.** Glass displays contain everything related to *bandoleros* from antique pistols to old, yellowed documents with ransom amounts scrawled across the top, to comic books of the late 1900s glorifying the thieves. You can cruise through this place in about 15 minutes, but if you're not really keen on checking out dressed up dummies and rusty rifles you can just breeze right by the entrance. *Calle Arminan 65.* ☎ *952-877-785. www.museobandolero.com. Admission 3€. Daily 10:30am–8pm.*

The "deer in the headlights" expression on their faces is priceless. While there are actual stuffed deer inside with looks on their mugs that might have been induced by a headlight or a shotgun barrel, I'm talking about the faces of tourists leaving this "museum." Like me, they were a tad stunned by the collection of stuffed carcasses on display at the **Museo de Caza** (aka the **Hunting Museum**). There are animals big and small, cute and ferocious but all are dead as a doornail. If all this gets you excited, you'll love the hunting store at the end. Buy your loved one or yourself a souvenir skinning knife. Me, I'd probably use it to gouge my eyes out afterwards. *Calle Arminán 59.* ☎ *952-877-862. Admission 1.50€. Daily 11am–6:30pm.*

the somewhat constricted passageway and rooms will give you a healthy respect for what went into building the enormous thing. *Puente Nuevo (Pl. España).* ☎ *620-340-148. Admission 2€. Mon–Fri 10am–6pm (until 7pm in spring/summer); Sat–Sun and holidays 10am–3pm.*

➔ **Palacio de Mondragón/Museo de la Ciudad** An important figure during the reign of Charles III used to call this place home. Visitors can check out just how good Mondragón had it in this opulent building with eye-catching Mudéjar influences in the courtyards and towers. After you've admired the gorgeous features of the place, including the extraordinary wooden ceilings of the Nobility Hall, you can learn a few things in the museum

inside. There you'll find displays and exhibits that chronicle the city's rich history. *Plaza de Mondragón s/n.* ☎ *952-878-450. Admission 2€. Mon–Fri 10am–6pm (until 7pm in spring/summer); Sat–Sun and holidays 10am–3pm.*

MTV Best ➔**Plaza El Toros de Ronda/Museo Taurino** ★★ The best way to experience the bullring is to go on off-hours (during lunch or right when it opens) and explore the actual ring when it's empty. Not only will you get some incredible photos, but there's an oddly surreal feeling when there's not a soul in sight. If you come with friends, you can have your own mock bullfight in the oldest bullring in Spain. Adjacent to the ring is a small museum, but you'll want to wait until the large tour groups leave before you dive in. It's not big by any means, but there are some interesting photos and old matador outfits that are worth investigating. You'll find quite a bit of memorabilia and information about one of the greatest bullfighters in Spanish history, Ronda-born Pedro Romero. *Virgen de la Paz 15.* ☎ *952-871-539. www.rmcr.org. Admission 5€. Nov–Feb daily 10am–6pm; Apr–Sept daily 10am–8pm; Mar and Oct daily 10am–7pm.*

Shopping

While there aren't many standout stores in Ronda, throughout the main shopping thoroughfare of **Carrera Espinel,** there's roughly one **shoe shop** every few yards. Sorry fellas, while the ladies will love the endless opportunities to window-shop, not many boutiques offer the latest in men's couture. You're better off exploring the **old town,** where you can pick up a few **souvenirs** and interesting **crafts** from the smaller stalls sprinkled around the streets.

Tarifa

I'll be blunt: Tarifa is windy. Ridiculously windy. It should be awfully apparent long before you even get to the city limits of Tarifa that you're going to be in for a string of bad hair days when you see the giant, mechanical forests of white windmills spinning ever so slowly in the distance, or when your bus gently swerves out of the firm control of your trusty driver. Even the trees outside of your window seem permanently bent at the trunk in a penitent position. It's no wonder that the blustery town has become an internationally renowned windsurfing and 🎬 Best ◐ **kite-surfing hot spot.** You only have to walk a few meters from the bus drop-off to realize the magnitude of the two sports' popularity with no less than four kite-surfing schools on each block. Throw in hundreds of surf shops, a carefree, hippie community to boot, and insane nightly street parties, and you're left with a town brimming with energetic pleasure-seekers and adrenaline junkies. Pack up your surfboard, some industrial strength hair gel, and get ready for a few crazy days of gusty gusto.

Getting There

BY FERRY

Once you've finished your weeklong bender in Morocco (p. 579) and managed to pry that hookah out of your hands, it's time to head back to Spain. Several ferry companies offer the hour-long trip from Tangiers to Tarifa with **FRS** (☎ **956-681-830;** www.frs.es) being one of the more reputable and popular names. The ferry leaves from Estación Maritima on the southeastern part of town. Consider bringing some Dramamine—it's one hell of a choppy ride.

BY BUS

Aside from renting a car, the only way to get to Tarifa is by bus. Given this fact, you'd think the town would have a decent bus station with a waiting area, multiple bus ports, and a line of ticket windows. What they have instead is a small white trailer alongside an even smaller roundabout on the corner of Calle Mar de Norte. **Transportes Generales** (☎ **902-199-208;** tgcomes.es), one of the main bus companies in Andalucia, frequently stops

Cuidado! Wind Advisory

Don't give in to temptation by buying a kite-surfing board. They're a pain to check-in on the plane and you'll look pretty stupid trying to catch a breeze in the calmer beaches in the States. What you might want to invest in however is a pair of sunglasses. You'll need to protect your eyes not only from the UV rays, but from the sadistic gusts of wind that kick up all sorts of nasty things. Take it from me, it's not fun walking around the last few weeks of your trip with a swollen eye. I unfortunately tried to brave the elements after buying some groceries and since my hands were holding two plastic bags, I couldn't protect my eyes from a small rock that somehow got airborne. If I had even a cheap pair of shades, it probably wouldn't have been able to cut the inside of my eyelid. Chicks dig scars—unfortunately only the ones they can see.

here from various locations. You can buy tickets from the clerk inside, but you'll have to settle for the curb as an uncomfortable cement waiting room while you try to determine if the incoming bus is yours or not. Its not the best setup in the world and it can get a little unsettling when it's not clear if your bus is late or if you simply just missed the sign on the bus window. Tarifa is one of the intermediate stops on the line going from Malaga to Cádiz (with stops made in Costa del Sol, La Linea de Concepcion, and the other beach towns) and vice versa, so to get to other destinations in Andalucia you'll probably have to go to either city first and leave from there.

Getting Around

With the **buses** running rather infrequently, you'll find yourself using the taxis in Tarifa quite a bit if you're crashing in one of the campgrounds and hostels outside of the city and want to party it up late at night in the city. A **taxi ride** from Puerta Jerez to the campgrounds a few kilometers away should never cost more than 10€. Even after several rounds of toasts with your new Tarifa pals, when you can't walk in a straight line or see how many fingers they're holding up, it's easy to spot the

shiny white cabs cruising around the main streets of Tarifa.

Tarifa Basics

Tarifa is so tiny that you could probably get around just fine without the help of a map—not to mention a strong gust is all it takes for your newly purchased map to go airborne. Brutal weather conditions aside, the ancient city walls to the east and the water to the south and west conveniently section off the *casco antiguo*, or historical area of Tarifa. So before you get terribly lost, you'll likely hit a 600-year-old stone slab or you'll end up smack up against the Mediterranean. Even if you have to backtrack numerous times, the town is small enough that you can explore its streets pretty thoroughly in an afternoon. You might want to explore the area outside of the walls, but the only thing worth visiting out there is the **Plaza de Toros,** which is a decent bullring by Andalusian and Spanish standards.

Recommended Website

○ **www.tarifa.costasur.com/en**: In addition to your run-of-the-mill tourist info, hotel links, and transportation details, the site also has some really useful tidbits about kite-surfing in Tarifa and where to get lessons or board rentals.

ANDALUCIA

Tarifa Nuts & Bolts

Currency   **ATMs** are mainly concentrated in the center of Casco Antiguo, around Calle San Francisco and the busy plazas.

Emergencies   For general emergencies throughout Spain, dial ☎ 112. To get in touch with the hospital, call ☎ 956-020-770. The police will help you if you've been a victim of a crime or if you want to report something. Call them at ☎ 092 or ☎ 062 (for Guardia Civil). Unique to Tarifa is surf rescue. If something happens to you or your buddy while you're out on the rough waters, the Maritime Rescue team (☎ 900-202-202) will respond to such emergencies when called upon.

Laundromats   For the most part, the hotels and higher quality hostels have laundry facilities or services offered to their guests. Otherwise, you'll be relieved to find that chains, like PressTo (www.pressto.com), offer laundry and dry-cleaning outlets here, as throughout the region.

Pharmacies   Like all other cities and towns in Spain, the place to go for strong medicines and ointments is the pharmacy. Along the sidewalks you'll usually find one neon green cross lit up every few blocks. You can stock up here on seasick medication for your upcoming trip to Morocco or maybe for some Pepto-Bismol-like stuff in case you come across some iffy food while you're over there.

Post Offices   For all your postal needs in Tarifa, head to the Correos office at Coronel Moscardo 9 (☎ 956-684-237).

Safety   Tarifa, especially around Casco Antiguo, is an incredibly safe place. If you do find that you're missing a few euro bills from your bag, it's more likely that the wind blew them away than anything else. Don't let your guard down, though, since small crimes like pickpocketing happen everywhere in Spain.

Sleeping

📺 Best 🌙 →**El Beaterio** ★★★ If it weren't for the small group of travelers waiting outside the building with piles of luggage, you'd never guess that the door, hidden by a jungle of leaves, leads to the incredible and perfectly located *hosteria* in Plaza del Angel. When you get to reception on the top level, guests are greeted by an old, crazy (in a very good way) woman flashing the warmest smile possibly. Say hello to Carmen. The lovely lady and her husband Verna run this amazing *hosteria*, treating all their guests as if they were extended family just visiting in Tarifa. If only all our aunts and uncles had homes like El Beaterio. Verna spent years converting the 16th-century monastery into a collection of spacious apartments with separate dining rooms, kitchens, and bedrooms. No two apartments are alike and they range in size from a single to a room for eight. Each is furnished with antique pieces from countries like Morocco and Germany and the walls are decorated with art made by previous guests. In the balconies overlooking the lobby, the art (of the crayon variety) is done by the couple's cute kids. When she's not charming guests with her incredibly quirky laugh, Carmen loves to make things that help people's health (like dentures) and their soul (like

2 Continents + 16 Hours = 1 Seasick Traveler

For many, a venture to Africa requires enough vaccinations and needles to make anyone feel like Iggy Pop, with a veiny and drugged out forearm taking a more psychedelic sort of trip. Forgo all the poking and puncturing by taking a day trip to **Tangiers,** one of North Africa's biggest tourist draws. You can easily spend the morning kite-surfing in Spain and waste the afternoon away smoking *shisha* in **Morocco.** It almost sounds too good to be true, but thanks to a few ferry companies it's perfectly feasible. Quite a number of ships shuttle back and forth across the Straight of Gibraltar from Morocco to three cities along Costa del Sol and Costa de la Luz: **Algeciras, Gibraltar,** and **Tarifa.** While Gibraltar might seem like the best choice, they have the most limited number of ferries leaving its ports for Morocco and it takes about 30 minutes longer than the one in Tarifa. The sleek jet-boat of **FRS** (Estación Marítima; ☎ **956-681-830;** www. frs.es; 1-day tour 56€, one-way ticket either direction 29€) is almost as fast as it looks. As advertised on the brochures and on the ship itself, the trip is supposed to take 35 minutes to reach North Africa. Unfortunately, it hardly ever cracks 40 minutes. For about an hour, the boat traverses the extremely choppy waters of the straight and docks in the busy port city of Tangier. It's highly recommended to take the company's 1-day tour of the city if you only plan on spending 12 hours in Morocco. Not only is it a decent value, but they'll bring you to places in the city that you'd either never reach by walking or to areas where you're sure to get lost. You'll also feel a lot more comfortable eating lunch in a recommended restaurant where you don't have to worry about those digestive nightmares you hear from everyone else coming back from Morocco. Two important pieces of advice: Bring **Dramamine** even if you never get seasick (the waters can get *extremely* rough), and make sure you get your **passport and documentation** stamped before you get off the boat and then again before you get back on. If you're interested in staying longer in Morocco, you can take off on your own once you arrive in Tangier. Just use caution when eating and exploring the crowded, narrow alleyways. Ladies, it's *highly* advisable to travel in pairs or groups. Never travel alone while going from city to city in Morocco.

beaded jewelry). After a few nights at El Beaterio, you'll realize that her hospitality and personality probably do a better job than even the beads or wooden teeth. *Plaza del Ángel 2.* ☎ *956-680-924 or 629-592-716. www.tarifa.net/beaterio. Single 35€, double 57€–77€. Amenities: Laundry, parking. In room: A/C, TV, fridge.*

→ **Misiana** The eye-candy in the tiny reception is indeed shiny, although lacking a bit of personality. Unfortunately, I'm not talking about the modern decorations. Instead the semi-inept folks behind the front desk have just enough brain cells and skill to match the name on your passport to the reservations on their calendar. Once you've gotten past Tweedle-dum and Tweedle-duh, Misiana is really a spiffy little hotel that seems a bit out of place in laid-back Tarifa. The guest rooms make it feel more like a loungey club with plush beds and attractive furnishings thrown in than a regular ol' hotel. If you want to visit an actual loungey club, you don't need to stray far from your ultracolorful room in Misiana—a cafe/restaurant/bar on the first floor (not directly accessible from the hotel) is just as stylish as the hotel. *Calle San Joaquin 2. ☎ 950-627-083. www.misiana. com. Double 75€. Amenities: Bar/restaurant.*

→**OTB Backpacker's Hostel** The OTB, likened to a Neverland for beach bums, is where hordes of ruddy, chiseled men and women come to roll out of bed at noon, splash around the Mediterranean until the sun goes down, and booze in the hostel bar until the sun pokes back up. Those divas who have a need to be pampered on holiday will likely suffer here while easygoing, low-maintenance travelers might have too much fun. OTB also has a bit of an identity crisis. It's half hostel and half kite-surfing school (lessons available), resulting in a bohemian getaway where caution, as well as responsibility, is thrown to the Tarifa wind. You'll see this manifested in things like their half-assed hostel BBQ's where you pay 6€ and they give you a plastic plate of raw meat to throw on the grill yourself. Need a shower? Hop into one of the outdoor shower stalls next to the folks still passed out in their open-air bungalows (little straw huts that sit on stilts with a mattress thrown in) from last night's bender. You'll likely wake them up with a hearty yelp when you find out that the outdoor showers only pump out cold water. The one indoor bathroom sometimes spits out lukewarm water, but it's a crapshoot. Falling asleep might be a problem for some: With the hostel's bar being extremely popular with outsiders, the stereo is costantly barraging the rooms' walls with massive bass. If that wasn't enough, the Tarifa wind can wreak havoc with the hall doors, forcing you to use your supreme MacGyver

skills to find a way to silence the slamming in complete darkness. Wind isn't the only thing that can mess with the doors. When you checked in, you probably thought that they just forgot to give you a set of keys. Actually, there are no locks anywhere in the place. The only thing that keeps it remotely secure is the hostel's location. It's just off the highway, almost in the middle of nowhere, a full kilometer from Tarifa. Getting there isn't too much of a hassle for guests though—a tiny, tanned Italian pixie in a shoddy minivan makes regular pick-ups from the bus station for free from 11am until 8pm. *Carretera Nacional 340 Km 81. ☎ 661-030-446. otb-tarifa@hotmail. com. Single bed 16€. Amenities: Bar, Internet point, shuttle service.*

Eating

→**Bar/Restaurante Morilla** SPANISH/ ANDALUSIAN   Call it shabby chic. Call it authentically rustic. Either way, the chipped tables and chairs under the breezy ceiling fan of the Restaurant Morilla are a fitting setting for the cheap, tasty, no-frills dishes on its menu. Locals come here in the morning to sip their *café con leche,* read their morning paper on the sidewalk terrace, and enjoy the view of the aging Iglesia San Mateo. Or they come during the lunch hour to scarf down a plate of the *pez espada a la plancha,* a well-prepared grilled swordfish steak, in the confines of the homey dining room. *Calle Sancho IV El Bravo 2. ☎ 956-681-757. Main course 5€– 14€. Daily 9am–late.*

→**Café Central** ★ CAFE   As good as they are, one cannot live on *churros* alone. That's why a place like Café Central is quite a find in Spain. In addition to the deep-fried delights, breakfasts also feature comfort foods that can temporarily soothe some cases of homesickness: bacon and eggs, omelets, and fresh-squeezed orange juice. Typical diner fare is served for lunch and dinner, but carnivores will especially love the various pork sirloins, beef filets, and steaks. *Calle Sancho El Bravo 10.* ☎ *956-680-590. Main courses 2€–13€. Breakfast, lunch, and dinner til close.*

→**Inti** MODERN SPANISH/INTERNATIONAL If the winds have caused you to drift south along the water, hop into one of the seaside eateries to wait until the gusts subside. Many of them, like the modern and trendy Inti, are excellent spots to try out the extremely fresh seafood that Tarifa provides. Definitely worth a try is the succulent grilled red tuna, prepared to perfection by the able chefs on staff. If you're strapped for cash, you can opt for the much more affordable spaghetti with sage and cherry tomatoes for just under 7€. *Calle Alcalde Juan Nunez L-8. Main courses 6€–18€. Kitchen daily 10am–11pm, main dining area open until late.*

Partying

For kite surfers, life doesn't get much better than on Tarifa's blustery beaches. The same goes for partiers within Tarifa's old city walls. The tiny area is filled with even smaller streets and alleyways that, by day, are usually lifeless and empty. Once night falls however, the quaint pathways begin to pulsate with life as the huge 20-something population wakes from its siesta and starts to roam the streets with a new supply of energy. At their disposal is the best collection of hip cafes and trendy bars possibly in all of Andalucia. All of them ooze the breezy, laid-back feel of the surfing community but are just as chic as the watering holes of SoHo, the Haight, or Barcelona. Many locals hop from bar to bar or cafe to cafe, but most spill out from the small

establishments onto the cobblestones. Every weekend in the summer one enormous block party swallows the entire town in a whirlwind of drinking and dancing.

BARS

MTV **Best ♀** →**Almedina** ★★★ If I'm ever in Tarifa, you'll probably find me here—either kicking back in the morning with my coffee and toast or later with a beer in hand, listening to some awesome tunes. You have to climb a few sets of stairs until the entrance pokes out on a landing halfway up, but it's worth the trip. The staff is incredibly friendly and chill, the dark orange walls are rife with kitschy art (the dartboard is a definite plus, as is the fantastic and funky iron light fixture in the back room), and the appropriate CDs are always in rotation (AIR in the morning, Toots and the Maytals in the afternoon). Every Thursday features live flamenco performances while various reggae and jazz acts come other nights for informal concerts. Take a quick glance above while you're ordering a drink at the bar—the gray stone arch that sticks out of its otherwise orange surroundings is actually a historical landmark: La Puerta del Castillo or La Entrada al Mundo Árabe. In other words, it was the original 15th-century gate to the city. It's a hard place to dislike: kickass ambience, live music, and some culture to boot. *Calle Almedina 3. No phone.*

→**Soul Café** You'll probably walk right by it a few times during the day, but the normally unassuming black wooden gate to Soul Café only opens up to throngs of clubbers at night. Before they head to the raucous La Ruina next door, they start the night off by kicking back in this chill lounge and taking in some excellent house and R&B. It's one of the hottest nightspots in Tarifa and it's also one of the most unpretentious. *Santisima Trinidad 9. No phone.*

NIGHTCLUB

📺 Best ☻ ➜ **Tanakas** ★★ Ask anyone in Tarifa where the best discothéque is and they'll usually bring up Tanakas whether they actually go there or not. For the past few years, the club has gained a ton of popularity with locals for its always excellent house/dance music. Almost everyone, young and old, in Tarifa shows up at Tanakas at some point in the weekend. During the day, it doubles as a cinema and an exhibition space. *Plaza San Hiscio s/n.* ☎ *956-680-327.*

Shopping

➜ **Tarifa Records** As a local music label, Tarifa Records distributes discs chock full of the whirring beats and shiny melodies that are synonymous with Euro-trance and electronica. Not surprisingly, many DJs come to this little outlet on Calle Jerez for the latest CDs that the label produces. If electronica isn't your cup of tea, choose from several funk, chill, and ambient discs as well as T-shirts with the label's logo. Grab a couple of compilations here, pop

wwwired

One of the better **Internet spots** is located just across from Café Central on Calle Sancho El Bravo s/n. The little **gift shop** has about a dozen relatively old, yet fast, terminals where you can **check your e-mail.** Their doors are open daily from 10am until 8pm for your surfing pleasure.

them in iTunes back home, and turn up the volume to relive those Tarifa nights with head-pounding trance and trip-hop tunes. *Calle Jerez 18b.* ☎ *956-680-340. www.tarifa records.com.es. No credit cards.*

➜ **Zas** Wander Tarifa for only 5 minutes and you'll probably come across half a dozen jewelry and souvenir shacks. For some reason, the necklaces in the tiny Zas and it's secluded location in a small alleyway caught my eye. Not one for draping things around my neck, I ended up buying a few for friends and myself. You can also get ethnic garb like shawls and shiny tops or you can stick to the selection of simple, cheap, and often eye-catching jewelry. *Calle Lorito 1.* ☎ *956-680-255. www.robapinzas.com.*

📺 Best ☻ Cadiz

Cadiz isn't your typical southern Spanish coastal town. Instead of the warm waters of the Mediterranean crashing on its shores, it's the more aggressive waves of the Atlantic that beach-goers dive into. Rather than rolling hills, you'll hit water walking in almost any direction since the city is essentially a small peninsula jutting out into the ocean. Even the demographic is unique. Thanks to an exchange program called Erasmus and a large, respectable university in the center of town, the streets are filled with young, energetic students

from all around the world and plenty of bars and restaurants that pander to these resident 20-somethings. Altogether, the picturesque seaside promenades, the energetic college kids, and an awesome laidback vibe create a unique Spanish paradise on the Costa de la Luz.

Getting There

BY TRAIN

If you really wanted to, you could take the bus from the cities to the north. However, you'd probably be much more comfortable using the rail system. All trains arrive in the **station** (☎ 902-240-202) located on Avenida del Puerto, adjacent to the ports of Cadiz. Cadiz is connected to Andalusian towns and cities like Jerez de la Frontera, Seville, and Cordoba by no less than a dozen trains that run that route. The trip from Cadiz to Cordoba takes about 3 hours, to Seville about 2 hours, and to nearby Jerez about 45 minutes. In reality, Jerez is served by quite a few more trains by Renfe's Cercanías system. The pseudo-public transportation system carries passengers to outlying towns for a small fare. Jerez just so happens to be connected to the Cercanías system of Cadiz with trains leaving roughly every 15 minutes throughout the day.

BY BUS

Unless you're traveling from the North, you'll likely arrive in Cadiz via motor coach. As with most cities in Andalucia and Costa del Sol, the main means of getting around is by bus. **Transportes Generales** (☎ 902-199-208; tgcomes.es) is the primary carrier, bringing several buses daily from eastern destinations like Tarifa, La Linea de Concepcion, and Malaga. The **main station** (Pl. de la Hispanidad 1; ☎ 956-227-811), located near Plaza de Espana, is roughly a 15- to 20-minute walk to Cadiz's train station. Close to a dozen buses from Seville arrive here as well, after a 2-hour drive. Buses from Madrid are run by **Secorbus** (☎ 956-257-415) and drop/pick-up passengers at Avenida José León de Carranza (N-20).

Getting Around

Public buses (1€) come in handy when you need to get to the bus or train station in a hurry and on the cheap. Although you won't find them very useful for getting around the heart of the city as most stick to the wider streets that surround the old part and cut through the newer section of Cadiz.

Cadiz Basics

The main **tourist office** (☎ 956-258-646) in Cadiz is located on Av. Ramón de la Carranza s/n. It's open 9am to 7pm Monday through Friday and 10am to 1:30pm on Saturdays.

The only way to really explore Cadiz is by walking. Never mind the fact that the **old town** of Cadiz is tiny. The gorgeous **seaside promenades** that outline the edges of the peninsula not only provide unforgettable views of the Atlantic Ocean and the Bay of Cadiz, but they're also populated with amazing gardens and parks. **Parque Genovés** and **Alameda Apodaca** are just two of the unique green spaces that contain intricately painted park benches, ancient trees, and relaxing fountains. Farther inland, the city is pretty easy to navigate. If you stay a couple of days, you'll figure out the primary arteries, **Calle Sacramento, Calle San Francisco,** and **Calle Sagasta,** as well as the landmark plazas, **Plaza de Mina, Plaza de Espana, Plaza San Juan de Dios,** and **Plaza San Francisco,** and you'll rarely have to pull out the map.

However, the minute you reach **Plaza de la Constitucion,** you'll see the scene change dramatically—this wide plaza is where Old Cadiz meets New Cadiz. Continuing to the south, Cadiz becomes a narrow strip of land full of commercial areas and more modern bars, clubs, and restaurants.

RECOMMENDED WEBSITE

⊙ **www.sol.com/cadiz**: Ooooh, a site full of all sorts of practical info! Get hotel details, write-ups on what's happening in the city, and other goodies from this useful website.

ANDALUCIA

cadiz Nuts & Bolts

Currency While **ATMs** are plentiful in Cadiz, you have your pick of the litter if you head to Avenida Ramón de Carranza. Some are usually out of service or vandalized to the point of not functioning, but you'll still have a dozen or so to choose from with every conceivable bank in Spain represented by a cash machine.

Emergencies The **local police** can be reached at ☎ 956-228-106 and the **Guardia Civil** ☎ 956-262-400. To get in touch with the **local hospital,** call ☎ 956-242-100.

Laundromats If your hostel doesn't have laundry facilities, you'll be relieved to find that **PressTo** (www.pressto.com) offers laundry and dry-cleaning outlets throughout the region.

Pharmacies You'll usually find one neon green cross lit up every few blocks along the sidewalks in Cadiz, as elsewhere in Spain.

Post Offices Locate the **El Corte Ingles** (☎ 956-253-498) on Avenida Cortes de Cadiz and you'll find a branch of Spain's **Correos,** or postal service. Stock up on postcard stamps or send home a parcel of your stuff to lighten your pack.

Safety Again, use common sense when traveling at night and when going into crowded plazas and markets. Keep your belongings in your sight and use extreme caution when approached by strangers. Pickpockets still exist and have gotten creative when it comes to distracting tourists. Be alert.

Sleeping

HOSTEL

➜ **Casa Caracol** Snail House. That's the translation though I'm still not quite sure why it's called that. Perhaps it hints at the extremely laid-back vibe and easy going pace of its guests. This startlingly Anglophone (many American Erasmus students work here) hostel is dangerously close to being called a hippie haven, especially with the cliquey feel that some guests (particularly those traveling solo) might come across and the outdoor hammocks on the roof that many people love. It could also point to the speed at which things travel through its plumbing. Although the bathrooms are usually clean, the lead pipes haven't been changed since the building was erected. What does this mean to you? Signs next to the john direct guests to not flush *any* toilet paper. It's also recommended to brush your teeth with bottled water. Rooms, on the other hand, fare slightly better. Rickety metal bunks have pillows that are as big and thick as a marble notebook. Sheets are oftentimes holey, but always clean. The biggest drawback is that all the dorms and rooms are never closed off from the balconies looking over the common room below. If you want to crash a little earlier than usual, you'll have to battle the idle chatter and intermittent guitar performances that come from below. It doesn't sound like an ideal place for a fledgling backpacker, but if you have absolutely no agenda while you're in Cadiz and you're an extremely laid-back, nocturnal person, chances are you'll have a blast. *Calle Suárez de Salazar 4.* ☎ *956-261-166. www.caracol casa.com. Single bed 17€. Amenities: Internet point, kitchen.*

CHEAP

→**Hostal San Francisco** Finding last-minute accommodations anywhere can be a royal pain and with the lack of youth hostels in town, you'd think it would be impossible in Cadiz. Though thanks to Hostal San Francisco's strange reservation policies, several rooms are available almost every night. Situated on the lovely Calle San Francisco, the hostel is smack dab in a commercial street, with a grocery right around the corner, little boutiques just down the block, and people always milling about. In contrast to the elegant *hospederia* across Calle San Francisco, the rooms at San Francisco are very modest, but reasonably comfortable. While air-conditioning is nowhere to be found, they do provide oscillating fans. Double-jointed backpackers and yoga instructors shouldn't have much of a problem with the clean, yet miniscule, bathrooms. Bath space aside, the hostel is a steal considering the price and comfort relative to location. *Calle San Francisco 12.* ☎ *956-221-842. Single 24€, double 49€. Amenities: TV.*

→**Hotel Puertatierra** Outside of the old town you'll find finer beaches, glitzier bars and clubs, and shinier hotels. One such hotel, the Puertatierra gives off the impression of being glamorous, but everything inside is a bit of a let down. Rooms look like they've robbed a Sheraton of all its furniture, and the service is shaky at best. Even if you're the only one at the reception, the staff behind the desk run around as if they're taking care of a dozen guests at a time. Brochures proudly boast having a tennis court, but I don't think I've seen that much crack since the plumber came over to fix my leaky sink; neglect has turned the court into a rundown patch of cement. Pitfalls aside, it's a decent hotel that offers reasonably priced rooms while just pretending to be swanky. *Av. Andalucia*

34. ☎ *956-272-111. www.hotelesmonte.com. Double 55€-100€. Amenities: Restaurant, bar, laundry service, tennis court. In room: A/C, TV, hair dryer, minibar, safe.*

SPLURGE

→**Hospederia Las Cortes** ★★★ When a hotel is brazen enough to forgo room numbers and to arrange their elevator buttons in a dizzying, asymmetrical pattern, you know you'll need to pony up some extra cash for all that cleverness. Despite the novel twists, Hospederia Las Cortes is a traditional luxury hotel at heart. The muted yellow walls, marble floors, and old-world accents make guests feel like they're being pampered in a 19th-century town house. As expected, each guest room is incredibly plush and unique. The name of some famous Spaniard or landmark is used for identifying which room is which (remember, no room numbers) and also sets the theme for the decor. Of the 36 rooms, you can choose from people like Francisco Isturis or of Cadizian structures like the Arco de la Rosa. *Calle San Francisco 9.* ☎ *956-220-489. Single 90€-105€, double 115€-130€. Amenities: Restaurant, bar, gym, mini-spa, rooftop sun terrace, room service. In room: A/C, TV, minibar.*

Eating
CHEAP

→**Avegades** SPANISH The faux marble may seem cheesy and cheap, but it actually fits the feel of this restaurant, an unpretentious eatery where the staff is laid-back and the menu is stocked with fish and meat dishes. If the prices weren't reasonable enough, most dishes are offered in half and full rations so you can save some money or some room for a hefty dessert later. Those with a couple extra euros should give the fresh monkfish filet baked with scallops and prawns and doused with manzanilla wine a whirl. *Calle Rosario (Marques de Valdeíñigo).*

☎ *956-265-788. www.avegades.com. Main courses (full rations) 7.50€–13€. Daily 10am–1am.*

SPLURGE

➔ **10 Veedor** MODERN SPANISH/SPANISH FUSION The decor is easy on the eyes, the octopus however isn't as attractive. Thankfully though, the dish more than compensates for its aesthetic shortcomings with its incredible flavor and taste. The *pulpo a la gallega* is just one of the excellent seafood dishes that the slick 10 Veedor offers. The usual pork offerings also grace the menu, but the restaurant's strength lies in what comes straight from the Atlantic Ocean. You don't have to sit down to a full meal to sample some of their food either. Sidle up to the bar and order from the tapas menu that includes yummy treats like empanadas. *Calle Veedor 10.* ☎ *956-225-222. Main courses 9€–17€. Daily 1–5pm and 8:30pm–12:30am.*

CAFES

➔ **Café/Bar El Terraza** ★★ While everyone was gazing at the gorgeous cathedral, my eyes were fixed on the Ben & Jerry's across the way. But the instant the waiters at Café El Terraza placed the aromatic seafood in front of my gaping maw, I forgot all about that Vermontian ice cream. El Terraza has been around for decades and it's no surprise why. The fish here is awesomely fresh and always prepared perfectly. The Mediterranean menu features savory dishes of dogfish and coated dory sinfully fried for your taste buds. A meal here is a fantastic precursor for that Cherry Garcia that awaits a few yards away. *Plaza de la Catedral de Cadiz.* ☎ *956-282-605. Main courses 8€–18€. Daily 11am–late.*

➔ **Cafeteria Chamara** What better place to start your day than Calle Ancha. Come down to Cafeteria Chamara for your morning caffeine fix and watch the lively and

picturesque pedestrian street buzz with early-bird activity. Students dart through crowds to get to classes, businesspeople leaf through the morning paper, and stores prepare their displays for the day ahead. Chamara sits in the middle of all this, serving potent cups of coffee and basic cafe fare. Try to score one of the few outdoor tables for the best people-watching perch on the whole block. *Calle Ancha 9.* ☎ *956-214-102. Daily 8am–late.*

➔ **Heladeria Artesanal Italiana** ★ I like to think of it as a *"botellón* for babies." Every summer evening, Plaza de Mina becomes overrun with little, hyper *niños* and *niñas* riding high on their sugar highs while their parents try to chase them around. Cádiz seems to have an inordinate number of candy stores, a few of which can be found not far from Plaza de Mina, but the main sugar supply comes from the little Heladeria Artesanal Italiana—hands down the best ice cream in Cádiz. It's impossible to choose the wrong flavor since every single one is incredibly rich and sweet. As evidenced by the smears of vanilla and chocolate on the little faces running and screaming around the plaza, Heladeria Artesanla Italiana is tops in Cadiz. *Plaza de Mina 15.* ☎ *956-212-880. No credit cards.*

Partying

While the summer nights get pretty rowdy, things really pick up when the students migrate back after break. In the fall and winter, everyone ditches the clubs and bars in the new part of Cadiz (extremely popular in the hotter months) and retreats to the awesome dives and lounges found within the older town center. To kick things off, most go to the town *botellón* for a warm-up. In the winter, the plaza of choice for the public event is Plaza de San Francisco. It's too small for the larger summer crowds though, so everyone tends to head to the beaches and plazas in the new town. Afterward, they plunder on to the clubs and bars near Playa de la Victoria in the summer, and the ones near Plaza de San Francisco in the winter.

BAR

MTV **Best ●** ➜ **Medussa** ★★★ If I had a choice, I'd definitely be an Erasmus student. Not only does it sound a whole lot cooler than "Rhodes Scholar" but I'd be kicking back in sunny Costa de la Luz rather than chilly old England. And I'd be able to hang out at Medussa nearly every day. The small bar near Plaza San Francisco is an indie and alt-crowd heaven for the students and locals of Cadiz. Each night, Medussa shows off her fantastic taste in music while doling out beers on the cheap. And I mean cheap. Come here Wednesday nights when—until 2am Thursday morning—the bar charges 1€ a bottle. During the weekends, DJs like RTF and Batusi bombard patrons' eardrums with every conceivable strain of rock from punk to shoegazer to '90s alternative. Tuesdays are when they show video concerts such as Morrissey's *Live in Manchester*, PJ Harvey's *Please Leave Quietly*, or Bowie's *Reality Tour*, the perfect way to unwind from a hectic day of classes or sightseeing. I'm filling out my Erasmus application as we speak. *Calle Beato Diego 10 (Manuel Rances). No phone. pubmedussa@ono.com.*

NIGHTCLUBS

➜ **Barabass** ★★ It doesn't really matter if you can't dance. Instead of bobbing your head in some dark corner, come to the über-popular Barabass a little earlier than usual to get a few pointers. Well, actually 92 hours earlier. Every Tuesday, the club holds free classes on merengue, cha-cha, and all sorts of salsa. Dudes will dig the female-to-male ratio as they learn some essential moves, but they might not be able to show off their new hip-swivels and spins that upcoming Friday night—the joint tends to stick to house and pop to get people on the dance floor. *Calle Muñoz Arenillas 4/6.* ☎ *956-079-026. www.barabass cadiz.com.*

➜ **Nahu** ★ This popular student haunt combines the African-themed art and patterns with a swanky lounge feel. You only have to stop by on Wednesdays to see why the kiddies love it. That's when Erasmus students guzzle down super cheap 1€ beers. Affordable booze aside, it's also extremely popular for the chill atmosphere and the awesome percussive beats coming from the speakers. *Calle Beato Diego de Cadiz 6.* ☎ *956-070-922. www.nahucadiz. com.*

Sightseeing

➜ **Casa del Obispo** Ambience is everything, and in the case of this converted palace, you might forget you're in an archaeology museum while you listen to Enya-esque chanting pouring out of the speakers overhead. Loosely translated as the Bishop's House, it was once home to said big guy back in the 16th century. Now, it's a permanent archaeological dig where disorienting glass walkways and stairs snake through the entire complex, allowing visitors to view the unearthed remnants of the building's 8th-century-B.C. past. Those with poor depth perception and balance just might get a closer than expected view of the ruins. *Plaza Fray Félix s/n.* ☎ *956-264-734. www.lacasadelobispo. com. Admission 4€ adults, 6€ combination ticket with Catedral. June 15–Sept 15 daily 10am–8pm; Sept 16–June 14 daily 10am–6pm. Closed Dec 25, Jan 1, and Jan 6.*

➜**Catedral/Torre de Poniente** Thanks to the narrow tunnel-like streets of Cadiz, you may not see the cathedral's golden dome and baroque/neoclassical architecture until you actually reach the busy plaza just in front of the 19th-century structure. It may look quite a bit older, but the city's cathedral was only completed in 1838. It was built from the riches found in the New World, but the most visited and photographed site is the tomb of legendary Spanish composer Manuel de Falla who was laid to rest here in the mid-1900s. Others come for the impressive view supplied by the adjacent tower, definitely worth the climb up the cramped winding ramp. Once visitors reach the top behind the giant bells hanging idly in the tower, they'll be treated to an incredible panorama of the city's mess of red roofs and white-washed buildings. *Plaza Catedral.* ☎ *956-286-154. Admission 4€ adults, 6€ combo ticket with Casa del Obispo. June 15–Sept 15 daily 10am–8pm; Sept 16–June 14 daily 10am–6pm.*

➜**Museo de Cadiz** Phoenicians, paintings, and puppets. I could be wrong, but I don't think many other museums in the world can boast all three. Part archaeology exhibit, part art gallery, and part disturbing puppet display, Museo de Cadiz is an attraction that's sure to have *something* to intrigue all carbon-based visitors. You'll find the usual pottery shards and artifacts encased in glass. However, the giant stone sarcophagi relaxing under a few spotlights will surely get your attention. Ditto the two big names proudly presented by the museum: Miró and Zurbarán. The latter is a permanent part of the museum, with numerous religious panels and canvases created by the Spanish master. Miró's exhibit, though a temporary one, takes up the main atrium and his works span the lengths of the walls on the ground floor. The floors above feature pieces from other European artists. Finally, there's the puppets. Oh, the creepy puppets. The museum has preserved the wooden likenesses and hung them either by themselves or in front of actual sets from puppet shows in the past. Most will retreat from Chuckie's ancestors to the Zurbaráns after a few minutes of horrified gaping. *Plaza de Mina s/n.* ☎ *956-212-281. www.juntadeandalucia. es/cultura. Admission 1.50€, free for students and on Sun. Tues 2:30–8:30pm, Wed–Sat 9am–8:30pm; Sun and holidays 9am–2:30pm. Closed Mon.*

➜**Oratorio de la Santa Cueva** ★ Oratorio de la Santa Cueva features two chapels, one downstairs (La Pasion) and one upstairs (the Holy Sacrament). If I were you, I wouldn't even bother going to the basement. Truth be told, it's a pretty creepy place. Walking through the dark, dim, rundown pews I was ready for Linda Blair to come out head spinning and bile spewing. Scamper up to the other chapel for the oratory's main tourist draw: the Goyas. It's almost impossible to fix your eyes on one particular feature, but the three Goya panels (the biggies depicting the feeding of the 5,000, the royal banquet, and the last supper) should stand out among the rest of the beautiful pieces. They're located just between the marble columns. For this chapel alone, you have to visit the Oratory of Santa Cueva—the power of MTV compels you! *Calle Rosario 10a.* ☎ *956-222-262. Admission 2€. Tues–Fri 10am–1pm and 5–8pm; Sat–Sun 10am–1pm. Closed Mon and holidays.*

→**Torre de Tavira** Citizens of Cadiz were once a particularly paranoid bunch. Back in the day, as many as 160 towers were erected to look over the harbor and make sure that all was well on the Costa de la Luz. Torre de Tavira now provides one of the best vantage points, with one cool trick up its sleeve to set it apart from the Torre de Poniente's spire: Inside, you'll find a camera obscura, a series of mirrors and periscopes that essentially condenses the panoramas surrounding the tower, allowing viewers to see the living and breathing city of Cadiz in its entirety. *Calle Marques del Real Tesoro 10.* ☎ *956-212-910. www.torretavira.com. Admission 3.50€ adults, 2.80€ students. Oct–May daily 10am–6pm; June–Sept daily 10am–8pm. Closed Dec 25 and Jan 1.*

Shopping

→**La Casa Sana** The great thing about college kids is that when they're not out pounding cans of Bud, they're probably recycling them. La Casa Sana is one of the haunts of the earth-friendly university kids. The little *tienda de productos ecológicos* sells products that are organic, made from recycled materials, and/or biodegradable—everything from fresh fruit and vegetables, to wines, candy, soaps, cleaning products, sunscreen, and even a few toys. The charming cashier welcomes everyone with a warm smile, a small and pleasant reward for helping save the planet. *Calle Veedor 12.* ☎ *856-070-559. casasanacadiz@hotmail.com. Closed Sun.*

🎵 Best● Jerez de la Frontera

Good things come in barrels. Like monkeys. And gallons of potent sherry. Jerez de la Frontera can thank Albariza soil for the awesome alcohol. If it weren't for the chalky dirt, the town would be nothing more than an inconvenient stop on the train from Cadiz to Seville. Instead, the juicy grapes that grow in the fertile soil have given Jerez de la Frontera immense renown as a sherry powerhouse. Truth be told though, sherry isn't exactly what you'll find kicking around college campuses. Jerez draws mostly large crowds of middle-aged and retired folks to its *bodegas,* or sherry factories. While sherry swillin' hasn't quite caught on with the co-eds, by your fourth bodega, you'll probably be showing your new octogenarian buddy the merits of sherry-shotgunning.

Getting There

BY AIR

For a small town, it's surprising that visitors can fly directly into its airport (☎ **956-150-000**) located 11km (7 miles) from Jerez. Yet, flights to and from other Spanish cities are available at this small hub. Iberia (☎ **902-400-500**; www.iberia.com), the primary carrier that flies to Jerez, connects the sherry town to places such as Barcelona, Zaragoza, and Madrid (four daily).

BY TRAIN

Coming in from Seville, the sight of the Harvey's bodega to the right of the train is the perfect introduction to Jerez. About a dozen trains leave Santa Justa Station and take roughly an hour and a half to get to Jerez's **train station** at Plaza de la Estación (☎ **902-240-202**) for around 6€. If you want to come straight from Madrid, the high-speed trains will get you to Jerez in about 4¹/₂ hours.

BY BUS

There are plenty of upsides to taking the bus to Jerez. Not only can you get there from more cities, but the location of the

ANDALUCIA

bus station (C. Cartuja; ☎ 956-345-207) won't require a 15-minute walk to the center of town. Around seven buses connect Jerez to Seviile and more than 15 from Cadiz.

Jerez de la Frontera Basics

Get your bearings and find those bodegas by snagging a map from the **tourist office** at Paul s/n (Edificio Senitium; ☎ 956-359-450; www.webjuarez.com). They're open 9:30am to 2:30pm and 4:30 to 6:30pm Monday through Friday and 9:30am to 3:30pm on Saturdays and Sundays. Jerez is a pretty small town. You can visit most of the popular **bodegas** without having to take the bus, but it's highly advisable to call in advance to get more detailed directions. The **buses** within Jerez run like clockwork and can be a great boon to travelers who are going a little further out.

RECOMMENDED WEBSITES

○ **www.jerez.org** and **www.turismo jerez.com**: Read up on bodegas, transportation info, hotel info, and all things Jerez before you come here. Both sites have a glut of information that'll prove useful while you're in town.

Jerez **Nuts & Bolts**

Currency Even if the sherry's affected your sense of direction, you'll have no problems locating a **cash machine.** They're everywhere in the town center, but much rarer when you venture to the farther bodegas. Hopefully you can still remember your PIN after the fourth tasting.

Emergencies For general emergencies throughout Spain, dial ☎ 112.

Post Offices Head to the **Correos** at Cerron 2 (☎ 956-326-733) to ship those heavy bottles of sherry and brandy.

Safety The sleepy town of Jerez, despite its size and laid-back atmosphere, still sees a fair share of petty crime. Use your head and you won't fall victim to a pickpocket or mugger.

Sleeping

Since there's nothing much else to do in Jerez than bodega-hop and sip sherry or brandy, you'll spend more time than usual crashing on your bed to sober up and regain your strength. Thankfully most of the budget hotels in town feature siesta-friendly beds and time-killers like TVs and Internet.

➔ **Hotel Avila** ★★ Given that there are no youth hostels whatsoever in Jerez, Hotel Avila is the best choice for backpackers and travelers on a budget. Though not spacious by any means, the small rooms contain simple beds and furnishings perfect for a cozy and restful night. Exhausted travelers who have been on the road for a while will especially like the hot water and high pressure provided by the showers, a rare find in cheap hotels anywhere in Spain. While the decor in the room isn't notable, the reception and the lounge have an extra bit of character, like the hookah-turned-vase and the antique operator's panel near the elevator. But you'll find the bulk of the hotel's charm in its staff. In the morning, while the extremely gracious and bespectacled man at the desk whips up a simple breakfast of tostadas, *café con leche,* and orange juice for a few extra euros, you can practice your linguistic skills—the friendly dude speaks French, Spanish, German, and English. *Calle Avila 3.* ☎ *956-334-808. www.hotelavilaonline.com. Single 35€–45€, double 55€–74€. Amenities: Cafeteria, Internet point, laundry service, lounge, parking nearby. In room: A/C, TV.*

➜**Hotel Joma** Maybe it was the receptionist's uncanny resemblance to John Turturro or it might have been the cigarette stench in the elevator, but I felt a little uneasy checking into Hotel Joma. While at first the beds weren't half bad, a functional TV hung above the bed, and the bathrooms were surprisingly tidy. Unfortunately, the decor in the entire building was disappointing. The bed sheets looked like they were cut from the same exact cloth as the curtains (which cover huge, shuttered windows that were near impossible to open), a shabby mirror was the only adornment on the walls, and the reception felt more fitting in an old vaudeville than in a contemporary hotel. For the price however, you can't really complain. *Calle Medina 28.* ☎ *956-349-689 or 956-322-811. www.hoteljoma.com. Single 36€–70€. Double 57€–96€. In room: TV, hair dryer.*

Eating

➜**Meson El Cabildo** SPANISH After a few bodega visits, the deep-fried johndory fish here can help sop up all the excess sherry swimming around your stomach. Although this little restaurant rarely gets full, locals and families frequent Meson El Cabildo for the hearty, seafood-laden lunch. Grab a seat next to them under the antique streetlamps hanging overhead and admire the different sherry labels framed on the wall while you wait for your order. Though your liver might not agree, it'll get you excited for the next bodega sampling. *San Dionisio 2.* ☎ *956-322-735. Main courses 4€–9€. Half portions offered. Daily 11am–5pm and 8pm–midnight.*

➜**Parilla La Pampa** STEAK/ARGENTINIAN They may share the same ocean, but Spain and Argentina have awfully different culinary tendencies. Parilla La Pampa lets you determine exactly how different by being one of the few Argentinian restaurants in the region. It's a venerable oasis of beef among the pork-heavy kitchens of Andalucia. The cowhides hanging on the wall and the barnlike wooden ceilings help prepare you for the succulent Argentine beef imported from across the Atlantic. Not sure whether to get the butterfly steak or sirloin? Try the beef filet with the blue cheese sauce instead. It's an extremely rich meal that should have you patting your belly before you can even finish the whole thing. The sight of ostrich loin on the menu will probably intrigue adventurous diners but the price might dissuade the tight-fisted from trying the bird (18€). *Calle Guadalete 24.* ☎ *956-341-749. Main courses 8.75€–20€. Mon–Sat 12:30–4:30pm and 8:30pm–midnight. Closed Sun.*

Partying

Unfortunately, a night out in Jerez feels more like a rowdy bingo night at a nursing home. I admit, this is a bit of an exaggeration but the tourist demographic shies away from MTV and leans more toward AARP. There is, thankfully, one nightspot where you won't exactly be ogling octogenarians all evening long.

➜**Jaipur** The majority of Jaipur's patrons are 30-somethings who want to forget

ANDALUCIA

about their long day in the office. Every so often, you'll come across a university student who's just tagging along with older friends but the bar is a pretty swanky spot no matter what the age of the crowd. An East Asian theme prevails throughout the entire space with dark woods accentuated with strategically placed lights and spiritual icons thrown here and there. If you're traveling in a group, it's a sweet place to sip cocktails and listen to rather chill music. Otherwise, pony up next to Richie Rich and see if you can score some free drinks. *Calle José Cádiz Salvatierra 4.* ☎ 956-331-569.

Sightseeing

In all, there are dozens of 📺 ⬤Best⬤ **bodegas** sprinkled around Jerez. After a while, and especially after several tastings, each bodega starts to feel exactly the same as the one before. It doesn't take a genius to realize that all the tours and tastings are part of an efficient and, at times, elaborate marketing ploy. Thankfully, it gives sightseers an excuse to be three sheets to the wind by three in the afternoon. The general plan of attack by these liquor companies goes like this: Tourist A forks over some dough for the entrance fee; tourist A watches a slickly produced promo video; guides show tourist A around the grounds; tourist A drinks more than they can handle in the tasting; tourist B brings tourist A to next bodega. Lather, rinse, and repeat. A fair share of bodegas, however, regulate exactly how much each guest can taste. Others keep bringing bottles out. Thankfully, while some require a small hike along the outlying highways, the majority are centrally located inside the town limits. Two of the most popular ones, **Domecq** (C. San Ildefonso 3; ☎ **956-151-500;** admission 7€) and **Gonzalez/Byass** (Manuel María González 12; ☎ **956-357-016;** admission

Hot to Trot in Andalucia

Every May, the strong smells of bitter sherry in Jerez is replaced by the pleasant aroma of horse poop. **Feria del Caballo** is a celebration involving parades of mounted men and equestrian exhibitions of the Carujana horse that's native to the area. The procession of men in black suits and white frills on their chest occurs annually to the delight of locals and sightseers in the region. If you miss the festival, you can still witness the majestic cousins of the Spanish horse in the **Escuela Andaluza del Arte Ecuestre,** Andalusian School of Equestrian Art (Av. Duque de Abrantes s/n; ☎ **956-319-635;** www. realescuela.org). The Dancing Horses of Jerez put on excellent displays that combine storytelling and equestrian performances. Tickets range from 17€ to 23€.

9€, 14€ with tapas) are only a few minutes from each other. The latter claims to be the largest distributor of sherry in the world and their act sure seems like it. To start the tour off, guests are brought aboard a Disney-esque choo-choo train and shuttled from site to site. The cheesy sheen lasts throughout the tour, from the makeshift theater in the warehouse to the gigantic circus tent where the tasting occurs. Small bottles are distributed to each table, ensuring sobriety for all paying customers. Domecq, owners of the famed Harvey's (and their legendary Bristol Cream), puts together a much more interesting and inebriating tour of its beautiful complex. After an informative video, guides bring you through the warehouses and gorgeous garden, explain the entire method of aging, and then leave you alone in their tasting room where you can imbibe sherry and brandy to your heart's content (and liver's demise).

Shopping

[MTV] (Best ●) → **Mala Musica** ★★★ Cádiz's loss is Jerez's gain. While the name couldn't be any more deceiving, Mala Musica has quite possibly the best selection in any CD store in southern Spain. Alvaro used to run two stores, one in Cadiz and one in Jerez, but for some strange reason the one in student-laden Cadiz didn't prosper. After shutting down that store, he put all his time and effort into the Jerez branch. The result is a music store with incredible albums from indie rock, electronica, and jazz. Aside from the new releases, the bulk of the discs are grouped into separate price groups. You won't find many worthwhile albums in the 3€ racks, but the 6€ rack is sprinkled with names like Idlewild, Stiff Little Fingers, and Bjork. Older releases by more obscure groups like Black Box Recorder, Clem Snide, and Blonde Redhead can have price tags ranging from 13€ to 16€. Alvaro is also a venerable source to get a heads up on upcoming concerts in the area—which should only help to enrich your nightlife when in town. *Calle Medina 10.* ☎ *956-325-543.*

ANDALUCIA

Costa del Sol

by Andre Legaspi

Costa del Sombra, or Coast of Shade, wouldn't sound like much of summer get-away. The Brits would surely agree and this is possibly why they, along with multitudes of Germans and Scandinavians, scurry over to the more alluring Costa del Sol on the southern shores of Spain. With the refreshing, clear waters of the Mediterranean Sea licking the heels of the country, life's always a beach on . . . well, the beaches of the Coast of Sun. Unlike the scorching inland cities of Seville and Cordoba, temperatures are significantly cooler and the occasional breeze brings much needed relief to sunbathers and surfers.

Not more than 60km (37 miles) from each other, the beach towns of Costa del Sol are so inundated with visitors from other parts of the European Union that it's easy to forget that you're right smack in the bottom of Spain: English restaurants serving kidney pie in Nerja, menus in Marbella written in German, and French madams and monsieurs conversing in a Torremolinos souvenir store. It's a venerable melting pot of the perfectly tanned and scantily clad.

It's almost hard to believe that the incredibly carefree and relaxing environment would also produce one of the most influential artists of the 20th century, Pablo Picasso. While a ludicrous number of people populate the beaches for a deeper tan, an equally as ludicrous number of people flock to Málaga for a deeper understanding of the storied painter. Both groups however seem to converge later in the day for the region's never-ending nocturnal activities.

When the sun plummets behind Portugal, a mass bacchanalian migration erupts from the sandy dunes to the *tascas,* bars, and clubs. Some stay behind and throw beach parties of various proportions, but inside the glittery discothèques and gritty bars is where the region gets its well deserved hedonistic reputation. Thank god Pablo got out when he was young. Instead of Minotaurs, harlequins, and self-portraits, we'd probably be staring at still-lifes of disco balls and 40s of Cruzcampo.

Best of Costa del Sol

- **Best Rock Venue: ZZ Pub.** For most of the week, the speakers here are constantly pumping out live music. A few local bands could easily call the place home with the frequency they play there. Thankfully though, they've got some great guitar chops and each one can carry a tune. When semi-famous alternative bands come to Málaga, don't be surprised to see them on the bill at ZZ Pub. See p. 603.

- **Best Hostel: Picasso's Corner Backpacker Hostel.** Okay, so there really aren't any other hostels in Málaga but even if 20 or so hostels popped up within the next year, Picasso's Corner would likely still be tops in the city. A friendly rotating cast of employees, central location next to Plaza Merced, and the nicest bathrooms this side of the Atlantic make the little hostel on Calle San Juan de Letran among the best in Spain. See p. 600.

- **Best Authentic Andalusian Food: Casa de la Era.** So you want to have that truly quintessential Spanish meal in that cozy little restaurant that epitomizes the "real" Spain. Casa de la Era is your guy. The seafood, the beef... whatever you order, it's sure to be the right choice at this little Andalusian gem. See p. 611.

- **Best Attraction: Museo Picasso.** Pablo's greatest works may live in Madrid at the Prado Museum and the Reina Sofía, but this converted 16th-century palace is also home to a number of Picasso's paintings and sketches. Don't leave the city without spending an afternoon in this excellent museum. See p. 606.

- **Best Hangout: Plaza de la Merced.** Follow the masses with their plastic bags full of wine, cola, booze, or all of the above to this outdoor dive bar. By 11pm or so the entire square is packed with pre-drinkers getting ready for the night's debauchery. Didn't bring along any beverages? Don't fret. There's a little hut that sells a few cocktails right in the plaza and several stores along the surrounding streets sell all sorts of beer, snacks, and other drinks. See p. 598.

- **Best Street for People-Watching: Calle Marques de Larios.** This wide, white marbled passageway is a pedestrian's dream. Flanked by upscale boutiques and popular clothing chains, Calle Marques de Larios is always busy with shoppers, diners, and, later in the evening, inebriated locals stumbling out of the *tascas* and bars in the small side streets. Park your rear on one of the marble benches and watch the parade unfold before you.

- **Best Diamond in the Rough: Cueva de Nerja.** History, culture, and nude sunbathing all within spitting distance of each other... what's not to like? Come for the prehistoric cave paintings, but stay for the secluded beaches nestled in dramatic rocky coves that might make you feel a little primal too. See p. 618.

○ **Best Tapas Bar: Pepa y Pepe.** With not much room to offer patrons, it only makes sense to come here a little earlier before the hungry masses come to Calle Caldereria. An early start in Pepa y Pepe means you'll have a headstart on the tasty tapas as well as the booze. The tasty hams and deep-fried seafood of the former are worth the mighty hangover of the latter in the morning. See p. 603.

○ **Best Club: Sala Karma.** An extremely easygoing vibe is felt throughout this crowded haunt. Whether you want to cut the rug with a pretty local or chat them up during a concert, Sala Karma is a prime spot to do either. See p. 604.

Málaga

Every Thursday, Friday, and Saturday night, plastic bags full of various beverages are brought to Plaza Merced, fueling the crowd before they slink into the nearby clubs and bars. Just over 120 years ago, amidst the chattering of locals and the pouring of wine in Plaza Merced (assuming things haven't changed much since the 1880s), you might also have been able to hear the squeal of a newborn artistic genius. Picasso, as it turns out, came out kicking and crying into the world right next to Málaga's current prime pre-drinking spot. Pablo didn't stick around for his first swig of *kalimotxo* (coke and wine) however, and left for greener, more inspiring, pastures. But thanks to Picasso's heirs, who endowed Málaga with a number of canvases and ceramics, the city is still an important site for art lovers.

Not interested in paintings and sketches from the Spaniard? Compared to the other towns along Costa del Sol, Málaga has plenty of culture to spare. The Alcazaba, Gibralfaro Castle, and the cathedral are all yours to explore. Relaxing after a day of staring at paintings and ruins couldn't be easier for the booze hounds and night owls. But the action doesn't just start and end with Plaza Merced. Instead, Málaga's streets and alleyways are filled with tasty *tascas*, truckloads of beats spilling from its discothèques, and sassy rock bars. Party on Wayne. Party on Pablo.

Getting There

BY AIR

Vacationers from all parts of Europe touch down on the runways of Málaga's airport. Located 8km (5 miles) west of Málaga, the airport is one of the country's busiest. It's currently constructing a new terminal to welcome the numerous direct flights from **Iberia Airlines** (☎ 800-772-4642; www.iberia.com). The charter airline Air Plus Comet (an offshoot of Aerolineas Argentinas) also has direct flights from London and New York.

BY TRAIN

The bulk of visitors usually arrive in Málaga via Spain's railways. Travelers from Madrid can choose from six trains that depart daily for the roughly 4½ hour trip to Málaga. Those in Seville can expect four or five trains leaving every day while Cordoba offers a few more with about seven or eight heading to Málaga daily. Check **RENFE** for times (☎ 902-240-202; www.renfe.es).

Costa del Sol

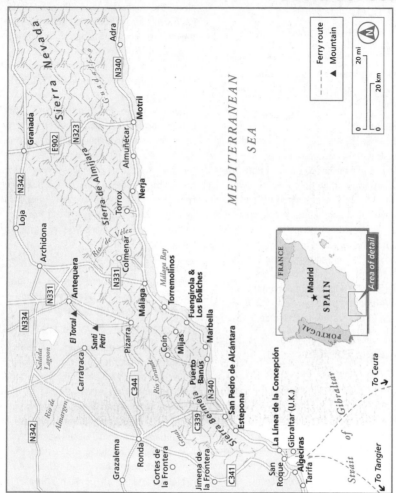

BY BUS

The only way to reach the other towns along Costa del Sol is to use the extensive bus system in southern Spain. Málaga's **bus station** can be found a few blocks south of the train station. Companies such as **Alsina Graells Sur** (☎ 952-348-023), **Automobiles Portillo** (☎ 952-360-191), and **Los Amarillos S.L.** (☎ 952-363-024) all offer coaches to various cities in Andalucia, Costa del Sol, and Costa de la Luz. Don't worry about the bus schedule if you're trying to get to one of the towns in this chapter. Buses from Málaga to Torremolinos leave every 15 minutes and there are about 20 that leave for Marbella daily. Just over 10 coaches depart Málaga for Nerja.

Getting Around

BY FOOT

Málaga is a relatively large city, at least compared to others in Costa del Sol. Fortunately though, the historic part of Málaga is small enough to explore without having to use public transportation or scooter.

BY BUS

They may not be able to squeeze through the tiny roads inside the main part of the city, but the buses of Málaga's public transportation system help bring townsfolk over the bridge and back as well as to the fringes of the city limits. A ride costs only 1€, which you pay directly to the driver. Although everything here is within walking distance, a scorching summer day is all that it takes to loosen that budget-traveler's death grip on that euro coin. The air-conditioned coach can get you from the train or bus station to Paseo del Parque in less than 15 minutes.

Málaga Basics

ORIENTATION

You can easily tackle the major attractions in Málaga in 1 hectic day with just a pair of broken-in running shoes and a decent map. Actually, even with a comprehensive map you'll likely get lost in the winding streets of Málaga. Just keep in mind that the heart of the city is closed off by the Rio Guadalmedina to the west and the gorgeous wide avenues of Paseo del Parque and Alameda Principal to the south. If all else fails, try locating the cathedral's tall towers to get your bearings. Before long you'll be back on the main commercial street of Calle de Marqués de Larios. The marbled avenue, lined with Málaga's best stores, cuts right through the middle of the historic center and ends at the Plaza de la Constitucion. Almost parallel to Calle Marqués de Larios, a little farther east and along the Alcazaba, is Calle Alcazabilla. Follow this street north and make a left at the end to get to Málaga's well-known ★ Best● **Plaza de la Merced**—Picasso's first home and the place where hundreds gather for the city's *botellón* (BYOB party in the plaza).

Every so often, you'll come across information booths strategically placed on various sidewalks throughout Málaga. A boon to backpackers, it's hard not to feel sorry for the sweating city employee stuck inside the cramped space. Despite the conditions, they're more than happy to help you find your way to the hotel or to whichever landmark you're trying to get to.

TOURIST OFFICE

The main tourist offices can be found at Pasajes Chinitas 4 (☎ 952-213-445) and in Avenida Cervantes (☎ 952-122-020).

RECOMMENDED WEBSITES

○ **www.estabus.emtsam.es**: Timetables, station information, and other useful transportation links are all found on the train station's website (Málaga).

○ **www.alsinagraells.es** and **www.ctsa-portillo.com**: The two main bus companies for shuttling between cities in southern Andalucia and Costa del Sol.

○ **www.malaga.com**: Basic info about Málaga and the surrounding area as well as little articles about what's going on in the city and what's coming to town in the future.

○ **www.andalucia.com**: Comprehensive site about Andalucia, including all cities in Costa del Sol. Incredible amount of information that can help you find a hotel, take up certain outdoor pursuits, or tie the knot with your drinking partner from last night (click on the "Marriage" link).

Costa del Sol Nuts & Bolts

Currency Finding a **cash machine** all along Costa del Sol shouldn't be much of a problem. ATMs from Deutchesbank, Caixa, and Unicaja, just to name a few, are plentiful within the center of each city.

Emergencies For various crises, you can phone Red Cross ☎ 952-443-545, Drug Help-line ☎ 900-161-515, or the AIDS hotline ☎ 900-111-000. Throughout the coast, you can dial ☎ 061 for an ambulance, ☎ 080 for fire officials, and ☎ 091 for the police. For other types of emergencies, one of the following numbers might be able to help you out: Sea Rescue ☎ 900-202-202, Málaga Health Center ☎ 952-604-266, Marbella Health Center ☎ 952-826-596, Nerja Health Center ☎ 952-520-935, Guardia Civil (Málaga) ☎ 952-391-900, First Aid (Torremolinos) ☎ 952-386-484.

Laundromats Walking around Málaga can get your clothes sweaty and stinky rather quickly. Before you scare off that hottie in Plaza de la Merced later in the evening, drop off your threads at **Tintoreria Lavanderia Pizarro** (Alda. Colón 18; ☎ 952-222-868) to get them fresh and clean. Seriously, you can only Febreeze your clothes for so long before the can runs out.

Post Offices The Spanish postal service is notoriously slow, but the letters and postcards do eventually make it to their destinations. Send larger parcels and bulky souvenirs or stock up on a roll of stamps by visiting the **post office** (☎ 952-364-380) on Av. Andalucia 1. They're open from 8:30am to 10:30pm on Mondays through Fridays and 9:30am to 2pm on Saturdays (closed Sun and holidays).

Restrooms You could be testing the limits of your bladder by downing massive amounts of *kalimotxo* in Plaza de la Merced or guzzling down gallons of water while you explore the Alcazaba, but don't worry about finding a place to empty your tank. Restaurants and bars generally let you use their *servicios* without giving you any sass. Be polite and smile when asking and your urinary tract will thank you.

Safety Generally, Málaga is a safe city. The common plagues of tourist-infested cities do exist here: pickpockets and petty theft, but it's not widespread in Málaga. When walking off your huge meal of octopus and swordfish, be smart and keep your valuables where you can see or feel them.

Sleeping

Thanks to Málaga's favorite son, a steady stream of tourists comes to the city and keeps the numerous hotels in business. While there are plenty of choices when it comes to hotels and *hostales,* there's only one true youth hostel in Málaga. Naturally, it gets booked more quickly than other places, but with the abundance of budget options scattered around the city you'll never be without a bed.

➜ **AC Málaga Palacio** ★★★ In town not to check out a Picasso, but to actually buy one? If that's the case, you'll have no problem footing the bill at the plush AC Málaga Palacio. Half of the luxurious rooms overlook the leafy Paseo del Parque below while the others on higher floors have more impressive vistas of the waterfront. The location can't be beat either: the cathedral a block and a half north, the Alcazaba just a few minutes to the east, and the Paseo del Parque at the hotel's doorstep. Not that you'd actually ever want to *leave* the AC Málaga Palacio. *Cortina del Muelle 1.* ☎ *952-215-185. www.ac-hoteles.com. Double 120€–180€; suite 147€–324€. Amenities: Restaurant, bar, dry cleaning, fitness center, laundry service, outdoor pool, room service, sauna. In room: A/C, TV, hair dryer, minibar.*

➜**Hostal Carlos V** It almost sits in the shadows of the nearby cathedral, but the sparsely furnished rooms let down the regal moniker of the hotel. The building's quaint exterior and almost modern lobby are slightly deceiving when you realize that the actual quarters aren't noteworthy. Simplicity aside, it's a good deal given its location and overall comfort. *Cister 10.* ☎ *952-215-120. Double 50€–65€. Amenities: Breakfast room. In room: A/C, TV.*

MTV **Best ●** ➜ **Picasso's Corner Backpacker Hostel** ★★ Picasso probably wouldn't have any objections pimping his name out to this hostel. While the artist tried to convey a sense of space and volume with the geometric shapes of Cubism, the hostel tries to convey a sense of relaxation and comfort with cozy areas where backpackers can unwind. Picasso's Corner can easily lay claim to having some of the nicest *servicios* in any Spanish hostel, with faux marble walls and floors. Throw in a clean, spacious shower and the prospect of bathing without flip-flops seems almost prudent. Rooms are equally as comfortable and are stocked with sturdy wooden bunks. As this book is going to press, the hostel is making changes to the rooms by adding walls for guests who want a tad

¡Cuidado! To Catch a Thief

One place where you need to exercise extra caution in Málaga is the area around **Gibalfaro**. The dark streets have been known to hide muggers and thieves, so try to limit your travel in the area to taxi and bus.

more privacy between dorms. Those looking for the complete opposite can chat up other travelers in the convivial common room and bar on the ground floor or in one of two terraces (one on the roof, the other adjacent to the kitchen on the first floor). Once night falls, the action moves from the hostel to nearby Plaza de la Merced where the town's *botellón* can sometimes be heard from some of the rooms in Picasso's Corner. *Calle San Juan de Letrán 9.* ☎ *952-212-287. www.picassoscorner.com. 18€ bed in dorm of 6, 19€ bed in dorm of 5 or 4, 22€ per person for a private double. Amenities: Bar, bike rental, breakfast, kitchen, laundry facilities. In room: Safe.*

➜ **Residencia Universitaria Santa Paula** ★ It's a great backup in case Picasso's Corner is all booked. While it may not be a true hostel, the beds are relatively cheap, rooms are clean, and it's in an excellent location in Málaga. Unlike backpacker's hostels, you won't have to squirm around in some uncomfortable bunk bed here. Instead, the mostly one-person rooms all have comfortable single beds. Oh and if you're worried about having a sketchy, old man as a temporary roommate you'll be happy to know that the Residencia Universitaria only allows students to snooze in their dorms. Make sure you bring along your student ID. *Calle Especerías 5.* ☎ *952-214-148. www.rsanta paula.com. Bed 24€. Breakfast included. Amenities: Free Internet access, laundry facilities.*

Eating

Whether you're munching on some tapas or sitting down for a candlelit dinner, seafood reigns supreme in Málaga and the rest of Costa del Sol. Fresh fish, octopus, shrimp, and shellfish are front and center on most, if not all, of the menus in Málaga's excellent restaurants. Meals in Costa del Sol are generally slightly cheaper than in the northern and central parts of Spain, but if you're on an extremely tight budget you can still get by with the abundance of small, cheap eateries that also feature less variety. You may not be sampling the finest seafood that Spain has to offer, but you'll save a pretty penny in the process.

HOT SPOT

➜ **El Chinitas** SPANISH/ANDALUSIAN As you walk down the busy Marqués de Larios, poke your head into the side street of Moreno Monroy. If the wind is just right, as soon as you get a glimpse of the vertical sign belonging to the restaurant, you'll also get a whiff of their sumptuous seafood dishes. Follow your nose, grab a seat either on the street or inside, and try to decide whether you should sample their incredible fried *aubergines* and honey or their fresh shrimp (locally caught from the bay of Málaga). In any case, you'll have to start your meal off with the *ajo blanco*. It's a cold garlic soup with raisins that, despite it's seemingly unappetizing combination, is actually refreshing and flavorful. Bowls will be tipped. *Moreno Monroy 4–6.* ☎ *952-210-972 or 952-226-440. www.chinitas.arrakis. es. Main courses 7€–14€. Daily noon–4pm and 8pm–midnight.*

TAPAS

➜ **Bar Logueno** Cheap, authentic tapas are surprisingly hard to find in and around Málaga. Many are touristy, cheesy, and overpriced. But Bar Logueno thankfully doesn't follow suit and provides patrons with awesome ambience (requisite hanging hams and wooden beer kegs? check and check) and incredibly affordable tapas (dishes start out at just around 1€). *Marín García 9.* ☎ *952-223-048. Hours vary, so call ahead.*

CHEAP

➜ **La Taperia Delicatessen** DELI/CAFE-TERIA When that trapezoid of a banana on Picasso's still life starts to make you hungry, you might want to find actual food once you leave the Picasso Museum. Luckily there's La Taperia not far from the entrance. Sandwiches and salads on the menu all cost less than 6€ while larger meals cost 10€ at most. Try their veggie and chicken *bocadillo*. The toasted whole grain baguette is surprisingly tasty and filling for a measly 5€. It's a much better deal than some crusty, oily, old Cubist piece of fruit. *Calle Granada 60.* ☎ *952-603-429. Main course 6€–10€. Mon–Sat noon–midnight. Closed Sun.*

➜ **Wok Noodle Bar** PAN-ASIAN I admit, the first thing that pops into the minds of hungry sightseers in Málaga during its steamy summer isn't a bowl of hot noodles. Fortunately, Wok Noodle Bar is chic enough, tasty enough, and cheap enough to draw a wide range of diners to its simple, minimalist wooden benches for lunch and dinner on even the hottest of days. See for yourself and order the beef option. Eight euros later, you'll find yourself inhaling the aroma of the steamed vegetables, beef, oyster sauce, teriyaki, and garlic rising from the pale noodles. You'll soon forget about the 100°F (38°C) weather. . . .

COSTA DEL SOL

at least until the sliding glass doors shut behind you on your way out. *Calle Alcazabilla 14.* ☎ *952-608-184. Main course 8€. Daily 1:30pm—12:30am.*

DOABLE

➔ **El Jardin** SPANISH/SEAFOOD   On the southeast corner of the cathedral is a small, winding walkway lined with a few souvenir stores and restaurants, but walk to the end and you'll find a fantastic spot right at Calle Cañón 1. Named for its location right next to the cathedral's garden, El Jardin is a breezy eatery where you can enjoy a refreshing seafood salad with salmon and squid and watch flamenco an hour later. Major foot stomping and guitar strumming takes place on Fridays and Saturdays at 9:30pm, although there are other visuals to keep your eyes occupied during the rest of the week. Aside from the cathedral that is visible from the large open doors and windows, the interior is full of vines hanging from the ceiling and skylight, with pseudo-gilded adornments on the bar. *Calle Cañón 1.* ☎ *952-220-419. Main courses 8€—15€. Daily 8am—11pm, until 2am on Fri and Sat.*

➔ **Lechuga** ★ SALADS   At first, Lechuga has the look and feel of a vegetarian or vegan joint. The menu, despite being almost completely made up of various salads, shows otherwise with ham and other meats playing prominent roles in some of their salads—and these aren't your normal tossed salads either. Constructed pleasantly with ingredients strategically and artistically distributed, the leafy plates are delicious and well portioned. Their *espagnola* salad is particularly excellent with a tasty tower of lettuce, cheese, and salty ham surrounded by a ring of peppers and apples. Unfortunately, the furnishings aren't as well thought out. The deliberately quirky tabletops are constructed of old

doors made of uneven planks with the handles and ironwork still on them. Still, the superb salads are worth the effort of the circus-worthy balancing act involving your dish and the table. *Plaza de la Merced 1.* ☎ *610-391-494. Main course 7€—10€. Daily 1pm—12:30am.*

CAFE

➔ **La Teteria** ★★ You could head here in the morning for its limited breakfast menu or for a spot of afternoon tea as well, but make sure you drop by when night falls and the street lamps flicker on. From the small wooden tables lining the cobblestone streets, you can see the cathedral's illuminated tower peeking through Calle San Agustin. While you take in the stunning view, sip one of their green or black teas served from small red kettles and pair it with a crepe—the selection ranges from bland (plain for 2.30€) to decadent (fruit/chocolate up to 8€), and you don't need to ask which one would I recommend. *San Agustin 9. No phone. Daily midday until 1am.*

Partying

As you already know, Plaza de la Merced is where the weekend really starts for hundreds of locals and backpackers. What you may not know is that after the *botellón* dies down, they all head to the area north of Plaza de la Constitucion to continue their nocturnal pursuits. There, the tiny streets come to life with people filing in and out of the bars and clubs until the early morning hours. Other areas like Plaza de Uncibay and the beaches near the city also get rowdy with hordes of drinkers and dancers. Like, and perhaps because of, the late dinner hour, the nightlife in Costa del Sol doesn't reach full tilt until after midnight. Bars rarely see people before 11pm and they might close around a modest 3am, but folks who pay a cover charge

ᴍᴛᴠ🆅 The University Scene

Although it doesn't feel like your traditional college town, the presence of around 30,000 university students gives the city a unique and youthful feel. And with the popular **University of Málaga** supplying the city with thousands of co-eds, there's never a dull night, especially during the school year. As the start of the semester nears, *botellones* get rowdier, clubs get more crowded, and the scene in Málaga becomes electric. The main campus is a 15-minute bus ride from the city, so you can't really check out the bulletin boards to see what events and parties are in store for the weekend. Instead, just hang around the main hot spots on Plaza de la Merced and around town and you can be sure tons of promoters will be handing out flyers and trying to draw as many 20-somethings as possible to their bar or club. And groups of kids will always be on hand after class, just having a pre-dinner beer and tapas.

anywhere as low as 4€ up to 16€ at dance clubs hear massive beats until sunrise.

BARS

➜ **Fraggle Rock** ★ Some of you reading this may not be old enough to remember the Fraggles and the rock they came in on. But these carefree Muppets brought happiness to thousands of children in the '80s, and this bar attempts to do the same for those "kids," now in their mid-20s. While the age group varies from night to night, 19-year-olds seem to have as good a time as the ones hitting 30. The AC/DC poster on one wall and blue New Jersey license plates on another perfectly match the mix of good ol' rock 'n' roll with cheesy tunes. Dance your cares away, worries for another day. Down in Fraggle Rock. . . . *Calle Comedias 10.* ☎ *610-222-772.*

ᴹᵀⱽ (Best ◉) ➜ **Pepa y Pepe** ★ If you're lucky, you just might be able to score a barrel on the street. The tiny tapas bar is one of the better places in town to scarf down those bite-size treats despite its size. A few tables populate the closetlike interior but most patrons opt for the handful of barrels and stools outside for a breezier setting. The menu is mostly made up of your standard tapas offerings, but they're extremely

tasty and, more importantly, cheap. Costing at most 1.30€, you can order as much *pipirrana de pulpo* (octopus) or *salchichas* as your stomach can handle without making much of a dent in your wallet. Just watch your alcohol intake. You want to score a barrel, not with one. *Calle Caldereria 9. No phone.*

➜ **Road House** It may not look like it, but the small bar on Calle Alamos is actually a hot spot for rock and indie music in Málaga. Although Road House doubles as a concert venue, an attractive alternative crowd is usually found downing cheap beer and listening to an impressive selection of funk, rock, and acid jazz tunes on days when the stage is empty. Check out Málaga's local paper *El Sur* to find out who's in town now. *Calle Alamos 45.* ☎ *952-229-850.*

ᴹᵀⱽ (Best ◉) ➜ **ZZ Pub** ★★ When university students want to catch a show or unwind after a day of mind-numbing lectures they head to ZZ Pub. The popular rock venue hosts at least three or four shows a week, two of them from a regular rotation of local bands in Málaga. On nights that the amps and microphones are silent, DJs make sure top-notch rock spills out of the speakers. It's an incredibly easygoing joint where you can catch some of the better regional rock acts in Spain or just kick back and shoot the breeze with the laid-back clientele. *Tejon y Rodriguez 6.* ☎ *952-441-595.*

NIGHTCLUBS

→ **Habana Café** ★ Uninspired techno and hip-hop tunes with seemingly identical beats can slowly make bumping and grinding in any club a little boring. Change the tempo and your dance moves in Habana Café. Don't know how to salsa? No worries, just come on Thursdays when they hold classes for novices and beginners. Other days, there are live bands for you to bust a Latin move to and you'll also have your pick of the litter for a dance partner. Folks that come to Habana Café range in age from the curious college student to the salsa seniors swingin' those new titanium hips. *Av. Carlos Haya 3.* ☎ *952-102-161.*

MTV Best → **Sala Karma** ★★ Another popular spot, particularly in the summer, is Sala Karma. The disco-bar that sometimes doubles as a music venue gets full fast but, like most other spots, never before midnight. The crowd inside the bar reflects the type of music that pours out of the PA: bubbly, upbeat, and carefree. *Calle Luis de Velazquez 5. No phone.*

→ **White Lounge** ★ On most nights, the White Lounge is where you'll hear some fine hip-hop and R&B. It's a popular club that pours tasty cocktails to its young and attractive clientele. On Wednesdays, the estrogen levels spike up with a raucous ladies night involving a male striptease and endless amounts of body shots. *Calle José Denis Belgrano 19.* ☎ *952-213-810.*

LIVE MUSIC

→ **Teatro Cervantes** While it may not look like it, this silvery building dates all the way back to the 19th century. Now home to performances by the Málaga Symphony Orchestra, Teatro Cervantes also hosts various kinds of concerts. On some days, you'll hear the distinct stomping and singing of flamenco artists on stage while other days will find the speakers spewing distorted guitar riffs from some rock band stopping in Málaga for their Spanish tour. Last summer, Erykah Badu, Wynton Marsalis, Wayne Shorter, Kings of Convenience, and Eric Burdon all came to Málaga to perform in this attractive theater. *Calle Ramos Marín s/n.* ☎ *952-224-109. www.teatrocervantes.com. Call or log on for showtimes.*

> **Board Talk**
>
> It's one of the few cities near the Mediterranean that features wide, asphalt streets, parks with solid benches, and large plazas where you can pull off manuals and kick-flips to your heart's content. To find the best skating spots, check with the folks at Japan (p. 608). They not only sell some basic parts for your board but they'll be able to point you to the places where the Guardia Civil won't cause you any grief.

Sightseeing

Aside from Nerja and its caves, Málaga is the only city in Costa del Sol that culture hounds will appreciate. Some painter brought fame to Málaga, but there are also a handful of landmarks that are worth checking out while you're not traipsing around the beaches.

MONUMENTS & ATTRACTIONS

→ **Alcazaba** Luckily, during the sweltering siesta hours of the summer, this fortress overlooking the Mediterranean sometimes drops the admission fee for visitors (only on Sun). Otherwise you can tour the dusty,

wwwired

Check out bus schedules, your e-mail, or if someone decided to buy your old toaster off of Craigslist in one of the spots near Plaza de la Merced. As this is being written, a swanky Internet cafe/bar/meet-market called **Red** is being built right next door to the Picasso's Corner Hostel. If they're still in the process of blinging it out, there's another Internet spot on the block over (across the street from Casa Natal): **Telsat** (C. Gomez Palette 7; no phone) has 25 computers in an air-conditioned environment so you can cruise the Web without sweating your butt off. It costs .60€ for each half-hour. At that rate, it's not a bad place just to cool down for a bit.

old palace grounds for a few euros. It's nowhere near as breathtaking as the Alhambra in Granada or the Alcázar in Seville, but it does provide perfect digital camera fodder with excellent views of the coast and of Málaga itself. *Plaza de la Aduana (Alcazabilla).* ☎ *952-216-005. Admission 1.90€, 3.10€ combined with Gibralfaro. Summer Tues–Sun 9:30am–8pm; winter Tues–Sun 8:30am–7pm. Closed Mon.*

➔**Cathedral** Aside from those in places like Seville and Cordoba, Spanish cathedrals often start to look like generic masses of concrete. The cathedral in Málaga, dark and cavernous and with few notable sights, is one such place but the external features make it a beautiful structure to view from the surrounding cafes and restaurants. But the 3.50€ to get in is a little overpriced. Rather, get the most of your money by using the 3.50€ that night toward a pot of fresh tea in La Teteria (p. 602) instead. This way you'll be able to

enjoy an amazing view of the cathedral—it is a national monument after all—with a cool, evening breeze and a refreshing cup of Earl Grey. *Plaza Obispo.* ☎ *952-215-917. Admission 3.50€. Mon–Sat 10am–6:30pm. Closed holidays.*

➔**Gibralfaro Castle** It's a bit of a hike to the top of the hill, but if you're in the area, a visit to these ruins is worth the 1.80€ admission fee. Lately, there have been reports of petty theft and muggings occurring near the castle, so that fee becomes more like 4€ or 5€ after you include the bus or taxi fare. Either way, just like the Alcazaba, there are some memorable views of Málaga and its surroundings to be found. *Cerro de Gibralfaro. No phone. Admission 1.80€. Open daily. Microbus 35 (from cathedral).*

MUSEUMS

FREE ➔**Centro de Arte Contemporáneo de Málaga** ★ Taking a few cues from the German Kunsthaus, Centro de Arte Contemporáneo (CAC) showcases some of the most cutting edge and creative artists of the 20th and 21st centuries. Not limited to just Spanish artists, CAC also displays many modern pieces by their North American counterparts. The bulk of the permanent collection is made up of works of Spanish painters in the 1980s. If you have some spare time, a visit to CAC Málaga is well worth it. *Calle Alemania s/n.* ☎ *952-120-055. www.cacmalaga.org. Free admission. Open 10am–8pm, Tues–Sun (until 9pm in summer). Closed Mon and 2–5pm in summer.*

➔**Fundación Picasso** I highly doubt that MTV Cribs would even bother doing a posthumous tour of Picasso's old digs, but even if they did the segment wouldn't last longer than a couple of minutes. Despite the small size of the "museum," there's no reason you shouldn't visit Fundación

Scissors Beat Paper, Rock Beats Scissors, Apes Poop on Rock

A Stopover in the Sunny, Sweltering . . . U.K.?

If you haven't already noticed from the pints of Newcastle in the pubs, fish and chips in the restaurants, and pale sunbathers on the beach, the British are well represented in Costa del Sol. At times, it may not even feel like you're in the middle of Spain. Travel farther west and you'll actually end up in the United Kingdom itself—well technically, at least. Back in 1704 (made official in 1713 by the Treaty of Utrecht), the British claimed the small sliver of land and still occupy what is now known as **Gibraltar.** Buses from Spain don't enter the territory, so travelers need to get off at La Linea de Concepción. Once there, they spot the Rock in the distance and follow it for about 5 minutes until they reach the border. After passing through Customs (a relatively quick and painless process), travelers walk across the one runway in Gibraltar's airport and into the English-speaking oasis sandwiched between Spain and North Africa.

For backpackers, especially those under 30, 1 day is plenty of time for you to explore Gibraltar. Any longer and your bank account, as well as mental state, will suffer quite a bit. In addition to the steep exchange rate, you'll find yourself spending almost twice as much on beer, food, and admission fees to the sights than you would in the rest of Spain. Speaking of attractions, there are a few worthwhile places to visit: **Casemates Square** and the adjacent **Main Street, The Rock** (reachable by cable car, £8–£10), **Europa Point** (take a bus, roads have almost nonexistent sidewalks and combined with the blind turns, is a recipe for disaster), and **St. Michaels Cave.** Oh, and then there's the macaques on the top of the Rock: These **Barbary Apes** are cute for roughly a

Picasso. The ground floor is used by the foundation and doubles as a library for art historians. The second floor is actually where Pablo's parents raised him for the first year and a half after his birth, moving from the city while he was still an infant. Unfortunately, the space on the second floor is kind of a buzz kill to the imagination. Except for the re-creation of a 19th-century studio room that contains a piece painted by Pablo's father, the home is void of any furniture or household objects. Instead, you'll find photos from different periods of Picasso's life hanging on the walls and a few works done by the artist on the first floor, including faces painted on ceramics and various lithographs. Be sure to check out *The Lobster* (1949) before you leave. The

wash-drawing created a fascinating and realistic effect on the crustacean's shell. *Plaza de la Merced 15.* ☎ *952-060-215. www.fundacionpicasso.es. Admission 1€ adults, free for students. Mon–Sat 10am–8pm; Sun 10am–2pm. Closed holidays.*

📺 ⬛Best❂ → **Museo Picasso** ★★★
Thanks to Pablo's daughter-in-law and grandson, Málaga still stands as an important landmark for fans of the artist. A slew of paintings, sketches, and ceramics were loaned and/or sold to the museum by Christine and Bernard Ruiz-Picasso, and visitors to the city can view the works that cover the breadth of Pablo's lifetime—from the *Little Girl with Doll*, which he painted when he was only 15 years old, to

split second but get too close and they'll ambush your noggin, rummage through your hair for munchies, and fill your nostrils with the stench that flies adore.

Here are three places where you can crash after a hard day of ape-dodging, runway crossing, and uphill hiking: **Emile Youth Hostel** (Line Wall Rd.; ☎ **350-51-106;** www.emilehostel.com) is the cheapest deal on the peninsula, with dorm beds for 15€ to 20€, singles for 20€ to 30€, and doubles for 30€ to 50€; breakfast is included in all prices. If you're lucky, you won't run into the 16-year-old twerp that sometimes runs the desk. Accommodations can be uncomfortable if you're traveling solo, especially with decor that looks like the owners stole some art and furnishings from their deranged grandma. Otherwise, stay here if you're in a group or if you're really desperate for an inexpensive bed.

Queens Hotel (1 Boyd St.; ☎ **350-74-000;** www.queenshotel.gi) is your best mid-range option (singles 50€–60€, doubles 65€–95€, triples 85€, and four-person "family rooms" for 90€). An excellent breakfast is included and the decidedly no-frills rooms provide a definitively restful night. Ask if they are offering any special student rates.

If you have the extra dough (160€–175€) and excellent quads and glutes—or want them (it's a rough incline leading to the hotel)—**The Rock Hotel** (3 Europa Rd.; ☎ **350-73-000;** www.rockhotelgibraltar.com) is the place for you. Even with the newer, glitzier O'Callaghan Hotel near the town center, The Rock Hotel is a better deal. Bigger pool area, friendlier staff, fantastic breakfast, and plush rooms will have you smiling the next morning. At least until your first run-in with those apes.

the puzzlelike *Woman in an Armchair* that was done in his 60s. In all, there are roughly 150 pieces in the entire collection, so devote at least a couple of hours to really appreciate the work of Málaga's most famous figure. *Calle San Agustin 8.* ☎ *952-127-600. Admission 6€ for permanent collection, 4.50€ temporary exhibitions, 8€ combination ticket. Reduced price (50%) for students under 26 (with valid ID). Tues–Thurs 10am–8pm; Fri–Sat 10am–9pm; Sun and holidays 10am–8pm. Tickets must be bought 30 min. prior to closing.*

Playing Outside

Unfortunately, there aren't really any parks or green spaces in Málaga. Your best bet is just to tackle the beaches.

Shopping

➔ **Candilejas** ★★ After hearing Alej (bartender/cook/jack-of-all-trades) in Picasso's Corner play some Maná one night, I went in search of a music store in the city to find a couple of their albums. What I found was Candilejas, a small yet comprehensive store staffed with helpful clerks who never look annoyed even when you ask for the cheesiest of CDs. There's a tiny jazz and flamenco section, but the store's strength lies in the rock genre. Classics like Television's Marquee Moon can be found in one bin while indie favorites like Spoon and Belle and Sebastian are well represented in others. *Calle Santa Lucia 9.* ☎ *952-225-593. Closed Sun.*

→ **ESC Outdoor Experience** ★ Floaties? Check. Quickset cement for stress-free sandcastle building? Check. Swim shorts and flip-flops? Oops. Next time you pack, you might want to rearrange your priorities. For now head to ESC on Callejones del Perchel. They have all the beach basics from wetsuits to flip-flops and even fins for your surfboard. Those heading to the mountains of the Pyrenees can also stock up on some climbing or hiking gear. So pick up a pair of board shorts and ditch the leopard print Speedos. Banana hammocks were *so* 5 minutes ago. *Calle Callejones del Perchel (Edificio Aurora 2).* ☎ *952-369-610. www.escexperience.com.*

→ **Japan** While the wide asphalt streets in Málaga make driving a little more enjoyable, it also means more skateboarders carving in between cars. When they're not doing kick-flips over scooters, they stock up on gear and clothes in Japan. Here, racks of Stussy and Split share space with decks, trucks, wheels, and skate shoes in the tiny but noteworthy store. *Calle Nosquera 2.* ☎ *952-212-958.*

→ **La Mar de Cosas** Málaga is chock full of stores that are chock full of everything. One such store is, fittingly enough, La Mar de Cosas aka "The Sea of Things." Quirky clocks, kitschy housewares, and other objects that wouldn't feel out of place in an Urban Outfitters make up the bulk of junk here, but it was the canvas/prints of a legendary starlet that almost had me forking over 9.95€ to the cashier. The illustrious Audrey Hepburn, represented as a pixilated figure on a canvas welcomes everyone that enters the store. Despite the unwieldy size of the canvas, the prospect of having Eliza Doolittle as a travel companion was awfully tempting. Luckily the prospect of checking that sucker in at the airport dissuaded me from leaving the store with Audrey. The sane in Spain would never put that on a plane. *Calle Mendez Nuñez 6.* ☎ *952-215-095. Closed Sun.*

→ **The Zpot** A couple doors down from ESC Outdoor Experience is the smaller Zpot. Less testosterone-y than ESC, Zpot is geared toward more of an alternative crowd and mainly sells clothing from various skate companies like DC, Element, and Dragon. *Calle Callejones del Perchel 2.* ☎ *952-245-793. www.thezpot.com. Closed Sun.*

MARKET

It looks more like some historical site than one of the biggest markets in Andalucia. That's because the archway in the main gate was one of the few structures preserved after the government decided to tear down what was once a shipyard and convent. Now, the **Ataranzas market** (Pl. de Arriola and Ataranzas) welcomes hundreds of food shoppers to its expansive space. Even if you're not there to buy any food, a walk through the famous landmark is worth the chaos of butchers peddling slabs of meat, grocers bartering with customers over the price of apples, and the acrid smell of shrimp and fish from the seafood section.

Marbella

When the condo in Biarritz is under renovation, affluent vacationers jump on their yachts, private jets, and Bentleys and head for one of the most popular destinations in not only Costa del Sol, but in all of Spain: Marbella. Thanks in part to the equally as swank Puerto Banús and a never-ending stream of international stars and millionaires, Marbella is an incredible, and expensive, vacation spot. Unlike Torremolinos to the east, you'll come across handsome, tanned 20-somethings, well-off couples

Marbella

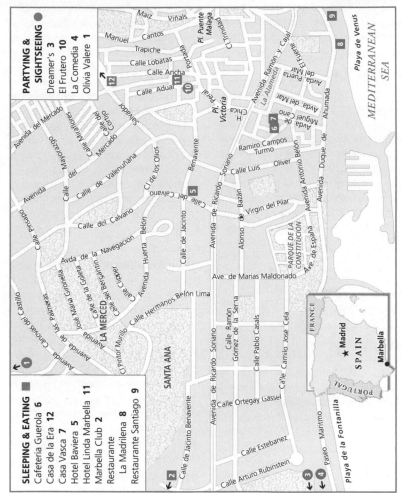

PARTYING & SIGHTSEEING ●

Dreamer's **3**
El Frutero **10**
La Comedia **4**
Olivia Valere **1**

SLEEPING & EATING ■

Cafeteria Guerola **6**
Casa de la Era **12**
Casa Vasca **7**
Hotel Baviera **5**
Hotel Linda Marbella **11**
Marbella Club **2**
Restaurante
  La Madrilena **8**
Restaurante Santiago **9**

with their spoiled kids, and loaded retirees with another handsome, tanned 20-something in tow. Thankfully you don't need a wad of 500€ bills to roll with the socialites in Marbella. There might be multi-million-dollar yachts parked in Puerto Banús, but you'll never have to pay more than 10€ to get into most of the discothèques and the excellent beaches are open to everyone from Bill Gates to Jose Schmoe.

As for the name that rolls off the tongue in an oddly gratifying way, "Marbaaaaaaaaaaay-uh," some give credit to Columbus's sugar mommy, Queen Isabella. On one visit she exclaimed, *"Qué mar tan bella!"* when she sailed into its ports. Others believe it to come from Marbil-la, when it was under Muslim rule hundreds of years ago. Myth or not, Queen Isabella was spot on. The scenic town is flanked by the looming Sierra Blanca to the north and a crystal blue Mediterranean that looks like the late Bob Ross painted it himself. It's up to you where to plant your happy little butt along its popular shores.

Getting There

Trains never stop in Marbella because . . . well, there isn't a train station anywhere in the city (the closest is in Fuengirola). Instead, travelers use Málaga as a transportation hub to reach the other towns in Costa del Sol. Roughly 20 buses shuttle back and forth on the 60km (37 miles) stretch of highway between Málaga and Marbella. The **bus station** is located in the northern part of town and it's a breeze finding your way into the city center—just head downhill and follow the scent of the salty sea.

Marbella Basics

ORIENTATION

The layout of Marbella couldn't be any more straightforward. There's one street that bisects the party town into a northern section (Casco Antiguo and the quieter side of Marbella) and the southern side (the beaches, clubs, and so on). The street starts out as Avenida Ricardo Soriano and turns into Avenida Ramón y Cajal and Avenida Severo Ochoa as it goes east. Casco Antiguo in the northern part is the place to be to relax and unwind in a quaint setting (head to Pl. Puente de Ronda). Also in the north is Parque de la Represa, a sleepy green space where you can escape the sun and stroll through the leafy paths.

TOURIST OFFICES

There are two tourist offices in Marbella. One is more centrally located in Plaza de los Naranjos (☎ **952-823-550**) while the other sits along the beach on Glorieta de la Fontanilla (☎ **952-771-442**). Both are open Monday through Friday 9:30am to 9pm and Saturday 10am to 2pm.

RECOMMENDED WEBSITE

◦ **www.marbella.com/eng**: Site chock full of information. Book your hotel from here and find details about various activities in Marbella.

Sleeping

Not everyone in Marbella goes to bed in some lavish beachside resort. There are some who get rocked gently to sleep in their multi-million-dollar yachts. For the rest of us, there are plenty of affordable options farther inland. Casco Antiguo in particular not only has cheap accommodations but they're usually in quiet areas— perfect for catching up on those much needed zzz's.

DOABLE

➔**Hotel Baviera** Hotels right along the beach can sometimes get away with cutting corners with some amenities while still being rather pricey. Hotel Baviera is halfway between the ocean and the bus station and is a decent option for budget travelers looking to crash for a couple of nights or for those not too keen on staying with throngs of tourists in the beachside hotels. Furnishings aren't spectacular, but at least you'll get to hang with the Sandman in relative peace. *Calle Calvario 4.* ☎ *952-772-950. Double 115€. Amenities: Parking garage. In room: A/C, minibar.*

➔**Hotel Linda Marbella** ★ Some of the best places in these beach resort towns aren't necessarily within spitting distance of the ocean. Casco Antiguo in Marbella is a perfect example. Little cafes and lively bars make the area a great alternative to the touristy shores. The 5-year-old Hotel Linda Marbella sits quietly in the middle of all this, providing affordable and comfortable accommodations. The 16 rooms, not spacious by any means, are simply furnished but with amenities not normally found in cheap hotels. And with its cozy

location, it's a great value. *Calle Ancha 21.*
☎ *952-857-171. Single 30€–55€, double 45€–
75€. In room: A/C, TV, safe.*

SPLURGE

➔ **Marbella Club** ★★★ It's the swankiest
of the swank in Marbella and, let's face it,
you're probably not going to have enough
cash to buy a bottle of water in Marbella
Club, let alone spend a night there. But, hey,
we thought you oughta know. The resort
opened its doors back in Eisenhower's day
and since then has been consistently welcoming people to Marbella more powerful
and richer than the ex-pres himself.
Everything from a private beach to acres of
leafy gardens help their affluent clientele
escape the paparazzi and screaming fans.
*Bulevar Principe Alfonoso von Hohenlohe
s/n.* ☎ *952-822-211. www.marbellaclub.com.
Double 250€–645€. Amenities: Restaurants,
bars, laundry service, massage, 2 outdoor
pools. In room: A/C, TV, hair dryer, minibar, safe.*

Eating

Marbella's cuisine is similar to that of the
other cities with a few differences. First,
it's slightly more expensive. Second, the
quality is a step above places like Málaga
and Torremolinos. Perhaps it's because
they serve the rich best seafood in the
region or it could very well be that the fatter, tastier fish are just attracted to the
massive amounts of bling.

HOT SPOTS

MTV **Best ◉** ➔ **Casa de la Era** ★★★
ANDALUSIAN If you're willing to walk to
the edge of Marbella, you'll be rewarded
handsomely in the form of amazing
Andalusian cuisine. This homey eatery
does almost as much with its ambience as
it does with its food. The hunks of ham
dangling from the ceiling and well worn
furniture create an amazingly warm environment that complements their tasty
dishes. You can't go wrong with anything

on their menu either. Their seafood dishes
are seasoned to perfection and their meats
are always tender enough to eat without a
knife. So, walk, crawl, or hail a cab if you
have to. Casa de la Era will make it worth
the little trip. *Finca El Chorraero-Noreste s/n.*
☎ *952-770-625. Main courses 9€–19€.
Reservations required. May–Oct Mon–Sat
1–4pm and 8pm–midnight; off season
Mon–Sat 1–4pm.*

CHEAP

➔ **Cafeteria Guerola** SPANISH A quiet
lunch in Marbella is hard to come by.
Beaches bustle with hordes of vacationers
with their bratty kids and the main streets
are full of roaring car engines and beeping
scooters. Somewhere in the middle of all
this, on the shady street of Padre Enrique
Cantos is Cafeteria Guerola. There you can
order a plate of their squid Bolognese
style, enjoy it in relative peace, and still
have enough cash for a post-meal drink
at their bar. *Calle Padre Enrique Cantos 1.*
☎ *952-770-007. Main course 7.50€–12€.
Open daily for lunch and dinner.*

➔ **Restaurante La Madrileña** SEAFOOD
Another great option along Paseo Maritimo, just in front of Hotel El Fuerte, is the
Restaurante La Madrileña. The slightly
more inexpensive seafood restaurant also
offers starving-student- and backpacker-
friendly options of pizza and pasta dishes,
most of which are priced under the 10€
mark. If you still can't decide on whether
to try their excellent seafood or not, you
can fork over 15€ for the menu of the day.
Paseo Marítimo, Edif Mediterráneo. ☎ *952-
828-484. www.lamadrilena.com. Main courses
7€–20€. Open daily for lunch and dinner.*

DOABLE

➔ **Casa Vasca** SPANISH/ANDALUSIAN
On the same street as Cafeteria Guerola,
Casa Vasca has a much better ambience
and menu. The lazy ceiling fans, dark
wooden furniture, and huge windows give

the eatery a breezy beach hut feel even if it is a few minutes away from the crashing waves of the sea. The menu features a range of Mediterranean and seafood options like hot spiced mussels, ratatouille *bibaine* style, and my favorite: *chorizo al infierno*. Translated on their menu, the "Spanish sausage from hell" will disappoint diners looking for a heartburn inducing, tongue numbing food. Instead, it most likely got its name by the way waiters bring the dish to your table—in a ceramic dish sizzling and crackling in a pool of oil, as if the personal chef of Lucifer had just pulled it off the stove. The sinful plate is still tasty however, with the sweet sausage packing a ton of flavor. *Padre Enrique Cantos 2.* ☎ *952-826-227. Main course 6.50€–15€. Daily noon–midnight.*

SPLURGE

➔**Restaurante Santiago** SEAFOOD The boardwalk on Paseo Maritimo is littered with concession stands hawking over-priced bottles of water, ice cream bars, and bags of chips. When the hunger pangs hit you hard skip the snacks and take advantage of the area's tasty seafood by checking out places like Restaurante Santiago. It may be quite a bit more expensive than, say, a bag of Lays, but their succulent oysters and perfectly prepared hake are worth the extra euro or two . . . or 12. More adventurous diners might want to sample the uncommon offering of barnacles (20€ for 100 grams). Not enticing enough? The veal terrine in red wine is a worthy alternative to the salty hull-sucking creature. *Paseo Maritimo 5.* ☎ *952-770-078 or 952-774-339. Main course 14€–30€. Open for lunch and dinner.*

Partying

Marbella might be home to some of the shiniest and most lavish clubs this side of the Mediterranean, but there's something for everyone in this coastal playground. Those looking to down a few mugs of beer, listen to some chill music, and hang out with an interesting mix of people should head to Marbella's **Casco Antiguo** near the center of town. The area truly comes to life at night when the quirky bars start to get full and the streets get noisier. Most of the dance clubs and discothèques are found in the city center, closer to the shore or in Puerto Banús. Getting there before 11pm will only result in disappointment since most bars and clubs don't open until a few hours after dinner (11ish) and stay open until early morning (2–3am for bars, 4–5am for clubs). While you might find some places with free or cheap admission (look for people passing out flyers) it goes without saying that the cover charges at some of the biggest clubs (such as Olivia Valere) can cause the biggest dent in your wallet (up to 20€).

BAR

➔**El Frutero** ★★ It may not look like much from the outside, but the three floors within El Frutero make it a favorite chill-out spot for a more alternative crowd in Marbella. The three levels, while each offering a little something different for patrons, overflow with energy and fantastic music. Grab some tapas on the ground floor, digest your *chorizo* on the plush couches on the second floor, and close out the night on the rooftop terrace. *Calle Aduar 5. No phone.*

NIGHTCLUBS

➔**Dreamer's** Leave the wad of singles (or in this case, a roll of euro coins) in your hotel. Even though the neon lights, barely clothed "employees," and strategically placed poles of Dreamer's may give it the look and feel of a gentleman's club or Rio's Carnavale, it's one of Marbella's biggest and most popular nightspots. Guest DJs

Estepona

Go West, Young Man ... & Take It All off

Most people experience **Estepona** from a bus headed to Algeciras or Cadiz. It's a shame since developers have hardly touched the budding resort town. Streets aren't cluttered with unsightly buildings and the quality beaches are almost always empty. Instead, the only thing spoiling the skyline are a few iron frameworks jutting into the sky. As this goes out to print, contractors are quickly erecting condos and resorts in Estepona but the **sandy shores** probably won't reach the overcrowded status of those in Torremolinos or Marbella until they're completed and well established. In the meantime, anyone who decides to get off the bus a few stops early can claim an area on the beach the size of Rhode Island for a little R&R. If you make it to Km 257 on N-340, you won't have to worry if you forgot your swimsuit. It's home to the **nude beach Costa Natura,** so you can literally hang out with other beachgoers in their birthday suits. Another great thing about the Estepona beaches are the existence of *chiringuitos*. Locals erect these little spots right on the sand and sell home-cooked seafood dishes for the hungry. After you're finished enjoying your newfound solitude or nude sunbathing, you can retreat to **Plaza de las Flores** for companionship. The square is home to several bars and is always humming with activity in the summer. It's just a matter of time until the same can be said about its beaches.

regularly make appearances here and the turntables are always spinning until the early morning hours. Whether you come here straight after dinner or right before sunrise, you'll always find an assortment of perfectly tanned 20-somethings slinking around on the dance floor. *Carretera Cadiz Km 175, Rio Verde (Puerto Banús).* ☎ *952-812-080. www.dreamers-disco.com.*

→**La Comedia** ★★ Long before bottles of Cristal were being cracked off the decks of the multi-million-dollar boats in Puerto Banús, the swank La Comedia was one of the most well known nightspots in the area. Thanks to constant reinvention however, it still is one of the favorites among locals as well as international celebrities. The former theater-themed restaurant has morphed into a loungey disco-bar where you're not constantly being drowned out by massive bass. The classy joint still plays fantastic music for their esteemed clientele, but they can easily switch from

having friendly banter to busting a move on the dance floor. Easily one of the best clubs in Marbella, La Comedia doesn't open its doors until midnight. *Plaza La Comedia (Puerto Banús).* ☎ *952-789-358.*

→**Olivia Valere** ★★★ Another disco-bar/restaurant that the famous frequent is this Alhambra-inspired club. Graceful archways, the colorful tiled bar and minifountain are all elements included by designer Oscar de la Pena. Combined with an incredibly attractive, rich, and well-dressed (leave the shorts and jeans at home—you don't need a suit, but dress smartly and you'll get in) clientele, it's no surprise that some of the biggest names in cinema, music, and fashion line up behind the velvet rope. Top DJs also make sure that those names are always bobbing their heads or shaking their hips to a great mix of tunes. Of course, drinks and everything else can get pretty expensive. No worries though; just nurse that one jack and coke until you find that sugar daddy or mommy to grab you another one. *Carretera De Istan Km 0,8.* ☎ *952-828-861. www.oliviavalere.com. Cover varies.*

Shopping

It's only natural that some of the most luxurious labels and designers such as Versace have outlets here and in Puerto Banús. Less glamorous yet fashionable Spanish clothing chains like Pull and Bear and Mango are also represented here. Aimed at the younger visitors to Marbella, they both have stores here on Avenida Ricardo Soriano. A few independent designers sell their threads straight off the mannequins and racks, but mostly middle-aged women spend their euros in the boutiques found sprinkled around the small side streets in the center of Marbella.

→ **The Ecotourism Shop** While they sell some T-shirts and fruit preserves, the Ecotourism Shop isn't much of a shop—at least in the conventional sense. The group organizes excursions to locations in Andalucia and Costa del Sol ranging from river adventures to hiking in the Sierra Nevada to horse riding trips. There are few places in the world, let alone Spain, where you can get new threads, an aquatic adrenaline rush, AND the perfect companion to your boring peanut butter sandwich. *Calle Ancha 7.* ☎ *952-820-579. www.daidin.com.*

Torremolinos

Torremolinos was once a vibrant destination for vacationers, and still is a viable option for beachgoers, but the glory years of the old fishing town are long gone. The streets are now full of dated souvenir stores, ugly buildings, and hordes of wrinkly vacationers that secretly ache for the Torremolinos of the '80s. The largely British, over-40 demographic has also turned Torremolinos into an aging Anglophone collective. As a result, the nightlife mostly panders to the middle-aged and retired with numerous pubs and tapas bars; and while there are a few exciting dance clubs, most aren't particularly noteworthy. You'll do less hip swiveling and more shoulder lending to the fella knee-deep in a mid-life crisis. The upside of the town's declining popularity is that the beaches aren't as crowded as überhot spots like Marbella or as glitzy as Puerto Banús. It's a 15-minute bus ride from Málaga, so bring along your sunscreen and shades but leave your mojo back in the hostel. Unless you're really into shakin' what your momma gave ya with . . . well, grandma.

Getting There

From Málaga, you have two options if you want to get to the beaches of Torremolinos: bus and train. For the former, a bus departs Málaga's **bus station** every 15 minutes for Torremolinos. While you may not see it listed as a destination on schedules, most buses headed west for places like Marbella make obligatory stops in Torremolinos. Another option is using **RENFE** Cercanías. This local train shuttles people from Málaga to nearby towns. Compared to the few euros that you'll have to pay for the bus, the 1.30€ fare for the pseudo-subway (it utilizes the aboveground rail of RENFE) is a rather good deal. While RENFE Cercanías drops you off in the center of Torremolinos in a plaza just off of Guetaria, one downside is that they don't run as often as a normal metro. You may have to wait 15 minutes between trains.

Torremolinos Basics

ORIENTATION

The closer you get to the shore, as a pedestrian, the more frustrating the walkways get in Torremolinos. From the main streets, you'll find little walkways and staircases filled with cheesy souvenir stores and touristy restaurants that descend toward the boardwalk (Paseo Maritimo).

TOURIST OFFICE

Head to Plaza de la Independencia (☎ 952-374-231; www.visitetorremolinos.com) for tourist information, maps, and brochures about Torremolinos. The office is open daily from 9:30am to 2pm.

Sleeping

➜**Hotel Castilla** If you somehow missed the last bus and train back to Málaga or are too exhausted from dodging old folk, Hotel Castilla is a perfectly decent place to crash for the night. The smallest rooms are twins, but even for solo travelers it's still relatively cheap when you absorb the bill for both beds. The old-fashioned decor in the lobby isn't indicative of the quarters themselves. Rooms are simply furnished and feature hospital-style TVs and an awkwardly placed sink in each. The staff is hit or miss when it comes to general friendliness, but they're never rude. If you stay there for at least 3 nights, they'll even provide you with a bike for cruising around Torremolinos . . . or for escaping to Málaga. *Calle Manila 3.* ☎ *952-381-050. www.hotelcastilla.net. Single 35€, double 47€. Amenities: Breakfast room. In room: TV.*

Eating

➜**El Velero Restaurante** SPANISH/ SEAFOOD Budget-minded backpackers usually are wise to avoid the pricey restaurants located right on the beach. The open-air El Velero is one exception. Decent seafood dishes like fried red snapper are offered on their menu and similar dishes never cost more than 15€. Chances are you won't be spending much on tip either. Waiters here can either be true space cadets or energetic to a fault. *Playa de Bajondillo.* ☎ *952-374-406. Main course 6.50€–15€. Daily 11:30am–11pm, bar until 2am.*

Partying

Torremolinos used to be a rip-roaring good time. Bars and clubs were incredibly popular, the crowd was young and sexed up, and it was common to see a procession of partiers coming in from Málaga every weekend. Unfortunately, things have died down and even though there's a plethora of nightspots still kicking around, they mostly draw the interest of older, middle-aged revelers. However, Torremolinos's gay scene (centered around La Nogalera) keeps the pulse of the town pumping and is one of the hottest places in Costa del Sol for gays and lesbians. There's one spot in particular that makes it worthy for a trip to Torremolinos.

➜**Abadia** It's no surprise that this electric bar is one of the best gay haunts in Costa del Sol. The good-looking crowd, a carefree atmosphere, an excellent bar, and an outdoor terrace make it incredibly popular among gay men. *La Nogalera 521. No phone.*

Shopping

➜**Danger Station** Losing your sunglasses on the beach can be frustrating. Losing your bathing suit in the Mediterranean can be life scarring. Both crises can thankfully be resolved in Danger Station, a store just outside of the town center. Update your surf wardrobe with board shorts, bathing suits, flip-flops, shoes, and sunglasses from familiar brands like Quiksilver, Reef, Oakley, Arnette, and Globe. *Calle Mercedes de las 16.* ☎ *952-050-863.*

COSTA DEL SOL

Nerja

If you were asked where the third most visited site in Spain was, you'd most likely stick to the obvious choices of Madrid, Barcelona, or even Granada for the Alhambra. Instead, you'd have to jump on a bus headed to the eastern end of Costa del Sol to find the **Cueva de Nerja.** Only the Prado Museum (Madrid) and the Alhambra (Granada) see more tourists and sightseers annually than the rocky prehistoric site. The unique beaches in Nerja also manage to draw a great number of vacationers from other parts of the European Union.

Thanks to a particularly craggy shoreline that also produced the amazing set of caves, the crystal clear blue Mediterranean crashes onto little sections of beach bookended by rocky outcroppings. As a result, sunbathers revel in the semi-seclusion of the seemingly less crowded shore. The sense of privacy also makes them less bashful. Walk to the gorgeous **Balcón de Europa,** an esplanade littered with palm trees and pedestrians that overlooks the beach, and look below—you'll find a few square inches of polyester barely qualifying as men's swimwear and women dropping their tops even though the practice is technically illegal. It's Costa del Sol's best display of nature's wonders: caves, coves, and cleavage.

Getting There

From Málaga, there are about 10 buses that go to Nerja daily. For most of these coaches, the final destination isn't Nerja, but the Cueva de Nerja. More ticket booth than station, **buses** arrive and depart from a corner on Avenida Pescia (☎ **952-521-504** for information and schedules) in the northern part of town.

Nerja Basics

ORIENTATION

The streets in Nerja are charming and easy to navigate. In contrast to the other towns in this chapter, they aren't a dense tangle of pathways. Instead, a handful of streets stretch from the main avenue of Avenida Pescia (where the small bus depot is located) to the Mediterranean Sea. One such street is the quaint Almirante Ferrandiz where little boutiques sit side-by-side with homey restaurants. As you reach the very southern end of Almirante Ferrandiz, you'll find the Balcon de Europa. This palm-lined promenade extends out over the beaches and gives visitors an incredible view of the shore and the sea.

TOURIST OFFICE

All your touristy needs can be satisfied in the office at Puerta del Mar 2 (☎ **952-521-531;** www.nerja.org). They're open Monday to Friday 10am to 2pm and 4:30 to 7:30pm and on Saturdays from 10am to 1pm.

RECOMMENDED WEBSITE

○ **www.nerja.org**: The municipal folks at Nerja whipped this site up to help visitors learn a bit more about the town's history and what it has to offer. Find all the info you need about its beaches, an excellent map, and details about the caves here.

Sleeping

While there are no youth hostels in Nerja, there are plenty of places for you to crash without breaking the bank. Like many of the stores and restaurants in Nerja, the hotels and hostels that you'll encounter are for the most part run by extremely friendly small-town folks. You'll find after a few nights in some of these places that it's the closest to home you'll get anywhere on the coast.

➔ **Hostal Azahara** ★★ After a long day of sunbathing and spelunking, nothing tastes better than an ice cold bottle of beer. Thankfully, you can chill your brown bottle of Cruzcampo in your room while you're out and about sightseeing in Nerja. The empty minibar might be a plus, but it's the gracious English and Spanish couple that runs the hostel, going to great lengths for their guests to make sure they're comfortable, that makes it a fantastic place to stay while you're in Nerja. Sometimes the only thing warmer than the atmosphere inside Hostal Azahara is the night air outside but fight the urge to keep the fridge open to cool down the room. While there's no air-conditioning, a fan placed in each room will help you sleep soundly on their super plush beds. *Av. de Pescia 1.* ☎ *952-520-426. www.hostalazahara.com. Single 22€–28€, double 30€–44€. Amenities: Breakfast, Internet point. In room: TV, fridge.*

➔ **Hostal San Miguel** Even if you only have 10 minutes to catch your bus back to Málaga, you can still take a dip, cool off, check out, *and* still have a couple of minutes to spare. Hostal San Miguel, conveniently located right around the corner from the bus depot, is one of the few budget places in town that offers services like a rooftop pool and free wireless Internet to its guests. A restful stay is guaranteed with sturdy beds, air-conditioning, and bathrooms that are simple, but clean. *Calle San Miguel 36.* ☎ *952-521-886. Double 50€. Amenities: Bar, terrace. In room: A/C, TV.*

Eating

Thanks to the presence of many English transplants and tourists, you'll notice a good number of street-side chalkboards advertising British staples such as fish and chips. If you'd rather stick to local fare, you're in luck. Nerja is also home to some incredible seafood joints. Places like Marisqueria La Marina (p. 618) whip up some mean servings of mussels and calamari that loyal locals enjoy on a daily basis.

➔ **The Cottage** ★ TRADITIONAL ENGLISH Those aching for homemade comfort foods should look no further than this cozy, English-speaking restaurant. Nerja's popularity with English vacationers is evident when you glance at The Cottage's menu. British classics like kidney pie are offered as well as more regional dishes such as deep fried hake, a coastal favorite. Food aside, the restaurant has an undeniable familial quality in its decor and ambience. Locals come in and bearhug the owners and staff while newcomers are greeted with an abundance of hospitality. *Calle Cristo 68.* ☎ *952-525-492. Main courses 6€–10€. Menu of the day 8.75€. Mon–Sat 6:30pm–late.*

➔ **Heladeria Cantarero** SNACKS Rather than wait for the bus in the direct sunlight in Nerja's "bus station," head to the fountain in Plaza Cantarero. In the middle of the small park are tables that belong to Heladeria Cantarero. The little store sells two sure-fire summer favorites: ice cream and ice cold beer. Order a few scoops of the cool treat or a few bottles of suds and wait for your bus in the relaxing plaza rather than in the baking hot sun next to what passes as the bus depot. *Plaza Cantarero 2.* ☎ *680-699-704. Daily 9:30am–11:30pm.*

→**Marisqueria La Marina** ★★★ ANDALUSIAN/SEAFOOD Like all other towns in Costa del Sol, seafood restaurants aren't hard to come by in Nerja. Locals, however, don't seem to care about that fact. Instead, they all seem to flock to one spot: the ultrapopular Marisqueria La Marina. Patrons chat over a plate of Galician-style octopus and steamed mussels while enjoying the easygoing surroundings. The restaurant opens up its windows and doors to reveal archways looking out onto the street and the adjacent Plaza Marina creating a cool, laid-back, and social atmosphere. *Av. Castilla Perez 20.* ☎ *952-521-299. Main courses 6€–12€. Daily noon–midnight.*

→**Trébol** ITALIAN/INTERNATIONAL It's within earshot of the parador in Nerja, but you might not find anyone staying there dining in the much too affordable Trébol. Instead, folks on limited budgets and backpackers will love the fact that most things on their menu can be had for under 7€. Enjoy cafeteria staples like pasta, pizza, and paella on the street-side tables looking out onto the roundabout and the fountain in the center. Trébol also has some decent breakfast options, making it a great stop for early risers. *Calle Almuñecar 2.* ☎ *952-523-176. Main courses 6€–11€. Daily 9am–1:30am.*

Partying

Compared to the other beach towns along Costa del Sol, unless there's a cache of ancient hidden dance clubs deep in the cave, the nightlife in Nerja isn't as lively and is in fact limited to a few tapas bars and a couple of discothèques. Nevertheless, there are a few places around the oddly named Plaza Tutti Frutti that do manage to keep the craggy town alive when the late-setting sun disappears. The little plaza hums with activity from the mass of bars

until the wee hours of the morning, when revelers stumble out of the clubs satisfied and starved.

→**Bar Redondo** ★ One of the most popular *tascas* in Nerja sits on the tiny Calle de la Gloria, just off the charming street of Almirante Ferrandiz. Locals flock to Bar Redondo for some friendly banter, a few pints, and tasty tapas. Those who come with a heartier appetite for solids can sit down for larger portions and order from a number of dishes that all cost less than 6€. *Calle de la Gloria 10.* ☎ *952-520-450.*

→**Jimmy's** Nerja's most popular nightclub consistently reels in the town's most attractive and liveliest crowd to its cavernous subterranean confines. Partiers don't have to worry about sweatin' to the oldies here since this air-conditioned scene is and always pumping out decent music ranging from modern pop to electronica and techno. Because of the presence of only a few quality dance clubs in the city, the weekend finds the enormous Jimmy's filled to capacity with tourists and locals. *Calle Antonio Millon. No phone. Cover less than 6€.*

Sightseeing

Throughout the entire region of Costa del Sol there are only a few cultural options to keep you interested when the weather doesn't want to cooperate with your beach-plans. Málaga is the prime spot for sightseeing, but not the only one. Nerja, thankfully, has something up its rocky sleeve.

📺 (Best ✿) →**Cueva de Nerja** ★★★ The rocky coast not only makes for breathtaking and intimate beach spots, but it's also responsible for the archaeological gem in the hills of Nerja. The cave wasn't discovered until the 1950s when a few boys stumbled upon it by accident. Visitors can now marvel at the enormous spaces within the cave as well as faint traces of life left behind by the former tenants of the cave: prehistoric paintings of horses and deer that adorn the incredibly high rock face. Buses from both Málaga and Nerja regularly leave for the cave every hour or so. *Carretera de Maro s/n.* ☎ *952-529-635. Admission 5€ adults. Daily 10am–2pm and 4–6:30pm.*

Shopping

➔ **Smiffs** Whether you need a new novel to leaf through on the beach or need to replace your well-worn copy of *MTV Spain,* Smiffs should have just what you're looking for. The English couple that runs the bookstore is a genuinely friendly duo that goes to great lengths to help anyone who enters their cozy store. Can't decide which novel to tackle, which hotel to stay in, or even which restaurant is serving the freshest seafood that week? Smiffs is your man. *Calle Almirante Ferrándiz 10.* ☎ *952-523-102. www.booksaboutspain.com.*

Appendix A: Spain in Depth

by Fernando Gayesky

Amazing beaches, sunny skies, endless nights. Thirteenth-century cities full of history, streets for you to get literally lost in. Little towns, where people live almost exactly as they did 100 years ago and the fish you eat was bought directly from the fishermen that morning.

Spain is a crossroad in times. People celebrate their festivals as they did hundreds of years ago, but under the shadow of 21st-century skyscrapers; while pilgrims walk through small, labyrinthine medieval streets alongside high-speed train rails on their way to their destination.

Spain is also a harmonious clash of cultures. A church might have been a mosque under the Moors, a Visigoth church before that, or even a pagan temple in advance of the Romans becoming Christian. Every region here has a distinctive culture, steeped in its own traditions and perhaps even its own language that may be counted among the oldest in the world. Yet, cities like Barcelona have become the kind of cosmopolitan places where the world's cultures mix with local flavor, creating a cultural paella that is truly unique to Spain. It is, after all, the second fastest growing economy in the E.U. With tourism as one of its biggest industries, Spain is rapidly becoming one of the most visited destinations in the world.

Spain Today

It's amazing to think that a little more than 30 years ago Spain was an ultra-Catholic country ruled with an iron fist by "Generalisimo" Franco after a civil war, one of the most awful conflicts a country can face. Luckily, although those kinds of scars never quite fade away, Spain has risen from the ashes and is becoming one of Europe's foremost countries. Spain is now part of the E.U., which means that pesetas have gone the way of the dinosaur, and its legal currency is the euro.

Although Spain is officially a democratic country fronted by a chosen parliament and prime minister, it also has a king, and a pretty liked one. Juan Carlos I was actually Franco's successor, but he rapidly distanced himself from that legacy. He is a hard-working king and has even earned the people's respect by taking a pretty low salary, for a king that is, earning less than one-tenth of what Queen Elizabeth II is reputed to earn in a year.

Under this political system Spain has continued to distance itself from the conservatism of Franco's dark ages. In this once extremely buttoned-down country, divorce has become legal, every woman has access to contraception and abortion, and—since 2005 when Spain became the third country in the world to legalize gay marriage—annual lesbian "kiss-ins" are celebrated at Madrid's Puerta del Sol.

Art, literature, and cinema are quite alive and well in modern Spain, reflecting the prosperity of the nation and the populace's confidence in their future. Following the footsteps of some of the most revolutionary artists of the 20th century, thousands of innovative artists pullulate through the streets of every big city. The living statues and street cartoonists bring elemental street art to the people, while the more well-known artists present their work in galleries and theaters to a sometimes more exclusive crowd.

History

Over the years Spain has been invaded and conquered by more men than Elizabeth Taylor can count as husbands. And, just like Liz did, Spain kept something from each of them.

The oldest set of bones discovered in Europe was found near Burgos, in la Sierra de Atapuerca. Archaeological research and findings tell us that Spain might have been populated as early as 780,000 years ago. The caves of Altamira show some signs of that. There we can find some of the most impressive prehistoric paintings in the world. Hunters used to depict themselves and the prey they hunted so they could relive the highlights, sort of like the first ESPN Web Gems ever.

Carthaginians & Rome

This first Iberian people traded with the Phoenicians and Greeks to the south and the Celts to the north. Eventually, a Carthaginian colony that was a branch of a former Phoenician colony from North Africa was established in Ibiza, replacing the Greeks and Phoenicians as the main power in the Mediterranean Sea. But like the school bully on the playground, their power went to their heads and they decided to start a conflict with some new guys who were starting to get busy in the Mediterranean: the Romans.

The conflict, known as the Punic Wars, was a huge rumble. Carthage brought its troops—complete with elephants—straight across Spain and over the Alps to attack Rome. Warriors who had never seen anything like an elephant shook in their boots as the hulking beasts charged them. The Punic Wars would make quite a summer blockbuster.

But by the end of the third Punic War, Carthage was destroyed. As a result, the Mediterranean belonged to the Romans who, in turn, set out to conquer the Iberian peninsula. It took them almost 200 years to subdue the fiercest local tribes, but when they finally did, they were able to hang onto control of the region for 600 years. By A.D. 50 all of "Hispania" had adopted the Roman way of life, which, for the times, was actually quite luxurious. They had roads, aqueducts, theaters and amphitheaters, temples, circuses, baths—and churches, since Romans introduced the peninsula to Christianity. The best places to see the remnants of the Roman presence in Spain are Empúries, Itálica, Mérida, Tarragona, and Segovia.

The Germanic Tribes

Around A.D. 410 the Vandals, a Germanic tribe displaced by the Huns, overran the peninsula and gave the boot to the Roman administration. The next to unify the peninsula under one regime were the Visigoths, another Germanic ethnic group. When the Western Roman Empire fell, the Visigoths were pushed from the Gault and into Hispania, where they settled, making Toledo their capital. It was difficult for them to rule the very sophisticated Hispanic-Romans, whose know-how was needed to run a bureaucratic state that the Visigoths didn't quite grasp. You can still see some Visigoth churches in northern Spain, including the oldest church in the country, which dates from 661.

The Advance of Islam

By 700 the Visigoth empire was falling apart, and the Islamic nation jumped in to sweep up. This was the turning point that forever distanced Spain from the rest of Europe. In 711, Tariq ibn Ziyad, the Muslim governor of Tangier, landed in Gibraltar with 10,000 men, and the Visigoths were decimated. In a matter of years, the Muslims took control of most of the peninsula, with the exception of some small areas to the north. They even tried to cross the Pyrenees, but were spanked and sent back by Charlemagne's grandfather, Carlos Martel.

Muslim Spain, known as Al-Andalus, was one of the most advanced cultures in medieval history. They even introduced soap in Europe—how smart was that?! And, perhaps more importantly, they gradually reintroduced all the ancient Greek knowledge and wisdom that had fled east, escaping the Western Roman Empire's debacle. In Toledo in the 13th century, a translation school was founded, where Moors, Jews, and Christians came together to translate the important thinkers of the day, like Aristotle, from Arabic to Latin. Without the Moors, Toledo's school of translation would never have existed, and those works that shaped our civilization might have been lost to the western world entirely.

Dateline

- **11th century B.C.** Phoenicians settle Spain's coasts.
- **650 B.C.** Greeks colonize the east.
- **600 B.C.** Celts cross the Pyrenees and settle in Spain.
- **6th–3rd century B.C.** Carthaginians make Cartagena their colonial capital, driving out the Greeks.
- **218–201 B.C.** Second Punic War: Rome defeats Carthage.
- **2nd century B.C.–A.D.** 2nd century Rome controls most of Iberia. Christianity spreads.
- **5th century** Vandals, then Visigoths, invade Spain.
- **8th century** Moors conquer most of Spain.
- **1214** More than half of Iberia is regained by Catholics.
- **1469** Ferdinand of Aragón marries Isabella of Castile.
- **1492** Catholic monarchs seize Granada, the last Moorish stronghold. Columbus lands in the New World.

Cordoba Emirate & Caliphate, Almoravids & Almohads, the Nasrid Emirate of Granada & Other Tongue Twisters

Initially Al-Andalus was part of the caliphate of Damascus, which lorded it over the Muslim world. But when Damascan rule ended in 752, a survivor of that dynasty established himself in Cordoba as the independent emir of Al-Andalus. At this time the Moorish territories in Spain were more or less unified and Al-Andalus reached its peak of power and beauty. Cordoba was the biggest and most impressive city in all of Western Europe, and the court of the caliph was frequented by Arab, Jewish, and Christian scholars alike. At this time the grand *mezquita* (mosque) of Cordoba was built.

In the 10th century, a ferocious Cordoban general, Al-Mansour, raided Santiago de Compostela and destroyed its cathedral, absconding with no less than the doors and bells, which were then integrated into the grand *mezquita.* After his death, the Caliphate disintegrated into dozens of *taifas,* or small kingdoms.

One of these *taifas,* the Sevilla branch, invited the Almoravid—a strict Muslim sect that had conquered North Africa—in 1091 to help them combat the growing Christian threat from the north. They invaded the peninsula and once again restored Al-Andalus's political unity. Although, it didn't last long, at least historically speaking; 70 years later a new sect came from North Africa and invaded Spain: the Almohads. Under their rule Sevilla had a cultural revival.

Prey of internal disputes and Christian advances, the Almohad's power disintegrated and Sevilla fell to the Christians in 1248. After that the only Muslim territory left in Spain was the Emirate of Granada ruled by the Nasrid dynasty. Granada saw the last blooming of Muslim culture in Spain, especially in the 14th century. You can still see where it left its mark in the splendors of the Alhambra.

During the 800 years that the Moorish occupation lasted in Spain, the frontiers of Al-Andalus were constantly changing. There were 8 centuries of war as the Christians tried to recover the peninsula from the north. Not only that, but the

- 1519 Cortés conquers Mexico. Charles I is crowned Holy Roman Emperor, as Charles V.
- 1556 Philip II inherits the throne and launches the Counter-Reformation.
- 1588 England defeats the Spanish Armada.
- 1700 Philip V becomes king. The War of Spanish Succession follows.
- 1713 Treaty of Utrecht ends the war. Spain's colonies are reduced.
- 1759 Charles III ascends throne.
- 1808 Napoleon places his brother Joseph on the Spanish throne.
- 1813 Wellington drives the French out of Spain; the monarchy is restored.
- 1876 Spain becomes a constitutional monarchy.
- 1898 Spanish-American War leads to Spain's loss of Puerto Rico, Cuba, and the Philippines.
- 1923 Primo de Rivera forms a military directorate.
- 1930 Right-wing dictatorship ends; Primo de Rivera exiled.

continues

Moors were also internally divided, and Christian Muslim alliances seethed from within as well.

The Muslim political and cultural center shifted during their reign. Originally in Cordoba, it then moved to Sevilla and finally to Granada. In these cities you can still see the amazing palaces, mosques, gardens, and universities that the Moors built.

La Reconquista

It took the Moors just a few short years to conquer most of the Iberian peninsula, but as soon as the Christians realized what had happened, they mounted a counter-offensive—only they were not quite as fast as the Moors had been. La Reconquista (the recovery) started as soon as 722 at Covadonga, Asturias, and it ended in 1492 with the fall of Granada. You do the math! Suffice to say, it was an incredibly long affair conducted against the Muslims by a series of Christian states that were just as often as not warring against each other too. For all the pains it took, though, the Moors were pushed to the south and eventually out of the country entirely as the northern kingdoms of Asturias, León, Navarra, Castile, and Aragón developed.

The Killer Saint

The cult of Santiago, one of the 12 apostles, was an essential part of the Reconquista. His tomb was supposedly discovered in A.D. 813 in Galicia. The whole town of Santiago de Compostela grew on the spot and became the third most popular pilgrimage destination in medieval times. Pilgrims would walk for miles through dangerous forests and other places dark and scary to get there—and they still do it today, although hotels with food and A/C have replaced caves and berries along the way.

During the Reconquista it is said that Christian generals had visions of Santiago, who was also known as Santiago Matamoros (Moor-slayer). Today, he is the patron saint of Spain.

The Catholic Monarchs

By 1476 the last enclave of the Moors was Granada, but they wouldn't be able to hold out for long against the combined forces of Castile and Aragón under the leadership of Catholic monarchs Isabella and Ferdinand. Much like Ozzy and Sharon, they were an unbeatable team. They got married in

- 1931 King Alfonso XIII abdicates; Second Republic is born.
- 1933–35 Falange party formed.
- 1936–39 Civil War between the governing Popular Front and the Nationalists led by Gen. Francisco Franco.
- 1939 Franco establishes dictatorship, which will last 36 years.

- 1941 Spain technically stays neutral in World War II, but Franco favors Germany.
- 1955 Spain joins the United Nations.
- 1975 Juan Carlos becomes king. Franco dies.
- 1978 New democratic constitution initiates reforms.
- 1981 Coup attempt by right-wing officers fails.

- 1982 Socialists gain power after 43 years of right-wing rule.
- 1986 Spain joins the European Community (now the European Union).
- 1992 Barcelona hosts the Summer Olympics; Seville hosts EXPO '92.
- 1996 A conservative party defeats the Socialist party, ending its 13-year rule. José

It Is ROUND, Coño!

By 1492 trade routes to the Orient were severed and Spain was in serious need of another route. So the kings decided to listen to this Genovese merchant who was pretty sure that the earth was round and that he could reach the east by traveling to the west. Pretty wise of them to do so, because this *loco*-sounding Genovese turned out to be Christopher Columbus, the most famous explorer ever. He set off from the port of Palos de la Frontera with three small ships and 120 men (most of them prisoners trying to commute their sentence—no one else would be so crazy as to go with him). They sailed west for over a month without seeing land whatsoever and, finally, when his crew was about to hang him and turn back, they reached the island of Guanahani in The Bahamas. Columbus made three more voyages and "discovered" some more Caribbean islands and even the mouth of the Orinoco in Venezuela.

This was the beginning of the golden age for Spain, but Columbus ended up betrayed by his comrades, doing some time, and then dying broke in Valladolid in 1506, convinced that he had reached Asia.

1469, Isabella succeeded to the Castilian throne in 1474, and Ferdinand got crowned in Aragon in 1479. In 1492 they snagged back Granada and it was curtains for the Muslim presence in Spain. That was the year, too, in which they decided to fund the expedition of a crazy guy who was pretty sure the earth was round . . . Ring any bells? Yes, the Catholic monarchs flashed their cash and became Christopher Columbus's Russell Simmons, officially underwriting his little mission.

Not all was roses during their reign, though. They also instituted that nasty thing known as the Spanish Inquisition. Besides being fodder for old Monty Python skits, it was a sort of religious police that would judge, torture, and convict (usually to death) anyone whom they thought was not practicing Christianity as they should. Inspired by the Grand Inquisitor Tomás de Torquemada, they expelled Jews from Spain and persecuted Muslims, eradicating anything that had to do with their culture. The Inquisición cost the lives and happiness of thousands of innocent people, who were targeted and killed for their religious beliefs.

María Aznar is chosen prime minister.
- 1998 The controversial Guggenheim Museum at Bilbao is inaugurated, and Madrid's opera house, Teatro Real, reopens.

- 2002 Spain gives up its historic currency, the peseta, and adopts the euro as its national currency.
- 2003 Basque terrorists continue a campaign of terror against the government.

- 2004 Al-Qaeda strikes Spanish trains in the deadliest terrorist attack in Europe since World War II.
- 2005 Gay marriage is legalized in Spain.

The Gold Rush

Ferdinand and Isabella married their kids off pretty well. As a result, when Carlos I, their grandson, inherited Spain's throne, he ended up being the ruler of Spain, the Low Countries, Austria, several Italian states, and parts of France and Germany— plus the colonies, of course. He was also the founder of the Habsburg dynasty. Those were the days for Spain and when people really knew how to make a living. Gold was pouring in from the colonies, conquerors like Cortés and Pizarro in America were adding chunks of territories the size of Europe every day—even Portugal was added when its king died in 1580, unifying not only the whole peninsula, but also two of the largest overseas empires. Folks like the Habsburgs, who weren't famous for their economic skills, used every penny they had to build churches, palaces, and monasteries to make sure they got their place in the sun too.

The last of the Habsburgs, though, were more concentrated in living *la vida loca* than in ruling. While perfect at house parties, that's never really good news for a country. They eventually lost Portugal, ended up flat broke, with revolts breaking out all over the country. When Carlos II failed to produce an heir (no Viagra back then) before he died, the war of the Spanish succession broke out. This 13-year struggle more or less molded Spain's actual borders, and the Bourbon dynasty, which is still in place today, emerged on top.

The Decline

Although the 18th century was known as the Age of Enlightenment for most of Europe, new ideas had real problems crossing the Pyrenees, since the Spanish Inquisition would arrest and, more often than not, execute the messenger, literally.

That's how Spain briefly stayed behind the rest of Europe, even declaring war on France during the French Revolution. However, a few years later they found themselves allied with Napoleon to divide Portugal between them. They let Napoleon's troops enter Spain on their way to Portugal—big mistake!—and the French decided to stay. It took 6 years to evict them.

During that time, some of Spain's colonies decided that they would not obey the puppet king whom Napoleon had set in place of Ferdinand VII, Spain's legitimate ruler. They began the process of independence that would, in the end, cost Spain almost all of its colonies in America.

On the home front, a national parliament in Cadiz wrote a new liberal constitution following the French and American models. This was the first spark of a fire that would rage in Spain for the next century. Very rapidly two sides formed: on one side of the ring, the liberals, who wanted the Cadiz constitution to be enforced, and on the other side, the church, the monarchy, and other conservative sectors weighed in. Ferdinand VII revoked the Libs's constitution as soon as he got back in power, prosecuting all the pro-constitutioners and reestablishing the Inquisition. And we thought it was bad between liberals and conservatives today.

The First Republic

Ferdinand was about as popular as Kevin after Britney dumped him, and, when he died, a war began for succession of his throne. It was known as the First Carlist War (1833–39) and was—not so shockingly with a name like that—only the first of many. Passing on the royal torch was not peaceful in this century as the church, the aristocracy, the military, and the liberals all kicked and scrummed to get their candidates on top. Between 1872 and 1876 the

Second Carlist War erupted, only ending when the parliament proclaimed Spain a federal republic made up of 17 states. But Spain was in too much turmoil for such a weak government to control it, and peacetime lasted only 11 months. At the end, the army propped up Alfonso, Ferdinand's grandson, in the throne as Alfonso XII and, in a coalition with the church and the landowners, set up a new constitution that recognized the monarchy and the parliament. And so the table was set for the supposed conservatives to have their say in the government.

Early 20th Century

Alfonso and his fat friends in the church, in the military, and among the rich landowners were finally happy; but on the other side of the social spectrum things were beginning to get agitated. A short period of prosperity allowed cities like Madrid, Barcelona, and some Basque cities to industrialize. This brought big money to some, but also big slums, as a new proletarian class formed, mainly from the large migrations from the countryside. Slowly, the pissed-off working class gravitated toward Marxism and anarchism.

The direct-action philosophy of the Russian anarchist Mikhail Bakunin quickly gained adepts among the impoverished peasants of Andalucía, Aragón, Catalonia, and northwestern Spain, and also in the slums of Barcelona and other big cities. Bakunin believed in a free society with no state in which everyone would openly collaborate with one another. In his arsenal was a series of strikes and revolts. At the beginning of the century, anarchists carried out some bombings, like the one that took the life of 24 people in Alfonso XIII's wedding, and finally organized themselves in the powerful Confederacion Nacional del Trabajo (CNT, National Confederation of Work).

Socialism's growth was more peaceful because of its less-extremist strategy of effecting steady change through parliamentary processes. Socialists congregated in the Union General de Trabajadores (UGT, General Union of Workers) and got most of their support in urban areas such as Madrid and Bilbao. As if it wasn't enough with the rise of the leftist anarchists and socialists, Basque and Catalonian separatism started to grow.

During WWI Spain stayed neutral and some members of society enjoyed an economic boom. But anarchist and socialist numbers continued to grow among the disenfranchised, and political violence and general mayhem continued, especially in Barcelona.

Primo de Rivera

In 1921, 10,000 Spanish soldiers were killed in Morocco. Everyone blamed King Alfonso, except for General Miguel Primo de Rivera, an eccentric Andalusian aristocrat. In 1923 he led an army rising in support of the king, only to swing the whole coup in his favor and launch his own mild dictatorship.

Allied with the UGT, Primo founded industries, improved roads, and built dams and power plants. But the entire economy went down the toilet with Wall Street's crash, which pretty much reverbed around the world, and Alfonso took the chance to return to power and get Primo out of the way.

The Second Republic

But monarchy was as well-received as Michael Moore at Camp David and, when the new republican movement won the municipal election in 1931, the king went into exile in Italy and the second republic was born.

Its government was mainly composed of socialists, republicans, and so-called radicals, but it had little, if any, worker representation and no one from the CNT. While they were in charge, however, quite a lot was done to secularize the state—separating it from the church, disbanding the Jesuits, and breaking their monopoly on education—and to promote a new constitution that, among other things, gave women the right to vote, legalized divorce in Spain, and gave Catalonia its own parliament.

Yet turbulence and political violence never quite ceased to grow, and in 1933 the right won the most seats in parliamentary elections. Violence broke out around the country. In 1934 UGT called for a general workers strike, Catalonia declared itself independent, and labor committees took over the mining regions of Asturias.

This was the cue for the protagonist of the recent not-so-happy history of Spain to appear: General Francisco Franco. He led the Spanish Foreign Legion (created to fight Moroccan tribes in the 1920s) in a violent campaign against the Asturian workers that polarized Spain into left and right quadrants for good.

Spanish Civil War

In February 1936 a left-wing coalition narrowly won the election. Extremist groups continued to grow on both sides and there seemed to be no stopping the violence. The revolt came from the right-wing supporters on July 1936. An army garrison in Melilla, North Africa, rose up against the government, followed by some garrisons on the mainland the day after.

The civil war was unavoidable now and it would rage through Spain pitting brother against brother, and leaving no family unscarred. It is easy to think of Franco as the bad guy, but in this case it's fair to say that both sides did awful things. They committed massacres and used death squads, killed their enemy's supporters by the

The WWII Dress Rehearsal

So, while the Spaniards ripped each other apart, did the world just stand there and watch? Of course not, they gave the Spaniards weapons! Nazi Germany and Fascist Italy gave support to the nationalists in the form of planes, weapons, and men (almost 100,000 between the both of them). The republicans received planes, tanks, artillery, and advisors from the Soviets.

In April 1937 German planes bombed the Basque town of Guernica causing an enormous amount of fatalities. Picasso immortalized this bombing in his touching painting with the name of the town, while the rest of the world watched.

thousands, and wreaked all the horrific collateral damage a war usually brings. Almost 350,000 Spaniards died as a consequence.

On the one side, the Nationalists, composed mainly of the army and civil guards, thought they were defending their country against the enemies of God. On the other side, the republicans, anarchists, socialists, and communists thought they were fighting for a better world and increased social justice.

From the beginning, the advance of the well-organized troops of the nationalists was slow but steady. In November 1936 Franco set Madrid under a siege that lasted almost 2 years. The government moved to Valencia and, eventually, to Barcelona from where it fled to France, when the city fell in January 1939. Madrid fell on March 28, and Franco called the war on the first of April.

The Dark Days

Franco was as merciless after the war as he was during it. One hundred thousand people were killed or died in prison in times of "peace," many of them intellectuals and teachers. Those who were able to avoid persecution fled to other countries. A whole generation of thinkers, artists, scientists, and educators was forced to disappear overnight.

And so Franco reigned unopposed. Parliament was a joke, simply legitimating Franco's whims. Any regional aspirations of autonomy were crushed. The Catholic orthodoxy was at its highest, and Jesuits ruled supreme in the schools. Workers had paid holidays, but no right to strike, and the only political organization was the Movimiento Nacional.

Although he had promised his support to Hitler, Franco remained officially neutral during WWII. In the end, Spain was excluded from the UN and NATO and had to cope with a UN-sponsored post-WWII reconstruction that left Spain out, spawning what Spaniards know as *los años de hambre* (the years of hunger). But during the Cold War, the American need to establish some bases on the Iberian peninsula bought Franco some relief and large sums of financial aid. Spain was accepted into the UN in 1955.

The Next Years

In 1959 Spain launched a plan that was able to bring an upswing in the economy. Modernization was funded by U.S. aid, but, more than anything, with tourism. By 1965, over 14 million tourists had arrived in Spain. They brought a remarkable amount of money, which was accompanied by a huge migration from impoverished rural regions to cities and tourist resorts.

Even though Spain was doing a lot better due to this rising service industry and experiencing what a lot of people called an "economic miracle," jails were packed with political prisoners, every major city was watched by a large garrison, and regional problems resurfaced. In 1959 the terrorist organization Euskadi Ta Batasuna (ETA) was born, and, over the years, it committed ferocious acts of terrorism and bombings. Franco's brutal police tactics won the ETA a lot of support, even with moderate Basques.

By the end of Franco's administration, discontent had been steadily rising among workers, universities, and even the army and the church. And when some reforms made by his prime minister, Carlos Arias Navarro, in July 1975, met with violent right-wing opposition, it seemed like chaos was starting all over again.

Back to Democracy

Franco died in November 1975 leaving as his successor prince Juan Carlos, grandson of Alfonso XIII. Juan Carlos I had sworn loyalty to Franco and the Movimiento Nacional, so he did not inspire any confidence in a people screaming for democracy. Luckily, he was a sheep in wolf's clothing. He fired Arias Navarro and appointed as prime minister Adolfo Suárez, another former Francoist; and, to everyone's surprise, he managed to get a new two-chamber parliamentary system approved by Franco's old parliament. By 1977 political parties, trade unions, and strikes were legal again and the Movimiento Nacional was abolished. Talk about a surprise comeback!

Suárez's party won more than half the seats in Parliament in 1977, and a year later Spain got a new constitution that made it a parliamentary monarchy with no official religion. By 1983 the country was divided in 17 autonomous communities, each one with its own regional government. Franco's centralism was finally undone.

It wasn't only politically that Spain was changing. A newborn live-and-let-live mentality has taken hold after the dark days of social oppression. Contraceptives, homosexuality, and divorce were legalized and, in these years, the counterculture of the Movida Madrileña was born. Lucky us! Thanks to this, we can go partying all night long.

The New Spain

Nineteen eighty-two marked the final break with Franco's regime. In that year the Partido Socialista Obrero Español (PSOE, Spain's Socialist Worker's Party) clearly won the elections. Felipe Gonzalez would be elected prime minister and would remain in office for the next 14 years.

Although unemployment rose in these years, the government allowed industries to become competitive and Spain to enter the E.U., which immersed the country in a general economic boom. Thanks to the PSOE's reforms, a huge middle class formed, women gained access to higher education and jobs, university populations soared to more than a million, and a new healthcare system was set in place.

But such a booming economy couldn't last forever. By 1992, in spite of Barcelona hosting the Olympics, and Seville the world's fair, the economy halted as unemployment reached 22.5%. Worse yet, the PSOE was involved on all sorts of scandals, from corruption to connections with a death squad that had assassinated 28 suspected ETA members (several of whom it turns out actually weren't).

In 1996 the Partido Popular (PP, or people's party), a center-right party, won the general elections and elected José María Aznar prime minister. The PP reduced state control, selling its enterprises and liberalizing various government sectors, and reformed Spain's employment system. As a result, by 2000 Spain had the fastest growing economy in the E.U., and unemployment had plummeted to 15%.

Aznar also adopted a hard line against Basque terrorism. He banned Batasuna, ETA's political wing, and refused to have any dealings with ETA until they deposed their arms. In 2002 and 2003, the administration made some high-profile arrests to prove it was on the business end of the game.

Following the September 11, 2001, terrorist attacks on the U.S., Aznar supported the U.S.-led invasion of Iraq and even sent troops, despite the fact that 90% of the population was against it.

Nevertheless the PP was stronger than ever and seemed ready to win the elections in 2004.

11M

Thursday, March 11, 2004, is one of those days that forever mark a country's history. Early in the morning, four crowded commuter trains were bombed in Madrid. One hundred ninety-two people were killed and over 1,800 were injured. Millions of Spaniards poured onto the streets the day after, coordinating demonstrations for peace and solidarity all over the country.

Government was quick to put the blame on ETA, in spite of evidence that pointed in Islamic extremists' direction. On Saturday, March 13, police in Madrid arrested three Moroccans and two Indians with suspected links to Al-Qaeda. The Spanish people perceived the government blaming ETA as an attempt to manipulate public opinion and decrease the focus on the PP's very unpopular Iraq policies.

The following day, the PSOE, which supposedly had no chance, won the election, led by José Luís Rodriguez Zapatero. Two weeks after taking office, Zapatero and his government pulled Spanish troops out of Iraq.

Eating

Eating in Spain is not a subject to be taken lightly. Spaniards like to eat well and, in fact, spend more money per capita on food than any other Europeans. You rarely hear the likes of "Let's grab a quick bite" in Spain. If you are with a Spaniard, you'll sit and have a real meal for lunch, or some tapas, but forget about the 30-minute lunch special. Whether it's over late-night drinks or a traditional family lunch, dining is a social event.

If you're a fussy eater, don't worry. Spain's cuisine is fairly simple. Adolf Loos said, "Ornament is a crime" and, as far as food goes, Spanish chefs live up to the saying, using lots of garlic and olive oil and few other spices and embellishments. This also means that you probably won't ever receive a half-full plate, with mounds of parsley and carved inedibles for garnish. Cooking is not necessarily a visual art here. Dishes are, first and foremost, unpretentious and generous, so you'll rarely be left wanting more.

Meals

BREAKFAST The only place where you'll find eggs and bacon for your breakfast will be in a hotel . . . a really fancy one, probably. In Spain, breakfast is not an important meal. It may even be reduced to a lonely cup of coffee before running to work or school. However, the most delicious Spanish breakfast you can get is *chocolate con churros. Churros* are a type of fried fingerlike doughnuts, and *chocolate* means thick and really tasty hot chocolate. As far as coffee goes, it's served hot and you can have it black, as a *café con leche* (half coffee and half milk), or a *cortado* (espresso with a little bit of milk). Be advised, Spanish coffee is not for the caffeine-challenged, though some places in Spain will serve you a diluted *Café Americano* if you are more Laurel than Hardy.

LUNCH Go crazy! This is it! The ultimate meal! The most important part of every Spaniard's day! Why do you think that shops usually close from 1 to 4pm? Lunch is the time for Spaniards to get together and share a meal with friends. It will usually begin with soup or a quite large portion of hors d'oeuvres. A fish or egg dish is usually served after that, then meat with vegetables, and finally some pastries, custard, or fruits as dessert, plus a coffee. Have you been counting? Yes, you need an Anna Nicole–size stomach to stay hungry after all of that! Food is always, but always accompanied with wine. Lunch is served between 1 and 4pm and may last up to 2 hours, leaving you time for a much-needed siesta after using all that energy to eat, talk, and drink.

TAPAS Every tourist resource in the world agrees: You haven't been to Spain if you had no tapas. Anything can be considered a tapa, a bit of ham and cheese, some mussels, a *tortilla española* (potato and onion omelet), anything that can be cut in small pieces and served with a glass of wine. The natural habitat of this, the most Spanish kind of place of them all, is the *tasca:* a bar especially dedicated to eating tapas, usually taken standing by the bar. Tapas are not only a food but a Spanish right to socialize and make friends.

DINNER Dinner is similar to lunch: soup, fish, meat, dessert, and coffee. Of course, since you probably had a serious lunch around 2pm you won't normally be down for dinner until 10pm. Most restaurants aren't even open before 8:30pm, but in most touristy areas you might be able to find *somewhere* to eat around 8pm. Restaurants will generally have their kitchens open until 11pm. In touristy places, you may have problems finding a table after 10pm during the high season, so try to make reservations or be there earlier.

The Cuisine

SOUPS & APPETIZERS If you want to be on the safe side, go for traditional gazpacho, our main recommendation for Spanish soup. Served chilled, gazpacho is really tasty and refreshing during the hellish heats of summer. Cucumbers, carrots, peppers, tomatoes, and, of course, garlic and olive oil, all puréed into a cold soup. You can even get it in the supermarket and it'll probably still be cheap and tasty. There are also quite a few varieties of fish soup, depending on where in Spain you are. Cheap soups often may be made from powdered envelope soups such as Knorr and Liebig, so if you have a lackluster experience, just try to move on.

Appetizers come in so many shapes and colors in Spain that you'll think you got sucked onto the 1968 set of *Barbarella*. But beware; if you get them in shady places you might be getting some leftovers from Altamira's caves. The best special secret places in a city are not discovered by playing it safe, but there are few things more annoying than losing a day on the beach because of indigestion. So choose wisely, my friend.

TORTILLAS Spaniards do have quite an imagination when it comes to serving an egg. The best of the countless ways they'll find to cook it is the *tortilla española,* an omelet with onions and potatoes. Your everyday omelet is called *tortilla francesa,* and you'll get what you know as a Spanish omelet (onions and peppers) if you order a *tortilla portuguesa.*

FISH As with almost every other food, fish recipes will vary from province to

province, but they are normally prepared with fish so fresh that it might have been swimming 15 minutes ago. You'll get a lot of *merluza* (sweet white hake) and probably the best *mejillones* (mussels) you'll ever taste. If you're passing through the Basque provinces do not forget to try the charcoal-broiled sardines. And though it looks kind of scary, the squid cooked in its own ink has a taste you won't forget easily.

PAELLA Ah paella. The most famous Spanish dish in the world. Like fish and chips in England or a juicy burger in the States, if you are only in Spain for a day, this has got to be on your meal itinerary. Brought directly from the kitchen to your table this steaming pan of saffron-flavored rice will rank high in your Spanish food gallery. It is usually served with shellfish, chicken, sausage, peppers, and lots of spices. Don't touch the *paellera,* the metal pan in which they cook and bring the paella to your table—it will be smokin' hot.

MEAT Pass the chicken and the steak, and go directly to the pork. It's all about the pig here, and Spaniards roast pork so well that it almost dissolves in your mouth. Be sure to try the *lomo de cerdo.*

VEGETABLES & SALADS Spain does have its share of fresh home-cultivated vegetables. Still, vegetarians will get sick of traditional salads pretty quickly. Mostly they'll be made of just tomatoes with lettuce, and sometimes, if you're lucky, some olives and fresh cheese. Potatoes and rice are very widely used. Potatoes appear fried, in tortillas, boiled, or mashed. Rice is the prime ingredient in paellas as well as plenty of other dishes if you need to load those carbs.

DESSERTS Desserts are not normally the focal point of the menu, and most Spaniards tend to enjoy fresh fruit instead. You can get a home-cooked egg custard called *flan* almost everywhere in Spain, as well as some basic ice creams. Even pastries are not as sweet as the teeth-melting Dunkin' Donuts and Little Debbies we might be used to.

Beverages

WATER Water in Spain is safe to drink for the most part. If you're playing Columbus and trying to discover a new land in the wilds, you'll be safer drinking bottled water. Otherwise, just ask for *agua mineral con gas,* if you want carbonated water, or *agua mineral sin gas,* for no bubbles.

SOFT DRINKS Our favorite summertime drink is the Spanish *horchata.* This milklike beverage is made of tiger nuts and sugar. You'll find it mostly in the regions of Catalonia and Valencia. If you want a bottle of *gaseosa* (soda), it's cheapest by the liter at the supermarket.

COFFEE & MILK We've said it once, we'll say it again: Coffee in Spain is not for lightweights. You can always try a *leche manchada,* or glass of milk with just a stain

of coffee. Bottled milk is easy to get in supermarkets in Spain. You might come across some unpasteurized milk products, especially cheese, in some remote areas. But otherwise, fresh local cheese and bread makes a lovely cheap meal.

BEER In hot sunny Spain, you'll find cold beer everywhere, even at the drive-thru at McDonald's. Bars and *tascas* always offer a variety of beer on tap. Ask for *caña,* if you want a small one, *jarra,* if you're thirsty, or *clara,* if you want it mixed with some lemon soda. Domestic brands are San Miguel, Mahou, Aguila, and Cruz Blanca; but around Plaza Santa Ana in Madrid you'll find a whole line of micro-breweries if you want a special treat.

WINE Wine is an important part of every meal in Spain. Spaniards start drinking wine in their most tender years, although the legal age for buying it is 18. But instead of growing up to be a nation of drunkards, they (eventually) develop responsible attitudes toward drinking. As far as table wines go, you can just ask for the *vino de la casa* (house wine). It's usually decent and it's the cheapest option. Nevertheless Valdepeñas and Rioja, from Castile, are our recommendations for the would-be connoisseur. One of the most famous nonwine drinks you'll find here is *vino de Jerez* (sherry), which was originally from Andalucía but is now available all over Spain. Spaniards drink it as an aperitif or as a refreshment. If you're ordering the variety of sherry called *vino de Manzanilla,* don't try to sound like you're in the know and ask for *manzanilla*—you will get a hot cup of herbal chamomile tea. Spain also has good sparkling wines, known as *cava;* if you want the most famous for your Kir Royale, try the Freixenet.

A Taste of Catálan Bubbly

Catalonia is famous for its *cava,* the local name for champagne. Throughout Barcelona champagne bars are called *xampanyerías.* For a fun night on the town, go on a champagne bar crawl sampling the local bubbly. Our favorites include **El Xampanyet** (Carrer Montcada 22; ☎ **933-197-003;** Metro: Jaume I), close to the Picasso Museum in the old town on an ancient street. Revelers go here to drink the champagne at marble tables and to feast on tapas. Open Tuesday to Saturday noon to 4pm and 7 to 11:30pm, Sunday noon to 4pm. Closed in August. Another favorite, **Xampanyería Casablanca** (Bonavista 6; ☎ **932-376-399;** Metro: Passeig de Gràcia or Diagonal), honors the World War II classic film starring Bogart and Ingrid Bergman. It offers four types of the house *cava* that can be purchased by the glass. Open Monday to Saturday 8am to 3pm. At the corner of Plaça de Tetuan is a final choice, **Xampú Xampany** (Gran Vía de les Corts Catalanes 702; ☎ **932-650-483;** Metro: Girona). Against a backdrop of abstract paintings, you can enjoy glass after glass of the bubbly Monday to Saturday 8pm to 1:30am.

SANGRIA Bear in mind that sangria was created as a way to use up bad wine. It's come a long way, however, and is now a very popular refreshing drink made from red wine, lemons, oranges, and sugar. Be careful with some sangria in touristy areas—it can be quite a sad affair.

WHISKEY & BRANDY Spain is not known for its whiskey, but its brandies and cognacs are pretty good if you're into that sort of thing. So consider buying local, instead of spending half your budget buying whiskeys imported from Kentucky or Tennessee.

Appendix B: Glossary

I t's so much easier to travel to a place where English is the mother tongue, but what's the fun in that? One of the best things about traveling is the opportunity to practice or learn a new language. Don't be mistaken, a different language is a different way of thinking and living. Try to immerse yourself in the country you are visiting by communicating with the natives. Make the most of the differences. In Spain, besides the numerous regional dialects, you'll find four major languages: **Catalán** in Catalunya, **Euskera** in the Basque country, **Gallego** in Galicia, and **Castilian** (or simply Español) everywhere else. Español is the main and official language in the country so everyone will understand it. Knowing a few basic phrases in Español will take you a long way. For more information on Euskera and Catalán, see p. 256 and 346.

English & Castilian Phrases

English	Castilian	Pronunciation
Good day	**Buenos días**	*bweh*-nohs *dee*-ahs
How are you?	**¿Cómo está?**	*koh*-moh es-*tah*
Very well	**Muy bien**	mwee byehn
Thank you	**Gracias**	*grah*-syahs
You're welcome	**De nada**	deh *nah*-dah
Goodbye	**Adiós**	ah-*dyohs*
Please	**Por favor**	pohr fah-*vohr*
Yes	**Sí**	see
No	**No**	noh
Excuse me	**Perdóneme**	pehr-*doh*-neh-meh

English	Castilian	Pronunciation
Give me	**Déme**	*deh*-meh
Where is ...?	**¿Dónde está ...?**	*dohn*-deh es-*tah*
the station	**la estación**	lah es-tah-*syohn*
a hotel	**un hotel**	oon oh-*tel*
a gas station	**una gasolinera**	*oo*-nah gah-so-lee-*neh*-rah
a restaurant	**un restaurante**	oon res-tow-*rahn*-teh
the toilet	**el baño**	el *bah*-nyoh
a good doctor	**un buen médico**	oon bwehn *meh*-dee-coh
the road to ...	**el camino a/hacia ...**	el cah-*mee*-noh ah/*ah*-syah
To the right	**A la derecha**	ah lah deh-*reh*-chah
To the left	**A la izquierda**	ah lah ees-*kyehr*-dah
Straight ahead	**Derecho**	deh-*reh*-choh
I would like	**Quisiera**	kee-*syeh*-rah
I want	**Quiero**	*kyeh*-roh
to eat	**comer**	ko-*mehr*
a room	**una habitación**	*oo*-nah ah-bee-tah-*syohn*
Do you have?	**¿Tiene usted?**	tyeh-neh oo-*sted*
a book	**un libro**	oon *lee*-broh
a dictionary	**un diccionario**	oon deek-syoh-*na*-ryo
How much is it?	**¿Cuánto cuesta?**	*kwahn*-toh *kwehs*-tah
When?	**¿Cuándo?**	*kwahn*-doh
What?	**¿Qué?**	keh
There is (Is there ...?)	**(¿)Hay (...?)**	aye
What is there?	**¿Qué hay?**	keh aye
Yesterday	**Ayer**	ah-*yehr*
Today	**Hoy**	oy
Tomorrow	**Mañana**	mah-*nyah*-nah
Good	**Bueno**	*bweh*-noh
Bad	**Malo**	*mah*-loh
Better (Best)	**(Lo) Mejor**	(loh) meh-*hor*
More	**Más**	mahs
Less	**Menos**	*meh*-nohs
No smoking	**Se prohibe fumar**	seh proh-*ee*-beh foo-*mahr*
Postcard	**Tarjeta postal**	tar-*heh*-tah pohs-*tahl*
Insect repellent	**Repelente contra insectos**	reh-peh-*lehn*-teh *cohn*-trah een-*sehk*-tohs

MORE USEFUL PHRASES

English	Castilian	Pronunciation
Do you speak English?	**¿Habla usted inglés?**	ah-blah oo-*sted* een-*glehs*
Is there anyone here who speaks English?	**¿Hay alguien aquí que hable inglés?**	eye *ahl*-gyehn ah-*kee* keh *ah*-bleh een-*glehs*

English	Castilian	Pronunciation
I speak a little Spanish.	**Hablo un poco de español.**	*ah*-bloh oon *poh*-koh deh es-pah-*nyol*
I don't understand Spanish very well.	**No (lo) entiendo muy bien el español.**	noh (loh) ehn-*tyehn*-doh mwee byehn el es-pah-*nyol*
The meal is good.	**Me gusta la comida.**	meh *goo*-stah lah koh-*mee*-dah
What time is it?	**¿Qué hora es?**	keh *oh*-rah es
May I see your menu?	**¿Puedo ver el menú (la carta)?**	*pweh*-do vehr el meh-*noo* (lah *car*-tah)
The check please.	**La cuenta por favor.**	lah *kwehn*-tah pohr fah-*vohr*
What do I owe you?	**¿Cuánto le debo?**	*kwahn*-toh leh *deh*-boh
What did you say?	**¿Mande?** (colloquial expression for American "Huh?")	*mahn*-deh
More formal:	**¿Cómo?**	*koh*-moh
I want (to see) a room	**Quiero (ver) un cuarto** *or* **una habitación**	*kyeh*-roh (vehr) oon *kwahr*-toh, *oo*-nah ah-bee-tah-*syohn*
for two persons.	**para dos personas.**	*pah*-rah dohs pehhr-*soh*-nas
with (without) bathroom.	**con (sin) baño.**	kohn (seen) *bah*-nyoh
We are staying here only	**Nos quedamos aquí solamente**	nohs keh-*dah*-mohs ah-*kee* soh-lah-*mehn*-teh
ɪ night.	**una noche.**	*oo*-nah *noh*-cheh
ɪ week.	**una semana.**	*oo*-nah seh-*mah*-nah
We are leaving tomorrow.	**Partimos (Salimos) mañana.**	pahr-*tee*-mohs (sah-*lee*-mohs) mah-*nya*-nah
Do you accept traveler's checks?	**¿Acepta usted cheques de viajero?**	ah-*sehp*-tah oo-*sted* *cheh*-kehs deh byah-*heh*-roh
Is there a laundromat near here?	**¿Hay una lavandería cerca de aquí?**	eye *oo*-nah lah-*vahn*-deh-*ree*-ah *sehr*-kah deh ah-*kee*
Please send these clothes to the laundry.	**Hágame el favor de mandar esta ropa a la lavandería.**	*ah*-gah-meh el fah-*vohr* deh mahn-*dahr* ehs-tah *roh*-pah a lah lah-*vahn*-deh-*ree*-ah

TRULY USEFUL PHRASES

English	Castilian	Pronunciation
Where is the best . . . ?	**¿Dónde está el (la) mejor . . . ?**	*dohn*-deh es-*tah* el (lah) *mehore* . . . ?
club	**discoteca**	*dees-caw-teh-cah*
party	**fiesta**	*fee-es-tah*
nightlife	**Marcha**	*mahr-chah*
I'm feeling sick.	**Me siento mal.**	meh see-en-taw mahl
Take me home.	**Llevame a casa.**	*yeh-bah-meh ah cah-sah*
You are beautiful.	**Eres muy guapa/o.**	eh-rehs mooy wah-pah/oh

English	Castilian	Pronunciation
Meet me at . . .	Te espero en . . .	teh ehs-pear-awe en . . .
What's your telephone number?	¿Cuál es tu número de teléfono?	koo-ahl ehs too noo-meh-roh deh te-leh-foh-noh?
May I buy you a drink?	¿Te puedo invitar un trago?	teh poo-eh-do in-vee-tahr uhn trah-goh?
Which way to the beach?	¿Hacia dónde está la playa?	ah-cee-ah dawn-deh ehs-tah lah plah-ya?
Do you want to dance?	¿Quieres bailar?	Kee-eh-rehs bah-ee-lahr?
Another beer	Otra cerveza	oh-trah sehr-beh-sah
What are you doing . . .	¿Qué harás . . .	keh ah-rahs . . .
tomorrow?	mañana?	mah-nya-na
tonight?	esta noche?	eh-stah naw-cheh?

LA JERGA (SLANG)

Spanish slang varies from town to town, but there are some terms that can make you sound cool (or at least funny) no matter where you are.

Cutre (coo-tray)	divvy
Hortera (ore-tayrah)	tacky
Pijo (pee-haw)	conservative
Marcha (mar-chah)	nightlife
Chungo (choon-gaw)	shady
Cojonudo, guay, mola	cool
Curro (coo-raw)	work
Mosquearse (maws-kay-ar say)	get pissed
Cogerse un pedo, ciego (caw-her-say oon pay-daw, see-ay-gaw)	get wasted
Porro, canuto, peta (paw-raw, cahn-oo-taw, pay-tah)	joint
Resacón (ray-sah-cawn)	hangover
Colega (caw-lay-gah)	mate
Ligar (lee-gar)	to hook up (or try at least)
Ser un plasta (sehr oon plah-stah)	be a pain
Flipar, fliparlo (fleep-ahr)	to be shocked, astonished
Gafe (gah-fay)	Killjoy
Chocolate, costo (caw-staw)	hash

NUMBERS

1	uno (oo-noh)		10	diez (dyehs)
2	dos (dohs)		11	once (ohn-seh)
3	tres (trehs)		12	doce (doh-seh)
4	cuatro (kwah-troh)		13	trece (treh-seh)
5	cinco (seen-koh)		14	catorce (kah-tohr-seh)
6	seis (says)		15	quince (keen-seh)
7	siete (syeh-teh)		16	dieciséis (dyeh-see-says)
8	ocho (oh-choh)		17	diecisiete (dyeh-see-syeh-teh)
9	nueve (nweh-beh)		18	dieciocho (dyeh-see-oh-choh)

19 **diecinueve** (dyeh-see-*nweh*-beh)
20 **veinte** (*bayn*-teh)
30 **treinta** (*trayn*-tah)
40 **cuarenta** (kwah-*rehn*-tah)
50 **cincuenta** (seen-*kwehn*-tah)
60 **sesenta** (seh-*sehn*-tah)
70 **setenta** (seh-*tehn*-tah)

80   **ochenta** (oh-*chehn*-tah)
90   **noventa** (noh-*behn*-tah)
100   **cien** (*syehn*)
200   **doscientos** (doh-*syehn*-tohs)
500   **quinientos** (kee-*nyehn*-tos)
1,000 **mil** (meel)

I

IAMAT (International
  Association for Medical
  Assistance to Travelers), 49
Iberia, 61
Ibiza, 486–506
  culture tips, 491
  eating, 494–496
  emergencies, 492
  getting around, 487–488
  hanging out, 497
  Internet access, 494
  orientation, 488, 490
  partying, 496–501
  pharmacies, 492
  playing outside, 501–503,
    505–506
  scooter rentals, 502
  shopping, 503–504
  sightseeing, 501
  sleeping, 492–494
  tourist offices, 490
  traveling to, 486–487
  12 hours in, 491
  websites and magazines,
    490–491
Ibiza Town, 488
Ice-skating, Jaca, 325–326
Iglesia de la Vera Cruz
  (Segovia), 237
Iglesia de Nuestra Señora del
  Azogue (Sanabria), 231
Iglesia de San Claudio de
  Olivares (Zamora), 231
Iglesia de San Esteban
  (Burgos), 215
Iglesia de San Juan (Cáceres),
  191
Iglesia de San Juan de Puerta
  Nueva (Zamora), 231
Iglesia de San Mateo
  (Cáceres), 191
Iglesia de San Nicolas
  (Burgos), 215
Iglesia de San Pablo
  (Valladolid), 208
Iglesia de San Pedro and San
  Ildefonso (Zamora), 231
Iglesia de Santa María
  Alicante, 449
  Fuenterrabía, 272
  Trujillo, 174
Iglesia de Santa María la
  Horta (Zamora), 231
Iglesia de Santiago de los
  Caballeros
  Cáceres, 191
  Zamora, 231
Iglesia de Santo Tomé
  (Toledo), 145

Iglesia de San Vicente
  (Zamora), 231
Iglesia San Martín (Trujillo),
  173
Igueldo, Monte, 271
Il Caffé di Roma (Toledo), 142
Immunizations, 49
In-line skating, Madrid, 126
Institute of International
  Education (IIE), 28
Instituto Valenciano de Arte
  Moderno (Valencia), 442
International Association for
  Medical Assistance to
  Travelers (IAMAT), 49
International driver's license,
  59–60
The International Ecotourism
  Society (TIES), 65
International Film Festival
  (San Sebastián), 73, 251,
  260, 271
The International Gay and
  Lesbian Travel Association
  (IGLTA), 63
International Jazz Festival
  (San Sebastián), 72, 251
International Music and
  Dance Festival
  (Granada), 71
International Society of
  Travel Medicine, 49
International Student
  Identity Card (ISIC), 61
International Youth Travel
  Card (IYTC), 61
Internet access, 53–55
  Barcelona, 345
  Bilbao, 277
  Cordoba, 557
  Girona, 392
  Ibiza, 494
  Madrid, 85
  Málaga, 605
  Menorca, 516
  Palma de Mallorca, 475
  Pamplona, 286, 288
  San Sebastián, 260–261
  Sevilla, 528
  Valencia (city), 434
  Zaragoza, 305
The Irish Rover Theater
  (Salamanca), 222
Isla Marina (Alicante), 448
Itineraries, multi-city, 43

J

Jaca, 318–326
Jaca Bowling, 326

Jaipur (Jerez de la Frontera),
  591–592
Jamboree (Barcelona), 373
J & J Books and Coffee
  (Madrid), 132
Japan (Málaga), 608
Jardín Botánico (Madrid), 130
Jardín de la Isla (Aranjuez),
  153
Jardín del Parterre
  (Aranjuez), 153
Jardín del Principe
  (Aranjuez), 153
Jardines de Alderdi-Eder (San
  Sebastián), 271
Jardines del Turia (Valencia),
  442
Jardins Rubio i Lluch
  (Barcelona), 383
Jazzaldia (San Sebastián), 271
Jazz and blues
  Barcelona, 373, 377
  Cadaqués, 406
  Girona, 397
  Madrid, 115–116
  Mérida, 183
  Salamanca, 222
  San Sebastián, 267
Jazz Bar (Mérida), 183
Jem Casey's (Figueres), 402
Jerez de la Frontera,
  2, 589–595
Jet lag, 47
Jimmy's (Nerja), 618
Johnnyjet.com, 36
Joies (Figueres), 402
José Alfredo's Cocktail
  Lounge (Madrid), 113
Juan Foronda (Sevilla), 548

K

Kame Café (San Lorenzo de
  El Escorial), 159
Kapital (Madrid), 117
Kayak.com, 36
Kayaking, Girona, 399
Kemwel Holiday Auto, 60
Kentucky (Barcelona),
  365, 368
KGB (Barcelona), 368
Khurp (Benasque), 334
Kite-surfing, in Tarifa,
  11–12, 576–579
KM DanceClub (Benidorm),
  454
Ku (Benidorm), 454–455
Kumharas (Ibiza), 504–505
Ku Playa (Benidorm), 454

INDEX

Notes